Mental Capacity: Law and Practice

Third Edition

Mental Capacity: Law and Practice

Third Edition

GENERAL EDITOR AND CONTRIBUTOR

Gordon R Ashton, OBE
Retired District Judge and Nominated Judge of the Court of Protection

CONTRIBUTORS

District Judge Marc Marin
Nominated Judge of the Court of Protection

Claire van Overdijk
Barrister, No 5 Chambers

Alex Ruck Keene
Barrister, 39 Essex Street, London

Martin Terrell
Partner, Thomson Snell & Passmore

Adrian D Ward MBE
Partner, TC Young LLP, Solicitors, Scotland

PAST CONTRIBUTORS

Penny Letts, OBE
Policy Consultant, Editor of Elder Law Journal

Laurence Oates
Official Solicitor to the Supreme Court 1999–2006

Published by
Jordan Publishing Limited
21 St Thomas Street
Bristol BS1 6JS

British Library Cataloguing-in-Publication Data

A catalogue record for this book is available from the British Library.

ISBN 978 1 78473 160 1

Typeset by Letterpart Ltd, Caterham on the Hill, Surrey CR3 5XL

Printed in Great Britain by Hobbs the Printers Limited, Totton, Hampshire SO40 3WX

DEDICATION

To the memory of

PAUL JOSEPH SCHOLES ASHTON

who died at the age of 28 years on 26 January 2004 before he could benefit from this much needed legislation.

PREFACE TO THE FIRST EDITION

It is 17 years since the Law Society's Mental Health Sub-Committee (as it then was) first drew public attention to the legal vacuum in which people who lacked mental capacity were obliged to exist. This provoked the Law Commission to take this topic on board and, after several years of consultation, recommendations were made for a statutory mental incapacity jurisdiction. Different governments then pursued further consultation whilst lacking the will to introduce legislation, but pressures to do so became overwhelming with the introduction of community care policies, disability discrimination laws and ultimately human rights legislation. The Mental Capacity Act 2005 is the result, but a consequence of the changed climate is that it must meet higher standards then were expected when the need was first identified.

This Act builds upon enduring powers of attorney and the existing jurisdiction of the Court of Protection, and follows most of the Law Commission's recommendations in creating a broad and viable framework. The devil will be in the detail that has yet to emerge through forms, Codes of Practice, regulations and Court rules. There is an inevitable tension between protection and empowerment, and inadequate support may lead to a denial of both. Those who complain that the jurisdiction is too controlling mat be the first to express outrage when abuse is not prevented. But we do not live in a 'nanny state' and there are issues as to who should fund the new jurisdiction. The existing Court of Protection can seek to be self-funding because it only opens its doors to those who have money. The new jurisdiction may find itself addressing the needs of some of the most financially disempowered people in the community. Is it in reality an extension of our health and social services notwithstanding that it functions through a Court? The legal rights of individuals who lack the capacity to pursue them must be addressed, but this can only be done in the context of support and care provision, which become the ultimate responsibility of the state.

No one should allow themselves to be fooled by the familiar terms 'Public Guardian' and 'Court of Protection'. The former is a new incarnation with a statutory role rather than a mere administrative body, and only time will tell how far this role will develop. The latter is a new regional court working within the mainstream courts and enjoying a wider jurisdiction exercised under different principles. Those already working within the existing system do not know how the new regime will develop, so for practitioners and others there must be an element of speculation.

This book is an attempt by four concerned authors who have throughout been committed to the reforms to explain what is going on and provide some insight into the issues that must be faced. Although the detailed law must be set out, however tedious this may be, we have endeavoured to breath life into the provisions and procedures. We have also tried to face up to some of the potential pitfalls and difficulties that will inevitably arise in implementing new legislation in this complex area.

I wish to thank my co-authors for their dedicated contributions, each being highly experienced in the topics that they have covered. As to the rest I must accept responsibility. We do not claim to be experts – who is in this field? – but for my part I have drawn on 28 years of general legal practice, 13 years as a generic judge and five years involvement within the existing Court of Protection. Above all, I have been influenced by my family experience of a child with severe learning disabilities and the insight this gave me into a different philosophy which should influence the legal system more in the future than it has in the past. I have campaigned for this jurisdiction from the inception and wish to see it improve the quality of life of those who lack capacity, their families and carers. Whether it does so will depend upon all those who play a part in the process, but by picking up this book you have indicated that you are one of those people. Thank you for your support.

Gordon R Ashton
Grange-over-Sands
January 2006

INTRODUCTION

As the Mental Capacity Act 2005 approaches its 10th anniversary our mental capacity jurisdiction faces four significant challenges. Two relate to Conventions so concern the international credibility of our once ground-breaking approach to these universal issues. The other two are more concerned with the credibility of our Court of Protection which has grown and matured over its first 7 years and hopefully now found a permanent home.

EUROPEAN CONVENTION ON HUMAN RIGHTS

It always seemed to me that the Human Rights Act 1998 created a climate in which legislation to facilitate decision-making for those who lacked the capacity to make their own decisions became a necessity. None of us realised that the need went further than this, and that any care arrangements that deprived the individual of their liberty would require a system of authorisation prescribed by law. This has provoked the hasty development of two very different procedures with an irrational basis of selection, each designed to satisfy society (and lawyers in particular) that the human rights of vulnerable adults are not being infringed. These processes dominate the Court of Protection and deplete the resources of social services authorities, but the DoLS procedure does not directly address the suitability or quality of the care package and the judicial *Re X* procedure may not do so on information provided solely by the applicant authority. It may not be the care plan but the way it is implemented that results in an inappropriate deprivation of liberty. In any event it may be fruitless for a judge to query best interests when only one care package is offered by the funding authority. What if judges, who are not well qualified to assess risk or care provision in the real world, have expectations that the authorities cannot afford to meet? As a lawyer I am protective of human rights, but my wife and I as parents of a disabled child whose liberty inevitably had to be curtailed became more concerned about the detailed care arrangements. I have often written about the delicate balance between empowerment and protection because it is seldom possible to achieve both at the same time, and this now seems to have evolved into tension between human rights and necessary care provision. Scarce resources that should be directed towards the delivery of quality care are being diverted into justification for that care.

UN CONVENTION ON THE RIGHTS OF PERSONS WITH DISABILITIES

I always regarded our mental capacity jurisdiction as a reasonable adjustment that, far from discriminating against mentally disabled people, enables them to enjoy a lifestyle comparable with that of people without this impairment. Previously they existed in a legal vacuum and their personal rights and freedoms were not recognised. There has since developed the notion that any form of differential treatment is discriminatory and this leads to two consequences.

The first is that the 'diagnostic threshold', inherited from the previous regime, should not be used as a pre-requisite for admission to the jurisdiction because it discriminates against disabled people. If it was removed those vulnerable adults now being protected by the enlarged inherent jurisdiction of the High Court could be dealt with by the Court of Protection, and that would surely be desirable. But has the Court continued to adopt too medical an approach to this concept? Might the 'impairment or disturbance of the mind' be a consequence not only of internal factors but also external forces such as fear, oppression or overwhelming cultural pressures? That interpretation would bring some, if not all, of the cases now being dealt with under the inherent jurisdiction within the ambit of the Court of Protection. It is a shame to create a specialised court to deal with vulnerable adults and then have to supplement it elsewhere.

The second is that supported decision-making must be the norm and delegated decisions on a best interests basis are unacceptable, but how far can support go and who should provide it? We are all subject to influences and it is only undue influence that the law seeks to control, but the threshold for what is undue reduces as the individual becomes more vulnerable. I see great dangers in insisting that support is given to an incapacitated individual to the extent that the decision reached is deemed to be that of the individual. It seems to me that this is inevitably the decision of the supporter so we end up with delegated decision-making without the framework of best interests. Would it not be sufficient for our jurisdiction to place even more emphasis on support in both the assessment of capacity and the determination of best interests, with the wishes of the individual to the extent ascertainable being a dominant factor? All of this could be achieved by judicial interpretation of our existing legislation. The best interests approach as now adopted would be retained for those instances where the individual remains quite unable to make a personal decision (the stage where the Convention offers little guidance).

LEGAL AID

The virtual withdrawal of public funding denies access to the Court of Protection for the majority of people and creates a challenge for the nominated judges. This is counter-productive because, even though the court is only the tip of a very large iceberg, an application to the court is the ultimate means whereby the effectiveness of the jurisdiction can be tested and controlled. It has become necessary for courts generally to adjust their procedures to accommodate a preponderance of unrepresented parties. These parties generally desire a local outcome in a timely and economical manner under a procedure they can understand and without inflaming an already confrontational situation. An early directions hearing, possibly by telephone to save expense but ideally with the parties present, may result in considerable progress and the allocation to track approach in the Civil Procedure Rules 1998 has much to commend it. There is also much to be gained by the new approaches being adopted for family cases. Inevitably there are situations where the law needs to be clarified but very few cases in the Court of Protection set a precedent or require an adversarial hearing, and an inquisitorial 'small claims' approach may be sufficient when lawyers are not involved for all parties. A contested hearing is the last resort, but the prospect frequently leads to alternative methods of dispute resolution and the Court should be given power to refer a case to the OPG for this purpose. The first Public Guardian did not see conciliation as part of his role but fortunately that attitude has changed and a mediation scheme is now being tried. But there are limitations – the objective is to identify the 'best interests' of the incapacitated person, and reaching agreement between members of a dysfunctional family vying for control may not achieve this.

THE 'SECRET COURT'

There will always be those who, having exhausted or rejected the appeal process, seek publicity as a means of expressing their dissatisfaction with the outcome. Inevitably they only put forward their side of the case and omit aspects that may have been seen by the court as determinative. Certain elements of the press are all too willing to present this, with some embellishment, as a serious injustice. Those newspapers that condemn the Court of Protection as a secret court interfering in the lives of decent people would, on another day, criticise a system that allowed a vulnerable person to be exploited or abused. They cannot have it both ways! Certainly judges must be prepared to make available reasoned judgments, anonymised in their discretion, but I am far from satisfied that public hearings are the answer. Restricted access by the press is now possible but cases will still be reported in an unbalanced way according to a pre-determined agenda. My experience in the civil courts is that the public find hearings boring and those who attend are generally supporters of one party, which can be intimidating to the other party. If I were involved in a family dispute about the future of my elderly parent or learning disabled son I would not wish this to take place in a public arena and would question the motives of anyone who did.

THE WAY FORWARD

Applying lofty principles with impeccable legal logic in a society with limited public resources may not be in the best interests of vulnerable people. It is simply not realistic to require judicial scrutiny on an annual basis of the care arrangements for every individual receiving intensive care and supervision or to assume that there are impartial supporters available who can facilitate decisions without influencing those whose capacity is impaired. My solution would be to direct the available resources into the delivery of care and rely upon a 'whistle blowing' regime with judicial resources being reserved for those situations where intervention may be required. That would avoid intrusive and unnecessary scrutiny of those situations where there is no cause for concern. It would be necessary to develop procedures whereby family and carers were aware of how to express their concerns and to expand the role of IMCAS to actively seek out those without this safeguard. It would be better for them to be employed and trained by a central government agency rather than the authorities whose conduct they may be required to question.

CONCLUSION

I have lived the world of the lawyer/advocate and then the judge, and am now moving towards the viewpoint of the consumer of the Mental Capacity legislation. We must never overlook the fact that it is for the benefit of that person, not the lawyers, that this valuable jurisdiction and the Court of Protection exist.

As always, I wish to thank my fellow contributors for their dedication and encouragement, and James Beck from the Office of the Official Solicitor for his contribution on the work of his office. We have endeavoured to present the law as at July 2015.

This is not the first book that I have produced over the past three decades – it all started with Mental Handicap and the Law in 1992 – but it may prove to be the last. I wish to thank the many readers who have expressed their interest and support. It remains my hope that my initiatives in these areas during the intervening years may be continued by other dedicated lawyers in the decades ahead. That would be a fulfilling legacy.

Gordon R Ashton OBE
Grange-over-Sands
July 2015

CONTENTS

TABLE OF CASES

References are to paragraph numbers.

[2014]
& AC. 896.

TABLE OF STATUTES

References are to paragraph numbers.

TABLE OF STATUTORY INSTRUMENTS

References are to paragraph numbers.

TABLE OF EUROPEAN MATERIALS

References are to paragraph numbers.

LIST OF ABBREVIATIONS

Statutes

AWI(S)A 2000	Adults with Incapacity (Scotland) Act 2000
CPA 2004	Civil Partnership Act 2004
DDA 1995	Disability Discrimination Act 1995
EPAA 1985	Enduring Powers of Attorney Act 1985
HRA 1998	Human Rights Act 1998
MCA 2005	Mental Capacity Act 2005
MHA 1983/2007	Mental Health Act 1983/2007
SGA 1979	Sale of Goods Act 1979

Statutory Instruments

2007 Regs	Lasting Powers of Attorney, Enduring Powers of Attorney and Public Guardian Regulations 2007
COPR 2001/2007	Court of Protection Rules 2001/2007
CPR	Civil Procedure Rules 1998

International Conventions

ECHR	European Convention on Human Rights and Fundamental Freedoms 1950

General

ADR	Alternative dispute resolution
ANH	Nutrition and hydration supplied by artificial means
CAFCASS	Children and Family Court Advisory and Support Service
CLS	Community Legal Service
Convention rights	ECHR rights
CTO	Community treatment order
DCA	Department for Constitutional Affairs
DHSS	Department of Health and Social Security
DSS	Department of Social Security
DWP	Department for Work and Pensions
ECT	Electro-convulsive therapy

EPA	Enduring power of attorney
FDR	Financial dispute resolution
GMC	General Medical Council
IMCA	Independent mental capacity advocate
JAC	Judicial Appointments Commission
JCHR	Joint Committee on Human Rights
JSB	Judicial Studies Board
LPA	Lasting power of attorney
MCIP	Mental Capacity Implementation Programme
MHRT	Mental health review tribunal
NHS	National Health Service
OPG	Office of the Public Guardian
PGO	(Old) Public Guardianship Office
PTO	Public Trust Office
PVS	persistent vegetative state
SDD	Social services departments of local authorities
section 5 act	Act which may be carried out with protection from liability under MCA 2005, s 5
SFE	Solicitors for the Elderly Limited

CHAPTER 1

BACKGROUND

PRELIMINARY

Overview

Issues

1.1　The *Concise Oxford Dictionary* defines a decision as 'a conclusion or resolution reached after consideration', and we all assume that fellow citizens are able to make their own decisions. Those who cannot do so depend upon the support of others and are vulnerable to abuse or neglect. A civilised society must make provision for such people in its laws, but this assumes that they can be properly identified.

Capacity

1.2　The assessment of capacity is not an easy matter for society. To deprive people who are capable of making their own decisions of the right to do so would be an abuse,[1] yet failure to recognise lack of capacity results in continuing vulnerability. It is possible to stigmatise a person as lacking capacity for a variety of reasons and our history provides many examples of this.[2] Is the objective to protect the individual or society? Is it to afford power to one section of society over another by categorising some people as being unable to make decisions? We accept that children may be denied capacity, especially during their formative years, but the age at which capacity becomes recognised by the law has progressively reduced during recent years. It is only within the past century that all people in our society have been recognised as equals, and this means that some objective justification must exist before personal capacity is denied to an adult. That justification is generally to be found in the diagnosis of some form of mental impairment.

1.3　Legal incompetence is thus to be found when there is lack of capacity due to a mental disability. It may arise for a variety of reasons and may be merely temporary or may be a permanent condition. The lack of capacity may be partial or total. Insofar as an individual does have capacity, any decisions that

---

[1]　It would also be a breach of the human rights of the individual if not justified and a proportionate response.

[2]　Women, felons and lunatics have all at some time been treated as incompetent. The Mental Deficiency Act 1913 extended to 'moral imbeciles' and thus unmarried mothers could be deprived of their liberty.

are made should be recognised and an 'all or nothing' approach should not be adopted. Some decisions require little thought and may be identified from a mere assent or even body language. Others require knowledge and understanding and need to be communicated in a reasoned manner.

Decision-making

1.4   When lack of capacity is temporary it may be possible to defer decisions until capacity is restored. But if it is of lasting duration or permanent, or if an urgent decision otherwise needs to be made, there must be some legally recognised procedure whereby necessary decisions can be made by some other person or body. The decision-maker must be identified so that any decision that is made will be recognised by others.

1.5   There are different types of decision that we all make. We have to manage our financial affairs, and those who enter into transactions with us must be satisfied that these are enforceable and not likely to be set aside due to lack of competence on our part or lack of authority on the part of the person who transacts them for us. Decisions about medical treatment may also need to be made and should not simply be left to doctors, especially if they could have a serious effect upon the rest of our lives. Many personal welfare decisions are trivial, but some may have implications for other persons and lead to disputes within families.[3] Each of these three types of decision-making needs to come within any jurisdiction afforded by the law.

1.6   If personal choices are to be made for us then there must be a recognised basis on which this should be done. Is the decision-maker free to make whatever decisions he or she thinks best, which might be subjective and influenced by personal interests, or is an objective basis to be adopted? What might that basis be? There seems to be general acceptance that the paternalistic approach adopted in respect of children is not appropriate for an adult.

1.7   It is not acceptable for one person to assume dominion over another without the facility for this to be questioned and it is a function of the law to provide this facility. Although various procedures may be devised to resolve disputes, as a last resort it is the courts that are usually relied upon to undertake this task. They need to be legally empowered to do so, but it is not only disputes that may need to be referred to the courts: where there is uncertainty as to what may be done or what would be lawful, the courts are usually expected to determine this.

Communication

1.8   There is no magic about decision-making: it merely means making a choice, but this does require the ability to identify the range of possible choices and the implications of each. It also requires the ability to communicate the

---

[3]   Compare decisions about what to wear and what to eat with decisions about where to live or with whom.

choice once this has been made. Communication is a two-way process: it is as important to ensure that the person understands what is being said to them as that their attempts to respond are understood. Impairment of communication does not necessarily indicate lack of mental capacity and, where there is doubt, a medical report may establish the capacity of the individual.

1.9   If we are to empower people we must not rely solely upon normal methods of communication, but should explore and adopt any method that will achieve effective communication.[4] This may involve using available aids or an interpreter where this will assist. If verbal dialogue is not possible, written notes or sign language may facilitate communication. A simple response to questions, such as movement of a finger, may be found reliable but in that event questions must be phrased so as to facilitate a range of responses.

Conclusion

1.10   These are the fundamental issues that should be addressed by any legal system, and other countries including Germany, the provinces in Canada and the states of the USA, Australia and New Zealand have through their legislation over the years developed adult guardianship laws. The Mental Capacity Act 2005 was an early attempt to remedy this shortcoming in England and Wales and contained some innovative features.[5] A slightly different approach had already been adopted in Scotland.[6]

Legal competence

1.11   The law assumes that an adult has the capacity to make and the ability to communicate personal decisions so there is a vacuum if someone is not able to do this. Concerns may also arise as to whether an individual is competent to make a particular decision or acquiesce in the decisions of others, even though he or she purports to do so. In a legal context we are assessing whether any choice would be recognised by the law.

1.12   When talking about competence we are considering the ability to understand, make a choice and then make this clear to others, even though assistance may be needed to carry the choice into effect. It follows that neither age nor physical or sensory impairment should by itself affect competence. Lack of legal competence may arise through mental incapacity, an inability to communicate or a combination of the two, but every effort should be made to overcome communication difficulties.

---

[4]   The phrase 'locked in syndrome' is used to describe a person who can reason and make decisions but is unable to communicate.

[5]   The implementation date was 1 October 2007 for England and Wales and it could be adopted in Northern Ireland by regulations (although it has not been).

[6]   Adults with Incapacity (Scotland) Act 2000; Mental Health (Care and Treatment) (Scotland) Act 2003; and Adult Support and Protection (Scotland) Act 2007.

Tests of mental capacity

1.13 Although the term 'mental incapacity' conveys a fairly consistent impression to most people it does not have a precise meaning. It would be convenient if there were a universal definition, so that we could readily identify those members of society who are eligible for special treatment, but this could never be the case because very few people are incapable in all things. Legal tests of capacity must vary according to the circumstances.

1.14 In some situations, specific tests have been developed by case-law so textbooks are able to identify testamentary capacity and the capacity required to sign an enduring power of attorney, enter into a marriage or make a gift. The classic definition of a 'patient'[7] which was found in the Mental Health Act 1983 and the various court rules was not interpreted by the appeal courts until the turn of the century.[8] Otherwise general principles must be relied upon, and these are now based upon function rather than the status of the person making the decision or the outcome of decisions. Furthermore, it is the individual's understanding rather than judgment that is relevant – we are all entitled to make unwise decisions.

Assessment of mental capacity

1.15 Doubts about capacity may arise for several reasons but these should not be confused with tests of capacity. Thus the status of the individual (such as being elderly and living in a nursing home), the outcome of a decision (viewed by others as illogical) or the appearance or behaviour of the individual may cause capacity to be questioned. Yet it is not unusual for outward appearances to create a false impression of incapacity and, conversely, the absence of any of these indications does not mean that the individual is capable. In all these situations a proper assessment should be made according to appropriate criteria.

1.16 One of the difficulties is that the various professionals who may be involved approach the question of capacity from different standpoints so often reach different conclusions. In case of dispute, capacity is a question of fact for the court to decide on the balance of probabilities with a presumption of capacity. The opinions of professionals will be admitted as 'expert' evidence but considered alongside factual evidence from those who know the individual and will only be persuasive if the experts have been given all relevant information and applied the appropriate legal test.

1.17 The medical profession tends to be concerned with diagnosis and prognosis rather than the severity and implications of mental disability. The doctor may well be able to identify the cause of the disability and indicate its likely future consequences, but what is in issue to the lawyer is the effect on the

---

[7]   'Incapable by reason of mental disorder of managing and administering his property and affairs.'

[8]   *Masterman-Lister v Brutton & Co and Jewell & Home Counties Dairies* [2002] EWCA Civ 1889, [2002] All ER (D) 297 (Dec).

individual at this moment in time.[9] Care workers classify people according to their degree of independence, which involves consideration of levels of competence in performing skills such as eating, dressing, communication and social skills. These skills may be affected by mental or physical causes and also enhanced by a learnt behaviour pattern. An assessment based upon a medical diagnosis is of little use to the care worker other than to explain the reason for the present impairment and indicate whether improvement or deterioration is to be expected. The carer may become concerned as to the vulnerability of the person cared for and the entitlement of others to take decisions on that person's behalf but vulnerability does not by itself signal a lack of capacity.

1.18 The lawyer wishes to establish whether the individual is capable of making a reasoned and informed decision, although there may be a need to assess the degree of dependence, for example, when considering what financial provision should be made for the individual. There can be no universally applied test because the capacity required will depend upon the nature of the decision to be made, but the medical diagnosis will be largely irrelevant except insofar as it points to the degree of capacity that may be anticipated and the carer's view may be helpful but will not be based on any particular legal test. Thus the lawyer may need to consult the doctor and carer (or social worker) but their views merely form part of the evidence when considering the question of legal capacity. Having gathered this evidence the lawyer is in the best position to form a considered view as to legal capacity or to refer the issue to a court for determination.

Incapacitated people

1.19 Children are adequately catered for under the law of England and Wales.[10] Those adults who may lack capacity fall into four main groups. The largest group comprises elderly people who are deprived of their capacity by senile dementia but have previously been able to manage their own affairs. At the other extreme are those with learning disabilities which may be so severe that they have never been able to enjoy personal autonomy. In between are those who encounter a period of mental illness or have an acquired brain injury rendering them incapable of making decisions that others should recognise. The situation is made more complicated by the fact that for some capacity may fluctuate and in every instance there is the potential for partial capacity.

Decision-making

1.20 Decisions fall into three broad categories: financial, personal welfare and health care. When an adult is incapable of making decisions special procedures should be available for these to be taken on his or her behalf if that is

---

[9] The Law Society and the British Medical Association have produced guidance in a book entitled *Assessment of Mental Capacity: Guidance for Doctors and Lawyers* (BMA, 1995; BMJ Books, 2nd edn, 2004; Law Society Publishing, 3rd edn, 2009).

[10] The Children Act 1989 contains the necessary powers for intervention by the courts and the High Court wardship jurisdiction remains.

appropriate. This raises the questions of when decision-making powers should be delegated, who should then be empowered to take the decisions and the basis on which they should be taken.

Delegated decision-making

1.21 Although under general legal principles a specific decision may be held to be invalid due to lack of competence this may be merely a 'one-off' situation[11] and something more is needed if decision-making powers are to be delegated. This criteria – which makes clear that there is an ongoing problem that needs to be addressed – is known as the 'diagnostic threshold'. It was previously the existence of a 'mental disorder' which caused the lack of capacity.

1.22 'Mental disorder' was defined in the Mental Health Act 1983 as: 'mental illness, arrested or incomplete development of mind, psychopathic disorder and any other disorder or disability of mind' but did not include the effect of alcohol or drugs.[12] This definition is extremely wide but provided a useful screening process because merely being eccentric should not be a basis for being deprived of one's rights. However, it was widely used in other contexts so was not ideal.

Decision-makers

1.23 There have in the past been various persons who might represent the interests of a mentally disabled individual to a greater or lesser extent. These included:[13]

• appointee for state benefits;
• receiver appointed by the former Court of Protection for financial affairs;
• attorney under an enduring power for financial affairs;
• trustees for financial affairs;
• litigation friend for civil proceedings;[14] or family proceedings;[15]
• next friend or guardian ad litem for family proceedings (now litigation friend);
• personal advocate – used in practice but not recognised in law.

Most of these roles still exist, but despite the length of this list the authority of such representatives extended to very few ordinary decisions for the individual and there were large gaps where no one had any power to make such decisions.

1.24 In a climate where many marriages end in separation or divorce and 'living together relationships' have become almost the norm, it would no longer

---

[11] The individual may be under the influence of alcohol or drugs at the time.
[12] Mental Health Act 1983, s 1(2) and (3).
[13] This list applies to England and Wales. A different list could be produced for Scotland.
[14] Civil Procedure Rules 1998, SI 1998/3132, Part 21.
[15] Family Procedure Rules 2010, SI 2010/2955, Part 15.

be acceptable for a spouse or designated blood relative to be given special status by the law as decision-maker. Preserving personal autonomy requires that the incapacitated individual has the opportunity to make the choice of decision-maker in advance (if then capable) and to influence that choice even after losing mental capacity to the extent that wishes can be ascertained. Introducing such flexibility creates its own problems but there must be a procedure whereby the appointment of a nominee can be challenged on established principles.

Best interests

1.25   There has been much debate about the basis on which delegated decisions are to be made. Should this be what the decision-maker thinks best or what the incapacitated individual would have decided had he or she been capable? The former is too paternalistic for contemporary society whereas the latter is not feasible for those who have never been able to express their own wishes. The concept of best interests has emerged, which is an attempt to combine respect for the wishes of the individual with the views of others in a climate of minimum intervention. But what exactly does this mean in practice?

A special jurisdiction

1.26   There is an increasing number of adults who lack mental capacity and have property or financial affairs that need to be dealt with. This is partly because the population is living longer with greater home ownership, and partly because more brain-damaged children survive – some with substantial damages awards. Former procedures allowed these affairs to be dealt with but there was a vacuum in our law for other forms of decision-making.

1.27   It was a nonsense that financial management should control personal welfare: none of us run our own lives in that way. We each decide what we wish to do and how we wish to conduct our lives and then temper this according to what we can afford. It was also unacceptable that uncertainty prevailed on issues such as where the individual should live, with whom he or she should have contact and what medical treatment should be given. It was inevitable that sooner or later legislation would have to be introduced to tackle this issue. The Mental Capacity Act 2005 now superimposes a procedure for decision-making on our existing law.

1.28   It has to be acknowledged that any jurisdiction whose role is to address the needs of 'adults with incapacity'[16] has little relevance to the work of most lawyers and, apart from an occasional high-profile case, is of little interest to the public at large. But to anyone who encounters a decline in the mental capacity of a loved one, and to the professionals involved, the manner in which

---

[16]   This is the terminology now creeping into use, based on the title to the Scottish legislation, but it is questionable. It may be thought that referring to those who 'lack capacity' is demeaning and to be discouraged, but it is illogical to refer to someone as being with something that they are without.

issues that arise are addressed is seen as a test of the integrity of the legal system. No one can afford to ignore reform in this area, because this is not a 'them and us' situation. Any of us may encounter a period when we lack capacity whether temporary, progressive or permanent, especially as we grow older. We and our loved ones then depend on the new jurisdiction established by the Mental Capacity Act 2005.

1.29 The new jurisdiction must also set standards for others to follow in the field of disability. Disabled people must be assured of equal access to justice and that the discrimination they still encounter in society will not be reproduced within the system of justice. This applies to the legal principles that are applied, the procedures that are followed, the facilities available and the attitudes of those involved. There will be many lessons to be learnt by the Public Guardian and the new Court of Protection, but hopefully these will be well learned and thereafter permeate throughout the legal system.[17]

Confidentiality

1.30 Doctors, lawyers, social workers and professional persons generally owe a duty of confidentiality to their patients or clients, which means that personal information should only be revealed to others with the consent of the patient or client.[18] This duty is not absolute and may be overridden where there is a stronger public interest in disclosure.[19] Where the individual lacks the mental capacity to consent to (or refuse) disclosure, it may be desirable to permit disclosure in certain circumstances. This has been expressed as follows:[20]

> 'C's interest in protecting the confidentiality of personal information about himself must not be underestimated. It is all too easy for professionals and parents to regard … incapacitated adults as having no independent interests of their own: as objects rather than subjects. But we are not concerned here with the publication of information to the whole wide world. There is a clear distinction between disclosure to the media with a view to publication to all and sundry and disclosure in confidence to those with a proper interests in having the information in question.'

1.31 During an assessment as to mental capacity it is essential that information is shared by the professionals involved. The individual's consent to this should be obtained wherever possible, but in the absence of this relevant disclosure may be permitted. However, this does not extend to confidential

---

[17] Guidance to judges is available from the Judicial College (formerly JSB) in the *Equal Treatment Bench Book*, which can be accessed at: www.judiciary.gov.uk/publications-and-reports/judicial-college/Pre+2011/equal-treatment-bench-book.

[18] This may be imposed by codes of professional conduct or by the law, eg Data Protection Act 1998 or European Convention on Human Rights, Art 8.

[19] *W v Egdell* [1990] Ch 359, at 419.

[20] *R (on the application of Ann Stevens) v Plymouth City Council and C* [2002] EWCA Civ 388, per Hale LJ.

information about the individual unrelated to the assessment. Disclosure will be based on a need-to-know and the overall test is the best interests of the individual.

1.32 Similar principles must apply in a family context. Parents may choose not to reveal their financial affairs to their children and the situation does not change simply because a parent ceases to be mentally capable. This can cause suspicion when one of the children is appointed to deal with those affairs, but the duty of confidentiality will apply to such child whether acting as attorney or deputy (formerly receiver) appointed by the Court of Protection. In appropriate circumstances that court may direct that some disclosure do take place (eg, of financial affairs) to dispel suspicion.

Undue influence

Assisted decision-making

1.33 One of the problems when dealing with individuals who are frail or of borderline mental capacity is undue influence. Some adults prefer to have many of their decisions made by others and tests of capacity encourage the acceptance of support from others even though this may amount to influence.[21] But there may be cause for concern if an individual is too easily influenced or becomes too much under the influence of another person. Also, understanding of relevant factors may be corrupted by the manner and selectivity in which information is provided. A person who is constantly given incomplete or even incorrect information is likely to make choices that they would not otherwise have made. The ability to make a choice may also be affected by threats, perceived or actual. Thus a decision which appears to have been competently made could be the outcome of at best a limited perception of the choices available or at worst fear of the consequences of making a different decision.

1.34 This problem is magnified by the fact that those seeking to challenge a decision may themselves be seeking to exert an influence over the individual. All too often these situations of conflict develop from a power struggle between otherwise concerned relatives with the vulnerable person becoming a pawn in the game. A tendency by this person to agree with the party who presently has their audience either because of a short-term desire for peace or the strength of that party's personality merely provides evidence which fuels the problem. Experience in the Court of Protection demonstrates that many of the disputes arise from the abuse of power or desire of another individual for control over the vulnerable individual.

1.35 Perhaps of more concern is the situation where undue influence is not recognised and financial or emotional abuse is taking place. An individual who needs assistance from others before making significant personal decisions is

---

[21] The real problem is likely to become undue influence of those whose capacity is impaired but not lacking. To what extent should one decide that an individual lacks capacity because they have become too susceptible to the influence of others?

vulnerable. There is a tendency to delegate decisions to others who demonstrate a willingness to take them over, and when those others are influenced by personal gain or improper motives there is likely to be abuse. The courts are prepared to set aside transactions adverse to an individual when these are the result of undue influence, but these matters can be expensive to litigate and the interaction between improper influence and mental capacity has yet to be fully developed.

The legal position

1.36   People may not be saved from their own foolishness but will be protected from being victimised by other people. The common law developed a principle of duress but equity supplemented this by enabling gifts and other transactions to be set aside if procured by undue influence or if they are otherwise unconscionable. The manner in which the intention to enter into the transaction was secured may be investigated and if produced by unacceptable means, the law will not permit the transaction to stand. There are thus three situations where transactions may be set aside:

- where duress or undue influence has been expressly used for the purpose of achieving a gift or benefit – the burden of proof is on the party alleging this;
- where undue influence is presumed – the burden is then on the other party to justify the transaction; and
- where a contract of an improvident nature has been made by a poor and ignorant person acting without independent advice, and the other party cannot show that it was fair and reasonable – this is a fall-back remedy for unconscionable conduct.

1.37   The law has appeared to approach the issue of undue influence according to the specific relationship between the parties but the question is whether one party has placed sufficient trust and confidence in the other, rather than whether the relationship between the parties is of a particular type.[22] However, a presumption may arise in two ways:

(1) *The type of relationship*: where there is a recognised relationship in which one party acquires influence over another who is vulnerable (eg client and solicitor, patient and doctor, beneficiary and trustee). There is then an irrebuttable presumption of influence and it is not necessary to establish that the relationship was based upon trust and confidence. If it appears that this influence has been inappropriately exercised then the party with influence must prove that this was not the case.

(2) *The evidential presumption*: where there is evidence that the relationship was based on trust and confidence in relation to the management of the complainant's financial affairs, coupled with a transaction giving rise to suspicions which must be addressed. There may then be a rebuttable

---

[22]   GH Treitel *The Law of Contract* (Sweet & Maxwell, 10th edn, 1999), at pp 380–381.

presumption of undue influence and it is for the other party to produce evidence to counter the inference which otherwise should be drawn.

1.38 There are thus two prerequisites to the burden of proof shifting to the other party. First, that trust and confidence was placed in the other party, or that party was in a position of dominance or control. Secondly, that the transaction is not readily explicable by the relationship of the parties. The mere existence of influence is not enough, but it is not essential that the transaction should be disadvantageous to the pressurised or influenced person, either in financial terms or in any other way.[23] However, questions of undue influence will not usually arise where the transaction is innocuous.[24]

Legal background

Historical

Parens patriae

1.39 Until 1959, the High Court and its predecessors had jurisdiction over the lives of incompetent adults pursuant to the rights of the Crown, known as the Royal Prerogative or parens patriae jurisdiction which was given statutory recognition in 1339.[25] In practice this meant state involvement in the financial affairs of the mentally incapacitated citizen and there was no equivalent of the modern welfare state or social services. The Mental Health Act 1959 abolished the delegation of the Royal Prerogative in respect of adults and established a completely statutory jurisdiction but, although this was not realised at the time, it deprived the courts of jurisdiction over personal welfare and health care decisions other than in the context of treatment for mental disorder. This became apparent after it was held that the statutory jurisdiction of the Court of Protection only extended to financial affairs.[26]

The declaratory jurisdiction

1.40 Nevertheless, the High Court found it necessary to facilitate decisions in extreme cases for incompetent adults (ie, where the individual lacked capacity) and did so by making *declarations* as to best interests, relying on its inherent jurisdiction. This was initially in respect of serious health care decisions[27] but subsequently this remedy was extended to personal welfare decisions. In 1995, Mrs Justice Hale not only applied the procedure to a personal welfare

---

[23] The label 'manifest disadvantage' adopted by Lord Scarman in *Morgan's Case* [1985] 1 All ER 821 can give rise to misunderstanding and should no longer be adopted – see the judgment of Lord Nicholls in *Bank of Scotland plc v Etridge (No 2)* [2001] UKHL 44, [2001] 4 All ER 430.

[24] *CIBC Mortgages plc v Pitt* [1993] 4 All ER 433, [1994] 1 AC 200, HL.

[25] Statute de Prerogativa Regis, 17 Edw II (1339) St I cc 9, 10. The earliest reference is to be found in a semi-official tract known as the *De Praerogativa Regis* ('On the King's Prerogative') dating from the reign of Edward 1 (1272–1307).

[26] *Re W* [1971] Ch 123; [1970] 2 All ER 502.

[27] This power was first recognised by the House of Lords in *F v West Berkshire Health Authority* [1989] 2 All ER 545 and confirmed in *Airedale NHS Trust v Bland* [1993] AC 789. See generally Chapter 5.

decision[28] but also backed it up with an injunction and this was upheld by the Court of Appeal.[29] In that same year the High Court held that the court had jurisdiction to grant a declaration that a child with cerebral palsy and learning difficulties was upon attaining majority entitled to choose where to live and with whom to associate, and to restrain the parents by injunction from interfering.[30] However, it should be noted that the making of a declaration or an injunction is a discretionary remedy and this procedure is inordinately expensive and scarcely available for everyday situations even though these do arise.

1.41 More recently the High Court has extended this power beyond incompetent adults to those who were vulnerable for other reasons. Thus it has been stated:[31]

> '... there is no doubt that the court has jurisdiction to grant whatever relief in declaratory form is necessary to safeguard and promote the vulnerable adult's welfare and interests.'

and subsequently:[32]

> '... the inherent jurisdiction remains alive, in appropriate cases, to meet circumstances unmet by the scope of the legislation'

So, the inherent jurisdiction continues notwithstanding that the Mental Capacity Act 2005 now provides a statutory decision-making jurisdiction for those who lack capacity according to the criteria specified in the Act.[33]

Terminology

1.42 Even if there was no need for decisions to be made on behalf of those who lacked capacity, it was necessary for the courts to decide whether decisions could be made by the individual or whether those purported to have been made were effective. There was confusion in the legal terms found in statutes and law reports well into the twentieth century which pointed to a general condition but did not assist in determining the specific implications. Undefined and

---

[28] *Re S (Adult Patient: Jurisdiction)* [1995] 1 FLR 302. An injunction was granted to stop the wife of an elderly, infirm man taking him abroad out of the care of his mistress.

[29] *Re S (Hospital Patient: Court's Jurisdiction)* [1996] Fam 1, [1995] 1 FLR 1075.

[30] *Re V (Declaration against Parents)* [1995] 2 FLR 1003, Johnson J.

[31] *Re PS* [2007] EWHC 623 (Fam), [2007] 2 FLR 1083, Munby J at para 13.

[32] *KC and Anor v City of Westminster Social and Community Services Department and Anor* [2008] EWCA Civ 198, [2009] Fam 11, Roderic Wood J at para 56.

[33] For a contrary view see Macur J in *LBL v RYJ and VJ* [2010] EWHC 2665 (COP): 'I reject what appears to have been the initial contention of this local authority that the inherent jurisdiction of the court may be used in the case of a capacitous adult to impose a decision upon him/her whether as to welfare or finance ... the relevant case law establishes the ability of the court, via its inherent jurisdiction, to facilitate the process of unencumbered decision-making by those who they have determined have capacity free of external pressure or physical restraint in making those decisions.' But, see now Chapter 10.

stigmatising phrases such as 'of unsound mind',[34] 'mentally defective' and 'mentally disordered' were sometimes used with little attempt to define or assess the implications in any particular case. These terms reflected the period when used rather than the interpretation that should now be placed on the words chosen.

Incapacity

1.43 Lawyers too frequently failed to distinguish mental illness, mental handicap (now known as learning disability) and brain injury or to realise that although any of these conditions may result in lack of mental capacity they did not inevitably do so. Their approach tended to concentrate upon the nature of the condition rather than its effect on the individual. Unless a status test applied lawyers relied on doctors to assess capacity and little guidance was given as to the specific test to be applied. An 'all or nothing' approach tended to be adopted rather than asking whether the individual was capable of making the particular decision in question. Thus there were people who were without doubt capable and those who clearly lacked capacity, but between these extremes was a grey area for the most part avoided by lawyers.

Legislation

Mental Health Acts

1.44 The Lunacy Act 1890 gave various powers to the Office of the Master in Lunacy (which was not renamed the Court of Protection until 1947) and these were the basis of the provisions contained in the Mental Health Act 1983, Part VII.[35] This former Court of Protection had powers over the property and affairs of an individual who was 'incapable, by reason of mental disorder, of managing and administering his property and affairs' but this was interpreted as relating to financial affairs only. Usually someone would be appointed as a *receiver* to handle those affairs under the supervision of the court, but a *short order* was available for small or straightforward cases.

Enduring Powers of Attorney Act 1985

1.45 Demand for a less expensive and simpler procedure of choice[36] coupled with the inability of the Court of Protection to cope with the financial affairs of all mentally incapacitated persons resulted in recommendations by the Law Commission in 1983[37] and the passing of the Enduring Powers of Attorney Act 1985. This overcame the problem with ordinary powers of attorney that they were revoked by the subsequent mental incapacity of the donor[38] under normal agency principles. Some formality was introduced into the

---

[34] This phrase is defined in the Trustee Act 1925 as 'incapable from infirmity of mind of managing his own affairs'. Typical of the 1925 property legislation this has stood the test of time.

[35] These largely re-enact the Mental Health Act 1959, Part VIII.

[36] Ie the choice of the person whose affairs are to be dealt with.

[37] *The Incapacitated Principal*, Law Com No 122, Cmnd 8977 (HMSO, 1983).

[38] Ie the person who granted the power.

documentation and an application had to be made to the Public Guardianship Office for the power to be registered with the Court of Protection upon the donor becoming mentally incapable but there was no supervision although the court had power to intervene.

1.46 Enduring powers have proved to be a great success but they have their limitations (only financial decisions can be dealt with in this way) and leave considerable scope for financial abuse. In terms of numbers they far surpassed receivership orders. The development of enduring powers into lasting powers dealing with a wider range of decision-making is considered in Chapter 3, but enduring powers that existed in October 2007 when the new jurisdiction was introduced remain valid under the former principles.

THE NEW CLIMATE

The social climate

General

1.47 There is now a new social and legal climate that emphasises personal autonomy, favours community care and disapproves of discrimination in any form. It should not be overlooked that those who lack mental capacity frequently have other physical or mental impairments as well, so the combined implications of mental and physical disabilities have to be considered.

Community care

1.48 New community care policies were introduced in 1993. There are many facets to community care, but of particular relevance to disabled people are the requirement for their needs to be assessed, the duty placed upon the social services departments of local authorities (subject to available funding) to ensure that these needs are met rather than expecting the individual to cope with whatever services are available and the move away from institutional care to care in the community. The consequence is that people with disabilities are more visible in society and both they and their family/carers have greater expectations as to how they will be treated. Their rights are increasingly being recognised and enforced, by others if not by themselves.

Discrimination

1.49 Discrimination is not always intentional. It may be due to pure ignorance or mere thoughtlessness (ie treating people in an insensitive way) but stereotyping and prejudice also give rise to discrimination. Unwitting or unconscious prejudice – demonstrating prejudice without realising it – is difficult to tackle. Ignorance of the cultures, beliefs and disadvantages of others encourages prejudices and these are best dispelled by greater awareness. For people with disabilities it is not just a question of avoiding these forms of discrimination because any special needs also have to be addressed. Providing equal treatment may involve different treatment so as to ensure equal opportunity.

1.50 Discrimination takes many forms: it may be actual or perceived and it may be direct or indirect. *Direct* discrimination occurs where a person is treated less favourably on grounds of race, colour, religion, gender, ethnic or national origin or disability than others would be in similar circumstance. *Indirect* discrimination occurs where a requirement is applied equally to all groups, but has a disproportionate effect on the members of one group because a considerably smaller number of members of that group can comply with it.

1.51 Discrimination may also be found in an entire organisation through its processes, attitudes and behaviour.[39] A culture of prejudice may have grown up within an organisation which is seen as acceptable by those involved and results in unquestioning behaviour that disadvantages a section of the community.[40] If this arises in the legal system or in any environment it should be addressed in an appropriate way.

1.52 Discrimination in any form is now disapproved of as it means being treated unfairly or denied opportunities. It should be avoided even if not intended. Indirect discrimination should not be tolerated unless it can be objectively justified by a legitimate aim and the means of achieving that aim are appropriate and necessary. Even if there is no discrimination, every effort should be made to avoid the perception that there has been.

Attitudes to disability

1.53 Attitudes to disability in general have also changed in three significant respects:

(1) We have moved away from the medical model of disability which concentrates on the limitations of the individual to a social model which identifies the barriers created in society. Thus lack of access to a building is not seen as being due to the fact that the individual is a wheelchair user but rather that the building has been constructed with steps but no ramp. In other words, don't blame the individual but blame the way society is structured. It is the barriers that should be removed (or not put there in the first place) rather than the individual that should be given special treatment.

(2) Stereotyping has been recognised as the most significant form of discrimination that affects people with disabilities. This is exhibited in the unjustified assumption that people who meet particular criteria will behave in a particular way. In other words, we must be careful not to

---

[39] This was one of the conclusions of *The Stephen Lawrence Inquiry – Report by Sir William Macpherson*, Cmnd 4264-1 (1999). 'Institutional racism' was identified in the police force.

[40] Eg failure to provide assistance to wheelchair users or to communicate in a friendly manner with people from ethnic minorities.

apply labels to people, often unconsciously, and then make assumptions based thereon. People who have a specific condition should not all be assumed to have the same limitations or approach to life – they should be treated as 'people first' rather than identified by their perceived disability.

(3)   There is a greater awareness of mental health problems and arguably less social stigma involved although it is still prevalent in certain sections of the community.[41] There are many myths about people with mental health problems, in particular that they are dangerous and violent, can't work and are incapable of making their own decisions. Contrary to popular belief, mental health problems are not rare and unusual. However, there remains a tension, reflected in the debate about reform of the Mental Health Act, between the need to protect society and the best interests of the individual. Society and politicians, fuelled by the media, still tend to be obsessed with those few cases where the individual has become a public danger when in the vast majority of cases any risk is purely to the individual.

Terminology

1.54 How we refer to people is important. Use of inappropriate terms can cause great offence to the individual and also demonstrates prejudicial attitudes towards disabled people. Also, if we attach labels to people there is a danger that we then use these, however inadvertently, to take away their rights by making assumptions that are not in fact justified. Comparisons should never be made with 'normal'[42] and we should avoid referring to 'the disabled' or 'the handicapped' as if these are a class of person.[43] Terminology that suggests a value judgment should also be avoided.[44] One of the difficulties is that defined medical or legal terms have over the years tended to become used in a derogatory manner[45] and then new neutral terms have to be found. Thus 'mental handicap' has been replaced by 'learning disability' and efforts are being made to find a new term for 'mentally ill'.[46]

1.55 Use of appropriate terminology is not just political correctness but is also an attitude of mind: we should recognise the person rather than any disability. Organisations such as People First[47] prefer that we state 'people with disabilities' for this reason. More recently the Disability Rights Commission

---

[41]   Stigma arises from negative stereotypes associated with the symptoms or diagnosis of mental health problems.

[42]   Instead refer to non-disabled or able bodied.

[43]   These terms are grammatically incorrect! Similarly 'the blind' or 'the deaf' – instead use 'people with impaired sight' or 'people with impaired hearing'.

[44]   Eg referring to someone as 'a victim of ...', 'suffering from ...', 'afflicted by ...' or 'wheelchair bound'.

[45]   Eg the terms *idiot, imbecile, lunatic, cretin, moron*, all of which have appeared in earlier legislation or medical textbooks. The Mental Deficiency Act 1913 used the defined terms 'idiot' and 'imbecile'.

[46]   MIND, the national organisation, tends to use 'people who experience mental distress' or 'people with mental health problems' but at one time the expression 'mentally challenged' was advocated.

[47]   There are many People First Groups – see www.peoplefirstltd.com.

opted for 'disabled people' because this emphasises that the individual is disabled by society (the social model of disability).[48]

Attitudes of minority ethnic communities

1.56 It has become apparent that some minority ethnic communities have a distrust of mental health authorities, try to deal with problems within the family and viewed the former Public Guardianship Office as 'interfering'. It is essential that our new mental capacity jurisdiction reaches out to such communities and recognises cultural norms. The problems that are faced may be illustrated by reference to two communities.

1.57 Asian communities in the UK have tended to be young, with the men mainly working and in consequence controlling the finances. This is changing as they move into the second and third generation, and as members become older more are presenting with senile dementia. There is a stigma associated with mental health problems which tend to be concealed with a consequent delay in accessing services. Many unwritten transactions take place within the community so incapacity issues are not being faced up to. There is a need to raise awareness of the legal position because families react with disbelief when told that they have no authority over the finances of an incapacitated member.

1.58 The Jewish community ranges across a religious spectrum from liberal to ultra-orthodox and increased numbers come from a range of racial groups, mainly Asian and African. They generally live in urban areas situated around local and regional centres close to religious, education and cultural venues. Some are assimilated into the general community but others lead segregated lives. Parents tend to request the continuation of a Jewish life and value base for their children, of whom they have high expectations. Jews have a different experience, both historically and culturally, from the mainstream population. They would define themselves as an ethnic minority and carry a shared past and present experience of persecution and discrimination.

National statistics tend to show a higher than average incidence of mental health problems in the Jewish community, especially in students and young people. This is coupled with a lack of knowledge and awareness of mental health issues and a feeling of stigma within families who have difficulty in accepting problems. In consequence these are often concealed and not regularly acknowledged as a Jewish issue. There are a large number of Jewish social care agencies and care tends to be segregated in the Jewish community with culturally specific services – kosher food, prayer facilities and religious activities.

---

[48] The Disability Rights Commission has now become part of the Equality and Human Rights Commission. The website is www.equalityhumanrights.com.

Role of the law

1.59 People with disabilities are vulnerable to neglect, abuse and exploitation and may need support, protection and empowerment.

Support

1.60 There have traditionally been three sources of support, all regulated by the law:

(1) DWP – the Department for Work and Pensions,[49] which through the *Benefits Agency* provided state benefits, generally on a weekly basis. These may be contributory, non-contributory[50] or a means-tested top-up to ensure that everybody has a minimum income to meet their requirements.[51] The Benefits Agency has since been replaced by *Job Centre Plus* (for adults of working age), the *Disability and Carers Service* (for disability-related benefits) and the *Pensions Service* (for people over pension age);

(2) SSD – the social services departments of local authorities,[52] which are responsible for providing or arranging community care services and services for disabled persons. These must generally be paid for, subject to a means test;

(3) NHS – the National Health Service which, largely now through NHS Trusts, provides free hospital and nursing care and general medical services.[53]

1.61 The respective roles of these providers are changing and overlapping, with social services applying means tests which may take away state benefit yet now providing cash to pay for services, whilst state benefits are withdrawn from those in 'hospital'.[54] In some areas, Care Trusts provide both health and social care services, particularly mental health and learning disability services and care for older people.

Protection

1.62 The law must also ensure protection and has done so by providing a representative in the form of an *appropriate adult* for police interviews and a *statutory guardian* or *nearest relative* for Mental Health Act functions. The authorities should investigate and intervene where there is a suspicion of abuse

---

[49] Formerly known as the Department of Social Security (DSS), and previously the Department of Health and Social Security (DHSS).

[50] For example, disability benefits. Contributory benefits are generally for earnings replacement, eg, retirement pension and incapacity benefit.

[51] Often referred to as 'welfare benefits'.

[52] Not all local authorities have such departments and reference is often now made to 'local authorities with social services responsibilities'.

[53] Older readers will remember the DHSS, when health and social security came within the same government department.

[54] The definition of 'hospital' for benefits purposes is wider than the generally recognised meaning.

but their powers are limited at present when compared with those under the Children Act 1989 and there is no duty to act – which means that often they do not do so despite conflict or perceived abuse. Some local authorities have set up adult protection procedures under the *No Secrets* guidance.[55]

Empowerment

1.63 Empowerment means enabling individuals to take decisions for which they are competent. There must be a proper assessment of capacity and any communication difficulties should be overcome. A suitable person should be empowered to take decisions for individuals who are not competent. At present we have a number of potential representatives but coverage is not comprehensive.

Problems

1.64 There have been four significant problems in the provision of services and in our present law and procedures:

(1) A lack of adequate public funding to cover the needs of disabled people and a lack of ring-fencing of the funds that could be available.

(2) Buck-passing between the DWP, local authorities and health authorities with the disabled individual becoming a pawn in the funding game, and money that could have been expended on unquestionable needs being wasted on the argument over which funder must provide. Many appeal decisions have sought to define responsibilities but to some extent the problem has been alleviated by the introduction of joint commissioning of services by health and social services.

(3) The delicate balance between protection and empowerment, because protection involves taking away the personal autonomy it is desired to preserve. This dilemma is frequently encountered when dealing with vulnerable persons and is especially apparent when seeking to identify the best interests of an incapacitated individual.

(4) No adequate legally authorised representative in many situations because of the piecemeal nature of our legal system, in particular the lack of procedures for personal and medical decision-making.

The new jurisdiction introduced by the Mental Capacity Act 2005 has addressed the third and fourth of these problems and assists family and carers to address the second, but will not assist where there is inadequate funding for care needs.

---

[55] Department of Health and Home Office 'No secrets: guidance on developing and implementing multi-agency policies and procedures to protect vulnerable adults from abuse', 20 March 2000. Available on the website at www.dh.gov.uk.

Role of lawyers

1.65 Lawyers have developed considerable skills in negotiating on behalf of, and promoting the rights of, individuals who for one reason or another are at a disadvantage in looking after their own interests. The lawyer can also act as a whistle-blower to draw attention to situations where the rights of a vulnerable person are being overlooked or abuse is taking place.

Who is the client?

1.66 It is essential for any adviser in these situations to start by identifying the client. The identity of the client does not change just because of communication difficulties or even lack of capacity. Undue reliance should not be placed on relatives or carers in identifying the wishes of the client especially where these persons may be affected by the outcome of any decision. Any potential conflicts of interest should be identified at an early stage and if appropriate independent legal advice recommended either for the would-be client or for the relatives or carers.

1.67 A solicitor receiving instructions from a third party on behalf of an individual who is or may become mentally incapacitated should at all times remember that this individual is the client, not the third party. This is so even if the third party has legal authority to represent the individual, whether as deputy appointed by the Court of Protection, attorney acting under a registered enduring power of attorney or donee of a lasting power of attorney. The third party is merely an agent with a duty to act in the best interests of the incapacitated principal, and any solicitor who accepts instructions shares this duty even if it brings them into conflict with the agent through whom they receive instructions.

The legal climate

General

1.68 Driven by these social forces the legal climate has changed too over the past decade. Lawyers and the courts are having to cope with the needs of infirm elderly and disabled people. Some practitioners concentrate upon this aspect of legal practice and have developed considerable expertise. There have also been significant legislative initiatives which provide the basis for the growth of legal activity and a wide range of new outcomes from the courts.

Legal publishing

1.69 A new approach to legal publishing and the practice of the law was also developing. In July 1992 *Mental Handicap and the Law*[56] was published with the aim of addressing the needs of people with learning disabilities and their families and carers. This was followed by further books by the same author

---

[56] G Ashton and AD Ward *Mental Handicap and the Law* (Sweet & Maxwell, 1992).

relating to elderly people[57] which represented a radical new approach to the law based on the needs of client groups rather than the coverage of legal topics as hitherto favoured by practitioners, authors and academics.

Elderly client practices

1.70 With the encouragement of the Law Society, solicitors have developed 'elderly client practices' providing a full range of services targeting the needs of older clients that go beyond the traditional wills, tax planning and enduring powers of attorney.[58] These developments have resulted in a wider range of legal services being available to the public thereby increasing expectations and creating a greater awareness of the weaknesses of our existing legal system in regard to incapacitated people.

Community Care

Background

1.71 Care in the community is not a new concept. For many it had been the reality for years, but meant living alone or being cared for by family with little support from the state in an indifferent society. The need became apparent to reduce institutional care and provide alternative services in a community setting, and increasing pressure from concerned people and organisations to recognise the rights and freedoms of people who need care or support found expression in policies which have become known as *community care*.

1.72 It was also recognised that this meant more than just the provision of a home in the community for former hospital patients: a whole range of support and services had to be provided for all persons needing care, including those already living in their own family homes. The emphasis should be upon enabling them to remain in their own homes or otherwise in the community when they, their family and friends could no longer cope without support. In the absence of a suitable range of services the only alternative had been long-term care in a residential home or hospital.

Reports

1.73 In 1986 the Audit Commission carried out a review of community-based care services and identified many problems which needed to be tackled. Resources, staffing and training were all directed towards the more institutional forms of care, organisation was fragmented and there was a lack of effective joint working and planning between the different agencies involved in the provision of services. The Commission regarded community care as providing

---

[57] C Bielanska and M Terrell (general eds), G Ashton (consultant ed) *The Elderly Client Handbook* (The Law Society, 1994; 4th edn, 2010); G Ashton *Elderly People and the Law* (1995; 2nd edn Jordans, 2014 by G Ashton and C Bielanska). Further books have followed by other authors.

[58] First advocated by this author at the Annual Conference of the Law Society in 1992. A new professional body, Solicitors for the Elderly Limited (SFE), now has 1,500 members, runs conferences and has a website at www.solicitorsfortheelderly.com.

clients with a full range of services, and a wide range of options; bringing services to people, rather than people to services; the adjustment of services to meet the needs of people, rather than the adjustment of people to meet the needs of services.[59]

1.74 A further review, *Community Care: Agenda for Action*, was published in 1988.[60] It acknowledged the need to promote 'the provision of services to individuals, developed from a multi-disciplinary assessment of their needs and made with proper participation of the individuals concerned, their families and other carers'. This was followed in 1989 by the publication of a White Paper *Caring for People: Community Care in the Next Decade and Beyond* in which it was stated:

> 'Community care means providing the services and support which people who are affected by problems of ageing, mental illness, mental handicap or physical or sensory disability need to be able to live as independently as possible in their own homes, or in homely settings in the community.'

1.75 Since the introduction of the new community care policies further changes have been implemented within social services and the NHS.[61] There have been many consultation papers and policy initiatives reflecting the need for fundamental change in the provision and funding of services. It has been recognised that people want greater control and choice over the services and support they receive and this has led to the introduction of direct payments and personal budgets. Following consultation two Green Papers were published: *Shaping the Future of Care Together* (Cm7673) and *Paying for Care in Wales*, identifying the need to provide early intervention or prevention services to avoid the need for more intensive care.[62]

Legislation

1.76 Although the legislation seen as introducing community care policies and procedures is the National Health Service and Community Care Act 1990, this devotes only nine sections[63] to the topic in England. The Act does not create new rights to new services, and although it imposes a new duty upon local authorities to assess anyone who appears to them to need a community care service which they may provide, it relied heavily on the following earlier legislation some of which had existed for many years:

- National Assistance Act 1948, Part III;
- Health Services and Public Health Act 1968;
- Chronically Sick and Disabled Persons Act 1970;

---

[59] Audit Commission Report *Making a Reality of Community Care* (1986).
[60] Report to the Secretary of State for Social Services by Sir Roy Griffiths (the *Griffiths Report*).
[61] See in particular the White Paper *Modernising Social Services* 1998, *The NHS Plan* (Cmd 4818-I) July 2000 and subsequent reports.
[62] The DoH White Paper *Building the National Care Service* (Cm7854) 2010 promoted joined up services with a national and portable needs assessment.
[63] See National Health Service and Community Care Act 1990, Part III.

- Housing Act 1985;
- National Health Service Act 1977;
- Disabled Persons Act 1981;
- Mental Health Act 1983;
- Health and Social Services and Social Security Adjudications Act 1983;[64] and
- Disabled Persons (Services Consultation and Representation) Act 1986.

1.77 The 1990 Act extended the role of local authorities in the provision of residential accommodation and welfare services, enabling them to make agency arrangements with other organisations and persons whilst restricting their powers to provide accommodation. It amended the provisions as to charges for residential accommodation and other community care services and dealt with recovery of such charges. Local authorities were required following consultation with health and housing authorities to prepare and publish a community care plan. They had to assess the care needs of any person who might appear to them to require community care services and decide what services needed to be provided. Disabled individuals were given a right to an assessment. Further provisions dealt with the inspection of certain premises used for community care services, access to information and the transfer of staff from health authorities to local authorities. Finally, local authorities had to provide a complaints procedure and comply with directions from the Secretary of State in carrying out their social services functions failing which default powers became available.

1.78 Further legislation has followed and this has proved a prolific area for litigation with many appeal cases contributing to the implementation of the policy. In particular the following legislation should be considered:[65]

- Carers (Recognition and Services) Act 1995;
- Housing Act 1996 Part VII (replacing the 1985 Act);
- Health Act 1999;
- Carers and Disabled Children Act 2000;
- Care Standards Act 2000 (to be replaced);
- Health and Social Care Act 2001, Part 4;
- National Health Service Reform and Health Care Professions Act 2002 Part 1;
- Community Care (Delayed Discharge, etc.) Act 2003;
- Carers (Equal Opportunities) Act 2004;
- National Health Service Act 2006;
- National Health Service (Wales) Act 2006;

---

[64] Known as the HASSASSA Act.
[65] For a useful introduction to this complex area see C Bielanska and M Terrell (general eds), GR Ashton (consultant ed) *The Elderly Client Handbook* (The Law Society, 1994; 4th edn, 2010).

- Work and Families Act 2006;
- Safeguarding Vulnerable Groups Act 2006;
- Health and Social Care Act 2008;
- Autism Act 2009;
- Health Act 2009;
- Personal Care at Home Act 2010.

Circulars and directions

1.79 The legislation is supplemented by government guidance and circulars, and by directions issued by the Secretary of State. A local authority may only be obliged to take account of advice contained in circulars and having done so may not be under a duty to comply,[66] though where an appeal to the Secretary of State is provided for it may be expected that he or she will follow his or her own advice. The policy documents of a local authority (including its community care plan) should reflect any directions and guidance in circulars and these are likely to be quoted in court proceedings and could form the basis for a legal challenge of an authority's action or inaction. The Secretary of State is empowered to issue directions to local authorities in regard to the exercise of their social services functions, and these must be observed with the sanction being the use of default powers.

Equality and discrimination

Background

1.80 People with impaired capacity are particularly susceptible to discrimination on account of their age or disabilities. During recent years certain forms of discrimination have been made unlawful and statutory remedies provided for a breach, more recently fuelled by European Directives. Standards have been set in these areas and enforced through the courts and tribunals. Failure to comply could lead to an expensive lesson but, whilst a few test cases achieved a high profile, discrimination remained rife in society without effective sanction. Article 14 of the European Convention on Human Rights, now part of UK law,[67] is particularly relevant because it provides:

> 'Prohibition of discrimination: the enjoyment of the rights and freedoms set forth in this Convention shall be secured without discrimination on any ground such as sex, race, colour, language, religion, political or other opinion, national or social origin, association with a national minority, property, birth or other status.'

This provision is not, however, freestanding and has to be joined to other Articles.

---

[66] Local Authority Social Services Act 1970, s 7. In this respect there may be a difference between general guidance and a direction, but the other view is that guidance is instruction that must be followed – see *R v North Yorkshire CC, ex p Hargreaves* (1994) *The Times*, 9 November.

[67] Under the Human Rights Act 1998.

1.81 Until recently we had a plethora of inconsistent yet overlapping legislation dealing with substantive law on discrimination.[68] The Equality Act 2006 established from October 2007 a new *Equality and Human Rights Commission* (EHRC)[69] which merged the three existing commissions.[70] The EHRC can tackle prejudice based on race, gender and sexual orientation and disability as well as human rights, and has wide powers to enforce legislation.

In February 2005, the Government set up the Discrimination Law Review to address long-term concerns about inconsistencies in the current discrimination law framework, and this was followed by consultation[71] and further papers.

Equality Act 2010

1.82 The outcome is this Act whose purpose is to harmonise discrimination law and strengthen the law to support progress on equality. It brings together and re-states all the existing anti-discrimination legislation and a number of other related provisions and most provisions were brought into effect from October 2010. It also extends the categories by identifying the following 'protected characteristics':

- age (section 5)
- disability (sections 6 and 15, and Schedule 1)
- gender reassignment (sections 7 and 16)
- marriage and civil partnership (section 8)
- race (section 9)
- religion or belief (section 10)
- sex (ie gender) (section 11)
- sexual orientation (section 12)

1.83 The definitions are similar to those that applied before,[72] but the application of disability discrimination is brought into line with the other categories. The Act also strengthens the law in a number of areas by:

- placing a new duty on certain public bodies to consider socio-economic disadvantage when making strategic decisions about how to exercise their functions;

---

[68] Sex Discrimination Act 1975, Race Relations Act 1976, Disability Discrimination Act 1995 and Employment Equality (Age) Regulations 2006.

[69] The website is: www.equalityhumanrights.com.

[70] Equal Opportunities Commission, Commission for Racial Equality and Disability Rights Commission.

[71] *A Framework for Fairness – Proposals for a Single Equality Bill for Great Britain* – a consultation paper, June 2007.

[72] The definition of a disabled person is complex but extends to mental impairments and includes an adult who lacks capacity.

- extending the circumstances in which a person is protected against discrimination, harassment or victimisation because of a protected characteristic;
- making it unlawful to discriminate against, harass or victimise a person when (a) providing a service (which includes the provision of goods or facilities), (b) exercising a public function or (c) disposing of (for example, by selling or letting) or managing premises;
- making it unlawful for associations (for example, private clubs) to discriminate against, harass or victimise members, associates or guests.
- requiring taxis, other private hire vehicles, public service vehicles (such as buses) and rail vehicles to be accessible to disabled people and to allow them to travel in reasonable comfort.

1.84 The Act creates a duty on listed public bodies when carrying out their functions and on other persons when carrying out public functions to have due regard to the need to:

- eliminate conduct which the Act prohibits;
- advance equality of opportunity between persons who share a relevant protected characteristic and those who do not; and
- foster good relations between people who share a relevant protected characteristic and people who do not.

Prohibited conduct

1.85 Several forms of conduct are now defined for the purpose of prohibition. Enforcement continues to be through the County Courts (in relation to services and public functions) and employment tribunals (in relation to work and related areas, and equal pay).

Direct discrimination

1.86 This occurs where the reason for a person being treated less favourably than another is a protected characteristic.[73] This definition is broad enough to cover cases where the treatment is because of the victim's association with someone who has that characteristic (for example, is disabled). For age, different treatment that is justified as a proportionate means of meeting a legitimate aim is not direct discrimination. In relation to disability it is not discrimination to treat a disabled person more favourably than a person who is not disabled.

Discrimination arising from disability

1.87 It is discrimination to treat a disabled person unfavourably not because of the person's disability itself but because of something arising from, or in

---

[73] Equality Act 2010, s 13. Thus excluding old people would be discrimination.

consequence of, his or her disability.[74] The perpetrator must know, or reasonably be expected to know, of the disability, and it is possible to justify such treatment if it can be shown to be a proportionate means of achieving a legitimate aim.[75]

Indirect discrimination

1.88 This would occur when a policy which applies in the same way for everybody has an effect which particularly disadvantages people with a protected characteristic.[76] Where a particular group is disadvantaged in this way, a person in that group is indirectly discriminated against if he or she is put at that disadvantage, unless the person applying the policy can justify it. Indirect discrimination can also occur when a policy would put a person at a disadvantage if it were applied and thus acts as a deterrent.[77]

The treatment of the claimant must be compared with that of an actual or a hypothetical person – the comparator – who does not share the same protected characteristic as the claimant but who is (or is assumed to be) in not materially different circumstances from the claimant.

Duty to make adjustments

1.89 Section 20 defines what is meant by the duty to make reasonable adjustments to the 'provision, criterion or practice' whereby things are done.[78] The duty comprises three requirements which apply where a disabled person is placed at a substantial disadvantage in comparison to non-disabled people:

- the first covers changing the way things are done (such as changing a practice);
- the second covers making changes to the built environment (such as providing access to a building); and
- the third covers providing auxiliary aids and services (such as providing special computer software or providing a different service).

For the second requirement, taking steps to avoid the disadvantage would include removing or altering the physical feature where it would be reasonable to do so. For the first and third a reasonable step might include providing information in an accessible format). Except where the Act states otherwise, it would never be reasonable for a person bound by the duty to pass on the costs of complying with it to an individual disabled person.

---

[74] Equality Act 2010, s 15. This would cover the need to have a guide dog.
[75] This is a new provision designed to overcome the problem caused by *London Borough of Lewisham v Malcolm* [2008] UKHL 43 explained above.
[76] Equality Act 2010, s 19. This would cover the need to have a guide dog.
[77] The extension of indirect discrimination to disability is new, coming after consultation following *London Borough of Lewisham v Malcolm* [2008] UKHL 43.
[78] This replaces with some changes provisions in the Disability Discrimination Acts.

1.90 A failure to comply with any one of the reasonable adjustment requirements amounts to discrimination against a disabled person to whom the duty is owed.[79]

Harassment

1.91 There are three types of harassment, but the one which applies to disability and age involves unwanted conduct which is related to the characteristic and has the purpose or effect of creating an intimidating, hostile, degrading humiliating or offensive environment for the complainant or violating the complainant's dignity.[80] There may be a need to balance the right of freedom of expression (as set out in Art 10 of the European Convention on Human Rights) against the right not to be offended in deciding whether a person has been harassed.

Victimisation

1.92 Victimisation takes place where one person treats another badly because he or she in good faith has done a "protected act" or is suspected of having done so or intending to do so.[81] This might include taking or supporting any action taken in relation to any alleged breach of the Act. Only an individual can bring a claim for victimisation and a person is not protected from victimisation where he or she maliciously makes or supports an untrue complaint.

Implications of conduct

1.93 Previous legislation provided some protection from discrimination, harassment and victimisation in the provision of services and the exercise of public functions. However, the protection was not uniform for the different protected characteristics. For example, there was no protection for discrimination on account of age, either in the provision of services or in the exercise of public functions. Section 29 replaces the provisions in previous legislation and extends protection so that it is generally uniform across all the protected characteristics.

It is unlawful to discriminate against or harass a person because of a protected characteristic, or victimise someone when providing services (which includes goods and facilities). The person is protected both when requesting a service and during the course of being provided with a service. It is also unlawful to discriminate against, harass or victimise a person when exercising a public function which does not involve the provision of a service. Examples of such public functions include law enforcement and revenue raising and collection. Public functions which involve the provision of a service, for example, medical treatment on the NHS, are covered by the provisions dealing with services. This

---

[79] Equality Act 2010, s 21. This replaces comparable provisions in the Disability Discrimination Acts.

[80] Equality Act 2010, s 26.

[81] Equality Act 2010, s 27. This is not really a form of discrimination.

section also imposes the s 20 duty to make reasonable adjustments in relation to providing services and exercising public functions.

Premises

1.94 There is protection from discrimination in the disposal and management of premises across all the protected characteristics with the exception of age and marriage and civil partnership, although other provisions may be relied on where they apply.[82] It is unlawful for a person who has the authority to dispose of premises (for example, by selling, letting or subletting a property) to discriminate against or victimise someone else in a number of ways including by offering the premises to them on less favourable terms; by not letting or selling the premises to them or by treating them less favourably. It is also unlawful for a person whose permission is needed to dispose of premises to discriminate against or victimise someone else by withholding that permission.

It is unlawful for a person who manages premises to discriminate against or victimise someone who occupies the property in the way he or she allows the person to use a benefit or facility associated with the property, by evicting the person or by otherwise treating the person unfavourably.

Associations

1.95 It is unlawful for an association to discriminate against, harass or victimise an existing or potential member, or an associate. This means that an association cannot refuse membership to a potential member or grant it on less favourable terms because of a protected characteristic. It does not, however, prevent associations restricting their membership to people who share a protected characteristic.[83] It is also unlawful to discriminate against, harass or victimise existing or potential guests. In particular, an association cannot refuse to invite a person as a guest because of a particular characteristic or invite that person on certain conditions which the association would not apply to other would-be guests. There is also a duty to make reasonable adjustments for disabled members and guests.

1.96 The courts are not exempted from these provisions: they provide legal services and may be in breach of this legislation if they do not take into account the needs of disabled people.[84] The Office of the Public Guardian and the Court of Protection must be fully conversant with these provisions both as regards the manner in which they deal with disabled people and the expectations that they have for incapacitated persons when dealing with their financial, social welfare and health care decisions.

---

[82] Equality Act 2010, ss 32–35. Similar protection was available in the previous legislation.
[83] Equality Act 2010, ss 100–103. Similar protection was available in the previous legislation.
[84] HM Courts Service has already found itself having to admit liability in a claim involving access to the courts for a hearing impaired person.

Human Rights Act 1998

The Convention

1.97   The European Convention on Human Rights[85] (ECHR) is a treaty of the Council of Europe.[86] It was signed in 1950 and ratified by the UK in 1951, which means that under international law the UK became obliged to abide by its terms, although the right of individual petition was only afforded in 1966. But this did not mean that Convention rights could be relied upon in proceedings in our courts. The treaty has subsequently been amended by Protocols which are either mandatory or optional, the latter only binding states that choose to ratify them.

The legislation

1.98   The long title to the Human Rights Act 1998 (HRA 1998) states that it is 'to give further effect to' the Convention rights and it was said to be 'bringing rights home' on the basis that individuals within the UK would be enabled to rely on their rights in their home courts,[87] although the right to bring a case in Strasbourg is not prevented. The Act is a compromise, representing an attempt to incorporate the ECHR into our law whilst still recognising the traditions of the common law and the sovereignty of Parliament. Every new Bill must, when introduced, be supported by a *statement of compatibility* by the Minister responsible.[88]

1.99   Only certain of the rights contained in the ECHR have been designated as 'Convention rights' for the purpose of HRA 1998,[89] but those omitted must no doubt be 'taken into account'. Those of particular relevance in the present context are:

- Article 2 – the right to life, which has implications for the health services and especially decisions as to whether to treat those who would otherwise die.

- Article 3 – the prohibition of inhuman or degrading treatment, which is of particular relevance to the abuse and neglect of vulnerable people.

- Article 5 – the protection of liberty, which may affect detention in a care home or hospital.

- Article 6 – the right to a fair trial, which concerns participation and ensuring an independent and impartial tribunal.

- Article 8 – respect for private and family life, home and correspondence, which extends to bodily integrity, access to information, confidentiality and sexual relations.

---

[85]   The full title is *Convention for the Protection of Human Rights and Fundamental Freedoms*.
[86]   This is a separate organisation from the European Union and now comprises more than 40 member states. For further information see www.coe.int.
[87]   See the White Paper *Bringing Rights Home*, Cm 3782 (1997).
[88]   HRA 1998, s 19.
[89]   HRA 1998, s 1. The text of these Articles is set out in HRA 1998, Sch 1.

- First Protocol, Art 2 – protection of property, which has implications for ownership, access to and control of property.

Some of these are 'absolute' in the sense that they do not include any qualification or allow for any derogation[90] by a ratifying country and others are qualified by some limitation or restriction.[91] Non-discrimination operates within all other rights pursuant to Art 14.[92]

Interpretation

1.100 The courts must interpret our primary and secondary legislation 'so far as it is possible to do so' in a way which is not incompatible with the ECHR whilst not having power to overrule any such legislation.[93] Where this cannot be done a *declaration of incompatibility* may be made[94] and it then becomes a matter for Parliament (which has a fast-track procedure for remedying the incompatibility[95]), although in the meanwhile the legislation must still be applied.[96] So legislation must henceforth be interpreted so as to give effect, if possible, to Convention rights.

1.101 It has been stated that an Act must receive a 'generous and purposive' interpretation to ensure that Convention rights are effective rather than illusory. Techniques may include 'reading down' (choosing between two possible interpretations and opting for the narrower) and 'reading in' (inserting words to make the statute compatible). Strasbourg jurisprudence must be 'taken into account' by our courts and tribunals,[97] which means that decisions of the European Court of Human Rights now become part of our case-law.

1.102 The European Court has recognised that the obligations of states under the ECHR are not limited to refraining from interfering with individual human rights. There is a positive obligation to ensure that one person's rights are protected from violation by another person and this has led to five duties being imposed on states in relation to Convention rights:

(1)   to have a legal framework providing effective protection;

(2)   to prevent breaches;

---

[90]   An exceptional limitation imposed by the ratifying country on a particular right in specified circumstances. It must be in accordance with the law, directed to a 'particular purpose' and 'necessary in a democratic society'.

[91]   This relates to some existing law of the country concerned which is not to be affected.

[92]   A breach of another Convention right does not need to be established, but the circumstances must fall within the ambit of an ECHR provision.

[93]   HRA 1998, s 3.

[94]   HRA 1998, s 4. This power is restricted to the High Court, Court of Appeal and House of Lords and the Crown is entitled to make representations.

[95]   HRA 1998, s 10. This procedure will also be appropriate when a finding of the European Court in proceedings against the UK renders a provision incompatible.

[96]   If subordinate legislation (eg a statutory instrument) is incompatible with Convention rights, and the incompatibility is not required by primary legislation, either the courts will find ways of interpreting it so as to be compatible or will set it aside.

[97]   HRA 1998, s 2(1).

(3) to provide information and advice;

(4) to respond to breaches; and

(5) to provide resources to individuals to prevent breaches.

Remedies

1.103 When a Convention right is found to have been breached (or is about to be breached) the court may grant such relief or remedy, or make such order, within its powers as it considers 'just and appropriate'.[98] The Act does not give additional powers and the normal routes of an appeal or judicial review apply. There can be no claim for damages in respect of a judicial act done in good faith except in the case of a breach of liberty.

New concepts

1.104 It follows that each branch of government (legislature, executive and judicial) is responsible for giving effect to Convention rights when exercising public powers. However, various concepts apply in the interpretation and application of Convention rights which will not be familiar to lawyers brought up on the common law and statute law:

(1) Not only can proceedings be brought against a public authority in relation to Convention rights (the 'vertical' effect), but as the courts are public authorities they must apply Convention rights when adjudicating on proceedings between private individuals (the 'horizontal' effect). So litigants can argue their human rights in the courts and these must be respected.

(2) To some extent the European Court adopts a hands-off approach to the way that individual countries apply Convention rights, although this 'margin of appreciation' has no application to national courts. This reflects the fact that those courts are in a better position to assess the needs and standards of their own society and the national authorities should be deferred to (especially in moral matters and social policy) as long as the whole process is fair and the outcome is true to the Convention.

(3) Where a state interferes with a Convention right, the means ('the limitation') must be balanced against the end ('the permitted purpose') and shown to be necessary. There must be a reasonable relationship between the goal pursued and the means employed. This follows from the fact that any limitation on a Convention right must be in accordance with law and 'necessary in a democratic society',[99] and has become the principle of 'proportionality'.

---

[98] HRA 1998, s 8(1).

[99] A 'democratic society' means a society which is pluralistic and tolerant. The interests of minorities and individuals must be carefully considered.

(4) A 'principle of legality' is derived from the use by the ECHR of the phrases 'in accordance with the law' and 'prescribed by law' and the use of the word 'lawful'. It has been stated to mean:[100]

   (a) the legal basis for any restriction on Convention rights must be identified and established by the domestic law;

   (b) that law must be accessible and not interpreted according to unpublished criteria; and

   (c) the law must be clear to those affected by it so that they can understand it, although it may allow some discretion as long as the limits are clear.

Application to the Court of Protection and Public Guardian

1.105 Not only must the courts apply Convention rights but rather than giving individuals personal rights HRA 1998 imposes a new statutory duty on 'public authorities' not to act in contravention thereof. This term is not defined but a function based test is to be applied. Courts and tribunals are expressly included, as is 'any person certain of whose functions are functions of a public nature' which would include the Public Guardian. It is 'unlawful for a public authority to act in a way which is incompatible with a Convention right'[101] and even a failure to act would be construed as non-compliance. An individual who claims that a public authority has acted in an incompatible way may bring proceedings against that authority either directly or within the context of other proceedings.[102]

1.106 Where the public body determining the civil rights or obligations is not a court or tribunal[103] a two-limbed test is applied: either that body must comply with the right to a fair hearing under ECHR, Art 6 or there must be a right of appeal or review from that body to a court or tribunal which fully complies. The previous right to apply for judicial review is not sufficient because the Administrative Court cannot make findings of fact.[104]

Comment

1.107 People who lack capacity do not lose their human rights, but the rights of others must also be respected. In delivering its services the new jurisdiction must not overlook the human rights of anyone, but there will be many situations when there is a conflict between the rights of those involved, whether it be the incapacitated individual, family members or others. An appropriate balance must then be achieved.

1.108 The ECHR is a living instrument so, unlike the common law where previous decisions of higher courts create precedents, it must be interpreted in

---

[100] K Starmer *European Human Rights Law* (Legal Action Group, 1999), at para 4.29.
[101] HRA 1998, s 6.
[102] HRA 1998, s 7.
[103] For example, a local housing authority, a health authority, social services and probably the Public Guardian.
[104] *W v UK* (1987) 10 EHRR 29, at para 82.

accordance with present-day conditions. This means that what was decided yesterday may be decided differently tomorrow, although this may be a whole generation later. The difficulty lies in determining what the contemporary standards are which merit protection. However, the ECHR is intended to guarantee rights that are practical and effective rather than theoretical and illusory.[105]

Civil Partnership Act 2004

Background

1.109 This legislation reflects more liberal social attitudes. It has become widely accepted that it is both logically and morally indefensible to prevent homosexual couples from access to formal recognition of their relationships and to the 'next of kin' rights and the tax, pension and other advantages that flow from marriage. Encouraging stability in relationships, whether heterosexual or homosexual, should involve the same sorts of protections as come with marriage, and the Civil Partnership Act 2004 (CPA 2004) addresses these issues in considerable detail.

The legislation

1.110 CPA 2004[106] introduces greater recognition for same-sex relationships in England and Wales, Scotland and Northern Ireland by an option of registration as 'civil partners'. A 'civil partnership' is defined as:[107]

> '... a relationship between two people of the same sex ... which is formed when they register as civil partners of each other ...'

It ends only on death, dissolution or annulment. Heterosexual couples are specifically excluded because they have the option of marriage. The general approach is to make detailed provision for the formation and ending of civil partnerships, and for the consequences that flow from them. It deals with these matters by treating civil partners in very much the same way as married couples.

1.111 To create a civil partnership a specific document is required, signed in the presence of each other and of a civil partnership registrar and two witnesses. No religious service is to be used during the registration formalities, and it cannot take place on religious premises. A couple cannot register if one is already married or a civil partner of someone else, nor if either is under 16 or within prohibited degrees of relationship.

1.112 The provisions for court proceedings to end partnerships[108] and as to children and finances in most cases mirror existing provisions for married

---

[105] _Artico v Italy_ A/37 (1980) 3 EHRR 1.
[106] It has 196 sections arranged in 8 Parts and there are 22 Schedules.
[107] CPA 2004, s 1.
[108] Including nullity, presumption of death and separation orders.

couples. In the case of disputes about property either civil partner may apply to the County Court, and the court may make such order with respect to the property as it thinks fit, including an order for sale. Contributions to property improvement if substantial and in money or money's worth are recognised.

1.113 Other amendments align civil partners with married persons, for example, in certain parts of the law relating to housing and tenancies, in domestic violence proceedings[109] and under the Fatal Accidents Act 1976. Interpretation of statutory references to step-relationships (eg stepson, stepmother etc), and the terms 'in-law' (eg brother-in-law and daughter-in-law) are amended to apply in civil partnerships. There are amendments to the sex discrimination, social security, child support and tax credits legislation. Civil partners will have an insurable interest in each other. Implementation involves significant changes in many areas, for example, in court rules, the registration service, training and guidance for employers. CPA 2004 does not address the problems in the legal treatment of those cohabitating without registration by marriage or by civil partnership.

Same sex marriage

1.114 More recent legislation enables a civil same sex marriage for those who desire more than civil partnership.[110]

Incapacity issues

1.115 Civil partnership is not merely a matter of contract but affects status and creates a completely new legal relationship. Clearly this has implications for a mental capacity jurisdiction. The civil partner must be recognised to the same extent as a spouse when decisions are to be made, whether relating to financial matters, personal welfare or health care. Comparable duties and responsibilities may also arise on the part of the civil partner.

1.116 The civil partner must also be afforded the same status as a spouse as regards participation in any of the procedures. This is not as radical as it may seem, because the new social attitudes have already resulted in domestic partners being involved in many situations, and this has included same-sex partners even in the absence of a civil partnership. To this extent there has been a move away from relationships of blood and marriage to de facto relationships. The Adults with Incapacity (Scotland) Act 2000 provided 'next of kin' rights to same-sex partners by including them within the definition of nearest relative whose views must be taken into account,[111] and the equivalent provision under the Mental Capacity Act 2005 includes 'anyone engaged in caring for the person or interested in his welfare' as well as 'anyone named by the person as someone to be consulted on the matter in question or matters of that kind'.[112]

---

[109] Under Family Law Act 1996, Part IV.
[110] Marriage (Same Sex Couples) Act 2013.
[111] Adults with Incapacity (Scotland) Act 2000, ss 1(4)(b) and 87(2).
[112] Mental Capacity Act 2005, s 4(7).

Access to justice

Background

1.117 Any court that seeks to protect and empower those who have mental impairments must set a good example to other courts and tribunals in ensuring equal access to justice, and the establishment of a new Court of Protection was an opportunity to get things right from the start.[113]

A change of culture

1.118 There has been a change of culture in the civil and family courts during the past two decades. Proceedings not only have to be fair, but also have to be seen as fair and it is the view of the public that is relevant rather than that of lawyers. No longer are litigants expected to cope with the court process and denied access to justice if unable to do so. There is an expectation, in a diverse and multi-cultural society, that judges will ensure that there is effective communication with all manner of persons and take into account their personal attributes and beliefs. This is the art of *Judgecraft* on which judges receive training through the Judicial College (formerly the Judicial Studies Board (JSB)).

1.119 An Equal Treatment Advisory Committee of the JSB[114] ensured that all training courses included this topic and produced an *Equal Treatment Bench Book* which is supplied to all judges including tribunal judges.[115] This identifies potential problem areas, offers information and guidance, and then concentrates upon the following areas of particular concern:

(1) minority ethnic communities;

(2) belief systems (different religions);

(3) gender issues;

(4) disability;

(5) children; and

(6) sexual orientation.

The issues of unrepresented parties and social exclusion are also addressed. Equal access to justice is not assured if people are too frightened to attend a hearing or unable to cope when they get there.

---

[113] The Mental Capacity Bill team set the standard for the Department for Constitutional Affairs by producing various documents in easy read format for their stakeholders with learning difficulties prior to Royal Assent. It also worked closely with the Disability Rights Commission and various representative disability groups.

[114] The author of this chapter was a member of that Committee.

[115] This is available on the Judicial College website: www.judiciary.gov.uk/publications/equal-treatment-bench-book.

Discrimination

1.120 There must be no discrimination in the delivery of legal services. A person who cannot cope with the facilities and procedures of the courts and the administration is as entitled to justice as those who have no such difficulty. It is fundamental to the delivery of justice that those involved are able to appear before and communicate with the relevant court or tribunal. It is equally important that judges understand what those who appear before them are endeavouring to say and that they in turn understand what the judge and any advocates are saying and have an adequate opportunity to consider this. Any misunderstanding may impair justice and it is not sufficient to say that this is the failing of the individual who must take the consequences – it is the responsibility of the court to ensure that communication is effective.

1.121 A further development is that those who appear before the courts are no longer expected to cope with whatever facilities happen to be available. The special needs of those with disabilities must be addressed in an effective way both by the administration in regard to the facilities made available and by the judge in the manner in which hearings are conducted. All courts and tribunals must comply with the Equality Act 2010 (formerly the Disability Discrimination Act 1995) and also ensure that the human rights of those who become involved in the justice system are respected.[116]

1.122 It follows that courts and tribunals must be accessible to those who appear before them. This is not merely a question of access to the building or the provision of disabled facilities within the courtroom, but also of proximity and the recent closure of many of the smaller courts makes it difficult for people in those areas to attend a hearing. A judge may, of course, hold a hearing or part of a hearing other than in the normal courtroom.

Unrepresented parties

1.123 Some litigants seek to represent themselves rather than instruct a lawyer[117] and everybody of full age and capacity is entitled to do so. This may be because they cannot afford a solicitor, distrust lawyers or believe that they will be better at putting their case across.

Disadvantages

1.124 Those who do exercise this right find that they are operating in an alien environment because the courts have not traditionally been receptive to their needs:[118]

> 'All too often the litigant in person is regarded as a problem for judges and for the court system rather than a person for whom the system of civil justice exists.'

---

[116] Before the European Convention on Human Rights became enforceable it was the principles of 'natural justice' that were invoked.
[117] Traditionally known as 'litigants in person'.
[118] Lord Woolf *Access to Justice*: Interim Report (June 1995).

They are likely to experience feelings of fear, ignorance, anger, frustration and bewilderment. Their cases will tend to dominate their thoughts and they will feel at a disadvantage. The aim of the judge should be to ensure that the parties leave with the sense that they have been listened to and have had a fair hearing – whatever the outcome.

1.125 Disadvantages stem from a lack of knowledge of the law and court procedure. For many their perception of the court environment will based on what they have seen on the television and in films. They:

- are likely to be unfamiliar with the language and specialist vocabulary of legal proceedings;
- have little knowledge of the procedures involved and find it difficult to apply the rules even if they do read them;
- tend to lack objectivity and emotional distance from their case;
- may not be skilled in advocacy and are unlikely to be able to undertake cross-examination or to test the evidence of an opponent;
- may be confused about the presentation of evidence; and
- are unlikely to understand the relevance of law and regulations to their own problem, or to know how to challenge a decision that they believe to be wrong.

1.126 The aim must be to ensure that unrepresented parties understand what is going on and what is expected of them at all stages of the proceedings. The court is therefore under an obligation to ensure that:

(1) the process is (or has been) explained to them in a manner that they can understand;

(2) they have access to appropriate information through books or websites;

(3) they are informed about what is expected of them in ample time for them to comply; and

(4) wherever possible they are given sufficient time according to their needs.

Personal assistance

1.127 A litigant who cannot arrange legal representation may request that someone be permitted to 'quietly assist' at the hearing (the role of the *McKenzie friend*). The court can refuse this and will do so if the friend is unsuitable.[119] Such assistance is less likely to be needed at a hearing in the Court of Protection because a more informal approach is adopted and the judge is more likely to provide explanations and assistance.

1.128 Alternatively the litigant may request that someone speak for him or her (known as a *lay representative*). There is no right of audience but the court has

---

[119] The 'friend' may be seeking to provide general advocacy services or pursuing a separate agenda the pursuit of which is not in the best interests of the litigant.

a discretion to allow such representation and it may be in the interests of justice to do so.[120] The litigant should normally justify the request and be present in court when personal interests are involved.[121] The doubt about the status of an attorney under a power of attorney has recently been resolved – there is still no right of audience.[122]

Physical and sensory impairments

Hearings

1.129 When it is known that a party or witness has a physical impairment, arrangements should be made for any hearing to take place where there are appropriate facilities.[123] These may extend beyond wheelchair access to the existence of disabled toilets and the loop system for those with hearing impairments. Ideally every regional venue of the Court of Protection will have suitable facilities but if these are inadequate for a particular hearing consideration should be given to conducting the hearing at a more suitable venue. When necessary justice should be taken to those who are unable to come to the court and the examination of a witness or even part of a hearing may take place elsewhere, for example, in a residential care home or mental hospital. A video link may assist where an infirm party cannot travel far.[124]

1.130 It may be appropriate to arrange hearings at particular times, keep them shorter or take more frequent breaks. Allowance should be made for the need to attend a toilet, take medication or otherwise recover concentration. This may result in a longer time estimate for the hearing.

Interpreters

1.131 Interpreters[125] are provided for a party or witness who does not speak the language of the court or has a hearing impairment, and the court must arrange one if the party cannot. Other communication difficulties may need to be addressed in a similar manner.[126] The interpreter should not be simply a relative or friend but needs to be independent and fully conversant with the individual's preferred method of communication. A witness will only need an

---

[120] Advocacy rights may be granted under the Courts and Legal Services Act 1990, s 27(2)(c) – see also Civil Procedure Rules 1998, SI 1998/3132, PD 27, para 3.2; Lay Representatives (Right of Audience) Order 1999, SI 1999/1225.

[121] *Clarkson v Gilbert & Ors* [2000] 2 FLR 839, CA; *Izzo v Phillip Ross & Co* [2002] BPIR 310.

[122] If this is an enduring power of attorney inquiry should be made as to whether it has been registered with the Public Guardianship Office, because if it has the litigant may be a protected party who needs a litigation friend.

[123] Seom guidance is available at www.justice.gov.uk/courts.

[124] The President of the Family Division adopted both these procedures in the *Re B* case when she attended at the hospital and then continued by video-link.

[125] The HMCTS website provides information as to the facilities available at particular courts – www.justice.gov.uk/courts.

[126] The special measures directions introduced by the Youth Justice and Criminal Evidence Act 1999, Part II to assist vulnerable and intimidated witnesses to give evidence in criminal proceedings refer to communicators rather than just language interpreters. These include the use of *intermediaries* and *communication aids*.

interpreter whilst giving evidence but a party may need one before, during and after the hearing. The interpreter should be provided with breaks at regular intervals.

THE (FORMER) COURT OF PROTECTION

Origins of the jurisdiction

1.132 The former Court of Protection existed to protect and manage the property and financial affairs of people in England and Wales (known as 'patients') who were incapable, by reason of mental disorder, of managing and administering their own affairs.[127] The origins of state involvement in the financial affairs of the mentally incapacitated citizen go back a long way.[128] Until 1960 the jurisdiction 'in Lunacy' was in part statutory and in part dependent on the inherent jurisdiction of the court derived from the Royal Prerogative which is often referred to as the parens patriae jurisdiction. Under the Lunacy Act 1890 the jurisdiction relating to the administration and management of patients' affairs was assigned to a Master in Lunacy, who operated under different titles[129] until 1947 when the term Court of Protection was established. The Mental Health Act 1959, Part VIII re-established the Court of Protection and its continuing existence was confirmed by the Mental Health Act 1983, Part VII. Further jurisdiction was conferred on the court by the Enduring Powers of Attorney Act 1985.

1.133 This was not a court as such but an office of the Supreme Court of Judicature (as it then was),[130] although in practice this was of little significance and some High Court judges were nominated to conduct its work. Headed by the Master and situated in London, much of the work was delegated to nominated officers appointed by the Lord Chancellor. The three senior ones adopted the courtesy title of Assistant Master and were given more authority including the conduct of hearings.[131] The Public Guardianship Office provided administrative support for the court and had a staff of several hundred, including those in the Judicial Support Unit who processed formal applications and appeals.

---

[127] Mental Health Act 1983, s 94(2).

[128] The earliest reference is to be found in a semi-official tract known as the *De Praerogativa Regis* ('On the King's Prerogative') dating from the reign of Edward 1 (1272–1307).

[129] Initially the 'Office of the Master in Lunacy' but this was changed to the 'Management and Administration Department' in 1934 (note the abbreviation MAD).

[130] Supreme Court Act 1981, s 1(1) – now the Senior Courts Act 1981.

[131] Mental Health Act 1983, ss 93(4) and 94(1). It is questionable whether and to what extent judicial powers should have been delegated in this way following the Human Rights Act 1998.

Practice and procedure

General

1.134 The procedure of the court was governed by the Court of Protection Rules 2001 (COPR 2001),[132] which were briefly compared with the Civil Procedure Rules 1998 (CPR).[133] Instead of a statement of objectives they started with an Interpretation clause in which reference was made to the Supreme Court Act 1981 for the meaning of expressions used: a 'direction' meant a direction or authority given under the seal of the court and an 'order' included a certificate, direction or authority of the court under the official seal of the court. A 'patient' was a person who was alleged to be or who the court had reason to believe might be 'incapable by reason of mental disorder of managing and administering his property and affairs'.

1.135 Any function of the court could be exercised by a nominated judge of the High Court, the Master or (to the extent authorised) a nominated officer and this might, except where COPR 2001 provided otherwise, be:

(1) without an appointment for a hearing;
(2) by the court of its own motion or at the instance or on the application of a person concerned;
(3) whether or not proceedings have been commenced with respect to the patient.

COPR 2001 then dealt with applications and hearings.

Applications

1.136 Provision was made as to the form of applications, but apart from those for the first appointment of a receiver there was considerable informality and a letter might be sufficient. Hearings were notified by letter and might be dispensed with where it was considered that the application could properly be dealt with without one. Special rules dealt with applications under the Trustee Act 1925, for settlement or a gift of a patient's property and for the execution of a will for a patient.

Short orders

1.137 COPR 2001, r 8 provided that where the property of the patient did not exceed a specified value[134] or it was otherwise considered appropriate, the court might instead of appointing a receiver make a short order or direction which authorised some suitable person to deal with the patient's property or affairs in the manner specified. This power came to be used increasingly where

---

[132] SI 2001/824. This update to the existing Rules was required following the demise of the Public Trust Office and the creation of the Public Guardianship Office from 1 April 2001. The authority for the rules was to be found in Mental Health Act 1983, s 106.
[133] SI 1998/3132.
[134] Latterly £16,000.

it was felt that intrusive supervision was not necessary. Not only might small estates be dealt with in this summary way but, for example, a tenancy could be authorised.

Service

1.138 COPR 2001 specified the persons who should be given notice, who included 'such other persons who appear to the court to be interested as the court may specify'. The mode of service was prescribed and far from antiquated, being personal service, first class post or document exchange and even fax or 'other electronic means'. Service on a solicitor and substituted service were provided for, and service on a person under a disability was to be on the parent or guardian (for a minor) and the receiver, registered attorney or 'person with whom he resides or in whose care he is' (for a patient).

Evidence

1.139 Except where COPR 2001 otherwise provided, evidence was by affidavit.[135] However, the court might accept such oral or written evidence as it considered sufficient even if not on oath. Persons who gave written evidence could be ordered by the court to attend and the oath might then be administered. Any such evidence could be used in other proceedings in the court relating to the same patient and, if authorised by the court, in proceedings in other specified courts.

Hearings

Conduct

1.140 Where appropriate the Master referred matters to a High Court judge who might refer any question back to the Master for inquiry and report.[136] Applications were heard in chambers (ie in private) unless, in the case of an application before a judge, the judge otherwise directed.[137] The Master and Assistant Masters had their own private hearing rooms. The court decided who attended any part of a hearing, although obviously certain persons needed to attend although they might be excluded for part of a hearing. A witness summons could be issued to require a person to attend and give oral evidence or produce any document.

1.141 The court had wide powers to require persons having conduct of proceedings to explain delay or other causes of dissatisfaction and to make orders for expediting proceedings. It could direct any person to make an application or carry out directions and even appoint the Official Solicitor (with his or her consent) to act as solicitor for a patient. There was also a valuable

---

[135] COPR 2001 did not introduce the concept of a statement containing a certificate of truth that now applies under the CPR.

[136] This mirrors the procedure in Chancery and insolvency proceedings in the High Court.

[137] This inevitably means a High Court judge.

power to require a patient to attend at a specified time and place for examination by the Master, a Visitor or any medical practitioner.

Reviews and appeals

1.142 Where a decision was made without an attended hearing, any aggrieved person could apply to have the decision reviewed and if still not satisfied apply for an attended hearing. Appeals from decisions made at attended hearing were heard by High Court judges of the Chancery or Family Division.

Fees and costs

Court fees

1.143 The court charged fees which were usually paid out of the estate of the patient, or by the donor in the case of a registered enduring power of attorney. A policy of full costs recovery applied and the fees were intended to reflect the actual cost of the service provided. There was power to remit or postpone the payment of the whole or part of any fee on grounds of hardship.

Legal costs

1.144 All costs incurred in relation to proceedings were at the discretion of the court, which could order them to be paid out of the estate of the patient (or donor in the case of an enduring power of attorney), or by an applicant, objector or any other person attending or taking part in the proceedings. Unlike proceedings in the civil courts, costs did not automatically follow the event and the court had an unlimited discretion to make whatever order it considered that the justice of the case required. In exercising its discretion the court had regard to all the circumstances of the case, including the relationship between the parties, their conduct, their respective means and the amount of costs involved.

1.145 Where an application was made in good faith, supported by medical evidence, in the best interests of the donor and without any personal motive, the applicant was generally awarded his or her costs, even if unsuccessful. However, in cases where the court considered an objection or application to have been made in bad faith, frivolous, malicious, vexatious or motivated by self-interest, it might order the applicant or objector to pay some or all of the costs. Similarly, where a person placed him- or herself in a hostile position to the donor, or where his or her conduct resulted in the costs of the proceedings being more expensive than they might otherwise have been, the court might consider it appropriate to penalise him or her as to costs.[138]

1.146 There was a range of procedures available to approve the costs including fixed costs, agreed costs and assessment of costs. The costs actually charged by solicitors had to be approved by the court before being paid from

---

[138] *Re Cathcart* [1893] 1 Ch 466.

the funds of a patient and although summary assessment was not allowed the court sometimes ordered the patient to pay a fixed contribution towards the costs of a party.

Venue

Background

1.147 Although in the early days inquisitions took place throughout the country and involved local people who knew the alleged patient, since its creation the Court of Protection sat in London despite having a jurisdiction extending to England and Wales. Following an extensive consultation[139] the Law Commission proposed that a reconstituted Court of Protection with jurisdiction over incapacity matters should have a regional presence, with designated judges throughout the country dealing with hearings locally. After further consultation the Lord Chancellor published the Government's proposals in October 1999 in the Report *Making Decisions* and these included a new Court of Protection with a regional presence. It thus became current policy to make the Court of Protection more accessible to the public by providing it with a regional presence.

1.148 The Court of Protection was not readily accessible to those in the North of England and other parts of the country. The cost to parties of travelling to and staying in London for a hearing was prohibitive and represented a denial of justice to those involved. In addition, solicitors in the provinces were discouraged from gaining 'hands-on' experience of the work of the court by attending hearings and therefore less able to give well-informed advice to their clients. Concerns were also expressed that the Master was the only human rights-compliant judge of the court, as the Assistant Masters did not have a judicial appointment.[140] In consequence it was proposed that even before the implementation of a new mental incapacity jurisdiction a few district judges based at carefully selected locations (eg one on each circuit) should be appointed as Deputy Masters to hear locally cases that were referred to them by the Master.[141]

Regional hearings

1.149 On 1 October 2001 District Judge Ashton was appointed a part-time Deputy Master of the Court of Protection to hear any case where it was more convenient for the parties to attend at Preston in Lancashire. Thereafter the 'Northern Court of Protection' operated as a 'satellite' of the Central Court in London and on certain days in each month hearings took place at Preston

---

[139] This is outlined below. The proposal of a tribunal for some types of case was rejected.

[140] The term Assistant Master was a courtesy title and they were in reality legally qualified civil servants in the Department of Constitutional Affairs who were 'nominated officers' under the Mental Health Act 1983, s 93(4).

[141] Supreme Court Act 1981, s 91 permitted the Lord Chancellor to appoint deputy judges if he considered that it was expedient to do so in order to facilitate the disposal of the business of the court. This has now been renamed the Senior Courts Act 1981.

Combined Court Centre. These were generally contested hearings (mainly disputes over enduring powers of attorney and the choice of receiver) and fund management hearings for large damages awards, but also hearings of applications for gifts, statutory wills and to be discharged from the jurisdiction due to recovery. This link with the civil and family courts led to the cross-fertilisation of ideas and resulted in more local practitioners becoming familiar with the work of this specialised but nonetheless essential jurisdiction. Based on experience at Preston the Court of Protection in London then introduced the recording of hearings, telephone conferences and attendance by video link.

1.150 The selection of venues and judges is crucial to the success of a regionalised Court of Protection. Having a centralised administration with satellite courts raises many problems. To a large extent these were tackled in the Preston pilot and workable solutions devised. Communication by email proved effective and the main problems proved to be access to the case file, uncertainty amongst parties and solicitors as to where to send documents and delay in receiving documents sent at a late stage to the Public Guardianship Office. There was a lack of administrative support because HM Courts Service staff had no involvement with the Public Guardianship Office. Experience showed that these difficulties could be overcome.

An evaluation of the Court of Protection

1.151 The former Court of Protection was the Cinderella of the judicial system, underfunded, unrecognised and only appreciated by those who knew it well. This has changed with generic judges becoming involved, a regional structure and the acquisition of jurisdiction for declarations previously dealt with by the High Court. There is more inter-dependence between the civil and family courts and the Court of Protection now it is no longer restricted to financial affairs.

1.152 How different is the Court of Protection from other courts? Which functions are truly judicial? How many judges should be nominated to the court and where should they be deployed? On what basis should the different levels of the judiciary be allocated cases? What procedural rules are appropriate? How should hearings be conducted and what human rights issues arise? To what extent and in what manner should judgments be reported? What right should individuals have to disclosure of information held about them by the court? What should be the relationship between the new Court of Protection and the Public Guardian? To what extent may the legal profession become involved and who funds the non-money cases? When should cases be publicly funded? These are all questions that had to be faced when the new Court of Protection was set up.

Court Rules

1.153 It will be seen from the above outline that COPR 2001 provided only the most basic structure for the conduct of applications and hearings, and much was left to the discretion of the Master, Deputy Master or Assistant Master dealing with the case. The lack of guidance to practitioners or the parties themselves as to the submission of applications and preparation for or conduct of hearings coupled with no requirement for active case management might be seen as an obstacle to justice. However, the issues that have to be tackled are very different from those in the civil courts, although a parallel may be drawn with proceedings relating to the welfare of children. Whilst a paternalistic approach is acceptable when considering the best interests of children, it must be avoided for adults. A Court of Protection is concerned to identify and safeguard the best interests of incapacitated adults rather than to impose what other persons think is best for them, and will be influenced more by the previous lifestyle and any expressed wishes of the individual. However, the former court only had power to do this through the management and administration of the individual's property and financial affairs.

Contested hearings

1.154 It is only when there is disagreement or conflict resulting in the need for an attended hearing that more prescriptive Rules are required to regulate the conduct of the parties involved. Under the former regime this might arise in the following situations, namely where:

(1)   there was uncertainty as to whether an individual was a patient within the jurisdiction of the court and this had to be resolved;

(2)   there was a dispute as to who should be appointed to act as receiver;

(3)   there was an unresolved challenge to the registration of an enduring power of attorney;

(4)   a receiver or registered attorney was not satisfied with the extent of any authority given or restriction imposed;

(5)   family, carers or other persons concerned with the welfare of the patient were in dispute; or

(6)   an application was made for a statutory will, gift or settlement.

Other hearings

1.155 Attended hearings were also required for the setting of broad policy where substantial compensation had been awarded for brain injury, typically following a clinical negligence claim. The family, who may have been the carers to date and contemplate the continued provision of a care environment, would be anxious to have authoritative guidance as to how they should handle the funding. There might be an enhancement in their own standard of living and judicial approval assuaged any feeling of guilt in a context where earning capacity was otherwise impaired.

1.156 These hearings or 'attendances' were generally friendly and constructive. The Master would look to the heads of loss in the civil claim as pointers to what should be considered but would not seek to impose these on the family. It was more appropriate to concentrate upon what was achievable with the personal and financial resources available whilst keeping an eye on the future when intensive family care may no longer be available. Headings that were discussed included:

(1) the provision of a suitable home and modifications to meet disability needs;

(2) transport (usually a personal vehicle which can accommodate any disability needs);

(3) the monthly personal and household budget;

(4) care provision and funding;

(5) holidays;

(6) disability aids and appliances (including computers); and

(7) the retention by the parents or family carers of a personal stake in the housing market where the shared home is purchased by the patient.

Investment policy then had to be determined for the contingency fund available after the provision of a home, although in some cases there would be an index-linked tax-free annuity for the life of the patient from a structured settlement. This type of support is less frequent under the new jurisdiction because there is more delegation to the deputies appointed by the court, but it could still be provided.

THE PUBLIC GUARDIANSHIP OFFICE

Background[142]

1.157 The former Court of Protection depended heavily upon the support that it received from its administrative arm, the Public Guardianship Office,[143] whose responsibilities extended across the whole of England and Wales.[144] That office supported the court in the same way that HM Courts and Tribunals Service now supports all other courts, but that was only a small part of its functions. The administration also provided services to promote the financial and social well-being of clients who were not able to manage their financial affairs because of mental incapacity (known as 'patients').

1.158 Support was provided for the families and advisers of the incapable person after someone had applied to the Court of Protection to manage that person's financial affairs. When the court had considered the application, it appointed a Receiver, to manage and administer the person's financial affairs whilst they were unable to do so themselves. The administration thus assisted and supported the Receiver in completing his or her duties and worked with the Receiver to promote the best interests of the patient (the 'Protection function').

---

[142] The evolution of the Public Guardianship Office from the former Public Trust Office is more fully described in the 2012 and previous volumes of this work.

[143] Previously the Public Trust Office.

[144] Separate arrangements existed for Scotland and Northern Ireland.

1.159 Sometimes the administration would act as Receiver through a designated official (the 'Receivership function'). This occurred only as a last resort when the Court of Protection could find no one else willing or suitable to become the Receiver. The staff would then be involved on a daily basis in the client's financial and legal affairs. As a result, the administrative arm developed and maintained very close working relationships with its clients, their families, carers and any other people or organisations involved in their welfare.

Other jurisdictions

1.160 There was a difference of approach to the need for and the services provided by a Public Guardian in the separate jurisdictions of the UK and Ireland.

Scotland

1.161 The Adults with Incapacity (Scotland) Act 2000 introduced a new jurisdiction for Scotland. This established with effect from 2 April 2001 a Public Guardian based in Falkirk with supervisory and support functions. She has published a useful range of forms, precedents and guidance notes.[145] There is also a Mental Welfare Commission which was established in 1960 and has been given additional functions under the Act. A 2-year review of the operation of this legislation was commissioned by the Scottish Executive in 2002 and the Report, *Learning from Experience*, was published in the Autumn of 2004. In broad terms the Adults with Incapacity (Scotland) Act 2000 was considered to be meeting its central aims, but there was concern about lack of publicity and knowledge as to how it may benefit incapacitated adults and their carers. This Report resulted in amendments to the Act by the Adult Support and Protection (Scotland) Act 2007. The jurisdiction in Scotland is outlined in Chapter 12.

Northern Ireland

1.162 There is at present no equivalent of a Public Guardian in Northern Ireland. All jurisdiction relating to incapacitated persons is vested in the High Court by virtue of s 28(1) of the Judicature (Northern Ireland) Act 1978 and carried out by the Office of Care and Protection, which is a part of the Family Division of the court. Judicial responsibility lies with the family judge (or another judge assigned by the Lord Chief Justice) and with the Master (Care and Protection). An assessment is presently being made of future needs and the additional functions which might be assigned to a Public Guardian. There is concern about a single organisation being both regulator and provider and a desire to relinquish last resort work. An advocacy service would be welcomed with a cadre of advocates to take on legal representation unless the Official Solicitor was engaged for this. The availability of funding is a crucial issue.

---

[145] These are available on the website: www.publicguardian-scotland.gov.uk.

Ireland

1.163   There is no equivalent of the Public Guardian in the Republic of Ireland and any intervention by the courts is based on the Wardship jurisdiction exercised by the President of the High Court, who has Medical Visitors at his disposal. There is a need for modernising legislation and it is likely that a comprehensive new jurisdiction will be introduced in the foreseeable future. The Office of the General Solicitor for Minors and Wards of Court assists the court.

THE LORD CHANCELLOR'S VISITORS

Historical

1.164   The office of Visitor dates from the Lunatics' Visitors Act 1833, which authorised the Lord Chancellor to appoint two physicians and a barrister to visit patients at least once a year – more often, if necessary – and to superintend, inspect and report on their care and treatment.[146] Under the Lunacy Regulation Act 1853 the Masters in Lunacy became ex officio Visitors.[147] The first Visitors were paid an annual salary, but only worked part-time and were allowed to remain in private practice. The Lunacy Regulation Act 1862 required them to visit on a full-time basis and increased their salary to compensate. Consequently, the post became both lucrative and prestigious and attracted some of the leading psychiatrists of the day.

1.165   Until 1981 all visits to Court of Protection patients were carried out by the Medical and Legal Visitors. The majority of these visits required a combination of social work, public relations and plain common sense, and did not warrant the expense of being made by an eminent psychiatrist or leading counsel. So, with effect from 1 October 1981, the Lord Chancellor created a panel of lay General Visitors, membership of which was initially drawn from the welfare officers in his own department.[148] The Medical Visitors and Legal Visitors subsequently ceased to be full-time employees of the Lord Chancellor's Department, and made their visits on an ad hoc basis. In March 2000 there were six General Visitors, each covering a particular region of England and Wales.

1.166   If the court considered that a patient should be visited for any reason, it sent one of the Lord Chancellor's Visitors and there was a strategy to ensure that visits were carried out in the most suitable cases. The visits were usually

---

[146]   3 & 4 Will IV, c 36. The Act also introduced a system of percentage, whereby patients were required to pay a percentage of their clear annual income to the court, in order to fund the Visitors' salaries. This is the origin of the present fee structure in the Court of Protection.

[147]   This provision could be found in the Mental Health Act 1983, s 103(7). The Master occasionally visited patients in their own home.

[148]   Supreme Court Act 1981, s 144 (now renamed the Senior Courts Act 1981).

carried out at the patient's place of residence, but the Visitors did not have automatic rights of entry and inspection, although anyone who obstructed a visit might commit an offence.[149]

Medical Visitors

1.167 A Medical Visitor had to be a 'registered medical practitioner who appears to the Lord Chancellor to have special knowledge and experience of cases of mental disorder'.[150] There were six and between them they conducted about one hundred visits each year. They were all senior consultant psychiatrists, mostly retired or semi-retired, and some also sat as medical members of Mental Health Review Tribunals. Each Medical Visitor covered a particular region of England and Wales, roughly approximating to the former court Circuits, but there were reserve Visitors who could be called upon when necessary

1.168 The reports by Medical Visitors addressed the particular issues they had been asked to investigate. Their principal function was to assess an individual's:

- capacity to manage and administer their property and financial affairs, either on entry into the jurisdiction or exit from it;
- capacity to create or revoke an enduring power of attorney, which nearly always requires a retrospective assessment; and
- testamentary capacity.

1.169 These visits were only commissioned where other medical evidence was conflicting, unsatisfactory or non-existent. The Medical Visitors also reported on a variety of other matters which the court might wish to consider before taking action, for example, a patient's life expectancy, which might be helpful for setting an investment strategy, or deciding whether an intended lifetime gift was likely to be effective for inheritance tax purposes. Occasionally a medical visit was abortive because the patient either refused to admit the Visitor into his or her home or was no longer available. Nevertheless, even though a visit was abortive, it might still be possible for the court to accept jurisdiction on the basis of the Visitor's examination of the patient's medical records alone. The court had an emergency jurisdiction which enabled it to intervene if it had *reason to believe* that a person may be incapable, by reason of mental disorder, of managing and administering his or her property and affairs, and it was of the opinion that it was *necessary* to make immediate provision in respect of that person's affairs.[151]

General Visitors

1.170 The General Visitors regarded themselves as 'the eyes and the ears of the court, and the voice of the patient'. The purpose of their visits was to enable the

---

[149] Mental Health Act 1983, s 129. This was also a contempt of court.
[150] MHA 1983, s 102(3)(a).
[151] MHA 1983, s 98.

court and the PGO to assess whether a patient's needs were being properly addressed and to alert them to any action needed to bring about improvements. Their reports might cover, for example, how money had actually been expended; the patient's or donor's present wishes and feelings, so far as they were ascertainable, as to who should manage their property and financial affairs during their incapacity; whether a proposed course of action was likely to be in a patient's best interests; the suitability of a patient's accommodation; whether a patient required residential care or specialist nursing care.

1.171 Additionally, the Visitors could show patients, receivers and carers that the court and the PGO were interested in their welfare and ready to discuss any particular difficulties or concerns. In most cases they represented the only face-to-face contact a patient or receiver had with the authorities. Occasionally, a General Visitor was asked to carry out a special visit when a particular problem arose. For example:

- where the relationship between a patient and his or her receiver, carers or family was strained or appeared to have broken down completely;

- where a receiver was behaving in a manner or proposing a course of action which the court had reason to believe might not be in the patient's best interests; or

- to assist in resolving some particular difficulty with the court or the PGO, for example, expenditure, accounts or investment strategy.

Enduring powers of attorney

1.172 Although there was provision[152] for the donors of enduring powers of attorney to be visited, in practice they were never visited by the General Visitors.[153] This was principally because the philosophy underlying the Enduring Powers of Attorney Act 1985 was that there should be minimal public intervention in the operation of the enduring powers of attorney scheme.

Confidentiality of reports

1.173 Visitors' reports were confidential: their contents could not be disclosed to anyone unless authorised by the Court of Protection.[154] However, the court might in its discretion allow the report, or part of it, to be disclosed and in that event there was provision for written questions to be submitted. The General Visitors were reluctant to have their reports routinely disclosed because this could inhibit their comments, but one way round this was for them to include an addendum with confidential comments which would not be disclosed. Some

---

[152] Enduring Powers of Attorney Act 1985, s 10(1)(a) and (2).
[153] The donor of an enduring power of attorney might be visited by a Medical Visitors when there was a conflict of evidence as to whether the donor had the capacity to create or revoke an enduring power, or whether an application to register the power was premature.
[154] MHA 1983, s 103(8). Any unauthorised disclosure is an offence. This goes further than the rules in relation to reports by CAFCASS (Children and Family Court Advisory and Support Service) Reporters in children cases which may only be disclosed to the parties and their legal advisers.

cases, though not all, held that the principles of natural justice must prevail over the Court of Protection's paternalistic jurisdiction.[155]

THE OFFICIAL SOLICITOR

Background

1.174   The state has for many centuries recognised the need for representation of an incapacitated person when a benevolent relative or friend cannot be found to act on his or her behalf. This function was undertaken on behalf of the Crown as parens patriae in various ways. The development of the functions of the Official Solicitor's office date back to the eighteenth century. The office of the Official Solicitor to the Supreme Court of Judicature was created by an Order of the Lord Chancellor on 6 November 1875 under the power given to him by the Supreme Court of Judicature Act 1873, s 84 to appoint officers to serve the Supreme Court generally. The Official Solicitor has been a civil servant since 1919. It was not until 1981 that this became a statutory office and was renamed the Official Solicitor to the Supreme Court (now the Official Solicitor to the Senior Courts).

Creation of the OSPT

1.175   The distinct office of the Public Trustee was created under the Public Trustee Act 1906. Since then trustee services have become more readily available in the private sector so the Public Trustee has tended to become a trustee of last resort. In the early 1980s the Court of Protection was relocated within the Public Trustee Office, which later became known as the Public Trust Office. Subsequently the Public Trustee was given the additional responsibilities of acting as receiver of last resort, performing judicial functions as authorised by the Court of Protection Rules and dealing with the registration of enduring powers of attorney.

1.176   The offices of the Official Solicitor and the Public Trustee were co-located from 1 April 2001 when the trust division of the PTO was abolished and some of the Official Solicitor's work was transferred to CAFCASS. The joint office of the Official Solicitor and Public Trustee is known as the OSPT. The OSPT is an 'arm's length body' which exists to support the work of the Official Solicitor and Public Trustee. The two office holders continue to have separate corporate functions and the Public Trustee is not involved in mental capacity issues.

---

[155]   *Re WLW* [1972] Ch 456, Goff J.

LAW REFORM

Origins

1.177 During the 1980s it became apparent that the law and procedures in England and Wales failed to address in a comprehensive manner the problems raised by those who were incompetent in the sense that they could not make their own decisions. The courts did not have adequate powers to fill the vacuum and such legislation as there had been was piecemeal and not based upon an underlying philosophy. Comprehensive reform became essential. This was first highlighted in a paper produced by the Law Society in 1989[156] which was followed by a conference when the speakers included Professor Brenda Hoggett who had recently been appointed as a Law Commissioner.[157]

The Law Commission

1.178 Prompted by this initiative the Law Commission of England and Wales embarked upon a consideration of the whole question of decision-making and mental incapacity.[158] Serious deficiencies were identified during a protracted consultation and it became clear that reform was badly needed.[159]

Consultation

1.179 The first consultation paper in March 1991[160] provided an invaluable overview of the present state of the law and its procedures. It recognised that the existing law was inadequate to cope with the range of decisions that needed to be made on behalf of mentally incapable people but that the issue was large and complex. Further consultation followed.

1.180 The second consultation paper in December 1992[161] dealt with private law aspects and proposed procedures whereby decisions relating to the personal care and financial affairs of incapacitated people could be made. A third consultation paper in March 1993[162] explored legal procedures whereby substitute decisions about medical treatment could be authorised at an

---

[156] *Decision-making and Mental Incapacity: A Discussion Document*: Memorandum by the Law Society's Mental Health Sub-Committee, January 1989.
[157] *Decision-making and Mental Incapacity*, The Law Society, 5 May 1989.
[158] A similar review was undertaken by the Law Commission of Scotland.
[159] Professor Brenda Hoggett, the Law Commissioner responsible, later became Mrs Justice Hale and rapidly progressed through the Court of Appeal to become the first lady to sit in the House of Lords (now the Supreme Court). In these capacities she has had the opportunity to shape the law in accordance with her previous thinking.
[160] *Mentally Incapacitated Adults and Decision-Making: An Overview*, Law Com No 119.
[161] *Mentally Incapacitated Adults and Decision-Making: A New Jurisdiction*, Law Com No 128.
[162] *Mentally Incapacitated Adults and Decision-Making: Medical Treatment and Research*, Law Com No 129.

appropriate level. The fourth consultation paper in April 1993[163] considered the powers of public authorities and was expanded to cover vulnerable as well as mentally incapacitated people.

Report

1.181 The Law Commission published its final Report in March 1995[164] with the almost unanimous support of charities and others concerned with the welfare of mentally incapacitated people. This set out comprehensive recommendations and included a draft Mental Incapacity Bill. It was recommended that there should be a single comprehensive piece of legislation[165] to make new provision for people who lack mental capacity. This should provide a coherent statutory scheme to which recourse could be had when any decision (whether personal, medical or financial) needed to be made for a person aged 16 or over who lacked capacity. Two concepts were identified as being fundamental to any new decision-making jurisdiction, namely capacity and best interests.[166]

1.182 The proposals included:

(1) a general authority to act reasonably;

(2) living wills to be given statutory authority subject to safeguards;

(3) the appointment of someone to take treatment decisions;

(4) independent supervision of certain medical and research procedures;

(5) 'continuing power of attorney' which could extend to a donor's personal welfare, health care and property and affairs;

(6) decision-making by the court and power to make declarations and one-off orders or appoint a manager with substitute decision-making powers;

(7) a new Court of Protection with a central registry in London and regional hearing centres;

(8) a code of practice; and

(9) public law protection of vulnerable adults.[167]

The Government's response

1.183 The Government announced that it did not intend to proceed with legislation 'in its present form' but would undertake further consultation on the Report. That consultation did not materialise until October 1997 when the new

---

[163] *Mentally Incapacitated and Other Vulnerable Adults: Public Law Protection*, Law Com No 130.

[164] *Mental Incapacity*, Law Com No 231.

[165] This would move these problems away from the Mental Health Act 1983 and facilitate a different approach to the needs of incapacitated persons from that of mental health professionals.

[166] These concepts have been further developed in the Mental Capacity Act 2005.

[167] These proposals, which went beyond the initial Law Commission brief, have not been adopted.

Lord Chancellor, Lord Irvine of Lairg, announced that he intended to issue a consultation paper seeking views on the Report.

'Who Decides?'

1.184 In December 1997, the Lord Chancellor's consultation document *Who Decides? Making Decisions on Behalf of Mentally Incapacitated Adults*[168] was published with a relatively short period for consultation. This was in addition to an ambitious programme of law reform which included a Human Rights Bill to give effect to the ECHR in the UK and the continuance of civil justice reforms following Lord Woolf's Report *Access to Justice*.

1.185 This Green Paper was structured to follow the Law Commission's Report *Mental Incapacity*. The Government accepted that there was a clear need for law reform in this area and contemplated that there would be codes of practice dealing with specific areas. Whilst emphasising that there would be no move towards euthanasia (which is illegal) the Government supported many of the Law Commission's recommendations and expressed the wish to consult further on how they might best be implemented and those that might be controversial.[169] Inevitably the issue of resources arose.

'Making decisions'

1.186 In October 1999, the Government's proposals were published in the Report *Making Decisions*. Much, but not all, of the Law Commission's recommendations survived.[170] The Lord Chancellor announced in November 1999 that there would be legislation 'when Parliamentary time allows' but much of the detail had still to be worked out. In the meanwhile some of the recommendations of the Law Commission were already finding their way into our law through decisions of the courts.

Legislation

Adults with Incapacity (Scotland) Act 2000

1.187 Scotland achieved legislation first. The Adults with Incapacity (Scotland) Act 2000, which followed recommendations of the Scottish Law Commission[171] and was widely welcomed as a significant and much-needed reform of the law, received Royal Assent on 16 May 2000 and came into force in stages.[172] It protects the rights and interests of adults in Scotland who are incapable of managing their own affairs, acknowledged to be one of the most

---

[168] Cm 3803, issued by the Lord Chancellor's Department.
[169] These included advance statements about health care and non-therapeutic research.
[170] In particular the proposals for public law protection have not been followed up.
[171] *Report on Incapable Adults*, Scot Law Com No 151 (July 1995).
[172] Available at www.opsi.gov.uk/legislation/scotland/s-acts.htm and also accessible through the Office of Public Sector Information website: www.opsi.gov.uk. Information about implementation, which is updated at intervals, is to be found on the Scottish Executive website: www.scotland.gov.uk.

vulnerable groups in society. There are regulations under the Act and codes of practice which provide guidance on the legislation itself and offer further practical information for those people and organisations that have functions given to them by the Act.

1.188 A number of different agencies are involved in supervising those who take decisions on behalf of the adult:

(1)   the Public Guardian has a supervisory role and keeps registers of attorneys, people who can access an adult's funds, guardians and intervention orders;

(2)   local authorities look after the welfare of adults who lack capacity; and

(3)   the Mental Welfare Commission protects the interests of adults who lack capacity as a result of mental disorder.

Mental Incapacity Bill

1.189 On 27 June 2003, the Government published a draft Mental Incapacity Bill which was then scrutinised by a joint committee of both Houses of Parliament which published its response in November 2003.[173] The Government commented on some of those recommendations.[174] The title was to be changed to the *Mental Capacity Bill* and it was considered that draft *Codes of Practice* should be available before the Bill was passed. The joint committee considered that priority should be given to the Bill so that account could be taken of its provisions when framing new mental health legislation.

Mental Capacity Act 2005

1.190 A Bill, duly called the Mental Capacity Bill and incorporating the desired changes to the draft Bill, was introduced in Parliament in June 2004. This Bill (as amended) was finally passed in April 2005 and extends to England and Wales only. It was intended to come into force on 1 April 2007 but this date was postponed to 1 October 2007 due to delays in the implementation process. The Mental Capacity Act 2005 (MCA 2005) does not provide all the answers but laid down the principles, creates a statutory framework and authorises rules, practice directions and codes of practice to be made.

Human rights compatibility

1.191 Explanatory notes[175] prepared by the Department for Constitutional Affairs and the Department of Health state that MCA 2005 meets the state's positive obligation under ECHR, Art 8 to ensure respect for private life.

---

[173] *Report of the Joint Committee on the Draft Mental Incapacity Bill*, HL Papers 189-1 and 189-II, HC 1083-1 and 1083-II) (TSO, 2003), vols I and II.

[174] *The Government's Response to the Scrutiny Committee's Report on the draft Mental Incapacity Bill*, Cm 6121 (TSO, 2004).

[175] These do not form part of MCA 2005 and have not been endorsed by Parliament.

1.192   The European Court of Human Rights has made it clear that there must be adequate involvement of the individual in the court process. A person of unsound mind must be allowed to be heard either in person or, where necessary, through some form of representation. He will play a double role in the proceedings: as an interested party, and, at the same time, the main object of the court's examination. Participation is therefore necessary not only to enable him to present his own case, but also to allow the judge to form a personal opinion about mental capacity. In one case it was held that despite the applicant's mental illness he had been a relatively autonomous person. In such circumstances it was indispensable for the judge to have at least a brief visual contact with the applicant, and preferably to question him. The decision of the judge to decide the case on the basis of documentary evidence, without seeing or hearing the applicant, was unreasonable and in breach of the principle of adversarial proceedings enshrined in Article 6.[176]

1.193   This analysis concentrates upon the rights of the incapacitated person. Procedures for decisions to be made on behalf of such persons may also have an impact upon the human rights of other persons, and especially members of the family. Experience of the former Court of Protection shows that there may be strong sibling rivalry for control over the financial affairs of a parent and that the person in control of the finances, although not legally empowered to make personal welfare decisions, has a strong influence over such decisions. This may impact upon the human rights of other members of the family to respect for family life. The new jurisdiction is better able to tackle these issues but must do so in a way that is human rights compliant for all concerned.

An initial assessment of the MCA 2005

1.194   At last there was in England and Wales a statutory jurisdiction for decision-making in respect of mentally incapacitated adults. The need for this had been clearly demonstrated and the legislation was overdue, but would it fill the vacuum in our legal system? The general principles contained in MCA 2005, s 1 were relatively innovative so far as UK legislation was concerned and were much praised. However, there followed complaints that the system is 'a legal and bureaucratic minefield' and that 'a secret court is seizing the assets of thousands of elderly and mentally impaired people and turning control of their lives over to the State – against the wishes of their relatives'.[177]

1.195   Of key importance are the statutory formulae for assessing a lack of capacity and determining best interests. The MCA 2005 set a benchmark against which people with a mental impairment are to be assessed and interventions must be justified. This should apply beyond the specialist jurisdiction of the Court of Protection and be adopted by all courts and tribunals when they encounter people with impaired capacity. There is the

---

[176] *Shtukaturov v Russia*, Application no 44009/05, 27/06/2008.
[177] *The Mail on Sunday* (25 October 2009). The editorial commented that the system assumed individuals to have suspect motives and treated them as potential thieves, and that this tendency should be reversed.

potential for the specialist judges to sit in a dual jurisdiction but the benchmark should become second nature to all professionals working in this field. There was also a developing awareness of the need to identify incapacity as a discrete area of law divorced from provisions that deal with the treatment of those who are mentally ill.

1.196   The new procedures to implement decision-making over a wider range of content are intended to empower those members of our families and society who lack capacity, but must also ensure that they are protected from abuse. This is a delicate balance and where that balance should be struck depends upon one's viewpoint and how one interprets the statistics. It should not be assumed that everyone is satisfied with the present balance.[178] There is a range of diversity within mental incapacity and a 'one size fits all' approach cannot be adopted. There is a world of difference between the needs of a wealthy senior citizen who develops Alzheimer's, an autistic young person dependent on means-tested benefits and a brain-injured individual who has recovered compensation of several million pounds. There is also a difference between the incapacitated adult with dedicated family carers and the similarly incapacitated adult who has been abandoned by family.

1.197   Those working in this field are concerned about vulnerability, but this does not feature in the test of mental capacity. In a decision of the Court of Appeal it was stated:[179]

> '... the courts have ample powers to protect those who are vulnerable to exploitation from being exploited; it is unnecessary to deny them the opportunity to take their own decisions if they are not being exploited. It is not the task of the courts to prevent those who have the mental capacity to make rational decisions from making decisions which others may regard as rash or irresponsible.'

Many practitioners working in this field would question the suggestion that the courts have ample powers to protect those who are vulnerable. However, where vulnerability is perceived it becomes appropriate to inquire why this should be so and a thorough investigation may reveal that the underlying cause is a mental impairment. Although there may be sufficient understanding, resulting personal qualities such as impulsiveness, recklessness and being easily manipulated may mean that there is an inability to make and implement decisions based on that understanding.

1.198   The procedures need to be publicly known and accessible. There is a role for the Office of the Public Guardian in this respect, but that role should extend to resolving uncertainties where these exist and assisting in facilitating the resolution of disputes as to best interests. We now have a specialist court

---

[178]   The Law Society paper of 1989 was concerned about protection and the Law Commission proposals were perhaps the high point of empowerment. The consultation appeared to swing back towards protection but the emphasis in MCA 2005 appears to be empowerment.

[179]   Chadwick LJ in *Masterman-Lister v Brutton & Co and Jewell & Home Counties Dairies* [2002] EWCA Civ 1889, [2003] 3 All ER 162. It is not clear what those 'ample powers' actually were.

charged with the responsibility of interpreting the statutory criteria and exercising the new jurisdiction, but although empowering a new court to make all types of decisions or to authorise other persons to do so is a *sine qua non*, delivering that which is needed depends upon those called upon to implement the new jurisdiction at all levels. Where will these people come from and how will they be trained? The success or failure of this much needed initiative depends on the guidance that is produced and the availability of professionals who are familiar with the new law and procedures.

1.199 Within the framework established by MCA 2005 there is the prospect of a ground-breaking improvement in the lives of those who have the misfortune to be unable to structure these for themselves. Whether that improvement actually takes place may depend upon those involved adopting a pragmatic approach rather than becoming rule-bound. The following questions were raised initially and would only be answered as the new jurisdiction reached maturity:

- Is a decision-specific assessment of capacity viable?
- Does a test based on understanding protect those who are mentally unstable or vulnerable to influence?
- Does the 'best interest' approach involving the need to consult create too much opportunity for disputes?
- Does a 'best interest' test for the incapacitated person infringe the human rights of others?
- Will the court be accessible and affordable to those who need it?
- Will the court become a battleground between families/carers and social services/health authorities?
- Will the court resolve disputes or address best interests?
- Will the new jurisdiction achieve the right balance between empowerment and protection?
- Is the new jurisdiction too complex and theoretical?
- Will HRA 1998, which made the new jurisdiction inevitable, now render it illusory?

The *ad hoc* Rules Committee

1.200 In response to public criticisms and concerns expressed by practitioners an *ad hoc* Rules Committee was set up early in 2010 to consider what improvements could be made. The following recommendations were made, but these have not been implemented although some administrative changes have been made:[180]

---

[180] The full Report is available at: www.judiciary.gov.uk/publications-and-reports/reports/family/court-of-protection.

1. The procedure and practice of the court should reflect the differences in the nature of the following categories of its work, namely (a) non-contentious property and affairs applications, (b) contentious property and affairs applications and (c) health and welfare applications.

2. This change should be implemented by (a) the introduction of new forms, and (b) relevant changes in the rules and practice directions.

3. The distinction between serving and notifying people who are or may be interested in making representations to the court should be preserved. But it should be better explained and some amendments to the present provisions relating to this process should be made.

4. The present position relating to the notification and participation of P should be retained (with some minor amendments).

5. Strictly defined and limited non-contentious property and affairs applications should be dealt with by court officers (eg, applications for a property and affairs deputy by local authorities and in respect of small estates that do not include defined types of property). The provisions will also have to provide for an automatic right to refer any such decision to a judge and internal monitoring and review by the judges.

6. Separate applications for permission should be abandoned and the application for permission should be incorporated into the main application form.

7. The detailed and minor changes set out in Annex 1 [to the Report] should be considered. It is recognised that on a detailed consideration some may be rejected and others added and this recommendation and annex is included to assist those who are performing that detailed exercise.

8. Issues as to whether and when the court should sit in public or permit its proceedings to be made public should be dealt with by the courts through decisions rather than any rule change.

9. The proposed new forms prepared by members of this committee should be 'tested' with a range of potential users before they are finalised and the relevant rules and practice directions are altered.

10. A Committee should be established to review and make recommendations relating to the procedure and practice of the Court of Protection.

House of Lords Select Committee Report

1.201 On 13 March 2014 after a mammoth evidence gathering exercise the House of Lords Committee appointed to consider the MCA 2005 provided a damning report upon its implementation.[181] The Committee was unanimous in its overall finding that the MCA 2005 is important – indeed visionary – legislation, with the potential to transform lives. However, they were equally clear that the Act is not working well, because people do not know about the Act and, where they do know about it, they do not understand it:

---

[181] www.publications.parliament.uk/pa/ld201314/ldselect/ldmentalcap/139/13902.htm.

'… [f]or many who are expected to comply with the Act it appears to be an optional add-on, far from being central to their working lives. The evidence presented to us concerns the health and social care sectors principally. In those sectors the prevailing cultures of paternalism (in health) and risk-aversion (in social care) have prevented the Act from becoming widely known or embedded. The empowering ethos has not been delivered. The rights conferred by the Act have not been widely realised. The duties imposed by the Act are not widely followed.'

In regard to the Deprivation of Liberty (DOLS) regime the conclusion was that:

'… [t]he provisions are poorly drafted, overly complex and bear no relationship to the language and ethos of the Mental Capacity Act. The safeguards are not well understood and are poorly implemented. Evidence suggested that thousands, if not tens of thousands, of individuals are being deprived of their liberty without the protection of the law, and therefore without the safeguards which Parliament intended. Worse still, far from being used to protect individuals and their rights, they are sometimes used to oppress individuals, and to force upon them decisions made by others without reference to the wishes and feelings of the person concerned. Even if implementation could be improved, the legislation itself is flawed.'

1.202 The main recommendations to ensure effective implementation of the Act are:

(1) Overall responsibility for the Act be given to an independent body whose task will be to oversee, monitor and drive forward implementation;

(2) The DOLS regime be ripped up and the Government goes back to the drawing board to draft replacement provisions that are easy to understand and implement, and in keeping with the style and ethos of the Mental Capacity Act;

(3) The Government works with regulators and the medical Royal Colleges to ensure the Act is given a higher profile in training, standard setting and inspections;

(4) The Government increases the staff resources at the Court of Protection to speed up handling of non-controversial cases;

(5) The Government reconsiders the provision of non-means tested legal aid to those who lack capacity, especially in cases of deprivation of liberty;

(6) Local authorities use their discretionary powers to appoint Independent Mental Capacity Advocates more widely than is currently the case;

(7) The Government addresses the poor levels of awareness and understanding of Lasting Powers of Attorney and advance decisions to refuse treatment among professionals in the health and social care sectors;

(8) The Government review the criminal law provision for ill-treatment or neglect of a person lacking capacity to ensure that it is fit for purpose.

The Government response

1.203 In its response[182] *Valuing every voice, respecting every right: Making the case for the Mental Capacity Act* the Government agreed with the Committee's overall finding and set out a system-wide programme of work over the coming year and beyond that should realise a real improvement in implementation of the Act.[183]

A New Ad Hoc Rules Committee

1.204 Another Rules Committee has now been formed to consider further and possibly more extensive changes to the Court of Protection Rules 2007 and it is the Government's intention to have the new Rules in place during 2015.

UN Convention on the Rights of Persons with Disabilities

Background

1.205 The *United Nations Convention on the Rights of Persons with Disabilities* (CRPD) was adopted by the UN General Assembly in 2006, came into force internationally in 2008, was ratified by the UK in 2009, and by the EU (on behalf of all member states) in 2010. The CRPD does not have the force of law in UK courts, but in ratifying the Convention the UK committed itself to revising domestic legislation as necessary to conform with CRPD standards. The *UN Committee on the Rights of Persons with Disabilities* (the Committee) was then established to implement the Convention and review compliance by signatory nations. In signing the CRPD's Optional Protocol, the UK agreed to have its domestic law and practice reviewed regularly by the Committee and the first such review is awaited although significant concerns are being raised[184] about the 'diagnostic threshold', substituted decision-making on a 'best interests' basis and the potential for discrimination against disabled persons due to differential treatment.

1.206 Of particular concern is Art 12 – 'Equal recognition before the law' which provides:

1. States Parties reaffirm that persons with disabilities have the right to recognition everywhere as persons before the law.

2. States Parties shall recognize that persons with disabilities enjoy legal capacity on an equal basis with others in all aspects of life.

3. States Parties shall take appropriate measures to provide access by persons with disabilities to the support they may require in exercising their legal capacity.

---

[182] See   www.gov.uk/government/publications/mental-capacity-act-government-response-to-the-house-of-lords-select-committee-report.

[183] The Government has now requested the Law Commission to consider the entire DOLs regime.

[184] An interesting *Discussion Paper* on the CRPD is available on the website of Thirty Nine Essex Street at: www.39essex.com/newsletters.

4. States Parties shall ensure that all measures that relate to the exercise of legal capacity provide for appropriate and effective safeguards to prevent abuse in accordance with international human rights law. Such safeguards shall ensure that measures relating to the exercise of legal capacity respect the rights, will and preferences of the person, are free of conflict of interest and undue influence, are proportional and tailored to the person's circumstances, apply for the shortest time possible and are subject to regular review by a competent, independent and impartial authority or judicial body. The safeguards shall be proportional to the degree to which such measures affect the person's rights and interests.

5. Subject to the provisions of this article, States Parties shall take all appropriate and effective measures to ensure the equal right of persons with disabilities to own or inherit property, to control their own financial affairs and to have equal access to bank loans, mortgages and other forms of financial credit, and shall ensure that persons with disabilities are not arbitrarily deprived of their property.

The right to legal capacity on an equal basis was thus identified as a subsidiary to the right to equal recognition before the law. It encompasses both a 'static' element (the right to be a person before the law and a holder of rights) and an 'active' element' (the right to be a legal agent whose decisions are respected and validated by the law).

The diagnostic threshold

1.207 The MCA 2005 adopts a 'functional test' of decision-making ability but also includes a second requirement. In order for an individual to be deemed lacking in mental capacity, the lack of decision-making ability must be because of 'an impairment of, or a disturbance in the functioning of the mind or brain'. It is this second component of the definition that has come to be known as the 'diagnostic threshold'. It is suggested that the diagnostic threshold constitutes a form of indirect discrimination against persons with disabilities because they are far more likely than are the general population to comply with this test. The functional tests then amount to indirect discrimination because many people without disabilities might fail if they were subjected to them, but only people with disabilities are required to take them and experience the consequences of failing them.

1.208 Differential treatment does not of itself constitute unlawful discrimination, but the Committee calls into question any system that denies legal capacity on the basis of disability or impairment or is indirectly discriminatory against people with disability. The Committee's aim is to ensure that legal capacity is de-coupled from prejudicial perceptions of an individual's 'mental capacity', and that regardless of an individual's level of decision-making skills, she or he is still respected as a person before the law and a legal agent. If intervention in legal decision-making does occur, it must be based on factors that all individuals could be subject to, not merely people who have a cognitive disability or are perceived as lacking decision-making skills.

Best interests

1.209 The CRPD requires states parties to ensure that legal principles and practices affecting the legal capacity of persons with disabilities are devised so as to provide safeguards that ensure 'respect for the rights, will and preferences' of disabled persons. Under the MCA 2005 the best interests decision-maker is only required to 'consider, so far as is reasonably ascertainable, the person's past and present wishes and feelings ... [and] the beliefs and values that would be likely to influence his decision if he had capacity' and an objective approach is adopted to the decision that in some cases override the wishes of the individual. The Committee considers that this pays insufficient 'respect' to the rights, will and preferences of the individual.

The functional test

1.210 The Act provides that 'A person is not to be treated as unable to make a decision unless all practicable steps to help him to do so have been taken without success' but there is little guidance as to what form this support should take, or who has the legal obligation to provide it. Compliance with the CRPD requires at the very least that this 'support principle' within the MCA 2005 be strengthened and developed.

The Committee provides guidance for States on the development of support for the exercise of legal capacity but does not provide a comprehensive list of examples of good practice so as to allow States to develop their own culturally and jurisdictionally specific practices. The MCA 2005 approach to support may not comply with the CRPD's approach in four key respects. The purpose is to help the person to exercise their legal capacity, rather than to pass a functional test of capacity, so support must be available regardless of mental capacity. The Committee's model of support is consensual: support cannot be imposed against a person's will, and 'must be based on the will and preference of the person, not on what is perceived as being in his or her objective best interests'. The requirement is for 'Legal recognition of the support person(s) formally chosen by a person' to 'be available and accessible', but the MCA 2005 affords no means for a person to designate a chosen and trusted individual to be recognised by others as their supporter.

Substituted decision-making

1.211 Although some of these failings could be resolved by adjusting the present law and practice, it is suggested that the MCA 2005 suffers from non-remediable forms of non-compliance with the CRPD. The Committee has stated that support systems for the exercise of legal capacity must replace regimes of substituted decision-making that deny legal capacity. There are problems in this approach. How do you distinguish support from influence and when does this become undue? The supporter may become the effective decision-maker, because a decision can be influenced by the provision of selective information. What if the person providing support is motivated by self-interest? There are dangers in treating a decision as that of the individual when in reality it has been dictated by the 'supporter'.

1.212 The Committee defined what constitutes a 'substituted decision-making regime' and the MCA 2005 meets all three elements of that definition. The provision for 'declarations of incapacity' and voiding a person's past or future decisions in the relevant area, meet the first element: the removal of legal capacity. The second element is also met because the Act allows for the appointment of a deputy, potentially against the will of the person concerned. In addition, once a person is found to 'lack capacity', a substitute decision-maker is empowered to make a best interest decision. Where a person objects to an 'informal' decision-maker making substitute decisions under the 'general defence' provided by s 5 this would also meet this second element, as informal decision-makers are empowered to make decisions whether or not the person wishes them to do so. Finally, the last element is met because 'best interests' decisions are made on the basis of 'objective' criteria, rather than the person's own will and preference.

Individuals who cannot be supported

1.213 There are cases where the individual cannot communicate or their will and preference is unclear, conflicting or impracticable and where there is concern of undue influence by another individual. It is contended that the CRPD addresses these situations but on the basis that there are clear distinctions with existing substitute decision-making systems by:

(1) using 'will and preference' as the guiding model as opposed to 'best interest,'

(2) not denying legal capacity to individuals with disabilities on a different basis, and

(3) not imposing outside decision-makers against the will of the individual.

1.214 Under the CRPD model, where significant attempts to provide support have failed, an outside decision-maker can make a decision on the individual's behalf in accordance with the 'best interpretation' of her or his will and preference, taking into account past expressed preferences, where available, knowledge gained from family and friends and any other evidence that is available. In this situation, the individual must be closely consulted to discover who she or he would like to appoint as a representative decision-maker. If she or he is communicating but not clearly expressing who she or he would like to make a decision on her or his behalf, then a decision-maker could be appointed, but again, could only make decisions that were in accordance with the best interpretation of her or his will and preference.

A view of the future

1.215 The MCA 2005 adopts a three-stage approach to decision-making:

(1) people with capacity make their own decisions – that fulfils their legal capacity;

(2) people with impaired capacity are required to be supported in making decisions, and will not be treated as lacking capacity unless and until all appropriate support has been tried – that enhances their legal capacity;

(3) people who lack mental capacity have decisions made for them in their best interests. By definition they could not make decisions of their own even with support and this is the process whereby the law implements legal capacity.

It may be that a re-interpretation of the Act would be sufficient to resolve most of the potential conflicts with the CRPD. Placing more emphasis on support as a pre-requisite to a finding of lack of mental capacity and as a preliminary to determining best interests would be a starting point, coupled with a recognition that the matters expressed in s 4(6) of the MCA 2005 represent the will and preference of the individual and must be adopted if ascertainable. However, a more specific shift from an objective to a subjective approach may be required and that would require legislation.

1.216 It then appears that the MCA 2005 definition of capacity is not wide enough, thereby requiring the inherent jurisdiction to fill a newly recognised vacuum, namely adults who 'are incapacitated by external forces – whatever they may be – outside their control from reaching a decision'. Is the retention of a diagnostic threshold an outdated approach inherited from the previous jurisdiction when this was the existence of a 'mental disorder'? Should the diagnostic threshold perhaps become: 'unable to make a decision due to an impairment of or disturbance in the decision-making process through internal or external factors beyond the control of the individual'? This change may not be necessary. The new definition now refers to both the mind and the brain, so have we continued to adopt too medical an approach? Might the impairment or disturbance of the mind be a consequence not only of internal factors but also external forces such as fear, oppression or overwhelming cultural pressures? That would bring some, if not all, of the cases now being dealt with under the inherent jurisdiction within the ambit of the Court of Protection – it is a shame to create a specialised court to deal with vulnerable adults and then have to supplement it elsewhere. This interpretation may also satisfy the concerns about direct discrimination against disabled people.

1.217 We were ahead of the game with the Mental Capacity Act 2005 but are perhaps now at a turning point where there is the opportunity to interpret the legislation in a manner that diminishes the need to rely upon the inherent jurisdiction and ensures that it complies with current international expectations. If we do not take advantage of this we may cease to be a leading jurisdiction in this field.

CHAPTER 2

THE MENTAL CAPACITY JURISDICTION

INTRODUCTION

2.1   The Mental Capacity Act 2005 (MCA 2005) was intended to establish a comprehensive statutory framework setting out how decisions should be made by and on behalf of adults whose capacity to make specific decisions is in doubt. It also clarifies what actions can be taken by others involved in the care or medical treatment of people lacking capacity to consent. The framework provides a hierarchy of processes, extending from informal day-to-day care and treatment, to decision-making requiring formal powers and ultimately to court decisions and judgments. The full range of processes was intended to govern the circumstances in which necessary acts of caring can be carried out, and necessary decisions taken, on behalf of those lacking capacity to consent to such acts or make their own decisions. Some decisions affecting vulnerable or incapacitated people may not fall clearly within the remit of MCA 2005 – those cases 'at the margins' of the MCA are dealt with in Chapter 11.

2.2   This chapter is in three parts:

- Part 1 gives a brief overview of the jurisdiction created by MCA 2005 and discusses the role and status of the Code of Practice which provides statutory guidance on its operation.

- Part 2 looks in detail at the guiding statutory principles that underpin MCA 2005's key messages and govern how the Act should be interpreted and implemented. The two fundamental concepts – capacity and best interests, which form the basis of the statutory framework – are discussed and their definitions explained.

- Part 3 looks at the provisions in MCA 2005 which permit actions to be taken in relation to the care and treatment of people lacking capacity to consent to those actions. Some types of decisions are excluded from the Act's provisions and these are explored. Finally, an explanation is given of the criminal offence created under the Act to deal with cases of ill-treatment or wilful neglect of people lacking capacity to protect themselves from such abuse.

PART 1: OVERVIEW

Key elements

General

2.3   MCA 2005 sets out a comprehensive integrated jurisdiction for the making of personal welfare decisions, health care decisions and financial decisions on behalf of people who may lack capacity to make specific decisions for themselves. The Act's starting point is to enshrine in statute the presumption at common law that an adult has full legal capacity unless it is established that he or she does not. It also includes provisions to ensure that people are given all appropriate help and support to enable them to make their own decisions or to maximise their participation in the decision-making process.

2.4   MCA 2005 also enshrines in statute best practice and former common law principles concerning people who lack capacity and those who take decisions on their behalf. The statutory framework is based on two fundamental concepts:[1] lack of capacity and best interests. For those who lack capacity to make particular decisions, the Act provides a range of processes, extending from informal arrangements to court-based powers, to govern the circumstances in which necessary decisions can be taken on their behalf and in their best interests.

Essential provisions

2.5   The essential provisions of MCA 2005 are intended to:

- set out five guiding principles to underpin the Act's fundamental concepts and to govern its implementation and operation;
- define people who lack decision-making capacity;
- set out a single clear test for assessing whether a person lacks capacity to take a particular decision at a particular time;
- establish a single criterion (best interests) for carrying out acts or taking decisions on behalf of people who lack capacity to consent to such acts or take those specific decisions for themselves;
- clarify the law when acts in connection with the care or treatment of people lacking capacity to consent are carried out in their best interests, without formal procedures or judicial intervention, but with clear restrictions on the use of restraint and, in particular, acts resulting in deprivation of liberty;[2]

---

[1]   A full discussion of the meaning of these concepts is set out in the Law Commission Report, *Mental Incapacity*, Law Com No 231 (HMSO, 1995), Part III. See also Part 2 of this chapter below.

[2]   MCA 2005 amended by the Mental Health Act 2007 to provide procedural safeguards in cases where someone lacking capacity may be deprived of their liberty in their best interests – see Chapter 7.

- extend the provisions for making powers of attorney which outlast capacity (lasting powers of attorney (LPA)) covering health and welfare decisions as well as financial affairs, with improved safeguards against abuse and exploitation;
- provide for a decision to be made, or a decision-maker (deputy) to be appointed, by a specialist Court of Protection;
- make statutory rules, with clear safeguards, for the making of advance decisions to refuse medical treatment;
- set out specific parameters for research involving, or in relation to, people lacking capacity to consent to their involvement;
- provide for the appointment of independent mental capacity advocates (IMCAs) to support people with no one to speak for them who lack capacity to make important decisions about serious medical treatment and changes of accommodation, and in some circumstances to support those lacking capacity who are involved in safeguarding adults procedures; and
- provide statutory guidance, in the form of a code (or codes) of practice, setting good practice standards for the guidance of people using the Act's provisions.

The public bodies

2.6   MCA 2005 also created two public bodies to support and implement the statutory framework:

(1)   a superior court of record, the Court of Protection, with jurisdiction relating to the whole of MCA 2005 and its own procedures and nominated judges; and

(2)   a Public Guardian, whose office is the registering authority for LPAs and deputies, with responsibility to supervise deputies and respond to any concerns raised about donees or deputies.

The Code of Practice

2.7   It has long been recognised that complex legislation of this sort requires an accompanying code (or codes) of practice for the guidance of practitioners using MCA 2005 and those affected by its provisions, and also to assist with interpretation and implementation of the Act.[3] Provision for such statutory guidance is made in the Act.[4] Following parliamentary pre-legislative scrutiny of the Draft Mental Incapacity Bill in 2003, the Joint Scrutiny Committee specifically recommended that the Bill should not be introduced into Parliament unless it could be considered alongside a draft code of practice.[5]

---

[3]   Law Com No 231, n 1 above, at para 2.53.
[4]   MCA 2005, s 42.
[5]   *Report of the Joint Committee on the Draft Mental Incapacity Bill, Vol 1*, HL 189-1, HC 1083-1 (TSO, 2003), at para 229.

2.8 Following Royal Assent of MCA 2005, a revised version of the draft Code was issued for formal public consultation during 2006. It was further revised in the light of responses to the consultation and the final version was laid before Parliament in February 2007. The Code of Practice[6] was formally issued in April 2007 and came fully into effect on 1 October 2007 as the statutory guidance for the entire MCA 2005 as originally enacted. A supplement to the Code[7] has since been issued separately to deal with the deprivation of liberty provisions inserted into MCA 2005 by the Mental Health Act 2007, which came into effect in April 2009 (see Chapter 7).

Application

2.9 The Lord Chancellor is required to prepare and issue one or more codes of practice and MCA 2005 specified the particular issues, as well as particular categories of people, that guidance in the Code(s) must address.[8] These are:

- persons involved in assessing capacity;
- persons acting in connection with the care or treatment of a person lacking capacity;
- donees of LPAs;
- deputies appointed by the Court of Protection;
- persons carrying out research involving people lacking capacity;
- independent mental capacity advocates (IMCAs);
- persons involved in using the deprivation of liberty procedures;
- representatives appointed for people deprived of their liberty;
- the provisions in the Act covering advance decisions to refuse treatment;
- any other matters concerned with the Act as the Lord Chancellor thinks fit.

2.10 The Government originally decided to issue one Code of Practice (sometimes referred to as the main Code) to include guidance on the whole of the MCA jurisdiction. However, the deprivation of liberty provisions subsequently inserted into MCA 2005 (which came into effect in 2009) are dealt with in a separate supplement.[9] The main Code is intended to give practical guidance and examples to illustrate the provisions of MCA 2005, rather than imposing any new legal or formal requirements. It was originally intended that the Code would be revised as and when required[10] but this has

---

[6] Mental Capacity Act 2005: Code of Practice (TSO, 2007). The Code is reproduced in Part VI of this book.

[7] Mental Capacity Act 2005: Deprivation of Liberty Safeguards – Code of Practice to supplement the main Mental Capacity Act 2005 Code of Practice (TSO, 2008). Also reproduced in Part VI of this book.

[8] MCA 2005, s 42(1), as amended by the Mental Health Act 2007, s 50(7), Sch 9, Part 1, paras 1, 8(1), (2).

[9] See n 7 above.

[10] MCA 2005, s 42(2).

not as yet happened. The Lord Chancellor may delegate the preparation or revision of the whole or any part of the Code as he considers expedient.[11]

2.11 Responsibility for the dissemination of the Code of Practice passed from the Ministry of Justice (MoJ) (formerly the Department for Constitutional Affairs, which published the Code) to the Office of the Public Guardian (OPG) although policy responsibility, including any updating, returned to the MoJ in 2011. Apart from the Code appearing on the Ministry of Justice website,[12] it appears that little effort has been made to promote the Code or to make sure that the people required by MCA 2005 to 'have regard' to it have it drawn to their attention.

2.12 In June 2013, the House of Lords established a Select Committee to 'consider and report on the Mental Capacity Act 2005'.[13] Perhaps surprisingly, the Code of Practice was the subject of remarkably little discussion before or by the Committee in its report.[14] The Government in its response,[15] *Valuing every voice, respecting every right: Making the case for the Mental Capacity Act,* stated its belief that the Code still represents a valuable and respected source of guidance for professionals. The Government committed itself to considering following a review carried out in the autumn of 2014 by the Social Care Institute for Excellence of MCA guidance to 'determining whether amendments or additions to the Code would be valuable;' as at the point of writing, no further steps have been taken in this regard. The Coalition Government ruled out carrying out major revisions to the deprivation of liberty supplement until the Law Commission has reported its findings in the summer 2017,[16] although it is now significantly out of step with the case-law developments discussed in Chapter 7. The Department of Health commissioned guidance from the Law Society to assist front-line professionals in identifying when deprivations of liberty may be occurring; this guidance, published in April 2015 and discussed in Chapter 7, may be regarded as an informal update to the Deprivation of Liberty Code of Practice, but does not have the same status and legal effect as that Code.

---

[11] MCA 2005, s 42(3).

[12] See www.justice.gov.uk/protecting-the-vulnerable/mental-capacity-act. Perhaps tellingly, that webpage is now, itself, archived

[13] See www.parliament.uk/business/committees/committees-a-z/lords-select/mental-capacity-act-2005.

[14] See www.publications.parliament.uk/pa/ld201314/ldselect/ldmentalcap/139/13902.htm.

[15] See www.gov.uk/government/publications/mental-capacity-act-government-response-to-the-house-of-lords-select-committee-report, at paras 5.6–5.8.

[16] Paragraph 7.31.

Legal effect

2.13   The Code of Practice is statutory guidance in that MCA 2005 imposes a duty on certain people to 'have regard to any relevant Code' when acting in relation to a person lacking capacity.[17] The specified people are those acting in one or more of the following ways:

(1)   as a donee of a LPA;

(2)   as a deputy appointed by the Court;

(3)   as a person carrying out research under the Act;

(4)   as an IMCA;

(5)   in exercising the procedures authorising deprivation of liberty;

(6)   as a representative of someone deprived of their liberty;

(7)   in a professional capacity; and/or

(8)   for remuneration.

In the context of considering the threshold test for the appointment of a deputy in *SBC v PBA and Others*,[18] Roderic Wood J held that the court should look at the 'unvarnished words' of the MCA 2005. There was no additional requirement to be derived from the Code of Practice, although the court may take account of the guidance in the Code in coming to its conclusions. He set out the following reasons for this interpretation (at [67]):

> '(i)   the words of the statute are the essential provisions laid down by Parliament;
> (ii)   whatever its genesis and weight, the Code of Practice is indeed only guidance;
> (iii) there is a reasonable expectation in the Code that its provisions should be followed;
> (iv) departure from it, if undertaken, should require careful explanation;
> (v)   ... [the Code] remains essentially guidance – however weighty and significant – and is not the source of the relevant power which is to be found only in the statutory provision.'[19]

2.14   The statutory duty to have regard to the Code therefore applies to those exercising formal powers or duties under MCA 2005, and to professionals (including lawyers, health and social care professionals) and others acting for remuneration (such as paid carers). The position of informal carers, such as family members, was considered by the Joint Committee on the Draft Bill:[20]

> 'The position is different with regard to guidance issued to assist non-professional or informal decision-makers, such as family members and unpaid carers acting under the general authority. It is essential that family members and carers carrying out such responsibilities are provided with appropriate guidance and assistance, both to promote good practice and also to impress upon them the seriousness of

---

[17]   MCA 2005, s 42(4), as amended by the Mental Health Act 2007, s 50(7), Sch 9, Part 1, paras 1, 8(3).

[18]   [2011] EWHC 2580 (Fam), [2011] COPLR Con Vol 1095.

[19]   See also *The Mental Health Trust & Ors v DD & Anor* [2014] EWCOP 11 at para 156.

[20]   Joint Committee Report, Vol I, n 5 above, at para 232.

their actions and the need to be accountable for them. However, we accept that it would be inappropriate to impose on them a strict requirement to act in accordance with the codes of practice.'

Sanctions for non-compliance

2.15 MCA 2005 provides that a provision of a code of practice, or a failure to comply with the guidance set out in a code, can be taken into account by a court or tribunal where it appears relevant to a question arising in any criminal or civil proceedings.[21] There is no liability for breach of the Code itself, but compliance or non-compliance may be an element in deciding the issue of liability for breach of some other statutory or common law duty. For example, the need to have regard to the Code is highly likely to be relevant to a question of whether someone has acted or behaved in a way which is contrary to the best interests of a person lacking capacity. Breach of the Code might also be relevant to an action in negligence or to a criminal prosecution (including, potentially, to a prosecution under the new care worker and care provider offences created by ss 20 and 21 of the Criminal Justice and Courts Act 2015 respectively (see further **2.226–2.228**)

2.16 This applies not only to those categories of people who have a duty to have regard to the Code of Practice, but also to those who are not under a duty. This is because informal carers still have an obligation to act in accordance with the principles of MCA 2005 and in the best interests of a person lacking capacity.[22] The provision therefore remains applicable where any such person is facing civil or criminal proceedings and the court or tribunal considers the Code to be relevant.

2.17 As no arrangements have been made to monitor compliance with the Code of Practice (or indeed the Act more generally),[23] it is next to impossible to gauge how it is being used in practice. An on-line survey of health and social care practitioners conducted in 2010–11 as part of research into '*Making Best Interests Decisions*' commissioned by the Department of Health found that only 16.2% of participants had used the Code of Practice as a source of information and guidance in relation to the particular decision described in the survey.[24] The Care Quality Commission as part of its strategy for 2013–16 has placed increased emphasis upon monitoring compliance with MCA 2005 as

---

[21] MCA 2005, s 42(5).

[22] See Part 2 at **2.19**ff below.

[23] A point made with some force in the House of Lords Select Committee's report: www.parliament.uk/business/committees/committees-a-z/lords-select/mental-capacity-act-2005 at paragraphs 35–36. By way of comparison, the Secretary of State for Health delegated to the Mental Health Act Commission (which in April 2009 became part of the Care Quality Commission) responsibility to monitor compliance with the Code of Practice to the Mental Health Act 1983 and to advise Ministers of any changes to the Code which the Commission feels might be appropriate.

[24] V Williams et al, *Making Best Interests Decisions: People and Processes*, (Mental Health Foundation, 2012), p 111.

part of its assessment of regulated providers,[25] and it is to be expected – or at least hoped – that this increased focus will see a commensurately increased awareness of the Code. Other professionals (such as lawyers) must monitor their own compliance with the Code.

Creation and revision

2.18 MCA 2005 sets out the procedures required for the preparation or revision of the Code(s) and for parliamentary approval.[26] In particular, there must be formal consultation with anyone whom the Lord Chancellor considers appropriate before a Code is prepared or revised.[27] Since health and social care responsibilities are devolved in relation to Wales, the National Assembly for Wales must specifically be consulted and involved in the preparation of the Codes.

A draft of the Code(s) must be laid before Parliament.[28] The Code takes effect after 40 days unless, within that time, either House has resolved not to approve it (known as the 'negative resolution' procedure).[29]

The Lord Chancellor is allowed considerable flexibility in arranging for the Codes to be produced in the most appropriate format and for bringing the guidance to the attention of everyone who needs to know about it.[30] It had been suggested that separate Codes should be produced for different types of decisions or aimed at different decision-makers, but this suggestion was not taken up. The prospects for revisions to the main Code and/or the DoLS supplement are discussed at **2.13** above.

PART 2: PRINCIPLES AND CONCEPTS

The principles

Background

2.19 Much of the evidence submitted to the Joint Committee undertaking pre-legislative scrutiny of the Draft Mental Incapacity Bill was concerned with the principles said to underlie the provisions of the Bill. In particular, commentators stressed the need for a clear statement of those principles to be set out on the face of the legislation.[31] Comparisons were made with s 1 of the Adults with Incapacity (Scotland) Act 2000 (AWI(S)A 2000), which sets out

---

[25] *Raising Standards, Putting People First*, available at www.cqc.org.uk/public/about-us/our-performance-and-plans/our-strategy-and-business-plan.
[26] MCA 2005, s 43.
[27] MCA 2005, s 43(1).
[28] MCA 2005, s 43(2).
[29] The 40-day period is defined in MCA 2005, s 43(4)–(5).
[30] MCA 2005, s 43(3).
[31] See in particular the evidence submitted by the Making Decisions Alliance, Joint Committee Report, Vol II, HL 198-II, HC 1083-II (TSO, 2003), at Ev 85.

five general principles to govern all 'interventions' in the affairs of an adult taken under or in pursuance of AWI(S)A 2000.[32]

2.20 It is important to note that while some of the specific provisions of AWI(S)A 2000 and the MCA 2005 are similar, there are significant differences in the underlying intentions and operation of both pieces of legislation as well as in the respective jurisdictions. Both are based on the recommendations of the respective Law Commissions, each of which adopted a different approach as a result of their separate consultation exercises. There are also differences in drafting styles.

2.21 The Joint Committee examined these differences in approach, and was persuaded that the statement of principles in AWI(S)A 2000 provided not only necessary protection for people with impaired capacity and a framework for ensuring that appropriate action is taken in individual cases, but also that the specified principles were extremely helpful in pointing the way to solutions in difficult or uncertain situations.[33] In conclusion, the Joint Committee commented:[34]

> '... we were struck by the absence of a specific statement of principles on the face of the Bill as an initial point of reference, as had been done in the Scottish Act. Although the principles of the draft Bill may be discernible to lawyers from the opening clauses of the draft Bill, they may not be so obvious to the majority of non-legal persons who will have to deal with the Bill in practice.'

The statement of principles

2.22 The Joint Committee's strong recommendations[35] that a statement of principles be incorporated on the face of MCA 2005 were accepted by the Government. MCA 2005, s 1 sets out five guiding principles designed to emphasise the underlying ethos of the Act, which is not only to protect people who lack capacity to make specific decisions, but also to maximise their ability to participate in decision-making. This section provides as follows:

> '(1) The following principles apply for the purposes of this Act.
> (2) A person must be assumed to have capacity unless it is established that he lacks capacity.
> (3) A person is not to be treated as unable to make a decision unless all practicable steps to help him to do so have been taken without success.
> (4) A person is not to be treated as unable to make a decision merely because he makes an unwise decision.
> (5) An act done, or decision made, under this Act for or on behalf of a person who lacks capacity must be done, or made, in his best interests.
> (6) Before the act is done, or the decision is made, regard must be had to whether the purpose for which it is needed can be as effectively achieved in a way that is less restrictive of the person's rights and freedom of action.'

---

[32] AWI(S)A 2000, s 1.
[33] *Evidence for the Law Society of Scotland*, Joint Committee Report, Vol II, n 31 above, at Ev 2.
[34] Joint Committee Report, Vol I, n 5 above, at para 39.
[35] Joint Committee Report, Vol I, n 5 above, Recommendations 4 and 5.

2.23 In his ministerial statement announcing the publication of the Mental Capacity Bill and its introduction into Parliament, David Lammy, the then Parliamentary Under Secretary of State for Constitutional Affairs said:[36]

> 'The overriding aim of the Bill is to improve the lives of vulnerable adults, their carers, families and professionals. It provides a statutory framework for decision making for people who lack capacity, making clear who can take decisions, in which situations and how they should go about this.
>
> The Bill is based on clearly defined principles. Its starting point is that everyone has the right to make his or her own decisions, and must be assumed to have capacity to do so unless it is proved otherwise. No-one should be labelled as incapable – each decision should be considered individually and everyone should be helped to make or contribute to making decisions about their lives. The Bill sets out clear guidelines for, and limits on, other people's role in decision making.'

2.24 The statement of principles was warmly welcomed, not only by voluntary and professional organisations involved with people who lack capacity,[37] but also by MPs and Peers commenting on the principles during the parliamentary debates. In particular, during the Bill's second reading in the House of Lords, the Lord Bishop of Worcester said:[38]

> 'The result is not just a Bill with important protections for vulnerable people; Clause 1 contains a statement about a vision of humanity and how humanity is to be regarded. I hope children in generations to come will study that as one of the clearest and most eloquent expressions of what we think a human being is and how a human being is to be treated ...
>
> I believe that [the Bill] states what is fundamentally right. In the course of Committee we shall no doubt improve and tighten some of the wording, but we shall never take away the powerful and eloquent statement in Clause 1. That should underlie our treatment of one another in all circumstances and for all purposes.'

2.25 The principles underpinning the Act were strongly endorsed in evidence given to and in the report produced by the House of Lords Select Committee appointed to consider MCA 2005.[39] The following paragraphs consider the origins of each of the key principles and their operation in practice.

Presumption of capacity

2.26 Practitioners will have been familiar with the presumption, at common law, that an adult has full legal capacity unless it is established that he or she does not. If a question of capacity comes before a court, the burden of proof is

---

[36] *Hansard*, HC Deb, vol 422 ser 6, col 67WS (18 June 2004).
[37] See eg Making Decisions Alliance *Briefing for 2nd Reading debate in House of Commons* (11 October 2004), at pp 7–9.
[38] *Hansard*, HL Deb, vol 668, ser 5, cols 53–54, 55 (10 January 2005).
[39] See www.publications.parliament.uk/pa/ld201314/ldselect/ldmentalcap/139/13902.htm at para 12.

generally on the person who is seeking to establish a lack of capacity and the matter is decided according to the usual civil standard, the balance of probabilities.

Law Commission proposals

2.27 Taking account of responses to consultation and in keeping with its proposal to establish a single comprehensive jurisdiction, the Law Commission recommended that the new statutory provisions should expressly include and re-state both the common law principle of presumption of capacity and the relevant standard of proof.[40]

The legislation

2.28 The Joint Committee also supported the principle of presumption of capacity and recommended that this principle should be given primacy of place in the legislation:[41]

> 'This is because it better reflects the positive nature of the Bill's purpose and will increase confidence in the operation of this legislation.'

The presumption of capacity therefore appears in MCA 2005, s 1(2) as the first principle relating to the Act.

The Code of Practice

2.29 The Code of Practice stresses that the starting point for assessing someone's capacity to make a particular decision is always the assumption that the individual does have capacity:[42]

> 'Some people may need help to be able to make a decision or to communicate their decision. However, this does not necessarily mean that they cannot make that decision – unless there is proof that they do lack capacity to do so.'

2.30 Capacity must then be judged in relation to the particular decision at the time that decision needs to be made, and the presumption of capacity may only be rebutted if there is acceptable evidence that the person is incapable of making the decision in question. In relation to most decisions in connection with the person's care and treatment, a 'reasonable belief' that the person lacks capacity is sufficient, so long as reasonable steps have been taken to establish this.[43]

2.31 Where the question of capacity is to be decided in proceedings before the Court of Protection, it has been held that the threshold for engagement of the court's powers (under MCA 2005, s 48) is lower than that of evidence sufficient

---

[40] Law Com No 231, n 1 above, at para 3.2. In Scotland, the presumption of capacity is established under common law and is not re-stated in AWI(S)A 2000.

[41] Joint Committee Report, Vol I, n 5 above, at paras 66–67.

[42] Mental Capacity Act 2005: Code of Practice, at para 2.5.

[43] MCA 2005, s 5(1). See **2.87–2.90**.

in itself to rebut the presumption of capacity. The proper test in such circumstances is whether there is evidence giving good cause for concern that the person may lack capacity in some relevant regard.[44] The operation of this threshold test was clearly illustrated in the decision in *Re SB*,[45] involving a woman with a history of bipolar disorder who wished to terminate her pregnancy at the 23rd week of its term, having previously shown signs of wanting to keep the baby. Permission was given for the NHS Trust treating her to apply to the Court of Protection for a determination of SB's capacity to make this decision since there was cause for concern that deterioration in her mental state had caused her to change her mind. Despite expert evidence to the contrary, Holman J found her to have capacity to make the decision herself:[46]

> '... even if aspects of the decision making are influenced by paranoid thoughts in relation to her husband and her mother, she is nevertheless able to describe, and genuinely holds, a range of rational reasons for her decision. When I say rational, I do not necessarily say they are good reasons, nor do I indicate whether I agree with her decision, for section 1(4) of the Act expressly provides that someone is not to be treated as unable to make a decision simply because it is an unwise decision. It seems to me that this lady has made, and has maintained for an appreciable period of time, a decision. It may be that aspects of her reasons may be skewed by paranoia. There are other reasons which she has and which she has expressed. My own opinion is that it would be a total affront to the autonomy of this patient to conclude that she lacks capacity to the level required to make this decision. It is of course a profound and grave decision, but it does not necessarily involve complex issues. It is a decision that she has made and maintains; and she has defended and justified her decision against challenge. It is a decision which she has the capacity to reach. So for those reasons I conclude that it has not been established that she lacks capacity to make decisions about her desired termination, and I will either make a declaration to that effect or dismiss these proceedings.'

Practicable steps to help decision-making

2.32 The second of MCA 2005's key principles[47] clarifies that a person should not be treated as unable to make a decision until everything practicable has been done to help the person make his or her own decision. All practicable steps to enable decision-making must first be shown to be unsuccessful before the person can be assessed as lacking capacity.

Law Commission proposals

2.33 The Law Commission had originally proposed that it would only be necessary for 'reasonable attempts' to be made to understand a person who has

---

[44] *Re F* [2009] EWHC B30 (Fam) [COPLR] Con Vol 390 at para 44.
[45] *Re SB (A patient; Capacity to consent to termination)* [2013] EWHC 1417 (COP), [2013] COPLR 445.
[46] Ibid at para 44.
[47] MCA 2005, s 1(3).

difficulty in communicating a decision.[48] However, many respondents to the consultation paper made the point that the reference to 'reasonable attempts' was too weak and, for people who are not simply unconscious, 'strenuous steps must be taken to assist and facilitate communication before any finding of incapacity is made'.[49] Other respondents stressed the need for help and support to maximise a person's potential to make their own decisions, not just those with communication difficulties.

The legislation

2.34 This requirement has now been translated into MCA 2005's guiding principles in s 1(3). Although the requirement is contained in the guiding principles, it is perhaps of note that s 1(3) represents the sole reference to support in the MCA 2005. The contrast to the Mental Capacity Bill under consideration in Northern Ireland[50] in this regard is noteworthy; that legislation which – in some regards – is very similar to MCA 2005, includes an entire clause (4) relating to support. Further, 'serious interventions' require a formal assessment of capacity where the assessor must specifically document what help and support has been given to enable P to make a decision (clause 13).

2.35 Perhaps because the Act contains no further reference to the need for support, the principle enshrined in s 1(3) can all too often be overlooked. It is striking, for instance, how rarely cases before the Court of Protection involve consideration of providing support to the person said to lack capacity to take the decision(s) in question: conversely, it is also striking how in the rare cases where judges have taken active measures to ensure compliance with s 1(3), findings of incapacity have been avoided. A particularly good example of this is *Wandsworth CCG v IA and TA*,[51] in which P had consistently failed to engage with those seeking to assess his capacity (who, in turn, concluded he lacked capacity to take material decisions). The court, however, the court directed that P be involved in the instruction of a psychiatric expert to report upon his capacity to take the material decisions; the evidence of that expert, with whom P engaged fully, was to the effect that he <u>had</u> the requisite decision-making capacity, evidence that the court accepted.

2.36 In addition, since the UK has formally ratified the United Nations Convention on the Rights of Persons with Disabilities (CRPD),[52] Art 12 of which calls on state parties to recognize the right of people with disabilities to 'enjoy legal capacity on an equal basis with others in all aspects of life', the

---

[48]   *Mentally Incapacitated Adults and Decision-Making: A New Jurisdiction*, Law Com Consultation Paper No 128 (HMSO, 1993), at para 3.41.

[49]   Law Com No 231, n 1 above, at para 3.21.

[50]   For a discussion of the earlier draft Bill and its contrasts with MCA 2005, see Alex Ruck Keene and Catherine Taggart: 'A brave new (fused) world? The draft Northern Irish Mental Capacity Bill' *Elder Law Journal*, Jordans, [2014] Eld LJ 395.

[51]   [2014] EWHC 990 (COP).

[52]   UN General Assembly, A/61/611.

need to maximise individual autonomy and promote supported decision-making would be minimum requirements in ensuring the law is CRPD compliant. For a further discussion of this requirements of the CRPD in this regard see **1.218–1.230**.

2.37 There are a number of ways in which people can be given help and support to enable them to make their own decisions, and these will vary depending on the decision to be made, the timescale for making the decision and the individual circumstances of the person wishing to make it. The practicable steps to be taken might include using specific communication strategies, providing information in an accessible form or treating an underlying medical condition to enable the person to regain capacity. However, those taking practicable steps to help someone make a decision must be careful to avoid subjecting the person to pressure or undue influence, possibly based on their own beliefs or their family or cultural obligations.[53]

The Code of Practice

2.38 The main Code of Practice devotes a whole chapter to provide guidance and prompt consideration of a range of practicable steps which may assist decision-making, although the relevance of the various factors will vary depending on each particular situation.[54] As a minimum, the following steps should be considered:

(1) Try to minimise anxiety or stress by making the person feel at ease. Choose the best location where the client feels most comfortable and the time of day when the client is most alert.

(2) If the person's capacity is likely to improve, wait until it has improved (unless the decision is urgent). If the cause of the incapacity can be treated, it may be possible to delay the decision until treatment has taken place.

(3) If there are communication or language problems, consider using a speech and language therapist or interpreter, or consult family members on the best methods of communication.

(4) Be aware of any cultural, ethnic or religious factors which may have a bearing on the person's way of thinking, behaviour or communication.

(5) Consider whether or not a friend or family member should be present to help reduce anxiety. But in some cases the presence of others may be intrusive.

---

[53] Undue influence can affect both those with or without capacity. See for example, *Re SA (Vulnerable Adult with Capacity: Marriage)* [2005] EWHC 2942. For consideration of the law relating to undue influence, see *V Hackett v CPS* [2011] EWHC 1170 (Admin).

[54] Mental Capacity Act 2005: Code of Practice, Chapter 3.

Unwise decisions

The legislation

2.39　The third principle underlying the Act, set out in MCA 2005, s 1(4), confirms that a person should not be treated as lacking capacity merely because he or she makes a decision that others consider to be unwise. The intention here is to reflect the nature of human decision-making. Different people will make different decisions because they give greater weight to some factors than to others, taking account of their own values and preferences. Some people are keen to express their own individuality or may be more willing to take risks than others. The diagnostic threshold requiring evidence of some mental impairment or disturbance[55] will to some extent ensure that the capacity of those who are merely eccentric is not challenged unnecessarily. However, people who have mental disabilities which could affect their decision-making capacity should not be expected to make 'better' or 'wiser' decisions than anyone else. What matters is the ability to make a decision – not the outcome.

Law Commission proposals

2.40　Originally, the Law Commission had suggested that it was unnecessary to make such provision in MCA 2005. The right to make unwise decisions has been part of the common law since at least 1850.[56] In a consultation paper the Law Commission argued:[57]

> 'If it is feared that a function test along these lines is not strong enough, interference in the lives of the merely deviant or eccentric could be expressly excluded. New Zealand law (Protection of Personal and Property Rights Act 1988, s 1(3)) provides that the fact that the client "has made or is intending to make any decision that a person exercising ordinary prudence would not have made or would not make is not in itself sufficient ground for the exercise of its jurisdiction by the court." A similar safeguard is proposed by the Scottish Law Commission, with a stipulation that "the fact that the person has acted or intends to act in a way an ordinary prudent person would not should not by itself be evidence of lack of capacity" (Discussion Paper No 94, para 4.40). We, however, doubt the need for any such stipulation, in the light of the definition we have proposed, which clearly directs an assessor to the decision-making process, rather than its outcome. We invite views on this.'

2.41　The views received by the Law Commission were strongly in favour of explicit provision being made in the legislation:[58]

> 'Those we consulted, however, overwhelmingly urged upon us the importance of making such an express stipulation. This would recognise that the "outcome" approach to capacity has been rejected, while recognising that it is almost certainly in daily use. We recommend that a person should not be regarded as unable to

---

[55]　See **2.60–2.61**.
[56]　*Bird v Luckie* (1850) 8 Hare 301.
[57]　Law Com Consultation Paper No 128, n 1 above, at para 3.25.
[58]　Law Com No 231, n 1 above, at para 3.19.

make a decision by reason of mental disability merely because he or she makes a decision which would not be made by a person of ordinary prudence.'

Evidence before the Joint Committee

2.42 During pre-legislative scrutiny of the draft Bill, the Joint Committee received evidence from some witnesses expressing concern that a person with apparent capacity may be able to make repeatedly unwise decisions that put him or her at risk or result in preventable suffering or disadvantage.[59] Particular concerns were raised by Denzil Lush, then Master of the Court of Protection (now Senior Judge of the Court of Protection), who drew attention to the distinction between decision-specific capacity and more general ongoing incapacity. He gave examples of cases where people had made unwise decisions, each of which they appeared capable of making, but where they in fact lacked an overall awareness or understanding of the implications of those decisions.[60] Senior Judge Lush explained his concerns as follows:[61]

> 'Even though they may be suffering from a condition that restricts their ability to govern their life and make independent choices, so long as they have the basic ability to consider the options and make choices, we must not intervene against their will. By intervening against their will, even for their own good, we show less respect for them than if we had allowed them to go ahead and make a mistake. This lack of inter-personal respect is potentially a more serious infringement of their rights and freedoms than allowing them to make an unwise decision.'

2.43 Some caution may therefore need to be applied in operating this principle in practice. Although as a general rule, capacity should be assessed in relation to each particular decision or specific issue, there may be circumstances where a person has an ongoing condition which affects his or her capacity to make a range of interrelated or sequential decisions. One decision on its own may make sense but the combination of decisions may raise doubts as to the person's capacity or at least prompt the need for a proper assessment. The Code of Practice suggests that further investigation (such as a formal assessment of capacity) may be needed if somebody:[62]

> '... repeatedly makes unwise decisions that put them at significant risk of harm or exploitation; or makes a particular unwise decision that is obviously irrational or out of character.'

For example, in *D v R (Deputy of S) v S*, having confirmed a person's right to act in an unwise, capricious or even spiteful manner, Henderson J said:[63]

---

[59]   Joint Committee Report, Vol I, n 5 above, at paras 72, 78.
[60]   Joint Committee Report, Vol II, n 32 above, at Ev 184, Q495–Q496.
[61]   Denzil Lush 'The Mental Capacity Act and the new Court of Protection' (2005) *Journal of Mental Health Law* 12, at p 34.
[62]   Mental Capacity Act 2005: Code of Practice, at para 2.11.
[63]   [2010] EWHC 2405 (COP) at para 40. A different approach was taken in the case of *Re SB* [2013] EWHC 1417 (COP), [2013] COPLR 445 where Holman J reached the conclusion that SB, a woman with bipolar disorder, had capacity to decide to terminate her pregnancy, despite her previously expressed wish of wanting to have the baby – see **2.31** above.

'The significance of section 1(4) must not, however, be exaggerated. The fact that a decision is unwise or foolish may not, without more, be treated as conclusive, but it remains in my judgment a relevant consideration for the court to take into account in considering whether the criteria of inability to make a decision for oneself in section 3(1) are satisfied. This will particularly be the case where there is a marked contrast between the unwise nature of the impugned decision and the person's former attitude to the conduct of his affairs at a time when his capacity was not in question.'

2.44 But equally, an unwise decision should not, by itself, be sufficient to indicate lack of capacity. For example, in *CC v KK and STCC*, Baker J concluded, against all the expert evidence, that KK had capacity to decide where to live, even though the local authority and the experts believed her decision to return to her bungalow was unwise:[64]

'There is, I perceive, a danger that professionals, including judges, may objectively conflate a capacity assessment with a best interests analysis and conclude that the person under review should attach greater weight to the physical security and comfort of a residential home and less importance to the emotional security and comfort that the person derives from being in their own home. I remind myself again of the danger of the "protection imperative" identified by Ryder J in *Oldham MBC v GW and PW* [2007] EWHC 136 (Fam). These considerations underpin the cardinal rule, enshrined in statute, that a person is not to be treated as unable to make a decision merely because she makes what is perceived as being an unwise one.'

In *PC and Anor v City of York Council*, concerning the capacity of a woman with learning disabilities to decide to resume cohabitation with her husband on his release from prison having been convicted of serious sexual offences, the Court of Appeal recognised that:[65]

'... the court's jurisdiction is not founded upon professional concern as to the 'outcome' of an individual's decision. There may be many women who are seen to be in relationships with men regarded by professionals as predatory sexual offenders. The Court of Protection does not have jurisdiction to act to "protect"these women if they do not lack the mental capacity to decide whether or not to be, or continue to be, in such a relationship. The individual's decision may be said to be "against the better judgment" of the woman concerned, but the point is that, unless they lack mental capacity to make that judgment, it is against their better judgment. It is a judgment that they are entitled to make. The statute respects their autonomy so to decide and the Court of Protection has no jurisdiction to intervene.

... there is a space between an unwise decision and one which an individual does not have the mental capacity to take and ... it is important to respect that space, and to ensure that it is preserved, for it is within that space that an individual's autonomy operates.'

---

[64] *CC v KK and STCC* [2012] EWHC 2136 (COP), [2012] COPLR 627 at para 65.
[65] *PC and Anor v City of York Council* [2013] EWCA Civ 478, [2013] COPLR 409 at paras 53–54 per McFarlane LJ.

Best interests

The Law Commission proposals

2.45 In seeking to establish a clear legal framework for making decisions with, or on behalf of people who lack capacity, the Law Commission proposed a single criterion to govern all decision-making:[66]

> 'Although decisions are to be taken by a variety of people with varying degrees of formality, a single criterion to govern any substitute decision can be established. Whatever the answer to the question "who decides?", there should only be one answer to the subsequent question "on what basis?".
>
> We explained in our overview paper that two criteria for making substitute decisions for another adult have been developed in the literature in this field: "best interests", on the one hand, and "substituted judgment", on the other. In Consultation Paper No 128 we argued that the two were not in fact mutually exclusive and we provisionally favoured a "best interests" criterion which would contain a strong element of "substituted judgment". It had been widely accepted by respondents to the overview paper that, where a person has never had capacity, there is no viable alternative to the "best interests" criterion. We were pleased to find that our arguments in favour of a "best interests" criterion found favour with almost all our respondents, with the Law Society emphasising that the criterion as defined in the consultation papers was in fact "an excellent compromise" between the best interests and substituted judgment approaches. We recommend that anything done for, and any decision made on behalf of a person without capacity should be done or made in the best interests of that person.'

2.46 It is notable that the Scottish Law Commission took a different approach in formulating proposals which led to AWI(S)A 2000:[67]

> 'We consider that "best interests" by itself is too vague and would require to be supplemented by further factors which have to be taken into account. We also consider that "best interests" does not give due weight to the views of the adult, particularly to wishes and feeling which he or she had expressed while capable of doing so. The concept of best interests was developed in the context of child law where a child's level of understanding may not be high and will usually have been lower in the past. Incapable adults such as those who are mentally ill, head injured or suffering from dementia at the time when a decision has to be made in connection with them, will have possessed full mental powers before their present incapacity. We think it is wrong to equate such adults with children and for that reason would avoid extending child law concepts to them. Accordingly, the general principles [of AWI(S)A 2000] are framed without express reference to best interests.'

---

[66] Law Com No 231, n 1 above, at paras 3.24–3.25.
[67] *Report on Incapable Adults*, Scot Law Com No 151 (Scottish Executive, 1995) para 2.50.

The Joint Committee's view

2.47 The Joint Committee on the draft Bill compared the two approaches and came down in favour of including the concept of best interests within the Act's key principles:[68]

> 'We heard evidence that the concept of best interests has been usefully developed by the courts and that its inclusion in statute would assist in promoting awareness and good practice, thereby ensuring some consistency in approach.'

The legislation

2.48 MCA 2005, s 1(5) establishes in statute the former common law principle that any act done, or any decision made, under MCA 2005 for or on behalf of a person who lacks capacity must be done, or made, in that person's best interests. This establishes 'best interests' as the single criterion to govern all decision making affecting people who lack capacity to make their own decisions. Further details on the meaning and determination of best interests are set out in the Act.[69] Whether the concept of 'best interests' is one that is – in and of itself – a concept that is fundamentally incompatible with the CRPD is a topic of increasingly hot debate: see in this regard the discussion at **1.218–1.230**.

Less restrictive alternative

The Law Commission proposals

2.49 The Law Commission originally proposed that the 'least restrictive alternative' principle should be included in the new legislation as one of the factors to be taken into account in determining the best interests of a person who lacks capacity.[70] The Commission considered that the principle had been developed over many years by experts in the field so as to become widely recognised and accepted.[71] The Draft Mental Incapacity Bill therefore included this principle in the proposed statutory checklist for best interests.[72]

The legislation

2.50 However, in response to the Joint Committee's recommendation[73] the Government agreed to incorporate in MCA 2005, s 1(6) the principle that, where possible, a *less* restrictive option should be chosen (rather than the *least* restrictive alternative). This became the fifth key principle to guide the use of MCA 2005 generally, rather than just one factor in the best interests checklist.

---

[68] Joint Committee Report, Vol I, n 5 above, at para 82.
[69] MCA 2005, s 4, and see **2.122–2.153**.
[70] Law Com No 231, n 1 above, at paras 3.28, 3.37.
[71] For a discussion of the origins and development of the principle of least restrictive alternative, see Denzil Lush 'The Mental Capacity Act and the new Court of Protection', n 61 above, at pp 37–38.
[72] Draft Mental Incapacity Bill, Cm 5859-I (TSO, 2003) cl 4(2)(e).
[73] Joint Committee Report, Vol I, n 5 above, at para 44.

2.51 Before any action is taken, or any decision is made under MCA 2005 in relation to a person lacking capacity, the person taking the action or making the decision must consider whether it is possible to act or decide in a way that is less restrictive of the person's rights and freedom of action. Where there is more than one course of action or a choice of decisions to be made, all possible options or alternatives should be explored (including whether there is a need for any action or decision at all) in order to consider which option would be less restrictive or intrusive. However, other options need only be considered so long as the desired purpose of the action or decision can still be achieved. In any event, the option chosen must be in the person's best interests, which may not in fact be the least restrictive.[74]

The Scottish approach

2.52 This formulation differs from the principles set out in AWI(S)A 2000, which starts with a specific 'no intervention' provision[75] – that there shall be no intervention in the affairs of an adult unless the intervention will benefit the adult and that such benefit cannot reasonably be achieved in any other way. This is then followed by the 'least restrictive option' principle.[76] The Joint Committee considered this approach, but took the view that the less restrictive alternative principle would involve decision-makers in having to consider whether any intervention at all was in fact necessary.[77] Experience has shown, however, that there may not be so great a difference in a difference in practice between the approaches ultimately adopted in the two jurisdictions.

Relevance to the Court of Protection

2.53 Although the Court of Protection is subject to the principles set out in MCA 2005, s 1,[78] including best interests and the less restrictive alternative, specific provision is made to limit the scope of any intervention where court proceedings are contemplated with the intention of ensuring that a less restrictive or interventionist approach is adopted. MCA 2005 requires the Court, in deciding whether to grant permission for an application to it (where permission is required), to consider the reasons for the application, the benefit to the person lacking capacity and whether the benefit can be achieved in any other way.[79] In addition, the Act imposes an obligation on the Court to make a single order in preference to appointing a deputy, and where the appointment of a deputy is considered necessary, that the powers conferred on the deputy should be as limited in scope and duration as possible.[80]

---

[74] Confirmed by Ryder J in *C v A Local Authority* [2011] EWHC 1539, [2011] COPLR Con Vol 972 at para 61. In other words, 'The "best interests" principle takes priority': *London Borough of Havering v LD & KD* [2010] EWHC 3876 (COP) at para 9.

[75] AWI(S)A 2000, s 1(2).

[76] AWI(S)A 2000, s 1(3).

[77] Joint Committee Report, Vol I, n 5 above, at para 96.

[78] MCA 2005, s 16(3).

[79] MCA 2005, s 50(3).

[80] MCA 2005, s 16(4).

Defining lack of capacity

The functional approach

2.54 Before MCA 2005 came into effect, the lack of a clear statutory definition of capacity (or lack of capacity) caused confusion and difficulty for all concerned, not least for professionals called on to assess someone's decision-making capacity. There were also significant differences in approach between legal and medical or psychological concepts of capacity.[81] Case-law offered a number of tests of capacity depending on the type of decision in issue.[82] The Law Commission recommended that, in order to provide certainty and clarity in using the new jurisdiction, a single statutory definition of capacity should be adopted.[83] Therefore, having set out the key principles governing its operation, MCA 2005 goes on to define the people affected by its provisions.

2.55 MCA 2005, s 2 sets out the definition of a person who lacks capacity. MCA 2005, s 3 sets out the test for assessing whether a person is unable to make a decision and therefore lacks capacity. By applying these together, MCA 2005 adopts a functional approach to defining capacity, requiring capacity to be assessed in relation to each particular decision at the time the decision needs to be made, and not the person's ability to make decisions generally. This means that individuals should not be labelled 'incapable' simply on the basis that they have been diagnosed with a particular condition, or because of any preconceived ideas or assumptions about their abilities due, for example, to their age, appearance or behaviour. Rather, it must be shown that they lack capacity for each specific decision, or type of decision, at the time the particular decision needs to be made. In *A, B and C v X and Z*, an important case demonstrating the approach taken by the court in determining capacity, Hedley J was required to decide whether X had capacity to (a) marry; (b) make a will; (c) revoke or grant an enduring or lasting power of attorney; (d) manage his property and affairs; (d) litigate; and (e) decide with whom to have contact (although the last issue was not currently for the court to decide). He stressed from the outset 'Each of those questions requires an answer, but each must be considered individually'.[84]

The following paragraphs consider in turn each element of the Act's definition and test of capacity.

---

[81] The Law Society and British Medical Association attempted to address this problem by providing much needed guidance in *Assessment of Mental Capacity: A Practical Guide for Doctors and Lawyers* (BMA, 1995; BMJ Books, 2nd edn, 2004; Law Society Publishing, 3rd edn, 2009). A further edition of this book is in production as at the time of writing.

[82] See **2.85–2.86**.

[83] Law Com No 231, n 1 above, at para 3.7.

[84] *A, B and C v X, Y and Z* [2012] EWHC 2400 (COP), [2013] COPLR 1 at paragraph 1. Note: permission was granted to A, B and C to appeal the decision in relation to X's capacity to marry, but the appeal lapsed when X subsequently died.

People who lack capacity

2.56 MCA 2005, s 2(1) sets out the definition of a person who lacks capacity as follows:

> 'For the purposes of this Act, a person lacks capacity in relation to a matter if at the material time he is unable to make a decision for himself in relation to the matter because of an impairment of, or a disturbance in the functioning of, the mind or brain.'

Capacity is therefore both decision-specific and time-specific. The inability to make the particular decision in question must be *because of* 'an impairment of, or a disturbance in the functioning of, the mind or brain' (ie a mental disability or disorder) and the causal link (that the impairment or disturbance directly causes the inability to make the decision) must be clearly demonstrated.[85] It does not matter whether the impairment or disturbance is permanent or temporary.[86] A person can lack capacity to make a decision even if the loss of capacity is partial or temporary or if his or her capacity fluctuates. In particular, a person may lack capacity in relation to one matter but not in relation to others.

2.57 There has been considerable legal debate, particularly in cases concerning capacity to marry or to consent to sexual relations as to whether the test of capacity is act-specific or person-specific (for further discussion, see Chapter 6). The Court of Appeal has now clarified that, unless the common law and/or the MCA 2005 expressly state otherwise, capacity is to be assessed in relation to the specific decision. It will depend on the character of the particular decision as to whether the information relevant to that decision relates to an act, to a particular person or to a specific set of circumstances:[87]

> 'The determination of capacity under MCA 2005, Part 1 is decision specific. Some decisions, for example agreeing to marry or consenting to divorce, are status or act specific. Some other decisions, for example whether P should have contact with a particular individual, may be person specific. But all decisions, whatever their nature, fall to be evaluated within the straightforward and clear structure of MCA 2005, ss 1 to 3 which requires the court to have regard to 'a matter' requiring 'a decision'. There is neither need nor justification for the plain words of the statute to be embellished. I do not agree with the Official Solicitor's submission[88] that absurd consequences flow from a failure to adopt either an act-specific or a person-specific approach to each category of decision that may fall for consideration. To the contrary, I endorse Mr Hallin's argument to the effect that

---

[85] This point was strongly made by the Court of Appeal in *PC & Anor v City of York Council* [2013] EWCA Civ 478, [2013] COPLR 409, as described in **2.59** below.

[86] MCA 2005, s 2(2).

[87] *PC & Anor v City of York Council* [2013] EWCA Civ 479, [2013] COPLR 409 at paragraph 35 per McFarlane LJ, approving the approach adopted by Hedley J in *CYC v PC and NC* [2012] COPLR 670 at para 19. See also **2.72–2.76** below.

[88] For an explanation of the Official Solicitor's submission in this case, see Alastair Pitblado, 'The decision of the Court of Appeal in *PC & NC v City of York*', *Elder Law Journal*, Jordans, [2013] Eld LJ 361.

removing the specific factual context from some decisions leaves nothing for the evaluation of capacity to bite upon. The MCA 2005 itself makes a distinction between some decisions (set out in s 27) which as a category are exempt from the court's welfare jurisdiction once the relevant incapacity is established (for example consent to marriage, sexual relations or divorce) and other decisions (set out in s 17) which are intended, for example, to relate to a 'specified person' or specific medical treatments.'

The two-stage test of capacity

2.58 In applying the test for capacity set out in ss 2–3 of the MCA 2005 to determine whether an individual has capacity to make a particular decision, the Code of Practice advises that a two-stage procedure must be applied:[89]

(1) it must be established that there is an impairment of, or disturbance in the functioning of, the person's mind or brain; and

(2) it must be established that the impairment or disturbance is sufficient to render the person unable to make that particular decision at the relevant time.

2.59 This approach to assessing capacity was based on the Law Commission's conclusion that considering first whether the 'diagnostic threshold' was met (see below) would serve to protect the autonomy of people who merely make unusual or unwise decisions. If there is no indication of impairment or disturbance in the mind or brain, the individual should be presumed to have capacity and his or her ability to make decisions should not be questioned. However, in *PC & Anor v City of York Council* the Court of Appeal appeared to hold that the test should be applied in the sequence set out in s 2(1), that is focussing first on the functional aspect of whether the person concerned is unable to make the decision in question, and if so, whether that inability is *because of* an impairment or disturbance:[90]

> 'There is, however, a danger in structuring the decision by looking to s 2(1) primarily as requiring a finding of mental impairment and nothing more and in considering s 2(1) first before then going on to look at s 3(1) as requiring a finding of inability to make a decision. The danger is that the strength of the causative nexus between mental impairment and inability to decide is watered down. That sequence – "mental impairment" and then "inability to make a decision"- is the reverse of that in s 2(1) – "unable to make a decision ... **because of** an impairment of, or a disturbance in the functioning of, the mind or brain" [emphasis added]. The danger in using s 2(1) simply to collect the mental health element is that the key words "because of" in s 2(1) may lose their prominence and be replaced by words such as those deployed by Hedley J: "referable to" or "significantly relates to".'

---

[89] Mental Capacity Act 2005: Code of Practice, pp 44-45.
[90] *PC & Anor v City of York Council* [2013] EWCA Civ 479, [2013] COPLR 409 at [58] per McFarlane LJ.

Although the passage cited above would appear to suggest that the Court of Appeal suggested that it was necessary to reverse the order in which the two limbs of the test are applied, there has been some considerable debate about this and Parker J in *NCC v PB and TB*[91] expressed the view that it had not. It may be, we suggest, that the question is one more of focus – in some settings (for instance the psychiatric hospital setting) the functional aspect will be more important; in some settings (for instance the community setting) the diagnostic element will be more important.

In all cases, however, the 'causative nexus' is crucial. Indeed, it is sufficiently important that it may – in practice – be prudent to proceed on the basis that there is a three-stage test. In other words, in all cases (and whether the diagnostic aspect is considered before the functional aspect or vice versa), the final question must always be whether there is a sufficient causative link between the identified impairment or disturbance and the identified functional inability to take the decision in question. It is undoubtedly the case that any *pro forma* capacity assessment tool that does not include such a question runs the risk of leading the assessor into error.

A *diagnostic threshold*

2.60 During its consultation processes, the Law Commission considered the finely balanced arguments for and against having a diagnostic threshold, requiring a 'mental disability' to be established before someone is deemed to lack capacity.[92] The Commission concluded that a diagnostic 'hurdle' would serve a useful gate-keeping function, to ensure that decision-making rights are not taken over prematurely or unnecessarily and to make the test of capacity stringent enough *not* to catch large numbers of people who make unusual or unwise decisions. It was felt that the protection offered by a diagnostic threshold outweighs any risk of prejudice or stigma affecting those who need help with decision-making.[93] It does however appear increasingly likely that the existence of a diagnostic threshold, thereby creating a link between legal capacity and mental capacity, brings the law into conflict with the UN Convention on the Rights of Persons with Disabilities (CRPD): see further **1.218–1.230.**

2.61 Instead of using the term 'mental disability', MCA 2005, s 2(1) refers to 'an impairment of, or a disturbance in the functioning of, the mind or brain'. This covers a wide range of conditions. For example, people taken to casualty requiring treatment for a physical disorder who are incapacitated in the short term through alcohol or drug misuse, delirium or following head injury may need urgent attention which cannot wait until their capacity has been restored. People in such situations are entitled to the protections and safeguards offered by the Act in the same way as those found to lack the capacity to make specific

---

[91]   [2014] EWCOP 14; [2015] COPLR 118.
[92]   The arguments are set out in Law Com Consultation Paper No 128, n 51 above, at paras 3.10–3.14.
[93]   Law Com No 231, n 1 above, at para 3.8.

financial, health or welfare decisions as a result, for example, of mental illness, dementia, learning disabilities or the long-term effects of brain damage.[94]

Principle of 'equal consideration'

2.62 During the Bill's Report stage in the House of Lords, an amendment was passed to make it clear that lack of capacity cannot be established merely by reference to a person's age or appearance, or any condition or aspect of his or her behaviour which might lead others to make unjustified assumptions about the person's capacity.[95] This amendment was originally proposed by the Making Decisions Alliance[96] as a 'principle of non-discrimination and equal consideration' which the Alliance sought to have included in MCA 2005's statement of principles, in order to ensure that people with impaired capacity are treated no less favourably than people with capacity:[97]

> 'Our concerns stem from evidence, anecdotal and otherwise, that prejudices and attitudes about the quality of life of a person with serious learning disabilities, mental health problem or a head injury or other condition that leads to loss of capacity can get in the way of supporting that person and how they are, what they want and what they need.'

2.63 While the Government was sympathetic to these concerns, the drafting of a broad 'equal consideration' principle proved unworkable. Instead the Government put forward two amendments, one relating to the definition of capacity and the second concerning best interests determinations[98] in order to:[99]

> '... reinforce the belief, shared across the House, that no-one should be assumed to lack capacity, excluded from decision-making, discriminated against or given substandard care and treatment simply, for example, as a result of disability.'

2.64 Section 2(3) of MCA 2005 therefore ensures that individuals should not be labelled 'incapable' because of their age or appearance, or because of any preconceived ideas or prejudicial assumptions about their abilities due to their particular condition or behaviour. The reference to 'condition' covers a range of factors, including both mental or physical disabilities, age-related illness and temporary conditions such as drunkenness. 'Appearance' is also deliberately broad, covering all aspects of physical appearance, visible medical problems or disfiguring scars, disabilities, skin colour, religious dress or simply being

---

[94] For a discussion on medical conditions which may impact on capacity, see Steven Luttrell, 'Impact of Dementia and Other Conditions Affecting Capacity' in *Elder Law Journal*, Jordans [2011] Eld LJ 403, reproduced as an Annex to this chapter.

[95] MCA 2005, s 2(3).

[96] A coalition of around 40 charities that campaigned for MCA 2005.

[97] Making Decisions Alliance *House of Lords Briefing*, Second Reading (10 January 2005), at p 3.

[98] See **2.130–2.131**.

[99] *Hansard*, HL Deb, vol 670, ser 5, col 1318 (15 March 2005).

unkempt or dishevelled. 'Behaviour' relates to ways of behaving that might seem unusual or odd to others, such as failing to make eye contact, talking to oneself or laughing inappropriately.

Qualifying age

2.65 It has always been the intention that the MCA jurisdiction should apply only to *adults* who lack capacity, leaving disputes about the care and welfare of children and young people to be resolved under the Children Act 1989. However, the Law Commission commented that a number of the statutory provisions in the Children Act 1989 do not apply to 16–18 year olds or only in 'exceptional' circumstances. The Law Commission concluded that:[100]

> 'If continuing substitute decision-making arrangements are needed for someone aged 16 or 17, this is likely to be because the young person lacks mental capacity and not because he or she is under the age of legal majority.'

2.66 It followed that the provisions of the MCA 2005, rather than the Children Act 1989, should apply in those circumstances for young people aged 16 or 17, and not just where there is no one available to exercise parental responsibility. For example, there may be circumstances where it is in the young person's best interests for someone other than a person with parental responsibility to be appointed as deputy to make financial or property decisions. Or it may be appropriate for the Court of Protection to make personal decisions, for example, where the young person should live, or medical treatment decisions concerning a young person lacking capacity where it is considered that those with parental responsibility are not acting in the young person's best interests. It was suggested that the resultant overlap would pose no great problems in practice.

2.67 MCA 2005, s 2(5) therefore makes it clear that the powers exercisable under MCA 2005 apply in general only to people lacking capacity who are aged 16 years or over. However, as was the case under the previous law, MCA 2005's powers to deal with property and financial affairs might be exercised in relation to a child whose disabilities will cause a lack of capacity to manage those affairs to continue into adulthood.[101]

2.68 In cases where legal proceedings are required to resolve disputes or make legally effective arrangements for someone aged 16 or 17, the Law Commission pointed out that it would not make sense to require two sets of legal proceedings to be conducted within a short period of time where the problems arising from the young person's incapacity are likely to continue after the age of 18. MCA 2005, therefore, makes provision for transfer from the Court of Protection to the family courts, and vice versa.[102] The choice of court will depend on what is 'just and convenient' in the particular circumstances of the

---

[100] Law Com No 231, n 1 above, at para 2.52.
[101] MCA 2005, ss 2(6) and 18(3).
[102] MCA 2005, s 21.

case.[103] In particular, in considering whether to transfer a case from a court having jurisdiction under the Children Act 1989 to the Court of Protection, the court must consider:[104]

> 'The extent to which any order made as respects a person who lacks capacity is likely to continue to have effect when that person reaches 18.'

2.69 The court should also take into account any other matters it considers relevant.[105] Some helpful guidance on what matters may often be relevant in such cases has been given by Hedley J in *B (A Local Authority) v RM, MM, and AM*:[106]

> 'One, is the child over 16? Otherwise of course, there is no power. Two, does the child manifestly lack capacity in respect of the principal decisions which are to be made in the Children Act proceedings? Three, are the disabilities which give rise to lack of capacity lifelong or at least long-term? Four, can the decisions which arise in respect of the child's welfare all be taken and all issues resolved during the child's minority? Five, does the Court of Protection have powers or procedures more appropriate to the resolution of outstanding issues than are available under the Children Act? Six, can the child's welfare needs be fully met by the exercise of Court of Protection powers? These provisional thoughts are intended to put some flesh on to the provisions of Article 3(3); no doubt, other issues will arise in other cases. The essential thrust, however, is whether looking at the individual needs of the specific young person, it can be said that their welfare will be better safeguarded within the Court of Protection than it would be under the Children Act.'

In that case, Hedley J concluded that the case should be transferred to the Court of Protection for the following reasons:[107]

> 'A) I think that there should be a Court determination as to U [residential placement] and the need for AM to stay there. B) I think the Court door should remain open during those delicate planning stages and potentially difficult decisions over the placement, even if the Court does not actively intervene in that process unless it is specifically invited so to do. C) I am far from satisfied that these matters will be resolved by the time of AM's 18th birthday. D) Her disabilities and acute care needs are lifelong. E) Declarations in the Court of Protection avoid all the negative consequences as I see them of making of a care order whilst at the same time, setting the necessary framework within which AM's needs can be addressed. F) Her lack of capacity on all relevant issues for decision is manifest. It follows, that I propose pursuant to Article 3(4)(a) to transfer on my own initiative having as required given my reasons for so doing. Accordingly, I propose to reconstitute as the Court of Protection and it would be quite unnecessary in these circumstances to have a separate hearing in the Court of Protection, because all the evidence and all the issues are before me and I am myself a judge of the Court of

---

[103] Mental Capacity Act 2005 (Transfer of Proceedings) Order 2007, SI 2007/1899, arts 2(2) and 3(2).
[104] Ibid, art 3(3)(c).
[105] Ibid, art 3(3)(d).
[106] [2010] EWHC 3802 (Fam) at [28], [2010] COPLR Con Vol 247.
[107] Ibid, at para 30.

Protection. Therefore, I propose to restrict myself to considering how what I have said in this judgment, can properly be given effect to by an order of the Court of Protection.'

The different concepts of 'competence' in relation to children under 16 years and 'capacity' applying to young people aged 16–17 are considered further below.[108]

Inability to make decisions

2.70   MCA 2005, s 2(1)[109] requires it to be shown that the person is unable to make the decision in question because of an impairment of, or disturbance in the functioning of, the person's mind or brain. The impairment or disturbance must be shown to cause the person to be unable to make that decision at the relevant time. MCA 2005, s 3 sets out the test for assessing whether a person is unable to make a decision for him or herself. This is a 'functional' test, focusing on the personal ability of the individual concerned to make a particular decision and the processes followed by the person in arriving at the decision – not on the outcome. A person is unable to make a decision if he or she is unable:[110]

'(a)   to understand the information relevant to the decision,
(b)   to retain that information,
(c)   to use or weigh that information as part of the process of making the decision, or
(d)   to communicate his decision (whether by talking, using sign language or any other means).'

If someone cannot undertake any one of these four aspects of the decision-making process, then he or she is unable to make the decision.[111] The fourth criterion in MCA 2005, s 3(1)(d) relates only to a residual category of people who are totally unable to communicate.[112]

Some guidance as to the interpretation of the functional test was given by Macur J (as she then was) in *LBL v RYJ*:[113]

'I read section 3 to convey, amongst other detail, that it is envisaged that it may be necessary to use a variety of means to communicate relevant information, that it is not always necessary for a person to comprehend all peripheral detail and that it is recognised that different individuals may give different weight to different factors.'

---

[108]   See **2.91–2.94**.
[109]   See **2.56 ff**.
[110]   MCA 2005, s 3(1).
[111]   *RT and LT v A Local Authority* [2010] EWHC 1910 (Fam) [2010] COPLR Con Vol 1061 at para 40.
[112]   See **2.83–2.84**.
[113]   [2010] EWHC 2665 (Fam) [2010] COPLR Con Vol 795 at para 24.

2.71 In *Re SB (A patient: Capacity to consent to termination)*, Holman J appeared to consider the question of being 'unable' to make a decision separately in relation to its ordinary meaning (whether SB had in fact made a decision) and its legal meaning by reference to MCA 2005, s 3 (whether she could understand, use or weigh the relevant information etc.):[114]

> 'Where I very respectfully differ from, and disagree with, the engaged psychiatrists is as to, what I might call, the level of the bar as to capacity. The relevant question under section 2 is whether she is "unable" to make a decision. There is absolutely no doubt whatsoever that this lady has, many weeks ago, made a decision. She persists in it, and she very, very strongly urges it upon me today. So there is no doubt that she has a capacity to "make" a decision and she has made one.'

While the judge went on to consider the clinical evidence in relation to s 3(1)(a)-(c) (at [39]), the evidence of SB herself was influential on the court's judgment that she had capacity to make the decision:[115]

> '... even if aspects of the decision making are influenced by paranoid thoughts in relation to her husband and her mother, she is nevertheless able to describe, and genuinely holds, a range of rational reasons for her decision ... It may be that aspects of her reasons may be skewed by paranoia. There are other reasons which she has and which she has expressed. My own opinion is that it would be a total affront to the autonomy of this patient to conclude that she lacks capacity to the level required to make this decision. It is of course a profound and grave decision, but it does not necessarily involve complex issues.'

Understand the information relevant to the decision

2.72 Information relevant to the decision includes the particular nature of the decision in question, the purpose for which the decision is needed and the likely effects of making the decision. It must also include the reasonably foreseeable consequences of deciding one way or another or of making no decision at all.[116]

2.73 Following lobbying by the Making Decisions Alliance, amendments were made to the Bill in both Houses of Parliament to require communication support, as is *appropriate* to meet individual needs, to be provided to help people with impaired capacity to express their views and, wherever possible, to make their own decisions.[117] As a result, MCA 2005[118] requires every effort to be made to provide an explanation of information relevant to the decision in question in a way that is appropriate to the circumstances of the person concerned and using the most effective means of communication (such as

---

[114] *Re SB (A patient: Capacity to consent to termination)* [2013] EWHC 1417 (COP), [2013] COPLR 445 at para 38.

[115] Ibid, (at para 44).

[116] MCA 2005, s 3(4).

[117] See eg *Re AK (Medical Treatment: Consent)* [2001] 1 FLR 129, where strenuous efforts were made to communicate with someone able only to move one eyelid.

[118] MCA 2005, s 3(2).

simple language, visual aids or any other means) to assist their understanding. Cursory or inadequate explanations are not acceptable unless the situation is urgent.

2.74 The threshold of understanding is quite low, requiring an ability to understand an explanation of what is proposed and any possible consequences given in broad terms and simple language – the 'salient details' but not necessarily 'all peripheral details'.[119] This approach is consistent with the desire to enable people to take as many decisions as possible for themselves, while also ensuring that the more serious the consequences of any decision, the greater the degree of understanding required. However, in an important case relating to the assessment of capacity *CC v KK and STCC*, Baker J criticised what he called the 'blank canvas' approach where the person being assessed was given little information about the choices she was being asked to make:[120]

> 'The person under evaluation must be presented with detailed options so that their capacity to weigh up those options can be fairly assessed. I find that the local authority has not identified a complete package of support that would or might be available should KK return home, and that this has undermined the experts' assessment of her capacity. The statute requires that, before a person can be treated as lacking capacity to make a decision, it must be shown that all practicable steps have been taken to help her to do so. As the Code of Practice makes clear, each person whose capacity is under scrutiny must be given 'relevant information' including 'what the likely consequences of a decision would be (the possible effects of deciding one way or another)'. That requires a detailed analysis of the effects of the decision either way, which in turn necessitates identifying the best ways in which option would be supported. In order to understand the likely consequences of deciding to re *A Local Authority v AK and Others* turn home, KK should be given full details of the care package that would or might be available.'

2.75 Identifying what is the specific decision in question, and the information relevant to the decision, is not always straightforward.[121] For example, in *Re S: D v R (Deputy of S) and S*,[122] in the context of assessing whether S had capacity to continue litigation commenced in his name by his property and affairs deputy, his daughter, to set aside gifts he had made to Mrs D, Henderson J commented:[123]

> 'At a superficial level, the nature of the decision may be simply stated ... it is whether to discontinue, or to continue to prosecute, the Chancery proceedings. But that decision cannot be taken, it seems to me, without at least a basic understanding of the nature of the claim, of the legal issues involved, and of the

---

[119] *LBL v RYJ* [2010] EWHC 2665 (COP), [2010] COPLR Con Vol 795 at paras 24 and 58.
[120] [2012] EWHC 2136 (COP) [2012] COPLR 627 at para 68.
[121] In *PC and Anor v City of York Council* [2013] EWCA Civ 478, [2013] COPLR 409, the Court of Appeal endorsed the approach taken by Hedley J at first instance in 'the fixing of attention upon the actual decision in hand', 'to articulate the question actually under discussion in the case and apply the statutory capacity test to that decision' which includes identifying the information relevant to the decision – see paras 13, 31, 35 and 56.
[122] *Re S: D v R (Deputy of S) and S* [2010] EWHC 2405 (COP), [2010] COPLR Con Vol 1112.
[123] Ibid, at [43].

circumstances which have given rise to the claim. It would be an over-simplification to say that the claim is just a claim to set aside or reverse the gifts which Mr S made to Mrs D, because in the ordinary way a gift is irrevocable once it has been made and perfected by delivery or transfer of the relevant assets. If a gift is to be set aside or recovered, some vitiating factor such as fraud, misrepresentation or undue influence has to be established; and if the donor is to decide whether or not to pursue a claim, he needs to understand, at least in general terms, the nature of the vitiating factor upon which he may be able to rely, and to weigh up the arguments for and against pursuing the claim. Provided that the donor is equipped with this information, and provided that he understands it and takes it into account in reaching his decision, it will not matter if his decision is an imprudent one, or one which would fail to satisfy the 'best interests' test in section 4. But if the donor is unable to assimilate, retain and evaluate the relevant information, he lacks the capacity to make the decision, however clearly he may articulate it.'

In this case, the decision was held to be 'a complex one which requires a good deal of detailed information and self-awareness'.[124]

2.76 Similarly, it may not always be easy to identify the 'reasonably foreseeable consequences' of deciding one way or another or making no decision at all, particularly in relation to a personal welfare decision. In *A Local Authority v Mrs A*, concerning the capacity of a woman to make decisions about contraceptive treatment, the local authority argued that 'the reasonably foreseeable consequences' included the ability to understand and envisage what would actually be involved in caring for and committing to a child, but this argument was rejected by the court:[125]

'Although in theory the "reasonably foreseeable consequences" of not taking contraception involve possible conception, a birth and the parenting of a child, there should be some limit in practice on what needs to be envisaged, if only for public policy reasons. I accept the submission that it is unrealistic to require consideration of a woman's ability to foresee the realities of parenthood, or to expect her to be able to envisage the fact-specific demands of caring for a particular child not yet conceived (let alone born) with unpredictable levels of third-party support. I do not think such matters *are* reasonably foreseeable: or, to borrow an expression from elsewhere, I think they are too remote from the medical issue of contraception. To apply the wider test would be to "set the bar too high" and would risk a move away from personal autonomy in the direction of social engineering. Further, if one were to admit of a requirement to be able to foresee things beyond a child's birth, then drawing a line on into the child's life would be nigh impossible.'

However, in financial transactions dealing with significant amounts of money, the reasonably foreseeable consequences may be more clearly identified.[126]

---

[124] Ibid, at [144].
[125] *A Local Authority v Mrs A* [2010] EWHC 1549 COP, [2010] COPLR Con Vol 138 at [63]. Further consideration of the issues involved in capacity to consent to sexual relations is given in Chapter 6.
[126] See for example, *Gorjat v Gorjat* [2010] EWHC 1537 (Ch)

Useful guidance as to the assessment of capacity to make financial decisions was commissioned by the Department of Health in 2014 and is now available online.[127]

Retain the information

2.77 The ability to retain information for a short period only should not automatically disqualify the person from making the decision.[128] The person must be able to retain the information for long enough to make a choice or take an effective decision and the length of time will therefore depend on what is necessary for the decision in question. The Code of Practice suggests that items such as notebooks, photographs, videos and voice recorders could be used to assist retention and recording of information.[129]

2.78 It has been suggested that MCA 2005's failure to define for how long the information must be retained may cause confusion for those seeking to assess a person's capacity, particularly, for example, a person suffering from dementia or other condition affecting his or her short-term memory. In *A Local Authority v AK & Ors*, a case concerning capacity to marry of a person whose brain injuries caused him to have severe memory problems, Bodey J commented:[130]

> 'The reference to the retention of information for 'a short period' in s 3(3) of the Act cannot seriously be interpreted to mean, in the context of the lifetime commitment of marriage, for so short a period as AK is able to recall whether he is married at all, or reliably (when he does remember) to whom.'

However, in *A, B and C v X and Z*, in making 'qualified' declarations regarding X's capacity to make a will and to create an LPA, the court has suggested a way forward in cases of borderline or fluctuating capacity where the ability to retain information may be in doubt. In weighing up the evidence demonstrating X's understanding and retention of the information relevant to these decisions as compared with medical evidence of a dramatic decline in his memory and executive functions, Hedley J concluded:[131]

> '... that I cannot make a general declaration that X lacks testamentary capacity, but that needs to be strongly qualified. There will undoubtedly be times when he does lack testamentary capacity. There will be many times when he does not do so. The times when he does lack such capacity are likely to become more frequent. It follows that, in my judgment, any will now made by X, if unaccompanied by contemporary medical evidence asserting capacity, may be seriously open to challenge.'

---

[127] See www.empowermentmatters.co.uk/Wordpress/wp-content/uploads/2014/09/Assessing-Capacity-Financial-Decisions-Guidance-Final.pdf.

[128] MCA 2005, s 3(3).

[129] Mental Capacity Act 2005: Code of Practice, at para 4.20.

[130] *A Local Authority v AK & Ors* [2012] EWHC B29 (COP), [2013] COPLR 163 at para 51.

[131] *A, B and C v X, Y and Z* [2012] EWHC 2400 (COP) [2013] COPLR 1 at para 37. Hedley J reached a similar conclusion in relation to X's capacity to make an LPA (at para 38). Note: permission was granted to A, B and C to appeal this decision, but the appeal lapsed when X subsequently died.

A similar 'qualified' declaration was made concerning X's capacity to make an LPA.

Use or weigh the information

2.79 Prior to MCA 2005 coming into effect, a number of cases came before the courts where the person concerned had the ability to understand information but where the effects of a mental health problem or disability prevented him or her from using that information in the decision-making process.[132] The Law Commission gave examples of certain compulsive conditions (such as anorexia) which cause people, who are quite able to absorb information, to make decisions which are inevitable (eg not to eat) regardless of the information and their understanding of it. To reflect these concerns, the Law Commission originally proposed that in order to have capacity, a person must be able to make a 'true choice'.[133] However, in its final report, the Commission recognised that:[134]

> 'Common to all these cases is the fact that the person's eventual decision is divorced from his or her ability to understand the relevant information. Emphasising that the person must be able to use the information which he or she has successfully understood in the decision-making process deflects the complications of asking whether a person needs to "appreciate" information as well as understand it. A decision based on a compulsion, the overpowering will of a third party or any other inability to act on relevant information as a result of mental disability is not a decision made by a person with decision-making capacity.'

2.80 The courts further defined the process as the ability to weigh all relevant information in the balance as part of the process of making a decision and then to use the information in order to arrive at a decision. MCA 2005, s 3(1)(c) translates this former common law provision into statute. The focus of this element of the test is on the personal ability of the individual concerned to make a particular decision (such as the ability to weigh up any risks involved) and the processes followed by the person in arriving at the decision, and not on the outcome.

2.81 Further guidance on applying this element of the capacity test was given in *The PCT v P, AH & The Local Authority* where Hedley J, noting – correctly – that it is the most difficult aspect of the test to apply, described it as 'the capacity actually to engage in the decision-making process itself and to be able to see the various parts of the argument and to relate the one to another'.[135] In assessing P's capacity to make a range of decisions concerning his care, residence and medical treatment, the judge concluded that, in addition to his

---

[132] See eg *Re MB* [1997] 2 FLR 426; *R v Collins and Ashworth Hospital Authority ex parte Brady* [2001] 58 BMLR 173.

[133] Law Com Consultation Paper No 128, n 1 above, at paras 3.31–3.35.

[134] Law Com No 231, n 1 above, at para 3.17.

[135] *The PCT v P, AH & The Local Authority* [2009] EW Misc 10 (COP), [2009] COPLR Con Vol 956 at para 35.

disabilities, P's relationship with his adoptive mother hindered his ability to 'use or weigh' information which conflicted in any way with his mother's views:[136]

> 'The reasons that I am persuaded that he lacks that capacity are the cumulative force of the following: (a) his epilepsy and its impact on his functioning, (b) his learning disability which is at the lower end of mild, (c) the enmeshed relationship that he has with AH [his adoptive mother] which severely restricts his perspective in terms of being able to think about his future, (d) his inability, frequently articulated by him to those who have interviewed him, to visualise any prospect of having a different view to his mother on any subject that matters and his inability to understand what the other aspects of the argument may be in relation to his expressed wishes simply to return and live undisturbed with his mother. Finally, I have regard to that which has emerged more recently ... namely some disparity between his words on the one hand and his actions and attitudes in his dealings with staff on the other ...

> No one of those matters by themselves would justify a finding of disability, but the cumulative effect of all of them is to satisfy me beyond a peradventure that at the present time he wants capacity to deal with the matters to which I have related.'

2.82　The provision of advice and support, or even some degree of constraint (for example, to overcome impulsivity) may be appropriate ways to enable someone to weigh up information and understand the consequences of any actions they might or might not take, and thus have capacity to make some types of decisions, such as capacity to litigate when assisted by family members and professional advisers.[137] However, in cases where the issue of capacity is finely balanced, it may be difficult to establish the extent to which the person can 'use or weigh' information in order to act on the advice given or understand when assistance was needed. In *Loughlin v Singh*,[138] a case concerning the assessment of damages in a personal injury claim of a young man who sustained brain injuries in a traffic accident, Parker J took account of a range of evidence, relying in particular on the evidence of one expert witness that, while the claimant may be able to respond to prompting or make a decision in a 'laboratory setting', he would be 'vulnerable in an unpredicted and unmanaged environment' and therefore lacked capacity to 'respond in an appropriate manner' in the real world.

2.83　In the case of *A Local Authority v E and Others*,[139] E, a 32-year-old woman suffered from severe anorexia and other adverse health conditions, had gone to great lengths to demonstrate her ability to use or weigh information and hence her capacity to make an advance decision to the effect that she

---

[136] Ibid, at paras 37–38.

[137] See for example, *V v R* [2011] EWHC 822 (QB).

[138] *Loughlin v Singh* [2013] EWHC 1641 (QB), [2013] COPLR 371 at paras 36 and 51. This case is discussed in more detail in Chapter 11.

[139] [2012] EWHC 1639 (COP), [2012] COPLR 441. To the extent that Peter Jackson J appeared to imply that the presumption of capacity was displaced in such cases, it is suggested that this was incorrect; rather, it is suggested that the correct approach is that raising a prima facie case that the decision was made without capacity shifts the burden to the person seeking to uphold the original decision. See also Chapter 6, at **6.35** and **6.63**.

wished to be allowed to die rather than be force fed. At the time of the hearing, E was near death, refusing food and taking only small amounts of water, and Peter Jackson J was satisfied that E then lacked capacity to consent to or refuse treatment (at para 49):

> '... there is strong evidence that E's obsessive fear of weight gain makes her incapable of weighing the advantages and disadvantages of eating in any meaningful way. For E, the compulsion to prevent calories entering her system has become the card that trumps all others. The need not to gain weight overpowers all other thoughts.'

But at the earlier time of making the advance decisions, E had been eating and had even put on some weight. The judge acknowledged that people with severe anorexia may be in a 'Catch 22 situation', that deciding not to eat is seen as proof of lack of capacity to decide at all. Nevertheless, on the balance of probabilities the judge concluded that E did not have capacity when she signed either of the two advance decisions she had made, saying (at para 65):

> 'Against such an alerting background, a full, reasoned and contemporaneous assessment evidencing mental capacity to make such a momentous decision would in my view be necessary. No such assessment occurred in E's case and I think it at best doubtful that a thorough investigation at the time would have reached the conclusion that she had capacity.'

Unable to communicate

2.84 The final criterion which would indicate an inability to make a decision is the fact that the person is *unable to communicate the decision* by any possible means.[140] There are obvious situations, such as unconsciousness, which would result in a person being unable to communicate a decision. Other types of cases may include people in a vegetative state[141] (previously referred to as a persistent or permanent vegetative state), a minimally conscious state or with the condition sometimes known as 'locked-in syndrome'. The Law Commission intended this to be very much a residual category affecting a minority of people:[142]

> 'This test will have no relevance if the person is known to be incapable of deciding (even if also unable to communicate) but will be available if the assessor does not know, one way or the other, whether the person is capable of deciding or not.'

Strenuous efforts must first be made to assist and facilitate communication before any finding of incapacity is made. Communication by simple muscle movements, such as blinking an eye or squeezing a hand, to indicate 'yes' or

---

[140] MCA 2005, s 3(1)(d).

[141] For elaboration as to the different diagnoses of vegetative state and minimally conscious state, see *W v M and S, and a NHS Primary Care Trust* [2011] EWHC 2443 (Fam); [2012] COPLR 222. See also the POST (Parliamentary Office of Science and Technology) Note on Vegetative and Minimally Conscious States published in March 2015, available at http://www.parliament. uk/briefing-papers/post-pn-489/vegetative-and-minimally-conscious-states.

[142] Law Com No 231, n 1 above, at para 3.20.

'no', can be sufficient to indicate that the person has the ability to communicate and therefore may have capacity.[143] The Code of Practice recommends that in cases of this sort, the involvement of speech and language therapists or professionals with specialist skills in verbal and non-verbal communication may be required to assist in the assessment.[144]

Common law tests of capacity

2.85　The definition and two-stage test of capacity set out in MCA 2005 are expressed to apply 'for the purposes of this Act'[145] and MCA 2005, Sch 6 makes consequential amendments to existing statutes, inserting the new statutory definition. There are also several *common law* tests of capacity set out in case-law before MCA 2005 came into effect.[146] Examples given in the Code of Practice are as follows:

- capacity to make a will;[147]
- capacity to enter into marriage;[148]
- capacity to make a gift;[149]
- contractual capacity;[150] and
- capacity to litigate.[151]

2.86　MCA 2005's definition of capacity is intended to build on, rather than contradict, the terms of pre-existing common law tests.[152] The Code of Practice suggests that, as cases come before the court, judges may adopt the statutory definition if they see fit and use it to develop common law rules in particular cases.[153]

- For example, the High Court has confirmed that the correct approach is to apply the MCA test for capacity in deciding whether a person has capacity to conduct litigation in proceedings to which the Civil Procedure Rules apply,[154] since those Rules were subsequently amended to conform with changes brought about by MCA 2005.

---

[143]　*Re AK (Adult Patient) (Medical Treatment: Consent)* [2001] 2 FCR 35, [2001] 1 FLR 129.
[144]　Mental Capacity Act 2005: Code of Practice, at para 4.24.
[145]　MCA 2005, s 2(1).
[146]　Details of the relevant common law tests of capacity can be found in BMA/Law Society *Assessment of Mental Capacity*, n 81 above. A further edition of this book is in production as at the time of writing.
[147]　*Banks v Goodfellow* (1870) LR 5 QB 549.
[148]　*Sheffield City Council v E & S* [2005] 1 FLR 965.
[149]　*Re Beaney (deceased)* [1978] 2 All ER 595.
[150]　*Boughton v Knight* (1873) LR 3 PD 64.
[151]　*Masterman-Lister v Brutton & Co and Jewell & Home Counties Dairies* [2003] 3 All ER 162, CA.
[152]　Law Com No 231, n 1 above, at para 3.23.
[153]　Mental Capacity Act 2005: Code of Practice at para 4.33
[154]　See *Saulle v Nouvet* [2007] EWHC 2902 (QB), [2008] WTLR 729 for an early decision under the new jurisdiction on capacity to litigate in regard to a brain-injured claimant. See also Chapter 11 for further discussion of the assessment of capacity of those 'at the margins of the

- In relation to testamentary capacity, in respect of wills made before MCA 2005 came into effect on October 2007, it is clear the question of capacity should be based on the common law test, without reference to the Act.[155] There have been conflicting conclusions as regards wills made before MCA 2005 came into force, and the question remains one that is ripe for consideration by the superior courts.[156]

It may, over time, be that the common law tests that continue to survive will assimilate more and more of the features of the statutory test under MCA 2005.[157]

Reasonable belief of lack of capacity

2.87 In most day-to-day decisions or actions involved in caring for someone, it will not be appropriate or necessary to carry out a formal assessment of the person's capacity. Indeed many informal carers or others exercising powers under MCA 2005 will not be equipped to carry out a detailed assessment. Rather, it is sufficient that they 'reasonably believe' that the person lacks capacity to make the decision or consent to the action in question,[158] but, if challenged, they must be able to point to objective reasons to justify why they hold that belief.

2.88 This is based on the Law Commission's explanation that:[159]

'It would be out of step with our aims of policy, and with the views of the vast majority of the respondents to our overview paper, to have any general system of certifying people as "incapacitated" and then identifying a substitute decision-maker for them, regardless of whether there is any real need for one. In the absence of certifications or authorisations, persons acting informally can only be expected to have reasonable grounds to believe that (1) the other person lacks capacity in relation to the matter in hand and (2) they are acting in the best interests of that person.'

2.89 Reasonable steps must be taken to establish the person's lack of capacity to make a particular decision. Responses to the consultation on the draft Code

---

MCA 2005', in particular the overlap with personal injury proceedings and consideration as to whether P is a 'protected party' (ie lacking capacity to litigate) and/or a 'protected beneficiary' (ie lacking capacity to manage any money recovered).

[155] *Scammell and Scammell v Farmer* [2008] EWHC 1100 (Ch), [2008] WTLR 1261 at 24–29.

[156] *Fischer v Diffley* [2013] EWHC 4567 (Ch) and *Bray v Pearce* (unreported, 6 March 2014) suggested that MCA 2005 should be applied; to contrary effect is *Re Walker* [2014] EWHC 71 (Ch), [2015] COPLR 348. In the context of gifts, see *Re Smith* [2014] EWHC 3926 (Ch), [2015] COPLR 284. For a discussion of some of the issues in this area, see Alex Ruck Keene and Annabel Lee, 'Testamentary Capacity' Elder Law Journal, Jordans [2013] Eld LJ 272 and Chapter 2 of Frost et al Testamentary Capacity: Law, Practice and Medicine (Oxford University Press, 2015).

[157] See for example, *MM (An Adult), Re; Local Authority X v MM and KM* [2007] EWHC 2003 (Fam), [2008] 3 FCR 788.

[158] MCA 2005, ss 4(8) and 5(1).

[159] Law Com No 231, n 1 above, at para 4.5.

of Practice requested additional guidance on what might be considered 'reasonable'. The Code confirms that:[160]

> '... the steps that are accepted as "reasonable" will depend on individual circumstances and the urgency of the decision. Professionals who are qualified in their particular field are normally expected to undertake a fuller assessment, reflecting their higher degree of knowledge and experience, than family members or other carers who have no formal qualifications.'

2.90   It goes on to suggest a number of steps that may be helpful in establishing a 'reasonable belief' of lack of capacity:

- 'Start by assuming the person has capacity to make the specific decision. Is there anything to prove otherwise?
- Does the person have a previous diagnosis of disability or mental disorder? Does that condition now affect their capacity to make this decision? If there has been no previous diagnosis, it may be best to get a medical opinion.
- Make every effort to communicate with the person to explain what is happening.
- Make every effort to try to help the person make the decision in question.
- See if there is a way to explain or present information about the decision in a way that makes it easier to understand. If the person has a choice, do they have information about all the options?
- Can the decision be delayed to take time to help the person make the decision, or to give the person time to regain the capacity to make the decision for themselves?
- Does the person understand what decision they need to make and why they need to make it?
- Can they understand information about the decision? Can they retain it, use it and weigh it to make the decision?
- Be aware that the fact that a person agrees with you or assents to what is proposed does not necessarily mean that they have capacity to make the decision.'

Competence and capacity: children and young people

Children under 16: 'Gillick competence'

2.91   MCA 2005 generally applies only to people aged 16 years and over.[161] Where welfare or healthcare decisions are required of a child aged under 16, any disputes may be resolved by the family courts under the Children Act 1989. In such cases, the common law test of *Gillick* competence applies:[162] whether the child has sufficient maturity and intelligence to understand the nature and implications of the proposed treatment.[163] *Gillick* competence is a developmental concept and will not be lost or acquired on a day-to-day or

---

[160]   Mental Capacity Act 2005: Code of Practice, at para 4.45.

[161]   See **2.65–2.69**.

[162]   For a thought-provoking suggestion that MCA 2005 should apply also to those under 16, see McFarlane LJ, 'Mental Capacity: One Standard for All Ages' *Family Law* Jordans [2011] Fam Law 479.

[163]   *Gillick v West Norfolk and Wisbech Area Health Authority* [1986] 1 AC 112.

week-by-week basis.[164] The understanding required for different treatments or decisions may vary, depending on the nature of the decision in question.

Young people aged 16 or 17: Capacity or competence?

2.92   The main provisions of MCA 2005 apply to adults, which includes young people aged 16 years or over. The starting point for assessing whether a young person aged 16 or 17 has capacity to make a specific decision is therefore the test of capacity in MCA 2005, having regard to the MCA principles. However, there may be circumstances where 16-17 year olds who are unable to make a decision for themselves will not be covered by the provisions of MCA 2005. A young person may be unable to make a decision either:

- because of an impairment of, or disturbance in the functioning of, their mind or brain (they lack capacity within the meaning of the MCA); or
- for reasons of immaturity (due to the person's age, they are unable to make the decision in question).

2.93   Young people aged 16 and 17 are presumed to have capacity in relation to any surgical, dental or medical treatment.[165] If a young person suffers from an impairment of, or a disturbance in the functioning of, the mind or brain which may affect their ability to make a particular healthcare decision, an assessment of capacity under MCA 2005 will be required, notwithstanding the presumption that the young person has capacity. However, if there is no such impairment or disturbance, MCA 2005 will not apply if it can be established that the young person's inability to make a decision is because:

- they do not have the maturity to understand fully what is involved in making the decision (ie they lack *Gillick* competence); or
- the lack of maturity means that they feel unable to make the decision for themselves (for example, where particularly complex or risky treatment is proposed, they may be overwhelmed by the implications of the decision).[166]

2.94   In cases where MCA 2005 applies, decisions about a young person's care or treatment may be made under the provisions of the MCA in the person's best interests (see below and Chapter 6), without the need to obtain parental consent, although those with parental responsibility for the young person should generally be consulted.[167]

---

[164] *Re R (A Minor) (Wardship: Consent to medical treatment)* [1992] 1 FLR 190 at 200.

[165] Family Law Reform Act 1969, s 8(1).

[166] Mental Capacity Act 2005: Code of Practice, at para 12.13. Specific guidance on assessing the ability of children and young people to make treatment decisions is given in National Institute for Mental Health in England (2009) *The Legal Aspects of the Care and Treatment of Children and Young People with Mental Disorder: A guide for professionals* (National Mental Health Development Unit), Chapter 2 (available online at www.nmhdu.org.uk).

[167] MCA 2005, s 4(7)(b).

The assessment of capacity

Background

2.95 By making a judgment on an individual's decision-making capacity, anyone with authority over that person can deprive him or her of civil rights and liberties enjoyed by most adults and now safeguarded by the Human Rights Act 1998. Alternatively, such a judgment could permit a person lacking capacity to do something, or carry on doing something, whereby serious prejudice could result, either putting that person at risk or causing harm or inconvenience to others. It is therefore essential that anyone called upon to assess another person's capacity must understand what they are being asked to judge and be prepared to justify their findings.

2.96 The Joint Committee on the Draft Mental Incapacity Bill received evidence from a number of organisations expressing concern that the Bill made no specific provisions for the assessment of capacity, despite the far-reaching implications of the outcome of assessment.[168] These concerns were discussed during the Bill's Committee stage in the House of Lords, when Lord Carter put forward a probing amendment, seeking to impose a statutory duty on public bodies to carry out a formal assessment of a person's capacity where it may be relevant in the context of any assessment of needs or the provision of services to meet those needs. The Minister responded:[169]

> 'This is important – I recognise that – but I am not sure that is something I want to see covered in primary legislation. The purpose of the Bill is to set out the broad principles and absolutes ... to be followed, but we cannot lay out on the face of the Bill the practical detail of how professionals should operate ... The details of the assessment procedure must be a matter for professional judgement in relation to the case, with support from the code of practice in training and guidance.'

2.97 The following sections draw on the guidance given in the Code of Practice and on the professional guidance for doctors and lawyers on assessment of mental capacity issued jointly by the BMA and the Law Society.[170] Attention is also drawn to the article by Dr Steven Luttrell, Consultant Geriatrician, 'Impact of Dementia and Other Conditions Affecting Capacity'[171] which includes some guidance on good practice in the assessment of capacity.

When should capacity be assessed?

2.98 According to the principles of MCA 2005, the starting point should be the presumption of capacity. Doubts as to a person's capacity may arise for a

---

[168] Joint Committee Report, Vol I, n 5 above, at para 242.

[169] *Hansard*, HL Deb, vol 668, ser 5, col 1230 (25 January 2005).

[170] BMA/Law Society *Assessment of Mental Capacity*, n 81 above. A further edition of this book is in production as at the time of writing.

[171] Steven Luttrell, 'Impact of Dementia and Other Conditions Affecting Capacity' [2011] Eld LJ 403, n 94 above, reproduced as an Annex to this chapter.

number of reasons, either because of the person's behaviour or circumstances, or through concerns raised by someone else, but any concerns must be considered specifically in relation to the particular decision which needs to be made. Where doubts are raised about a person's decision-making abilities, the following questions should first be considered:

(1) Does the person have all the relevant information needed to make the decision in question? If there is a choice, has information been given on any alternatives?

(2) Could the information be explained or presented in a way that is easier for the person to understand?

(3) Are there particular times of day when the person's understanding is better, or particular locations where they may feel more at ease? Can the decision be put off until the circumstances are right for the person concerned?

(4) Can anyone else help or support the person to make a choice or express a view, such as an advocate or someone to assist communication?

2.99 If all these steps have been taken without success in helping the person make a decision, an assessment of their capacity to make the decision in question should be made.

Who should assess capacity?

2.100 In keeping with the functional approach, the question of who assesses an individual's capacity will depend on the particular decision to be made, but will in general be the person who needs the decision to be made. For most day-to-day decisions in connection with the person's care or treatment, the carer most directly involved with the person at the time the decision has to be made assesses his or her capacity to make the decision in question. Carers acting informally are not expected to be experts in assessing capacity, but they must be able to show they have reasonable grounds for believing that the person lacks capacity to make the decision or do the act in question, at that particular time.[172] Formal processes are rarely required unless the assessment is challenged, for example, by the person whose capacity is being assessed or by another family member. In such circumstances, the assessor must be able to point to objective reasons as to why they believe the person lacks capacity to make the decision in question.

2.101 Where consent to medical treatment or examination is required, the doctor or healthcare professional proposing the treatment must decide whether the patient has capacity to consent and should record the assessment process and findings in the person's medical notes.[173] Where a legal transaction is involved, such as making a will or a power of attorney, the solicitor handling the transaction must be satisfied that their client has the capacity to give them

---

[172] MCA 2005, ss 4(8) and 5(1). See **2.87–2.90** above.
[173] Doctors must in this regard have in mind the heightened requirements as to the information to

the necessary instructions. This may require the solicitor to assess whether the client has the required capacity to satisfy the relevant legal test, perhaps assisted by an opinion from a doctor.[174] The position is less clear where the decision relates to the provision of social care services – the assessment of capacity may be carried out by a social worker or care manager, depending on the particular circumstances. The Code of Practice advises:[175]

'There are also times when a joint decision might be made by a number of people. For example, when a care plan for a person who lacks capacity to make relevant decisions is being put together, different healthcare or social care staff might be involved in making decisions or recommendations about the person's care package. Sometimes these decisions will be made by a team of healthcare or social care staff as a whole. At other times, the decision will be made by a specific individual within the team.'

2.102 The more serious the decision, the more formal the assessment of capacity may need to be, but whoever assesses capacity must be prepared to justify their findings. Ultimately, if a person's capacity to do something is disputed, it is a question for the court to decide.[176] Cases referred to the Court of Protection will require formal evidence of the assessment of capacity, either to enable the court to make a declaration as to whether the person has or lacks capacity to make a specific decision or to confirm that the court has jurisdiction to deal with the matter in question.[177] While such evidence will usually be provided by a registered medical practitioner or psychiatrist, other professionals are now recognised as having the ability to provide such evidence.[178] Other types of evidence may also be relevant to the court in considering someone's capacity.[179] In *CC v KK and STCC* the court received both written and oral

---

be provided to all patients (whether or not it is thought that they may lack capacity) imposed upon them following the judgment of the Supreme Court in *Montgomery v Lanarkshire Health Board* [2015] UKSC 11, [2015] 2 WLR 768.

[174] In *Hill v Fellowes Solicitors LLP* [2011] EWHC 61 (QB), the court confirmed (at para 77): 'there is plainly no duty upon solicitors in general to obtain medical evidence on every occasion upon which they are instructed by an elderly client just in case they lack capacity. Such a requirement would be insulting and unnecessary.' In the contentious probate case of *Hawes v Burgess* [2013] EWCA Civ 74, it was held that (at para 60): 'the courts should not too readily upset, on grounds of lack of mental capacity, a will that has been drafted by an experienced independent lawyer.' However, see also **2.106** and **2.120** below, for a discussion on when a medical opinion should be obtained and pitfalls to be avoided when solicitors undertake capacity assessments.

[175] Mental Capacity Act 2005: Code of Practice, para 5.11.

[176] In *Baker Tilly v Makar* [2013] EWHC 759 (QB); [2013] COPLR 245 it was held that the absence of medical evidence cannot be a bar to the court making a finding of lack of capacity, but in such cases the court must be cautious before concluding that the presumption of capacity had been rebutted.

[177] See Chapters 4 and 6.

[178] Court of Protection Rules 2007 (SI 2007/1744 (L.12)), r 64(c). The Court of Protection Form COP3 'Assessment of Capacity', was revised in 2013 to this effect, making clear that, for instance, social workers can provide the necessary evidence upon capacity for purposes of making an application to the court.

[179] In *Masterman-Lister v Brutton & Co* [2003] 3 All ER 163, the court gave detailed consideration to diaries, letters and computer documents; in *Saulle v Nouvet* [2007] EWHC 2902 (QB), the court took into account evidence from family members as well as home videos.

evidence from KK, an 82-year-old woman alleged to lack capacity, which helped Baker J to conclude, against all the expert evidence, that she had capacity to decide where to live:[180]

> 'I remind myself that the court must be careful when weighing up the evidence of someone in KK's position against expert opinion evidence. Nonetheless, I found her to be clear and articulate. She betrayed relatively few signs of the dementia which, I accept, afflicts her. Furthermore, I agree ... that she demonstrated an understanding of and insight into her care needs and the reality of life if she returned home. ... I found her to be broadly realistic as to her physical limitations. My conclusion on this point is that, whilst KK may have underestimated or minimised some of her needs, she did not do so to an extent that suggests that she lacks capacity to weigh up information.'

The need for formal assessment

2.103 For certain more complex or serious decisions, a formal assessment of capacity may be required, sometimes involving different professionals. Doctors are generally regarded as experts in the assessment of capacity,[181] and in many cases all that may be needed is an opinion from the person's GP or family doctor. Where the person has been diagnosed with a particular condition or disorder, it may be more appropriate to seek an opinion from a specialist, such as a consultant psychiatrist or psychologist who has extensive clinical experience of the disorder and is familiar with caring for patients with that condition. In some cases, a multi-disciplinary approach is best, using the skills and expertise of different professionals. A professional opinion may help to justify a finding about capacity, but the decision as to whether someone has or lacks capacity must be taken by the potential decision-maker, and not the professional who is merely there to advise.[182]

2.104 Doctors or other experts should never express an opinion without first conducting a proper assessment of the person's capacity to make the decision in question and applying the appropriate test of capacity. Solicitors requesting a professional opinion should send full letters of instruction, setting out details of the decision in question, the requisite test of capacity[183] and how this should be applied in relation to the client's particular circumstances.[184] However, a

---

[180] *CC v KK and STCC* [2012] EWHC 2136 (COP), [2012] COPLR 627 at para 64.

[181] In *Ali v Caton & Anor* [2013] EWHC 1730 (QB), Stuart-Smith J acknowledged (at [296]) that 'other experts tended to defer to the neuropsychologists' but he did not accept that other experts were unable to provide assistance on the issue of capacity.

[182] *Bailey v Warren* [2006] EWCA Civ 51, [2006] WTLR 753 at [87].

[183] In *SC v BS and Anor* [2012] COPLR 567 the opinion of an expert in autism was discounted as he was unfamiliar with the MCA test of capacity, referring instead in his report to 'unfitness to plead'.

[184] Sample letters have been provided in BMA/Law Society *Assessment of Mental Capacity*, n 81 above and Denzil Lush et al *Elderly Clients: A Precedent Manual* (Jordans, 4th edn, 2013). In *D v R (Deputy of S) and S* [2010] EWHC 2405 (COP), [2010] COPLR Con Vol 1112, Henderson J made a number of critical comments about the expert evidence, and in particular the inadequate instructions given to the expert asked by D to report on S's capacity (at for

doctor's opinion may not necessarily be given greater weight than other relevant evidence, such as the views of a solicitor where capacity to undertake a legal transaction is involved.[185]

Legal or professional requirements

2.105 In some cases it is a requirement of the law, or good professional practice, that a formal assessment of capacity be carried out. These include the following situations:

(1) where a doctor or other expert witness certifies a legal document (such as a will) signed by someone whose capacity could be challenged (the so-called 'golden rule' established in *Kenward v Adams*[186] – see below);

(2) to establish that a particular person requires the assistance of the Official Solicitor or other litigation friend in civil proceedings;[187]

(3) to establish that a particular person comes within the jurisdiction of the Court of Protection;[188]

(4) where the court is required to determine a person's capacity to make a particular decision;[189] and

(5) if there may be legal consequences of a finding of capacity (eg in the settlement of damages following a claim for personal injury) (see **2.121** below and Chapter 11 for further details).

The 'Golden Rule'

2.106 There are particular circumstances where the courts have strongly advised that a doctor should witness a person's signature on a legal document such as a will, thereby providing medical evidence as to the person's capacity. In *Kenward v Adams* Templeman J set out what he called 'the golden if tactless rule' that, where a will has been drawn up for an elderly person or for someone who is seriously ill, it should be witnessed or approved by a medical practitioner, who should make a formal assessment of capacity and fully record the examination and findings. The need to observe this 'golden rule' was restated in subsequent cases,[190] albeit balanced with acknowledgement that

---

example paragraphs 109 and 147), subsequently resulting in an award of costs against D and her advisers – see *D v R (Deputy of S) and S* [2010] EWHC 3748 (CoP) at paras 29–30.

[185] *Richmond v Richmond* (1914) 111 LT 273; *Birkin v Wing* (1890) 63 LT 80; *Hawes v Burgess* [2013] EWCA Civ 74, [2013] WTLR 453.

[186] (1975) *The Times*, November 29.

[187] Civil Procedure Rules 1998, SI 1998/3132, r 21.1.

[188] MCA 2005, ss 15(1), 16(1). See Form COP3 – *Assessment of Capacity* reproduced in Part VII of this book.

[189] *Masterman-Lister v Brutton & Co and Jewell & Home Counties Dairies* [2002] EWCA Civ 1889, [2003] 3 All ER 162, at para 54.

[190] The advice to observe the 'golden rule' was repeated in *Re Simpson (Deceased)*, *Schaniel v Simpson* (1977) 121 SJ 224; *Buckenham v Dickinson* [1997] CLY 661; and more forcefully in *Great Ormond Street Hospital v Pauline Rushie* (unreported) 19 April 2000, in which the solicitor was strongly criticised for failing to follow the 'golden rule'.

failure to observe the 'golden rule' would not necessarily invalidate the will.[191] More recently in *Key v Key*, the 'golden rule' was again reinforced and the solicitor involved strongly criticised for failing to follow it:[192]

> '[The solicitor's] failure to comply with what has come to be well known in the profession as the Golden Rule has greatly increased the difficulties to which this dispute has given rise and aggravated the depths of mistrust into which his client's children have subsequently fallen ...
>
> Compliance with the Golden Rule does not, of course, operate as a touchstone of the validity of a will, nor does non-compliance demonstrate its invalidity. Its purpose, as has repeatedly been emphasised, is to assist in the avoidance of disputes, or at least in the minimisation of their scope. As the expert evidence in the present case confirms, persons with failing or impaired mental faculties may, for perfectly understandable reasons, seek to conceal what they regard as their embarrassing shortcomings from persons with whom they deal, so that a friend or professional person such as a solicitor may fail to detect defects in mental capacity which would be or become apparent to a trained and experienced medical examiner, to whom a proper description of the legal test for testamentary capacity had first been provided.'

2.107 Some commentators have argued that attempted compliance with the so-called 'golden rule' can in fact cause more practical problems than non-compliance, because of the practical difficulties, consequent delay and increased costs that may be involved in obtaining an in-depth specialist assessment of capacity before accepting instructions even for a straightforward will or gift.[193] As noted above, the courts have also not always been consistent as to their approach to the rule, and, in the case of dispute, have shown a preference for the contemporaneous of the solicitor in question over retrospective evidence from a medical expert as to capacity, as demonstrated by the Court of Appeal in the contentious probate case of *Hawes v Burgess*, where Mummery LJ said:[194]

> 'If, as here, an experienced lawyer has been instructed and has formed the opinion from a meeting or meetings that the testatrix understands what she is doing, the will so drafted and executed should only be set aside on the clearest evidence of lack of mental capacity. The court should be cautious about acting on the basis of evidence of lack of capacity given by a medical expert after the event, particularly when that expert has neither met nor medically examined the testatrix, and

---

[191] *Buckenham v Dickinson* [1997] CLY 661; *Hoff v Atherton* [2005] WTLR 99; *Cattermole v Prisk* [2006] 1 FLR 693. The 'golden rule' was also considered in some detail in *Scammell and Scammell v Farmer* [2008] EWHC 1100 (Ch) at paras 117–123.

[192] *Key v Key* [2010] EWHC 408 (Ch) at paras 6 and 8.

[193] See for example, Stephen Lawson, 'The Golden Rule: Time to move on' in *Trusts Quarterly Review* (TQR, Vol 8, Issue 3), (STEP, Sept 2010) and Barbara Rich 'The Assessment of Mental Capacity for Legal Purposes' in *Elder Law Journal*, Jordans [2011] Eld LJ 39). See also *Re S* [2010] EWHC 2405 (COP), [2010] COPLR Con Vol 1112 for an illustration of the costs and complexity that may be involved.

[194] *Hawes v Burgess* [2013] EWCA Civ 74, [2013] WTLR 453 at [60].

particularly in circumstances when that expert accepts that the testatrix understood that she was making a will and also understood the extent of her property.'

Ultimately, it is perhaps best to see the so-called 'golden rule' as an aspect on the duty on the solicitor taking the client's instructions to be satisfied as to the person's capacity and understanding of the decision in question, and to keep a proper record and attendance notes of the steps taken and the evidence on which they base their conclusions.[195]

Other expert assessments

2.108 In other cases, a judgment will need to be made as to whether the particular circumstances make it appropriate or necessary to seek a formal assessment of capacity by obtaining a professional opinion from a doctor or other expert. The Code of Practice suggests that any of the following factors might indicate the need for a professional to be involved in the assessment:[196]

- the decision that needs to be made is complicated or has serious consequences;
- an assessor concludes a person lacks capacity, and the person challenges the finding;
- family members, carers and/or professionals disagree about a person's capacity;
- there is a conflict of interest between the assessor and the person being assessed;
- the person being assessed is expressing different views to different people – they may be trying to please everyone or telling people what they think they want to hear;
- somebody might challenge the person's capacity to make the decision – either at the time of the decision or later (eg a family member might challenge a will after a person has died on the basis that the person lacked capacity when they made the will);
- somebody has been accused of abusing a vulnerable adult who may lack capacity to make decisions that protect them;
- a person repeatedly makes decisions that put them at risk or could result in suffering or damage.

How capacity is assessed

2.109 Where there are doubts about capacity, it is important that people are assessed when they are at their highest level of functioning because this is the only realistic way of determining what they may or may not be capable of

---

[195] See the discussion in Frost et al *Testamentary Capacity: Law, Practice and Medicine* (Oxford University Press, 2015), at paragraphs 6.13–6.120.
[196] Mental Capacity Act 2005: Code of Practice, at para 4.53.

doing. Many of the practicable steps which can be taken to enable a person to make his or her own decisions[197] may also be helpful in creating the best environment for capacity to be assessed. Once this has been done, the test of capacity set out in MCA 2005, ss 1–3[198] must then be applied, to determine whether the person is unable to make a decision *because of* an impairment of, or a disturbance in the functioning of, the mind or brain.

2.110 In many cases, it may be obvious whether there is any impairment or disturbance which could affect the person's ability to make a decision. For example, there may have been a previous diagnosis of an ongoing mental illness or learning disability, or recognisable symptoms to indicate the recurrence of illness or the disabling effects of a head injury. However, in other cases, such as dementia, the onset of debilitating illness is gradual and the point at which capacity is affected is hard to define. During the period when capacity is borderline, a medical opinion may be required. It should be noted that this is both to allow appropriate decision-making by others as at the point of assessment (if the individual is considered to lack capacity) and to prevent retrospective challenges to the decisions of the individual (where the individual is considered to have capacity at the time, but their decisions are questioned later).[199]

2.111 People should not be considered 'incapable' simply on the basis that they have a particular diagnosis or condition, but the impairment of, or disturbance in the functioning of, the person's mind or brain must be shown to cause the person to be unable to make a decision at the time the decision needs to be made.[200] The following questions must be considered:

(1) Does the person have a general understanding of what the decision is and why he or she is being asked to make it?

(2) Does the person have a general understanding of the consequences of making, or not making, this decision?

(3) Is the person able to understand and weigh up the information relevant to the decision as part of the process of arriving at it?

In borderline cases, or where there is any element of doubt, the person doing the assessment must be able to show that it is more likely than not that the answer to the above questions is 'No'.

Confidentiality

2.112 Carrying out an assessment of capacity requires the sharing of information about the personal circumstances of the person being assessed. Yet

---

[197] Mental Capacity Act 2005: Code of Practice, Chapter 3. See **2.36–2.39** above.

[198] See **2.58–2.59** above.

[199] See in this regard *A, B and C v X and Z* [2012] EWHC 2400 (COP), [2013] COPLR 1.

[200] The way in which different conditions and disabilities may impact on an individual's decision-making abilities, and hence their capacity, is discussed in the article by Steven Luttrell, n 94 above reproduced as an Annex to this chapter.

doctors, lawyers and other professionals are bound by a duty of confidentiality towards their clients, imposed through their professional ethical codes and reinforced by law.[201] As a general principle, personal information may only be disclosed with the client's consent, even to close relatives. However, there are circumstances when disclosure is necessary in the absence of consent.[202]

2.113 In relation to people who lack capacity to consent to (or refuse) disclosure, a balance must be struck between the public and private interests in maintaining confidentiality and the public and private interest in permitting, and occasionally requiring, disclosure for certain purposes. Some guidance has been offered in the case of *S v Plymouth City Council and C*, which established:[203]

> '… a clear distinction between disclosure to the media with a view to publication to all and sundry and disclosure in confidence to those with a proper interest in having the information in question.'

A similar balancing act must be carried out by professionals seeking or undertaking assessments of capacity. It is essential that information concerning the person being assessed which is directly relevant to the decision in question is made available to ensure that an accurate and focused assessment can take place. Every effort must first be made to obtain the person's consent to disclosure by providing a full explanation as to why this is necessary and the risks and consequences involved. If the person is unable to consent, relevant disclosure – that is the minimum necessary to achieve the objective of assessing capacity – may be permitted where this is in the person's best interests.[204] However, this does not mean that everyone has to know everything.

2.114 When matters come to court, the position is somewhat different, in light of the demands of open justice – in other words that parties to proceedings should be entitled to see all material relevant to the determination by the court of the application before it. In *C v C (Court of Protection: Disclosure)*,[205] Sir James Munby P considered whether an unredacted psychological report and social worker statements should be disclosed to a birth mother who sought the reintroduction of indirect contact with her adopted 20-year-old daughter who lacked capacity to consent, either to the requested contact or to disclosure of the reports. Applying principles derived from cases involving children, Sir James

---

[201] In particular, solicitors must comply with *The Solicitors' Code of Conduct 2011* (Solicitors Regulation Authority, SRA Handbook, 2011), O (4.1).

[202] *W v Egdell and others* [1990] 1 All ER 835, at p 848.

[203] [2002] EWCA Civ 388, at [49].

[204] Further guidance is given in the Code of Practice, Chapter 16. See also William East, 'The Court of Protection: No Longer the 'Secret' Court?' in Jordans *Elder Law Journal* [2011] Eld LJ 415 for a discussion of the Court of Protection's approach to balancing the right to privacy against the principle of open justice. The President of the Court of Protection has also issued Practice Guidance: 'Transparency in the Court of Protection – Publication of Judgments', [2014] Eld LJ 113 aimed at improving transparency whilst protecting the personal privacy of vulnerable adults. See www.judiciary.gov.uk/Resources/JCO/Documents/Guidance/transparency-in-the-cop.pdf.

[205] [2014] 1 WLR 2731.

Munby P held that the test for denying disclosure was one of strict necessity, requiring consideration of the following points:

- The court should first consider whether disclosure of the material would involve a real possibility of significant harm to the child.

- If it would, the court should next consider whether the overall interests of the child would benefit from non-disclosure, weighing on the one hand the interest of the child in having the material properly tested, and on the other both the magnitude of the risk that harm will occur and the gravity of the harm if it does occur.

- If the court is satisfied that the interests of the child point towards non-disclosure, the next and final step is for the court to weigh that consideration, and its strength in the circumstances of the case, against the interest of the parent or other party in having an opportunity to see and respond to the material. In the latter regard the court should take into account the importance of the material to the issues in the case.

He noted, further, that consideration should always be given to the fact that disclosure is never a binary exercise, and a proper evaluation and weighing of the various interests may lead to the conclusion that (i) there should be disclosure but (ii) the disclosure needs to be subject to safeguards such as limits to the use that may be made of the documents, in particular so as to limit the release into the public domain of intensely personal information about third parties. Further, the position initially arrived at is never set in stone and that it may be appropriate to proceed one step at a time. In a conclusion that may we suggest be tested further in a suitable case, Sir James Munby P also endorsed the potential limitation of disclosure to a party's legal representatives, albeit that he noted there were obviously practical difficulties to such an approach, chief amongst them being the requirement that such disclosure cannot take place without the consent of the lawyers to whom the disclosure is to be made; and they may find themselves, for reasons they may be unable to communicate to the court, unable to give such consent. Moreover, as the President noted, the lawyers cannot consent unless satisfied that they can do so without damage to their client's interests.

Refusal to be assessed

2.115 There may be circumstances in which a person whose capacity is in doubt refuses to undergo an assessment of capacity or refuses to be examined by a doctor. It will usually be possible to persuade someone to agree to an assessment if the consequences of refusal are carefully explained. For example, it should be explained to people wishing to make a will that the will could be challenged and held to be invalid after their death, while evidence of their capacity to make a will would prevent this from happening.

2.116 If the person lacks capacity to consent to or refuse assessment, it will normally be possible for an assessment to proceed so long as the person is compliant and this is considered to be in the person's best interests. In many situations, a 'reasonable belief' of lack of capacity will be sufficient.[206] However, where a formal assessment is needed, no one can be forced to undergo an assessment of capacity in the face of an outright refusal.[207] For example, entry to a person's home cannot be forced and a refusal to open the door to the doctor may be the end of the matter. Where there are serious concerns about the person's mental health, an assessment under mental health legislation may be warranted, but only so long as the statutory grounds are fulfilled.[208] If there are proper grounds to believe that the person's refusal to undergo the assessment is due to the influence of a third party, then it may be possible to invoke the inherent jurisdiction of the High Court (see **11.3**) to seek injunctions requiring that third party to allow access to the person. Note, finally, that it may in some cases be necessary for a court to take steps to circumvent a refusal by an individual to undergo an assessment of capacity to litigate so that appropriate steps can be taken to appoint a litigation friend.[209]

Recording assessments of capacity

2.117 The majority of decisions made on behalf of people lacking capacity will be informal day-to-day decisions and, as such, those caring for them on a daily basis will be able to assess their capacity and carry out acts in connection with their care and treatment in accordance with MCA 2005, s 5.[210] No formal assessment procedures or recorded documentation will be required. However, if the carer's assessment is challenged, they must be able to point to the steps they have taken to establish the person's capacity to make the decision in question and the grounds which justified a reasonable belief of lack of capacity.[211]

Professional records

2.118 Where professionals are involved, it is a matter of good practice that a proper assessment of capacity is made and the findings recorded in the relevant professional records. This includes, for example:

---

[206] See **2.87–2.90** above.

[207] See for example *Baker Tilley v Makar* [2013] EWHC 759 (QB), [2013] COPLR 245, in which the court held that a Costs judge was wrong to conclude that M lacked capacity to litigate on the basis of a single incident even though she had refused to undergo a capacity assessment or allow access to her medical records.

[208] Mental Health Act 1983, ss 2, 3. A refusal to be assessed is in no way sufficient grounds for assessment under the Mental Health Act 1983.

[209] In *Re RGS* [2012] EWHC 4162 (COP), for instance, the court found itself able to reach conclusions as to the capacity of P's son to conduct the litigation on the basis of evidence before the court from professional witness and the son's own account, even though the son declined to undertake a formal medical assessment. Obiter comments in *Bennett v Compass Group* [2002] EWCA Civ 642, [2002] CP Rep 58 could also be read as suggesting that a court might be able to go so far (in an exceptional case) as making an order requiring a GP or hospital to disclose medical records without the consent of the person in question.

[210] See **2.158–2.173** below.

[211] See **2.87–2.90** above.

(1)   an assessment of a patient's capacity to consent to medical treatment made by the doctor proposing the treatment and recorded in the patient's clinical notes;

(2)   an assessment of a client's capacity to instruct a solicitor to carry out a legal transaction (where necessary supported by a medical opinion) made by the solicitor and recorded in a clear attendance note on the client's file; and

(3)   an assessment of a person's capacity to consent to or agree the provision of services should be made as part of the care planning processes for health or social care needs and should be recorded in the relevant documentation.

Formal reports or certificates of capacity

2.119   In some cases, a more detailed report or certificate will be required, for example:

(1)   for use in court or other legal proceedings;

(2)   as required by regulations made under MCA 2005;

(3)   as required by the Court of Protection Rules.

Assessments by solicitors

2.120   Two cases in the former Court of Protection highlight the pitfalls for solicitors concerning capacity assessments when asked by an expectant attorney to take instructions for the preparation of an EPA from a donor. In his first judgment Deputy Master Ashton stated:[212]

'The assessment of an experienced solicitor must be taken very seriously by the Court provided that adequate enquiry has been made and all appropriate information obtained. In this case the solicitor's assessment does not stand up to scrutiny for the following reasons:

1.   the interview note is brief and the solicitor was only able to give evidence as to what she would have done because she could not remember;

2.   the interview lasted 30 minutes which included getting to know the new clients, explaining the wisdom of signing enduring powers of attorney, making a choice of attorney, considering any limitations or conditions, preparing and going through the documentation (which would be a slow process as [the donor] was hard of hearing) and arranging for the safe custody of the documents. There was thus little time for an effective mental health assessment;

3.   despite the age of the client there is no indication that enquiry was made as to [his] mental health or a letter sought from [his] own GP. The solicitor was not informed of mental health problems and did not suspect these because of the demeanour of the client who was being 'led' by the daughter. Had the solicitor been more circumspect and insisted on the most basic enquiry, or insisted upon a second interview at a later date with the client on his own, the true position would almost certainly have emerged.'

---

[212]   *Re AS and DS* (2004) Case No. 2120091/2.

In the subsequent case the Deputy Master stated:[213]

> '... the solicitor did not carry out a proper assessment of mental capacity of the client (the Donor) for the following reasons:
>
> 1. instructions were taken from the daughter and son-in-law who wished to be appointed as attorneys and there was no independent corroboration of any of the information that they provided (eg. as to the existence of other members of the family or the nature of the task involved);
> 2. the interview was conducted on the basis of explanations by the solicitor of the particular document involved, with remarkably little communication by the client other than apparent nods of assent. There should have been an initial 'getting to know the client' discussion at which he was encouraged to do most of the talking, with a few questions designed to test his knowledge and the depth of his understanding;
> 3. there was no preliminary assessment of capacity as such – the understanding of the client was perceived rather than tested. There was merely a basic interview lasting half-an-hour which appears to have progressed on the assumption that there was capacity. This assumption was based upon the client's responses as the interview progressed to the explanations being given whereas these may merely have been manifestations of a learnt behaviour pattern;
> 4. despite the fact that the intended donor was elderly and in hospital no prior approach was made to the medical staff as to his diagnosis and present condition. This would have revealed that he had advanced Alzheimer's dementia and was under the care of a psychiatrist who considered that he did not have capacity to sign any documents.
> 5. I find that the half hour interview would not (and did not) reveal the true state of understanding of the client. It was not searching at all and relied solely upon the impression gained by a solicitor with little experience in this area whilst explaining a legal document.'

Assessments for civil courts

2.121 Uncertainty sometimes arises during high value personal injury claims as to whether a brain damaged claimant is a protected party (CPR, r 21.1(d)) and, if so, also a protected beneficiary (CPR, r 21.1(e)) (see Chapter 11 for further details). Consideration was given to the approach to these issues and the implications of the MCA in *Saulle v Nouvet*.[214] The Court of Protection can assist, as illustrated by the following judgment:[215]

> 'This is an application to the new Court of Protection for a declaration pursuant to the Mental Capacity Act 2005, section 15 as to [P]'s capacity:
>
> a) to conduct his civil claim (which is now well advanced); and
> b) to manage his property and affairs (which will include damages of up to £400,000).

---

[213] *Re HW* (2005) Case No. 2122208.
[214] [2007] EWHC 2902 (QB), Andrew Edis QC sitting as a deputy judge.
[215] *In the matter of GS* [2008] CoP Case No: 11582024, 10 July 2008, DJ Ashton.

If he lacks capacity to do the former a litigation friend will need to be appointed for him in the civil proceedings although this would normally be any deputy already appointed. If he lacks capacity to do the latter his financial affairs will come under the jurisdiction of this Court and a financial deputy will need to be appointed for him. The calculation of compensation in the personal injury proceedings may in consequence be affected by the need to appoint such a deputy.

... [The decision in *Saulle v Nouvet*] identifies a weakness of dealing with the issue of capacity in the civil court. That court can make a definitive decision as to capacity to litigate but it cannot make a decision as to capacity to manage financial affairs that will be binding on the Court of Protection. Conversely, the Court of Protection has a statutory power to make declarations as to capacity which may relate to both litigation and management of financial affairs and any such declarations are likely to be followed by a civil court. In substantial personal injury claims where the quantum of damages may be affected by the involvement of the Court of Protection there are therefore advantages in the civil court referring both issues of capacity to the Court of Protection for determination. However, where the amount of money involved would not normally trigger the intervention of the Court of Protection it is proportionate and desirable for the civil court to adjudicate on both aspects of capacity (ie to decide whether the litigant is a protected party and if so then whether he or she is also a protected beneficiary).'

Determining best interests

Background

2.122 Before MCA 2005 came into effect, the principle of acting in the best interests of a person who lacks capacity had become well established in the common law and the concept had been developed by the courts in cases relating to incapacitated adults, mainly those concerned with the provision of medical treatment.[216] MCA 2005, s 1(5) enshrines this principle in statute as the overriding principle that must guide all actions done for, or all decisions made on behalf of, someone lacking capacity.[217] MCA 2005, s 4 goes on to describe, for the purposes of this Act, the steps that must be taken in determining what is in a person's best interests.

2.123 Given the wide range of decisions and acts covered by this legislation and the varied circumstances of the people affected by its provisions, the concept of best interests is not defined in MCA 2005. In considering the need for a definition, the Law Commission acknowledged that:[218]

'... no statutory guidance could offer an exhaustive account of what is in a person's best interests, the intention being that the individual person and his or her individual circumstances should always determine the result.'

---

[216] See eg *Re A (Male Sterilisation)* [2000] 1 FLR 549; *Re S (Sterilisation: Patient's Best Interests)* [2000] 2 FLR 389; *Re F (Adult Patient: Sterilisation)* [2001] Fam 15.

[217] See **2.45–2.48** above.

[218] Law Com No 231, n 1 above, at para 3.26.

2.124 Instead, the Law Commission recommended that statute should set out a checklist of common factors which should always be taken into account. It also set out some important considerations as to how a statutory checklist should be framed:[219]

> 'First, a checklist must not unduly burden any decision-maker or encourage unnecessary intervention; secondly it must not be applied too rigidly and should leave room for all considerations relevant to the particular case; thirdly, it should be confined to major points, so that it can adapt to changing views and attitudes.'

2.125 The Joint Committee on the Draft Mental Incapacity Bill agreed with this approach:[220]

> 'We agree that no list of "best interest" factors can ever be comprehensive or applicable in all situations. We therefore endorse the approach recommended by the Law Commission that a checklist of common factors to be considered in all cases should be set out in statute. However, it should be made clearer in the Bill that in addition to these common factors, all other matters relevant to the incapacitated individual and the decision in question must also be considered.'

Both as a result of recommendations made by the Joint Committee and amendments made during the parliamentary process, the best interests checklist contained in MCA 2005, s 4 was extended and made more prescriptive in relation to certain types of decisions, in particular, those involving end-of-life decisions. The specific requirements for determining best interests are considered in detail in the following paragraphs.

The best interests checklist

2.126 Under MCA 2005, a person's capacity to make the decision or take the action in question must first be assessed. MCA 2005, s 4 only comes into play once it has been established (or there are reasonable grounds for believing) that the person lacks capacity to make the decision in question and needs someone else to decide or act on his or her behalf. It then sets out a checklist of factors which must be considered in deciding what is in a person's best interests aimed at identifying those issues most relevant to the individual who lacks capacity (as opposed to the decision-maker or any other persons). The particular factors in the checklist can be broadly summarised as follows:

- equal consideration and non-discrimination;
- considering all relevant circumstances;
- regaining capacity;
- permitting and encouraging participation;
- special considerations for life-sustaining treatment;
- the person's wishes and feelings, beliefs and values;

---

[219] Ibid, at para 3.28.
[220] Joint Committee Report, Vol I, n 5 above, at para 85.

- the views of other people.

Not all the factors in the checklist will be relevant to all types of decisions or actions, but they must still be considered if only to be disregarded as irrelevant to that particular situation. It is also important always to be clear before applying the checklist whether the decision to be taken is actually a best interests decision for purposes of MCA, s 1(5). The fact that a person may lack capacity to take decisions (for instance regarding their care arrangements) does not mean that every decision taken in relation to them – in particular by public bodies discharging their statutory obligations – is a best interests decision. This is discussed further at **11.19–11.24**, but a sensible rule of thumb is always to ask whether the decision in question is one that the individual in question could take for themselves if they had capacity. If so, then the best interests checklist will need to be applied by whoever is to take the decision on their behalf.[221] If not, then it is more likely than not that MCA 2005, s 1(5) and the best interests checklist in MCA 2005, s 4 will have no application.

2.127 The serious nature of this task of determining best interests was recognised by the Joint Committee:[222]

> 'We acknowledge that consideration of best interests requires flexibility, by allowing and encouraging the person [lacking capacity] to be involved to the fullest possible extent but also enabling the decision-maker to take account of a variety of circumstances, views and attitudes which may have a bearing on the decision in question. This flexibility is particularly important in cases of partial or fluctuating capacity. Determining best interests is a judgement, requiring consideration of what will often be conflicting or competing concerns, while seeking to achieve a consensus approach to decision-making.'

2.128 There is an increasing discussion as to the extent to which there is a hierarchy in the checklist. In *Re M, ITW v Z*, applying the statutory scheme under MCA 2005 ss 1 and 4, Munby J (as he then was) held that there was no hierarchy, and summarised three points derived from experience in other jurisdictions:[223]

> '(i)   The first is that the statute lays down no hierarchy as between the various factors which have to be borne in mind, beyond the overarching principle that what is determinative is the judicial evaluation of what is in P's "best interests".
>
> (ii)   The second is that the weight to be attached to the various factors will, inevitably, differ depending upon the individual circumstances of the particular case. A feature or factor which in one case may carry great, possibly even preponderant, weight may in another, superficially similar, case carry much less, or even very little, weight.

---

[221] The precise identity of the decision-maker is – deliberately – not set out in MCA 2005. See further **2.174** and the discussion of MCA 2005, s 5.

[222] Ibid, at para 89.

[223] *Re M, ITW v Z & Ors* [2009] EWHC 2525 (Fam), [2009] COPLR Con Vol 828 at para 32.

(iii) The third, following on from the others, is that there may, in the particular case, be one or more features or factors which, as Thorpe LJ has frequently put it, are of "magnetic importance" in influencing or even determining the outcome: see, for example, *Crossley v Crossley*,[224] at para [15] (contrasting "the peripheral factors in the case" with the "factor of magnetic importance") and *White v White*[225] where at page 314 he said "Although there is no ranking of the criteria to be found in the statute, there is as it were a magnetism that draws the individual case to attach to one, two, or several factors as having decisive influence on its determination." Now that was said in the context of section 25 of the Matrimonial Causes Act 1973 but the principle, as it seems to me, is of more general application.'

2.129 However, and as discussed further in this regard at **2.148–2.149**, the case-law does not all speak with one voice as regards the status of P's wishes and feelings. It should also be noted that while 'the right to private and family life' confirmed by ECHR Article 8 will always be a relevant factor in determining a person's best interests, it should not be 'the starting point' or given priority over other relevant factors, not least because 'there may well be a conflict between the incapacitated person's right to family life and that person's right to private life'.[226]

Principle of equal consideration

2.130 Similar to the 'equal consideration' requirement imposed as an amendment to the definition of people who lack capacity,[227] MCA 2005, s 4(1) begins with a clear statement that a determination of someone's best interests must not be based merely on the person's age or appearance, or any condition or aspect of his or her behaviour which might lead others to make unjustified assumptions about the person's best interests. As in MCA 2005, s 2(3), the reference here to 'condition' covers a range of factors, including both mental or physical disabilities and age-related illness as well as temporary conditions, such as drunkenness. 'Appearance' is also deliberately broad, covering all aspects of physical appearance, visible medical problems or disfiguring scars, disabilities, skin colour, religious dress and so on. 'Behaviour' relates to ways of behaving that might seem unusual or odd to others, such as failing to make eye contact or laughing inappropriately.

2.131 This is intended to ensure that people with impaired capacity are treated no less favourably than people with capacity. Thus, decisions about best interests must not be based on any preconceived ideas or negative assumptions, for example, about the value or quality of life experienced by older people or people with mental or physical disabilities who now lack capacity to make decisions for themselves.

---

[224] *Crossley v Crossley* [2007] EWCA Civ 1491, [2008] 1 FLR 1467.
[225] [1999] Fam 304 (affirmed, [2001] 1 AC 596).
[226] *K v LBX & Ors* [2012] EWCA Civ 79; [2012] COPLR 411 at para 30.
[227] See **2.62–2.64** above.

All relevant circumstances

2.132 A determination of a person's best interests involves identifying those issues most relevant to the individual who lacks capacity in the context of the decision in question. The statutory checklist sets out the minimum necessary considerations but all other matters relevant in the particular situation must also be taken into account. MCA 2005, s 4(2) therefore requires the person making the determination to consider 'all the relevant circumstances' as well as following the steps set out in the checklist. In *Re M, ITW v Z*, Munby J (as he then was) gave the following example:[228]

> '... the use of the words "engaged in caring" in section 4(7)(b), which would seem to connote only someone who is currently caring and to exclude someone whose caring has come to an end, does not mean that the views of a past carer are irrelevant. The effect of section 4(7)(b) may be to limit the decision-maker's duty to consult to current carers, but the views of a past carer if known are nonetheless part of the circumstances which have to be taken into account under section 4(2).'

2.133 It is recognised that the person making the determination may not be in a position to make exhaustive inquiries to investigate every issue which may have some relevance to the incapacitated person or the decision in question. Therefore relevant circumstances are defined in MCA 2005 as those:[229]

(a)   of which the person making the determination is aware; and

(b)   which it would be reasonable to regard as relevant.

For example, in decisions about the living arrangements of a person who lacks capacity to decide where to live, the courts have confirmed that 'the right to private and family life' under ECHR Art 8 will always be a relevant factor in determining the person's best interests.[230]

Regaining capacity

2.134 Following further consultation on the checklist suggested by the Law Commission for the determination of best interests, the Government proposed an additional factor – whether the person is likely to regain capacity.[231] One of MCA 2005's key principles is that before a person is found to be incapable of making a decision, all practicable steps must be taken to help the person make that decision.[232]

2.135 In keeping with this approach, when looking at best interests, it is important to consider whether the individual concerned is likely to have

---

[228]   *Re M, ITW v Z & Ors* [2009] EWHC 2525 (Fam), [2009] COPLR Con Vol 828 at para 36.
[229]   MCA 2005, s 4(11).
[230]   *Hillingdon v Neary* [2011] EWHC 1377 (COP), [2011] COPLR Con Vol 632 at [24]; *FP v GM and A Health Board* [2011] EWHC 2778 (COP) at [20]; *K v LBX & Ors* [2012] EWCA Civ 79, [2012] COPLR 411 at para 52 per Lady Justice Black.
[231]   Lord Chancellor's Department *Making Decisions*, Cm 4465 (TSO, 1999), at para 1.12.
[232]   MCA 2005, s 1(3). See **2.32–2.38** above.

capacity to make that particular decision in the future and, if so, when that is likely to be.[233] It may be possible to put off the decision until the person can make it him or herself. This delay may allow further time for additional steps to be taken to restore the person's capacity or to provide support and assistance which would enable the person to make the decision.

2.136 The Code of Practice suggests some factors which may indicate that a person may regain capacity:[234]

- 'the cause of the lack of capacity can be treated, either by medication or some other form of treatment or therapy;
- the lack of capacity is likely to decrease in time (for example, where it is caused by the effects of medication or alcohol, or following a sudden shock);
- a person with learning disabilities may learn new skills or be subject to new experiences which increase their understanding and ability to make certain decisions;
- the person may have a condition which causes capacity to come and go (such as some forms of mental illness) so it may be possible to arrange for the decision to be made during a time when they do have capacity;
- a person previously unable to communicate may learn a new form of communication.'

Permitting and encouraging participation

2.137 MCA 2005, s 4(4) requires that, even where a person does not have capacity to make an effective decision, he or she should be both permitted and encouraged to participate, or to improve his or her ability to participate as fully as possible, in the decision-making process or in relation to any act done for him or her. It will always be important to consult the person on the particular act or decision to be made and to try to seek their views, not only to encourage the development of decision-making skills, but also as an important contribution in determining best interests. The practicable steps to enable decision-making will also be relevant here.[235] The importance of involving the person in the decision-making process has been reinforced by the Court of Protection (*C v V, Re S and S (Protected Persons)*).[236]

Life-sustaining treatment

2.138 A specific best interests factor relates to decisions concerning the provision (or withdrawal) of life-sustaining treatment, which is defined as treatment which a person providing health care regards as necessary to sustain life, usually the life of a person lacking capacity to consent to that treatment.[237] MCA 2005, s 4(5) clarifies that in determining whether the treatment is in the

---

[233] MCA 2005, s 4(3).
[234] Mental Capacity Act 2005: Code of Practice, at para 5.28.
[235] See **2.33–2.38** above.
[236] [2008] EWHC B16 (Fam), [2008] COPLR Con Vol 1074 at paras 54–55.
[237] MCA 2005, s 4(10). In parliamentary debate, it was also clarified that 'in the case of a pregnant woman we want to ensure that the life of the baby, not only the life of the mother, must be considered': *Hansard*, HL Deb, vol 668, ser 5, col 1184 (25 January 2005). However,

best interests of someone who lacks capacity to consent to it, the person making the determination must not be motivated by a desire to bring about the individual's death.

2.139 A great deal of the debate in both Houses of Parliament concerned life and death decisions affecting people who lack capacity to make those decisions for themselves. In order to provide clarity and reassurance on these very difficult issues, the Government agreed to a number of amendments introducing specific statements in the legislation. In particular, MCA 2005, s 62 confirms that the Act does not have the effect of authorising or permitting unlawful killing (including euthanasia) or assisted suicide. Secondly, in relation to decisions about whether the provision or continuance of life-sustaining treatment would be in a person's best interests, MCA 2005, s 4(5) clarifies that the decision-maker must not be motivated by a desire to bring about the person's death.

2.140 This particular factor was introduced as an amendment in the House of Lords after an undertaking was given in correspondence between the Lord Chancellor and the Roman Catholic Archbishop of Cardiff, Peter Smith, that MCA 2005 would make this point absolutely clear. Commenting on a situation where no advance decision has been made about whether treatment should be continued or refused, the Lord Chancellor said:[238]

> 'The decision about whether to continue to give life-sustaining treatment will then fall to be taken by the doctor, acting with an attorney who has relevant powers ... In some cases a decision ... will still be taken by the court. The Bill preserves the jurisdiction exercised in the Tony Bland case and restates the principles applied in that case. These are very difficult decisions, even for a court. In making them the decision-maker must act in the best interests of the patient. Above all, he must make an objective assessment. The decision cannot simply be the personal value judgement of the decision-maker – the decision-maker cannot say "If I were in the patient's position, I would want to die" – nor can it be motivated by the desire to bring about the death of the patient.'

2.141 Any decision about life-sustaining treatment for a person lacking capacity will take as its starting point the assumption that it is in the person's best interests for life to continue. This was confirmed by the Court of Protection in *W v M*, where Baker J held:[239]

---

an unborn child does not have an independent set of interests to be weighed against the mother's best interests (*St George's Healthcare NHS Trust v S* [1998] 3 All ER 673).

[238] *Hansard*, HL Deb, vol 668, ser 5, cols 14–15 (10 January 2005).

[239] *W v M & Ors* [2011] EWHC 2443 (Fam), [2012] COPLR 222 at para 7. The strong presumption in favour of preserving life can 'tip the balance' despite the person's known wishes to die: *A Local Authority v E* [2012] EWHC 1639 (COP), [2012] COPLR 441 at para 140. See, however, the decision in *United Lincolnshire Hospitals NHS Trust v N* [2014] EWCOP 16, [2014] COPLR 660 for a different approach where the known wishes of a patient in an MCS were given significant weight in declaring that it was not in her best interests for PEG feeding to be re-introduced where (whether by reflex or otherwise) she consistently pulled out her feeding tube.

'The factor which does carry substantial weight, in my judgment, is the preservation of life. Although not an absolute rule, the law regards the preservation of life as a fundamental principle. As another judge has said: "there is a very strong presumption in favour of taking all steps which will prolong life and, save in exceptional circumstances, or where the person is dying, the best interests of the patient will normally require such steps to be taken".'

However, there will be some cases, for example, in the final stages of terminal illness or for some patients in a vegetative state,[240] where treatment is futile, overly burdensome or intolerable for the patient or where there is no prospect of recovery, where it may be in the best interests of the patient to withdraw or withhold treatment or to give palliative care that might incidentally shorten life.[241] All the factors in the best interests checklist must be considered, but the person determining best interests must not be motivated in any way by the desire to bring about the person's death.[242]

The person's wishes and feelings, beliefs and values

2.142 A particularly important element of the best interests checklist is the consideration, so far as these can be ascertained, of:

'(a) the person's past and present wishes and feelings (and in particular, any relevant written statements made by him when he had capacity),

(b) the beliefs and values that would be likely to influence his decision if he had capacity, and

(c) the other factors that he would be likely to consider if he were able to do so.'

This places the focus firmly on the person lacking capacity, taking into account the issues most important to him or her and what he or she would have wanted to achieve and in the words of the Supreme Court in *Aintree University Hospitals NHS Foundation Trust v James*[243] requiring the decision-maker: 'to consider matters from the patient's point of view'. It also reflects the need to

---

[240] It has been confirmed that the court also has jurisdiction to hear applications for the withdrawal of artificial nutrition and hydration (ANH) from a patient in a minimally conscious state: *W v M & Ors*, ibid. In his judgment, Baker J made some observations (at paras 256–261), which have been approved by the President of the Court of Protection, designed to assist in future applications for the withdrawal of ANH from a person in a vegetative state or minimally conscious state.

[241] Mental Capacity Act 2005: Code of Practice, paras 5.31–5.33. See for example *Re CW; A Primary Care Trust v CW* [2010] EWHC 3448 (COP). See also Chapter 6 for further details concerning best interests in relation to the provision or withdrawal of life-sustaining treatment, including discussion of the Supreme Court's decision in *Aintree University NHS Hospitals Trust v James* [2013] UKSC 67, [2013] 3 WLR 1299; [2013] COPLR 492.

[242] In *Aintree University NHS Hospitals Trust v James* [2013] 3 WLR 1299; [2013] COPLR 492, the Supreme Court held that 'decision-makers must look at [the patient's] welfare in the widest sense, not just medical but social and psychological' and then set out the various factors that must be considered (at [39]). The British Medical Association has published specific guidance on the provision or withdrawal of life-sustaining treatment (Withholding and withdrawing life-prolonging medical treatment: Guidance for decision making, BMA, 3rd edn, 2007). The General Medical Council has also issued guidance for doctors (*Treatment and care towards the end of life: good practice in decision making*, GMC, 2010).

[243] [2013] UKSC 67, [2013] COPLR 492, SC at para 45.

make every effort to find out whether the person has expressed any relevant views in the past, whether verbally, in writing or through behaviour or habits, as well as trying to seek his or her current views.

2.143 The reference to written statements was included as a Government amendment in the House of Lords in response to lobbying by the Making Decisions Alliance and other stakeholder organisations. Those organisations had requested that advance statements, particularly those expressing wishes about medical treatment, should be given some form of statutory recognition and should specifically be taken into account in determining a person's best interests. The Minister for Constitutional Affairs, Baroness Ashton, confirmed:[244]

> '... the purpose of this amendment is to clarify that if someone with capacity has written down their wishes and feelings in respect of a matter, including positive preferences, those must be explicitly taken into account in a best interests determination.
>
> Patients do not have a right to demand and receive treatment, so advance requests cannot have the same legal effect as advance decisions to refuse treatment. However, the amendment makes clear that preferences about any aspect of a person's life, including treatment, should be respected and taken into account ... The more specific and well thought out the statement, the more likely it will be persuasive in determining best interests.'

An example of such a case is *PS v LP*,[245] concerning whether LP should have contact with her husband and family whom she had left to live with her lover, shortly before suffering a cerebral aneurism which robbed her of capacity to make her own decision. HHJ Cardinal considered that LP's clear expression of her wishes not to have any contact with her family, which she had set out in a hand-written will and a signed 'letter of wishes', was a magnetic factor in the case. After weighing all the relevant matters, he concluded that it was not in the best interests of LP to see her family unless there was a change in LP's situation at some point in the future.

2.144 The Draft Mental Incapacity Bill published in 2003 made no mention of the person's 'beliefs and values' but this was added to the Bill in response to a recommendation of the Joint Committee:[246]

> 'The Medical Ethics Alliance suggested to us that the factor involving the need to consider the incapacitated person's "past and present wishes and feelings" should also contain reference to that person's values. Others suggested that specific reference should be made to social, psychological, cultural, spiritual and religious

---

[244] *Hansard*, HL Deb, vol 670, ser 5, cols 1441–1442 (17 March 2005).

[245] *PS v LP* [2013] EWHC 1106 (COP). See also *RGB v Cwm Taf Health Board* [2013] EWHC B23 (COP), [2014] COPLR 83 (advance statement by wife as to contact with her estranged husband determinative of question of whether it was in her best interests for them to have contact in a care facility).

[246] Joint Committee Report, Vol I, n 5 above, at para 90.

issues. It is anticipated that the need to consider a wide range of issues, in particular religious and cultural concerns, will be spelt out in the Code of Practice. We seek reassurance that the form of words used in the Bill will require a person's values to be given due weight.'

2.145 The reference to factors the person 'would be likely to consider' if able to do so provides the 'substituted judgment' element of the best interests checklist, as previously reflected in case-law in relation to the powers exercised by the previous Court of Protection to make a statutory will, where:[247]

> '... subject to all due allowances ... the court must seek to make the will which the actual patient, acting reasonably, would have made if notionally restored to full mental capacity, memory and foresight.'

2.146 MCA 2005, s 4(6)(c) extends this notion as a factor to consider for all decisions or actions, whether or not the person concerned ever had capacity in relation to the matter in question. Prior to implementation of MCA 2005, the courts had held that the possible wider benefits to a person lacking capacity, arising for example from emotional support from close relationships, are important factors which the person would be likely to consider if able to do so, and are therefore relevant in determining the person's own best interests.[248] The Court of Protection has since upheld the significance of the 'emotional dimension' of the best interests analysis:[249]

> 'There is of course more to human life than [physical care needs], there is fundamentally the emotional dimension, the importance of relationships, the importance of a sense of belonging in the place in which you are living, and the sense of belonging to a specific group in respect of which you are a particularly important person.'

Or in the words of Munby J (as he then was) 'What good is it making someone safer if it merely makes them miserable?'[250] For a further, very powerful, example of the application of this principle, see *Re M (Best Interests: Deprivation of Liberty).*[251]

2.147 The Code of Practice suggests that such emotional factors might include altruistic motives, such as 'the effect of the decision on other people, obligations to dependants or the duties of a responsible citizen'.[252] In the case of *Re G (TJ)*, Morgan J considered whether it was in Mrs G's best interests to continue to pay a regular sum for the maintenance of her adult daughter. In considering the

---

[247] *Re D (J)* [1982] 2 All ER 37, at p 43.
[248] See eg *Re Y (Mental Incapacity: Bone marrow transplant)* [1996] 2 FLR 787; *Re A (Male Sterilisation)* [2000] 1 FLR 549.
[249] *FP v GM and A Health Board* [2011] EWHC 2778 (COP) at para 21.
[250] *X v MM & KM* [2007] EWHC 2003 (Fam) at [120].
[251] [2013] EWHC 3456 (COP), [2014] COPLR 35.
[252] Mental Capacity Act 2005: Code of Practice, at para 5.47.

difference between substituted judgment and best interests, he reviewed the relevant cases (summarised below) and reached the following conclusions:[253]

'The best interests test involves identifying a number of relevant factors. The actual wishes of P can be a relevant factor: section 4(6)(a) says so. The beliefs and values which would be likely to influence P's decision, if he had capacity to make the relevant decision, are a relevant factor: section 4(6)(b) says so. The other factors which P would be likely to consider, if he had the capacity to consider them, are a relevant factor: section 4(6)(c) says so. Accordingly, the balance sheet of factors which P would draw up, if he had capacity to make the decision, is a relevant factor for the court's decision. Further, in most cases the court will be able to determine what decision it is likely that P would have made, if he had capacity. In such a case, in my judgment, P's balance sheet of factors and P's likely decision can be taken into account by the court. This involves an element of substituted judgment being taken into account, together with anything else which is relevant. However, it is absolutely clear that the ultimate test for the court is the test of best interests and not the test of substituted judgment. Nonetheless, the substituted judgment can be relevant and is not excluded from consideration. As Hoffmann LJ said in the *Bland* case, the substituted judgment can be subsumed within the concept of best interests. That appeared to be the view of the Law Commission also.

Further, the word 'interest' in the best interests test does not confine the court to considering the self interest of P. The actual wishes of P, which are altruistic and not in any way, directly or indirectly self-interested, can be a relevant factor. Further, the wishes which P would have formed, if P had capacity, which may be altruistic wishes, can be a relevant factor. It is not necessary to establish that P would have been aware of the fact that P's wishes were carried into effect. Respect for P's wishes, actual or putative, can be a relevant factor even where P has no awareness of, and no reaction to, the fact that such wishes are being respected.'

The weight to be given to P's wishes and feelings

2.148 There is an increasing debate as to whether it is necessary to give particular weight to P's wishes and feelings in the application of MCA 2005, s 4[254] and the case-law reveals something of a split. At one end of the spectrum is the decision of Munby J (as he then was) in In *Re M, ITW v Z and others*, a statutory will application in a case in which an elderly woman had been the

---

[253] *In the Matter of G (TJ)* [2010] EWHC 3005 (COP), [2010] COPLR Con Vol 403 at paras 55–56. *Re X, Y and Z* [2014] EWHC 87 (COP), [2014] COPLR 364 (in P's best interests for funds awarded her in compensation for personal injuries to be used to provide care to her children).

[254] See for a discussion of some of these issues Alex Ruck Keene and Cressida Auckland, 'More Presumptions, Please: Wishes, Feelings and Best Interests Decision-Making' Elder Law Journal, Jordans, [2015] Eld LJ forthcoming. The relevant paragraphs (5.37–5.48) in the Mental Capacity Act 2005 Code of Practice remain of importance but need to be read in light of the developing body of case-law.

victim of financial abuse by a neighbour. When considering the weight and importance to be attached to the person's (P's) wishes and feelings, he made the following observations:[255]

'i)   First, P's wishes and feelings will always be a significant factor to which the court must pay close regard: see *Re MM; Local Authority X v MM (by the Official Solicitor) and KM* [2007] EWHC 2003 (Fam), [2009] 1 FLR 443, at paras [121]–[124].

ii)   Secondly, the weight to be attached to P's wishes and feelings will always be case-specific and fact-specific. In some cases, in some situations, they may carry much, even, on occasions, preponderant, weight. In other cases, in other situations, and even where the circumstances may have some superficial similarity, they may carry very little weight. One cannot, as it were, attribute any particular *a priori* weight or importance to P's wishes and feelings; it all depends, it must depend, upon the individual circumstances of the particular case. And even if one is dealing with a particular individual, the weight to be attached to their wishes and feelings must depend upon the particular context; in relation to one topic P's wishes and feelings may carry great weight whilst at the same time carrying much less weight in relation to another topic. Just as the test of incapacity under the 2005 Act is, as under the common law, 'issue specific', so in a similar way the weight to be attached to P's wishes and feelings will likewise be issue specific.

iii)   Thirdly, in considering the weight and importance to be attached to P's wishes and feelings the court must of course, and as required by section 4(2) of the 2005 Act, have regard to *all* the relevant circumstances. In this context the relevant circumstances will include, though I emphasise that they are by no means limited to, such matters as:

    (a) the degree of P's incapacity, for the nearer to the borderline the more weight must in principle be attached to P's wishes and feelings: *Re MM; Local Authority X v MM (by the Official Solicitor) and KM,*[256] at para [124];

    (b) the strength and consistency of the views being expressed by P;

    (c) the possible impact on P of knowledge that her wishes and feelings are not being given effect to: see again *Re MM; Local Authority X v MM (by the Official Solicitor) and KM,*[257] at para [124];

    (d) the extent to which P's wishes and feelings are, or are not, rational, sensible, responsible and pragmatically capable of sensible implementation in the particular circumstances; and

    (e) crucially, the extent to which P's wishes and feelings, if given effect to, can properly be accommodated within the court's overall assessment of what is in her best interests.'

2.149   To contrary effect could be seen to be the judgment in *C v V, Re S and S (Protected Persons))* when HHJ Hazel Marshall QC held that there is a presumption in favour of implementing the person's wishes unless they are irrational, impractical, or irresponsible (with reference to resources), or there is

---

[255]   *Re M, ITW v Z & Ors* [2009] EWHC 2525 (Fam), [2009] COPLR Con Vol 828 at para [35]. See also *PS v LP* [2013] EWHC 1106 (COP).

[256]   [2007] EWHC 2003 (Fam), [2009] 1 FLR 443.

[257]   Ibid.

a sufficiently countervailing consideration.[258] Further, it is entirely possible to read the decision in *Aintree v James*[259] as suggesting that the individual's wishes and feelings (where it is possible reliably to identify them) as having an especial status,[260] and Senior Judge Lush has also noted, in placing weight upon the views expressed by P in the form of a will, that '[a]lthough it has been said that there is no hierarchy of factors in the checklist in section 4 of the Mental Capacity Act, I attach weight to EO's views, because section 4(6)(a) refers "in particular" (my emphasis) to "any relevant written statement made by him when he had capacity."'[261] Further, as discussed at **1.218–1.230**, it would seem that construing the Act so as to allow particular weight to be placed upon the individual's wishes and feelings is likely to be necessary as a step towards achieving compliance with the CRPD (as well as the right to autonomy enshrined in Art 8 of the ECHR). This, though, raises problems of its own, including, but not limited to:

- The potential for a conflict between the person's past and present wishes;

- Situations in which complying with the person's wishes carry potentially profoundly adverse consequences for them or others, which requires a particularly acute sensitivity to the (sometimes competing) obligations imposed upon the decision-maker by the European Convention on Human Rights and, in the majority of cases, is likely to be an indicator that the matter should be brought to the Court of Protection for either a declaration or a decision;

- The fact that – as with those with capacity – it is not always possible for the incapacitated adult to get what they want.[262] In proceedings before the Court of Protection, this highlights the importance of establishing at an early stage what options are actually before the court: see also in this regard **11.19–11.25**.

The views of other people

2.150 For the first time, MCA 2005 ensured that carers, family members and other relevant people are consulted on decisions affecting the person lacking capacity to make those decisions for themselves. People who must be consulted include anyone previously named by the person who now lacks capacity as

---

[258] [2008] EWHC B16 (Fam), [2008] COPLR Con Vol 1074 at paras 57–58, 87. In the later case of *Re P*, in the context of a statutory will application, Lewison J complimented HHJ Marshall QC for considering the MCA 2005 'in a most impressive and sensitive judgment', the broad thrust of which he agreed with, but he thought she 'may have slightly overstated the importance to be given to P's wishes' and he preferred 'not to speak in terms of presumptions': *In the matter of P* [2009] EWHC 163 (Ch), [2009] COPLR Con Vol 906 at [40] and [41]. Senior Judge Lush has recently referred to HHJ Marshall's approach in approving terms in – unusually – dismissing the application of the Public Guardian to revoke and cancel the registration of an EPA, in part on the basis of the wishes and feelings expressed by the adult in question: *Re DT* [2015] EWCOP 10 at [44]–[46].

[259] *Aintree University Hospitals NHS Foundation Trust v James* [2013] UKSC 67, [2013] COPLR 492, SC.

[260] See para 45 in particular.

[261] *Re BM; JB v AG* [2014] EWCOP B20 at para 58.

[262] See in this regard *Aintree v James* at para 45.

someone they would wish to be consulted, carers and anyone interested in the person's welfare, donees and deputies.[263] Any person who is determining the best interests of someone lacking capacity is required to take into account the views of these key people, but only if it is 'practicable and appropriate' to consult them. Further, the Senior Judge of the Court of Protection has held that where consultation is likely to be unduly onerous, contentious, futile or serve no useful purpose, it is not 'practicable or appropriate'.[264]

2.151   The Code of Practice suggests:[265]

> 'Decision-makers must show they have thought carefully about who to speak to. If it is practical and appropriate to speak to the above people, they must do so and must take their views into account. They must be able to explain why they did not speak to a particular person – it is good practice to have a clear record of their reasons.'

Consultation with all relevant people must be 'undertaken at a time when proposals are still formative, with sufficient reasons for proposals ... and adequate time to allow intelligent consideration and response to be given'[266] and taken into account in making the decision.

2.152   The consultation is limited to two matters – first, what those people consider to be in the person's best interests on the matter in question and, secondly, whether they can provide any information on the wishes, feelings, values or beliefs of the person lacking capacity.[267] If, prior to losing capacity, the person concerned has nominated someone whom he or she would like to be consulted, the named person is more likely to have that information. People who are close to the person lacking capacity, such as relatives, partners and other carers, may also be able to assist with communication or interpret signs which give an indication of the person's present wishes and feelings. In *Re M, ITW v Z* Munby J suggested that in determining best interests, it may be appropriate to consult with former carers and to take into account oral statements made to them by the person who lacks capacity.[268]

2.153   The requirement for consultation must be balanced against the right to confidentiality of the person lacking capacity. That right should be protected so that consultation only takes place where relevant and with people whom it is

---

[263]   MCA 2005, s 4(7).
[264]   *Re Allen* [2009] (CoP No 11661992) (unreported).
[265]   Mental Capacity Act 2005: Code of Practice, at para 5.51.
[266]   *R (W) v LB Croydon* (2011) EWHC 696 (Admin) at para 39.
[267]   See in this regard *Aintree v James* at para 39 per Lady Hale: the decision-maker 'must consult others who are looking after him or interested in his welfare, in particular for their view of what his attitude would be.' In *Re DE, A NHS Trust v DE* [2013] EWHC 2562 (Fam), [2013] COPLR 531, concerning whether it was in the best interests of an incapacitated learning disabled young man to have a vasectomy as a method of contraception, while it was clearly appropriate to consult DE's parents, it appears that their own feelings of distress caused by his unexpected fathering of a child and their views of the disruption that a further pregnancy would cause, were given undue weight.
[268]   *Re M, ITW v Z and Ors* [2009] EWHC 2525 (Fam), [2009] COPLR Con Vol 828 at para 36.

appropriate to consult. For example, it is unlikely to be appropriate to consult anyone whom the person had previously indicated should not be involved. However, there may be occasions where it is in the person's best interests for specific information to be disclosed, or where the public interest in disclosure may override the person's private interest in maintaining confidentiality.[269] If professionals are involved in the determination of best interests, they will also need to comply with their own duties of confidentiality in accordance with their professional codes of conduct.

Duty to apply the best interests principle

2.154 The principle set out in MCA 2005, s 1(5) confirms that any act done, or any decision made, on behalf of a person lacking capacity must be done in his or her best interests. MCA 2005, s 4(8) confirms that the best interests principle, and the duties to be carried out in determining best interests, also apply in certain circumstances where the person concerned may not in fact lack capacity in relation to the act or decision in question. This applies in relation to any powers which:

(1) are exercisable under a lasting power of attorney;

(2) are exercisable by a person under MCA 2005 where he or she 'reasonably believes' that another person lacks capacity.

Reasonable belief

2.155 The second situation reflects the position that in most day-to-day decisions or actions involved in caring for someone, it will not be appropriate or necessary to carry out a formal assessment of the person's capacity. Rather, it is sufficient for there to be a 'reasonable belief' that the person lacks capacity to make the decision or consent to the action in question.[270]

2.156 Similarly, MCA 2005, s 4(9) confirms that, in cases where the Court is not involved, carers (both professionals and family members) and others who are acting informally can only be expected to have reasonable grounds for believing that what they are doing or deciding is in the best interests of the person concerned, but they must still, so far as possible, apply the best interests checklist and therefore be able to point to objective reasons to justify why they hold that belief.[271]

2.157 MCA 2005, s 4(9) also applies to donees and deputies appointed to make welfare or financial decisions, as well as to those carrying out acts in connection with the care and treatment of a person lacking capacity. In deciding

---

[269] *S v Plymouth City Council and C* [2002] EWCA Civ 388, at para 49. See **2.112–2.114**.

[270] See **2.87–2.90** above.

[271] In *Commissioner of Police for the Metropolis v ZH* [2013] EWCA Civ 69, [2013] COPLR 332, the Court of Appeal upheld the decision at first instance that the police had failed to provide objective evidence to demonstrate that the actions they had taken in forcibly removing ZH from a swimming pool were in ZH's best interests. See **2.177** below for further discussion on this case.

what is 'reasonable' in any particular case, higher expectations are likely to be placed on those appointed to act under formal powers and those acting in a professional capacity than on family members and friends who are caring for a person lacking capacity without any formal authority.

PART 3: GENERAL POWERS AND DUTIES

Acts in connection with care or treatment – background

The problem

2.158 Until MCA 2005 came into effect, legislation has been silent about what actions could lawfully be taken by carers in looking after the day-to-day personal or health care needs of people who lack capacity to consent to those actions. These actions may include helping individuals to wash, dress and attend to their personal hygiene, feeding them, taking them out for walks and leisure activities, taking them to the doctor or dentist or providing necessary treatment.

2.159 In consequence, doctors, dentists and other health care professionals were hesitant about carrying out examinations, treatment or nursing care on patients unable to consent to those medical procedures. In the absence of any clear statutory provision, it was left to the courts to establish the former common law 'principle of necessity', setting out the circumstances in which actions and decisions could lawfully be taken on behalf of adults who lack capacity.[272]

2.160 The courts confirmed that where the principle of necessity applied (ie that it was necessary to act in relation to the well-being of a person lacking capacity to consent), and the action taken was reasonable and in the person's best interests, that action which would otherwise amount to a civil wrong, or even a crime (eg of battery or assault) would in fact be lawful. The principle of necessity is *not* equivalent to having consent but may constitute a defence if an action is subsequently challenged.

2.161 Such actions might involve touching or interfering with the person's bodily integrity, or using or interfering with the person's property or possessions. In such cases, the lack of capacity of the people concerned means that they cannot give their informed consent and therefore the proposed actions, if they were to take place, could potentially be unlawful unless the principle of necessity applied.

The Law Commission proposal

2.162 The Law Commission acknowledged that within the new jurisdiction it proposed, there should remain scope for caring actions to take place, and for

---

[272] *Re F (Mental Patient: Sterilisation)* [1990] 2 AC 1, at 75.

some informal decision-making 'without certifications, documentation or judicial determinations'.[273] However, the Commission recognised that the common law 'principle of necessity' was not widely understood and there was therefore a need to clarify the confused state of the law governing such actions:[274]

> 'We suggested in our consultation papers that there was a strong case for clarifying in statute the circumstances in which decisions can be taken for people who lack capacity, but without anyone having to apply for formal authorisation. We did not envisage this as conferring any new power on anyone, but rather as a clarification of the uncertain "necessity" principle. Respondents gave an enthusiastic welcome to our provisional proposals. There was very broad agreement that a statutory provision would be invaluable in dispelling doubt and confusion and setting firm and appropriate limits to informal action.'

The general authority

2.163 The Law Commission proposed a new statutory authority, which it called the 'general authority to act reasonably', to codify in statute what had become practice under common law and to clarify the 'principle of necessity'. It was intended that the general authority would provide legal authorisation for acts connected with the personal welfare or health care of a person lacking capacity to consent if it is reasonable in the particular circumstances for the act to be done by the person who does it. The legal authorisation would apply to different people acting at different times, so long as it was appropriate for them to do the act in question and they were acting reasonably and in the best interests of the person lacking capacity.

The views of the Joint Committee

2.164 However, the clauses in the Draft Mental Incapacity Bill making provision for the 'general authority'[275] caused significant concerns and confusion to a number of witnesses giving evidence to the Joint Committee on the Bill:[276]

> 'A number of the concerns which have been brought to our attention seem to be premised on a misunderstanding of the general authority as it is set out in the draft Bill. The extent of the misunderstandings apparent in the evidence we have received suggests that the drafting of this provision is not sufficiently clear. Many interested parties appear to be under the erroneous impression that the general authority would be assumed by a single individual who would then take all decisions on behalf of an incapacitated individual. In fact the general authority is for the relevant person, in the context of a specific decision or action, at a particular point in time, so long as it is reasonable for that person to act. Others have suggested that the general authority may be used by carers to justify taking decisions for which they would otherwise need formal authorisation. In fact the

---

[273] Law Com No 231, n 1 above, at para 4.1.
[274] Ibid, at para 4.2.
[275] Draft Mental Incapacity Bill, cls 6–7.
[276] Joint Committee Report, Vol I, n 5 above, at paras 109–110.

general authority is not intended to convey any new powers on anyone but rather to clarify the uncertain principle of "necessity".

We have come to the conclusion that the term "general authority" itself has contributed to the misinterpretations apparent within the evidence we have received. The word "authority" implies an imposition of decision making upon an incapacitated individual rather than an enabling process designed to enact decisions taken in their best interests. This may have contributed to perceptions of the general authority as likely to promote "over-paternalistic attitudes" towards incapacitated individuals. We are convinced that semantic issues are important in affecting public perceptions of the draft Bill as well as in determining legal interpretations of the provisions it contains.'

2.165 The Joint Committee recommended radical redrafting to clarify the legislative intent of the 'general authority' and the use of alternative terminology to avoid its misleading connotations. The Government's response was to recast the provisions to allow for a limitation of liability for people who need to act in connection with the care or treatment of a person lacking capacity to consent. Offering protection from liability is intended to enable caring actions to take place in the absence of consent, but also to make clear that anyone acting unreasonably, negligently or not in the person's best interests would forfeit that protection.

Acts in connection with care or treatment – the legislation

Protection from liability

2.166 MCA 2005, s 5 makes provision to allow carers (both informal carers, such as family members, and paid carers) and health and social care professionals to carry out certain acts in connection with the personal care, health care or treatment of a person lacking capacity to consent to those acts. These provisions are intended to give legal backing, in the form of protection from liability, for actions which are essential for the personal welfare or health of people lacking capacity to consent to having things done to or for them. Such actions can be performed as if the person concerned had capacity and had given consent.[277] There is no need to obtain any formal powers or authority to act.

2.167 In introducing the Bill into the House of Commons, the Under Secretary of State for Constitutional Affairs, David Lammy explained:[278]

'Clause 5, entitled "Acts in connection with care and treatment", is an important clarification of the law surrounding what someone can do to or for a person lacking mental capacity who is unable to give consent. The current law is based on the poorly understood and obscure "doctrine of necessity". Hon. Members will know of constituents who are worried and uncertain about what they are allowed to do, because they do not understand the law. For example, a nurse may want to restrain someone who is having an epileptic fit. Someone caring for an elderly

---

[277] MCA 2005, s 5(2).
[278] *Hansard*, HC Deb, vol 425, ser 6, col 29 (11 October 2004).

patient at home may need to help them to use the toilet. Someone whose daughter suffers from bipolar disease may want to go to her house to cook for her and to help her to eat because she is in too much distress.

It is not right that people in such situations should have to rely on what seems to them to be an outdated and obscure legal concept. Clause 5 explains what they can do. It provides that one is protected from liability when the person cannot consent, provided that one takes reasonable steps to establish whether that person lacks mental capacity in relation to the matter in question, that one reasonably believes that the person lacks capacity in relation to the matter, and that what one does is in the person's best interests.'

Section 5 acts

2.168 The types of acts which may be carried out with protection from liability under MCA 2005, s 5 (sometimes referred to as 'section 5 acts') are those carried out *in connection with the care or treatment* of a person who is believed to lack capacity in relation to the matter in question, at the time the act needs to be carried out. The Code of Practice provides examples (but not an exhaustive list) as follows:[279]

'Personal care

- helping with washing, dressing or personal hygiene
- helping with eating and drinking
- helping with communication
- helping with mobility (moving around)
- helping someone take part in education, social or leisure activities
- going into a person's home to drop off shopping or to see if they are alright
- doing the shopping or buying necessary goods with the person's money
- arranging household services (for example, arranging repairs or maintenance for gas and electricity supplies)
- providing services that help around the home (such as homecare or meals on wheels)
- undertaking actions related to community care services (for example, day care, residential accommodation or nursing care)
- helping someone to move home (including moving property and clearing the former home)

Healthcare and treatment

- carrying out diagnostic examinations and tests (to identify an illness, condition or other problem)
- providing professional medical, dental and similar treatment
- giving medication
- taking someone to hospital for assessment or treatment
- providing nursing care (whether in hospital or in the community)
- carrying out any other necessary medical procedures (for example, taking a blood sample) or therapies (for example, physiotherapy or chiropody)
- providing care in an emergency.'

---

[279] Mental Capacity Act 2005: Code of Practice, at para 6.5.

As a general rule, a 'section 5 act' is one where consent (either explicit or implied) would normally be required from a person of full capacity for the particular act to be carried out. Only acts or arrangements involving minimum legal formality are covered, since more formal legal transactions (particularly those requiring written documentation) would require more than the person's 'consent'.

Serious acts relating to medical treatment or welfare

2.169 In a briefing on the Mental Capacity Bill, the Making Decisions Alliance expressed concern that the scope of MCA 2005, s 5 'remains unclear and is too wide'. It argued that the legislation should:[280]

> '... establish a clear hierarchy of safeguards which reflect the seriousness of the action taken and the consequences for that individual. The MDA recommends that some actions taken under section 5 require additional safeguards to counter against its inappropriate use. For example, we think it is important that a person has the support of an independent advocate when moving home which would involve a change of carer. Similarly, we think that there should be an independent second medical opinion, in relation to serious medical treatment.'

2.170 The Government recognised that some acts in connection with care or treatment may cause major life changes with significant consequences for the person concerned, particularly those involving a change of residence (eg into a care home or nursing home) or major decisions about serious medical treatment. The Code of Practice, therefore, gives detailed guidance aimed at ensuring that the decision in question is made in accordance with the principles of MCA 2005 and is in the person's best interests.[281] The best interests checklist must therefore be carefully applied and particular consideration must be given to whether there is any other choice that would be less restrictive of the person's rights and freedom of action (under MCA 2005, s 1(6)). The Act itself also imposes some limitations on the scope of MCA 2005, s 5, described below.[282]

2.171 If a proposed move to a hospital or care home would have the effect of depriving the person of their liberty, the protection afforded by s 5 will not be available.[283] Instead, authorisation for the deprivation of liberty will be required using the deprivation of liberty safeguards (DOLS) (see Chapter 7) or by order of the Court of Protection. In *A Local Authority v A (Re A (Adult) and Re C (Child))*, Munby LJ gave guidance to local authorities as to the exercise of their powers in respect of the welfare of adults lacking capacity to consent. He stressed that:[284]

> 'People in the situation of A and C, together with their carers, look to the State – to a local authority – for the support, the assistance and the provision of the

---

[280] Making Decisions Alliance *Mental Capacity Bill: Briefing for 2nd Reading* (11 October 2004).
[281] Mental Capacity Act 2005: Code of Practice, at paras 6.7–6.19.
[282] See **2.178ff**.
[283] See **2.185–2.189** below and Chapter 7.
[284] [2010] EWHC 978 (Fam) at [52].

services to which the law, giving effect to the underlying principles of the Welfare State, entitles them. They do not seek to be "controlled" by the State or by the local authority. And it is not for the State in the guise of a local authority to seek to exercise such control. The State, the local authority, is the servant of those in need of its support and assistance, not their master.'

He warned against the 'mindset' of some local authorities seeking to exercise control, citing examples of the removal of incapacitated adults from the care of their relatives into residential accommodation, without the sanction of the court and, therefore in some cases, without any legal authority. Further criticism of a local authority abusing its powers was given in *Hillingdon London Borough Council v Neary & Ors*,[285] in which Peter Jackson J set out some guidance on the responsibilities of public authorities and when matters should be referred to the court for a decision regarding residence. In *CC v KK and STCC*, Baker J reminded himself of the danger of the 'protection imperative' identified by Ryder J in *Oldham MBC v GW and PW*, whereby:[286]

> '... professionals, including judges, may objectively conflate a capacity assessment with a best interests analysis and conclude that the person under review should attach greater weight to the physical security and comfort of a residential home and less importance to the emotional security and comfort that the person derives from being in their own home.'

The importance of ensuring that steps that give rise to a deprivation of liberty are not taken in the purported best interests of the individual without due consideration was emphasised by Baker J in *Re AJ (Deprivation of Liberty Safeguards)*,[287] discussed further in Chapter 7.

2.172 In relation to serious medical treatment, the Code of Practice confirms that the previous case-law requirement to seek a declaration from the Court in cases where particularly serious forms of medical treatment are proposed, is unaffected by MCA 2005.[288] The Court of Protection Rules, supplemented by Practice Directions, confirm that such cases must always be heard before the President of the Court of Protection or another High Court judge nominated by him or her.[289] This includes the withdrawal or withholding of life-sustaining treatment from patients in a vegetative or minimally conscious state, the proposed non-therapeutic sterilisation of a person lacking capacity or other cases involving an ethical dilemma in an untested area which may well involve doubts as to the person's best interests and such cases should therefore continue to be referred to the Court.[290] One such case, *DH NHS Foundation Trust v PS*, came before Sir Nicholas Wall, then President of the Court of Protection, who held that it was in the best interests of PS, who lacked capacity to agree to

---

[285] [2011] EWHC 1377, [2011] COPLR Con Vol 632 at para 33.
[286] [2012] EWHC 2136 (COP), [2012] COPLR 627 at para 65.
[287] [2015] EWCOP 5, [2015] COPLR 167.
[288] Mental Capacity Act 2005: Code of Practice, at para 6.18. See also Chapter 6.
[289] Court of Protection Rules 2007, SI 2007/1744, r 86, supplemented by PD 12A *Court's Jurisdiction to be exercised by Certain Judges*.
[290] Ibid. See also Practice Direction 9E *Applications relating to Serious Medical Treatment*.

medical treatment due to her learning difficulties and her phobia of needles and hospitals, to undergo treatment for cancer. Since she had previously both failed and refused to attend hospital for treatment, the President authorised the use of force if necessary to sedate her and convey her to hospital and to detain her in hospital during the period of post-operative recovery.[291] In *A Local Authority v E & Others*,[292] a complex case concerning a young woman with severe anorexia who wanted to be allowed to die and was only accepting end-of-life palliative care, Peter Jackson J declared that E lacked capacity to make decisions about life-sustaining treatment, and that it was lawful and in her best interests for her to be fed, forcibly if necessary. These issues are discussed further in Chapter 6 (see in particular **6.30–6.36**).

2.173 An additional safeguard is provided where serious medical treatment or a change of residence is proposed for a person lacking capacity, but *only* where the person concerned has no family or friends available to be consulted or to speak up on his or her behalf. In such cases, MCA 2005 makes provision for an independent mental capacity advocate (IMCA) to be appointed to support and represent the person.[293] In these and any other cases where there is a doubt or dispute about whether a particular s 5 act is in the person's best interests, and the matter cannot be resolved through negotiation or other means of dispute resolution, the Court of Protection has ultimate jurisdiction to resolve the matter.

Who can act in connection with care or treatment?

2.174 There is no intention that MCA 2005, s 5 applies to a single identifiable person involved in the care or treatment of a person lacking capacity, nor does it convey any powers on anyone to make substitute decisions or to give consent on behalf of the person lacking capacity. The intention is to allow carers, health and social care professionals to do whatever is necessary to safeguard and promote the welfare and health of individuals who lack capacity to consent, so long as it is appropriate for the particular carer or professional to take the action in question and the act is in the best interests of the incapacitated person. Some guidance on the limits of MCA 2005 s 5 was given by Baker J in *G v E*:[294]

> 'The Act and Code are ... constructed on the basis that the vast majority of decisions concerning incapacitated adults are taken informally and collaboratively by individuals or groups of people consulting and working together. It is emphatically not part of the scheme underpinning the Act that there should be one individual who as a matter of course is given a special legal status to make decisions about incapacitated persons. Experience has shown that working together is the best policy to ensure that incapacitated adults such as E receive the highest quality of care. This case is an example of what can go wrong when people do not work together. Where there is disagreement about the appropriate care and

---

[291] *DH NHS Foundation Trust v PS* [2010] EWHC 1217 (Fam), [2010] COPLR Con Vol 346.
[292] [2012] EWHC 1639 (COP), [2012] COPLR 441.
[293] MCA 2005, ss 35–41. See Chapter 6.
[294] [2010] EWHC 2512 (COP), [2010] COPLR Con Vol 470 at para 57.

treatment, (which cannot be resolved by the methods suggested in Chapter 15 [of the Code]) or the issue is a matter of particular gravity or difficulty, the Act and Code provide that the issue should usually be determined by the court. The complexity and/or seriousness of such issues are likely to require a forensic process and formal adjudication by an experienced tribunal.'

2.175 Before doing anything, the person wishing to take action in connection with the care or treatment of another person must take 'reasonable steps' to establish whether the person concerned has capacity in relation to the matter in question.[295] This does not necessarily require a formal assessment of capacity, although professional practice may require this, for example, in respect of medical treatment. In any event, steps must be taken to look for objective reasons which would justify a reasonable belief of lack of capacity.[296] If it is found that the person has capacity, his or her consent to the action will be required to provide protection from liability.

2.176 Anyone proposing to carry out an act under MCA 2005, s 5 must also take account of the MCA 2005's key principles set out in s 1.[297] This includes starting with the presumption of capacity and taking all practicable steps to enable the person to express a view about the proposed action. If it is believed the person lacks capacity, the 'less restrictive alternative' principle requires consideration of whether the act is needed at all and if so, whether the purpose for which the act is needed can be achieved in a way less restrictive of the person's future choices or would allow him or her the most freedom.

In addition, the person wishing to act must 'reasonably believe' that what they are doing is in the best interests of the person lacking capacity.[298] Again, they must be able to point to objective reasons to justify that belief. They must be able to show that they have taken account of all relevant circumstances, including those set out in the best interests checklist.[299] If their judgment of best interests is challenged, they will be protected if they can show that it was reasonable in all the circumstances of that particular case for them to have arrived at that judgment. Where professionals are involved, their professional skills and levels of competence will be taken into account in determining what would be considered 'reasonable'.

2.177 As recognised by the Court of Appeal *in Commissioner of Police for the Metropolis v ZH*, '[a]striking feature of the statutory defence (provided by MCA 2005, s 5) is the extent to which it is pervaded by the concepts of reasonableness, practicality and appropriateness'.[300] The Court of Appeal upheld the decision of Sir Robert Nelson at first instance that the police had not taken appropriate steps or been able to point to objective reasons that they

---

[295] MCA 2005, s 5(1)(a).
[296] See **2.87–2.90** above.
[297] See **2.19–2.53** above.
[298] MCA 2005, s 5(1)(b)(ii).
[299] See **2.122–2.153** above.
[300] *Commissioner of Police for the Metropolis v ZH* [2013] EWCA Civ 69, [2013] COPLR 332, at para 40 per Lord Dyson.

were acting in ZH's best interests, nor had they considered a less restrictive approach, when they had forcibly removed ZH, a severely autistic 16 year old who suffered from epilepsy, from a swimming pool and subsequently restrained him. Lord Dyson commented:[301]

> '... the MCA does not impose impossible demands on those who do acts in connection with the care or treatment of others. It requires no more than what is reasonable, practicable and appropriate. What that entails depends on all the circumstances of the case. As the judge recognised, what is reasonable, practicable and appropriate where there is time to reflect and take measured action may be quite different in an emergency or what is reasonably believed to be an emergency.'

No protection in cases of negligence

2.178 Professionals and other carers may have duties of care which, if breached, give rise to liability in the tort of negligence. Consent is not a defence to a claim of negligence. Similarly in relation to people who lack capacity to consent, MCA 2005, s 5(3) clarifies that protection from liability does not extend to situations where the person taking the action has acted negligently, whether in carrying out the act or by failing to act in breach of duty. Therefore, there is no protection excluding a person's civil liability for any loss or damage, or his or her criminal liability, resulting from his or her negligence in carrying out or failing to do an act.

Effect on advance decisions to refuse treatment

2.179 In cases where an advance decision to refuse treatment is known to exist, is clear and unambiguous and is valid and applicable in the circumstances which have arisen, any health professionals who knowingly provide treatment contrary to the terms of the advance decision may be liable to legal action for battery or assault, or for breach of the patient's human rights.[302] The provisions of MCA 2005, s 5 do not provide protection from liability in these circumstances, since s 5(4) specifically excludes the operation of advance decisions to refuse treatment.

Limitations on permitted acts

2.180 MCA 2005, s 6 imposes two important limitations on the acts which can be carried out with protection from liability under s 5. The first relates to acts intended to restrain a person who lacks capacity and the second to situations where the act might conflict with a decision made by a donee of a lasting power of attorney or a deputy appointed by the court.

---

[301] Ibid at para 49. This approach was endorsed by Sir James Munby P in *JO v Go & Ors* [2013] EWHC 3932 (COP), [2014] COPLR 62, in which the President reaffirmed the doctrine of necessity, and held that there is (at para 18): 'nothing in the 2005 Act to displace this approach'.

[302] MCA 2005, ss 24–26. See also Chapter 6.

Restraint

2.181 As a general rule, any act that is intended to restrain a person lacking capacity will not attract protection from liability[303] and any carer or professional using restraint could be liable to legal action and will be personally accountable for their actions. In particular, no protection from liability is offered to people who use or threaten violence in order to carry out any action in connection with the care or treatment of a person lacking capacity or to force that person to comply with the carers' actions. However, the practicalities of caring for and providing protection for people who are unable to protect themselves are also recognised. MCA 2005 therefore permits the use of some form of restraint or physical intervention in limited circumstances in order to protect the person from harm.[304]

2.182 An individual restrains a person lacking capacity if he or she (a) uses, or threatens to use, force to secure the doing of an act which the person resists or (b) restricts that person's liberty of movement, whether or not there is resistance.[305] Restraint may take many forms. It may be verbal or physical and may vary from shouting at someone, to holding them down, to locking them in a room. It may also include the prescribing of a sedative or other chemical restraint which restricts liberty of movement.

2.183 MCA 2005 permits restraint to be used *only* where two conditions are satisfied:[306]

(1) the person using it must reasonably believe that it is necessary to do the act in order to prevent harm to the person lacking capacity; and

(2) the restraint used must be a proportionate response both to the likelihood of the person suffering harm and the seriousness of that harm.

MCA 2005 does not define 'harm', since this will vary according to individual circumstances. The restraining act must be 'necessary' to avert harm – not simply to enable the carer or professional to do something more quickly or easily. Similarly, what is likely to be a 'proportionate response' to harm, both in scale and nature, will depend on the seriousness of the particular circumstances and the desired outcome. However, where there are objective reasons for believing that restraint is necessary to prevent the person from coming to any harm, only the minimum necessary force or intervention may be used and for the shortest possible duration.

2.184 In *R (on the application of Sessay) v South London and Maudsley NHS Foundation Trust*, the court confirmed that MCA 2005, s 6 did not extend to

---

[303] MCA 2005, s 6(1).
[304] MCA 2005, s 6(2).
[305] MCA 2005, s 6(4).
[306] MCA 2005, s 6(2) and (3).

giving the police powers to remove someone lacking capacity to consent to hospital or other place of safety and endorsed the following statement which had been agreed by the parties:[307]

> 'Sections 135 and 136 of the Mental Health Act 1983 are the exclusive powers available to police officers to remove persons who appear to be mentally disordered to a place of safety. Sections 5 and 6 of the Mental Capacity Act 2005 do not confer on police officers authority to remove persons to hospital or other places of safety for the purposes set out in sections 135 and 136 of the Mental Health Act 1983.'

This decision was applied in the case of *ZH v Commissioner of Police for the Metropolis* where the court gave detailed consideration to the provisions of s 6 of the MCA 2005 in the context of awarding damages against the police as a result of their actions in forcibly removing a young man with severe autism and learning disabilities from a swimming pool and subsequently restraining him, without having first consulted his carers, informed themselves of the nature of his disabilities or considered any less restrictive options. In that case, Sir Robert Nelson concluded that it was not necessary for the police officers to know the relevant sections of MCA 2005, or indeed to know about the Act itself, but rather:[308]

> 'What they must reasonably believe at the material time are the facts which determine the applicability of the Mental Capacity Act. Thus, at the material time they need to believe that the Claimant lacked capacity to deal with and make decisions about his safety at the swimming pool, that when they carried out the acts that they did, they believed that the Claimant so lacked capacity, and that they believed that it was in the Claimant's best interests for them to act as they did. A belief that the situation created a need for them to act in order to protect the Claimant's safety and prevent him from severely injuring himself would in my judgment be sufficient to satisfy the Act, provided of course that the belief was reasonable under sections 5 and 6 and a proportionate response under section 6 of the Act. It is also necessary for the Police to have considered whether there might be a less restrictive way of dealing with the matter under section 1(6) and, if practicable and appropriate to consult the carers, to take into account their views. These are not only matters which they must have in mind when they carry out the acts of touching, grabbing or restraint but are matters which they must have had regard to before carrying out such acts.'

Deprivation of liberty

2.185 The provisions of s 6 (as originally drafted) attracted some criticism from the Joint Committee on Human Rights (JCHR) in two of its reports on

---

[307] [2011] EWHC 2617 (QB). [2012] QB 760 at para 4.
[308] [2012] EWHC 604 (QB), [2012] COPLR 588, QBD at [40]. Sir Robert Nelson's judgment was upheld in its entirety by the Court of Appeal in *Commissioner of Police for the Metropolis v ZH* [2013] EWCA Civ 69, [2013] COPLR 332, CA – see also para **2.177** above.

the human rights implications of the Mental Capacity Bill.[309] The Committee was concerned that use of these provisions could lead to deprivations of liberty which are not compatible with Art 5(1) of the European Convention on Human Rights, and in particular could lead to involuntary placement in hospital of a person lacking capacity and thereby deprive them of the procedural safeguards available if they had been detained under Mental Health Act powers:[310]

'Although clauses 5 and 6 contain important safeguards against the inappropriate use of restraint ... the combined effect of the two clauses appears to be to authorise (in the sense of protect against liability for) the use of force or the threat of force to overcome an incapacitated person's resistance in certain circumstances, or restrict their liberty of movement, in order to avert a risk of harm. For example, the power in clause 5 could be used to secure the admission into hospital of a person lacking capacity who is resisting such admission, where the person using or threatening force reasonably believes that the person lacks capacity in relation to his treatment, that it is in his best interests for him to be admitted to hospital for treatment and that it is necessary to admit the person in order to prevent harm to himself.

We have written to the minister asking why the Government has not adopted the recommendation of the Joint Committee [on the Draft Mental Incapacity Bill] that the use or threat of force or other restriction of liberty of movement be expressly confined to emergency situations. Without such an express limitation on the face of the Bill, it appears to us that these provisions are likely to lead to deprivations of liberty which are not compatible with Article 5(1) ECHR, because they do not satisfy the Winterwerp requirements that deprivations of liberty be based on objective medical expertise and are necessary in the sense of being the least restrictive alternative. The Bill as drafted therefore does not appear to contain sufficient safeguards against arbitrary deprivation of liberty.'

2.186 The response from the Under Secretary of State, Baroness Ashton, confirmed that: 'It has never been the Government's policy that acts in connection with care and treatment in clause 5 might amount to a deprivation of liberty.'[311] The Government therefore moved a series of amendments in the House of Lords to address the Committee's concerns:[312]

'The committee wanted the Bill to confirm expressly that actions amounting to deprivation of liberty do not fall within the definition of "restraint" used in the Bill. The amendments achieve this ... This means that no-one acting in connection with care or treatment under Clause 5, nor an attorney or deputy, may deprive a person who lacks capacity of his liberty. "Restraint" includes only restrictions of liberty.'

2.187 One amendment introduced by the Government (previously MCA 2005, s 6(5) now repealed) expressly confirmed that someone carrying out an act

---

[309] JCHR, Twenty-third Report of Session 2003–04 *Scrutiny of Bills: Final Progress Report*, HL Paper 210, HC 1282, Part 2; JCHR, Fourth Report of Session 2004–05 *Scrutiny: First Progress Report*, HL Paper 26, HC 224, Part 4.

[310] JCHR, Twenty-third Report of Session 2003–04, at paras 2.22–2.23. See also Chapter 7.

[311] JCHR, Fourth Report of Session 2004–05, Appendix 4, at para 11.

[312] *Hansard*, HL Deb, vol 670, ser 5, col 1468 (17 March 2005).

under MCA 2005, s 5 will do more than 'merely restrain' a person lacking capacity if he or she deprives that person of liberty within the meaning of Art 5(1). This applied not only to public authorities covered by the Human Rights Act 1998 but to anyone carrying out acts in connection with care or treatment under s 5. Subsequent amendments to the Act introducing the 'deprivation of liberty safeguards' (DOLS) made these provisions redundant, but confirm that specific authorisation is required to deprive someone of their liberty. These amendments have now been recognised as failing to meet their desired purpose, and the Law Commission has been charged with preparing draft legislation to put in place a proper framework for the authorisation of deprivation of liberty in this context (see further Chapter 7).[313]

2.188 There is clearly a fine line to be drawn between *restriction* of liberty, permitted under the definition of restraint, and *deprivation* of liberty under Art 5(1).[314] This was considered by the European Court of Human Rights in *HL v The United Kingdom* (the so-called *Bournewood* case) which said:[315]

> '... in order to determine whether there has been a deprivation of liberty, the starting point must be the specific situation of the individual concerned and account must be taken of a whole range of factors arising in the particular case such as the type, duration, effects and manner of implementation of the measure in question. The distinction between a deprivation of, and restriction upon, liberty is merely one of degree or intensity and not one of nature or substance ...

> ... the Court considers the key factor in the present case to be that the health care professionals treating and managing the applicant exercised complete and effective control over his care and movements ...'

2.189 The judgment in this case was delivered at a very late stage in the parliamentary passage of the Mental Capacity Bill. It identified serious deficiencies (known as the '*Bournewood* gap') in that the law provided insufficient safeguards against unlawful deprivation of liberty of people lacking capacity to consent. The Government promised further safeguards, which have now been introduced into MCA 2005 by the Mental Health Act 2007 (MHA 2007). MHA 2007, s 50 repealed MCA 2005, s 6(5) and substituted complex provisions and procedures allowing for the lawful deprivation of liberty of a person with mental disorder who lacks capacity to consent, where that is in the person's best interests.[316] The interface between MCA 2005 and mental health legislation, and the Deprivation of Liberty Safeguards introduced in response to the European Court judgment, are considered in more detail in Chapter 7.

---

[313] It remains possible for the court to authorise a deprivation of liberty: see *DH NHS Foundation Trust v PS* [2010] EWHC 1217 (Fam), [2010] COPLR Con Vol 346, in which the President of the Court of Protection authorised the use of force if necessary to sedate PS and convey her to hospital for cancer treatment and to detain her in hospital during the period of post-operative recovery.

[314] Some guidance is given in the Mental Capacity Act 2005: Code of Practice, at paras 6.49–6.53.

[315] *HL v The United Kingdom* [2004] 40 EHRR 761, at paras 89 and 91.

[316] These provisions and procedures were implemented in April 2009 accompanied by guidance in a supplement to the Code of Practice.

Decisions of donees or deputies

2.190 The provisions of MCA 2005, s 5 provide protection from liability to carers and professionals in circumstances where no formal decision-making powers are required. However, where formal powers already exist, for example, under a lasting power of attorney or through an order made by the Court of Protection, these formal decision-making powers will take precedence. Thus, MCA 2005, s 6(6) confirms that the provisions of s 5 do not authorise a person to do an act which conflicts with a decision made by a donee of a lasting power of attorney previously granted by the person lacking capacity, or by a deputy appointed by the Court, so long as the donee or deputy is acting within the scope of their authority. Anyone acting contrary to a decision of a donee or deputy will not have protection from liability.

2.191 In cases of dispute, for example, when carers or health professionals feel that a donee or deputy is acting outside the scope of his or her authority, or contrary to the incapacitated person's best interests, an application may be made for permission to apply to the Court of Protection to resolve the matter. Where the dispute involves serious health care decisions, MCA 2005, s 6(7) clarifies that life-sustaining treatment, or treatment necessary to prevent a serious deterioration in the person's condition, can be given pending a ruling from the Court.[317]

Paying for goods, services and other expenditure

Background

2.192 Before implementation of MCA 2005, the law already made provision for the enforceability of contracts, including contracts to purchase goods, which were made 'with' a person who lacked capacity or whose mental capacity was in doubt. In such cases, the courts have had to balance two important policy considerations. One is a duty to protect those who are incapable of looking after themselves, and the other is to ensure that other people are not prejudiced by the actions of persons who lack capacity to contract but who appear to have full capacity. So, people without contractual capacity are bound by the terms of a contract they have entered into, even if it was unfair, unless it can be shown that the other party to the contract was aware of their lack of capacity or should have been aware of this.[318] If the other party knows, or must be taken to have known, of the lack of capacity the contract is voidable.

2.193 The Sale of Goods Act 1979 (SGA 1979) modified this rule when applied to contracts for 'necessaries'. A person without mental capacity who agrees to pay for goods which are necessaries is legally obliged to pay a reasonable price for them. Although SGA 1979 applies to goods, similar common law rules were believed to apply to essential services.

---

[317] Issues around life-sustaining treatment are dealt with in Chapter 6.
[318] *Imperial Loan Company v Stone* [1892] 1 QB 599.

The legislation

2.194 These rules are now brought together and given statutory force under MCA 2005, s 7. This clarifies that the obligation to pay a reasonable price applies to both the supply of necessary goods and the provision of necessary services to a person without capacity to contract for them, and it is the person who lacks capacity who must pay.

2.195 The definition of 'necessary' set out in MCA 2005, s 7(2) is based on that in SGA 1979,[319] meaning goods and services which are suitable to the person's condition in life (ie his or her place in society, rather than any mental or physical condition) and his or her actual requirements at the time of sale and delivery (eg ordinary drink, food and clothing or the provision of domiciliary or residential care services).

2.196 During parliamentary debate of these provisions, Lord Goodhart put forward some probing amendments to try to protect people with impaired capacity from entering into contracts which may be disadvantageous to them, for example, through abusive doorstep selling:[320]

> 'These amendments have been proposed by the CAB [Citizens Advice Bureau] which is concerned with the number of cases in which businesses have entered into contracts with people who lack capacity, and those contracts were unduly disadvantageous to those people. At present under English law, though not under the law of Scotland, a contract entered into by a person lacking capacity can be set aside only if the other party to that contract was aware of the incapacity. The CAB amendment alters this, and it wants to apply to England the rule in Scotland which is that a contract can be set aside on grounds of incapacity even if the other party was not aware of the incapacity.'

The amendments were resisted by the Government on the ground that they may have unintended consequences, either by disempowering people with impaired capacity with whom traders may be reluctant to contract, or by allowing the possibility of abuse by people claiming incapacity in order to avoid being bound by a contract. However, the Minister committed the Government to further work during implementation of the Act to ensure that 'policy development … on consumer strategy, credit and indebtedness is sensitive to the needs of consumers who lack capacity'.[321]

---

[319] SGA 1979, s 3(3).

[320] *Hansard*, HL Deb, vol 668, ser 5, col 1396 (27 January 2005). See also HL Deb, vol 670, ser 5, cols 1469–1472 (17 March 2005).

[321] *Hansard*, HL Deb, vol 670, ser 5, col 1472 (17 March 2005). The Office of Fair Trading has issued guidance for creditors on granting credit to people who may lack capacity to make informed borrowing decisions: *Mental Capacity: OFT guidance for creditors* (OFT, September 2011), available online at: www.oft.gov.uk/about-the-oft/legal-powers/legal/cca/mental-capacity-guidance/#.UK_MBYbI-8F.

Responsibility to pay for necessary goods and services

2.197 MCA 2005 confirms that the legal responsibility for paying for necessary goods and services lies with the person for whom they are supplied even though that person lacks the capacity to contract for them.[322] The obligation is to pay 'a reasonable price' for them[323] so this provision cannot be used to enforce a contract which involves gross overcharging for goods or services. In the case of *Wychavon District Council v EM (HB)*[324] concerning entitlement to Housing Benefit of a woman with profound physical and mental disabilities who lacked capacity to enter into a tenancy agreement, the Upper Tribunal overturned its previous decision that Housing Benefit was not payable because there was no valid tenancy agreement. When the provisions of s 7 of the MCA 2005 were brought to the attention of Judge Mark, he reconsidered his original decision. He expressed some doubt as to whether 'services' in s 7 of the MCA 2005 is wide enough to cover the provision of accommodation, but even if it was not, the common law doctrine of necessities would apply, obliging the claimant to pay for the necessary accommodation with the assistance of Housing Benefit. He held (at para 30):

> 'Neither section 7 nor the common law imposed on her any liability under the terms of any putative tenancy agreement, whether for rent or under any repairing or other covenants. So far as long term decisions are concerned, it is clear that suitable accommodation is a necessary at common law, and I see no reason why, so long as it being provided, either accommodation or any other necessary should be excluded from either the common law requirements or those of the 2005 Act, whichever is applicable.'

It was suggested that matters such as a tenancy ought to be dealt with through the Court of Protection and that was eventually done in this case.[325] Judge Mark took a pragmatic view that during the course of an application to the Court of Protection, a person lacking capacity ought not to be left without necessaries (including accommodation), which, as the judge pointed out, will only be supplied if there is confidence that they will be paid for.[326]

2.198 Where the person also lacks the capacity to arrange for payment to be made, the carer who has arranged for the provision of goods and services necessary for the person's care or treatment may also have to arrange settlement of the bill. The Law Commission described the problem as follows:[327]

---

[322] See also in this regard, and for a discussion of s 7 more generally, *Aster Healthcare* [2014] EWHC 77 (QB), [2014] COPLR 397, upheld on appeal ([2014] EWCA Civ 1350, [2014] PTSR 1507).

[323] MCA 2005, s 7(1).

[324] [2012] UKUT 12 (AAC).

[325] The Court of Protection has issued guidance on 'Applications to the Court of Protection in relation to tenancy agreements' (February 2012), available online at: www.mentalhealthlaw.co.uk/File:COP_guidance_on_tenancy_agreements_February_2012.pdf.

[326] Note that, for s 7 to be applicable, the supplier of the necessaries must intend to impose a liability upon the individual lacking capacity: see *Aster Healthcare* at parah 30.

[327] Law Com No 231, n 1 above, at para 4.7.

'We are not here concerned with ways in which a person may gain access to another person's income or assets. Where assets are held by a bank or other institution, specific authority will certainly be required before they can be transferred to anyone other than the legal owner. We are concerned, rather, with the situation where a carer arranges for something which will cost money to be done for a person without capacity. Family members often arrange for milk to be delivered, or for a hairdresser, gardener or chiropodist to call. More costly arrangements might be roof repairs, or for an excursion or holiday. In many cases it may be reasonable for a family member to arrange such matters, if it is done in the best interests of the person without capacity. Such actions could therefore fall within the confines of the general authority to provide for the person's welfare and care recommended above. Who, however, is to pay the provider of the goods or services supplied?'

2.199   Where it is appropriate for carers to arrange such matters, and so long as the arrangements made are in the best interests of the person lacking capacity, the carers' actions are therefore likely to be considered 'acts in connection with care or treatment' under MCA 2005, s 5, providing them with some protection from liability if their actions were to be challenged. However, some further arrangements may need to be made to meet the costs involved or to pay the provider of the goods or services supplied.

Expenditure

2.200   In such cases where necessary goods or services must be paid for, provision is made under MCA 2005, s 8 to meet the expenditure involved. This may be done in any one of three ways, described in the Code of Practice as follows (with footnotes added):[328]

- 'If neither the carer nor the person who lacks capacity can produce the necessary funds, the carer may promise that the person who lacks capacity will pay.[329] A supplier may not be happy with this, or the carer may be worried they may be held responsible for any debt. In such cases the carer must follow the formal steps ... below.
- If the person who lacks capacity has cash, the carer may use that money to pay for goods or services[330] (for example, to pay the milkman or the hairdresser).
- The carer may choose to pay for the goods or services with their own money. The person who lacks capacity must pay them back.[331] This may involve using cash in the person's possession or running up an IOU. (This is not appropriate for paid care workers, whose contracts might stop them handling their clients' money.) The carer must follow formal steps to get money held in a bank or building society account.'

2.201   The intention of these provisions is to make it possible for ordinary but necessary goods and services to be provided for people who lack the capacity to

---

[328] Mental Capacity Act 2005: Code of Practice, at para 6.61.
[329] 'The carer may pledge the credit of the person who lacks capacity': MCA 2005, s 8(1)(a).
[330] MCA 2005, s 8(1)(b).
[331] MCA 2005, s 8(2).

organise and pay for them, but without requiring carers to invoke expensive and time-consuming court proceedings to obtain authority to do so. However, MCA 2005, s 8 does not give any authorisation to a carer to gain access to the incapacitated person's income or assets or to sell the person's property. A distinction is drawn between the use of available cash already in the possession of the person lacking capacity, on the one hand, and the removal of money from a bank account or selling valuable items of property, on the other. Where a carer has promised that the person lacking capacity will pay for the goods or services supplied (ie has pledged the person's credit), formal authority may then need to be obtained before that promise can be put into effect. Similarly, formal arrangements may need to be made before a carer can be reimbursed if a large amount of expenditure is involved.

2.202 Some carers (such as family members) may already have such formal authority, for example, under an enduring or lasting power of attorney, as a deputy appointed by the Court of Protection or as a social security 'appointee' (although the precise scope of authority of such an appointee is not absolutely clear). MCA 2005, s 8(3) makes clear that these arrangements are not affected or changed by the above provisions allowing carers to arrange and pay for necessary goods and services on behalf of a person lacking capacity to make their own arrangements. However, as confirmed by s 6(6), an informal carer cannot make arrangements for goods or services to be provided for someone lacking capacity if this conflicts with a decision made by a donee or deputy acting within the scope of their authority.

Excluded decisions

Background

2.203 The Law Commission recognised the need to place some restrictions on carers and others acting under its proposed 'general authority' (now s 5 acts) without the need to apply for formal powers:[332]

> 'One benefit of setting out a clear general authority in statute is that the statute can then specify which matters fall outside the scope of that general authority. The general law already provides that certain acts can only be effected by a person acting for himself or herself. Examples would be entering into marriage or casting a vote in a public election. For the avoidance of doubt, our draft Bill lists certain matters which must be done by a person acting for him or herself ... In many areas, however, it is at present quite unclear whether action may be lawfully taken on behalf of a person without capacity. If no-one is sure what can lawfully be done, then no-one can be sure what must and must not be done.'

The legislation

2.204 MCA 2005 therefore seeks to make clear what can and cannot be done by someone else in relation to a person lacking capacity. There are certain acts

---

[332] Law Com No 231, n 1 above, at para 4.29.

which cannot be done and certain decisions which can never be made on behalf of a person who lacks capacity to consent to those actions or to make those decisions for him or herself, either because they are so personal to the individual concerned or because they are governed by other legislation. In ss 27–29, the Act lists those specific decisions which are excluded and cannot be made under MCA 2005, whether by a carer or professional acting under MCA 2005, s 5, a donee under a lasting power of attorney, a deputy or by the Court of Protection itself.

Family relationships etc

2.205 MCA 2005, s 27 excludes the following decisions on family relationships from being taken on behalf of a person lacking capacity to make the decision:

'(a) consenting to marriage or civil partnership,
(b) consenting to have sexual relationships,
(c) consenting to a decree of divorce being granted on the basis of two years' separation,
(d) consenting to a dissolution order being made in relation to a civil partnership on the basis of two years' separation,
(e) consenting to a child's being placed for adoption by an adoption agency,
(f) consenting to the making of an adoption order,
(g) discharging parental responsibilities in matters not relating to a child's property,
(h) giving a consent under the Human Fertilisation and Embryology Act 1990.'

However, the Court of Protection retains the power to make declarations under MCA 2005, s 15 with regard to the person's capacity to consent to the matters set out above.[333]

2.206 Where a person lacking capacity becomes involved in divorce or dissolution proceedings on any basis other than 2 years' separation, or where someone loses capacity during the course of such proceedings, a litigation friend will be appointed under the Family Procedure Rules 2010 to give instructions and otherwise act on their behalf in relation to the proceedings.[334] Where a decision needs to be made about placing a child for adoption, if the birth parent lacks capacity to consent to an adoption order, the rules relating to dispensing with consent in adoption legislation apply.[335] Matters concerned with the discharging of parental responsibilities not related to a child's property are dealt with under the Children Act 1989.

Mental Health Act matters

2.207 MCA 2005, s 28 states that the Act's decision-making powers cannot be used to give or to consent to treatment for mental disorder if the treatment is

---

[333] See **2.56ff** above. See also Chapter 6 for consideration of the test of capacity to consent to sexual relations.
[334] Family Procedure Rules 2010, SI 2010/2955, Part 15.
[335] Adoption and Children Act 2002, s 52.

regulated by the Mental Health Act (MHA) 1983, Part 4. The purpose of Part 4 is to clarify the extent to which treatment for mental disorder can be imposed on detained patients in hospital and to provide specific statutory safeguards concerning the provision of treatment without consent.[336] Section 28 ensures that where a person lacking capacity to consent to treatment is detained in hospital under the long term provisions of MHA 1983, the powers available under MHA 1983, Part 4 would 'trump' the decision-making powers under MCA 2005 in relation to treatment for mental disorder.

2.208 This means that the safeguards and procedures of MHA 1983 (as amended by MHA 2007) relating to treatment for the person's mental disorder cannot be avoided by reference to MCA 2005, s 5 or by the consent or refusal of treatment by a donee or deputy. However, depending on the scope of their authority, a welfare attorney or deputy may apply to a mental health tribunal, or to the hospital managers, for the patient's discharge where the patient lacks capacity to make the application. For all other decisions affecting that person, the principles and provisions of MCA 2005 would apply. Moreover, the existence of a valid advance decision to refuse medical treatment (as to which, see further Chapter 6) must be taken into account when considering whether to impose forced treatment under the provisions of Part 4 and has been said to 'weigh most heavily in the scales' upon an application for a declaration that a decision not to impose such treatment was lawful where the consequences were potentially life-threatening.[337]

2.209 Provisions in the Mental Health Act 2007 amended MCA 2005, s 28 to take account of the new provisions in the amended MHA 1983 relating to the use of electro-convulsive therapy (ECT)[338] and those introducing compulsory community treatment orders (CTOs – also referred to as supervised community treatment) for patients previously detained in hospital who are now living in the community, but who continue to need treatment for their mental disorder.[339] The new MHA 1983, s 28(1A)[340] removes the exclusion in relation to patients aged 16–17 years who lack capacity to consent to ECT, thus allowing ECT to be given to informal patients aged 16-17 under MCA 2005, s 5 rather than under the amended provisions of MHA 1983, where such patients lack capacity to consent, so long as the treatment is in their best interests, it is being given in circumstances that do not amount to a deprivation of their liberty and a Second Opinion Appointed Doctor considers ECT to be appropriate. Where a patient subject to a CTO (known as a 'community patient'[341]) is being treated under Part 4A of the amended 1983 Act,

---

[336] MHA 1983, ss 57–58.
[337] *Nottinghamshire Healthcare NHS Trust v RC* [2014] EWCOP 1317; [2014] COPLR 468 at para 30 (whether blood transfusion – falling within the scope of the compulsory treatment provisions of MHA 1983, s 63 – should be imposed upon a self-harming capacitous patient refusing such transfusion).
[338] MHA 1983, s 58A, inserted by MHA 2007, s 28(6).
[339] MHA 1983, ss 17A–17G, inserted by MHA 2007, s 32(1), (2).
[340] Inserted by MHA 2007, s 28(10).
[341] MHA 1983, s 17A(7).

MCA 2005, s 28(1B)[342] prohibits that treatment being given under s 5, so that powers under the 1983 Act must be used. However, MHA 1983, Part 4A provides authority for attorneys or deputies with relevant powers to consent to treatment on behalf of a community patient.[343]

2.210   During the two pre-legislative scrutiny exercises carried out – on the draft Mental Incapacity Bill in 2003 and on the draft Mental Health Bill in 2004–05, both Joint Committees expressed concern about the interrelation between the two pieces of legislation and the potential for overlap and confusion between them.[344] These concerns were also raised frequently during the parliamentary debates on the Mental Capacity Bill. Of particular concern were the need to:

(1)   provide appropriate safeguards in relation to the treatment of adults lacking capacity who are compliant with their care and treatment as required by the European Court judgment in *HL v The United Kingdom*;[345] and

(2)   ensure that health professionals are clear about which law should be used to provide treatment for serious mental disorder for those lacking capacity to consent.

Several years after the amendments to both Acts were introduced, the interface between them is still causing considerable problems for practitioners and for both courts and tribunals.[346] These matters are considered further in Chapter 7.

Voting rights

2.211   The final category of excluded decisions concerns voting rights. MCA 2005, s 29 confirms that no one can make a decision on voting or cast a vote at an election or a referendum on behalf of a person lacking capacity to vote (for example through a proxy, or where acting as a deputy or donee of a Lasting Power of Attorney). A proxy vote can only be cast on behalf of a person who has capacity to nominate someone as their proxy voter. The precise test for capacity to appoint a proxy has yet to be established. It is very important to understand that since the coming into force of the Electoral Administration Act 2006, s 73, a person's mental health problems or learning disabilities cannot, by themselves, constitute a ground to disqualify them from voting. There is therefore, in law, no test of 'mental capacity to vote.' A person

---

[342]   Inserted by MHA 2007, s 35(4), (5).

[343]   MHA 1983, s 64B(3)(b)(ii).

[344]   Joint Committee on the Draft Mental Incapacity Bill, Vol I, HL Paper 189-I, HC 1083-I, Chapter 12; Joint Committee on the Draft Mental Health Bill, Vol I, HL Paper 79-I, HC 95-I, Chapter 4.

[345]   *HL v The United Kingdom* [2004] 40 EHRR 761. MCA 2005 was amended by MHA 2007 to introduce the Deprivation of Liberty Safeguards (DOLS) which have been widely criticised as unworkable and 'not fit for purpose' – see Chapter 7.

[346]   See for example, *An NHS Trust v Dr A* [2013] EWHC 2442 (COP), [2013] COPLR 605; *AM v South London & Maudsley NHS Foundation Trust & Secretary of State for Health* [2013] UKUT 0365 (AAC), [2013] COPLR 510.

registered on the relevant electoral roll cannot be refused a ballot paper, or in other words be excluded from voting, on the grounds of mental incapacity.

Ill-treatment or neglect

Background

2.212 MCA 2005 created a number of ways in which someone can acquire powers over another person who lacks some decision-making capacity. For this reason the Law Commission concluded that:[347]

> 'It is right that a person with such powers should be subject to criminal sanction for ill-treating or wilfully neglecting the other person concerned.'

2.213 The Government was not at first 'persuaded that the creation of a new offence would be the best way of tackling abuse'.[348] However, a number of high-profile cases concerning abuse and ill-treatment of vulnerable people resulted in such an offence being included in the Draft Mental Incapacity Bill. This proposed the creation of an offence of ill-treatment or neglect with a maximum penalty of two years' imprisonment.[349]

2.214 The original impetus for the creation of a specific offence was the *Longcare* case, in which more than 50 adults with learning difficulties were abused at two care homes in South Buckinghamshire between 1983 and 1993. Despite the severity of abuse (which included rape, assault, over-sedation, starvation and neglect over a period of 10 years) existing law meant those responsible only received light sentences. The *Independent Longcare Inquiry*, the report of which was published in 1998,[350] recommended that the Government introduce a new, arrestable offence of harming or exploiting a vulnerable adult, with a maximum penalty of 10 years in prison. Lack of action in implementing any changes led to a campaign called 'Justice for Survivors' launched in 2003 by the journal *Disability Now* and supported by leading disability organisations and charities.

Criminal offence

2.215 MCA 2005, s 44 addressed some of these concerns by creating a specific criminal offence of ill-treatment or wilful neglect of a person who lacks, or is believed to lack, capacity by any person involved in caring for that person or in a position of trust or power over the person. The penalty will vary according to the seriousness of the offence, ranging from a fine to a term of imprisonment, but the maximum penalty has been increased to 5 years' imprisonment.[351] This has the effect of making it an 'arrestable offence' under the Police and Criminal

---

[347] Law Com No 231, n 1 above, at para 4.38.
[348] Lord Chancellor's Department *Making Decisions*, Cm 4465 (1999), at para 1.37.
[349] Draft Mental Incapacity Bill, cl 31.
[350] Tom Burgner *Independent Longcare Inquiry* (Buckingham County Council, 1998).
[351] MCA 2005, s 44(3)(b).

Evidence Act 1984, s 2. It also reflects the potential severity of the crime, with sentences in parallel with those for serious assaults on individuals, including the offences of inflicting grievous bodily harm and assault occasioning actual bodily harm under the Offences Against the Person Act 1861, which both carry maximum sentences of 5 years. For example, after acts of neglect and abuse at Winterbourne View private hospital were uncovered by BBC Panorama, subsequent prosecutions under MCA 2005, s 44 resulted in six out of 11 care workers being given sentences ranging from 6 months' to 2 years' imprisonment and the other five were given suspended sentences.[352]

Scope of the offence

2.216 The criminal offence has a wide application to 'anyone who has the care of' a person who lacks, or is reasonably believed to lack, capacity.'[353] This includes not only family carers, but also health and social care staff in hospital or care homes (including the owner or manager of the care home) or those providing domiciliary care. It also applies to donees of a lasting power of attorney or attorneys of an enduring power of attorney previously made by the person now lacking capacity[354] and to any deputy appointed by the Court of Protection for that person.[355] No lower age limit is specified, so the offence also applies to the ill-treatment or wilful neglect of children under 16 whose lack of capacity is caused by an impairment of, or disturbance in the functioning of, the mind or brain, not solely by the immaturity of youth.

2.217 During the parliamentary stages, amendments were put aimed at extending the application of the new offence to appointees, appointed by the Department for Work and Pensions (DWP) to collect and manage social security benefits on behalf of claimants unable to do so for themselves. The Minister clarified that:[356]

> '... it is clear that noble Lords are still concerned that because DWP appointees are handling only financial matters they might not be considered as having "care of the person" and, as such, would fall outside the scope of the offence. Again, we made clear during the Report stage in the other place that, in the majority of cases, the appointee will have care of the person and will therefore be covered by the offence.'

2.218 The Minister also confirmed that DWP officials were considering ways of introducing more effective monitoring of appointees. In 2011, the DWP carried out an equality impact assessment on the Government's intention to introduce an 'appointee review system', both to meet the requirements of the

---

[352] BBC News at: www.bbc.co.uk/news/uk-england-bristol-20092894.

[353] MCA 2005, s 44(1)(a). The section does not specify which particular decision the person lacks capacity to make – see **2.219–2.220** on its interpretation by the courts. See also Neil Allen, 'Criminal Care: ill-treatment and wilful neglect', *Elder Law Journal*, Jordans [2012] Eld LJ 71-75, for further consideration of this point and on who should be prosecuted.

[354] MCA 2005, s 44(1)(b).

[355] MCA 2005, s 44(1)(c).

[356] *Hansard*, HL Deb, vol 669, ser 5, col 746 (8 February 2005).

Equality Act 2010 and to satisfy Art 12.4 of the UN Convention on the Rights of Persons with Disabilities (CRPD).[357] When ratifying the CRPD, the UK Government entered a reservation stating that the UK was actively working towards introducing a proportionate system of review for appointees, but no date has yet been set for implementing the review system to enable the Government to lift the reservation.

Person who lacks capacity

2.219 In *R v Dunn*,[358] the court considered the meaning of 'a person who lacks capacity' since this is not defined further within MCA 2005, s 44. Dunn had been convicted of four counts of ill-treating a person without capacity contrary to MCA 2005 s 44 against three victims at the residential care home of which she was manageress. The judge in the Crown Court had directed that 'a person without capacity' meant a person unable to make decisions for himself because of a disturbance or impairment of function of the mind or brain, that a diagnosis of dementia was not enough, that 'impairment' could be permanent or temporary, that capacity was presumed unless disproved on the balance of probabilities, and that this direction applied to all three victims. The defendant appealed on the basis that the direction on 'a person without capacity' was inadequate, failed to focus on the capacity of each victim to make a decision at the relevant time, and failed to identify the questions required by MCA 2005, s 3. The appeal was dismissed on the following grounds:[359]

'(1) The legislation, including MCA 2005 s 2, was convoluted and did not appropriately define the elements of the offence (including 'matter' and 'disturbance or impairment').

(2) Lack of capacity had to be decided on the balance of probabilities.

(3) There was a disconnect between MCA 2005, s 44 (referring to 'persons without capacity') and the elaborate definition sections (MCA 2005, ss 2 and 3), but it was open for the jury to conclude that the decisions regarding care (the 'matter') had been made because the victims lacked capacity.

(4) It was unnecessary for the judge to complicate matters by referring to MCA 2005 s 3, and the conviction was safe.'

2.220 his matter was considered again by the Court of Appeal in the case of *R v Hopkins; R v Priest* where the court observed:[360]

'Unconstrained by authority, this court would be minded to accept the submission made on behalf of the appellants that Section 44 (1) (a), read together with Section 2 (1) of the Mental Capacity Act 2005, is so vague that it fails the test of sufficient certainty at common law and under Article 7.1, ECHR. However this court has made a decision upon Section 44 of the Act which binds this court.'

---

[357] Department for Work and Pensions, Appointee Review: Integrated equality impact assessment, (September 2011), available at www.dwp.gov.uk/docs/appointee-review.pdf.

[358] *R v Dunn* (2010) All ER (D) 250 (Nov), [2010] EWCA Crim 2935.

[359] Ibid, at paras 22–23. Based on the All ER (D) summary.

[360] [2011] EWCA Crim 1513 at para 40.

The judgment then quotes at length from *R v Dunn*, confirming (at para 43) that 'the matter in respect of which capacity was required to be lacking for the purposes of s 44 was the person's ability to make decisions concerning his or her own care.' This approach was followed in the Court of Appeal cases culminating in *Ligaya Nursing v R*.[361]

Ill-treatment

2.221 A single act is sufficient to show ill-treatment.[362] For a conviction of ill-treatment, it is necessary to show deliberate conduct by the accused which could properly be described as ill-treatment, whether or not it had caused or was likely to cause harm. The accused must either realise that he or she is inexcusably ill-treating the other person or be reckless as to whether he or she is doing so.[363]

Wilful neglect

2.222 Ill-treatment and neglect are separate offences.[364] Neglect relates to a failure to provide nourishment, fluid, shelter, warmth or medical attention to a dependant person.[365] The meaning of 'wilful neglect' may vary according to the circumstances, but is generally taken to mean that there has been an intentional or deliberate omission that the person in question knows s/he has a duty to do.[366] In the context of the offence of wilfully neglecting a child in a manner likely to cause unnecessary suffering or injury to health (under the Children and Young Persons Act (CYPA) 1933, s 1), it has been held that neglect cannot be described as *wilful* unless the person:[367]

- either had directed his or her mind to whether there was some risk (although it might fall far short of a probability) that the child's health might suffer from the neglect, and had made a conscious decision to refrain from acting; or

- had so refrained because he or she did not care whether the child might be at risk or not.

2.223 However, by contrast to the offence under CYPA 1933, s 1 which specifies acting 'in a manner likely to cause unnecessary suffering or injury to health', s 44 makes no such reference. In *R v Patel*,[368] concerning a conviction for wilful neglect of a nurse who failed to carry out cardiopulmonary resuscitation (CPR) on an elderly resident in a nursing home, the nurse appealed on the ground that judge had wrongly directed the jury that neglect could be established even if it was unlikely that the appellant's inaction caused

---

[361] [2012] EWCA Crim 2521.
[362] *R v Holmes* [1979] Crim LR 52.
[363] *R v Newington* (1990) 91 Cr App R 247, CA.
[364] *R v Newington* (1990) 91 Cr App R 247, CA.
[365] *R v Humberside and Scunthorpe Coroner, ex parte Jamieson* [1994] 3 All ER 972, 990–991.
[366] *De Maroussem v Commissioner of Income Tax* [2005] STC 125, PC.
[367] *R v Sheppard* [1981] AC 394, [1980] 3 All ER 899, HL.
[368] *R v Patel* [2013] EWCA Crim 965 at para 34.

any adverse consequence. The Court of Appeal held the *actus reas* of the offence under MCA 2005, s 44 is complete if the nurse (or a medical practitioner) neglects to do an act which should be done in the treatment of the patient. The court also noted the clear distinction between the offence of neglect under MCA 2005, s 44 and the (much more serious) offence of gross negligence manslaughter, where causation would be an issue.

The nurse also contended that the judge had failed to direct the jury properly about the meaning of 'wilful', objecting in particular to his direction that if the appellant acted out of stress or panic that would not constitute a defence. The Court of Appeal held that:[369]

> '... neglect is wilful if a nurse or medical practitioner knows that it is necessary to administer a piece of treatment and deliberately decides not to carry out that treatment, which is within their power but which they cannot face performing ... if the appellant was acting at a time of stress, that would be a matter which the judge could take into account at the time of sentence.'

2.224 In *R v Hopkins*, the Court of Appeal confirmed that 'Neglect may be an instant or a continuing phase. We note that s 44 does not require proof of any particular harm or proof of the risk of any particular harm.'[370] That case related to the prosecution of the owner and manager of a care home concerning a number of incidents of 'systematic incompetence' and substandard care of residents. However, the court was critical of the trial judge's inadequate direction to the jury as to the law relating to wilful neglect, and in particular, his lack of explanation of *R v Sheppard*, suggesting that a short, unambiguous statement of the law and a 'written route to verdict' was needed to assist the jury:[371]

> 'By way of example, returning to count 1 which alleged wilful neglect of [a resident], the prosecution relied on several alleged failings. The jury needed to ask in respect of each one (1) are we sure lack of care is proved?; (2) if so, are we sure that it amounted to neglect?; (3) if so, are we sure either (i) that the defendant knew of the lack of care and deliberately or recklessly neglected to act, or (ii) that the defendant was unaware of the lack of care and deliberately or recklessly closed her mind to the obvious? We do not suggest that this is the form of question required in every case. But in this case the appellants were persons whose primary responsibility was supervision and management rather than hands-on care. The issue whether or not either or both of them was aware of the failing was a principal fact about which the jury required direction or, in the alternative, if unaware of that failing, whether the jury were sure that it was the consequence of a deliberate or reckless closing of the eyes to the obvious. The judge did not explain the concept of wilful neglect as it applied to each defendant in the circumstances of her role in the care plan. Neither did he relate the requirement for wilful neglect to any of the failings which, it was alleged, applied to any particular count.'

---

[369] Ibid at para 42.
[370] *R v Hopkins; R v Priest* [2011] EWCA Crim 1513 at para 49.
[371] Ibid at paras 57–60.

In this case, the verdicts were considered unsafe and the appeals against conviction were allowed, although the care home had since been closed down.

2.225 In *Ligaya Nursing v R*, the Court of Appeal acknowledged the difficulties involved in cases of alleged wilful neglect, in that evidence purporting to establish wilful neglect was often 'elusive'. However, the court set out some key principles in relation to such cases:[372]

> 'The purpose of s 44 of the Act is clear. Those who are in need of care are entitled to protection against ill-treatment or wilful neglect. The question whether they have been so neglected must be examined in the context of the statutory provisions which provide that, to the greatest extent possible, their autonomy should be respected. The evidential difficulties which may arise when this offence is charged do not make it legally uncertain within the principles in *Mirsa* [2005] 1 Cr App R 328 and *R v Rimmington: R v Goldstein* [2006] 1 AC 459. On analysis, the offence created by s 44 is not vague. It makes it an offence for an individual responsible for the care of someone who lacks the capacity to care for himself to ill-treat or wilfully to neglect that person. Those in care who still enjoy some level of capacity for making their own decisions are entitled to be protected from wilful neglect which impacts on the areas of their lives over which they lack capacity. However s 44 did not create an absolute offence. Therefore, actions or omissions, or a combination of both, which reflect or are believed to reflect the protected autonomy of the individual needing care do not constitute wilful neglect. Within these clear principles, the issue in an individual prosecution is fact specific.'

Courts and Criminal Justice Act 2015

2.226 With respect to incidents occurring on or after 13 April 2015, the provisions of the Courts and Criminal Justice Act 2015 have made it an offence (under s 20) for an individual who has the care of another individual by virtue of being a care worker to ill-treat or wilfully to neglect that individual. A 'care worker' is an individual who, as paid work, provides health care for an adult or a child (with certain exceptions), or social care for an adult. Significantly, a care worker also includes those with managerial responsibility and directors (of equivalents) of organisations providing such care.

2.227 There is also a separate offence (under s 21) relating to care providers. A care provider will commit this offence where:

- an individual who has the care of another individual by virtue of being part of the care provider's arrangements ill-treats or wilfully neglects that individual,
- the care provider's activities are managed or organised in a way which amounts to a gross breach of a relevant duty of care owed by the care provider to the individual who is ill-treated or neglected, and
- in the absence of the breach, the ill-treatment or wilful neglect would not have occurred or would have been less likely to occur.

---

[372] [2012] EWCA Crim 2521 at [18].

It should perhaps be noted in relation that this offence is not relevant to service users who are receiving direct payments.

2.228 It is likely that that use will be made wherever possible of two new offences, which do not depend upon the capacity (or otherwise) of the individual to whom care is being provided. However, the offence under MCA 2005, s 44 will remain of importance to cover instances of ill-treatment or wilful neglect by family members or others falling outside the category of paid care workers or care providers. In the circumstances, it is to be regretted that the opportunity was not taken in this Bill also to revisit MCA 2005, s 44 and the flawed approach adopted there to capacity.

ANNEX

Impact of Dementia and Other Conditions Affecting Capacity

Dr Steven Luttrell

Consultant Geriatrician and General Physician, Barrister at law

Conditions Affecting Capacity

A wide range of medical conditions cause mental impairments and affect mental capacity. These include conditions causing an acute deterioration of brain function, those causing a progressive deterioration and those causing a range of specific psychiatric symptoms. The pattern of deterioration and impact on the person's capacity to make decisions varies between and within these groups. This paper sets out further details about this range of conditions and their impact on mental capacity.

Acute Brain Injury

This group of conditions result in a rapid deterioration of brain function. The causes of acute deterioration are varied and include:

- external trauma;
- internal vascular impairment such as a clot or thrombosis within a cerebral artery resulting in a stroke;
- intracerebral haemorrhage;
- metabolic dysfunction such as a rapid reduction in the supply of oxygen as a result of a cardiac arrest;
- delirium resulting from infection or other illness.

The brain is sensitive to metabolic or physical changes and function will deteriorate within minutes of significant trauma or change in metabolic state. Irreversible damage will rapidly follow and the window of opportunity for action to correct the underlying problem is short. For example thrombolytic drugs which reverse the impaired blood supply in thrombotic stroke have a benefit only if given within the first few hours of symptoms.

The impairments resulting from acute brain injury include physical, sensory, cognitive and language dysfunctions and behavioural problems. About half of stroke survivors are left with some degree of physical or cognitive impairment (A Di Carlo, 'Human and economic burden of stroke' (2009) 38 *Age and Ageing* 4–5). Impairments relating to cognitive, language and behavioural function may impact on mental capacity and impairments of physical or sensory function may make it more difficult for a person to use the residual mental abilities that they possess. The interplay of the range of disabilities may make it difficult for an affected person to participate in decision making.

Whilst traumatic brain injury, stroke and metabolic disturbances can rapidly cause irreversible brain damage, the resulting impairments will for many people improve with time. Recovery is in general more marked for younger people and is enhanced by participation in multi-professional rehabilitation programmes. Recovery for most people is in part related to 'neuroplasticity', an ability of brain tissue to remodel, and in part due to compensatory adaptation. Recovery may continue for up to and beyond one year, particularly in younger people. However most recovery is likely to be seen within the first few months following injury.

Delirium is an acute deterioration in cognitive function, particularly orientation, caused by acute medical conditions such as a severe infection. This condition is increasingly recognised in hospital admissions although the true prevalence is unknown (A Teodorczuk et al, 'Education, hospital staff and the confused older patient' (2009) 38 *Age and Ageing* 252–253). Older people and people with pre-existing dementia appear to be particularly susceptible to delirium. In most cases cognitive function will recover to previous levels following treatment of the causative medical condition. However, recovery may be delayed by several weeks or months following recovery from the physical condition, and some people may be left with residual deficits.

Neuro-Degenerative Conditions

This group includes a range of conditions associated with a slow decline in cognitive abilities often over many years. It includes the Alzheimer's dementia, vascular dementia, diffuse Lewy body disease, Parkinson's disease and multiple sclerosis. The onset is usually insidious and in many instances, particularly in older people, a formal diagnosis is not made until the illness is fairly advanced.

Alzheimer's disease and vascular dementia are characterised by progressive global cognitive decline over a period of many years. Whilst there is evidence that some medications will slow the decline in Alzheimer's disease, the effect is limited and not curative (J Cerejeira and E Mukqetova-Ladinska, 'Treating dementia – will the NICE guidance 2006 change our clinical practice?' (2007) 36 *Age and Ageing* 605–606).

Parkinson's disease is characterised by progressive slowing of physical movements. However the disease is also associated with significant cognitive decline. The incidence of dementia is five times that in an unaffected population and in many patients there will be some evidence of cognitive dysfunction at the time of diagnosis (J Hindle, 'Ageing, neurodegeneration and Parkinson's disease' (2010) 39 *Age and Ageing* 156–161). The later stages of the disease include impairments of memory, language function and hallucinations.

Multiple sclerosis is a condition of mainly younger people characterised by episodic focal neurological deficits often involving physical or sensory functions. Early in the disease episodes tend to resolve leaving little residual disability. However for some people repeated episodes are associated with incomplete resolution and a progressive decline in neurological function. In the later stages of the disease this will for many also include a decline in global cognitive abilities.

The pathological causes of most neuro-degenerative conditions remain ill understood and on the whole treatment options which slow the progression of these diseases are limited in effectiveness.

Psychiatric Conditions

Many psychiatric conditions in their more severe forms will affect mental capacity as a result of symptoms which render the individual unable to make judgments. For example, a person with severe depression or anxiety may be unable to form a judgment on a particular issue because their thoughts are so clouded by nihilistic ideas or overwhelming fear. Depression is an increasingly recognised problem in older people and is associated with poor self-rating of general health (Huang Chang-Quan et al, 'Health status and risk for depression amongst the elderly: a meta-analysis of published literature' (2010) 39 *Age and Ageing* 23–30). Medical treatments and psychological management of psychiatric conditions have improved considerably over recent years. However for many patients the medical treatment options continue to cause a significant burden of side effects.

Issues Associated with Multiple Pathology and Complexity

In the UK and many other countries increased wealth and improved medical and nursing care has been associated with a significant increase in lifespan. The number of older people has grown along with the number of people with complex comorbidities including combinations of medical conditions along with significant physical, sensory and mental disabilities. Hospital and community health services are looking after an increasing number of people who have cognitive impairments resulting from a variety of medical causes for example dementia, stroke and depression. In such circumstances mental capacity can be difficult to assess. Recovery patterns can be difficult to predict and will relate to the relative contribution and prognosis of each underlying condition and their responsiveness to treatment or rehabilitation.

Many older people discharged from hospital are now on large numbers of medications and have complex and increasingly expensive care needs. Whilst the UK population continues to enjoy free health care at the point of delivery through the National Health Service, social care is means tested and provided by local authorities. The complexity and cost of social care provision creates a substantial burden for a number of older people who have disabilities affecting their mental capacity. Fragmentation of family units has created increased levels of social isolation for many older people whose social networks may not be resilient enough to manage the many health, social care and financial decisions which can be required during periods of deteriorating health.

Cognitive Disabilities and Impact on Mental Capacity

Mental capacity is determined by an assessment of an individual's:

- ability to understand the information relevant to the decision;
- retain that information;
- use and weigh that information as part of the process of making the decision; and
- communicate the decision.

Both acute brain injury and neuro degenerative conditions can affect mental capacity as a result of a range of mental disabilities including impairments of:

- short and long term memory;
- orientation for time, place and person;
- ability to manage numbers and undertake numerical calculations;
- ability to manage language, both understanding words and using them to communicate;
- visuo-spatial skills;
- executive functions (initiating, planning and undertaking sequences of tasks);
- judgment;
- insight; and
- interpretation of emotion and appropriate emotional responses.

In addition, a significant number of people suffering acute or progressive neurological conditions will also suffer other mental health conditions such as anxiety or depression which may further impede their capacity for decision making.

Change in Capacity with Time

The change in mental disability with time varies with the type of condition. Following an acute brain injury a person may become rapidly mentally incapable but may recover some function over the ensuing weeks or months. In contrast in neuro-degenerative conditions there is a pattern of progressive and irreversible decline in cognitive abilities. Within these general patterns mental capabilities may fluctuate significantly from week to week or from one part of the day to another.

Case Example: Alzheimer's Disease

Alzheimer's disease is characterised by a global and progressive decline in cognitive abilities and patients pass through a number of stages as the disease progresses:

(i) Mild Cognitive Impairment

During the initial years the person has subtle deficits including memory impairment, difficulty organising more complex tasks, reduced work performance and difficulties mastering new skills. Triebel's recent study of people with mild cognitive impairment found evidence of declining financial skills in the year before conversion to Alzheimer's disease (K Triebel et al, 'Declining financial capacity in mild cognitive impairment: A 1-year longitudinal study' (2009) 73 *Neurology* 928–934). If not called on to undertake more complex social or work related tasks, neither the person nor their relatives or friends may be aware of the decline in function until it is fairly advanced. During this phase mental capacity for more complex financial, work related or social decisions may become impaired, but go unrecognised.

(ii) Mild Alzheimer's Disease

This phase of the disease is characterised by a further reduction in ability to manage the more complex elements of daily living including preparing meals, shopping, managing finances and organising social activities. Short term memory will often be impaired and although the person may be aware of some of the difficulties he/she may avoid seeking help. Mental capacity for financial decisions or more complex social decisions will deteriorate but the person may continue to function independently, adopting a variety of strategies to compensate for the decline in cognitive ability.

(iii) Moderate Alzheimer's Disease

In its moderate stage the person will have more substantial difficulties with basic activities of daily living including day to day judgements about social activities, meal preparation, clothing and finances. Memory problems will have become more significant and basic arithmetical calculations may be impaired. Difficulties may be such that the person is unable to live independently. Mental capacity for a range of social decisions will become significantly impaired as the person increasingly lacks insight into the extent of their disability and its effects.

(iv) Severe Alzheimer's Disease

In this phase it is increasingly difficult for the person to remain safe without significant support. The person will be unable to manage simple activities of daily living without assistance, such as washing and dressing, toileting and simple meal preparation. There may be evidence of increasing physical disabilities such as incontinence. Memory and calculations are severely impaired and the person may exhibit emotional and behavioural problems including apathy and aggression. As the disease progresses cognitive, language function, swallowing and mobility will deteriorate and the person will become increasingly prone to intercurrent medical conditions. During this final phase the person will become mentally incapable of most health and social care decisions.

Range of Decisions

For people with conditions affecting cognitive function or mental capacity there are often a range of difficult decisions to be made. These can become increasingly complex and urgent during periods of acute deterioration in function. For example, it is not unusual for older patients and their carers and relatives to be faced with decisions about the provision of health care, social care and financial matters during the period following an admission to hospital with delirium or a stroke or a deterioration in physical function against a background of dementia. These include decisions about:

- driving;
- management of financial affairs including paying household bills;
- long term care options including home care or nursing home care;
- adaptations to the home;
- sale of properties or other assets;
- health care decisions such as artificial feeding or the treatment of life threatening infections;
- advance care planning including advance decisions about potential future treatments such as cardiopulmonary resuscitation.

Case Example: Person Suffering a Stroke

Ms X is admitted to hospital following a stroke. She was previously living at home but had become increasingly socially isolated. There was some evidence of self-neglect prior to the stroke.

The stroke has affected her ability to use language. She has difficulty understanding more complex sentences and difficulty finding some words. In addition there is evidence of impairments of cognitive function including short term memory, executive function and judgment. Ms X has difficulty with simple arithmetical calculations, planning simple activities and undertaking tasks which involve sequences of actions such as the preparation of a very simple meal. Her stroke has caused a variety of physical impairments affecting her mobility and swallowing. However, as part of her cognitive disability, she lacks insight into the extent of both her physical and cognitive disabilities and their effect on her ability to undertake basic activities of daily living such as transferring from bed to chair, washing, dressing and meal preparation. Associated with these disabilities and a failure to make significant improvements with rehabilitation Ms X has become withdrawn and depressed. The depression has responded to a limited degree to a combination of input from a clinical psychologist and the use of an antidepressant medication.

Ms X has complex cognitive, language and mental health impairments relating to a combination of probable pre stroke dementia, the stroke itself and post stroke depression. Following the conclusion of the rehabilitation programme the multi professional team looking after Ms X has undertaken a variety of assessments. In collaboration with Ms X's family and her limited number of friends, the team concluded that:

- Ms X is not able to manage simple financial matters and has limited insight into her physical and cognitive disabilities.

- There are substantial risks associated with a return to living at home even with social care support. Ms X is mentally incapable of making a decision about her place of future residence as a result of a range of cognitive impairments involving memory, judgement, insight and executive function. The decision will be made in her best interests involving her near relatives, friends and social worker.

- Ms X has repeatedly articulated a desire to return home and refuses to consider a nursing home as an option. If the best interest decision about future place of residence, taking into account Mrs X's previous and present wishes and least restrictive options, concludes that this is a nursing home, the team will continue to discuss options and safety issues with Ms X and her family in the hope of reaching a solution which all feel able to support. However the team and family will also consider the deprivation of liberty safeguards.

- Ms X is mentally capable of a variety of less complex decisions relating to day to day care and is capable of making decisions about her healthcare needs such as whether to have artificial feeding to supplement her oral nutrition.

Decisions and the Person with Dementia

A recent qualitative study undertaken by Gill Livingston and colleagues (G Livingston et al, 'Making decisions for people with dementia who lack capacity; qualitative study of family carers in UK' (2010) 341 *British Medical Journal* c4181) highlighted some of the common decisions made by families and carers on behalf of people with dementia and the facilitators and barriers to decision making. The study highlighted a range of consistent problems including the resistance of the person with dementia and the changes in family roles. Many decisions provoked considerable difficulties. Decisions about care homes were problematic particularly if the carer was aware that the person with dementia would never have wanted to live in a care home and the carer felt obliged to act against this knowledge. Financial matters caused considerable concerns with carers worried about vulnerability to exploitation, along with worries that they might be perceived as exploitative. Decisions related to end of life healthcare issues were difficult particularly if there were family disagreements. Decisions such as instituting artificial nutrition were particularly difficult and complex. The study concluded that: 'Family cohesion alleviated emotional conflicts and facilitated decisions, as did professionals' support, information sharing and the use of their "authority" to advocate helpful interventions.'

Good Practice in the Assessment of Capacity and Management of Decision Making

Good practice in the care of people with medical conditions resulting in lack of capacity includes the use of multi-professional decision making, consideration of social and cultural context and the increasing use of advance care plans.

Multi-Professional Assessment and Decision Making

For patients with deteriorating cognitive functions health care will often be provided by multi professional care teams including medical and nursing staff, physiotherapists, occupational therapists, speech and language therapists, clinical psychologists and social workers. Such teams will undertake assessments of mental capacity for particular decisions coming to jointly agreed conclusions and will work with families, carers and advocates to form views on best interests for those who have impaired capacity. Although various assessment tools are used there is a recognition that decisions need to be made on an individual basis and that no one tool is helpful in all circumstances. A recent review of the mini-mental status examination, a widely used 30 point assessment tool, suggested that it has poor sensitivity and that reliance on scores above 19 will frequently lead to misclassification and incorrect assumptions about decision making abilities (A Pachet et al, 'Clinical utility of the mini-mental status examination when assessing decision-making capacity' (2010) 23(1) *Journal of Geriatric Psychiatry and Neurology* 3–8). Conversely, a study of the use of a semi structured clinical interview for financial capacity concluded that this is a tool which clinicians could use to reliably evaluate financial capacity in cognitively impaired older adults (D Marsden, 'Clinical interview assessment of financial capacity in older adults with mild cognitive impairment and Alzheimer's disease' (2009) 57 *Journal of the American Geriatrics Society* 806–814). Assessing mental capacity can be particularly difficult in acute situations, where the availability of expert advice and support is essential. (B Brody, 'Who has capacity?' (2009) 361 *New England Journal of Medicine* 232)

Cultural Context

For all professional teams there is a need to be aware of the cultural context within which decisions are usually made. The Mental Capacity Act Code of Practice (TSO, 2007) recognises that language, cultural and religious belief can influence the applicability of the Act. In professional assessments there is a need to have due regard to the use of interpreters, attention to dialects, the use of female interpreters for women and the cultural influences on decisions. For example elders from some religious or cultural groups may be expected to disengage from a range of economic, social and domestic responsibilities passing these to other members of the family (A Shah and C Heginbotham,

'The Mental Capacity Act: some implications for black and minority ethnic elders' (2008) 37 *Age and Ageing* 242–243).

Advance Care Planning

Increasingly people with conditions which follow a deteriorating course are encouraged to make advance decisions so that more individualised future health and social care decisions can be better planned. Knowing the views of the person held before losing capacity helps family members in their ability to make decisions. Decisions are best made whilst the person retains cognitive capacity and reduced abilities are associated with an impaired ability to participate in advance care planning (see T Stewart et al, 'Advance care planning in care homes for older people – qualitative study of the views of staff and families' (2011) 40 *Age and Ageing* 330–335; and M Luppa et al, 'Prediction of institutionalisation in the elderly, a systematic review' (2010) 39 *Age and Ageing* 31–38). However, the extent to which individuals wish to participate in such advance care planning varies, particularly with regard to decisions about end of life issues in dementia.

CHAPTER 3

LASTING POWERS OF ATTORNEY

BACKGROUND

Powers of attorney

3.1   A power of attorney is simply a formal arrangement, undertaken by deed, whereby one person ('the donor') entrusts to another person ('the attorney' or 'the donee') authority to act in his or her name and on his or her behalf. A power of attorney is a form of agency which has been recognised at common law and used for centuries to enable the affairs of the donor (the principal) to be conducted on his or her behalf by an attorney (the agent) while the donor is away on business, overseas or physically unwell.

3.2   Common law principles of agency apply to powers of attorney, although the law relating to powers of attorney has been developed by statute, beginning with the Powers of Attorney Act 1971.[1] This short statute confirmed that a power of attorney must be made by deed[2] and provided for the protection of the attorney and a third person where they act in good faith without knowledge of revocation of the power.[3]

3.3   Notwithstanding the introduction of statutory rules governing their operation, common law principles concerning the creation, operation and revocation continue to apply, and in particular the principle that a power of attorney is revoked by the supervening incapacity of the donor. The rationale behind this principle is quite straightforward. An act carried out by an attorney is treated in law as an act carried out by the donor. The attorney can only do what the donor can give authority for him or her to do and if the donor lacks capacity then the donor cannot give that authority. The attorney and any third party dealing with the attorney can therefore assume, in the absence of any evidence to the contrary, that the donor is able to know and approve of what is being done on his or her behalf. The only exception to this cardinal rule is where the power of attorney is made in a prescribed statutory form. The Mental Capacity Act 2005 (MCA 2005), Sch 1 (Lasting Powers of Attorney) or

---

[1]   This implemented the recommendations of the Law Commission's report *Powers of Attorney (1970)* Law Com No 30 (HMSO, 1970).
[2]   Law of Property (Miscellaneous Provisions) Act 1989, s 1.
[3]   Powers of Attorney Act 1971, ss 1 and 5.

Sch 4 (Enduring Powers of Attorney) provide for the powers made in a prescribed form to continue notwithstanding the supervening incapacity of the donor.

Limitations

3.4   Any power of attorney has to be understood in the context of the common law principles of agency and their limitations, which underpin the further statutory obligations imposed by MCA 2005. A power of attorney confers rights on the attorney as well as responsibilities. And while an attorney may, if authorised, do anything that can lawfully be done by the donor, this is not an open-ended right to deal with the donor's property as the attorney wishes.[4] In particular:

- an attorney owes a fiduciary duty to the donor and cannot act so as to benefit him or herself or any other person to the detriment of the donor or the donor's estate.[5] The attorney must act in good faith, keep accounts and disclose any conflict of interest;[6]

- an attorney contracts in the name of the donor and while not personally liable under the contract, any property acquired or money held as attorney should be kept in the donor's name and must be kept separate from the attorney's own estate;[7]

- an attorney owes a duty of skill and care commensurate with the degree of expertise offered by him or her and whether he or she is acting gratuitously or for reward;[8]

- an attorney owes a duty of confidentiality to the donor and cannot disclose information unless authorised or to the extent required by the agency. This duty survives the operation of the power;

---

[4]   The relevance of the common law principles to the role of an attorney under a modern LPA was eloquently restated by Senior Judge Lush in the case of *Re Harcourt: the Public Guardian v A* [2013] COPLR 69.

[5]   The Code of Practice issued under MCA 2005 defines an attorney's fiduciary duty as follows: 'A fiduciary duty means attorneys must not take advantage of their position. Nor should they put themselves in a position where their personal interests conflict with their duties. They must also not allow any other influences to affect the way in which they act as an attorney. Decisions should always benefit the donor, and not the attorney. Attorneys must not profit or get any personal benefit from their position, apart from receiving gifts where the Act allows it, whether or not it is at the donor's expense' (7.60).

[6]   An attorney must be prepared to produce accounts or depending on the size and nature of the estate, financial records. See *Gray v Haig* (1855) 20 Beav 219.

[7]   If the attorney holds property of the donor then he or she holds it as trustee. See *Henry v Hammond* [1913] 2 KB 515. For a recent case where an attorney was criticized for intermingling his own money with that of the donor, see the decisions of Senior Judge Lush in *Re PC: the Public Guardian v AC and JC* [2014] EWCOP 41 and *Re OL: Public Guardian and DA, YS and ES* [2015] EWCOP 41.

[8]   See e g *Chaudhry v Prabhakar* [1988] 3 All ER 718. See also the decision of Senior Judge Lush in *Re Buckley: The Public Guardian v C* [2013] COPLR 39.

- an attorney cannot generally delegate his or her authority to another person;[9]
- an attorney is chosen to exercise personal skill and cannot appoint a successor in the same way as a trustee can appoint a new or replacement trustee;
- a power of attorney may be revoked by the donor by a deed or other act inconsistent with the continued operation of the power, which must include the giving of notice to the attorney;[10]
- the authority of the attorney is revoked by the death, incapacity or bankruptcy of the attorney;[11]
- the attorney may disclaim the power at any time;
- the attorney may only do such things as may lawfully be done by an attorney. Thus an attorney cannot perform an act which can only be performed personally, such as swearing an affidavit[12] or executing a will.[13] Neither can an attorney perform an act arising by virtue of the donor's office[14] or which is of a personal nature;[15]
- Rules of Court do not permit an attorney, in that role, to conduct legal proceedings in the name of the donor;[16] and
- a power of attorney is revoked by the incapacity of the donor.[17]

The incapable donor

3.5   It is the last limitation that has been regarded as having the largest impact for most people. A power of attorney made using common law principles or under the Powers of Attorney Act 1971 was adequate for businessmen or families going abroad leaving a relative or solicitor to manage their property. It would also help where a donor was physically unable to manage his or her affairs.[18] However, it was of no assistance in the increasingly frequent cases

---

[9]   Delegation may be permitted if authorised by the instrument or by statute, if it is purely administrative, it is usual practice in the business of the donor or the attorney or if it is due to necessity. For example, directors of a company may delegate powers to an attorney or agent who may in turn delegate all or any of his or her powers (Art 71 of Table A).

[10]   Thus the creation of a new power does not operate to revoke an earlier one, in contrast to a will under the Wills Act 1837, s 20.

[11]   In respect of lasting powers of attorney, see MCA 2005, s 13(6). A welfare lasting power of attorney is not, however, revoked by the bankruptcy of the donee: s 13(8).

[12]   *Clauss v Pir* [1988] 1 Ch 267.

[13]   Wills Act 1837, s 9.

[14]   For example, the attorney of a judge cannot pass a sentence nor the attorney of a bishop ordain a priest.

[15]   Thus an attorney cannot, eg, sit an exam, drive a car, marry or vote on behalf of the donor. These last two circumstances are specifically excluded from the scope of an attorney's authority under a lasting power of attorney by MCA 2005, ss 27 and 29.

[16]   See *Gregory v Turner* [2003] EWCA Civ 183. The appointment of a litigation friend for a 'protected party' is dealt with by the Civil Procedure Rules 1998, SI 1998/3132, Part 21.

[17]   See *Drew v Nunn* (1879) 4 QBD 661, CA; *Yonge v Toynbee* [1910] 1 KB 215, CA.

[18]   Such powers of attorney can still be made and are often used for those specific situations; especially if a power of attorney needs to be used immediately and there would otherwise be a delay in completing a Lasting Power of Attorney.

where a person had become incapable and had property and affairs that required administration. There were only three ways of responding to that situation. Either the person's affairs were neglected, were dealt with under a potentially invalid power of attorney or the Court of Protection would appoint a receiver to manage that person's property and affairs.[19]

3.6   The traditional power of the Court to appoint a receiver was reviewed by the Law Commission in its report *The Incapacitated Principal* (1983).[20] This drew attention to the fact that the slow and bureaucratic procedures of the Court of Protection and the Public Trust Office (which administered the property and affairs of persons under the Court's jurisdiction) might not be necessary or appropriate in every situation where an incapable person's property and affairs needed to be administered. Surely if a person could plan ahead and choose who would administer their property and affairs in the event of their incapacity, that person should be allowed to do just that without having to undergo a formal judicial process. In such cases a loving spouse or mature and sensible children could look after the affairs of the incapable person without having to go to the expense and indignity of accounting for their conduct. It was also assumed that the existing judicial and administrative framework would not be able to cope with the increasing demands placed upon it by an ageing population.

Statutory powers of attorney

Enduring powers of attorney

3.7   In response to the Law Commission report *The Incapacitated Principal*, Parliament enacted the Enduring Powers of Attorney Act 1985 (EPAA 1985) which came into force on 10 March 1986.[21] This created a new type of power of attorney, known as an enduring power of attorney (EPA), which would function in the same way as a conventional power of attorney but which, subject to a basic registration process, would continue or 'endure' beyond the onset of incapacity.[22] So long as that formality was complied with, a third party dealing with the attorney could assume that the attorney had a valid form of authority from the donor.[23] Although EPAs have since 1 October 2007 been superseded by new Lasting Powers of Attorney (LPAs) created under the MCA 2005, EPAs created before that date remain valid and need to be understood in their own terms.[24] Furthermore, LPAs cannot be fully understood without reference to this earlier history.

---

[19] First under the Mental Health Act 1959 and then under the Mental Health Act 1983. Under MCA 2005, the Court has power to appoint a deputy.

[20] Law Com No 122.

[21] Enduring Powers of Attorney Act 1985 (Commencement Order) 1986, SI 1986/125.

[22] EPAA 1985, s 1(1)(a); MCA 2005, Sch 4, para 1.

[23] EPAA 1985, s 9(3); MCA 2005, Sch 4, para 18(3).

[24] See **3.17** below.

3.8   An attorney acting under an EPA would still be subject to the laws and principles governing the relationship between the donor and the attorney, except in so far as they were altered by statute. Thus an attorney acting under an EPA would be able to make gifts or provide for the needs of someone the donor might be expected to provide for.[25] For example, a husband looking after an incapable wife would be able to make gifts at Christmas to grandchildren on behalf of their grandmother and an attorney could use the donor's estate to maintain a disabled child or pay a grandchild's school fees.[26]

3.9   EPAA 1985 further provided a number of safeguards for the protection of donors of EPAs and placed the EPA jurisdiction under the authority of the Court of Protection. However, such safeguards were the result of a compromise between two competing objectives: on the one hand, individuals should be able to entrust their affairs to someone with as little interference from the state as possible; on the other, the vulnerable would need protection from the unscrupulous as well as the inefficient. Any system of protection would also have to be simple to operate, cost effective and largely self-financing.

3.10   The result of this tension was a simple system of protection which would operate on two levels. On the first level, there would be an administrative process of registration which would involve the donor and his or her next of kin being notified of an intention to register the EPA and therefore having an opportunity to object. The onus would be on the donor and his or her family to alert the Court of Protection in the event of misuse. On the second level, the civil law would apply to acts carried out by an attorney who was acting beyond the scope of his or her authority, particularly if the donor were incapable and the power was not registered. Acts carried out by an attorney would be invalid and provide the donor or his or her estate with a form of redress.[27]

3.11   The level of protection offered by an EPA, reflecting two opposing ideals, represented an imperfect compromise.[28] EPAA 1985 (which is largely incorporated in MCA 2005, Sch 4 insofar as existing EPAs are concerned, and which governs the operation of EPAs made prior to 1 October 2007) would provide the following safeguards:

- The power of attorney must be in a prescribed form[29] and must be executed by the donor and attorney.

- The prescribed form contains a brief explanation of the nature and effect of the power.

---

[25]   EPAA 1985, s 3(4), (5); MCA 2005, Sch 4, paras 2, 3. The donor of an EPA could restrict this additional power but could not extend it.

[26]   *Re Cameron* [1999] Ch 386, [1999] 2 All ER 924.

[27]   Although a Scottish case and not directly involving EPAs, this principle was applied in *McDowall v Inland Revenue* [2003] UKSC SPC00382 (26 June 2003). Ironically the beneficiary of this case was not the donor's estate but the Inland Revenue.

[28]   Problems with the EPA jurisdiction are considered in more detail at **3.15**.

[29]   EPAA 1985, s 2(1)(a); MCA 2005, Sch 4, para 2(1).

- The attorney or attorneys must undertake a process of official validation or registration when they believe that the donor is or is becoming mentally incapable of managing their property and affairs.[30] The EPA is registered by the Public Guardian, the registration providing a degree of protection for the donor and for third parties dealing with the attorney.

- Before applying for registration the attorney or attorneys must notify the donor of their intention and also at least three relatives in a prescribed order of classes of relatives.[31] All the members of a class must be notified, even if there are more than three persons, so that if a donor has one child, one sibling and six grandchildren all eight relatives must be notified.

- The donor must be given notice personally of the intention to register.[32]

- Any notices must be in a prescribed form and provide the recipient with details of the applicant and the grounds on which an objection can be made.[33]

- Any person notified of an application to register an EPA, and any other person at any other time (with the leave of the Court), may apply to the Court to refuse registration or to revoke the EPA.

- The Court shall refuse to register a power or cancel the registration of a power if satisfied that the donor has revoked the power, the donor remains capable, the donor has died or become bankrupt, that fraud or undue influence was used to create the power or 'having regard to all the circumstances and in particular the attorney's relationship or connection with the donor, the attorney is unsuitable to be the donor's attorney'.[34]

- If no valid notice of objection is received within five weeks of the last notice being given, the EPA is registered.[35]

- The Court of Protection has powers to intervene generally on behalf of the incapable or potentially incapable donor of the EPA. Thus the Court may exercise its powers to determine whether the EPA is effective,[36] and give directions as to the management of the donor's affairs and the rendering of accounts or the making of gifts.[37] In addition the Court retains its powers under MCA 2005 to intervene in the affairs of a person who lacks capacity so that there is an overlap between the two jurisdictions.

---

[30] EPAA 1985, s 4(1); MCA 2005, Sch 4, paras 4(1) and 23. Notwithstanding the implementation of MCA 2005, the Mental Health Act 1983 definition of 'mental disorder' is preserved in relation to existing EPAs.

[31] EPAA 1985, Sch 1, para 2(1); MCA 2005, Sch 4, paras 5 and 6.

[32] EPAA 1985, Sch 1, para 4(1) and Court of Protection (Enduring Power of Attorney) Rules 2001, SI 2001/825, r 15(1); MCA 2005, Sch 4, para 8.

[33] The current notices are set out in the Lasting Powers of Attorney, Enduring Powers of Attorney and Public Guardian Regulations 2007, SI 2007/1253, Sch 7.

[34] EPAA 1985, ss 6(5) and 8(4); MCA 2005, Sch 4, paras 9 and 16(4).

[35] EPAA 1985, s 6(4)(a); MCA 2005, Sch 4, para 13(4).

[36] EPAA 1985, ss 5 and 8; MCA 2005, Sch 4, para 16(2)(a).

[37] EPAA 1985, s 8(2); MCA 2005, Sch 4, para 16(2)(e).

Success of enduring powers

3.12 That the EPA responded to a legal and social need is evident from the substantial number of EPAs in place. Because EPAs were often made for use prior to the onset of incapacity or as an insurance against incapacity, there remains no reliable method of knowing how many EPAs have been created. Those that can be measured are those which been registered with the Court of Protection or Public Guardian and the number of registrations has increased steadily each year since the first such powers were registered in 1986. In 2004, 16,314 EPAs were registered.[38] Even though no new EPAs could be made from October 2007, the number of registrations has remained relatively stable, although modest when compared to the large number of LPAs being registered. As time goes on their number will diminish. In 2009/2010 over 20,000 applications to register an EPA were received by the Public Guardian.[39] In 2010/2011, 19,000 applications were made. In 2012/2013 there were 18,000 applications and 16,000 applications in 2013/2014.[40]

3.13 While the number of registered EPAs has increased, the number of incapable persons whose affairs are subject to the traditional jurisdiction of the Court of Protection has also continued to increase, to around 50,000. Thus, without the introduction of EPAs (and their successors, LPAs), it would not have been possible for the existing judicial and administrative system to manage without a significant increase in resources.

3.14 There is no doubt that EPAs have, by the measure of their popularity alone, proved useful. They were seen as simple documents and therefore inexpensive to create. Forms could be obtained from stationers and online. The registration process was – and remains – easy to operate, with registration forms available from the Public Guardian and a one-off fee of £110 payable on an application for registration.[41]

Problems with enduring powers

3.15 Despite the widespread acceptance and use of EPAs, the EPA jurisdiction had several clear drawbacks. It is important not to lose sight of these. Not only so these still exist with EPAs which are still valid but they also have also

---

[38] National Audit Office *Protecting and promoting the financial affairs of people who lose capacity*, HC 27 (Session 2005–6). Under MCA 2005, the Public Guardian is the registration authority for EPAs: see Sch 1.

[39] The number of registrations contrasts with the much higher number of LPAs registered. It is however impossible to compare with LPAs, which are generally registered while the donor has capacity; EPAs by their nature remain unregistered while the donor has capacity.

[40] Annual Report of the Office of the Public Guardian 2012/2013, HC345 and Annual Report of the Office of the Public Guardian 2013/2014, HC334. In this last period, there were 295,000 applications to register LPAs, an increase of 22% on the previous year's figure of 242,000 applications.

[41] Public Guardian (Fees, etc) Regulations 2007, SI 2007/2051 as amended by the Public Guardian (Fees, etc) (Amendment) Regulations 2013, SI 2013/1748. The prescribed fee was increased from £120 to £130 from 1 October 2011, and reduced to £110 from 1 October 2013.

influenced the new legislation relating to LPAs. Furthermore the benefits and failings of LPAs can be measured against them. The main drawbacks of the EPA jurisdiction can be summarised as follows

- An EPA relates only to the property and affairs of the donor. The attorney therefore has no authority over the personal welfare of the incapable donor, covering matters such as where the donor should live, what care he or she should receive or whether a particular treatment can be given or withheld. This is despite the fact that an attorney acting in the best interests of the incapable donor needs to take account of the welfare of the donor. The donor's estate cannot, in practice, be dealt with in isolation from the actual needs of the donor.

- The EPA jurisdiction rests on the principle that the donor's autonomy and right to choose the person to manage his or her affairs needs to be respected, so that the attorney can operate with as little official intervention as possible. This delays and limits such intervention, which is to protect the incapable person who is by the nature of his or her situation vulnerable and at risk from abuse. The Senior Judge of the Court of Protection had estimated that financial abuse took place in about 10–15% of cases.[42] This substantial proportion included not just cases of actual fraud but also cases of misuse where, for instance, an attorney was acting beyond the scope of his or her authority, and may have been overly optimistic in view of the extent to which unregistered EPAs were often used beyond the onset of incapacity.[43]

- That fraud or misuse takes place so extensively is due to the very limited degree of official supervision provided. There is no means of knowing that a particular EPA is being used, let alone that it is being used correctly. The Court of Protection relies on misuse being notified to it, but this in turn presupposes that an attorney who registers an EPA correctly notifies relatives and they in turn file an objection with the Court of Protection. In one case the manager of a nursing home was attorney for several residents and systematically defrauded them of their savings over a couple of years. The residents had no relatives and, in any event, the EPAs were not registered. An improper benefit claim brought the fraud to light. Although the Court of Protection revoked the EPA, the civil and criminal laws offered little recompense for the victims. Recovery of the stolen assets was impossible as these had been dissipated and a criminal prosecution was made difficult by the fact that the witnesses could not give evidence for themselves.[44] The failure of the system to protect vulnerable adults was recognised officially in 1999 by the Quinquennial Review of the then Public Trust Office:[45]

---

[42] This bold assertion was first made by Denzil Lush in 'Taking Liberties: Enduring Powers of Attorney and financial abuse' (1998) *Solicitors Journal*, 11 September, at p 808 but has been restated by Denzil Lush in *Cretney & Lush on Enduring Powers of Attorney* (Jordans, 5th edn, 2001) at p 133 and see also oral evidence given by Master Lush to the Joint Committee on the Draft Mental Incapacity Bill, HL Paper 189-1l, HC 1083-1l, at p 188.

[43] This may be less of an issue today as the EPAs still in existence and which are now being

'An EPA bestows virtually unfettered control of someone's finances once it is brought into force. While its objective (to put someone's financial affairs into the hands of an individual they have pre-selected, rather than surrendering to the Court of Protection) fits entirely with the objective of keeping the state out of family affairs unless there is no alternative, if an EPA goes wrong the results can be catastrophic for the person concerned. Although comparatively rare, there are plenty of instances where the system has been deliberately or accidentally abused and getting the position rectified through the Court is a long and difficult process ...'

- In view of these difficulties, the choice of attorney is crucial to the success or failure of a person's EPA. Unfortunately, many EPAs are made long before they are needed and the donor is unable to foresee changes in his or her circumstances that might otherwise have led him or her to choose a different attorney. The knowledge of the donor and the advice received at the time the EPA was made are therefore of utmost importance. However, the prescribed form of EPA was easy to obtain and complete and offered little effective protection. The form only required a signature by the donor and one witness whereupon it is presumed to have been validly executed.[46] There is furthermore no requirement that the donor has any form of legal or independent advice or that there be any assessment of the donor's capacity to create the power. Thus the ability to misuse the EPA is instituted quite easily at the time the form is created.

- EPAs have proved a victim of their own success. They were designed to be simple to complete and the forms could be obtained from stationers or from the internet. Many solicitors prepared EPAs for a nominal cost, often in connection with another matter such as a will. The problem, however, was that many such EPAs were prepared too quickly, without proper care, and without proper thought being given to problems that might arise in the future. A carefully prepared EPA would take account of family dynamics, the donor's capacity, conditions and restrictions available to the donor and the nature of his or her estate: in too many cases advice on such matters was not available.[47]

- An attorney is required to register an EPA once he or she 'has reason to believe that the donor is or is becoming mentally incapable'.[48] Therefore once the EPA has been registered, it appears to anyone dealing with the

---

registered were prepared some years ago and have remained dormant, and only activated by the attorneys as the requirement to use them and therefore register them has arisen.

[44] In this tragic example, although the Crown prosecuted the former manager, it accepted an admission of liability in respect of only certain counts where the victims were capable of giving evidence. Where the victims were incapable or had subsequently died, there was no conviction in their individual cases, making civil recovery very difficult to pursue.

[45] Ann Chant CB *The Public Trust Office of the Lord Chancellor's Department: A Quinquennial Review* (November 1999), at para 47.

[46] *Re W (enduring power of attorney)* [2001] Ch 609, [2001] 4 All ER 88.

[47] The Law Society published detailed Guidance in 1995 (revised in 1995) on EPAs and while this was very detailed and encouraged best practice among solicitors, it was not always followed and of course not all EPAs were professionally prepared.

[48] EPAA 1985, s 4(1). Notwithstanding the implementation of MCA 2005, this is still the case for existing EPAs; see MCA 2005, Sch 4, para 4(1).

attorney that the donor is mentally incapable and thereby incapable, by reason of mental disorder, of managing and administering his or her property and affairs.[49] The presumption arises therefore that once the EPA is registered, the donor is unable to manage or administer the full extent of his or her property and affairs. This sits uneasily with the principle, now enshrined in MCA 2005, that capacity is function specific and that a person may have capacity or lack capacity in respect of different functions.[50] Thus a donor could be prevented from making decisions in respect of which he or she had capacity. For example, a donor might be able to manage small amounts of money or collect his pension, but his bank or pension administrator would assume, from the fact that the EPA had been registered, that he could not and would therefore deny him any rights whatsoever over his own estate.

Abolition of enduring powers

3.16 The Law Commission considered these inherent failings in the EPA jurisdiction in the context of a review of the law relating to mental incapacity in its report *Mental Incapacity* (1995).[51] This review of the law, considered in more detail in Chapter 1, led to the passing of MCA 2005 in April 2005 which came into force on 1 October 2007.

3.17 Although no new EPAs may be made after 1 October 2007, all existing EPAs made prior to that date, even though not registered, continue to remain effective. The Law Commission had proposed converting all existing EPAs to new-style powers of attorney. However, EPAs have been made in good faith to comply with a different statutory framework and for many of those powers there is no means for the persons who made them to change them. Therefore instead of cancelling or converting existing EPAs into new lasting powers of attorney (LPAs), MCA 2005 provides for existing EPAs to continue to operate under the same legal basis as they were created, but within the framework of the new 2005 Act. MCA 2005 does, however, impose one further set of obligations on an attorney making decisions for a donor who lacks capacity. The attorney must act in the donor's best interests within the meaning of MCA 2005, s 4 and must also comply with the statutory Code of Practice.[52]

3.18 The provisions of the new Act relating to existing EPAs are contained in MCA 2005, Sch 4. Apart from a few small changes, Sch 4 incorporates the provisions of EPAA 1985 into the new Act.[53]

---

[49]   EPAA 1985, s 13. This is now set out in MCA 2005, Sch 4, para 23(1).
[50]   *Re Beaney* (deceased)[1978] 2 All ER 595, [1978] 1 WLR 770 and see generally Chapter 2.
[51]   Law Com No 231.
[52]   MCA 2005, s 1(4). The 'best interests' requirements are dealt with at **2.127–2.157** and the Code of Practice is dealt with at **2.7–2.22**.
[53]   Forms and procedures are dealt with by provisions issued under MCA 2005, such as the Lasting Powers of Attorney, Enduring Powers of Attorney and Public Guardian Regulations 2007, SI 2007/1253.

Lasting Powers of Attorney

3.19 MCA 2005 provides expressly for the revocation of the EPAA 1985,[54] and for the creation of a new type of Lasting Power of Attorney (LPA).[55]

3.20 LPAs and MCA 2005 jurisdiction cannot, however, be comprehended without reference to EPAs:

- EPAs made before MCA 2005 came into force will continue to operate in accordance with the same legal principles as existed as when they were made, although within the framework of the 2005 Act.[56] Thus different procedures as well as laws will operate side by side for many years to come.

- The Public Guardian and the Court of Protection will be responsible for administering the two sets of procedures and laws.

- A LPA, like an EPA, is a statutory form of power of attorney that builds on existing common law and statutory principles. Thus decisions of the courts affecting EPAs as well as practical and professional experience gained in their use will have a bearing on the use and understanding of LPAs.

- Attorneys acting under LPAs and EPAs are, where the donor lacks capacity, bound by the same requirements to act in the donor's best interests under MCA 2005, s 4.

- The principle requirement of the LPA is to address problems inherent in the EPA jurisdiction. It therefore needs to be measured against that standard.

NATURE OF LASTING POWER OF ATTORNEY

Character of lasting power of attorney

3.21 A LPA is defined by MCA 2005, s 9 as 'a power of attorney' under which one party (the donor) confers on another (the donee) authority to make certain decisions.[57] A LPA is therefore at heart 'a power of attorney' so that the principles governing the relationship in law between principal and agent apply to it. As with the EPA, the scope of such a power is both restricted and extended by statute.

---

[54] MCA 2005, s 66(1)(b).
[55] MCA 2005, s 9.
[56] See **3.132**.
[57] MCA 2005 generally refers to a 'donee' in the context of LPAs and an 'attorney' in the context of EPAs. The author has used the term 'attorney' as a generic term that applies to a person to whom authority has been delegated under a power of attorney, whether it be an ordinary, enduring or lasting power.

3.22 Under a LPA the donor may confer authority on the attorney to make decisions, including decisions in circumstances where the donor no longer has capacity in relation to all or any of:

- the donor's personal welfare or specified matters concerning the donor's personal welfare; and
- the donor's property and affairs or specified matters concerning the donor's property and affairs.[58]

3.23 The essential character of the LPA is that it respects the presumption contained in MCA 2005, ss 1 and 2, that a person must be assumed to have capacity unless it can be established that he or she lacks capacity and that capacity is only relative to the matter and at the time that capacity needs to be determined. The LPA of itself is silent as to the capacity of the donor.[59] The LPA therefore must work in tandem with the ability of the donor to make decisions in person over a range or spectrum of matters for which decisions might be made. At one end of the spectrum, the donor continues to make all decisions in person, with the attorney having no role to play (waiting in the background to be called upon to act); further along the spectrum, the donee carries out specific functions such as the sale of a property and the investment of the proceeds. The donor may or may not have capacity to make these decisions in person. At the other end of the spectrum, the attorney makes all the decisions which can be made by an attorney.

3.24 A LPA therefore functions at several different levels, applying different principles according to the circumstances in which the power is being operated. Thus:

- the LPA operates, in respect of property and affairs, as an ordinary power of attorney so that the attorney acts with the implied knowledge and approval of the donor;
- the LPA operates, in respect of property and affairs, in relation to matters which the donor lacks capacity to determine for him or herself;
- in respect of welfare decisions, the LPA only operates where the donor lacks capacity to make decisions; and
- where the attorney makes decisions on behalf of the donor which the donor lacks capacity to make, the attorney must also act in the donor's best interests, applying the criteria laid down in MCA 2005, s 4 as well as the Code of Practice.

3.25 This holistic approach to the requirements of the donor obviates the need for an attorney to register the LPA specifically on the onset of incapacity. Although registration might be delayed until that point is reached, the lack of capacity of itself does not trigger the registration process required to complete

---

[58] MCA 2005, s 9(1).
[59] By contrast with EPAs whose registration is triggered by a defined medical state which therefore creates a presumption that the donor lacks capacity (see **3.15**).

or validate the power. The existence of a completed LPA thereby avoids a presumption, as is the case with an EPA, that the donor is incapable of managing the full extent of his or her property and affairs.[60] Thus to any third party dealing with the property and affairs of the donor are concerned, the state of mind of the donor is irrelevant and the donor is not labelled or stigmatised as being incapable.

3.26 This approach is not followed where the power relates to welfare matters. Although the LPA can be registered at any time irrespective of the capacity of the donor, when the LPA comes to be used, it can only be used where the donor lacks capacity to make the decision in question.[61] For obvious reasons, the capable donor's right to make decisions over his or her own welfare takes precedence over another person's judgment, and in practice a doctor or carer will obtain consent or refusal to treatment from the donor in person so long as the donor has capacity. Only if the donor clearly lacks capacity does the LPA come into play.

Problems in practice with 'presumption of capacity'

3.27 While it is obviously sensible to allow people autonomy over their own affairs to the extent possible without making presumptions about a lack of capacity, this can cause practical difficulties. Any third party dealing with the attorney acting under a LPA is not 'on notice' that the donor lacks capacity. This may cause problems if there are conflicting instructions or the LPA is being used fraudulently. It may, for instance, be possible for the attorney to arrange the sale of the donor's property against the donor's wishes. Will anyone check with the donor that the donor wants the property sold? Or take the case of a donor who makes regular withdrawals from his account to pay a friendly tradesman, even though there is a LPA in place and registered with the bank. In both cases the status of the LPA does not of itself provide any greater degree of protection for either party than an ordinary power of attorney.

3.28 The protection afforded by the LPA is in the making and registration of the power. Once those steps have been taken and the LPA is in place, there is no further formal protection for the donor. The status of the LPA and the statutory presumption of capacity may well make it easier for the confused and the vulnerable to make mistakes which will be harder to detect in practice. Although LPAs may be drafted to ensure that they will only operate on the onset of incapacity (in the same way as an EPA), this does not appear to be common in practice (although the new prescribed forms introduced on 1 July 2015 now include this as an option).[62] Where a LPA is restricted in this way, the donor ends up reversing the statutory presumption in favour of capacity

---

[60] This follows the recommendation of the Law Commission, see Law Com No 231 (see **3.16**), at para 7.31.

[61] MCA 2005, s 11(7)(a).

[62] See the Lasting Powers of Attorney, Enduring Powers of Attorney and Public Guardian (Amendment) Regulations 2015, SI 2015/1899. See further **3.77**. Problems caused by the policy of early registration are considered in more detail at **3.117**.

intended by Parliament to benefit the donor. Restrictions also cause their own difficulties in terms of drafting, evidence and defining the actual trigger for registration.[63] Should for instance the LPA be used if the donor is physically incapable but mentally capable? Should it be used if the donor needs the attorneys to act (in relation to property and affairs) while he has capacity? What sort of medical evidence should be presented and to whom, before the LPA can be used? Should registration be delayed until the condition has been satisfied? There is then a danger in delaying registration until a triggering condition has arisen, as the registration process takes time and the LPA may need to be used at short notice.[64] Experience suggests that most LPAs are drafted on the basis that there should be flexibility to make decisions for the donor when they need to be taken and the donees should be trusted to act accordingly.

Scope of lasting power of attorney

3.29   The scope of the attorney's authority is very extensive. Principles concerning powers of attorney tend to be drafted in quite wide terms, and then refined or limited for particular situations. For example, an attorney may do anything that may lawfully be done by the donor. There are then things an attorney cannot do, such as make gifts or receive a benefit. But there are cases in which a benefit may be received. A LPA may consist of a web of interconnected powers and limitations, as well as interventions, involving one or more of the following:

(1)   *The donor.* The donor may limit the authority of the attorney so that the power relates only to specified matters or operates in certain circumstances.[65] For example, a power may provide that it only relates to property and affairs or that it will only operate if the donor becomes incapable. Limitations in the form of the power are considered in more detail at **3.76**.

(2)   *Common law.* There are certain personal acts that cannot be delegated to an attorney and an attorney cannot act to benefit him or herself or delegate his or her authority. These and other restrictions, including duties imposed on the attorney by law, such as a duty of care and a fiduciary duty not to benefit from the role, are considered in more detail at **3.4**.[66]

---

[63]   The Law Society Practice Note of 8 December 2011 discourages such a condition, pointing out that: '… as a registered property and financial affairs LPA can be used while the donor retains capacity, restrictions that attempt to limit the attorney's power to use the LPA while the donor still has capacity are difficult to draft'.

[64]   The prescribed period which must expire before the Public Guardian can register an LPA where there are no objections is 6 weeks (Lasting Powers of Attorney, Enduring Powers of Attorney and Public Guardian Regulations 2007, SI 2007/1253, reg 12).

[65]   MCA 2005, s 9(4)(b) and see **3.77**.

[66]   See also the recent case of *Re Harcourt the Public Guardian v A* [2013] COPLR 69 for an illustration of the application of common law principles to a modern LPA. The fiduciary role of the attorney of an attorney (or deputy) is robustly stated in the Code of Practice at para 7.60.

(3) *Statute.* MCA 2005 includes some crucial extensions to these restrictions. Subject to the formalities of the Act being complied with, a LPA is not revoked by the lack of capacity of the donor and in certain circumstances a power can be used to make gifts, delegate trustee functions and make decisions concerning personal welfare matters. MCA 2005 also sets out limits on the scope of the 2005 Act itself and limits on the attorney's authority.[67] For instance an attorney's power to make gifts is defined by MCA 2005, s 12.[68]

(4) *The Court.* The Court of Protection has powers to intervene in the operation of the power. The court can cancel the power in favour of an attorney, attach conditions to the power or provide the attorney with authority to make a decision which is beyond the scope of the attorney's authority within the LPA.[69] The court can also make decisions of its own concerning the property and affairs and welfare of the donor.[70]

Property and affairs

3.30 MCA 2005 does not define in any detail the extent or scope of an attorney's powers over a person's property and affairs. MCA 2005, s 9(1) describes a LPA as 'a power of attorney' which confers authority on a donee to make decisions about 'all or any of' the donor's property and affairs or specified matters concerning the donor's property and affairs. What is peculiar to a LPA (as opposed to an ordinary power of attorney) is that the LPA includes authority to make such decisions in circumstances where the donor no longer has capacity.

3.31 The wording used for the attorney's authority under a LPA is similar, if not as clearly defined as it is under an EPA. Under an EPA, where a donor has conferred general authority, the power 'operates to confer, subject to the restriction [relating to the making of gifts] ... and to any conditions or restrictions contained in the instrument, authority to do on behalf of the donor anything which the donor can lawfully do by an attorney'.[71] Thus the EPA refers back to common law principles. MCA 2005, Sch 4, para 1(2) also provides a useful reminder of an attorney's limited but essential authority to 'maintain the donor or prevent loss to his estate' which can operate when an application for registration has been made and the power has not been registered. The attorney acting under an EPA also has authority to make gifts and provide for the needs of any other person if the donor might be expected to provide for that person's needs.[72]

---

[67] MCA 2005, ss 27–29.
[68] See **3.37–3.43** below.
[69] MCA 2005, s 23. As to the role of the Court of Protection in making decisions concerning LPAs , see **3.138** et seq.
[70] MCA 2005, ss 15–17.
[71] MCA 2005, Sch 4, para 3(1).
[72] MCA 2005, Sch 4, para 3(2) and (3). Curiously, the specific reference to a power to provide for another person's needs is not repeated in the provisions of the MCA 2005 dealing with LPAs. See **3.35** below.

3.32   Nevertheless, a LPA is a power of attorney and must also be understood in terms of the common law relationship between principal and agent. MCA 2005, s 9(1) defines the scope of the attorney's authority in expansive terms, referring to 'all or any' of the donor's property and affairs.' As there is a clear distinction between separate LPAs created for personal welfare and for property and affairs, the latter can only be understood in terms of 'business matters, legal transactions and other dealings of a similar kind.'[73] The attorney has a fiduciary duty to act as the donor's agent and secure the proper management of the donor's estate, for the benefit of the donor.[74] MCA 2005 however takes the attorney into a new area of responsibility, requiring the attorney to make decisions where the donor lacks capacity, and which must be in accordance with the best interests criteria of the Act.[75] The attorney must therefore take into account matters such as the donor's past and present wishes and feelings, beliefs and values, the views of anyone specified as a person to be consulted or caring for the donor or interested in the welfare of the donor as well as the other factors the donor would be likely to consider if he or she had capacity.

Acting in the best interests of the donor

3.33   The importance of the application of 'best interests' to the attorney's role is more than a restatement of the common law duty of an agent to act in the best interests of his or her principal. Neither is the attorney necessarily doing what the donor would have done and making a substituted decision on his behalf. The attorney must act in the best interests of the donor, taking account of a whole range of factors, only one of which might be the actual or likely wishes of the donor.

3.34   The extended test of best interests requires an attorney to possess an appropriate understanding of the character and circumstances of the donor. It may though be difficult to reconcile this with an objective responsibility towards the donor's estate. For example, a donor may have been determined to live in his own home, notwithstanding a worrying degree of self-neglect.[76] Or a donor may have been profligate or lived beyond his means, without an appreciation of his limited resources. The donor may have chosen to make unwise decisions with his lifestyle, property and investments. An attorney may however have to make a tactful compromise between these personal circumstances and his or her responsibilities to the estate (and its preservation for the long-term benefit of the donor). There is often an inherent tension between making the decision which the donor would make (the substituted judgment test) and the decision which is financially prudent or morally correct

---

[73]   *F v West Berkshire HA* [1989] 2 All ER 545, per Lord Brandon at 554.

[74]   The attorney's common law duties are summarised at 3.4 above.

[75]   MCA 2005, s 4(7) and also s 9(4).

[76]   A person acting in a fiduciary role should not replicate the unwise decision which would have been made by the principal. See *Re P* [2009] EWHC 163 (Ch), [2009] COPLR Con Vol 906 (para 42) and in the context of an attorney acting under a LPA see *Re Buckley: The Public Guardian v C* [2013] COPLR 39. In exceptional circumstances, it may be in a person's best interests to have an unwise unwise decision made by a court, see the decision of Hedley J in *CYC v PC and NC* [2012] COPLR 670.

(the objective test). In trying to make the decision which the donor would make, if capable, the attorney may have to assume that the donor could appreciate his predicament as one of the 'other factors he would be likely to consider if he were able to do so'. This dilemma was addressed by Her Honour Judge Marshall QC in the case of *Re S and S*.[77] Although this case related to the wishes of a donor of an EPA (that the attorneys should act jointly and if they could not act jointly a professional deputy should be appointed), the judge explained that the donor's wishes should where possible have priority over other considerations. Although the donor's wishes in this case could be adhered to, they are not by themselves binding. They are a factor that must be considered, and one to which a great deal of weight must be given. But they remain just one of several factors in the balancing act that the attorney must perform when acting in the donor's best interests. As the judge pointed out (at paras 57 and 58):[78]

'... where P can and does express a wish or view which is not irrational (in the sense of being a wish which a person with full capacity might reasonably have), is not impracticable as far as its physical implementation is concerned, and is not irresponsible having regard to the extent of P's resources (ie whether a responsible person of full capacity who had such resources might reasonably consider it worth using the necessary resources to implement his wish) then that situation carries great weight, and effectively gives rise to a presumption in favour of implementing those wishes, unless there is some potential sufficiently detrimental effect for P of doing so which outweighs this.

That might be some extraneous consequence, or some other unforeseen, unknown or unappreciated factor. Whether this further consideration actually should justify overriding P's wishes might then be tested by asking whether, had he known of this further consideration, it appears (from what is known of P) that he would have changed his wishes. It might be further tested by asking whether the seriousness of this countervailing factor in terms of detriment to P is such that it must outweigh the detriment to an adult of having one's wishes overruled, and the sense of impotence, and the frustration and anger, which living with that awareness (insofar as P appreciates it) will cause to P. Given the policy of the Act to empower people to make their own decisions wherever possible, justification for overruling P and "saving him from himself" must, in my judgment be strong and cogent. Otherwise, taking a different course from that which P wishes would be likely to infringe the statutory direction in s 1(6) of the Act, that one must achieve any desired objective by the route which least restricts P's own rights and freedom of actions.'

Where there is a conflict between different objectives, it is important that an attorney should not be exposed to liability. It must be remembered that an attorney under a property and affairs LPA is also acting in a fiduciary role and has been appointed to act on that basis. It is not the role of the attorney to

---

[77] [2008] EWHC B16 (Fam).

[78] This approach was followed in the High Court decisions of Lewison J in the case of *Re P* [2009] EWHC 163 (Ch) and Morgan J in the case of *Re G (TJ)* [2010] EWHC 3005 (COP). It has been applied more recently in similar circumstances, in respecting the donor's wishes concerning who should manage his estate, in the case of *Re DT; the Public Guardian and IT and others* [2015] EWCOP 10.

speculate with the donor's assets or determine alone how or where the donor should be cared for. This point was emphasised in the case of *Re Buckley, the Public Guardian v C*, where the attorney's justification for making an unusual investment (in a reptile breeding business) was that she was doing what the donor would have wanted. Senior Judge Lush was keen to dismiss this approach:[79]

> 'Managing your own money is one thing. Managing someone else's money is an entirely different matter. People who have the capacity to manage their own financial affairs are generally not accountable to anyone and don't need to keep accounts or records of their income and expenditure. They can do whatever they like with their money, and this includes doing nothing at all. They can stash their cash under the mattress, if they wish and, of course, they are entitled to make unwise decisions. None of these options are open to an attorney acting for an incapacitated donor, partly because of their fiduciary obligations and partly because an attorney is required to act in the donor's best interests. The Mental Capacity Act 2005, section 1(5), states that, "an act done, or decision made, under this Act for or on behalf of a person who lacks capacity must be done, or made, in his best interests."'

Thus, not only does the attorney have a fiduciary duty to the donor's estate, exercising this responsibility correctly is also on the best interests of the donor. In practice, it may still be difficult to reconcile the attorney's wishes and doing what the donor would have wanted. Sometimes this can be resolved with tact and good judgment. There may be a range of options, one of which may be close to the donor's wishes. For example, a donor may wish to be generous and make gifts to his children. The attorney can give effect to the sentiment, but the amounts that can be given are limited.[80] Sometimes, there will be a degree of uncertainty or risk that may need to be justified in terms of the donor's best interests. For example, the donor's estate may not be able to manage the cost of a desired level of care. So long as the attorney is not being extravagant or reckless, possibly a degree of has to be accepted to preserve the donor's quality of life. The question for the attorney is: can I do what the donor is expecting me to do, within an acceptable level of risk? If this dilemma still cannot be resolved, then the objective best interests of the donor should prevail. If there is any prospect of the attorney acting beyond the scope of the authority conferred by the donor, or the attorney may be inclined to make an unwise decision, then an application should be made to the Court of Protection.[81]

Power to maintain others

3.35 It is a basic fiduciary duty of an attorney to use the property under his or her control for the benefit of the donor, and not to benefit in person or to benefit a third party. However, the donor may have commitments to other dependents or objects which need to continue beyond the onset of incapacity,

---

[79]   [2013] EWCOP 2965; [2013] COPLR 39.
[80]   See **3.37** below.
[81]   For an example of a case in which the Court of Protection authorised the making of an unwise decision, see the decision of Hedley J in *CYC v PC and NC* [2012] COPLR 670.

and which therefore the donor cannot authorise in person. This difficulty was recognised by the Law Commission in its report *Mental Incapacity*, which recommended that attorneys should have a limited authority to maintain others, subject to any express restriction specified by the donor.[82] Thus the attorney acting under a registered EPA 'may so act in relation to himself or in relation to any other person if the donor might be expected to provide for his or that person's needs respectively; and ... may do whatever the donor might be expected to do to meet those needs'.[83] This power provides some very useful flexibility in practice, especially where a donor has a pre-existing commitment to maintain a spouse or disabled child.[84] This power is distinct from the power to make gifts, which is dealt with at **3.37** below.

3.36 By contrast with the EPA framework, where LPAs are concerned, MCA 2005 makes no reference to the maintenance of another party. In the absence of such an express power, a benefit to the attorney or a third party, is inconsistent with the attorney's fiduciary duty the donor.

In its report *Mental Incapacity* the Law Commission took the view that the power to act in a donor's 'best interests' was more flexible and wider than the power of an attorney at common law, because:[85]

> '... it requires the attorney to consider the wishes and feelings of the donor and the factors he or she would have taken into account, the attorney would in appropriate cases be quite able to meet another person's needs (including the attorney's own needs) or make seasonal or charitable gifts, while still acting within the best interests duty.'

However, this rather sweeping assumption is implicitly contradicted by MCA 2005, s 12, which expressly prohibits an attorney from making gifts, except to the limited extent permitted:

> 'Where a lasting power of attorney confers authority to make decisions about P's property and affairs, it does not authorise a done ... to dispose of the donor's property by making gifts except to the extent permitted by subsection (2).'

This is further emphasised by s 23(4), which provides that any gifts not within the scope of that section must be authorised by the Court of Protection. A benefit to another person of necessity involves a disposition of property and the making of a gift, irrespective of the desirability or necessity of the act. For Inheritance Tax purposes, there is no distinction between maintenance and

---

[82] Law Com No 122, paras 4.23 to 4.30.
[83] MCA 2005, Sch 4, para 3(2); formerly covered by EPAA 1985, s 3(4).
[84] The extent of the EPAA 1985 power was illustrated in the case of *Re Cameron (deceased), Phillips v Cameron* [1999] Ch 386, [1999] 2 All ER 924. In the more recent case of *Re DT; the Public Guardian and IT and others* [2015] EWCOP 10 the attorneys were acting within their authority is using the donor's pension to maintain the donor.
[85] Law Com No 231, at para 7.11.

gifts, which are invariably classed as transfers of value.[86] If the attorney had such wide powers on a wide interpretation of the attorney's ability to act in the donor's best interests, then there would be no need for an express provision dealing solely with gifts and then to a clearly limited extent only.[87] There is no corresponding provision addressing maintenance. While it can be argued that a distinction should be made between the provision of maintenance and the making of a gift, there must be some uncertainty as to whether the attorney can – or the extent to which the attorney should – benefit another person without the sanction of the Court of Protection.[88] The Court takes this approach, but will make a pragmatic exception for a spouse, civil partner or child under the age of 18.[89]

The clear wishes of the donor expressed on the face of the LPA cannot provide assistance, although they may serve as evidence of the donor's wishes. In a case where the donor of a LPA purported to extend the attorney's authority to 'continue to make contributions to my grandchildren's Child Trust Funds and any other saving/pension plans that I fund for their benefit' the Court severed the provision from the instrument.[90] Guidance that 'I hereby express the wish that my Attorneys will continue to pay my contribution to the school fees of my granddaughters, A and B, as per my previous pattern of contributions' was likewise severed.[91] However, the Court has accepted a provision which authorised the attorney to maintain the donor's wife. This was however accepted on the basis that the attorney was simply carrying out the donor's legal obligation to maintain his spouse and not because of an express or implied power in MCA 2005.[92]

---

[86] Inheritance Tax Act 1984, s 3 (although s 11 allows a limited exception for maintenance for a spouse. Civil partner or child who is under the age of 18 or in full time education.

[87] MCA 2005, s 12 and see **3.37–3.43**. The draft Bill prepared by the Law Commission made no reference to gifts or to maintenance, perhaps assuming that all such gifts could be permitted so long as they were within the donor's best interests.

[88] It might be argued that maintenance in return for consideration such as the care of the donor is not the same as a gift. But unless the recipient is actually providing care whose value can be measured, there is bound to be some uncertainty as to what is bounty and what is value. The Court has accepted that the maintenance of a spouse is a legal obligation which an attorney may – or indeed, must – implement (see *Re Bloom*, referred to below). However, unless such an exception exists, an attorney would be acting appropriately in referring such a matter to the Court of Protection.

[89] See guidance 'Avoiding Invalid Provisions in a Lasting Power of Attorney' published on the Government website under www.gov.uk/government/publications/lasting-power-of-attorney-avoid-invalid-provisions. The wording here seems to reflect the wording used by Inheritance Tax Act 1984, s 11 although without reference to a child in full time education. This may be an unlikely situation where most LPAs are made by older people and the Court of Protection decisions on this point involve a donor and a donor's spouse.

[90] See the decision in the case of *Re Wheatley* (an order of the Senior Judge dated 31 January 2011). The decision is no longer reported on the Ministry of Justice website, but is referred to in the guidance on severing invalid provisions (see note above). For severance of provisions in an LPA see **3.62**.

[91] See the decision in *Re Forrest* (an order of the Senior Judge made on 2 March 2012).

[92] See the decision in *Re Bloom* (an order of the Senior Judge made on 16 March 2012). The LPA included the following direction: 'I direct my attorneys to use such of my capital and income as they shall at their discretion deem necessary to make provision for my wife's maintenance and

Where the attorney is also the person whom the donor might be expected to provide for there is a further conflict of interest which the attorney, as a fiduciary, cannot resolve in that role. In the case of *Re Buckley: the Public Guardian v C*, Senior Judge Lush stated emphatically that (subject to a sensible *de minimis* exception), any gift that exceeds the scope of the attorney's authority under s 23 as well as loans to the attorney or attorney's family or any other transaction involving a conflict of interest must be approved by the Court of Protection.[93]

Limited power to make gifts

3.37 MCA 2005, s 12 restates the principle that an attorney cannot make gifts, but allows gifts to be made in certain limited circumstances. The donor can limit this authority, but cannot extend it.[94] Subject to any limitation contained in the power, the donee may make gifts:[95]

'(a) on customary occasions to persons (including himself) who are related to or connected with the donor, or

(b) to any charity to whom the donor made or might have been expected to make gifts,

if the value of each such gift is not unreasonable having regard to all the circumstances and, in particular, the size of the donor's estate.'

3.38 MCA 2005 therefore imposes four basic conditions on an attorney before a gift can be made:

(1) there must be no restriction in the power itself which prevents the gift from being made;

(2) the gift must be made on a 'customary occasion';

(3) an individual must be related to or connected with the donor, while a charity must be one which has benefited or might be expected to benefit from the donor; and

---

benefit.' The Court severed the reference to 'benefit' but allowed the reference to 'maintenance' to remain in place. The Court also confirmed its understanding that the attorney's authority to maintain the donor's spouse rested on the donor's own common law duties to his wife. This approach was queried in the later case of *Re Strange* (an order of the senior judge made on 21 May 2012). Even if there is no common law obligation of one spouse to maintain the other, other statutes impose maintenance obligations. For example a donor's estate can be required to provide for the maintenance of a spouse under the Inheritance (Provision for Family and Dependants) Act 1975.

[93] *Re Buckley: The Public Guardian v C* [2013] COPLR 39.

[94] See the decision in the case of *Re Baker* (an order of the Senior Judge made on 12 November 2010). An LPA included the following provision: 'I authorise my Attorneys to make gifts from my assets on such terms and conditions as they think fit, for the purposes of inheritance tax planning, including but not restricted to the making of gifts in line with the annual lifetime gift allowance'. On the application of the Public Guardian the provision was severed on the grounds that it contravened s 12 of the MCA 2005.

[95] MCA 2005, s 12(2).

(4)   the value of any gift must not be unreasonable having regard to all the circumstances and especially to the value of the donor's estate.

3.39   'Customary occasion' is defined by MCA 2005, to allow for all types of family, seasonal or religious events which justify the making of a gift, as:[96]

'(a)   the occasion or anniversary of a birth, a marriage or the formation of a civil partnership, or
(b)   any other occasion on which presents are customarily given within families or among friends or associates.'

3.40   The attorney cannot therefore make a gift at a time that is not a 'customary occasion' such as the beginning or end of a tax year, or to make gifts of surplus income at the end of a tax year.[97] For the attorney to make a valid gift as part of a tax-planning exercise, it must also be of a 'customary occasion'. An attorney who wishes to make a series of small gifts to the donor's children and grandchildren cannot therefore make simultaneous payments on 6 April. The payments would need to be made on each birthday, or may be made at the same time at Christmas.

3.41   Although any gift made by an attorney on behalf of a donor should be in the donor's best interests, MCA 2005, s 12 contains an express provision that where the gift is to a charity, the charity must be one 'to whom the donor made or might have been expected to make gifts'. This would, for instance, allow an attorney to continue an established pattern of giving, for example, maintaining standing orders to charities. This power is therefore meant to be used to continue existing arrangements or to reflect past associations and interests of the donor, rather than to reflect new wishes and interests.

3.42   Consideration of the donor's best interests is consistent with the attorney's responsibilities to act prudently in relation to the donor's estate. A donor who had in the past been very generous may now have a commitment to funding long term care costs. The sale of the donor's property may mean that gifts are now affordable. These are factors that the donor would consider if he had capacity. The gift must in any event comply with MCA 2005, s 12 and be reasonable 'having regard to all the circumstances and, in particular, the size of the donor's estate'. The attorney cannot avoid a fiduciary duty to the estate and could not make a gift which the donor could not afford to make. It is for the attorney to exercise his or her judgment in measuring the appropriate value of a gift. There is no fixed limit as to what is reasonable or not. Different recipients may have greater or lesser needs or be more or less deserving of a gift. A wealthy donor may be able to afford a gift of several thousand pounds, although a gift of £20,000 was treated as beyond the scope of an attorney's authority under an EPA.[98] A donor with limited capital and in receipt of

---

[96]   MCA 2005, s 12(3).
[97]   See the case of *Re PC: the Public Guardian v AC and JC* [2014] EWCOP 41 where a LPA was revoked due to excessive gifts made by attorneys, ostensibly to mitigate Inheritance Tax.
[98]   See *Re W (Enduring Power of Attorney)* [2001] Ch 609, [2001] 4 All ER 88 and in particular

benefits may, by contrast, only be able to afford a gift of a few pounds. In any event, an attorney acting under an LPA should have regard to the guidance given by Senior Judge Lush in the case of *Re GM* [2013] COPLR 290. Although this judgment referred to the conduct of a deputy, the deputy's authority in this case – as in most cases – reflects the statutory wording used to define an attorney's attorney. The judge stated that gifts beyond a *de minimis* level should not be made without the express authority of the court. The *de minimis* exception could be construed as covering use of the annual IHT exemption of £3,000 and use of the annual small gifts exemption of £250 per person, up to a maximum of, say, 10 people where P has a life expectancy of less than 5 years, has an estate in excess of the IHT nil rate band, the gifts are affordable by P and there is no evidence that P would be opposed to gifts of this magnitude. Gifts which are potentially exempt transfers or which are made from surplus income to avoid Inheritance Tax should only be made on the authority of the court.

3.43 Where there is any doubt about the attorney's authority to make the gift or it is clear that a proposed gift exceeds the attorney's authority under the LPA, the Court of Protection can authorise the gift under MCA 2005, s 23, which deals with the court's powers in relation to the operation of LPAs. Under this power, the Court can authorise the making of gifts which are not permitted by s12(2). The court cannot, however, ignore an express limitation in the power itself. This section would not allow the Court to ignore an express restriction relating to the making of gifts.[99] In this situation, the attorney or any other person who may apply, may request the court to authorise a gift under MCA 2005, s 18(1)(b).[100] However, the court would be required to have regard to the restriction in the LPA which would stand as a 'relevant written statement' in determining the donor's best interests.[101]

---

the comments of the judge at first instance, Jules Sher QC [2000] 1 All ER 175 at p 181 and [2000] Ch 343 at p 349. At the time of the hearing, and allowing for three gifts of £20,000 each to the three children of the donor, the estate was worth approximately £260,000. Apart from the value of the gifts, they were made following the sale of a property. The facts that the donor had the resources and that the gifts would potentially reduce liability to inheritance tax ensured that the gifts were sufficient to render them beyond the scope of the attorney's authority.

[99] See *Re R (enduring power of attorney)* [1990] Ch 647, [1990] 2 All ER 893 where the EPA contained an express restriction that the attorney could not make gifts to friends or relatives. The position should not be different where an LPA is in issue. This does not prevent a person applying to the Court of Protection for an order for a gift under MCA 2005, s 18(1)(b). Although the Court is not bound by a restriction on the face of the LPA, this would be a factor that the court would have to take into account.

[100] Unless the LPA expressly prevents the making of gifts, the attorney has a choice between ss 23(4) and 18(1)(b). There are therefore two similar provisions that can be used. This may be due to the fact that EPAA 1985 provided authority for the Court to authorise gifts by attorneys (which is now contained in MCA 2005, Sch 4, para 16(e)) so that attorneys would have their own legislative framework.

[101] MCA 2005, s 4(6)(a).

The donor as trustee

3.44 A LPA confers the same rights as an EPA in favour of an attorney who is a trustee of land. An attorney acting under a LPA has no power to act as a trustee unless the power complies with the Trustee Act 1925, s 25 or the provisions of the Trustee Act 1925, s 36 apply. This latter provision saves most domestic situations where a property is owned by husband and wife under a trust for land. One of the owners, who is also a trustee for land becomes incapable. To fulfil the 'two trustee' rule, the attorney of the incapable trustee – acting under a registered power[102] – can appoint a new trustee to act on the sale and give a valid receipt for capital monies.[103] An appointment of a new trustee in place of the donor by the donee of a LPA may however have to be accompanied by medical evidence of the lack of capacity, as the fact of registration is not evidence that the trustee lacks capacity to exercise his functions as a trustee for the purposes of the Law of Property Act 1925, s 22.

The donor as a litigant

3.45 A person's right or standing to conduct proceedings is governed by the relevant Rules of Court in which those proceedings take place. Civil proceedings in the High Court and County Court are governed by the Civil Procedure Rules 1998 (CPR).[104] The issue of whether a person has capacity to conduct or settle proceedings is the very matter for which capacity is required. A person may therefore have capacity to issue and then settle proceedings even though he or she might otherwise be unable to administer his or her property and affairs.[105] CPR Part 21 therefore distinguishes between the person conducting proceedings who is the 'protected party' and the person who is in receipt of a damages award who is the 'protected beneficiary'.

3.46 The litigation friend can be appointed to act by the Court of Protection[106] but if the Court of Protection is not involved in the affairs of the person who lacks capacity, a suitable representative can nominate him or herself as litigation friend. The litigation friend must be someone capable of acting in the protected party's best interests with no conflict of interest in the matter and whose role is limited to the proceedings in question.

3.47 An attorney acting under a LPA has no standing as an attorney to bring or defend proceedings on behalf of the donor who lacks capacity.[107] There is no

---

[102] 'Registered power' is defined as an 'Enduring Power of Attorney or Lasting Power of Attorney registered under the Mental Capacity Act 2005' (Trustee Act 1925, s 36(6C)).

[103] Trustee Act 1925, s 36(6A).

[104] SI 1998/3132.

[105] *Masterman-Lister v Jewell* [2002] EWHC 417 (QB), [2002] All ER 247 (Mar); on appeal sub nom *Masterman-Lister v Jewell* [2002] EWCA Civ 1889, [2003] 3 All ER 162, [2003] 1 WLR 1511.

[106] MCA 2005, s 18(1)(k).

[107] The Law Commission's draft Bill proposed giving the attorney power over 'all matters relating to the donor's property or affairs, including the conduct of legal proceedings' (clause 16(1) of the draft Bill set out as Appendix A to Law Com No 231 (see **3.16**)). There is no corresponding reference in MCA 2005.

reference in the CPR to an attorney. There is therefore no change to the established procedure whereby if the donor lacks capacity, the attorney – if he or she wishes to act in the proceedings – must demonstrate his or her suitability to act as a litigation friend or obtain the express authority of the Court of Protection to conduct the proceedings.[108]

Welfare matters

3.48 The donor of a personal welfare LPA may authorise the attorney to make decisions on behalf of the donor about his or her personal welfare or specified matters concerning personal welfare. This appears at first sight an extensive power to make vitally important decisions such as where and how the donor shall live and to give or refuse consent to treatment.[109] In certain circumstances, the attorney's authority may even extend to giving or refusing consent to life-sustaining treatment.

3.49 The principle application of this authority is to enable those providing health care or treatment for a person who lacks capacity to obtain consent to what they propose to do in that person's best interests. A doctor performing a hip replacement or a dentist fitting a denture can be assured of having formal consent to an invasive treatment rather than having to rely on his or her own judgment about the necessity of the treatment and whether it is covered by MCA 2005, s 5.[110] A LPA also gives an attorney certain rights, in particular:

- a person or body determining whether a proposed act is in the best interests of the incapable person must take into account the views of, and if possible consult, the donee of the LPA (MCA 2005, s 4(7));

- an act performed in connection with 'care or treatment' under MCA 2005, s 5 is not authorised by that section if it conflicts with a decision of an attorney acting within the scope of his or her power (MCA 2005, s 6(6)(a));

- a LPA made after an advance decision conferring authority in respect of treatment to which the advance decision relates takes precedence over the refusal of consent contained in the advance decision (MCA 2005, s 25(2)(b)); and

- the attorney may apply to the Court of Protection for the exercise of any of its powers under MCA 2005 without seeking prior permission (MCA 2005, s 50(1)(b)).

Limits on welfare matters

3.50 The scope of an attorney's authority in welfare matters is more limited than may at first be apparent. The principal limitations are as follows:

---

[108] See *Gregory v Turner* [2003] EWCA Civ 183. Although this case concerned an action conducted by an attorney acting under an EPA, the principle will be the same where a LPA is concerned.

[109] MCA 2005, s 11(7)(c).

[110] Acts in connection with care or treatment are dealt with at **2.158ff**.

- Any act performed by an attorney must be in accordance with the donor's best interests (MCA 2005, ss 1(5) and 4)).

- There is no power to make decisions if the donor has capacity to make decisions for him or herself (MCA 2005, s 11(7)(a)). The fact that there is a valid registered LPA in place does not of itself authorise the person treating the donor to take instructions directly from the attorney. The carer or clinician must also be satisfied that the donor lacks capacity.

- A LPA does not authorise the attorney to restrain the donor unless the attorney reasonably believes that it is necessary to prevent harm to the donor and the act of restraint is a proportionate response to the likelihood of the donor suffering harm and the seriousness of that harm (MCA 2005, s 11(3) and (4)).

- Any restraint of the donor cannot deprive the donor of his or her liberty within the meaning of Art 5(1) of the European Convention on Human Rights (MCA 2005, s 11(6)). This may be at odds with the power to restrain the donor which by its nature deprives the donor of his or her liberty. In the light of the *Bournewood* case, it is likely that the power to 'restrain' under MCA 2005 will be interpreted narrowly, for use in emergencies or as a very temporary measure.[111] A longer-term detention of a person who cannot consent to it or detention for the purposes of treatment, must either be authorised by the Court of Protection under MCA 2005, s 16(2)(a) or by one of the bodies empowered by MCA 2005, Sch 1A using the Deprivation of Liberty Safeguards.[112]

- The donor's authority to consent to care or treatment is subject to a valid and applicable advance decision made after the LPA.[113]

- The attorney only has authority to give or refuse consent to life-sustaining treatment if this is expressly allowed by the LPA and this authority is furthermore subject to any restrictions or conditions in the power.[114] This power of 'life and death' is considered in more detail below, but is in its turn subject to two further safeguards:
  - a person considering whether a life-sustaining treatment is in a person's best interests must not be motivated by a desire to bring about that person's death;[115] and

---

[111] *HL v United Kingdom* (2004) 5 October (the Strasbourg proceedings arising out of the decision of the House of Lords in *R v Bournewood Community and Mental Health NHS Trust ex p L* [1999] 1 AC 458, [1998] All ER 303).

[112] For a more detailed consideration of the powers of restraint in MCA 2005 in the light of the European Convention on Human Rights, see Chapter 6. The Act has been considerably amended by the Mental Health Act 2007, which introduced new safeguards dealing with the deprivation of liberty.

[113] MCA 2005, ss 11(7)(b) and 25(7).

[114] MCA 2005, s 11(8).

[115] MCA 2005, s 4(5). This was a late amendment to the Mental Capacity Bill, first referred to in a letter from the Lord Chancellor to Archbishop Smith on 14 December 2004 and subsequently incorporated in an amendment introduced in the House of Lords by Baroness Ashton of Upholland.

- the declaration in MCA 2005, s 62 that the existing law relating to murder or manslaughter is not affected by anything contained in MCA 2005.

- An attorney acting under a welfare LPA cannot compel the carrying out of a particular treatment or decision. An attorney may give or refuse consent to treatment, but if a doctor is unwilling to carry out a treatment, the attorney cannot force another person to make a decision which he or she believes is contrary to the donor's best interests.[116]

- MCA 2005 confers no authority on any person or body to make decisions in respect of:
  - family relations, including consent to a marriage or civil partnership, sexual relations, divorce (based on 2 years' separation) and parental responsibilities relating to a child's welfare;[117]
  - MCA 2005 matters, where medical treatment is required for mental disorder as defined by the Mental Health Act 1983;[118] and
  - voting rights where the election is for any public office or at a referendum.[119]

3.51 It is unclear therefore how useful or widespread welfare LPAs have become since MCA 2005 came into force. The majority of LPAs appear to be restricted to property and affairs.[120] Even where welfare LPAs are made, they are not necessarily used in practice. They are made at a time when the donor has capacity and to bring peace of mind, even if they do not need to be used. Even when they do need to be used, it is not necessarily the case that a lay attorney must make a complex welfare decision. It may be that beyond giving the donor peace of mind, they ensure that a person named by the donor has authority to act as a 'consultee' or advocate at a time when the donor lacks capacity, thus someone who can speak for the donor when the donor can no longer speak for him or herself. Experience of the operation of the new LPA forms indicates that they are of limited popularity or applicability where personal welfare matters are concerned. The length and complexity of the statutory forms acts as a deterrent to all but the most determined of donors. Many donors appreciate the usefulness of a property and affairs LPA and can contemplate the circumstances in which the LPA will be used. It is harder to anticipate the circumstances in which a personal welfare LPA will be needed unless the donor is suffering a long running condition and is concerned about the making of day to day decisions. Even then, the clearly expressed wishes of

---

[116] See *AVS v a NHS Foundation Trust* [2011] EWCA Civ 7, [2011] COPLR Con Vol 219.

[117] MCA 2005, s 27.

[118] MCA 2005, s 28 and see also Mental Health Act 1983, s 1(2), which defines 'mental disorder' as 'mental illness, arrested or incomplete development of mind, psychopathic disorder and any other disorder or disability of mind'.

[119] MCA 2005, s 29. The Act makes no reference to voting as a member of any other association such as a political party or unincorporated association.

[120] The Office of the Public Guardian Annual Report does not distinguish between property and affairs LPAs and welfare LPAs. It is thought that approximately 90% of all LPAs are property and affairs LPAs. This is supported by anecdotal and practical experience. Furthermore, many welfare LPAs are made as a form of insurance, without necessarily being used.

the potential donor should inform a decision maker acting at a time when capacity is lacking, so that there are alternative ways of addressing these concerns.[121]

3.52 The provisions of MCA 2005 relating to LPAs and life-sustaining treatment are both confusing and controversial.[122] How, for instance, is the authority of an attorney to refuse consent to 'life-sustaining treatment' reconciled with the requirement that 'best interests' cannot include a desire to bring about the death of the donor? These provisions of the Act appear mutually inconsistent, but the Act does clearly allow the donor to authorise the attorney to make these decisions on his or her behalf. The only way of giving effect to this requirement is to ensure that a decision to withhold treatment can be made on the basis that it is unduly burdensome or futile and it is not in the best interests of the donor to continue treatment. The motive of the attorney is to relieve pain and suffering and not primarily or exclusively to bring about the death of the donor.[123]

3.53 The problem remains therefore that LPAs may be easy to abuse.[124] The attorney may well end up as sole arbiter of whether a refusal of a treatment is in the donor's 'best interests'. This gives rise to several potential problems:

- MCA 2005 does not address the fundamental question of who is making the decision. The attorney is still exercising his or her judgment as to what is in the donor's best interests;[125]

- doctors and other carers may find that the permission of an attorney to withdraw life-sustaining treatment avoids the inconvenience of a more detailed or independent assessment of the donor's best wishes;

- the fiduciary character of a power of attorney is more difficult to apply to a power which relates to welfare. Many attorneys will have an obvious conflict of interest as potential beneficiaries of the donor's estate. While an attorney (who is a beneficiary) should not benefit from his or her dealings with the property and affairs of the donor, there is no equivalent safeguard to dealings with the welfare of the donor;

- a person may be deemed to lack capacity because he or she is unable to communicate a decision;[126]

- an attorney acting in respect of a donor's welfare will generally be a relative or friend, and is unlikely to be a professional person with a

---

[121] See **3.55** below.

[122] An article in the *Daily Mail* of 8 December 2004 by Melanie Philips, headed 'A barbaric Bill that would destroy the value of life', was not untypical of some of the press coverage of the Bill at the time of its passage in the House of Commons.

[123] See Mental Capacity Act 2005: Code of Practice, at para 5.31.

[124] The scope for abuse in the creation of LPAs is considered at **3.84**.

[125] Much of the controversy around this question is based on the assumption that the attorney will bring about the death of the donor when the donor might not have wished that outcome. But the reverse scenario might also cause concern, where the attorney refuses consent to the withdrawal of treatment which prolongs the life of a donor who has no desire to go on living.

[126] MCA 2005, s 3(1)(d).

professional duty of care. It is unclear therefore what skill or judgment a lay attorney may be expected to exercise in making welfare decisions;

- an attorney acting in the best interests of the donor must take account of the views of anyone caring for the donor, so may be expected to act on medical advice where this is appropriate. But a decision to treat or not to treat can only be informed by medical advice – the actual decision remains with the attorney. The attorney makes what he or she believes to be the right decision and is protected by MCA 2005 so long as the attorney 'reasonably believes that what he does or decides is in the best interests of the person concerned'.[127]

3.54 Although LPAs will be of use to some people in some circumstances, these concerns and the extent of the attorney's powers will need to be addressed carefully by donors when executing LPAs. The drafting and execution of LPAs will therefore be a relatively painstaking process, involving clear professional advice from solicitors and doctors. This will affect the costs involved and either deter potential donors from making LPAs or encourage the making of such powers without proper advice or assistance.

Alternatives to welfare lasting powers of attorney

3.55 While there are situations in which LPAs are necessary and useful, many people who might benefit from their provision will be put off by the length and complexity of the forms. If they seek professional assistance, they may be further deterred by the costs involved. They may therefore consider whether a LPA is really necessary and whether their objectives can be achieved in other ways:

- MCA 2005, s 5 provides a defence for a person who carries out an act in connection with the care or treatment of a person lacking capacity so long as the act carried out is in that person's best interests. Most day to day acts of care and treatment of persons who lack capacity are carried out by carers and doctors without the permission of an attorney or deputy or order of the Court of Protection, relying on this provision.

- Any determination of P's best interests requires the person making the determination to take into account the views of 'anyone named as someone to be consulted' as well as the views of anyone engaged in caring for P or interested in his or her welfare.[128] Many people worry that when they lack capacity their loved ones will have no rights and that they will be abandoned to painful and pointless treatment. Although in practice it would be unethical for a physician to treat a patient lacking capacity without consulting the views of family and carers and MCA 2005 gives

---

[127] MCA 2005, s 4(9).
[128] MCA 2005, s 4(7).

carers rights to be consulted.[129] However, such rights are not binding or prescriptive and are may be just one of many factors to be taken into account.

- MCA 2005 gives statutory recognition to an advance refusal of treatment.[130] The difference between an advance refusal and a LPA is that the former represents the decision of the person made at a time when he or she has capacity for use when he or she subsequently lacks capacity; the LPA, by contrast, requires the attorney to make the decision at the relevant time. While the LPA has the benefit of being a flexible document, an advance directive is easier to complete. So long as it is clear in its purpose, there is no prescribed form. Only an advance refusal of life-sustaining treatment must be in writing and witnessed.[131] It may well be that many individuals who are primarily concerned at being over-treated will find that a simple advance refusal of treatment will meet those concerns.

- While an advance decision may appear overly inflexible or prescriptive, a person may also provide a 'relevant written statement' which must be considered by anyone making a decision on behalf of such person while lacking capacity. This might not necessarily be an advance directive. For instance, a statement expressing a wish not to be resuscitated or kept alive in certain circumstance might not be too vague to be applicable or not signed and witnessed and thus not valid. However, many people will be satisfied knowing that their wishes will be taken into account but that there will be some flexibility to take account of other considerations.[132]

FORM OF LASTING POWER OF ATTORNEY

Who can give a lasting power of attorney?

3.56 Any person who has reached the age of 18 and who has capacity to do so, may grant a LPA.[133] For a LPA to be effective, it must be made in a prescribed form and in a prescribed manner, must comply with certain requirements as to the appointment of an attorney and must be registered.

Prescribed forms

3.57 No instrument can be effective as a LPA unless it is in the prescribed form.[134] The principle of using a standard statutory form is the same that applied to an EPA made prior to 1 October 2007. However, the 2007

---

[129] See, eg, the General Medical Council Guidelines considered in the case of *R (on the application of Burke) v General Medical Council* [2005] EWCA Civ 1003.

[130] MCA 2005, ss 24–26.

[131] MCA 2005, s 25(6).

[132] See for example the consideration given to the wishes expressed by M in the case of *W v M & S* [2011] EWHC 2443 (Fam). For a more detailed account of advance decisions and their relevance see Chapter 5.

[133] For capacity to grant a LPA, see **3.109–3.110**.

[134] MCA 2005, Sch 1, Part 1.

Regulations provide for two different prescribed forms depending on whether the power relates to personal welfare or property and affairs. The forms that accompanied the MCA 2005 have been revised and replaced with new forms introduced on 1 October 2009 and 1 July 2015. The current forms are prescribed by the Lasting Powers of Attorney, Enduring Powers of Attorney and Public Guardian (Amendment) Regulations 2015.[135]

Use of different prescribed forms

3.58 Because different powers may be given for different purposes, there are two prescribed forms, one for personal welfare matters and one for property and affairs.[136]

3.59 The same donor may therefore give two LPAs dealing respectively with personal welfare matters and property and affairs respectively. Different considerations apply to the requirements and content of each power, different attorneys may be appointed for different purposes and the powers may be registered at different times. For instance, a donor may want a solicitor to act as an attorney in respect of property and affairs but a relative to act in respect of personal welfare matters. The former power can also be used at any time after it has been registered and without reference to the capacity of the donor; a power dealing with personal welfare matters only extends to making decisions in circumstances where the donor lacks capacity.[137] The LPAs may also be made at different times. A donor may create a LPA when he or she has capacity and requires assistance and then makes a welfare power later to anticipate medical treatment. The donor may already have made an EPA and now requires a separate welfare LPA.

Defective forms

3.60 At first sight, MCA 2005 appears unequivocal about a LPA being in the prescribed form. Thus s 9(3) clearly states that an instrument which does not comply with the relevant sections 'confers no authority'. When it comes to registration, Sch 1, para 11(1) states that the Public Guardian must not register an instrument (unless directed to do so by the court) if it appears to him that the instrument is not made in accordance with Sch 1. The role of the Public Guardian is to register the instrument and act as the gatekeeper or guardian of the system. Registration confers formal validity on the power. It is therefore vital for the integrity of the system that a defective form is not registered and therefore the Public Guardian is obliged to refuse registration of a defective

---

[135] SI 2015/899. The 2015 Regulations amend the 2007 Regulations, SI 2007/1253. The original prescribed forms issued under the 2007 Regulations could be used until 1 April 2011. New forms were introduced on 1 October 2009 by the Lasting Powers of Attorney, Enduring Powers of Attorney and Public Guardian (Amendment) Regulations 2009, SI 2009/1884. These remain valid until 31 December 2015.

[136] Although MCA 2005, Sch 1, Part 1, para 1(2) allows for an instrument dealing with *both* welfare matters and property and affairs, a hybrid form has not been prescribed. The measure requiring the prescribed forms is contained in the Lasting Powers of Attorney, Enduring Powers of Attorney and Public Guardian Regulations 2007, SI 2007/1253, reg 5.

[137] MCA 2005, s 11(7)(a).

instrument, 'if it appears to the Public Guardian' that the instrument has not been made in accordance with schedule 1 of the Act.[138]

On receipt of an application to register an instrument that is potentially defective, the Public Guardian has a limited number of options. He may:

- Reject the application and return the papers to the applicant. The applicant may then either correct the LPA or apply to the Court of Protection to exercise its powers relating to the validity of the LPA.
- The Public Guardian has a limited power to register a LPA if there is a minor error or 'slip'. Sch 1, para 3(1) 'if an instrument differs in an immaterial respect in form or mode of expression from the prescribed form, it is to be treated by the Public Guardian as sufficient in point of form and expression.[139]
- Apply to the court to exercise its powers. Under Sch 1, para 11(2) the Public Guardian must refer to the court an instrument which contains a provision which prevents it from operating as an LPA, for the court to sever the provision. If it appears to the Public Guardian that the LPA may be valid but there is a doubt for instance over the capacity of the donor, then the Public Guardian will refer it to the court.

3.61 The Court of Protection has a number of powers under MCA 2005 to determine questions relating to the validity or form of a LPA:

- Under s 23(1) the court may 'determine any question as to the meaning or effect of a lasting power of attorney or an instrument purporting to create one.'
- Under Sch 1, para 3(2) the court may 'declare that an instrument which is not in the prescribed form is to be treated as if it were, if it is satisfied that the persons executing the instrument intended it to create a lasting power of attorney.'
- Under s 23(1) and Sch 1, para 11(4) the court may sever a provision from an instrument which prevents it operating as a valid LPA.

3.62 The interaction of the Public Guardian's responsibility to register an LPA and the court's authority to determine the validity of the power, whether by a declaration or severance of a provision which would otherwise invalidate the power is illustrated by a number of cases reported by way of short summaries on the website of the Public Guardian. Many of these cases relate to restrictions

---

[138] MCA 2005, Sch 1, para 11(1).

[139] This might be used where there is a clerical error where the content or meaning in the power can be readily inferred from other evidence. For example, an inconsistency in an address, a crossing out and correction or a box has been ticked incorrectly or not ticked. For example, the pre-2009 forms required a certificate provider to tick the box marked 'I am 18 or over'. Where the certificate provider also states his qualification as a consultant psychiatrist or solicitor, ticking this box might be considered immaterial.

or conditions that are inconsistent either with the status of an attorney or the appointment of more than one attorney. For example:

- In the case of *Re Davies* (an order of the Senior Judge made on 5 July 2010), the donor appointed two attorneys, A and B, to act jointly and severally. He then imposed the following restriction: 'If in the unlikely event of A and B not being wholly in agreement, B is to defer to the wishes of A.' On the application of the Public Guardian the court severed the restriction as being incompatible with a joint and several appointment.

- In the case of *Re Clarke* (an order of the Senior Judge made on 18 November 2009) the donor appointed three attorneys, A (his wife), B, and C, to be his attorneys. They were appointed to act jointly in some matters and jointly and severally in others. He then stated that the attorneys were to act independently for transactions not exceeding £5,000 'but together in respect of all other decisions subject to my wife A's opinion prevailing in the event that my attorneys are not unanimous in any decision involving property or expenditure exceeding £5,000'. On the application of the Public Guardian, the words 'subject to my wife A's opinion ...' onwards were severed on the ground that they purported to allow one of the three attorneys to act independently in relation to matters that had been specified as subject to the joint decision making powers of the attorneys.

- In the case of *Re Moore* (an order of the Senior Judge made on 26 October 2010) the donor appointed three attorneys to act jointly. She then imposed the following restriction: 'At least two attorneys to act on any transactions'. On the application of the Public Guardian the court severed the restriction as being incompatible with a joint appointment.

- In the case of *Re Weyell* (an order of the senior Judge made on 2 December 2010) the donor appointed three attorneys, A, B and C, to act jointly for some decisions and jointly and severally for others. He then imposed the following restrictions:
  '(a) Two out of three of my attorneys must act jointly in relation to any transaction with a value in excess of £5,000 and my attorneys may act jointly and severally in relation to everything else.
  (b) I direct that when acting jointly and severally where possible my attorneys are to act in the following order of priority: firstly A, then B and then C.'

On the application of the Public Guardian the first restriction was severed as being incompatible with the joint aspect of the appointment. As to the second restriction, the Public Guardian submitted that a direction that attorneys appointed to act jointly and severally must act in an order of priority would normally be regarded as incompatible with a joint and several appointment, the addition of the words 'where possible' made the direction in effect a statement of wishes only. The court accepted this submission and did not sever the second restriction.

- In the case of *Re Sykes* (an order of the Senior Judge made on 9 July 2009), the donor of a property and affairs LPA imposed a restriction stating that no gifts of any of her assets should be made other than 'annual or monthly gifts already being made by me at the date of my signing this LPA by regular bank standing orders or direct debits'. On the application of the Public Guardian the Court severed this restriction on the ground that the gifts envisaged by the donor exceeded the attorney's authority to make gifts as set out in MCA 2005, s 12.[140]

- In the case of *Re Begum* (an order of the Senior Judge made on 24 April 2008), the court directed the severance from a Property and Affairs LPA instrument of the following clauses, on the ground that they were ineffective as part of an LPA:
    (a) 'All decisions about the use or disposal of my property and financial resources must be driven by what my Personal Welfare Lasting Power of Attorney(s) believe will support my long term interests.
    (b) Any decisions affecting assets (individually or together) worth more than £5,000 at any one time must be discussed and agreed with Dr X.
    (c) In the event of there being any disagreement between my Personal Welfare Lasting Power of Attorney(s) and/or Dr X this should be resolved by these parties appointing an independent advocate to adjudicate.'

- In the case of *Re Kittle* (a judgment of the Senior Judge given on 1 December 2009), the court was asked to consider whether a first cousin was prevented from acting as a certificate provider. Regulation 8(3) of the LPA, EPA and PG Regulations 2007 sets out categories of persons who cannot act in this role, who include 'a family member' of the donor or of the attorney (or of the owner, director, manager or employee of any care home in which the donor is living when the instrument is executed). The Public Guardian declined to register the instrument on the ground that a first cousin was a family member of the donor. The court ruled that a first cousin is not a family member, and so the LPA was valid.

- In *Re Forrest* (a decision of the Senior Judge made on 2 March 2012) in *Re Bloom* (an order of the Senior Judge made on 16 March 2012) the Court of Protection severed respectively guidance and a special condition concerning an attorney's power to provide for the maintenance or benefit of another person, which was outside the scope of MCA 2005, s 12.[141]

- In the case of *Re Goodwin* (an order of the Senior Judge made on 17 June 2013) the donor appointed three attorneys and two replacements. Regarding the replacements, she directed that if one ceased to act the other could act alone, and added: 'She should also make every effort to find one or two replacement attorneys to take over her responsibilities in the event of her own death, or if she no longer has the mental capacity to carry on, so that there is a continuing "Lasting Power of Attorney" in place during

---

[140] The clearly defined and limited authority of a donor to make gifts is dealt with at **3.37** above.

[141] These cases are dealt with in more detail at **3.36** above in the context of an attorney's authority to make gifts under the MCA 2005.

the donor's lifetime.' On the application of the Public Guardian this provision was severed on the ground that MCA 2005, s 10(8)(a) invalidates any provision in an LPA giving an attorney power to appoint a substitute or successor.

3.63 It is not, however, always for the court to remedy a failing on the part of the donor or a solicitor and there is a limit as to how far the court will go in assisting a party in these circumstances. It is likely that the circumstances will determine the outcome. There will for instance be cases where the donor no longer has capacity and there is no possibility of a new LPA being prepared. In general, the Public Guardian and the court will assist where possible, especially where the LPA was prepared without professional support or there is a disproportionate burden on the parties to complete a new LPA. In the case of *Re Nazran*, the certificate provider had not completed the first two boxes in Part B of the instrument to confirm that he was acting independently of the donor, was not ineligible to provide a certificate, and was aged 18 or over.[142] The Public Guardian refused to register the instrument. As the donor was suffering a wasting illness and could not make a new LPA, the attorneys applied to the court for a declaration that the instrument was a valid LPA or, alternatively, that the instrument was to be treated as valid under MCA 2005, Sch 1, para 3(2). The court, in the exercise of its discretion under Sch 1, para 3(2), declared that the instrument was to be treated as if it were an LPA and registered accordingly.

Content of LPA

3.64 The current prescribed forms are up to 24 pages long with continuation sheets and the application to register the power (which is part of the prescribed form) and at first sight somewhat daunting.[143] Large parts of the LPA form consists of boxes and fields which may or may not be relevant. A lot of space is taken up by guidance which makes it difficult to distinguish essential details, options and the core provisions of a power of attorney. The wording which distinguishes the form as a power of attorney is almost concealed at section 9 on page 10, amidst the guidance for the donor and the witness to sign. Where there is insufficient space in the form, then supplementary pages need to be added. The 2007 and 2009 forms (the latter of which remain valid to 31 December 2015) could be broken down into their component parts, which reflected the sequence in which they would be completed:

- The Prescribed Information – set out in pages 1–2, which the donor, certificate provider(s) and any attorney(s) are required to read or have read or have read to them;

---

[142] An order of the Senior Judge made on 27 June 2008. This case related to a LPA made using the 2007 prescribed form. This sort of problem is unlikely to occur where the prescribed form is used, as there are fewer fields or boxes for a certificate provider to complete and therefore less scope for errors being made on the face of the document.

[143] As prescribed by the Lasting Powers of Attorney, Enduring Powers of Attorney and Public Guardian (Amendment) Regulations 2015, SI 2015/899.

- Part A – the Donor's Declaration – setting out the powers granted by the donor;
- Part B – the Certificate Provider's Declaration; and
- Part C – the Attorney's Declaration.

The current forms are not so clearly divided and are set out in fifteen sections as follows:

- Section 1 – Donor's details;
- Section 2 – Attorneys' details. There are spaces for up to four attorneys; if further attorneys are to be appointed, a continuation sheet is required;
- Section 3 – Showing how the attorneys are appointed, whether jointly or jointly and severally or jointly for some purposes and jointly and severally for others;
- Section 4 – Replacement attorneys' details. There are spaces for two replacement attorneys; if further replacement attorneys are to be appointed, a continuation sheet is required; a continuation sheet is also required if the power is to specify when or how then may act;
- Section 5 – the property and affairs form allows the donor to specify when the attorneys can make decisions, thus whether the power can be utilised immediately or on the onset of incapacity; the personal welfare power allows the donor to select whether the attorneys can give or refuse consent to life sustaining treatment;
- Section 6 – Showing the names of persons to be notified;
- Section 7 – Preferences and instructions. There is limited space only for preference and instructions and a continuation sheet for this part of the form may be added;
- Section 8 – the Prescribed Information – now headed 'Everyone signing the LPA must read this information';
- Section 9 – Execution by donor;
- Section 10 – certificate of capacity;
- Section 11 – Execution by attorneys or replacement attorneys. The prescribed form incorporates four pages, one for each attorney; more forms can be added if necessary;
- Section 12 – Details of person making application to register the instrument;[144]
- Section 13 – Correspondent's details (where the registered instrument should be returned to)
- Section 14 – Payment details for the application fee; and
- Section 15 – Declaration by person applying to register the instrument.

---

[144] It is assumed that the instrument will be registered as part of the same process and therefore dealt with at the same time. Thus, early registration of the LPA is to be encouraged.

Section 1 – The donor's details

3.65 The prescribed form provides space for the donor to write or print his or her name and address and date of birth. The benefit of the new form is that the donor's details are shown on the very first page of the form, making it easier to use in practice (earlier versions showed the prescribed information at the front of the form, so the user would have to find the third page to identify the donor).

Section 2 – Choice of attorney

3.66 A donor may appoint any person or, in the case of a power relating to property and affairs, a trust corporation, to act as his or her attorney. Apart from where a trust corporation is appointed, the appointment of an attorney is personal and an attorney cannot be appointed by reference to an office or title.[145]

3.67 Where an individual is appointed then he or she must have reached 18 and must not be a bankrupt.[146] If the attorney subsequently becomes bankrupt, then his or her appointment as an attorney is terminated.

3.68 Clearly the choice of attorney is essential to the effective operation of a LPA. And because a LPA may be made many years before it is used, the donor may need some insurance against the risk of an attorney becoming unable to act due to death, divorce, bankruptcy, incapacity or disclaimer. MCA 2005 therefore allows the donor to appoint two or more attorneys and also allows for the appointment of replacement attorneys.

Section 3 – More than one attorney

3.69 MCA 2005, s 10(4) allows the donor to appoint more than one attorney provided that the attorneys are appointed to act 'jointly' or 'jointly and severally'. The Act uses the terms 'jointly' or 'jointly and severally' whereas the 2007 forms use the terms 'together' or 'together and separately'. The current forms use the statutory terminology. Section 10 also permits attorneys to be appointed jointly in respect of some matters and jointly and severally in respect of others. Thus, a donor is able to appoint attorneys to act jointly and severally in respect of his or her investments, but require them to act jointly where a major decision was required, for instance, to sell the donor's home or, in a welfare power, to withhold consent to life-sustaining treatment.[147] If it is

---

[145] The Law Commission assumed that an officeholder could be appointed under existing law (Law Com No 231 (see **3.16**), at para 7.21) but recommended a specific provision authorising an attorney to be described as 'the holder for the time being or a specified office or position'. This provision was not included in MCA 2005, and contrasts with the power of the court to appoint 'the holder for the time being or a specified office or position' as a deputy (MCA 2005, s 19(2)).

[146] MCA 2005, s 10(1).

[147] Care needs to be taken to prevent rendering a joint and several appointment ineffective. See for instance the decision of the Senior Judge in the case of *Re P* where the donor appointed three

unclear whether attorneys are appointed jointly or jointly and severally, the appointment is construed in favour of their being appointed jointly.[148]

3.70 A joint appointment of attorneys clearly provides a greater degree of protection, as the attorneys must act unanimously in any act carried out under the power. For example, a contract for a care home or even a cheque drawn on the donor's bank account must be signed by both attorneys. The disadvantages are that the LPA may be cumbersome to operate in practice and that the LPA is terminated if the appointment of any one attorney fails.[149] These difficulties inherent in a joint appointment can be remedied by limiting the scope of the joint appointment to certain decisions or by appointing a replacement attorney to act on the failure of the joint appointment. Where these issues are addressed, careful drafting is required.

3.71 Where two or more attorneys are appointed *jointly and severally*, each attorney may act independently of the other. Most LPAs which appoint more than one attorney to deal with a person's property and affairs provide for the attorneys being appointed jointly and severally. It is simply more practical for attorneys to work separately, either with a clear division of responsibility between them or on the understanding that one will take a lead role and another will act as a spare or default attorney. However, any potential conflict or discord between the attorneys will make the power extremely difficult to operate in practice. Care must be taken to address the issue of how they are to act at the time the instrument is made, rather than leave matters to wishful thinking. If the authority of one attorney to act independently of another is limited, there is a danger that the 'joint and several' nature of the appointment will be fatally compromised.[150] Where one of the attorneys is a professional attorney, it will also be important for the donor to define the extent to which the professional attorney is expected to be actively involved in the administration of the donor's affairs or the supervision of the other attorney.

---

attorneys to act jointly and severally, and imposed the following restriction: 'I require that two attorneys must act at any one time so that no attorney may act alone.' On the application of the Public Guardian the court severed the restriction on the ground that it was ineffective as part of an LPA. The requirement for a majority or quorum was ineffective as being neither a joint appointment nor a jointly and several appointment for the purposes of s (10)(4). See the Ministry of Justice website, and see also the case of *Re Moore*, described at **3.62** above.

[148] This avoids the problem created by EPAA 1985, s 11(1), where an EPA had to appoint attorneys either jointly or jointly and severally to be valid as an EPA. An instrument that was unclear might therefore be defective. See also *Re E (Enduring Power of Attorney)* [2001] Ch 364, sub nom *Re E, X v Y* [2000] 3 All ER 1004.

[149] MCA 2005, s 10(6).

[150] For instance in the case of *Re Bratt* (an order made by the Senior Judge on 14 September 2009) the donor appointed two attorneys, A and B, to act jointly and severally, and directed that 'B is only to act as attorney in the event of A being physically or mentally incapable of acting in this capacity'. On the application of the Public Guardian this provision was severed as being inconsistent with a joint and several appointment. See also the cases referred to at **3.62** above.

Section 4 – Replacement attorneys

3.72 The top of Section 4 contains the words: 'this section is optional, but we recommend you consider it. Replacement attorneys are a backup in case one of your original attorneys can't make decisions for you any more'. The appointment of a replacement attorney is often desirable, especially as attorneys are often appointed several years before they may need to act. Attorneys cannot appoint their own successors in the same way that trustees can.[151] This preserves the distinction between an attorney and a trustee in that the attorney is the agent of the donor and is appointed personally in his or her own right.[152] MCA 2005 provides expressly for the appointment of a replacement attorney, so that a new attorney, who has also been chosen by the donor, may replace the old attorneys, but only on the failure of the earlier appointment on one of the grounds specified in s 13(6)(a)–(d).[153] Thus if the appointment of the first attorney should fail on the disclaimer, death, divorce, bankruptcy or incapacity of that attorney, a new attorney is appointed, within the same instrument, to act in that event. The replacement attorney is only appointed on the failure of the prior appointment on one of the specified grounds. If, for example, the first appointed attorney is removed by the court for failure to act in the donor's best interests, then the condition that allows the replacement attorney to act is not satisfied.

3.73 A replacement attorney will often be appointed to cover the failure of a joint appointment of attorneys. Where joint attorneys are appointed there will be an obvious concern that the appointment of all the attorneys will fail if the appointment of just one will fail. However this can also give rise to some unintended consequences. For example, a donor may appoint his children A and B to act jointly. Aware of the risk of a joint appointment, the donor takes advantage of the prescribed form to appoint his solicitor C as a replacement attorney. If A dies or becomes bankrupt, then the appointment of both A and B fails and C will then be appointed as sole attorney.[154] Care therefore needs to be taken in drafting as, in this scenario, the donor may well have preferred to have C act with B. The donor therefore needs to appoint three replacement attorneys. On the basis that he could not know which of his children might become unable to act, he would have to re-appoint A, B and C as replacement attorneys, jointly and severally. It is not, however, straightforward re-appointing the same persons in different capacities within the same

---

[151] MCA 2005, s 10(8)(a).

[152] A trust by contrast is a distinct legal entity that may need to be administered for much longer and the trustees owe their primary duty to the beneficiaries.

[153] There was no equivalent provision in the Enduring Powers of Attorney Act 1985. A donor could achieve the same result by creating more than one EPA, with the later being conditional on the failure of the first. See **3.74** below.

[154] See the case of *Re Druce* (an order of the Senior Judge dated 31 May 2011) where the donor made LPAs appointing A and B as her attorneys, to act jointly, and C and D to be her replacement attorneys. She then imposed the following restriction: 'Both C and D should jointly replace the first attorney who needs replacing so that on the first replacement there will be three acting attorneys. No further replacements will be needed.' On the application of the Public Guardian the court severed the restriction as being incompatible with the principle that the survivor of joint attorneys cannot act.

instrument. In the case of *Re Miles*, Senior Judge Lush severed a clause re-appointing attorneys, as the prescribed form did not provide a page for specifying how those attorneys would act, and recommended that a separate conditional LPA should be made. However, this case was based on the 2009 forms.[155] The new forms provide at the end of Section 4 a tick-box and link to a continuation sheet to show 'how replacement attorneys step in and act.' Continuation Sheet 2 then has a tick-box for use where it is to be used in conjunction with Section 4. This can be used to confirm that the replacement attorneys are appointed to act jointly and severally. It can also be used to replace one attorney. For example if the donor appoints A and B jointly and severally, the donor can also appoint C as a replacement for A and D as a replacement for B.

3.74 While it makes sense for a donor to cover as many eventualities as possible within the same instrument, this can give rise to another unexpected complication, whereby the donor does not receive all the protection afforded by the registration process. The practice with EPAs and which was recommended for LPAs by Senior Judge Lush in the case of *Re Miles*, had been for a donor to create separate instruments, with the replacement power taking effect on the failure of the first. In this way, if the first power failed, the attorneys under the second or replacement power would apply to register that instrument. As the new power of attorney could only take effect on the failure of the first, evidence of its failure would need to be produced to register the new EPA and once it was registered, no further explanation would be needed. The protection afforded by the registration process would come into play, even if the first EPA had been registered previously. It was, however, cumbersome to prepare two instruments for use in situations that might not arise and the practice arose of appointing successor attorneys within the same instrument.[156] This would, after all, only reflect the practice used in will drafting. However, as EPAs were usually made long before they would be used, it was anticipated that registration would be effected just once by the first attorney. It was never established what would happen if the EPA was registered by the first attorney who died or became unable to act, leaving the successor attorney appointed on the face of the instrument.[157]

3.75 MCA 2005, s 10(8)(b) provides for a replacement attorney being appointed in the same instrument. In most such cases the first attorney will accept the appointment. The attorney (or donor) sends out the notices in the

---

[155] [2015] EWCOP 40. The case illustrates how complicated LPAs can become when planning for different eventualities.

[156] The practice was shown in *Elderly Clients: A Precedent Manual* (Jordans, 2005) edited by the Master (now Senior Judge) of the Court of Protection, Denzil Lush, and is based on a simple application of existing legal principles. See also Law Com No 231 (see **3.16**), at p 114. This approach was approved in the decision of Lewison J in the case of *Re J (Enduring Power of Attorney)* [2009] EWHC 436 (Ch).

[157] Take the case of a donor who appointed A as his attorney and B as his replacement attorney; on losing capacity, A applied to register the EPA. Some time later, A dies. Presumably B step into his shoes and carry out the functions of an attorney. B should then notify the Public Guardian so that the EPA is noted with the death of A.

usual way and the named persons are satisfied that the attorney is acting in the donor's best interests.[158] Form LPA3 is given to the named persons, but this only shows the names of the original attorneys. Subsequently the authority of the first attorney is terminated. The replacement attorney has already been appointed, but no new registration is required. Although the Public Guardian must be notified, no one else is notified of the existence of a different attorney who unlike the first attorney may be wholly unsuitable for the role.[159] The named person will have no knowledge that a replacement attorney has been appointed, let alone of that attorney's identity. A further difficulty may arise if there is a delay in registration, as the replacement. In many cases, the replacement attorney is also someone who will be concerned for the best interests of the donor. A donor may, for instance, appoint one child as an attorney in the first instance and another child as a replacement attorney. The second child cannot be a named person and is not given notice by the Public Guardian and may be unaware that the instrument is being registered.[160] In contrast, a co-attorney who did not join in making the application for the purposes of the notification requirements is automatically notified.[161]

Section 5 – Limiting when attorneys can make decisions (property and affairs)

3.76 Whereas a welfare LPA can only operate when the donor lacks capacity, a property and affairs LPA is capable of being used at any time as soon as it has been registered. As has been mentioned, this can give rise to problems, especially when combined with a policy which encourages early registration.[162] Many donors wish to remain in control of their affairs for as long as possible and will be concerned that their LPAs may be used prematurely. The new prescribed form for a property and affairs LPA introduced on 1 July 2015 incorporates a provision that expressly deals with this concern. This is set out at Section 5 where the donor is asked: 'When do you want your attorneys to make decisions?' and is then provided with a choice of two options, each with its own tick-box. The first allows the LPA to be used as soon as it has been registered, thus while the donor still has capacity; the second allows the LPA only to be used when the donor lacks capacity.

3.77 It may appear sensible to encourage donors to consider when their LPAs might be used. However, such a provision may also create hostages to fortune. Therefore while donors are encouraged to consider this option, they are also

---

[158] The continued role and effectiveness of persons named as persons to be notified are considered at **3.82ff**.

[159] It is of course open to a donor to create two LPAs with separate appointments, the second taking effect on the failure of the first. But, given the complexity of the forms, it is unlikely that many donors will realistically complete two LPAs to deal with their property and affairs.

[160] This also contrasts with the principle applied in the registration of EPAs where a class of relatives is notified, and a replacement attorney would be notified if within the prescribed class. See MCA 2005, Sch 4, Part 3, para 6(2). The inclusion of named persons and the problems associated with their role is dealt with in more detail at **3.82ff**.

[161] MCA 2005, Sch 1, para 8(2).

[162] See **3.28**.

discouraged from exercising it! The second option, to make use of the LPA conditional on a lack of capacity, is followed by the words 'Be careful – this can make your LPA a lot less useful. Your attorneys might be asked to prove you do not have mental capacity each time they try to use this LPA.' Clearly use of the second option is impractical. Any third party relying on the LPA, such as a bank or building society, will need evidence of the donor's lack of mental capacity to address the decision in issue. Different tests of capacity may be required for different decisions. Furthermore, the use of such a policy sits uncomfortably with the ethos of the property and affairs LPA which is to avoid questions of capacity, so that use of the LPA does not label the donor as incapable and prevent the donor from making decisions which he or she retains capacity to make. The main benefit of this new provision is to force the donor to address the issue of when the LPA should be used. However, the tick-boxes provided only allow for two choices. For such a provision to work, careful consideration needs to be given to how this will work in practice. For instance how will a lack of capacity be proved when the attorney comes to operate the LPA? More detailed instructions need to be set out elsewhere in the form, at Section 7. At which point, consideration should also be given to whether the attorneys are trustworthy and can be relied upon to act at the right time. There may also be simpler and less restrictive ways of using the LPA such as leaving the original with a solicitor who can only release the document if satisfied that it needs to be used, or delaying registration.

Section 6 – Life-sustaining treatment (welfare LPA)

3.78 The authority of an attorney under a welfare LPA does not extend to 'giving or refusing of consent to the carrying out or continuation of life-sustaining treatment' unless the instrument so permits.[163] MCA 2005 does therefore contain a default provision so that a LPA should not deal with issues of life-sustaining treatment unless this is positively specified. The prescribed form departs from this presumption by setting out two choices and requiring the donor to specify one of them, which is contained in Section 5 of the welfare LPA. Thus the donor must sign the box beside Option A or Option B specifying as follows:

A   I want to give my attorney(s) authority to give or refuse consent to life-sustaining treatment;

B   I **do not** want to give my attorney(s) authority to give or refuse consent to life-sustaining treatment.

3.79 As a further safeguard and to prevent the donor signing the wrong box in error, the signature beside the chosen box must be signed in the presence of a witness, who must sign and complete the boxes at the foot of the same page. The form does not specify who can witness this statement. The guidance notes

---

[163] MCA 2005, s 11(8).

on the form merely state that 'the witness must not be an attorney or replacement attorney appointed under this LPA, and must be aged 18 or over.'[164]

Section 7 – Named persons to be notified or told

3.80 LPAs, in the same way as EPAs, are designed as a simple and accessible means of providing a legal basis for future decision-making on behalf of a person who lacks capacity. By exercising a choice over the attorney, the donor of a power of attorney obviates the need for a formal court-based process or official supervision. This does not, however, mean that there is no protection available to a donor and there are in effect three levels of protection:

- the creation of the power of attorney;
- the notification of specified persons on registration; and
- the registration process which allows time for objections to be made by the donor and the persons notified, as well as allowing the registration authority to ensure that the documentation is all correct.

3.81 MCA 2005 improved the protection provided at the first of these levels, as a LPA requires a certificate of capacity from an independent person who can confirm that the donor understands the scope and purpose of the power. However, at the second of these levels, the notification procedure has been reduced in importance. On registration of an EPA, the attorney must notify prescribed members of a class of relatives.[165] By contrast, the donor of a LPA may specify in the instrument the names of one of more persons to be notified of an application to register the LPA. This follows on from the principle that the donor should be free to make his or her own choice of persons to be notified. That principle is taken a stage further, as the donor is also free to specify that there should be no such persons to be notified.[166] Prior to new prescribed forms being introduced on 1 July 2015, the only limit on the donor's freedom of choice was that a named person could not be a donee of the power (including a replacement donee), that there were a maximum of five named persons and that if there were no named persons, then two certificates of capacity must be provided.[167] The new prescribed forms introduced on 1 July 2015 provides space for persons to be notified, but only as an option. This satisfies the literal wording of MCA 2005 which allows the donor to state 'that there are no persons whom he wishes to be notified of any such application.'

---

[164] The declaration concerning life-sustaining treatment is in effect a separate advance statement within the LPA and complies with MCA 2005, s 25(5) and (6).

[165] EPAA 1985, Sch 1, Part 1, para 2(1). The same provisions apply to EPAs registered after 1 October 2007: MCA 2005, Sch 4, Part 3, para 6. Safeguards in the EPA jurisdiction are considered at **3.11**.

[166] MCA 2005, Sch 1, Part 1, para 2(1)(c).

[167] MCA 2005, Sch 1, Part 1, para 2(2)(b). The certificate of capacity is considered in more detail at **3.90ff**.

3.82   The right of the donor to choose or not choose persons to be notified of the application to register the LPA differs significantly from the requirements of EPAA 1985, which requires prescribed members of a class of relatives to be notified. This has proved controversial, but embodies a recommendation of the Law Commission,[168] which was critical of the statutory list of notifiable relatives which:

> '... makes no acknowledgement that close and important relationships may exist outside of legal marriage and blood ties. It conflicts with the autonomy principle to require, regardless of the donor's wishes, that certain relatives must be notified of a private arrangement to govern future decision making.'

3.83   This approach was actively supported by the Government in the long legislative process that led to the passing of MCA 2005. In the Report Stage of the Bill in the House of Lords, the Minister of State, Baroness Ashton provided the following justification:[169]

> 'I said that families are different. I did not say that they were not very important. I simply said that families are not what they used to be. We have lots of different kinds of families. People have many strong relationships – for example, half-siblings, step-children, and different situations within families ...
>
> I am also very clear that this provision is about the donor making a choice. Ultimately, the donor should say who they would like to have notified. It could be a relative, but there may not be any relatives around or the donor may be estranged from his or her family – so there would be little point in notifying a relative. Just because someone is related does not necessarily mean that he will care anything for the donor. He may even have his own selfish motives for showing an interest in trying to object to the donor's chosen attorney.
>
> So the Bill provides freedom of choice, but it does not lose sight of protection. My noble friend has made it clear that he is worried about the coercion or pressure that could be put on someone to give a decision-making power to a person through a lasting power of attorney.
>
> That is why the Bill provides that all applications to register a lasting power of attorney must be accompanied by a certificate from a person of prescribed description that, in his opinion, the donor understands what he is doing and that no fraud or undue pressure is being used to induce the donor to create that lasting power of attorney. It goes one step further than that. Where there is no named person, regulations may require two certificates of that kind to be provided. This is the balance that I feel we have struck within the Bill: freedom and protection working in tandem.'

3.84   The obligation to give notice of an intention to register the power is therefore a key safeguard against abuse. But the then Government's approach was political as much as functional, as concerned with reflecting its particular view of society as protecting the donor. However well-intentioned was this

---

[168]   Law Com No 231 (see **3.16**), at para 7.37.

[169]   *Hansard*, HL Deb, vol 670, ser 5, col 1316 (15 March 2005).

approach, it assumed that the competent donor putting his or her affairs in order is acting with a complete understanding of all the relevant factors and will choose sensibly those persons who might actually be in a position to protect his or her interests in the event of abuse or a future change in circumstances. The benefit inherent in a prescribed list of relatives is lost. Disputes concerning EPAs often come to light when relatives are notified. Sometimes relatives will conduct their own disputes with each other at the expense of the donor, but there are also many cases where the attorney was in a position of trust and confidence at the time the power was made. The attorney may have abused that position of trust to influence a power of attorney in his or her favour; but there are other more innocent but equally difficult cases where at the time the power was made, the choice of attorney seemed sensible. The trusted friend may subsequently have had financial difficulties or have fallen out with the donor; or the favourite nephew may have moved away and become less helpful. Problems may arise with second marriages where the spouse may be appointed to act as an attorney without any notice being given to the donor's children. When preparing a LPA a donor will be under the influence of the circumstances that exist at that time and the persons named will reflect that. By choosing who should be notified or indeed by not notifying anyone, the creation of the LPA can be a purely private act, limited to the persons involved in the process. While it may be good practice for a donor to let other relatives, friends or professional advisers know of the LPA, there is absolutely no requirement for this to be the case.

3.85 In practice, therefore, the act of notifying named persons has added very little value to the registration system. In the absence of any notification of a party who is not connected to the LPA, the registration process does not provide any greater degree of protection. This contrasts with the EPA and the registration requirements that have been carried into MCA 2005, Sch 4 which apply if there is no person capable of being notified. In this case, the Public Guardian cannot register the EPA and 'must undertake such inquiries as he thinks appropriate in all the circumstances.' While such inquiries may be a formality, at least there is some sort of delay that requires an enquiry to be made.

Section 8 – Preferences and instructions

3.86 The authority of an attorney is not only subject to the limitations imposed by MCA 2005 but also any conditions or restrictions specified in the instrument.[170] In view of the wide-ranging scope of a LPA, the donor needs to consider very carefully how the LPA can be 'tailored' to meet his or her requirements and provide the right level of compromise between function and protection. Although the forms are designed with plenty of space for donors to insert their own conditions, there is a danger that instructions made without proper advice will prove unworkable in practice.[171]

---

[170] MCA 2005, s 9(4)(b).
[171] Although the forms are intended for completion without professional help, not every donor

Instructions

3.87 Special instructions that a donor might add, in respect of property and affairs, to the prescribed form include:

- A right to remuneration by a professional attorney. An attorney acts as a fiduciary role and should not benefit from his or her so acting without the consent of the donor. It is therefore advisable for this to be expressly provided for in the instrument.

- Authority for the delegation of investment powers to a professional fund manager. An attorney cannot generally delegate his or her functions except where he or she cannot be expected to attend to them personally.[172]

- Requiring the attorney to keep accounts or to render an account to a co-attorney or to a third party such as another member of the family, a solicitor or accountant. Although an attorney has a common law duty to keep accounts, this is not always followed in practice. The Court of Protection has authority to require an attorney to deliver an account, but it is unlikely that this authority will be widely exercised.[173] Many of the disputes that arise around EPAs and LPAs have been caused by a lack of awareness of what an attorney is doing: a duty or power to disclose information and/or account to another party or to an independent professional often provides an adequate degree of reassurance in such cases.[174]

- Authorising disclosure of personal financial information. An attorney owes a duty of confidentiality and may have concerns about providing other family members with information about the donor's estate. A careful donor should consider whether, when and to what extent information should be disclosed. Family arguments may often be avoided if attorneys are authorised (and therefore encouraged) to disclose information to other family members.

- Restricting the operation of the LPA to use in specified circumstances. The LPA can be used – subject to registration – at any time by the attorney. Many donors will be unhappy with going through the formalities and expense of registration when the power only needs to be used for a limited time or purpose. They may also be unhappy with the prospect of the LPA being used while they still have capacity. Section 5 allows a donor to

---

will be able to deal with this unaided. The Guidance Notes LP12 provides some assistance, and a long list of useful precedents, but not every donor will work through the 48 pages of notes to find the right advice and even this concludes: 'we are not able to provide you with wording for restrictions or conditions. In any particular situation, you may want to seek further advice from a legal or financial professional such as a solicitor or accountant' (at p 38).

[172] The Guidance Notes provide some useful precedents, but not for this case. The notes state, somewhat unhelpfully: 'The only circumstances in which you must write an instruction is in a financial LPA if you have investments managed by a bank and you want that to continue. Contact the Office of the Public Guardian (OPG) or a legal adviser if you want advice on the wording.'

[173] MCA 2005, s 23(3)(a).

[174] See, for instance, the case of *Public Guardian and CS and PL* [2015] EWCOP 30, where the lack of co-operation between the attorneys made it impossible for the LPA to function.

specify that the LPA can only be used when he or she lacks capacity. This may need clarification as to what evidence should be produced. Although this is allowed by s 5 and is referred to in the guidance notes, such a condition does contradict the spirit of a property and affairs LPA which is that the LPA itself is neutral as to the donor's capacity.[175]

- Restricting the power to make gifts under MCA 2005, s 12 by setting a maximum amount for gifts or prohibiting the making of gifts without the consent of the court or a third party.

- Restricting the amount of capital which can be applied or limiting the value of transactions that may be entered into by the attorney.

- Giving authority to the attorney to receive the donor's Will (or a copy). An attorney may need to refer to a Will when dealing with the property and affairs of a donor who lacks capacity sometime after the LPA has been created. The Will remains a privileged document and should not ordinarily be disclosed by a person holding the Will without the express consent of the donor (which may be in the LPA or by the Court of Protection).[176]

- Restricting the scope of the LPA so that it does not apply to a particular asset, for instance, that it should not apply to the sale of the family home.

Great care needs to be taken in drafting instructions, as there is a danger in making the power unworkable in practice or even invalidating it. Curiously, the 2015 prescribed forms refer to instructions rather than conditions. There is a danger of taking this too literally and making an instruction overly prescriptive and undermine the attorney's ability to exercise his or her own skill and judgment or end up requiring the attorney to do something that is contrary to his or her authority. An attorney cannot for example be authorised to make gifts that go beyond what is permitted by MCA 2005, s 12 or to maintain another person. It may appear safer to refer to conditions and therefore specify when the LPA cannot be used, thus the attorneys have the authority available to them as attorneys, except where there is restricted. But this also gives rise to problems where for instance conditions are attached that require attorneys appointed jointly and severally to act together and therefore jointly. Furthermore, conditions may be unworkable in practice. For instance, a LPA may give effect to the sensibilities of an elderly donor who is determined to stay in his own home and restrict the power accordingly. The attorney then finds he or she lacks authority to sell the property when inevitably the donor needs to go

---

[175] The current guidance states (at page 30): 'If you have opted (in section 5 of the LPA form) for your attorneys to act under your financial LPA only if you've lost mental capacity, you might add instructions about how your mental capacity should be assessed. For example, you might write: "This lasting power of attorney only applies if a doctor confirms in writing that I don't have the capacity to make decisions about my finances."' Such provisions can create their own difficulties. For an example of the complications such a clause can create, see the case of *Re XZ; XZ v the Public Guardian* [2015] EWCOP 35. See also **3.28** above.

[176] See the Law Society Practice Note of 8 December 2011 at para 11.5. It should be noted that while the attorney may be authorised to inspect or retain the donor's Will, there is some uncertainty as to whether this can compel a third party to act on this. If this might be a concern, then the donor should separately authorise the third party to release this information in specified circumstances.

into a care home. Likewise, a condition that prevents use while the donor has capacity, may prevent the LPA being used when it is needed if the donor becomes physically incapable, but still has capacity It may be far safer and more useful to address these concerns of the donor in the form of preferences, whether recorded in the LPA or separately (see **3.79** below).

Welfare instructions

3.88 Where the welfare of the donor is concerned, the same restrictions as to when and with what evidence the LPA is created may be applicable. A welfare LPA is perhaps a more personal and subjective instrument than its financial counterpart. It may need careful consideration and discussions with the attorneys, family members, carers and doctors. The donor may need to address a particular set of circumstances the LPA is required to address, such as a terminal illness. The donor may have strong views as to how he or she should be treated and whether or not the LPA extends to the giving or refusing of consent to life-sustaining treatment. Special conditions might include:

- restricting the right to 'give or refuse consent to life-sustaining treatment' so that the attorney may only give such consent (and not refuse consent);
- qualifying the right to refuse consent to life-sustaining treatment so that it does not include the right to refuse artificial nutrition and hydration or that such a decision should be subject to the consent of other relatives or medical experts.

The guidance notes provide the following examples of instructions that might be used this this type of LPA:

> 'My attorneys must not decide I am to move into residential care unless, in my doctor's opinion, I can no longer live independently.'

> 'My attorneys must not consent to any medical treatment involving blood products, as this is against my religion.'

> 'My attorneys must ensure I am given only vegetarian food.'

Preferences (guidance)

3.89 The prescribed forms also contain space for the donor to set out preferences or guidance for the attorney. A LPA should if possible provide an attorney with discretion and autonomy, in that trust and confidence are at the heart of the appointment. It goes against the nature of the relationship between donor and attorney to be overly prescriptive. However, attorneys may well benefit from a record of the donor's wishes and concerns. While these may not be binding in the same way as express instructions, the attorney will be obliged to take them into account as a relevant written statement in determining the donor's best interests. The importance of written preferences or guidance should not be underestimated as it can be used to allow other parties to be involved and provide a remedy where there are concerns about the conduct of an attorney. For instance a donor may record as guidance his wish that his attorneys should consult with his other children over certain decisions or obtain professional advice when taking certain decisions; a failure to do so would not invalidate their decisions. It would however give the other children the ability to apply to the Court of Protection on the grounds that the attorney is failing to act in the best interests of the donor under s 22(3)(b) of the MCA 2005. Preferences need not be contained in the instrument itself and could be set out in a separate letter or memorandum, as this will have to be considered in any assessment of the donor's best interests. The guidance provided by the Public Guardian sets out the following examples of preferences:

'I prefer to live within five miles of my sister.'

'I'd like to be prescribed generic medicines where they are available.'

'I would like to take exercise at least three times a week whenever I am physically able to do so. Whether or not I am mobile, I would like to spend time outdoors at least once a day.'

'I'd like my pets to live with me for as long as possible – if I go into a care home, I'd like to take them with me.'

'I'd like to have regular haircuts, manicures and pedicures.'

(for a health and welfare LPA)

'I like to reinvest all interest from each year's investments into next year's ISA allowance.'

'I would like to maintain a minimum balance of £1,000 in my current account.'

'I prefer to invest in ethical funds.'

'I'd like my attorneys to consult my doctor if they think I don't have the mental capacity to make decisions about my house.'

'I would like to donate £100 each year to Age UK.'

(for a Property and financial affairs LPA)

Section 9 – Prescribed information

3.90 For a LPA to comply with MCA 2005, Sch 1, para 2(1) the instrument must include 'prescribed information about the purpose of the instrument and the effect of a lasting power of attorney.' This is set out at s 8 so that it follows the previous sections which set out the details of the parties and the terms of the attorney's appointment (the 2007 and 2009 prescribed forms showed this information at the beginning of the form on the basis that it would be read before the donor commenced preparing the form).[177] The prescribed information is to be read by the donor, as well as any attorney, and contains the following essential information:

> 'Everyone signing the LPA must read this information. In sections 9 to 11, you, the certificate provider, all your attorneys and your replacement attorneys must sign this lasting power of attorney to form a legal agreement between you (a deed).
>
> By signing this lasting power of attorney, you (the donor) are appointing people (attorneys) to make decisions for you.
>
> LPAs are governed by the Mental Capacity Act 2005 (MCA), regulations made under it and the MCA Code of Practice. Attorneys must have regard to these documents. The Code of Practice is available from www.gov.uk/opg/mca-code or from The Stationery Office.
>
> Your attorneys must follow the principles of the Mental Capacity Act:
>
> 1.   Your attorneys must assume that you can make your own decisions unless it is established that you cannot do so.
> 2.   Your attorneys must help you to make as many of your own decisions as you can. They must take all practical steps to help you to make a decision. They can only treat you as unable to make a decision if they have not succeeded in helping you make a decision through those steps.
> 3.   Your attorneys must not treat you as unable to make a decision simply because you make an unwise decision.
> 4.   Your attorneys must act and make decisions in your best interests when you are unable to make a decision.
> 5.   Before your attorneys make a decision or act for you, they must consider whether they can make the decision or act in a way that is less restrictive of your rights and freedom but still achieves the purpose.
>
> Your attorneys must always act in your best interests. This is explained in the Application guide, part A8, and defined in the MCA Code of Practice.
>
> Before this LPA can be used:
>
> •   it must be registered by the Office of the Public Guardian (OPG)
> •   it may be limited to when you don't have mental capacity, according to your choice in section 5
>
> Cancelling your LPA: You can cancel this LPA at any time, as long as you have mental capacity to do so. It doesn't matter if the LPA has been registered or not. For more information, see the Guide, part D.

---

[177] Rule 9(3) of the Lasting Powers of Attorney, Enduring Powers of Attorney and Public Guardian Regulations 2007, SI 2007/1253 as amended implies that the donor must first read the prescribed information and then complete Sections 1 to 7 – even though it follows on in Section 8. Thus the punctilious donor should first read Section 8 and then go back to Section 1.

Your will and your LPA: Your attorneys cannot use this LPA to change your will. This LPA will expire when you die. Your attorneys must then send the registered LPA, any certified copies and a copy of your death certificate to the Office of the Public Guardian.'

Section 10 – Execution by donor

3.91   Once the donor has read the prescribed information, the donor executes the instrument as a deed, therefore in the presence of a witness. the donor may not witness any signature required for the power and an attorney may not witness any signature required for the power apart from that of another attorney.

This part of the form also confirms the core legal structure of the power of attorney. Thus for the property and affairs LPA the donor confirms as follows: 'I appoint and give my attorneys authority to make decisions about my property and financial affairs, including when I cannot act for myself because I lack mental capacity, subject to the terms of this LPA and to the provisions of the Mental Capacity Act 2005.' For the welfare LPA the declaration is similar, save that it explicitly states that the LPA only applies if the donor lacks capacity: ' I appoint and give my attorneys authority to make decisions about my health and welfare, when I cannot act for myself because I lack mental capacity, subject to the terms of this LPA and to the provisions of the Mental Capacity Act 2005.

If the donor is unable to sign in person, then the form can be signed on behalf of the donor by another signatory, provided there are two independent witnesses.[178] If the LPA is being executed in this way then Continuation Sheet 3 must be used.

Section 11 – The certificate provider's statement

3.92   One of the principal objections to EPAs was that they were completed too readily, without the extent of the donor's capacity being addressed. The presumption would then arise that the EPA had been validly executed and as it might be several years before the problem came to light, there was no contemporaneous evidence to address the issue one way or the other. To address this particular problem and to add a further safeguard, the LPA must also contain a certificate of capacity. This added level of protection is all the more important where the LPA relates to welfare decisions, which may include decisions concerning life-sustaining treatment.

3.93   The LPA instrument therefore requires a certificate to be given by a person of a prescribed description, who is not a donee of the power, stating that in his or her opinion, at the time the donor executes the instrument:[179]

---

[178] Lasting Powers of Attorney, Enduring Powers of Attorney and Public Guardian Regulations 2007, SI 2007/1253, reg 9(7).

[179] Capacity to create a LPA is considered in more detail at **3.109** below.

(a) the donor understands the purpose of the instrument and the scope of the authority given under it;

(b) no fraud or undue pressure is being used to induce the donor to create a LPA; and

(c) there is nothing else which would prevent a LPA from being created.[180]

3.94 The certificate provider's statement constitutes Section 10 of the prescribed form, and must be completed after Sections 1 to 7 and 9 have been completed. There is set no time-limit in which the certificate must be completed, although the instrument cannot be registered until it has been completed. Clearly, the longer the gap between execution and the giving of the certificate, the harder it is for the certificate provider to be able to certify the facts required by MCA 2005. All that the legislation actually requires is that the certificate of capacity is completed 'as soon as reasonably practicable' after the preceding steps (the execution of the instrument) have been carried out.[181] However, it can be argued that any gap between the two events makes it impossible for the certificate to be given, as the certificate provider is addressing a prior event of which he or she had no actual knowledge. To address this difficulty, the certificate provider should if at all possible be a witness to the LPA or be present when the LPA is executed.

3.95 The prescribed forms do not prevent the witness to the donor's signature also completing the certificate of capacity. This may therefore reflect standard practice among solicitors, where the LPA is professionally prepared. Any professional who has prepared a LPA for a client and can witness the client's solicitor should also be satisfied that the client can give instructions and is able to understand the contents of the instrument.[182] If the solicitor is unsure of the client's capacity then another professional may be asked to give a certificate of capacity. This should complement the solicitor's understanding of the client's capacity, and is not a substitute for the solicitor's own judgment. Where a solicitor obtains advice as to capacity it is essential that the person giving the advice understands the relevant tests of capacity and that the solicitor is therefore able to rely on that advice.

3.96 The certificate of capacity is an important safeguard provided by MCA 2005; but it is not intended to be so onerous that it deters potential donors from making LPAs. To encourage completion of LPAs, the certificate can be given by a wide class of persons, who need not necessarily be professionally qualified. A certificate may therefore be given by:[183]

---

[180] MCA 2005, Sch 1, Part 1, para 2(1)(e).

[181] Lasting Powers of Attorney, Enduring Powers of Attorney and Public Guardian Regulations 2007, SI 2007/1253, reg 9(4).

[182] This was common when solicitors prepared EPAs for clients, although the problem was that many EPAs were created too quickly without sufficient attention to the donor's capacity. See further **3.15**.

[183] Lasting Powers of Attorney, Enduring Powers of Attorney and Public Guardian Regulations 2007, SI 2007/1253, reg 8(1).

'(a)   someone the donor has known personally for two years;

[OR]

(b)   someone who because of their relevant professional skills and expertise, considers themselves able to provide the certificate.'

3.97   The 2007 and 2009 prescribed forms required the certificate provider to specify whether he or she was acting in a personal or a professional capacity and then provide some evidence to support this. There is no requirement for the lay certificate provider to show any particular level of expertise or experience. The Regulations refer to 'a person chosen by the donor as being someone who has known him personally for the period of at least two years which ends immediately before the date on which that person signs the LPA certificate'.[184] There is no way of showing or indeed requiring the certificate provider to show that he or she understands the concept of capacity in the light of MCA 2005 as well as the nature and effect of the form. The onus is on the donor to choose – and the Regulations deliberately use the words 'chosen by the donor' – a suitable certificate provider who can if called upon to do so, show that he understood what he was doing and more importantly, that he understood what the donor was doing at the relevant time.

3.98   There is no prescriptive definition of who can be a professional certificate provider. The Regulations refer to:

'... a person chosen by the donor who, on account of his professional skills and expertise, reasonably considers that he is competent to make the judgments necessary to certify the matters set out in paragraph (2)(1)(e) of Schedule 1 to the Act.'

As with choosing a lay certificate provider, the onus is on the donor to choose a suitable certificate provider but it also rests on the certificate provider to consider that he or she is competent. As to who may or may not be competent, the Regulations merely provide the following examples of persons who can act ascertificate providers, namely:[185]

- a registered health care professional;
- a barrister, solicitor or advocate called or admitted in any part of the United Kingdom;
- a registered social worker; or
- an independent mental capacity advocate.

3.99   This list is not exhaustive, and the defined skills are provided as examples only. Although the Regulations refer to the 'professional skills' of the certificate

---

[184] Lasting Powers of Attorney, Enduring Powers of Attorney and Public Guardian Regulations 2007, SI 2007/1253, reg 8(1).
[185] Lasting Powers of Attorney, Enduring Powers of Attorney and Public Guardian Regulations 2007, SI 2007/1253, reg 8(2).

provider, the prescribed form requires the certificate provider to complete two tests. He must state his profession and then state his particular skills. Clearly a certificate provider acting in a professional capacity must have a profession; it must also be a relevant profession. A solicitor may for instance be a professional person but may specialise in commercial litigation and have no experience of assessing capacity and understanding the nature and effect of the LPA. A solicitor experienced in this area of law should state this in the box in provided for the certificate provider to place this information on record.[186]

3.100   There are, however, some persons who cannot provide a certificate.[187] A certificate provider must be over 18.[188] A donee of a power – including a replacement donee as well as the donee of another LPA or EPA given by the same donor – cannot be a certificate provider. A certificate provider must be acting 'independently' and must not be a relative of the donor or the attorney, a business partner or paid employee, or anyone involved in the care home in which the donor lives.[189] This may cause difficulties where the donor wishes to appoint a professional attorney. A donor appointing a professional attorney will not be able to have the certificate given by a partner or employee of the attorney's firm. The donor will need to find someone else to complete the certificate or else take it to a doctor or another solicitor. By contrast, however, the certificate provider can be an employer of the donee. There is also nothing to prevent a named person or the witness to the donor's signature being a certificate provider.[190]

3.101   A professional certificate provider will furthermore need to consider carefully matter such as:[191]

- the identity of the client and the extent of the instructions or retainer;[192]
- whether the donor(s) should provide proof of their identity;

---

[186] The prescribed form refers to a consultant specializing in geriatric care as an example of the particular skills of a professional certificate provider.

[187] Lasting Powers of Attorney, Enduring Powers of Attorney and Public Guardian Regulations 2007, SI 2007/1253, reg 8(3).

[188] The forms prescribed by the 2007 Regulations contained a box requiring the certificate provider to confirm that he or she was over 18. The 2009 forms require the certificate provider to sign the declaration 'I confirm that I act independently of the attorneys and of the donor and I am aged 18 or over.'

[189] In the case of *Re Kittle* referred to at **3.62** above and reported on the Ministry of Justice website, it was held that a first cousin was not a 'relative' for the purposes of preventing a person from acting as a certificate provider.

[190] It may in fact be good practice for a doctor or solicitor who knows the donor sufficiently well to give a certificate of capacity and also to act as a named person, especially if the donor has few close friends or relatives.

[191] It is unclear what responsibility or duty a non-professional person has in giving a certificate of capacity. However, there is no doubt that a professional person will have a greater responsibility and this will be reflected in the fee he or she will be obliged to charge, thereby making it more likely that LPAs will not be certified appropriately.

[192] A solicitor who prepares a LPA for a client needs to be satisfied that on the balance of probabilities the client has the mental capacity to make a LPA (see the Law Society's Practice Note of 8 December 2011 at para 4).

- the time that has passed between execution of the instrument and the certificate of capacity;
- whether the contents of the instrument give rise to any queries or concerns;
- whether, if he or she is not medically qualified, medical advice is required;
- whether, if he or she is not legally qualified, legal advice is required;
- what records should be kept and for how long; and
- that if the power is given by one spouse (or civil partner) to the other, the donor in each case must be interviewed separately.

3.102 Notwithstanding these considerations, the three tests set out in MCA 2005, Sch 1, para 1(e) are ostensibly quite limited. It should quickly be established that there is no fraud or undue pressure and that there is nothing else to prevent the instrument taking effect as a LPA. It is the first of the statutory requirements – that 'the donor understands the purpose of the instrument and the scope of the authority given under it' – that in practice requires the greatest degree of attention. But the certificate provider is not primarily concerned with the content of the instrument or the wisdom or lack of wisdom in the decisions being made by the donor, or even the capacity of the donor to make his own decisions. All the Act requires is an assessment that the donor understands the purpose of the instrument – that it is a power of attorney, who the attorneys are and when they may act and the scope of the power – that it extends to property and affairs or welfare matters.[193] Clearly the certificate provider should be alert to a lack of understanding of the proposed LPA, but neither is he or she conducting a separate examination on the subject, or expecting the donor to go through the same set of instructions twice.

3.103 The certificate of capacity is intended to provide an important safeguard, to protect the donor from undue influence of abuse and also to avoid subsequent doubts about the validity of the power. This will therefore reinforce the presumption that already exists in the due execution of an EPA, that a LPA which has been properly executed and contains such a certificate is a valid power.[194] A certificate of capacity will, to most persons dealing with the LPA, serve as a badge of authenticity that will make it that much harder to query or object to the power, although this is less prominent on the 2015 forms which do not provide any space for the certificate provider to set out his or her qualifications, whether acting in a personal capacity or a professional capacity. This will widen the scope for abuse where a certificate of capacity is procured fraudulently or without proper consideration for the importance of the subject

---

[193] The donor must show that he or she understands the 'purpose' and 'scope' of the instrument. Most definitions of capacity to perform a legal act refer to 'nature' and 'effect' and it is arguable that the former requires a lesser degree of understanding. See the decision of the Senior Judge of the Court of Protection in the case of *Re Collis* (27 October 2010) reported on the website of the Ministry of Justice under the heading 'other orders of interest made by the Court of Protection since 1 October 2007'.

[194] *Re W (Enduring Power of Attorney)* [2001] Ch 609, [2001] 4 All ER 88.

matter. Only when the validity of the LPA or the conduct of the attorneys is queried and addressed by the Court of Protection will it become obvious that the certificate of capacity is only as good as the person giving the certificate.

3.104 In the event that the donor does not require any person to be notified of registration of the instrument, the instrument must contain two such certificates.[195] The prescribed forms therefore have space for two certificates to be given.

Section 12 – The attorney's statement

3.105 The final section of the form is the Attorney's Statement, which must be completed after the Donor and the Certificate Provider have completed their respective sections of the form.[196] As with the prescribed form of EPA, the prescribed form must also contain a statement by the attorney that he or she is prepared to take on the role of attorney and understands his or her obligations. Although often completed as a mere addendum to the main part of the document, it serves as a useful reminder of the attorney's core duties and a solicitor preparing a LPA should emphasise to the attorney that by signing this part of the form, these obligations are imposed on the attorney. Thus to act as an attorney under a LPA (for property and affairs), each attorney must make a statement in the following terms:[197]

> '• I am aged 18 or over
> • I have read this lasting power of attorney (LPA) including section 8 "Your legal rights and responsibilities", or I have had it read to me
> • I have a duty to act based on the principles of the Mental Capacity Act 2005 and to have regard to the Mental Capacity Act Code of Practice
> • I must make decisions and act in the best interests of the donor
> • I must take into account any instructions or preferences set out in this LPA
> • I can make decisions and act only when this LPA has been registered and at the time indicated in section 5 of this LPA.'

Curiously the 2015 forms omit the following wording from the attorney's declaration which was contained on the 2007 and 2009 forms:[198]

> '•   I can spend money to make gifts but only to charities or on customary occasions and for reasonable amounts [property and affairs power only]

---

[195] MCA 2005, Sch 1, Part 1, para 2(2)(b). The space for two certificates adds to the length and complexity of the form. There can be no demand for two certificates as it is hardly a hindrance to name at least one person to be notified on registration, especially as the persons named can be complete strangers.

[196] Lasting Powers of Attorney, Enduring Powers of Attorney and Public Guardian Regulations 2007, SI 2007/1253, reg 9(5).

[197] MCA 2005, Sch 1, Part 1, para 2(1)(d) which requires a statement that the donee 'has read the prescribed information or a prescribed part of it (or has had it read to him), and understands the duties imposed on a donee of a lasting power of attorney under sections 1 (the principles) and 4 (best interests).'

[198] This wording does however appear in the form for use by a trust corporation.

- I have a duty to keep accounts and financial records and produce them to the Office of the Public Guardian and/or the Court of Protection on request [property and affairs power only]'

3.106 The same form is used for a replacement attorney and should be completed in the same way, although clearly the replacement attorney is also endorsing the words on the form: 'I understand that I have the authority to act under this LPA only after an original attorney's appointment is terminated. I must notify the Public Guardian if this happens.' As we have seen, it is easy for the appointment of a replacement attorney to be overlooked on registration and subsequently when he is called upon to act.[199] Therefore in the event of a triggering event arising – namely the disclaimer, death, divorce, bankruptcy or incapacity of the first attorney – the replacement attorney will notify the Public Guardian and return the original LPA to the Public Guardian. This serves two important purposes:

- The Public Guardian has notice of an event that has occurred which not only triggers the appointment of the replacement attorney but which also allows him to update his records.
- The original LPA can be endorsed so that the replacement attorney can produce this (or a certified copy) of his authority to act.

3.107 Under a welfare LPA the attorney's statement is modified to make it clear that the attorney understands that he or she can only act where the power has been registered and the donor lacks mental capacity.

3.108 MCA 2005 refers to the duties imposed on an attorney under Sections 1 (the principles) and 4 (best interests) in the same way as they are imposed on any person or body who makes decisions which another person lacks capacity to make. This is however a minimum requirement, as the attorney may well have other duties. A donee of a property and affairs LPA for instance, has other common law or fiduciary obligations when dealing with property and affairs.[200] A professional attorney or an attorney who has been appointed on account of a particular expertise is likely to have a higher duty of care. The sensible aim of the forms is to ensure that an attorney makes a positive commitment to carry out his or her legal obligations (and provides a measure against which performance can be judged in the future) and no attorney should undertake the role without careful consideration. Nevertheless, it is likely that many attorneys will sign a form without thinking too carefully about what they are signing, but at least there is a record of what they should be thinking about when signing the forms.

---

[199] See **3.72**.
[200] See **3.4**.

CREATION OF LASTING POWER OF ATTORNEY

A lasting power of attorney is created in two stages

3.109 A power of attorney intended to be a LPA for the purposes of MCA 2005 must be made in two stages for it to be valid as a LPA: the drawing up and execution of the instrument followed by its formal registration by the Public Guardian. The terminology can cause some confusion. Until both stages have been completed, a properly completed and duly executed instrument has no legal effect.[201] A completed document headed 'Lasting Power of Attorney' is not therefore a LPA until both stages have been completed. Until that has been done, the document is a worthless piece of paper, of no legal effect whatsoever. MCA 2005, s 9(2) describes the unregistered form somewhat clumsily as 'an instrument conferring authority of the kind mentioned in subsection (1)'; thereafter it is referred to as an instrument 'intended to create a lasting power of attorney' or, more commonly, simply as an 'instrument'.

THE FIRST STAGE: COMPLETING SECTIONS 1 TO 11

3.110 The first stage is the completion and execution of the prescribed form. This involves a number of steps, which may or may not be taken at some distance in time from each other, although the Regulations assume that each step will be taken 'as soon as reasonably practicable' after the previous step.[202] The steps must however be taken in the correct sequence.[203] Thus:

(1) The donor reads the prescribed information.

(2) The donor completes the provisions of the instrument that pertain to him or her (Sections 1 to 10) and executes the instrument, by signing Section 9 in the presence of a witness.[204] Although MCA 2005 refers to the time when the donor 'executes the instrument' there is no mention in the Act to execution as a deed.[205] A power of attorney, however, is regarded as a deed and a LPA complies with the Law of Property (Miscellaneous Provisions) Act 1989, s 1.[206] The original prescribed forms introduced by the 2007 Regulations made no reference to the document being a deed; this is now made clear in the 2009 and 2015 forms.

(3) A welfare LPA also requires Section 5, dealing with life-sustaining treatment, to be completed and that page must therefore be signed separately in the presence of a witness.

---

[201] MCA 2005, s 9(2).

[202] Lasting Powers of Attorney, Enduring Powers of Attorney and Public Guardian Regulations 2007, SI 2007/1253, reg 9(1).

[203] This is a simple trap for the unwary. It is not unusual for donors and donees (especially if they are a close family) to complete their parts first and then organise a certificate of capacity. If the forms are completed in the wrong order, an application for registration will be rejected.

[204] Lasting Powers of Attorney, Enduring Powers of Attorney and Public Guardian Regulations 2007, SI 2007/1253, reg 9(9).

[205] MCA 2005, s 9(2)(c).

[206] Powers of Attorney Act 1971, s 1.

(4) The Certificate of Capacity (Section 10) is signed by a person of a prescribed description confirming that in his or her opinion, at the time the donor executes the instrument:[207]

> '(i)   the donor understands the purpose of the instrument and the scope of the authority conferred under it,
> (ii)   no fraud or undue pressure is being used to induce the donor to create a lasting power of attorney, and
> (iii) there is nothing else which would prevent a lasting power of attorney from being created by the instrument.'

(5) A statement (Part C) is made by the donee or by each donee to the effect that he or she:[208]

> '(i)   I have read the prescribed information (the section called 'information you must read on page 2), and
> (ii)   I understand the role and responsibilities under this lasting power of attorney ...'

3.111 Only when all these steps have been completed can the instrument be registered by the Public Guardian. It is this second stage which 'creates' the power in its registration with the Public Guardian and until the instrument is actually registered, it is ineffective as a power of attorney.[209] The registration procedure is described in more detail below.

Capacity to create a power

3.112 A person's capacity to execute a LPA is specific to that matter at the material time.[210] Although MCA 2005 sets out a framework for assessing capacity, and expects a certificate provider to certify that the donor 'understands the purpose of the instrument and the scope of the authority conferred under it', existing case-law will assist in determining questions concerning capacity to grant a LPA.

3.113 The principle that capacity to create an EPA required its own test which was distinct from that of managing property and affairs was considered in the case of *Re K, Re F*.[211] Registration of an EPA was objected to on the grounds that the power had been made immediately before an application was made for its registration – on the basis that the donor lacked capacity to manage her property and affairs. Hoffman J confirmed the validity of the power, it being a specific legal act at the time it was made and therefore distinct from the donor's ability to manage or not manage her property and affairs. He set out four basic requirements as to what the donor should understand:[212]

---

[207] MCA 2005, Sch 1, para 2(1)(e). The Certificate of Capacity is dealt with at **3.89ff**.
[208] MCA 2005, Sch 1, para 2(1)(d). See **3.102** above for the complete declaration.
[209] MCA 2005, s 9(2)(b).
[210] MCA 2005, s 2(1).
[211] [1988] Ch 310, [1988] 1 All ER 358.
[212] [1988] 1 All ER 358, at p 363.

'... first, if such be the terms of the power, that the attorney will be able to assume complete authority over the donor's affairs; second, if such be the terms of the power, that the attorney will in general be able to do anything with the donor's property which the donor could have done; third, that the authority will continue if the donor should be or become mentally incapable; fourth, that if he should be or become mentally incapable, the power will be irrevocable without confirmation by the court.'

3.114 The test of capacity to create an EPA will be different for an LPA made under MCA 2005. In the case of *Re Collis* Senior Judge Lush suggested the following modifications to the tests set out in *Re K, Re F*:[213]

- '• the donor would need to understand that the LPA cannot be used until it is registered by the Public Guardian.
- • the donor would need to understand that the attorney under an LPA for personal welfare can only make decisions that the donor is contemporaneously incapable of making.
- • unlike an EPA, the donor can revoke an LPA at any time when he or she has the capacity to do so without the court having to confirm the revocation.
- • the authority conferred by an LPA, unlike an EPA, is subject to the provisions of the Mental Capacity Act 2005 and, in particular, sections 1 (the principles) and section 4 (best interests).'

The last requirement sets a high threshold for the donor, as it requires an understanding of information that is beyond the scope of the form or merely summarised in the form. Thus the donor needs some understanding of the basis on which the attorneys must act if the donor lacks capacity. There are also matters that are specific to the LPA such as the choice of attorneys or the restrictions and guidance contained in the instrument. The donor must also understand the consequences of deciding one way or another, or failing to make the decision.[214] In the context of an LPA this might include the consequences of not appointing a particular person as an attorney or not including guidance as well as the consequences of not making an LPA. There is no doubt that the complexity of the form and the registration process, the options available to the donor and additional information the donor needs to understand set a high threshold for capacity.

3.115 As with an EPA, a properly executed LPA will create a presumption of due execution. The certificate of capacity alone places a very strong burden on anyone objecting to registration on the grounds that the power is invalid. The Public Guardian furthermore has a positive duty to register a LPA unless he receives a valid objection to registration within the prescribed period or an objection is made to the court.[215] The court can only revoke the power if it is satisfied that one of the limited grounds allowed by MCA 2005 has been

---

[213] Reported on the website of the Ministry of Justice. See also **3.99**. Capacity to create a LPA was also considered briefly by Hedley J in the case of *A, B & C v X & Z* (a judgment of given on 30 July 2012).

[214] MCA 2005, s 3(4).

[215] MCA 2005, Sch 1, Part 2, para 5.

established.[216] Thus, unless the court is satisfied that the ground for revocation has been established, it cannot prevent the LPA from being registered. This approach is the same applied by the Court of Protection in the context of registration of EPAs.[217] The evidential burden is weighted against the objector, which in practice makes it very difficult for the court to revoke an EPA on the grounds of its invalidity. Unless there is clear and compelling evidence that the donor lacked capacity at the time of execution or that there was fraud or undue influence, the court must register the EPA. An even greater burden of proof will apply on anyone seeking to challenge the validity of the LPA.

THE SECOND STAGE: REGISTRATION

The requirement of registration

3.116 A LPA is not effective as a power of attorney unless and until it is registered with the Public Guardian in accordance with MCA 2005, Sch 1.[218] The aim of the Act is to encourage early registration of LPAs, so that the process of validation and supervision is started as soon as the power is used. However, a welfare power – which has in any event already been registered – can only operate in respect of those decisions which the donor lacks capacity to make.[219]

3.117 An attorney operating a welfare power must therefore pass two separate thresholds before he or she can make a decision: the first is that the power must be registered; the second is that the donor lacks capacity. Any clinician or other person treating or caring for a person and seeking to take instructions from the attorney must likewise ensure that the two thresholds are passed, checking that there is a registered LPA in place and also verifying that the donor lacks capacity.

3.118 Unless it has been restricted, a property and affairs LPA is by contrast more straightforward as it can operate notwithstanding the capacity of the donor. This has three practical benefits:

(1) It avoids misuse of the power where the attorney continues to act notwithstanding the revocation of the power on the incapacity of the donor. As often happens with EPAs the power is used by an attorney where it should be registered with the result that the donor's interests are not protected and the attorney (even though he or she may be acting in good faith) is acting beyond the scope of his or her authority.

---

[216] MCA 2005, s 22(3).
[217] *Re W* [2001] Ch 609, [2001] 4 All ER 88, [2001] 1 FLR 832.
[218] MCA 2005, s 9(2)(b).
[219] MCA 2005, s 11(7)(a).

(2)   The attorney is not required to conduct a medical assessment of the donor's capacity. He or she does not need to take responsibility for or undergo the awkwardness of asserting that the donor is mentally incapable.

(3)   No other person is entitled to make an assessment based on the fact, that by virtue of registration, the donor is incapable of managing all his or her property and affairs. Thus, the fact of registration does not give rise to a presumption of incapacity.

Problems with capacity not being relevant to registration

3.119   While the benefits of avoiding the issue of capacity on registration of a LPA are self-evident, there are also several disadvantages. A third party dealing directly with the donor of the LPA cannot make any assumption as to the donor's lack of capacity, but must make his or her own assessment of the donor's capacity at the relevant time. While this respects the integrity of the donor, the third party's position is less clear. A bank, for example, cannot rely on the fact of registration to prevent the donor from using his or her account, where, for instance, there are large or frequent withdrawals from the account. Likewise, a solicitor selling a property on the authority of the attorney of a LPA cannot assume that the donor is incapable and the property is being sold to pay for nursing care. The donor therefore may have less protection against financial abuse than the donor of an EPA.

Problems with early registration

3.120   Although the aim of MCA 2005 is to encourage early registration of LPAs, it should not be assumed that all donors and attorneys will follow this in practice. A capable donor may well feel stigmatised by the fact of registration but is more likely to resent the expense and inconvenience of registration as well as the perception that this restricts his or her freedom. Of course the donor can revoke the LPA but he or she must still go through the process of having the registration cancelled. There is no prescribed form or procedure for a donor who has revoked a LPA to cancel registration. A donor who has capacity or who recovered capacity and wishes to revoke the LPA needs to provide the Public Guardian with sufficient evidence to cancel the registration.[220] This may cause not only inconvenience, expense, embarrassment or family discord, but also force the donor to demonstrate to the Public Guardian that he or she is capable of revoking the power. Moreover if the revocation is contested or the donor's evidence of revocation is contested, then the matter must be referred to the Court of Protection for determination.[221]

3.121   Following the implementation of the MCA 2005, the practice appears to be for instruments to be registered even though there is no intention to use

---

[220] Lasting Powers of Attorney, Enduring Powers of Attorney and Public Guardian Regulations 2007, SI 2007/1253, reg 21.
[221] MCA 2005, Sch 1, para 18(b).

them.[222] The donor and the attorneys have the benefit of knowing that the LPA has been properly completed and any disputes can be addressed early on while the donor is still capable of being consulted.

3.122 Early registration can also cause practical problems where the LPA is registered long in advance of its use. The donor's circumstances may have changed and the protection afforded by registration is no longer available. Furthermore, once the LPA is registered it can be used; not every donor will want it to be used but an attorney who is insensitive or dishonest can still operate the LPA unless and until the donor takes active steps to revoke the LPA. A donor may include a special condition limiting registration of operation to a time when capacity is lacking, but this creates its own problems in drafting as well as in timing as a restriction may delay registration at the time it is needed. However, if registration is delayed, the benefits of early registration are also lost.[223]

Procedure for registration – Sections 12 to 15

3.123 The procedure for registration of a LPA is relatively straightforward, and should not therefore deter attorneys from taking on their responsibilities to register and act under the LPA. This is facilitated and encouraged by incorporating the application for registration in the body of the form. In contrast to the procedure for registration of an EPA, the application may be made by the donor as well as by the attorney.

3.124 Application to register a LPA can be made by the donor or donee or by one of two or more donees appointed to act jointly and severally. Where the attorneys are appointed jointly and the attorneys rather than the donor make the application, then all the attorneys must make the application. Application must be made using Sections 12 to 15 of the prescribed forms. These are short and self-explanatory and contain sufficient information about the donor, the donee or donees and service of notices to enable the Public Guardian to deal with the registration process. The applicant for registration will also need to submit the original LPA and the prescribed fee of £110.[224]

3.125 Where the donor has created separate LPAs in respect of property and affairs and welfare matters, then they will need to be registered separately. It will often be the case that different attorneys are appointed for different purposes or the powers need to be registered at different times. There is therefore no obvious mechanism for registering the two powers by the same

---

[222] This does perhaps explain why applications for registration, which amounted to 7,500 in September 2008, was higher than expected (Bridget Prentice MP, addressing the Public Guardian Board General Meeting, 7 October 2008). This is more than double the level predicted and may account in part for some of the administrative problems faced by the Public Guardian in the early period the new regime.

[223] The role of notified persons and the problems of early registration are also considered at **3.87**.

[224] MCA 2005, Sch 1, para 4(3). The actual fees prescribed are set out in the Public Guardian (Fees, etc) Regulations 2007, SI 2007/2051, as amended by the Public Guardian (Fees, etc) (Amendment) Regulations 2013, SI 2013/1748.

process. An attorney registering welfare and financial powers for his elderly parents will have to make four applications and pay four separate fees each of £130. It is therefore possible that a separate fee for each process may deter attorneys from registering LPAs – especially welfare powers – until the last moment.[225]

Status of attorney prior to registration

3.126 A LPA has no legal effect until it is registered.[226] As the document is not a power of attorney, there is no legal basis on which an attorney can act or the Court of Protection can assist. MCA 2005 does not therefore provide any interim or limited authority for the attorney to act after the application has been made but before the power has been registered.[227] Where a donor has become incapable of carrying out an act for which authority is urgently required by the donee, the donee has no ability to act under the LPA, even though an application to register the power has been made.

3.127 This omission from MCA 2005 may cause difficulties for an attorney who needs to administer the donor's affairs while the power is being registered. It may be that a short delay will not prejudice the donor's interests, but the situation is more complicated if registration is delayed for perhaps several months while there is a dispute over the validity of the power or the conduct of the attorney. If the attorney requires authority in this period, he or she must either apply to the court for a specific order under MCA 2005, s 18 or rely on the provisions of MCA 2005, ss 7 and 8. Thus an attorney who needs to access the donor's bank account to pay for nursing home fees must either apply to the Court of Protection for an order, or spend his or her own money and be reimbursed by the donor subsequently.[228]

3.128 Where the donee wishes to resolve any queries concerning the validity of the power, he or she can apply to the Court of Protection for a determination under MCA 2005, s 22(2).

---

[225] The unintended consequence may prove positive: a welfare LPA is only intended as a 'last resort' and may well not need to be registered. Many donors whose property and affairs are dealt with by an attorney will carry on being cared for informally without the need for intervention by an attorney. Thus a welfare power will not be registered as a matter of course on incapacity, but may be held back until there is a dispute or contentious treatment that requires the authority of an attorney to resolve. This should not, however, be used to overlook the risk of the power being needed urgently and its use is delayed by registration.

[226] MCA 2005, s 9(2)(b).

[227] Compare the provisions of MCA 2005, Sch 4, para 1(2). An EPA is already a power of attorney when it is made.

[228] It has therefore been suggested by some practitioners that a donor who does not want his or her LPA used immediately should also complete a simple power of attorney in accordance with the Powers of Attorney Act 1971, s 10 to operate while the donor has capacity and before the LPA is registered.

Notices

3.129 The person applying to register the LPA (who may be the donor or the donee) must notify any person named in the LPA for that purpose of his or her intention to register the power.[229] Notification is made in the prescribed form LPA3.[230]

3.130 The applicant is only obliged to notify the persons named in the LPA for that purpose of his or her intention to register the power. There is no requirement for one attorney where there is more than one attorney to notify the other attorney(s). The Public Guardian is responsible for notifying:

- the donee or donees where the application is made by the donor, using form LPA003A;[231]

- the donor where the application is made by the donee or donees, using form LPA003B;[232] and

- a donee where two or more donees have been appointed jointly and severally and who has not applied to register the power (using form LPA003A).[233]

Service of notices

3.131 MCA 2005, Sch 1 refers to the applicant having to 'notify' a person; the Lasting Powers of Attorney, Enduring Powers of Attorney and Public Guardian Regulations 2007, regs 10 and 13 refer to notices being 'given'. Even form LPA003A and LPA003B must be 'given' by the Public Guardian. There is, however, no reference in the legislation to the mode of service of documents.[234] Form LPA3 refers to the form being 'received' by the recipient, but makes no reference to how it has come to be received. Likewise the guidance from the Public Guardian refers to notices being sent.[235]

---

[229] MCA 2005, Sch 1, para 6. The rationale for notifying only named persons is dealt with at **3.84–3.85.** There is no requirement for the donee to notify any close relatives or persons involved in the care and welfare of the donor unless they have been actually named by the donor for this purpose.

[230] Lasting Powers of Attorney, Enduring Powers of Attorney and Public Guardian Regulations 2007, SI 2007/1253, reg 10 and Sch 2 (as amended by SI 2015/899).

[231] MCA 2005, Sch 1, para 7.

[232] MCA 2005, Sch 1, para 8(1).

[233] MCA 2005, Sch 1, para 8(2).

[234] Compare the Court of Protection (Enduring Power of Attorney) Rules 2001, SI 2001/825, rr 15 and 16 which applied to the registration of EPAs prior to 1 October 2007. A notice of intention to register an EPA must also be served personally on the donor: Lasting Powers of Attorney, Enduring Powers of Attorney and Public Guardian Regulations 2007, SI 2007/1253, reg 23(3). It is difficult to see how the sending of a form by post to a donor will provide a greater degree of protection.

[235] 'Guidance for people who want to register a lasting power of attorney' at page 4.

Dispensing with notice

3.132 Only the court can direct that service of a notice on a named person be dispensed with.[236] However, the court must first be satisfied that no useful purpose would be served by giving notice. There is no corresponding power for the court to dispense with the requirement for the Public Guardian to notify the donor.

3.133 There is no provision in MCA 2005 or regulations which allows the person who is applying to register the LPA to dispense with the service of notice without reference to the court. This is an unlikely event given that most LPAs are registered at the time they are drawn up and notified persons are chosen as people who can be readily notified at the time, if indeed they are notified at all. The 2015 forms no longer make notification a requirement so it will become unusual for anyone to receive formal notice in this way. However, in the unlikely event that notification was required and the named person cannot be located, has died or is incapable, the court must first agree to notice being dispensed with before the application to register the power is made.[237] If that is the approach of the court, and a formal application needs to be made to dispense with notice (with a fee payable), then it is likely that many applicants in such cases will simply send the notice to the address on the form. They can claim to have 'notified' the named persons at their last known address.

Completion of registration

3.134 Unless there is a valid objection to registration of the LPA, the Public Guardian must register the power at the end of the prescribed period.[238] There is therefore a positive duty on the Public Guardian to register the power unless there is a defect in the power or a valid objection is received.

3.135 Once the LPA is registered, the Public Guardian must notify the donor and attorney(s) of the fact of registration in form LPA004.[239] While the original LPA will be endorsed with details of the registration and returned to the applicant or his or her solicitor, MCA 2005, s 16(1) provides authority for office copies to be conclusive evidence of the fact of registration and the contents of the power.

---

[236] MCA 2005, Sch 1, para 10.

[237] In contrast to the donee of an EPA who does not need to notify a relative if his or her name or address is not known to the attorney and cannot reasonably be ascertained or the attorney believes that the relative is aged under 18 or mentally incapable (EPAA 1985, Sch 1, para 2(2)).

[238] MCA 2005, Sch 1, para 5. The Lasting Powers of Attorney, Enduring Powers of Attorney and Public Guardian Regulations 2007, SI 2007/1253, reg 12 specifies a period of 4 weeks, from the date of the last notice given to a person required to be notified (the prescribed period was reduced from 6 weeks to 4 weeks from 1 April 2013 by the Lasting Powers of Attorney, Enduring Powers of Attorney and Public Guardian (Amendment) Regulations 2013, SI 2013/506).

[239] Lasting Powers of Attorney, Enduring Powers of Attorney and Public Guardian Regulations 2007, SI 2007/1253, reg 17(5) and Sch 5.

Objections to registration

The role of the Public Guardian

3.136 The registration authority is the Public Guardian who must register the LPA unless:

- it appears to the Public Guardian that the LPA is not a valid power, in which case the power cannot be registered unless directed by the court;[240]
- the Court of Protection has already appointed a deputy and it appears to the Public Guardian that the powers conferred on the deputy would conflict with the powers conferred on the attorney, in which case the power cannot be registered unless directed by the court;[241]
- it appears to the Public Guardian that there is a provision in the instrument which would be ineffective as part of a LPA or which would prevent the power from operating as a LPA, in which case the power must be referred to the court for determination;[242]
- the Public Guardian receives a notice of objection from the donee or named person on one of the specified grounds and it appears to the Public Guardian that the ground for making the objection is satisfied, in which case the Public Guardian must not register the power unless directed by the court;[243] or
- the Court of Protection receives a notice of objection from the donee or named person on one of the prescribed grounds, in which case the Public Guardian must not register the power unless directed by the court.[244]

Objections made to the Public Guardian

3.137 The Public Guardian's authority to refuse registration of the LPA is limited to cases where there is a defect of form in the power, which is either apparent from the facts or which is brought to the Public Guardian's attention by a named person who is objecting to registration of the power. Although MCA 2005 provides for the Public Guardian to be notified by means of an objection, it would be more appropriate to describe this process as a technical or procedural notice. The notice form given to a named person (LPA3) or by the Public Guardian to a co-attorney who is not applying to register the LPA (LPA003A) refer to these grounds as the 'factual grounds'.

---

[240] MCA 2005, Sch 1, para 11(1). For example, where the power was made using the incorrect form or there was a technical defect in the form which prevented it from operating as a valid LPA.

[241] MCA 2005, Sch 1, para 12.

[242] MCA 2005, Sch 1, para 11(2) and (3).

[243] MCA 2005, Sch 1, para 13(1) and (2). These are the narrow or factual grounds defined in s 13(3) and (6)(a)–(d) on which the Public Guardian can refuse to register the power without reference to the court. See **3.134**.

[244] MCA 2005, Sch 1, para 13(3) and (4). This part of the Act refers to prescribed grounds and these are not defined. It can be assumed that these are the wider or substantive grounds defined in s 22(3) whereby the court can direct that the power is not to be registered or revoke the power.

3.138　An objection to proposed registration on one of the 'factual' grounds can only be made to the Public Guardian by the donor, an attorney or named person, before the expiry of the period of 3 weeks beginning with the date on which the notice is given.[245] An attorney or named person must file their objection with the Public Guardian using form LPA007. The 'factual' or specified grounds on which a named person or a donee (where the application is made by the donor or the other donee) can 'object' in this way are limited to the following cases:[246]

- insofar as the LPA relates to the property and affairs of the donor, the bankruptcy of the donor or the donee or, where the donee is a trust corporation, its winding up or dissolution;
- the LPA has been disclaimed by the attorney;
- the death of the attorney;
- the dissolution or annulment of the donor's marriage or civil partnership between the donor and the donee (unless the power excludes revocation in these circumstances); or
- the attorney lacks capacity.

3.139　On receipt of an objection on the factual grounds, the Public Guardian will simply stop the registration process. It is then for the applicant to accept the situation or apply to the Court of Protection to consider the matter and require the Public Guardian to register the power. The onus here is very much on the person applying for registration to take further steps to proceed with the application.[247]

3.140　If the donor objects to registration, he or she simply gives notice to the Public Guardian in form LPA006. The Public Guardian must refuse to register the LPA unless the Court of Protection is satisfied that the donor lacks capacity to object to the registration.[248] However, it would be unlikely for the Public Guardian to refer the case immediately to the Court of Protection and it will be for the attorneys – if they wish – to persist with their application and refer the matter to the court.

The role of the Court of Protection

3.141　Where a donee or a named person receives a notice of registration and objects on one of the 'prescribed grounds' the Public Guardian cannot register the LPA until directed to do so by the court.[249] The 'prescribed grounds' on

---

[245] Lasting Powers of Attorney, Enduring Powers of Attorney and Public Guardian Regulations 2007, SI 2007/1253, reg 14. The prescribed period was reduced from 5 weeks from 1 April 2013 by the Lasting Powers of Attorney, Enduring Powers of Attorney and Public Guardian (Amendment) Regulations 2013, SI 2013/506.
[246] MCA 2005, s 13(3) and (6)(a) to (d).
[247] MCA 2005, Sch 1, para 13 (2).
[248] MCA 2005, Sch 1, para 14.
[249] MCA 2005, Sch 1, para 13(3) and (4).

which a person can object to registration are not defined by MCA 2005 but mirror the substantive grounds on which the court can revoke a power under MCA 2005, s 22.

3.142 The court's powers are not limited to the period of registration, but can be exercised at any time after a person has executed a power or a power has been registered as a LPA. However, an objection to registration made after the power has been registered will require a formal application to the court.[250]

3.143 The court may in such cases either refuse to register the LPA or, if the donor lacks capacity, revoke the LPA.[251] MCA 2005 does not, however, allow the court to revoke the LPA if the donor retains capacity, although registration can be refused or cancelled. Thus if the power has already been registered where the donor has capacity and the court is satisfied that undue pressure was used to create the power, it appears that the court cannot interfere with the donor's choice of attorney.

Whether the requirements for the creation of the power have been met

3.144 The court can determine any question relating to whether or not any of the requirements for creating or revoking a lasting power have been met.[252] This power covers not just the formal requirements of completing and executing the power, but also covers the ability or capacity of the donor to grant the power.

3.145 Although the court may determine any question relating to the validity of the power, where an application to register is made, the Public Guardian is obliged to register the power unless one of the grounds for objection exists. This is consistent with EPAA 1985, which imposes a positive obligation to register an EPA unless a valid ground for objection is established to the satisfaction of the court, thereby placing the evidential burden of proof on the objector.[253] The court will assume that a LPA which has been correctly executed and which contains a certificate of capacity has been validly executed and that alone will place a strong burden of proof on the objector seeking to establish that the donor lacked capacity.

Whether the power has been revoked

3.146 The Court may determine any question relating to whether the power has been revoked or otherwise come to an end.[254] This power enables the court to determine whether the power has been revoked by the donor. The donor

---

[250] COPR 2007, r 67. Permission is not required where the applications concerns 'a lasting power of attorney which is, or purports to be created under the Act.' MCA 2005, s 50(2) and COPR 2007, r 51(2)(b). See further **3.154** below.

[251] MCA 2005, s 22(4). The power to refuse registration or revoke the power is without prejudice to the court's powers to give directions under s 22.

[252] MCA 2005, s 22(2).

[253] EPAA 1985, s 6(6) and see *Re W* [2001] 1 FLR 832.

[254] MCA 2005, Sch 1, para 18.

must not only demonstrate capacity to revoke the instrument, but must also communicate to the donee an intention to revoke the power. If the court determines the power has been revoked, it will direct the Public Guardian to cancel registration of the power.

3.147 The role of the court to determine such matters is in addition to a separate power of the Public Guardian to cancel registration if he receives notice of revocation and is satisfied 'that the donor has taken such steps as are necessary in law to revoke it'.[255]

That fraud or undue pressure was used to induce the donor to create the power

3.148 If the use of fraud is alleged, the objection will be considered very carefully with the court expecting all available evidence to be placed before it. Although the Court of Protection has wide powers to summon witnesses and cross-examine them, it is not an appropriate venue for a detailed investigation into an alleged fraud. If the LPA has been used improperly to commit a fraud then the police should be notified and the court may revoke the power. If fraud is alleged, this usually comes to light when the LPA is being used fraudulently. At that point, the manner in which the LPA was made may be academic. The grounds for revocation are established by the conduct of the donee, who is clearly acting contrary to the donor's best interests. Revocation on these grounds is considered below at **3.147**.

3.149 Similar considerations arise where 'undue pressure' is alleged. Pressure may be brought which is not 'undue pressure', for instance, where an elderly client is regularly advised by a solicitor or concerned relative that he or she should make a power of attorney. 'Undue pressure' is a matter of degree and requires a subjective assessment of whether the pressure was extreme or disproportionate to the extent that the donor could not have executed the power of his or her own free will.

That the donee has behaved, is behaving or proposes to behave in a way that contravenes his or her authority or contrary to the donor's best interests

3.150 The court's power to intervene in the absence of fraud or undue influence being used to procure the LPA, is limited to two grounds only:

(1) the donee has behaved, is behaving or proposes to behave in a way that contravenes his or her authority; or

(2) the donee has behaved, is behaving or proposes to behave in a way that is not or would not be in the donor's best interests.

---

[255] Lasting Powers of Attorney, Enduring Powers of Attorney and Public Guardian Regulations 2007, SI 2007/1253, reg 21. This does appear to confer on the Public Guardian a judicial discretion to consider evidence and either cancel or refuse to cancel registration of the LPA.

3.151 These two grounds represent a limitation in the court's powers to intervene in the conduct of an attorney. The first ground, where the attorney contravenes his or her authority, can only cover acts which are illegal or in breach of the attorney's fiduciary duty to the donor. Thus they are acts which are actionable in their own right and for which there would be a civil or criminal remedy. For instance, an attorney who causes loss to the donor's estate may be liable to remedy the loss and an attorney who uses the donor's funds for his own benefit or ill-treats the donor may be guilty of a criminal offence.[256]

3.152 It is the second of these two grounds that may be problematic in practice. The difficulty for the court is that the court must impose its own view of what is in the donor's 'best interests' when there is no objective measure of a person's best interests. If the attorney takes account of the factors and consults with the persons referred to in MCA 2005, s 4, then he or she has complied with the requirements of MCA 2005 if he or she 'reasonably believes that what he does or decides is in the best interests of the person concerned'. There has been some uncertainty as to how the court will measure the attorney's belief against attorney's statutory and fiduciary duties. The court has recently taken a robust approach to this issue and applying an objective standard to the attorney's duties. Where an attorney has failed to account for funds under her control in breach of her fiduciary duties to the donor, the court had no hesitation in finding that her conduct was not in the donor's best interests.[257] Where the attorney used the donor's property to invest in her own business, despite a reasonable belief that she was doing what the donor would have wanted, the Senior Judge had no hesitation in finding that the clear breach of a fiduciary duty was contrary to the donor's best interests and revoking the LPA.[258]

3.153 A person challenging a LPA on this ground also has to cross a high evidential threshold in showing that an action (let alone a proposed action) is contrary to a person's 'best interests'. Unless there is a clear act of negligence or breach of fiduciary duty on the part of the attorney, such cases are likely to centre around a different and subjective views of 'best interests.' For instance an allegation that the attorney is acting contrary to the donor's best interests in paying for an inferior care home or paying too much for care may involve the court being asked to make a welfare decision on a matter such as where the donor should live rather than on the operation of the LPA.

---

[256] A dramatic instance of financial abuse was reported in the Daily Mail on 6 October 2013 and concerned a donee who used a LPA to steal £471,000 from an elderly relative, most of which was spent on clothes.

[257] See *Re Harcourt: the Public Guardian v A* [2013] COPLR 69 (31 July 2012) which involved a failure to account on the part of the attorney acting under an LPA. Senior Judge Lush held that the donor was entitled to expect 'that her property and financial affairs should be managed competently, honestly and for her benefit' (para 60). By failing to pay care costs on time, account for her actions or co-operate with an investigation by the Public Guardian, the donee was not acting in the donor's best interests and the LPA was revoked.

[258] See *Re Buckley: The Public Guardian v C* [2013] COPLR 39.

3.154 By contrast with EPAA 1985 and MCA 2005, Sch 4, the court may refuse to register an enduring power or cancel such a power if satisfied that:[259]

> '... having regard to all the circumstances and in particular the attorney's relationship to or connection with the donor, the attorney is unsuitable to be the donor's attorney.'

3.155 The 'unsuitability' ground ostensibly gives the court more discretion to intervene in cases where it might be difficult to prove, on the balance of probabilities, that an act or proposed act is not in a person's best interests. There are cases where an attorney is unsuitable despite ostensibly acting in the donor's best interests. For example:

- two attorneys are in conflict and both claim to be acting in the donor's best interests;

- the attorney's financial dealings with the donor's estate give rise to a potential conflict of interest or require further investigation, even though there is no evidence or it is very difficult to prove any actual wrongdoing.

- the attorney may act diligently in connection with the donor's estate but refuses to discuss the donor's welfare with close relatives who have an interest in this.

3.156 The reason for changing the basis on which the Court of Protection can intervene is that the court's powers should be consistent with MCA 2005 generally and applied in the context of the attorney's duty to act in the best interests of the donor.[260] However, an attorney who may otherwise be unsuitable by reason of his conduct is unlikely, on a close examination of the circumstances, to be acting in the donor's best interests. The MCA 2005 simply requires a careful assessment of the facts and a review of the 'best interests' criteria rather than using 'unsuitability' as a catch-all ground on which an attorney can be removed.

Procedure

3.157 The process for objection is not defined by MCA 2005. The separate roles of the Public Guardian as the registration authority and the Court of Protection as the judicial authority cause some confusion and the procedure for dealing with objections and further proceedings falls between the Lasting Powers of Attorney, Enduring Powers of Attorney and Public Guardian Regulations 2007[261] and the Court of Protection Rules 2007.[262] A person who has been notified of an application and who wishes to object on one of the substantive grounds therefore has quite an arduous responsibility. It is not possible for a concerned relative to write to the Public Guardian setting out his

---

[259] MCA 2005, Sch 4, Part 4, para 9(e).
[260] This follows the recommendation of the Law Commission: see Law Com No 231 (at **3.16**), at para 7.58.
[261] SI 2007/1253.
[262] SI 2007/1744.

or her concerns. Not only must a formal application be made to the Court of Protection, but the Public Guardian must also be notified so that the application for registration is suspended.[263] The objector must, within the prescribed period of 3 weeks (beginning with the date on which the notice is given):

- file a formal application for objection in form COP7 with the Court of Protection; and
- notify the Public Guardian in form LPA008.

3.158 Form COP7 serves as the formal application to the Court of Protection (instead of form COP1). This form is issued by the court and must be served on the donor and attorneys as soon as practicable and in any event within 21 days of issue. Each application form must be accompanied by a form for acknowledging service (COP5) and a certificate of service (COP20) must be filed with the court within 7 days of service.

3.159 A person who is not a person named for notification and who wishes to object to registration of the LPA or who if the LPA has already been registered wishes to apply to have power cancelled must apply directly to the Court of Protection in form COP1, paying an application fee and using the procedure under the Court of Protection Rules, Part 9. Applications to the Court of Protection and its procedures are dealt with in more detail in Chapter 4. An attorney also has standing to make applications to the Court of Protection where the donor lacks capacity and will use the same procedures as any other person who has standing to make an application. These are also dealt with in Chapter 4.

ENDURING POWERS OF ATTORNEY

The future of existing powers

3.160 MCA 2005 repeals EPAA 1985 and provides for a new type of power of attorney, the LPA. No new EPAs can therefore be created.[264] There will, however, remain in place countless numbers of EPAs.[265] There is no reliable record of how many EPAs have been made and what proportion of them should be registered or might in future need to be registered on the grounds that the donor lacks capacity. Those EPAs which are registrable as well as the thousands which have already been registered cannot be replaced by new powers of attorney. Not only does the donor lack capacity to grant a new power, but it would be contrary to public policy to require donors – who have in good faith provided for the management of their property and affairs in the event of

---

[263] MCA 2005, Sch 4, Part 2, para 13(3).
[264] MCA 2005, Sch 7.
[265] There is no reliable record of how many EPAs have actually been created. Probably tens if not hundreds of thousands have been created as 'insurance policies' and remain in deed boxes and solicitors' offices across the country.

incapacity – to go to the effort and expense of making new powers of attorney. Neither was it considered appropriate to alter the terms on which a person was appointed to act.[266] MCA 2005 therefore addresses the status of those EPAs, registered and unregistered, made before its commencement. These transitional provisions are considered in Chapter 9.[267] The procedure for registering EPAs is set out in the Lasting Powers of Attorney, Enduring Powers of Attorney and Public Guardian Regulations 2007[268] and the prescribed forms set out in the Schedules thereto.

3.161　EPAs are dealt with in more detail above and a detailed account of the rules and principles applicable to their operation is beyond the scope of this work.[269] However, practitioners will need to be able to advise on and administer two distinct types of statutory power of attorney and apply different principles and procedures to each one. Debate over whether one is better than the other will no doubt continue, until a new form of power of attorney is introduced that replaces them both. In the meantime, the inevitable result is the complexity of comprehending two different jurisdictions and two procedures applicable to persons in similar circumstances. Given the difficulties faced by the Court of Protection and Public Guardianship Office in operating one jurisdiction, it must be hoped that the new Court of Protection and Public Guardian will fare better than its predecessor in the operation of two jurisdictions.

---

[266] The Law Commission had proposed that unregistered EPAs could be converted to new-style powers of attorney, but that the expectations of donors should continue to be met. See Law Com No 231 (at **3.16**), at para 7.59.

[267] See MCA 2005, Sch 4.

[268] SI 2007/1253.

[269] See **3.7–3.18**. The topic is covered in greater and better detail in *Cretney & Lush on Lasting and Enduring Powers of Attorney* (Jordans, 6th edn, 2009) which will remain the definitive work on the subject. See also *Heywood & Massey: Court of Protection Practice* (Sweet & Maxwell). The same law and procedure will apply to existing EPAs, only different statutory provisions will apply to their operation.

CHAPTER 4

POWERS OF THE COURT

PRELIMINARY

4.1   The Mental Capacity Act 2005 (MCA 2005) only sets out the basic powers of the new Court of Protection and one must look at the Court of Protection Rules 2007[1] and Practice Directions to see how these are to be implemented. In addition to explaining the court's jurisdiction an attempt is made here to address some of the issues that must be faced. The manner in which the court conducts its business is dealt with in Chapter 8.

4.2   A helpful summary of the court's approach to the exercise of its powers is to be found in *G v E and others*.[2] The following extracts from the judgment of Mr Justice Baker are worth setting out as an introduction to this chapter:

'(i)   The vast majority of decisions about incapacitated adults are taken by carers and others without any formal general authority. That was the position prior to the passing of the MCA under the principle of necessity ... In passing the MCA, Parliament ultimately rejected the Law Commission's proposal of a statutory general authority and opted for the same approach as under the previous law by creating in section 5 a statutory defence to protect all persons who carry out acts in connection with the care or treatment of an incapacitated adult, provided they reasonably believe that it will be in that person's best interests for the act to be done. Crucially, however, all persons who provide such care and treatment are expected to look to the Code ...

(ii)   The Act and Code are therefore constructed on the basis that the vast majority of decisions concerning incapacitated adults are taken informally and collaboratively by individuals or groups of people consulting and working together. It is emphatically not part of the scheme underpinning the Act that there should be one individual who as a matter of course is given a special legal status to make decisions about incapacitated persons.

(iii)   It will usually be the case that decisions about complex and serious issues are taken by a court rather than any individual. In certain cases, as explained in paragraphs 8.38 and 8.39 of the Code, it will be more appropriate to appoint a deputy or deputies to make these decisions. But because it is important that such decisions should wherever possible be taken collaboratively and informally, the appointments must be as limited in scope and duration as is

---

[1]   SI 2007/1744.
[2]   [2010] EWHC 2042 (COP) (Fam). An earlier judgment on an emergency application in this case was reported as *G v E and Others* [2010] EWHC 621 (Fam).

reasonably practicable in the circumstances. ... the appointment of deputies is likely to be more common for property and affairs than for personal welfare.

(iv)   It is axiomatic that the family is the cornerstone of our society and a person who lacks capacity should wherever possible be cared for by members of his natural family, provided that such a course is in his best interests and assuming that they are able and willing to take on what is often an enormous and challenging task. That does not, however, justify the appointment of family members as deputies simply because they are able and willing to serve in that capacity.'

4.3   Applying this approach to the facts of the particular case Baker J stated:

'(v)   ... the application for the appointment of F and G as personal welfare deputies is, in my judgment, misconceived. The routine decisions concerning E's day-to-day care, including decisions about holidays and respite care can be taken by F as his carer. Decisions about his education should be taken collaboratively by F, G, his teacher, and other relevant professionals. Decisions about possible medical treatment should be taken by his treating clinicians, who will doubtless consult both F and G and others as appropriate. If there is any disagreement about any of these matters, an application can be made to the Court of Protection. Decisions about who should look after E in the event that F is no longer able to do so should equally be considered (when the need arises) in a collaborative way and only referred to the court for endorsement if required or if there is any disagreement. That is an issue for the very long term and it would be wholly inappropriate to appoint a deputy or deputies now to make that decision ...

(vi)   I am also unpersuaded that the appointment of deputies for property and affairs is justified at this point. Currently, E's income consists of state benefits alone and his savings are less than one thousand pounds. ... the management of his independent budget ... do not justify the appointment of a financial deputy. I recognise that an appointment of a deputy for property and affairs would become appropriate were E to acquire assets of a size that required the sort of management decisions described in section 18. That might occur, for example, were he to be awarded a significant sum of damages as a result of his forthcoming claim ...'

DECLARATIONS

Background

4.4   In regard to serious medical treatment and welfare decisions the High Court found it necessary to make declarations as to both capacity and then best interests when there was uncertainty or dispute over these issues in relation to an individual.[3] The High Court then enforced these declarations when necessary. The court had to do this under its inherent powers because the courts did not have power to make decisions on behalf of those who lacked capacity.

---

[3]   For the case-law and a further explanation, see Chapter 5.

4.5   However, the MCA 2005 filled the legal vacuum in the law which was left to the inherent jurisdiction of the High Court and instead allowed the court to make a wide range of orders and decisions relating to P. Nevertheless, the inherent jurisdiction still remains for vulnerable adults who do not lack capacity and who therefore fall outside the scope of the MCA 2005.

4.6   Traditionally, the civil and family courts struggled when doubt was raised as to the mental capacity of a party because generic judges had little experience in this area. However, the increase of awareness of the MCA 2005 and more judges being nominated to hear Court of Protection cases especially in the Regional Courts, judges faced with issues of capacity are either able to address the issues in the case themselves or they have colleagues nearby who can do so.

General powers of the court

4.7   The new Court of Protection may make declarations as to:

(1)   whether a person has or lacks capacity to make a decision specified in the declaration;

(2)   whether a person has or lacks capacity to make decisions on such matters as are described in the declaration;

(3)   the lawfulness or otherwise of any act done, or yet to be done, in relation to that person.

In this respect an 'act' includes an omission and a course of conduct.[4] There is a clear distinction here, which has always applied at common law, between a declaration as to capacity and a declaration as to the lawfulness of an act. But one follows from the other – if the person does not lack capacity it will not be appropriate for the court to make a declaration as to the lawfulness of an act. What is lawful will generally be what is in the best interests of the individual applying the statutory criteria.

Declarations as to capacity

4.8   The previous jurisdiction under the Mental Health Acts required the former Court of Protection to make an initial decision as to whether the individual was a patient and thus within its jurisdiction. That decision was seldom reconsidered thereafter, and usually a receiver would be appointed to manage the patient's property and financial affairs under fairly close supervision unless there was so little involved that a short order could be made delegating everything to a suitable person without continuing supervision. The emphasis was thus on protection.

4.9   Under the MCA 2005's jurisdiction there is a need to reassess capacity in regard to different decisions and at different times. The emphasis is on empowerment, with protection when necessary. This power to make

---

4   MCA 2005, s 15.

declarations as to capacity in regard to a particular decision or range of decisions is of considerable importance. In every case the court will need to make a decision about capacity before it exercises its jurisdiction although it may not need to make a declaration in each instance.[5]

4.10   As the judges of the Court of Protection either sit full-time in the court at the Central Registry in London or are nominated from amongst circuit and district judges and sit on a regional basis, it has become possible for them to be treated as specialists in capacity issues. Colleagues may refer to the regional judges for guidance or even transfer cases to them when difficult issues as to capacity arise. This may be helpful not only for case management but also for substantive decisions. There is the potential for these judges not only to make declarations as to capacity in the Court of Protection (which may be treated as binding within particular proceedings in another court) but also to sit in a dual jurisdiction.

Declarations as to medical treatment

4.11   The Code of Practice provides that certain types of medical decision should be brought before the court.[6] Although the court may actually make decisions concerning medical treatment under its new statutory powers, it is likely that in serious or developing situations a declaration as to the lawfulness of treatment will be preferred because this delegates to the medical profession the decision as to whether treatment is appropriate in the circumstances.

4.12   For situations where the treatment will definitely be provided if it is authorised (eg non-therapeutic dental treatment or cosmetic surgery for a learning disabled adult) there is no reason why the court should not exercise its power to make the treatment decision.

MAKING DECISIONS AND APPOINTING DEPUTIES

Powers of the Court

4.13   If a person ('P') lacks capacity in relation to a matter or matters concerning his or her personal welfare, or his or her property and affairs, the Court is given certain powers, but these are subject to the provisions of MCA 2005 and, in particular, to s 1 (the principles) and s 4 (best interests).[7] In these situations the court may:[8]

(1)   by making an order, make the decision or decisions on P's behalf in relation to the matter or matters; or

---

[5]   See **4.12** for an elaboration of this.
[6]   See paras 8.18–8.24 of the Code.
[7]   These are dealt with in Chapter 2.
[8]   MCA 2005, s 16.

(2)   appoint a person (a 'deputy') to make decisions on P's behalf in relation to the matter or matters.

An order of the court may be varied or discharged by a subsequent order.

4.14   It is a pre-requisite of the jurisdiction of the court that the person to whom the proceedings relate (now referred to as 'P') lacks capacity. In an early case it was held that since the Act laid down that mental capacity was to be presumed, there was no jurisdiction to make an order for directions unless and until this presumption was rebutted.[9] This therefore raised issues of the correct test to be applied for the court to assume jurisdiction under s 48 of the MCA, to make 'interim orders and directions'. On appeal it was held that the 'gateway' test for the engagement of the court's powers under s 48 must be lower than that of evidence sufficient, in itself, to rebut the presumption of capacity. It was held that the proper test for the engagement of s 48 in the first instance is whether there is evidence giving good cause for concern that P may lack capacity in some relevant regard. Once that is raised as a serious possibility, the court then moves on to the second stage to decide what action, if any, it is in P's best interests to take before a final determination of his capacity can be made.

Making decisions

General

4.15   Instead of making the decision in question the court may decide to appoint a deputy with powers to make decisions both now and in the future. The appointment of deputies is dealt with below.[10]

Children

4.16   Some flexibility has been provided in regard to people under the age of 18 years. The Lord Chancellor may by order make provision as to the transfer of proceedings relating to a person under 18, in such circumstances as are specified in the order:

(1)   from the Court of Protection to a court having jurisdiction under the Children Act 1989; or

(2)   from a court having jurisdiction under that Act to the Court of Protection.[11]

---

[9]   *Re F* [2009] EWHC B30 (Fam).
[10]   See **4.25** et seq.
[11]   MCA 2005, s 21. See the Mental Capacity Act 2005 (Transfer of Proceedings) Order 2007, SI 2007/1899.

Personal welfare

4.17 The powers as respects P's personal welfare extend in particular to:[12]

(1) deciding where P is to live;

(2) deciding what contact, if any, P is to have with any specified persons;

(3) making an order prohibiting a named person from having contact with P;

(4) giving or refusing consent to the carrying out or continuation of a treatment by a person providing health care for P; and

(5) giving a direction that a person responsible for P's health care allows a different person to take over that responsibility,

but this is subject to the restrictions on deputies set out at **4.25**ff.

Property and affairs

4.18 The powers as respects P's property and affairs extend in particular to:[13]

(1) the control and management of P's property;

(2) the sale, exchange, charging, gift or other disposition of P's property;

(3) the acquisition of property in P's name or on P's behalf;

(4) the carrying on, on P's behalf, of any profession, trade or business;

(5) the taking of a decision which will have the effect of dissolving a partnership of which P is a member;

(6) the carrying out of any contract entered into by P;

(7) the discharge of P's debts and of any of P's obligations, whether legally enforceable or not;

(8) the settlement of any of P's property, whether for P's benefit or for the benefit of others;

(9) the execution for P of a will;

(10) the exercise of any power (including a power to consent) vested in P whether beneficially or as trustee or otherwise; and

(11) the conduct of legal proceedings in P's name or on P's behalf.

4.19 The powers as respects matters relating to P's property and affairs may be exercised even though P has not reached 16, if the court considers it likely that P will still lack capacity to make decisions in respect of that matter when he or she reaches 18. Once again, restrictions apply to deputies as set out at **4.25**ff.

Wills

4.20 The court can thus, if P is an adult, make an order or give directions requiring or authorising a person (the 'authorised person') to execute a will on

---

[12]   MCA 2005, s 17.
[13]   MCA 2005, s 18.

behalf of P. The restrictions prevent this being done by a deputy or if P has not reached 18.[14] However, the approach of the court to the terms of the will has changed. It is no longer a question of seeking to make the will that the testator would have made if acting reasonably on competent legal advice and notionally restored to full mental capacity, memory and foresight.[15] The court must now act in the best interests of the testator in accordance with the statutory formula, and this will include consideration of how the testator would be remembered after his death.[16] It seems that the best interests approach may justify the court authorising a statutory will when there is doubt as to the validity of the last will due to concerns as to testamentary capacity or undue influence.[17]

4.21 There are further provisions in respect of wills in MCA 2005, Sch 2. The will may make any provision (whether by disposing of property or exercising a power or otherwise) which could be made by a will executed by P if he or she had capacity to make it. The will must:

(1) state that it is signed by P acting by the authorised person;
(2) be signed by the authorised person with the name of P and his or her own name in the presence of two or more witnesses present at the same time;
(3) be attested and subscribed by those witnesses in the presence of the authorised person; and
(4) be sealed with the official seal of the court.

4.22 If a will has been so executed the Wills Act 1837 has effect in relation to the will as if it were signed by P by his or her own hand, except that the Wills Act 1837, s 9 (requirements as to signing and attestation) does not apply, and in the subsequent provisions of the Act any reference to execution in the manner required by the previous provisions is to be read as a reference to execution as stated above.

4.23 The will then has the same effect for all purposes as if P had had the capacity to make a valid will, and the will had been executed by him or her in the manner required by the Wills Act 1837. But this does not apply in relation to the will insofar as:

(1) it disposes of immovable property outside England and Wales; or
(2) it relates to any other property or matter if, when the will is executed, P is domiciled outside England and Wales, and under the law of P's domicile,

---

[14] It has been held that the approach is the best interests of the testator, which is different from the enquiry as to what the testator 'might be expected to have done' under the former jurisdiction – see *In the Matter of P* [2009] EWHC 163 (Ch).

[15] The test expounded by Megarry J in *Re D (J)* [1982] 2 All ER 37.

[16] *In the Matter of P* [2009] EWHC 163 (Ch), Lewison J; *In the Matter of M* [2009] EWHC 2525 (Fam), [2009] COPLR Con Vol 828, Munby J.

[17] *Re D (Statutory Will)* [2010] EWHC 2159 (Ch), HHJ Hodge QC sitting as a nominated judge.

any question of his or her testamentary capacity would fall to be determined in accordance with the law of a place outside England and Wales.

Settlements

4.24 Special provisions in regard to settlements are also to be found in MCA 2005, Sch 2. The court may make vesting or other orders as required, and may vary or revoke a settlement in certain circumstances. The court may also order that investments be vested in a suitable curator outside England and Wales.[18] This provision is sometimes used to facilitate personal injury settlements in the case of brain injury awards, thereby by-passing the statutory procedures for the management of financial affairs where there is a lack of capacity. Such settlements were common under the former regime, but now need to be justified because the primary jurisdiction is that of the Court of Protection. Supervision and intervention is more difficult in the cases of a settlement and would involve expensive Chancery proceedings, whereas the decisions of a deputy can readily be examined by the Court of Protection and the Public Guardian and costs are more closely monitored.

Miscellaneous

4.25 Further provisions enable the court to preserve the interests of others (eg under a will or in intestacy) in property disposed of on behalf of the person lacking capacity. This might involve transferring the interest to a replacement property. There can also be a charge imposed for P's benefit on property that has been improved at P's expense.[19]

Deputies

Appointment

4.26 As stated above, instead of making decisions itself the court may appoint a person (a 'deputy') to make decisions on P's behalf in relation to matters concerning P's personal welfare, or P's property and affairs, or both.[20] A deputy is to be treated as P's agent in relation to anything done or decided by the deputy within the scope of his or her appointment and in accordance with MCA 2005.

4.27 When deciding whether it is in P's best interests to appoint a deputy, the court must have regard (in addition to the matters mentioned in MCA 2005, s 4[21]) to the principles that:

(1) a decision by the court is to be preferred to the appointment of a deputy to make a decision; and

---

[18] MCA 2005, Sch 2, paras 5, 6 and 7.
[19] MCA 2005, Sch 2, paras 8 and 9.
[20] MCA 2005, s 19.
[21] This defines the concept of best interests – see generally Chapter 2.

(2)   the powers conferred on a deputy should be as limited in scope and duration as is reasonably practicable in the circumstances.

The Code of Practice gives examples of decisions that it may be appropriate for the court to make[22] and also of situations where it may be appropriate to appoint a welfare deputy.[23]

4.28   The court may make such further orders or give such directions, and confer on a deputy such powers or impose on him or her such duties, as it thinks necessary or expedient for giving effect to, or otherwise in connection with, an order or appointment made by it. The court may make the order, give the directions or make the appointment on such terms as it considers are in P's best interests, even though no application is before the court for an order, directions or an appointment on those terms.

Who may be appointed?

4.29   A deputy appointed by the court must be an individual who has reached 18, but for powers in relation to property and affairs the deputy could be a trust corporation. A person may not be appointed as a deputy without his or her consent, but the court may appoint an individual by appointing the holder for the time being of a specified office or position.

4.30   The court may appoint two or more deputies to act jointly, jointly and severally, or jointly in respect of some matters and jointly and severally in respect of others. The court may also appoint one or more other persons to succeed the existing deputy or deputies in such circumstances, or on the happening of such events, as may be specified by the court and for such periods as may be so specified.[24]

Control of the deputy

4.31   The court may require a deputy:

(1)   to give to the Public Guardian such security as the court thinks fit for the due discharge of his or her functions; and

(2)   to submit to the Public Guardian such reports at such times or at such intervals as the court may direct.

4.32   The levels of supervision by the Public Guardian are considered in Chapter 9.

---

[22]   See paras 8.27–8.28 of the Code.
[23]   See paras 8.38–8.39 of the Code. For different views as to whether a personal welfare deputy should be appointed see *Re P* [2010] EWHC 1592 (Fam), Hedley J, and *G v E* [2010] EWHC 2512 (COP) (Fam), Baker J.
[24]   For guidance as to the appointment of family members see *Re P* [2010] EWHC 1592 (Fam), Hedley J.

Powers

4.33 The court may confer on a deputy's powers to take possession or control of all or any specified part of P's property and to exercise all or any specified powers in respect of it, including such powers of investment as the court may determine.[25]

4.34 The deputy is entitled to be reimbursed out of P's property for his or her reasonable expenses in discharging his or her functions and, if the court so directs when appointing him or her, to remuneration out of P's property.[26]

4.35 There are various restrictions on the powers of deputies appointed by the court and indeed of the powers that the court may give to deputies[27] and these are dealt with under the following headings. The authority conferred on a deputy is always subject to the provisions of MCA 2005 and, in particular, s 1 (the principles) and s 4 (best interests).[28]

Conditional on lack of capacity

4.36 A deputy does not have power to make a decision on behalf of P in relation to a matter if he or she knows or has reasonable grounds for believing that P has capacity in relation to the matter.

Powers that cannot be given

4.37 A deputy may not be given power:

(1) to prohibit a named person from having contact with P;
(2) to direct a person responsible for P's health care to allow a different person to take over that responsibility;
(3) with respect to the settlement of any of P's property, whether for P's benefit or for the benefit of others;
(4) with respect to the execution for P of a will; or
(5) with respect to the exercise of any power (including a power to consent) vested in P whether beneficially or as trustee or otherwise.

Medical treatment

4.38 A deputy may not refuse consent to the carrying out or continuation of life-sustaining treatment in relation to P.

Conflict with an attorney

4.39 A deputy may not be given power to make a decision on behalf of P which is inconsistent with a decision made, within the scope of his or her

---

[25] MCA 2005, s 19(8).
[26] MCA 2005, s 19(7).
[27] See MCA 2005, s 20.
[28] These are dealt with in Chapter 2.

authority and in accordance with MCA 2005, by the donee of a lasting power of attorney granted by P (or, if there is more than one donee, by any of them).

Restraint

4.40 A deputy may not do an act that is intended to restrain P unless the following four conditions are satisfied:[29]

(1) in doing the act, the deputy is acting within the scope of an authority expressly conferred on him or her by the court;

(2) P lacks, or the deputy reasonably believes that P lacks, capacity in relation to the matter in question;

(3) the deputy reasonably believes that it is necessary to do the act in order to prevent harm to P; and

(4) the act is a proportionate response to the likelihood of P's suffering harm, or the seriousness of that harm.

4.41 A deputy will be treated as having restrained P if he or she uses, or threatens to use, force to secure the doing of an act which P resists, or restricts P's liberty of movement, whether or not P resists, or if he or she authorises another person to do any of those things. But a deputy does more than merely restrain P if he or she deprives P of his or her liberty within the meaning of Art 5(1) of the European Convention on Human Rights (whether or not the deputy is a public authority).[30]

Revocation of appointment

4.42 The court may revoke the appointment of a deputy or vary the powers conferred on him or her if it is satisfied that the deputy:

(1) has behaved, or is behaving, in a way that contravenes the authority conferred on him or her by the court or is not in P's best interests; or

(2) proposes to behave in a way that would contravene that authority or would not be in P's best interests.

How will the court exercise these powers?

The court's approach

4.43 The court has a wide range of options for decision-making on behalf of the incapacitated person ('P'). It may make supervised or non-supervised single orders, or may appoint a deputy to make all decisions or a specified range of decisions in regard to personal welfare matters and/or financial affairs. The

---

[29] MCA 2005, s 20(7)–(11).
[30] MCA 2005, s 19(13). This provision has been repealed by the Mental Health Act 2007, s 55, Sch 11, Part 10 upon the introduction of the deprivation of liberty safeguards.

Court has a duty to take into account P's best interests as now defined but also to act in a way that is least restrictive of P's rights and freedom of action.

4.44 There is also a desire to deal with matters so that they do not need to be repeatedly referred back to the court, although there are some cases where this is necessary such as where deprivation of P's liberty is in issue and review of arrangements is appropriate. Often, however, a one-off decision will suffice on one of many issues the court has to deal with; perhaps about the grant of a tenancy or minor medical treatment for a person with learning disabilities

4.45 The bulk of the work of the court relates to P's financial affairs, and the judiciary have devised a lot of standard orders which are available to the profession in various publications and online in the hope that its approach can be understood and to generally assist practitioners.

What happened to receiverships?

The past regime

4.46 Unless a short order was appropriate, the standard outcome had been to appoint a receiver who administered the financial affairs of the patient under the supervision of the court. This was costly and bureaucratic, and although control over day-to-day finances might be delegated to the patient there was reluctance by receivers to allow this in case they were later criticised.

The present regime

4.47 Existing receivers have been replaced by a deputy, but with wider delegated powers. The court may also be inclined, especially in the case of professional deputies, to give them powers similar to those exercisable by donees under lasting powers of attorney dealing with financial affairs. There is a greater willingness in some cases to approve settlements rather than retain funds, although the statutory jurisdiction of the Court of Protection is often preferred for substantial brain injury awards.

4.48 A key criterion will be whether the continued involvement of the Office of the Public Guardian provides added value. This may depend upon an assessment of the family and other persons involved and of the risks involved in permitting more delegation. To some extent this risk can be minimised by requiring insurance bonds to be in place. The levels of supervision by the Public Guardian are considered in Chapter 9.

4.49 The approach to investment of funds has also changed, with the deputy being expected to seek advice from an independent financial adviser, and the special account which for many years has provided a high interest return but now provides interest below market rates may ultimately cease to be a viable option.

CONTROL OF LASTING POWERS OF ATTORNEY

Court's powers to intervene

General

4.50 Lasting powers of attorney (LPAs) introduced by MCA 2005, s 9 are dealt with in more detail in Chapter 3. Until the registration of a LPA is revoked by a donor with capacity or by the court on any of the specified grounds, the attorney (in MCA 2005 referred to as 'the donee') can continue to act with all the powers of an attorney subject to any restrictions and conditions contained in the power.[31] The court, however, retains the following powers which are exercisable at any time, not just to revoke or cancel the power or attach conditions to the donee's conduct, but also to guide the donee or provide authority where the donee requires this to carry out his or her duties under the power.[32]

4.51 All these powers which are specific to the operation of LPAs are in addition to the court's general powers which are exercisable in respect of any matter in which a person lacks capacity, whether or not the donee has authority to act in respect of the same matter. Thus the court has power to make a declaration of capacity under MCA 2005, s 15, decisions in respect of personal welfare under s 17 and decisions concerning a person's property and affairs under s 18.

4.52 In most cases, the court will be required to exercise its powers where these are needed to supplement the donee's powers under the LPA. For example, if the power is restricted to property and affairs the donee may apply to the Court of Protection for a decision concerning medical treatment or personal welfare. A LPA furthermore does not authorise the donee to make a will or settlement. Equally the court may need to supplement the powers of an attorney under a registered enduring power of attorney.

4.53 Conflicts between the authority of the court and the authority of the donee should be rare. If the donee has authority to carry out an act under the LPA then there is no need for the court to intervene unless there are grounds for overruling the donee, for instance, if the donee is acting contrary to the best interests of the donor. There may also be cases where the donee simply requires the assistance of the court to confirm that a proposed act may be carried out.

Specific powers

Creation and revocation

4.54 The court may determine any question relating to whether the requirements for the creation of the power have been met or the power has

---

[31] See generally Chapter 3.
[32] These matters are considered in greater detail in Chapter 3.

been revoked or come to an end.[33] There is concern that although there is a prescribed form which must be adopted, the Public Guardian is to ignore an immaterial difference and the court:[34]

> '... may declare that an instrument which is not in the prescribed form is to be treated as if it were, if it is satisfied that the persons executing the instrument intended it to create a lasting power of attorney.'

4.55 There is always a fear that the Office of the Public Guardian and the court will be faced with numerous applications to permit registration of otherwise defective forms. A relaxed response would encourage a sloppy approach to these important documents, whereas refusal to register will generally result in an application for the appointment of a deputy.

4.56 Unless a hearing is needed these applications are dealt with 'on paper' by a judge at the Central Registry rather than sent to regional judges.[35] Whilst the view may be taken that in the absence of objections it is preferable to empower the donor by registering the power, how will the intention of the donor be known? Defective forms are most likely to arise where there has been no proper professional advice and these are the very situations where lack of capacity or undue pressure tends to arise. To some extent the certificate of capacity on the form provides a safeguard, but at this stage this will merely be a signature on the form. The absence of such a certificate would be a fatal defect and the court may adopt a policy of requiring further information from the maker of the certificate before accepting a defective form.

Capacity

4.57 The court's power to determine any question relating to whether the requirements for the creation of the power have been met extends to whether the donor had the capacity to execute it.[36] Lack of capacity at the time of execution is often alleged in dysfunctional family cases, but the onus is on an objector to establish this and it is difficult to do so retrospectively in the absence of contemporary medical evidence. The objectors must therefore turn to one of the grounds on which registration of the power may be refused.

Registration

4.58 The court may refuse registration or revoke an otherwise valid lasting power if satisfied that:

---

[33] MCA 2005, s 22(2).
[34] MCA 2005, Sch 1, Part 1, para 3(2).
[35] Significant decisions are reported on the Justice website – commence a search at www.justice.gov.uk/guidance/protecting-the-vulnerable/mental-capacity-act/orders-made-by-the-court-of-protection/index.htm.
[36] MCA 2005, s 9(2)(c).

(1)   fraud or undue pressure was used to induce the donor to create the power;[37] or

(2)   the donee (or, if more than one, any of them) has behaved, is behaving or proposes to behave in a way that contravenes his or her authority or is not in the donor's best interests.[38]

4.59   If there is more than one donee the court may revoke the power so far as it relates to any of them thus allowing it to be registered as regards another.[39] Presumably if fraud or undue pressure is established the whole power must fail (although MCA 2005 appears to provide otherwise), but it is not clear whether the court is empowered to remove one misbehaving donee under a joint power (as distinct from a joint and several power).[40]

4.60   The approach to fraud or undue pressure is unlikely to differ from that previously adopted in relation to enduring powers of attorney. Fraud does not require further comment, but in the case of dysfunctional families (and even where a solicitor has been involved) there is generally an objection on the basis of undue pressure in the execution of the power. There can be no objection to mere influence – it is undue pressure that is objectionable, but the boundaries may be difficult to define.[41]

4.61   The new certificate of capacity on the LPA form should assist in these cases as the makers of these certificates can be asked to attend a hearing to give evidence as to the manner in which they have formed their opinion that the donor understood the purpose of the instrument and the scope of the authority given under it, and that execution was not induced by fraud or undue pressure.[42]

In the dysfunctional family cases it will generally also be necessary for the Court to decide whether one or more of the attorneys has behaved, is behaving or intends to behave in a way that contravenes his or her authority or is not in the donor's best interests.[43]

4.62   Even if such a finding is made there will be a discretion on the part of the court to overlook the behaviour, taking into account all the circumstances. This differs from the equivalent ground under enduring powers of attorney, which is (and remains for those powers yet to be registered):[44]

---

[37]   MCA 2005, s 22(3)(a).

[38]   MCA 2005, s 22(3)(b). The criteria for refusing to register or revoking an enduring power of attorney are slightly different – see Chapter 3.

[39]   MCA 2005, s 22(5).

[40]   Reference should be made to MCA 2005, s 10(6) in this context.

[41]   There may be no difference between 'undue pressure' as now defined and the previous term 'undue influence' in respect of which there is considerable case-law.

[42]   The limited extent to which solicitors who have acted in the preparation of enduring powers of attorney are presently called to give evidence in support of the power does not provide an encouraging precedent.

[43]   See MCA 2005, s 22(3)(b) and also Sch 1, Part 3.

[44]   See MCA 2005, Sch 4, Part 4, para 13(9)(e).

'... that, having regard to all the circumstances and in particular the attorney's relationship to or connection with the donor, the attorney is unsuitable to be the donor's attorney.'

4.63 A test based on behaviour is very different from one based upon suitability and this can provoke the need for the court to make findings of fact. If past behaviour is relied upon and the donor knew about this when the LPA was executed, it may be difficult to argue that such behaviour, or the propensity for such behaviour in the future, is not in the donor's best interests. This approach demonstrates a move away from a paternalistic approach towards empowerment of the donor, whose choice of donee must be respected. It will shift the emphasis when objections are raised from suitability of the donees to the validity of the power and the presumption of validity may dictate the outcome in many cases. There will be cases where, despite genuine concerns as to the manner in which an LPA was procured and the intentions of the donee, family members cannot establish an objection to registration.

Meaning and effect of the power

4.64 The court may determine any question as to the meaning or the effect of the LPA (or an instrument purporting to create a LPA). The court may therefore clarify any uncertainty as to the form of the power or the scope of the donee's authority.[45]

Directions to the attorney

4.65 The court may, if the donor lacks capacity, give directions with respect to decisions the donee has authority to make or give any consent or authorisation to act which the donee would have to obtain from a mentally capable donor.[46] Thus a donee who is unsure about whether he or she has authority to act can obtain prior approval from the court before acting. A donee who might otherwise need to obtain the consent of the donor to a proposed act, where, for instance, he or she may benefit from the act or the act is subject to the express agreement of the donor, can also obtain the prior approval of the court.

Rendering accounts etc

4.66 The Court may, if the donor lacks capacity, give directions to the donee with respect to the rendering of accounts or production of records, require the donee to supply information or produce documents,[47] and give directions with regard to remuneration or expenses.[48] These are useful powers and mirror those for enduring powers of attorney.[49]

---

[45] MCA 2005, s 23(1).

[46] MCA 2005, s 23(2).

[47] For example, the deeds to a property or a testamentary document where it is a confidential document.

[48] MCA 2005, s 23(3)(a), (b) and (c).

[49] Cf Enduring Powers of Attorney Act 1985, s 8(2)(c), now reproduced in MCA 2005, Sch 4, para 16(2).

4.67 In some cases the court may authorise the production of accounts, whether to the court or to a third party,[50] and the power can be useful to dispel mistrust and suspicion within families in regard to financial management. An objection to registration may be withdrawn if the court is prepared to require basic financial disclosure to an objector whose intervention might be justifiable, and the power must then be registered. This is sometimes viewed as preferable to revocation of an enduring power and the imposition of a professional receiver under the former jurisdiction and a similar approach is likely to be adopted towards the appointment of a deputy as an alternative to registration of a lasting power. There is a difficult balance to be achieved between maintaining confidentiality in regard to the donor's financial affairs, which should not automatically be disclosed to family members on the onset of mental incapacity, and avoiding the suspicion and mistrust that arises when a financial manager is unduly secretive, especially when all involved are potential beneficiaries of the donor's estate.

Relieving the attorney of liability

4.68 The court has power, if the donor lacks capacity, to relieve the donee wholly or partly from any liability which he or she has or may have incurred on account of a breach of his or her duties as attorney.[51] Although this power is included in MCA 2005 with those set out under the above heading it is fundamentally different in nature, being retrospective in nature. Where financial shortcomings are involved it may be difficult to find that relief for the attorney is in the best interests of the donor. Where a liability has been incurred to a third party, which could presumably be for breach of contract or negligence, relieving the attorney of liability would presumably involve requiring the donor to provide an indemnity because this provision is not intended to take away the rights of third parties. Nevertheless, this provision enables the court to provide relief where the donor would have so done if capable.

Gifts

4.69 The court may authorise the making of any gift which is beyond the scope of the donor's limited authority under MCA 2005, s 12(2).[52]

Applying to the court

4.70 Following creation by registration, any person who wishes to apply to the court to invoke its powers dealing with the validity and operation of a LPA must apply directly to the court in form COP1. A donee or other party who wishes to apply for an order for a gift or authority for any decision not within the scope of the donee's authority must use the same formal procedure. The

---

[50] Re C *(Power of Attorney)* [2000] 2 FLR 1 provides one example of an account being required.

[51] MCA 2005, s 23(3)(d). For enduring powers see MCA 2005, Sch 4, para 16(2)(f).

[52] MCA 2005, s 23(4). For enduring powers see MCA 2005, Sch 4, paras 3(3) and 16(2)(e).

formalities of an application are governed by Court of Protection Rules 2007[53] made pursuant to MCA 2005, s 51(1), as supplemented by Practice Directions.

4.71 A donor or donee under a LPA does not require permission from the court to make an application for the exercise of any of its powers.[54] Neither does MCA 2005 appear to prevent the court from exercising its powers of its own volition, for instance, in response to a report made to it by the Public Guardian or a Visitor. Although permission may be required for another person to make an application to the court, this does not apply in respect of disputes about enduring or lasting powers of attorney.[55]

4.72 Instead of applying to the court directly a concerned relative or other body may make a complaint to the Public Guardian about the conduct of the donee and then leave the Public Guardian to make inquiries or take action directly or through the Court of Protection.[56]

4.73 If the applicant knows or has reasonable grounds for believing that the donor lacks capacity, then the procedure for notifying P under the Court of Protection Rules 2007, Part 7 applies to the donor. Any person making such an application must proceed on the basis that the court has no existing record of the case and cannot assume that P lacks capacity. Clearly the fact that the LPA is operational does not in any way indicate that the donor lacks capacity. Each application must stand alone and be justified on its own merits and with its own evidence, including medical evidence. Only in very straightforward cases covered by PD9D is this procedural burden relaxed.

The role of the Public Guardian

4.74 The role of the Public Guardian has been considered in more detail in Chapter 9 in the context of his or her principle role of registering LPAs. The Public Guardian is also responsible for registering enduring powers of attorney (EPAs) created before the coming into force of MCA 2005.[57] However, the Public Guardian has a distinct legal personality as well as an important administrative role, dealing with most routine applications to the Court of Protection.[58]

4.75 Where LPAs are concerned, the Public Guardian is the main administrative focus for all applications and inquiries, whether contentious or non-contentious. Thus the Public Guardian will be able to determine whether applications need to be forwarded to the court or can be addressed through correspondence by the Public Guardian.

---

[53] SI 2007/1744.
[54] MCA 2005, s 50(1)(c).
[55] See Court of Protection Rules 2007, SI 2007/1744, Part 8 and in particular r 51.
[56] MCA 2005, s 58(1)(h).
[57] MCA 2005, Sch 4, para 4(2). See Chapter 8.
[58] The powers and responsibilities of the Public Guardian are considered in more detail in Chapter 7.

4.76 The Public Guardian therefore has the following statutory functions:[59]

(1) establishing and maintaining registers of LPAs and EPAs;

(2) directing Court of Protection Visitors to visit the donee of a LPA and making reports on such matters as the Public Guardian may direct;

(3) receiving reports from donees of LPAs;[60]

(4) reporting to the Court of Protection on such matters as the court requires; and

(5) dealing with representations (including complaints) about the way in which a donee is exercising his or her powers.

4.77 The Secretary of State may by regulations confer other functions in connection with MCA 2005 upon the Public Guardian or make provision in connection with the discharge of his functions.[61] It is clear that the Public Guardian's role is being developed beyond the scope of the former Public Guardianship Office, so that through his office he can take a more proactive role in monitoring the operation of LPAs. In view of the likely volume of transactions it is unlikely that there will be much scope for routine investigation, but where there are complaints or concerns are expressed about the conduct of a donee (or an attorney), the Public Guardian will be able to respond and make inquiries. In most cases a call for a report from a public body such as the Public Guardian and some discrete correspondence or negotiation may be sufficient to address the particular concern. In other cases the Public Guardian will be expected to advise and involve the Court to ensure that action is taken.

CHALLENGES FACED BY THE COURT

Overview

4.78 People who lack mental capacity fall into four broad groups:

(1) The largest group comprises elderly people who are deprived of capacity due to senile dementia, a condition that tends to be irreversible. They have enjoyed personal autonomy in the past and may have a personal income and savings that require management, but are no longer able to conduct their own lives.

(2) People with learning disabilities[62] form the second distinct group. They may never have matured to the stage where they can live a totally

---

[59] MCA 2005, s 58.
[60] The Public Guardian receives the report but only the court can direct a report: see MCA 2005, ss 23(3)(a) and 49(2).
[61] MCA 2005, s 58.
[62] Referred to in an educational context as 'learning difficulties' and previously known as 'mental handicap'.

independent and self-supporting life, and in consequence do not have significant savings or income unless they have come into an inheritance.

(3) Some people are deprived of mental capacity for a period or periods of their lives due to a mental illness which might be treatable. They will need to be supported and protected when the illness is acute but at other times can make their own decisions and may be financially successful.

(4) The fourth group comprises people who have had an acquired brain injury which affects their ability to make decisions. This is seldom treatable and may be linked with physical disabilities. Large sums of compensation may need to be managed to finance a comprehensive care plan.

4.79 Each of these groups presents different challenges as regards both financial and care management, and some people overlap these groups. Those working in this jurisdiction must be sensitive to this diversity and there can be no standard approach.

4.80 The old Court of Protection was only concerned with financial management, but the court now has to contend with a mixture of financial and welfare issues and the myriad issues this brings through its doors.

Property and affairs

4.81 The management of financial affairs is not a new concept for a Court of Protection and statutory criteria have been imposed, and in particular a 'best interests' approach. In human terms, however, the court still adjudicates on struggles for control, whether this be the appointment of a donee or a deputy, to approve gifts and wills and to make policy decisions in regard to large damages awards. The change is the availability of a wider range of possible outcomes and the requirement for minimum intervention.

Personal welfare

4.82 However, some may say the the court's real test is in the making of personal welfare decisions, especially when the need for these arises through conflict within families or between families, carers and professionals. A simple decision may have wider implications. The issue is always the best interests of the incapacitated individual, but the process whereby this is addressed may differ according to whether the court is required to resolve a dispute or an uncertainty. The Official Solicitor will generally be involved to represent the incapacitated individual, although public funding issues and a heavy workload can stand in the way of his involvement in some cases, leaving P without representation and hence a voice in the proceedings. This in turn has led to amendments to the court rules, which are discussed in Chapter 8.

Health care

4.83 The Family Division of the High Court was accustomed to identifying best interests in regard to serious medical treatment, often in controversial and high-profile situations. Little changes following the transfer of this work to the new Court of Protection and the same judges are nominated to hear these cases, but instead of doing so under the inherent jurisdiction they do so under a statutory framework. Again, the challenge for the Family Division is more one of resources with an ever increasing workload generally.

4.84 Applications relating to less serious medical treatment and health care issues that do not need to be dealt with by High Court judges will tend to be resolved in the same way as other personal welfare issues, although expert medical evidence will be required. These applications do not necessarily result from disputes but may arise due to uncertainty, such as a proposal for non-therapeutic dental treatment or cosmetic surgery.

Personal care

4.85 The issues arising under this heading encompass the full range of decisions, from where to live and with whom to have contact down to holiday arrangements, mode of dress and choice of diet. Any issue that parents cannot agree in respect of their adult child with severe learning disabilities or siblings cannot agree in respect of their parent with senile dementia has the potential to be referred to the court. Professional carers may also wish to validate their plans for vulnerable individuals, such as participation in adventure holidays that carry some degree of risk.

4.86 'Adult contact' disputes are becoming more common and previously could only be resolved in the High Court at disproportionate expense, but the seniority of that court discouraged the type of application that is now the norm for the Court of Protection. Hearings in these cases now are usually before a nominated district judge who spends much of his or her time deciding such issues in respect of children and is best placed to hear such cases.

4.87 These cases cannot all be treated as litigation to be resolved on an adversarial basis. In some instances findings of fact are required, but otherwise the hearing will be more of an inquiry with input from family, friends, carers and professionals – and, of course, the incapacitated person to the extent that a contribution is meaningful. The parties may seek to bring issues before the court yet fail to address the best interests of this person. In such cases it may be appropriate for the incapacitated person to be made a party with a litigation friend and a legal representative (unless one professional such as the Official Solicitor can act in both capacities) or for the Court to obtain a report from a Visitor to ascertain the situation on the ground.[63]

---

[63] Such representation may be required in any event so as not to infringe the human rights of the incapacitated person, but the manner in which the proceedings are conducted must be proportionate to the matters in issue and funding may not be available for independent legal representation. See Court of Protection Rules 2007, SI 2007/1744, r 73, which gives the court discretion as to whether the incapacitated person is made a party.

4.88 Applications for 'adult care orders' are also becoming frequent where a child with learning disabilities has been placed in care under the Children Act 1989 and is approaching legal majority. The local authority may consider it necessary to continue to prevent or restrict a relationship with the parents and an application to the Court of Protection is then required. This may coincide with a transfer of responsibility from child services to adult services with a different approach from the social workers involved. The best interests approach under the MCA 2005 differs from the more paternalistic 'welfare of the child' approach under the Children Act 1989.

4.89 A new and perhaps unwanted challenge presented itself to the court in 2014 in the form of deprivation of liberty cases. Following the decision in *P v Cheshire West and Chester Council* [2014] UKSC 19, the definition of deprivation of liberty was held to be wider than was previously thought. Consequently, it was appreciated that the court would face a flood of applications in the tens of thousands seeking approval of arrangements that fell within the Supreme Court's definition of deprivation of liberty. This prompted the President of the Court of Protection to formulate a streamlined procedure to allow cases where there was no challenge to the deprivation of liberty to pass through the court speedily to receive approval. This exercise is recorded in two judgments in *Re X and others (Deprivation of Liberty)* [2014] EWCOP 25 and [2014] EWCOP 37. However, certain aspects of the decision have been appealed and the Court of Appeal judgment is awaited. This may result in the streamline procedure being aborted and potential chaos for the court.

THE FUTURE

4.90 In 2014, the House of Lords Select Committee on the Mental Capacity Act published its first report and the Government replied. The report made a large number of recommendations including that the overall responsibility for implementation of the Mental Capacity Act be given to a single independent body. The report stated that this would not remove ultimate accountability for its successful implementation from ministers, but it would locate within a single independent body the responsibility for oversight, co-ordination and monitoring of implementation activity across sectors, which is currently lacking. This new responsibility could be located within a new or existing body. The new independent body would make an annual report to Parliament on the progress of its activities.

The report also addressed the need for more awareness of the MCA and LPAs; the role of IMCAs; the need for consideration of the deprivation of liberty safeguard provisions; the provision of legal aid; the need to increase resources at the Court of Protection and the need for changes to the rules. This latter recommendation brought about the setting up of the Ad Hoc Rules Committee in 2014. The report set a wide agenda and it will be interesting to see how in the next year its proposals are taken on board. But if they are, then the Court of Protection will face challenging times.

4.91 Meanwhile, in the first quarter of 2015, the Ad Hoc Rules Committee completed its first tranche of reforms to the rules and by 1 July 2015, all these changes will be operative. These changes are discussed in Chapter 8.

However, it is the results of the second tranche of work that will be interesting as the Ad Hoc Rule Committee grapples with the more serious issues of transparency and the need to manage cases in a court with more litigants in person, far less legal aid and, where some cases incur heavy costs, which many feel disproportionate.

CHAPTER 5

GIFTS, STATUTORY WILLS AND SETTLEMENTS

PRELIMINARY

The statutory framework

5.1   The statutory framework set out in MCA 2005 extends beyond just making decisions for the direct benefit of the incapable person. Decisions that a person lacks capacity to make in person and that may need to be made include the making of gifts or other provisions for the benefit of another person. Where such decisions are delegated to an attorney or deputy, they are permitted by MCA 2005 as an exception to the common law principle that a fiduciary cannot dispose of property for the benefit of a third party, let alone for his or her own benefit. MCA 2005 enshrines this principle and makes it clear that no such decisions can be made unless they are permitted by the court (whether by the court directly or delegated to a deputy) or by the Act itself.

Decisions that can be made for the benefit of another party and that are permitted by MCA 2005 fall into the following categories:

- Small gifts and the provision of maintenance that may be made by an attorney acting under an Enduring Power of Attorney (MCA 2005, Sch 4, paras 3(2) and 3(3));
- Small gifts that may be made by an attorney acting under a Lasting Power of Attorney (MCA 2005, s 12(2));
- Small gifts and the provision of maintenance that may be made by a deputy within the scope of the authority conferred on the deputy (MCA 2005, s 19(8)(b));
- Gifts (and the provision of maintenance) that may only be permitted by express order of the Court (MCA 2005, s 18(1)(c) and that fall within the scope of PD9D);[1]
- Gifts (and the provision of maintenance) that may only be permitted by express order of the court (MCA 2005, s 18(1)(c) and that fall outside the scope of PD9D);

---

[1]   The Court of Protection also has power under MCA 2005, Sch 4 para 16(2)(e), in respect of a registered EPA to 'authorise the attorney to act so as to benefit himself or other persons than the donor otherwise than in accordance with para 3(2) and (3). In practice, an attorney would be expected to use s 18 of the Act.

- The making of a settlement or will for a person that may only be permitted by express order of the court (MCA 2005, ss 18(1)(h), 18(1)(i), 20(3)).

GIFTS NOT REQUIRING THE COURT'S AUTHORITY

Enduring powers of attorney

5.2 MCA 2005, Sch 4, paras 3(2) and 3(3) allow an attorney to benefit another person (or the attorney directly) but only in certain circumstances. These provide as follows:

> '(2) Subject to any conditions or restrictions contained in the instrument, an attorney under an enduring power, whether general or limited, may (without obtaining any consent) act under the power so as to benefit himself or other persons than the donor to the following extent but no further –
>> (a) he may so act in relation to himself or in relation to any other person if the donor might be expected to provide for his or that person's needs respectively, and.
>> (b) he may do whatever the donor might be expected to do to meet those needs.
> (3) Without prejudice to sub-paragraph (2) but subject to any conditions or restrictions contained in the instrument, an attorney under an enduring power, whether general or limited, may (without obtaining any consent) dispose of the property of the donor by way of gift to the following extent but no further –
>> (a) he may make gifts of a seasonal nature or at a time, or on an anniversary, of a birth, a marriage or the formation of a civil partnership, to persons (including himself) who are related to or connected with the donor, and,
>> (b) he may make gifts to any charity to whom the donor made or might be expected to make gifts,
> provided that the value of each such gift is not unreasonable having regard to all the circumstances and in particular the size of the donor's estate.'

5.3 The provisions of MCA 2005 relating to gifts made by an attorney acting under an EPA do not distinguish between a donor who has capacity and a donor who lacks capacity. Clearly, an attorney would be acting contrary to his authority if he acted contrary to the wishes of the capable donor. If the donor lacks capacity, then any decision made by the attorney must be made in the donor's best interests under MCA 2005, s 1(5). The authority of the attorney is further limited by Sch 4, paras 3(2) and 3(3):

- The power is subject to any conditions or restrictions in the instrument. While the donor cannot extend these powers, the donor may have limited these powers by an express condition or restriction.
- The provision for the maintenance or benefit for the attorney or other person is limited to doing what the donor 'might be expected to do' to meet that person's needs. Thus there must be a 'need' that is being

addressed. This power cannot be used as a way of making a gift by other means. The attorney must also aim to do what the donor might be expected to do, thus exercising a substituted judgment. There is also a sense that the attorney is carrying out a moral obligation, doing something that the particular donor is expected to do. Thus a husband may be expected to provide for his wife.

- Gifts can only be made to persons who are related to or connected to the donor. This is not defined more closely, but there must be a relationship or some connection between donor and donee.

- Gifts must be of a seasonal or anniversary nature or made on a special occasion such as a wedding. Thus gifts may be made on a birthday, wedding anniversary or at Christmas. Gifts cannot be made arbitrarily or by reference to a tax period.

- Gifts to a charity must be to a charity where there is a record of past donation or which the donor might be expected to provide for. The attorney cannot indulge a generous whim or choose a charity that is supported by the attorney.

- The value of each gift must not be unreasonable having regard to all the circumstances and in particular the size of the donor's estate.

5.4   Where the attorney acting under an EPA wishes to make a gift that is outside the scope of his or her authority, whether because of an express limitation in the power of because it goes beyond what is permitted by MCA 2005, then a formal application must be made to the Court.

Lasting powers of attorney

5.5   The authority of an attorney to make gifts while acting under a LPA is dealt with in more detail at **3.35–3.43**. The attorney has limited authority to make gifts under MCA 2005, s 12 and, as with an EPA, any gifts that exceed this authority must be approved by the court.[2] However, there is no express authority conferred on the attorney to maintain a person whom the donor may be expected to provide for, as there is for an attorney acting under an EPA. In these cases, the approval of the court should be sought unless there is a contractual or other obligation that is enforceable in a court of law against the donor. For example, the donor's spouse who is financially dependent on the donor would have a claim for financial provision against the donor.

Deputy appointed by the court

5.6   When appointing a deputy, the Court of Protection can confer on the deputy powers to 'exercise all or any specified powers in respect of [all or any part of P's property] including such powers of investment as the court may determine'. The court has a very wide discretion to confer powers on a deputy, so long as these are not the powers that are reserved to the court under

---

[2]   See *Re Buckley: The Public Guardian v C* [2013] COPLR 39 at [43].

MCA 2005, s 20(3). In practice, the court will, in the majority of orders appointing a deputy, provide authority to make gifts in the following terms:

> 'The deputy may (without obtaining any further authority from the court) dispose of [P]'s money or property by way of gift to any charity to which he/she made or might have been expected to make gifts and on customary occasions to persons who are related to or connected with him/her, provided that the value of each such gift is not unreasonable having regard to all the circumstances and, in particular, the size of his/her estate.'

5.7   The Court will also use its powers to allow a deputy authority to provide maintenance. Most orders appointing a deputy include the following provisions:

> 'The deputy may make provision for the needs of anyone who is related or connected with [P], if he/she provided for or might be expected to provide for that person's needs, by doing whatever he/she did or might reasonably be expected to do to meet those needs.'

The wording used in such orders is derived from the wording used in MCA 2005, Sch 4, paras 3(2) and 3(3) regarding the authority of an attorney under an EPA.[3]

The provisions relating to maintenance and gifts to charity require a degree of substituted judgment. The deputy must aim to stand in P's shoes and either continue what P has been doing or do what P might have been expected to do. There is no such proviso in relation to the making of gifts. Such gifts can only be made on customary occasions and the value of each gift must be reasonable. Clearly such gifts must also be made in the best interests of P.

The deputy's authority is exercised subject to MCA 2005, s 1(5) that any act done on behalf of a person who lacks capacity must be done in that person's best interests. The deputy is further constrained by the proviso in s 20(1) that no decision can be made on behalf of P if the deputy knows or has reasonable grounds for believing that the person has capacity to make the decision in person.

Value of gifts not requiring the court's authority

5.8   The statutory wording used for EPAs and LPAs and the authority conferred on a deputy are intentionally vague where maintenance and gifts are concerned. This is because each person's circumstances are different and some discretion or judgment has to be allowed to the individual attorney or deputy to act appropriately. In most cases it is self-evident what can or cannot be done. For a pensioner about to go into care whose estate is no more than a few thousand pounds, a gift of £100 to a child at Christmas may be unreasonable;

---

[3]   This in turn uses the wording first set out in the Enduring Powers of Attorney Act 1985, s 3.

for a millionaire with a private pension, a gift of several thousand pounds that utilises the annual Inheritance Tax allowance may be quite reasonable.

Guidance on what constitutes a reasonable gift was provided by the Court of Protection in *Re GM* [2013] COPLR 290. The 'gifts' made by the deputies purportedly in accordance with their authority were so excessive that they were set aside by the Court. The estate of GM had been worth approximately £500,000 (£300,000 had been bequeathed to her by her only daughter who had died intestate). Following their appointment as deputies, MJ and JM took it upon themselves to interpret their authority, which included the usual provision for the making of small gifts and maintenance, to make gifts to themselves and their families, as well as charities. These did not come to light until a routine meeting with a Court of Protection Visitor, who (according to the judgment) had 'recommended that the applicants apply to the court for the retrospective approval of the money they had given away on GM's behalf'. A report prepared by the Public Guardian under MCA 2005, s 49 disclosed gifts of £231,259 (of which £57,532 were to charitable organisations) and expenses of £46,552. Gifts included a Rolex watch valued at £18,275 and a ring valued at £16,500. Expenses for each of the deputies included a car and computer equipment. Obviously the purported gifts were excessive and were in large part set aside. But what gifts should have been made or could have been made, without being considered excessive? In a very helpful judgment, the Senior Judge laid down some very helpful guidelines (at [85]):

> 'The wording of the order appointing deputies for property and affairs envisages a threshold, albeit an imprecise one, beyond which any gifting by them could be regarded as unreasonable. For convenience, I shall call it the "reasonableness threshold".'

The reasonableness threshold differs from case to case depending on the individual circumstances. In *Re Buckley: The Public Guardian v C* [2013] COPLR 39, at para [43], I said that:

> '... subject to a sensible de minimis exception, where the potential infringement is so minor that it would be disproportionate to make a formal application to the court, an application must be made to the court for an order under section 23 of the Mental Capacity Act 2005 in any of the following cases:
>
> (a)   gifts that exceed the limited scope of the authority conferred on attorneys by section 12 of the Mental Capacity Act ...'

Re Buckley involved an LPA but the same principle would apply to a deputyship, where the wording of the order appointing the deputies is virtually identical to that in s 12 of the Mental Capacity Act 2005.

Being both proportionate and pragmatic, and to prevent the court from being overwhelmed with applications, with which it does not have the resources to cope, this *de minimis* exception can be construed as covering the annual IHT exemption of £3,000 and the annual small gifts exemption of £250 per person, up to a maximum of, say, 10 people in the following circumstances:

(a)   where P has a life expectancy of less than 5 years;

(b)   their estate exceeds the nil rate band for Inheritance Tax (IHT) purposes, currently £325,000;

(c)   the gifts are affordable having regard to P's care costs and will not adversely affect P's standard of care and quality of life, and

(d)   there is no evidence that P would be opposed to gifts of this magnitude being made on their behalf.

The *de minimis* exception referred to in the preceding paragraph does not apply to potentially exempt transfers, or to the use of the normal expenditure out of income exemption, where the authorisation of the court is required under ss 18(1)(b) and 23(4) of, and para 16(2)(e) of Sch 4 to, the Mental Capacity Act 2005.

The guidance given in the case of *GM* should apply equally to cases involving enduring and lasting powers of attorney, and this case has been referred to as well in Chapter 3 where gifts by attorneys acting under LPAs are considered in more detail in their own context.[4]

Maintenance not requiring the court's authority

5.9   It is not uncommon for a person who lacks capacity to have commitments to maintain another person. The most obvious example is that of the elderly husband who has historically been the main bread-winner with a pension that has been used to support himself and his wife in their retirement. On losing capacity and perhaps requiring full-time nursing care for himself, his deputy or attorney may continue to maintain his wife who continues to live in the family home. There are many other examples of a person lacking capacity also being or becoming responsible for maintaining another person. For example:

•   a parent may be maintaining an adult child who is disabled;

•   a parent may have been helping an adult child with living costs;

•   a grandparent has been helping an adult child with family costs or paying school fees;[5]

•   a disabled child has received a personal injury settlement which is used to acquire a property which is also lived in by the child's parents who are also caring for the child. The parents have no other employment.

---

[4]   By suggesting that gifts should be measured by reference to the Inheritance Tax allowances, the court has taken a more restrictive approach to the making of gifts. By comparison, in the 2000 case of *Re W*, the judge did not consider gifts of £20,000 to each of three children to be unreasonable. See **3.42** and note 89.

[5]   See the EPA case of *Re Cameron (deceased), Phillips v Cameron* [1999] Ch 386, [1999] 2 All ER 924.

An attorney acting under an EPA may, as mentioned above, authority under MCA 2005, Sch 4, para 3(2), to act in relation to any other person (including himself) if the donor might be expected to provide for his or that person's needs respectively, and may do whatever the donor might be expected to do to meet those needs. There is no equivalent provision conferred on the donee of a LPA, although the Court of Protection has allowed some leeway where there is a legal obligation to provide maintenance (see **3.36** above). Where a deputy is appointed, then the deputy is in effect exercising a power conferred on the deputy by the court. The court has a very wide discretion to confer such powers and, as mentioned at **5.7** above, these powers will usually include authority to maintain someone who has been maintained by P or whom P might be expected to maintain.

5.10 As with the making of gifts, there is no clear guidance as to when provision should be made and as to what level of provision should be provided. Clearly, there is a public policy to ensure that decisions that are necessary and often moral should be taken by those involved in implementing them and without putting unnecessary strain on themselves or on the court system. Often the sums in issue may be considerable, for instance where a personal injury award is maintaining a family in a property and covers property running costs, food, holidays and transport. The fact that there is conflict of interest is not of itself a barrier to this authority being exercised. For example, it is not uncommon for a deputy or attorney to be living in P's property. The deputy, or the attorney acting under an Enduring Power of Attorney, must act in P's best interests and apply common sense. A careful consideration of the relevant factors should lead to a satisfactory decision; if it might not or if there is any doubt of conflict, then an application should be made to the court.

Factors that a deputy may need to take into account:

- The wishes and feelings of P, to the extent that these can be ascertained;
- The nature of the relationship, for example a husband who has looked after his wife for many years or the parents of a disabled child who are totally dependent on the child's personal injury award;
- The extent to which the maintenance is affordable (whether relative to the value of the estate or any budget set by the court) as well as in the context of P's own wishes and feelings;
- Whether the maintenance confers a benefit on P, whether material or personal;
- Whether there is a conflict of interest. The deputy, or attorney, may be the beneficiary of the maintenance. This may be necessary and affordable, but care needs to be taken in measuring the level of maintenance being provided. A deputy in this position may consult with P (if P is able to assist) and other relatives, or obtain professional advice.

GIFTS REQUIRING THE COURT'S APPROVAL

Application required

5.11 Where the value of the proposed gift falls beyond the scope of the attorney's or deputy's authority, then an application must be made to the Court of Protection. The procedure is the same for any formal application and the generic steps to be taken are dealt with in more detail in Chapter 7. Thus, the application may be made by the attorney or deputy or by a person who is a beneficiary under a will or intestacy or who may be a person 'for whom P might be expected to provide if he had capacity to do so'.[6] Persons adversely affected may need to be served with the application as respondents (unless the 'short procedure' applies, see **5.13** below). The court will have to consider the application judicially, thus taking account of evidence of P's capacity and best interests and then making the order sought. The similar procedure involving an application for a statutory will is described at **5.30** below.

5.12 A gift authorised by the court may not necessarily be by a reference to a fixed sum being given to a particular person. A 'gift' in this context is any disposition that creates a transfer of value from P's estate to another's estate during P's lifetime or that confers a benefit on another party to P's detriment.[7] The maintenance of another person is technically a gift where it represents a transfer from P's estate to another's estate, although this may not necessarily be a transfer of value for Inheritance Tax purposes.[8] An application may need to be made to the Court of Protection where the gift is:

- A chattel – a valuable picture or item of jewellery may not be the sort of gift that is made on customary occasions;
- The making of gifts for Inheritance Tax planning, for example to use the annual exemptions outside of customary occasions, or to make gifts out of surplus income;
- To be made pursuant to a general power or authority to make gifts into the future (for example, a power to make gifts out of surplus income may be exercised over several years, likewise a commitment to pay care home fees or school fees may involve significant expenditure over many years);
- To provide for the maintenance of a relative or someone whom P might be expected to provide for, where the amounts involved are significant or controversial;
- The variation of an entitlement under a will or intestacy, so as to comply with Inheritance Act 1984, s 142;

---

[6]   COPR 2007, rr 51(2)(a), r 52(4).

[7]   The creation of a settlement may also constitute a 'gift' and transfer of value, and similar principles apply in measuring P's best interests. However, the statutory authority for creating a settlement is contained in MCA 2005, s 18(1)(h). See also **5.62** below.

[8]   Inheritance Tax Act 1984, s 11(3): 'A disposition is not a transfer of value if it is made in favour of a dependent relative of the person making the disposition and is a reasonable provision for his care or maintenance.'

- The making of a loan on favourable terms or a loan to the deputy or attorney or a member of his or her family; or
- The sale of property to the deputy or attorney or a member of his or her family.

Gifts using the 'short procedure'

5.13   In the context of making gifts, one of the problems caused by MCA 2005 is that in formal terms a gift must be either one which can be made by an deputy or attorney under his or her own authority or one which must be authorised by the Court of Protection. In the latter case, it will involve the court's jurisdiction and all the effort (and expense) of a formal application. However, in practice there is a vast difference between on the one hand a major tax planning exercise involving several hundred thousand pounds and on the other hand, a gift of a few thousand pounds which is not made on a customary occasion.

It is recognised in practice that not all applications require the same amount of time, effort and expense. Practice Direction 9D therefore provides a simplified or short procedure for routine and simple applications by existing deputies and as attorneys. This sets out a list of cases where the 'short procedure' would be appropriate. The cases involving a gift, include:

- applications for regular payments from P's assets to the deputy in respect of remuneration;
- applications seeking minor variations only as to the expenses that can be paid from P's estate;
- applications in relation to the sale of property owned by P, where the sale is non-contentious;
- applications to make a gift or loan from P's assets, provided that the sum in question is not disproportionately large when compared with the size of P's estate as a whole;

5.14   Paragraphs 6 and 7 of the Practice Direction go on to specify the following situations where (in the context of making gifts) the short procedure is not appropriate:

- where the sum in question is disproportionately large when compared with the size of P's estate as a whole;
- the application is likely to be contested;
- the application concerns large sums of money when compared with the size of P's estate

5.15   An application within the scope of PD9D still requires a formal application. However, there is no requirement to file medical evidence or give notice to P or any other person unless specifically directed to do so by the court. The applicant should not, however, assume that the court has any information about the case and should, therefore, provide the court with some up-to-date background information about P's estate, P's physical condition and any other recent decisions made by P or on P's behalf. As a matter of good practice, the court should, therefore, be provided with an up-to-date form COP1A and recent medical evidence, especially where the case involves a power of attorney (as registration will not have involved obtaining formal medical evidence).

STATUTORY WILLS[9]

Background

5.16 A statutory will is the term commonly used where a will is made on behalf of a *person who lacks capacity to make a will*[10] pursuant to an order of the Court of Protection under MCA 2005, s 18(1). The making of a will is one of the most distinctive and important decisions that can be made for a person who lacks capacity. This decision is, however, one that cannot be delegated to a deputy; it is expressly reserved to the Court of Protection, so that no will can be made without a formal application and consideration by a judge.[11] A will made in this way is no different to a will made by an adult testator who has testamentary capacity, save that it cannot apply to immovable property outside England and Wales.[12]

5.17 The statutory will jurisdiction is an unusual one and around 400 such applications are made each year. A will is a powerful expression of a person's autonomy. A person has a right to make a will or not to make a will, and this should not be interfered with lightly. However, there are cases where a carefully made will cannot foresee future events or the making of a will is put off and good intentions are cut off by incapacity. There are also cases where a person has never had an opportunity to make a will or the consequences of an intestacy would be unjust or even harmful. Examples of when a statutory will should be considered include situations where:

---

[9]   The commentary relating to statutory wills has been adapted from the commentary by the same author in *Elderly Clients: A Precedent Manual* (Jordans 2013).

[10] MCA 2005, s 2(1) defines such a person who lacks capacity in relation to a matter if at the material time he is unable to make a decision for himself in relation to the matter because of an impairment of, or a disturbance in the functioning of, the mind or brain.

[11] MCA 2005, s 20(3)(b). Practice Direction 9A expressly limits the authority of nominated officers acting under r 7A of the Court of Protection Rules 2007 to the making of certain decisions, which do not include the making of a will.

[12] MCA 2005, Sch 2, paras (3) and (4).

- there has been a major change in a person's status or circumstances such as a marriage, which has the effect of revoking any earlier will,[13] or an inheritance or personal injury award, which has the effect of altering the nature of the estate;[14]

- a legacy in an existing will adeems, for example where a property that is a specific gift in a will is sold to pay for care home fees;[15]

- there has been a major change in the personal circumstances of the beneficiaries, or any major change in P's relationship with them;[16]

- the effects of an existing will or intestacy might prejudice the interests of a beneficiary, for example where the beneficiary is a child or someone who is also disabled and where their interests can be better protected within a trust;

- there are concerns over the validity of an existing will. While a statutory will application cannot be used to conduct an examination into the validity of an earlier act, a new will might avoid future conflict and allow beneficiaries and claimants to resolve their differences in the context of P's best interests;[17]

- an existing will, or an intestacy, fails to make provision for a person or organisation for whom a person 'might be expected to provide' if he had capacity;[18]

- there are substantial legacies that cannot now be satisfied because P's financial circumstances have been diminished through care fees;

- there is a tax planning advantage to a new will. The right of everyone 'if he can, to arrange his affairs so that the tax attaching under the appropriate Acts is less than it otherwise would be'[19] is not confined to those who are capable of arranging their affairs in the most tax-efficient manner. One of the principal reasons for creating the statutory will jurisdiction in the first place was to facilitate tax planning, even though such an exercise is not directly for P's benefit but for the greater advantage

---

[13] As in *Re Davey (Deceased)* [1981] 1 WLR 164. See the summary of this case below. When making a new will in a person's best interests, the fact of a marriage and its consequences in terms of an intestacy are 'other factors' that P would be likely to consider for the purposes of MCA 2005, s 4(6)(c).

[14] Such as where a parent is left alone to care for a severely disabled child; under an intestacy, both parents will inherit in equal measure even where one parent has played little or no part in the child's life. While the parent who is a dependant may have a claim following death, see *Bouette v Rose* [2000] 1 FCR 385, the parent must live with uncertainty and the prospect of litigation throughout the child's lifetime.

[15] As in *Re D (J)* [1982] Ch 237, [1982] 2 WLR 373. See the summary of this case below.

[16] As in *Re HMF* [1976] Ch 33, [1975] 3 WLR 395, where the patient began to take a renewed interest in her two nephews with whom she had previously lost contact. See the summary of this case below.

[17] See *Re D, VAC v JAD* [2010] EWHC 2159 (COP), [2010] COPLR Con Vol 302. See the summary of this case below.

[18] As in *Re C (Spinster and Mental Patient)* [1991] 3 All ER 866. See the summary of this case below. Although MCA 2005 does not refer to persons for whom P 'might be expected to provide', the interests or claims of such persons are a legitimate consideration of P's best interests.

[19] *IRC v Duke of Westminster* [1936] AC 1, per Lord Tomlin.

of P's beneficiaries.[20] This does not, however, allow P's interests to be prejudiced and taken advantage of; a tax advantage for beneficiaries must be in P's best interests in the same way as any other increased benefit created by a new will.

- there is actual or potential financial abuse, and there is a possibility that a new will may have been executed in suspicious circumstances. While it is not for the Court to determine the validity of an existing will, it may be in P's best interests to make a new statutory will that resolves any potential uncertainty over the provisions of a will.[21]

The testator

5.18   The Court of Protection can only order the execution of a statutory will on behalf of a person ('P') who is:

- aged 18 or over;[22]
- lacks capacity to make a will. Under MCA 2005, s 2: 'a person lacks capacity in relation to a matter [the making of a will] if at the material time he is unable to make a decision for himself in relation to the matter because of an impairment of, or a disturbance in the functioning of, the mind or brain'; and
- there is property in England and Wales capable of being disposed of by a will.[23]

The court can also order the execution of a statutory will on behalf of the donor of an enduring power of attorney, or lasting power of attorney provided that he or she satisfies the above criteria.[24]

Medical evidence

5.19   A person's capacity to make any decision under MCA 2005 is function-specific. Capacity to make a will must, therefore, be assessed on its own terms and in the context of the individual testator's circumstances. The requirements of testamentary capacity will differ from other decisions or functions under MCA 2005. Capacity to manage and administer property and affairs require a different level of understanding. Even if a person lacks capacity to manage property and affairs and a deputy has been appointed or a registered EPA or LPA is in place, the same person may be perfectly capable of making a

---

[20]   Christopher Sherrin, *op cit.*

[21]   See *Re D, VAC v JAD* [2010] EWHC 2159 (COP), [2010] COPLR Con Vol 302.

[22]   MCA 2005, s 18(2), The court can, however, order the settlement of property belonging to a person who is a minor; s 18(3). It may therefore be advisable to consider an application for a revocable lifetime settlement for a minor who is unlikely to reach the age of 18 and where an intestacy might cause an unjust result.

[23]   MCA 2005, Sch 2, para 4(4). If the testator is domiciled outside of England and Wales then property in England and Wales may be disposed of by a statutory will if the law of the testator's domicile permits this.

[24]   MCA 2005, s 16(1).

valid will.[25] Thus, the court cannot approve a will for a person unless it has up-to-date primary medical evidence addressing that person's lack of capacity to make a will.

5.20 Medical evidence must be provided in form COP3 to comply with PD9A. The making of a will for someone who lacks capacity represents a significant assumption of power over an individual's autonomy. It is therefore essential to provide the Court with the reassurance that it can make this decision on behalf of another person. Form COP3 is, therefore, designed to address the nature of the decision being made, the medical diagnosis and the inability to make the decision in question. Thus the form is set out in two parts: the first part is for the applicant to complete and sets out the nature of the application and explains the decision that the court is being asked to make; the second part is for 'the practitioner' to complete and addresses the question of capacity to make that decision.

5.21 Form COP3 need not necessarily be completed by a medical practitioner, although it must be given by someone professionally qualified and able to give expert evidence on this subject. The guidance notes state that the form may be given by:

'... a registered medical practitioner, psychologist or psychiatrist who has examined and assessed the capacity of the person to whom the application relates. In some circumstances it might be appropriate for a registered therapist, such as a speech therapist or occupational therapist, to complete the form.'

5.22 If P has a particular disability, for instance one that prevents communication (which is evidence of an inability to make a decision), then the applicant may consider submitting a separate COP3 from a speech therapist or linguistic psychologist who can address this aspect of capacity. In practice, where P's capacity is complex, it is likely that the application will be accompanied by medical reports addressing capacity – or even specific aspects of capacity – in detail.

5.23 The quality of the medical evidence given to the court rests on the medical expert having a clear understanding of how the legal test of capacity is to be applied to the circumstances of the individual concerned. There is little point asking a doctor whether a patient has testamentary capacity or not, without the doctor knowing the requirements for capacity and, therefore, the information that is relevant to the decision. It is also important that the right practitioner is asked to complete the certificate. A busy GP or hospital doctor may not have the time or the necessary skills to deal with this adequately, and it is not unusual to request an assessment from a consultant psychiatrist or geriatrician or a neuropsychologist especially where capacity is borderline.

---

[25] See *A, B and C v X, Y and Z* [2012] EWHC 2400 (COP).

5.24 In the context of a will, the 'information relevant to the decision' includes:[26]

- the nature and effect of a will;
- the extent of the assets being disposed of;
- the claims to which P ought to give effect (which encompasses anyone whose interest under an existing will is reduced); and
- the consequences of deciding one way or the other or failing to make a decision (which would include understanding what would happen if no will were made).[27]

5.25 A medical practitioner who is asked to complete Form COP3 needs, therefore, to have some background information about P's property and affairs. He or she will also need some information about P's existing testamentary history and current intentions, if these can be ascertained.[28] It is probably unnecessary to disclose a copy of a current will, but a practitioner should be informed that for instance P is currently intestate or that there is a will in place that provides for a particular person and why it appears to be in P's best interests to alter those provisions.

5.26 Practice Direction 9F also asks for evidence in the application of 'an up to date report of P's present medical condition, life expectancy, likelihood of requiring increased expenditure in the foreseeable future, and testamentary capacity'. This information is not expressly requested in Form COP3 and the practitioner completing the form should be asked to provide this information while completing the certificate. The space for general comments (Box 7.9) in the form can be used for this purpose.[29]

The applicant

5.27 Section 50 of MCA 2005 sets out the general rule that permission is required to make an application to the Court of Protection, which is followed by a number of exemptions. Thus permission is not required if the application is made by:

- P;
- if P is under 18, anyone with parental responsibility;
- the donor or donee of an LPA to which the application relates;

---

[26]   The statutory test of testamentary capacity is consistent with the approach set out by Cockburn CJ in *Banks v Goodfellow* LR 5 QB 549, at 565.

[27]   MCA 2005, s 3(4).

[28]   The disclosure of confidential information about a person's property and affairs as well as family dynamics raises an ethical dilemma. Ideally, the consent of the P should be obtained whenever P is capable of giving consent. On the question of confidentiality generally, see Solicitors Regulation Authority's Solicitor's Code of Conduct, s 4.05(a).

[29]   If the case is particularly complicated then this information may be given in a separate witness statement.

- a deputy appointed by the court for a person to whom the application relates;
- a person named in an existing order of the court, if the application relates to the order; or
- a person permitted to make an application under the Court of Protection Rules 2007.

5.28 Rule 51 of the Court of Protection Rules 2007, provides further exemptions to the general rule. Permission is not required if the application:

- is made by the Official Solicitor;
- is made by the Public Guardian;
- concerns an LPA which is, or purports to be, created under the Act;
- concerns an instrument which is, or purports to be, an EPA;
- is made within existing proceedings in accordance with Part 10;
- where a person files an acknowledgment of service or notification, for any order proposed that is different from that sought by the applicant; or
- concerns P's property and affairs, unless the application is of a kind specified in r 52.

5.29 Rule 52 goes on to state that permission is in fact required in any application seeking the exercise of the court's jurisdictions under s 18(1)(b) (the making of a gift of P's property), s 18(1)(h) (settlement of property) or s 18(1)(i) (execution of a will) of the Act, but then is not required, if it is made by a person:

- who has made an application for the appointment of a deputy for which permission has been granted but which has not yet been determined;
- who, under any known will of P or under his intestacy, may become entitled to any property of P or any interest in it;
- who is an attorney appointed under an EPA that has been registered in accordance with the Act or the regulations referred to in Sch 4 to the Act;
- who is a donee of an LPA that has been registered in accordance with the Act; or
- for whom P might be expected to provide if he had capacity to do so.[30]

The aim of these provisions is simply to ensure that applications are only made by people with a genuine interest in the application. Any other person would have to make a separate application to the court for permission to make an application, using form COP2.

---

[30] For example, a beneficiary under an existing will whose legacy has adeemed: see *Re D (J)* [1982] Ch 237, summarised below.

The application

5.30 The following documents should be sent to: the Court of Protection, PO Box 70185, First Avenue House, 42–49 High Holborn, LONDON WC1A 9JA or DX 160013 Kingsway 7:

- general form of application (Form COP1) in duplicate;
- if the applicant needs permission, COP2;
- medical certificate (Form COP3);
- a statement of truth in support of the application, plus exhibits; and
- a cheque for £400, being the application fee, payable to 'HMCTS'.[31]

5.31 To assist an applicant in setting out the evidence required, PD9F specifies the information required by the court in support of an application. Paragraph 6 provides as follows:

> 'In addition to the application form COP1 (and its annexes) and any information or documents required to be provided by the Rules or another practice direction, the following information must be provided (in the form of a witness statement, attaching documents as exhibits where necessary) for any application to which this practice direction applies:
>
> (a) where the application is for the execution of a statutory will or codicil, a copy of the draft will or codicil, plus one copy;
> (b) a copy of any existing will or codicil;
> (c) any consents to act by proposed executors;
> (d) details of P's family, preferably in the form of a family tree, including details of the full name and date of birth of each person included in the family tree;
> (e) a schedule showing details of P's current assets, with up to date valuations;
> (f) a schedule showing the estimated net yearly income and spending of P;
> (g) a statement showing P's needs, both current and future estimates, and his general circumstances;
> (h) if P is living in National Health Service accommodation, information on whether he may be discharged to local authority accommodation, to other fee-paying accommodation or to his own home;
> (i) if the applicant considers it relevant, full details of the resources of any proposed beneficiary, and details of any likely changes if the application is successful;
> (j) details of any capital gains tax, inheritance tax or income tax which may be chargeable in respect of the subject matter of the application;
> (k) an explanation of the effect, if any, that the proposed changes will have on P's circumstances, preferably in the form of a "before and after" schedule of assets and income;
> (l) if appropriate, a statement of whether any land would be affected by the proposed will or settlement and if so, details of its location and title number, if applicable;
> (m) where the application is for a settlement of property or for the variation of an existing settlement or trust, a draft of the proposed deed, plus one copy;

---

[31] A further fee of £500 is payable on an attended hearing.

(n)   a copy of any registered enduring power of attorney or lasting power of attorney;

(o)   confirmation that P is a resident of England or Wales; and

(p)   an up to date report of P's present medical condition, life expectancy, likelihood of requiring increased expenditure in the foreseeable future, and testamentary capacity.'

5.32 The Practice Direction sets out the essential background to the application. The application also needs to show why the proposed will is P's best interests and this needs to be explained in the applicant's witness statement.[32] Where possible, additional evidence should be enclosed with the application. For example, close friends or relatives may provide evidence of P's past and present wishes and feelings, beliefs and values. The applicant should try to take into account the views of anyone engaged in caring for P or interested in P's welfare. Nevertheless, it is always important to distinguish evidence as to P's best interests from argument or speculation, which can all too easily over-complicate a statutory will application. The application may also need to be accompanied by expert reports dealing with capacity, care needs or finances.

5.33 Although an application should be as complete as possible, it is also likely that not all the evidence will be available to the applicant. There may be other evidence that is not produced until respondents file their own evidence, whether supporting or opposing the application. The applicant may not have access to evidence such as an earlier will, medical records, a solicitors' file or private correspondence.[33]

5.34 Where the applicant or other party needs the court to take further action unilaterally to assist the application, a separate or application notice (form COP9) should be filed with the court at the earliest opportunity. This may be necessary for instance where:

•   the application is urgent and needs to be expedited;

•   the applicant does not have access to confidential documents or information;

•   the applicant is unsure who should be a respondent owing to the number of the respondents or if they cannot be traced. Respondents may themselves be under a disability and require the appointment of a litigation friend;

•   considerable costs need to be incurred in tracing or serving respondents. An elderly testator may have no immediate relatives and the beneficiaries on the intestacy may be the issue of the parents' next of kin, where contact was lost several decades previously. A genealogist may need to be

---

[32]   See for example *Re P* [2009] EWHC 163 (Ch) and the other cases summarised below for examples of wills made in a the best interests of P.

[33]   The Official Solicitor plays an invaluable role in identifying where further evidence might be needed. It is also common for Official Solicitor staff to visit P.

instructed, and if the costs are likely to be high or more than an applicant can afford, an application should be made to authorise the research and the expenditure from P's estate;[34]

- further evidence to assist in determining P's best interests and cannot provide this, an application notice (form COP9) should be filed with the court at the earliest opportunity.

5.35 The application notice should be accompanied by any evidence required to explain the proposed decision. For example, a request to expedite the application should be accompanied by medical evidence and a request for a will or file from a solicitor should be accompanied by a letter from the solicitor confirming that this information is in the firm's custody. A person required to act in accordance with a proposed order such as a solicitor holding confidential records (who is not a party to the main application) should be named as a respondent in the application notice.

Respondents and persons who must be notified of an application

5.36 Upon receipt of the papers, the court will ensure that they are in order and allocate a case number. The application form is then issued, which is the point at which proceedings are started.[35] The issued application form is returned to the applicant who is responsible for serving a copy on any named respondent, together with copies of any documents filed with the application and a form for acknowledging service (COP5).[36] Service must be affected within 21 days of the application form being issued and the applicant must file a certificate of service (form COP20B) within 7 days.[37]

5.37 It is the responsibility of the applicant to identify and name in the application form any respondents and persons to be notified. The Court of Protection Rules and Practice Directions distinguish between the two categories of person. Rule 63(c)(iii) describes a respondent as 'any person (other than P) whom the applicant reasonably believes to have an interest which means that he ought to be heard in relation to the application'. Practice Direction 9F explains that in the context of a statutory will application, the following must be named as a respondent:

(a) any beneficiary under an existing will or codicil who is likely to be materially or adversely affected by the application;

(b) any beneficiary under a proposed will or codicil who is likely to be materially or adversely affected by the application; and

---

[34] While the costs will generally be recoverable from P's estate, this should not be taken for granted, especially if the application is unsuccessful or the costs disproportionately high. A lay applicant or solicitor's office account may also struggle to fund the considerable costs that may be involved.

[35] Court of Protection Rules 2007, r 62(1).

[36] Court of Protection Rules 2007, r 66(1).

[37] Court of Protection Rules 2007, r 66(2). Practice Direction 6A provides for service by fax, electronic means or by post.

(c)   any prospective beneficiary under P's intestacy where P has no existing will.

5.38   The reference to someone who is 'materially or adversely' affected covers two types of people. It is often assumed that a statutory will application only affects someone who stands to receive less under the new will than under an existing will or intestacy. However, someone 'materially' affected is also someone who stands to receive more under the proposed will as well as someone who stands to receive the same. That person has a material interest in the outcome and may wish to submit further evidence as to P's best interests. Likewise, a person who may inherit on a contingency may also be said to have a material interest in the outcome, especially if the original beneficiary is elderly and likely to predecease P. Generally, the court will interpret these requirements strictly, as a person with a legitimate interest in the outcome should be able to respond.[38] Unfortunately, the Practice Direction provides no threshold as to whether any particular interest might be *de minimis*. In practice, the court will generally overlook the interests of legatees or proposed legatees where the legacies are small in themselves or relative to the value of the estate, and do not affect the substantive provisions of the will.[39]

5.39   Practice Direction 9B identifies other people who should be notified of an application. The main distinction is that a person notified does not have a material interest in the outcome; he or she does not, therefore, receive all the documents filed with the application but only a short summary of the application (form COP15) and a form for acknowledgement of service (COP5). The onus is then on the notified person to apply to be a party to the application. The role of notified persons is usually considered when making an application to appoint a deputy (where there are no respondents who have a material interest in the outcome). Nevertheless, the status of notified persons should not be overlooked on a statutory will application. In most cases there will be an overlap between the two in that a respondent will also comply with the description of family members to be notified in PD9B. However, this is not always going to be the case. For example where the beneficiaries under an existing will or proposed statutory will are charities or friends, and P has relatives, then at least three relatives (or all the members of the appropriate class of relatives) should be notified of the application.

5.40   The Court of Protection Rules do not assume that P will be a party, and P should not be named as a respondent in the application.[40] It is up to the

---

[38]   See *Re B (Court of Protection: notice of proceedings)* [1987] 2 All ER 475. In one case dealt with by Brian Bacon of Thomson Snell & Passmore, where P was intestate, the applicant identified 77 residuary beneficiaries, all of whom were respondents to the application. The parties included over 30 of the residuary beneficiaries who responded as well as six proposed charities, a legatee, the applicant and the Official Solicitor.

[39]   There is no reason why a proposed legatee should not be notified of the application and therefore informed of what is being proposed. It would then be for the proposed legatee to apply to be a party if he or she felt that the proposed legacy was inappropriate.

[40]   Court of Protection Rules 2007, r 73(4).

Court to decide whether P should be joined as a party.[41] The person most directly connected with the outcome is of course, P, and therefore PD9F requires the Court to consider at the earliest opportunity whether P should be joined as a party to the proceedings and, if he is so joined, whether the Official Solicitor should be invited to act as a litigation friend, or whether some other person should be appointed as a litigation friend.[42] In most cases involving a statutory will, P will be joined as a party and the Official Solicitor asked to act as litigation friend.[43] Where P is joined as a party, the application form and other papers must be served on the litigation friend. P does not need to be notified in person.[44]

Subsequent procedure and final hearing

5.41   Once the court has issued an application, it must then consider how to deal with it.[45] On a statutory will application, the current practice is to issue initial or case management directions at an early stage and then return these to the applicant together with the issued application form. This will allow the court to address any missing evidence, confirm the appointment of P as a party and direct service on the respondents, including the Official Solicitor (subject to his agreement to act as a litigation friend). The court may also set a date for a hearing. Depending on the complexity of this case, this may be a directions hearing (which may be a telephone hearing) or a final hearing. This hearing date may be adjourned if more time is needed or disposed of if the case can be agreed on the papers.

5.42   The timeframe set by the court will allow for the respondents and P to be served with the application papers and to respond to the application. Any respondent or notified person who wishes to be a party to the application must file an acknowledgement of service (form COP5) within 21 days of being served with the application.[46] A respondent is automatically a party if he files an acknowledgement of service.[47] A person notified is only a respondent if he files an acknowledgement of service and the court agrees to make such person a party.[48]

---

[41]   Court of Protection Rules 2007, r 73(2).

[42]   At para 10. The Official Solicitor is usually invited to act as litigation friend, but this is not necessarily done in every case. Where a professional deputy has no personal interest in the case then it may be possible for the deputy to act as litigation friend.

[43]   If case is straightforward, for instance if it simply involves a codicil to change executors, then it may be possible to avoid joining P as a party. In almost every case, P is joined as a party and the Official Solicitor is appointed as litigation friend. If the Official Solicitor has a conflict of interest (for instance the Official Solicitor is already acting for P's spouse) then another solicitor will be appointed to take on this role.

[44]   Court of Protection Rules 2007, r 40(2).

[45]   Court of Protection Rules 2007, r 84(1).

[46]   Court of Protection Rules 2007, r 72(2).

[47]   Court of Protection Rules 2007, r 73(1)(b).

[48]   Court of Protection Rules 2007, r 72(8).

5.43   The requirement to respond to an application within 21 days may be unduly harsh especially if the application is complicated and the respondent needs time to consider the application, take legal advice and prepare evidence in response. In view of the timeframe laid down in the Court of Protection Rules, unless the time for service has already been extended by the initial directions order, a respondent who needs more time to file evidence should file an acknowledgement of service (Form COP5) within the time limit as well as a request for an extension of time to file further evidence.[49]

5.44   The period of time before a hearing takes place allows the parties to exchange evidence and deal with additional information that may not have been supplied in the application. The Official Solicitor will also need time to review the application, any responses filed and where possible, meet P.[50] To save the time and expense of an attended hearing, the parties are expected to attempt to settle the papers or, where agreement cannot be reached, to establish the level of consensus that can be achieved. Negotiations may be conducted through the Official Solicitor who may act as a lead party in applying to the court for further directions or with the terms of a proposed agreement. If there is an agreement and this is supported by the Official Solicitor as P's litigation friend, the court may make a final order on the papers, without an attended hearing.

5.45   If the case is complex and likely to proceed to an attended hearing, the directions order may require an applicant to file and serve complete trial bundles and the parties to circulate skeleton arguments.

5.46   Where the application proceeds to a hearing, this will be before a judge. Most cases are heard before a district judge or the Senior Judge (at First Avenue House); however, depending on the complexity of the case (especially if extensive cross-examination is required or the case must deal with an important point of legal principle), a hearing may be referred to a circuit judge or puisne judge.[51] An attended hearing imposes a considerable burden on all the parties, especially the applicant, to ensure that all the evidence is available to the parties and the judge, in the form of an agreed bundle. Unless the court has directed otherwise, an agreed bundle must be prepared by the applicant and served on the parties at least 5 days before the hearing and lodged with the court at least 3 days before the hearing. Skeleton arguments must be lodged with the court by at least 11am on the day before the hearing.[52]

5.47   Parties will be expected to attend in good time before the time listed for a hearing and it is not uncommon for discussions to take place at the courtroom

---

[49]   This should be included in form COP5.
[50]   Even if P lacks capacity to provide any insight into his or her present wishes, it is useful for P's representative to establish that this is the case and observe P's natural environment. Seeing how P is cared for and talking to carers may also help complete a picture of P's character and circumstances.
[51]   Practice Direction 13A.
[52]   Practice Direction 13B.

door in a final attempt to limit the issues between the parties. A judge will expect the parties to have used their best efforts to reduce the scope of disagreement as far as possible and concentrate the court's time only on those matters that remain in issue. No further evidence can be produced without the court's permission.[53] Any evidence already given in writing stands as a witness's final evidence, although a witness may be cross-examined on his evidence. Parties or their representatives will also be allowed to make submissions on the legal principles the court is being asked to resolve.

5.48 Unless judgment is reserved or the hearing is adjourned, the judge will make the order at the hearing that will authorise the applicant or some other person to execute the statutory will in the form approved by the court. Usually, the judge will agree the terms of the statutory will and direct the applicant or the Official Solicitor to file an agreed final draft. A draft will approved by the judge will be referred to in the final order.

5.49 Whether or not the order is made at the hearing, it will also provide for the costs of the applicant, the Official Solicitor and any other party who was legally represented to be assessed and paid from P's estate and for the safe custody of the will.

Execution of a statutory will

5.50 After the order has been made, it will be drawn up, sealed and entered. Sealed copies will be sent to all the parties to the application. However, the order is effective immediately it is made. In an emergency, a statutory will can be engrossed and executed immediately after the order has been made by the judge and before the order has been drawn up and sealed.

5.51 It is the responsibility of the applicant to engross the will that has been approved by the judge. The will is expressed to be signed by P acting by the *authorised person* (usually the applicant or the deputy):

- signed by the authorised person with the name of P, and with his or her own name, in the presence of two or more witnesses present at the same time;
- attested and subscribed by those witnesses in the presence of the authorised person; and
- sealed with the official seal of the Court of Protection.

5.52 As the authorised person is signing the statutory will on behalf of P and is not a witness as such, he or she will not be barred from benefiting under the will by virtue of the Wills Act 1837, s 15 (gifts to an attesting witness, or to the spouse or civil partner of an attesting witness, to be void). In all other respects, a statutory will is to be treated in the same way as a will made by P in accordance with the Wills Act 1837. Therefore, no beneficiary named in the

---

[53]   Court of Protection Rules 2007, r 96(4).

statutory will, nor a spouse or civil partner of such a beneficiary may act as a witness.[54] The statutory will also serves to revoke all earlier wills and is revoked in the event of P's marriage.

5.53 Once a statutory will has been executed, the applicant must send the original and two copies of the will to the court for sealing. The court will seal the original document and return this to the applicant or the applicant's solicitor for safe custody.[55] The will is effective on being executed; the requirement that it be sealed is confirmation that the will has been executed under MCA 2005.[56]

URGENT APPLICATIONS

5.54 The average time-span between lodging an application and a final hearing is about 5 months and can be longer if there are any extensions of time to obtain further evidence or comply with other directions. If, however, there is evidence that P is critically ill and may die before the hearing date, an application notice may be filed requesting an expedited hearing. However, this must be accompanied by medical evidence that directly addresses P's illness and life expectancy. The applicant must also explain to the court why the application could not have been made earlier and whether anyone will be prejudiced by the application being dealt with urgently. Any other respondent as well as the Official Solicitor should be notified as soon as possible and provided with any evidence that has already been lodged, even if the application has not yet been issued. The court should also be provided with a draft will.

5.55 The court will aim to be as helpful as it can and in extreme cases the application may be heard by telephone within a matter of days. The judge may authorise the applicant's solicitor or the Official Solicitor to execute the statutory will so that this can be done immediately after the order has been made.

5.56 The court does not favour urgent applications because they have a tendency to be weighted procedurally in favour of the applicant. An order made without proper notice to an affected party would breach Art 6 of the European Convention on Human Rights – the right to a fair trial. In *Re R* [2003] WTLR 1051, Ferris J declined to approve a statutory will for a patient (under the Mental Health Act 1983) as the emergency did not allow the court enough time to consider the application fully, especially in view of the 'procedural prejudice'

---

[54] MCA 2005, Sch 2, para 4(2) states that: 'The Wills Act 1837 has effect in relation to the will as if it were signed by P in his own hand, except that [s 9 of that Act shall not apply].'

[55] It is no longer the practice of the court to require a receipt and undertaking for the original will. Once it has been returned for safe custody, it is the responsibility of the custodian to hold the document safely to the order of P. Thus the Will should not be released without the further order of the Court of Protection during P's lifetime and for as long as P lacks capacity.

[56] *Re Hughes* (1999) *The Times*, January 8. See below.

suffered by the adversely affected party. In this case, the applicant had delayed making the application and therefore any adverse consequences of the delay would fall on the applicant. It is important that where there are concerns about P's health and life-expectancy, no time is lost in making the application and giving as much notice as possible to the other parties.

5.57 Where time is limited and there is any risk of prejudice to P or another party, the court will proceed with great care. It will also have regard to the principle in MCA 2005, s 1(6) that the decision should be the least restrictive of P's rights and freedom of action. Therefore, if the court does approve an 'emergency will', this should depart as narrowly as possible from the provisions of an existing will or intestacy. The court will often approve a holding or temporary will that deals with administrative matters such as the appointment of professional executors, which may make a great difference to the efficient winding up of P's estate. The will might also deal with matters that are unlikely to be uncontroversial. Small legacies could for instance be included to acknowledge a moral debt and that are unlikely to affect the substantive provisions of the existing intestacy. If the will is likely to be complicated or involve parties who have not yet been identified or given adequate time to respond, the court may approve a discretionary will. The court would, however, need to be persuaded that such a will did not represent an abdication of its powers but a decision that can be properly made in P's best interests. There would have to be some record of the basis on which trustees might be expected to exercise their discretionary powers; for instance, that they should provide for the needs of a dependent but otherwise follow an existing intestacy.[57]

Costs

5.58 Costs[58] incurred in any proceedings are governed by Pt 19 of the Court of Protection Rules in addition to Pts 44, 47 and 48 of the Civil Procedure Rules 1998. Court of Protection Rules, r 156 sets out the following general rule:

> 'Where the proceedings concern P's property and affairs the general rule is that the costs of the proceedings or of that part of the proceedings that concerns P's property and affairs, shall be paid by P or charged to his estate.'

5.59 As a statutory will relates to P's property and affairs, the court will usually follow the general rule. The general rule is not inflexible and can be avoided by the court. Rule 159 provides the court with power to depart from the general rule 'if the circumstances so justify'. The court must have regard to all the circumstances, including the conduct of the parties, whether a party has

---

[57]   Although the Court cannot approve a letter of wishes for P, a record of P's likely wishes setting out the understanding between the parties as to how the discretionary powers should be applied, could be recorded on the face of the will.

[58]   See, generally, Court of Protection Rules 2007, rr 155–168.

succeeded on part of his case, even if he has not been wholly successful; and the role of any public body involved in the proceedings. Rule 159(2) defines conduct of the parties as including:

(a) conduct before, as well as during, the proceedings;

(b) whether it was reasonable for a party to raise, pursue or contest a particular issue;

(c) the manner in which a party has made or responded to an application or a particular issue; and

(d) whether a party who has succeeded in his application or response to an application, in whole or in part, exaggerated any matter contained in his application or response.

5.60 To depart from the general rule does, therefore, involve an allocation of blame that the court generally tries to avoid. In many statutory will cases, the court will look to a solution that respects the *bona fides* of the parties. Where the parties have made genuine attempts to compromise and present P's best interests fairly, there are no winners or losers. The right will has been made in P's best interests. To deprive a party of costs or to award costs against a party involves a finding of blame. This will involve further argument, with parties making further representations and having a right to be heard (especially if the order was made without a hearing). It is often taken for granted that in property and affairs cases costs are payable from the estate as a matter of course. However, exceptions to the general rule do arise from time to time and can be illustrated by the following examples:

• An application was made by for a deed of variation redirecting the estate of P's deceased husband to his son (P's stepson). The stepson was a party to the proceedings and the main beneficiary of the variation that was approved by the court. He was ordered to pay half of the applicant's costs in the proceedings.

• In a statutory will application, one party produced a homemade will, which she claimed was P's last will and which should be upheld by the court. The court would not make a finding on the validity of this earlier will, but the party had caused delays in producing the will and was evasive and inconsistent in cross-examination. No order for costs was made in favour of that party.

• In a lengthy statutory will hearing before the High Court, it was argued by the successful applicant that the respondent had needlessly asked for a second day's hearing. No further material evidence was disclosed on the second day. The respondent's costs were limited to the first day of the hearing only.

5.61 The final order will provide authority for a party to recover costs from P's estate. A solicitor will, however, still have to submit these costs for detailed assessment in the same way as any other costs that are payable from P's estate that are not covered by fixed costs.

SETTLEMENTS

When necessary

5.62 The Court of Protection may approve a settlement under MCA 2005, s 18(1)(h). The approval of a settlement, as with a statutory will, is a decision reserved specifically to the court. These are not common procedures and generally a settlement will involve a benefit for another party. They may be appropriate in the following circumstances:

- where a direct gift to an individual is inappropriate but a transfer of property from P's estate should still be made, for example where the proposed beneficiary is a minor or has special needs;

- where P is a beneficiary under an existing will or settlement and P does not require an absolute interest or interest in possession that will be charged to inheritance tax on P's death. Rather than complete a deed of variation giving P's interest to another beneficiary absolutely, it may be appropriate to create a new settlement on discretionary trusts that include P as a discretionary beneficiary.

- where P is a recipient of a substantial damages award or other sum of money and it can be shown to the Court of Protection that it is in P's best interests for such money to be more effectively managed within a trust than through a deputyship. For instance, parents may prefer the flexibility of a private trust as a means of maintaining a severely disabled child, especially where the award is limited and their involvement may help reduce the costs of administering the estate while allowing some professional input from a professional trustee (see the detailed judgment of Hazel Marshall QC in *SM v HM* [2012] COPLR 187.

- where P is a beneficiary of an existing settlement that needs to be varied. If the beneficiaries of the settlement are not all of full age then the matter must also be dealt with under the Variation of Trusts Act 1958.

Procedure

5.63 An application for the approval of a settlement must be dealt with as a formal application to the Court of Protection in Form COP1. The application is similar to an application for a statutory will and is covered by PD9D in the same way (see **5.30** above).

CHAPTER 6

HEALTH CARE AND WELFARE, IMCAS, ADVANCE DECISIONS AND RESEARCH[1]

PRELIMINARY

6.1   A number of issues can arise under the Mental Capacity Act 2005 (MCA 2005) in regard to welfare and health care. For example, as to health care, first, what medical treatment should be provided for an adult who cannot make choices; secondly, how can the adult before losing capacity influence decisions about subsequent treatment; thirdly, to what extent should medical research be permitted; and, fourthly, whether the adult should make a donation of their body tissues or organs? Similar issues as the first two can arise in relation to such a person's more general welfare, for example, where they should live or with whom they should have contact. The welfare issue may be linked to a health care issue, but may be quite separate. Whilst questions of health care and welfare in relation to an incapacitated adult are fully integrated into the statutory framework provided by the MCA 2005, the pre-existing common law remains relevant to an understanding of these provisions as they apply in relation to these issues, and a brief overview is therefore provided at the outset of this chapter.

THE PRE-EXISTING COMMON LAW

Medical treatment

6.2   The starting point at common law was that any 'invasive' or 'intrusive' medical treatment constituted an unlawful act unless authorised by statute, done under the doctrine of necessity (see below) or with the consent of the person concerned.[2] A competent adult had an unfettered right at common law to refuse medical treatment; conversely an 'incompetent'[3] adult could not consent to treatment, nor did the common law recognise the ability of anyone else to give consent on their behalf.

---

[1]   The first edition of this work contained significantly more material regarding the position under the common law. This has, however, been pruned in light of the passage of time since the enactment of the MCA 2005. The contribution of James Beck from the Official Solicitor's office to the material under this heading is gratefully acknowledged.

[2]   Such consent being capable of being provided by an adult parent on behalf of a child, or by a child over the age of 16: Family Law Reform Act 1969, s 8.

[3]   This term was the consistent term used prior to the enactment of MCA 2005; whilst it would not now be used, for clarity's sake, it is retained in this part of the chapter.

6.3   From an early time, however, the common law allowed the High Court to make medical treatment decisions for children and for adults without the mental capacity to decide for themselves. Originally the judges of the High Court exercised the Crown's prerogative power as parens patriae. This power still exists in relation to children. Although it was excluded in relation to adults by the enactment of a succession of Mental Health Acts, the practical effect of this was limited by the dramatic development in the last decade of the 20th century of the declaratory jurisdiction of the High Court. Starting in 1990 with *Re F (Mental Patient: Sterilisation)*,[4] a series of decisions established clearly that the High Court retained an inherent jurisdiction to make declarations as to what was lawful as being in the best interests of an incompetent adult.

6.4   Substantially prior to 2007, therefore, it had become one of the many roles of the Family Division of the High Court of Justice in England and Wales to decide whether medical procedures should or should not be carried out on an adult who was unable to consent to the treatment in question. Such cases tended to divide into three main types, namely where medical opinion was that:

- A particular course of treatment would save life, for example, a blood transfusion or a Caesarean section;[5]

- A particular procedure should be carried out to enhance the patient's quality of life or prevent physical or mental deterioration, for example, a liver transplant or sterilisation;[6]

- Life-prolonging treatment should either be withheld or withdrawn to allow the patient to die with dignity.[7]

Welfare

6.5   Parallel to the development of the inherent jurisdiction in the medical realm, the High Court developed a similar declaratory jurisdiction in respect of decisions regarding the welfare of incompetent adults.[8] Indeed, prior to the enactment of MCA 2005, one High Court judge had already commented:[9]

'... we have come a long way since the decision in *In Re F*. The courts have created and now exercise what is, in substance and reality, a jurisdiction in relation to

---

[4]   [1990] 2 AC 1.

[5]   *HE v A Hospital NHS Trust* [2003] 2 FLR 408 (blood transfusion); *St George's Healthcare NHS Trust v S* [1999] Fam 26 (Caesarean section).

[6]   *Re T (A Minor) (Wardship: Medical Treatment)* [1997] 1 WLR 242 (kidney transplant); *Re A (Male Sterilisation)* [2000] 1 FLR 549; and eg *Re S (Adult Patient: Sterilisation)* [2001] Fam 16.

[7]   *Airedale NHS Trust v Bland* [1993] AC 789.

[8]   See eg *Re F (Mental Patient: Sterilisation)* [1990] 2 AC 1; *Re C (Mental Patient: Contact)* [1993] 1 FLR 940; *Re F (Adult: Court's Jurisdiction)* [2000] Fam 38; and *A v A Health Authority, Re J (a child), R (on the application of S) v Secretary of State for the Home Department* [2002] Fam 213.

[9]   *E (By her litigation friend the Official Solicitor) v Channel Four; News International Ltd and St Helens Borough Council* [2005] 2 FLR 913, at [55], per Munby J (as he then was).

incompetent adults which is for all practical purposes indistinguishable from its well-established *parens patriae* or wardship jurisdiction in relation to children.'

Injunctive relief

6.6 Prior to the enactment of MCA 2005, there was a distinction in principle between the adult jurisdiction to declare what is lawful and the power under the Children Act 1989 to make orders in children's cases. But this became more apparent than real as it was established that injunctive relief (where permissible) in support of a declaration could be granted.[10] However, the principle remained that doctors could not be compelled personally to undertake a treatment they did not, in their clinical judgment, wish to provide; in some circumstances, though, the NHS Trust responsible for the treatment might be required to transfer the patient to the care of other doctors who would treat as the patient wanted or in his or her best interests.[11]

Capacity

6.7 As set out further in Chapter 2 above, the common law test of capacity was specific to the decision in question. In the medical context, for instance, it depended on whether the patient fully understood the nature of the proposed intervention, the reasons and the consequences of submitting or not submitting to it, and could weigh these in the balance and reach and communicate a decision.[12]

6.8 Prior to the enactment of MCA 2005, the courts had developed a clear principle that it was necessary to attempt to reach an objective view of what was in the best interests of the incompetent adult in the light of all the relevant circumstances and evidence available to it. In medical cases, this went considerably further than medical considerations, to embrace emotional and all other welfare issues. In a seminal judgment in *Re A (Male Sterilisation)*, Lord Justice Thorpe held that the court should draw up a checklist of the actual benefits and disadvantages and the potential gains and losses, including physical and psychological risks and consequences, and should reach a balanced conclusion as to what is right from the point of view of the individual concerned.[13]

---

[10] See eg *A Local Authority v A* [2004] 2 WLR 926; and *Re SA (Vulnerable Adult With Capacity: Marriage)* [2005] EWHC 2942 (Fam), [2006] 1 FLR 867.

[11] *Re J (A Minor) (Child in Care: Medical Treatment)* [1993] Fam 15; *Re B (Consent to Treatment: Capacity)* [2002] 1 FLR 1090; and *R (Burke) v GMC and Others* [2005] QB 424, at [180]–[194], per Munby J.

[12] *Re MB (Medical Treatment)* [1997] 2 FLR 426.

[13] *Re A (Male Sterilisation)* [2000] 1 FLR 549.

THE POSITION UNDER THE MENTAL CAPACITY ACT 2005

General

6.9　Adult cases relating to a health care or welfare issue concerning someone who cannot choose for him or herself are dealt with by the Court of Protection under the jurisdiction granted it by MCA 2005.[14] No power under the Act may be exercised in relation to a child under 16, whose personal welfare is exclusively covered by the Children Act 1989. Cases concerning children of 16 or 17 may be started under either jurisdiction, and there is power for the court to transfer a case to whichever jurisdiction in the particular circumstances is more appropriate.[15]

6.10　The general provisions of MCA 2005 relating to capacity, inability to make decisions, best interests and acts in connection with care or treatment apply to medical treatment and welfare issues as to all other areas. They are dealt with in detail in Chapters 1 and 2; for present purposes, space is devoted to three topics which have revealed themselves to be of particular importance (and difficulty) in the health and welfare context: (1) the issue-specific nature of capacity; (2) the problem of fluctuating capacity; and (3) the question of capacity to consent to sexual relations.

The issue-specific nature of capacity in the health and welfare context

6.11　In the health and welfare context, it is of particular importance to identify with precision the issue the person is said to lack the capacity to decide, and also to identify what information is relevant to consideration of that issue for purposes of s 3(1)(a) of the MCA 2005.[16] The basis of the approach to be taken, and the reason why it is so important, was succinctly set out by Hedley J thus:

---

[14]　See Chapter 2. In some cases, where the remedy sought is not within the repertoire of remedies afforded by MCA 2005, relief may nonetheless be granted by way of the parallel exercise by the High Court of its inherent jurisdiction: see *XCC v AA and Others* [2012] EWHC 2183 (COP), [2012] COPLR 730 and the discussion in Chapter 11 at **11.5–11.9**.

[15]　Mental Capacity Act 2005 (Transfer of Proceedings) Order 2007, SI 2007/1899 made under MCA 2005, s 21. In relation to a child aged 16 or 17, the Children Act 1989 should in general only be invoked if the matter is capable of resolution prior to the child's 18th birthday. Guidance as to when proceedings in respect of 16- and 17-year-olds should be brought in the Court of Protection was given by Hedley J in *B (A Local Authority) v RM, MM and AM* [2010] EWHC B31 (Fam), [2010] COPLR Con Vol 247, the most important questions being whether the matters in respect of which relief is sought are likely to be long-lasting and extend beyond the child's majority. It should also be noted that s 31(2) of the Children's Act 1989 prevents a care or supervision order being made if a child has already reached the age of 17 or if married has reached the age of 16.

[16]　In *LBL v RYJ* [2010] EWHC 2665 (Fam), [2010] COPLR Con Vol 795, Mrs Justice Macur referred to the necessity that 'the person under review must comprehend and weigh the salient details relevant to the decision to be made' (emphasis added).

'... what the statute requires is the fixing of attention upon the actual decision in hand. It is the capacity to take a specific decision, or a decision of a specific nature, with which the Act is concerned. Sometimes that will most certainly be generic. Can this person make any decision as to residence or contact or care by reason of, for example, their dementia? Or does this person have any capacity to consent to sexual relations by reason of an impairment of mind which appears to withdraw all the usual restraints that are in place? Such generic assessments will often be necessary in order to devise effective protective measures for the benefit of the protected person, but it will not always be so. There will be cases, for example, in relation to medical treatment where attention is centred not only on a specific treatment or action but on the specific circumstances prevailing at the time of the person whose decision making capacity is in question. The hysteric resisting treatment in the course of delivering a child is an example from my own experience. Accordingly, I see no reason why in the construction of the statute in any particular case the question of capacity should not arise in relation to an individual or in relation to specific decision making relating to a specific person. In my judgment, given the presumption of capacity in section 1(2) this may indeed be very necessary to prevent the powers of the Court of Protection, which can be both invasive and draconian, being defined or exercised more widely than is strictly necessary in each particular case.'[17]

By way of further example, the contention is frequently advanced that 'X lacks the capacity to make decisions regarding her care needs'. Framed too widely, especially in the context of a person who is close to the threshold of having such capacity, proceeding on the basis could deprive the person in question of important autonomy over day-to-day 'micro' decisions about specific care being provided to them. Drawing the question too narrowly, conversely, could prevent appropriate consideration being given to whether the person fully understands (for instance) that they are only able to remain at home given the continuation of a specific care package.

Fluctuating capacity

6.12 Experience has shown that particular problems can arise where a person has fluctuating capacity to make decisions regarding medical treatment and/or their welfare needs. An example is a 'needle phobic' case where the adult understands and retains the relevant information to make a capacitous decision (and may give consent in advance) but whose ability to weigh in the balance is impaired when confronted with the sight of the needle which caused them to withdraw their consent. In practice (and as set out below), serious medical treatment cases are restricted to judges from the Family Division of the High Court[18] and where necessary such a judge will choose to sit in a dual jurisdiction; they have also shown themselves willing to be robust in their

---

[17] *CYC v PC and NC* [2012] COPLR 670 at paragraph 19. These dicta were approved on appeal by the Court of Appeal sub nom *PC & Anor v City of York Council* [2013] EWCA Civ 478, [2013] COPLR 409, at para 35 per McFarlane LJ, although the Court of Appeal allowed the decision on the facts of the particular case.

[18] All Queen's Bench Division judges are now nominated, but it is suggested that it would be unlikely were such a judge to be allocated a serious medical treatment case (save in the event of dire emergency).

interpretation of their mandate under MCA 2005 so as to ensure that whenever the person in question's capacity has decreased sufficiently they are brought within the protective scope of the Act. By way of one example within the author's experience, the court has been prepared to make 'contingent' declarations (on an interim basis) as to the circumstances under which a person would lack the capacity to make decisions as to medical treatment, and as to what would be in their best interests in such circumstances.[19]

6.13 Under the common law, the courts had shown themselves on at least one occasion to be creative in their approach to be taken to fluctuating capacity in welfare cases. In the pre-MCA case of *Re G*,[20] Bennett J made declarations as to the best interests of the person concerned in circumstances where, essentially as a result of the prior protective measures that had been put in place by the Court, she had at the time of the final hearing regained the capacity to make the relevant decisions. Bennett J concluded that it would be a:

> '... sad failure were the law to determine that I had no jurisdiction to investigate and if necessary make declarations as to G's best interests to ensure that the continuing protection of the court put in place with effect from 11 March 2004 is not summarily withdrawn simply because she has now regained her mental capacity in respect of the matters referred to, given the likely consequences to G if the court withdrew its protection'[21]

He therefore held that, on a proper analysis, G did not have the relevant capacity, such that he retained jurisdiction to make declarations as to her best interests and grant injunctions to give effect to those declarations. The approach taken in *Re G* does not at first blush sit easily with the presumption of capacity enshrined in s 1(2) of the MCA 2005; it is also the case that (as the Code of Practice recognises[22]) it necessary always to ensure that care is taken to identify whether the person in question is under a temporary disability which may lift (especially with the taking of appropriate steps by a person responsible for their care). However, it is suggested that the <u>result</u> reached in *Re G* can continue to be justified in appropriate cases where it is sufficiently clear that it is only because of the imposition of a sufficient protective framework on the part of the court that the person in question has regained (or can retain) the relevant capacity. On a proper analysis, though, the <u>route</u> to the result may well now be by way of the exercise by the High Court of its residual inherent jurisdiction to protect vulnerable adults who fall outside the scope of the

---

[19]   A decision of McFarlane J (as he then was) in March 2009. The circumstances of this case were very unusual, it being held by the court that the individual in question suffered from a particularly acute form of PTSD which would be triggered by certain clearly identifiable events linked to the prospect of hospital admission and would render her incapable of taking decisions as to whether she required such admission in the event of medical emergency. It is therefore a limited foundation upon which to build a general statement of principle, but it is submitted that the decision was one that was entirely sound in law.

[20]   [2004] EWHC 2222 (Fam), [2004] All ER (D) 33 (Oct).

[21]   Paragraph 103.

[22]   Paragraphs 4.26–427.

MCA 2005 (as to which see Chapter 11 below), but this is an untested area of the law, upon which judicial clarification will be required.

Capacity to consent to sexual relations

6.14 The question of the appropriate test to apply when determining whether a person has capacity to consent to sexual relations has been one of the most vexed issues before the courts since the enactment of MCA 2005. A detailed study of the principles and issues involved is outside the scope of this work,[23] but for those involved in applications before the court, it is vital to have in mind a number of considerations, set down below.

6.15 Section 27(1)(b) of the MCA 2005 provides expressly that nothing in the Act permits any person to consent on behalf of any other person to have sexual relations. Unlike many other questions regarding P's capacity, questions of capacity to consent to sexual relations are ones that (in principle) afford of a binary 'yes'/'no' answer, with no consequent ability on the part of a decision-maker to go on to consider whether it is in P's best interests to have sexual relations.

6.16 Perhaps the thorniest question is whether capacity to consent to sexual relations is act-specific or person (or situation)-specific: in other words, is the relevant information for purposes of s 3(1) solely information relevant to the proposed act (and its consequences), or does the information also include information about the proposed sexual partner? Prior to the enactment of MCA 2005, it had been established by Munby J (as he then was) that the question was act-specific.[24] However, the law was then thrown into doubt by the powerful dicta of Baroness Hale in *R v C*[25] (with which the balance of the House associated themselves), in which she made it clear her view that it was:

> '... difficult to think of an activity which is more person- and situation-specific than sexual relations. One does not consent to sex in general. One consents to this act of sex with this person at this time and in this place.'

6.17 A number of attempts were made by first instance judges to reconcile the incompatible views of Munby J and Baroness Hale.[26] Mostyn J in *D Borough Council v AB*[27] and Hedley J in *A Local Authority v H*,[28] essentially abandoned any attempt so to do. In *D Borough Council*, Mostyn J concluded[29] that the capacity to consent to sex remained act-specific and required an understanding

---

[23] For a discussion of the issues involved which is now slightly out of date as regards the law but remains of assistance, see *Assessment of Mental Capacity: A Practical Guide for Doctors and Lawyers* (3rd Edition, BMA/Law Society, 2010).

[24] *X City Council v MB, NB and MAB* [2006] EWHC 168 (Fam), [2006] 2 FLR 968 and *Local Authority X v MM and KM* [2007] EWHC 2003 (Fam), [2009] 1 FLR 443.

[25] [2009] 1 WLR 1786. The case concerned the criminal provisions contained in the Sexual Offences Act 2003, rather than the common law (or MCA 2005) test for capacity to consent.

[26] The most comprehensive attempt was that of Roderic Wood J in *D County Council v LS* [2010] EWHC 1544 (Fam), [2010] COPLR Con Vol 331.

[27] [2011] EWHC 101 (COP), [2011] COPLR Con Vol 313.

and awareness of: (a) the mechanics of the act; (b) that there are health risks involved, particularly the acquisition of sexually transmitted and sexually transmissible infections; and (c) that sex between a man and a woman may result in the woman becoming pregnant. In *A Local Authority v H*, Hedley J identified the same factors, but also (of his own motion) considered whether capacity also needed 'in some way to reflect or encompass the moral and emotional aspect of human sexual relationships'.[30] He concluded with relative ease that the moral aspect played no specific role in the test, but had more difficulty with the emotional aspect. Hedley J recognised that it remained 'an important, some might argue the most important, component [and that] certainly it is the source of the greatest damage when sexual relations are abused'; however, acknowledging the difficulty inherent in articulating the component into a workable test, he concluded that one could do no more than ask the question whether 'the person whose capacity is in question understand[s] that they do have a choice and that they can refuse'[31].

6.18 The matter came before the Court of Appeal in *IM v LM & Ors*[32] in November 2013. In this judgment, the Court of Appeal reconciled the apparent clash between the approaches of Munby J and of Baroness Hale by noting that the criminal law bites only retrospectively, to ask whether particular conduct, in particular circumstances, and with the knowledge or understanding of the particular participants, contravened the law; the civil law, by contrast, requires prospective assessment in light of the particular circumstances of the affected individual. The Court of Appeal therefore found that 'the fact that a person either does or does not consent to sexual activity with a particular person at a fixed point in time, or does or does not have capacity to give such consent, does not mean that it is impossible, or legally impermissible, for a court assessing capacity to make a general evaluation which is not tied down to a particular partner, time and place' (emphasis in original). Indeed, it went on:

> '... it would be totally unworkable for a local authority or the Court of Protection to conduct an assessment every time an individual over whom there was doubt about his or her capacity to consent to sexual relations showed signs of immediate interest in experiencing a sexual encounter with another person. On a pragmatic basis, if for no other reason, capacity to consent to future sexual relations can only be assessed on a general and non-specific basis.'[33]

---

[28] [2012] EWHC 49 (COP), [2012] COPLR 305. A further decision *A Local Authority v TZ* [2013] EWHC 2322 (COP) was handed down whilst this work was at the proofing stage. It is to similar effect as the decisions in *AB and H*.

[29] Paragraph 42.

[30] Paragraph 24.

[31] Paragraph 26; this approach was also endorsed by Mostyn J in *LB Tower Hamlets v TB* [2014] EWCOP 53 who stated that he had been persuaded that the more nuanced approach adopted by Hedley in *Re H* was to be preferred to the approach that he himself had adopted in *Re AB*, and that this more nuanced approach aligned the civil and criminal law.

[32] [2014] EWCA Civ 37, [2014] COPLR 246.

[33] *IM* at para [77] per Sir Brian Leveson giving the judgment of the court.

6.19 The Court of Appeal, further, emphasised that: 'The requirement for a practical limit on what needs to be envisaged as "reasonably foreseeable consequences" [of the sexual act in question] derives not just from pragmatism but from the imperative that the notional decision-making process attributed to the protected person with regard to consent to sexual relations should not become divorced from the actual decision-making process carried out in that regard on a daily basis by persons of full capacity. That process, as Ms Richards [on behalf of the Official Solicitor] observes, is largely visceral rather than cerebral, owing more to instinct and emotion than to analysis.' In holding that the ability to use and weigh information is unlikely to loom large in the evaluation of capacity to consent to sexual relations, the Court of Appeal emphasised that 'the information typically, and we stress typically, regarded by persons of full capacity as relevant to the decision whether to consent to sexual relations is relatively limited. The temptation to expand that field of information in an attempt to simulate more widely informed decision-making is likely to lead to … both paternalism and a derogation from personal autonomy.'[34]

In light of this judgment the focus in the area of capacity to consent to sexual relations is now on the question of whether the person has capacity to decide on contact with a particular person.[35] It is also noteworthy that concern has been expressed with regards to the outcome of the Court of Appeal's decision, particularly in *Derbyshire CC v AC, EC and LC*[36] where Cobb J stated:

> 'I have not heard detailed argument on this aspect of the case, as the parties were not in disagreement about it; but I must record my small misgivings about the conclusion reached. The distinguished line of judges sitting in the jurisdictions of the Family Division and Court of Protection who have opined on the question of what "relevant information" should inform the test of capacity in this vexed area have not sought to include within the scope of information the understanding of "P" that she (or he) may at any time change her (or his) mind about consenting to sexual relations. Hedley J. considered that it would be legitimate to ask the question whether "the person whose capacity is in question understand[s]that they do have a choice and that they can refuse." The evidence in this case reveals that AC may not always fully understand that she does have a choice, and/or that she can change her mind in relation to consent to sex; given the extent to which she has been exploited this gives me considerable anxiety. However, on the established test as it stands the professional consensus (with which I do not feel I should disagree) is that the criteria (summarised above) are established in relation to this issue at this time. Accordingly, I conclude that AC currently has capacity in this regard although, given the fluctuating nature of her capacity in this respect, I urge those who have continued responsibility for AC to keep this issue under careful review.'

---

[34]   *IM* at paras [80] and [82].
[35]   *A Local Authority v TZ (No 2)* [2014] EWHC 973 (COP).
[36]   [2014] EWCOP 38 at para 36.

PRACTICE AND PROCEDURE

6.20 The practice and procedure of the Court of Protection generally is dealt with in detail in Chapter 8. This section limits itself to considerations specific to welfare and medical treatment cases. As was recognised by the work of the Rules Review Committee established by the then-President,[37] these considerations are not always the same as those prevailing in property and affairs cases. Notwithstanding the fact that the Court of Protection is a unified jurisdiction, it is likely that the trend will be towards an increasing recognition of the different case-management approaches that are required to the different categories of case.

Serious medical treatment cases

Definition

6.21 The President's Practice Direction 'Applications Relating to Serious Medical Treatment'[38] makes special provision for these cases. 'Serious medical treatment' is defined for this purpose as treatment which involves providing, withdrawing or withholding treatment in circumstances where:

- (If a single treatment is proposed) there is a fine balance between its benefits and burdens and risks;
- (If there is a choice) a decision as to which treatment is finely balanced; or
- The treatment, procedure or investigation would be likely to involve serious consequences for the patient.

6.22 The Practice Direction first spells out that there are certain decisions which should be regarded as serious medical treatment decisions and should be brought to the court. It also gives examples of other decisions which should be considered serious medical treatment (see also **6.24** below).[39] It provides that in these cases the person bringing the application will always be a party to the proceedings, as will a respondent named in the application form who files an acknowledgment of service, and the organisation providing clinical or caring services should usually be named as a respondent (if not the applicant). Whether or not 'P' is to be joined as a party is to be determined at the first directions hearing (as is the question of who should be appointed as that person's litigation friend: the Official Solicitor or some other person). In practice, however, the increasing trend (at least where time allows) is that such

---

[37] See the Press Release issued by the Judicial Communications Office on 29 July 2010 available at www.judiciary.gov.uk/media/media-releases/2010/news-release-2210.

[38] Practice Direction 9E.

[39] As at the date of writing, there remains outstanding a proposal (from the Rules Review Committee referred to in the footnote above) that this Practice Direction be amended so as to make it clear that serious medical treatment can encompass treatment which is not in and of itself serious, but where the consequence of administering/not administering it would be serious. The current President of the Court of Protection has indicated his intention to press ahead with implementing in full the recommendations of the Committee.

questions – along with any questions of permission – are determined on paper by the court in advance of that hearing.

When should serious medical treatment cases be brought to court?

6.23   The Practice Direction in large part reflects the position that had been reached at common law as to when a serious medical treatment decision should be decided by the court. The first category concerns decisions to withhold or withdraw artificial nutrition and hydration ('ANH').[40] This covers people in a Persistent Vegetative State or a Minimally Conscious State. Prior to the enactment of MCA 2005, it had been established[41] that, as a matter of good practice, all cases where it was proposed to withdraw ANH from a patient in Persistent Vegetative State should go to court. This was partly a reflection of the importance of the decision for the individual and also provides a reassurance to the public as to how these decisions are taken. This is now buttressed by the Practice Direction, which also covers withholding or withdrawal of ANH in cases where a person is in a Minimally Conscious State.[42]

6.24   The second category of case set out in the Practice Direction is organ or bone marrow donation by a person who lacks capacity to consent. The third is non-therapeutic sterilisation (whether of a woman or a man by way of a vasectomy).[43] Other examples of 'serious medical treatment' given in the Practice Direction which should be taken to the Court of Protection are:

- Certain termination of pregnancy cases, where there is a dispute over capacity or the patient may regain capacity during her pregnancy, any lack of unanimity, where the procedures under the Abortion Act 1967, s 1 have not been followed, where the patient or members of her immediate family have opposed a termination, or where there are other exceptional circumstances (including that this may be the patient's last chance to bear a child, following Coleridge J's decision in *D v An NHS Trust (Medical Treatment: Consent)* cited at **6.25** below);

---

[40]   In all such cases reference should now be made to the guidelines issued by the Royal College of Physicians in December 2013 on 'Prolonged disorders of consciousness', available at: www.rcplondon.ac.uk/prolonged-disorders-consciousness-national-clinical-guidelines.

[41]   In *Airedale NHS Trust v Bland* [1993] AC 789. However, the existing terminology used in PD9E has not yet been updated to reflect the terminology used in the 2013 guidelines, where for instance 'ANH' is now referred to as 'CANH' (clinically assisted nutrition and hydration).

[42]   That such matters must be brought before the Court of Protection was reaffirmed in *W (by her Litigation Friend) v (1) M (by her Litigation Friend the Official Solicitor) (2) S and (3) A NHS Primary Care Trust* [2011] EWHC 2443 (Fam), [2012] COPLR 222 at para 257, per Baker J (in observations specifically endorsed by the President). It is a moot point as to whether section 2 of the Royal College of Physicians 2013 Guidelines comply with the observations of Baker J at para 259 of his judgment as to the formal testing required before a diagnosis can safely be reached for the purposes of withdrawing ANH from patients in a vegetative or minimally conscious state.

[43]   See in this regard *A Local Authority v K and Others* [2013] EWHC 242 (COP), [2013] COPLR 194 (female sterilisation) and *An NHS Trust v DE & Ors* [2013] EWHC 2562 (Fam), [2013] COPLR 531 (male sterilisation).

- Other medical treatment for the purpose of a donation to someone else;[44]
- Treatment which requires a degree of force to restrain the person concerned;[45]
- Treatment which is experimental or innovative; and
- Cases involving an ethical dilemma in an untested area.

6.25 These situations apart, there may be other procedures or treatments which can be regarded as serious medical treatment (because of the circumstances and consequences) and which, if so, may be brought to court. Where the decision as to the appropriate treatment is finely balanced either as to its benefit or the choice of treatment, testing whether it is in the best interests of the person concerned through Court of Protection proceedings may well be appropriate. The general principle is that the court's jurisdiction should be invoked whenever there is a serious justiciable issue requiring a decision by a court:

> 'In cases of controversy and cases involving momentous and irrevocable decisions, the courts have treated as justiciable any genuine question as to what the best interests of a patient require or justify.'[46]

Specific and detailed guidance as to when and how applications should made where a treating Trust is concerned that pregnant woman lacks, or may lack, the capacity to take decisions about her antenatal, perinatal and post natal care as a result of an impairment of, or a disturbance in, the functioning of her mind or brain resulting from a diagnosed psychiatric illness is set out by Keehan J in *NHS Trust & Ors v FG*.[47] It may be the case that this important guidance will feed through into a revision of PD9E in due course, both in terms of the circumstances under which applications should be brought and in terms of the procedure that should be adopted.

---

[44] Hedley J in *A NHS Trust v P* [2013] EWHC 50 (COP) recommended that the case be explicit. It is referred to as guidance in all serious medical treatment cases concerning the termination of pregnancies.

[45] Examples of the levels of restraint that have been permitted by the Court of Protection include covert sedation and the use of force if required to transport P to hospital for purposes of undergoing surgery (*DH NHS Foundation Trust v PS* [2010] EWHC 1217, [2010] COPLR Con Vol 346); restraining P for 18 hours a day for 5 days to ensure she received an intravenous immunosuppressant drug (*Re SB*); and restraining P for 3 hours every fortnight for 6 months (*Re KA*). The latter two cases were only reported by way of press reports. In *An NHS Trust v (1) K (2) Another Foundation Trust* [2012] EWHC 2922 (COP), [2012] COPLR 694, CP, Holman J authorised the use of mild sedation so as to render P more likely to be compliant in advance of an operation, but declined to authorise physical restraint because of the risks that it would pose to P.

[46] Coleridge J in *D v An NHS Trust (Medical Treatment: Consent)* [2004] 1 FLR 1110. See also *North Somerset Council v LW & Others* [2014] EWCOP 3 where an adverse costs order was made where the NHS trust failed to make an application to the Court of Protection.

[47] [2014] EWCOP 30.

Allocation, urgency and case management

6.26 The Practice Direction makes provision for the allocation of serious medical treatment cases. Where the application relates to the lawfulness of withholding or withdrawing ANH from a person in a Persistent Vegetative State or a Minimally Conscious State or it is a case involving an ethical dilemma in an untested area then the whole proceedings (including the permission stage) must be conducted by the President or a judge nominated by the President. All other serious medical treatment cases or cases in which a declaration of incompatibility is sought pursuant to the Human Rights Act 1998, s 4 must be conducted by the President, the Chancellor or a High Court judge (nominated to sit as a Court of Protection judge). However, there have been instances of High Court judges subsequently transferring such cases for determination by circuit and district judges sitting as nominated judges of the Court of Protection. Whether the Practice Direction covers a case is a matter for the Senior Judge of the Court of Protection or a judge nominated by him or her. In practice, this has meant that applications lodged at the court which have not been made on an urgent basis are referred to a district judge to make a decision as to allocation (for urgent cases see **6.27**). In a case requiring to be allocated to a High Court Judge which is not urgent (in the sense that P's life or health is not at immediate risk) but which nonetheless needs a speedy process (such as where P needs to be given treatment for cancer and any significant delay is likely to prejudicial), it is advisable before issue to alert the court's Listing and Appeals team to the application and the need for it to be processed and issued quickly.

6.27 The practice to be followed in urgent cases is set out in PD10B. The Practice Direction suggests that for urgent applications brought during office hours contact should be made with the Court of Protection. However, in serious medical treatment cases the practice which has developed is to go direct to the Clerk of the Rules of the High Court Family Division to seek an urgent hearing before the first available Family Division judge and giving an undertaking to issue the proceedings at the Court of Protection within the next working day.[48] That judge will determine the allocation of the case. When it is not possible to apply within court hours contact should be made with the security officer at the Royal Courts of Justice, who will invariably refer the matter to the Family Division High Court judge covering urgent out-of-hours business. It should be noted that the Official Solicitor does not operate an out-of-hours service. Where an application is brought out of normal court hours the court will normally strive to make the most limited order possible until such point as the matter can be brought back with P legally represented (invariably through the appointment of the Official Solicitor as litigation

---

[48] Difficulties can be encountered when listing a return date for the application after the urgent hearing has occurred as the Clerk of the Rules usually requires a case number, which is not always issued immediately. It is advisable to phone the listings office at the Court of Protection to ensure that they are aware of the urgency of the application and the need for it to be promptly issued. It is worth noting that the Clerk of the Rules office has clerks with specific responsibility for dealing with Court of Protection cases who can be very helpful to speak to in urgent cases.

friend). This will also generally be the case where the urgency of the application means that the litigation friend is unable to attend.[49] However, where a decision needs to be made without even the shortest delay, the court can make a decision on the spot without the assistance of the Official Solicitor.[50]

6.28 In *Aintree University NHS Hospitals Trust v James*,[51] the Supreme Court confirmed in relation to the timing of applications relating to the withholding of life-sustaining treatment that if clinicians bring an application too early, there is a risk that the court may be unable to say that when the treatments are needed that they will not be in the best interests of the patient. Unfortunately, the Supreme Court did not provide further assistance as to precisely when such applications should be brought, but did emphasise that it is necessary to be precise in the framing of the declarations sought.

6.29 Case management in serious medical treatment cases is subtly different to that of other less serious health and welfare cases, in that (1) the presumption is that P will be joined as the party; (2) that the Official Solicitor will invariably be appointed to act as P's litigation friend; and (3) the presumption is that the application will be heard in public, with suitable restrictions to be imposed in respect of the publication of information about the proceedings.[52] The President of the Family Division issued in January 2014 guidance upon the publication of judgments in cases before the Court of Protection, which preserves and extends the position in relation to such medical treatment cases, and suggests that, where a judge authorises publication of a judgment: public authorities and expert witnesses should be named in the judgment approved for publication, unless there are compelling reasons why they should not be so named; (ii) the person who is the subject of proceedings in the Court of Protection and other members of their family should not normally be named in the judgment approved for publication unless the judge otherwise orders; (iii) anonymity in the judgment as published should not normally extend beyond protecting the privacy of the adults who are the subject of the proceedings and other members of their families, unless there are compelling reasons to do so.

---

[49] See, for example, *Nottinghamshire Healthcare NHS Trust v RC* [2014] EWCOP 1137, [2015] COPLR (forthcoming).

[50] See *Newcastle-upon-Tyne Hospitals Foundation Trust v LM* [2014] EWHC 454 (COP). See also guidance given by Theis J in *Sandwell and West Birmingham Hospitals NHS Trust v CD & Ors* [2014] EWCOP 23.

[51] [2013] UKSC 67, [2013] 3 WLR 1299, [2013] COPLR 492.

[52] Practice Direction 9E; for a discussion of the principles underpinning the making of reporting restrictions in such cases, see *W (by her Litigation Friend, B) v M, S, an NHS PCT and Times Newspapers Ltd* [2011] EWHC 1197 (COP), [2011] Con Vol 1206. The former judgment provides very helpful guidance as to the form of order which can be sought in high profile cases, preventing the door stepping of P's family and other press intrusion which may be distressing to them or which may directly impact on P.

Best interests in medical treatment cases: life sustaining treatment

6.30 Whilst space precludes a detailed consideration of the specific evidential matters that arise in the context of serious medical treatment cases,[53] one matter that does call for particular attention in the determination of P's best interests is MCA 2005 s 4(5), which specifically relates to life-sustaining treatment and provides that:

> 'Where the determination relates to life-sustaining treatment *[the decision-maker]* must not, in considering whether the treatment is in the best interests of the person concerned, be motivated by a desire to bring about his death.'[54]

Given the importance accorded by both Houses of Parliament during the Parliamentary Debates on the MCA 2005 to issues related to withholding or withdrawing life-sustaining treatment, a short commentary drawing some of the threads together is appropriate. Two of the leading cases (both pre-dating MCA 2005) are *Bland* and *Burke*.[55]

6.31 In *Bland* the House of Lords decided that, where there is no continuing duty on doctors to sustain life through medical treatment, including the provision of ANH, because of the futility of doing so in the case of a patient in Persistent Vegetative State, it would be lawful to withhold or withdraw that treatment. It has subsequently been held that this decision is compatible with the incorporation of the European Convention on Human Rights in our law[56] and the decision has been re-affirmed in *Pretty v UK*.[57] It is the basis for the distinction in this jurisprudence between omissions and positive acts causing death.

6.32 The *Burke* case was a judicial review concerning the lawfulness of guidelines issued by the General Medical Council (GMC)[58] and was brought by a competent adult who feared that the guidance would not adequately protect him from doctors' withholding or withdrawing ANH at a time when, as a result of his wasting disease, he would need it to be kept alive. The case provided the opportunity, taken by Munby J (as he then was), for a judgment covering a number of important issues, although the Court of Appeal in its judgment, allowing the GMC's appeal and setting aside the declarations made at first

---

[53] Detailed consideration of the specific issues that arise in serious medical treatment cases can be found in Johnston et al, *Medical Treatment: Decisions and the Law* (Bloomsbury, 2010).

[54] Section 62 further provides that nothing in MCA 2005 is to be taken as affecting the law relating to murder, manslaughter or assisted suicide.

[55] *Airedale NHS Trust v Bland* [1993] AC 789; *R (Burke) v General Medical Council (Official Solicitor and others intervening)* [2004] EWHC 1879 (Admin), [2005] QB 424 (at first instance); [2005] EWCA 1003, [2006] 1 QB 273 (Court of Appeal).

[56] *NHS Trust A v H* [2001] 2 FLR 501.

[57] (2002) 35 EHRR 1.

[58] *Withholding and Withdrawing Life-prolonging Treatments: Good Practice in Decision-making* (August 2002). With effect from 1 July 2010, this guidance was replaced by *Treatment and care towards the end of life: good practice in decision making*, which expressly incorporates reference to *Burke* and is available at: www.gmc-uk.org/End_of_life.pdf_32486688.pdf.

instance, approached the case very more narrowly. The Court of Appeal recognised that, whilst the duty to keep a patient alive by administering ANH or other life-prolonging treatment is not absolute, the only exceptions are either where a competent patient refuses to receive it or where it is not considered to be in the best interests of an incompetent patient artificially to be kept alive. This latter circumstance covers patients in Persistent Vegetative State and where the patient's continued life involves an extreme degree of pain, discomfort or indignity and he or she has not shown a wish to be kept alive.[59]

6.33 In relation to Mr Burke's own situation, the Court of Appeal robustly declared:[60]

> 'Indeed, it seems to us that for a doctor deliberately to interrupt life-prolonging treatment in the face of a competent patient's expressed wish to be kept alive, with the intention of thereby terminating the patient's life, would leave the doctor with no answer to a charge of murder.'

and:[61]

> 'Where life depends upon the continued provision of ANH there can be no question of the supply of ANH not being clinically indicated unless a clinical decision has been taken that the life in question should come to an end. That is not a decision that can lawfully be taken in the case of a competent patient who expresses the wish to remain alive.'

6.34 That the MCA 2005 has not fundamentally altered the position reached at the common law in respect of the withdrawal or withholding of life-sustaining treatment was put beyond doubt in *W v M and S and A NHS Primary Care Trust*.[62] This decision is of significance not just for its comprehensive review of the domestic (and Strasbourg) jurisprudence, but also because it concerned – for the first time – an application for the withdrawal of ANH from a patient in a Minimally Conscious State.[63]

6.35 A final consideration is the tension that can sometimes arise between what may appear to have been the past wishes of the person and what might now appear objectively to be in their best interests. This tension (discussed

---

[59] This issue also arises in severely damaged baby cases: see eg *Re J (a Minor)(Wardship: Medical Treatment)* [1991] Fam 33.

[60] *R (Burke) v General Medical Council (Official Solicitor and others intervening)* [2006] 1 QB 273 at 297.

[61] Ibid, at 301.

[62] [2011] EWHC 2443 (Fam).

[63] A detailed discussion of this case lies outside the remit of this book; suffice it to say for these purposes that Baker J held (contrary to the submissions of the Official Solicitor) that the 'conventional' balance sheet approach applies to the withdrawal of ANH in such circumstances, and hence that as a matter of logic there are circumstances under which the person's best interests would be satisfied by its withdrawal. Applying the balance sheet, Baker J concluded that it was not in M's best interests for ANH to be withdrawn. See also the recent decision of Pauffley J in *United Lincolnshire Hospital Trust v N* [2014] EWCOP 16, discussed in para **6.36** below.

further in Chapter 2) can be particularly stark in the context of life-sustaining treatment, and was the subject of detailed judicial scrutiny in the *W v M* case outlined above. In this case, the incapacitated adult had made no formal advance decision[64] as to medical treatment, but had expressed views to relatives about the matter in conversations prior to their suffering the viral infection which led to their loss of capacity. However, whilst acknowledging the accuracy of M's views relayed by her relatives, Baker J concluded that:

> 'Given the importance of the sanctity of life, and the fatal consequences of withdrawing treatment, and the absence of an advance decision that complied with the requirements previously specified by the common law and now under statute, it would be in my judgment be wrong to attach significant weight to those statements made prior to her collapse.'[65]

The decision was perhaps even more finely balanced in the case of *A Local Authority v E and Others*.[66] In this case, discussed further at **6.65** below, Peter Jackson J had to consider the case of young woman, E, who was suffering from severe anorexia nervosa and who wished to refuse all food and drink. In circumstances where: (1) in consequence of her severe anorexia nervosa E 'above all [did] not want to eat or be fed;' and (2) she had sought twice – unsuccessfully – to make advance decisions refusing life-sustaining treatment, Peter Jackson J noted that the case 'raised for the first time in my experience[67] the real possibility of life-sustaining treatment not being in the best interests of a person who, while lacking capacity, is fully aware of her situation'. In particular given the high respect that had to be afforded to the view of E, an intelligent and articulate adult, he found that the competing factors were almost exactly in equilibrium; but he ultimately found the balance 'tip[ped] slowly but unmistakably in the direction of life-preserving treatment'. In the end, the presumption in favour of the preservation of life was not displaced.[68]

6.36   In *Aintree University NHS Hospitals Trust v James*[69] the Supreme Court held that:

> 'The purpose of the best interests test is to consider matters from the patient's point of view. That is not to say that his wishes must prevail, any more than those of a fully capable patient must prevail. We cannot always have what we want. Nor will it always be possible to ascertain what an incapable patient's wishes are. Even if it is possible to determine what his views were in the past, they might well have changed in the light of the stresses and strains of his current predicament. In this case, the highest it could be put was, as counsel had agreed, that "It was likely that Mr James would want treatment up to the point where it became hopeless". But insofar as it is possible to ascertain the patient's wishes and feelings, his beliefs and

---

[64]   Advance decisions are discussed further at **6.53ff** below.
[65]   Paragraph 230.
[66]   [2012] EWHC 1639 (COP), [2012] COPLR 441.
[67]   And, indeed to the author's knowledge.
[68]   To contrasting effect, see the decision of Eleanor King J in case concerning a young woman, L, who also suffered from anorexia nervosa: *The NHS Trust v L & Ors* [2012] EWHC 2741 (COP), [2013] COPLR 139.
[69]   [2013] UKSC 67, [2013] 3 WLR 1299, [2013] COPLR 492 at para [45] per Baroness Hale.

values or the things which were important to him, it is those which should be taken into account because they are a component in making the choice which is right for him as an individual human being.'

It will of interest to see whether these strong dicta give rise to decisions in the medical treatment sphere in which the balance is tipped further away from protective decision-making.

However, the balance has tipped further away from protective decision making as a result of the recent decision of Pauffley J in *United Lincolnshire Hospital Trust v N* [2014] EWCOP 16 in which the court went further than any case before involving a protected party in a minimally conscious state by declaring that it was not in N's best interests for the Trust to make any further attempts to establish and maintain a method for providing N with artificial nutrition.

N's case is distinguishable from the *W v M* case on the facts; in particular, M's case was about withdrawal of ANH rather than sanctioning the decision not to keep offering ANH. Further, the facts demonstrate that M did not manifest the same resistance as N to the provision of ANH. However, legally, both were held to be in the same position of minimal consciousness and, importantly, Pauffley J did not, as she could have done, seek to ascribe to N wishes and feelings based on her actions. Rather she focused on N's earlier expression (recounted by N's adult daughter) that she would not like to continue life in a reduced capacity in the event of a road traffic accident. Even though N's comments were of a similar level of generality to those expressed by M, and the views expressed by the families of the two women as to what they would have wished were materially identical, it seems that in N's case they were given very significant weight, but in M's case they were not.

Health and welfare cases

6.37 Outside the category of serious medical treatment cases addressed, in most instances it will be perfectly proper to proceed upon the basis of the authority given by MCA 2005, s 6.[70] It must be a decision to be taken in the circumstances of an individual case whether the protection of seeking a decision from the court should be obtained. Similarly, more general welfare decisions may be taken in the best interests of the person concerned without going to court. This point was strongly emphasised by Baker J in *G v E*,[71] where (in the context of refusing an application for a welfare deputy to be appointed) he emphasised that:

---

[70] See also Chapter 2 of this work.

[71] [2010] EWHC 2512 (COP) (Fam), [2010] COPLR Con Vol 470. NB, this was not the same *G v E* judgment as the more well-known one addressing questions of deprivation of liberty, discussed in Chapter 7.

'The Act and Code are ... constructed on the basis that the vast majority of decisions concerning incapacitated adults are taken informally and collaboratively by individuals or groups of people consulting and working together.'[72]

However, there may be a dispute which cannot be resolved by any other means, for example, between a close family member and the local authority's social services or between family members or between treating clinicians and/or other professionals involved in a person's care, as to what those best interests are: 'Ultimately, if all other attempts to resolve the dispute have failed, the court might need to decide what is in the person's best interests.'[73]

6.38   When any health and welfare cases need to be taken to the court (and, if required, permission is granted) the court decides who is to hear the case and gives directions as to the procedure to be followed. It determines who the parties are to be, and in particular whether the person concerned is to be made a party and, if so, who the litigation friend is to be, or whether it can reach a decision on the basis of the information made available to it (as well, potentially, as a report from the Public Guardian or Visitor or social or health services under MCA 2005, s 49). It also considers such matters as permission to obtain independent expert evidence, obtaining disclosure from third parties (e.g., medical records, social services' files, care home records, financial documents) and the filing of statements. Whilst Rule 90(1) of the Court of Protection Rules 2007 provides that 'the general rule is that a hearing should be held in private,'[74] the court is also increasingly likely to consider whether to allow the case to proceed in public (subject to appropriate reporting restrictions): the President of the Court of Protection, Sir James Munby, recently indicating that he considers to be 'compelling' the arguments in favour of allowing accredited journalists to attend hearings unless proper grounds for excluding them can be established on narrowly defined grounds.[75] Where there is a possibility that the court will wish to consider the grant of relief that does not lie within the repertoire of remedies that are afforded it by MCA 2005, consideration will also be given to whether the matter should be transferred to be heard before a High Court judge so that they can (in parallel) grant relief under the inherent jurisdiction.[76]

6.39   The Court of Appeal in *MN (An Adult)* [2015] EWCA Civ 411 provided important guidance on the approach the Court of Protection should adopt

---

See also *JO v GO & Ors* [2013] EWHC 3932 (COP) at para 26 per Sir James Munby P.

[73]   Code of Practice, para 5.68. Note akin to that which was promulgated in relation to proceedings under the inherent jurisdiction ([2006] 2 FLR 373, attaching to it the Practice Note from the Official Solicitor: "Declaratory Proceedings: Medical and Welfare Decisions for Adults who Lack Capacity.") The central themes of that guidance remain as pertinent today as they did in 2006.

[74]   See also *Independent News Media v A* [2010] EWCA Civ 343, [2010] 1 WLR 2262.

[75]   Sir James Munby P, 'The Court of Protection – the Way Forward?' (2013) ELJ 221. See also *Hillingdon LBC v Neary* [2011] EWHC 413 (COP), [2011] COPLR Con Vol 677.

[76]   See *XCC v AA and Others* [2012] EWHC 2183 (COP), [2012] COPLR 730, *An NHS Trust v Dr A* [2013] EWHC 2442 (COP) [2013] COPLR 605 and the discussion in Chapter 11 at **11.5–11.9**.

when a care provider is unwilling to provide, or to fund, the care sought, whether by the patient or by the patient's family. In particular, it was held that the Court of Protection, like the family court and the Family Division, can explore the care plan being put forward by a public authority and, where appropriate, require the authority to go away and think again. However, the Court of Protection cannot compel a public authority to agree to a care plan which the authority is unwilling to implement. In support of this the Court of Appeal stated that it is not the proper function of the Court of Protection to embark upon a factual inquiry into some abstract issue the answer to which cannot affect the outcome of the proceedings before it. Nor is it a proper function of the Court of Protection (nor of the family court of the Family Division) to embark upon a factual inquiry designed to create a platform or springboard for possible future proceedings in the Administrative Court. Such an exercise runs the risk of confusing the very different perspectives and principles which govern the exercise by the Court of Protection of its functions and those which govern the exercise by the public authority of its functions, and also runs the risk of exposing the public authority to impermissible pressure.

INDEPENDENT MENTAL CAPACITY ADVOCATES

Establishment

6.40 MCA 2005 imposes a duty on the Secretary of State (in practice the Secretary of State for Health) in England and the Welsh Assembly in Wales to make arrangements to enable independent mental capacity advocates (IMCAs) to be available to represent and support incapacitated persons in circumstances defined in the Act.[77] These arrangements must be designed to achieve the laudable principle that:[78]

'... a person to whom a proposed act or decision relates should, so far as practicable, be represented and supported by a person who is independent of any person who will be responsible for the act or decision.'

6.41 This adopts the conclusion of the Joint Parliamentary Committee scrutinising the draft Bill which was accepted by the Government that:[79]

'We are convinced that independent advocacy services play an essential role in assisting people with capacity problems to make and communicate decisions; helping them to enforce their rights and guard against unwarranted intrusion into their lives; providing a focus on the views and wishes of an incapacitated person in the determination of their best interests; providing additional safeguards against abuse and exploitation; and assisting in the resolution of disputes.'

---

[77] MCA 2005, s 36.
[78] MCA 2005, s 35(4).
[79] Joint Committee on the Draft Mental Incapacity Bill, Session 2002–2003, HL 189-1, HC 1083, para 297.

6.42 MCA 2005 empowers the Secretary of State (or Welsh Assembly) to discharge this duty by making Regulations providing for the circumstances and conditions under which such an advocate may act and as to his or her appointment. This he has done (in England) in the Mental Capacity Act 2005 (Independent Mental Capacity Advocates) (General) Regulations 2006.[80]

Appointment, functions and role

6.43 The IMCA service is locally based (commissioned by the relevant local authority). The qualifying conditions for a person to be an IMCA are that he or she is (or belongs to a class of persons) approved by the local authority, and that he or she has appropriate experience or training, is a person of integrity and good character and is able to act independently of any person who instructs him or her.

6.44 The Regulations provide for the functions of such advocates and the steps to be taken for the purposes of:[81]

- providing support so the person whom he or she has been instructed to represent may participate as fully as possible in any relevant decision;
- obtaining and evaluating relevant information;
- ascertaining what the person's wishes and feelings would be likely to be and the beliefs and values likely to influence that person;
- ascertaining what alternative courses of action are available; and
- obtaining a further medical opinion.

6.45 The IMCA's functions are to:

(1) verify that the instructions were issued by an authorised person;

(2) to the extent it is practicable and appropriate, interview the patient and examine relevant health, social services or care home records;

(3) to the extent practicable and appropriate, consult the professional carers and other persons in a position to comment on the patient's wishes, feelings, beliefs or values;

(4) take all practicable steps to obtain information about the patient, or the proposed act or decision;

(5) evaluate all the information he or she has obtained so as to ascertain the extent of the support provided to enable the patient to participate in the decision and what the patient's wishes and feelings would likely be and the beliefs and values likely to influence the patient, what alternative courses of action are available and where medical treatment is proposed whether the patient would benefit from a further medical opinion; and

---

[80] SI 2006/1832.
[81] MCA 2005, s 36.

(6) prepare a report for the person who instructed him or her, to include such submissions as he or she considers appropriate.

An IMCA who has been instructed also has power to challenge the decision taken as if he or she were someone engaged in caring for the patient or interested in the patient's welfare.

The duty to instruct

NHS bodies

6.46 An NHS body is under a duty to instruct such an advocate and to take into account any information given or submissions made by that advocate before providing 'serious medical treatment' (as defined in the Regulations in a similar way to that subsequently adopted in the President's Practice Direction as described at **6.21**ff) when there is no one else for the provider of the treatment to discuss it with.[82] This will occur when there is neither a person in the specified list[83] who can speak for the person – namely, a person nominated by the person, an attorney under a lasting power of attorney or pre-existing enduring power of attorney, or a deputy – nor a non-professional carer or friend whom it is appropriate to consult.[84] If the treatment has to be provided as a matter of urgency it may be provided even though no advocate has been instructed.

6.47 A similar duty arises where it is proposed that an incapacitated person should be accommodated in long-stay accommodation in a hospital or care home, or should transfer to another hospital or care home, where this accommodation is provided or arranged by the NHS.[85] If the accommodation is to last more than 28 days in a hospital or 8 weeks in a care home an advocate is to be instructed when there is no other person to discuss it with. The role of the advocate is again to support and represent the person concerned and any information and submissions from the advocate must be taken into account.

---

[82] Not being treatment regulated by the Mental Health Act 1983, Part 4: MCA 2005, s 37.

[83] This is set out in MCA 2005, s 40.

[84] Paragraph 10.69 of the Code of Practice refers to IMCAs being available to people who have no family or friends who are available and appropriate to support or represent them. There is currently no case law on what factors would prevent a family member or friend from being an 'appropriate adult'. Clearly concerns as to such a person having a conflict of interest or mental health problems would seem a reasonable basis to exclude their involvement as an appropriate adult but – for instance – would the fact that such a person may hold strong religious views sufficient to deem them to be not appropriate. The author has been informed of cases where IMCAs have been appointed where there are dissenting family members who simply have strong moral objections to the proposed provision or withholding of treatment. The IMCA should only accept appointment where satisfied that that person is not appropriate. The author is further aware of a recent case where the IMCA declined to report where she considered the husband of P was an appropriate adult for the NHS Trust to consult in a serious medical treatment case.

[85] MCA 2005, s 38.

This does not apply if the accommodation arises as a result of an obligation under the Mental Health Act 1983 nor when it is being arranged as a matter of urgency.[86]

Local authorities

6.48 Matching provisions are made in respect of, and a duty imposed, on a local authority in relation to long-stay accommodation arranged by that authority.[87] These apply to residential accommodation provided in accordance with the National Assistance Act 1948, s 21 or 29 or following discharge under the Mental Health Act 1983, s 117. The accommodation may be in a care home, nursing home, ordinary or sheltered housing, housing association or other registered social housing, or in private sector housing provided by a local authority or in hostel accommodation. Similar exceptions are made where the person concerned is required to live in the accommodation in question under the Mental Health Act 1983 or in relation to urgent placements.[88]

Expansion of role

6.49 Separate Regulations were made in 2006[89] expanding the role, adjusting the obligation to make arrangements and prescribing different circumstances in which an advocate may be instructed to act. In consequence, an NHS body or local authority may instruct an IMCA (if satisfied it would be beneficial to the person to be so represented) when reviewing accommodation arrangements or proposing to take protective measures to minimise the risk of abuse or neglect.

Powers of the IMCA

6.50 An IMCA may, for the purpose of enabling him or her to carry out his or her functions:

- interview in private the person he or she has been instructed to represent; and
- examine and take copies of any health record, social services record or care home record which the person holding the record considers may be relevant to the advocate's investigation.[90]

---

[86] Provision is made to ensure that an advocate is involved in relation to people whose residence is initially intended to be less than the 28 days or 8 weeks if the period is later extended beyond the applicable period (MCA 2005, s 38(4)).

[87] MCA 2005, s 39.

[88] MCA 2005, s 39(3) and (4).

[89] These are the Mental Capacity Act 2005 (Independent Mental Capacity Advocates) (Expansion of Role) Regulations 2006 SI 2006/2883.

[90] MCA 2005, s 35(6).

Comment

6.51 IMCAs are a valuable part of the machinery provided by MCA 2005.[91] Their primary role is to support someone where there are no family members or friends (except where protective measures are being considered) – particular examples include older people with dementia who have lost contact with all friends and family, or people with severe learning disabilities or long-term mental health problems who have been in residential institutions for long periods and lack outside contacts. It is clear, however, from the fifth annual report issued by the Department of Health on the IMCA service[92] that significant problems remain with the implementation of the provisions. The numbers of IMCA instructions have more than doubled in the 5 years that the service began (when there were 5,266 cases). However, there are still wide disparities in the rate of IMCA instructions across different local areas which cannot wholly be explained by population differences. As the Department of Health notes: '[i]t is likely that in some areas the duties under the MCA are still not well embedded. The duty to refer people who are eligible to IMCAs is still not understood in all parts of the health and social care sector.'[93] Worryingly, the first decrease was noted in the year 2011–12 in cases where IMCAs were appointed to represent people subject to safeguarding procedures; moreover, as the Department notes, there is only one care review referral for each four accommodation referrals, which raises the question of why, if an IMCA has been involved in the decision to move a person, why three quarters of them are not invited to support and represent the person in subsequent reviews (assuming that such care reviews are in fact being undertaken after moves).

6.52 The House of Lords Select Committee appointed to consider and report upon MCA 2005 took extensive oral evidence upon the operation of the IMCA service,[94] it also specifically called for evidence upon the safeguards. In its report published in March 2014[95] the Committee recommended that consistency of the service be ensured through national standards and mandatory training in the MCA 2005 and the IMCA Role. The Committee further recommended that local authorities use their discretionary powers to appoint IMCAs more widely than is currently the case and that the Government consider the establishment of a form of self-referral for IMCA services to prevent the damaging delay that occurred in the *Neary* case. The Government has accepted these recommendations in its response to the Committee report.[96]

---

[91] See, for instance John Williams, Sarah Wydell and Alan Clarke, 'Protecting Older Victims of Abuse: the Role of the Independent Mental Capacity Advocate' [2013] Eld LJ 167.

[92] Covering the period 2011–2, but also including an overview of the first 5 years of their operation. Available at: www.gov.uk/government/uploads/system/uploads/attachment_data/file/158009/Independent-Mental-Capacity-Service-fifth-annual-report.pdf.

[93] Ibid at p 6.

[94] See www.parliament.uk/business/committees/committees-a-z/lords-select/mental-capacity-act-2005.

[95] 'Mental Capacity Act 2005: post-legislative scrutiny' (13 March 2014) at paras 164–178.

[96] 'Valuing every voice, respecting every right: Making the case for the Mental Capacity Act' (June 2014) at paras 6.38–6.44.

ADVANCE DECISIONS

Preliminary: the position at common law

6.53 Advance decisions play so significant part in the framework established by MCA 2005 for making of medical decisions that they merit separate consideration, starting with a brief *tour d'horizon* of the position that had been reached at common law prior to the enactment of the Act.

The starting point: the principle of adult autonomy

6.54 Whether as Munby J (as he then was) analysed it in *Burke*[97] that the adult is the arbiter of his or her own best interests or it is purely a matter of adult autonomy irrespective of best interests; the court has no basis or jurisdiction to investigate a competent adult's best interests. The principle of adult autonomy is determinative.

Refusal of treatment

6.55 At common law, it was clear that advance refusals[98] to consent to particular treatments were an aspect of a competent adult's autonomy. An advance refusal of medical treatment was required to be given binding effect if, but only if:

(1)   made at a time when the adult had capacity to make a decision of such a nature;

(2)   intended to apply when that person was incapable;

(3)   it related to the circumstances which had arisen;

(4)   the maker understood the nature and consequences of his or her decision; and

(5)   there was no undue influence or coercion by a third party.

6.56 No particular form was needed, and such a refusal could be revoked in any way or as a result of a change in relevant circumstances. The courts had to be satisfied that the advance refusal remained valid and applicable to the particular circumstances; it there was doubt, that doubt was to be resolved in favour of the preservation of life and the best interests test applied.[99] The greatest difficulty in practice was whether from the drafting of an advance directive it could be clearly inferred that such a refusal was intended to apply in the circumstances which had arisen; and it was clear that there was not always consistency of practice amongst medical professionals in their interpretation of the application of the facts to the directive before them.

---

[97]   *R (Burke) v GMC and Others* [2005] QB 424.
[98]   Documents setting out wishes as to medical treatment were initially described as 'living wills'.
[99]   *HE v A Hospital NHS Trust* [2003] 2 FLR 408.

The relationship with suicide

6.57 Well prior to 2007, it was settled law that whilst no one had the right to ask for and be given treatment which constituted a positive act (such as the administration of an excessive dose of diamorphine) to assist in their suicide, they could refuse the provision or continuation of life-sustaining treatment such as ANH even when the inevitable consequence was death.[100]

Requests for treatment

6.58 An advance directive could request rather than seek to refuse treatment. There was (and is) at common law no general right for a person to require, either at the time or in an advance decision, that a particular form of medical treatment be given. This was reaffirmed in robust terms by the Court of Appeal in its judgment in *Burke*.[101]

ADVANCE DECISIONS UNDER THE MENTAL CAPACITY ACT 2005

Recognition

6.59 MCA 2005, ss 24–26 give statutory recognition to, and govern the applicability and effect of, advance decisions to refuse specified treatments made by an adult when they have capacity to consent to or refuse medical treatment which are to have effect when the adult loses that capacity. A number of conditions are laid down which must be met before such a decision is to be valid and applicable. These replicate the common law position in a number of respects in relation to refusals of treatment, and in some modify it by providing additional safeguards as indicated below.

Advance refusals of treatment

6.60 These provisions of MCA 2005 in their terms only apply to advance refusals of specified treatments. It is necessary to specify the treatment which is to be refused, although this does not have to be done in medical language and can be expressed in layman's terms.[102] The circumstances in which the refusal is to apply may also be specified. Such a decision may be subsequently withdrawn

---

[100] Reaffirmed in *Pretty v United Kingdom* (2002) 35 EHRR 1. In deciding whether effect must be given to an advance refusal of life-sustaining treatment it is not necessary to inquire into the motives of the person making it. The Catholic Bishops Conference of England and Wales submitted to the Court of Appeal in *Burke* that adult autonomy is limited by an inability to refuse treatment motivated by a suicidal intent. It is suggested that this was not established in existing case-law as at that point, and remains the case at present.

[101] *R (Burke) v General Medical Council* [2006] 1 QB 273.

[102] MCA 2005, s 24(1)(a) and (2).

or altered when the maker of the decision has capacity to do so. This need not be in writing unless the altered decision is a decision to refuse life-sustaining treatment.[103]

Advance requests for treatment and care arrangements

6.61 Advance requests for treatment are dealt with differently under MCA 2005. They are treated as a relevant written statement which, if made when the person had capacity, must be considered by the decision-maker in determining best interests.[104] They cannot be determinative if, taking into account all relevant factors, that treatment would not in P's best interests. This would also apply to an advance statement relating to care arrangements, for instance as to where P would wish to live or with whom they would wish to have contact, statements which find no express place in the scheme of MCA 2005 but which can be useful tools for individuals who either have fluctuating capacity or are aware that their capacity is likely to diminish over time, but who wish to have some say in arrangements to be made for them when they lack capacity.

6.62 To have the effect prescribed in MCA 2005 an advance decision to refuse a treatment must have been made by a person after he or she has reached the age of 18 and at a time when he or she had capacity to do so. It loses its validity if:[105]

- the person has withdrawn the decision (by any means) at a time when he or she had capacity to do so;
- he or she has created a lasting power of attorney after the decision was made in which he or she gives the donee of the power the authority to give or refuse consent to the treatment in question; or
- he or she has since the decision was made acted inconsistently with that being his or her fixed intention.[106]

Applicability

6.63 An advance decision is not applicable if:[107]

- at the time the provision of the treatment is in question the person has the capacity to give or refuse consent to it;
- the treatment falls outside the treatment specified in the decision;

---

[103] MCA 2005, s 24(5).
[104] MCA 2005, s 4(6).
[105] MCA 2005, s 25(2).
[106] See *HE v A Hospital NHS Trust* [2003] 2 FLR 408 as a good example (a previous Jehovah's Witness who had become betrothed to a Muslim and was professing she would live by the principles of that faith). This was a pre-MCA 2005 case but it is suggested that the same outcome would prevail under the Act.
[107] MCA 2005, s 25(3) and (4).

- any circumstances specified in the decision are absent; or
- there are reasonable grounds for believing that circumstances exist which the maker of the advance decision did not anticipate at the time of its making and which would have affected his or her decision had he or she anticipated them.

Life-sustaining treatment

6.64 In addition to these conditions, there are statutory conditions for the applicability of advance decisions refusing life-sustaining treatment. These are that:[108]

- the decision includes a statement by the maker that it is to apply to the life-sustaining treatment even if his or her life is at risk;
- the decision is in writing; and
- it is signed by or under the direction and in the presence of its maker and that signature is made or acknowledged in the presence of a witness who signs or acknowledges his or her signature in the presence of the maker of the decision. Peter Jackson J confirmed in *An NHS Trust v D* that the absence of a witness rendered invalid an advance decision refusing life-sustaining treatment.[109]

Effect

6.65 A valid and applicable advance decision has effect as if the maker had made it, and had the capacity to make it, at the time the question arises whether the treatment specified in it should be carried out or continued. In *A Local Authority v E and Others*,[110] Peter Jackson J held that for 'an advance decision relating to life-sustaining treatment to be valid and applicable, there should be clear evidence establishing on the balance of probability that the maker had capacity at the relevant time. Where the evidence of capacity is doubtful or equivocal it is not appropriate to uphold the decision.'[111]

6.66 If the person providing treatment withholds or withdraws the treatment when he or she reasonably believes that an advance decision refusing the treatment exists which is valid and applicable to the treatment, he or she is

---

[108] MCA 2005, s 25(5) and (6). The first and third of the requirements do not apply in the case of an advance decision made prior to 1 October 2007 where P has at all stages subsequent to that point lacked capacity to make a new advance decision. See Art 5 of the Mental Capacity Act 2005 (Transitional and Consequential Provisions) Order 2007/1898. A pre-October 2007 decision must be in written form in order for it to be applicable in such situations.

[109] [2012] EWHC 885 (COP) [2012] COPLR 493. It is not entirely clear whether Peter Jackson J was also of the view that the advance decision failed to comply with the requirement in MCA, s 25(5)(a) that it was to apply even if life was at risk. On the facts of the case, however, Peter Jackson J was able to conclude that withdrawal of treatment from D (who was in a permanent vegetative state) was in his best interests.

[110] [2012] EWHC 1639 (COP), [2012] COPLR 441.

[111] Paragraph 56. See also **6.35** above.

protected from legal liability in doing so.[112] Conversely, a person does not incur liability for carrying out or continuing treatment unless or until he or she is satisfied that an advance decision exists which is valid and applicable to the treatment.[113]

Doubt or disagreement

6.67 If there is any doubt or disagreement over whether an advance decision exists, is valid or is applicable to a treatment, an application can be made to the Court of Protection for it to make a declaration.[114] By way of example, in an unreported case in 2009 where P's family claimed that a valid written advanced decision was given to paramedics during air ambulance evacuation and subsequently lost, the court heard oral evidence and made a finding that a valid and applicable advance decision existed refusing the use of blood or blood products in P's treatment. While a decision is being sought, those treating the person concerned are entitled to take nothing in the advance decision as preventing them providing life-sustaining treatment or doing any act they reasonably believe to be necessary to prevent a serious deterioration in that person's condition.[115] The importance of bringing matters relating to the validity of an advance decision to Court as quickly as possible has recently been emphasised in the cases of *A Local Authority v E and Others* (discussed above at **6.35** and **6.64**) and *X Primary Care Trust v XB* (discussed further below at **6.69**).

The Code of Practice

6.68 Chapter 9 of the Code of Practice contains valuable guidance and suggestions for best practice in this area, and has been the subject of specific judicial endorsement.[116] In particular, Chapter 9 suggests that, whilst there is no set form for written advance decisions, it is helpful to include the following information:[117]

- full details of its maker, including date of birth, home address and any distinguishing features (so that eg an unconscious person might be identified);

- the name and address of general practitioner and whether they have a copy;

---

[112] MCA 2005, s 26(3).

[113] MCA 2005, s 26(2).

[114] MCA 2005, s 26(4).

[115] MCA 2005, s 26(5).

[116] *X Primary Care Trust v XB* [2012] EWHC 1390 (Fam), [2012] COPLR 577, Theis J endorsing (at para 34) the guidance at paras 9.10–9.23 of the Code of Practice as to what should be included.

[117] Code of Practice, para 9.19. See also *Nottinghamshire Healthcare NHS Trust v RC* [2014] EWCOP 1317 and *A NHS Foundation Trust v Ms X (By Her Litigation Friend, the Official Solicitor)* [2014] EWCOP 35 as recent and interesting illustrations of the court's consideration of the validity of advanced decisions.

- a statement that the document should be used if the maker lacks capacity to make treatment decisions;

- a clear statement of the decision, the treatment to be refused and the circumstances in which the decision will apply;

- the date the document was written (or reviewed); and

- the person's signature (or that of the person signing in their presence on their behalf) and the signature of a witness (if there is one).

6.69 In addition, if the decision relates to life-sustaining treatment, it must contain a clear statement that the decision is intended to apply even if the treatment in question is necessary to sustain life (and there must be a witness to the signature).

A cautionary tale: *X Primary Care Trust v XB*

6.70 The danger of using pro forma advance decisions was graphically illustrated by the case of *X Primary Care Trust v XB*,[118] the first reported case in which the Court of Protection was asked to make a declaration under the provisions of MCA 2005 s 26(4). As it also stands as a cautionary tale in a number of other respects, the case merits more than a passing mention.

6.71 XB, who suffered from Motor Neurone Disease, sought to make an advance decision that he wished life-sustaining treatment to be withdrawn as at the point when he was no longer able to communicate his needs or have control over his decisions as to his care and management. As he was unable to write (or indeed to communicate other than moving his eyes) at the material time, it was necessary for the advance decision to be completed on his behalf. The advance decision was recorded on a form downloaded from the internet. The form included a box to enter a date upon which it was to be reviewed; it also included a box to enter a date against the cryptic entry 'valid until.'

6.72 Doubt having arisen as to the circumstances under which XB had made the advance decision and in particular, as to whether he given his express consent by moving his eyes, the Primary Care Trust investigated and ultimately brought the matter before the Court of Protection. However, as it had taken over a month to investigate the circumstances, the matter did not come before the Court until days before the 'valid until' date upon the form. XB's condition had by that stage progressed to the point where he lacked the capacity to communicate (and hence, prima facie, the decision would be applicable). The Court had to decide in very short order[119] whether the advance decision had been properly made and (if so) whether the words 'valid until' in fact meant what on their face they did. If the decision was properly made but the words meant what they appeared to mean, then XB – who was no longer in a position to make a fresh advance decision but was still conscious and alert – would have

---

[118] [2012] EWHC 1390 (Fam), [2012] COPLR 577.
[119] The matter first came before the Court on a Friday; a 2-day hearing was concluded by close of play on the Tuesday (the 'valid until' date being the Wednesday).

been in the position where; (1) his original decision would have expired and those near to him could no longer lawfully act upon it; (2) in light of the case-law upon withdrawal of life-sustaining treatment,[120] his wishes as contained in the original decision could not have been determinative of the question, and there would there therefore have been a very real prospect that the court would have found that withdrawal was not in XB's best interests; and (3) XB would have been aware that his wishes as contained in the decision were not being acted upon in precisely the circumstances in which he sought them to be honoured.

6.73 Fortuitously (if that is the correct word in such a situation), Theis J was able to find upon the facts before her that the 'valid until' date had been entered by one of the professionals attending XB at the point at which the advance decision had been made without discussing it with him and without XB's consent, such XB had not intended to time-limit his advance decision. Evidence having been received which allayed the earlier concerns as to the circumstances under which the decision had been made, Theis J was therefore able to make a declaration that the advance decision had properly been made and was not time-limited. Unsurprisingly, Theis J emphasised for the future that (1) in the event that an issue is raised as to the circumstances in which an advance decision has been made, this should be investigated as a matter of urgency by the relevant statutory body; and (2) organisations producing pro forma documents might wish to look again at the merits of including a 'valid until' date.

Comment: striking a balance

6.74 The statutory provisions on advance decisions are designed to strike a balance between, on the one hand, recognition of a competent adult's autonomy and, on the other, the fears expressed during the parliamentary debates on the Bill[121] that a person could be locked into an advance refusal he or she would wish to change but can no longer do so. The main way in which they have sought to strike this balance has been by placing a particular emphasis (in the case of life-sustaining treatment) upon the advance refusal taking the form specified by statute; the serious consequences of failure to comply with these requirements have been emphasised by the courts in decisions handed down since the enactment of the Act.[122]

---

[120] See **6.35** above.
[121] See eg, *Hansard*, HC Deb, vol 425, ser 6, cols 37–102 (11 October 2004); *Hansard*, HC Official Report, SC A (Mental Capacity Bill), 28 October 2004, vol 1, HL Paper 79-1, HC Paper 95-1; and *Hansard*, HL Deb, vol 668, ser 5, cols 11–26 and 42–106 (10 January 2005), 1396–1432 and 1443–1512 (27 January 2005), vol 670, cols 1276–1324 (15 March 2005) and vol 671, cols 412–459 (24 March 2005).
[122] *W v M and S and A NHS Primary Care Trust* [2011] EWHC 2443 (Fam), [2012] COPLR 222 and *Re D* [2012] EWHC 885 (COP), [2012] COPLR 493. See also the discussion at **6.35** above.

The alternative of a lasting power of attorney

6.75 It is a matter of individual choice whether a person wishes to plan in advance for possible future lack of capacity by indicating a refusal of specified treatments. An alternative is to create a lasting power of attorney with the authority for the person chosen as donee to take health care decisions. If it is intended that the attorney should have the power to refuse life-sustaining treatment, this power must be expressly granted in the instrument (and the grant witnessed); a box to this effect appears in the prescribed form.[123] The power would also be subject to any conditions or restrictions in the instrument.[124]

Decisions by health care professionals

6.76 In the absence of either an advance decision or a lasting power of attorney, decisions will be taken by the health care professionals in the person's best interests.[125] A written statement which does not amount to an advance decision will be taken into account,[126] but it will depend on the facts of the case at the time what the overall best interests are. Where life-sustaining treatment is in question, significant weight may be attached to views even if they are expressed in a form which does not comply with the statutory requirements.[127]

6.77 Those taking treatment decisions when faced with an advance refusal of the treatment will need to take a view on the validity and applicability of the decision. For example, they will need to make an assumption as to the person's capacity at the time the decision was made (to which the statutory presumption of capacity will apply). In most instances there may be no doubt. The formalities around making an advance decision refusing life-sustaining treatment may make it easier to make this assumption in such a case. In some instances, however, where it is thought possible that the advance decision may be challenged in the future and there may be some doubt as to capacity, it may be helpful for the maker to obtain evidence confirming his or her capacity at the time.

6.78 Of greater difficulty may be (now as under the common law) whether the maker of the decision really had in mind the circumstances which have arisen and intended it to apply in those circumstances; or whether relevant circumstances have changed (eg the prospect of a new cure) so as to invalidate

---

[123] MCA 2005, s 11(8)(a).

[124] MCA 2005, s 11(8)(b).

[125] In the context of decisions made at the end of life, reference should be made to the decision of the Supreme Court in *Aintree University NHS Hospitals Trust v James*. See **6.36** above.

[126] See, by analogy, *RGB v Cwm Taf Health Board & Ors* [2013] EWHC B23 (COP) (advance statement made by wife regarding contact with husband). MCA 2005, s 4(6).

[127] See *Aintree University NHS Hospitals Trust v James, United Lincolnshire Hospital Trust v N* and the discussion at **6.34–6.36** above.

the decision. As the Code of Practice states, particular care will need to be taken for advance decisions which do not appear to have been reviewed or updated for some time.[128]

MEDICAL RESEARCH

Common law position

The regulation of research

6.79　It is beyond the scope of this chapter to delve deeply into the different types of research – for example, therapeutic, non-therapeutic and observational – and the volume of current learning on what is or is not permissible in accordance with modern ethical principles. There is in place a system of Local Research Ethics Committees and Multi-Centre Research Ethics Committees to regulate research carried out in an NHS body. This came into existence to relate to research involving patients who are fully informed and freely give their consent.

General principles

6.80　As a general principle it can be stated that medical research which involves some invasion of bodily integrity on a person who is not able to consent to it is not permissible under the existing common law, as it cannot be justified under the doctrine of necessity. A court might declare therapeutic research lawful if done in that person's best interests, although this has not been tested in court and often the point of research is not to benefit the particular individual but others who might in the future be suffering from a similar condition.

6.81　The closest the common law came to recognising benefits to others as a factor in the best interests equation arose in the cases in which the taking of samples from one sibling for the potential benefit of another were authorised as benefiting the child, or incapacitated adult, to contribute to the family's welfare in this way.[129] This is not a precedent justifying research. Nor is the decision in *Simms v Simms; A v A (a child)*[130] in which experimental and innovative treatment was authorised to victims of vCJD (Variant Creutzfeldt-Jakob disease), not by way of research, but as medical treatment in their best interests as in the circumstances being the only hope for them in slowing down the decline in their condition.

Clinical Trials Regulations

6.82　Therapeutic research in the form of clinical trials on medicinal products for human use is now authorised and regulated under and in accordance with

---

[128]　Code of Practice, para 9.51.
[129]　*Re Y (Mental Patient: Bone Marrow Donation)* [1997] Fam 110.
[130]　[2003] Fam 83.

the Medicines for Human Use (Clinical Trials) Regulations 2004[131] made under
the authority given by the European Union Directive on Good Clinical Practice
in Clinical Trials.[132] The Regulations govern such trials in relation to both those
who can provide informed consent and those who cannot.

6.83 The general principles underlying these Regulations are that:

- the clinical trial must have the approval of the relevant ethics committee
  and be authorised by the appropriate minister as licensing authority;

- the anticipated therapeutic and public health benefits must justify the
  risks; and

- informed consent must be given (which must be written, signed and dated)
  after an interview with a member of the investigating team.[133]

6.84 The involvement of an adult who lacks capacity to consent requires the
informed consent of his or her 'legal representative' and is subject to the
following additional conditions:

- the research is essential to validate data obtained in clinical trials on
  persons able to give consent and relates directly to a life-threatening or
  debilitating clinical condition from which the incapacitated adult suffers;
  and

- the trial has the potential to produce a benefit to the patient which
  outweighs the potential risks.

6.85 For the purposes of the Regulations, an incapacitated participant's legal
representative is either:

(1) a person close to the patient (a 'personal legal representative'); or, where
    no one can act in that capacity,

(2) someone such as the doctor responsible for the care of the patient or other
    person nominated by the health care provider, being someone not involved
    in the conduct of the trial (a 'professional legal representative').

---

[131] SI 2004/1031. These Regulations came into force on 1 May 2004 and have been subsequently
       amended on numerous occasions.

[132] Directive 2001/20/EC. The Regulations now also incorporate the requirements of Directive
       2005/28/EC setting down (inter alia) principles and detailed guidelines for good clinical
       practice as regards investigational medicinal products for human use.

[133] There is an exception in the case of urgency where treatment is being or is about to be provided
       for an incapacitated adult as a matter of urgency, and it is also necessary to take action for the
       purposes of the clinical trial as a matter of urgency but it is not reasonably practicable to obtain
       such informed consent; in such instances, the action required for the purposes of the clinical
       trial can be carried out if it is in accordance with a procedure approved by an Ethics Committee
       (or by an appeal panel considering an appeal against an unfavourable decision of an Ethics
       Committee): Sch 1 to the Regulations, paras 6 and 7.

6.86   The legal representative may withdraw the subject from the trial at any time.[134] If an adult prior to the onset of incapacity has refused to give his or her consent, he or she cannot be included as a subject.

Research authorised by the Mental Capacity Act 2005

Background

6.87   The draft Mental Incapacity Bill presented to Parliament in June 2003 did not contain any provisions on research. The Joint Scrutiny Committee on this Bill, in response to evidence it received from the British Medical Association, the Royal College of Psychiatrists, the British Psychological Society and The Law Society, concluded that if properly regulated research involving people who may lack capacity was not possible then treatment for incapacitating disorders would not be developed. It recommended, therefore, that clauses should be included to enable strictly controlled medical research to explore the causes and consequences of mental incapacity and to develop effective treatment for such conditions. It further recommended that these clauses should set out the key principles governing such research and the protections against exploitation or harm.[135]

6.88   As a result, provisions were included in the Mental Capacity Bill as presented to Parliament, and these were refined through various amendments made during the course of the Bill's consideration. They now form MCA 2005, ss 30–34.[136]

Application of the Act

6.89   The provisions of ss 30–34 apply to any intrusive research carried out on, or in relation to, a person who lacks capacity to consent to it other than a clinical trial subject to the Medicines for Human Use (Clinical Trials) Regulations 2004 (because they already make provision for trials involving participants who lack capacity). They are based upon long-standing international standards such as those laid down by the World Medical Association (originally in the Helsinki Declaration in 1964 and updated since) and in the Council of Europe Convention on Human Rights and Biomedicine.

Pre-condition to authorisation

6.90   The pre-condition to the authorisation of research under these provisions is that a committee established to advise on the ethics of intrusive research in relation to people who lack capacity to consent to it and recognised for this

---

[134] Subject to the 'urgency' exemption set out at fn 132 above.

[135] See recommendations 81–88, HL Paper 189-1 HC Paper 1083-1 (Session 2002–03).

[136] See Chapter 11 of the Code of Practice for a general explanation of and guide to these provisions.

purpose by the Secretary of State for Health (in relation to research in England) or the Welsh Assembly (in relation to Wales) has approved the research project.[137]

6.91 That approval can only be given in relation to a person who lacks capacity to consent if:[138]

- the research is connected with the person's impairing condition or its treatment;
- there are reasonable grounds for believing that research of comparable effectiveness cannot be carried out if the project is confined to persons who can consent;
- the research has the potential to benefit the person without imposing a disproportionate burden or it is intended to provide knowledge of the causes or treatment of, or the care of persons affected by, the same or a similar condition;
- in the case of research which falls only in the latter category, there are reasonable grounds for believing that the risk to the individual in taking part is negligible and anything done to that person will not interfere with his or her freedom of action or privacy in any way or be unduly invasive or restrictive; and
- there are arrangements in place to ensure the particular conditions (referred to below) will be met.

Pre-conditions relating to the individual

6.92 Before a person who lacks capacity to consent can take part in an approved research project, particular conditions relating to his or her participation must be met.

6.93 These conditions relate first to the requirement for a researcher to consult a carer (someone not professionally interested in the person's welfare) or, if a carer who is prepared to be consulted cannot be identified, a person not connected with the research project whom, in accordance with guidance to be issued by the Secretary of State (or the Welsh Assembly), the researcher has nominated as the person prepared to be consulted (eg a general practitioner or specialist engaged in the person's treatment).[139]

6.94 The regime established here is the equivalent of that provided for under the Clinical Trials Regulations outlined above. It includes provision for the consultee advising that the person concerned would not have wanted to take part, in which event that person is not to be included, or if already taking part,

---

[137] MCA 2005, s 30.

[138] MCA 2005, s 31.

[139] MCA 2005, s 32. The Secretary of State and Welsh Ministers have, in accordance with MCA 2005 s 32(3), issued 'Guidance on nominating a consultee for research involving adults who lack capacity to consent' (February 2008).

must be withdrawn. It also includes provision relating to treatment being provided as a matter of urgency and carrying on necessary research associated with that treatment.

6.95   Secondly, additional safeguards are provided that:

- nothing may be done in the course of the research to which the person appears to object (except where what is being done is intended to protect the person or reduce his or her pain or discomfort) or would be contrary to any known advance decision of that person or current statement of wishes;

- the person's interests must be assumed to outweigh those of science and society; and

- if the person lacking capacity indicates in any way that he or she wishes to be withdrawn he or she must be withdrawn, as he or she must be if any of the conditions for the approval of the research project cease to be met (although any treatment being given to which the research is associated may continue if there is a significant risk to health if discontinued).[140]

6.96   Regulations have been made (by the Secretary of State and the Welsh Assembly) covering the continuation of a research project in relation to a person who had consented to take part in it before these provisions were brought into force and who loses capacity to consent to continuing to take part in it before the conclusion of the project.[141]

Comment

6.97   These provisions, which have yet to be the subject of any decisions (either reported, or, to the best of the author's knowledge, unreported), cover the whole range of research activities which would require a person's consent if that person had capacity, which includes research involving them, their tissue or their data.[142] The provisions strike a careful balance between allowing intrusive procedures when not necessarily of direct benefit to that person and facilitating research into an impairing condition. They are also designed to cater for situations where the research is but one aspect of the clinical or professional care of the person who lacks capacity (which will be governed by the best interests test).

---

[140] MCA 2005, s 33.

[141] See Mental Capacity Act 2005 (Loss of Capacity During Research Project) (England) Regulations 2007, SI 2007/679 and Mental Capacity Act 2005 (Loss of Capacity during Research Project) (Wales) Regulations, SI 2007/837, both made under MCA 2005, s 34.

[142] Research on anonymised medical data or tissue may be possible outside the terms of MCA 2005, although subject to controls under the Data Protection Act 1998 or the Human Tissue Act 2004 respectively.

CHAPTER 7

DEPRIVATION OF LIBERTY SAFEGUARDS

BACKGROUND

7.1 With effect from 1 April 2009, the Mental Capacity Act 2005 (MCA 2005) was substantively amended by the Mental Health Act 2007 (MHA 2007) to provide mechanisms for authorising, subject to safeguards, the deprivation of liberty of a person who cannot consent when that is necessary in their best interests for their care or treatment.[1] The Mental Health Act 1983 (MHA 1983), as amended by the MHA 2007, contains its own compulsory powers for the detention, assessment or treatment of patients for their mental disorder. Whilst it is beyond the scope of this book to set out any detailed description or analysis of the mental health legislation, there are some interesting parallels and comparisons with the MCA 2005, particularly in relation to some health care issues discussed in Chapter 6. These set the scene and provide the context for a more detailed explanation of the deprivation of liberty safeguards.

THE MENTAL HEALTH ACT 1983, AS AMENDED BY THE MENTAL HEALTH ACT 2007

Powers of admission, detention and treatment

7.2 The MHA 1983, as amended by the MHA 2007, is principally concerned with the admission of patients to hospital for assessment and treatment for their mental disorder. However, the MHA 2007 extended powers of compulsion by introducing compulsory community treatment orders (also referred to as supervised community treatment) for patients previously detained in hospital who are now living in the community, but who continue to need treatment for

---

[1] Prior to that date under the MCA 2005 as originally enacted a person acting in connection with the care or treatment in the best interests of an incapacitated person could restrain that person if it was to prevent harm to that person and was a proportionate response but could not deprive them of their liberty (ss 5 and 6 – see Chapter 2). The High Court could make an order under its inherent jurisdiction which had the effect of depriving the person concerned of their liberty putting in place as many safeguards as practicable, including provision for review (see *Re PS (Incapacitated or Vulnerable Adult)* [2007] EWHC 623 (Fam), [2007] 2 FLR 1083 and *Salford City Council v GJ, NJ and BJ (by their litigation friends)* [2008] EWHC 1097 (Fam), [2008] 2 FLR 1295). That the inherent jurisdiction to grant such an order survives in an appropriate situation was confirmed by Baker J in *An NHS Trust v Dr A* [2013] EWHC 2442 (COP), [2013] COPLR 605, discussed further at **7.46** below.

their mental disorder. Mental disorder is defined as any disorder or disability of the mind (MHA 1983, s 1(2), as amended by MHA 2007). MHA 1983 enables compulsory powers of detention and treatment to be used when the statutory conditions for 'sectioning' the patient are met. In the case of admission for assessment, the patient must be suffering from mental disorder of a nature or degree which warrants the detention of the patient in a hospital for assessment, and:[2]

> '... he ought to be so detained in the interests of his own health or safety or with a view to the protection of other persons.'

7.3　　In the case of admission for treatment, the grounds need to be established that:[3]

> '(a)　he is suffering from mental disorder of a nature or degree which makes it appropriate for him to receive medical treatment in a hospital; and
>
> ...
>
> (c)　it is necessary for the health or safety of the patient or for the protection of other persons that he should receive such treatment and it cannot be provided unless he is detained under this section; and
>
> (d)　appropriate medical treatment is available for him.'

7.4　　The relevant criteria for community treatment orders are that:[4]

> '(a)　the patient is suffering from mental disorder of a nature or degree which makes it appropriate for him to receive medical treatment;
>
> (b)　it is necessary for his health or safety or for the protection of other persons that he should receive such treatment;
>
> (c)　subject to his being liable to be recalled as mentioned in para (d) below, such treatment can be provided without his continuing to be detained in a hospital;
>
> (d)　it is necessary that the responsible clinician should be able to exercise the power ... to recall the patient to hospital; and
>
> (e)　appropriate medical treatment is available for him.'

7.5　　MHA 1983 sets out the conditions and procedures for use of these powers. These include that the application for admission (either for assessment or treatment) must be made on the recommendation in the prescribed form of two registered medical practitioners. The Act also provides for patients to be received into guardianship, giving the appointed guardian (usually a local authority) the power to require a patient in the community to reside at a specified place and attend for treatment. The 2007 Act broadened the powers of the guardian by introducing a new power to take and convey a person subject to guardianship to their required place of residence (MHA 2007, Sch 3, para 3(5)).

---

[2]　　MHA 1983, s 2(2).

[3]　　MHA 1983, s 3(2), as amended by MHA 2007.

[4]　　MHA 1983, s 17A(5), as amended by MHA 2007.

Review and appeals

7.6 MHA 1983 then provides the procedures for review and appeals to the Health, Education and Social Care Chamber of the First-tier Tribunal (prior to 3 November 2008 the independent mental health review tribunals (MHRT)) in relation to the use, or continued use, of the compulsory powers.[5] The MHRT for Wales remains as a separate devolved tribunal. There is a right of appeal on a point of law from both tribunals to the Upper Tribunal.

Purpose

7.7 The purpose of MHA 1983 is to provide the statutory framework for the compulsory care and treatment of people for their mental disorder when they are unable or unwilling to consent to that care and treatment, and when it is necessary for that care and treatment to be given to protect themselves or others from harm.

7.8 The key point for the exercise of these powers is the inability or unwillingness of the patient who suffers from a mental disorder to consent to the relevant care and treatment. This encompasses people who, notwithstanding their mental disorder, have capacity to do so – and it is entirely possible for someone detained under the MHA 1983 to have capacity in relation to a treatment decision.[6] Inability to consent will also include people who do not have capacity, but the question whether an individual patient has or does not have decision-making capacity is not the key determinant of whether the powers conferred by MHA 1983 should be used.

COMPARISONS

7.9 The Mental Capacity Act 2005 (MCA 2005) is based wholly on a capacity test. Its provisions have no application to people who have the capacity to make their own decisions. Some who lack capacity will not come within the definition of those for whom compulsory powers under MHA 1983 can be exercised. People with learning difficulties, for example, who may thereby not be able to give their consent to treatment, will not generally be subject to the compulsory powers of MHA 1983, unless they are also abnormally aggressive or seriously irresponsible. Other examples are people in a persistent vegetative state or anyone suffering from 'locked-in' syndrome, which prevents them from communicating, persons with brain injuries or temporarily unconscious, drunk or under the influence of drugs.

---

[5] Tribunals, Courts and Enforcement Act 2007, Part 1.
[6] See, for a clear pre-MCA 2005 example, *Re C (Adult: Refusal of Treatment)* [1994] 1 WLR 290.

Differences

7.10   It can be seen that the differences between these two approaches are that:

(1)   MCA 2005 relates to a person's functioning – incapacity to make a particular decision – whereas MHA 1983 relates to a person's status, as someone diagnosed as having a mental disorder within the meaning of the Act and subject to its powers;

(2)   MCA 2005 covers all decision-making, whereas MHA 1983 is, to a very large degree, limited to decisions about care in hospital and medical treatment for mental disorder;

(3)   MHA 1983 authorises detention, but this was specifically excluded under MCA 2005 as originally enacted;[7] and

(4)   MCA 2005 specifically excludes[8] anyone giving a patient medical treatment for mental disorder, or consenting to a patient being given medical treatment for mental disorder, if the patient is, at the relevant time, already detained and subject to the compulsory treatment provisions of MHA 1983, Part 4.

Overlaps

7.11   There are areas of overlap. For example:

(1)   people who are detained in hospital under MHA 1983 and who also lack capacity to make financial decisions may be subject to the provisions of MCA 2005 when it comes to the taking of such decisions; and, equally,

(2)   an elderly person, for example, with Alzheimer's disease, whose day-to-day life is managed in accordance with the provisions of MCA 2005, may be made subject to MHA 1983 if it is no longer possible to care for such a person at home and he or she requires treatment for the mental disorder and is resisting being admitted to hospital.

THE DEPRIVATION OF LIBERTY SAFEGUARDS

The 'Bournewood Gap'

7.12   The great majority of people with a mental disorder are not treated under the MHA 1983. That Act specifically provides that nothing in that Act is to be treated as preventing the informal admission of a patient requiring treatment for mental disorder to any hospital or registered establishment.[9] Moreover, there are those people being treated or living in hospitals or care homes who

---

[7]   See MCA 2005, s 6, which provides the conditions under which a person may 'restrain' a person whilst remaining within the protection given by s 5, but this protection is not available if there is a deprivation of liberty. The provisions introduced into MCA 2005 by MHA 2007 allow deprivation of liberty in specific circumstances – see **7.17ff**.

[8]   See MCA 2005, s 28.

[9]   MHA 1983, s 131.

suffer from a mental disorder but are not there to be treated for their mental disorder and are not within scope of the MHA 1983. They may not have resisted nor objected to their admission nor to their continued stay in the hospital or care home. This does not give rise to any issue of particular concern when they have capacity and it is their choice. However, it can be seen that questions can arise as to how such patients should be dealt with who may be compliant but who do not have the capacity to reach their own decisions about what is happening to them. This is particularly the case so far as they are deprived of their liberty.[10] That there were no safeguards in relation to the deprivation of their liberty was characterised as 'the Bournewood gap'. The 'Bournewood gap' takes its name from, and achieved prominence as a result of, the decision of the European Court of Human Rights in *HL v UK*.[11]

The decisions of the domestic courts

7.13 Mr HL, an autistic man, was readmitted to the Bournewood Hospital after a period in the community with paid carers, but the decision was taken not to section him under MHA 1983 as he had not resisted admission. The ensuing dispute between the carers and the hospital over his care and treatment was first litigated in judicial review proceedings in the domestic courts. The carers lost at first instance and ultimately in the House of Lords, in the latter case essentially on the ground that the circumstances were covered by the common law doctrine of necessity. This reversed the decision of the Court of Appeal, which had upheld their claim that Mr HL had been unlawfully detained.[12]

European Court of Human Rights

7.14 The case was then taken to the European Court of Human Rights. The unanimous decision was:

(1)   that Mr HL had been deprived of his liberty contrary to Art 5(1) of the European Convention on Human Rights (ECHR);

(2)   that detention was arbitrary and not in accordance with a procedure prescribed by law; and

(3)   the procedures available to Mr HL did not comply with the requirements of Art 5(4) as there was no procedure under which he could seek a merits review of whether the conditions for his detention remained applicable.

---

[10]   This is not a new problem. The Mental Health Act Commission, established to keep under review the care and treatment of patients detained under MHA 1983, identified in its *First Biennial Report (1983–1985)* (HMSO, 1985) the lack of safeguards for 'de facto' detained patients.

[11]   Application no 45508/99, judgment on the merits given on 5 October 2004 [2004] 1 FLR 1019.

[12]   *R v Bournewood Community and Mental Health NHS Trust ex parte L* [1999] AC 458, HL; [1998] 2 WLR 764, CA.

7.15   The specific criticisms the European Court made, and the contrast it drew between the safeguards available to a person detained under MHA 1983 and an informal patient in Mr HL's position, related to the lack of any formal procedures as to:

- who could authorise an admission;
- the reasons needing to be given for that admission (whether it was for treatment or assessment);
- the need for continuing clinical assessment and review; and
- who could represent the patient and be able to seek a review in an independent tribunal as to the lawfulness of the continued detention.

7.16   The discussion in the court related to the position under the inherent jurisdiction as it was at the time these events occurred (1997). The enactment of MCA 2005, notably the creation of the Independent Mental Capacity Advocacy Service, dealt with some of the points raised. However, the decision in the case came too late for the Government to deal with it fully in MCA 2005 as enacted and it was recognised that it did not fill the gap. Following a period of consultation, the Government brought forward a new scheme enacted in the MHA 2007, amending MCA 2005 so that it can be lawful to deprive a compliant patient of their liberty other than through activating the MHA 1983 powers if the conditions of the scheme are met.

THE MCA SOLUTION

7.17   MHA 2007, s 50 and Schs 7 and 8 amended MCA 2005 so as to render it lawful to deprive a person of their liberty either if it is a consequence of giving effect to an order of the Court of Protection on a personal welfare matter or, if the deprivation of liberty is in a hospital or care home, if a standard or urgent authorisation (under the provisions of MCA 2005, Sch A1) is in force.[13] The Court of Appeal confirmed in *G v E*[14] that the scheme enacted by these amendments is both compliant with Art 5(1) ECHR and plugs the 'Bournewood Gap.'

Meaning of deprivation of liberty

7.18   For the purposes of these provisions deprivation of liberty is defined as having the same meaning as in Art 5(1) of the ECHR.[15] The starting principles are clearly established in the Strasbourg jurisprudence:

---

[13]   The amendments came into force on 1 April 2009 (The Mental Health Act 2007 (Commencement No 10 and Transitional Provisions) Order 2009, SI 2009/139.

[14]   [2010] EWCA Civ 822, [2010] COPLR Con Vol 431.

[15]   Section 64(5) MCA 2005. The ECHR cases relating to deprivation of liberty in the context with which we are concerned can be divided into two parts. The 'canon' is made up of *Guzzardi v Italy* (1980) 3 EHRR 333; *Ashingdale v UK* (1985) 7 EHRR 528; *Nielson v Denmark* (1988) 11 EHRR 175; *HM v Switzerland* (2002) 38 EHRR 314; *HL v UK* (2004) 40 EHRR 761; and *Storck v Germany* (2005) 43 EHRR 97. There was then something of a

- There are three elements necessary for there to be a deprivation of liberty falling within the scope of Art 5(1): an objective element of a person's confinement in a particular restricted space for a non-negligible length of time;[16] a subjective element, namely that the person has not validly consented to the confinement in question;[17] and that the deprivation of liberty must be imputable to the State.[18]

- The difference between restricting a person and depriving them of their liberty is one of degree or intensity rather than of nature or substance.[19]

- In order to determine whether there is a deprivation of liberty there must be an assessment of the specific factors in each case, such as the type, duration, effects and manner of implementation of the measure in question and its impact on the person.[20]

- Not all restrictions on a person's liberty will constitute a deprivation of liberty.[21]

7.19 While the DOLS Code of Practice provides guidance on identifying a deprivation of liberty,[22] the domestic courts have struggled to identify principles by which it may be determined where restrictions have crossed the line to amounting to deprivation of a person's liberty.[23] However, the Supreme Court's

---

pause, before a recent flurry of activity in Strasbourg resulting in resulting in *Stanev v Bulgaria* (2012) 55 EHRR 22; *DD v Lithuania* [2012] MHLR 209; *Austin v United Kingdom* (2012) 55 EHRR 14; *Kędzior v Poland* (Application No. 45026/07, decision of 16 October 2012); and more recently in *Stankov v Bulgaria* (Application No. 25820/07, decision of 17 March 2015). For a detailed discussion of the recent Strasbourg jurisprudence, see the paper by Alex Ruck Keene entitled 'Tying ourselves into (Gordian) knots?' available from: www.39essex.com/resources/article_listing.php?id=748.

[16] *Storck v Germany* (2005) 43 EHRR 96, at para 74.

[17] Ibid at para 74. There is some suggestion in the recent Strasbourg jurisprudence that it may in some circumstances be possible for 'substituted' consent to be given: *Stanev v Bulgaria* at para 130. However, the recent decision of *Stankov v Bulgaria* confirmed that, in asking whether a person has the capacity to consent to their confinement for social care purposes, the same approach is to be taken as in relation to placement for psychiatric treatment purposes. Thus, the consent of a person (and their ability to understand the consequences of this) can only be considered valid if determined through a fair procedure in which all necessary information concerning the placement and the proposed treatment is provided (paragraph 90). This is in essence consistent with the approach suggested by Baker J in *A PCT v LDV* [2013] EWHC 272 (Fam).

[18] Ibid at para 89.

[19] *Guzzardi v Italy* (1980) 3 EHRR 333 at para 92.

[20] *HL v UK* (2004) 40 EHRR 761 at para 89.

[21] *Guzzardi v Italy* (1980) 3 EHRR 333 at para 92.

[22] See Chapter 2; in addition to the DOLS Code of Practice, practical guidance on the law on deprivation of liberty for lawyers and health and social care professionals has recently (April 2015) been published by The Law Society: https://www.lawsociety.org.uk/support-services/advice/articles/deprivation-of-liberty/

[23] One consequence of this is the wide variation in the use of authorisations under Sch A1 of the MCA 2005. In significant part in reaction to widespread criticism of the way in which the amendments to MCA 2005 to bring in the DOLS safeguards were drafted, on 1 October 2014 the Scottish Law Commission published a Report on Adults with Incapacity including a draft Bill (Scot Law Com No 240). The Commission recommends that the Adults with Incapacity (Scotland) Act 2000 should be amended to include a legal process to authorise measures preventing an adult from going out of a hospital and a more detailed legal process for the

landmark decision in the linked appeals of *P (by his litigation friend the Official Solicitor) v Cheshire West and Cheshire Council and Another*, and *P and Q (by their litigation friend the Official Solicitor) v Surrey Council* [2014] UKSC 19, [2014] 2 WLR 642, (2014) 17 CCLR 5 clarifies the meaning of deprivation of liberty. The decision concerned the living arrangements of three disabled people: P, MIG and MEG.

7.20 P, a man with cerebral palsy and Down's Syndrome, lived in a staffed bungalow with other residents near his home and had one-to-one support to enable him to leave the house frequently for activities and visits. He needed 24-hour care including prompting with activities of daily living including hygiene and continence. Intervention was sometimes required when he exhibited challenging behaviour. He wore a 'bodysuit' and required invasive interventions including 'fingersweep' to the mouth to stop him ingesting harmful substances. Baker J held that these arrangements did deprive him of his liberty but that it was in P's best interests for them to continue.[24] The Court of Appeal substituted a declaration that the arrangements did not involve a deprivation of liberty, after comparing his circumstances with another person of the same age and disabilities as P.[25]

7.21 MIG and MEG (otherwise known as P and Q) were sisters who became the subject of care proceedings in 2007 when they were respectively 16 and 15. Both suffered from learning disabilities. MIG was placed with a foster mother to whom she was devoted and went to a further education unit daily. She never attempted to leave the foster home by herself but would have been restrained from doing so had she tried. MEG was moved from foster care to a residential home for learning disabled adolescents with complex needs. She sometimes required physical restraint and received tranquillising medication. When the care proceedings were transferred to the Court of Protection, Parker J held that these living arrangements were in the sisters' best interests and did not amount to a deprivation of liberty.[26] This finding was upheld by the Court of Appeal.[27]

7.22 The Supreme Court unanimously overruled the Court of Appeal in P and overruled the Court of Appeal in MIG and MEG's case by a majority of 4 to 3. The ultimate question before the Supreme Court was summarised by Lady Hale at para 33:

---

scrutiny of significant restriction of liberty of an adult in a care home or other placement in the community. Further, the Act should also be amended to provide for a right to apply to the sheriff court for release of an adult who may lack capacity from unlawful detention in certain care settings. The report can be found at www.scotlawcom.gov.uk/law-reform-projects/adults-with-incapacity.

24 *Cheshire West and Chester Council v P* [2011] EWHC 1330 (Fam).
25 *Cheshire West and Chester Council v P* [2011] EWCA Civ 1257, (2012) 15 CCLR 48, [2012] COPLR 37; Munby LJ, who delivered the lead judgment, adopted the 'relative normality' approach, considering that P was not deprived of his liberty because his life was no more restricted than that which anyone with his disabilities and difficulties might be expected to lead.
26 *Re MIG and MEG* [2010] EWHC 785 (Fam).
27 *Re P and Q* [2011] EWCA Civ 190.

'The first and most fundamental question is whether the concept of physical liberty protected by article 5 is the same for everyone, regardless of whether or not they are mentally or physically disabled.'

Lady Hale had no hesitation in holding that it was:

'45. [I]t is axiomatic that people with disabilities, both mental and physical, have the same human rights as the rest of the human race. It may be that those rights have sometimes to be limited or restricted because of their disabilities, but the starting point should be the same as that for everyone else. This flows inexorably from the universal character of human rights, founded on the inherent dignity of all human beings, and is confirmed in the United Nations Convention on the Rights of Persons with Disabilities. Far from disability entitling the state to deny such people human rights: rather it places upon the state (and upon others) the duty to make reasonable accommodation to cater for the special needs of those with disabilities.

46. Those rights include the right to physical liberty, which is guaranteed by article 5 of the European Convention. This is not a right to do or to go where one pleases. It is a more focussed right, not to be deprived of that physical liberty. But, as it seems to me, what it means to be deprived of liberty must be the same for everyone, whether or not they have physical or mental disabilities. If it would be a deprivation of my liberty to be obliged to live in a particular place, subject to constant monitoring and control, only allowed out with close supervision, and unable to move away without permission even if such an opportunity became available, then it must also be a deprivation of the liberty of a disabled person. The fact that my living arrangements are comfortable, and indeed make my life as enjoyable as it could possibly be, should make no difference. A gilded cage is still a cage.'

Lord Kerr, who agreed with Lady Hale and Lord Neuberger, noted at para 76 that:

'Liberty means the state or condition of being free from external constraint. It is predominantly an objective state. It does not depend on one's disposition to exploit one's freedom. Nor is it diminished by one's lack of capacity.'

7.23 Lady Hale conducted an analysis of the European Court of Human Rights case law in this area[28] and identified the twin ingredients of a deprivation of liberty where there is no valid consent to the living arrangements as:

(a) the person is not free to leave; and

(b) under continuous supervision and control.

---

[28] *HL v UK* (2004) 40 EHRR 761, *Stanev v Bulgaria* (2012) 55 EHRR 696, *DD v Lithuania* (App No 13469/06, 12 February 2012, *Kedzior v Poland* (App No 45026/07, 16 October 2012), *Mihailovs v Latvia* (App No 35939/10).

This is identified as the 'acid test' for whether or not a person is deprived of their liberty to avoid the minute examination of the living arrangements of each mentally incapacitated person for whom the state makes arrangements which might otherwise be required.

At para 50, Lady Hale also identified as irrelevant factors:

- P's compliance or lack of objections;
- the relative normality of the placement; and
- the reasons/purpose behind the placement.

7.24 Applying this test to the facts of these cases, the majority held that all three appellants were deprived of their liberty. Lords Hodge, Carnwath and Clarke dissented in MIG and MEG's case, taking the view that the sisters were not deprived of their liberty.

7.25 The Supreme Court's decision effectively restores the classical interpretation of what constitutes a deprivation of liberty and reiterates that deprivation of liberty safeguards also apply to locations other than hospitals and care homes. There is now an acid test as set out by Lady Hale. Further, at para 63, Lord Neuberger considered the essential ingredients of a deprivation of liberty to be 'continuous supervision and control and lack of freedom to leave' as well as 'the area and period of confinement'. At para 78 Lord Kerr said that the duration of the restriction was paramount.

7.26 While the judgment sets out what factors are irrelevant when applying the acid test, no further guidance is given as to the parameters of this test and, for example, when supervision does not amount to control and when supervision and control are not complete or continuous. Nor is there analysis of what it means to be 'free to leave' or how to determine the area and period of confinement. Until these issues are further tested before the courts, it would appear that the best guidance currently available on these issues is way in which the Supreme Court applied the acid test to the P and MIG and MEG.

7.27 It is also apparent that the concepts of relative normality and a disabled comparator are no longer applicable. The concept of relative normality originates from ECHR jurisprudence[29] and was embraced in the P & Q proceedings. The more controversial concept of disabled normality originated in the *Cheshire West* proceedings.[30]

7.28 As regards the role of a comparator in determining whether there is a deprivation of liberty, their Lordships expressed differing views. Lady Hale did not consider that comparing the lives of MIG and MEG with the ordinary lives

---

[29]   *Engel & Ors v The Netherlands* (Application no. 5100/71; 5101/71; 5102/71; 5354/72; 5370/72) of 8 June 1976.

[30]   However, none of the parties in the appeals to the Supreme Court supported a disabled comparator test.

that young people of their ages might live to answer the question and was of the view that the relative normality of the placement (whatever the comparison made) is not relevant (para 50). At para 46 Lady Hale went on to suggest that an appropriate comparator ought to be herself: 'if it would be a deprivation of my liberty ... then it must also be a deprivation of liberty of a disabled person'.

At para 80 Lords Carnwath and Hodge recognised that the comparator should in principle be a person with unimpaired health and capacity. Lord Kerr on the other hand considered that it was necessary to compare the person's age and 'station in life'. Thus, for MIG and MEG the relevant comparator was 'a teenager of the same age and familial background as them'. Lord Clarke, by contrast, expressly endorsed the approach of Parker J, which was to consider the sisters' lives as dictated by their own cognitive limitations.

In this context, Lady Hale has recently commented on what she considered the case had decided:

> 'We all held that the man had been deprived of his liberty, but three members of the court held that the sisters had not been deprived of their liberty, while the majority held that they had. The acid test was whether they were under the complete control and supervision of the staff and not free to leave. Their situation had to be compared, not with the situation of someone with their disabilities, but with the situation of an ordinary, normal person of their age. This is because the right to liberty is the same for everyone. The whole point about human rights is their universal quality, based as they are upon the ringing declaration in article 1 of the Universal Declaration of Human Rights, that "All human beings are born free and equal in dignity and rights".'[31]

7.29   Finally, P's objection or lack of objection is now irrelevant as the right to liberty is deemed to be too important for a person to lose the benefit of protection because he may have given himself up to detention. This is a departure from both domestic and Strasbourg jurisprudence, which has often referred to the relevance of the person's objections and the 'effect' of the measure as a relevant criteria to be taken into account.

7.30   As an illustration of the difficulties this area of law continue to present for practitioners and the judiciary, reference is made to a decision handed down by Mostyn J on 18 November 2014 in the case of *Rochdale MBC v KW* [2014] EWCOP 45 in which Mostyn J essentially attempted to take on the Supreme Court in *Cheshire West* and demanded that it 'reconsider' the application of Article 5 ECHR in the context of deprivation of liberty at home. Although Mostyn J's judgment has since been successfully appealed to the Court of Appeal (see further below), the facts of this case are worthy of mention. The case concerned a 52-year-old woman who has cognitive and mental health problems, epilepsy and physical disability as a result of a subarachnoid haemorrhage sustained during a medical operation many years previously. At

---

[31]   See www.supremecourt.uk/docs/speech-141031.pdf for the speech made by Lady Hale at the Lord Rodger Memorial Lecture on 31 October 2014.

the time that the matter came before Mostyn J, she was cared for in her own home with a package of 24-hour care funded jointly by Rochdale MBC and the local CCG. Both the local authority and KW (by her litigation friend) agreed that the decision of the majority in *Cheshire West* compelled the conclusion that KW was deprived of her liberty. However, Mostyn J decided to the contrary, holding at para 7 that he:

> '[found] it impossible to conceive that the best interests arrangement for Katherine, in her own home, provided by an independent contractor, but devised and paid for by Rochdale and CCG, amounts to a deprivation of liberty within Article 5. If her family had money and had devised and paid for the very same arrangement this could not be a situation of deprivation of liberty. But because they are devised and paid for by organs of the state they are said so to be, and the whole panoply of authorisation and review required by Article 5 (and its explications) is brought into play. In my opinion this is arbitrary, arguably irrational, and a league away from the intentions of the framers of the Convention.'

In order to reach this conclusion, Mostyn J embarked upon his own analysis of the meaning of Art 5 and of the concept of liberty, holding that the first question he had to ask was what the concept of 'liberty' was for KW. In doing so he considered what J S Mill had to say on the subject. He considered it 'inconceivable' that Mill would have found that the provision of care to KW in her own home involved an encroachment on her liberty and that he would have taken the same view of each the of three cases that were before the Supreme Court in *Cheshire West*.

Somewhat controversially, Mostyn J considered that 'freedom to leave' in the objective test of confinement did not mean 'wandering out of the front door' but leaving in the sense of permanently removing oneself to live where and with whom one likes.[32] Further, the conception of freedom relied upon by Mostyn J is fundamentally predicated upon a concept of liberty that is dependent upon a person's ability to exercise that right, either themselves or by another. He considered that a person who is severely physically disabled, and therefore house-bound, could not be considered to be deprived of their liberty. Such a conception is extremely difficult to square with the conclusion of Lady Hale (with whom Lord Kerr agreed) that liberty must mean the same for all, regardless of whether they are mentally or physically disabled.

The Court of Appeal allowed KW's appeal against Mostyn's decision on 30 January 2015 by endorsing a consent order without a hearing. This led to a further decision by Mostyn J where he held that the Court of Appeal procedurally erred in permitting the appeal by consent without delivering a

---

[32] See para 20, which relies upon the dicta of Munby J in *JE v DE and Surrey County Council* [2006] EWHC 3459 (Fam), [2007] 2 FLR 1150 (per Munby J at para 115), which Mostyn J considered to have been 'implicitly approved' in the Supreme Court at para 40. In the speech noted at fn 31 above, Lady Hale, explaining the decision, noted that P, MIG and MEG 'were under the complete control of the people looking after them and were certainly not free to go, either for a short time or to go and live somewhere else' (emphasis added). It is therefore far from clear that Mosytn J's definition of freedom to leave is the same as that of the majority.

judgment as the question of whether or not KW was deprived of her liberty required judicial determnation (*Rochdale MBC v KW* [2015] EWCOP 13). Thus, Mostyn J considered that there should have been a full hearing with a judgment. He concluded by saying that:

> 'In this difficult and sensitive area, where people are being looked after in their own homes at the state's expense, the law is now in a state of serious confusion.'

Regardless, it is clear that in light of the Court of Appeal's endorsement of the consent order, Mostyn J's conclusions as to what 'freedom to leave' means now ought to be treated with an abundance of caution. Although it is hoped that the philosophical questions raised by Mostyn J as to the meaning of liberty will fall to be considered in the Law Commission review of the area.

7.31 There can be no doubt that one of the practical implications of the judgment of the Supreme Court is a significant increase in deprivation of liberty applications to the Court of Protection. In *Re X and Others (Deprivation of Liberty)* [2014] EWCOP 25, the President of the Court of Protection devised a streamlined process to seek to enable the court to deal with deprivation of liberty cases in a timely, just, fair and ECHR-compatible way. This first judgment[33] handed down on 7 August 2014 sets out the broad framework. This was followed by the second judgment handed down on 16 October 2014, [2014] EWCOP 37, which elaborates on the reasons for the implementation of the streamlined process.[34] The streamlined process[35] is based on the following principles:

- Deprivation of liberty authorisations must be judicial and not administrative.

- There are circumstances in which an authorisation for the deprivation of someone's liberty can be determined on the papers, but there must still be an unimpeded right to request a speedy review.

- The 'triggers' for deciding whether an oral hearing is necessary include whether P is objecting to the deprivation of liberty, whether there is any dispute around the care arrangements and whether there is any dispute around whether the patient lacks capacity to decide where to live.

- Evidence in support of an application for a deprivation of liberty authorisation must include professional medical opinion but should be 'succinct and focussed' and the evidence and supporting material should not ordinarily exceed 50 pages.

---

[33] Permission was sought by three of the parties to appeal certain aspects of this judgment, including the President's conclusion that P did not need to be a party in all cases. The appeals were heard on 17 and 18 February 2015 and judgment from the Court of Appeal was handed down on 16 June 2015: *Re X (Court of Protection Practice)* [2015] EWCA Civ 599 (see below).

[34] A third judgment is awaited addressing three remaining matters of the 25 identified by the court, particularly relating to the possible extension of urgent authorisations by the court.

[35] A new process came into effect on 17 November 2014 on a pilot basis to implement the judgments.

- There is no requirement that P be joined as a party to deprivation of liberty proceedings. P should always be given the opportunity to be joined if he wishes and, whether joined as a party or not, must be given the support necessary to express views about the application and to participate in the proceedings to the extent that they wish.[36] Typically P will also need some form of representation, which should be professional though not necessarily always legal.

- P can participate and be represented in proceedings in the Court of Protection without being a party and if P is participating other than as a party there is no need for a litigation friend. Therefore, P could be represented without one.

- If P is a party, then there is no reason in principle why the rules cannot be amended to allow P to act without a litigation friend.[37] However, at present rule 141(1) requires P, if a party, to have a litigation friend. The President indicated that this is a matter that requires consideration by the ad hoc Rules Committee convened to review the Court of Protection Rules.

- A litigation friend does not need to act through a solicitor to conduct litigation, but requires the permission of the court to act as an advocate on behalf of P.[38]

- Reviews should be annually unless otherwise required. They must be judicial and may take place on the papers, whether or not there has been an earlier oral hearing, raising the possibility of a process where there is no hearing at all and where P would not have the benefit of legal aid which requires an oral hearing.

- 'Bulk' deprivation of liberty applications are unlawful. Each application must be individual so that it can be considered separately and on its own merits.

A new process came into effect on 17 November 2014 (on a pilot basis) to implement the streamlined procedure set out by the President of the Court of Protection in *Re X and Others (Deprivation of Liberty)*,[39] which seeks to enable the court to deal with deprivation of liberty cases in a timely, just, fair

---

[36] The President used the analogy of wardship proceedings, where wards do not always have to be a party. Drawing on his conclusions in *RC v CC (By Her Litigation Friend the Official Solicitor) and X Local Authority* [2014] EWCOP 131, [2014] COPLR 351, namely that the principles of disclosure in the family division also applied in the Court of Protection, and the essentially welfare-based nature of Court of Protection proceedings, he concluded that there is no distinction to be drawn between the need to join P in a Court of Protection case and the need to join a child who is a ward. Further, the President noted P's entitlement to the safeguards of Art 5(4) and the UNCRPD, and concluded that Article 6 requires that P be able to participate in the proceedings in such a way as to enable P to present his case 'properly and satisfactorily': see *Airey v Ireland* (1979) 2 EHRR 305, para 24.

[37] The President noted that the requirement to have a litigation friend is compliant with, but not mandated by, the ECHR: *RP v United Kingdom* [2013] 1 FLR 744. The ECHR requirement is to ensure that P's interests are properly represented and that does not, of itself, require the appointment of a litigation friend.

[38] *Gregory v Turner* [2003] EWCA Civ 183; [2003] 1 WLR 1149.

[39] Her Majesty's Courts and Tribunal Service have indicated that they intend to review the

and ECHR-compatible way. This is founded on a new form,[40] which is accompanied by a new Practice Direction.[41] A model form of order has also been made available which will be made – on the papers – if all the necessary criteria are satisfied.[42] It is very likely, however, that this new process will need to be fundamentally overhauled in light of the judgment of the Court of Appeal in *Re X* handed down on 16 June 2015 where all three members of the Court took the clear view that both fundamental principles of domestic law and the requirements of the ECHR demand that P be a party to proceedings for authorisation of deprivation of liberty. It is not presently known what the future holds for the *Re X* procedure although, at the very least, it is anticipated that immediate amendments will be required to ensure that P is joined in each case. The President made clear in his judgment that there is much work to be done by the Ad Hoc Rules Committee, which has been meeting since the summer. It is hoped that the Committee's findings will be available for discussion in the next edition of this book.

Court of Protection powers

7.32   Under MCA 2005, s 4A (inserted by MHA 2007, s 50) the Court of Protection has the power by making an order under MCA 2005, s 16(2)(a) to make the decision which has the effect of lawfully depriving a person of their liberty.[43] It cannot, however, do so if the patient is ineligible to be deprived of their liberty under that Act as amended by MHA 2007 because they are or should be detained under the Mental Health Act powers.[44] A person may lawfully deprive someone of their liberty whilst a decision is sought from the

---

process once it has been up and running for a while, and would be grateful for any feedback on how it works in practice. Comments can be emailed to the DoL Team: COPDOLS/S16@hmcts. gsi.gov.uk.

[40]   COP DOL 10.

[41]   Practice Direction A: Deprivation of Liberty Applications. Part 1 addresses the procedure to be followed in applications to the court for orders under s 21A of the Mental Capacity Act 2005 relating to a standard or urgent authorisation under Sch A1 of that Act to deprive a person of his or her liberty; or proceedings (for example, relating to costs or appeals) connected with or consequent upon such applications. Part 2 addresses the procedure to be followed in applications under s 16(2)(a) of that Act to authorise deprivation of liberty under s 4A(3) and (4) pursuant to a streamlined procedure. Part 3 makes provision common to applications under both Parts 1 and 2.

[42]   Broadly speaking, this will be the case where all the factors point to the situation being a 'state' deprivation of liberty that is incontrovertibly in P's best interests requiring authorisation because they are unable to give the requisite consent.

[43]   There is an interesting debate as to the precise effect of the decision, and whether such decision amounts to the giving of consent by the court on the part of the person. This was largely an academic debate until recently, but may now assume more relevance in light of the possibility that 'substituted' consent could nullify what would otherwise be a deprivation of liberty (see fn 17 above). There is also an interesting, if largely academic, debate as to whether the court can also authorise a deprivation of liberty by way of a declaration under s 15 of the MCA 2005. Given the wording of s 4A, it is suggested that the route of a decision under s 16(2)(a) is to be preferred.

[44]   MCA 2005, s 16A, as inserted by MHA 2007, s 50(3); and see *W PCT v TB (an adult by her litigation friend the Official Solicitor)* [2009] EWHC 1737 (Fam), [2009] COPLR Con Vol 1193, *GJ v The Foundation Trust* [2009] EWHC 2972 (Fam), [2009] COPLR Con Vol 567 and *AM v South London & Maudsley NHS Foundation Trust & Secretary of State for Health*

court if there is a question about whether that person may be lawfully deprived of their liberty and the deprivation is necessary to enable life-sustaining treatment to be given or any treatment believed necessary to prevent a serious deterioration in their condition.[45]

7.33   Where the Court of Protection has been seized of a matter concerning the welfare of an individual,[46] the questions can sometimes arise: (1) as to whether that individual is deprived of their liberty; and (2) how such deprivation of liberty is to be authorised thereafter. As regards the first question, the court will either have to endorse an agreed position that the person is or is not deprived of their liberty or, failing such agreement, determine[47] that issue. As regards the second question, the answer will depend upon whether the person is detained in hospital or care home (and hence they are within the scope of Sch A1 to MCA 2005). If they are not, then it is suggested that the court will have to retain the case on an ongoing basis so that it can oversee the regular reviews that are necessary to satisfy the requirements of Art 5 of the ECHR.[48] If the person is within the scope of Sch A1, then it is suggested that the appropriate course of action is for the court to authorise (by way of a s 16(2)(a) decision) the deprivation of liberty for a limited period of time to enable the grant of a standard authorisation by the relevant supervisory authority.[49] The court, it is suggested, should then relinquish its supervisory jurisdiction in favour of the regime established by Parliament.[50]

[2013] UKUT 0365 (AAC) [2013] COPLR 510. See also **7.46** below for a discussion of *An NHS Trust v Dr A* [2013] EWHC 2442 (COP), [2013] COPLR 605.

[45]   MCA 2005, s 4B, as inserted by MHA 2007, s 50(2).

[46]   Other than by way of an application under MCA 2005, 21A.

[47]   The cases would suggest that such should be done by way of a declaration under s 15 MCA of the 2005, as occurred (for instance) in *P and Q* [2011] EWCA Civ 90, [2011] COPLR Con Vol 931.

[48]   See in this regard *P and Q* at para 4. The Court of Appeal, following *Salford City Council v GJ, NJ and BJ (by their litigation friends)* [2008] EWHC 1097 (Fam), [2008] 2 FLR 1295, considered that the review would be at least annual and would require independent representation of the detained person; Wilson LJ considered (para 4) that such reviews could be on paper unless requested otherwise.

[49]   But what then happens (as the author has experience of happening) if the best interests assessor determines that the person in question is not deprived of their liberty? It is suggested that, akin to the position that prevails in relation to the decisions of the First Tier Tribunal (Mental Health), namely that clinicians or other professionals involved in the care of an individual can only proceed in a way incompatible with that decision if they reasonably and in good faith consider that they have information, unknown to the court, which put a significantly different complexion on the case: see *R (Von Brandenburg) v East London and City NHS Trust* [2004] 2 AC 280. Otherwise, the proper course of action would be for the public authority to seek to appeal the determination of the court that there is a deprivation of liberty.

[50]   The proposition that if the DOLS regime applies, or would apply if there is a deprivation of liberty, it should be used in preference to authorisation and review by the court has been endorsed by Charles J: *LBL v PB and P* [2011] EWHC 2675 (COP), [2012] COPLR 1 at para 64(iii); see also *Re HA* [2012] EWHC 1068 (COP), [2012] COPLR 534 at para 8, where he noted that the DOLS regime had 'checks and balances that generally should be preferred to review by the court'.

Deprivation of liberty in a hospital or care home

7.34 The managing authority of a hospital or care home is able lawfully to deprive a patient or resident of their liberty if they are detained for the purpose of being given care or treatment and a standard or urgent authorisation is in force which relates to the relevant person and to the hospital or care home in which they are detained. In this event the managing authority is put in the same position as if the resident had capacity to consent and had consented to their detention (no liability is incurred for the deprivation of liberty but there is no protection for any negligence).[51] The authorisation also extends to cover (1) any deprivation of liberty that occurs during transport of P to and from contact sessions;[52] and (2) the ability of the managing authority to return P to the establishment at which he resides upon any outing from there.[53] It is suggested that it cannot cover any deprivation of liberty which may occur during the course of P's initial journey to the hospital or care home mentioned in the authorisation (and hence a separate authorisation from the court will be required[54]). The authorisation under these procedures does not extend to the treatment to which the patient cannot consent, to which MCA 2005, s 5 will continue to apply.

7.35 In *Hillingdon London Borough Council v Neary*[55] Peter Jackson J made it very clear that it is unlawful for a public authority to use the procedure provided for under Sch A1 to foreclose a genuine dispute about where it is in the incapacitated adult's best interests to reside. In setting out the purpose of authorisations under Sch A1, he commented as follows:

> 'Significant welfare issues that cannot be resolved by discussion should be placed before the Court of Protection, where decisions can be taken as a matter of urgency where necessary. The DOL scheme is an important safeguard against arbitrary detention. Where stringent conditions are met, it allows a managing authority to deprive a person of liberty at a particular place. It is not to be used by a local authority as a means of getting its own way on the question of whether it is in the person's best interests to be in the place at all. Using the DOL regime in that way turns the spirit of the Mental Capacity Act 2005 on its head, with a code designed to protect the liberty of vulnerable people being used instead as an instrument of confinement. In this case, far from being a safeguard, the way in which the DOL process was used masked the real deprivation of liberty, which was the refusal to allow Steven to go home.'[56]

---

[51] MCA 2005, Sch A1, Part 1, inserted by MHA 2007, Sch 7.

[52] *DCC v KH* (2009) CoP Case No 11729380.

[53] Unreported decision of Mostyn J of June 2010 brought to the author's attention by the Official Solicitor's office.

[54] See para 2.15 of the Deprivation of Liberty Safeguards Code of Practice, although it is not the author's experience that deprivations of liberty in the initial transport are necessarily as exceptional as the Code of Practice envisages. The judgment of Charles J in *GJ v The Foundation Trust* [2009] EWHC 2972 (Fam), [2009] COPLR Con Vol 567 supports the proposition that an authorisation cannot cover transport: see para 75.

[55] [2011] EWHC 1377 (COP), [2011] COPLR Con Vol 632.

[56] Paragraph 33.

7.36   In similar vein, in *LBL v PB and P*,[57] a decision handed down before that of the Supreme Court in *Cheshire West* (and therefore to be read subject to that decision), Charles J expressed the strong view that debates about whether circumstances amounted to a deprivation of liberty could all too easily lead to a loss of focus about the real question, namely whether the placement and care arrangements were in P's best interests and subjected him or her to the least possible restrictions. He expressed the view that in such circumstances, it would frequently be appropriate to put in place a standard authorisation on an essentially precautionary basis, ie by resolving any doubt as to whether there was a deprivation of liberty in favour of there being such a deprivation. Charles J reached a similar conclusion, albeit in a different context, in his subsequent decision in *AM v South London & Maudsley NHS Foundation Trust & Secretary of State for Health*,[58] in which he confirmed that the DOLS regime 'applies when there may be a deprivation of liberty in the sense that [the regime] applies when it appears that judged objectively there is a risk that cannot sensibly be ignored that the relevant circumstances amount to a deprivation of liberty.'[59]

The authorisation procedure

7.37   The authorisation procedure usually begins with a request by the managing authority (generally the managers of a hospital or care home where the person is, or may be, deprived of their liberty) to the supervisory body (see **7.50**). Before a standard authorisation can be obtained, the supervisory body arranges for assessments to be carried out to determine whether the following requirements are met in relation to the detained resident.[60]

The age requirement

7.38   The person must be 18 or over. Note in this regard that a parent cannot authorise restrictions upon the liberty of their child which amount to a deprivation of that child's liberty;[61] if such restrictions amount to a deprivation of liberty, authorisation must be obtained other than under the provisions of Sch A1.

The mental health requirement

7.39   The person must be suffering from a mental disorder within the meaning of MHA 1983, as amended (which includes for these purposes a learning disability whether or not associated with abnormally aggressive or seriously irresponsible conduct). The importance in this context of ensuring that there is

---

[57]   [2011] EWHC 2675 (COP), [2012] COPLR 1.
[58]   [2013] UKUT 0365 (AAC) [2013] COPLR 510. See further **7.44** below.
[59]   Paragraph 59.
[60]   MCA 2005, Sch A1, Part 3; the DOLS forms applicable to the authorisation procedure have recently been reviewed and are available at http://www.adass.org.uk/mental-health-Drugs-and-Alcohol/key-documents/New-DoLS-Forms/.
[61]   *RK v BCC & Ors* [2011] EWCA Civ 1305, [2012] COPLR 146.

evidence of a mental disorder which is both current and given on the basis of objective medical expertise (and that such evidence is periodically reviewed) has recently been emphasised by the European Court of Human Rights in *KC v Poland*.[62]

The mental capacity requirement

7.40 The person must lack capacity in relation to the question whether or not they should be accommodated in the hospital or care home for the purpose of being given the care or treatment concerned. This question must be assessed in accordance with MCA 2005, ss 1–3, and the question is the same whether consideration is being given for purposes of an authorisation or a court order.[63]

The best interests requirement

7.41 It must be in the person's best interests to be a detained resident and the deprivation of liberty must be necessary to prevent harm and be a proportionate response to the likelihood and seriousness of that harm. In this context, the European Court of Human Rights has emphasised that detention in a care home is 'such a serious measure that it is only justified where other, less severe measures have been considered to be insufficient to safeguard the individual or public interest which might require the person concerned be detained.'[64]

The eligibility requirement

7.42 A person is ineligible if already subject to MHA 1983 through being:

- detained in hospital under MHA 1983 powers or meeting the criteria for detention and objecting to being detained in the hospital or to some or all of the treatment (ie in those circumstances MHA 1983 powers should be used if the person is to be detained);[65]
- on leave of absence or subject to guardianship, a community treatment regime or conditional discharge and subject to a measure which would be inconsistent with an authorisation if granted; or

---

[62] [2014] ECHR 1322.

[63] *A Primary Care Trust v LDV* [2013] EWHC 272 (Fam) [2013] COPLR 204 at para 29 per Baker J.

[64] See *Stanev v Bulgaria* (2012) 55 EHRR 22 at para 143. See also *KC v Poland* [2014] ECHR 1322.

[65] This was considered by Roderic Wood J in *W PCT v TB (an adult by her litigation friend the Official Solicitor)* [2009] EWHC 1737 (Fam), [2009] COPLR Con Vol 1193 and by Charles J in *GJ v The Foundation Trust* [2009] EWHC 2972 (Fam), [2009] COPLR Con Vol 567 and *AM v South London & Maudsley NHS Foundation Trust & Secretary of State for Health* [2013] UKUT 0365 (AAC), [2013] COPLR 510.

- on leave of absence or subject to a community treatment regime or conditional discharge and the authorisation if granted would be for deprivation of liberty in a hospital for the purpose of treatment for mental disorder.[66]

7.43   The presence of the eligibility requirement gives rise to the question of whether MHA 1983 is intended to have primacy over MCA 2005 (or vice versa). In *GJ v The Foundation Trust*[67], Charles J expressed the view that MHA 1983 had primacy over MCA 2005 in the following terms:[68]

> '45. In my judgment, the deeming provisions alone,[69] and together with that view on assessments, are strong pointers in favour of the conclusions that (1) the Mental Health Act 1983 is to have primacy when it applies, and (2) the medical practitioners referred to in sections 2 and 3 of the 1983 Act cannot pick and choose between the two statutory regimes as they think fit having regard to general considerations (eg the preservation or promotion of a therapeutic relationship with P) that they consider render one regime preferable to the other.'

7.44   However, in *AM v South London & Maudsley NHS Foundation Trust & Secretary of State for Health*,[70] Charles J, sitting as the Chamber President of the Upper Tribunal (Administrative Appeals Chamber), revisited his earlier decision.[71] He confirmed[72] that (1) general propositions in respect of issues that arise concerning the interrelationship between MHA 1983 and MCA 2005 are 'dangerous;' and (2) his references to 'primacy' in his earlier decision were made in and should be confined to the position where the person was within the scope of MHA 1983. Whilst strictly of persuasive effect only before the Court of Protection,[73] it is suggested that that this decision, reached after full argument and by the judge in charge of the Court of Protection, should carry significant weight before that latter court.

7.45   The decision in *AM* is also of importance for the confirmation given by Charles J as to the approach that should be adopted by decision-makers responsible for determining whether a person who requires assessment or treatment as an in-patient in a psychiatric hospital in circumstances amounting

---

[66]   The details of 'Persons ineligible' are set out in MCA 2005, Sch 1A, as inserted by MHA 2007, Sch 8. A person ineligible to be deprived of their liberty by virtue of the operation of Sch 1A cannot be deprived of their liberty by way of the procedure contained in Sch A1 or by way of a court order under s 16 (see s 16A(1)).

[67]   [2009] EWHC 2972 (Fam).

[68]   Paragraph 45.

[69]   In MCA 2005, Sch 1A, para 12.

[70]   [2013] UKUT 0365 (AAC) [2013] COPLR 510.

[71]   In light of a decision of Upper Tribunal Judge Jacobs in *DN v Northumberland Tyne & Wear NHS Foundation Trust* [2011] UKUT 327 (AAC), and a letter provided by the Department of Health in that case setting out the policy intentions behind MCA 2005, Sch 1A.

[72]   Paragraph 78.

[73]   See, by analogy, *Secretary of State for Justice v RB* [2010] UKUT 454 (AAC). Weight was placed upon the decision in *Northamptonshire Healthcare NHS Foundation Trust and Others v ML and Others* [2014] EWCOP 2, although Hayden J then – rather curiously – held that MHA 1983 was 'magnetic north' in cases falling within Case E.

to a deprivation of liberty should be detained under the provisions of MHA 1983 or whether the provisions of MCA 2005, Sch A1 should be used.[74] He set out three questions that such decision-makers need to ask:

(1)   does the person have capacity to consent to admission as an informal patient?[75]

(2)   might the hospital be able to rely upon the provisions of MCA 2005 lawfully to assess or treat the person (most importantly, would the person be compliant with the arrangements, as a non-compliant patient who is within the scope of MHA 1983 can only be detained under the provisions of that Act[76])?

(3)   if there is a choice between reliance on MHA 1983 and MHA 2005, Sch A1, which is the least restrictive way of best achieving the proposed assessment or treatment?

Charles J emphasised[77] that the answer to the last of these questions of necessity requires the exercise of a value judgment and a consideration of all the circumstances, including the actual availability of the MCA 2005 regime and a comparison of its impact, if it were used, with the impact of detention under MHA 1983.

7.46   If further proof were needed that the DOLS provisions are unwieldy and capable of producing potentially absurd results, in *An NHS Trust v Dr A*[78] Baker J has recently identified a further lacuna in the statutory schemes provided for by MHA 1983 and MCA 2005. That lacuna arose where a person unable to make decisions about their medical needs and subject to detention under MHA 1983 is to be treated in a way outwith the treatment provided under that Act for his mental disorder and that treatment involves a deprivation of liberty. Such a person would be ineligible to be deprived of their liberty (whether by way of a standard authorisation or by way of a court order).[79] If the treatment could not properly be said to be treatment falling within the compulsory provisions of MHA 1983, s 63, then the MHA 1983 would not afford a route to authorise the administration of such treatment and any ancillary deprivation of liberty:

> 'To take a stark example: if someone detained under section 3 is suffering from gangrene so as to require an amputation in his best interests and objects to that operation, so that it could only be carried by depriving him of his liberty, that process could not prima facie be carried out either under the MHA or under the

---

[74]   Charles J's judgment encompassed situations other than those amounting to a deprivation of liberty, but for present purposes the discussion is limited to those which either do or are likely to amount to such a deprivation.

[75]   As to which, see also *A Primary Care Trust v LDV* [2013] EWHC 272 (Fam) [2013] COPLR 204.

[76]   Footnote 59 above.

[77]   Paragraphs 72–4.

[78]   [2013] EWHC 2442 (COP), [2013] COPLR 605.

[79]   Ie they would be within Case A of MCA 2005, Sch Al. See also **7.42** above.

MCA. This difficulty potentially opens a gap every bit as troublesome as that identified in the Bournewood case itself.'[80]

In the case before Baker J, it was clear (a) that the adult lacked the capacity to decide whether to consent to forcible feeding; (b) that such forcible feeding would involve a deprivation of their liberty; (c) that it was in the adult's best interests; but that (d) the forcible feeding could not be said to be medical treatment for the mental disorder from which he suffered so as to fall within the provisions of MCA 2005, s 63. After an exhaustive analysis of the statutory provisions and the authorities, Baker J held that he could not read into the prohibition in MCA 2005, s 16A(1) against welfare orders being made depriving ineligible adults of their liberty the words 'save where such provision is necessary to uphold the person's right to life under Art 2 of the European Convention on Human Rights,' but that he could authorise forcible feeding and the ancillary deprivation of liberty by way of the exercise of the inherent jurisdiction.[81] The inherent jurisdiction of the High Court is discussed further at **11.5ff**.

7.47   Another potential lacuna that falls to be resolved is where the eligibility assessor considers that the adult is within scope of MHA 1983 (and therefore ineligible to be deprived of their liberty by way of MCA 2005), but where either the relevant doctors are not willing to make the statutory recommendations for admission under MHA 1983 or, as anecdotally appears not to be uncommon, the Approved Mental Health Professional ('AMHP') is not willing to make the application for admission. If such a stand-off cannot be resolved, then it is suggested that steps be taken as a matter of some urgency to bring the matter to the court so that the deprivation of the person's liberty can be authorised.[82] It is further suggested that:

- the Court of Protection is the ultimate arbiter of whether a person is or is not eligible to be deprived of their liberty under MCA 2005;

- the Court of Protection cannot, however, dictate to either clinicians or AMHPs how they are to discharge their duties under MHA 1983, such that, especially if the bar to application is the unwillingness of an AMHP to make an application for admission, it may be necessary to consider whether that unwillingness amounts to a public law error capable of being challenged by way of judicial review proceedings;

- pending the resolution of the question of eligibility and the taking of appropriate steps to authorise the deprivation of liberty under either MHA 1983 or MCA 2005, and by way of analogy with *An NHS Trust v Dr A*, the High Court can properly authorise the deprivation of liberty by way of the exercise of the inherent jurisdiction if satisfied that (a) the individual in

---

[80]   Paragraph 67.
[81]   Paragraph 96.
[82]   As happened in *A Primary Care Trust v LDV* [2013] EWHC 272 (Fam) [2013] COPLR 204, in which the matters considered in this paragraph fell for determination. Matters then evolved in such a way that the issue fell away, although it is clear that they will need to be determined sooner rather than later.

question suffers from a mental disorder; and (b) it is in their best interests to be deprived of their liberty for purposes of receiving care and treatment at the relevant facility. Appropriate mechanisms would need to be put in place so as to allow the court to review the deprivation of liberty.[83]

7.48 Finally in this regard, it should be noted that it is possible for an authorisation to be granted under Sch A1 in respect of a person currently detained under MHA 1983 in anticipation of the person's discharge so that suitable arrangements are in place upon their arrival; in other words, merely because a person is, in fact, detained under MHA 1983 does not necessarily mean that they are therefore to be considered ineligible for a future authorisation under Sch A1.[84]

The no refusals requirement

7.49 There must not be a valid and effective advance decision by the detained resident refusing the treatment in question, nor a valid refusal of the proposed care or treatment by a deputy or donee of a lasting power of attorney (LPA) within the scope of their authority.

STANDARD AUTHORISATIONS

7.50 A standard authorisation is an authorisation given by the supervisory body after it has been requested to do so and once the procedure set out below has been followed.[85] With effect from 1 April 2013, and as a result of amendments made by the Health and Social Care Act 2012 to reflect the abolition of Primary Care Trusts in England and Wales,[86] the supervisory body is:

- in the case of a care home in England or Wales, the local authority where the person is ordinarily resident or where the care home is situated; or

- in the case of a hospital in England, the local authority for the area in which the person is ordinary resident;

- in the case of a hospital in Wales, the National Assembly for Wales or the local health board if the care is commissioned by it (this also applies if the

---

[83] *An NHS Trust v Dr A* at para 94, citing Munby J (as he then was) in *Re BJ (Incapacitated Adult)* [2009] EWHC 3310 (Fam), [2010] 1 FLR 1373.

[84] *DN v Northumberland Tyne & Wear NHS Foundation Trust* [2011] UKUT 327 (AAC). In this regard, note also that para 12(3) of Sch 1A directs the attention of the decision-maker to the circumstances which are expected to apply at the time the authorisation is expected to come into effect.

[85] See generally MCA 2005, Sch A1, Part 4. Provisions relating to the suspension of a standard authorisation are in Part 6, a change in supervisory responsibility in Part 7, review in Part 8 and generally relating to assessments in Part 9. Part 10 provides for the relevant person's representative and Part 11 for the role of independent mental capacity advocates.

[86] The material amendments being contained in the Health and Social Care Act 2012, Sch 5, para 136(3).

hospital is in England but the care is commissioned by the National Assembly for Wales or a local health board);

- in the case of a hospital in England where the person is not ordinarily resident in England or Wales or their ordinary residence cannot be determined, the local authority for the area where the hospital is situated.

The Department of Health afforded limited additional funding to local authorities to support them in the extension of their statutory role, emphasising in so doing that:

> '... [h]ospitals will remain responsible as managing authorities for compliance with the DOLS legislation, for understanding DOLS and knowing when and how to make referrals. Hospitals remain responsible for ensuring that all staff in hospitals are Mental Capacity Act (MCA) compliant. Clinical Commissioning Groups (CCGs) will oversee these responsibilities; and be responsible for training and MCA compliance. All CCGs must have a named MCA lead and MCA policies to support their responsibilities.'[87]

7.51 The managing authority must request a standard authorisation if it is accommodating a detained resident who appears to meet all the qualifying requirements or is likely to do so within the next 28 days or if it will be so accommodating or detaining the person up to 28 days in advance of its doing so. In *AM v South London & Maudsley NHS Foundation Trust & Secretary of State for Health*,[88] Charles J considered the meaning of the phrase 'likely – at some time within the next 28 days – to be a detained resident' in Sch 1A, para 24(2) and (3), and agreed with the Secretary of State's submission that 'the DOLS regime applies when there may be a deprivation of liberty in the sense that [the regime] applies when it appears that judged objectively there is a risk that cannot sensibly be ignored that the relevant circumstances amount to a deprivation of liberty.' The relevant managing authority must also make a request if there is, or is to be, a change in the place of detention.

7.52 An authorisation cannot be given unless assessments have been commissioned by the supervisory body which conclude that all the qualifying requirements are met. Regulations[89] specify who can carry out assessments, covering the need for more than one assessor, the professional skills, training and competence required and independence from decisions about providing or commissioning care to the person concerned and the timeframe within which

---

[87] See www.dh.gov.uk/health/files/2012/09/Deprivation-of-Liberty-Safeguards_Funding-Fact-Sheet-for-2013-14.pdf, page 4.

[88] [2013] UKUT 0365 (AAC) [2013] COPLR 510. See also *AJ (Deprivation of Liberty Safeguards)* [2015] EWCOP 5 (Baker J) where it was emphasised at [113] that 'the scheme of the DOLS is that, in the vast majority of cases, it should be possible to plan in advance so that a standard authorisation can be obtained before the deprivation of liberty begins. It is only in exceptional cases, where the need for the deprivation of liberty is so urgent that it is in the best interests of the person for it to begin while the application is being considered, that a standard authorisation need not be sought before the deprivation begins.' See also **7.44–7.45** above.

[89] The Mental Capacity (Deprivation of Liberty: Standard Authorisations, Assessments and Ordinary Residence) Regulations 2008, SI 2008/1858, as amended by SI 2009/827.

the assessments must be completed. The mental health and best interests assessments must be carried out by different assessors. It is the responsibility of the supervisory body to appoint eligible and suitable assessors. Anyone carrying out assessments (other than the age assessment) must have undergone specific training.

7.53 The best interests assessor must first decide whether a deprivation of liberty is occurring or is likely to occur. The assessment must take account of any relevant needs assessment or care plan, and of the opinion of the mental health assessor on the impact of the proposed course of action on the person's mental health. The assessor must consult the managing authority and take into account the views of anyone named by the person, anyone engaged in caring for the person or interested in their welfare, any donee of a LPA granted by the person or deputy appointed by the court. If the person does not have anyone to speak for them who is not paid to provide care an independent mental capacity advocate (IMCA) must be appointed to support and represent them during the assessment process.

7.54 In determining whether a deprivation of liberty is justified as being in the person's best interests, it is suggested that the best interests assessor is carrying out a public law function and their decision would be open to challenge upon standard public law principles. By way of example, in *Re MB*,[90] a best interests assessor had concluded that the best interests requirement was not met in the case of an elderly lady in a residential home, even though there was no practical alternative accommodation for her to go to. Charles J found, however, that the assessor's reasoning was flawed because she did not compare and contrast viable and practically available alternative placements.

7.55 The best interests assessor is required to record the name and address of every interested person consulted (as they will be entitled to information about the outcome). If that assessor concludes that deprivation of liberty is not in the person's best interests but becomes aware that they are already being deprived of their liberty, the assessor must draw this to the attention of the supervisory body. If the assessment recommends authorisation the assessor must state the maximum authorisation period, which may not be for more than a year.[91] The assessor may also recommend conditions to be attached to the authorisation. Whilst not expressly stated in Sch A1, it would appear that the only conditions which can be imposed are those over the implementation of which the relevant managing authority has a degree of control.[92] The best interests assessor must also identify someone to recommend for appointment as representative of the person being deprived of their liberty.

---

[90] [2010] EWHC 2508 (COP), [2010] COPLR Con Vol 65.

[91] The period starting either at the exact time on the day when it was granted or on any later time specified in the document giving the authorisation: *Re MB* [2010] EWHC 2508 (COP), [2010] COPLR Con Vol 65 at para 45. The maximum period that can be included in the authorisation should be calculated by including the whole of the day on which the authorisation is given (or expressed to start) and on the basis that it ends at the end of the last day: para 47.

[92] This flows from the wording of Sch A1, para 53(3), which has the effect that conditions cannot

7.56 If existing equivalent assessments have been carried out within the past year they may be used if the supervisory body is satisfied there is no reason that they may no longer be accurate.[93] If any of the assessments conclude that the person does not meet the criteria the supervisory body must turn down the request for authorisation and inform all persons with an interest. If all the assessments recommend it, the supervisory body must give the authorisation and:

- set the period of the authorisation, which may not be longer than the maximum period identified in the best interests assessment;

- issue the authorisation in writing, stating the period for which it is valid, the purpose for which it is given and the reason why each qualifying requirement is met;

- if appropriate, attach conditions;

- appoint someone to act as the person's representative during the term of the authorisation;

- provide a copy of the authorisation to the managing authority, the person being deprived of their liberty and their representative, any IMCA who has been involved and any other interested person consulted by the best interests assessor (in due course notifying them when the authorisation ceases to be in force); and

- keep written records.

7.57 In *LB Hillingdon v Neary & Ors*[94] Peter Jackson J emphasised the importance of the role of the supervisory authority thus:

> 'The granting of DOL standard authorisations is a matter for the local authority in its role as a supervisory body. The responsibilities of a supervisory body, correctly understood, require it to scrutinise the assessment it receives with independence and a degree of care that is appropriate to the seriousness of the decision and to the circumstances of the individual case that are or should be known to it. Where, as here, a supervisory body grants authorisations on the basis of perfunctory scrutiny of superficial best interests assessments, it cannot expect the authorisations to be legally valid.'[95]

---

be imposed which are directed solely against third parties (for instance, by way of providing that other statutory bodies should undertake assessments). In practice, this can significantly limit the utility of conditions, although where a supervisory body takes the view that a deprivation of liberty can only be authorised subject to a condition falling outside the scope of para 53, such is a clear indication that the supervisory body should be taking appropriate steps to obtain an authorisation from the Court of Protection by way of an order under MCA, s 17.

[93] It is suggested that particular caution must be exercised to ensure that the mental health assessment is subject to periodic review in light of the decision of the European Court of Human Rights in *Kędzior v Poland* (Application No. 45026/07, decision of 16 October 2012) and the emphasis placed by the court in the decision upon the importance of there being evidence of a mental disorder which is both current and given on the basis of objective medical expertise. See also in this regard *KC v Poland* [2014] ECHR 1322.

[94] [2011] EWHC 1377 (COP), [2011] COPLR Con Vol 677.

[95] Paragraph 3.

Expanding upon this later in his judgment, Peter Jackson J held as follows:

> '174. Although the framework of the Act requires the supervising body to commission a number of paper assessments before granting a standard authorisation, the best interests assessment is anything but a routine piece of paperwork. Properly viewed, it should be seen as a cornerstone of the protection that the DOL safeguards offer to people facing deprivation of liberty if they are to be effective as safeguards at all.
>
> 175. The corollary of this, in my view, is that the supervisory body that receives the best interests assessment must actively supervise the process by scrutinising the assessment with independence and with a degree of care that is appropriate to the seriousness of the decision and the circumstances of the individual case that are or should be known to it.
>
> 177. Paragraph 50 provides that a supervisory body must give a standard authorisation if all assessments are positive. This obligation must be read in the light of the overall scheme of the schedule, which cannot be to require the supervisory body to grant an authorisation where it is not or should not be satisfied that the best interests assessment is a thorough piece of work that adequately analyses the four necessary conditions.
>
> 177. In support, I refer to the fact that the supervisory body has control over the terms of the authorisation in relation to its length and any conditions that should be attached. It does not have to follow the recommendations of the best interests assessor on those issues. It would not be possible for the supervisory body to make decisions of this kind rationally without having a sufficient knowledge base about the circumstances of the person affected. In all cases, it is open to the supervisory body to go back to the best interests assessor for discussion or for further enquiries to be made.'

7.58 If the supervisory body knows or ought to know that a best interests assessment is inadequate, it is not obliged to follow the recommendation.

> 'On the contrary it is obliged to take all necessary steps to remedy the inadequacy, and if necessary bring the deprivation of liberty to an end, including by conducting a review under Part 8 or by applying to the court.'[96]

7.59 If an authorisation is granted the supervisory body must appoint a person to be the detained resident's representative,[97] this being someone who the supervisory body considers will maintain contact with the resident and support and represent them in relation to the authorisation, including requesting review or appealing to the Court of Protection on their behalf. The representative has a right of access to the court (any person other than the detained resident would require the permission of the Court to bring a case).[98] The managing authority in acting on the authorisation must:

---

[96] Ibid, para 80.

[97] See the Mental Capacity (Deprivation of Liberty: Appointment of Relevant Person's Representative) Regulations 2008 (SI 2008/1315), as amended by SI 2008/2368.

[98] In *AB v LCC (A Local Authority) and the Care Manager of BCH* [2011] EWHC 3151 (COP), [2012] COPLR 314, Mostyn J reviewed the role of the RPR in bringing proceedings to the Court of Protection, and emphasised that, prima facie, there is no reason why an RPR cannot act as litigation friend for P in proceedings under MCA 2005, s 21A (as to which, see further 7.71 below).

- ensure that any conditions are complied with;

- take all practicable steps to ensure that the detained resident understands the effect of the authorisation, their right of appeal to the Court of Protection and their right to request a review;

- give the same information to the person's representative; and

- keep the person's case under consideration and request a review if necessary.

7.60 The supervisory body may review a standard authorisation at any time and must do so if requested by the detained resident, their representative or the managing authority. The managing authority must request a review if it appears that there has been a change in the person's circumstances. The relevant person or their representative may make a request at any time. The supervisory body must decide whether any of the qualifying requirements appear to be reviewable and, if so, commission review assessments. A review may lead to the authorisation being terminated, a change in the recorded reasons or a change in the conditions attached to the authorisation. When the review is complete the supervisory body must inform the managing authority, the relevant person and their representative of the outcome.

7.61 A managing authority may apply for a further authorisation to begin when an authorisation expires. In this event, the full assessment process is repeated.

Urgent authorisations

7.62 Urgent authorisations[99] may be given by the managing authority of a care home or hospital to provide a lawful basis for a deprivation of liberty whilst a standard authorisation is being obtained when it is urgently required and the qualifying requirements appear to be met. The managing authority must record the urgent authorisation in writing, giving its reasons for giving the authorisation. The managing authority is to take all practicable steps (verbally and in writing) to ensure the person understands the effect of the authorisation and their right of appeal to the Court of Protection and to notify any IMCA who has been involved.

7.63 An urgent authorisation takes effect at the exact time that it was given on a particular day.[100] It can only last for a maximum of 7 days,[101] unless extended for up to a further 7 days by the supervisory body if there are exceptional reasons why it has not been possible to decide on a request for standard authorisation and it is essential that the detention continues. Absent such

---

[99]   MCA 2005, Sch A1, Part 5.
[100] *Re MB* [2010] EWHC 2508 (COP), [2010] COPLR Con Vol 65, at para 35.
[101] Calculated by including the whole of the day upon which the authorisation was granted. The maximum period for which the authorisation can run extends to the end of the relevant day upon which the authorisation expires: *Re MB* at para 43. The same goes for the calculation of any extended period: para 41.

exceptional circumstances, an urgent authorisation can only be extended by a standard authorisation or a court order. In any event, it is only possible for one urgent authorisation to be given in respect of any one period of deprivation of liberty.[102]

The Standard Authorisations, Assessments and Ordinary Residence Regulations

7.64 The Mental Capacity (Deprivation of Liberty: Standard Authorisations, Assessments and Ordinary Residence) Regulations 2008[103] fill out the detail of obtaining standard authorisations and who the assessors are to be.

7.65 The eligibility requirements for people who are to carry out the assessments are that:

- all assessors are adequately insured[104] and the supervisory body (primary care trust or local authority) is satisfied that they have suitable skills and have undergone a Criminal Record Bureau check (reg 3);

- mental health assessments can only be carried out by medical practitioners who have been approved under MHA 1983, s 12[105] or are registered medical practitioners who have at least 3 years' post-registration experience in the diagnosis or treatment of mental disorder and have completed the relevant training[106] (reg 4));

- best interests assessments can only be carried out by mental health practitioners approved under MHA 1983, s 114(1)[107] or certain health practitioners (nurses, occupational therapists or psychologists) with the relevant skills and specialism, or social workers, all of whom must have had at least 2 years' post-registration experience, and have completed the required training (reg 5);

- mental capacity assessments can only be carried out by people who are eligible to carry out a mental health or best interests assessment (reg 6);

- eligibility assessments can only be carried out by medical practitioners approved under MHA 1983, s 12 and eligible to carry out a mental health

---

[102] Ibid at paras 59–77, construing para 77 of Sch A1. Charles J also indicated that, where the best interests assessor upon an application for a standard authorisation following an urgent authorisation reaches the view that the best interests requirement was no longer met, it could in some circumstances nonetheless still be in the person's best interests for them to be subject to a short further period of deprivation of liberty pending changes to arrangements and/or the assistance of the court. Such a period could only be authorised by the grant of a standard authorisation, rather than the grant of a second urgent authorisation.

[103] SI 2008/1858, as subsequently amended.

[104] This has been amended by SI 2009/827 to include assessors covered by an indemnity arrangement.

[105] Medical practitioners eligible to recommend the admission of a patient to hospital under MHA 1983.

[106] A Mental Health Assessors training programme made available by the Royal College of Psychiatrists.

[107] Approved mental health professionals appointed under MHA 1983 by a local social services authority.

assessment or an approved mental health professional eligible to carry out a best interests assessment (reg 7); and

- age assessments and no refusals assessments can only be carried out by people who are eligible to carry out a best interests assessment (regs 8 and 9).

7.66 The Regulations provide some limitations on who a supervisory body may select as assessors (even if otherwise eligible) by preventing the selection of:

- a person who is a relative of the relevant person or a person or relative of someone who has a financial interest in that person's care (regs 10 and 11); and

- a person to carry out a best interests assessment who is involved in the care of the person to be assessed or who is employed by the supervisory body where the managing authority and supervisory body are the same (reg 12).

7.67 All assessments for a standard authorisation are to be completed within 21 days or where an urgent authorisation is in force during the period of that authorisation (reg 13) and assessments to decide whether or not there is an unauthorised deprivation of liberty within 7 days (reg 14). When the eligibility and best interests assessors are not the same person the former may require the latter to provide any relevant information as to eligibility they have (reg 15).

7.68 Regulation 16 specifies the information to be provided in a request for a standard authorisation (the text of this regulation is reproduced in Part IV of this book). The Regulations also provide the mechanism for resolving a dispute over which local authority is the supervisory body where there is a question as to the relevant person's ordinary residence).[108]

The Appointment of Relevant Person's Representative Regulations

7.69 MCA 2005, Sch A1, para 139 requires that the supervisory body appoints a representative, selected for that purpose, to represent a person in respect of whom a standard authorisation has been issued. That representative is to maintain contact and to support and represent the person in matters relating to their deprivation of liberty. The Mental Capacity (Deprivation of Liberty: Appointment of Relevant Person's Representative) Regulations 2008[109] provide for the selection and appointment of representatives by:

- detailing the eligibility requirements for appointment as a representative (reg 3);

---

[108] MCA 2005, Sch A1, para 182(2).

[109] SI 2008/1315, as amended by SI 2008/2368; for a fuller discussion on the interpretation of these regulations see *AJ (Deprivation of Liberty Safeguards)* [2015] EWCOP 5 (Baker J) at paras [52] to [91].

- enabling the best interests assessor to determine whether the relevant person has capacity to select a person to be their representative (reg 4);

- enabling the relevant person to select a family member, friend or carer to be their representative where they have capacity to make that decision (reg 5);

- enabling a donee of a LPA (granting welfare powers) or a deputy appointed by the Court of Protection to select themselves or a family member, friend or carer to be the representative where the scope of their authority permits it (reg 6);

- requiring the best interests assessor to confirm the eligibility of the person selected by the relevant person or donee or deputy, and if so to recommend that appointment but if not to invite a further selection (reg 7);

- where no selection has been made by the relevant person, donee or deputy, enabling the best interests assessor to select a relevant person's family member, friend or carer (reg 8);

- enabling the supervisory body to select and pay for a person in a professional capacity to be a representative (regs 9 and 15); and

- requiring that the process of appointing a representative begins as soon as a best interests assessor is selected upon a request for a standard authorisation or as soon as an existing representative's appointment is about to terminate (reg 10).

7.70 The formalities of appointment and termination of appointment of a representative are detailed in regs 12–14.

REVIEW BY THE COURT OF PROTECTION

7.71 A person who has been deprived of their liberty or their representative may apply to the Court of Protection for a review of the lawfulness of their detention.[110] Where a standard authorisation has been given, the Court of Protection may determine any question relating to:

(1) whether the person meets any of the qualifying requirements;

(2) the period for which the standard authorisation is to be in force;

(3) the purpose for which it has been given; or

(4) the conditions subject to which it has been given,

---

[110] MCA 2005, s 21A, as inserted by MHA 2007, Sch 8, para 2. See also Court of Protection (Amendment) Rules 2009 (SI 2009/582) which inserted Part 10A to the Court of Protection Rules 2007. In *AB v LCC (A Local Authority) and the Care Manager of BCH* [2011] EWHC 3151 (COP), [2012] COPLR 314, Mostyn J reviewed the role of the RPR in bringing proceedings to the Court of Protection, and emphasised that, prima facie, there is no reason why an RPR cannot act as litigation friend for P in proceedings under MCA 2005, s 21A. An RPR may therefore bring a case as an applicant in his own name, or as litigation friend for P. This is consistent with the findings of the President of the Court of Protection in *Re X and Others (Deprivation of Liberty)*.

and may make an order terminating or varying the authorisation, or requiring the supervisory body to do so. A new process came into effect on 17 November 2014 on a pilot basis to implement the streamlined process set out by the President of the Court of Protection in *Re X and Others (Deprivation of Liberty)*. However, it remains to be seen what the impact of the Court of Appeal's judgment in *Re X* will be (see **7.31**).

7.72 Where an urgent authorisation has been given, the court may determine:

(1)   whether the urgent authorisation should have been given;

(2)   the period during which the urgent authorisation is to be in force; or

(3)   the purpose for which it is given,

and may make an order terminating or varying the authorisation, or requiring the managing authority to do so.

7.73 Once an application is made to the court under MCA 2005, s 21A, the court's powers are not confined simply to determining that question. Once its jurisdiction is invoked, the court has a discretionary power under MCA 2005, s 15 to make declarations as to (a) whether a person has or lacks capacity to make a decision specified in the declaration; (b) whether a person has or lacks capacity to make decisions on such matters as are described in the declaration, and (c) the lawfulness or otherwise of any act done, or yet to be done, in relation to that person. Where P lacks capacity, the court has wide powers under MCA 2005, s 16 to make decisions on P's behalf in relation to matters concerning his personal welfare or property or affairs.[111]

7.74 In *Re UF*,[112] Charles J expressed the view that, where an application is made under MCA 2005, s 21A, the court can either: (1) take control of the matter itself and grant interim relief and authorisations under MCA 2005, ss 15–16; or (2) reach effectively the same result under s 21A, by continuing in force the relevant authorisation, or otherwise bringing about the result that a standard authorisation is in existence.[113] Charles J held that the court has the power 'to vary an existing standard authorisation by extending (or shortening) it and that if and when it exercises that power it would normally be sensible for the court to give consideration to whether it should then exercise its powers under ss 6) and (7) or give directions concerning its future exercise of those powers,' but doubted that the court would have the power to extend a standard authorisation beyond the possible maximum period of one year. In the judgment he also recorded[114] concessions by the Ministry of Justice and the Legal Aid Agency that, despite the wording of reg 5(1)(g) of the Civil Legal Aid (Financial Resources and Payment for Services) Regulations 2013 to apparently

---

[111]   See *CC v KK and STCC* [2012] EWHC 2136 (COP), [2012] COPLR 627 at para 16 per Baker J.

[112]   [2013] EWHC 4289 (COP), [2014] COPLR forthcoming.

[113]   *UF* at para [33].

[114]   *UF* at para [32].

contrary effect, the 'taking control' by the court of the authorisation of a deprivation of liberty by the making of orders under MCA 2005, s 16 and the consequent coming to an end of any existing standard authorisation would not be regarded as a contrivance giving rise to the removal of non-means-tested public funding (see further **8.110–13**).

7.75 In approaching questions relating to the deprivation of P's liberty (including as to whether P is deprived of his liberty at all), it would appear that the Court of Protection is engaged in an inquisitorial process, such that questions of burdens of proof do not arise.[115] When making orders under MCA 2005, s 21A, the court may also consider a person's liability for any act done in connection with the standard or urgent authorisation before its variation or termination, including making an order excluding a person from liability.

MONITORING

7.76 The operation of these provisions is monitored and is reported on by the Care Quality Commission.[116] To this end, both hospitals and care homes must notify the Commission about any application to deprive a person of their liberty and about the outcome of that application.[117] The Commission has now published four reports, the most recent covering the period 2011–13.[118] This report is discussed further below at **7.69** but it is clear that there has been significant under-reporting to the Commission in relation to the operation of the provisions, especially by care homes.[119]

STATISTICS

7.77 Prior to the decision of the Supreme Court in *Cheshire West*, the rate of increase in applications has started to slow: 11,890 were made in the year to 31 March 2013 as opposed to 11,380 for the year to 30 June 2012.[120] More than half of applications completed in 2012–13 resulted in an authorisation being granted,[121] continuing a trend from previous years that remains well above the

---

[115] See *Chester West and Cheshire Council v P* [2011] EWHC 1330 (Fam), [2011] COPLR Con Vol 273 at para 45 per Baker J (this aspect of the decision not being appealed to the Court of Appeal). But see the discussion at **11.53–11.55**.

[116] See the Mental Capacity (Deprivation of Liberty: Monitoring and Reporting; and Assessments – Amendment) Regulations 2009 (SI 2009/827).

[117] Regulations 18(1) and (4A) of the Care Quality Commission (Registration) Regulations 2009 (SI 2009/3112). This obligation applies both to an application for a standard authorisation and for an application to the Court of Protection for an order under MCA 2005, s 16(2)(a).

[118] Available at: www.cqc.org.uk/public/publications/reports/deprivation-liberty-safeguards-2012/13.

[119] Ibid at pp 20–21.

[120] Health and Social Care Information Centre: Mental Capacity Act 2005, Deprivation of Liberty Safeguards Assessments, England: 2012–13, Annual report, available at www.hscic.gov.uk/article/3401/Mental-Health-Use-of-Deprivation-of-Liberty-Safeguards-continues-to-rise.

[121] Ibid, showing that 55% of applications resulted in an authorisation being granted; where an

Department of Health's expectation that less than a quarter of applications would result in an authorisation being granted.[122]

However, this landscape is subject to significant change. The effect of the acid test identified by the Supreme Court in *Cheshire West* is that many 'ordinary' placements may amount to a deprivation of liberty. This has far-reaching implications. According to the Alzheimer's Society,[123] there are 200,000 people with dementia in care homes in England and Wales. In addition, between 2012 and 2013 there were over 28,000 people aged 18–64 with learning disability in care and nursing homes. It would seem that all of those unable to give valid consent are now likely to be deprived, necessitating a deprivation of liberty authorisation. The impact also extends to hospitals, supported living and shared lives schemes. All disabled and vulnerable adults lacking the relevant capacity who receive care or support funded by, or arranged by, a public body may now need to be reviewed to see if the acid test satisfied. Further, foster carers, children in local authority care, and family members receiving support from health or social services may now be acting unlawfully unless the procedural and substantive safeguards in Art 5 are met. Only time will tell how the statistics will pan out post *Cheshire West* and whether the recent streamlined process implemented by the Court of Protection will be effective in managing the significantly increased workload.

COMMENT

7.78 There is rising groundswell of opinion that the deprivation of liberty safeguards have not achieved the (laudable) aims for which they were introduced. In its post-legislative scrutiny of MHA 2007 published in August 2013,[124] the House of Commons Health Select Committee considered the deprivation of liberty safeguards, and found them profoundly wanting. Evidence was received from (inter alia) the Department of Health, the Care Quality Commission and the Mental Health Alliance, and the Committee concluded thus:

'106. The Committee found the evidence it received about the effective application of deprivation of liberty safeguards (DOLS) for people suffering from mental incapacity profoundly depressing and complacent. The Department itself described the variation as "extreme". People who suffer from lack of mental capacity are

---

application was not granted, this was in 80% of cases because the supervisory body considered that the best interests requirement had not been met.

[122] See https://catalogue.ic.nhs.uk/publications/mental-health/legislation/m-c-a-2005-dep-lib-saf-ass-eng-2011-12/m-c-a-2005-dep-lib-saf-ass-eng-2011-12-rep.pdf at pp 4 and 9, citing the Department of Health's Impact Assessment of the Mental Capacity Act 2005 Deprivation of Liberty Safeguards to accompany the Code of Practice and regulations, now available at webarchive.nationalarchives.gov.uk/20130107105354/http://www.dh.gov.uk/en/Publicationsandstatistics/Publications/PublicationsLegislation/DH_084982. That impact assessment also predicted that applications would fall at a constant rate between 2009–10 and 2015–16.

[123] See www.alzheimers.org.uk.

[124] See www.publications.parliament.uk/pa/cm201314/cmselect/cmhealth/584/584.pdf.

among the most vulnerable members of society and they are entitled to expect that their rights are properly and effectively protected. The fact is that despite fine words in legislation they are currently widely exposed to abuse because the controls which are supposed to protect them are woefully inadequate.

107. Against this background, the Committee recommends that the Department should initiate an urgent review of the implementation of DOLS for people suffering from mental incapacity and calls for this review to be presented to Parliament, within twelve months, together with an action plan to deliver early improvement.'

7.79 The House of Lords Select Committee appointed to consider and report upon MCA 2005 took extensive oral evidence upon the operation of the DOLS safeguards,[125] the tenor of which was largely to the effect that the safeguards were complex and unwieldy and of questionable effectiveness in discharging the purpose for which they were enacted. In its final report,[126] the Select Committee pulled no punches:

'The intention behind the safeguards – to provide protection in law for individuals who were being deprived of their liberty for reasons of their own safety – was understood and supported by our witnesses. But the legislative provisions and their operation in practice are the subject of extensive and wideranging criticism. The provisions are poorly drafted, overly complex and bear no relationship to the language and ethos of the Mental Capacity Act. The safeguards are not well understood and are poorly implemented. Evidence suggested that thousands, if not tens of thousands, of individuals are being deprived of their liberty without the protection of the law, and therefore without the safeguards which Parliament intended. Worse still, far from being used to protect individuals and their rights, they are sometimes used to oppress individuals, and to force upon them decisions made by others without reference to the wishes and feelings of the person concerned.

The only appropriate recommendation in the face of such criticism is to start again. We therefore recommend a comprehensive review of the Deprivation of Liberty Safeguards with a view to replacing them with provisions that are compatible in style and ethos to the rest of the Mental Capacity Act.'[127]

7.80 No immediate legislative change is forthcoming. However, the Law Commission has been asked to consider how deprivation of liberty should be authorised and supervised in hospitals, care homes and community settings, where it is possible that Art 5 rights would otherwise be infringed. This includes considering the legislation underpinning Sch A1 in its entirety. The Law Commission aims to produce a consultation paper in the summer of 2015, with recommendations for reform and a draft Bill, in summer 2017.[128]

---

[125] See www.parliament.uk/business/committees/committees-a-z/lords-select/mental-capacity-act-2005.
[126] See www.publications.parliament.uk/pa/ld201314/ldselect/ldmentalcap/139/139.pdf.
[127] Ibid, summary, p 7 (emphasis in the original).
[128] See: http://lawcommission.justice.gov.uk/areas/capacity-and-detention.htm.

7.81 In the interim, the system is under huge pressure, both as regards the need to authorise deprivations of liberty under Sch A1 in respect of those who satisfy the 'acid test', and to bring applications to the Court of Protection for those deprivations of liberty taking place outside care homes and hospitals. There is a real risk that, under this pressure, we will lose sight of the reason why questions of deprivation of liberty is so important in this context. It is not so that boxes can be ticked and forms completed. Rather, it is because those who are deprived of their liberty for purposes of providing care and treatment – and who lack capacity to consent to such deprivation– are, by definition, intensely vulnerable. They need, as Lady Hale was at pains to emphasise in *Cheshire West*, regular independent scrutiny of the arrangements made for them to ensure that they are in their best interests.[129]

7.82 We can certainly legitimately ask the question whether looking at matters through the prism of Art 5 ECHR is the best way in which to achieve this policy aim; at the very least, all can probably agree that the debates of the past few years as to what constitutes a deprivation of liberty have not been of the slightest assistance to those most affected. We would therefore urge readers of this work to engage with the Law Commission's consultation process to seek to develop a better way in which to give meaningful protection to the rights of such individuals both under Article 5 and Article 8 of the ECHR.

---

[129] *Cheshire West* at para 57.

CHAPTER 8

COURT PRACTICE AND PROCEDURE

PRELIMINARY

Role of the Lord Chancellor

8.1   In the Mental Capacity Act 2005 (MCA 2005) and, thus, the paragraphs that follow, references are made to the Lord Chancellor, who was given various powers. These references must be interpreted in the light of the constitutional reforms that overlapped with the Act before Parliament, so an overview of the impact of those reforms is needed.[1]

8.2   In June 2003, abolition of the office of Lord Chancellor was announced as part of a suite of constitutional reforms which also included the establishment of an independent Judicial Appointments Commission and a new Supreme Court. The overall aim of these reforms was to put the relationship between the executive, legislature and judiciary on a modern footing, respecting the separation of powers between the three. On 26 January 2004 the Government announced proposals which included the transfer of the Lord Chancellor's judiciary-related functions, and these were effected within the reforms by the Constitutional Reform Act 2005.[2]

8.3   Following concerns expressed by the judiciary a Concordat was established between the Lord Chancellor and the Lord Chief Justice.[3] So far as is relevant to the new mental capacity jurisdiction the roles become as follows. The Lord Chancellor is:

- under a duty to ensure that there is an efficient and effective system to support the carrying on of the business of the courts in England and Wales, as set out in the Courts Act 2003, Part 1;[4]

---

[1]   The consequential amendments have been made by statutory instrument under the Constitutional Reform Act 2005.

[2]   The title Lord Chancellor was to be abolished in favour of Secretary of State for Constitutional Affairs but the Bill was amended to retain that title although the role and functions of the office are substantively recast.

[3]   The Concordat is 'an essential tool for protecting the independence of the judiciary, as a blueprint governing the relations between the judiciary and the government for the long-term and as providing a much-needed, non-contentious way of appointing and disciplining the judiciary', per Lord Woolf CJ.

[4]   This includes the provision and allocation of resources which include financial, material and human resources.

- accountable to Parliament for the overall efficiency and effectiveness of the administration of the court system, including the proper use of public resources voted by Parliament;

- responsible for ensuring that the public interest is served in decisions taken on matters affecting the judiciary in relation to the administration of justice; and

- responsible for supporting the judiciary in enabling them to fulfil their functions for dispensing justice.

8.4   The Lord Chief Justice is responsible for ensuring that appropriate structures are in place to ensure the well-being of and training and provision of guidance for the judiciary, and for the deployment of individual members of the judiciary and the allocation of work within the courts.

8.5   The Lord Chancellor, in consultation with the Lord Chief Justice, is responsible for the efficient and effective administration of the court system including setting the framework for the organisation of the courts system (such as geographical and functional jurisdictional boundaries). This includes determining the number of judges required for each jurisdiction and region and the number required at each level of the judiciary; also the provision of the courts, their location and sitting times and consequent administrative staffing to meet the expected business requirement.

Judiciary

8.6   The majority of judicial appointments fall within the remit of the Judicial Appointments Commission (JAC). The Lord Chief Justice is responsible, after consulting the Lord Chancellor, for determining which individual judge should be assigned to which court and the authorisation of individual members of the judiciary to sit in particular levels of court. Also for deciding the level of judge appropriate to hear particular classes of case (including the issuing of Practice Directions in that regard) and the nominations of judges to particular posts including those that provide judicial leadership not formal promotion.

8.7   The Lord Chief Justice is responsible for the provision and sponsorship of judicial training within the resources provided by the Lord Chancellor, but responsibility for assessing the need for and providing training of professional judicial office-holders remains with the Judicial College (formerly the Judicial Studies Board).

Rules and Practice Directions

8.8   In general, functions relating to the allowing of procedural Rules of Court remain with the Lord Chancellor. The making of such rules and Practice

Directions will rest with the relevant rule committees where such a committee exists, and otherwise will be exercised by the Lord Chief Justice, with the concurrence of the Lord Chancellor.[5]

STATUS OF THE COURT OF PROTECTION

Preliminary

8.9 MCA 2005, Part 2, comprising ss 45–56, deals with the creation of the new Court of Protection and its powers.

The Court

Name and venue

8.10 MCA 2005 created a new superior court of record[6] with an official seal known as the Court of Protection and the former office of the Supreme Court (as it was then known) called the Court of Protection ceased to exist. The functions of the new court are described in Chapter 4.

8.11 The court has a central office and registry at a place appointed by the Lord Chancellor. This was originally at Archway Tower, Junction Road, London N19. In January 2012 the court moved to the Thomas Moore Buildings at the Royal Courts of Justice, and in December 2013 the court moved again to its present home at First Avenue House where it joined what was then known as the Principal Registry of the Family Division and what is now called the Central Family Court. The Court of Protection remains separate and retains its individual identity and staff. The court may also sit at any place in England and Wales, on any day and at any time and a number of courts have been designated as regional courts.

Administration

8.12 The court is managed by HM Courts and Tribunals Service. Prior to 2009, the Office of the Public Guardian managed the court and was also responsible for its funding. This arrangement was not good. The OPG had never been responsible for a court and this created difficulties and it was also felt that as the Public Guardian is a common litigant in the Court of Protection, it was not appropriate that he should also be running and funding the court. It was therefore against this background that HMCTS (or rather its predecessor HM Courts Service) took over the running of the court.

---

[5]   MCA 2005 makes no provision for a Rules Committee.
[6]   Thus able to establish precedent unlike the former Court.

Forms

8.13 The forms used by the former Court of Protection were reviewed and rewritten so as to be fit for purpose and align with other court forms. As might be expected of a court of this nature, the applications and acknowledgment of service forms inquire whether the party needs any special assistance or facilities at an attended hearing. This information should be volunteered in advance for any other person who attends a hearing.

There has been criticism of the court's forms as requests for the same information are repeated on some forms and they can be awkward to complete. COP 20 has been amended and work was undertaken to produce more user friendly forms. The result is that new forms for application are expected to be introduced by the summer of 2015.

Judges

8.14 MCA 2005 also provides that, subject to the Court of Protection rules, the jurisdiction of the new court shall be exercisable by a number of judges nominated for that purpose by the Lord Chancellor.[7] The judges who may be nominated are the President of the Family Division, the Chancellor of the Chancery Division,[8] puisne judges of the High Court,[9] circuit judges and district judges. There was originally no provision for part time judges such as Recorders, deputy district judges or tribunal judges to sit in the Court of Protection. This denied the court the important resource of judges who could sit in place of full time judges on annual or sick leave, a pool of potential future appointees to the court and crucially extra judicial resources when needed to cope with the ever increasing work load. This issue was finally resolved by the Crime and Courts Act 2013 which allowed a large number of full time and part time judges from across the judicial spectrum to sit in the court. Indeed, these provisions proved to be vital recently. After the decision of the Supreme Court in *P v Cheshire West and Chester Council*[10] it became clear that the court would not be able to deal with the high volume of applications to authorise deprivation of liberty. These provisions have allowed the court to nominate judges from tribunals to assist with these cases. This is in fact the first time there has been judicial cross fertilization.

8.15 In October 2007 the Lord Chancellor appointed the then President of the Family Division, Sir Mark Potter, as President of the Court of Protection. On his retirement, Sir Nicholas Wall took over until December 2012, to be

---

[7]   The references in this and the following paragraph to the Lord Chancellor may be interpreted as being to the Lord Chief Justice after consulting the Lord Chancellor – see **8.1ff**.

[8]   The Senior Judge of the Chancery Division whose title was previously the Vice-Chancellor.

[9]   This is no longer reserved to judges of the Family or Chancery Division although no judges of the Queen's Bench Division have yet been nominated.

[10]   [2014] UKSC 19.

followed by the present incumbent Sir James Munby. The Vice-President is Mr Justice Charles who was appointed in December 2013.[11]

The former Master of the old Court of Protection, Denzil Lush, was appointed to be Senior Judge.

In addition, all judges of the Family and Chancery Divisions were originally nominated as judges of the Court of Protection although now, only certain Chancery Division judges are nominated. In 2011, the President nominated all judges of the Queen's Bench Division but it is understood that they are only used as a resource when other High Court Judges are unavailable.

In the High Court, it is the Family Division that really shoulders the bulk of the responsibility for Court of Protection work. At one point, it was said that approximately 10% of the Family Division's work derives from the Court of Protection which led one judge to complain that urgent attention needed to be given to increasing the resources of the Family Division to accommodate this work.[12] This level of work is only increasing.

There are five full time district judges at the main registry at First Avenue House and one district judge who sits part time in the court, spending the rest of his time in the Family and County Courts. They are regularly joined by district judges who sit in the regional courts who wish to gain experience from sitting at the main registry and who are a valuable resource to ensure cases can be properly processed.

In 2011, a decision was taken to appoint Mr Justice Charles as Judge in Charge of the Court of Protection. Now that he is Vice President of the court, that position is really redundant as the Vice President carries out the same role which is effectively to lead the court and ensure it runs smoothly.

Regional judges

8.16   District judges and circuit judges specialising in chancery or family work have been nominated to sit in the court on a regional basis.[13].

One of the advantages of regionalisation is that more provincial solicitors and barristers will appear before the 'local' Court of Protection and thereby gain experience with which they may better advise their clients.

Allocation of cases

8.17   MCA 2005 provides for three levels of the judiciary to be nominated to sit in the Court, thus following the practice in the civil and family courts where

---

[11]   MCA 2005, s 46.
[12]   See *G v E* 2010 EWHC 621 (Fam) per Baker J at paras 4 and 5.
[13]   In Scotland the new jurisdiction was given to every Sheriff but this has not proved to be ideal because some have little experience or interest in the jurisdiction.

the Rules and Practice Directions allocate cases between these levels.[14] The rules as recently amended refer to judges as being in tiers so Tier 1 are district judges and first tier tribunal judges, Tier 2 are circuit judges and upper tribunal judges and Tier 3 are High Court Judges.

However, the reality is that the majority of the court's work is undertaken by district judges. Serious medical treatment decisions are heard by High Court judges, though sitting in the Court of Protection rather than as Family Division judges. Other personal welfare decisions are allocated to district judges who will either hear the case or send it to a circuit judge or High Court Judge if that is more appropriate. Financial management decisions tend to be heard at first instance by district judges although appeals from them lie to circuit judges.

Transfer of cases

8.18   In the case of a mentally incapacitated person under the age of 18 years the Lord Chancellor may by order make provision as to transfer of proceedings from the Court of Protection to a court with jurisdiction under the Children Act 1989, or vice versa.[15]

Powers

General

8.19   The Court has in connection with its jurisdiction the same powers, rights, privileges and authority as the High Court.[16] It must be emphasised that the powers may only be exercised within the Court's jurisdiction, so although it may resolve disputes or uncertainty concerning the personal welfare, health care or financial management of the mentally incapacitated person, the Court has no jurisdiction to resolve disputes between that person and other persons. Similarly it has no power to order a local authority to provide a particular care plan or to resolve a dispute between two authorities as to responsibility based upon ordinary residence. In such instances the Court of Protection may need to authorise the conduct of proceedings in another court which has the appropriate jurisdiction.

8.20   Office copies of orders made, directions given or other instruments issued by the Court and sealed with its official seal are admissible in all legal proceedings as evidence of the originals without further proof.[17]

---

[14]   Circuit judges (unlike district judges) do not sit in the High Court unless specifically authorised to do so on a case-by-case basis under Senior Courts Act 1981 (formerly Supreme Court Act 1981), s 9.

[15]   MCA 2005, s 21. See the Mental Capacity Act 2005 (Transfer of Proceedings) Order 2007, SI 2007/1899.

[16]   MCA 2005, s 47(1). The Law of Property Act 1925, s 204 (orders of High Court conclusive in favour of purchasers) will apply in relation to orders and directions of the court as it applies to orders of the High Court.

[17]   MCA 2005, s 47(3).

Interim orders and directions

8.21 The court may, pending the determination of an application to it in relation to a person, make an order or give directions in respect of any matter if:[18]

(1) there is reason to believe that this person lacks capacity in relation to the matter;

(2) the matter is one to which its powers under MCA 2005 extend; and

(3) it is in the person's best interests to make the order, or give the directions, without delay.

The proper test for the involvement of the court in the first instance is whether there is evidence giving good cause for concern that P may lack capacity in some relevant regard. Once that is raised as a serious possibility, the court then moves on to the second stage to decide what action, if any, it is in P's best interests to take before a final determination of his capacity can be made.[19]

Reports

8.22 The court may, where in proceedings brought in respect of a person it is considering a question relating to that person:[20]

(1) require a report to be made to it by the Public Guardian or by a Court of Protection Visitor; or

(2) require a local authority, or an NHS body,[21] to arrange for a report to be made by one of its officers or employees, or such other person as the authority, or the NHS body, considers appropriate.

8.23 The report must deal with such matters relating to the person, and be made in writing or orally, as the court may direct.[22]

8.24 When preparing a report the Public Guardian or a Court of Protection Visitor[23] may, at all reasonable times, examine and take copies of any health record, any record of or held by, a local authority and compiled in connection with a social services function, and any record held by a person registered under the Care Standards Act 2000, Part 2 so far as the record relates to the person. When making a visit the Public Guardian or a Court of Protection Visitor may interview the person in private.

---

[18] MCA 2005, s 48.
[19] *Re F (Interim Declarations)* [2009] COPLR Con Vol 390, HHJ Hazel Marshall QC.
[20] MCA 2005, s 49.
[21] As defined in the Health and Social Care (Community Health and Standards) Act 2003, s 148.
[22] Court of Protection Rules may specify matters which, unless the court directs otherwise, must also be dealt with in the report.
[23] The status and role of the Public Guardian and the Visitors is considered in Chapter 8.

8.25 A Special Visitor when making a visit may, if the court so directs, carry out in private a medical, psychiatric or psychological examination of the person's capacity and condition.

THE COURT RULES

Court of Protection Rules 2007[24] (COPR 2007)

8.26 The Lord Chancellor is empowered to make Rules of Court with respect to the practice and procedure of the court,[25] and these may, in particular, make provision:

(1) as to the manner and form in which proceedings are to be commenced;

(2) as to the persons entitled to be notified of, and be made parties to, the proceedings;

(3) for the allocation, in such circumstances as may be specified, of any specified description of proceedings to a specified judge or to specified descriptions of judges;

(4) for the exercise of the jurisdiction of the court, in such circumstances as may be specified, by its officers or other staff;

(5) for enabling the court to appoint a suitable person (who may, with his consent, be the Official Solicitor) to act in the name of, or on behalf of, or to represent the person to whom the proceedings relate;

(6) for enabling an application to the court to be disposed of without a hearing;

(7) for enabling the court to proceed with, or with any part of, a hearing in the absence of the person to whom the proceedings relate;

(8) for enabling or requiring the proceedings or any part of them to be conducted in private and for enabling the court to determine who is to be admitted when the court sits in private and to exclude specified persons when it sits in public;

(9) as to what may be received as evidence (whether or not admissible apart from the rules) and the manner in which it is to be presented; and

(10) for the enforcement of orders made and directions given in the proceedings.

COPR 2007 may, instead of providing for any matter, refer to provision made by directions.

---

[24] SI 2007/1744.

[25] MCA 2005, s 51. The reference to the Lord Chancellor should be interpreted as being to the Lord Chief Justice with the concurrence of the Lord Chancellor. There is no provision for a Rules Committee.

8.27 The Court of Protection Rules 2001[26] and their predecessors were brief and left much to judicial discretion. This may have been useful in a jurisdiction of where the objective was to address the best interests of the incapacitated person rather than personal disputes between members of their families, carers and other concerned persons. But it was not easy for practitioners to know how they should prepare or conduct their cases.

8.28 An Informal Rules Group was set up to consider the content of the first Rules of the new Court of Protection and these were made on 24 June 2007 and came into force on 1 October 2007.[27]

8.29 In December 2009, an Ad Hoc and Informal Rules Committee was set up with a view to seeing how the rules worked and whether change was necessary. The Committee held a number of meetings and published a report which recommended many changes in July 2010. Although the President of the Court of Protection accepted the Committee's proposals, save for one exception, nothing was done to implement the recommendations.

8.30 The exception was a new r 7A which allows authorised court officers to undertake certain work.

However, the rule went beyond the intention of the rules committee which was to allow court officers to only undertake a very limited scope of work. The Practice Direction for this rule reveals a far greater scope of work being devolved on the authorised court officer than was ever imagined.

The Senior Judge monitored the situation for the first 6 months and thereafter, the scheme seems to have worked well in practice with the authorised court officers readily referring cases to a judge if they have a query and feel the case is better handled at a higher level.

In March 2014, the House of Lords Select Committee on the MCA 2005 published its report and this lead to another Ad Hoc Rules Committee being set up in July 2014.

The Committee reported on the first tranche of its work in early 2015 and amendments were proposed to the rules which were accepted by the Lord Chancellor and the President of the Court of Protection. These rules took effect in July 2015.

However, this is not the end of the Committee's work. Whereas the first tranche of amendments were largely uncontroversial being designed to remedy problems in the working of the rules, tranche two will comprise a fundamental consideration of the working of the rules and processes and consideration of issues such as case management and transparency. No date has been fixed for a

---

[26] SI 2001/824.
[27] The COPR 2007, SI 2007/1744. The 2001 Rules were revoked along with the Court of Protection (Enduring Powers of Attorney) Rules 2001, SI 2001/825.

final report although it is understood that the Committee is working as quickly as possible to draw its conclusions together.

Practice Directions

8.31 The President of the Court of Protection may, with the concurrence of the Lord Chancellor, give directions as to the practice and procedure of the court. No such directions may be given by anyone else without the approval of the President and the Lord Chancellor, but this does not prevent the President from giving directions which contain guidance as to law or making judicial decisions.[28] Thus, the rules are supplemented by a large number of practice directions which fill out the rules.

One recent amendment to the rules is r 9A. This allows a practice direction to be made to operate a pilot scheme for a specified period and in respect of certain parts of the country. Furthermore, a practice direction may now modify or disapply a rule. It will be interesting to see how this is used although one possible use could be to pilot proposed changes the Ad Hoc Rules Committee recommend to ascertain if they are workable or not.

Practice Guidance

8.32 In May and June 2013, the President issued two Practice Guidance documents relating to contempt of court applications.

However, although there was a fear that the issue of such documents might be the start of a new practice, it is suggested that with the new r 9A may obviate the need for guidance documents in the future especially as it is questionable how a Practice Guidance document fits into the scheme of the rules and also whether such documents are desirable, the preferred route for change being through a change to the rules or amendment to a practice direction.

In July 2013, a draft Practice Guidance was issued on the subject of transparency and reporting of judgments of the court which was introduced formally in May 2014. One positive effect of this is that a large number of decisions of the Senior Judge on property and affairs cases are now available on the Bailli website which some practitioners feel has helped them to understand the court's approach to a variety of issues.

---

[28]   MCA 2005, s 52. The references to the Lord Chancellor may be interpreted as being to the Lord Chief Justice though with the concurrence of the Lord Chancellor.

Interface with other rules

8.33 Provision is made in the rules to apply the CPR or the Family Procedure Rules 2010 including their practice directions.[29] This gives the court flexibility to incorporate other rules into Court of Protection proceedings if they will assist.

The overriding objective

General

8.34 COPR 2007 commence in Part 2 with a statement of the 'overriding objective', borrowed from the original Civil Procedure Rules 1998[30] (CPR) in which context it has proved extremely successful.

The objective is to enable the court to deal with cases justly, having regard to the principles contained in MCA 2005, and the court will seek to give effect to the overriding objective when it exercises any power or interprets any rule or Practice Direction. The present version of the CPR, however, talks about the need to deal with a case at proportionate cost. This part of the CPR has not been incorporated into the COPR 2007 although it remains to be seen if any future change will do so.

8.35 Dealing with a case justly includes, so far as is practicable, ensuring that it is dealt with expeditiously and fairly, that the parties are on an equal footing and that the incapacitated person's interests and position are properly considered. Also dealing with the case in ways which are proportionate to the nature, importance and complexity of the issues, saving expense and allotting to it an appropriate share of the court's resources, while taking account of the need to allot resources to other cases.

Duties of the court and parties

8.36 The court is expected to further the overriding objective by actively managing cases, which means encouraging the parties to co-operate with each other in the conduct of the proceedings. It should identify the issues at an early stage, including who should be parties, and then decide which issues need a full investigation and hearing and which do not, and the procedure to be followed. In the process the court will decide the order in which issues are to be resolved and fix timetables or otherwise control the progress of the case. The parties are required to help the court to further the overriding objective.

8.37 The parties will be encouraged to use an alternative dispute resolution procedure when appropriate. The court will also consider whether the likely benefits of taking a particular step justify the cost, deal with as many aspects of the case as it can on the same occasion and where possible without the parties

---

[29] COPR 2007, r 9.
[30] SI 1998/3132.

needing to attend. All of this involves giving directions to ensure that the case proceeds quickly and efficiently and making use of technology.

The court must now also consider whether a hearing should be held in public and if any document should be made public.

An important amendment to the rules is r 3A. This rule obliges the court to consider how P can participate in the proceedings. Until now, the court only had to ensure that P's interests and position were considered but now, right at the very start of the proceedings, the court has to tackle the issue of how P is involved in a case.

The rule allows for P to be a party as well as not being a party. It also creates two new roles, that of an accredited legal representative and a representative. The former will be chosen from a panel which has yet to be set up and approved), the latter can be anyone such as a family member, a friend or IMCA.

Rule 4 has also been completely amended to require the parties not only to help the court further the overriding objective but to co-operate with each other, adhere to timetables set by the court and to comply with all rules, orders and directions. The rule also contains a warning that if without reasonable excuse, a party fails to satisfy the requirements of r 4, the court may depart from the general costs rule under r 159.

Interpretation

8.38 COPR 2007, Part 3 contains an interpretation clause and also makes provision for computation of time. In order to fill any gaps the CPR (and Practice Directions) are to be applied with any necessary modifications.[31]

Case management powers

General

8.39 COPR 2007, Part 5[32] deals with the Court's general powers of case management. The court may take any step or give any direction for the purpose of managing the case and furthering the overriding objective, and in particular:

(1) extend or shorten the time for compliance with any rule, Practice Direction, or court order or direction (even if an application is made out of the time);

(2) adjourn or bring forward a hearing;

(3) require the incapacitated person or a party (including the legal representative or litigation friend) to attend court;

---

[31]   COPR 2007, rr 6–8.
[32]   COPR 2007, rr 25–28.

(4) hold a hearing and receive evidence by telephone or any other method of direct oral communication;

(5) stay any proceedings or judgment generally or until a specified date or event;

(6) consolidate proceedings;

(7) hear two or more applications on the same occasion;

(8) direct a separate hearing of any issue;

(9) decide the order in which issues are to be heard;

(10) exclude an issue from consideration;

(11) dismiss or give judgment on an application after a preliminary decision; and

(12) direct a party to file and serve an estimate of costs.

8.40 The court will take into account whether or not a party has complied with any rule or Practice Direction.

Security for costs

8.41 The rules have been amended to incorporate[33]new rules which specifically allow an application for security for costs to be made if the court is satisfied that having regard to all the circumstances of the case, it is just to make the order and certain conditions are satisfied.

Court's own initiative

8.42 The court may make (or vary or revoke) any order, even if a party has not sought that order, dispense with the requirement of any rule and generally exercise its powers on its own initiative without hearing the parties. But if it proposes to make an order on its own initiative it may give the parties and any person it thinks fit an opportunity to make representations and, where it does so, it will specify the time by which, and the manner in which, the representations must be made. If the court proposes to hold a hearing it will give the parties and any other person likely to be affected by the order at least 3 days' notice.

8.43 An error of procedure will not invalidate any step taken unless the court so orders and the court may waive the error or require it to be remedied or make such other order as appears just.

Human rights

8.44 A party who seeks to rely upon any provision of or right arising under the Human Rights Act 1998 or who seeks a remedy available under that Act must inform the court in the manner set out in the relevant Practice Direction

---

[33] COPR 2007 rr 81A–81D.

specifying the Convention right which it is alleged has been infringed and details of the alleged infringement, and the remedy sought and whether this includes a declaration of incompatibility.[34] The court may not make a declaration of incompatibility unless 21 days' notice, or such other period of notice as the court directs, has been given to the Crown, and a minister or other permitted person will then be joined as a party on filing an application.[35]

PRACTICE AND PROCEDURE

Court documents

8.45 COPR 2007, Part 4 deals with court documents.[36] The documents used in proceedings include application forms application notices and other documents referred to in Practice Directions. An application form is used to commence proceedings, and an application notice will relate to an application within existing proceedings.[37] The usual slip rule enables the court to correct any clerical mistakes in an order or direction or any error arising in an order or direction from any accidental slip or omission, but an endorsement shall show that this has been done.[38]

Statements of truth

8.46 When submitted by a party such documents, and also witness statements, may need to be verified by a 'statement of truth', which is the modern form of oath. This is a statement that the party putting forward the document (or litigation friend on that person's behalf) believes that the facts stated therein are true. The statement must be signed by the party or litigation friend (or legal representative on such person's behalf) or the witness. If this is not done the document may not be relied upon without the court's permission, and it would be contempt of court to make a false statement.[39] A position statement does not need to be verified by a statement of truth.[40]

Personal details

8.47 Where a party does not wish to reveal a home address or telephone number, or other personal details, those particulars must be provided to the Court but will not be revealed to any other person unless the Court so directs. Nevertheless a party must provide an address for service within the jurisdiction.[41]

---

[34]   Ie under the Human Rights Act 1998, s 4.
[35]   COPR 2007, Part 11, r 83. A Practice Direction (PD 11A) deals with this.
[36]   A Practice Direction (PD 4A) deals with court documents.
[37]   COPR 2007, Pts 9 and 10 respectively.
[38]   COPR 2007, rr 23–24.
[39]   COPR 2007, rr 11–14. A Practice Direction (PD 4B) deals with statements of truth.
[40]   COPR 2007, r 11A.
[41]   COPR 2007, r 15.

Access to documents

8.48 Unless the court orders otherwise, a party may inspect or obtain a copy of any filed document and any communication with the court in the proceedings. A non-party may generally inspect or obtain a copy of a judgment or order given or made in public, and the court may authorise further disclosure (with or without editing). There are restrictions on the use of such documents in other proceedings.[42] Further provisions deal with the Public Guardian's access to court documents.[43]

Service of documents

8.49 COPR 2007, Part 6[44] makes general provision for service which includes both the service of documents and notifying the issue of an application form, but other rules may make different provision or the court may order otherwise. The rules have also been amended to include provisions for service out of the jurisdiction.[45]

Who serves?

8.50 An order or judgment, an acknowledgment of service or notification and a notice of hearing (other than for committal) will generally be served by the court. Any other document is to be served by the party seeking to rely upon it, except where the court directs or a rule or Practice Direction provides otherwise.

How is service effected?

8.51 Several methods of service are allowed. Unless a solicitor is acting the document may be delivered to the person personally or his or her last known home address. It may also be sent to that address by first class post (or by an alternative method of service which provides for delivery on the next working day). Otherwise documents will be served on a solicitor who has stated that he or she is authorised to accept service unless personal service is required. COPR 2007 confirms when a document is deemed to have been served, deals with service out of the jurisdiction and makes provision for a certificate of service (or non-service).

8.52 The court may direct that service be effected by another method (including substituted service) where there is good reason for this and will then specify the method of service and the date when the document will be deemed to be served. It may also dispense with service. Special provision is made for service of documents on children and protected parties (which will include the

---

[42] COPR 2007, rr 16–19.
[43] COPR 2007, rr 20–21.
[44] COPR 2007, rr 29–39. A Practice Direction (PD 6A) deals with service of documents.
[45] COPR 2007, rr 39–39H.

incapacitated person to whom the proceedings relate), the aim being to reach a responsible person who will arrange representation for the child protected party.

Notifying the incapacitated person

8.53   Clearly the person alleged to be incapacitated and thereby the subject of the proceedings should be notified of the steps being taken and given an opportunity to intervene or contribute, unless clearly unable to do so. Even then it may be that this person should be notified in case someone in close contact needs to know and thereby have an opportunity to become involved. Part 7 of the COPR 2007 which makes appropriate provision to achieve this aim.[46] If the incapacitated person is made a party (see below) other provisions then apply.

8.54   Notification must be given when an application form has been issued or withdrawn, of the date of any hearing to dispose of the application and on the appointment of a litigation friend, accredited legal representative or representative.[47] This will be done by the applicant or his or her agent, or such other person as the court directs, and appropriate explanations must be given.[48] Final orders and appeals are similarly dealt with, and the court may direct notification on other occasions. The manner of notification is prescribed in COPR 2007 and provision made for a certificate of notification to be filed, although the court may dispense with or vary any of these requirements.

Permission to apply

Who may apply?

8.55   It has in the past been found necessary to control those who may bring applications to the Court of Protection. The rules as originally drafted sought to ensure that genuine applications were not be discouraged but that a screening process was in place to prevent those who seek to interfere without justification from causing inconvenience and expense to others. However, the rules governing permission have been amended to allow far more applications to be made without the requirement of permission being granted. One such example are cases involving deprivation of liberty. The rules also now provide that the application for permission is made when making the application.[49]

---

[46]   COPR 2007, rr 40–49. A Practice Direction (PD 7A) deals with notifying P.
[47]   COPR 2007, rr 41A and 3A.
[48]   These are specified in COPR 2007, r 42.
[49]   COPR 2007, r 54.

Starting proceedings

Initial steps

8.56 COPR 2007, Part 9[50] and its Practice Directions[51] cover the procedure for starting new proceedings. The appropriate forms must be used and may need to be varied, but not so as to omit any information or guidance which the form gives to the intended recipient. Proceedings are started when the court issues an application form at the request of the applicant but this will not be done until any required permission is granted. The date will be entered on the application form by the court. The rules and Practice Directions prescribe the information to be contained in the form and the documents to be filed with it.[52]

8.57 Within 14 days of issue the applicant must serve a copy of the application form on the named respondents, together with copies of any filed documents and a form for acknowledging service. A certificate of service must then be filed within 7 days. Specific requirements are then specified in respect of applications relating to lasting and enduring powers of attorney.

8.58 As stated above, the incapacitated person must be notified in accordance with COPR 2007, Part 7 that an application form has been issued, unless the requirement to do so has been dispensed with. The applicant must also within 14 days of issue notify the persons specified in the relevant Practice Direction of the application whether it relates to property and affairs or personal welfare, or to both, and the orders sought. A form for acknowledging service should be attached and a certificate of service must then be filed within seven days of service.

Responding to an application

8.59 A person who is served with or notified of an application form and wishes to take part in proceedings must within 14 days file an acknowledgment of service or notification providing an address for service within the jurisdiction and stating the interest in the proceedings and whether he or she wishes to be joined as a party. The court then serves this on the applicant and on anyone else who has filed an acknowledgment. The acknowledgment or notification must also state whether the person consents to or opposes the application, and if so the grounds for doing so, and if a different order is sought what that order is. A witness statement should in those events accompany the form containing any evidence upon which the person intends to rely. The court will then consider whether to join this person as a party and make any appropriate order.

---

[50] COPR 2007, rr 61–76.
[51] In particular they cover the application form (PD 9A); notifying other persons (PD 9B); responding to an application (PD 9C); applications by deputies, attorneys and donees relating to property and affairs (PD 9D); applications relating to serious medical treatment (PD 9E); applications relating to statutory wills and gifts (PD 9F); applications relating to trustees (PD 9G); and applications relating to registration of enduring powers of attorney (PD 9H).
[52] PD 9A contains a table setting out the documents that must be filed.

Parties

8.60 The court addresses the best interests of vulnerable incapacitated individuals so will not be concerned to resolve disputes between members of the family which may have continued for years and resurface in the context of a struggle for control over the incapacitated member and his affairs.

This has implications as to who is, or may be, party to the proceedings. In this respect the court differs from the civil courts whose purpose is to resolve disputes between parties who select themselves. The approach is more akin to the family courts when addressing the best interests of children. In reality the court is often called upon to make a decision following an application by a party and will only do so after giving other persons with a relevant interest the opportunity to state their case. Treating these persons as parties introduces an unnecessarily adversarial approach to the hearing, yet those persons may expect this.

8.61 The court now has an obligation to consider P's involvement in the proceedings and whether P should be joined as a party or represented in some other way.[53]

The new r 3A introduces an accredited legal representative. This is defined in r 6 as a legal representative authorised pursuant to a scheme of accreditation approved by the President to represent persons meeting the definition of P in the COPR 2007. So far, no scheme has been made or approved. The rule came into effect in July 2015, and it remains to be seen how use of this rule will develop. If the court is minded to appoint an accredited legal representative, that person must consent and P does not have to be a party to the proceedings.

However, it is hoped that the r 3A(2)(c) representative will be useful. This could enable P to play a part in proceedings without being a party but having a family member, friend, IMCA or some other appropriate person to represent his interests to the court.

With the ever increasing workload of the Official Solicitor and the lack of legal aid, it is hoped that these alternative representatives will be of use in court proceedings.

8.62 Any person with sufficient interest may apply to be joined as a party and this is done by filing an application notice within the proceedings which will state the applicant's full name and address, his or her interest in the proceedings and the further information required when responding to an application including, where appropriate, a statement in support. The court will serve this on all parties make an order joining the person if it decides to do so. A person who wishes to be removed as a party must apply for an order to that effect.

---

[53]   See **8.38** and COPR 2007, r 3A.

Applications within proceedings

8.63 The procedure in COPR 2007, Part 10 is used for these applications.[54] The court may grant an interim remedy before an application form has been issued only if the matter is urgent or it is otherwise necessary to do so in the interests of justice. The applicant must file an application notice with the evidence upon which he relies (unless such evidence has already been filed) unless any rule or Practice Direction permits an application without or the court dispenses with the requirement. If the applicant makes an application without giving notice, the evidence in support must state why notice has not been given.

8.64 An application notice must state the order or direction that the applicant is seeking, the brief grounds relied on and such other information as may be required by any rule or a Practice Direction. The court will issue the application notice and, if there is to be a hearing, give notice of the date to the applicant. The applicant must within 21 days serve a copy of the application notice together with the notice of hearing and evidence relied upon on anyone named as a respondent (if not otherwise a party to the proceedings), every party and any other person that the court may direct. The applicant must then file a certificate of service within 7 days.

Applications without notice

8.65 Where the court has dealt with an application made without notice and made an order, whether granting or dismissing the application, the applicant must, as soon as practicable or within such period as the court may direct, serve a copy of the application notice, the court's order and any evidence filed with the application on the respondent, the parties and any other peron as the court may direct.[55] A person affected by the order may ask for it to be reconsidered.[56]

Interim remedies

8.66 The court may grant an interim injunction, declaration or any other interim order it considers appropriate. Unless the court orders otherwise, a person on whom a new application is served or who is given notice of such an application may not apply for an interim remedy before filing an acknowledgment of service or notification.

---

[54] COPR 2007, rr 77–82. Practice Directions deal with such applications (PD 10A), and also urgent and interim applications (PD 10B).

[55] COPR 2007, r 81.

[56] COPR 2007, r 89.

Dealing with applications

8.67 COPR 2007, Part 12[57] explains how the court deals with applications. As soon as practicable after any application has been issued the court considers how to deal with it and may do so at a hearing or without a hearing. In considering whether it is necessary to hold a hearing, the court has regard to:

(1)   the nature of the proceedings and the orders sought;

(2)   whether the application is opposed by a person who appears to the court to have an interest in matters relating to the incapacitated person's best interests;

(3)   whether the application involves a substantial dispute of fact;

(4)   the complexity of the facts and the law;

(5)   any wider public interest in the proceedings;

(6)   the circumstances of the incapacitated person and of any party, in particular, as to whether their rights would be adequately protected if a hearing were not held;

(7)   whether the parties agree that the court should dispose of the application without a hearing; and

(8)   any other matter specified in the relevant Practice Direction.

8.68 Where the court considers that a hearing is necessary, it gives notice of the date to the parties and any other person it directs and will state what is to be dealt with at the hearing, including whether the matter is to be disposed of at that hearing.

Directions

8.69 The court may give directions in writing or set a date for a directions hearing and do anything else required by a Practice Direction. The rule sets out a long list of things the court might do, including requiring a report, joining or removing parties, and setting a timetable (eg for disclosure of documents and witness statements). In fact the court may give directions at any time on its own initiative or on the application of a party.

8.70 The court will always be concerned to approach a case in a way that ensure that it is heard as quickly as possible and having regard to proportionality. Thus, it will carefully scrutinise requests for expert evidence, limit disclosure only to the documents required and impose a timetable. As stated above, the Ad Hoc Rules Committee is looking at the whole case management process and it is likely that changes will be made to achieve these aims especially as there have been examples of cases where the costs have been wholly disproportionate to the issues in dispute.[58]

---

[57]   COPR 2007, rr 84–89. Practice Directions deal with the exercise of the jurisdiction by certain judges (PD 12A) and the procedure for disputing the court's jurisdiction (PD 12B).

[58]   See *Cases A and B (Court of Protection: Delay and Costs)* [2014] EWCOP 48.

Allocation

8.71   The court will also consider whether the application is of a type that must under a Practice Direction be dealt with by a particular level of judge and generally who is the best judge to hear a case.

Disputing the court's jurisdiction

8.72   A person who wishes to dispute the court's jurisdiction or argue that the court should not exercise its jurisdiction may apply to the court at any time for an appropriate order. The appropriate form should be used and the application must be supported by evidence. The consequence may be the setting aside of the original application, the discharge of any order made and a stay of the proceedings.

Hearing the incapacitated person

8.73   It has already been noted that the new r 3A obliges the court to consider how to involve P in a case. Outside whether P should be a party or not, however, the court will readily agree if appropriate to hear P or to allow P to observe the proceedings[59] or take part in some other meaningful way by allowing P to address the court or write a letter to the judge.

Reconsideration

8.74   Where the court makes an order without a hearing or without notice to any person who is affected by it, that order must contain a statement of the right to apply for reconsideration. A party or person affected by the order (including the incapacitated person) may then apply, within 21 days of service or such other period as the court may direct, for reconsideration of the order. The court will reconsider the order without a hearing or arrange a hearing for this purpose, and may affirm, set aside or vary the order. Any judge of the court may do this, including the judge who made the first decision, but any further challenge must be by appeal.

Hearings

8.75   The court is anxious not to exclude any person with a legitimate interest but also conscious that personal information concerning the incapacitated individual is to be discussed and there should not be any unnecessary intrusion into this person's right to privacy. COPR 2007, Pt 13[60] deals with hearings, which are to be in private unless the court orders otherwise for the whole or part of the hearing, in which event it may exclude any person, or class of persons, from attending. A private hearing is a hearing which only the parties, their legal representatives, the incapacitated person, any litigation friend and

---

[59]   See, for example, *London Borough of Redbridge v G, C and F* [2014] EWHC 485 (COP).
[60]   COPR 2007, rr 90–93. A Practice Direction (PD 4B) deals with the privacy of hearings and reporting restrictions.

court officers are entitled to attend, but the judge may authorise other persons to attend or exclude any person from attending in whole or in part.

8.76 The court may also impose restrictions on the publication of any information or the identity of any party (including the incapacitated person even if not a party), witness or other person. Conversely, the court may make an order authorising the publication of information. Such orders may be made only where it appears to the court that there is good reason for doing so.

8.77 How formal should hearings be? Options include the formality of a courtroom trial, the relative informality of a chambers hearing or around the table conference. The proceedings are now recorded so transcripts can be obtained where appropriate.[61] Telephone conferences and video links may be utilised as part of the hearing process.[62] Should evidence be taken on oath? Should the public be admitted and how far should the existing rules on publishing case reports be extended? These issues are now the subject of debate and it is likely that further changes will occur.

Types of case

8.78 One of the challenges faced by the court is how to approach the different types of cases. A judge can be confronted with heavily contested personal welfare cases involving medical or ethical issues that require careful deliberation, disputes between public authorities and families about P's care and residence or about financial management and investment of P's property and money and who is to be responsible for financial management. Cases can involve the difficult issue of deprivation of liberty and disputes surrounding Enduring and Lasting Powers of Attorney.

Moreover, some cases raise public law issues which overlap with the Administrative Court and others may interface with other jurisdictions such as personal injury claims.

All this challenges the court to ensure the right judge hears the case and to ensure that the case is properly managed.

Evidence

8.79 COPR 2007, Part 14[63] and several Practice Directions deal with the delivery of evidence. In contrast to the regimes for civil and family proceedings, which have express statutory provisions concerning the admissibility of hearsay evidence, neither the MCA 2005 nor the COPR 2007 directly refer to hearsay

---

[61]   This also protects the judge from allegations of inappropriate behaviour by a disaffected party.
[62]   There should be consistency so these facilities need to be available at all regional hearing centres.
[63]   COPR 2007, rr 94–118. The Practice Directions deal with written evidence (PD 14A); depositions (PD 14B); fees for examiners (PD 4C); witness summons (PD 14D); and s 49 reports (PD 4E).

evidence. Nevertheless, it has been held that proceedings in the Court of Protection fall within the wide definition of 'civil proceedings' under the Civil Evidence Act 1995, s 11 and hearsay evidence will be admissible in accordance with the provisions of that Act.[64]

Admissions

8.80 A party may admit the truth of the whole or part of another party's case by giving notice in writing, and the court may allow a party to amend or withdraw an admission.

Witnesses' evidence

8.81 The court may control the evidence by giving directions as to the issues on which it is required, the nature of the evidence and the way in which the evidence is to be placed before the court. In so doing it may exclude evidence that would otherwise be admissible, allow or limit cross-examination and admit such evidence, whether written or oral, as it thinks fit. The court may admit such evidence, whether written or oral as it thinks fit[65] and admit, accept and act upon such information, whether oral or written from P as the court considers sufficient whether or not it would be admissible in a court of law apart from under the COPR 2007.[66] The court may allow a witness to give evidence through a video link or by other communication technology.

8.82 A witness statement is a written statement of the evidence which that person would be allowed to give orally, and it must contain a statement of truth and be in proper form.[67] A party may not rely upon written evidence unless it has been duly filed, or this is expressly permitted by the Rules or a Practice Direction or the court gives permission. The court will give directions about the service of witness statements including the order in which they are to be served. A witness giving oral evidence at the final hearing may, if there is good reason for this and the court permits, amplify his or her witness statement and give evidence in relation to new matters which have arisen since the witness statement was made.

8.83 The court may allow or direct any party to issue a witness summons requiring the person named in it to attend before the court and give oral evidence or produce any document to the court. Provision is made in COPR 2007 for applications of this nature. Where a party has access to information which is not reasonably available to the other party, the court may direct that party to prepare and file a document recording the information.

---

[64] See the decision of McFarlane J in *London Borough of Enfield v SA* [2010] EWHC 196 (Admin).

[65] COPR 2007, r 95.

[66] COPR 2007, r 95(e).

[67] In some instances an affidavit may be required. A witness summary may be permitted to be served where for some reason the statement is going to be late.

Depositions

8.84 A party may apply for an order for a person (the 'deponent') to be examined on oath before a judge or other person nominated by the court prior to the hearing. Documents may be ordered to be produced at such examination. Provision is made in COPR 2007 for applications of this nature. The resulting deposition may be put in evidence at a hearing unless the court orders otherwise. There are further provisions concerned with taking evidence outside the jurisdiction.[68]

Reports

8.85 Where the court orders a report pursuant to MCA 2005, s 49, it is the duty of the person who is required to make the report to help the court on the matters within his or her expertise. COPR 2007 spells out further the duty of this person to:

(1) contact or seek to interview such persons as he or she thinks appropriate or as the court directs;

(2) ascertain what the incapacitated person's wishes and feelings are, and the beliefs and values that would be likely to influence him or her if he or she had the capacity to make a decision in relation to the matter to which the application relates;

(3) describe the incapacitated person's circumstances; and

(4) address such other matters as are required in a Practice Direction or as the court may direct.

8.86 The court may, on the application of any party, permit written questions to be put to the maker of the report and send a copy of the replies to the parties and to such other persons as the court may direct. Unless the court directs otherwise, the maker of the report may examine and take copies of any document in the court records.[69]

Experts

8.87 COPR 2007, Part 15[70] deals with expert evidence. In this context an expert is one who has been instructed other than pursuant to MCA 2005, s 49 to give or prepare evidence for the purpose of proceedings. No person may file expert evidence unless the court or a Practice Direction permits, or if it is filed with the permission or application form[71] and is evidence that the incapacitated person is a person who lacks capacity to make a decision in relation to the

---

[68] See generally PD 14B.

[69] See generally PD 14E.

[70] COPR 2007, rr 119–131. A Practice Direction (PD 15A) deals with expert evidence.

[71] COPR 2007, r 64(a) requires the applicant to file any evidence upon which he or she wishes to rely with the application form, and r 54 requires certain documents to be filed with the application for permission form.

matter to which the application relates or as to his or her best interests. An applicant may only rely upon such evidence to the extent and for the purposes that the court allows.

8.88 Expert evidence is generally given in a written report. It is the duty of the expert to help the court on the matters within his or her expertise, and expert evidence will be restricted to that which is reasonably required (a lower threshold than the requirement of necessity in family proceedings) to resolve the proceedings. When a party applies for directions as to expert evidence he or she must identify the field and, where practicable, the expert and also provide any other material information about the expert with a draft letter of instruction. The court when giving directions will confirm such matters and also deal with service of the report on the parties and on persons.

8.89 In a simple or non-controversial situation a single expert may be allowed or appointed. Where each party instructs their own expert there may be a direction for these experts to communicate with one another and produce a joint statement of issues on which they are agreed and issues on which they disagree, with reasons. There are also provisions for 'single joint experts' who will be instructed by the parties jointly. An expert may request directions from the court to clarify his or her function, and the court may allow the parties to put written questions to an expert on his or her report. Where a party has disclosed an expert's report, any party may use this as evidence at any hearing in the proceedings.

8.90 The expert's report must state the substance of all material instructions, whether written or oral, on the basis of which it was written and conclude with a statement that the expert understands his or her duty to the court and has complied with that duty. Unless the court otherwise directs, and subject to any final costs order, the instructing party is responsible for the payment of the expert's fees and expenses, including the cost of answering questions put by any other party.

Disclosure

8.91 Disclosure of documents means stating that documents exist or have existed, and is dealt with in COPR 2007, Part 16.[72] A party's duty to disclose documents by producing a list is limited to documents which are or have been in his or her control.[73] The list must indicate separately the documents in respect of which the party claims a right or duty to withhold inspection and those that are no longer in his or her control, stating what has happened to them. There is a need to balance the incapacitated persons right to privacy against the need for adequate disclosure to enable best interests to be addressed. For example, in property and affairs applications the court must consider whether it is necessary to disclose the contents of the last Will.

---

[72] COPR 2007, rr 132–139.
[73] This means that he or she has or has had physical possession of them or the right to inspect or take copies of them.

8.92 The court may either on its own initiative or on the application of a party make an order to give general or specific disclosure. Any party to whom the order applies is under a continuing duty to provide such disclosure until the proceedings are concluded. General disclosure relates not only to documents that are to be relied upon but also to those that adversely affect the party's own case, or adversely affect or support another party's case. Specific disclosure relates to specified documents or classes of documents and may include carrying out a search to the extent stated in the order. There is no equivalent to the provision in the Civil Procedure Rules 1998 for pre-action disclosure.

Inspection

8.93 A party has a right to inspect any document disclosed to him or her except where it is no longer in the control of the party who disclosed it, or the party disclosing the document has a right or duty to withhold inspection of it. An opportunity must be given for inspection and a copy of the document may be requested on payment of reasonable copying costs. A timetable is usually laid down for this process. Where documents are withheld the party wishing to inspect may apply to the court to decide whether this should be upheld. A party may not without the permission of the court rely upon any document which he or she fails to disclose or in respect of which he or she fails to permit inspection.

Litigation friends and representatives

8.94 A party will normally need a litigation friend to conduct the proceedings on his or her behalf if he or she is a child[74] or a 'protected party' (ie lacks capacity to conduct the proceedings) although in *Re X (Deprivation of Liberty) Number 2*[75] the court stated that there is no fundamental principle of law that dictates that P must have a litigation friend. It is simply that court rules demand it. COPR 2007, Part 17[76] and a Practice Direction make detailed provision for this. A person may act as a litigation friend if he or she satisfies two conditions, namely he or she can fairly and competently conduct proceedings on behalf of the incapacitated party and he or she has no interests adverse to those of that person.

8.95 The incapacitated person, if made a party, may also need a litigation friend but this will generally be the Official Solicitor because the persons who might otherwise provide such support are likely to be parties themselves or have an adverse interest. In other words, a person who should really be a party may not hijack the incapacitated person's case.

8.96 The court has full control over the appointment and removal of litigation friends. It may make an order appointing the Official Solicitor or some other person to act as a litigation friend either on its own initiative or on the

---

[74] The court may allow a child to proceed without a litigation friend if of sufficient understanding.
[75] [2014] EWCOP 37.
[76] COPR 2007, rr 140–149 and PD 17A. Part 17 was completely amended on 1 July 2015.

application of any person, but only with the consent of the person to be appointed. A deputy with the power to conduct legal proceedings on the protected party's behalf is entitled to be the litigation friend of that party but otherwise, if no one has been appointed by the court, a person who wishes to act as a litigation friend must file a certificate of suitability and serve this on the child or protected party. The certificate states that he or she satisfies the above two conditions.

8.97 Specific provision is made for the situation where the appointment of a litigation friend comes to an end and where the incapacitated person who is the subject of proceedings ceases to lack capacity.

Consequent upon the introduction of the r 3A representative, the rules have been amended in Part 17 to address the appointment of the representative. The court must be satisfied that the representative can fairly and competently discharge his or her functions on behalf of P.[77] The court now has power to direct a person may not act as a representative.[78]

Representation

8.98 The procedure to be followed when there is a change of solicitor is dealt with in COPR 2007, Part 18.[79] A notice of the change must be filed with the court and served on all other parties, and the new address for service must be stated. A solicitor may apply for an order declaring that he or she has ceased to be the solicitor acting for a party.

Costs

8.99 The costs of and incidental to all proceedings are in the court's discretion but the MCA 2005 requires the Rules to make detailed provision for regulating those costs.[80] The court has full power to determine by whom and to what extent the costs of any proceedings are to be paid, and to disallow costs or order the legal or other representatives[81] concerned to meet the whole or part of any wasted costs. 'Wasted costs' means any costs incurred by a party:

(1) as a result of any improper, unreasonable or negligent act or omission on the part of any legal or other representative or any employee of such a representative; or

(2) which, in the light of any such act or omission occurring after they were incurred, the court considers it is unreasonable to expect that party to pay.

---

[77] COPR 2007, r 147.
[78] COPR 2007, r 148B.
[79] COPR 2007, rr 150–154. A Practice Direction (PD 18A) deals with change of solicitor.
[80] MCA 2005, s 55.
[81] This expression means any person exercising a right of audience or right to conduct litigation on behalf of a party to proceedings.

This enables unreasonable conduct by representatives to be controlled by costs sanctions.

8.100 COPR 2007 may make provision:[82]

(1) as to the way in which, and funds from which, fees and costs are to be paid;

(2) for charging fees and costs upon the estate of the person to whom the proceedings relate; and

(3) for the payment of fees and costs within a specified time of the death of the person to whom the proceedings relate or the conclusion of the proceedings.

8.101 A charge on the estate of a person created by this provision does not cause any interest of the person in any property to fail or determine or to be prevented from recommencing.

8.102 COPR 2007, Part 19[83] and a Practice Direction deal with costs and incorporate much of the regime for assessment of the CPR which is accordingly reproduced in Part IV of this volume (including the Practice Direction on costs).

The general rule

8.103 Where the proceedings concern the incapacitated person's property and affairs, the general rule is that the costs of the proceedings or of that part of the proceedings that concerns his or her property and affairs shall be paid by him or her or charged to his or her estate. Where the proceedings concern the incapacitated person's personal welfare, the general rule is that there will be no order as to the costs of the proceedings or of that part of the proceedings that concerns his or her personal welfare. Where the proceedings concern both property and affairs and personal welfare, the court, insofar as practicable, will apportion the costs as between the respective issues.

8.104 The court may depart from the general rule if the circumstances so justify, and in deciding whether departure is justified the court will have regard to all the circumstances, including the conduct of the parties, whether a party has succeeded on part of his or her case, even if he or she has not been wholly successful, and the role of any public body involved in the proceedings. The conduct of the parties includes conduct before, as well as during, the proceedings and whether it was reasonable for a party to raise, pursue or contest a particular issue. Also the manner in which a party has made or responded to an application or a particular issue, and whether a party who has succeeded in his or her application or response to an application, in whole or in

---

[82] MCA 2005, s 56.
[83] COPR 2007, rr 155–168. The Practice Directions deal with costs generally (PD 19A) and fixed costs (PD 19B).

part, exaggerated any matter contained in his or her application or response. Costs can even be awarded against non-parties but appropriate procedures must be followed.

Assessment

8.105 The court may order fixed costs or the payment of a contribution to the costs. It may also where appropriate carry out a summary assessment of the costs, but where the court orders costs to be assessed by way of detailed assessment, this takes place in the High Court. Where the court orders that a deputy, donee or attorney is entitled to remuneration out of the incapacitated person's estate for discharging his or her functions, the court may make such order as it thinks fit, including an order that he or she be paid a fixed amount, he or she be paid at a specified rate or the amount of the remuneration shall be determined in accordance with the schedule of fees set out in the relevant Practice Direction. Alternatively, the court may order a detailed assessment of such remuneration by a costs officer.

Fees

8.106 It has been Government policy that the existing Court of Protection (like the other courts) be self-funding, raising its income from court fees, although some subsidy is necessary for those who cannot afford the fees. Such subsidy is likely to be enhanced and increased for the new enlarged jurisdiction because many applications relate to situations where there is no money available or involved.

8.107 The Lord Chancellor may with the consent of the Treasury by order prescribe fees payable in respect of anything dealt with by the court.[84] Such order may (and does) contain provision as to scales or rates of fees, exemptions from and reductions in fees and remission of fees in whole or in part.[85] Before making an order the Lord Chancellor must consult the President and Vice-President and the Senior Judge of the Court of Protection. Such steps as are reasonably practicable must then be taken to bring information about fees to the attention of persons likely to have to pay them. The fees will be recoverable summarily as a civil debt.

Appeals

8.108 MCA 2005 provides some flexibility as to how appeals may be dealt with.[86] COPR 2007, Part 20[87] makes detailed provision for appeals. Judges are defined by reference to tiers. Tier 1 comprises district judges and certain first

---

[84] MCA 2005, s 54. Following the constitutional reforms this remains the responsibility of the Lord Chancellor.
[85] See Court of Protection Fees Order 2007, SI 2007/1745.
[86] MCA 2005, s 53.
[87] COPR 2007, rr 169–182. A Practice Direction (PD 20A) deals with Appeals.

tier tribunal judges, Tier 2 comprises the Senior Judge, circuit judges and Upper Tribunal Judges and Tier 3 are High Court Judges. Appeal is normally to the next tier of judge.

8.109 The court may deal with an appeal or any part of an appeal at a hearing or without a hearing, having regard to the same matters as on reconsideration of orders made without a hearing or without notice to a person.[88] An appeal will generally be limited to a review of the decision of the first instance judge although there is some discretion. The appeal judge has all the powers of the first instance judge whose decision is being appealed and may affirm, set aside or vary any order made by the first instance judge, refer any issue to that judge for determination or order a new hearing as well as making a costs order. But authorisation is not limited to cases concerning medical treatment and may extend to decisions which would have the effect of depriving a person who lacked capacity to consent of their liberty.

Permission to appeal

8.110 COPR 2007 provides that permission is required to appeal against a decision of the court (other than an order for committal to prison) and prescribes how this is obtained, the requirements to be satisfied and the considerations to be taken into account. An application for permission to appeal may be made by an 'appellant's notice' or a 'respondent's notice' to the first instance judge or the appeal judge, and where it is refused by the first instance judge, a further application for permission may be made to a specified higher judge. There are time-limits but these may be varied on application.

8.111 Permission to appeal will be granted only where the court considers that the appeal would have a real prospect of success, or there is some other compelling reason why the appeal should be heard. Where a higher judge of the court makes a decision on an appeal, no appeal may be made to the Court of Appeal from that decision unless the Court of Appeal considers that the appeal would raise an important point of principle or practice, or there is some other compelling reason for the Court of Appeal to hear it.

Enforcement

8.112 The court's powers of enforcement are much more extensive than may at first appear. The court has in connection with its jurisdiction the same powers, rights, privileges and authority as the High Court,[89] which means that it may fine or commit to prison for contempt, grant injunctions, summons witnesses and order production of evidence. COPR 2007, Part 21 makes further provision,[90] while the relevant Practice Direction (PD 21A) and Practice Guidance notes deals with contempt of court. Applications for enforcement

---

[88]   See COPR 2007, r 89.
[89]   MCA 2005, s 47(1).
[90]   COPR 2007, rr 183–194.

may be made and the CPR relating to third party debt orders and charging orders apply. The rules have now been amended to ensure that the enforcement provisions incorporate the latest version of the CPR which was extensively amended recently.

8.113 The court may direct that a penal notice is to be attached to any order warning the person on whom the copy of the order is served that disobeying the order would be a contempt of court punishable by imprisonment or a fine. An application relating to the committal of a person for contempt of court can be made to a judge (which includes a district judge) by filing an application notice, stating the grounds of the application, and must be supported by an affidavit made in accordance with the relevant Practice Direction. COPR 2007 makes further provision. In addition, the court may make an order for committal on its own initiative against a person guilty of contempt of court, which may include misbehaviour in the face of the court.

Transitional provisions

8.114 These are to be found in COPR 2007, Part 22.[91] They include the transition from receiver to deputy and the nomination of officers to deal with such matters thereby implementing MCA 2005, Sch 5, Part 1.

Miscellaneous provisions

8.115 Provision is made in COPR 2007, Part 23[92] for the giving of security by deputies, references to the court by the Public Guardian following objections to the registration of an enduring power of attorney and disposal of property where an incapacitated person ceases to lack capacity. Practice Directions deal with certain objections to the registration of enduring powers of attorney (PD 23A) and the procedure where 'P' ceases to lack capacity or dies (PD 23B).

PRACTICAL POINTS

The workload

Volume of cases

8.116 With a wide range of cases relating not only to financial management but also to social welfare and health care – in fact the entire range of personal decision-making for adults who lack capacity, the consequence is an ever increasing volume of cases for the Court of Protection to cope with which shows no sign of abatement. The withdrawal of legal aid in family work and a

---

[91] COPR 2007, rr 195–199. Practice Directions deal with transitional provisions (PD 22A); transitory provisions (PD 22B); and certain specified appeals (PD 22C).
[92] COPR 2007, rr 200–202.

general downturn in the economy means that more solicitors and barristers are looking to the Court of Protection as a source of work which is to be encouraged.

The court also faces a major challenge (if not its biggest administrative challenge) following the decision in *P v Cheshire West and Chester Council*[93] and the need for more types of situations involving deprivation of liberty to be authorised by the court. No exact figure is known for the likely number of applications but tens of thousands have been mentioned. This prompted the President to convene a hearing to consider the best process to manage such cases (see *Re X and others (Deprivation of Liberty)*[94] and *Re X and others (Deprivation of Liberty) (Number 2)*.[95] As a result, a streamlined *Re X* procedure was developed, although parts of this are the subject of an appeal to the Court of Appeal although as explained in Chapter 4; the appeal process has brought yet further challenge to the court.

Cases under the court's jurisdiction

8.117   The following are examples of situations that the court can encounter and illustrate the need for local dispute resolution by a nominated district or circuit judge as to the best interests of the person lacking capacity.

- *Residential care dispute* – Dispute between a son and daughter who live some distance apart as to which residential care or nursing home their mother should move to. She has Alzheimer's disease and is incapable of participating in the decision but has adequate funds to meet the fees.

- *Contact disputes* – There may be a preliminary issue as to whether the adults in the following examples have capacity to decide whom they wish to have contact with. The court may wish to decide this first and only proceed to an intrusive best interests inquiry if capacity to make the decision is lacking.
    - (a)   A daughter from an Asian background has married outside her ethnic origins and adopted a way of life that results in her being cut off by her family. She still wishes to visit her learning disabled brother but the family prevent this.
    - (b)   Older parents with a learning disabled son became involved in a bitter divorce which results in father being excluded from the matrimonial home where mother continues to care for this son. A daughter who has sided with father is then denied access to her brother.

---

[93]   [2014] UKSC 19.
[94]   [2014] EWCOP 25.
[95]   [2014] EWCOP 37.

- *Adult care dispute* – A child with learning disabilities has been placed in care under the Children Act 1989 and the social workers involved are concerned about the role of the parents upon the child attaining majority.[96]

- *Adult protection issues* – Social services respond to allegations of abuse by moving a senile elderly person into a care home and restricting access by family carers who then challenge this intervention.[97]

- *Activities* – A charity providing outdoor adventure holidays for adults with learning disabilities wishes to take an individual on a mountaineering course but mother (who may be over-protective) thinks it is too dangerous and objects. Care workers and a personal advocate support this opportunity for personal development. The charity seeks reassurance that this is in the best interests of the individual so that it would only be vulnerable to legal proceedings if negligent (and not irrespective of fault in the event of an accident).[98]

- *Education* – Father wants his 19-year-old son with severe learning disabilities to attend a residential training college and has arranged funding. Mother prefers him to live with her but has made no arrangements for his daytime activities. The local authority has offered a place at the local training centre and is very concerned that mother will not allow him to attend. A local nominated judge could see the parties, consider welfare reports and make a decision (if an attempt at mediation did not result in the deadlock being resolved).

- *Minor medical decisions* – Parents wish to arrange for their 23-year-old daughter with Down's syndrome to have some dental treatment which will improve her appearance but is not otherwise necessary. She appears to want this treatment but there is doubt as to whether she can legally consent so the dentist is unwilling to proceed, perhaps because there is some element of risk. A local nominated judge could resolve this.

- *Sexual relationships* – Care workers are concerned as to whether a resident with learning disabilities being supported in a group living arrangement is competent to enter into a sexual relationship with another resident. They seek a declaration from the court.[99]

Integration with other courts

Judicial support

8.118 Historically there has been little liaison between the former Court of Protection and the civil or family courts, although there were occasions when

---

[96] Such cases have become quite common.
[97] Ideally the local authority should initiate proceedings to justify its intervention but there have been cases where the family members have had to apply to the court.
[98] This type of activity may well be covered under MCA 2005, s 5 and not require Court of Protection authority.
[99] The court does not have power to consent on a person's behalf to a sexual relationship: MCA 2005, s 27(1)(b).

one must refer to the other. Now that there are generic judges spread throughout the country nominated to sit in the new Court of Protection there is proving to be more integration of an informal nature, with judicial colleagues seeking support and guidance on capacity issues and cases raising issues that require Court of Protection input. Cases with a capacity element may be transferred to, or listed before, the local nominated judge because of their additional expertise. For example:

- *Financial remedies* – Following a divorce between an elderly couple financial claims are made which include the future of the former matrimonial home. At a financial dispute resolution hearing the husband makes proposals under which the wife may remain in the home for life. The lawyers involved agree that these proposals are more beneficial to the wife than she is likely to achieve at a contested hearing. She cannot grasp the implications and refuses to accept. The district judge is in a dilemma because if she persists in refusing the offer she is in danger of paying all the costs and losing the home. The judge questions whether she lacks mental capacity and should be treated as a 'protected party' with a 'next friend' appointed to conduct the proceedings on her behalf (often the Official Solicitor), but she refuses to be medically examined. A nominated judge to whom the case is transferred could tackle all the issues and resolve them locally with minimum delay and expense.

- *Possession* – A landlord or mortgagee brings a possession claim for non-payment of sums due and the elderly tenant or mortgagor attends but appears confused and unable to cope. Doubts arise as to mental capacity and the judge is in great difficulty knowing how to proceed. If this defendant is a protected party a litigation friend must be appointed but a separate application would have to be made to the Court of Protection for the appointment of a deputy. The case could be referred to a nominated judge who could deal with the capacity issue, the need for practical support and the merits of the possession claim all in the same series of hearings, invoking the jurisdiction of the Court of Protection if necessary.

- *Contract* – A local shopkeeper sues a customer with learning disabilities who has been placed 'in the community' for non-payment of bills for normal provisions. Support from social services (who set up this living arrangement) has evaporated with everyone passing the buck. A district judge dealing with the matter as a 'small claim' in the County Court will be in difficulty, but could pass the case to a nominated judge who would have the powers (under a dual jurisdiction if necessary) and experience to deal with it.

Dual jurisdiction

8.119 There are situations where it might be helpful for a nominated judge to sit in a dual capacity, namely in the Court of Protection and also the civil or family court. The following examples illustrate both the need for local dispute resolution and an overlap with the existing role of the civil or family courts:

(1) Following a divorce between elderly parents there is a dispute as to which parent is to continue to care for their 40-year-old mentally disabled child and the future of the matrimonial home may depend on this. *A nominated district judge could simultaneously deal with the care issue under the new jurisdiction and the ancillary relief claims in the County Court, these being interdependent.*[100]

(2) There is a dispute between parents relating to contact by father with their two children, the older of whom has learning disabilities but is by now an adult. *An application in the County Court under the Children Act 1989 relating to the younger child could be linked with an application to the Court of Protection in respect of the older child and heard together by a nominated district judge.*

(3) Older parents with a learning disabled adult son became involved in a bitter divorce which results in father being excluded from the matrimonial home where mother continues to care for the son. A daughter who has sided with father is then denied access to her brother and seeks to establish that it is in his best interests to see her on a regular basis. *A nominated district judge could resolve the issue under the new jurisdiction in the context of the divorce proceedings thereby having an overview of the whole family situation.*

(4) A local authority has made a decision about the placement of an incapacitated adult, and it may be necessary, if that decision is to be challenged, to proceed both by way of proceedings for judicial review and a best interests claim under the new Court of Protection jurisdiction. *A nominated High Court judge could deal with both matters together.*

8.120 If a case requires transfer in whole or part to the Court of Protection, if a judge is also nominated to sit in the Court of Protection, he can reconstitute himself as a Court of Protection judge and make appropriate orders to bring the case within that court. He may also dispense with the need to make an application. Some judges prefer an application to be made although the overriding objective would suggest that the most economical and expeditious method of transfer of a case should be adopted especially when the same judge will continue to hear it. If a case is being transferred by a judge who is not nominated to sit in the Court of Protection, he can order that the case is transferred and the court file will be sent to the Court of Protection's main registry in the normal way of transfer of any case. On arrival, a judge will give appropriate directions.

---

[100] If the child had not yet attained majority the residence and ancillary relief claims would have been amalgamated in the County Court.

CHAPTER 9

THE PUBLIC GUARDIAN AND SUPPORTING SERVICES

INTRODUCTION

9.1   The mental capacity jurisdiction, and in particular the Court of Protection, is supported by a range of statutory and other bodies, and other professional individuals. This chapter considers the nature of such resources and their purpose or role.

THE PUBLIC GUARDIAN[1]

9.2   The Mental Capacity Act 2005[2] (MCA 2005) established a new a statutory office-holder appointed by the Lord Chancellor[3] and known as the Public Guardian.

Office of the Public Guardian[4]

9.3   The Lord Chancellor[5] may, after consulting the Public Guardian, provide him with such officers and staff, or enter into such contracts with other persons for the provision (by them or their subcontractors) of officers, staff or services, as the Lord Chancellor thinks necessary for the proper discharge of the Public Guardian's functions. Any functions of the Public Guardian may, to the extent authorised by him or her, be performed by any of his officers. So the Office of the Public Guardian ('OPG'), an agency of the Ministry of Justice, is itself recognised by and funded under the authority of Parliament.[6]

---

[1]   See www.justice.gov.uk/about/opg. For the background to this Office see Chapter 1 at para 1.162.1.
[2]   MCA 2005, s 57.
[3]   For the meaning in this context see Chapter 7 at **7.1**ff.
[4]   The assistance of Joan Goulbourn from the Office of the Public Guardian with the material under this heading is gratefully acknowledged.
[5]   For the meaning in this context see Chapter 7 at **7.1**ff.
[6]   MCA 2005, s 57(4), (5).

Functions

9.4   The Public Guardian has the following basic functions:[7]

(1)   establishing and maintaining a register of lasting powers of attorney;[8]

(2)   establishing and maintaining a register of orders appointing deputies;

(3)   supervising deputies appointed by the court;

(4)   directing a Court of Protection Visitor to visit (i) a donee of a lasting power of attorney, (ii) a deputy appointed by the court, or (iii) the person granting the power of attorney or for whom the deputy is appointed, and to make a report to the Public Guardian on such matters as he or she may direct;

(5)   receiving security which the court requires a person to give for the discharge of his or her functions;

(6)   receiving reports from donees of lasting powers of attorney and deputies appointed by the court;

(7)   reporting to the court on such matters relating to proceedings under MCA 2005 as the court requires;

(8)   dealing with representations (including complaints) about the way in which a donee of a lasting power of attorney or a deputy appointed by the court is exercising his or her powers;

(9)   publishing, in any manner the Public Guardian thinks appropriate, any information he or she thinks appropriate about the discharge of his or her functions.

9.5   These functions thus fall into three categories: registration, supervision and investigation. With the exception of the first one they may be discharged in co-operation with any other person who has functions in relation to the care or treatment of the incapacitated person. The Public Guardian works closely with organisations such as local authorities, care providers and NHS Trusts, and can request information from them under this provision. The Lord Chancellor[9] may by regulations make provision conferring on the Public Guardian other functions in connection with MCA 2005 or in connection with the discharge by the Public Guardian of his or her functions. In particular, regulations may make provision as to:[10]

•   the giving of security by deputies appointed by the court and the enforcement and discharge of security so given;

•   the fees which may be charged by the Public Guardian;

•   the way in which, and funds from which, such fees are to be paid;

---

[7]   MCA 2005, s 58.

[8]   He must also continue the Register of enduring powers of attorney: MCA 2005, Sch 4, Pt 4, para 14.

[9]   For the meaning in this context see Chapter 7 at **7.1**ff.

[10]   MCA 2005, s 58(3) and (4). See Lasting Powers of Attorney, Enduring Powers of Attorney and Public Guardian Regulations 2007, SI 2007/1253.

- exemptions from and reductions in such fees;
- remission of such fees in whole or in part;
- the making of reports to the Public Guardian by deputies appointed by the court and others who are directed by the court to carry out any transaction for a person who lacks capacity.

This provides considerable scope for development of the operation and services of the OPG as experience is gained under the new jurisdiction. In particular it is hoped that the Public Guardian will be able to address some of the abuse that takes place by attorneys and others.

9.6   The OPG may be contacted at:

Office of the Public Guardian

PO Box 16185

Birmingham B2 2WH

DX 744240 Birmingham 79

Tel: 0300 456 0300 (Phone lines are open Monday–Friday 9am–5pm (Except Wednesday 10am–5pm))

Fax: 0870 739 5780

Textphone: 0115 934 2778

Powers

9.7   For the purpose of enabling him to carry out his functions, the Public Guardian may, at all reasonable times, examine and take copies of any health record, any record of (or held by) a local authority and compiled in connection with a social services function and any record held by a person registered under the Care Standards Act 2000, Part 2 so far as the record relates to the client. He (or his officers) may also for that purpose interview the incapacitated person in private.[11] The Public Guardian is empowered to apply to the court of Protection in connection with his functions under the Act in such circumstances as he considers it necessary or appropriate to do so.[12]

Fees

9.8   Annual fees are charged for the supervision of deputies payable annually in arrears on 31 March.[13] Following a Consultation in February 2011, the OPG fee regime has been changed. With effect from 1 October 2011, one flat fee of £320 is being charged under Type I, Type IIa and II supervision and there is a

---

[11]   MCA 2005, s 58(5) and (6).
[12]   2007 Regulations, reg 43.
[13]   Public Guardian (Fees etc) Regulations 2007, SI 2007/2051 and Public Guardian (Fees etc) (Amendment) Regulations 2007, SI 2007/2616.

one-off fee of £100 on the appointment.[14] The fees are revised at intervals and are to be found on the OPG website.[15] There is a fee of £35 for Type III supervision. Each case will be reviewed regularly and the type of supervision allocated may change as circumstances change. Supervision fees will be calculated on a pro-rata basis if:

- there has been more than one type of supervision applied in a 1-year period; or
- supervision has been in place for less than 1 year; or
- the person lacking capacity or the deputy dies. (Fees are payable up to the date of death).

Fees are also charged for the registration of enduring powers of attorney and lasting powers of attorney. In certain circumstances fee exemption or remission may apply.[16]

Annual Report

9.9 The Public Guardian must make an annual report to the Lord Chancellor[17] about the discharge of his or her functions.[18]

The Office of the Public Guardian Board

9.10 The Office of the Public Guardian Board provides strategic leadership on the broad direction for the agency and supports the delivery of the aims and objectives agreed within the Business Plan. It consists of executive and non-executive board members. The Board operates within Ministry of Justice/OPG governance and its members take decisions collectively and not as representatives of any business area or interest.

Panel of Deputies

9.11 OPG maintains a panel of deputies for use by the court in 'last resort' cases; that is, cases where there is no one else willing, suitable, or able to act as deputy. As part of the terms of membership a panel deputy must agree to accept any appointment as deputy at the request of the Court of Protection unless they have a valid reason not to do so. The panel appointed in April 2011 was comprised mainly of solicitors who have deputyship experience and relevant specialist skills. Currently most deputies are family members but the panel is a useful facility especially where there are continuing disputes within the family or there is no one suitable to accept appointment. Panel deputies are generally

---

[14] Previously £800 for Type I and £350 (£175 at lower rate) for Type II. There was no fee for Type III supervision.

[15] See www.gov.uk/government/organisations/office-of-the-public-guardian.

[16] Refer to www.gov.uk/government/publications/deputy-fees-remission-or-exemption.

[17] For the meaning in this context see Chapter 7 at **7.1**ff.

[18] MCA 2005, s 60. The Annual Reports and Accounts are available at: www.justice.gov.uk/publications/corporate-reports/office-of-the-public-guardian.

only appointed for property and affairs because they charge professional fees. Many local authorities also provide deputyship services but on the basis of fixed costs and these services are therefore subsidised.

9.12 In an attempt to widen the pool of potential deputies the Public Guardian launched a consultation in late 2011 on the appointment of not-for-profit organisations as deputies which it has used to inform the recruitment for the refreshment of the panel for 2015. A greater representation of different organisation types on the panel increases the options available to the court ensuring that the most appropriate deputy can be appointed in each case. For example, in straightforward cases it may be more appropriate for the person's affairs to be managed by a deputy who is not a solicitor and whose charges would therefore be lower, or the person who lacks capacity may benefit from having a deputy who can provide advocacy and support services as part of their package of services.

Challenges ahead

9.13 The OPG is fundamentally different in status and functions from its predecessor, the PGO, despite a similarity of name. It has a statutory existence with supervisory and regulatory functions.[19] It is hoped that the Public Guardian (through his or her senior staff to whom he or she can delegate his or her powers) will act fearlessly and independently, becoming a mediator and problem-solver as well as performing administrative functions and investigating abuse.

Public Guardian's role

9.14 The Public Guardian has three distinct roles: administrative, supervisory and policy-making. He or she must:

(1) be a supporter of incapacitated persons and their families and carers;
(2) be a supporter of good attorneys and deputies;
(3) provide guidance on, and as part of the investigation process monitor standards in decision-making for vulnerable adults that everyone is expected to follow;
(4) establish procedures for investigating allegations of abuse; and
(5) work with local authorities and other agencies who have an interest in safeguarding vulnerable adults, such as the Police, Care Quality Commission, Care and Social Services Inspectorate Wales, and regulators such as the Solicitors Regulation Authority.

The new OPG places emphasis on promoting the concept of the assumption of capacity and being dedicated to ensure that appointed decision makers only

---

[19] It also provided the administrative arm of the Court of Protection until this function was transferred to HM Courts Service (now HM Courts and Tribunals Service) on 1 April 2009.

become involved in decisions when necessary and always act in the best interests of the client. Partnerships must be developed with social services and health authorities and agencies and also those charitable organisations working in this area.

Dispute resolution

9.15 OPG is looking at ways in which it can establish its own dispute resolution procedures. It must not be overlooked that the objective is to address the best interests of the incapacitated individual rather than resolve disputes between other persons, especially when these persons are not addressing this individual's welfare. In the case of many dysfunctional families the issue becomes control over rather than the welfare of the vulnerable member and involving an outsider may be the appropriate solution. A pilot mediation scheme is running until April 2015, following which OPG will evaluate the results and merits of continuing such a scheme.

Investigating abuse

9.16 An Investigations Unit was established at the PGO and lessons were learnt as to how such a unit may best function. The OPG has drawn on this experience. Internal procedures for referring cases have been developed and other procedures agreed for external referrals. A protocol has been agreed by the OPG with local authorities on how to work with them to safeguard vulnerable adults. Publicity is necessary if this is to function effectively and a dedicated helpline is in place, together with a programme for raising awareness. Cases may be referred by safeguarding staff in local authorities and OPG has consulted with the Association of Directors of Social Services on a Working Protocol. Referrals may now extend beyond financial abuse and include other forms of abuse. If OPG does not have the jurisdiction to investigate a case it will ensure that the person raising the concern is signposted to the relevant authority or OPG may contact the relevant authority itself. In some instances a new deputy will be appointed following an application to the court and instructed to take appropriate action. The Public Guardian can also apply to the court for an attorney to be removed from acting under an LPA. If this still leaves other attorneys then the LPA will remain in force. If it means that there are no longer any attorneys or replacement attorneys then an application will be made to court to appoint a deputy.

The Public Guardian's jurisdiction is to investigate representations and complaints about the way in which an attorney of an LPA or a deputy appointed by the court is exercising his powers.[20] As LPAs can be registered before the donor loses capacity, the Public Guardian is obliged to consider representations about the actions of an LPA donee even if the donor has capacity. However, the practice adopted is to firstly investigate the donor's

---

[20]   Under MCA, s 58(1)(h). This is extended to attorneys acting under a registered EPA by Reg 48 of the LPA, EPA and PG Regs.

capacity and ability to address the concerns himself, and the Public Guardian will generally only take forward a full investigation if the donor lacks capacity or is otherwise unable to address the concerns.

Use of technology

9.17 OPG is developing its use of technology as one of MoJ's 'digital exemplars' which form part of the Government's digital by default strategy. In September 2014, OPG published its first digital strategy outlining its programme of transformation up to 2018 and its plans to be a digital by default agency by 2015. In May 2014 a digital service was launched to aid the process of completing the LPA forms. The forms can be completed without the need to enter details multiple times and embedded help and guidance helps users avoid common administrative errors.

Partnerships

9.18 OPG is proactive in developing partnerships. These include working with voluntary and third sector organisations, the legal sector, the Financial Ombudsman, the Financial Conduct Authority, the British Banking Association and individual banks and utility companies. It also works closely with other government departments and agencies including the Department for Work and Pensions, the Department of Health, HM Revenue and Customs, the police and the Criminal Records Bureau.

Funding

9.19 Separate fees are now charged for the work of OPG as distinct from the Court of Protection (as they are now statutorily separate bodies). OPG has a regime of fees in place which ensure that 100% of the costs of the organisation (other than remissions and exemptions) are met from the fees paid. There is a remissions and exemptions policy in place to ensure that those with lower incomes are not eligible to pay fees. At times, OPG has looked to increase its fees to cover the cost of transformation but the fee for registering an LPA is currently lower than it has been at any time since OPG came into being.

Relationship with the Court of Protection

9.20 The Court of Protection deals with disputes that require a hearing and may be the ultimate decision-maker when matters cannot be resolved by the Public Guardian. The court also retains a considerable volume of paper-based decision-making which is to some extent delegated to nominated officers with any challenges being referred to the nominated district judges. Recourse to the court for the resolution of disputes should be regarded as a last resort. The extent to which the Public Guardian may ultimately act on his own initiative will be dictated by decisions of the Court of Protection on references and appeals, and no doubt by the High Court in the event of judicial reviews. But OPG will have a more authoritative role than the former PGO as it is a separate statutorily defined body.

9.21 This enhanced role for the Public Guardian leads to a change in the relationship with the Court of Protection. It was questioned whether, if the OPG was to act independently from the Court of Protection, it should also administer the court in the same way as HM Courts Service administered the civil and criminal courts. There was a need to demonstrate the distinction between administrative and judicial functions and to maintain judicial independence, yet there were significant advantages in maintaining a link between the court and the OPG. Master Lush had identified a need to 'disentangle the close relationship that exists between the Court of Protection and the PGO in a way that achieves a proper distinction between the two organisations, whilst retaining the positive aspects of the present close working arrangements' but the former Chief Executive of the PGO had concerns as to how that close relationship might be maintained.

9.22 The list of functions conferred by MCA 2005 does not expressly include the PGO's previous function of processing originating applications to the Court of Protection. Initially there were two separate administrations, in separate offices within Archway but both under the control of the Public Guardian, with the court having its own staff. The concern that the Public Guardian, who may be a party to court proceedings and appeal orders of the judges, also administered the Court has now been resolved. During 2009 the administration of the court was transferred to HM Courts Service (now HM Courts and Tribunals Service) and much of the work of the OPG has been moved to Birmingham and Nottingham.[21]

Transforming the services of the OPG

9.23 In August 2014 OPG published a consultation 'Transforming the services of the Office of the Public Guardian: enabling Digital by Default'. The consultation paper considered the next phase of the OPG transformation programme, as well as exploring some of the future changes that OPG may seek to make within the next few years. The consultation included proposed improvements to the design of the paper forms for creating a LPA, fees for a new combined form, access to the OPG registers and changes to the supervision of court appointed deputies.

9.24 It also considered the bigger picture and proposals for future changes, in line with MoJ's Transforming Justice agenda and the Government's commitment for more public services to be digital by default. Initial proposals for the delivery of a fully digital method of creating and registering LPAs were outlined which would require primary legislation in the future. The proposals

---

[21] The postal address is now Office of the Public Guardian, PO Box 16185, Birmingham B2 2WH (DX 744240 Birmingham 79).

were designed to ensure that OPG is able to deal effectively with future volumes across all areas of its business and deliver services that are more effective, less costly and more responsive for its users. The response to the consultation was published in August 2014.

COURT OF PROTECTION VISITORS

Background

9.25 For the history of the role of the Lord Chancellor's Visitors and the proposals for reform prior to the MCA 2005 reference should be made to Chapter 1 at **1.188** et seq.

The new regime

Appointment

9.26 For the purpose of the new jurisdiction there are two panels of Court of Protection Visitors[22] appointed by the Lord Chancellor:[23] a panel of Special Visitors and a panel of General Visitors.[24] They are appointed to carry out visits and produce reports in much the same way as previously although the brief may be wider. There is not seen to be the need for a Legal Visitor under the new regime. It is the OPG practice to recruit by open competition rather than private invitation. Visitors are appointed for such term and subject to such conditions, and may be paid such remuneration and allowances, as the Lord Chancellor may determine. The OPG administers the panel of visitors but the Court can draw on this as a resource.

General Visitors

9.27 A General Visitor need not have a medical qualification. Many have social work, welfare or experience in mental capacity backgrounds but more recently there has been recruitment from new areas such as local authority finance teams and those with legal and medical experience. It is unlikely that outsourcing to bodies such as other government agencies, local authorities or NHS organisations would be adopted because this would lack the transparent independence of the Visitors Service. In some cases the court needs a report because of conflict between family and such bodies. There is a statutory power to request reports from these bodies when that is thought appropriate, but in most instances the judges will seek a report from their own reporting service just as they turn to CAFCASS in children cases. Outsourcing to the not-for-profit sector may not be desirable because consistent training might not be available and uniform standards would be difficult to impose and enforce. It is essential for the Public Guardian to maintain his or her own independent

---

[22] This title replaces 'Lord Chancellor's Visitors'.
[23] All references to the Lord Chancellor should be read in the light of the constitutional reforms – see Chapter 7 at **7.1**ff.
[24] MCA 2005, s 61(1)–(4).

'eyes and ears' and for this facility to be available to the court. Mental capacity issues represent a discrete area where a body of experience needs to be developed, and the role of the Visitors is so important that a specialist service needs to be established and maintained.

9.28 There is now a core of a small number of General Visitors employed by the OPG supported by casuals. The employed full-timers are based at home and operate on a regional basis. In order to maintain a sufficient reserve of visiting services a panel of self-employed casual General Visitors are retained who can be commissioned to prepare reports. An employment basis for the General Visitors may be preferred because this allows for more central control and frees the way for more training, the provision of standard facilities (including laptop computers with appropriate pro formas) and access to networked or secure email communication. But this must not be at the expense of a loss of independence. The Visitors may be accountable to the Public Guardian as employees but are accountable to the court when delivering reports requested directly by the court. They may be required to attend hearings to give evidence and in that respect are vulnerable to cross-examination. So their approach to the reporting process and any constraints placed upon them will become apparent.

9.29 A high proportion of the visiting carried out for the OPG is still done by the enlarged body of self-employed visitors supplementing the small employed group. This has enabled the Public Guardian to guarantee a rapid response if necessary but also to deploy some very experienced or more specialist Visitors within the wider group for particular visits. Reporting timescales have been greatly shortened to only 6 weeks or less from the time of visits being commissioned, and the Public Guardian can also get a visit done the same day if need be.

Frequency of visiting, including the decision whether there will be a visit at all, is now tied to supervision levels (from 1 to 3) allocated after the order is received from the Court. Only Type 1 cases are routinely visited and repeat visited. Type 2A has been introduced as an intermediate level for new lay deputies largely but also to address other short term situations and these also generally receive a visit. Prior to implementation and this 'risk based' approach to supervision and visiting, the OPG had aimed to have some level of visiting to almost all its clients although it never fully achieved this. Many clients will now not be visited at all in this model but they should have been assessed first as low risk/'light touch'.

9.30 The OPG no longer directs all its visiting to the client – in many cases the Visitor is instructed to interview the deputy only, or to ensure that the deputy is seen as well as the client. OPG operates a system of 'assurance visits' to professional deputies and local authorities, who are visited to discuss several clients at the same time, following a visit to a sample of their clients. There is a new emphasis on regulation and ensuring that principles of the Act and the

Code of Practice are complied with, for example that clients are seen by the deputy or their representative and that as far as possible efforts are made to consult with them.

Special Visitors

9.31 A Special Visitor must be a registered medical practitioner (or appear to the Lord Chancellor to have other suitable qualifications or training), and must also appear to the Lord Chancellor to have special knowledge of and experience in cases of impairment of or disturbance in the functioning of the mind or brain. This is the main distinction between the Special and General Visitors. The scale of remuneration is also different and the method of recruitment may differ as these are specialist appointments, but fundamentally the funding mechanism and the process of recruitment is the same with both groups of visitors. A small number of suitably experienced psychiatrists (or in some instances psychologists) are appointed on a consultancy basis and called upon when the need arises.

9.32 The role of the Special Visitors is largely restricted to reporting in two areas. First, they are by reason of their qualification and experience well placed to provide reports expressing an opinion on capacity. Secondly, they are able to assist in cases where there are communication difficulties and to report on the wishes and feelings of the incapacitated individual when others have difficulty in doing so. It may be that, other than in these two respects, the Court will not seek a report from a Special Visitor in health and welfare cases because where guidance is needed that will be the role of experts' evidence. The use of Special Visitors in serious medical treatment involving the withholding and withdrawal of treatment is likely to be exceptional. It would appear that there is potential for Special Visitors to be used more widely, particularly in cases where there are problems funding independent experts. They have been used relatively frequently in personal welfare cases to deal with issues relating to P's capacity, such as where a number of parties are unrepresented and there is no local authority involvement (eg, a dispute amongst family members as to residence and contact) and where perhaps P has not been joined as a party due to problems over funding his or her legal representation.

Reports by Visitors

9.33 Under MCA 2005 the Court of Protection may require a report to be made to it by a Visitor, in writing or orally, on such matters as may be specified.[25] The Public Guardian may also direct a Visitor to visit a donee of a lasting power of attorney, a deputy or the incapacitated person and make a report on such matters as may be directed.[26] The jurisdiction now extends to personal welfare and health care decisions affecting mentally incapacitated adults, in addition to the former jurisdiction over their property and financial affairs. Accordingly, the Visitors may now be required to report on matters

---

[25] MCA 2005, s 49.
[26] MCA 2005, s 58(1)(d).

relating to where a patient should live and whether a decision should be made to withhold or withdraw medical treatment.

9.34 The demand for reports is unlikely to reduce from the previous level for financial affairs, and to this are now added health and welfare reports of a more specific nature. There may of course be an overlap. However, the Official Solicitor is appointed to represent the incapacitated person in many personal welfare cases and a report is unlikely to be required then from a General Visitor. Where there is an issue as to mental capacity and the evidence from medical experts is felt by the court to be insufficient, a report from a Special Visitor who has reviewed the existing evidence is often a process of great value.

Powers

9.35 For the purpose of carrying out their functions in relation to a person who lacks capacity, Court of Protection Visitors may, at all reasonable times, examine and take copies of:

(1) any health record;

(2) any record of, or held by, a local authority and compiled in connection with a social services function; and

(3) any record held by a person registered under the Care Standards Act 2000, Part 2 so far as the record relates to the person who lacks capacity.

They may also for that purpose interview the person who lacks capacity in private.[27]

The changed climate

9.36 It has been recognised that changes are required in the relationship between the Public Guardian and the new panels of Visitors compared with that of the PGO, which dealt with the former Visitors as self-employed contractors. There is a need to ensure that Visitors are adequately protected financially and legally, with health and safety checks (especially in respect of lone visits), public liability insurance, and clearly defined job roles, skills sets and person specifications. The Public Guardian has established increased levels of accountability in terms of quality standards, reporting timescales, professional updating and training.

Association of Independent Visitors

9.37 After October 2007 clients of the court were no longer certain to receive a periodic visit from a Court of Protection Visitor or their successors. Some solicitors and local authorities regretted the loss of the useful independent monitoring and advice this gave them about their clients. They saw the need to commission such visits themselves to fill this gap and to address Mental

---

[27] MCA 2005, s 61(5)–(6).

Capacity Act issues and the good practice requirements enshrined in the Code of Practice. One new resource which can assist in this area is the *Association of Independent Visitors* which was set up by a group of experienced former and current Court Visitors following the implementation of the Act. Its members emphasise that their private work is, as the name suggests, completely independent of the OPG or the court.[28]

THE OFFICIAL SOLICITOR[29]

Status and function

9.38   The Official Solicitor to the Senior Courts is an independent statutory officer holder appointed by the Lord Chancellor under the Senior Courts Act 1981, s 90.[30] His main function is to represent parties to proceedings who are without capacity, deceased or unascertained when no other suitable person or agency is able and willing to do so. The purpose is to prevent a possible denial of justice and safeguard the welfare, property or status of the party. Such proceedings may be in the family proceedings court, County Court, High Court or Court of Protection.

9.39   The Official Solicitor can as at 1 January 2014 be contacted at:

Victory House

30–34 Kingsway

London WC2B 6EX

DX 141423 Bloomsbury[31]

Tel: 020 3681 2751 (Health & Welfare); 020 3681 2758 (Property & Affairs)[32]

Fax: 020 3681 2762

Email: inquiries@offsol.gsi.gov.uk

Website: www.justice.gov.uk/about/ospt.htm

---

[28]   They can be contacted via their website www.aivuk.org.uk which enables the enquirer to find the visitor covering every area of the country according to postcode.

[29]   The extensive contribution of James Beck from the Official Solicitor's office to the material under this heading is gratefully acknowledged.

[30]   Following the creation of a new Supreme Court to replace the House of Lords as the ultimate appeal court, from October 2009 his title changed from Official Solicitor to the Supreme Court. Constitutional Reform Act 2005, Sch 11, para 26. The Supreme Court Act 1981 was also renamed the Senior Courts Act 1981.

[31]   Official Solicitor's office moved in August 2013 from 81 Chancery Lane, London WC2A 1DD.

[32]   There is no single enquiry number for the Office. Telephone numbers for enquiries concerning Civil Litigation and family proceedings please consult the website.

The present office

9.40 The joint office of the Official Solicitor and Public Trustee is known as the OSPT. The OSPT is an 'arm's length body' which exists to support the work of the Official Solicitor and Public Trustee.[33] The two office holders continue to have separate corporate functions and the Public Trustee is not involved in mental capacity issues. Functionally the Official Solicitor is part of the judicial system of England and Wales (that is, excluding Scotland and Northern Ireland), while the Public Trustee is a separate and independent statutory body. The office is currently administered as part of the Ministry of Justice. At the time of writing the Official Solicitor to the Senior Courts is Alastair Pitblado and the Public Trustee is Eddie Bloomfield.

9.41 For the financial year 2014–15, the office has an agreed compliment equivalent to 136 full time staff.[34] All the staff are civil servants who specialise in different areas of work. As at September 2014, the Official Solicitor employed 22 lawyers (including part time and agency) amongst his staff. About 40 of his other staff are caseworkers who are not employed as lawyers but who are responsible for managing litigation friend cases on behalf of the Official Solicitor. Their primary role is to discharge the Official Solicitor's duties as litigation friend in the cases they manage, which will usually involve the appointment of a private firm of solicitors to act for the incapacitated party, ensuring that funding arrangements are in place to pay those solicitors and providing instructions to them for the duration of the proceedings. The caseworkers have access to in-house legal advice where appropriate and sometime conduct litigation themselves under the direct supervision of a lawyer.

During the financial year 2013–14 the Official Solicitor had around 1,020 cases referred to him in proceedings in the Court of Protection with over 680 relating to property and affairs and over 330 relating to healthcare and welfare (of which 23 related to potential serious medical treatment).[35]

9.42 Both the Official Solicitor and the Public Trustee have such powers and perform such duties as may be conferred on them by statute and by Rules of Court, and, in the case of the Official Solicitor, also at common law. The Official Solicitor's role in court proceedings is recognised by the Court Rules,[36] and the Court of Protection Rules 2007[37] and Practice Directions make specific provision for his involvement.[38] By way of guidance he issued Practice Notes

---

[33] For the background to the Office see Chapter 1.

[34] OSPT Annual Delivery Agreement 2014-15.

[35] This information is provisional and is subject to confirmation in the next Official Solicitor and Public Trustee Annual Report for 2013–14.

[36] See the Civil Procedure Rules 1998, SI 1998/3132, PD 21, para 3.4 and the Family Procedure Rules 2010, SI 2010/2955, r 15.6(1)(b) and PD 15A, paras 4.44.5.

[37] SI 2007/1744.

[38] Practice Direction 9E, para 8 and para 14(b) in respect of serious medical treatment applications, PD 9F, para 10 in respect of applications relating to statutory wills, codicils, settlements and other dealings with P's property and PD 17A para 4(c) in respect of the appointment of a litigation friend.

dealing with medical and welfare decisions for incapacitated adults,[39] including sterilisation[40] and persistent vegetative state (PVS) cases.[41] These are no longer of direct application following the implementation of the MCA 2005 but a Practice Note relating to the Official Solicitor's Appointment in Family Proceedings and Proceedings under the Inherent Jurisdiction in relation to Adults was issued in March 2013 which will be applicable in some adult welfare cases which fall outside the MCA 2005.[42]

Vision Statement

9.43 The vision statement of the Official Solicitor and Public Trustee' is:

> '[to] ... be a modern dynamic organisation delivering high quality and efficient client-focused services for vulnerable persons, where those services need to be provided by the public sector .

> ... [and] to achieve justice for those who need our services, to protect the legal, welfare and financial interests of our clients through specialist services designed to meet their needs, and to deliver those services efficiently and effectively to provide value for money to our clients and the taxpayer.'

Acceptance policy

9.44 The Official Solicitor requires three criteria[43] to be met before he will accept appointment as litigation friend:

- there must be evidence (or a finding by the court) that the party (or intended party)
- lacks capacity to conduct the proceedings
- there is no one else suitable and willing to act as litigation friend[44]
- that there is security for the costs which the Official Solicitor will incur in providing legal representation for the incapacitated party or the case falls in one of the classes in which, exceptionally, the Official Solicitor funds the costs of litigation out of his budget, in accordance with long standing practice. In practice this means that either the incapacitated party will be eligible for legal aid, or have the means to pay for such costs out of income and/or capital or there is some third party willing to agree to pay such costs. The category of cases that Official Solicitor is likely to fund in part

---

[39] Practice Note: *Medical and Welfare Decisions for Adults* [2001] 2 FLR 158 and Practice Note: *Family Division: Incapacitated Adults* (2002) *The Times*, 4 January.

[40] Practice Note: *Sterilisation Cases* [2001] 2 FLR 155.

[41] Practice Note: *PVS Cases* [2001] 2 FLR 155.

[42] This replaces the Practice Note dated 2 April 2001.

[43] See Official Solicitor's Note dated 21 February 2012 'Court of Protection: Acceptance of Appointment as Litigation Friend', which is available on the MoJ website.

[44] However, in the Court of Protection property and affairs cases referred to in PD 9F it has been long established practice for the Official Solicitor to act as both litigation friend and solicitor on record. It is open to the Court of Protection to appoint a lay litigation friend who could choose to instruct a different solicitor but to date there has been no change to this practice.

or in whole from his budget is usually limited to cases where he agrees to act as advocate to the court, or where he is joined in a case as an interested party (usually one of wide pubic importance such as in *R v Burke*) or cases in the Court of Protection concerning serious medical treatment (where half his costs are met from his own and the remaining half is usually paid by the NHS body or bodies or local authority which brought, or should have brought, the proceedings).

9.45 Once appointed as litigation friend the Official Solicitor will decide whether the solicitor's role is handled in-house or external solicitors are to be instructed. In practice external solicitors are instructed in almost all cases except those in the Court of Protection which concern property and affairs or serious medical treatment and some divorce main suit cases (but rarely financial proceedings). The Official Solicitor operates to a fixed budget and has to consider how his costs in litigation to which he may become a party are to be funded. Depending on the circumstances, this may be out of the incapacitated party's own estate;[45] where external solicitors are used their costs may be met through legal aid where available; or he can seek an undertaking as to costs, or an order for all or some of his costs, from another party to the litigation.[46]

The incapacity work of the Official Solicitor

Giving advice

9.46 Inquiries are frequently made by the judiciary and members of the legal profession, IMCAs, members of the medical profession, managers of care homes and social workers. It is important to note that the advisory role is necessarily limited to the role of the Official Solicitor in respect of the proceedings and not to the law generally. Members of the general public are usually encouraged to obtain the advice of their own solicitor, or perhaps consult their local Citizens Advice Bureau.

Representing adults who lack capacity

9.47 An order of the Court, appointing the Official Solicitor to act as a representative in a civil court case for a person who lacks capacity, will either be made with his prior consent or will only take effect if his consent is obtained. The Official Solicitor needs to be satisfied that that there is no suitable

---

[45] The Official Solicitor's current policy in Court of Protection personal welfare cases is that he will generally not accept appointment where the incapacitated party has insufficient liquid capital to pay a lump sum of £20,000 on account of the costs to any solicitors to be instructed by him on behalf of that party (unless there is a realistic prospect that an incapacitated party would become eligible for legal aid where there liquid capital takes them slightly over the eligibility level and is likely to be used in initial legal costs).

[46] Undertakings are quite frequently used in civil proceedings where the claimant requires the defendant to be represented in order to proceed with the litigation, such as in possession claims. They are also sometimes used in Court of Protection personal welfare cases where a local authority urgently requires P to be represented in the proceedings but the Official Solicitor has not yet been able to conclude his enquiries in respect of the funding of the costs of P's legal representation.

alternative person who is willing to act as litigation friend and that there is a satisfactory funding arrangement available to meet his charges and expenses of providing legal representation for the incapacitated person before agreeing to act.

9.48 It may be desirable that the Official Solicitor be consulted about a proposed application which seeks his involvement in any proceedings before a court in England and Wales (this is particularly the case with regard to serious medical treatment cases and other cases involving urgent applications).[47] In proceedings before the Court of Protection, particularly with regard to personal welfare applications, the Official Solicitor will have to first establish that his acceptance criteria are met. The time required by the Official Solicitor to carry out such financial enquiries should not be underestimated, particularly if the incapacitated party's financial circumstances are complicated or where a relative or partner is managing those finances and are obstructive.[48] Where a public body such as a local authority is bringing proceedings the Official Solicitor will encourage the public body concerned to carry out its own enquiries as to the availability of an alternative litigation fund and as to the incapacitated party's financial resources. It is now the Official Solicitor's practice where his appointment as litigation friend is sought to request that the Court makes directions which will allow his staff (and the staff of any public body acting as applicant) to obtain financial information from third parties and public bodies about the incapacitated party and allow for that party's costs to be obtained from legal aid where eligible.[49] The Official Solicitor's lawyers may provide precedent draft orders to facilitate his involvement and to expedite acceptance of appointment where this is appropriate.

9.49 Failure to provide any obtainable financial and personal information about the incapacitated party (such as their National Insurance Number) may result in avoidable delay. Where it is established that the incapacitated party is required to fund the costs of legal representation from his/her own financial resources, it is likely that the Official Solicitor will require a further detailed order to be made which will facilitate the payment of the costs of legal representation, including a payment on account of costs and provision for the payment of interim bills and disbursements. This is particularly likely if the incapacitated party does not have a financial deputy or an attorney who could make such payments. The need for a further order may cause further delay as the Official Solicitor will not usually consent to act until fully satisfied over the funding arrangements and a case will not even be placed on his waiting list for acceptance until this criterion is satisfied.

---

[47] See PD 9E, para 8 and *Sandwell and West Birmingham Hospitals NHS Trust v CD & Ors* [2014] EWCOP 23 (1 August 2014) Theis J at para 39.

[48] For example, as at 25 February 2013 the Official Solicitor had 68 Court of Protection personal welfare cases which were being investigated by his staff to establish whether they met his criteria for acceptance – see Official Solicitor's letter to the 39 Essex Street Chambers Court of Protection Newsletter dated 25 February 2013.

[49] Orders relating to third party disclosure should be drawn as separate orders so as to avoid giving private and confidential information about P's proceedings to such third parties – Ibid.

9.50   The Official Solicitor will, if necessary act for two (and potentially more) incapacitated parties in the same court proceedings. In such cases special arrangements are put in place to prevent any conflict of interest and to preserve confidentiality of communications between the litigation friend case manager and the instructed solicitors and counsel. Accordingly each incapacitated party has a separate case manager and, if applicable, separate lawyer at the office. A strict conflict of interest information barrier is maintained to prevent privileged information being disclosed within the office to the staff responsible for the case management of the other incapacitated party or parties. Before accepting appointment for a second or further incapacitated party the Official Solicitor will seek the court's approval of these arrangements.

The Official Solicitor is unable to act as solicitor to individual members of the general public as though he were a solicitor in private practice, nor will he respond to inquiries from individuals who are seeking free legal advice for their own benefit.

Assisting the civil and family courts

9.51   The Official Solicitor may also be called on to give confidential advice to judges and invited to instruct counsel to appear before a judge to assist the court as advocate to the court, or to investigate any matter on which the court needs a special report.[50] This has happened where for instance the court has difficulties in ascertaining the mental capacity of a party to proceedings before the court. A special report might also be requested by the court from the Official Solicitor when the judge feels he or she needs help to ascertain facts or information relevant to the case which would not otherwise be made available to the court. It is probably a contempt of court to interfere with an investigation by the Official Solicitor.

Assisting the Court of Protection

9.52   The Official Solicitor may bring an application without the permission of the court. Subject to his consent, the Official Solicitor may be appointed to act as litigation friend for an incapacitated party (whether P or a Protected Party) in any proceedings.[51] He is invariably asked to assist the court in applications for statutory wills or authority to make gifts or other dispositions. He may be appointed to represent the incapacitated party because the deputy or attorney has a personal interest in the outcome. This work is undertaken in-house and costs are generally payable from the incapacitated party's estate. In serious medical treatment cases the Official Solicitor usually acts in-house both as litigation friend and solicitor. In such cases the Official Solicitor does not seek to fund his costs either from public funding or from the incapacitated party's own estate. Instead the current practice is that he seeks half his costs from the NHS body or other public body seeking the court's decision and funds the

---

[50]   Known as a *Harbin v Masterman* inquiry [1896] 1 Ch 351.
[51]   Court of Protection Rules 2001, rr 11 and 13.

balance from his own budget.[52] In most personal welfare proceedings in the Court of Protection the Official Solicitor will instruct an external firm of solicitors to act for the incapacitated party and the proceedings will be funded by legal aid or from the incapacitated party's own financial resources.

9.53 Due to the rise in Court of Protection healthcare and welfare cases the Official Solicitor operated from early 2012 until October 2013 a waiting list in relation to his acceptance of invitations to act in personal welfare cases under the MCA 2005. The waiting list has now been discontinued. Although there continues to be a high volume of cases and the resources of the Official Solicitor remain limited by public spending restraints, it is currently the Official Solicitor's practice to allocate immediately to his case managers those cases which meet his criteria for acceptance.

9.54 In cases involving a challenge to a DOLS authorisation under s 21A of MCA 2005, the Official Solicitor will where the Relevant Person's Representative (RPR) is the applicant, write to the RPR to check whether s/he will remain the applicant and that P does not need to be made a party. Where the RPR is not the applicant and P has already been joined as a party, the Official Solicitor will also write to the RPR to establish if the RPR is willing and able to act as P's litigation friend.[53]

9.55 The Official Solicitor currently has two separate teams at his office which undertake work in respect of the Court of Protection:

1. The *Court of Protection Property and Affairs Division* which acts both as litigation friend and solicitor principally in applications for statutory Wills and other proceedings referred to in PD 9F, is led by a senior lawyer who is also a Deputy Official Solicitor and currently has a further six lawyers (one of whom currently works part time in team)

2. The *Healthcare and Welfare Division* which undertakes all work in relation to personal welfare applications is currently led by a Senior lawyer who is also a Deputy Official Solicitor and has a further lawyers and a number of paralegal case managers who undertake litigation friend task. In addition, three lawyers who principally undertake family law cases also case manage a limited number of personal welfare cases in the Court of Protection (often those where there are related family proceedings such as care proceedings involving P's children, forced marriage or where P was previously the subject of Children Act orders).

15.5

---

[52] Most recently approved by Peter Jackson J in *Re D (Costs)* [2012] EWHC 88, [2012] COPLR 499 which followed judgment of the former President, Sir Mark Potter, in *A Hospital v SW and A PCT* [2007] EWHC 425 (Fam). See generally Chapter 5.

[53] See *AB v LCC (A Local Authority)* [2011] EWHC3151 (COP) (06 December 2011) in which Mostyn J approved of the appointment of a RPR as litigation friend in such cases. A transcript of the judgment is available on BAILII.

Adult personal welfare declarations including serious medical treatment

9.56 The Official Solicitor is invariably appointed as litigation friend of P whenever there are serious medical treatment cases in the court unless an urgent out-of-hours decision[54] is made which does not require any further hearing or exceptionally where there is a suitable and willing alternative litigation friend. The most common cases involving serious medical treatment cases in which the Official Solicitor acts have been those involving the use of significant restraint including sedation, the withholding of life-sustaining treatment, disputes concerning DNAR notices, the termination of pregnancy, those where there is uncertainty as to capacity. Other cases less commonly handled are those concerning donation of organs or bone marrow and sterilisation (both male[55] and female) and the validity, applicability or existence of advanced decisions. The Official Solicitor is also often appointed to act as litigation friend in other personal welfare cases. These commonly involve disputes either within families or between families and local authorities or NHS bodies. They invariably relate to disputes concerning capacity, residence, contact and or care provision. Some are challenges to authorisations made under the DOLS. Others are brought by local authorities and NHS bodies to enable P to be deprived of their liberty in locations not covered by DOLS (such as supported living tenancies or foster home placements).[56]

9.57 Where the Official Solicitor is appointed to act, he will wish to play a full role in the proceedings and to have an opportunity to properly investigate the case. The Official Solicitor will invariably wish to instruct, on a sole or joint basis, one or more experts to advise on capacity and/or best interests. When drafting directions orders prior to the Official Solicitor accepting appointment, care should be taken to ensure that as far as possible the timetable for his involvement is realistic and allows sufficient time for investigations, including the selection and instruction of independent experts.[57]

Other jurisdictions

9.58 Although there should be a clear definition of the range of services to be provided by the Official Solicitor, there is a diversity of services available in the jurisdictions of the UK and Ireland.

---

[54] The Official Solicitor has not provided an out-of-hours service with lawyers on duty to cover such applications since 15 December 2011.

[55] See *An NHS Trust v DE & Ors* [2013] EWHC 2562 (Fam) for the first decision made in respect of a male sterilisation under MCA 2005.

[56] The number of these deprivation of liberty cases falling outside DOLS which require a litigation friend may fall significantly following the guidance provided by the President in *Re X and others (Deprivation of Liberty)* [2014] EWCOP 25 (7 August 2014).

[57] Neither the Official Solicitor nor his staff are social care or mental health experts and that they rely on the use of such experts to obtain expert evidence independent from that provided by any local authority or NHS body which may be a party to the proceedings.

Scotland

9.59   There is no equivalent of the Official Solicitor in Scotland and the Office of the Public Guardian has no recourse to a professional legal service other than in response to its own departmental administrative requirements. However, in a case where the incapacitated party had been moved to Scotland it was possible through liaison with the relevant Scottish local authority to obtain a mirror order from the local Sheriff's Court under the Adults with Incapacity (Scotland) Act 2000 to confirm and implement an earlier decision of the Court of Protection relating to residence and contact.

Northern Ireland

9.60   Northern Ireland also has an Official Solicitor with a similar role to that of the Official Solicitor to the Senior Courts in England and Wales. The contact details are:

Official Solicitor's Office

Royal Courts of Justice

Chichester Street

Belfast

BT1 3JF

Tel: 028 9072 5940

Fax: 028 9023 1759

Ireland

9.61   The equivalent of the Official Solicitor in the Republic of Ireland is the Office of the General Solicitor for Minors and Wards of Court situated in Dublin. Its origins lie in Chancery practice but it was brought within the public service in 1969. There is no equivalent of the Public Guardian. The General Solicitor may assist the High Court to arrange medical examinations, act as guardian ad litem of a ward (or a minor) and act as a Committee of the Estate (or of the Person) of last resort. In many ways this latter role appears similar to that of a social worker but with a legal or administrative bias and legal services may be provided.

Office of the General Solicitor for Minors and Wards of Court

2nd Floor

15/24 Phoenix Street North

Smithfield

Dublin 7

Phone +353 (0) 1 888 6231

Fax +353 1 872 2681

Email GenSol@courts.ie

For more information see: www.courts.ie

Current and future issues[58]

9.62 Funding of litigation in the Court of Protection has been a cause of concern for the Official Solicitor since the inception of the MCA 2005. Increasing numbers of incapacitated parties are ineligible for legal aid but often lack significant capital other than the equity in their homes. Whilst it is technically possible to fund litigation by way of charging such property this has not proven to be a practical solution due to the staff resources required to secure such funding and the fact that there is inevitably a long delay in recovering the expenditure on legal representation from an incapacitated party's property and a degree of risk over recovery (in that a charge cannot be registered until the case has concluded and P's legal costs have been agreed or assessed by the Senior Courts Costs Office). It is therefore unlikely that the Official Solicitor will agree to fund cases by way of deferred charge on the incapacitated party's estate. Where there is a lack of liquid capital the Official Solicitor has in some cases agreed to act only where a public body, such as a local authority, has undertaken to pay his legal costs (with the provision that the public body is then authorised to recoup these costs from the incapacitated party's estate at the conclusion of the case). There will inevitably also be cases where although a protected party is ineligible for legal aid they have no realistic means of paying for their costs due to the fact that their ineligibility arises from having income only marginally above qualifying levels. In such cases the Official Solicitor is again unlikely to be willing to consent to act as it will not comply with the funding criterion relating to his acceptance of appointment.[59] These funding problems have increased following the implementation on 1 April 2013 of the changes introduced by the Legal Aid, Sentencing and

---

[58] The material under this heading has been contributed by James Beck from the Official Solicitor's Office.

[59] In his outline judgment the President in *Re X and others (Deprivation of Liberty)* [2014] EWCOP 25 (7 August 2014) at para 26 confirmed that a litigation friend could conduct litigation on behalf of P even if the litigation friend lacks the right of audience provided he has the permission of the court to act as advocate. This may perhaps be the only option where there are no means to pay for P's legal representation and it is necessary to join P as a party to the proceedings.

Punishment of Offenders Act 2012 in April 2013. Legal Aid reforms have also presented problems in the conduct of cases themselves particularly around the instruction of independent experts.[60]

9.63　The number of personal welfare cases has grown at a considerable pace from a mere 42 as at 1 April 2008, to 216 cases as at 1 April 2009, 368 cases as at 1 April 2010, 438 cases as at 1 April 2011 and a peak of 582 cases as at April 2012.[61] The level of new referrals and cases in hand appears to have plateaued with there being 546 personal welfare cases as at 1 April 2013.[62] Given demographic trends and the increasing awareness of the Mental Capacity Act 2005 amongst the general public the volume of new cases is unlikely to reduce significantly for the foreseeable future. Some cases currently require quite lengthy involvement by the Official Solicitor, such as deprivation of liberty cases which require annual reviews as a consequence of falling outside the DOLS scheme. In particular there has been the question of how the Official Solicitor would be able to deal with the significant increase in deprivation of liberty cases which inevitably would arise from the Supreme Court decision in (1) *P v Cheshire West and Chester Council and another*; (2) *P and Q v Surrey County Council*.[63] Given the current economic climate and the reductions in public spending, the Official Solicitor will probably have to devise new strategies to allow his current staffing levels to cover the continuing high number of invitations to act.

The Official Solicitor has been particularly involved in several important areas of litigation in recent years concerning the Mental Capacity Act 2005 before the Court of Protection and the High Court. These related to the following areas:

- Cases concerned with whether P was being deprived of his liberty for the purposes of Art 5 of the European Convention on Human Rights. This is of importance not only to those detained under DOLS but also those in placements not covered by DOLS, such as supported tenancies and foster home placements. It has included restraint beyond the limits permitted by the Mental Health Act 1983.[64]

---

[60]　See Transforming Legal Aid: Developing a more credible and effective system. Ministry of Justice Consultation Paper CP14/2013 – Response of the Official Solicitor 04.6.2013.

[61]　The Official Solicitor and Public Trustee Annual Report 2011–12. The numbers have slightly fallen during the last financial year but this may be largely due to the waiting list rather than any significant fall in the number of applications being made.

[62]　The Official Solicitor and Public Trustee Annual Report 2012–13. This also shows the level of new cases accepted fell slightly from 358 in 2011–12 to 333 in 2012–13 However these figures may reflect that the waiting list was in place for much of the relevant period.

[63]　The number of cases may now fall significantly following the President's guidance in *Re X and others (Deprivation of Liberty)* [2014] EWCOP 25 (7 August 2014).

[64]　Which have included *R v A Local Authority and Ors* [2011] EWHC 1539, [2011] COPLR Con Vol 972; *London Borough of Hillingdon v Steven Neary* [2011] EWHC 413 (COP); *P (otherwise known as MIG) and Q (otherwise known as MEG) v (1) Surrey County Council (2) CA (3) LA and Equality and Human Rights Commission, intervener* [2011] EWCA Civ 190, [2011] COPLR Con Vol 931; *Cheshire West and Chester Council v P* [2011] EWCA Civ 1257

- Cases concerning capacity to consent to sexual relations, particularly in the light of Baroness Hale's comments in *R v C* [2009] 1 WLR 1786.[65]
- Cases concerning capacity to marry.[66]
- Cases concerning the power of the court to review the decisions made by local authorities in the allocation of their resources on best interests grounds.[67]
- The power of the court to award damages under the Human Rights Act 1998.[68]
- Media access to private court proceedings and restrictions on media reporting of open court proceedings which concerned the countervailing rights to protection and privacy under Art 8 of those lacking mental capacity.[69]
- The limits upon the levels of restraint which can be justified in providing medical treatment to a person lacking capacity.[70]
- Whether it can ever be lawful and in the best interests of a person in the minimally conscious state to have artificial nutrition and hydration withdrawn or withheld if they are not in the dying process.[71]
- Whether an advanced decision was lawful and applicable.[72]
- Whether the placement of a DNAR notice is in the best interests of a person and other cases concerning the withholding or withdrawal of intensive care and other life sustaining treatment.[73]

---

and *RK v (1) BCC (2) YB and (3) AK* [2011] EWCA Civ 1305. (1) *P v Cheshire West and Chester Council and another*; (2) *P and Q v Surrey County Council* [2014] UKSC 19.

[65] *D County Council v LS* [2010] EWHC 1544 (Fam), [2010] COPLR Con Vol 331; *D Borough Council v AB* [2011] EWHC 101 (COP), [2011] 2 FLR 72, COPLR Con Vol 313; *A Local Authority v TZ* [2013] EWHC 2322 (COP); *IM v LM and Others* [2014] EWCA CIV 37.

[66] *A, B and C v X, Y and Z* [2012] EWHC 2400 (COP) in respect of which an appeal to the Court of Appeal was due to be heard in 2013 but 'P' died after permission had been granted. *Sandwell Metropolitan Borough Council v RG & Ors* [2013] EWHC 2373 (COP); *YLA v PM and MZ* [2013] EWHC 3622 (Fam).

[67] *AH v (1) Hertfordshire Partnership NHS Foundation Trust and (2) Ealing Primary Care trust* [2011] EWHC 276, [2011] COPLR Con Vol 195 and *A Local Authority v PB and P* [2011] EWHC 2675 (COP), [2012] COPLR 1.

[68] *YA (F) v A Local Authority (2) YA(M) (3) A NHS trust and (4) A Primary Care Trust* [2010] EWHC 2770 (Fam); *TheLocal Authority v Mrs D and Mr D* [2013] EWCOP B34.

[69] *P v Independent Print Ltd* [2011] EWCA Civ 756, [2012] COPLR 110 and *W v M* [2011] EWHC 1197 (COP), [2011] COPLR Con Vol 1205; *RGS (No. 3), Re* [2014] EWHC B12 (COP).

[70] *Re D* [2010] EWHC 2535 (COP); *The Mental Health Trust/The Acute Trust & The Council v DD and BC (Number 1 and Number 2)* [2014] EWCOP 11 & [2014] EWCOP 13.

[71] *W v M and Ors* [2011] EWHC 2443 (Fam), [2012] COPLR 222.

[72] *Primary Care Trust v XB* [2012] EWHC 1390 (Fam), [2012] COPLR 577; *Nottinghamshire Healthcare NHS Trust v RC* [2014] EWCOP 1136 (9 April 2014) and *Nottinghamshire Healthcare NHS Trust v RC* [2014] EWCOP 1317 (1 May 2014).

[73] *Aintree University Hospitals NHS Foundation Trust v James & Ors* [2013] UKSC 67, [2013] 3 WLR 1299, [2013] COPLR 492 (the Official Solicitor was not involved in the subsequent appeal to the Supreme Court). *A NHS Hospital Trust v M and K* [2013] EWHC 2402; *An NHS Foundation trust v VT and A* [2013] EWHC 826 (Fam).

- ECHR Art 8 – right to family and right to privacy and its applicability in respect of an incapacitated person's bests interests regarding care and residence.[74]
- Whether the taking of a DNA sample for the purposes of a Statutory Will notice is in the best interests of P.[75]
- Whether it can be in the best interests of a man to be sterilised.[76]
- The correct test for capacity to cohabit with a spouse.[77]
- The correct test for capacity to make decision about contact to others.[78]
- Whether it was appropriate to withhold disclosure of statements and and un-redacted reports.[79]
- Whether P has capacity to consent to the requisite medical treatment.[80]
- The interface between the Mental Capacity Act and Inherent Jurisdiction.[81]
- The basis for dispensing with service in statutory will cases.[82]
- Providing inter vivos gifts to parents.[83]

COURT FUNDS OFFICE

Background

9.64 The Court Funds Office provides investment and banking administration services for clients whose money is held under the control of the civil courts of England and Wales, including the Court of Protection (COP). The practice of holding funds 'in-court' on behalf of litigants goes back several hundred years but an Act of Parliament was passed in 1726, creating the post now known as the Accountant General of the Senior Courts and giving him responsibility for safeguarding funds in court.

9.65 Under the Administration of Justice Act 1982 (AJA), the Court Funds Office, which operates as an arm's length body of the Ministry of Justice, is responsible for administering £3.7bn (£3.5bn in cash and £0.2bn in securities)

---

[74] *K v LBX & Ors* [2012] EWCA Civ 79, [2012] COPLR 411.
[75] *LG v DK* [2011] EWHC 2453 (COP), [2012] COPLR 80.
[76] *Re DE* [2013] EWHC 2409.
[77] *PC and NC v City of York* [2013] EWCA Civ 478.
[78] *PC & Anor v City of York Council* [2013] EWCA Civ 478 (01 May 2013) and *A Local Authority v TZ (No. 2)* [2014] EWCOP 973 (1 April 2014).
[79] *RC v CC and X Local Authority* [2013] EWHC 1424 (COP).
[80] *Heart of England NHS Foundation Trust v JB* [2014] EWHC 342 (COP) – amputation; *Re SB* [2013] EWHC 1417 (COP) – termination of pregnancy.
[81] *An NHS Trust v Dr A* [2013] EWHC 2442 (COP); *Great Western Hospitals NHS Foundation Trust v AA, BB, CC, DD* [2014] EWHC 132 (Fam); *The London Borough of Redbridge v G, C and F* [2014] EWHC 485 (COP); *The London Borough of Redbridge v G & Ors (No 2)* [2014] EWCOP 959; Nottinghamshire Healthcare NHS Trust cases referred to at fn 72 above.
[82] *Re AB* [2013] EWHC B39 (COP).
[83] *Re AK (gift application)* [2014] EWHC B11 (COP).

held in court on behalf of over 140,000 clients. The money held by Court Funds Office originates primarily from three sources:[84]

(1) Damages awarded to children represented by litigation friends as a result of civil legal action and held on their behalf until majority (18 years of age);

(2) Damages awarded to adults represented by litigation friends as a result of civil legal action and held on their behalf because they are 'protected beneficiaries' and the amount does not justify an application to the Court of Protection;

(3) Assets belonging to people who lack the capacity to manage their own financial affairs where the Court of Protection has appointed a deputy to manage their affairs.

A 'protected beneficiary' is as a party who lacks capacity to conduct proceedings who also lacks capacity to manage and control any money recovered by him or on his behalf or for his benefit in the proceedings.[85]

The Mental Capacity Act 2005 now provides greater choice for the deputy and only some Court of Protection clients have to keep money at the Court Funds Office.

Court Funds Rules 2011

9.66 The Court Funds Office has been working in partnership with National Savings & Investments (NS&I) to modernise the service it provides to clients. The Court Funds Rules 2011 came into force on 3 October 2011.[86] They govern the manner in which the Accountant General may accept funds into, hold and pay funds out of court. The new Rules were introduced to make the procedures clearer, less confusing and more user friendly. They restate, clarify and modernise the former Rules rather than alter their substantive effect.

9.67 Part 1 of the new Rules contains provisions for interpreting the Rules and also prescribes the courts to which the Rules apply. Part 2 sets out which documents are required to deposit funds in court and how funds may be deposited. Part 3 deals with investment options for a fund in court, who may make investment decisions and when investments may be made. Part 4 deals with payment out of a fund in court, including which documents are required for payment out and the circumstances in which a fund can be released where the person entitled to the fund has died. Part 5 deals with unclaimed funds. Part 6 contains miscellaneous provisions including how to obtain information about a fund in court.

---

[84] Only the second and third sources are considered here.
[85] Civil Procedure Rules 1998, r 21.1(2)(e).
[86] Replacing the Court Funds Rules 1987.

Investments on behalf of protected beneficiaries

9.68 The Accountant General may only invest money in a common investment fund if it amounts to £10,000 or more and it is held on behalf of a person lacking capacity who a court, deputy or investment manager has reason to believe will require the investment to be held for 5 years or more.[87]

9.69 The Court Funds Office has introduced a new investment framework on behalf of protected beneficiaries where the sum to be invested is more than £10,000 but less than £30,000. In these cases, following the hearing of an application for the approval of a settlement or compromise, the judge completes form CFO 320PB[88] and indicates which investment policy is to apply from one of the following four options:

- Capital growth only – where no income is likely to be required from the fund for over 10 years;
- Capital growth and income – where some income is likely to be required from the fund within 5 to 10 years;
- Maximum income – where income is likely to be required from the fund within 5 years;
- Place all funds on special - where there is less than £10,000 to invest, the funds are likely to be invested for less than 5 years, there is a specific request not to invest or the protected beneficiary is 80 years of age or more.

Court staff then complete form CFO 212 and on receipt the Court Funds Office apply the investment framework set out in the following table:[89]

Capital growth only	65%
Capital growth and income	50%
Maximum income	Special
Place all funds on special	Special

The percentage figure represents investment in the Equity Index Tracker Fund.

9.70 An annual review is undertaken of all cases where funds have been invested in the Equity Index Tracker Fund to ensure that the percentage split between the equity and cash components remains appropriate.

---

[87] Court Funds Rules 2011, r 14(2).
[88] Form CFO 320PB is available via: www.justice.gov.uk/global/forms/cfo.htm.
[89] Where the court has not selected an investment policy the money will be placed to the special account.

An application must be made to the Court of Protection for the appointment of a deputy where the award is £30,000 or more, unless a deputy or attorney has already been appointed as required by the relevant Practice Direction.[90]

Contacting the CFO

9.71   The CFO has for many years been based at Kingsway, London but from 5 December 2011 moved to:

Court Funds Office, Glasgow, G58 1AB

DX: 501757 Cowglen

Email: enquiries@cfo.gsi.gov.uk

Tel: 0845 223 8500

Fax: 0141 636 4398

INDEPENDENT MENTAL CAPACITY ADVOCATE SERVICE

Advocates

9.72   Advocacy involves helping people to express their views and wishes, access information and services, explore choices and options, and secure their rights. In some situations an advocate may need to represent another person's interests. This is called non-instructed advocacy, and is used when a person is unable to communicate their views.

An advocate is someone who supports a person so that their views are heard and their rights are upheld especially when decisions are being made about their life. An advocate will support a person to speak up for themselves or, in some situations, will speak on a person's behalf. Advocates are independent: they are not connected to the carers or services that are involved in supporting the person.

IMCAs

9.73   Independent Mental Capacity Advocates (IMCAs) provide a new type of statutory advocacy introduced by the MCA 2005.[91] Some people who lack capacity have a right to receive support from an IMCA and responsible bodies, the NHS and local authorities all have a duty to make sure that IMCAs are

---

[90]   Civil Procedure Rules 1998, PD 21, para 10.2.

[91]   See MCA 2005, ss 35–36 and The Mental Capacity Act 2005 (Independent Mental Capacity Advocates) (General) Regulations 2006. The DH and OPG produced a booklet called Making decisions: The Independent Mental Capacity Advocate (IMCA) service [OPG606], which can be downloaded at: www.dh.gov.uk/prod_consum_dh/groups/dh_digitalassets/documents/digitalasset/dh_095893.pdf.

available to represent them.[92] IMCA services are provided by organisations that are independent from those authorities.[93]

The majority of service users who access the IMCA service are people with learning disabilities, older people with dementia, people who have an acquired brain injury or people with mental health problems. If the person is unable to communicate their views and wishes relating to the decision to be made, an advocate uses non-instructed advocacy.

> 'Non-instructed advocacy is taking affirmative action with or on behalf of a person who is unable to give a clear indication of their views or wishes in a specific situation. The non-instructed advocate seeks to uphold the person's rights; ensure fair and equal treatment and access to services; and make certain that decisions are taken with due consideration for their unique preferences and perspectives.' (Action for Advocacy, 2006.)

The advocate goes to meetings on the person's behalf and actively probes the process by which service providers reach a decision and causes them to think about why they are making the specific decision and to justify the actions proposed.

Who can be an IMCA?

9.74 Individual IMCAs must have relevant experience and receive IMCA training. They must have integrity and a good character[94] and be able to act independently.

How do IMCAs challenge a decision?

9.75 The IMCA may initially use informal methods to challenge decisions and ask for a meeting with the decision-maker to explain any concerns and request a review of the decision. Where there are serious concerns about the decision made, an IMCA may decide to use formal methods to challenge the decision. These include using the relevant complaints procedure, approaching the Official Solicitor and referring the case to the Court of Protection. They may also seek legal advice on the incapacitated person's behalf and consider applying for a judicial review.

---

[92] For an explanation of the appointment, functions and role of IMCAs and the duty to instruct them refer to Chapter 5 at para 5.42 et seq.
[93] Local authorities have commissioned IMCA services in England and local health boards have commissioned them in Wales.
[94] They must have enhanced checks with the Criminal Records Bureau that show no areas of concern.

CHAPTER 10

MISCELLANEOUS

ENDURING POWERS – TRANSITIONAL (MENTAL CAPACITY ACT 2005, SCH 4)

10.1 The Mental Capacity Act 2005 (MCA 2005) repealed the Enduring Powers of Attorney Act 1985 (EPAA 1985) so no new enduring powers of attorney (EPAs) can now be created.[1] There remain in place countless numbers of EPAs, some already registered but perhaps the majority unregistered and held in deed boxes and solicitors' offices across the country as 'insurance policies' in case of future incapacity. The registered EPAs cannot be replaced by new lasting powers of attorney (LPAs) because the donors will invariably lack capacity to grant a new power. Although it may be prudent for those who have already executed an enduring power to replace this with a new lasting power, many simply will not do so and it would be contrary to public policy to require donors – who have in good faith provided for the management of their property and affairs in the event of incapacity – to go to the effort and expense of making new LPAs. The status of these EPAs, registered and unregistered, has therefore been addressed.

10.2 MCA 2005, Sch 4 provides for the recognition and operation of EPAs made before the commencement of the Act. Although EPAA 1985 is repealed, all EPAs made prior to the commencement of MCA 2005 remain effective and operate as EPAs. The provisions of Sch 4 replicate the provisions of EPAA 1985. MCA 2005 therefore confirms that an EPA is a power of attorney, which has been executed in the prescribed form and which is not revoked on the onset of incapacity provided it is registered with the Public Guardian.[2] The attorney must, as soon as is practicable, make an application to register the EPA if he or she has reason to believe that the donor is or is becoming mentally incapable.[3] The attorney must, furthermore, notify a prescribed class of relatives before applying to register the LPA.

---

[1]   MCA 2005, Sch 7.

[2]   This preserves, for existing EPAs, a 'diagnostic threshold' which has to be attained before the power can be registered and as a result, a presumption that the donor is incapable of managing his or her property and affairs. MCA 2005, s 1 does not therefore apply (MCA 2005, Sch 4, para 1(1)).

[3]   MCA 2005, Sch 7, Part 2, para 4(1). MCA 2005, Sch 7, Part 8 defines 'mentally incapable' in the context of the management of the donor's property and affairs.

10.3 EPAs are dealt with in more detail in Chapter 3 and a detailed account of the rules and principles applicable to their operation is beyond the scope of this work.[4] However, practitioners will need to be able to advise on and administer two distinct types of statutory power of attorney and apply different principles and procedures to each one. There will no doubt be endless debate over whether one is better than the other, but the inevitable result will be the complexity of two different jurisdictions applicable to persons in identical circumstances.

TRANSITIONAL PROVISIONS (MENTAL CAPACITY ACT 2005, SCH 5)

10.4 MCA 2005, Sch 5[5] deals with transitional provisions and savings in two Parts. Part 1 covers the repeal of the Mental Health Act 1983, Part VII (which established the jurisdiction of the previous Court of Protection) and Part 2 covers the repeal of EPAA 1985 (which established EPAs).

Mental Health Act 1983, Part VII

10.5 A receiver under the former regime is in effect converted into a deputy under the new jurisdiction from its commencement but with the same functions as he or she had as receiver. Application may be made to the court to end the appointment, to make a decision not authorised or for the court to exercise its powers. Any existing order or appointment, direction or authority will continue to have effect despite the repeal of the Mental Health Act 1983, Part VII.

10.6 Any pending application for the exercise of a power under the Mental Health Act 1983, Part VII was treated, insofar as a corresponding power is exercisable, as an application for the exercise of that power.[6] An appeal which had not been determined continued to be dealt with under the former regime. All fees and other payments which, having become due, had not been paid were to be paid to the new Court of Protection after the commencement day.

10.7 The records of the former Court of Protection are to be treated as records of the new Court of Protection and the Public Guardian for the purpose of exercising any of his or her functions has access thereto. The new Court of Protection Rules may provide that former receivers must continue to render accounts.

---

[4] The topic is covered in greater and better detail in *Cretney & Lush on Enduring Powers of Attorney* (Jordans, 5th edn, 2001), which will remain the definitive work on the subject. The same law and procedure will apply to existing EPAs, only different statutory provisions will apply to their operation.

[5] MCA 2005, s 66(4).

[6] An application for the appointment of a receiver will be treated as an application for the appointment of a deputy.

Enduring Powers of Attorney Act 1985

10.8 Any order or determination made, or other thing done, under EPAA 1985 continues to have effect under the new jurisdiction from its commencement and insofar as it could have been done under MCA 2005, Sch 4[7] is so treated. Any instrument registered under EPAA 1985 is to be treated as having been registered by the Public Guardian under Sch 4.

10.9 Any pending application for the exercise of a power under EPAA 1985 was treated, insofar as a corresponding power was exercisable under MCA 2005, Sch 4, as an application for the exercise of that power. Special provisions apply to powers given by trustees. An appeal which had not been determined continued to be dealt with under the former regime.

CONSEQUENTIAL AMENDMENTS AND REPEALS (MENTAL CAPACITY ACT 2005, SCH 6)

10.10 It is inevitable that there is a long list of minor and consequential amendments to earlier legislation and these are to be found in MCA 2005, Sch 6. They date from the Fines and Recoveries Act 1833 and include amendments to the following legislation:

- Trustee Act 1925;
- Law of Property Act 1925;
- Administration of Estates Act 1925;
- National Assistance Act 1948, s 49;
- Intestates' Estates Act 1952;
- Variation of Trusts Act 1958;
- Administration of Justice Act 1960;
- Industrial and Provident Societies Act 1965;
- Compulsory Purchase Act 1965;
- Leasehold Reform Act 1967;
- Medicines Act 1968;
- Family Law Reform Act 1969;
- Local Authority Social Services Act 1970;
- Local Government Act 1972;
- Matrimonial Causes Act 1973;
- Consumer Credit Act 1974;
- Sale of Goods Act 1979;
- Limitation Act 1980, s 38;
- Mental Health Act 1983;

---

[7] See above.

- Insolvency Act 1986;
- Public Trustee and Administration of Funds Act 1986;
- Child Support Act 1991;
- Social Security Administration Act 1992;
- Leasehold Reform, Housing and Urban Development Act 1993;
- Disability Discrimination Act 1995;
- Trusts of Land and Appointment of Trustees Act 1996;
- Adoption and Children Act 2002; and
- Licensing Act 2003.

10.11 In addition, specific repeals of earlier legislation are to be found in MCA 2005, Sch 7. The following wholesale repeals are noteworthy:

- Mental Health Act 1983, Part VII; and
- Enduring Powers of Attorney Act 1985.

10.12 With effect from 1 October 2009 numerous amendments were made by the Mental Capacity Act 2005 (Transitional and Consequential Provisions) Order 2007[8] to various Statutory Instruments. These are set out in Schedule 1 and include such diverse regulations and court rules as:

- National Savings Bank Regulations 1972;
- Premium Savings Bond Regulations 1972;
- National Savings Stock Register Regulations 1976;
- Motor Vehicles (Tests) Regulations 1981;
- Mental Health Review Tribunal Rules 1983;
- Road Vehicles (Construction and Use) Regulations 1986;
- Insolvency Rules 1986;
- Non-contentious Probate Rules 1987;
- Savings Certificates Regulations 1991.

In the present context the most significant amendment is that to the Insolvency Rules 1986 whereby the new definition of 'lacks capacity' is adopted for incapacitated persons. Similar changes were made by amendments to the Civil Procedure Rules 1998 and the Family Procedure Rules 2010.

---

[8] SI 2007/1898.

CHAPTER 11

THE MARGINS OF THE MCA[1]

PRELIMINARY

11.1 In this chapter, we highlight four areas at the fringes of the jurisdiction of the Court which are of particular significance to practitioners:

- the inherent jurisdiction of the High Court;
- the overlap with judicial review;
- the overlap with civil proceedings; and
- the jurisdiction of the Court of Protection to grant declarations and award damages for breaches of the European Convention on Human Rights.

In each case, a health warning should be given. The precise boundaries and interrelationship between the Court of Protection and other courts are not fixed by statute; they are therefore subject to evolution and what is set out below of necessity therefore represents a snapshot as at the time of writing.

THE INHERENT JURISDICTION

Background

11.2 It is now clear that the inherent jurisdiction of the High Court has survived the implementation of MCA 2005 so as to remain of relevance in two distinct ways when considering the position of adults requiring the protection of the courts:

- To protect vulnerable persons who require such protection but do not fall within the categories of incapacitated persons covered by MCA 2005. A number of cases determined since the enactment of MCA 2005 had suggested that this was so, but the matter was put definitively beyond doubt in *DL v A Local Authority and Others*,[2] at least insofar as it concerns those who require protection from the baleful influence of third parties;

---

[1] Parts of this chapter first appeared in Alex Ruck Keene *'The Inherent Jurisdiction: Where are we now?'* (2013) 1 Elder Law Journal; it also draws upon case summaries included in the 39 Essex Chambers Mental Capacity Law newsletter (available at www.copcasesonline.com).

[2] [2012] EWCA Civ 253, [2012] COPLR 504.

- To enable a High Court judge, exercising the inherent jurisdiction, to afford protection to <u>incapacitated</u> adults where the remedy sought does not fall within the remedies provided for in MCA 2005.

Both of these are discussed in turn. At **11.10ff** is discussed a third potential way in which the inherent jurisdiction has survived, namely to afford protection in the case of an adult unable to take a decision for themselves but who does not suffer from an impairment of or disturbance in the functioning of the mind such as to fall within MCA 2005, s 2(1).

Vulnerable adults

11.3 The precise scope of the High Court's powers under the inherent jurisdiction in respect of those who are not considered to lack capacity within the meaning of MCA 2005 but who require its protection against third parties has still to be finally tested, but it is suggested that the following points are uncontroversial:

- The jurisdiction can only be exercised by High Court judges (most usually of the Family Division) sitting in their capacity as such, rather than as judges of the Court of Protection. The Court of Protection only has jurisdiction over those who lack capacity within the meaning of MCA 2005, and the powers exercised over the capacitous but vulnerable are therefore powers of the High Court;
- For these purposes, 'vulnerable' adults includes those who, even if not incapacitated by mental disorder or mental illness, are, or are reasonably believed to be, either (i) under constraint or (ii) subject to coercion or undue influence or (iii) for some other reason deprived of the capacity to make the relevant decision, or disabled from making a free choice, or incapacitated or disabled from giving or expressing a real and genuine consent;[3]
- The test for engaging the inherent jurisdiction of the High Court is whether the proposed intervention is necessary and proportionate;[4]
- The High Court will in the first instance seek to exercise the inherent jurisdiction so as to facilitate the process of unencumbered decision-making by the adult, rather than taking the decision for or on behalf of the adult;[5]

---

[3] Per Munby J (as he then was) in *A Local Authority v (1) MA (2) NA and (3) SA* [2005] EWHC 2942, para 77, the seminal case in which the jurisdiction of the High Court was identified. To this end the term 'vulnerable adult' retains a specific meaning even if in the context of safeguarding and the Care Act 2014 the term is no longer one that has currency.

[4] *DL* at paras 66 (per McFarlane LJ) and 76 (per Davis LJ).

[5] See in this regard, in particular, *LBL v RYJ and VJ* [2010] EWHC 2665 (COP), [2010] COPLR Con Vol 795 and the dicta of Macur J in that case as to the 'facilitative, rather than dictatorial, approach of the court' to the exercise of the inherent jurisdiction in the case of vulnerable adults, her dicta being expressly endorsed by the Court of Appeal in *A Local Authority v DL & Ors* (above, fn 2, at para 67, per McFarlane LJ).

- However, the inherent jurisdiction of the High Court is not limited solely to affording a vulnerable adult a temporary 'safe space' within which to make a decision free from any alleged source of undue influence.[6] The High Court could therefore impose long-term injunctive relief to protect the vulnerable adult (for instance, by making orders without limit of time prohibiting third parties from taking steps to remove the adult from the jurisdiction).

11.4 A difficult question which has yet definitively to be answered is whether the High Court in the exercise of its inherent jurisdiction in respect of a vulnerable adult can grant relief which goes further than that aimed against third parties. For instance, could the High Court require that the adult be removed from the environment in which they are subject to coercion? In the author's experience, the courts have sought vigorously to explore all steps short of this, and have fought shy of granting such relief. In very significant part, this is because whilst it is conceptually easy to formulate effective relief against a third party or parties so as to protect the vulnerable adult, it is much less easy to formulate relief directed against the vulnerable adult in such a way that it does not become dictatorial rather than facilitative. However, it is suggested that in a sufficiently extreme case the High Court could properly take the view that the welfare of the vulnerable adult required their removal.[7] It is suggested that this could only ever be justified where it could be shown all other protective measures had failed and where there was a realistic possibility that the removal would put the adult in a position to make a free choice about the matter or matters in respect of which it was considered that their will was being overborne. This, though, is subject to the caveat that steps amounting to a deprivation of liberty can only be taken where one of the bases for such deprivation contained in Art 5(1) of the ECHR is made out; the most obvious being where the adult suffers from a 'mental disorder' so as to come within the scope of Art 5(1)(e) of the ECHR.[8] In *NCC v PB and TB*,[9] Parker J expressed the view – obiter – that the inherent jurisdiction extended so as to allow a vulnerable adult to be deprived of their liberty in circumstances where they strongly objected to such a course of action. It is respectfully suggested that

---

[6]   DL at para 68 per McFarlane LJ. For an example of the type of relief that may be granted, see the decision of Baker J in *O v P* [2015] EWHC 935 (Fam).

[7]   A comparison with the position in relation to Scotland is instructive: the interested reader is directed to the paper by Alex Ruck Keene available at http://www.39essex.com/inherent-jurisdiction-note/, which considers the extent to which the High Court could or should model the relief that it grants under the inherent jurisdiction upon the relief available under the Adult Support and Protection Act 2007.

[8]   That the High Court can grant relief under the inherent jurisdiction which involves the deprivation of liberty of an adult suffering from a mental disorder was confirmed in *An NHS Trust v Dr A* [2013] EWHC 2442 (COP), [2013] COPLR 605. It may not be necessary to have medical evidence of such a disorder in advance in a true emergency: *Winterwerp v The Netherlands* (1979) 2 EHRR 387 at paragraph 39 and *X v United Kingdom (Application No 7215/75*, decision of 5 November 1981) at paras 41 and 45), but evidence of such disorder must be obtained as soon as practicable.

[9]   [2014] EWCOP 14, [2015] COPLR 118.

these obiter observations should be approached with caution, especially the analysis of the interaction between the inherent jurisdiction and Art 5(1)(e).[10]

Incapacitated adults

11.5 In *XCC v AA & Anor*,[11] Parker J emphasised a point which (although made by the Court of Appeal early in the life of MCA 2005) has sometimes been overlooked, namely that there remains the possibility that the High Court can grant relief under the inherent jurisdiction in respect of a person who is incapacitated within the meaning of MCA 2005, but where such relief does not lie within the gift of the Court of Protection under the powers granted it by MCA 2005. The decision of Parker J is also of some importance – and potentially no little difficulty – as regards how the High Court will exercise the inherent jurisdiction in such circumstances.

11.6 In *XCC*, Parker J was concerned with the question of whether she had power under MCA 2005 to make a declaration that a marriage entered into in and recognised as valid in Bangladesh was to be recognised under the law of England and Wales in circumstances where P had lacked the capacity to marry. She held that the repertoire of declarations available to the Court of Protection in MCA 2005, s 15 expressly circumscribed and limited the power of the Court under that Act and did not extend to the making of such a 'non-recognition declaration.' She did not therefore have the power, as a Court of Protection judge, to make such a declaration.[12] Importantly, however, she went on to hold that:

> 'The protection or intervention of the inherent jurisdiction of the High Court is available to those lacking capacity within the meaning of the MCA 2005 as it is to capacitous but vulnerable adults who have had their will overborne, and on the same basis, where the remedy sought does not fall within the repertoire of remedies provided for in the MCA 2005. It would be unjustifiable and discriminatory not to grant the same relief to incapacitated adults who cannot consent as to capacitous adults whose will has been overborne.'[13]

---

[10]   Whilst 'P' in the case before Parker J had a recognised psychiatric condition, it is suggested that it is very far from obvious how such a condition could be said to be such as to warrant detention applying the strict criteria set down in *Winterwerp* (n 8 above). Further, Parker J's statement that 'deprivation of liberty is specifically authorised under the 2005 Act in cases of incapacity without reference to unsoundness of mind' (para 118) is not easy to square with the conclusion of the *President in Re X & Ors (Deprivation of Liberty)* [2014] EWCOP 25, [2014] COPLR 674 that an application for judicial authorisation of a deprivation of liberty requires evidence not just of lack of capacity to consent to the care arrangements but also of unsoundness of mind (see paras 14 and 35(v)). Although the Court of Appeal held that the President had not, in fact, made any binding decision in this case ([2015] EWCA Civ 599), no party challenged these obiter remarks, nor did the Court of Appeal cast any doubt upon them.

[11]   [2012] EWHC 2183 (COP), [2012] COPLR 730.

[12]   Paragraph 48.

[13]   Paragraph 54.

There being a lacuna in the law, in the form of the absence of a power under MCA 2005 to make a non-recognition declaration, Parker J held that she had the jurisdiction – as a High Court judge – to make such a declaration under the inherent jurisdiction.

11.7 In reaching this conclusion, Parker J noted that she considered the Court of Appeal decision in *City of Westminster v IC and KC and NN*[14] to be binding authority for the proposition that she had jurisdiction to make such a declaration under the inherent jurisdiction. This may be doubted, because the question of why the Court of Appeal felt it had to proceed under the inherent jurisdiction when making such a declaration had not been considered by that court.[15] In any event, however, the decision in *XCC* would seem to put the question of whether it was necessary to use the inherent jurisdiction beyond doubt.

11.8 Finally in this regard, it should also be noted that Parker J proceeded in *XCC* on the basis that, in considering whether to grant a non-recognition declaration, the court was not confined to making a decision dictated only by considerations as to best interests, whether those set out in MCA 2005 s 4 or more general welfare considerations.[16] She therefore found that she was entitled to take into account public policy considerations and – specifically – that the marriage had been arranged for the purpose of engineering the entry of P's spouse into this country so as to allow him to work here. This is in very clear contrast to the position that prevails under MCA 2005: see *Sandwell Metropolitan Borough Council v RG & Ors*,[17] in which Holman J declined to declare (under MCA 2005) that it was in P's best interests that steps be taken to annul a marriage which was voidable as he had not had capacity to enter into it. He considered *XCC*, but noted that there was – for purposes of decisions being made under MCA 2005 – no place for policy considerations.

11.9 It is important to note, however, that where 'policy' considerations are not in issue, the court is likely to proceed as if it were conducting a best interests analysis governed by MCA 2005, s 5. In *An NHS Trust v Dr A*,[18] Baker J held that force-feeding and the ancillary deprivation of liberty required to bring about such feeding was in the best interests of the incapacitated adult in question, but that it could not be authorised save under the inherent jurisdiction because (a) the adult was detained under the Mental Health

---

[14]   [2008] EWCA Civ 198, [2008] 2 FLR 267.

[15]   The earlier case is also somewhat curious in that Wall LJ appeared (at paras 54–55) to entertain the possibility that there was no power under MCA 2005 to take steps to prevent an incapacitated adult being removed from the jurisdiction. Thorpe LJ proceeded on the basis that there was such a power, contained in MCA 2005, s 17(1)(a) (para 13). Hallett LJ agreed with both judgments without explaining which analysis she preferred. The author would respectfully suggest that the approach of Thorpe LJ is to be preferred, and indeed has been in (unreported) cases in which the Court of Protection has made 'non-removal' orders so to ensure that 'P' remains at an identified location in England and Wales.

[16]   Above, footnote 11 at para 56.

[17]   [2013] EWHC 2373 (COP), [2013] COPLR 643.

[18]   *An NHS Trust v Dr A* [2013] EWHC 2442 (COP).

Act 1983 and therefore ineligible to be deprived of his liberty under MCA 2005,[19] but (b) force-feeding could not properly be considered to be medical treatment for a mental disorder which could be compulsorily administered under the provisions of the MHA 1983. Baker J, following Parker J in *XCC*, identified that there was a lacuna, and deployed the provisions of the inherent jurisdiction so as to authorise the treatment and the ancillary deprivation of the adult's liberty.[20]

Adults lacking capacity for a reason outside MCA 2005

11.10 It is important to remember that there are those who lack the capacity to take decisions but for a reason which does not satisfy the diagnostic threshold set down in MCA 2005, s 2, and whose lack of capacity does not depend upon the overbearing influence of a third party. They are likely to be relatively few in number, but a possible example of such a person (drawn from an unreported case in the author's experience) might be someone born deaf and deprived of access to signing throughout their childhood. Such a combination can lead to language deprivation, resulting in concrete thinking, limited theory of mind and poor problem solving. Whilst fundamentally impacting upon a person's ability to make choices, it is not necessarily the case that such a combination of difficulties (flowing from the consequences of physical disability combined with the deleterious circumstances of the individual's childhood) would satisfy the diagnostic criteria contained in MCA, s 2(1). This category of person was not discussed by the Court of Appeal in *DL*.[21] However, the definition given by Munby J in *Re SA* of the 'vulnerable' included those 'for some other reason ... incapacitated or disabled from giving or expressing a real and genuine consent.'

11.11 The definition given by Munby J of the 'vulnerable' in *Re SA* was expressly endorsed by the Court of Appeal in *DL*.[22] It is further suggested that it is wide enough to capture the category under discussion and, indeed, logic would dictate that if they do not fall to be considered by reference to the MCA 2005, they either fall to be protected by reference to the inherent jurisdiction or fall not to be protected at all. The tenor of both *DL* and *XCC* is very firmly that the courts can and should be flexible and creative in deploying the inherent jurisdiction, so long as its deployment is not inconsistent with the MCA 2005. Taking this approach would not, it is suggested, be incompatible with the MCA 2005, and it is therefore suggested that such persons would fall – in an appropriate case – to benefit from the protection of the High Court by

---

[19] By virtue of Sch 1A, paras 1 and 2 to and s 16A of MCA 2005. See also Chapter 7.

[20] A similar approach was adopted in *A Local Health Board v AB* [2015] EWCOP 31. Note, however, that the parties and the court appear to have proceeded on a misunderstanding in this case as to the proper operation of Sch 1A, and – as discussed in Chapter 7 – this was not, in fact, a case in which the inherent jurisdiction was required.

[21] Above, footnote 2. See also **11.3–4**.

[22] Above, footnote 2 at para 56.

the exercise of the inherent jurisdiction even if their inability to make a choice does not arise because they are subject at the material time to the baleful influence of a third party.

11.12   In such a case, a very real question would arise as to whether the High Court should exercise its inherent jurisdiction as if it were exercising its powers under MCA 2005 ss 15-6. It is suggested that there is no logical objection in principle to such an approach. Indeed, in such a case, limiting the grant of relief to injunctive relief against third parties would not necessarily serve any purpose, not least as there may well be no third party involved at all.

11.13   It is likely, though, that in the event that the High Court is considering the exercise of its inherent jurisdiction in the circumstances outlined in the paragraphs above:

- The High Court will take very considerable care to reassure itself that the person is not, in fact, materially incapacitated within the meaning of ss 2–3 of the MCA 2005;[23]
- The High Court will be likely to wish to limit itself in the first place to the grant of relief designed – if possible – to improve the adult's autonomy in decision-making. In other words, the High Court will – and should – be slow to use the inherent jurisdiction in this regard as a simple fall-back in the event that the public authority in question is unable to make good an application founded upon the MCA 2005.[24]
- The High Court can only grant relief which involves a deprivation of the adult's liberty if they suffer a mental disorder so as to bring them within Art 5(1)(e) of the ECHR.[25]

11.14   It is further suggested that, if the High Court were to be exercising the inherent jurisdiction in such a case, it should proceed <u>as if</u> it were bound by the principles contained in (in particular) s 4 of the MCA 2005. In other words, it should not adopt the approach taken by Parker J in *XCC* (above, **11.5**). That approach could in any event be distinguished because Parker J there was not exercising the inherent jurisdiction to take a decision on behalf of the adult

---

[23]   In *LBL v RYJ and VJ* (above, footnote 5), for instance, Macur J noted that '[i]f I were to have found that [RYJ's] vulnerability was exceptional/greater by reason of her limited intellectual functioning and age, these factors would need to have been considered in reaching my decision concerning capacity. If she is unable to withstand external pressure of "normal/everyday" degree, whether emotional or physical, it seems to me that it would necessarily inform the answer to the question posed at s 3(1)(c) of the Act' (para 64). In the case discussed at **11.10** above for instance, a further report produced by a psychiatrist (as opposed to a psychologist) identified a material impairment which satisfied the diagnostic criteria under MCA 2005, s 2(1).

[24]   A course of action Macur J deprecated in *LBL*. This case can be distinguished from the situation under consideration here because it was common ground that RYJ satisfied the diagnostic criteria in s 2(1); we are concerned here with the position where the individual's material inability to take the decision in question stems from a situation where they do not so satisfy the criteria.

[25]   See **11.4** and fn 8 above.

before her; rather, she was using it to grant a declaration which lay outside the suite of remedies that were provided for in MCA 2005.

Statutory reform

11.15 Responding both to the Law Commission's report upon Adult Social Care[26] and the report of the Dilnot Commission,[27] the Coalition Government enacted a new Care Act to modernise the entirety of adult social services law. The Act started to come in force in April 2015 and impacts upon the issues under discussion in this section in two ways.

11.16 First, the Care Act repealed s 47 of the National Assistance Act 1948, which gave a notional power to local authorities to remove someone from his or her home in certain circumstances. It had been very rarely used, in large part because of concerns as to its compatibility with Art 5(1)(e) of the ECHR.

11.17 Second, the Care Act imposes, for the first time, a statutory duty upon authorities to make enquiries where there is a safeguarding concern in respect of an adult in its area who satisfies a number of criteria.[28] In such a case, the local authority 'must make (or cause to be made) whatever enquiries it thinks necessary to enable it to decide whether any action should be taken (whether under [the Act] or otherwise]) and, if so, what and by whom.'[29] The Department of Health had previously consulted upon whether there should be a new power of entry enacted to support this duty, enabling the local authority to speak to someone with mental capacity who they think could be at risk of abuse or neglect, in order to ascertain that they are making their decisions freely. Equivalent powers in Scotland in the Adult Support and Protection (Scotland) Act 2007[30] and in Wales.[31] To the considerable consternation of many groups such as Action on Elder Abuse, the Department declined to include such a power in the Bill. This means that recourse is likely to be required regularly to the inherent jurisdiction to enable local authorities to discharge their statutory safeguarding functions.

---

[26] Available at: http://lawcommission.justice.gov.uk/publications/1460.htm.

[27] Available at: www.dilnotcommission.dh.gov.uk/.

[28] Namely (1) that they have needs for care and support (whether or not the authority is meeting any of those needs); (2) is experiencing, or is at risk of, abuse or neglect; and (2) as a result of those needs is unable to protect himself or herself against the abuse or neglect or the risk of it.

[29] Section 42.

[30] Section 7. The Scottish powers, in fact, extend significantly further: for a discussion of the powers and their use, see Michael Preston-Shoot and Sally Cornish, 'Paternalism or proportionality? Experiences and outcomes of the Adult Support and Protection (Scotland) Act 2007,' *The Journal of Adult Protection*, Emerald Publishing, [2014] JAP 5.

[31] The Social Services and Well-Being (Wales) Act 2014, s 127 (adult support and protection orders).

OVERLAP WITH JUDICIAL REVIEW

The approach of the Court of Protection

11.19 The procedure described in the main body of this work works well when the public body responsible for the wellbeing of the person concerned (whether in a medical context or in the context of their welfare more generally) either brings proceedings to seek a decision from the court or is a party to the proceedings and is willing to abide by the result. However, there may be cases in which the public body has already taken a decision and the question then arises how that decision can appropriately be challenged. Alternatively, the public body may decide in the currency of Court of Protection proceedings that it does not wish to put before the Court a particular option for consideration. For instance, a local authority may contend that a placement to which P has been moved in discharge of its community care functions sufficiently meets their needs that they are not prepared to incur the substantially greater expenditure that may be required to allow them to move home. The question that then arises is as to the extent the Court of Protection is able to compel a public authority to discharge its statutory functions in a certain way or to make a specific funding decision. Put another way, how and when will parallel public law proceedings be required in such situations?

11.20 Cases decided prior to the enactment of MCA 2005 suggested that, in the event of an impasse of the nature described above, it would be necessary to proceed by way of judicial review in order to challenge the decision of the public authority.[32] In May 2015, the Court of Appeal confirmed in *Re MN*[33] that this remains the position. Sir James Munby P, giving the sole reasoned judgment of the court, held that:

> '80. The function of the Court of Protection is to take, on behalf of adults who lack capacity, the decisions which, if they had capacity, they would take themselves. The Court of Protection has no more power, just because it is acting on behalf of an adult who lacks capacity, to obtain resources or facilities from a third party, whether a private individual or a public authority, than the adult if he had capacity would be able to obtain himself. [...] The Court of Protection is thus confined to choosing between available options, including those which there is good reason to believe will be forthcoming in the foreseeable future.

> 81. The Court of Protection, like the family court and the Family Division, can explore the care plan being put forward by a public authority and, where appropriate, require the authority to go away and think again. Rigorous probing, searching questions and persuasion are permissible; pressure is not. And in the final analysis the Court of Protection cannot compel a public authority to agree to a care plan which the authority is unwilling to implement. I agree with the point Eleanor King J made in her judgment (para 57):

---

[32] See, in particular, *A v A Health Authority* [2002] Fam 213 and *Re S (Vulnerable Adult)* [2007] 2 FLR 1095.

[33] [2015] EWCA Civ 411, [2015] COPLR forthcoming.

"In my judgment, such discussions and judicial encouragement for flexibility and negotiation in respect of a care package are actively to be encouraged. Such negotiations are however a far cry from the court embarking on a 'best interests' trial with a view to determining whether or not an option which has been said by care provider (in the exercise of their statutory duties) not to be available, is nevertheless in the patient's best interest."'

The Court of Appeal in *Re MN* also upheld the approach of the judge below in respect of the application of HRA 1998. Eleanor King J had held that, exceptionally, and where a properly pleaded case is raised under HRA 1998, s 7(1)(b), the court must consider a hypothetical option for purposes of determining whether a public authority has acted in a way that is disproportionate and incompatible with a Convention right. This will, however, be very much the exception rather than the norm.

11.21   The following procedural matters arise in consequence:

- It is necessary to grapple early and clearly with whether the case in question is one in which this thorny issue arises. It may well be the case that the public authority, for good reason, may well not wish to commit itself to a stark statement that 'option A is not available' so as to allow room for discussion and the maintenance of a working relationship. However, if the reality is that it is not, it is likely to be better for this to be established sooner rather than later;

- Before deciding whether to issue parallel proceedings, the parties should consider whether the public authority has genuinely put one option before the court to the exclusion of all others or has simply indicated its preference. If it is a question of preference, parallel public law proceedings may not be required – it may suffice to seek a direction from the court that the public authority offers an alternative;

- If there is a disagreement between the parties as to how P's best interests should be met, the party/parties advancing a contrary position to that of the public authority should adduce their own evidence as to how those interests can properly be met;

- Where the decision under challenge is clearly one in which the public authority has exercised its discretion in such a way as expressly (or by necessary implication) to seek to balance P's interests against the funding implications for others, then it is more likely than not that the proper forum to such a challenge will be in the Administrative Court. The public law challenge should be expedited such that the Court of Protection's best interests analysis can be conducted in light of the available options on the ground (see, by analogy: *Re S*[34]);

- As in the earlier cases determined in relation to children and vulnerable adults, there can frequently be room for creative negotiation between the parties and between (in a loose sense) the parties and the court even if the

---

[34]   See above, fn 32.

result can, on occasion, be a stand-off which affords of no proper resolution save a public law challenge;

- If a party does intend to rely upon the provisions of the ECHR to seek to persuade the court to adopt a specific approach to the decision(s)s that fall to be taken in respect of P, this must be pleaded in detail at the earliest possible stage. The position where a party wishes to raise a claim for declarations and/or damages for a breach of rights under the ECHR is addressed at **11.50** below.

The approach of the Administrative Court

11.22 The Administrative Court will be astute to ensure that cases that should properly be determined within the four walls of the Court of Protection remain there. In *R (DO) v LBH*,[35] permission was refused to the sister of 'P' in concurrent Court of Protection proceedings to bring judicial review applications against decisions of the local authority which had the effect of removing her from caring for her brother and making decisions as to his care arrangements. HHJ Jarman QC (sitting as a Deputy High Court Judge) noted[36] that such questions were ones which the Court of Protection with its expertise was particularly suited to deal with and that judicial review was only a remedy of last resort which should only be deployed where (for instance) an application or appeal within Court of Protection proceedings was not available.

11.23 Of even greater importance is the decision in *R (Chatting) v Viridian Housing*,[37] in which the court was asked to consider a contention that the local authority had erred by not making reference to the claimant's best interests when deciding as to arrangements made for her accommodation under the National Assistance Act 1948. Rejecting that submission, Nicholas Paines QC (sitting as a Deputy High Court Judge) noted (it is suggested entirely accurately) that:

> '99 ... Plainly they would have erred in law if they had regarded Miss Chatting's best interests as an irrelevance, because they would have been in breach of their duty under section 21(2) of the 1948 Act to have regard for her welfare. But the fact that Miss Chatting is mentally incapacitated does not import the test of "what is in her best interests?" as the yardstick by which all care decisions are to be made.

> 100 Section 1(5) of the Act applies to "an act done, or decision made ... for or on behalf of a person who lacks capacity". Its decision-making criteria and procedures are designed to be a substitute for the lack of independent capacity of the person to act or take decisions for him or herself. They come into play in circumstances where a person with capacity would take, or participate in the taking of, a decision. In deciding not to press for the registration of Miss Chatting's flat as a residential home for one person and in deciding (as they appear to have

---

[35] [2012] EWHC 4044 (Admin), available on the www.mentalhealthlaw.co.uk website.
[36] Paragraphs 18–19.
[37] [2012] EWHC 3595 (Admin), [2013] COPLR 108.

done) to agree to a novation of their section 26 arrangements for Miss Chatting so as to substitute Gold Care for Viridian, Wandsworth Borough Council were taking decisions that fell to them to take, with due regard for her welfare. They could rationally conclude that the decisions were compatible with her welfare. They did not as a matter of law require Miss Chatting's assent to these decisions; no decision, or participation in a decision was involved on her part.'

The approach adopted by the Deputy Judge was specifically endorsed by the Court of Appeal in *Re MN*.[38]

11.24 In light of the decision in *Chatting*, it is suggested that practitioners would be well-advised to proceed on the basis that the Administrative Court in deciding whether a public body has discharged the obligations imposed upon it by the relevant community care legislation in respect of an incapacitated adult will therefore:

- proceed by reference to that legislation (and any obligations imposed, for instance, by the Human Rights Act 1998), rather than by asking itself whether the decision is in the incapacitated adult's best interests; and
- be very cautious before reading into any consultation requirements imposed (for instance) by the Care Act 2014 any additional obligations imposed by MCA 2005.

11.25 It is, though, important to note that the Administrative Court is likely to adopt an 'intense' standard of review of public law decisions taken in respect of those without capacity to take material decisions. This is not because of their lack of capacity per se, but because their lack of such capacity is likely to indicate their vulnerability. In such cases, following *R (KM) v Cambridgeshire County Council, National Autistic Society and others intervening*,[39] it is likely that the Administrative Court will consider that the impact of the decision upon the service user is sufficiently profound as to call for a high intensity of review.

OVERLAP WITH PERSONAL INJURY PROCEEDINGS

Overview

11.26 Prior to the introduction of MCA 2005, there was a very close link between the Court of Protection and personal injury litigants in that the court's approval was required in cases involving settlements out of court on behalf of incapacitated claimants. That approval is no longer required, and the automatic link therefore largely severed. However, there remain an important number of areas in which coordination will be required between the Court of Protection

---

[38] See **11.20**.
[39] At para 36 per Lord Wilson SCJ (with whom Lords Phillips, Walker, Brown, Kerr and Dyson SCJJ agreed).

and the civil courts as regards personal injury claimants. Four main areas give rise to points of sufficient importance to practitioners to warrant coverage in this chapter:

- The assessment of P's capacity in civil proceedings, both to litigate and to manage and control any money received;
- The approach to assessment of P's needs in personal injury proceedings contrasted to assessment of P's best interests in proceedings before the Court of Protection;
- The approach that the Court of Protection will take to approving proposals for the management of any monies recovered by P by way of compensation;
- The approach taken by the Court of Protection to steps in the civil proceedings aimed at preventing double recovery.[40]

Assessment of capacity

11.27 It is not unusual for an issue to arise in civil proceedings as to whether P (the claimant) is a protected party (ie lacking capacity to conduct the proceedings[41]) or a protected beneficiary (ie lacking capacity to managing and control any money recovered[42]). The former is important because if the claimant is a protected party any proceedings conducted without a litigation friend will be invalid. The latter is important because an additional head of damages will arise if the damages have to be administered by a deputy appointed by the Court of Protection (see further **11.41** below).

11.28 In *Saulle v Nouvet*,[43] Andrew Edis QC, sitting as a deputy High Court judge, confirmed that the High Court was required for purposes of civil proceedings to consider the question of whether P is either a protected party or a protected beneficiary by applying the test set down in MCA 2005.[44] Whilst in that case the Court resolved for itself the questions of the claimant's status for purposes of the CPR, in some circumstances it is suggested that it will be appropriate for the questions of P's capacity to litigate and/or to manage his financial affairs to be transferred to the Court of Protection. As identified by District Judge Ashton:[45]

> [The decision in *Saulle v Nouvet*] identifies a weakness of dealing with the issue of capacity in the civil court. That court can make a definitive decision as to capacity

---

40 The contribution of Simon Edwards of 39 Essex Chambers to material under this heading is gratefully acknowledged.
41 Civil Procedure Rules 1998 (CPR), r 21.1(2)(d).
42 CPR, r 21.1(2)(e).
43 [2007] EWHC 2902 (QB).
44 Although he made it clear that this because he was required to do so by virtue of the CPR, the MCA 2005 strictly only establishing the definition of capacity for purposes of that Act, and not regulating the conduct of any court other than the Court of Protection. See, in particular, para 21.
45 *In the matter of GS* – CoP Case No: 11582024, Preston County Court, 10 July 2008.

to litigate but it cannot make a decision as to capacity to manage financial affairs that will be binding on the Court of Protection. Conversely, the Court of Protection has a statutory power to make declarations as to capacity which may relate to both litigation and management of financial affairs and any such declarations are likely to be followed by a civil court. In substantial personal injury claims where the quantum of damages may be affected by the involvement of the Court of Protection there are therefore advantages in the civil court referring both issues of capacity to the Court of Protection for determination. However, where the amount of money involved would not normally trigger the intervention of the Court of Protection it is proportionate and desirable for the civil court to adjudicate on both aspects of capacity (ie to decide whether the litigant is a protected party and if so then whether he or she is also a protected beneficiary).'

11.29 Transferring questions of capacity to the Court of Protection will bring its own problems, not least because it may well take longer to convene a hearing than it would in the Queen's Bench Division. However, if questions of P's capacity to litigate and/or to manage his financial affairs are transferred to the Court of Protection, it is suggested that it would be appropriate for the defendant to the civil proceedings to participate in the proceedings before the Court of Protection, if for no other reason that this will facilitate the introduction of all the medical evidence from the civil proceedings. It is suggested that as a discrete issue in the civil proceedings has been delegated for decision to the Court of Protection the defendant to those proceedings would have a sufficient interest to satisfy r 75 of the Court of Protection Rules 2007, and their joinder would be desirable for purposes of r 73 (and thus the position would be different to that contemplated by Bodey J in *Re SK* discussed at **11.35 ff** below).[46]

11.30 Difficult issues can, though, arise where the question of capacity to manage property and affairs is properly before both the Court of Protection and a court considering a civil claim. Whilst District Judge Ashton in *GS* noted that declarations as to capacity made by the Court of Protection are likely to be followed by the civil court, that this will not necessarily be the case can be seen from the decision in *Loughlin v Singh & Ors*.[47] This case represents something of a cautionary tale, so merits consideration in a little detail.

11.31 Mr Loughlin, the claimant in personal injury proceedings, had already had a deputy appointed to manage his property and affairs. That deputy had been appointed upon the application of the Court of Protection department of the solicitors instructed on his behalf in the personal injury proceedings. The defendant to the personal injury proceedings contended that, in fact, the claimant had the capacity to manage his property and affairs, and for the purposes of the personal injury proceedings, Kenneth Parker J therefore embarked upon a full-fledged determination of the question with the assistance

---

[46] A defendant was joined for these purposes by District Judge Ashton in *In the matter of AKP* (COP) Case No: 10185666, Preston County Court, 1 November 2007, although to the extent that the Court took into account that the defendant had a financial interest in the outcome, that must now be read subject to the dicta of Bodey J in *Re SK*.

[47] [2013] EWHC 1641 (QB), [2013] COPLR 371.

of expert evidence called by both parties. In the civil proceedings, it emerged that the claimant's solicitors' Court of Protection department had in fact had evidence that he <u>had</u> capacity to manage his property and affairs, but had not put this evidence before the District Judge when making the application for the appointment of a deputy, relying instead upon evidence subsequently commissioned (independently) by the same firm's litigation department. That evidence was, itself, unsatisfactory because the expert providing it had initially considered that the claimant had had capacity, but then changed his mind without apparent good reason. However, only the later of the expert's reports was put before the Court of Protection, and it was on the basis of that report that it appears that the District Judge made the appointment upon the papers.

11.32 Whilst Kenneth Parker J found, on a fine balance, that the claimant had at all material times lacked capacity to manage his property and affairs, such that the appointment of the deputy had, in fact, been appropriate, he was, understandably, highly critical of the approach adopted by the claimant's solicitors,[48] noting that this was a case in which all available medical evidence relating to the question of capacity should have been disclosed to the Court of Protection. Kenneth Parker J made it clear that he considered that:

> '... the lamentable failures that occurred here, and the invidious position in which the judge in the Court of Protection was unwittingly placed, must never be repeated. The issue of capacity is of very great importance, and all involved must ensure that the Court of Protection has all the material which, on proper reflection, is necessary for a just and accurate decision.'[49]

Kenneth Parker J held that, had all the medical evidence in the possession of the claimant's solicitors been put before the Court of Protection at the time of applying for the appointment of a deputy, it would then have been 'almost certain' that the District Judge considering the application would have insisted on an oral hearing. He further noted that the possibility could not be ruled out that the court might have found at that hearing that the claimant <u>had</u> capacity, a finding which 'although not unreasonable, would have been incorrect.'

11.33 Most likely because of the curious and unsatisfactory way in which the Court of Protection had appointed the deputy, Kenneth Parker J did not anywhere ask himself the question of whether the defendant was entitled to put in issue before him the question of whether the claimant had capacity to make decisions as to the management of his property and affairs. On one view, it might be said that to do so amounted to a collateral attack upon the decision of the Court of Protection, and the proper course of action would have been for the defendant to seek to take steps before the Court of Protection to put the evidence disclosed in the civil proceedings before the Court of Protection and invite it to take appropriate steps to revisit its decision. On the other hand, it

---

[48] His criticisms are contained in a separate annex to the judgment explaining, inter alia, why he was unable to place any weight upon the evidence of the claimant's expert who had changed his mind.

[49] Paragraph 15 of the Annex.

could also be said that (as per, for instance *Re SK*[50]) the two courts were considering the question of the claimant's capacity for two different purposes,[51] and that the civil court was entitled to reach a different conclusion upon the totality of the evidence as it stood before it. On balance, it is suggested that there is no necessary bar upon the issue of capacity being determined in both jurisdictions, although whichever court is the later in time to consider the matter should be astute to give clear reasons as to why it is conducting a separate investigation. It is likely, though, that this procedural question will ultimately have to be the subject of judicial determination.

11.34 Finally, it should be noted that a claimant may already, for entirely unrelated reasons, be subject to the jurisdiction of the Court of Protection, and in that event will (very likely) be a protected beneficiary and (almost inevitably) a protected party for purposes of civil proceedings. However, because capacity is decision specific, it is possible to contemplate a claimant with very substantial property and affairs who is a protected beneficiary for purposes of personal injury proceedings yet not a protected party for the purposes of a simple claim dealt with under the small claims procedure.

Best interests

11.35 An examination of the way in which the civil courts determine damages in cases where P lacks capacity to determine questions of care and residence is outside the scope of this work.[52] The approach that the Court of Protection should take has, however, been the subject of detailed consideration by Bodey J and therefore merits standalone discussion in this chapter.

11.36 In *Re SK*,[53] Bodey J was confronted with a complicated factual matrix. In essence, there was on foot a personal injury claim concerning a man who had sustained a brain injury in a road traffic accident for which a bus company had been liable. The bus company wished to participate in Court of Protection proceedings brought subsequently (but before the personal injury proceedings had been concluded), in which the question of where SK should reside and what level of rehabilitation he required was in issue.[54]

11.37 In his decision upon the defendant bus company's application to intervene in the Court of Protection proceedings, Bodey J confirmed that the Court of Protection is unable to take a judicial review approach, such that

---

[50] See **11.38** below.

[51] Before the Queen's Bench Division, the issue was whether the Claimant was entitled to recover for the past and future costs associated with the fact that his property and affairs had been (and were for the future to be) managed by a professional deputy.

[52] The reader is directed in this regard, inter alia, to McGregor on Damages (19th Edition, Sweet & Maxwell), paras 38.183–38.194. See also **11.45–11.49** below for a discussion of the specific issues which arise as regards the avoidance of double recovery in such cases.

[53] *Re SK* [2012] EWHC 1990, [2012] COPLR 712.

[54] SK's brother, who acted as his litigation friend in the personal injury proceedings, also wished to be joined to the Court of Protection proceedings. His application was ultimately less contentious and is not discussed further here.

where the only candidates for funding are statutory authorities, the Court is 'largely restricted' to the options advanced by the statutory authorities.[55] However, where another source of potential funding is available (in SK's case, a judgment against an insured tortfeasor), Bodey J made it clear that he considered that the Court of Protection should be able to make a decision between all options where there is a reasonable prospect of funding being secured from an accessible funding source.

11.38 Bodey J recognised the pragmatic attraction to having one hearing to determine the question of where SK should live and with what level of rehabilitation. However, Bodey J ultimately decided that this pragmatic attraction could not outweigh the fact that:

> '... the underlying issue in the two sets of proceedings, however similar, is not the same. The jurisdiction of the Court of Protection is as to best interests and that of the Queen's Bench is compensatory. The tests to be applied, although very similar ('best interests' as against 'reasonable needs') are not the same.'[56]

In the circumstances, he considered that a defendant who had not been a party to Court of Protection proceedings would not be bound at a hearing as to quantum in the damages proceedings by any Court of Protection declaration as to that person's best interests; by the same token, the judge hearing the damages claim would not be bound to follow any such declaration, but would rather decide the issue according to the applicable principles relating to the assessment of damages. The bus company's particular interests would therefore be heard and protected according to law in a different forum, namely the personal injury proceedings.

11.39 Separately, Bodey J also held that a defendant to personal injury proceedings brought by P would unlikely to be a person with a sufficient interest in Court of Protection proceedings concerning P's residence to fall within r 75 of the Court of Protection Rules, as any interest they would have would be a commercial one as opposed to an interest in the ascertainment of P's best interests.[57] Finally, Bodey J emphasised that, wherever possible, P should be represented by the same litigation friend in both civil and Court of Protection proceedings so as to ensure that differently held opinions are not reached as to where their interests may lie in the different proceedings.

---

[55] Paragraph 20. See also the second judgment in the proceedings, [2013] COPLR 458, at paras 11–12. *SK* was endorsed by the Court of Appeal in *Re M*: see **11.99ff**.

[56] Paragraph 37. A similar theme was developed by Senior Judge Lush in the case of *Re Reeves* discussed at **11.48** below (*Re Reeves* not being cited to Bodey J).

[57] Paragraph 41. He also found that, on the facts of the case, joining the defendant would not satisfy the requirement in r.73 that such addition would be desirable for the purpose of dealing with the application in the Court of Protection. See **11.27ff** for a discussion of the different position that may pertain if the sole issue the Court of Protection is asked to determine is P's capacity to litigate and/or manage his property and affairs.

11.40 Whilst the facts of *SK* are unusual,[58] it stands as a reminder that proceedings before the Court of Protection have a special character and proceed upon a particular basis the focus of which is – and is legitimately – different to proceedings before other courts. Conversely, it stands also as a reminder that the position of P in proceedings before other courts will be considered primarily by reference to the principles applied in those courts to the tasks assigned them, rather than by reference to the fact that P does not have capacity to take the relevant decisions.

Management of monies received by P in civil proceedings

11.41 Where a person lacks capacity to manage property and affairs, it is usually the case that the Court of Protection will appoint a deputy. In some cases, however, there is an argument that a person's estate can be dealt with more effectively through the creation of a trust. Trusts are often created for claimants in personal injury cases to protect an award from being treated as capital when assessing entitlement to means-tested benefits.[59] Prior to the introduction of MCA 2005, such trusts were often created by the Court of Protection for persons who lacked capacity, often on the grounds that a trust would be cheaper and more flexible to administer compared to a receivership. Clear guidance was given by HHJ Marshall QC in *Re HM*[60] as to the approach that the 'new' Court of Protection is likely to take to such an application.

11.42 *Re HM* originated in an application for a personal injury award to be placed in trust. Liability was limited on causation and therefore there was only partial recovery. It was contended by the applicant that a trust with HM's mother and a solicitor acting as trustees would be cheaper in the long run, and thus would be in the best interests of HM. The application was refused by District Judge Ashton. The matter was put for reconsideration to HHJ Marshall QC so that a 'guiding judgment' could be obtained.[61]

---

[58] In part because, for reasons which need not detain us here, it was not possible for SK's brother to act as his litigation friend in the Court of Protection proceedings. It would be very rare for the Official Solicitor to act as litigation friend in personal injury proceedings, so the normal course of events in the case of parallel proceedings would be for the litigation friend in such proceedings to act as litigation friend in the Court of Protection proceedings. It should perhaps be noted that an appeal against the decision at Bodey J was launched and the single judge (Munby LJ) gave permission. At the last minute, though, the appeal was withdrawn.

[59] In *Newcastle City Council v PV and Criminal Injuries Compensation Authority* [2015] EWCOP 22, Senior Judge Lush held that, where the Criminal Injuries Compensation Authority ('CICA') makes it a condition of an award that there is a trust, then the Court of Protection, where the applicant lacks capacity so to do, should set up the trust and an application must be made to the Court of Protection for an order under MCA 2005 s 18(1)(h). Aspects of this decision is under appeal at the time of writing, but it is not understood that these include his conclusion, as the result of the fact that there is no equivalent to CPR Part 21 in the rules governing applications to the CICA, an application to the CICA by an adult who lacks mental capacity should be made by the holder of a property and affairs EPA or LPA or a deputy or person specifically authorised so to do by the Court of Protection.

[60] *SM v HM (by the Official Solicitor as her Litigation Friend)* [2012] COPLR 187.

[61] Paragraph 2.

11.43 HHJ Marshall QC concluded that, whilst every application had to be considered on its merits, the facts of the case before her would allow a trust to be created. She identified three factors 'without which [she] would not have been prepared to authorise the creation of the relevant settlement,'[62] namely:

- The administration of a trust, on the evidence before her, would be cheaper than a deputyship (there would for instance be no security bond premium or Public Guardian supervision fee);

- HM's mother was 'a competent, forceful, well-educated and responsible person'[63] and her presence as a trustee would provide a means of monitoring legal costs (in the absence of the procedure for detailed assessment required by a deputy); and

- The proposed professional trustee had agreed that his firm's costs would be limited to the guideline rates that would be allowed on detailed assessment.

It should also be noted that it was of particular importance in the case before HHJ Marshall QC that the degree of benefit to HM which could be achieved by only a modest saving in costs was significant, because she had under-recovered in her damages claim. In other words, although the saving was a slight one in monetary terms, it was (in context) a very valuable one. The case does not therefore represent authority for the proposition (which may have had held sway under the old regime) that any little saving can justify the endorsement of a trust.

11.44 In light of the decision in *Re HM*, it should not be assumed that an application for a trust to be created will automatically be endorsed. A party proposing a trust must complete a detailed analysis of the costs and benefits of a trust compared to a deputyship and show that the former will be materially more cost effective without prejudicing the safety of the trust assets. Evidence will also need to be produced of the professional trustee's charges and commitment to a charging policy as well as to the lay trustee's competence. The Official Solicitor will also need to be instructed. In the circumstances, therefore, the process of obtaining authorisation for the creation of a trust is now significantly riskier, and more expensive, than it was prior to the introduction of MCA 2005, and it is even more important that applications are prepared with care.

Double recovery and the Court of Protection

11.45 The civil courts have grappled for some time with finding a principled basis upon which to assess damages for personal injury where the claimant's care needs resulting from the injury are such that they could properly look to the state for those needs to be met. In such circumstances, the civil courts have been particularly astute to identify ways in which to ensure that there is no

---

[62] Paragraph 172.
[63] Paragraph 169.

element of double recovery – ie that the claimant recovers damages from the tortfeasor on the basis that those damages will go towards their care costs, but that then all or part of the costs of care are, in fact, ultimately met by the state. That gives rise to particular complications where the claimant lacks the capacity to manage his property and affairs (and/or take decisions about his health and welfare), and therefore gives rise to the question of what – if any – role the Court of Protection is required to play.

11.46 In *Peters v East Midlands Strategic Health Authority*,[64] an action for damages for personal injury, the Court of Appeal accepted an undertaking from the Deputy appointed to manage P's property and affairs that she would (inter alia) seek from the Court of Protection (a) a limit on the authority whereby no application for public funding of the claimant's care under National Assistance Act 1948, s 21 could be made without further order, direction or authority from the Court of Protection and (b) provision for the defendants to be notified of any application to obtain authority to apply for public finding of the claimant's care under s 21 and be given the opportunity to make representations in relation thereto. The Court of Appeal held that this was:

> '... an effective way of dealing with the risk of double recovery in cases where the affairs of the claimant are being administered by the Court of Protection. It places the control over the Deputy's ability to make an application for the provision of a claimant's care and accommodation at public expense in the hands of a court. If a Deputy wishes to apply for public provision even where damages have been awarded on the basis that no public provision will be sought, the requirement that the defendant is to be notified of any such application will enable a defendant who wishes to do so to seek to persuade that the Court of Protection should not allow the application to be made because it is unnecessary and contrary to the intendment of the assessment of damages. The court accordingly accepts the undertaking that has been offered.'[65]

11.47 The decision in *Peters* and, in particular, the approach that deputies should take in consequence, was the subject of detailed consideration by Senior Judge Lush in *Re Reeves*.[66] In that case, the local authority which was prima facie liable to contribute towards the costs of Mr Reeves' care at a rehabilitation unit wrote to his Deputy, noting that he had been awarded a personal injury award on the basis that he would be paying for future care himself, and formally requesting (on the basis of *Peters*), that the Deputy apply to the Court of Protection for authority to make a request of St Helen's Council to provide public funding for future care. The Deputy did so. Senior Judge Lush found, however, that the application was misconceived, not least in seeking to apply the *Peters* decision retrospectively to a personal injury claim resolved some 6 years prior to *Peters*.

---

[64] [2010] QB 48.
[65] Paragraph 65.
[66] *In the Matter of Reeves*: CoP Case No: 99328848, 5 January 2011. The decision in *Peters* and its consequences has also been the subject of critical commentary by Robert Glancy QC: 'Reverse Indemnities – whether and when to give them,' (2012) Journal of Personal Injury Law 3, 54–159.

11.48 Senior Judge Lush noted that Mr Reeves' Deputy had a duty to act in his best interests, including 'claiming all state benefits to which Mr Reeves may entitled and, if appropriate to do so, applying to a local authority under the National Assistance Act 1948.' He found that, in most cases, the order appointing a Deputy would give sufficient general authority to them to allow them to apply for social security benefits and to a local authority for a care needs assessment without having to obtain specific authorisation; indeed, Senior Judge Lush considered that it was implicit in the judgment in *Peters* that the Deputy had such authority – the purpose of the undertaking given in Peters was therefore to remove this authority from the Deputy and give it to the Court. Senior Judge Lush considered that the *Peters* undertaking was specific to that case, and noted that no such undertaking had been given in Mr Reeves' case; further 'there is no obligation upon the Court of Protection to adjudicate as between the claimant and defendant, or the claimant and local authority on the issue of double recovery.' Senior Judge Lush continued:

> 'Notwithstanding the undertaking that was approved in *Peters* and other undertakings of a similar nature, I am of the view that the Court of Protection is no longer really the appropriate forum to adjudicate on matters of this kind. Its primary function is to act in the best interests of a protected beneficiary and, even though it would strive to be impartial, there may be a perception of bias for this reason. Furthermore, the close links which the court had with personal injury litigants generally were effectively severed when the Mental Capacity Act 2005 came into force on 1 October 2007, and the court's approval was no longer required in cases involving settlements out of court on behalf of incapacitated claimants.[67] Additionally, the court no longer supervises deputies: that is one of the functions of the Office of the Public Guardian.
>
> In the absence of any order of the Court of Protection restricting the authority of a claimant's deputy from applying for public funding of the claimant's care under section 21 of the National Assistance Act, the correct procedure would seem to be for the deputy to apply to the local authority and, if he is dissatisfied with the response he receives, to consider the merits of an application for judicial review.'

11.49 There is perhaps something of a tension between the approach adopted by the Court of Appeal in *Peters* and that of Senior Judge Lush in *Re Reeves*;

---

[67] Whilst Senior Judge Lush did not cite it, the case of *Eeeles v Cobham Hire Services Ltd* [2009] EWCA Civ 204 [2010] 1 WLR 409 emphasises this point. In giving guidance as to the proper approach to the award of interim payments in personal injury proceedings, the Court of Appeal emphasised that the judge need have no regard to what a claimant intends to do with money awarded him, that being a matter (in the case of a claimant unable to manage his property and affairs) for the Court of Protection. At para 45, the Court of Appeal noted by way of example, 'where the request is for money to buy a house, [the judge] must be satisfied that there is a real need for accommodation now (as opposed to after the trial) and that the amount of money requested is reasonable. He does not need to decide whether the particular house proposed is suitable; that is a matter for the Court of Protection.' Senior Judge Lush confirmed in *Newcastle City Council v PV and Criminal Injuries Compensation Authority* [2015] EWCOP 22 that the approval of the Court of Protection is not required for awards made by the Criminal Injuries Compensation Authority to be accepted by an individual lacking capacity in the material domains. The decision in *PV* was under appeal at the time of writing; this aspect of the decision is not understood to be challenged.

the former clearly envisaged the Court of Protection playing a potentially important role in preventing double recovery, the latter had considerable reservations as to whether this is appropriate. It is suggested that (at least as regards the duties imposed upon deputies, which was not specifically addressed by the Court of Appeal in *Peters*) the approach of Senior Judge Lush is to be preferred, and that deputies should always be astute to ensure that monies received by P by way of compensation for personal injuries should be maximised by seeking such assistance from the state as is properly open to them.

THE EUROPEAN CONVENTION ON HUMAN RIGHTS

11.50 Almost every application brought under MCA 2005 will involve consideration of the rights under the European Convention on Human Rights ('ECHR') of the person without capacity and, very often, of his or her family members. Further, the Court of Protection is required itself to act compatibly with the Convention by Human Rights Act 1998, ss 6(1) and 6(3). We are concerned here not with the duty to have regard to those rights for purposes of making the substantive decisions relating to P (see **11.20ff**), but with the situation where the suggestion is that those rights have been breached in some way by a public authority and declarations and/or damages are sought to reflect that breach.[68] The rights most likely to have been breached (at least in applications concerning P's health and welfare) are those arising under Art 5(1) (the right to liberty) and Art 8(1) (the right to respect for private and family life).

11.51 It was for some considerable period of time after October 2007 unclear whether in such a situation the Court of Protection had the power to grant relief by way of a declaration or damages, or whether it was necessary for the affected person to bring a standalone action under s 7 of the Human Rights Act 1998. However, in *YA (F) v A Local Authority & Ors*[69], Charles J concluded that the Court of Protection has jurisdiction:

- To make declarations as to breaches of the ECHR rights of P himself;

- To make declarations as to breaches of the ECHR rights of a person other than P who can claim to be a victim of such a breach (in the case before him, P's mother), where those breaches are said to arise out of acts done in relation to P;[70] and

- To grant damages under s 8(1) of the Human Rights Act 1998 to reflect either category of breach (subject to the statutory caveat in s 8(3) that such damages must be necessary to afford the person affected just satisfaction.

---

[68] And that the public authority in so doing has acted contrary to s 6 of the Human Rights Act 1998.

[69] [2010] EWHC 2770 (COP); [2010] COPLR Con Vol 1226.

[70] The same approach was taken subsequently (albeit without reference to this case) by HHJ Moir in *City of Sunderland v MM (by her litigation friend, the Official Solicitor), RS, SB, MP and SA* [2009] COPLR Con Vol 881.

11.52 The judgment is a complex one, and Charles J acknowledged that his conclusions were 'possibly against the instinct of a number of lawyers dealing with a welfare jurisdiction',[71] a tacit acknowledgment that others may differ. Until an appellate court provides a binding decision, the position is therefore not entirely free from doubt. However, the approach adopted by Charles J accords with both the language and purpose of MCA 2005, together with the wider policy goal of minimising the need that would otherwise arise for parallel proceedings. Further, there is a now an increasing body of first instance decisions from the Court of Protection providing (most commonly by endorsing consent orders) for declarations and/or damages in respect of breaches of the ECHR.[72] That body of decisions represents the tip of an iceberg of unreported cases in which claims have been settled.

11.53 An interesting issue which has yet to be subject of judicial determination is as to whether the conventional rules as to the burden of proof in relation to claims raising Convention rights apply when such claims are brought in the Court of Protection. In *Cheshire West and Chester Council v P*,[73] Baker J rejected a contention that it was for the individual contending that they were deprived of their liberty to establish that fact; rather, he found that, as the processes of the Court of Protection were essentially inquisitorial rather than adversarial, 'the question of whether or not the circumstances as a whole amount to a deprivation of liberty is not one which falls to be determined by application of a burden or standard of proof.'[74] This would suggest that the Court of Protection would approach other situations engaging Convention rights on the same inquisitorial basis.

11.54 However, claims under the HRA conventionally require the victim to prove that they have suffered a breach of their Convention rights (the burden then lying upon the State to establish that any interference with the right in question was justified).[75] Moreover, in *Lumba v Secretary of State for the Home Department*,[76] Lord Dyson made it clear that the same approach applied

---

[71] Paragraph 45. This case was not cited to Eleanor King J in *ACCG & Anor v MN & Anor* [2013] EWHC 3859 (COP), but she independently reached the conclusion that Court of Protection could consider claims based upon HRA 1998, s 7(1)(b) brought within the currency of welfare proceedings, a position endorsed by the Court of Appeal in *Re MN*: see **11.20** above.

[72] Summarised in *Essex County Council v RF* [2015] EWCOP 1. This has no precedent value, being the decision of a District Judge, but contains a helpful summary of the case-law and also an indication of a 'tariff' of damages for an unlawful deprivation of liberty of between £3,000 and £4,000 per month where the individual would not have been detained had the public authority in question acted lawfully. Where the public authority can show the proper application of MCA 2005 would have led inevitably to the detention of the individual, only nominal damages are likely to flow: see, by analogy, *Bostridge v Oxleas NHS Foundation Trust* [2015] EWCA Civ 79.

[73] [2011] EWHC 1330 (Fam), [2011] COPLR Con Vol 273. This part of his judgment was not appealed or the subject of any consideration by the Court of Appeal upon appeal and therefore stands unchallenged.

[74] Paragraph 52.

[75] See Clayton & Tomlinson (eds), *The Law of Human Rights* (2nd Edn, OUP 2009), para 6.187.

[76] [2011] 1 AC 245.

in the context of domestic false imprisonment claims.[77] It does not appear that *Lumba* was cited to Baker J in *Cheshire West*.

11.55   The tension between these two approaches (and the possibility that two different Courts would take different evidential approaches to the question – for instance – of whether P has been deprived of his liberty depending upon where he brought his claim) has yet to be resolved. The author would respectfully suggest that – at least where the Court of Protection is being asked to determine whether a breach of a Convention right has taken place – the better approach is the conventional one applicable to Convention cases, such that the burden of proof lies with the person making the assertion to establish a breach (subject to the person resisting the assertion establishing that any interference with P's Convention right was justified).

---

[77]   Paragraph 53.

CHAPTER 12

OTHER JURISDICTIONS

Introduction

12.1 Previous chapters deal with the mental capacity jurisdiction in England and Wales, but all too often knowledge of this law and procedure is not sufficient. Each country or state has, or fails to have, its own mental capacity jurisdiction which may be applicable or overlap in the particular circumstances. Principles of private international law may also need to be applied. It may be the law of another country or state that applies or must be resorted to.

Cross-border issues

12.2 Cross-border issues arise whenever someone holds assets in more than one jurisdiction, encounters capacity issues whilst living or present in another jurisdiction or has a factor, such as domicile, habitual residence or nationality linking them with another jurisdiction. It is increasingly rare to find a person, who does not have such connections, for example:

(1) property abroad, whether a holiday home or other investments,

(2) present and receiving medical attention in another jurisdiction away from their normal residence in England and Wales, even because of an accident or emergency when on holiday,

(3) a child who is now living and working in a different jurisdiction,

(4) a parent, spouse, partner or cohabitee who was born overseas or who has a different nationality.

Any of these facts can raise cross-border issues and we need to understand the consequences.

12.3 In relation to any capacity or other legal issue, the first questions should always be:

(1) do the courts of England and Wales have jurisdiction?

(2) if so, which law will they apply? Will it be that of England and Wales or another state?

(3) if not, where does jurisdiction lie and what is the relevant law?

Clients are often puzzled to learn that the laws in Scotland are different to those in England and Wales and different again to those in Northern Ireland, so that cross-border issues arise even within the United Kingdom. Although the Hague

Convention (see para **12.8**) has simplified some issues, it remains difficult to determine jurisdiction and ascertain the relevant applicable law in non-Convention countries and yet with increased tourism and home ownership abroad (especially for retired people) capacity issues arise quite frequently.

Private International Law

12.4

> 'Private international law is that part of law which comes into play when the issue before the court is so closely connected with a foreign system of law as to necessitate recourse to that system'[1]

Private international law deals primarily with the application of laws in space and time. The local jurisdiction at a particular time is sovereign and can define as it wishes, and place a boundary at that or any other time as it thinks appropriate. Unlike garden fences, the boundaries created by separate jurisdictions are rarely co-terminous, and can be in different places at different times. Each jurisdiction has its own separate and distinct private international law rules which do not necessarily mesh with that of another state.

12.5 It is common in all private international law to consider separately issues of:

(1) Jurisdiction – do the courts of a state consider that they have jurisdiction in the first place?
(2) Applicable Law – if they do, which state's laws will be applied?
(3) Recognition and Enforcement – if the courts of a state make a particular order, will that order be recognised in the courts of a different state?[2]

12.6 English private international law in the area of capacity of adults has in the past been very uncertain. Mental capacity is really a particular requirement for many separate and different legal acts, each with their own test and different connecting factor. Other states have completely different private international law rules. Many states with law based on a civil code hold that issues to do with questions of capacity are governed by the personal law of the person. This is often governed by the law of either nationality or by domicile in a civil law sense rather than habitual residence.

This chapter

12.7 In this chapter we consider a relevant Convention and the specific provisions contained in the Mental Capacity Act 2005. Then we draw attention to recent developments in Northern Ireland and the Republic of Ireland. These

---

[1]   Private International Law – Cheshire, North and Fawcett 14th Edition.
[2]   For example, will an Enduring or Lasting Power of Attorney that is valid in England also be valid and accepted in another country? Will the appointment of a Deputy be recognised?

are instructive because they represent the next generation of mental capacity jurisdictions, it being now a decade since the ground-breaking Mental Capacity Act 2005 was enacted for England and Wales following consultation which commenced a quarter of a century ago. Finally the equally mature but significantly different Scottish jurisdiction is summarised. The lessons to be learnt are that there is more than one way to tackle a common challenge, each with its own advantages and disadvantage, and this is an area of law that must evolve according to the social climate and international expectations which are still being debated.

AVAILABLE LAW

The Convention on the International Protection of Adults

12.8 The Hague Conference on Private International Law seeks to establish international agreements to reduce conflicts of law and to lay down rules to determine jurisdiction and related matters. Under its auspices the Convention on the International Protection of Adults ('the Convention') was concluded on 13 January 2000. It applies to the protection in international situations of 'adults who, by reason of an impairment or insufficiency of their personal faculties, are not in a position to protect their interests'.[3]

12.9 The Convention came into force on 1 January 2009, the requisite three countries: the UK (in relation to Scotland[4]), Germany and France having ratified it. It has subsequently been ratified by Switzerland, Finland, Estonia, the Czech Republic and Austria.

Mental Capacity Act 2005, Sch 3

12.10 England and Wales has not yet ratified the Convention, but by making provision for it in Schedule 3 of the Mental Capacity Act 2005[5] the UK gives effect to the Convention internally in relation to England and Wales, so far as it can.[6] This sets out new uniform private international law rules for Convention states to establish questions of jurisdiction, applicable law, recognition and enforcement of measures for the protection of adults and of applicable law for powers of representation. This simplifies the position for Convention states.

12.11 Paragraph 35 of Sch 3 excepts the application of some provisions. Some experts express the view that this meant that the excepted sections only had effect when the Convention comes into force in England and Wales. Others believe that since the Convention has come into force in other jurisdictions, the

---

[3]   See www.hcch.net/index_en.php?act=conventions.pdf&cid=7 for the text of the Convention.
[4]   Instrument of ratification of 1 April 2003.
[5]   See MCA 2005, s 63 and Sch 3. This has been fully in force since 1 January 2009.
[6]   The provisions of the Schedule are intended to be compatible with the Adults with Incapacity (Scotland) Act 2000, Sch 3, which gave effect to the Convention in Scotland.

excepted sections are now in force in England and Wales.[7] Subject to this Sch 3 provides private international law rules to govern jurisdictional issues within the United Kingdom between Scotland and England and Wales and Northern Ireland. It also provides private international law rules for England and Wales with all other jurisdictions, and is not limited to those rules in relation to jurisdictions that have ratified the Convention.[8] In any event, unless or until the UK Government ratifies the Convention in relation to England and Wales, there cannot be full reciprocity in these countries – the UK Government has not yet, for example, designated the Central Authority for England and Wales under the Convention.[9]

12.12 Schedule 3 to the MCA 2005 extends the Convention in two ways. Firstly, the Convention applies to adults over the age of 18 whereas the MCA 2005 applies to persons over the age of 16 (other than children to whom either the Hague Protection of Children Convention XXXIV or Brussels IIbis apply[10]). Secondly, the Convention only applies to adults who, by reason of an impairment or insufficiency of their personal faculties, are not in a position to protect their interests, whilst the MCA 2005 also applies to the donors of powers of attorney even if not impaired or insufficient.

Schedule 3, para 33 specifically disapplies the Convention in relation to the matters set out in Art 4 of the Convention including trusts and succession. The jurisdiction of the Court of Protection in relation to these matters may therefore be limited.

Application of the law

12.13 These provisions cater for cross-border issues. Here are two potential examples:

(1) A senior citizen resident in England acquires a second home in, say, France. If he became incapacitated and a deputy was appointed here, that representative might have had to gain a separate authority in France before he or she could dispose of the property in France.[11] Under the Convention that would not be necessary.

(2) A person from, say, British Colombia, has under applicable provincial law made a health care representation agreement appointing a health care proxy. If that citizen is injured in Wales and unable to consent to medical

---

[7] The former view is supported in the judgment of Sir James Munby P in *The Matter of PO* [2013] EWHC 3932 (COP) at [9].

[8] Austria, Czech Republic, Estonia, Finland, France, Germany, Scotland or Switzerland.

[9] So Art 38 Certificates cannot yet be produced and Arts 7 and 8 cannot be invoked.

[10] Regulations 1(2) and 17 of The Parental Responsibility and Measures for the Protection of Children (International Obligations) (England and Wales and Northern Ireland) Regulations 2010.

[11] This would be so unless domestic private international law in France allowed foreign appointments to be recognised without further procedure (much as if the Convention already applied). This book cannot be taken as authority on the domestic law of France.

treatment, under the Convention the Canadian proxy would have the legal authority to give substitute consent in Wales.

12.14 The provisions are thus a useful clarification of the private international law rules which are to apply, by countries which ratify the Convention, and within the UK by England and Wales and Scotland, but not by Northern Ireland.

Jurisdiction and habitual residence

12.15 In place of the traditional connecting factor of domicile, the Convention and Sch 3 now use habitual residence as the relevant connecting factor. Thus Sch 3, paras 7 and 8 give the Court jurisdiction to exercise its powers in respect of:

(1) an adult habitually resident in England and Wales in relation to him and his worldwide property;

(2) an adult's property in England and Wales;

(3) an adult present in England and Wales or who has property there, if the matter is urgent;

(4) an adult present in England and Wales, if a protective measure which is temporary and limited in its effect to England and Wales is proposed in relation to him.

12.16 In addition the Court can have jurisdiction for:

(1) the worldwide property and the person of an adult present in England and Wales whose habitual residence cannot be ascertained, is a refugee, or has been displaced as a result of disturbance in the country of his habitual residence;

(2) a British citizen and his worldwide property, who has a closer connection with England and Wales than with Scotland or Northern Ireland, and Art 7 of the Convention has, in relation to the matter concerned, been complied with;

(3) a person and his worldwide property, for whom the jurisdiction of habitual residence is available and the UK Minister of Justice agrees that the matter is better dealt with in England as the state of nationality, of former residence or where property is situated, and Art 8 of the Convention has, in relation to the matter concerned, been complied with.

12.17 The case of *Marinos v Marinos*[12] is a helpful summary as to the definition of habitual residence for the purposes of European legislation. It is not clear as to whether the definition for Hague Convention purposes might in some circumstances be different.

---

[12] *Marinos v Marinos* [2007] EWHC 2047 and see also *Ikimi v Ikimi* [2001] EWCA Civ 873 upheld in *Mark v Mark* [2005] UKHL 42, *Mercredi v Chaffe (C-497/10)* [2012] Fam 22, *In the*

Applicable law

12.18 Generally each court is to apply its own law unless it considers that there is a substantial connection with another state, in which case it may apply the internal law of that other state.[13]

12.19 In relation to 'Lasting Powers'[14] the law applicable is:

(1) that of the country of the donor's habitual residence

(2) that of a country of which he is a national, or in which he has formerly been habitually resident or in which he has property (but only in respect of that property), if the donor specifies that law in writing,[15] (even if that applicable law does not itself accept such powers).

Clearly there can be problems here if the applicable law is that of another state which does not accept such a power or it was created in English form, when it should have been created in the form of another state.

Recognition and enforcement

12.20 England and Wales will now recognise protective measures[16] taken in another state provided that the relevant adult is habitually resident in that other state.[17] Recognition can be refused on limited grounds if the English Court finds that:

(1) the case in which the measure was taken was not urgent and the adult was not given an opportunity to be heard and the omission was in breach of the rules of natural justice; or

(2) recognition would be contrary to public policy; or

(3) the measure would be inconsistent with a mandatory provision in England and Wales; or

(4) the measure is inconsistent with a protective measure in England and Wales; or[18]

(5) Article 33 has not been complied with in relation to cross-border placement.[19]

---

matter of A (Children) (AP) [2013] UKSC 60, *In re L (A Child) (Habitual Residence)* [2013] UKSC 75 and *In the matter of LC (Children)* [2014] UKSC 1.

[13] MCA 2005, Sch 3, para 11.

[14] Defined as Lasting Powers of Attorney, Enduring Powers of Attorney and other powers having a like effect.

[15] MCA 2005, Sch 3, para 13.

[16] Defined by MCA 2005, Sch 3, para 5.

[17] MCA 2005, Sch 3, para 19(1) and *Re MN* [2010] EWHC 1926 (Fam).

[18] MCA 2005 Sch 3, para 19(3) & (4).

[19] MCA 2005 Sch 3, para 19(5).

There are provisions under paras 20 and 22 for interested persons to apply to the Court for a declaration as to whether a protective measure taken under the law of another state is to be recognised or enforced.

Protective measures

12.21 Protective measures have a very wide definition both under the Convention and under para 5.1 of Sch 3 and may also include an order for a Statutory Will, subject to the special rules of Sch 2, but do not extend to Lasting Powers of Attorney.

Within the United Kingdom

12.22 Schedule 3 applies these private international law rules to dealings with Scotland and Northern Ireland in the same way as to other states. An order of the Court of Protection will therefore be recognised in Scotland unless a Scottish guardian has been appointed.

The position in Northern Ireland is somewhat more complex until it too introduces private international law rules similar to the Convention.

The position in Non-Convention Countries

12.23 Although the Court of Protection may have jurisdiction under Sch 3 of the MCA 2005, traditionally it would not make an order directly affecting property in another state if such an order would not be recognised in that other state or if it would infringe another court's jurisdiction. If the Convention does not apply there are no universal rules if a person who lacks capacity is resident in a non-Convention state or has assets which are situated in such a state. Many states do, however, have authorities for the management of the property and affairs of people who lack capacity, similar to those in the UK.

12.24 In the same way that the Court of Protection will take jurisdiction in relation to assets in England and Wales belonging to a person resident in another state, the courts of other states may recognise the authority of their counterparts. This is consistent with the principles of many private international laws which provide that the capacity of a person is determined by the person's personal law. Some jurisdictions may therefore apply similar principles to those contained in the Convention.

12.25 If a person who lacks capacity and who is habitually resident in England and Wales has assets in another state, the requirements of that state will be different in each case and an agent in that state will need to be instructed. Many states will require a formal application to the local court. The possible requirements may include:

(1) a sealed and certified copy of the order appointing the deputy and also authorising the action in the other state, plus an explanation of the

deputy's authority to act and the arrangements made for the protection of the property and affairs in England and Wales;

(2) a sealed and certified copy of the relevant enduring, lasting, durable or continuing power of attorney;[20]

(3) details of the assets for which authority is required and whether they are movable or immovable;

(4) confirmation that no person has been appointed to administer those assets in the state where they are situated.

The court in the other state is likely either to confirm the deputy's authority, provide the deputy with authority to act or appoint a local guardian with authority to remit assets back to the deputy or the Court of Protection. In the event of dispute, the assets are likely to be retained in the other state until the dispute is resolved.

12.26 It remains difficult to determine jurisdiction and ascertain the relevant law in non-Convention countries and yet with increased tourism and home ownership abroad (especially for retired people) capacity issues arise quite frequently. An attempt has been made in the annual volume *Court of Protection Practice* (Jordans) to lead a pathway through this jungle by reproducing the responses to Questionnaires completed for many other jurisdictions.[21]

NORTHERN IRELAND

Existing law

12.27 The Mental Capacity Act 2005 was not introduced into Northern Ireland and the law relating to adults without capacity has continued to be governed by the Mental Health (Northern Ireland) Order 1986 (SI 1986/595). Part VIII deals with the property and affairs of a person ('the patient') who is 'incapable, by reason of mental disorder, of managing and administering his property and affairs'. This is similar to the previous law in England and Wales found in Part VII of the Mental Health Act 1983, save that its powers have been exercised by the Office of Care and Protection, part of the Northern Ireland Courts and Tribunals Service.

---

[20] This has been problematic, since there was no mechanism for the OPG to produce such a copy, but it is understood that this issue is currently being addressed.

[21] The most comprehensive analysis of the law in this area is to be found in Frimston, Ruck Keene, van Overdijk and Ward *The International Protection of Adults* (OUP, 2015) ISBN 978-0-19-872725-5.

The Office of Care and Protection
Room 2.2A, Second Floor
Royal Courts of Justice
Chichester Street
Belfast
BT1 3JF
Telephone (028) 9072 4733
Fax (028) 9032 2782
www.courtsni.gov.uk

12.28 A person appointed in Northern Ireland to make decisions in respect of a patient's property and affairs is a Controller. The Enduring Powers of Attorney (Northern Ireland) Order 1987 [SI 1987 No. 1627 (N.I. 16)] still subsists, so that Northern Ireland Enduring Powers of Attorney remain valid and can still be made. The legal vacuum in regard to personal welfare decisions has not yet been addressed.

Mental Capacity Bill

12.29 The review of Northern Irish legislation has lagged behind that in Scotland and England and Wales. The Bamford Review, published in November 2007, suggested a new comprehensive legislative model. A Mental Capacity Bill has now been published which places greater emphasis on the need to support people to exercise their capacity to make decisions where they can. If, on the other hand, it is established that a person lacks capacity to make a specific decision at a particular time, the Bill provides alternative decision making mechanisms. This approach goes part way to meeting the expectations of the Committee to the UN Convention on the Rights of Persons with Disabilities in regard to supported decision-making.

12.30 The Bill is likely to be dealt with by the Northern Ireland Assembly during 2015. Until then, Northern Irish private international law remains similar to that of England and Wales before the Mental Capacity Act 2005.[22]

IRELAND

Existing law

12.31 There has been no mental capacity legislation in Ireland hitherto and an all or nothing status approach involving a Ward of Court procedure has continued to be utilised.[23] This was inherited from the inherent jurisdiction of the High Court in England and Wales derived from the Royal prerogative notwithstanding that Ireland became a Republic. Agency arrangements under

---

[22] The draft Mental Capacity Bill is available as part of the consultation on: www.dhsspsni.gov.uk/mental_capacity_bill_consultation_paper.pdf.
[23] Lunacy Regulation (Ireland) Act 1871.

social welfare legislation are available but other agencies cease if the principal becomes mentally incapable, and trusts have been used as a means of advance financial planning for older people. However, enduring powers of attorney have been introduced similar to those that formerly applied in England and Wales,

12.32 Nevertheless, Ireland has been closely involved during recent years in conferences with counterparts in England and Wales, Scotland and Northern Ireland, and law reform is now being pursued.

Legislation

12.33 The Assisted Decision-Making (Capacity) Bill 2013 has been published and the Explanatory Memorandum states:

> 'The purpose of the Bill is to reform the law and to provide a modern statutory framework that supports decision-making by adults and enables them to retain the greatest amount of autonomy possible in situations where they lack or may shortly lack capacity.

> The Bill changes the existing law on capacity, shifting from the current all or nothing status approach to a flexible functional one, whereby capacity is assessed on an issue- and time-specific basis. The Bill replaces the Wards of Court system with a modern statutory framework to assist persons in exercising their decision-making capacity.

> The Bill provides a statutory framework enabling formal agreements to be made by persons who consider that their capacity is in question, or may shortly be in question, to appoint a trusted person to act as their decision-making assistant to assist them in making decisions or as a co-decision-maker who will make decisions jointly with them.

> The Bill also provides for the making of applications to court in respect of persons whose capacity may be in question to seek a declaration as to whether those persons lack capacity and for the making of consequent orders approving co-decision-making agreements or appointing decision-making representatives.

> The Bill provides for protection from liability for informal decision-makers in relation to personal welfare and healthcare decisions made on behalf of a person with impaired capacity where such decisions are necessary and where no formal decision-making arrangements are in place. It modernises the law relating to enduring powers of attorney.

> The Bill also provides for the establishment of a new statutory office, the Office of the Public Guardian. The Office of the Public Guardian will supervise decision-making assistants, co-decision- makers, decision-making representatives and persons holding enduring powers of attorney.

> Reform of the law on decision-making capacity is one of the actions required to enable the State to ratify the United Nations Convention on the Rights of Persons with Disabilities.

The Bill gives effect in the State to the Hague Convention on the International Protection of Adults.'

Comment

12.34 On first reading this appears to replicate the approach and objectives of the Mental Capacity Act 2005, but closer examination of the Bill reveals a desire to comply with the latest thinking emerging through the UN Convention on the Rights of Persons with Disabilities. The reference to decision-making assistants, co-decision-makers and decision-making representatives reflects the desire to adopt a supported decision-making approach as distinct from delegated decision-making under the best interests criteria which has been rejected by the Committee to the UN Convention. Only time will prove whether this approach is feasible in practice and does not create more opportunity for abuse.

SCOTLAND

Background

12.35 Legal practice reflects the society which it serves. Estimates by the Alliance which campaigned for passage of the Adults with Incapacity (Scotland) Act 2000, and referred to during the parliamentary proceedings, indicated that at any one time an estimated 100,000 Scots have impairments of capacity of potential significance in law. More recent estimates, taken cumulatively, would suggest a figure well above that. Modern private client practice accordingly encompasses a significant amount of adult incapacity work. Inevitably, that work can involve significant links outside Scotland, reflecting the multiplicity of connections between Scottish society and the present and past countries of the Commonwealth, the United States of America, Europe and elsewhere; and above all the other jurisdictions of the British Isles.

12.36 Inward and outward mobility is traditional. Many well-established Scottish families have interests elsewhere. An interim order in Scottish guardianship proceedings allowed spouse's consent to be given to the sale of property in Italy.[24] Modern travel and communications now counteract many of the previous consequences of distance. The attorney in London can in most practical ways be close to her elderly aunt in Edinburgh. The only son in California, whose job takes him worldwide, visited his father in Scotland with sufficient regularity to satisfy statutory criteria for appointment as his guardian.[25]

12.37 Also new is the mobility of people with impairments of capacity, sometimes to access specialist provision, sometimes to follow or return to their families or for similar reasons of convenience; and sometimes moved by others

---

[24] *C*, 23 Sept, 2009, Kilmarnock Sh Ct.
[25] *H*, 6 May, 2008, Dunoon Sh Ct.

for questionable motives. An elderly lady returned to her native Northern Ireland for nursing home care: a Scottish guardian was appointed to deal with her property in Scotland.[26] Another lady, subject to an order and proceedings in France, went to Scotland and a day after her arrival there purported to grant a Scottish POA.[27]

12.38 The relevant private international law of England and Wales, including from that perspective the Hague Convention on the International Protection of Adults, is described earlier in this chapter. From here on it outlines salient points of Scots law from the viewpoint of practitioners and others in England and Wales.

12.39 Be warned at the outset that Scots law is different. It is different in its fundamentals and structures. It does not contain full descriptions, and is referenced only selectively, in the more recent experience leading to the introduction of modern incapacity provision, and in the content of that provision. Do not assume that similar terminology has the same meaning, or that relevant provisions of Scots law can be understood simply by translating terminology. Where concepts are substantially the same, terminology sometimes differs to indicate Englishness or Scottishness, such as 'social services' in England and 'social work' in Scotland – hence the Social Work (Scotland) Act 1968 ('SW(S)A 1968'); a 'substitute attorney' is the same as a 'replacement attorney'; and the Judicial Institute fulfils the same function as the Judicial Studies Board, to give a few random examples. However, each jurisdiction has its own Public Guardian without any differentiation in titles, and surprisingly only the Scottish Public Guardian – though established first – makes clear (on her website and email addresses, for example) which one she is.

Scots law

12.40 Scots law is based on Roman law,[28] emphasising principles rather than precedents, and thus in its fundamentals is akin to European rather than Anglo-American systems. While foreign law lacks legitimacy as a formal source of law, Roman law is always potentially or actually Scots law. The influence of English law has been so great that Scots law is now often described as a hybrid system. However, the development of Scottish adult incapacity law continues to be driven mainly by the application of principles, hence the central importance of the principles stated in s 1 of Adults with Incapacity (Scotland) Act 2000[29] as exemplified by the development, without any express statutory provision, of a power to make and alter Wills,[30] and the methodology adopted by the courts in resolving matters of fundamental importance.[31]

---

[26]　*H, Applicant*, 2007 SLT (Sh Ct) 5.
[27]　*F v S* 2012 SLT (Sh Ct) 189.
[28]　Cairns and du Plessis 'Ten years of Roman Law in Scottish Courts' 2008 SLT News 191.
[29]　See **12.70**.
[30]　See **12.121**.
[31]　See for example *Muldoon, Applicant*, 2005 SLT (Sh Ct) 52; 2005 SCLR 611; 2005 GWD 5-57; and *North Ayrshire Council v JM*, 2004 SCLR 956, Sh Ct.

12.41 From 1707 to 2000 Scotland lacked its own separate legislature. The perpetual tendency for the needs of vulnerable people to slip down the order of priorities was compounded by the failure of the UK Parliament to meet the needs of law reform in Scotland. For many Scots lawyers, the establishment by the Scotland Act 1998 of a devolved Scottish Parliament was valued more as a means to address a serious backlog of essential law reform, rather than for any nationalistic or party political significance. 'Parliament' refers to the UK Parliament at Westminster, 'the Parliament' to the Scottish Parliament at Holyrood. The legislative competence of the Scottish Parliament is limited to matters devolved to it by the Scotland Act. At time of writing, following the rejection of independence for Scotland in a referendum on 18 September 2014, devolution of further matters is proposed. Legislation incompatible with ECHR is ultra vires. Acts of the pre-1707 Parliament of Scotland are designated APS (Act of the Parliament of Scotland) and those of 'the Parliament' asp (Acts of the Scottish Parliament). Note the distinction between SI (Statutory Instrument, which includes Instruments of solely Scottish application made under Westminster legislation) and SSI (Scottish Statutory Instrument, made under legislation of the Scottish Parliament).

12.42 Within its first decade the Parliament comprehensively reformed land tenure and related matters in Scotland. Even before that, as its first and highest priority, it produced the Adults with Incapacity (Scotland) Act 2000 ('AWI(S)A 2000'). Legislation to cover the three overlapping areas of adult incapacity, mental health and vulnerable adults continued with the Mental Health (Care and Treatment) (Scotland) Act 2003 ('MH(CT)(S)A 2003') and the Adult Support and Protection (Scotland) Act 2007 ('ASP(S)A 2007'), both of which included amendments to AWI(S)A 2000, in the latter case following review of experience of the working of AWI(S)A 2000 as originally enacted. AWI(S)A 2000 has also been amended by the Regulation of Care (Scotland) Act 2001, the Smoking, Health and Social Care (Scotland) Act 2005 and various SI's and SSI's. See **12.54** for proposals for further amendment. In October 2014 the Scottish Law Commission published its conclusions and recommendations following further review, concentrating on issues of deprivation of liberty. The Public Guardian has initiated debate on the need for review of guardianship procedures.[32] The Essex Autonomy Project, which reviewed the compliance of MCA 2005 with the UN Convention on the Rights of Persons with Disabilities, is at time of writing being extended to cover Scotland (and Northern Ireland).

The Scottish courts

12.43 In civil matters Scotland has two tiers of courts of first instance, the Court of Session, which sits only in Edinburgh, and the Sheriff Court. Lords Ordinary sit singly in the Outer House of the Court of Session. Appeal lies from them to the Inner House, which usually sits in divisions comprising at least

---

[32] Both the Public Guardian and the Mental Welfare Commission have proposed systems of graded guardianship; see paper on Graded Guardianship on the Public Guardian's website (**12.64**) and comments thereon on the website of the Law Society of Scotland www.lawscot.org.uk.

three judges, though a larger court may be convened for matters of particular importance. In a few matters the Inner House hears cases at first instance, examples being exercise of the nobile officium, which is an inherent jurisdiction to address matters not previously provided for in Scots law, and the parens patriae jurisdiction. Although that jurisdiction was invoked in *Morris, Petitioner*, 1986, the Inner House declared that future applications for appointment of tutors could be presented in the Outer House, and in *Law Hospital NHS Trust v Lord Advocate*,[33] the Inner House declared similarly in relation to applications to authorise withdrawal of treatment. Appeal lies from the Inner House to the Supreme Court (previously the House of Lords).

12.44 Sheriffs frequently hear cases of substantial value and great importance. There is no general upper financial limit to their civil jurisdiction. They have exclusive jurisdiction in low-value cases. Relatively few matters are excluded from their jurisdiction. There are six Sheriffdoms, each led by a Sheriff Principal. Apart from Glasgow, the Sheriffdoms are divided into Sheriff Court Districts, each with its own Sheriff Court of which there are 39 altogether, five of them on islands. Courthouses range from small buildings in locations such as Lochmaddy to massive ones in the main cities. With a few exceptions, up until now the first level of appeal has been to the Sheriff Principal of that Sheriffdom, thence to the Inner House of the Court of Session, and thence to the Supreme Court (formerly House of Lords). Sheriffs have been bound by precedents set by their own Sheriff Principal, but not by those of other Sheriffs Principal or other Sheriffs. Sheriffs Principal are not bound by the precedents of their own predecessors. All are bound by precedents set by the Inner House of the Court of Session and the Supreme Court.

12.45 The Courts Reform (Scotland) Act 2014 will however introduce (with effect from January 2016 in civil matters) a single Scotland-wide Sheriffs Principal Appeals Court, in which more than one Sheriff Principal will sit. It will also introduce two tiers at first instance, of Sheriffs and Summary Sheriffs; designation of specialisms to which particular Sheriffs would be assigned; and appointment of all-Scotland specialist Sheriffs.

12.46 Scotland has no Court of Protection, or equivalent separate court, nor an Official Solicitor (though since 2007 the Public Guardian may now initiate or enter proceedings as described in **12.64**).[34] Much information is available at www.scotcourts.gov.uk. For decisions under AWI(S)A 2000 go to 'Library', then 'Court Judgments', then 'Sheriff Courts Search' and search for 'Adults with Incapacity'. The Mental Health Tribunal for Scotland was established by MH(CT)(S)A 2003 s21 and has jurisdiction under that Act, but not (as yet) in incapacity matters. At time of writing it is understood that consideration is being given to utilising the reforms described in **12.45** to introduce, perhaps progressively during the course of implementation of the reforms, shrieval specialisation in the adult incapacity jurisdiction.

---

[33] 1996 SC 301; 1996 SLT 848; [1996] 2 FLR 407; (1998) 39 BMLR 166; [1996] Fam Law 670, IH.

[34] AWI(S)A 2000, s 6(2)(da).

Development of adult incapacity law prior to 2000

12.47 Fifteen years prior to AWI(S)A 2000 it was generally believed (though not universally accepted) that Powers of Attorney ceased to have effect upon the incapacity of the granter. Prior to AWI(S)A 2000 the only general form of financial management for adults lacking relevant capacity was to appoint a curator bonis, whereupon the adult was deprived of all management capacity, even to decide and manage matters of which the adult was in fact capable; and the only available form of welfare guardianship was Mental Health Act guardianship, with fixed and limited powers, which, under the Mental Health (Scotland) Act 1984, were similar to those under Mental Health Act 1983.

12.48 To the demand for Powers of Attorney that would indisputably be operable following the granter's incapacity, Westminster responded simplistically in the Law Reform (Miscellaneous Provisions) (Scotland) Act 1990, s 71, under which – for a decade – Powers of Attorney automatically remained in force in the event of subsequent incapacity of the granter, unless the document explicitly provided otherwise. Scotland thus experienced continuing Powers of Attorney with no effective regulation or control. The majority met a clear need and worked well, due to the sense and integrity of appointed attorneys rather than anything in relevant legislation; but inevitably there were many horror stories, such as the hospital patient who purportedly granted three Powers of Attorney in rapid succession to three different relatives; large numbers of Powers of Attorney granted by residents in a care home to the proprietor and operated dubiously; and so forth. Powers of Attorney granted during that decade remain valid, but become subject to many of the provisions of AWI(S)A 2000.

12.49 The most positive progress was achieved by going back to the tutors to adults originating in Roman law, reviving first the tutor-dative[35] and then the tutor-at-law.[36] Tutors-dative, as revived, were appointed as guardians with specific welfare powers, tailored to need in each individual case, and usually for a limited period. Joint appointments were permitted, and common. Tutors-dative were also appointed for limited purposes in relation to property and financial affairs, such as approving and executing a deed of family arrangement (for example, to establish a family discretionary trust following the death of a parent). Tutors-at-law had plenary financial and welfare powers, and were generally appointed to displace a curator bonis. In *Britton* (see footnote 36),the first modern case, the curator bonis was a professional who had never met his ward and allowed her an income – from a substantial award of damages – less than if she had been dependent solely upon state benefits.

12.50 As noted in **12.43**, in 1996 procedure was established for dealing with applications under the *parens patriae* jurisdiction to deal with proposed discontinuance of treatment in cases of persistent vegetative state.

---

[35] *Morris, Petitioner*, 1986; see Ward 'Revival of Tutors-Dative' 1987 SLT News 69.
[36] *Britton v Britton's curator bonis*, 1992 SCLR 947.

Particular characteristics of Scots law

12.51 In addition to experience of the developments in the years leading up to AWI(S)A 2000, described in the previous section, two well-established characteristics of Scots law, unchanged by AWI(S)A 2000, are relevant to the understanding of Scottish incapacity law. Firstly, in Scotland if an adult lacks adequate capacity for a particular act or transaction, it will be void, regardless of whether any other party was at the time aware of the incapacity. With a few exceptions such as purchase of 'necessaries', the position in law is the same as if the purported act or transaction had not taken place. Secondly, for most practical purposes adulthood in Scotland begins at 16. For example, it has always been possible, without parental consent, to marry at 16. Some special provisions apply to young people aged 16-18, but for adult incapacity legislation to commence at 16 fits easily with other statutes such as the Age of Legal Capacity (Scotland) Act 1991. In cross-border and international matters this does not fit so easily with commencement of adulthood at 18 under the Hague Convention on the International Protection of Adults 2000.[37] This issue is addressed in Chapter 12 of Frimston et al *International Protection of Adults*, OUP, 2015. A guardianship application may be lodged up to three months prior to the young person's 16th birthday, but the guardianship comes into force no earlier than that birthday (s 79A).

Literature

12.52 On adult incapacity law in Scotland, see Ward *Adult Incapacity* (2003) and *Adults with Incapacity Legislation* (2008), which updates *Adult Incapacity* and contains the updated text of AWI(S)A 2000. Together, the two volumes reproduce all relevant Statutory Instruments. See also Chapter 12 (by Ward) of Frimston et al *International Protection of Adults* (2015). On mental health law, see Franks and Cobb *Mental Health (Care and Treatment) (Scotland) Act 2003* – the text of the Act with annotations. On ASP(S)A 2007 and related topics, see Patrick and Smith *Adult Protection and the Law in Scotland* (2010). For a wider-ranging text on relevant subjects, see Patrick *Mental Health, Incapacity and the Law in Scotland* (2006). On private international law issues see *International Protection of Adults* (see footnote 21). Several Codes of Practice have been issued under AWI(S)A 2000. For useful websites see **12.46** and **12.64**.

Adults with Incapacity (Scotland) Act 2000

General

12.53 AWI(S)A 2000 (also referred to as 'the Act' in this section) is a co-ordinated and integrated, but non-exclusive, code of provision for adults with incapacity in Scotland. The topics covered differ from those in MCA 2005. As noted above, adults are persons over 16. During the law reform

---

[37] Converse issues will arise if a state where the age of majority is higher than 18 should ratify the Convention.

process, 'Incapable Adults' was used, but only as a working title. The title eventually adopted was a contraction of 'adults with impairments of capacity'. In practice, 'the adult' has been almost universally adopted to refer to the person whose capacity is, or may be, impaired.

12.54 The Act follows a similar overall pattern to several reformed jurisdictions. Gateway definitions of adult and incapacity give access to the Act's provisions. Guided by principles, procedures enable solutions to be selected from a flexible range of possibilities, and tailored to individual need. Implementation of those solutions is also guided by principles, and is subject (generally but not always) to supervision, accountability and re-assessment. AWI(S)A 2000 has been amended on various occasions, as narrated in **12.42**. Further amendment is to be expected following upon the Scottish Law Commission Report mentioned in **12.118**, and the process of engagement with the UN Committee on the Rights of Persons with Disabilities regarding compliance with the Convention of that name.

Jurisdiction and roles

12.55 Practitioners in England and Wales may choose not to instruct a city solicitor in a matter in which Lerwick Sheriff Court has jurisdiction; nor to instruct a Stornoway solicitor when the Court of Session in Edinburgh has jurisdiction; nor to instruct any Scottish solicitor where the judicial and administrative authorities of some other country have jurisdiction, or more appropriately have jurisdiction; and they may choose to attend themselves to matters dealt with by the Public Guardian upon submission of appropriate forms, without court process.

12.56 The jurisdiction and private international law provisions of AWI(S)A 2000 are set out in Sch 3, based on the Hague Convention on the International Protection of Adults of 13 January 2000. For description and discussion of them see Frimston et al *International Protection of Adults*, OUP, 2015 (in particular Chapter 12, by Ward). The Convention applies among jurisdictions in respect of which it has been ratified, currently Scotland, Austria, Czech Republic, Estonia, Finland, France, Germany and Switzerland. As explained in **12.10–12.12** it also, to an extent, in effect applies as between Scotland and England and Wales, by virtue of MCA 2005, Sch 3, notwithstanding that the Convention has not yet been ratified in respect of England and Wales. The Central Authority for Scotland under the Hague Convention is the Scottish Government's Constitution, Law and Courts Directorate, EU and International Law Branch, Civil Law Division, The Scottish Government, 2 West, St Andrew's House, Regent Road, Edinburgh EH1 3DG, Tel: 0131 244 2417.

The Courts

The Sheriff Court

12.57 The main jurisdiction under AWI(S)A 2000 rests with the Sheriff Court, and allocation to Sheriffdom is governed by similar rules to those in the Convention. Accordingly, the Sheriff having jurisdiction is the Sheriff in whose Sheriffdom:

(a) the adult is habitually resident;[38]

(b) relevant property is situated;

(c) the adult, or property belonging to the adult, is present in urgent cases where the adult is not habitually resident in Scotland;

(d) the adult is present, when the intervention sought is temporary and its effect limited to Scotland; and

(e) the adult is present, where the Sheriff considers it necessary in the adult's interests to take the proposed measure immediately.[39]

The Sheriff has jurisdiction to vary or recall intervention and guardianship orders[40] made by that Sheriff if no contracting state under the Convention (other than the United Kingdom) has jurisdiction and either:

(a) no other court or authority has jurisdiction; or

(b) another court or authority has jurisdiction but (i) it would be unreasonable to expect an applicant to invoke that jurisdiction or (ii) that court or authority has declined to exercise jurisdiction.[41]

The sheriff also has jurisdiction to determine applications to register international measures, the register itself being maintained by the Public Guardian.[42]

12.58 Note that the qualification 'other than the United Kingdom' means that recall or variation will be by the French courts where they have jurisdiction, but not automatically by the English courts even after ratification in respect of England. If the Scottish courts have jurisdiction, but no particular Sheriffdom is identified by the relevant rules, the fall-back Sheriff is the Sheriff at Edinburgh.

12.59 The Sheriff has jurisdiction to grant intervention and guardianship orders, to give directions to persons exercising functions under the Act,[43] to

---

[38] A change of habitual residence is not immediately effected by removal of an adult lacking relevant capacity from one jurisdiction to another – see *F v S*, referred to in **12.37** (footnote 27).

[39] AWI(S)A 2000, Sch 3, paras 2(1) and (3).

[40] See **12.120**.

[41] AWI(S)A 2000, Sch 3, para 2(2).

[42] See chapter XXIV 'International Protection of Adults' of the Act of Sederunt (Summary Applications, Statutory Applications and Appeals etc. Rules) 1999, as amended.

[43] Under AWI(S)A 2000, s 3(3): for examples see: *Application by Public Guardian for Directions*

hear appeals against decisions as to incapacity and appeals against any decision under the Act as to the medical treatment of an adult[44] (but not under the procedure described at **12.109**), and a wide range of remits and appeals under the Act. Unlike the position in England and Wales, the Act does not provide for stand-alone declaratory powers, but the powers to give directions and to determine appeals against decisions as to incapacity may in some cases have similar effect. For the sheriff's powers in relation to Powers of Attorney, including non-Scottish Powers of Attorney, see **12.98**; and for powers in relation to non-Scottish equivalents of guardians see **12.120**.

12.60 'Which forum?' was a major issue during the law reform process. The Law Society of Scotland recommended that the primary jurisdiction should rest with the Sheriff Court, but that individual Sheriffs should be designated to deal with adult incapacity matters. That suggestion was adopted by the Scottish Law Commission in the draft Bill annexed to its *Report on Incapable Adults*.[45] Sadly, that proposal was not included in the Act, with inconsistent and uncoordinated results. In Glasgow and Edinburgh Sheriff Courts the designated sheriff concept has been informally adopted. Many of the leading judgments which have developed this jurisdiction are those of Sheriff John Baird at Glasgow, who retired in April 2015. In many other Sheriff Courts, several Sheriffs exercise this jurisdiction in a consistent and appropriate way. Overall, however, there is often a lack of the case management which such a jurisdiction requires and there are inconsistencies which would have been less likely with designated sheriffs. In difficult cases where there is a possible choice of jurisdiction, it might be wise to seek advice about the particular Sheriff Court.[46] See **12.46** as to the possible introduction of shrieval specialisation in the adult incapacity jurisdiction under the provisions of the Courts Reform (Scotland) Act 2014.

The Court of Session

12.61 The role of the Court of Session as the first court to which a matter under the Act may be taken is limited to certain medical matters. See **12.100**.

Other functions under the Act

Public Guardian[47]

12.62 Scotland has its own entirely separate Public Guardian. In this chapter 'the Public Guardian' refers to Scotland's Public Guardian except where otherwise indicated. The Office of the Public Guardian has extensive

---

(Glasgow Sh. Ct. 30 June 2010), *Morton, Minuter for Directions* (Edinburgh Sh. Ct. 21 July 2010) and, as an ancillary matter, *Y W v Office of the Public Guardian* (Peterhead Sh. Ct. 25 June 2010).

44 With further appeal to the Court of Session, bypassing the Sheriff Principal.
45 Report No 151, published September 1995.
46 Also disappointing is the reluctance of the Sheriff Court Rules Council to address the requirements and consequences of this jurisdiction adequately.
47 AWI(S)A 2000, ss 6 and 7.

registration functions (including notification of registration), administers the scheme of Access to Funds (see **12.110** et seq), supervises guardians and appointees under intervention orders with financial powers, has investigative powers in relation to property and financial matters, and other powers and functions; but does not act as guardian, or have any other management functions, for any individual adults.

12.63 The Public Guardian's investigative functions include investigating, in relation to property and financial matters, complaints against continuing attorneys and non-Scottish equivalents, against guardians and non-Scottish equivalents, against appointees under intervention orders, and concerning the Access to Funds provisions of Part 3 of the Act. Certificates issued by the Public Guardian are conclusive evidence of their contents. They include certificates of registration of continuing and welfare Powers of Attorney ((CPA's) and (WPA's) respectively), various certificates under the Access to Funds scheme, and certificates of appointment under intervention and guardianship orders.

12.64 The Public Guardian has statutory duties to provide information and advice in property and financial matters, on request, to guardians, appointees under intervention orders, continuing attorneys and withdrawers under the Access to Funds scheme; and will generally provide helpful advice and guidance in response to reasonable requests from others, though the considerable information available on the Public Guardian's website should be checked before making an enquiry. The Public Guardian must investigate where she becomes aware of circumstances in which the property or financial affairs of an adult seem to be at risk. The Public Guardian may initiate or enter 'any proceedings before a court' where she considers that necessary to safeguard the property or financial affairs of an adult who lacks relevant capacity. Fees chargeable by the Public Guardian are prescribed by regulations and have been increased substantially.[48] Much useful information is available on her website (www.publicguardian-scotland.gov.uk) and the links which it provides.

Mental Welfare Commission[49]

12.65 The Mental Welfare Commission for Scotland exercises independent protective functions in relation to the rights, welfare and interests of adults with mental disorders in Scotland, including those with impairments of capacity. Many of the Commission's functions and powers are contained in MH(CT)(S)A 2003. Under AWI(S)A 2000 the Commission's functions include providing information and advice in personal welfare matters to guardians, welfare attorneys and appointees under intervention orders; and investigating complaints where either a local authority has failed to investigate, or the Commission is not satisfied with a local authority investigation. The Commission's investigative functions include investigating, in relation to personal welfare matters, complaints against welfare attorneys and non-Scottish equivalents, guardians and non-Scottish equivalents, and

---

[48] See Ward 'Out of the wrong pocket' 2008 JLSS 9.
[49] AWI(S)A 2000, s 9.

appointees under intervention orders. Important examples include the 'JL Report' referred to in **12.80** (footnote 67) and the 'D Report',[50] referred to in **12.77** and **12.90**.

Local authorities[51]

12.66 The functions of local authorities under the Act include supervising guardians in relation to welfare functions, investigating circumstances where the personal welfare of an adult appears to be at risk, and initiating applications for intervention or guardianship orders (in both personal welfare and property and financial matters) where this appears to be required and no-one else is taking action. The local authority supervises welfare guardians; supervises persons authorised under intervention orders and welfare attorneys where that has been ordered by the court; and has a duty to provide information and advice in welfare matters, when asked, to all of the foregoing.

Other Incapacity Act roles

12.67 The Act confers significant roles on an adult's primary carer[52] and nearest relative.[53] Others with roles include any named person[54] and any person providing independent advocacy services.[55]

Limitation of liability

12.68 The Act exempts certain persons exercising roles under the Act from liability for any breach of any duty of care or fiduciary duty owed to the adult. The exemption applies only if the person has acted reasonably and in good faith, and in accordance with the Act's general principles (see **12.70**), or has failed to act and the failure was reasonable and in good faith, and in accordance with the general principles. The persons protected by this provision are guardians, including non-Scottish equivalents, continuing and welfare attorneys and non-Scottish equivalents, appointees under intervention orders, withdrawers under the Access to Funds scheme, and managers of establishments acting under Part 4 of the Act.[56]

Ill treatment and wilful neglect

12.69 It is an offence under the Act for any person exercising powers under the Act in relation to an adult's personal welfare to ill-treat or wilfully neglect that adult. The maximum penalties are 2 years' imprisonment or a fine, or both.[57]

---

[50] The Commission's report on 'An investigation into the response by statutory services and professionals to concerns raised in respect of Mr and Mrs D' (published 13 February, 2012).
[51] AWI(S)A 2000, ss 10, 53(3) and 57(2).
[52] AWI(S)A 2000, s 87(1).
[53] MH(CT)(S)A 2003, s 254; AWI(S)A 2000, s 4.
[54] MH(CT)(S)A 2003, s 329.
[55] AWI(S)A 2000, s 3(5A) and (5B); MH(CT)(S)A 2003, s 259(1).
[56] AWI(S)A 2000, s 82.
[57] AWI(S)A 2000, s 83.

The principles

12.70 The Act commences with a statement of principles[58] which have proved to be invaluable, and which have been subject to minor consequential amendment but no calls for significant alteration. This Scottish experience led to the strong recommendation, described in **Chapter 2**, that legislation for England and Wales should likewise be governed by general principles. Scotland rejected a 'best interests' test for the reasons explained by the Scottish Law Commission in the passage quoted in **2.46**. The Scottish principles, with brief comments in ensuing paragraphs, are as follows:

> '1.(1) The principles set out in subss (2) and (4) shall be given effect to in relation to any intervention in the affairs of an adult under or in pursuance of this Act, including any order made in or for the purpose of any proceedings under this Act for or in connection with an adult.
>
> (2) There shall be no intervention in the affairs of an adult unless the person responsible for authorising or effecting the intervention is satisfied that the intervention will benefit the adult and that such benefit cannot reasonably be achieved without the intervention.
>
> (3) Where it is determined that an intervention as mentioned in subs(1) is to be made, such intervention shall be the least restrictive option in relation to the freedom of the adult, consistent with the purpose of the intervention.
>
> (4) In determining if an intervention is to be made and, if so, what intervention is to be made, account shall be taken of–
>
> > (a) the present and past wishes and feelings of the adult so far as they can be ascertained by any means of communication, whether human or by mechanical aid (whether of an interpretative nature or otherwise) appropriate to the adult;
> > (b) the views of the nearest relative, named person and the primary carer of the adult, in so far as it is reasonable and practicable to do so;
> > (c) the views of –
> > > (i) any guardian, continuing attorney or welfare attorney of the adult who has powers relating to the proposed intervention; and
> > > (ii) any person whom the sheriff has directed to be consulted, in so far as it is reasonable and practicable to do so; and
> > (d) the views of any other person appearing to the person responsible for authorising or effecting the intervention to have an interest in the welfare of the adult or in the proposed intervention, where these views have been made known to the person responsible, in so far as it is reasonable and practicable to do so.
>
> (5) Any guardian, continuing attorney, welfare attorney or manager of an establishment exercising functions under this Act or under any order of the sheriff in relation to an adult shall, in so far as it is reasonable and practicable to do so, encourage the adult to exercise whatever skills he has concerning his property, financial affairs or personal welfare, as the case may be, and to develop new such skills.'

---

[58] AWI(S)A 2000, s 1(1)–(5).

12.71 In AWI(S)A 2000 'intervention' has a wide meaning, and encompasses a decision not to do something. It may mean an intervention affecting a second adult in the course of proceedings initiated in relation to another.[59]

12.72 In s 1(2) 'benefit' can include anything which the adult would have done if capable, including something gratuitous, such as making gifts or participating in non-therapeutic medical research – both of which are expressly provided for in the Act.[60] In *G v West Lothian Council*,[61] Sheriff Principal Stephen controversially offered the novel proposition that the benefit principle was 'the essential principle' which should be addressed before consideration is given to the other principles. That would appear to equate 'benefit' with a 'best interests test' notwithstanding that the latter approach was expressly rejected for the purposes of AWI(S)A 2000 –see quotation in **2.46**. That approach would also appear to be inconsistent with the obligations undertaken by the United Kingdom under the UN Convention on the Rights of Persons with Disabilities. For criticism of the Sheriff Principal's approach, see Mental Capacity Law Newsletter, April 2015, Scotland section, p 9.

12.73 Section 1(3) requires not the simplest or cheapest option, nor even – without qualification – the least restrictive option, but 'the least restrictive option in relation to the freedom of the adult, consisting with the purpose of the intervention'. The exercise of quasi-guardianship powers without assessment, judicial procedure or procedure subject to judicial control, or appropriate supervision and accountability, can never be the least restrictive option under this definition.

12.74 Section 1(4)(a), unlike the following provisions of s 1(4), is not limited to 'in so far as it is reasonable and practicable to do so'. The obligation is unqualified. The sheriff (only) must take account of the adult's wishes and feelings so far as expressed by a person providing independent advocacy services.[62]

12.75 Section 1(4)(c)(i) includes similar appointments under the law of any country, but in the case of guardianship only if the guardianship is recognised by the Law of Scotland.[63]

Definitions of adult, incapable and incapacity

12.76 These definitions are contained in s 1(6), which is in the following terms:

'(6) For the purposes of this Act, and unless the context otherwise requires –

---

[59] See Ward 'Two "adults" in one incapacity case? – thoughts for Scotland from an English deprivation of liberty decision', 2013 SLT (News) 239-242.

[60] AWI(S)A 2000, ss 66 and 51 respectively.

[61] 2014, GWD 40-730 (see also case commentary by Eccles and Watson at 2015 SLT (News) 35).

[62] AWI(S)A 2000, s 3(5A).

[63] AWI(S)A 2000, s 1(7).

"adult" means a person who has attained the age of 16 years;
"incapable" means incapable of –
    (a)   acting; or
    (b)   making decisions; or
    (c)   communicating decisions; or
    (d)   understanding decisions; or
    (e)   retaining the memory of decisions,
as mentioned in any provision of this Act, by reason of mental disorder[64] or of inability to communicate because of physical disability; but a person shall not fall within this definition by reason only of a lack or deficiency in a faculty of communication if that lack or deficiency can be made good by human or mechanical aid (whether of an interpretative nature or otherwise); and
"incapacity" shall be construed accordingly.'

12.77 The initial words of s 1(6) mean that the above definition does not necessarily apply for other purposes, where other tests of incapacity may apply. This element of 'acting' in (a) broadens the scope of the definition significantly beyond decision-making, and includes (for example) acting to assert and safeguard the adult's own rights and interests; acting in accordance with decisions otherwise competently made; and acting to resist undue influence – see the 'D Report' referred to in **12.65**. Element (e) is usually interpreted as meaning memory to a degree, and for a duration, appropriate to the matter in question. As with s 1(4)(a) (see **12.70** and **12.74**), the requirement to facilitate communication is not subject to the qualification 'in so far as it is reasonable and practicable to do so'. Compliance with the UN Convention on the Rights of Persons with Disabilities is likely to require extension of this important exception to require provision of any necessary support where that will enable competent decision-making; though robust safeguards against undue influence will be necessary.

12.78 In modern Scottish usage, and in accordance with the above definition, 'incapacity' is the noun from 'incapable', referring to factual impairments of the ability to act or decide with legal effect. It does not refer to the consequences of any process of 'incapacitation', which is unknown in Scots law, nor to any outmoded (in Scotland) usages of 'legal capacity' to refer to elements of legal personality, rights and status, which all Scottish adults have regardless of any intellectual disabilities.[65]

12.79 On the one hand, capacity is function-specific. For example, AWI(S)(A) 2000, s 57(1) expressly recognises and provides that an adult may be capable of himself making application for appointment of a guardian to deal with matters of which that same adult is incapable.[66]

---

[64] See **12.82**.
[65] There is potential confusion, in relation to Scots law, in the terminology of Art 12 of the UN Convention on the Rights of Persons with Disabilities, which uses 'legal capacity' in a much wider sense, and even more so in the terminology of the pronouncements of the UN Committee on the Rights of Persons with Disabilities.
[66] Such an application was granted in *H*, Kilmarnock Sheriff Court, January 27, 2010.

12.80 On the other hand, a broad rather than narrow view is taken in assessing capacity for a particular purpose. In *Application by the Public Guardian re DC*, Glasgow Sheriff Court, August 14, 2012 (a decision upheld on appeal by the Sheriff Principal on December 6, 2012), an adult's decision to revoke a POA might on a narrow view have been considered competent, but his mental disorder – as to which he lacked any insight – prevented him from comprehending that his purpose, which was to return home to the care of his wife from the care home in which his attorney had placed him, was a practical impossibility which if attempted would have had dire consequences. The sheriff held that the adult lacked capacity to make a valid revocation, and directed the Public Guardian not to register it. Whether that same adult was in consequence unlawfully deprived of his liberty was an issue in subsequent separate proceedings before the Court of Session in which interim liberation was ordered (that action was settled without final determination by the court). Clear and consistently repeated articulation of a decision does not necessarily mean that it was competent.[67]

12.81 On whether an adult could be capable of decisions about use of contraception but not about having sexual relations, and related issues, see *Application for directions by West Lothian Council in respect of LY*, Livingston Sheriff Court, 30 May 2014 (judgment on scotcourts website).

12.82 The relevant definition of mental disorder is contained in s 328 of MH(CT)(S)A 2003, and is as follows:

'(1) Subject to subs (2) below, in this Act "mental disorder" means any – (a) mental illness; (b) personality disorder; or (c) learning disability, however caused or manifested; and cognate expressions shall be construed accordingly.

(2) A person is not mentally disordered by reason only of any of the following – (a) sexual orientation; (b) sexual deviancy; (c) transsexualism; (d) transvestism; (e) dependence on, or use of, alcohol or drugs; (f) behaviour that causes, or is likely to cause, harassment, alarm or distress to any other person; (g) acting as no prudent person would act.'

At time of writing there is debate as to whether this 'diagnostic threshold' is compatible with the UN Convention on the Rights of Persons with Disabilities.

Powers of Attorney (Part 2)

Terminology

12.83 Continuing and welfare Powers of Attorney are governed principally by the s 1 principles, and by Part 2, of AWI(S)A 2000. A continuing Power of Attorney ('CPA') is a Power of Attorney ('POA') in respect of the financial and property affairs of the granter (not 'donor') capable of operation after loss of

---

[67] Scottish Law Commission Report 'Left alone – the end of life support and treatment of Mr JL', 8th July 2014.

relevant capacity. A welfare Power of Attorney ('WPA') confers powers in relation to personal welfare, which term includes healthcare matters, operable during relevant incapacity.

Overview

12.84　No POA other than a CPA or WPA granted in accordance with the Act's provisions, and registered by the Public Guardian, may be operated after loss of relevant capacity of the granter. Careful compliance with the Act's provisions is essential: see *Application for guardianship in respect of* NW, referred to in **12.89**. A human rights based system of incapacity law emphasises the importance of autonomy and self-determination, and thus encourages the granting of such POA's while granters have the capacity to do so, or by people with some impairments of capacity who are nevertheless capable of granting POA's.[68] In Scotland large, and increasing, numbers of such POA's have been granted.[69] Granting of such POA's has become as much recommended, as a matter of prudence, as making a Will, and for reasons including speedier transfer of hospital patients ready for discharge was promoted in an advertising campaign which commenced in 2013 and continued in 2014 and 2015.[70] On the cross-border status of Powers of Attorney see **12.96**.

12.85　Procedural requirements contain necessary safeguards but avoid such difficulty and complexity as might be a deterrent to prospective granters or attorneys. Under the principles of autonomy and self-determination, it is for the granter to decide whom to appoint, with what powers, when the POA should be registered, and in what circumstances the powers which are conferred may be exercised. However, welfare powers may only be exercised during relevant incapacity (or while the attorney reasonably believes that there is relevant incapacity), and a welfare attorney may not place the granter in hospital for treatment of a mental disorder against the granter's will, consent on behalf of the granter to forms of treatment specified by regulations, or take other specified steps generally in relation to healthcare matters.[71] These are minimum statutory limitations. The granter may – and often will – further limit the powers conferred, and further limit the circumstances in which they may be operated (such as by requiring written medical certification as a prerequisite for operation).

12.86　The competence of authorising a deprivation of liberty in a WPA was an issue before the Court of Session (in a case brought by the adult, *DC*, see **12.80**), even although that is not among the statutory exclusions. That case settled and the point was not determined. However, anything contrary to the

---

[68]　See Council of Europe Recommendation on Principles concerning Powers of Attorney and Advance Directives for Incapacity and relative explanatory memorandum R (2009) 11.

[69]　Rising every year from 5,592 registrations in the first year after Part 2 came into force to 55,527 in the year to 31 March 2015.

[70]　'Begin the Conversation', promoted by Glasgow City Council, NHS Greater Glasgow and Clyde, and TC Young LLP, Solicitors.

[71]　See AWI(S)A 2000, s 16(6).

presumed purpose of a WPA would, as with a CPA,[72] require explicit provision even if competent. In *McDowall's Executors v IRC* [2004] STC (SCD) 22 it was held that making gifts was contrary to the presumed purpose of conserving the granter's estate, and therefore required explicit power. It would probably be held that the presumed purpose of a WPA would include safeguarding the granter's liberty.

Underlying law, the POA document

12.87   As in England and Wales the general law of POA's applies, subject only to the particular provisions of AWI(S)A 2000 if the POA is to be operable following loss of relevant capacity. A basic rule, applicable also to CPA's and WPA's, is that the attorney has no powers other than those conferred in the document. None are implied. No standard form is provided by or under the Act. A common form of POA document will contain a general power to do everything which may be competently done by such an attorney, followed by a list – often a long list – of specific powers conferred without prejudice to the general power. Some POA documents contain only specific powers, and no general power: in these cases the specific powers are strictly construed, and may be held not to have covered actions actually taken by the attorney.[73]

Formalities

12.88   This and the following paragraphs **12.89–12.93** apply only to CPA's and WPA's granted on or after 2 April 2001.[74] For POA's granted before that date, see **12.95**. CPA's and WPA's must be in writing and subscribed by the granter. They need not be witnessed, but usually are, such witnessing making them 'self-proving'. They must expressly state the granter's intention that they shall be a CPA or WPA (or both). Where a CPA is to be exerciseable only during relevant incapacity of the granter, the document must state that the granter has considered how such incapacity is to be determined, and all WPA's must contain such a statement. Curiously, the granter must state that he has considered this, but is not expressly required to include the outcome of such consideration! This requirement was introduced by ASP(S)A 2007 and accordingly is not reflected in the styles offered in Ward *Adult Incapacity* (see **12.52**).

12.89   In *Application for guardianship in respect of* NW, 2014 SLT (Sh Ct) 83, Sheriff Baird held that a CPA did not comply with the requirements described in either of the preceding sentences, and in consequence was invalid. The document was in accordance with a bank's standard form, which in turn was similar to a 'sample' which appeared on the Public Guardian's website until removed following issue of Sheriff Baird's decision. In *B v H*, 2014 SLT (Sh Ct) 160 Sheriff Murray, upon the facts of that case, came to the opposite

---

[72]   In *McDowall's Executors v IRC* [2004] STC (SCD) 22 it was held that making gifts was contrary to the presumed purpose of conserving the granter's estate, and therefore required explicit power.

[73]   See *McDowall's Executors* above and *M, Applicant* 2007 SLT (Sh Ct) 24; 2006 GWD 19–418.

[74]   When Part 3 of AWI(S)A 2000 was brought into force.

conclusion to Sheriff Baird in *NW* regarding a not dissimilar power of attorney document, but commented: 'I do not dispute that the deed could have been better drafted'. Sheriff Murray took into account extraneous evidence of the granter's intentions including as to whether the document should indeed be a CPA and WPA. In *Great Stuart Trustees Limited v Public Guardian*, 2015, SLT 115, a Special Case decided by an Extra Division of the Inner House of the Court of Session, the validity of yet another similar power of attorney document was considered. The court rejected the reasoning of Sheriff Baird and preferred that of Sheriff Murray. The Scottish Parliament had chosen not to prescribe any particular form of document. No particular form of words was accordingly essential, provided that the granter's intention was clear. In *Application in respect of S*, 2013 SLT (Sh Ct) 65, Sheriff Baird held that a POA document was not fit for purpose. In both that case and *NW* he granted guardianship orders. There is no reason for concern about the validity of a carefully drawn CPA or WPA, but as Scots law does not provide prescribed forms granters may well opt to engage appropriate professional expertise in drafting such documents.

12.90 The document must incorporate a certificate in prescribed form by a practising solicitor (which means a practising Scottish solicitor), practising advocate or registered medical practitioner. The certificate confirms that:

(a) the certifier has interviewed the granter immediately before the granter subscribed the POA,

(b) the certifier is satisfied that the granter understood the nature and extent of the POA document, either from the certifier's own knowledge of the granter or because the certifier has consulted a person, named in the certificate, who has knowledge of the granter, and

(c) the certifier has no reason to believe that the granter is acting under undue influence or that the granting of the POA is otherwise vitiated.

For a case where neither the solicitor who prepared POA's, nor the medical practitioner who certified them, identified pernicious undue influence which had grave consequences for the granters, see the "D Report" referred to in **12.65**. In implementation of one of the recommendations in that Report, the Law Society of Scotland issued two sets of professional guidance, and continues to update guidance in the light of experience. See 'Guidance on Continuing and Welfare Powers of Attorney' and 'Vulnerable Clients Guidance', both available on the Society's website www.lawscot.org.uk.

12.91 CPA's and WPA's may only be operated after registration. The form of application for registration is prescribed, and is available from the Public Guardian's website.[75] If they are registered before loss of relevant capacity, there is no provision for further registration upon loss of relevant capacity. However, the granter may state in the document a prerequisite for registration, such as medical certification of loss of capacity, though in practice it appears

---

[75] See **12.64**.

that relatively few granters do so, probably because of fear that it would then be too late to rectify if some defect caused the Public Guardian to refuse to register. The POA document should be checked for prerequisites for operation, as opposed to prerequisites for registration.

12.92 If a CPA or WPA is produced for use in England and Wales, it is essential to see a certificate of registration (or official copy thereof) and either an official copy of the POA document issued by the Public Guardian; or a copy certified in accordance with the Powers of Attorney Act 1971; or an official extract registered copy of the document registered in the Books of Council and Session which, in accordance with s 4 of the Evidence and Powers of Attorney Act 1940, is evidence of the contents thereof 'in any part of the United Kingdom, without further proof'.

12.93 If the POA document has not been registered with the Public Guardian, it is not (yet) operable, regardless of what it may say, and even if it has been registered the attorney may only exercise powers conferred by the document, and may only exercise those powers subject to any provisions in the document as to the circumstances in which they may be exercised.

Revocation and termination

12.94 The formalities for revocation are similar to those for granting, and include similar certification and registration of a revocation notice. No liability is incurred by persons acting in good faith in ignorance of the revocation. However, in matters of any significance it is prudent to check with the Office of the Public Guardian that the POA has not been revoked, and that no other termination of the POA or of the attorney's authority has been registered. Where the Public Guardian receives *prima facie* credible representations that a purported revocation, or a revocation coupled with a fresh POA, presented to her for registration may be invalid, it is her practice to seek directions under s 3(3) from the sheriff with primary jurisdiction as to whether she should register.[76]

POA's executed before 2 April 2001

12.95 Doubts remain as to whether any Scottish POA executed before 1 January 1991 may be operated following the granter's loss of capacity. See **12.47**. It would be wise to take Scottish advice before acting in reliance on such a POA if the granter lacks relevant capacity. In the case of Scottish POA's granted from 1 January 1991 to 1 April 2001, the position is the opposite, as explained in **12.48**. Unless the document specifies that it shall not be operable during the granter's incapacity, it may be relied upon (subject to its actual terms, and except in welfare matters) without enquiry as to whether the granter still has capacity or not. The formalities described in **12.88** do not apply, though the same rules of interpretation do apply. Under the transitional

---

[76] The sheriff directed the Public Guardian not to register in *Public Guardian, Applicant,* 2011 SLT (Sh Ct.) 66 and in *Application by Public Guardian re DC*: see **12.80**.

provisions of AWI(S)A 2000 such POA's are however now described as CPA's or WPA's or both, and several of the provisions of AWI(S)A 2000, including the powers of the sheriff described in **12.98**, apply to them. Commonly, what will be presented will be an official extract from the Books of Council and Session of the POA document (see **12.92**).

Non-Scottish Powers of Attorney

12.96 Subject to the next paragraph, the law governing the existence, extent, modification and extinction of CPA's, WPA's and non-Scottish equivalents is the law of the habitual residence of the granter at time of granting, unless the granter specified in writing the law of a jurisdiction in which the granter had previously been habitually resident; or the law of the jurisdiction where property is situated, but only as regards that property; or, in the case of a non-British granter, the law of the state of the granter's nationality. Where a non-Scottish POA or equivalent is exercised in Scotland, the manner of exercise is governed by Scots law. A transaction entered in Scotland between an attorney or equivalent and a third party is not challengeable on the grounds that the attorney was not entitled to enter it by the law of some other country, unless the third party knew or ought to have known that the attorney's entitlement to act was governed by the law of that other country.[77] In *C, Applicant*,[78] it was held that an English Enduring Power of Attorney had automatic recognition in Scotland under AWI(S)A 2000 and had the same effect as a Scottish CPA. As an interim measure pending resolution of the unacceptable uncertainty regarding POAs in both directions between England and Scotland, the Public Guardian offers a non-statutory certificate which may be downloaded from her website (see **12.64**) in the following terms:

> 'I, Sandra McDonald, Public Guardian for Scotland, hereby advise that interpretation of Scottish legislation suggests a non-Scottish Power of Attorney is automatically valid in Scotland. There is no provision for having a non-Scottish Power of Attorney endorsed for use in Scotland; this action being unnecessary.'

12.97 The provisions described in **12.96** are subject to the powers of the sheriff described in **12.98**. Also, they do not displace any enactment or rule of law which has mandatory effect for the protection of an adult with incapacity in Scotland, whatever law would otherwise be applicable; and no provision of the law of any country other than Scotland may be applied so as to produce a result manifestly contrary to public policy.

Powers of the sheriff

12.98 The powers of the sheriff described in this paragraph may be exercised under AWI(S)A 2000, s 20 in relation to CPA's, WPA's and non-Scottish equivalents. The law applicable to exercise of these powers is Scots law, but the sheriff must to the extent possible take into account the law which governs the

---

[77] AWI(S)A 2000, Sch 3, para 4.
[78] Airdrie Sheriff Court, 2 April 2013, unreported.

POA under the rules described in **12.96**.[79] The sheriff's powers may be exercised upon application by anyone claiming an interest in the property, financial affairs or personal welfare of the granter. The prerequisites for granting an order under s 20 are that the sheriff is satisfied that the granter is incapable in relation to relevant matters and that the order is necessary to safeguard or promote the granter's interests in those matters. Under CPA's, the sheriff may order supervision by the Public Guardian, and/or may order the attorney to submit accounts for any specified period for audit by the Public Guardian. In relation to WPA's, the sheriff may order supervision by the local authority, and/or may order the welfare attorney to give a report to the sheriff as to the manner in which the attorney has exercised the attorney's powers during any specified period. In relation to both CPA's and WPA's, the sheriff may revoke any of the powers granted by the CPA or WPA, or may revoke the appointment of an attorney. Where there are joint attorneys, the sheriff may thus revoke the appointment of one of them. Revocation may be appealed, but the other orders under s 20 are final. Orders under s 20 are subject to provisions for registration with, and intimation by, the Public Guardian. The sheriff's powers under s 20 are in addition to the sheriff's general powers, including the power to give directions described in **12.59**.

Accounts and funds (Part 3)

Joint accounts

12.99 AWI(S)A 2000, s 32 is the only provision of Part 3 of the Act which has remained unaltered since original enactment. It effected the simple but important reform that where one holder of a joint account loses relevant capacity, any other joint holder may continue to operate the account, unless the terms of the account provide otherwise or the court has barred the joint holder from operating it. Many accounts are now operated under this provision, which often renders any other intervention unnecessary.

'Access to funds'

12.100 The remainder of Part 3, replaced in its entirety with effect from 1 April 2008,[80] provides a scheme of limited financial guardianship under the jurisdiction of the Public Guardian rather than the sheriff (except where the Public Guardian refers a Part 3 application to the sheriff for determination[81]). Where applicable, Part 3 administration must be utilised rather than financial guardianship under Part 6.[82] Under the core provisions of Part 3, 'authority to intromit' is given to a 'withdrawer' who opens an operating account called the 'designated account', which receives funds of the adult held by 'fundholders',

---

[79] AWI(S)A 2000, Sch 3, para 3(3).
[80] The original Part 3 was the only Part of the Act which was not a success, and under-utilised. Usage has almost doubled since it was replaced: rising to a peak of 491 in the year to 31 March 2012, then dwindling; compared with 195 and 197 in the two preceding years.
[81] AWI(S)A 2000, s 27F.
[82] AWI(S)A 2000, s 58(1)(b).

and from which the withdrawer makes payments for the adult's benefit[83] in accordance with a budget approved by the Public Guardian. 'Intromit' covers dealing with funds, mainly receiving, paying out or investing them.

12.101 The scheme allows for individual or joint withdrawers, reserve (ie replacement) withdrawers, and organisations as withdrawers.[84] The scheme is operated by various types of application on prescribed forms to the Public Guardian,[85] who issues certificates of authority. Preliminary application may be made to obtain information from fundholders about the adult's assets, and to authorise release of information by the fundholder for that purpose. Authority may be obtained to open an 'adult's current account' to receive the adult's income to 'feed' the withdrawer's 'designated account', if the adult does not have an existing account suitable for that purpose.

12.102 Authority may also be obtained to open an 'adult's second account', normally a savings-type account to hold surplus funds at a better rate of interest than the current account.[86] Other possibilities include authority to transfer funds between different accounts in the adult's name, to terminate existing standing orders and direct debits, to close existing accounts, and to authorise payment of lump sums in addition to the regular budgeted expenditure. The budget may be amended.

Procedure

12.103 Applications for authority to provide information about the adult's funds, to open accounts, and to intromit with the adult's funds must be accompanied by a medical certificate of incapacity in prescribed form by any medical practitioner. All or any of these applications may be made on a single combined form with a single medical certificate. Those applications, and also applications to add a joint withdrawer, except where the applicant is an organisation rather than one or more individuals, must also be countersigned by someone who has known the adult for at least a year,[87] and who confirms that he or she believes (a) that the information in the application form is true; and (b) that the applicant is a fit and proper person to intromit with the adult's funds. Intimation (notification) requirements are dealt with by the Public Guardian upon receipt of the application.[88] Where there are joint withdrawers, or a withdrawer and a reserve, a countersignatory's certificate is required for each. Authority to intromit is usually granted for three years, but the Public Guardian may reduce or extend the period of validity of the withdrawal certificate.

---

[83] See AWI(S)A 2000, s 24A for the purposes for which the withdrawer may intromit with the adult's funds.
[84] Organisations cannot be financial guardians under Part 6.
[85] The various forms are designated ATF (Access to Funds), which may be downloaded from the Public Guardian's website: see **12.64**.
[86] That at least was the intention, before interest rates plummeted.
[87] See AWI(S)A 2000, s 27A(1)(b) for persons not permitted to countersign.
[88] See AWI(S)A 2000, s 27C.

Transition from guardianship

12.104 The procedural requirements are simplified for transition to Part 3 administration from financial guardianship under Part 6. If the Part 3 applicant is the financial guardian, countersignature is not required. The Public Guardian has discretion to dispense with the requirement for a medical certificate.

Part 3 scheme inapplicable or inappropriate

12.105 An application may not be made under Part 3 where, in relation to the funds in question, a guardian or continuing attorney has powers, or an intervention order has been granted. Circumstances in which Part 3 administration is inappropriate include 'where the adult has financial assets of a complex nature, for example, stocks and shares, investment bonds, etc. to be managed';[89] where heritable property[90] requires to be dealt with, or where a tenancy is to be given up; where a claim for compensation or other remedies require to be pursued, or there is other litigation; where a business is to be dealt with; and where tax-planning arrangements are contemplated.

Management of residents' finances (Part 4)

12.106 Part 4 of AWI(S)A 2000 provides a procedure for the management of the finances of an adult resident in an 'authorised establishment' by the managers of that establishment. Authorised establishments are NHS hospitals, for which the supervisory body for the purposes of Part 4 is the relevant health board, and independent hospitals, care homes and other services registered with the Care Inspectorate, for which the Inspectorate is the supervisory body. The procedure requires consideration of options by the managers of the establishment, medical examination, issue of a medical certificate of incapacity, and various intimation and notification requirements.

12.107 The consent of the supervisory body is required to manage funds in excess of £10,000. Subject to limitations, the managers may for the resident's benefit claim, receive, hold and spend funds, may hold moveable[91] property, and may dispose of moveable property (but only up to a cumulative value of £100 except with consent of the supervisory body). The supervisory body may authorise a named manager to withdraw funds from an existing account of the resident. An establishment registered with the Care Inspectorate may opt out of the Part 4 scheme, and the supervisory body may revoke the power of a particular establishment to operate the scheme. The Part 4 scheme is not available when relevant powers are in force under a CPA, or a guardianship or intervention order.

---

[89] Access to Funds Revised Code of Practice.
[90] Land and buildings.
[91] Property which is not land or buildings.

Medical treatment and research (Part 5)

12.108 Medical treatment, with some limited exceptions, may be authorised by a certificate of incapacity by a medical practitioner, dental practitioner, ophthalmic optician or registered nurse.[92] Certificates may be issued for up to 3 years where incapacity is unlikely to improve because of severe or profound learning disability, dementia or a severe neurological disorder. Otherwise the maximum duration is one year. Authorisation is limited to treatment to preserve life or prevent serious deterioration when the certifier is aware of a pending application for a guardianship or intervention order with relevant powers.

12.109 The certification procedure may be followed when an appointee under a WPA, guardianship order or intervention order has relevant powers, but treatment is only authorised if the appointee consents or by reference of disagreement to a practitioner nominated by the Mental Welfare Commission, subject to appeal to the Court of Session. Some other disputes about medical treatment may also be appealed to the Court of Session; otherwise they may be appealed to the sheriff, and thence, with leave of the sheriff, to the Court of Session.

12.110 Persons with impaired capacity may also be treated on grounds of necessity; and they may be treated under relevant provisions of MH(CT)(S)A 2003. There is statutory provision for advance statements in MH(CT)(S)A 2003, but not in AWI(S)A 2000, nor is there statutory provision for withholding and withdrawing treatment.[93]

Guardianship and intervention orders (Part 6)

12.111 A guardian is the approximate equivalent of a deputy in England and Wales. Guardianship orders have increased in each successive year since Part 6 came into force, from 288 in 2002–03 to 2,534 in 2014–15. Intervention orders have risen in most years, to 340 or more in each of the three years to 2014–15. The procedure for both guardianship and intervention orders is substantially the same. They are granted by the sheriff upon an application supported by three reports, two of them medical reports. One medical report must be produced by a 'relevant medical practitioner', usually a practitioner approved by a (Scottish) health board as having special experience in the diagnosis and treatment of mental disorder, though where the adult is not present in Scotland the term covers a medical practitioner with similar qualifications and experience who has consulted the Mental Welfare Commission about the report.[94] The other medical report may be provided by any medical practitioner, who need not be a Scottish medical practitioner.[95] The third report is provided by a mental health officer (a specialised social worker) where the

---

92 Regulations may specify other categories of certifiers.
93 Still regulated under the *nobile officium*: see **12.43**.
94 Other categories of 'relevant medical practitioners' may be specified by regulations.
95 *H, Applicant*, 2007 SLT (Sh Ct) 5; 2006 GWD 21-447.

powers sought are or include welfare powers, and by a 'person who has sufficient knowledge' where only property and financial powers are sought.

12.112 Procedure includes requirements for intimation (giving notice in accordance with relevant procedural requirements) and a hearing. The sheriff may only dispense with intimation to the adult if satisfied that this would be likely to pose a serious risk to the adult's health. Where property and financial powers are given, the sheriff may order that caution[96] be obtained or other security given. Once the order has been made and any requirement for caution met, the Public Guardian issues a certificate of appointment. The certificate is the document which should be inspected to ascertain details of the appointment, including the powers conferred. Where the order confers powers in relation to heritable property,[97] it must be recorded or registered in the appropriate property register.[98] The local authority must apply for an order if it appears to be necessary and no-one else is applying or likely to apply.

12.113 Until 2009 some guardians had no certificate of appointment, because they were originally appointed as curators bonis, tutors-dative or tutors-at-law under previous law and became guardians under the transitional provisions of AWI(S)A 2000. All such appointments still in force have now been renewed under the Act. The deadline for lodgement of renewal applications – for appointments otherwise still in force – was 5 October 2009. There could however be a small number of remaining transitional guardians originally appointed to children who have still not yet reached age 18.

Intervention orders

12.114 An intervention order may either authorise action specified in the order, or authorise a person to take action or make decisions as may be specified. The order may cover a single act such as signing a document, or a series of acts and decisions, such as giving up the lease of the adult's home and arranging all aspects of a transition to residential care. With limited exceptions, an intervention order can authorise anything which the adult, if capable, could have done in relation to the adult's personal welfare and/or property and financial affairs. An intervention order is the appropriate (though not the only) way to pursue or defend civil proceedings on behalf of an adult with impaired capacity, unless ongoing guardianship powers are likely to be required.

12.115 A guardianship order may not be granted where an intervention order will suffice, and the sheriff may grant an intervention order where guardianship has been applied for (but not vice versa). However, there is no rigid dividing line. Generally, an intervention order will be preferred for a self-limiting matter or series of matters, and guardianship where ongoing management may be

---

[96] Pronounced 'kay-shun', a guarantee bond covering loss through default which the appointee fails to make good.
[97] Land and buildings.
[98] The Land Register of Scotland, or for properties not yet registered in the Land Register, the General Register of Sasines.

required. However, while an intervention order was previously preferred for transactions such as selling a house when the proceeds were to be managed under Part 3, guardianship may now be preferred in such cases because the simplified transition to Part 3 administration described in **12.104** applies only to guardianship, and not to intervention orders.

Guardianship

12.116 Guardianship may be plenary or partial. The categories of powers which may be conferred are set out in s 64(1) as follows:

> '(a) power to deal with such particular matters in relation to the property, financial affairs or personal welfare of the adult as may be specified in the order;
>
> (b) power to deal with all aspects of the personal welfare of the adult, or with such aspects as may be specified in the order;
>
> (c) power to pursue or defend an action of declarator of nullity of marriage, or of divorce or separation in the name of the adult;
>
> (d) power to manage the property or financial affairs of the adult, or such parts of them as may be specified in the order;
>
> (e) power to authorise the adult to carry out such transactions or categories of transactions as the guardian may specify.'

Unless otherwise ordered by the sheriff, the guardian is the adult's legal representative within the scope of the powers conferred. See s 64(2) for matters excluded from a guardian's powers. For a case where guardianship powers were sought to make decisions about engagement in sexual relations, see *LY*, **12.81**. The status of consent on behalf of a patient by a guardian for the purposes of MH(CT)(S)A 2003 is unclear in statute and was addressed in *Petition by PW and AW*, Court of Session, 18 December 2013.

12.117 The sheriff may appoint an individual guardian, joint guardians (guardians jointly exercising the same powers), dual guardians (such as one guardian exercising welfare powers and another exercising financial powers, though the term 'dual guardian' is not used in the Act), one or more substitute (ie replacement) guardians, permutations of the foregoing, and the chief social work officer as welfare guardian. No other office holder may be appointed as such, nor may any trust, corporation or other entity. Financial guardians are under the supervision of the Public Guardian, to whom they must normally submit an inventory of estate and management plan following appointment, and annual accounts thereafter. Welfare guardians are supervised by local authorities.

Deprivation of Liberty

12.118 There are no specific provisions for deprivation of liberty cases, but the Scottish Law Commission has made proposals, including for a new Part 5A in AWI(S)A 2000, in that regard in Report No 240 on Adults with Incapacity

(October 2014).[99] It is generally considered that an order of a sheriff under AWI(S)A 2000, s 70 ordering compliance with a guardian's decision (see **12.120**) could authorise a deprivation of liberty. That procedure is not available to attorneys or appointees under an intervention order.

Provisions applicable to guardians and non-Scottish equivalents

12.119 The provisions of Part 6 described in this paragraph apply both to Scottish guardians and to non-Scottish equivalents. Guardians and equivalents with welfare powers may exercise their powers whether or not the adult is in Scotland at the time.[100] Guardians and equivalents are personally liable under any transaction which they enter outwith the scope of their authority; and when they act without disclosing that they do so as guardians, they are also personally liable but (if not otherwise in breach of the Act) are entitled to be reimbursed from the adult's estate.[101]

12.120 Guardians and equivalents with welfare powers may obtain an order from the sheriff in the event of non-compliance with their decisions: orders can ordain the adult to comply; authorise a constable to enter premises, apprehend and remove the adult to a place specified by the guardian (or equivalent); and order compliance in the event of a person other than the adult failing to comply with a decision which 'that person might reasonably be expected to comply with'.[102] The sheriff has powers, upon application, to replace or remove a guardian or equivalent, or to recall a guardianship order or equivalent.[103] Guardianship and equivalent orders cease on the adult's death, though there is protection for persons acting in good faith and unaware of the adult's death.[104]

Wills and related matters

12.121 Scots law has always lacked any specific statutory procedure for making a Will for an incapable adult. However, a line of precedents has applied the s 1 principles in appropriate cases to confirm the competence of using intervention orders, and guardianship orders, to renounce inheritance rights, execute a codicil amending an existing Will, or execute a new Will.[105] In *Application by Adrian Douglas Ward*, 2014 SLT (Sh Ct) 15, the Sheriff Principal of North Strathclyde upheld an appeal against a refusal by a Sheriff at first instance to authorise execution of a Will but, despite the mandatory requirement of AWI(S)A 2000 in terms of s 1(1) to determine any decision

---

[99] See https://s3-eu-west-1.amazonaws.com/tcylandingpages/AWI/AWI+-+Proposed+Law+Reform+-+2014.pdf for a description of the provisions proposed in that Report.

[100] AWI(S)A 2000, s 67(3).

[101] AWI(S)A 2000, s 67(4).

[102] AWI(S)A 2000, s 70.

[103] AWI(S)A 2000, s 71, which contains the criteria for recall, considered in *City of Edinburgh Council v D*, 30 September 2010 (scotcourts website).

[104] AWI(S)A 2000, s 77.

[105] *B, Applicant*, 2005 SLT (Sh Ct) 95; 2005 GWD 19-334; *T, Applicant*, 2005 SLT (Sh Ct) 97; 2005 GWD 26-501; *M, Applicant*, 2007 SLT (Sh Ct) 24; 2006 GWD 19-418; *G, Applicant*, 2009 SLT (Sh Ct) 122.

under that Act by reference to the s 1 principles, controversially declined to do so and held that evidence of competent testamentary intention was required 'in such a case'. Those words may have been intended to limit that aspect of the decision to the situation in that case that the evidence indicated that the adult's incapacity included an inability actually to commit to implementation of a decision, the implication being that aspects of the decision-making process were severable and could be competent in isolation.

Ademption

12.122 If a testator bequeaths an asset by Will but subsequently disposes of it, the bequest is adeemed, that is to say treated as revoked. Questions arise as to whether a disposal by an attorney, guardian or appointee under an intervention order is ademptive. Whereas in England this depends upon whether the disposal was authorised, in Scotland the test is necessity; so that if an attorney has no option but to sell an asset to pay for accommodation and care costs, a bequest of an asset is adeemed. The reason for that outcome is that if the adult had been capable, the adult would likewise have had no option but to sell and adeem. This rule was confirmed in *Turner v Turner*;[106] the sale of a house 'was a prudent act of administration but not a necessary act in the relevant sense', therefore a bequest of the house was not adeemed. That case arose after the death of the testator. Having made that finding, the judge proceeded to determine what provision should be made in favour of the legatee in place of the house which was no longer part of the deceased's estate. Where this issue arises during the testator's lifetime, but after loss of relevant capacity, it can be addressed by procedure under Part 6 of AWI(S)A 2000.[107]

Measures outwith the Incapacity Act

12.123 While Scottish law of trusts is distinct from that of England and Wales, trusts are frequently used in relation to incapacity in similar ways. Rules for administration of state benefits, vaccine damage payments and criminal injuries compensation payments are similar. Provisions for administration of sums awarded by the courts exist but have not been properly updated since the passing of AWI(S)A 2000. There is no Scottish equivalent to s 5 of MCA 2005, but the principle of necessity remains available to authorise some interventions.

---

[106] 2012 SLT 877.
[107] In *T, Applicant*, 2005 SLT (Sh Ct.) 97, the sheriff authorised execution of a codicil replacing a bequest of a house with a legacy equal to the net proceeds of sale of the house.

APPENDIX 1

MENTAL CAPACITY ACT 2005

PART 1
PERSONS WHO LACK CAPACITY

The principles

1 The principles

(1) The following principles apply for the purposes of this Act.

(2) A person must be assumed to have capacity unless it is established that he lacks capacity.

(3) A person is not to be treated as unable to make a decision unless all practicable steps to help him to do so have been taken without success.

(4) A person is not to be treated as unable to make a decision merely because he makes an unwise decision.

(5) An act done, or decision made, under this Act for or on behalf of a person who lacks capacity must be done, or made, in his best interests.

(6) Before the act is done, or the decision is made, regard must be had to whether the purpose for which it is needed can be as effectively achieved in a way that is less restrictive of the person's rights and freedom of action.

Preliminary

2 People who lack capacity

(1) For the purposes of this Act, a person lacks capacity in relation to a matter if at the material time he is unable to make a decision for himself in relation to the matter because of an impairment of, or a disturbance in the functioning of, the mind or brain.

(2) It does not matter whether the impairment or disturbance is permanent or temporary.

(3) A lack of capacity cannot be established merely by reference to –

  (a) a person's age or appearance, or
  (b) a condition of his, or an aspect of his behaviour, which might lead others to make unjustified assumptions about his capacity.

(4) In proceedings under this Act or any other enactment, any question whether a person lacks capacity within the meaning of this Act must be decided on the balance of probabilities.

(5) No power which a person ('D') may exercise under this Act –

    (a) in relation to a person who lacks capacity, or
    (b) where D reasonably thinks that a person lacks capacity,

is exercisable in relation to a person under 16.

(6) Subsection (5) is subject to section 18(3).

3 Inability to make decisions

(1) For the purposes of section 2, a person is unable to make a decision for himself if he is unable –

    (a) to understand the information relevant to the decision,
    (b) to retain that information,
    (c) to use or weigh that information as part of the process of making the decision, or
    (d) to communicate his decision (whether by talking, using sign language or any other means).

(2) A person is not to be regarded as unable to understand the information relevant to a decision if he is able to understand an explanation of it given to him in a way that is appropriate to his circumstances (using simple language, visual aids or any other means).

(3) The fact that a person is able to retain the information relevant to a decision for a short period only does not prevent him from being regarded as able to make the decision.

(4) The information relevant to a decision includes information about the reasonably foreseeable consequences of –

    (a) deciding one way or another, or
    (b) failing to make the decision.

4 Best interests

(1) In determining for the purposes of this Act what is in a person's best interests, the person making the determination must not make it merely on the basis of –

    (a) the person's age or appearance, or
    (b) a condition of his, or an aspect of his behaviour, which might lead others to make unjustified assumptions about what might be in his best interests.

(2) The person making the determination must consider all the relevant circumstances and, in particular, take the following steps.

(3) He must consider –

    (a) whether it is likely that the person will at some time have capacity in relation to the matter in question, and
    (b) if it appears likely that he will, when that is likely to be.

(4) He must, so far as reasonably practicable, permit and encourage the person to participate, or to improve his ability to participate, as fully as possible in any act done for him and any decision affecting him.

(5) Where the determination relates to life-sustaining treatment he must not, in considering whether the treatment is in the best interests of the person concerned, be motivated by a desire to bring about his death.

(6) He must consider, so far as is reasonably ascertainable –

    (a) the person's past and present wishes and feelings (and, in particular, any relevant written statement made by him when he had capacity),

    (b) the beliefs and values that would be likely to influence his decision if he had capacity, and

    (c) the other factors that he would be likely to consider if he were able to do so.

(7) He must take into account, if it is practicable and appropriate to consult them, the views of –

    (a) anyone named by the person as someone to be consulted on the matter in question or on matters of that kind,

    (b) anyone engaged in caring for the person or interested in his welfare,

    (c) any donee of a lasting power of attorney granted by the person, and

    (d) any deputy appointed for the person by the court,

as to what would be in the person's best interests and, in particular, as to the matters mentioned in subsection (6).

(8) The duties imposed by subsections (1) to (7) also apply in relation to the exercise of any powers which –

    (a) are exercisable under a lasting power of attorney, or

    (b) are exercisable by a person under this Act where he reasonably believes that another person lacks capacity.

(9) In the case of an act done, or a decision made, by a person other than the court, there is sufficient compliance with this section if (having complied with the requirements of subsections (1) to (7)) he reasonably believes that what he does or decides is in the best interests of the person concerned.

(10) 'Life-sustaining treatment' means treatment which in the view of a person providing health care for the person concerned is necessary to sustain life.

(11) 'Relevant circumstances' are those –

    (a) of which the person making the determination is aware, and

    (b) which it would be reasonable to regard as relevant.

4A Restriction on deprivation of liberty

(1) This Act does not authorise any person ('D') to deprive any other person ('P') of his liberty.

(2) But that is subject to —

(a) the following provisions of this section, and
(b) section 4B.

(3) D may deprive P of his liberty if, by doing so, D is giving effect to a relevant decision of the court.

(4) A relevant decision of the court is a decision made by an order under section 16(2)(a) in relation to a matter concerning P's personal welfare.

(5) D may deprive P of his liberty if the deprivation is authorised by Schedule A1 (hospital and care home residents: deprivation of liberty).

4B Deprivation of liberty necessary for life-sustaining treatment etc

(1) If the following conditions are met, D is authorised to deprive P of his liberty while a decision as respects any relevant issue is sought from the court.

(2) The first condition is that there is a question about whether D is authorised to deprive P of his liberty under section 4A.

(3) The second condition is that the deprivation of liberty –

(a) is wholly or partly for the purpose of –
  (i)   giving P life-sustaining treatment, or
  (ii) doing any vital act, or
(b) consists wholly or partly of –
  (i)   giving P life-sustaining treatment, or
  (ii) doing any vital act.

(4) The third condition is that the deprivation of liberty is necessary in order to –

(a) give the life-sustaining treatment, or
(b) do the vital act.

(5) A vital act is any act which the person doing it reasonably believes to be necessary to prevent a serious deterioration in P's condition.

5 Acts in connection with care or treatment

(1) If a person ('D') does an act in connection with the care or treatment of another person ('P'), the act is one to which this section applies if –

(a) before doing the act, D takes reasonable steps to establish whether P lacks capacity in relation to the matter in question, and
(b) when doing the act, D reasonably believes –
  (i)   that P lacks capacity in relation to the matter, and
  (ii) that it will be in P's best interests for the act to be done.

(2) D does not incur any liability in relation to the act that he would not have incurred if P –

(a) had had capacity to consent in relation to the matter, and
(b) had consented to D's doing the act.

(3) Nothing in this section excludes a person's civil liability for loss or damage, or his criminal liability, resulting from his negligence in doing the act.

(4) Nothing in this section affects the operation of sections 24 to 26 (advance decisions to refuse treatment).

6 Section 5 acts: limitations

(1) If D does an act that is intended to restrain P, it is not an act to which section 5 applies unless two further conditions are satisfied.

(2) The first condition is that D reasonably believes that it is necessary to do the act in order to prevent harm to P.

(3) The second is that the act is a proportionate response to –

    (a) the likelihood of P's suffering harm, and
    (b) the seriousness of that harm.

(4) For the purposes of this section D restrains P if he –

    (a) uses, or threatens to use, force to secure the doing of an act which P resists, or
    (b) restricts P's liberty of movement, whether or not P resists.

(5) ...

(6) Section 5 does not authorise a person to do an act which conflicts with a decision made, within the scope of his authority and in accordance with this Part, by –

    (a) a donee of a lasting power of attorney granted by P, or
    (b) a deputy appointed for P by the court.

(7) But nothing in subsection (6) stops a person –

    (a) providing life-sustaining treatment, or
    (b) doing any act which he reasonably believes to be necessary to prevent a serious deterioration in P's condition,

while a decision as respects any relevant issue is sought from the court.

7 Payment for necessary goods and services

(1) If necessary goods or services are supplied to a person who lacks capacity to contract for the supply, he must pay a reasonable price for them.

(2) 'Necessary' means suitable to a person's condition in life and to his actual requirements at the time when the goods or services are supplied.

8 Expenditure

(1) If an act to which section 5 applies involves expenditure, it is lawful for D –

    (a) to pledge P's credit for the purpose of the expenditure, and
    (b) to apply money in P's possession for meeting the expenditure.

(2) If the expenditure is borne for P by D, it is lawful for D –

    (a) to reimburse himself out of money in P's possession, or

    (b) to be otherwise indemnified by P.

(3) Subsections (1) and (2) do not affect any power under which (apart from those subsections) a person –

    (a) has lawful control of P's money or other property, and

    (b) has power to spend money for P's benefit.

Lasting powers of attorney

9 Lasting powers of attorney

(1) A lasting power of attorney is a power of attorney under which the donor ('P') confers on the donee (or donees) authority to make decisions about all or any of the following –

    (a) P's personal welfare or specified matters concerning P's personal welfare, and

    (b) P's property and affairs or specified matters concerning P's property and affairs,

and which includes authority to make such decisions in circumstances where P no longer has capacity.

(2) A lasting power of attorney is not created unless –

    (a) section 10 is complied with,

    (b) an instrument conferring authority of the kind mentioned in subsection (1) is made and registered in accordance with Schedule 1, and

    (c) at the time when P executes the instrument, P has reached 18 and has capacity to execute it.

(3) An instrument which –

    (a) purports to create a lasting power of attorney, but

    (b) does not comply with this section, section 10 or Schedule 1,

confers no authority.

(4) The authority conferred by a lasting power of attorney is subject to –

    (a) the provisions of this Act and, in particular, sections 1 (the principles) and 4 (best interests), and

    (b) any conditions or restrictions specified in the instrument.

10 Appointment of donees

(1) A donee of a lasting power of attorney must be –

    (a) an individual who has reached 18, or

    (b) if the power relates only to P's property and affairs, either such an individual or a trust corporation.

(2) An individual who is bankrupt or is a person in relation to whom a debt relief order is made may not be appointed as donee of a lasting power of attorney in relation to P's property and affairs.

(3) Subsections (4) to (7) apply in relation to an instrument under which two or more persons are to act as donees of a lasting power of attorney.

(4) The instrument may appoint them to act –

(a) jointly,
(b) jointly and severally, or
(c) jointly in respect of some matters and jointly and severally in respect of others.

(5) To the extent to which it does not specify whether they are to act jointly or jointly and severally, the instrument is to be assumed to appoint them to act jointly.

(6) If they are to act jointly, a failure, as respects one of them, to comply with the requirements of subsection (1) or (2) or Part 1 or 2 of Schedule 1 prevents a lasting power of attorney from being created.

(7) If they are to act jointly and severally, a failure, as respects one of them, to comply with the requirements of subsection (1) or (2) or Part 1 or 2 of Schedule 1 –

(a) prevents the appointment taking effect in his case, but
(b) does not prevent a lasting power of attorney from being created in the case of the other or others.

(8) An instrument used to create a lasting power of attorney –

(a) cannot give the donee (or, if more than one, any of them) power to appoint a substitute or successor, but
(b) may itself appoint a person to replace the donee (or, if more than one, any of them) on the occurrence of an event mentioned in section 13(6)(a) to (d) which has the effect of terminating the donee's appointment.

11 Lasting powers of attorney: restrictions

(1) A lasting power of attorney does not authorise the donee (or, if more than one, any of them) to do an act that is intended to restrain P, unless three conditions are satisfied.

(2) The first condition is that P lacks, or the donee reasonably believes that P lacks, capacity in relation to the matter in question.

(3) The second is that the donee reasonably believes that it is necessary to do the act in order to prevent harm to P.

(4) The third is that the act is a proportionate response to –

(a) the likelihood of P's suffering harm, and
(b) the seriousness of that harm.

(5) For the purposes of this section, the donee restrains P if he –

  (a) uses, or threatens to use, force to secure the doing of an act which P resists, or
  (b) restricts P's liberty of movement, whether or not P resists,

or if he authorises another person to do any of those things.

(6) ...

(7) Where a lasting power of attorney authorises the donee (or, if more than one, any of them) to make decisions about P's personal welfare, the authority –

  (a) does not extend to making such decisions in circumstances other than those where P lacks, or the donee reasonably believes that P lacks, capacity,
  (b) is subject to sections 24 to 26 (advance decisions to refuse treatment), and
  (c) extends to giving or refusing consent to the carrying out or continuation of a treatment by a person providing health care for P.

(8) But subsection (7)(c) –

  (a) does not authorise the giving or refusing of consent to the carrying out or continuation of life-sustaining treatment, unless the instrument contains express provision to that effect, and
  (b) is subject to any conditions or restrictions in the instrument.

12 Scope of lasting powers of attorney: gifts

(1) Where a lasting power of attorney confers authority to make decisions about P's property and affairs, it does not authorise a donee (or, if more than one, any of them) to dispose of the donor's property by making gifts except to the extent permitted by subsection (2).

(2) The donee may make gifts –

  (a) on customary occasions to persons (including himself) who are related to or connected with the donor, or
  (b) to any charity to whom the donor made or might have been expected to make gifts,

if the value of each such gift is not unreasonable having regard to all the circumstances and, in particular, the size of the donor's estate.

(3) 'Customary occasion' means –

  (a) the occasion or anniversary of a birth, a marriage or the formation of a civil partnership, or
  (b) any other occasion on which presents are customarily given within families or among friends or associates.

(4) Subsection (2) is subject to any conditions or restrictions in the instrument.

13 Revocation of lasting powers of attorney etc

(1) This section applies if –

   (a) P has executed an instrument with a view to creating a lasting power of attorney, or

   (b) a lasting power of attorney is registered as having been conferred by P,

and in this section references to revoking the power include revoking the instrument.

(2) P may, at any time when he has capacity to do so, revoke the power.

(3) P's bankruptcy, or the making of a debt relief order (under Part 7A of the Insolvency Act 1986) in respect of P revokes the power so far as it relates to P's property and affairs.

(4) But where P is bankrupt merely because an interim bankruptcy restrictions order has effect in respect of him or where P is subject to an interim debt relief restrictions order (under Schedule 4ZB of the Insolvency Act 1986), the power is suspended, so far as it relates to P's property and affairs, for so long as the order has effect.

(5) The occurrence in relation to a donee of an event mentioned in subsection (6) –

   (a) terminates his appointment, and

   (b) except in the cases given in subsection (7), revokes the power.

(6) The events are –

   (a) the disclaimer of the appointment by the donee in accordance with such requirements as may be prescribed for the purposes of this section in regulations made by the Lord Chancellor,

   (b) subject to subsections (8) and (9), the death or bankruptcy of the donee or the making of a debt relief order (under Part 7A of the Insolvency Act 1986) in respect of the donee or, if the donee is a trust corporation, its winding-up or dissolution,

   (c) subject to subsection (11), the dissolution or annulment of a marriage or civil partnership between the donor and the donee,

   (d) the lack of capacity of the donee.

(7) The cases are –

   (a) the donee is replaced under the terms of the instrument,

   (b) he is one of two or more persons appointed to act as donees jointly and severally in respect of any matter and, after the event, there is at least one remaining donee.

(8) The bankruptcy of a donee or the making of a debt relief order (under Part 7A of the Insolvency Act 1986) in respect of a donee does not terminate his appointment, or revoke the power, in so far as his authority relates to P's personal welfare.

(9) Where the donee is bankrupt merely because an interim bankruptcy restrictions order has effect in respect of him or where the donee is subject to an interim debt relief restrictions order (under Schedule 4ZB of the Insolvency Act 1986), his appointment and the power are suspended, so far as they relate to P's property and affairs, for so long as the order has effect.

(10) Where the donee is one of two or more appointed to act jointly and severally under the power in respect of any matter, the reference in subsection (9) to the suspension of the power is to its suspension in so far as it relates to that donee.

(11) The dissolution or annulment of a marriage or civil partnership does not terminate the appointment of a donee, or revoke the power, if the instrument provided that it was not to do so.

14 Protection of donee and others if no power created or power revoked

(1) Subsections (2) and (3) apply if –

 (a) an instrument has been registered under Schedule 1 as a lasting power of attorney, but
 (b) a lasting power of attorney was not created,

whether or not the registration has been cancelled at the time of the act or transaction in question.

(2) A donee who acts in purported exercise of the power does not incur any liability (to P or any other person) because of the non-existence of the power unless at the time of acting he –

 (a) knows that a lasting power of attorney was not created, or
 (b) is aware of circumstances which, if a lasting power of attorney had been created, would have terminated his authority to act as a donee.

(3) Any transaction between the donee and another person is, in favour of that person, as valid as if the power had been in existence, unless at the time of the transaction that person has knowledge of a matter referred to in subsection (2).

(4) If the interest of a purchaser depends on whether a transaction between the donee and the other person was valid by virtue of subsection (3), it is conclusively presumed in favour of the purchaser that the transaction was valid if –

 (a) the transaction was completed within 12 months of the date on which the instrument was registered, or
 (b) the other person makes a statutory declaration, before or within 3 months after the completion of the purchase, that he had no reason at the time of the transaction to doubt that the donee had authority to dispose of the property which was the subject of the transaction.

(5) In its application to a lasting power of attorney which relates to matters in addition to P's property and affairs, section 5 of the Powers of Attorney

Act 1971 (protection where power is revoked) has effect as if references to revocation included the cessation of the power in relation to P's property and affairs.

(6) Where two or more donees are appointed under a lasting power of attorney, this section applies as if references to the donee were to all or any of them.

General powers of the court and appointment of deputies

15 Power to make declarations

(1) The court may make declarations as to –

(a) whether a person has or lacks capacity to make a decision specified in the declaration;

(b) whether a person has or lacks capacity to make decisions on such matters as are described in the declaration;

(c) the lawfulness or otherwise of any act done, or yet to be done, in relation to that person.

(2) 'Act' includes an omission and a course of conduct.

16 Powers to make decisions and appoint deputies: general

(1) This section applies if a person ('P') lacks capacity in relation to a matter or matters concerning –

(a) P's personal welfare, or

(b) P's property and affairs.

(2) The court may –

(a) by making an order, make the decision or decisions on P's behalf in relation to the matter or matters, or

(b) appoint a person (a 'deputy') to make decisions on P's behalf in relation to the matter or matters.

(3) The powers of the court under this section are subject to the provisions of this Act and, in particular, to sections 1 (the principles) and 4 (best interests).

(4) When deciding whether it is in P's best interests to appoint a deputy, the court must have regard (in addition to the matters mentioned in section 4) to the principles that –

(a) a decision by the court is to be preferred to the appointment of a deputy to make a decision, and

(b) the powers conferred on a deputy should be as limited in scope and duration as is reasonably practicable in the circumstances.

(5) The court may make such further orders or give such directions, and confer on a deputy such powers or impose on him such duties, as it thinks necessary or expedient for giving effect to, or otherwise in connection with, an order or appointment made by it under subsection (2).

(6) Without prejudice to section 4, the court may make the order, give the directions or make the appointment on such terms as it considers are in P's best interests, even though no application is before the court for an order, directions or an appointment on those terms.

(7) An order of the court may be varied or discharged by a subsequent order.

(8) The court may, in particular, revoke the appointment of a deputy or vary the powers conferred on him if it is satisfied that the deputy –

    (a) has behaved, or is behaving, in a way that contravenes the authority conferred on him by the court or is not in P's best interests, or

    (b) proposes to behave in a way that would contravene that authority or would not be in P's best interests.

16A Section 16 powers: Mental Health Act patients etc

(1) If a person is ineligible to be deprived of liberty by this Act, the court may not include in a welfare order provision which authorises the person to be deprived of his liberty.

(2) If—

    (a) a welfare order includes provision which authorises a person to be deprived of his liberty, and

    (b) that person becomes ineligible to be deprived of liberty by this Act,
the provision ceases to have effect for as long as the person remains ineligible.

(3) Nothing in subsection (2) affects the power of the court under section 16(7) to vary or discharge the welfare order.

(4) For the purposes of this section —

    (a) Schedule 1A applies for determining whether or not P is ineligible to be deprived of liberty by this Act;

    (b) 'welfare order' means an order under section 16(2)(a).

17 Section 16 powers: personal welfare

(1) The powers under section 16 as respects P's personal welfare extend in particular to –

    (a) deciding where P is to live;

    (b) deciding what contact, if any, P is to have with any specified persons;

    (c) making an order prohibiting a named person from having contact with P;

    (d) giving or refusing consent to the carrying out or continuation of a treatment by a person providing health care for P;

    (e) giving a direction that a person responsible for P's health care allow a different person to take over that responsibility.

(2) Subsection (1) is subject to section 20 (restrictions on deputies).

18 Section 16 powers: property and affairs

(1) The powers under section 16 as respects P's property and affairs extend in particular to –

(a) the control and management of P's property;
(b) the sale, exchange, charging, gift or other disposition of P's property;
(c) the acquisition of property in P's name or on P's behalf;
(d) the carrying on, on P's behalf, of any profession, trade or business;
(e) the taking of a decision which will have the effect of dissolving a partnership of which P is a member;
(f) the carrying out of any contract entered into by P;
(g) the discharge of P's debts and of any of P's obligations, whether legally enforceable or not;
(h) the settlement of any of P's property, whether for P's benefit or for the benefit of others;
(i) the execution for P of a will;
(j) the exercise of any power (including a power to consent) vested in P whether beneficially or as trustee or otherwise;
(k) the conduct of legal proceedings in P's name or on P's behalf.

(2) No will may be made under subsection (1)(i) at a time when P has not reached 18.

(3) The powers under section 16 as respects any other matter relating to P's property and affairs may be exercised even though P has not reached 16, if the court considers it likely that P will still lack capacity to make decisions in respect of that matter when he reaches 18.

(4) Schedule 2 supplements the provisions of this section.

(5) Section 16(7) (variation and discharge of court orders) is subject to paragraph 6 of Schedule 2.

(6) Subsection (1) is subject to section 20 (restrictions on deputies).

19 Appointment of deputies

(1) A deputy appointed by the court must be –

(a) an individual who has reached 18, or
(b) as respects powers in relation to property and affairs, an individual who has reached 18 or a trust corporation.

(2) The court may appoint an individual by appointing the holder for the time being of a specified office or position.

(3) A person may not be appointed as a deputy without his consent.

(4) The court may appoint two or more deputies to act –

(a) jointly,
(b) jointly and severally, or
(c) jointly in respect of some matters and jointly and severally in respect of others.

(5) When appointing a deputy or deputies, the court may at the same time appoint one or more other persons to succeed the existing deputy or those deputies –

    (a) in such circumstances, or on the happening of such events, as may be specified by the court;

    (b) for such period as may be so specified.

(6) A deputy is to be treated as P's agent in relation to anything done or decided by him within the scope of his appointment and in accordance with this Part.

(7) The deputy is entitled –

    (a) to be reimbursed out of P's property for his reasonable expenses in discharging his functions, and

    (b) if the court so directs when appointing him, to remuneration out of P's property for discharging them.

(8) The court may confer on a deputy powers to –

    (a) take possession or control of all or any specified part of P's property;

    (b) exercise all or any specified powers in respect of it, including such powers of investment as the court may determine.

(9) The court may require a deputy –

    (a) to give to the Public Guardian such security as the court thinks fit for the due discharge of his functions, and

    (b) to submit to the Public Guardian such reports at such times or at such intervals as the court may direct.

20 Restrictions on deputies

(1) A deputy does not have power to make a decision on behalf of P in relation to a matter if he knows or has reasonable grounds for believing that P has capacity in relation to the matter.

(2) Nothing in section 16(5) or 17 permits a deputy to be given power –

    (a) to prohibit a named person from having contact with P;

    (b) to direct a person responsible for P's health care to allow a different person to take over that responsibility.

(3) A deputy may not be given powers with respect to –

    (a) the settlement of any of P's property, whether for P's benefit or for the benefit of others,

    (b) the execution for P of a will, or

    (c) the exercise of any power (including a power to consent) vested in P whether beneficially or as trustee or otherwise.

(4) A deputy may not be given power to make a decision on behalf of P which is inconsistent with a decision made, within the scope of his authority and in

accordance with this Act, by the donee of a lasting power of attorney granted by P (or, if there is more than one donee, by any of them).

(5) A deputy may not refuse consent to the carrying out or continuation of life-sustaining treatment in relation to P.

(6) The authority conferred on a deputy is subject to the provisions of this Act and, in particular, sections 1 (the principles) and 4 (best interests).

(7) A deputy may not do an act that is intended to restrain P unless four conditions are satisfied.

(8) The first condition is that, in doing the act, the deputy is acting within the scope of an authority expressly conferred on him by the court.

(9) The second is that P lacks, or the deputy reasonably believes that P lacks, capacity in relation to the matter in question.

(10) The third is that the deputy reasonably believes that it is necessary to do the act in order to prevent harm to P.

(11) The fourth is that the act is a proportionate response to –

(a) the likelihood of P's suffering harm, and
(b) the seriousness of that harm.

(12) For the purposes of this section, a deputy restrains P if he –

(a) uses, or threatens to use, force to secure the doing of an act which P resists, or
(b) restricts P's liberty of movement, whether or not P resists,

or if he authorises another person to do any of those things.

(13) ...

21 Transfer of proceedings relating to people under 18

(1) The Lord Chief Justice, with the concurrence of the Lord Chancellor, may by order make provision as to the transfer of proceedings relating to a person under 18, in such circumstances as are specified in the order –

(a) from the Court of Protection to a court having jurisdiction under the Children Act 1989, or
(b) from a court having jurisdiction under that Act to the Court of Protection.

(2) The Lord Chief Justice may nominate any of the following to exercise his functions under this section –

(a) the President of the Court of Protection;
(b) a judicial office holder (as defined in section 109(4) of the Constitutional Reform Act 2005).

Powers of the court in relation to Schedule A1

21A Powers of court in relation to Schedule A1

(1) This section applies if either of the following has been given under Schedule A1 —

    (a)   a standard authorisation;

    (b)   an urgent authorisation.

(2) Where a standard authorisation has been given, the court may determine any question relating to any of the following matters—

    (a)   whether the relevant person meets one or more of the qualifying requirements;

    (b)   the period during which the standard authorisation is to be in force;

    (c)   the purpose for which the standard authorisation is given;

    (d)   the conditions subject to which the standard authorisation is given.

(3) If the court determines any question under subsection (2), the court may make an order —

    (a)   varying or terminating the standard authorisation, or

    (b)   directing the supervisory body to vary or terminate the standard authorisation.

(4) Where an urgent authorisation has been given, the court may determine any question relating to any of the following matters —

    (a)   whether the urgent authorisation should have been given;

    (b)   the period during which the urgent authorisation is to be in force;

    (c)   the purpose for which the urgent authorisation is given.

(5) Where the court determines any question under subsection (4), the court may make an order—

    (a)   varying or terminating the urgent authorisation, or

    (b)   directing the managing authority of the relevant hospital or care home to vary or terminate the urgent authorisation.

(6) Where the court makes an order under subsection (3) or (5), the court may make an order about a person's liability for any act done in connection with the standard or urgent authorisation before its variation or termination.

(7) An order under subsection (6) may, in particular, exclude a person from liability.

Powers of the court in relation to lasting powers of attorney

22 Powers of court in relation to validity of lasting powers of attorney

(1) This section and section 23 apply if –

    (a)   a person ('P') has executed or purported to execute an instrument with a view to creating a lasting power of attorney, or

    (b) an instrument has been registered as a lasting power of attorney conferred by P.

(2) The court may determine any question relating to –

    (a) whether one or more of the requirements for the creation of a lasting power of attorney have been met;

    (b) whether the power has been revoked or has otherwise come to an end.

(3) Subsection (4) applies if the court is satisfied –

    (a) that fraud or undue pressure was used to induce P –

        (i) to execute an instrument for the purpose of creating a lasting power of attorney, or

        (ii) to create a lasting power of attorney, or

    (b) that the donee (or, if more than one, any of them) of a lasting power of attorney –

        (i) has behaved, or is behaving, in a way that contravenes his authority or is not in P's best interests, or

        (ii) proposes to behave in a way that would contravene his authority or would not be in P's best interests.

(4) The court may –

    (a) direct that an instrument purporting to create the lasting power of attorney is not to be registered, or

    (b) if P lacks capacity to do so, revoke the instrument or the lasting power of attorney.

(5) If there is more than one donee, the court may under subsection (4)(b) revoke the instrument or the lasting power of attorney so far as it relates to any of them.

(6) 'Donee' includes an intended donee.

23 Powers of court in relation to operation of lasting powers of attorney

(1) The court may determine any question as to the meaning or effect of a lasting power of attorney or an instrument purporting to create one.

(2) The court may –

    (a) give directions with respect to decisions –

        (i) which the donee of a lasting power of attorney has authority to make, and

        (ii) which P lacks capacity to make;

    (b) give any consent or authorisation to act which the donee would have to obtain from P if P had capacity to give it.

(3) The court may, if P lacks capacity to do so –

    (a) give directions to the donee with respect to the rendering by him of reports or accounts and the production of records kept by him for that purpose;

(b) require the donee to supply information or produce documents or things in his possession as donee;

(c) give directions with respect to the remuneration or expenses of the donee;

(d) relieve the donee wholly or partly from any liability which he has or may have incurred on account of a breach of his duties as donee.

(4) The court may authorise the making of gifts which are not within section 12(2) (permitted gifts).

(5) Where two or more donees are appointed under a lasting power of attorney, this section applies as if references to the donee were to all or any of them.

Advance decisions to refuse treatment

24 Advance decisions to refuse treatment: general

(1) 'Advance decision' means a decision made by a person ('P'), after he has reached 18 and when he has capacity to do so, that if –

(a) at a later time and in such circumstances as he may specify, a specified treatment is proposed to be carried out or continued by a person providing health care for him, and

(b) at that time he lacks capacity to consent to the carrying out or continuation of the treatment,

the specified treatment is not to be carried out or continued.

(2) For the purposes of subsection (1)(a), a decision may be regarded as specifying a treatment or circumstances even though expressed in layman's terms.

(3) P may withdraw or alter an advance decision at any time when he has capacity to do so.

(4) A withdrawal (including a partial withdrawal) need not be in writing.

(5) An alteration of an advance decision need not be in writing (unless section 25(5) applies in relation to the decision resulting from the alteration).

25 Validity and applicability of advance decisions

(1) An advance decision does not affect the liability which a person may incur for carrying out or continuing a treatment in relation to P unless the decision is at the material time –

(a) valid, and

(b) applicable to the treatment.

(2) An advance decision is not valid if P –

(a) has withdrawn the decision at a time when he had capacity to do so,

(b) has, under a lasting power of attorney created after the advance decision was made, conferred authority on the donee (or, if more than one, any of them) to give or refuse consent to the treatment to which the advance decision relates, or

(c) has done anything else clearly inconsistent with the advance decision remaining his fixed decision.

(3) An advance decision is not applicable to the treatment in question if at the material time P has capacity to give or refuse consent to it.

(4) An advance decision is not applicable to the treatment in question if –

(a) that treatment is not the treatment specified in the advance decision,

(b) any circumstances specified in the advance decision are absent, or

(c) there are reasonable grounds for believing that circumstances exist which P did not anticipate at the time of the advance decision and which would have affected his decision had he anticipated them.

(5) An advance decision is not applicable to life-sustaining treatment unless –

(a) the decision is verified by a statement by P to the effect that it is to apply to that treatment even if life is at risk, and

(b) the decision and statement comply with subsection (6).

(6) A decision or statement complies with this subsection only if –

(a) it is in writing,

(b) it is signed by P or by another person in P's presence and by P's direction,

(c) the signature is made or acknowledged by P in the presence of a witness, and

(d) the witness signs it, or acknowledges his signature, in P's presence.

(7) The existence of any lasting power of attorney other than one of a description mentioned in subsection (2)(b) does not prevent the advance decision from being regarded as valid and applicable.

26 Effect of advance decisions

(1) If P has made an advance decision which is –

(a) valid, and

(b) applicable to a treatment,

the decision has effect as if he had made it, and had had capacity to make it, at the time when the question arises whether the treatment should be carried out or continued.

(2) A person does not incur liability for carrying out or continuing the treatment unless, at the time, he is satisfied that an advance decision exists which is valid and applicable to the treatment.

(3) A person does not incur liability for the consequences of withholding or withdrawing a treatment from P if, at the time, he reasonably believes that an advance decision exists which is valid and applicable to the treatment.

(4) The court may make a declaration as to whether an advance decision –

    (a) exists;
    (b) is valid;
    (c) is applicable to a treatment.

(5) Nothing in an apparent advance decision stops a person –

    (a) providing life-sustaining treatment, or
    (b) doing any act he reasonably believes to be necessary to prevent a serious deterioration in P's condition,

while a decision as respects any relevant issue is sought from the court.

Excluded decisions

27 Family relationships etc

(1) Nothing in this Act permits a decision on any of the following matters to be made on behalf of a person –

    (a) consenting to marriage or a civil partnership,
    (b) consenting to have sexual relations,
    (c) consenting to a decree of divorce being granted on the basis of two years' separation,
    (d) consenting to a dissolution order being made in relation to a civil partnership on the basis of two years' separation,
    (e) consenting to a child's being placed for adoption by an adoption agency,
    (f) consenting to the making of an adoption order,
    (g) discharging parental responsibilities in matters not relating to a child's property,
    (h) giving a consent under the Human Fertilisation and Embryology Act 1990,
    (i) giving a consent under the Human Fertilisation and Embryology Act 2008.

(2) 'Adoption order' means –

    (a) an adoption order within the meaning of the Adoption and Children Act 2002 (including a future adoption order), and
    (b) an order under section 84 of that Act (parental responsibility prior to adoption abroad).

28 Mental Health Act matters

(1) Nothing in this Act authorises anyone –

    (a) to give a patient medical treatment for mental disorder, or
    (b) to consent to a patient's being given medical treatment for mental disorder,

if, at the time when it is proposed to treat the patient, his treatment is regulated by Part 4 of the Mental Health Act.

(1A) Subsection (1) does not apply in relation to any form of treatment to which section 58A of that Act (electro-convulsive therapy, etc) applies if the patient comes within subsection (7) of that section (informal patient under 18 who cannot give consent).

(1B) Section 5 does not apply to an act to which section 64B of the Mental Health Act applies (treatment of community patients not recalled to hospital).

(2) 'Medical treatment', 'mental disorder' and 'patient' have the same meaning as in that Act.

29 Voting rights

(1) Nothing in this Act permits a decision on voting at an election for any public office, or at a referendum, to be made on behalf of a person.

(2) 'Referendum' has the same meaning as in section 101 of the Political Parties, Elections and Referendums Act 2000.

Research

30 Research

(1) Intrusive research carried out on, or in relation to, a person who lacks capacity to consent to it is unlawful unless it is carried out –

   (a)   as part of a research project which is for the time being approved by the appropriate body for the purposes of this Act in accordance with section 31, and
   (b)   in accordance with sections 32 and 33.

(2) Research is intrusive if it is of a kind that would be unlawful if it was carried out –

   (a)   on or in relation to a person who had capacity to consent to it, but
   (b)   without his consent.

(3) A clinical trial which is subject to the provisions of clinical trials regulations is not to be treated as research for the purposes of this section.

(3A) Research is not intrusive to the extent that it consists of the use of a person's human cells to bring about the creation in vitro of an embryo or human admixed embryo, or the subsequent storage or use of an embryo or human admixed embryo so created.

(3B) Expressions used in subsection (3A) and in Schedule 3 to the Human Fertilisation and Embryology Act 1990 (consents to use or storage of gametes, embryos or human admixed embryos etc.) have the same meaning in that subsection as in that Schedule.

(4) 'Appropriate body', in relation to a research project, means the person, committee or other body specified in regulations made by the appropriate authority as the appropriate body in relation to a project of the kind in question.

(5) 'Clinical trials regulations' means –

(a) the Medicines for Human Use (Clinical Trials) Regulations 2004 and any other regulations replacing those regulations or amending them, and

(b) any other regulations relating to clinical trials and designated by the Secretary of State as clinical trials regulations for the purposes of this section.

(6) In this section, section 32 and section 34, 'appropriate authority' means –

(a) in relation to the carrying out of research in England, the Secretary of State, and

(b) in relation to the carrying out of research in Wales, the National Assembly for Wales.

31 Requirements for approval

(1) The appropriate body may not approve a research project for the purposes of this Act unless satisfied that the following requirements will be met in relation to research carried out as part of the project on, or in relation to, a person who lacks capacity to consent to taking part in the project ('P').

(2) The research must be connected with –

(a) an impairing condition affecting P, or

(b) its treatment.

(3) 'Impairing condition' means a condition which is (or may be) attributable to, or which causes or contributes to (or may cause or contribute to), the impairment of, or disturbance in the functioning of, the mind or brain.

(4) There must be reasonable grounds for believing that research of comparable effectiveness cannot be carried out if the project has to be confined to, or relate only to, persons who have capacity to consent to taking part in it.

(5) The research must –

(a) have the potential to benefit P without imposing on P a burden that is disproportionate to the potential benefit to P, or

(b) be intended to provide knowledge of the causes or treatment of, or of the care of persons affected by, the same or a similar condition.

(6) If the research falls within paragraph (b) of subsection (5) but not within paragraph (a), there must be reasonable grounds for believing –

(a) that the risk to P from taking part in the project is likely to be negligible, and

(b) that anything done to, or in relation to, P will not –

    (i) interfere with P's freedom of action or privacy in a significant way, or

    (ii) be unduly invasive or restrictive.

(7) There must be reasonable arrangements in place for ensuring that the requirements of sections 32 and 33 will be met.

32 Consulting carers etc

(1) This section applies if a person ('R') –

    (a) is conducting an approved research project, and

    (b) wishes to carry out research, as part of the project, on or in relation to a person ('P') who lacks capacity to consent to taking part in the project.

(2) R must take reasonable steps to identify a person who –

    (a) otherwise than in a professional capacity or for remuneration, is engaged in caring for P or is interested in P's welfare, and

    (b) is prepared to be consulted by R under this section.

(3) If R is unable to identify such a person he must, in accordance with guidance issued by the appropriate authority, nominate a person who –

    (a) is prepared to be consulted by R under this section, but

    (b) has no connection with the project.

(4) R must provide the person identified under subsection (2), or nominated under subsection (3), with information about the project and ask him –

    (a) for advice as to whether P should take part in the project, and

    (b) what, in his opinion, P's wishes and feelings about taking part in the project would be likely to be if P had capacity in relation to the matter.

(5) If, at any time, the person consulted advises R that in his opinion P's wishes and feelings would be likely to lead him to decline to take part in the project (or to wish to withdraw from it) if he had capacity in relation to the matter, R must ensure –

    (a) if P is not already taking part in the project, that he does not take part in it;

    (b) if P is taking part in the project, that he is withdrawn from it.

(6) But subsection (5)(b) does not require treatment that P has been receiving as part of the project to be discontinued if R has reasonable grounds for believing that there would be a significant risk to P's health if it were discontinued.

(7) The fact that a person is the donee of a lasting power of attorney given by P, or is P's deputy, does not prevent him from being the person consulted under this section.

(8) Subsection (9) applies if treatment is being, or is about to be, provided for P as a matter of urgency and R considers that, having regard to the nature of the research and of the particular circumstances of the case –

    (a) it is also necessary to take action for the purposes of the research as a matter of urgency, but

    (b) it is not reasonably practicable to consult under the previous provisions of this section.

(9) R may take the action if –

(a)   he has the agreement of a registered medical practitioner who is not involved in the organisation or conduct of the research project, or

(b)   where it is not reasonably practicable in the time available to obtain that agreement, he acts in accordance with a procedure approved by the appropriate body at the time when the research project was approved under section 31.

(10) But R may not continue to act in reliance on subsection (9) if he has reasonable grounds for believing that it is no longer necessary to take the action as a matter of urgency.

33 Additional safeguards

(1) This section applies in relation to a person who is taking part in an approved research project even though he lacks capacity to consent to taking part.

(2) Nothing may be done to, or in relation to, him in the course of the research –

(a)   to which he appears to object (whether by showing signs of resistance or otherwise) except where what is being done is intended to protect him from harm or to reduce or prevent pain or discomfort, or

(b)   which would be contrary to –
(i)   an advance decision of his which has effect, or
(ii)   any other form of statement made by him and not subsequently withdrawn,

of which R is aware.

(3) The interests of the person must be assumed to outweigh those of science and society.

(4) If he indicates (in any way) that he wishes to be withdrawn from the project he must be withdrawn without delay.

(5) P must be withdrawn from the project, without delay, if at any time the person conducting the research has reasonable grounds for believing that one or more of the requirements set out in section 31(2) to (7) is no longer met in relation to research being carried out on, or in relation to, P.

(6) But neither subsection (4) nor subsection (5) requires treatment that P has been receiving as part of the project to be discontinued if R has reasonable grounds for believing that there would be a significant risk to P's health if it were discontinued.

34 Loss of capacity during research project

(1) This section applies where a person ('P') –

(a)   has consented to take part in a research project begun before the commencement of section 30, but

(b)   before the conclusion of the project, loses capacity to consent to continue to take part in it.

(2) The appropriate authority may by regulations provide that, despite P's loss of capacity, research of a prescribed kind may be carried out on, or in relation to, P if –

(a) the project satisfies prescribed requirements,

(b) any information or material relating to P which is used in the research is of a prescribed description and was obtained before P's loss of capacity, and

(c) the person conducting the project takes in relation to P such steps as may be prescribed for the purpose of protecting him.

(3) The regulations may, in particular, –

(a) make provision about when, for the purposes of the regulations, a project is to be treated as having begun;

(b) include provision similar to any made by section 31, 32 or 33.

Independent mental capacity advocate service

35 Appointment of independent mental capacity advocates

(1) The responsible authority must make such arrangements as it considers reasonable to enable persons ('independent mental capacity advocates') to be available to represent and support persons to whom acts or decisions proposed under sections 37, 38 and 39 relate or persons who fall within section 39A, 39C or 39D.

(2) The appropriate authority may make regulations as to the appointment of independent mental capacity advocates.

(3) The regulations may, in particular, provide –

(a) that a person may act as an independent mental capacity advocate only in such circumstances, or only subject to such conditions, as may be prescribed;

(b) for the appointment of a person as an independent mental capacity advocate to be subject to approval in accordance with the regulations.

(4) In making arrangements under subsection (1), the responsible authority must have regard to the principle that a person to whom a proposed act or decision relates should, so far as practicable, be represented and supported by a person who is independent of any person who will be responsible for the act or decision.

(5) The arrangements may include provision for payments to be made to, or in relation to, persons carrying out functions in accordance with the arrangements.

(6) For the purpose of enabling him to carry out his functions, an independent mental capacity advocate –

(a) may interview in private the person whom he has been instructed to represent, and

(b) may, at all reasonable times, examine and take copies of –

    (i)   any health record,

    (ii) any record of, or held by, a local authority and compiled in connection with a social services function, and

    (iii) any record held by a person registered under Part 2 of the Care Standards Act 2000 or Chapter 2 of Part I of the Health and Social Care Act 2008,

which the person holding the record considers may be relevant to the independent mental capacity advocate's investigation.

(6A) In subsections (1) and (4), 'the responsible authority' means –

    (a) in relation to the provision of the services of independent mental capacity advocates in the area of a local authority in England, that local authority, and

    (b) in relation to the provision of the services of independent mental capacity advocates in Wales, the Welsh Ministers.

(6B) In subsection (6A)(a), 'local authority' has the meaning given in section 64(1) except that it does not include the council of a county or county borough in Wales.

(7) In this section, section 36 and section 37, 'the appropriate authority' means –

    (a) in relation to the provision of the services of independent mental capacity advocates in England, the Secretary of State, and

    (b) in relation to the provision of the services of independent mental capacity advocates in Wales, the National Assembly for Wales.

36 Functions of independent mental capacity advocates

(1) The appropriate authority may make regulations as to the functions of independent mental capacity advocates.

(2) The regulations may, in particular, make provision requiring an advocate to take such steps as may be prescribed for the purpose of –

    (a) providing support to the person whom he has been instructed to represent ('P') so that P may participate as fully as possible in any relevant decision;

    (b) obtaining and evaluating relevant information;

    (c) ascertaining what P's wishes and feelings would be likely to be, and the beliefs and values that would be likely to influence P, if he had capacity;

    (d) ascertaining what alternative courses of action are available in relation to P;

    (e) obtaining a further medical opinion where treatment is proposed and the advocate thinks that one should be obtained.

(3) The regulations may also make provision as to circumstances in which the advocate may challenge, or provide assistance for the purpose of challenging, any relevant decision.

37 Provision of serious medical treatment by NHS body

(1) This section applies if an NHS body –

    (a) is proposing to provide, or secure the provision of, serious medical treatment for a person ('P') who lacks capacity to consent to the treatment, and

    (b) is satisfied that there is no person, other than one engaged in providing care or treatment for P in a professional capacity or for remuneration, whom it would be appropriate to consult in determining what would be in P's best interests.

(2) But this section does not apply if P's treatment is regulated by Part 4 or 4A of the Mental Health Act.

(3) Before the treatment is provided, the NHS body must instruct an independent mental capacity advocate to represent P.

(4) If the treatment needs to be provided as a matter of urgency, it may be provided even though the NHS body has not been able to comply with subsection (3).

(5) The NHS body must, in providing or securing the provision of treatment for P, take into account any information given, or submissions made, by the independent mental capacity advocate.

(6) 'Serious medical treatment' means treatment which involves providing, withholding or withdrawing treatment of a kind prescribed by regulations made by the appropriate authority.

(7) 'NHS body' has such meaning as may be prescribed by regulations made for the purposes of this section by –

    (a) the Secretary of State, in relation to bodies in England, or

    (b) the National Assembly for Wales, in relation to bodies in Wales.

38 Provision of accommodation by NHS body

(1) This section applies if an NHS body proposes to make arrangements –

    (a) for the provision of accommodation in a hospital or care home for a person ('P') who lacks capacity to agree to the arrangements, or

    (b) for a change in P's accommodation to another hospital or care home,

and is satisfied that there is no person, other than one engaged in providing care or treatment for P in a professional capacity or for remuneration, whom it would be appropriate for it to consult in determining what would be in P's best interests.

(2) But this section does not apply if P is accommodated as a result of an obligation imposed on him under the Mental Health Act.

(2A) And this section does not apply if –

(a) an independent mental capacity advocate must be appointed under section 39A or 39C (whether or not by the NHS body) to represent P, and

(b) the hospital or care home in which P is to be accommodated under the arrangements referred to in this section is the relevant hospital or care home under the authorisation referred to in that section.

(3) Before making the arrangements, the NHS body must instruct an independent mental capacity advocate to represent P unless it is satisfied that –

(a) the accommodation is likely to be provided for a continuous period which is less than the applicable period, or

(b) the arrangements need to be made as a matter of urgency.

(4) If the NHS body –

(a) did not instruct an independent mental capacity advocate to represent P before making the arrangements because it was satisfied that subsection (3)(a) or (b) applied, but

(b) subsequently has reason to believe that the accommodation is likely to be provided for a continuous period –

    (i)   beginning with the day on which accommodation was first provided in accordance with the arrangements, and

    (ii) ending on or after the expiry of the applicable period,

it must instruct an independent mental capacity advocate to represent P.

(5) The NHS body must, in deciding what arrangements to make for P, take into account any information given, or submissions made, by the independent mental capacity advocate.

(6) 'Care home' has the meaning given in section 3 of the Care Standards Act 2000.

(7) 'Hospital' means –

(a) in relation to England, a hospital as defined by section 275 of the National Health Service Act 2006; and

(b) in relation to Wales, a health service hospital as defined by section 206 of the National Health Service (Wales) Act 2006 or an independent hospital as defined by section 2 of the Care Standards Act 2000.

(8) 'NHS body' has such meaning as may be prescribed by regulations made for the purposes of this section by –

(a) the Secretary of State, in relation to bodies in England, or

(b) the National Assembly for Wales, in relation to bodies in Wales.

(9) 'Applicable period' means –

(a) in relation to accommodation in a hospital, 28 days, and

(b) in relation to accommodation in a care home, 8 weeks.

(10) For the purposes of subsection (1), a person appointed under Part 10 of Schedule A1 to be P's representative is not, by virtue of that appointment, engaged in providing care or treatment for P in a professional capacity or for remuneration.

39 Provision of accommodation by local authority

(1) This section applies if a local authority propose to make arrangements –

    (a) for the provision of residential accommodation for a person ('P') who lacks capacity to agree to the arrangements, or

    (b) for a change in P's residential accommodation,

and are satisfied that there is no person, other than one engaged in providing care or treatment for P in a professional capacity or for remuneration, whom it would be appropriate for them to consult in determining what would be in P's best interests.

(2) But this section applies only if the accommodation is to be provided in accordance with –

    (a) section 21 or 29 of the National Assistance Act 1948, or

    (b) section 117 of the Mental Health Act,

as the result of a decision taken by the local authority under section 47 of the National Health Service and Community Care Act 1990.

(3) This section does not apply if P is accommodated as a result of an obligation imposed on him under the Mental Health Act.

(3A) And this section does not apply if —

    (a) an independent mental capacity advocate must be appointed under section 39A or 39C (whether or not by the local authority) to represent P, and

    (b) the place in which P is to be accommodated under the arrangements referred to in this section is the relevant hospital or care home under the authorisation referred to in that section.

(4) Before making the arrangements, the local authority must instruct an independent mental capacity advocate to represent P unless they are satisfied that –

    (a) the accommodation is likely to be provided for a continuous period of less than 8 weeks, or

    (b) the arrangements need to be made as a matter of urgency.

(5) If the local authority –

    (a) did not instruct an independent mental capacity advocate to represent P before making the arrangements because they were satisfied that subsection (4)(a) or (b) applied, but

(b) subsequently have reason to believe that the accommodation is likely to be provided for a continuous period that will end 8 weeks or more after the day on which accommodation was first provided in accordance with the arrangements,

they must instruct an independent mental capacity advocate to represent P.

(6) The local authority must, in deciding what arrangements to make for P, take into account any information given, or submissions made, by the independent mental capacity advocate.

(7) For the purposes of subsection (1), a person appointed under Part 10 of Schedule A1 to be P's representative is not, by virtue of that appointment, engaged in providing care or treatment for P in a professional capacity or for remuneration.

39A Person becomes subject to Schedule A1

(1) This section applies if –

(a) a person ('P') becomes subject to Schedule A1, and
(b) the managing authority of the relevant hospital or care home are satisfied that there is no person, other than one engaged in providing care or treatment for P in a professional capacity or for remuneration, whom it would be appropriate to consult in determining what would be in P's best interests.

(2) The managing authority must notify the supervisory body that this section applies.

(3) The supervisory body must instruct an independent mental capacity advocate to represent P.

(4) Schedule A1 makes provision about the role of an independent mental capacity advocate appointed under this section.

(5) This section is subject to paragraph 161 of Schedule A1.

(6) For the purposes of subsection (1), a person appointed under Part 10 of Schedule A1 to be P's representative is not, by virtue of that appointment, engaged in providing care or treatment for P in a professional capacity or for remuneration.

39B Section 39A: supplementary provision

(1) This section applies for the purposes of section 39A.

(2) P becomes subject to Schedule A1 in any of the following cases.

(3) The first case is where an urgent authorisation is given in relation to P under paragraph 76(2) of Schedule A1 (urgent authorisation given before request made for standard authorisation).

(4) The second case is where the following conditions are met.

(5) The first condition is that a request is made under Schedule A1 for a standard authorisation to be given in relation to P ('the requested authorisation').

(6) The second condition is that no urgent authorisation was given under paragraph 76(2) of Schedule A1 before that request was made.

(7) The third condition is that the requested authorisation will not be in force on or before, or immediately after, the expiry of an existing standard authorisation.

(8) The expiry of a standard authorisation is the date when the authorisation is expected to cease to be in force.

(9) The third case is where, under paragraph 69 of Schedule A1, the supervisory body select a person to carry out an assessment of whether or not the relevant person is a detained resident.

39C Person unrepresented whilst subject to Schedule A1

(1) This section applies if –

(a) an authorisation under Schedule A1 is in force in relation to a person ('P'),
(b) the appointment of a person as P's representative ends in accordance with regulations made under Part 10 of Schedule A1, and
(c) the managing authority of the relevant hospital or care home are satisfied that there is no person, other than one engaged in providing care or treatment for P in a professional capacity or for remuneration, whom it would be appropriate to consult in determining what would be in P's best interests.

(2) The managing authority must notify the supervisory body that this section applies.

(3) The supervisory body must instruct an independent mental capacity advocate to represent P.

(4) Paragraph 159 of Schedule A1 makes provision about the role of an independent mental capacity advocate appointed under this section.

(5) The appointment of an independent mental capacity advocate under this section ends when a new appointment of a person as P's representative is made in accordance with Part 10 of Schedule A1.

(6) For the purposes of subsection (1), a person appointed under Part 10 of Schedule A1 to be P's representative is not, by virtue of that appointment, engaged in providing care or treatment for P in a professional capacity or for remuneration.

39D Person subject to Schedule A1 without paid representative

(1) This section applies if –

    (a) an authorisation under Schedule A1 is in force in relation to a person ('P'),

    (b) P has a representative ('R') appointed under Part 10 of Schedule A1, and

    (c) R is not being paid under regulations under Part 10 of Schedule A1 for acting as P's representative.

(2) The supervisory body must instruct an independent mental capacity advocate to represent P in any of the following cases.

(3) The first case is where P makes a request to the supervisory body to instruct an advocate.

(4) The second case is where R makes a request to the supervisory body to instruct an advocate.

(5) The third case is where the supervisory body have reason to believe one or more of the following –

    (a) that, without the help of an advocate, P and R would be unable to exercise one or both of the relevant rights;

    (b) that P and R have each failed to exercise a relevant right when it would have been reasonable to exercise it;

    (c) that P and R are each unlikely to exercise a relevant right when it would be reasonable to exercise it.

(6) The duty in subsection (2) is subject to section 39E.

(7) If an advocate is appointed under this section, the advocate is, in particular, to take such steps as are practicable to help P and R to understand the following matters —

    (a) the effect of the authorisation;

    (b) the purpose of the authorisation;

    (c) the duration of the authorisation;

    (d) any conditions to which the authorisation is subject;

    (e) the reasons why each assessor who carried out an assessment in connection with the request for the authorisation, or in connection with a review of the authorisation, decided that P met the qualifying requirement in question;

    (f) the relevant rights;

    (g) how to exercise the relevant rights.

(8) The advocate is, in particular, to take such steps as are practicable to help P or R –

    (a) to exercise the right to apply to court, if it appears to the advocate that P or R wishes to exercise that right, or

    (b) to exercise the right of review, if it appears to the advocate that P or R wishes to exercise that right.

(9) If the advocate helps P or R to exercise the right of review –

    (a) the advocate may make submissions to the supervisory body on the question of whether a qualifying requirement is reviewable;

(b) the advocate may give information, or make submissions, to any assessor carrying out a review assessment.

(10) In this section –

'relevant rights' means –

(a) the right to apply to court, and
(b) the right of review;

'right to apply to court' means the right to make an application to the court to exercise its jurisdiction under section 21A;
'right of review' means the right under Part 8 of Schedule A1 to request a review.

39E Limitation on duty to instruct advocate under section 39D

(1) This section applies if an advocate is already representing P in accordance with an instruction under section 39D.

(2) Section 39D(2) does not require another advocate to be instructed, unless the following conditions are met.

(3) The first condition is that the existing advocate was instructed –

(a) because of a request by R, or
(b) because the supervisory body had reason to believe one or more of the things in section 39D(5).

(4) The second condition is that the other advocate would be instructed because of a request by P.

40 Exceptions

(1) The duty imposed by section 37(3), 38(3) or (4), 39(4) or (5), 39A(3), 39C(3) or 39D(2) does not apply where there is –

(a) a person nominated by P (in whatever manner) as a person to be consulted on matters to which that duty relates,
(b) a donee of a lasting power of attorney created by P who is authorised to make decisions in relation to those matters, or
(c) a deputy appointed by the court for P with power to make decisions in relation to those matters.

(2) A person appointed under Part 10 of Schedule A1 to be P's representative is not, by virtue of that appointment, a person nominated by P as a person to be consulted in matters to which a duty mentioned in subsection (1) relates.

41 Power to adjust role of independent mental capacity advocate

(1) The appropriate authority may make regulations –

(a) expanding the role of independent mental capacity advocates in relation to persons who lack capacity, and
(b) adjusting the obligation to make arrangements imposed by section 35.

(2) The regulations may, in particular –

    (a) prescribe circumstances (different to those set out in sections 37, 38 and 39) in which an independent mental capacity advocate must, or circumstances in which one may, be instructed by a person of a prescribed description to represent a person who lacks capacity, and

    (b) include provision similar to any made by section 37, 38, 39 or 40.

(3) 'Appropriate authority' has the same meaning as in section 35.

Miscellaneous and supplementary

42 Codes of practice

(1) The Lord Chancellor must prepare and issue one or more codes of practice –

    (a) for the guidance of persons assessing whether a person has capacity in relation to any matter,

    (b) for the guidance of persons acting in connection with the care or treatment of another person (see section 5),

    (c) for the guidance of donees of lasting powers of attorney,

    (d) for the guidance of deputies appointed by the court,

    (e) for the guidance of persons carrying out research in reliance on any provision made by or under this Act (and otherwise with respect to sections 30 to 34),

    (f) for the guidance of independent mental capacity advocates,

    (fa) for the guidance of persons exercising functions under Schedule A1,

    (fb) for the guidance of representatives appointed under Part 10 of Schedule A1,

    (g) with respect to the provisions of sections 24 to 26 (advance decisions and apparent advance decisions), and

    (h) with respect to such other matters concerned with this Act as he thinks fit.

(2) The Lord Chancellor may from time to time revise a code.

(3) The Lord Chancellor may delegate the preparation or revision of the whole or any part of a code so far as he considers expedient.

(4) It is the duty of a person to have regard to any relevant code if he is acting in relation to a person who lacks capacity and is doing so in one or more of the following ways –

    (a) as the donee of a lasting power of attorney,

    (b) as a deputy appointed by the court,

    (c) as a person carrying out research in reliance on any provision made by or under this Act (see sections 30 to 34),

    (d) as an independent mental capacity advocate,

    (da) in the exercise of functions under Schedule A1,

    (db) as a representative appointed under Part 10 of Schedule A1,

    (e) in a professional capacity,

    (f) for remuneration.

(5) If it appears to a court or tribunal conducting any criminal or civil proceedings that –

(a) a provision of a code, or
(b) a failure to comply with a code,

is relevant to a question arising in the proceedings, the provision or failure must be taken into account in deciding the question.

(6) A code under subsection (1)(d) may contain separate guidance for deputies appointed by virtue of paragraph 1(2) of Schedule 5 (functions of deputy conferred on receiver appointed under the Mental Health Act).

(7) In this section and in section 43, 'code' means a code prepared or revised under this section.

43 Codes of practice: procedure

(1) Before preparing or revising a code, the Lord Chancellor must consult –

(a) the National Assembly for Wales, and
(b) such other persons as he considers appropriate.

(2) The Lord Chancellor may not issue a code unless –

(a) a draft of the code has been laid by him before both Houses of Parliament, and
(b) the 40 day period has elapsed without either House resolving not to approve the draft.

(3) The Lord Chancellor must arrange for any code that he has issued to be published in such a way as he considers appropriate for bringing it to the attention of persons likely to be concerned with its provisions.

(4) '40 day period', in relation to the draft of a proposed code, means –

(a) if the draft is laid before one House on a day later than the day on which it is laid before the other House, the period of 40 days beginning with the later of the two days;
(b) in any other case, the period of 40 days beginning with the day on which it is laid before each House.

(5) In calculating the period of 40 days, no account is to be taken of any period during which Parliament is dissolved or prorogued or during which both Houses are adjourned for more than 4 days.

44 Ill-treatment or neglect

(1) Subsection (2) applies if a person ('D') –

(a) has the care of a person ('P') who lacks, or whom D reasonably believes to lack, capacity,
(b) is the donee of a lasting power of attorney, or an enduring power of attorney (within the meaning of Schedule 4), created by P, or
(c) is a deputy appointed by the court for P.

(2) D is guilty of an offence if he ill-treats or wilfully neglects P.

(3) A person guilty of an offence under this section is liable –

    (a) on summary conviction, to imprisonment for a term not exceeding 12 months or a fine not exceeding the statutory maximum or both;

    (b) on conviction on indictment, to imprisonment for a term not exceeding 5 years or a fine or both.

PART 2
THE COURT OF PROTECTION AND THE PUBLIC GUARDIAN

The Court of Protection

45 The Court of Protection

(1) There is to be a superior court of record known as the Court of Protection.

(2) The court is to have an official seal.

(3) The court may sit at any place in England and Wales, on any day and at any time.

(4) The court is to have a central office and registry at a place appointed by the Lord Chancellor, after consulting the Lord Chief Justice.

(5) The Lord Chancellor may, after consulting the Lord Chief Justice, designate as additional registries of the court any district registry of the High Court and any county court office.

(5A) The Lord Chief Justice may nominate any of the following to exercise his functions under this section –

    (a) the President of the Court of Protection;

    (b) a judicial office holder (as defined in section 109(4) of the Constitutional Reform Act 2005).

(6) The office of the Supreme Court called the Court of Protection ceases to exist.

46 The judges of the Court of Protection

(1) Subject to Court of Protection Rules under section 51(2)(d), the jurisdiction of the court is exercisable by a judge nominated for that purpose by –

    (a) the Lord Chief Justice, or

    (b) where nominated by the Lord Chief Justice to act on his behalf under this subsection –

        (i) the President of the Court of Protection; or

        (ii) a judicial office holder (as defined in section 109(4) of the Constitutional Reform Act 2005).

(2) To be nominated, a judge must be –

    (a) the President of the Family Division,

    (b) the Chancellor of the High Court,

(c) a puisne judge of the High Court,

(d) a circuit judge,

(e) a district judge,

(f) a District Judge (Magistrates' Courts).

(g) a judge of the First-tier Tribunal, or of the Upper Tribunal, by virtue of appointment under paragraph 1(1) of Schedule 2 or 3 to the Tribunals, Courts and Enforcement Act 2007,

(h) a transferred-in judge of the First-tier Tribunal or of the Upper Tribunal (see section 31(2) of that Act),

(i) a deputy judge of the Upper Tribunal (whether under paragraph 7 of Schedule 3 to, or section 31(2) of, that Act).

(j) the Chamber President, or Deputy Chamber President, of a chamber of the First-tier Tribunal or of a chamber of the Upper Tribunal,

(k) the Judge Advocate General,

(l) a Recorder,

(m) the holder of an office listed in the first column of the table in section 89(3C) of the Senior Courts Act 1981 (senior High Court Masters etc),

(n) a holder of an office listed in column 1 of Part 2 of Schedule 2 to that Act (High Court Masters etc),

(o) a deputy district judge appointed under section 102 of that Act or under section 8 of the County Courts Act 1984,

(p) a member of a panel of Employment Judges established for England and Wales or for Scotland,

(q) a person appointed under section 30(1)(a) or (b) of the Courts-Martial (Appeals) Act 1951 (assistants to the Judge Advocate General),

(r) a deputy judge of the High Court,

(s) the Senior President of Tribunals,

(t) an ordinary judge of the Court of Appeal (including the vice-president, if any, of either division of that court),

(u) the President of the Queen's Bench Division,

(v) the Master of the Rolls, or

(w) the Lord Chief Justice.

(3) The Lord Chief Justice, after consulting the Lord Chancellor, must –

(a) appoint one of the judges nominated by virtue of subsection (2)(a) to (c) to be President of the Court of Protection, and

(b) appoint another of those judges to be Vice-President of the Court of Protection.

(4) The Lord Chief Justice, after consulting the Lord Chancellor, must appoint one of the judges nominated by virtue of subsection (2)(d) to (q) to be Senior Judge of the Court of Protection, having such administrative functions in relation to the court as the Lord Chancellor, after consulting the Lord Chief Justice, may direct.

Supplementary powers

47 General powers and effect of orders etc

(1) The court has in connection with its jurisdiction the same powers, rights, privileges and authority as the High Court.

(2) Section 204 of the Law of Property Act 1925 (orders of High Court conclusive in favour of purchasers) applies in relation to orders and directions of the court as it applies to orders of the High Court.

(3) Office copies of orders made, directions given or other instruments issued by the court and sealed with its official seal are admissible in all legal proceedings as evidence of the originals without any further proof.

48 Interim orders and directions

The court may, pending the determination of an application to it in relation to a person ('P'), make an order or give directions in respect of any matter if –

    (a)   there is reason to believe that P lacks capacity in relation to the matter,
    (b)   the matter is one to which its powers under this Act extend, and
    (c)   it is in P's best interests to make the order, or give the directions, without delay.

49 Power to call for reports

(1) This section applies where, in proceedings brought in respect of a person ('P') under Part 1, the court is considering a question relating to P.

(2) The court may require a report to be made to it by the Public Guardian or by a Court of Protection Visitor.

(3) The court may require a local authority, or an NHS body, to arrange for a report to be made –

    (a)   by one of its officers or employees, or
    (b)   by such other person (other than the Public Guardian or a Court of Protection Visitor) as the authority, or the NHS body, considers appropriate.

(4) The report must deal with such matters relating to P as the court may direct.

(5) Court of Protection Rules may specify matters which, unless the court directs otherwise, must also be dealt with in the report.

(6) The report may be made in writing or orally, as the court may direct.

(7) In complying with a requirement, the Public Guardian or a Court of Protection Visitor may, at all reasonable times, examine and take copies of –

    (a)   any health record,
    (b)   any record of, or held by, a local authority and compiled in connection with a social services function, and

(c) any record held by a person registered under Part 2 of the Care Standards Act 2000 or Chapter 2 of Part 1 of the Health and Social Care Act 2008,

so far as the record relates to P.

(8) If the Public Guardian or a Court of Protection Visitor is making a visit in the course of complying with a requirement, he may interview P in private.

(9) If a Court of Protection Visitor who is a Special Visitor is making a visit in the course of complying with a requirement, he may if the court so directs carry out in private a medical, psychiatric or psychological examination of P's capacity and condition.

(10) 'NHS body' has the meaning given in section 148 of the Health and Social Care (Community Health and Standards) Act 2003.

(11) 'Requirement' means a requirement imposed under subsection (2) or (3).

Practice and procedure

50 Applications to the Court of Protection

(1) No permission is required for an application to the court for the exercise of any of its powers under this Act –

(a) by a person who lacks, or is alleged to lack, capacity,
(b) if such a person has not reached 18, by anyone with parental responsibility for him,
(c) by the donor or a donee of a lasting power of attorney to which the application relates,
(d) by a deputy appointed by the court for a person to whom the application relates, or
(e) by a person named in an existing order of the court, if the application relates to the order.

(1A) Nor is permission required for an application to the court under section 21A by the relevant person's representative.

(2) But, subject to Court of Protection Rules and to paragraph 20(2) of Schedule 3 (declarations relating to private international law), permission is required for any other application to the court.

(3) In deciding whether to grant permission the court must, in particular, have regard to –

(a) the applicant's connection with the person to whom the application relates,
(b) the reasons for the application,
(c) the benefit to the person to whom the application relates of a proposed order or directions, and
(d) whether the benefit can be achieved in any other way.

(4) 'Parental responsibility' has the same meaning as in the Children Act 1989.

51 Court of Protection Rules

(1) Rules of court with respect to the practice and procedure of the court (to be called 'Court of Protection Rules') may be made in accordance with Part 1 of Schedule 1 to the Constitutional Reform Act 2005.

(2) Court of Protection Rules may, in particular, make provision –

(a) as to the manner and form in which proceedings are to be commenced;
(b) as to the persons entitled to be notified of, and be made parties to, the proceedings;
(c) for the allocation, in such circumstances as may be specified, of any specified description of proceedings to a specified judge or to specified descriptions of judges;
(d) for the exercise of the jurisdiction of the court, in such circumstances as may be specified, by its officers or other staff;
(e) for enabling the court to appoint a suitable person (who may, with his consent, be the Official Solicitor) to act in the name of, or on behalf of, or to represent the person to whom the proceedings relate;
(f) for enabling an application to the court to be disposed of without a hearing;
(g) for enabling the court to proceed with, or with any part of, a hearing in the absence of the person to whom the proceedings relate;
(h) for enabling or requiring the proceedings or any part of them to be conducted in private and for enabling the court to determine who is to be admitted when the court sits in private and to exclude specified persons when it sits in public;
(i) as to what may be received as evidence (whether or not admissible apart from the rules) and the manner in which it is to be presented;
(j) for the enforcement of orders made and directions given in the proceedings.

(3) Court of Protection Rules may, instead of providing for any matter, refer to provision made or to be made about that matter by directions.

(4) Court of Protection Rules may make different provision for different areas.

52 Practice directions

(1) Directions as to the practice and procedure of the court may be given in accordance with Part 1 of Schedule 2 to the Constitutional Reform Act 2005.

(2) Practice directions given otherwise than under subsection (1) may not be given without the approval of –

(a) the Lord Chancellor, and
(b) the Lord Chief Justice.

(3) The Lord Chief Justice may nominate any of the following to exercise his functions under this section –

(a) the President of the Court of Protection;

(b) a judicial office holder (as defined in section 109(4) of the Constitutional Reform Act 2005).

53 Rights of appeal

(1) Subject to the provisions of this section, an appeal lies to the Court of Appeal from any decision of the court.

(2) Court of Protection Rules may provide that, where a decision of the court is made by a specified description of person, an appeal from the decision lies to a specified description of judge of the court and not to the Court of Appeal.

(3) (*Omitted*)

(4) Court of Protection Rules may make provision –

  (a) that, in such cases as may be specified, an appeal from a decision of the court may not be made without permission;
  (b) as to the person or persons entitled to grant permission to appeal;
  (c) as to any requirements to be satisfied before permission is granted;
  (d) that where a judge of the court makes a decision on an appeal, no appeal may be made to the Court of Appeal from that decision unless the Court of Appeal considers that –
    (i) the appeal would raise an important point of principle or practice, or
    (ii) there is some other compelling reason for the Court of Appeal to hear it;
  (e) as to any considerations to be taken into account in relation to granting or refusing permission to appeal.

Fees and costs

54 Fees

(1) The Lord Chancellor may with the consent of the Treasury by order prescribe fees payable in respect of anything dealt with by the court.

(2) An order under this section may in particular contain provision as to –

  (a) scales or rates of fees;
  (b) exemptions from and reductions in fees;
  (c) remission of fees in whole or in part.

(3) Before making an order under this section, the Lord Chancellor must consult –

  (a) the President of the Court of Protection,
  (b) the Vice-President of the Court of Protection, and
  (c) the Senior Judge of the Court of Protection.

(4) The Lord Chancellor must take such steps as are reasonably practicable to bring information about fees to the attention of persons likely to have to pay them.

(5) Fees payable under this section are recoverable summarily as a civil debt.

55 Costs

(1) Subject to Court of Protection Rules, the costs of and incidental to all proceedings in the court are in its discretion.

(2) The rules may in particular make provision for regulating matters relating to the costs of those proceedings, including prescribing scales of costs to be paid to legal or other representatives.

(3) The court has full power to determine by whom and to what extent the costs are to be paid.

(4) The court may, in any proceedings –

    (a) disallow, or
    (b) order the legal or other representatives concerned to meet,

the whole of any wasted costs or such part of them as may be determined in accordance with the rules.

(5) 'Legal or other representative', in relation to a party to proceedings, means any person exercising a right of audience or right to conduct litigation on his behalf.

(6) 'Wasted costs' means any costs incurred by a party –

    (a) as a result of any improper, unreasonable or negligent act or omission on the part of any legal or other representative or any employee of such a representative, or
    (b) which, in the light of any such act or omission occurring after they were incurred, the court considers it is unreasonable to expect that party to pay.

56 Fees and costs: supplementary

(1) Court of Protection Rules may make provision –

    (a) as to the way in which, and funds from which, fees and costs are to be paid;
    (b) for charging fees and costs upon the estate of the person to whom the proceedings relate;
    (c) for the payment of fees and costs within a specified time of the death of the person to whom the proceedings relate or the conclusion of the proceedings.

(2) A charge on the estate of a person created by virtue of subsection (1)(b) does not cause any interest of the person in any property to fail or determine or to be prevented from recommencing.

The Public Guardian

57 The Public Guardian

(1) For the purposes of this Act, there is to be an officer, to be known as the Public Guardian.

(2) The Public Guardian is to be appointed by the Lord Chancellor.

(3) There is to be paid to the Public Guardian out of money provided by Parliament such salary as the Lord Chancellor may determine.

(4) The Lord Chancellor may, after consulting the Public Guardian –

  (a) provide him with such officers and staff, or
  (b) enter into such contracts with other persons for the provision (by them or their sub-contractors) of officers, staff or services,

as the Lord Chancellor thinks necessary for the proper discharge of the Public Guardian's functions.

(5) Any functions of the Public Guardian may, to the extent authorised by him, be performed by any of his officers.

58 Functions of the Public Guardian

(1) The Public Guardian has the following functions –

  (a) establishing and maintaining a register of lasting powers of attorney,
  (b) establishing and maintaining a register of orders appointing deputies,
  (c) supervising deputies appointed by the court,
  (d) directing a Court of Protection Visitor to visit –
      (i)   a donee of a lasting power of attorney,
      (ii) a deputy appointed by the court, or
      (iii) the person granting the power of attorney or for whom the deputy is appointed ('P'),
      and to make a report to the Public Guardian on such matters as he may direct,
  (e) receiving security which the court requires a person to give for the discharge of his functions,
  (f) receiving reports from donees of lasting powers of attorney and deputies appointed by the court,
  (g) reporting to the court on such matters relating to proceedings under this Act as the court requires,
  (h) dealing with representations (including complaints) about the way in which a donee of a lasting power of attorney or a deputy appointed by the court is exercising his powers,
  (i) publishing, in any manner the Public Guardian thinks appropriate, any information he thinks appropriate about the discharge of his functions.

(2) The functions conferred by subsection (1)(c) and (h) may be discharged in co-operation with any other person who has functions in relation to the care or treatment of P.

(3) The Lord Chancellor may by regulations make provision –

  (a) conferring on the Public Guardian other functions in connection with this Act;
  (b) in connection with the discharge by the Public Guardian of his functions.

(4) Regulations made under subsection (3)(b) may in particular make provision as to –

(a) the giving of security by deputies appointed by the court and the enforcement and discharge of security so given;
(b) the fees which may be charged by the Public Guardian;
(c) the way in which, and funds from which, such fees are to be paid;
(d) exemptions from and reductions in such fees;
(e) remission of such fees in whole or in part;
(f) the making of reports to the Public Guardian by deputies appointed by the court and others who are directed by the court to carry out any transaction for a person who lacks capacity.

(5) For the purpose of enabling him to carry out his functions, the Public Guardian may, at all reasonable times, examine and take copies of –

(a) any health record,
(b) any record of, or held by, a local authority and compiled in connection with a social services function, and
(c) any record held by a person registered under Part 2 of the Care Standards Act 2000 or Chapter 2 of Part 1 of the Health and Social Care Act 2008,

so far as the record relates to P.

(6) The Public Guardian may also for that purpose interview P in private.

59 Public Guardian Board

(*Repealed*).

60 Annual report

(1) The Public Guardian must make an annual report to the Lord Chancellor about the discharge of his functions.

(2) The Lord Chancellor must, within one month of receiving the report, lay a copy of it before Parliament.

Court of Protection Visitors

61 Court of Protection Visitors

(1) A Court of Protection Visitor is a person who is appointed by the Lord Chancellor to –

(a) a panel of Special Visitors, or
(b) a panel of General Visitors.

(2) A person is not qualified to be a Special Visitor unless he –

(a) is a registered medical practitioner or appears to the Lord Chancellor to have other suitable qualifications or training, and

(b) appears to the Lord Chancellor to have special knowledge of and experience in cases of impairment of or disturbance in the functioning of the mind or brain.

(3) A General Visitor need not have a medical qualification.

(4) A Court of Protection Visitor –

(a) may be appointed for such term and subject to such conditions, and
(b) may be paid such remuneration and allowances,

as the Lord Chancellor may determine.

(5) For the purpose of carrying out his functions under this Act in relation to a person who lacks capacity ('P'), a Court of Protection Visitor may, at all reasonable times, examine and take copies of –

(a) any health record,
(b) any record of, or held by, a local authority and compiled in connection with a social services function, and
(c) any record held by a person registered under Part 2 of the Care Standards Act 2000 or Chapter 2 of Part 1 of the Health and Social Care Act 2008,

so far as the record relates to P.

(6) A Court of Protection Visitor may also for that purpose interview P in private.

PART 3
MISCELLANEOUS AND GENERAL

Declaratory provision

62 Scope of the Act

For the avoidance of doubt, it is hereby declared that nothing in this Act is to be taken to affect the law relating to murder or manslaughter or the operation of section 2 of the Suicide Act 1961 (assisting suicide).

Private international law

63 International protection of adults

Schedule 3 –

(a) gives effect in England and Wales to the Convention on the International Protection of Adults signed at the Hague on 13 January 2000 (Cm. 5881) (in so far as this Act does not otherwise do so), and
(b) makes related provision as to the private international law of England and Wales.

General

64 Interpretation

(1) In this Act –

'the 1985 Act' means the Enduring Powers of Attorney Act 1985,
'advance decision' has the meaning given in section 24(1),
'authorisation under Schedule A1' means either –

    (a) a standard authorisation under that Schedule, or
    (b) an urgent authorisation under that Schedule;

'the court' means the Court of Protection established by section 45,
'Court of Protection Rules' has the meaning given in section 51(1),
'Court of Protection Visitor' has the meaning given in section 61,
'deputy' has the meaning given in section 16(2)(b),
'enactment' includes a provision of subordinate legislation (within the meaning of the Interpretation Act 1978),
'health record' has the meaning given in section 68 of the Data Protection Act 1998 (as read with section 69 of that Act),
'the Human Rights Convention' has the same meaning as 'the Convention' in the Human Rights Act 1998,
'independent mental capacity advocate' has the meaning given in section 35(1),
'lasting power of attorney' has the meaning given in section 9,
'life-sustaining treatment' has the meaning given in section 4(10),
'local authority', except in section 35(6A)(a) and Schedule A1, means –

    (a) the council of a county in England in which there are no district councils,
    (b) the council of a district in England,
    (c) the council of a county or county borough in Wales,
    (d) the council of a London borough,
    (e) the Common Council of the City of London, or
    (f) the Council of the Isles of Scilly,

'Mental Health Act' means the Mental Health Act 1983,
'prescribed', in relation to regulations made under this Act, means prescribed by those regulations,
'property' includes anything in action and any interest in real or personal property,
'public authority' has the same meaning as in the Human Rights Act 1998,
'Public Guardian' has the meaning given in section 57,
'purchaser' and 'purchase' have the meaning given in section 205(1) of the Law of Property Act 1925,
'social services function' has the meaning given in section 1A of the Local Authority Social Services Act 1970,
'treatment' includes a diagnostic or other procedure,
'trust corporation' has the meaning given in section 68(1) of the Trustee Act 1925, and
'will' includes codicil.

(2) In this Act, references to making decisions, in relation to a donee of a lasting power of attorney or a deputy appointed by the court, include, where appropriate, acting on decisions made.

(3) In this Act, references to the bankruptcy of an individual include a case where a bankruptcy restrictions order under the Insolvency Act 1986 has effect in respect of him.

(3A) In this Act references to a debt relief order (under Part 7A of the Insolvency Act 1986) being made in relation to an individual include a case where a debt relief restrictions order under the Insolvency Act 1986 has effect in respect of him.

(4) 'Bankruptcy restrictions order' includes an interim bankruptcy restrictions order.

(4A) 'Debt relief restrictions order' includes an interim debt relief restrictions order.

(5) In this Act, references to deprivation of a person's liberty have the same meaning as in Article 5(1) of the Human Rights Convention.

(6) For the purposes of such references, it does not matter whether a person is deprived of his liberty by a public authority or not.

65 Rules, regulations and orders

(1) Any power to make rules, regulations or orders under this Act, other than the power in section 21 –

    (a)   is exercisable by statutory instrument;
    (b)   includes power to make supplementary, incidental, consequential, transitional or saving provision;
    (c)   includes power to make different provision for different cases.

(2) Any statutory instrument containing rules, regulations or orders made by the Lord Chancellor or the Secretary of State under this Act, other than –

    (a)   regulations under section 34 (loss of capacity during research project),
    (b)   regulations under section 41 (adjusting role of independent mental capacity advocacy service),
    (c)   regulations under paragraph 32(1)(b) of Schedule 3 (private international law relating to the protection of adults),
    (d)   an order of the kind mentioned in section 67(6) (consequential amendments of primary legislation), or
    (e)   an order under section 68 (commencement),

is subject to annulment in pursuance of a resolution of either House of Parliament.

(3) A statutory instrument containing an Order in Council under paragraph 31 of Schedule 3 (provision to give further effect to Hague Convention) is subject to annulment in pursuance of a resolution of either House of Parliament.

(4) A statutory instrument containing regulations made by the Secretary of State under section 34 or 41 or by the Lord Chancellor under paragraph 32(1)(b) of Schedule 3 may not be made unless a draft has been laid before and approved by resolution of each House of Parliament.

(4A) Subsection (2) does not apply to a statutory instrument containing regulations made by the Secretary of State under Schedule A1.

(4B) If such a statutory instrument contains regulations under paragraph 42(2)(b), 129, 162 or 164 of Schedule A1 (whether or not it also contains other regulations), the instrument may not be made unless a draft has been laid before and approved by resolution of each House of Parliament.

(4C) Subject to that, such a statutory instrument is subject to annulment in pursuance of a resolution of either House of Parliament.

(5) An order under section 21 –

    (a) may include supplementary, incidental, consequential, transitional or saving provision;

    (b) may make different provision for different cases;

    (c) is to be made in the form of a statutory instrument to which the Statutory Instruments Act 1946 applies as if the order were made by a Minister of the Crown; and

    (d) is subject to annulment in pursuance of a resolution of either House of Parliament.

66 Existing receivers and enduring powers of attorney etc

(1) The following provisions cease to have effect –

    (a) Part 7 of the Mental Health Act,

    (b) the Enduring Powers of Attorney Act 1985.

(2) No enduring power of attorney within the meaning of the 1985 Act is to be created after the commencement of subsection (1)(b).

(3) Schedule 4 has effect in place of the 1985 Act in relation to any enduring power of attorney created before the commencement of subsection (1)(b).

(4) Schedule 5 contains transitional provisions and savings in relation to Part 7 of the Mental Health Act and the 1985 Act.

67 Minor and consequential amendments and repeals

(1) Schedule 6 contains minor and consequential amendments.

(2) Schedule 7 contains repeals.

(3) The Lord Chancellor may by order make supplementary, incidental, consequential, transitional or saving provision for the purposes of, in consequence of, or for giving full effect to a provision of this Act.

(4) An order under subsection (3) may, in particular –

(a) provide for a provision of this Act which comes into force before another provision of this Act has come into force to have effect, until the other provision has come into force, with specified modifications;

(b) amend, repeal or revoke an enactment, other than one contained in an Act or Measure passed in a Session after the one in which this Act is passed.

(5) The amendments that may be made under subsection (4)(b) are in addition to those made by or under any other provision of this Act.

(6) An order under subsection (3) which amends or repeals a provision of an Act or Measure may not be made unless a draft has been laid before and approved by resolution of each House of Parliament.

68 Commencement and extent

(1) This Act, other than sections 30 to 41, comes into force in accordance with provision made by order by the Lord Chancellor.

(2) Sections 30 to 41 come into force in accordance with provision made by order by –

(a) the Secretary of State, in relation to England, and
(b) the National Assembly for Wales, in relation to Wales.

(3) An order under this section may appoint different days for different provisions and different purposes.

(4) Subject to subsections (5) and (6), this Act extends to England and Wales only.

(5) The following provisions extend to the United Kingdom –

(a) paragraph 16(1) of Schedule 1 (evidence of instruments and of registration of lasting powers of attorney),
(b) paragraph 15(3) of Schedule 4 (evidence of instruments and of registration of enduring powers of attorney).

(6) Subject to any provision made in Schedule 6, the amendments and repeals made by Schedules 6 and 7 have the same extent as the enactments to which they relate.

69 Short title

This Act may be cited as the Mental Capacity Act 2005.

SCHEDULES

Schedule A1
Hospital and Care Home Residents: Deprivation of Liberty

PART 1
AUTHORISATION TO DEPRIVE RESIDENTS OF LIBERTY ETC

Application of Part

1 (1) This Part applies if the following conditions are met.

(2) The first condition is that a person ('P') is detained in a hospital or care home –for the purpose of being given care or treatment –in circumstances which amount to deprivation of the person's liberty.

(3) The second condition is that a standard or urgent authorisation is in force.

(4) The third condition is that the standard or urgent authorisation relates –

    (a) to P, and
    (b) to the hospital or care home in which P is detained.

Authorisation to deprive P of liberty

2 The managing authority of the hospital or care home may deprive P of his liberty by detaining him as mentioned in paragraph 1(2).

No liability for acts done for purpose of depriving P of liberty

3 (1) This paragraph applies to any act which a person ('D') does for the purpose of detaining P as mentioned in paragraph 1(2).

(2) D does not incur any liability in relation to the act that he would not have incurred if P –

    (a) had had capacity to consent in relation to D's doing the act, and
    (b) had consented to D's doing the act.

No protection for negligent acts etc

4 (1) Paragraphs 2 and 3 do not exclude a person's civil liability for loss or damage, or his criminal liability, resulting from his negligence in doing any thing.

(2) Paragraphs 2 and 3 do not authorise a person to do anything otherwise than for the purpose of the standard or urgent authorisation that is in force.

(3) In a case where a standard authorisation is in force, paragraphs 2 and 3 do not authorise a person to do anything which does not comply with the conditions (if any) included in the authorisation.

PART 2
INTERPRETATION: MAIN TERMS

Introduction

5 This Part applies for the purposes of this Schedule.

Detained resident

6 'Detained resident' means a person detained in a hospital or care home – for the purpose of being given care or treatment – in circumstances which amount to deprivation of the person's liberty.

Relevant person etc

7 In relation to a person who is, or is to be, a detained resident –

'relevant person' means the person in question;
'relevant hospital or care home' means the hospital or care home in question;
'relevant care or treatment' means the care or treatment in question.

Authorisations

8 'Standard authorisation' means an authorisation given under Part 4.

9 'Urgent authorisation' means an authorisation given under Part 5.

10 'Authorisation under this Schedule' means either of the following –

(a) a standard authorisation;
(b) an urgent authorisation.

11 (1) The purpose of a standard authorisation is the purpose which is stated in the authorisation in accordance with paragraph 55(1)(d).

(2) The purpose of an urgent authorisation is the purpose which is stated in the authorisation in accordance with paragraph 80(d).

PART 3
THE QUALIFYING REQUIREMENTS

The qualifying requirements

12 (1) These are the qualifying requirements referred to in this Schedule –

(a) the age requirement;
(b) the mental health requirement;
(c) the mental capacity requirement;
(d) the best interests requirement;
(e) the eligibility requirement;
(f) the no refusals requirement.

(2) Any question of whether a person who is, or is to be, a detained resident meets the qualifying requirements is to be determined in accordance with this Part.

(3) In a case where –

(a) the question of whether a person meets a particular qualifying requirement arises in relation to the giving of a standard authorisation, and

(b) any circumstances relevant to determining that question are expected to change between the time when the determination is made and the time when the authorisation is expected to come into force,

those circumstances are to be taken into account as they are expected to be at the later time.

The age requirement

13 The relevant person meets the age requirement if he has reached 18.

The mental health requirement

14 (1) The relevant person meets the mental health requirement if he is suffering from mental disorder (within the meaning of the Mental Health Act, but disregarding any exclusion for persons with learning disability).

(2) An exclusion for persons with learning disability is any provision of the Mental Health Act which provides for a person with learning disability not to be regarded as suffering from mental disorder for one or more purposes of that Act.

The mental capacity requirement

15 The relevant person meets the mental capacity requirement if he lacks capacity in relation to the question whether or not he should be accommodated in the relevant hospital or care home for the purpose of being given the relevant care or treatment.

The best interests requirement

16 (1) The relevant person meets the best interests requirement if all of the following conditions are met.

(2) The first condition is that the relevant person is, or is to be, a detained resident.

(3) The second condition is that it is in the best interests of the relevant person for him to be a detained resident.

(4) The third condition is that, in order to prevent harm to the relevant person, it is necessary for him to be a detained resident.

(5) The fourth condition is that it is a proportionate response to –

(a) the likelihood of the relevant person suffering harm, and

(b) the seriousness of that harm,

for him to be a detained resident.

The eligibility requirement

17 (1) The relevant person meets the eligibility requirement unless he is ineligible to be deprived of liberty by this Act.

(2) Schedule 1A applies for the purpose of determining whether or not P is ineligible to be deprived of liberty by this Act.

The no refusals requirement

18 The relevant person meets the no refusals requirement unless there is a refusal within the meaning of paragraph 19 or 20.

19 (1) There is a refusal if these conditions are met –

(a) the relevant person has made an advance decision;
(b) the advance decision is valid;
(c) the advance decision is applicable to some or all of the relevant treatment.

(2) Expressions used in this paragraph and any of sections 24, 25 or 26 have the same meaning in this paragraph as in that section.

20 (1) There is a refusal if it would be in conflict with a valid decision of a donee or deputy for the relevant person to be accommodated in the relevant hospital or care home for the purpose of receiving some or all of the relevant care or treatment –

(a) in circumstances which amount to deprivation of the person's liberty, or
(b) at all.

(2) A donee is a donee of a lasting power of attorney granted by the relevant person.

(3) A decision of a donee or deputy is valid if it is made –

(a) within the scope of his authority as donee or deputy, and
(b) in accordance with Part 1 of this Act.

PART 4
STANDARD AUTHORISATIONS

Supervisory body to give authorisation

21 Only the supervisory body may give a standard authorisation.

22 The supervisory body may not give a standard authorisation unless –

(a) the managing authority of the relevant hospital or care home have requested it, or

(b) paragraph 71 applies (right of third party to require consideration of whether authorisation needed).

23

The managing authority may not make a request for a standard authorisation unless –

(a) they are required to do so by paragraph 24 (as read with paragraphs 27 to 29),

(b) they are required to do so by paragraph 25 (as read with paragraph 28), or

(c) they are permitted to do so by paragraph 30.

Duty to request authorisation: basic cases

24 (1) The managing authority must request a standard authorisation in any of the following cases.

(2) The first case is where it appears to the managing authority that the relevant person –

(a) is not yet accommodated in the relevant hospital or care home,

(b) is likely – at some time within the next 28 days – to be a detained resident in the relevant hospital or care home, and

(c) is likely –
    (i) at that time, or
    (ii) at some later time within the next 28 days,
    to meet all of the qualifying requirements.

(3) The second case is where it appears to the managing authority that the relevant person –

(a) is already accommodated in the relevant hospital or care home,

(b) is likely – at some time within the next 28 days – to be a detained resident in the relevant hospital or care home, and

(c) is likely –
    (i) at that time, or
    (ii) at some later time within the next 28 days,
    to meet all of the qualifying requirements.

(4) The third case is where it appears to the managing authority that the relevant person –

(a) is a detained resident in the relevant hospital or care home, and

(b) meets all of the qualifying requirements, or is likely to do so at some time within the next 28 days.

(5) This paragraph is subject to paragraphs 27 to 29.

Duty to request authorisation: change in place of detention

25 (1) The relevant managing authority must request a standard authorisation if it appears to them that these conditions are met.

(2) The first condition is that a standard authorisation –

(a) has been given, and
(b) has not ceased to be in force.

(3) The second condition is that there is, or is to be, a change in the place of detention.

(4) This paragraph is subject to paragraph 28.

26 (1) This paragraph applies for the purposes of paragraph 25.

(2) There is a change in the place of detention if the relevant person –

(a) ceases to be a detained resident in the stated hospital or care home, and
(b) becomes a detained resident in a different hospital or care home ('the new hospital or care home').

(3) The stated hospital or care home is the hospital or care home to which the standard authorisation relates.

(4) The relevant managing authority are the managing authority of the new hospital or care home.

Other authority for detention: request for authorisation

27 (1) This paragraph applies if, by virtue of section 4A(3), a decision of the court authorises the relevant person to be a detained resident.

(2) Paragraph 24 does not require a request for a standard authorisation to be made in relation to that detention unless these conditions are met.

(3) The first condition is that the standard authorisation would be in force at a time immediately after the expiry of the other authority.

(4) The second condition is that the standard authorisation would not be in force at any time on or before the expiry of the other authority.

(5) The third condition is that it would, in the managing authority's view, be unreasonable to delay making the request until a time nearer the expiry of the other authority.

(6) In this paragraph –

(a) the other authority is –
  (i)   the decision mentioned in sub-paragraph (1), or
  (ii) any further decision of the court which, by virtue of section 4A(3), authorises, or is expected to authorise, the relevant person to be a detained resident;
(b) the expiry of the other authority is the time when the other authority is expected to cease to authorise the relevant person to be a detained resident.

Request refused: no further request unless change of circumstances

28 (1) This paragraph applies if –

(a) a managing authority request a standard authorisation under paragraph 24 or 25, and

(b) the supervisory body are prohibited by paragraph 50(2) from giving the authorisation.

(2) Paragraph 24 or 25 does not require that managing authority to make a new request for a standard authorisation unless it appears to the managing authority that –

(a) there has been a change in the relevant person's case, and

(b) because of that change, the supervisory body are likely to give a standard authorisation if requested.

Authorisation given: request for further authorisation

29 (1) This paragraph applies if a standard authorisation –

(a) has been given in relation to the detention of the relevant person, and

(b) that authorisation ('the existing authorisation') has not ceased to be in force.

(2) Paragraph 24 does not require a new request for a standard authorisation ('the new authorisation') to be made unless these conditions are met.

(3) The first condition is that the new authorisation would be in force at a time immediately after the expiry of the existing authorisation.

(4) The second condition is that the new authorisation would not be in force at any time on or before the expiry of the existing authorisation.

(5) The third condition is that it would, in the managing authority's view, be unreasonable to delay making the request until a time nearer the expiry of the existing authorisation.

(6) The expiry of the existing authorisation is the time when it is expected to cease to be in force.

Power to request authorisation

30 (1) This paragraph applies if –

(a) a standard authorisation has been given in relation to the detention of the relevant person,

(b) that authorisation ('the existing authorisation') has not ceased to be in force,

(c) the requirement under paragraph 24 to make a request for a new standard authorisation does not apply, because of paragraph 29, and

(d) a review of the existing authorisation has been requested, or is being carried out, in accordance with Part 8.

(2) The managing authority may request a new standard authorisation which would be in force on or before the expiry of the existing authorisation; but only if it would also be in force immediately after that expiry.

(3) The expiry of the existing authorisation is the time when it is expected to cease to be in force.

(4) Further provision relating to cases where a request is made under this paragraph can be found in –

   (a) paragraph 62 (effect of decision about request), and
   (b) paragraph 124 (effect of request on Part 8 review).

Information included in request

31 A request for a standard authorisation must include the information (if any) required by regulations.

Records of requests

32 (1) The managing authority of a hospital or care home must keep a written record of –

   (a) each request that they make for a standard authorisation, and
   (b) the reasons for making each request.

(2) A supervisory body must keep a written record of each request for a standard authorisation that is made to them.

Relevant person must be assessed

33 (1) This paragraph applies if the supervisory body are requested to give a standard authorisation.

(2) The supervisory body must secure that all of these assessments are carried out in relation to the relevant person –

   (a) an age assessment;
   (b) a mental health assessment;
   (c) a mental capacity assessment;
   (d) a best interests assessment;
   (e) an eligibility assessment;
   (f) a no refusals assessment.

(3) The person who carries out any such assessment is referred to as the assessor.

(4) Regulations may be made about the period (or periods) within which assessors must carry out assessments.

(5) This paragraph is subject to paragraphs 49 and 133.

Age assessment

34 An age assessment is an assessment of whether the relevant person meets the age requirement.

Mental health assessment

35 A mental health assessment is an assessment of whether the relevant person meets the mental health requirement.

36 When carrying out a mental health assessment, the assessor must also –

(a) consider how (if at all) the relevant person's mental health is likely to be affected by his being a detained resident, and
(b) notify the best interests assessor of his conclusions.

Mental capacity assessment

37 A mental capacity assessment is an assessment of whether the relevant person meets the mental capacity requirement.

Best interests assessment

38 A best interests assessment is an assessment of whether the relevant person meets the best interests requirement.

39 (1) In carrying out a best interests assessment, the assessor must comply with the duties in sub-paragraphs (2) and (3).

(2) The assessor must consult the managing authority of the relevant hospital or care home.

(3) The assessor must have regard to all of the following –

(a) the conclusions which the mental health assessor has notified to the best interests assessor in accordance with paragraph 36(b);
(b) any relevant needs assessment;
(c) any relevant care plan.

(4) A relevant needs assessment is an assessment of the relevant person's needs which –

(a) was carried out in connection with the relevant person being accommodated in the relevant hospital or care home, and
(b) was carried out by or on behalf of –
(i) the managing authority of the relevant hospital or care home, or
(ii) the supervisory body.

(5) A relevant care plan is a care plan which –

(a) sets out how the relevant person's needs are to be met whilst he is accommodated in the relevant hospital or care home, and
(b) was drawn up by or on behalf of –
(i) the managing authority of the relevant hospital or care home, or
(ii) the supervisory body.

(6) The managing authority must give the assessor a copy of –

(a) any relevant needs assessment carried out by them or on their behalf, or
(b) any relevant care plan drawn up by them or on their behalf.

(7) The supervisory body must give the assessor a copy of –

(a) any relevant needs assessment carried out by them or on their behalf, or
(b) any relevant care plan drawn up by them or on their behalf.

(8) The duties in sub-paragraphs (2) and (3) do not affect any other duty to consult or to take the views of others into account.

40 (1) This paragraph applies whatever conclusion the best interests assessment comes to.

(2) The assessor must state in the best interests assessment the name and address of every interested person whom he has consulted in carrying out the assessment.

41 Paragraphs 42 and 43 apply if the best interests assessment comes to the conclusion that the relevant person meets the best interests requirement.

42 (1) The assessor must state in the assessment the maximum authorisation period.

(2) The maximum authorisation period is the shorter of these periods –

(a) the period which, in the assessor's opinion, would be the appropriate maximum period for the relevant person to be a detained resident under the standard authorisation that has been requested;
(b) 1 year, or such shorter period as may be prescribed in regulations.

(3) Regulations under sub-paragraph (2)(b) –

(a) need not provide for a shorter period to apply in relation to all standard authorisations;
(b) may provide for different periods to apply in relation to different kinds of standard authorisations.

(4) Before making regulations under sub-paragraph (2)(b) the Secretary of State must consult all of the following –

(a) each body required by regulations under paragraph 162 to monitor and report on the operation of this Schedule in relation to England;
(b) such other persons as the Secretary of State considers it appropriate to consult.

(5) Before making regulations under sub-paragraph (2)(b) the National Assembly for Wales must consult all of the following –

(a) each person or body directed under paragraph 163(2) to carry out any function of the Assembly of monitoring and reporting on the operation of this Schedule in relation to Wales;
(b) such other persons as the Assembly considers it appropriate to consult.

43 The assessor may include in the assessment recommendations about conditions to which the standard authorisation is, or is not, to be subject in accordance with paragraph 53.

44 (1) This paragraph applies if the best interests assessment comes to the conclusion that the relevant person does not meet the best interests requirement.

(2) If, on the basis of the information taken into account in carrying out the assessment, it appears to the assessor that there is an unauthorised deprivation of liberty, he must include a statement to that effect in the assessment.

(3) There is an unauthorised deprivation of liberty if the managing authority of the relevant hospital or care home are already depriving the relevant person of his liberty without authority of the kind mentioned in section 4A.

45 The duties with which the best interests assessor must comply are subject to the provision included in appointment regulations under Part 10 (in particular, provision made under paragraph 146).

Eligibility assessment

46 An eligibility assessment is an assessment of whether the relevant person meets the eligibility requirement.

47 (1) Regulations may –

(a) require an eligibility assessor to request a best interests assessor to provide relevant eligibility information, and
(b) require the best interests assessor, if such a request is made, to provide such relevant eligibility information as he may have.

(2) In this paragraph –

'best interests assessor' means any person who is carrying out, or has carried out, a best interests assessment in relation to the relevant person;
'eligibility assessor' means a person carrying out an eligibility assessment in relation to the relevant person;
'relevant eligibility information' is information relevant to assessing whether or not the relevant person is ineligible by virtue of paragraph 5 of Schedule 1A.

No refusals assessment

48 A no refusals assessment is an assessment of whether the relevant person meets the no refusals requirement.

Equivalent assessment already carried out

49 (1) The supervisory body are not required by paragraph 33 to secure that a particular kind of assessment ('the required assessment') is carried out in relation to the relevant person if the following conditions are met.

(2) The first condition is that the supervisory body have a written copy of an assessment of the relevant person ('the existing assessment') that has already been carried out.

(3) The second condition is that the existing assessment complies with all requirements under this Schedule with which the required assessment would have to comply (if it were carried out).

(4) The third condition is that the existing assessment was carried out within the previous 12 months; but this condition need not be met if the required assessment is an age assessment.

(5) The fourth condition is that the supervisory body are satisfied that there is no reason why the existing assessment may no longer be accurate.

(6) If the required assessment is a best interests assessment, in satisfying themselves as mentioned in sub-paragraph (5), the supervisory body must take into account any information given, or submissions made, by –

    (a) the relevant person's representative,
    (b) any section 39C IMCA, or
    (c) any section 39D IMCA.

(7) It does not matter whether the existing assessment was carried out in connection with a request for a standard authorisation or for some other purpose.

(8) If, because of this paragraph, the supervisory body are not required by paragraph 33 to secure that the required assessment is carried out, the existing assessment is to be treated for the purposes of this Schedule –

    (a) as an assessment of the same kind as the required assessment, and
    (b) as having been carried out under paragraph 33 in connection with the request for the standard authorisation.

Duty to give authorisation

50 (1) The supervisory body must give a standard authorisation if –

    (a) all assessments are positive, and
    (b) the supervisory body have written copies of all those assessments.

(2) The supervisory body must not give a standard authorisation except in accordance with sub-paragraph (1).

(3) All assessments are positive if each assessment carried out under paragraph 33 has come to the conclusion that the relevant person meets the qualifying requirement to which the assessment relates.

Terms of authorisation

51 (1) If the supervisory body are required to give a standard authorisation, they must decide the period during which the authorisation is to be in force.

(2) That period must not exceed the maximum authorisation period stated in the best interests assessment.

52 A standard authorisation may provide for the authorisation to come into force at a time after it is given.

53 (1) A standard authorisation may be given subject to conditions.

(2) Before deciding whether to give the authorisation subject to conditions, the supervisory body must have regard to any recommendations in the best interests assessment about such conditions.

(3) The managing authority of the relevant hospital or care home must ensure that any conditions are complied with.

Form of authorisation

54 A standard authorisation must be in writing.

55 (1) A standard authorisation must state the following things –

    (a)   the name of the relevant person;
    (b)   the name of the relevant hospital or care home;
    (c)   the period during which the authorisation is to be in force;
    (d)   the purpose for which the authorisation is given;
    (e)   any conditions subject to which the authorisation is given;
    (f)   the reason why each qualifying requirement is met.

(2) The statement of the reason why the eligibility requirement is met must be framed by reference to the cases in the table in paragraph 2 of Schedule 1A.

56 (1) If the name of the relevant hospital or care home changes, the standard authorisation is to be read as if it stated the current name of the hospital or care home.

(2) But sub-paragraph (1) is subject to any provision relating to the change of name which is made in any enactment or in any instrument made under an enactment.

Duty to give information about decision

57 (1) This paragraph applies if –

    (a)   a request is made for a standard authorisation, and
    (b)   the supervisory body are required by paragraph 50(1) to give the standard authorisation.

(2) The supervisory body must give a copy of the authorisation to each of the following –

    (a)   the relevant person's representative;
    (b)   the managing authority of the relevant hospital or care home;
    (c)   the relevant person;
    (d)   any section 39A IMCA;
    (e)   every interested person consulted by the best interests assessor.

(3) The supervisory body must comply with this paragraph as soon as practicable after they give the standard authorisation.

58 (1) This paragraph applies if –

(a)   a request is made for a standard authorisation, and

(b)   the supervisory body are prohibited by paragraph 50(2) from giving the standard authorisation.

(2) The supervisory body must give notice, stating that they are prohibited from giving the authorisation, to each of the following –

(a)   the managing authority of the relevant hospital or care home;

(b)   the relevant person;

(c)   any section 39A IMCA;

(d)   every interested person consulted by the best interests assessor.

(3) The supervisory body must comply with this paragraph as soon as practicable after it becomes apparent to them that they are prohibited from giving the authorisation.

Duty to give information about effect of authorisation

59 (1) This paragraph applies if a standard authorisation is given.

(2) The managing authority of the relevant hospital or care home must take such steps as are practicable to ensure that the relevant person understands all of the following –

(a)   the effect of the authorisation;

(b)   the right to make an application to the court to exercise its jurisdiction under section 21A;

(c)   the right under Part 8 to request a review;

(d)   the right to have a section 39D IMCA appointed;

(e)   how to have a section 39D IMCA appointed.

(3) Those steps must be taken as soon as is practicable after the authorisation is given.

(4) Those steps must include the giving of appropriate information both orally and in writing.

(5) Any written information given to the relevant person must also be given by the managing authority to the relevant person's representative.

(6) They must give the information to the representative as soon as is practicable after it is given to the relevant person.

(7) Sub-paragraph (8) applies if the managing authority is notified that a section 39D IMCA has been appointed.

(8) As soon as is practicable after being notified, the managing authority must give the section 39D IMCA a copy of the written information given in accordance with sub-paragraph (4).

Records of authorisations

60

A supervisory body must keep a written record of all of the following information –

    (a) the standard authorisations that they have given;

    (b) the requests for standard authorisations in response to which they have not given an authorisation;

    (c) in relation to each standard authorisation given: the matters stated in the authorisation in accordance with paragraph 55.

Variation of an authorisation

61

(1) A standard authorisation may not be varied except in accordance with Part 7 or 8.

(2) This paragraph does not affect the powers of the Court of Protection or of any other court.

Effect of decision about request made under paragraph 25 or 30

62 (1) This paragraph applies where the managing authority request a new standard authorisation under either of the following –

    (a) paragraph 25 (change in place of detention);

    (b) paragraph 30 (existing authorisation subject to review).

(2) If the supervisory body are required by paragraph 50(1) to give the new authorisation, the existing authorisation terminates at the time when the new authorisation comes into force.

(3) If the supervisory body are prohibited by paragraph 50(2) from giving the new authorisation, there is no effect on the existing authorisation's continuation in force.

When an authorisation is in force

63 (1) A standard authorisation comes into force when it is given.

(2) But if the authorisation provides for it to come into force at a later time, it comes into force at that time.

64 (1) A standard authorisation ceases to be in force at the end of the period stated in the authorisation in accordance with paragraph 55(1)(c).

(2) But if the authorisation terminates before then in accordance with paragraph 62(2) or any other provision of this Schedule, it ceases to be in force when the termination takes effect.

(3) This paragraph does not affect the powers of the Court of Protection or of any other court.

65 (1) This paragraph applies if a standard authorisation ceases to be in force.

(2) The supervisory body must give notice that the authorisation has ceased to be in force.

(3) The supervisory body must give that notice to all of the following –

    (a) the managing authority of the relevant hospital or care home;
    (b) the relevant person;
    (c) the relevant person's representative;
    (d) every interested person consulted by the best interests assessor.

(4) The supervisory body must give that notice as soon as practicable after the authorisation ceases to be in force.

When a request for a standard authorisation is 'disposed of'

66 A request for a standard authorisation is to be regarded for the purposes of this Schedule as disposed of if the supervisory body have given –

    (a) a copy of the authorisation in accordance with paragraph 57, or
    (b) notice in accordance with paragraph 58.

Right of third party to require consideration of whether authorisation needed

67 For the purposes of paragraphs 68 to 73 there is an unauthorised deprivation of liberty if –

    (a) a person is already a detained resident in a hospital or care home, and
    (b) the detention of the person is not authorised as mentioned in section 4A.

68 (1) If the following conditions are met, an eligible person may request the supervisory body to decide whether or not there is an unauthorised deprivation of liberty.

(2) The first condition is that the eligible person has notified the managing authority of the relevant hospital or care home that it appears to the eligible person that there is an unauthorised deprivation of liberty.

(3) The second condition is that the eligible person has asked the managing authority to request a standard authorisation in relation to the detention of the relevant person.

(4) The third condition is that the managing authority has not requested a standard authorisation within a reasonable period after the eligible person asks it to do so.

(5) In this paragraph 'eligible person' means any person other than the managing authority of the relevant hospital or care home.

69 (1) This paragraph applies if an eligible person requests the supervisory body to decide whether or not there is an unauthorised deprivation of liberty.

(2) The supervisory body must select and appoint a person to carry out an assessment of whether or not the relevant person is a detained resident.

(3) But the supervisory body need not select and appoint a person to carry out such an assessment in either of these cases.

(4) The first case is where it appears to the supervisory body that the request by the eligible person is frivolous or vexatious.

(5) The second case is where it appears to the supervisory body that –

    (a) the question of whether or not there is an unauthorised deprivation of liberty has already been decided, and

    (b) since that decision, there has been no change of circumstances which would merit the question being decided again.

(6) The supervisory body must not select and appoint a person to carry out an assessment under this paragraph unless it appears to the supervisory body that the person would be –

    (a) suitable to carry out a best interests assessment (if one were obtained in connection with a request for a standard authorisation relating to the relevant person), and

    (b) eligible to carry out such a best interests assessment.

(7) The supervisory body must notify the persons specified in sub-paragraph (8) –

    (a) that the supervisory body have been requested to decide whether or not there is an unauthorised deprivation of liberty;

    (b) of their decision whether or not to select and appoint a person to carry out an assessment under this paragraph;

    (c) if their decision is to select and appoint a person, of the person appointed.

(8) The persons referred to in sub-paragraph (7) are –

    (a) the eligible person who made the request under paragraph 68;

    (b) the person to whom the request relates;

    (c) the managing authority of the relevant hospital or care home;

    (d) any section 39A IMCA.

70 (1) Regulations may be made about the period within which an assessment under paragraph 69 must be carried out.

(2) Regulations made under paragraph 129(3) apply in relation to the selection and appointment of a person under paragraph 69 as they apply to the selection of a person under paragraph 129 to carry out a best interests assessment.

(3) The following provisions apply to an assessment under paragraph 69 as they apply to an assessment carried out in connection with a request for a standard authorisation –

    (a) paragraph 131 (examination and copying of records);

    (b) paragraph 132 (representations);

    (c) paragraphs 134 and 135(1) and (2) (duty to keep records and give copies).

(4) The copies of the assessment which the supervisory body are required to give under paragraph 135(2) must be given as soon as practicable after the supervisory body are themselves given a copy of the assessment.

71 (1) This paragraph applies if –

    (a) the supervisory body obtain an assessment under paragraph 69,

    (b) the assessment comes to the conclusion that the relevant person is a detained resident, and

    (c) it appears to the supervisory body that the detention of the person is not authorised as mentioned in section 4A.

(2) This Schedule (including Part 5) applies as if the managing authority of the relevant hospital or care home had, in accordance with Part 4, requested the supervisory body to give a standard authorisation in relation to the relevant person.

(3) The managing authority of the relevant hospital or care home must supply the supervisory body with the information (if any) which the managing authority would, by virtue of paragraph 31, have had to include in a request for a standard authorisation.

(4) The supervisory body must notify the persons specified in paragraph 69(8) –

    (a) of the outcome of the assessment obtained under paragraph 69, and

    (b) that this Schedule applies as mentioned in sub-paragraph (2).

72 (1) This paragraph applies if –

    (a) the supervisory body obtain an assessment under paragraph 69, and

    (b) the assessment comes to the conclusion that the relevant person is not a detained resident.

(2) The supervisory body must notify the persons specified in paragraph 69(8) of the outcome of the assessment.

73 (1) This paragraph applies if –

    (a) the supervisory body obtain an assessment under paragraph 69,

    (b) the assessment comes to the conclusion that the relevant person is a detained resident, and

    (c) it appears to the supervisory body that the detention of the person is authorised as mentioned in section 4A.

(2) The supervisory body must notify the persons specified in paragraph 69(8) –

    (a) of the outcome of the assessment, and

    (b) that it appears to the supervisory body that the detention is authorised.

PART 5
URGENT AUTHORISATIONS

Managing authority to give authorisation

74 Only the managing authority of the relevant hospital or care home may give an urgent authorisation.

75 The managing authority may give an urgent authorisation only if they are required to do so by paragraph 76 (as read with paragraph 77).

Duty to give authorisation

76 (1) The managing authority must give an urgent authorisation in either of the following cases.

(2) The first case is where –

    (a) the managing authority are required to make a request under paragraph 24 or 25 for a standard authorisation, and

    (b) they believe that the need for the relevant person to be a detained resident is so urgent that it is appropriate for the detention to begin before they make the request.

(3) The second case is where –

    (a) the managing authority have made a request under paragraph 24 or 25 for a standard authorisation, and

    (b) they believe that the need for the relevant person to be a detained resident is so urgent that it is appropriate for the detention to begin before the request is disposed of.

(4) References in this paragraph to the detention of the relevant person are references to the detention to which paragraph 24 or 25 relates.

(5) This paragraph is subject to paragraph 77.

77 (1) This paragraph applies where the managing authority have given an urgent authorisation ('the original authorisation') in connection with a case where a person is, or is to be, a detained resident ('the existing detention').

(2) No new urgent authorisation is to be given under paragraph 76 in connection with the existing detention.

(3) But the managing authority may request the supervisory body to extend the duration of the original authorisation.

(4) Only one request under sub-paragraph (3) may be made in relation to the original authorisation.

(5) Paragraphs 84 to 86 apply to any request made under sub-paragraph (3).

Terms of authorisation

78 (1) If the managing authority decide to give an urgent authorisation, they must decide the period during which the authorisation is to be in force.

(2) That period must not exceed 7 days.

Form of authorisation

79 An urgent authorisation must be in writing.

80 An urgent authorisation must state the following things –

(a) the name of the relevant person;
(b) the name of the relevant hospital or care home;
(c) the period during which the authorisation is to be in force;
(d) the purpose for which the authorisation is given.

81 (1) If the name of the relevant hospital or care home changes, the urgent authorisation is to be read as if it stated the current name of the hospital or care home.

(2) But sub-paragraph (1) is subject to any provision relating to the change of name which is made in any enactment or in any instrument made under an enactment.

Duty to keep records and give copies

82 (1) This paragraph applies if an urgent authorisation is given.

(2) The managing authority must keep a written record of why they have given the urgent authorisation.

(3) As soon as practicable after giving the authorisation, the managing authority must give a copy of the authorisation to all of the following –

(a) the relevant person;
(b) any section 39A IMCA.

Duty to give information about authorisation

83 (1) This paragraph applies if an urgent authorisation is given.

(2) The managing authority of the relevant hospital or care home must take such steps as are practicable to ensure that the relevant person understands all of the following –

(a) the effect of the authorisation;
(b) the right to make an application to the court to exercise its jurisdiction under section 21A.

(3) Those steps must be taken as soon as is practicable after the authorisation is given.

(4) Those steps must include the giving of appropriate information both orally and in writing.

Request for extension of duration

84 (1) This paragraph applies if the managing authority make a request under paragraph 77 for the supervisory body to extend the duration of the original authorisation.

(2) The managing authority must keep a written record of why they have made the request.

(3) The managing authority must give the relevant person notice that they have made the request.

(4) The supervisory body may extend the duration of the original authorisation if it appears to them that –

    (a) the managing authority have made the required request for a standard authorisation,

    (b) there are exceptional reasons why it has not yet been possible for that request to be disposed of, and

    (c) it is essential for the existing detention to continue until the request is disposed of.

(5) The supervisory body must keep a written record that the request has been made to them.

(6) In this paragraph and paragraphs 85 and 86 –

    (a) 'original authorisation' and 'existing detention' have the same meaning as in paragraph 77;

    (b) the required request for a standard authorisation is the request that is referred to in paragraph 76(2) or (3).

85 (1) This paragraph applies if, under paragraph 84, the supervisory body decide to extend the duration of the original authorisation.

(2) The supervisory body must decide the period of the extension.

(3) That period must not exceed 7 days.

(4) The supervisory body must give the managing authority notice stating the period of the extension.

(5) The managing authority must then vary the original authorisation so that it states the extended duration.

(6) Paragraphs 82(3) and 83 apply (with the necessary modifications) to the variation of the original authorisation as they apply to the giving of an urgent authorisation.

(7) The supervisory body must keep a written record of –

    (a) the outcome of the request, and

    (b) the period of the extension.

86 (1) This paragraph applies if, under paragraph 84, the supervisory body decide not to extend the duration of the original authorisation.

(2) The supervisory body must give the managing authority notice stating –

(a) the decision, and
(b) their reasons for making it.

(3) The managing authority must give a copy of that notice to all of the following –

(a) the relevant person;
(b) any section 39A IMCA.

(4) The supervisory body must keep a written record of the outcome of the request.

No variation

87 (1) An urgent authorisation may not be varied except in accordance with paragraph 85.

(2) This paragraph does not affect the powers of the Court of Protection or of any other court.

When an authorisation is in force

88 An urgent authorisation comes into force when it is given.

89

(1) An urgent authorisation ceases to be in force at the end of the period stated in the authorisation in accordance with paragraph 80(c) (subject to any variation in accordance with paragraph 85).

(2) But if the required request is disposed of before the end of that period, the urgent authorisation ceases to be in force as follows.

(3) If the supervisory body are required by paragraph 50(1) to give the requested authorisation, the urgent authorisation ceases to be in force when the requested authorisation comes into force.

(4) If the supervisory body are prohibited by paragraph 50(2) from giving the requested authorisation, the urgent authorisation ceases to be in force when the managing authority receive notice under paragraph 58.

(5) In this paragraph –

'required request' means the request referred to in paragraph 76(2) or (3);
'requested authorisation' means the standard authorisation to which the required request relates.

(6) This paragraph does not affect the powers of the Court of Protection or of any other court.

90 (1) This paragraph applies if an urgent authorisation ceases to be in force.

(2) The supervisory body must give notice that the authorisation has ceased to be in force.

(3) The supervisory body must give that notice to all of the following –

(a) the relevant person;
(b) any section 39A IMCA.

(4) The supervisory body must give that notice as soon as practicable after the authorisation ceases to be in force.

PART 6
ELIGIBILITY REQUIREMENT NOT MET: SUSPENSION OF STANDARD AUTHORISATION

91 (1) This Part applies if the following conditions are met.

(2) The first condition is that a standard authorisation –

(a) has been given, and
(b) has not ceased to be in force.

(3) The second condition is that the managing authority of the relevant hospital or care home are satisfied that the relevant person has ceased to meet the eligibility requirement.

(4) But this Part does not apply if the relevant person is ineligible by virtue of paragraph 5 of Schedule 1A (in which case see Part 8).

92 The managing authority of the relevant hospital or care home must give the supervisory body notice that the relevant person has ceased to meet the eligibility requirement.

93 (1) This paragraph applies if the managing authority give the supervisory body notice under paragraph 92.

(2) The standard authorisation is suspended from the time when the notice is given.

(3) The supervisory body must give notice that the standard authorisation has been suspended to the following persons –

(a) the relevant person;
(b) the relevant person's representative;
(c) the managing authority of the relevant hospital or care home.

94 (1) This paragraph applies if, whilst the standard authorisation is suspended, the managing authority are satisfied that the relevant person meets the eligibility requirement again.

(2) The managing authority must give the supervisory body notice that the relevant person meets the eligibility requirement again.

95 (1) This paragraph applies if the managing authority give the supervisory body notice under paragraph 94.

(2) The standard authorisation ceases to be suspended from the time when the notice is given.

(3) The supervisory body must give notice that the standard authorisation has ceased to be suspended to the following persons –

(a) the relevant person;
(b) the relevant person's representative;
(c) any section 39D IMCA;
(d) the managing authority of the relevant hospital or care home.

(4) The supervisory body must give notice under this paragraph as soon as practicable after they are given notice under paragraph 94.

96 (1) This paragraph applies if no notice is given under paragraph 94 before the end of the relevant 28 day period.

(2) The standard authorisation ceases to have effect at the end of the relevant 28 day period.

(3) The relevant 28 day period is the period of 28 days beginning with the day on which the standard authorisation is suspended under paragraph 93.

97 The effect of suspending the standard authorisation is that Part 1 ceases to apply for as long as the authorisation is suspended.

PART 7
STANDARD AUTHORISATIONS: CHANGE IN SUPERVISORY RESPONSIBILITY

Application of this Part

98 (1) This Part applies if these conditions are met.

(2) The first condition is that a standard authorisation –

(a) has been given, and
(b) has not ceased to be in force.

(3) The second condition is that there is a change in supervisory responsibility.

(4) The third condition is that there is not a change in the place of detention (within the meaning of paragraph 25).

99 For the purposes of this Part there is a change in supervisory responsibility if –

(a) one body ('the old supervisory body') have ceased to be supervisory body in relation to the standard authorisation, and
(b) a different body ('the new supervisory body') have become supervisory body in relation to the standard authorisation.

Effect of change in supervisory responsibility

100 (1) The new supervisory body becomes the supervisory body in relation to the authorisation.

(2) Anything done by or in relation to the old supervisory body in connection with the authorisation has effect, so far as is necessary for continuing its effect after the change, as if done by or in relation to the new supervisory body.

(3) Anything which relates to the authorisation and which is in the process of being done by or in relation to the old supervisory body at the time of the change may be continued by or in relation to the new supervisory body.

(4) But –

(a) the old supervisory body do not, by virtue of this paragraph, cease to be liable for anything done by them in connection with the authorisation before the change; and

(b) the new supervisory body do not, by virtue of this paragraph, become liable for any such thing.

PART 8
STANDARD AUTHORISATIONS: REVIEW

Application of this Part

101 (1) This Part applies if a standard authorisation –

(a) has been given, and
(b) has not ceased to be in force.

(2) Paragraphs 102 to 122 are subject to paragraphs 123 to 125.

Review by supervisory body

102 (1) The supervisory body may at any time carry out a review of the standard authorisation in accordance with this Part.

(2) The supervisory body must carry out such a review if they are requested to do so by an eligible person.

(3) Each of the following is an eligible person –

(a) the relevant person;
(b) the relevant person's representative;
(c) the managing authority of the relevant hospital or care home.

Request for review

103 (1) An eligible person may, at any time, request the supervisory body to carry out a review of the standard authorisation in accordance with this Part.

(2) The managing authority of the relevant hospital or care home must make such a request if one or more of the qualifying requirements appear to them to be reviewable.

Grounds for review

104 (1) Paragraphs 105 to 107 set out the grounds on which the qualifying requirements are reviewable.

(2) A qualifying requirement is not reviewable on any other ground.

Non-qualification ground

105 (1) Any of the following qualifying requirements is reviewable on the ground that the relevant person does not meet the requirement –

    (a) the age requirement;
    (b) the mental health requirement;
    (c) the mental capacity requirement;
    (d) the best interests requirement;
    (e) the no refusals requirement.

(2) The eligibility requirement is reviewable on the ground that the relevant person is ineligible by virtue of paragraph 5 of Schedule 1A.

(3) The ground in sub-paragraph (1) and the ground in sub-paragraph (2) are referred to as the non-qualification ground.

Change of reason ground

106 (1) Any of the following qualifying requirements is reviewable on the ground set out in sub-paragraph (2) –

    (a) the mental health requirement;
    (b) the mental capacity requirement;
    (c) the best interests requirement;
    (d) the eligibility requirement;
    (e) the no refusals requirement.

(2) The ground is that the reason why the relevant person meets the requirement is not the reason stated in the standard authorisation.

(3) This ground is referred to as the change of reason ground.

Variation of conditions ground

107 (1) The best interests requirement is reviewable on the ground that –

    (a) there has been a change in the relevant person's case, and
    (b) because of that change, it would be appropriate to vary the conditions to which the standard authorisation is subject.

(2) This ground is referred to as the variation of conditions ground.

(3) A reference to varying the conditions to which the standard authorisation is subject is a reference to –

    (a) amendment of an existing condition,
    (b) omission of an existing condition, or

(c) inclusion of a new condition (whether or not there are already any existing conditions).

Notice that review to be carried out

108 (1) If the supervisory body are to carry out a review of the standard authorisation, they must give notice of the review to the following persons –

    (a) the relevant person;
    (b) the relevant person's representative;
    (c) the managing authority of the relevant hospital or care home.

(2) The supervisory body must give the notice –

    (a) before they begin the review, or
    (b) if that is not practicable, as soon as practicable after they have begun it.

(3) This paragraph does not require the supervisory body to give notice to any person who has requested the review.

Starting a review

109 To start a review of the standard authorisation, the supervisory body must decide which, if any, of the qualifying requirements appear to be reviewable.

No reviewable qualifying requirements

110 (1) This paragraph applies if no qualifying requirements appear to be reviewable.

(2) This Part does not require the supervisory body to take any action in respect of the standard authorisation.

One or more reviewable qualifying requirements

111 (1) This paragraph applies if one or more qualifying requirements appear to be reviewable.

(2) The supervisory body must secure that a separate review assessment is carried out in relation to each qualifying requirement which appears to be reviewable.

(3) But sub-paragraph (2) does not require the supervisory body to secure that a best interests review assessment is carried out in a case where the best interests requirement appears to the supervisory body to be non-assessable.

(4) The best interests requirement is non-assessable if –

    (a) the requirement is reviewable only on the variation of conditions ground, and
    (b) the change in the relevant person's case is not significant.

(5) In making any decision whether the change in the relevant person's case is significant, regard must be had to –

    (a) the nature of the change, and

(b) the period that the change is likely to last for.

Review assessments

112 (1) A review assessment is an assessment of whether the relevant person meets a qualifying requirement.

(2) In relation to a review assessment –

(a) a negative conclusion is a conclusion that the relevant person does not meet the qualifying requirement to which the assessment relates;
(b) a positive conclusion is a conclusion that the relevant person meets the qualifying requirement to which the assessment relates.

(3) An age review assessment is a review assessment carried out in relation to the age requirement.

(4) A mental health review assessment is a review assessment carried out in relation to the mental health requirement.

(5) A mental capacity review assessment is a review assessment carried out in relation to the mental capacity requirement.

(6) A best interests review assessment is a review assessment carried out in relation to the best interests requirement.

(7) An eligibility review assessment is a review assessment carried out in relation to the eligibility requirement.

(8) A no refusals review assessment is a review assessment carried out in relation to the no refusals requirement.

113 (1) In carrying out a review assessment, the assessor must comply with any duties which would be imposed upon him under Part 4 if the assessment were being carried out in connection with a request for a standard authorisation.

(2) But in the case of a best interests review assessment, paragraphs 43 and 44 do not apply.

(3) Instead of what is required by paragraph 43, the best interests review assessment must include recommendations about whether –and, if so, how –it would be appropriate to vary the conditions to which the standard authorisation is subject.

Best interests requirement reviewable but non-assessable

114 (1) This paragraph applies in a case where –

(a) the best interests requirement appears to be reviewable, but
(b) in accordance with paragraph 111(3), the supervisory body are not required to secure that a best interests review assessment is carried out.

(2) The supervisory body may vary the conditions to which the standard authorisation is subject in such ways (if any) as the supervisory body think are appropriate in the circumstances.

Best interests review assessment positive

115 (1) This paragraph applies in a case where –

   (a) a best interests review assessment is carried out, and
   (b) the assessment comes to a positive conclusion.

(2) The supervisory body must decide the following questions –

   (a) whether or not the best interests requirement is reviewable on the change of reason ground;
   (b) whether or not the best interests requirement is reviewable on the variation of conditions ground;
   (c) if so, whether or not the change in the person's case is significant.

(3) If the supervisory body decide that the best interests requirement is reviewable on the change of reason ground, they must vary the standard authorisation so that it states the reason why the relevant person now meets that requirement.

(4) If the supervisory body decide that –

   (a) the best interests requirement is reviewable on the variation of conditions ground, and
   (b) the change in the relevant person's case is not significant,

they may vary the conditions to which the standard authorisation is subject in such ways (if any) as they think are appropriate in the circumstances.

(5) If the supervisory body decide that –

   (a) the best interests requirement is reviewable on the variation of conditions ground, and
   (b) the change in the relevant person's case is significant,

they must vary the conditions to which the standard authorisation is subject in such ways as they think are appropriate in the circumstances.

(6) If the supervisory body decide that the best interests requirement is not reviewable on –

   (a) the change of reason ground, or
   (b) the variation of conditions ground,

this Part does not require the supervisory body to take any action in respect of the standard authorisation so far as the best interests requirement relates to it.

Mental health, mental capacity, eligibility or no refusals review assessment positive

116 (1) This paragraph applies if the following conditions are met.

(2) The first condition is that one or more of the following are carried out –

(a) a mental health review assessment;
(b) a mental capacity review assessment;
(c) an eligibility review assessment;
(d) a no refusals review assessment.

(3) The second condition is that each assessment carried out comes to a positive conclusion.

(4) The supervisory body must decide whether or not each of the assessed qualifying requirements is reviewable on the change of reason ground.

(5) If the supervisory body decide that any of the assessed qualifying requirements is reviewable on the change of reason ground, they must vary the standard authorisation so that it states the reason why the relevant person now meets the requirement or requirements in question.

(6) If the supervisory body decide that none of the assessed qualifying requirements are reviewable on the change of reason ground, this Part does not require the supervisory body to take any action in respect of the standard authorisation so far as those requirements relate to it.

(7) An assessed qualifying requirement is a qualifying requirement in relation to which a review assessment is carried out.

One or more review assessments negative

117 (1) This paragraph applies if one or more of the review assessments carried out comes to a negative conclusion.

(2) The supervisory body must terminate the standard authorisation with immediate effect.

Completion of a review

118 (1) The review of the standard authorisation is complete in any of the following cases.

(2) The first case is where paragraph 110 applies.

(3) The second case is where –

(a) paragraph 111 applies, and
(b) paragraph 117 requires the supervisory body to terminate the standard authorisation.

(4) In such a case, the supervisory body need not comply with any of the other provisions of paragraphs 114 to 116 which would be applicable to the review (were it not for this sub-paragraph).

(5) The third case is where –

- (a) paragraph 111 applies,
- (b) paragraph 117 does not require the supervisory body to terminate the standard authorisation, and
- (c) the supervisory body comply with all of the provisions of paragraphs 114 to 116 (so far as they are applicable to the review).

Variations under this Part

119 Any variation of the standard authorisation made under this Part must be in writing.

Notice of outcome of review

120 (1) When the review of the standard authorisation is complete, the supervisory body must give notice to all of the following –

- (a) the managing authority of the relevant hospital or care home;
- (b) the relevant person;
- (c) the relevant person's representative;
- (d) any section 39D IMCA.

(2) That notice must state –

- (a) the outcome of the review, and
- (b) what variation (if any) has been made to the authorisation under this Part.

Records

121 A supervisory body must keep a written record of the following information –

- (a) each request for a review that is made to them;
- (b) the outcome of each request;
- (c) each review which they carry out;
- (d) the outcome of each review which they carry out;
- (e) any variation of an authorisation made in consequence of a review.

Relationship between review and suspension under Part 6

122 (1) This paragraph applies if a standard authorisation is suspended in accordance with Part 6.

(2) No review may be requested under this Part whilst the standard authorisation is suspended.

(3) If a review has already been requested, or is being carried out, when the standard authorisation is suspended, no steps are to be taken in connection with that review whilst the authorisation is suspended.

Relationship between review and request for new authorisation

123 (1) This paragraph applies if, in accordance with paragraph 24 (as read with paragraph 29), the managing authority of the relevant hospital or care home make a request for a new standard authorisation which would be in force after the expiry of the existing authorisation.

(2) No review may be requested under this Part until the request for the new standard authorisation has been disposed of.

(3) If a review has already been requested, or is being carried out, when the new standard authorisation is requested, no steps are to be taken in connection with that review until the request for the new standard authorisation has been disposed of.

124 (1) This paragraph applies if –

(a) a review under this Part has been requested, or is being carried out, and
(b) the managing authority of the relevant hospital or care home make a request under paragraph 30 for a new standard authorisation which would be in force on or before, and after, the expiry of the existing authorisation.

(2) No steps are to be taken in connection with the review under this Part until the request for the new standard authorisation has been disposed of.

125 In paragraphs 123 and 124 –

(a) the existing authorisation is the authorisation referred to in paragraph 101;
(b) the expiry of the existing authorisation is the time when it is expected to cease to be in force.

PART 9
ASSESSMENTS UNDER THIS SCHEDULE

Introduction

126 This Part contains provision about assessments under this Schedule.

127 An assessment under this Schedule is either of the following –

(a) an assessment carried out in connection with a request for a standard authorisation under Part 4;
(b) a review assessment carried out in connection with a review of a standard authorisation under Part 8.

128 In this Part, in relation to an assessment under this Schedule –

'assessor' means the person carrying out the assessment;
'relevant procedure' means –
(a) the request for the standard authorisation, or
(b) the review of the standard authorisation;

'supervisory body' means the supervisory body responsible for securing that the assessment is carried out.

Supervisory body to select assessor

129 (1) It is for the supervisory body to select a person to carry out an assessment under this Schedule.

(2) The supervisory body must not select a person to carry out an assessment unless the person –

(a) appears to the supervisory body to be suitable to carry out the assessment (having regard, in particular, to the type of assessment and the person to be assessed), and

(b) is eligible to carry out the assessment.

(3) Regulations may make provision about the selection, and eligibility, of persons to carry out assessments under this Schedule.

(4) Sub-paragraphs (5) and (6) apply if two or more assessments are to be obtained for the purposes of the relevant procedure.

(5) In a case where the assessments to be obtained include a mental health assessment and a best interests assessment, the supervisory body must not select the same person to carry out both assessments.

(6) Except as prohibited by sub-paragraph (5), the supervisory body may select the same person to carry out any number of the assessments which the person appears to be suitable, and is eligible, to carry out.

130 (1) This paragraph applies to regulations under paragraph 129(3).

(2) The regulations may make provision relating to a person's –

(a) qualifications,

(b) skills,

(c) training,

(d) experience,

(e) relationship to, or connection with, the relevant person or any other person,

(f) involvement in the care or treatment of the relevant person,

(g) connection with the supervisory body, or

(h) connection with the relevant hospital or care home, or with any other establishment or undertaking.

(3) The provision that the regulations may make in relation to a person's training may provide for particular training to be specified by the appropriate authority otherwise than in the regulations.

(4) In sub-paragraph (3) the 'appropriate authority' means –

(a) in relation to England: the Secretary of State;

(b) in relation to Wales: the National Assembly for Wales.

(5) The regulations may make provision requiring a person to be insured in respect of liabilities that may arise in connection with the carrying out of an assessment.

(6) In relation to cases where two or more assessments are to be obtained for the purposes of the relevant procedure, the regulations may limit the number, kind or combination of assessments which a particular person is eligible to carry out.

(7) Sub-paragraphs (2) to (6) do not limit the generality of the provision that may be made in the regulations.

Examination and copying of records

131 An assessor may, at all reasonable times, examine and take copies of –

(a) any health record,
(b) any record of, or held by, a local authority and compiled in accordance with a social services function, and
(c) any record held by a person registered under Part 2 of the Care Standards Act 2000 or Chapter 2 of Part 1 of the Health and Social Care Act 2008,

which the assessor considers may be relevant to the assessment which is being carried out.

Representations

132 In carrying out an assessment under this Schedule, the assessor must take into account any information given, or submissions made, by any of the following –

(a) the relevant person's representative;
(b) any section 39A IMCA;
(c) any section 39C IMCA;
(d) any section 39D IMCA.

Assessments to stop if any comes to negative conclusion

133 (1) This paragraph applies if an assessment under this Schedule comes to the conclusion that the relevant person does not meet one of the qualifying requirements.

(2) This Schedule does not require the supervisory body to secure that any other assessments under this Schedule are carried out in relation to the relevant procedure.

(3) The supervisory body must give notice to any assessor who is carrying out another assessment in connection with the relevant procedure that they are to cease carrying out that assessment.

(4) If an assessor receives such notice, this Schedule does not require the assessor to continue carrying out that assessment.

Duty to keep records and give copies

134 (1) This paragraph applies if an assessor has carried out an assessment under this Schedule (whatever conclusions the assessment has come to).

(2) The assessor must keep a written record of the assessment.

(3) As soon as practicable after carrying out the assessment, the assessor must give copies of the assessment to the supervisory body.

135 (1) This paragraph applies to the supervisory body if they are given a copy of an assessment under this Schedule.

(2) The supervisory body must give copies of the assessment to all of the following –

(a)   the managing authority of the relevant hospital or care home;
(b)   the relevant person;
(c)   any section 39A IMCA;
(d)   the relevant person's representative.

(3) If –

(a)   the assessment is obtained in relation to a request for a standard authorisation, and
(b)   the supervisory body are required by paragraph 50(1) to give the standard authorisation,

the supervisory body must give the copies of the assessment when they give copies of the authorisation in accordance with paragraph 57.

(4) If –

(a)   the assessment is obtained in relation to a request for a standard authorisation, and
(b)   the supervisory body are prohibited by paragraph 50(2) from giving the standard authorisation,

the supervisory body must give the copies of the assessment when they give notice in accordance with paragraph 58.

(5) If the assessment is obtained in connection with the review of a standard authorisation, the supervisory body must give the copies of the assessment when they give notice in accordance with paragraph 120.

136 (1) This paragraph applies to the supervisory body if –

(a)   they are given a copy of a best interests assessment, and
(b)   the assessment includes, in accordance with paragraph 44(2), a statement that it appears to the assessor that there is an unauthorised deprivation of liberty.

(2) The supervisory body must notify all of the persons listed in sub-paragraph (3) that the assessment includes such a statement.

(3) Those persons are –

(a) the managing authority of the relevant hospital or care home;
(b) the relevant person;
(c) any section 39A IMCA;
(d) any interested person consulted by the best interests assessor.

(4) The supervisory body must comply with this paragraph when (or at some time before) they comply with paragraph 135.

PART 10
RELEVANT PERSON'S REPRESENTATIVE

The representative

137 In this Schedule the relevant person's representative is the person appointed as such in accordance with this Part.

138 (1) Regulations may make provision about the selection and appointment of representatives.

(2) In this Part such regulations are referred to as 'appointment regulations'.

Supervisory body to appoint representative

139 (1) The supervisory body must appoint a person to be the relevant person's representative as soon as practicable after a standard authorisation is given.

(2) The supervisory body must appoint a person to be the relevant person's representative if a vacancy arises whilst a standard authorisation is in force.

(3) Where a vacancy arises, the appointment under sub-paragraph (2) is to be made as soon as practicable after the supervisory body becomes aware of the vacancy.

140 (1) The selection of a person for appointment under paragraph 139 must not be made unless it appears to the person making the selection that the prospective representative would, if appointed –

(a) maintain contact with the relevant person,
(b) represent the relevant person in matters relating to or connected with this Schedule, and
(c) support the relevant person in matters relating to or connected with this Schedule.

141 (1) Any appointment of a representative for a relevant person is in addition to, and does not affect, any appointment of a donee or deputy.

(2) The functions of any representative are in addition to, and do not affect –

(a) the authority of any donee,
(b) the powers of any deputy, or
(c) any powers of the court.

Appointment regulations

142 Appointment regulations may provide that the procedure for appointing a representative may begin at any time after a request for a standard authorisation is made (including a time before the request has been disposed of).

143 (1) Appointment regulations may make provision about who is to select a person for appointment as a representative.

(2) But regulations under this paragraph may only provide for the following to make a selection –

(a) the relevant person, if he has capacity in relation to the question of which person should be his representative;
(b) a donee of a lasting power of attorney granted by the relevant person, if it is within the scope of his authority to select a person;
(c) a deputy, if it is within the scope of his authority to select a person;
(d) a best interests assessor;
(e) the supervisory body.

(3) Regulations under this paragraph may provide that a selection by the relevant person, a donee or a deputy is subject to approval by a best interests assessor or the supervisory body.

(4) Regulations under this paragraph may provide that, if more than one selection is necessary in connection with the appointment of a particular representative –

(a) the same person may make more than one selection;
(b) different persons may make different selections.

(5) For the purposes of this paragraph a best interests assessor is a person carrying out a best interests assessment in connection with the standard authorisation in question (including the giving of that authorisation).

144 (1) Appointment regulations may make provision about who may, or may not, be –

(a) selected for appointment as a representative, or
(b) appointed as a representative.

(2) Regulations under this paragraph may relate to any of the following matters –

(a) a person's age;
(b) a person's suitability;
(c) a person's independence;
(d) a person's willingness;
(e) a person's qualifications.

145 Appointment regulations may make provision about the formalities of appointing a person as a representative.

146 In a case where a best interests assessor is to select a person to be appointed as a representative, appointment regulations may provide for the variation of the assessor's duties in relation to the assessment which he is carrying out.

Monitoring of representatives

147

Regulations may make provision requiring the managing authority of the relevant hospital or care home to –

(a) monitor, and
(b) report to the supervisory body on,

the extent to which a representative is maintaining contact with the relevant person.

Termination

148 Regulations may make provision about the circumstances in which the appointment of a person as the relevant person's representative ends or may be ended.

149 Regulations may make provision about the formalities of ending the appointment of a person as a representative.

Suspension of representative's functions

150 (1) Regulations may make provision about the circumstances in which functions exercisable by, or in relation to, the relevant person's representative (whether under this Schedule or not) may be –

(a) suspended, and
(b) if suspended, revived.

(2) The regulations may make provision about the formalities for giving effect to the suspension or revival of a function.

(3) The regulations may make provision about the effect of the suspension or revival of a function.

Payment of representative

151 Regulations may make provision for payments to be made to, or in relation to, persons exercising functions as the relevant person's representative.

Regulations under this Part

152 The provisions of this Part which specify provision that may be made in regulations under this Part do not affect the generality of the power to make such regulations.

Effect of appointment of section 39C IMCA

153 Paragraphs 159 and 160 make provision about the exercise of functions by, or towards, the relevant person's representative during periods when –

(a)   no person is appointed as the relevant person's representative, but
(b)   a person is appointed as a section 39C IMCA.

PART 11
IMCAS

Application of Part

154 This Part applies for the purposes of this Schedule.

The IMCAs

155 A section 39A IMCA is an independent mental capacity advocate appointed under section 39A.

156 A section 39C IMCA is an independent mental capacity advocate appointed under section 39C

157 A section 39D IMCA is an independent mental capacity advocate appointed under section 39D.

158 An IMCA is a section 39A IMCA or a section 39C IMCA or a section 39D IMCA.

Section 39C IMCA: functions

159 (1) This paragraph applies if, and for as long as, there is a section 39C IMCA.

(2) In the application of the relevant provisions, references to the relevant person's representative are to be read as references to the section 39C IMCA.

(3) But sub-paragraph (2) does not apply to any function under the relevant provisions for as long as the function is suspended in accordance with provision made under Part 10.

(4) In this paragraph and paragraph 160 the relevant provisions are –

(a)   paragraph 102(3)(b) (request for review under Part 8);
(b)   paragraph 108(1)(b) (notice of review under Part 8);
(c)   paragraph 120(1)(c) (notice of outcome of review under Part 8).

160 (1) This paragraph applies if –

(a)   a person is appointed as the relevant person's representative, and
(b)   a person accordingly ceases to hold an appointment as a section 39C IMCA.

(2) Where a function under a relevant provision has been exercised by, or towards, the section 39C IMCA, there is no requirement for that function to be exercised again by, or towards, the relevant person's representative.

Section 39A IMCA: restriction of functions

161 (1) This paragraph applies if –

(a) there is a section 39A IMCA, and
(b) a person is appointed under Part 10 to be the relevant person's representative (whether or not that person, or any person subsequently appointed, is currently the relevant person's representative).

(2) The duties imposed on, and the powers exercisable by, the section 39A IMCA do not apply.

(3) The duties imposed on, and the powers exercisable by, any other person do not apply, so far as they fall to be performed or exercised towards the section 39A IMCA.

(4) But sub-paragraph (2) does not apply to any power of challenge exercisable by the section 39A IMCA.

(5) And sub-paragraph (3) does not apply to any duty or power of any other person so far as it relates to any power of challenge exercisable by the section 39A IMCA.

(6) Before exercising any power of challenge, the section 39A IMCA must take the views of the relevant person's representative into account.

(7) A power of challenge is a power to make an application to the court to exercise its jurisdiction under section 21A in connection with the giving of the standard authorisation.

PART 12
MISCELLANEOUS

Monitoring of operation of Schedule

162 (1) Regulations may make provision for, and in connection with, requiring one or more prescribed bodies to monitor, and report on, the operation of this Schedule in relation to England.

(2) The regulations may, in particular, give a prescribed body authority to do one or more of the following things –

(a) to visit hospitals and care homes;
(b) to visit and interview persons accommodated in hospitals and care homes;
(c) to require the production of, and to inspect, records relating to the care or treatment of persons.

(3) 'Prescribed' means prescribed in regulations under this paragraph.

163 (1) Regulations may make provision for, and in connection with, enabling the National Assembly for Wales to monitor, and report on, the operation of this Schedule in relation to Wales.

(2) The National Assembly may direct one or more persons or bodies to carry out the Assembly's functions under regulations under this paragraph.

Disclosure of information

164 (1) Regulations may require either or both of the following to disclose prescribed information to prescribed bodies –

   (a) supervisory bodies;
   (b) managing authorities of hospitals or care homes.

(2) 'Prescribed' means prescribed in regulations under this paragraph.

(3) Regulations under this paragraph may only prescribe information relating to matters with which this Schedule is concerned.

Directions by National Assembly in relation to supervisory functions

165 (1) The National Assembly for Wales may direct a Local Health Board to exercise in relation to its area any supervisory functions which are specified in the direction.

(2) Directions under this paragraph must not preclude the National Assembly from exercising the functions specified in the directions.

(3) In this paragraph 'supervisory functions' means functions which the National Assembly have as supervisory body, so far as they are exercisable in relation to hospitals (whether NHS or independent hospitals, and whether in Wales or England).

166 (1) This paragraph applies where, under paragraph 165, a Local Health Board ('the specified LHB') is directed to exercise supervisory functions ('delegated functions').

(2) The National Assembly for Wales may give directions to the specified LHB about the Board's exercise of delegated functions.

(3) The National Assembly may give directions for any delegated functions to be exercised, on behalf of the specified LHB, by a committee, sub-committee or officer of that Board.

(4) The National Assembly may give directions providing for any delegated functions to be exercised by the specified LHB jointly with one or more other Local Health Boards.

(5) Where, under sub-paragraph (4), delegated functions are exercisable jointly, the National Assembly may give directions providing for the functions to be exercised, on behalf of the Local Health Boards in question, by a joint committee or joint sub-committee.

167 (1) Directions under paragraph 165 must be given in regulations.

(2) Directions under paragraph 166 may be given –

(a) in regulations, or
(b) by instrument in writing.

168 The power under paragraph 165 or paragraph 166 to give directions includes power to vary or revoke directions given under that paragraph.

Notices

169 Any notice under this Schedule must be in writing.

Regulations

170 (1) This paragraph applies to all regulations under this Schedule, except regulations under paragraph 162, 163, 167 or 183.

(2) It is for the Secretary of State to make such regulations in relation to authorisations under this Schedule which relate to hospitals and care homes situated in England.

(3) It is for the National Assembly for Wales to make such regulations in relation to authorisations under this Schedule which relate to hospitals and care homes situated in Wales.

171 It is for the Secretary of State to make regulations under paragraph 162.

172 It is for the National Assembly for Wales to make regulations under paragraph 163 or 167.

173 (1) This paragraph applies to regulations under paragraph 183.

(2) It is for the Secretary of State to make such regulations in relation to cases where a question as to the ordinary residence of a person is to be determined by the Secretary of State.

(3) It is for the National Assembly for Wales to make such regulations in relation to cases where a question as to the ordinary residence of a person is to be determined by the National Assembly.

PART 13
INTERPRETATION

Introduction

174 This Part applies for the purposes of this Schedule.

Hospitals and their managing authorities

175 (1) 'Hospital' means –

(a) an NHS hospital, or

   (b) an independent hospital.

(2) 'NHS hospital' means –

   (a) a health service hospital as defined by section 275 of the National Health Service Act 2006 or section 206 of the National Health Service (Wales) Act 2006, or

   (b) a hospital as defined by section 206 of the National Health Service (Wales) Act 2006 vested in a Local Health Board.

(3) 'Independent hospital' –

   (a) in relation to England, means a hospital as defined by section 275 of the National Health Service Act 2006 that is not an NHS hospital; and

   (b) in relation to Wales, means a hospital as defined by section 2 of the Care Standards Act 2000 that is not an NHS hospital.

176 (1) 'Managing authority', in relation to an NHS hospital, means –

   (a) if the hospital –

      (i) is vested in the appropriate national authority for the purposes of its functions under the National Health Service Act 2006 or of the National Health Service (Wales) Act 2006, or

     (ii) consists of any accommodation provided by a local authority and used as a hospital by or on behalf of the appropriate national authority under either of those Acts,

     the Local Health Board or Special Health Authority responsible for the administration of the hospital;

 (aa) in relation to England, if the hospital falls within paragraph (a)(i) or (ii) and no Special Health Authority has responsibility for its administration, the Secretary of State;

   (b) if the hospital is vested in a National Health Service trust or NHS foundation trust, that trust;

   (c) if the hospital is vested in a Local Health Board, that Board.

(2) For this purpose the appropriate national authority is –

   (a) in relation to England: the Secretary of State;

   (b) in relation to Wales: the National Assembly for Wales;

   (c) in relation to England and Wales: the Secretary of State and the National Assembly acting jointly.

177 'Managing authority', in relation to an independent hospital, means –

   (a) in relation to England, the person registered, or required to be registered, under Chapter 2 of Part 1 of the Health and Social Care Act 2008 in respect of regulated activities (within the meaning of that Part) carried on in the hospital, and

   (b) in relation to Wales, the person registered, or required to be registered, under Part 2 of the Care Standards Act 2000 in respect of the hospital.

Care homes and their managing authorities

178 'Care home' has the meaning given by section 3 of the Care Standards Act 2000.

179 'Managing authority, in relation to a care home, means –

   (a) in relation to England, the person registered, or required to be registered, under Chapter 2 of Part 1 of the Health and Social Care Act 2008 in respect of the provision of residential accommodation, together with nursing or personal care, in the care home, and

   (b) in relation to Wales, the person registered, or required to be registered, under Part 2 of the Care Standards Act 2000 in respect of the care home.

Supervisory bodies: hospitals

180 (1) The identity of the supervisory body is determined under this paragraph in cases where the relevant hospital is situated in England.

(2) If the relevant person is ordinarily resident in the area of a local authority in England, the supervisory body are that local authority.

(3) If the relevant person is not ordinarily resident in England and the National Assembly for Wales or a Local Health Board commission the relevant care or treatment, the National Assembly are the supervisory body.

(4) In any other case, the supervisory body is the local authority for the area in which the relevant hospital is situated.

(4A) 'Local authority' means –

   (a) the council of a county;
   (b) the council of a district for which there is no county council;
   (c) the council of a London borough;
   (d) the Common Council of the City of London;
   (e) the Council of the Isles of Scilly.

(5) If a hospital is situated in the areas of two (or more) local authorities, it is to be regarded for the purposes of sub-paragraph (4) as situated in whichever of the areas the greater (or greatest) part of the hospital is situated.

181 (1) The identity of the supervisory body is determined under this paragraph in cases where the relevant hospital is situated in Wales.

(2) The National Assembly for Wales are the supervisory body.

(3) But if the relevant person is ordinarily resident in the area of a local authority in England, the supervisory body are that local authority.

(4) 'Local authority' means –

   (a) the council of a county;
   (b) the council of a district for which there is no county council;
   (c) the council of a London borough;

    (d) the Common Council of the City of London;
    (e) the Council of the Isles of Scilly.

Supervisory bodies: care homes

182 (1) The identity of the supervisory body is determined under this paragraph in cases where the relevant care home is situated in England or in Wales.

(2) The supervisory body are the local authority for the area in which the relevant person is ordinarily resident.

(3) But if the relevant person is not ordinarily resident in the area of a local authority, the supervisory body are the local authority for the area in which the care home is situated.

(4) In relation to England 'local authority' means –

    (a) the council of a county;
    (b) the council of a district for which there is no county council;
    (c) the council of a London borough;
    (d) the Common Council of the City of London;
    (e) the Council of the Isles of Scilly.

(5) In relation to Wales 'local authority' means the council of a county or county borough.

(6) If a care home is situated in the areas of two (or more) local authorities, it is to be regarded for the purposes of sub-paragraph (3) as situated in whichever of the areas the greater (or greatest) part of the care home is situated.

Supervisory bodies: determination of place of ordinary residence

183 (1) Subsections (5) and (6) of section 24 of the National Assistance Act 1948 (deemed place of ordinary residence) apply to any determination of where a person is ordinarily resident for the purposes of paragraphs 180, 181 and 182 as those subsections apply to such a determination for the purposes specified in those subsections.

(2) In the application of section 24(6) of the 1948 Act by virtue of subparagraph (1) to any determination of where a person is ordinarily resident for the purposes of paragraph 182, section 24(6) is to be read as if it referred to a hospital vested in a Local Health Board as well as to hospitals vested in the Secretary of State and the other bodies mentioned in section 24(6).

(3) Any question arising as to the ordinary residence of a person is to be determined by the Secretary of State or by the National Assembly for Wales.

(4) The Secretary of State and the National Assembly must make and publish arrangements for determining which cases are to be dealt with by the Secretary of State and which are to be dealt with by the National Assembly.

(5) Those arrangements may include provision for the Secretary of State and the National Assembly to agree, in relation to any question that has arisen, which of them is to deal with the case.

(6) Regulations may make provision about arrangements that are to have effect before, upon, or after the determination of any question as to the ordinary residence of a person.

(7) The regulations may, in particular, authorise or require a local authority to do any or all of the following things –

(a) to act as supervisory body even though it may wish to dispute that it is the supervisory body;
(b) to become the supervisory body in place of another local authority;
(c) to recover from another local authority expenditure incurred in exercising functions as the supervisory body.

Same body managing authority and supervisory body

184 (1) This paragraph applies if, in connection with a particular person's detention as a resident in a hospital or care home, the same body are both –

(a) the managing authority of the relevant hospital or care home, and
(b) the supervisory body.

(2) The fact that a single body are acting in both capacities does not prevent the body from carrying out functions under this Schedule in each capacity.

(3) But, in such a case, this Schedule has effect subject to any modifications contained in regulations that may be made for this purpose.

Interested persons

185 Each of the following is an interested person –

(a) the relevant person's spouse or civil partner;
(b) where the relevant person and another person are not married to each other, nor in a civil partnership with each other, but are living together as if they were a married couple: that other person;
(d) the relevant person's children and step-children;
(e) the relevant person's parents and step-parents;
(f) the relevant person's brothers and sisters, half-brothers and half-sisters, and stepbrothers and stepsisters;
(g) the relevant person's grandparents;
(h) a deputy appointed for the relevant person by the court;
(i) a donee of a lasting power of attorney granted by the relevant person.

186 (1) An interested person consulted by the best interests assessor is any person whose name is stated in the relevant best interests assessment in accordance with paragraph 40 (interested persons whom the assessor consulted in carrying out the assessment).

(2) The relevant best interests assessment is the most recent best interests assessment carried out in connection with the standard authorisation in question (whether the assessment was carried out under Part 4 or Part 8).

187 Where this Schedule imposes on a person a duty towards an interested person, the duty does not apply if the person on whom the duty is imposed –

    (a)   is not aware of the interested person's identity or of a way of contacting him, and

    (b)   cannot reasonably ascertain it.

188 The following table contains an index of provisions defining or otherwise explaining expressions used in this Schedule –

age assessment	paragraph 34
age requirement	paragraph 13
age review assessment	paragraph 112(3)
appointment regulations	paragraph 138
assessment under this Schedule	paragraph 127
assessor (except in Part 8)	paragraph 33
assessor (in Part 8)	paragraphs 33 and 128
authorisation under this Schedule	paragraph 10
best interests (determination of)	section 4
best interests assessment	paragraph 38
best interests requirement	paragraph 16
best interests review assessment	paragraph 112(6)
care home	paragraph 178
change of reason ground	paragraph 106
complete (in relation to a review of a standard authorisation)	paragraph 118
deprivation of a person's liberty	section 64(5) and (6)
deputy	section 16(2)(b)
detained resident	paragraph 6
disposed of (in relation to a request for a standard authorisation)	paragraph 66
eligibility assessment	paragraph 46
eligibility requirement	paragraph 17
eligibility review assessment	paragraph 112(7)
eligible person (in relation to paragraphs 68 to 73)	paragraph 68

Schedule 1
Lasting Powers of Attorney: Formalities

Section 9

PART 1
MAKING INSTRUMENTS

General requirements as to making instruments

1 (1) An instrument is not made in accordance with this Schedule unless –

(a) it is in the prescribed form,
(b) it complies with paragraph 2, and

(c) any prescribed requirements in connection with its execution are satisfied.

(2) Regulations may make different provision according to whether –

(a) the instrument relates to personal welfare or to property and affairs (or to both);
(b) only one or more than one donee is to be appointed (and if more than one, whether jointly or jointly and severally).

(3) In this Schedule –

(a) 'prescribed' means prescribed by regulations, and
(b) 'regulations' means regulations made for the purposes of this Schedule by the Lord Chancellor.

Requirements as to content of instruments

2 (1) The instrument must include –

(a) the prescribed information about the purpose of the instrument and the effect of a lasting power of attorney,
(b) a statement by the donor to the effect that he –
  (i) has read the prescribed information or a prescribed part of it (or has had it read to him), and
  (ii) intends the authority conferred under the instrument to include authority to make decisions on his behalf in circumstances where he no longer has capacity,
(c) a statement by the donor –
  (i) naming a person or persons whom the donor wishes to be notified of any application for the registration of the instrument, or
  (ii) stating that there are no persons whom he wishes to be notified of any such application,
(d) a statement by the donee (or, if more than one, each of them) to the effect that he –
  (i) has read the prescribed information or a prescribed part of it (or has had it read to him), and
  (ii) understands the duties imposed on a donee of a lasting power of attorney under sections 1 (the principles) and 4 (best interests), and
(e) a certificate by a person of a prescribed description that, in his opinion, at the time when the donor executes the instrument –
  (i) the donor understands the purpose of the instrument and the scope of the authority conferred under it,
  (ii) no fraud or undue pressure is being used to induce the donor to create a lasting power of attorney, and
  (iii) there is nothing else which would prevent a lasting power of attorney from being created by the instrument.

(2) Regulations may –

(a) prescribe a maximum number of named persons;

(b) provide that, where the instrument includes a statement under
sub-paragraph (1)(c)(ii), two persons of a prescribed description must
each give a certificate under sub-paragraph (1)(e).

(3) The persons who may be named persons do not include a person who is
appointed as donee under the instrument.

(4) In this Schedule, 'named person' means a person named under
sub-paragraph (1)(c).

(5) A certificate under sub-paragraph (1)(e) –

(a) must be made in the prescribed form, and
(b) must include any prescribed information.

(6) The certificate may not be given by a person appointed as donee under the
instrument.

Failure to comply with prescribed form

3 (1) If an instrument differs in an immaterial respect in form or mode of
expression from the prescribed form, it is to be treated by the Public Guardian
as sufficient in point of form and expression.

(2) The court may declare that an instrument which is not in the prescribed
form is to be treated as if it were, if it is satisfied that the persons executing the
instrument intended it to create a lasting power of attorney.

PART 2
REGISTRATION

Applications and procedure for registration

4 (1) An application to the Public Guardian for the registration of an
instrument intended to create a lasting power of attorney –

(a) must be made in the prescribed form, and
(b) must include any prescribed information.

(2) The application may be made –

(a) by the donor,
(b) by the donee or donees, or
(c) if the instrument appoints two or more donees to act jointly and
severally in respect of any matter, by any of the donees.

(3) The application must be accompanied by –

(a) the instrument, and
(b) any fee provided for under section 58(4)(b).

(4) A person who, in an application for registration, makes a statement which
he knows to be false in a material particular is guilty of an offence and is
liable –

(a) on summary conviction, to imprisonment for a term not exceeding 12 months or a fine not exceeding the statutory maximum or both;

(b) on conviction on indictment, to imprisonment for a term not exceeding 2 years or a fine or both.

5 Subject to paragraphs 11 to 14, the Public Guardian must register the instrument as a lasting power of attorney at the end of the prescribed period.

Notification requirements

6 (1) A donor about to make an application under paragraph 4(2)(a) must notify any named persons that he is about to do so.

(2) The donee (or donees) about to make an application under paragraph 4(2)(b) or (c) must notify any named persons that he is (or they are) about to do so.

7 As soon as is practicable after receiving an application by the donor under paragraph 4(2)(a), the Public Guardian must notify the donee (or donees) that the application has been received.

8 (1) As soon as is practicable after receiving an application by a donee (or donees) under paragraph 4(2)(b), the Public Guardian must notify the donor that the application has been received.

(2) As soon as is practicable after receiving an application by a donee under paragraph 4(2)(c), the Public Guardian must notify –

(a) the donor, and
(b) the donee or donees who did not join in making the application,

that the application has been received.

9 (1) A notice under paragraph 6 must be made in the prescribed form.

(2) A notice under paragraph 6, 7 or 8 must include such information, if any, as may be prescribed.

Power to dispense with notification requirements

10 The court may –

(a) on the application of the donor, dispense with the requirement to notify under paragraph 6(1), or
(b) on the application of the donee or donees concerned, dispense with the requirement to notify under paragraph 6(2),

if satisfied that no useful purpose would be served by giving the notice.

Instrument not made properly or containing ineffective provision

11 (1) If it appears to the Public Guardian that an instrument accompanying an application under paragraph 4 is not made in accordance with this Schedule, he must not register the instrument unless the court directs him to do so.

(2) Sub-paragraph (3) applies if it appears to the Public Guardian that the instrument contains a provision which –

  (a) would be ineffective as part of a lasting power of attorney, or
  (b) would prevent the instrument from operating as a valid lasting power of attorney.

(3) The Public Guardian –

  (a) must apply to the court for it to determine the matter under section 23(1), and
  (b) pending the determination by the court, must not register the instrument.

(4) Sub-paragraph (5) applies if the court determines under section 23(1) (whether or not on an application by the Public Guardian) that the instrument contains a provision which –

  (a) would be ineffective as part of a lasting power of attorney, or
  (b) would prevent the instrument from operating as a valid lasting power of attorney.

(5) The court must –

  (a) notify the Public Guardian that it has severed the provision, or
  (b) direct him not to register the instrument.

(6) Where the court notifies the Public Guardian that it has severed a provision, he must register the instrument with a note to that effect attached to it.

Deputy already appointed

12 (1) Sub-paragraph (2) applies if it appears to the Public Guardian that –

  (a) there is a deputy appointed by the court for the donor, and
  (b) the powers conferred on the deputy would, if the instrument were registered, to any extent conflict with the powers conferred on the attorney.

(2) The Public Guardian must not register the instrument unless the court directs him to do so.

Objection by donee or named person

13 (1) Sub-paragraph (2) applies if a donee or a named person –

  (a) receives a notice under paragraph 6, 7 or 8 of an application for the registration of an instrument, and

(b) before the end of the prescribed period, gives notice to the Public Guardian of an objection to the registration on the ground that an event mentioned in section 13(3) or (6)(a) to (d) has occurred which has revoked the instrument.

(2) If the Public Guardian is satisfied that the ground for making the objection is established, he must not register the instrument unless the court, on the application of the person applying for the registration –

(a) is satisfied that the ground is not established, and
(b) directs the Public Guardian to register the instrument.

(3) Sub-paragraph (4) applies if a donee or a named person –

(a) receives a notice under paragraph 6, 7 or 8 of an application for the registration of an instrument, and
(b) before the end of the prescribed period –
    (i) makes an application to the court objecting to the registration on a prescribed ground, and
    (ii) notifies the Public Guardian of the application.

(4) The Public Guardian must not register the instrument unless the court directs him to do so.

Objection by donor

14 (1) This paragraph applies if the donor –

(a) receives a notice under paragraph 8 of an application for the registration of an instrument, and
(b) before the end of the prescribed period, gives notice to the Public Guardian of an objection to the registration.

(2) The Public Guardian must not register the instrument unless the court, on the application of the donee or, if more than one, any of them –

(a) is satisfied that the donor lacks capacity to object to the registration, and
(b) directs the Public Guardian to register the instrument.

Notification of registration

15 Where an instrument is registered under this Schedule, the Public Guardian must give notice of the fact in the prescribed form to –

(a) the donor, and
(b) the donee or, if more than one, each of them.

Evidence of registration

16 (1) A document purporting to be an office copy of an instrument registered under this Schedule is, in any part of the United Kingdom, evidence of –

(a) the contents of the instrument, and
(b) the fact that it has been registered.

(2) Sub-paragraph (1) is without prejudice to –

   (a) section 3 of the Powers of Attorney Act 1971 (proof by certified copy), and
   (b) any other method of proof authorised by law.

PART 3
CANCELLATION OF REGISTRATION AND NOTIFICATION OF SEVERANCE

17 (1) The Public Guardian must cancel the registration of an instrument as a lasting power of attorney on being satisfied that the power has been revoked –

   (a) as a result of the donor's bankruptcy or a debt relief order (under Part 7A of the Insolvency Act 1986) having been made in respect of the donor, or
   (b) on the occurrence of an event mentioned in section 13(6)(a) to (d).

(2) If the Public Guardian cancels the registration of an instrument he must notify –

   (a) the donor, and
   (b) the donee or, if more than one, each of them.

18 The court must direct the Public Guardian to cancel the registration of an instrument as a lasting power of attorney if it –

   (a) determines under section 22(2)(a) that a requirement for creating the power was not met,
   (b) determines under section 22(2)(b) that the power has been revoked or has otherwise come to an end, or
   (c) revokes the power under section 22(4)(b) (fraud etc).

19 (1) Sub-paragraph (2) applies if the court determines under section 23(1) that a lasting power of attorney contains a provision which –

   (a) is ineffective as part of a lasting power of attorney, or
   (b) prevents the instrument from operating as a valid lasting power of attorney.

(2) The court must –

   (a) notify the Public Guardian that it has severed the provision, or
   (b) direct him to cancel the registration of the instrument as a lasting power of attorney.

20 On the cancellation of the registration of an instrument, the instrument and any office copies of it must be delivered up to the Public Guardian to be cancelled.

PART 4
RECORDS OF ALTERATIONS IN REGISTERED POWERS

Partial revocation or suspension of power as a result of bankruptcy

21 If in the case of a registered instrument it appears to the Public Guardian that under section 13 a lasting power of attorney is revoked, or suspended, in relation to the donor's property and affairs (but not in relation to other matters), the Public Guardian must attach to the instrument a note to that effect.

Termination of appointment of donee which does not revoke power

22 If in the case of a registered instrument it appears to the Public Guardian that an event has occurred –

(a) which has terminated the appointment of the donee, but
(b) which has not revoked the instrument,

the Public Guardian must attach to the instrument a note to that effect.

Replacement of donee

23 If in the case of a registered instrument it appears to the Public Guardian that the donee has been replaced under the terms of the instrument the Public Guardian must attach to the instrument a note to that effect.

Severance of ineffective provisions

24 If in the case of a registered instrument the court notifies the Public Guardian under paragraph 19(2)(a) that it has severed a provision of the instrument, the Public Guardian must attach to it a note to that effect.

Notification of alterations

25 If the Public Guardian attaches a note to an instrument under paragraph 21, 22, 23 or 24 he must give notice of the note to the donee or donees of the power (or, as the case may be, to the other donee or donees of the power).

Schedule 1A
Persons Ineligible to be Deprived of Liberty by this Act

PART 1
INELIGIBLE PERSONS

Application

1 This Schedule applies for the purposes of –

(a) section 16A, and
(b) paragraph 17 of Schedule A1.

Determining ineligibility

2 A person ('P') is ineligible to be deprived of liberty by this Act ('ineligible')
if –

    (a) P falls within one of the cases set out in the second column of the
        following table, and

    (b) the corresponding entry in the third column of the table – or the
        provision, or one of the provisions, referred to in that entry – provides
        that he is ineligible.

	Status of P	*Determination of ineligibility*
Case A	P is – (a) subject to the hospital treatment regime, and (b) detained in a hospital under that regime.	P is ineligible.
Case B	P is – (a) subject to the hospital treatment regime, but (b) not detained in a hospital under that regime.	See paragraphs 3 and 4.
Case C	P is subject to the community treatment regime.	See paragraphs 3 and 4.
Case D	P is subject to the guardianship regime.	See paragraphs 3 and 5.
Case E	P is – (a) within the scope of the Mental Health Act, but (b) not subject to any of the mental health regimes.	See paragraph 5.

Authorised course of action not in accordance with regime

3 (1) This paragraph applies in cases B, C and D in the table in paragraph 2.

(2) P is ineligible if the authorised course of action is not in accordance with a
requirement which the relevant regime imposes.

(3) That includes any requirement as to where P is, or is not, to reside.

(4) The relevant regime is the mental health regime to which P is subject.

Treatment for mental disorder in a hospital

4 (1) This paragraph applies in cases B and C in the table in paragraph 2.

(2) P is ineligible if the relevant care or treatment consists in whole or in part of medical treatment for mental disorder in a hospital.

P objects to being a mental health patient etc

5 (1) This paragraph applies in cases D and E in the table in paragraph 2.

(2) P is ineligible if the following conditions are met.

(3) The first condition is that the relevant instrument authorises P to be a mental health patient.

(4) The second condition is that P objects –

    (a)   to being a mental health patient, or
    (b)   to being given some or all of the mental health treatment.

(5) The third condition is that a donee or deputy has not made a valid decision to consent to each matter to which P objects.

(6) In determining whether or not P objects to something, regard must be had to all the circumstances (so far as they are reasonably ascertainable), including the following –

    (a)   P's behaviour;
    (b)   P's wishes and feelings;
    (c)   P's views, beliefs and values.

(7) But regard is to be had to circumstances from the past only so far as it is still appropriate to have regard to them.

PART 2
INTERPRETATION

Application

6 This Part applies for the purposes of this Schedule.

Mental health regimes

7 The mental health regimes are –

    (a)   the hospital treatment regime,
    (b)   the community treatment regime, and
    (c)   the guardianship regime.

Hospital treatment regime

8 (1) P is subject to the hospital treatment regime if he is subject to –

    (a)   a hospital treatment obligation under the relevant enactment, or
    (b)   an obligation under another England and Wales enactment which has the same effect as a hospital treatment obligation.

(2) But where P is subject to any such obligation, he is to be regarded as not subject to the hospital treatment regime during any period when he is subject to the community treatment regime.

(3) A hospital treatment obligation is an application, order or direction of a kind listed in the first column of the following table.

(4) In relation to a hospital treatment obligation, the relevant enactment is the enactment in the Mental Health Act which is referred to in the corresponding entry in the second column of the following table.

Hospital treatment obligation	Relevant enactment
Application for admission for assessment	Section 2
Application for admission for assessment	Section 4
Application for admission for treatment	Section 3
Order for remand to hospital	Section 35
Order for remand to hospital	Section 36
Hospital order	Section 37
Interim hospital order	Section 38
Order for detention in hospital	Section 44
Hospital direction	Section 45A
Transfer direction	Section 47
Transfer direction	Section 48
Hospital order	Section 51

Community treatment regime

9 P is subject to the community treatment regime if he is subject to –

    (a) a community treatment order under section 17A of the Mental Health Act, or

    (b) an obligation under another England and Wales enactment which has the same effect as a community treatment order.

Guardianship regime

10 P is subject to the guardianship regime if he is subject to –

    (a) a guardianship application under section 7 of the Mental Health Act,

    (b) a guardianship order under section 37 of the Mental Health Act, or

    (c) an obligation under another England and Wales enactment which has the same effect as a guardianship application or guardianship order.

England and Wales enactments

11 (1) An England and Wales enactment is an enactment which extends to England and Wales (whether or not it also extends elsewhere).

(2) It does not matter if the enactment is in the Mental Health Act or not.

P within scope of Mental Health Act

12 (1) P is within the scope of the Mental Health Act if –

(a) an application in respect of P could be made under section 2 or 3 of the Mental Health Act, and

(b) P could be detained in a hospital in pursuance of such an application, were one made.

(2) The following provisions of this paragraph apply when determining whether an application in respect of P could be made under section 2 or 3 of the Mental Health Act.

(3) If the grounds in section 2(2) of the Mental Health Act are met in P's case, it is to be assumed that the recommendations referred to in section 2(3) of that Act have been given.

(4) If the grounds in section 3(2) of the Mental Health Act are met in P's case, it is to be assumed that the recommendations referred to in section 3(3) of that Act have been given.

(5) In determining whether the ground in section 3(2)(c) of the Mental Health Act is met in P's case, it is to be assumed that the treatment referred to in section 3(2)(c) cannot be provided under this Act.

Authorised course of action, relevant care or treatment & relevant instrument

13 In a case where this Schedule applies for the purposes of section 16A –

'authorised course of action' means any course of action amounting to deprivation of liberty which the order under section 16(2)(a) authorises;
'relevant care or treatment' means any care or treatment which –
(a) comprises, or forms part of, the authorised course of action, or
(b) is to be given in connection with the authorised course of action;
'relevant instrument' means the order under section 16(2)(a).

14 In a case where this Schedule applies for the purposes of paragraph 17 of Schedule A1 –

'authorised course of action' means the accommodation of the relevant person in the relevant hospital or care home for the purpose of being given the relevant care or treatment;
'relevant care or treatment' has the same meaning as in Schedule A1;
'relevant instrument' means the standard authorisation under Schedule A1.

15 (1) This paragraph applies where the question whether a person is ineligible to be deprived of liberty by this Act is relevant to either of these decisions –

(a) whether or not to include particular provision ('the proposed provision') in an order under section 16(2)(a);
(b) whether or not to give a standard authorisation under Schedule A1.

(2) A reference in this Schedule to the authorised course of action or the relevant care or treatment is to be read as a reference to that thing as it would be if –

(a) the proposed provision were included in the order, or
(b) the standard authorisation were given.

(3) A reference in this Schedule to the relevant instrument is to be read as follows –

(a) where the relevant instrument is an order under section 16(2)(a): as a reference to the order as it would be if the proposed provision were included in it;
(b) where the relevant instrument is a standard authorisation: as a reference to the standard authorisation as it would be if it were given.

Expressions used in paragraph 5

16 (1) These expressions have the meanings given –

'donee' means a donee of a lasting power of attorney granted by P;
'mental health patient' means a person accommodated in a hospital for the purpose of being given medical treatment for mental disorder;
'mental health treatment' means the medical treatment for mental disorder referred to in the definition of 'mental health patient'.

(2) A decision of a donee or deputy is valid if it is made –

(a) within the scope of his authority as donee or deputy, and
(b) in accordance with Part 1 of this Act.

Expressions with same meaning as in Mental Health Act

17 (1) 'Hospital' has the same meaning as in Part 2 of the Mental Health Act.

(2) 'Medical treatment' has the same meaning as in the Mental Health Act.

(3) 'Mental disorder' has the same meaning as in Schedule A1 (see paragraph 14).

Schedule 2
Property and Affairs: Supplementary Provisions

Section 18(4)

Wills: general

1 Paragraphs 2 to 4 apply in relation to the execution of a will, by virtue of section 18, on behalf of P.

Provision that may be made in will

2 The will may make any provision (whether by disposing of property or exercising a power or otherwise) which could be made by a will executed by P if he had capacity to make it.

Wills: requirements relating to execution

3 (1) Sub-paragraph (2) applies if under section 16 the court makes an order or gives directions requiring or authorising a person ('the authorised person') to execute a will on behalf of P.

(2) Any will executed in pursuance of the order or direction –

(a) must state that it is signed by P acting by the authorised person,

(b) must be signed by the authorised person with the name of P and his own name, in the presence of two or more witnesses present at the same time,

(c) must be attested and subscribed by those witnesses in the presence of the authorised person, and

(d) must be sealed with the official seal of the court.

Wills: effect of execution

4 (1) This paragraph applies where a will is executed in accordance with paragraph 3.

(2) The Wills Act 1837 has effect in relation to the will as if it were signed by P by his own hand, except that –

(a) section 9 of the 1837 Act (requirements as to signing and attestation) does not apply, and

(b) in the subsequent provisions of the 1837 Act any reference to execution in the manner required by the previous provisions is to be read as a reference to execution in accordance with paragraph 3.

(3) The will has the same effect for all purposes as if –

(a) P had had the capacity to make a valid will, and

(b) the will had been executed by him in the manner required by the 1837 Act.

(4) But sub-paragraph (3) does not have effect in relation to the will –

(a) in so far as it disposes of immovable property outside England and Wales, or

(b) in so far as it relates to any other property or matter if, when the will is executed –

(i) P is domiciled outside England and Wales, and

(ii) the condition in sub-paragraph (5) is met.

(5) The condition is that, under the law of P's domicile, any question of his testamentary capacity would fall to be determined in accordance with the law of a place outside England and Wales.

Vesting orders ancillary to settlement etc

5 (1) If provision is made by virtue of section 18 for –

(a) the settlement of any property of P, or

(b) the exercise of a power vested in him of appointing trustees or retiring from a trust,

the court may also make as respects the property settled or the trust property such consequential vesting or other orders as the case may require.

(2) The power under sub-paragraph (1) includes, in the case of the exercise of such a power, any order which could have been made in such a case under Part 4 of the Trustee Act 1925.

Variation of settlements

6 (1) If a settlement has been made by virtue of section 18, the court may by order vary or revoke the settlement if –

(a) the settlement makes provision for its variation or revocation,
(b) the court is satisfied that a material fact was not disclosed when the settlement was made, or
(c) the court is satisfied that there has been a substantial change of circumstances.

(2) Any such order may give such consequential directions as the court thinks fit.

Vesting of stock in curator appointed outside England and Wales

7 (1) Sub-paragraph (2) applies if the court is satisfied –

(a) that under the law prevailing in a place outside England and Wales a person ('M') has been appointed to exercise powers in respect of the property or affairs of P on the ground (however formulated) that P lacks capacity to make decisions with respect to the management and administration of his property and affairs, and
(b) that, having regard to the nature of the appointment and to the circumstances of the case, it is expedient that the court should exercise its powers under this paragraph.

(2) The court may direct –

(a) any stocks standing in the name of P, or
(b) the right to receive dividends from the stocks,

to be transferred into M's name or otherwise dealt with as required by M, and may give such directions as the court thinks fit for dealing with accrued dividends from the stocks.

(3) 'Stocks' includes –

(a) shares, and
(b) any funds, annuity or security transferable in the books kept by any body corporate or unincorporated company or society or by an instrument of transfer either alone or accompanied by other formalities,

and 'dividends' is to be construed accordingly.

Preservation of interests in property disposed of on behalf of person lacking capacity

8 (1) Sub-paragraphs (2) and (3) apply if –

(a) P's property has been disposed of by virtue of section 18,

(b) under P's will or intestacy, or by a gift perfected or nomination taking effect on his death, any other person would have taken an interest in the property but for the disposal, and

(c) on P's death, any property belonging to P's estate represents the property disposed of.

(2) The person takes the same interest, if and so far as circumstances allow, in the property representing the property disposed of.

(3) If the property disposed of was real property, any property representing it is to be treated, so long as it remains part of P's estate, as if it were real property.

(4) The court may direct that, on a disposal of P's property –

(a) which is made by virtue of section 18, and

(b) which would apart from this paragraph result in the conversion of personal property into real property,

property representing the property disposed of is to be treated, so long as it remains P's property or forms part of P's estate, as if it were personal property.

(5) References in sub-paragraphs (1) to (4) to the disposal of property are to –

(a) the sale, exchange, charging of or other dealing (otherwise than by will) with property other than money;

(b) the removal of property from one place to another;

(c) the application of money in acquiring property;

(d) the transfer of money from one account to another;

and references to property representing property disposed of are to be construed accordingly and as including the result of successive disposals.

(6) The court may give such directions as appear to it necessary or expedient for the purpose of facilitating the operation of sub-paragraphs (1) to (3), including the carrying of money to a separate account and the transfer of property other than money.

9 (1) Sub-paragraph (2) applies if the court has ordered or directed the expenditure of money –

(a) for carrying out permanent improvements on any of P's property, or

(b) otherwise for the permanent benefit of any of P's property.

(2) The court may order that –

(a) the whole of the money expended or to be expended, or

(b) any part of it,

is to be a charge on the property either without interest or with interest at a specified rate.

(3) An order under sub-paragraph (2) may provide for excluding or restricting the operation of paragraph 8(1) to (3).

(4) A charge under sub-paragraph (2) may be made in favour of such person as may be just and, in particular, where the money charged is paid out of P's general estate, may be made in favour of a person as trustee for P.

(5) No charge under sub-paragraph (2) may confer any right of sale or foreclosure during P's lifetime.

Powers as patron of benefice

10 (1) Any functions which P has as patron of a benefice may be discharged only by a person ('R') appointed by the court.

(2) R must be an individual capable of appointment under section 8(1)(b) of the 1986 Measure (which provides for an individual able to make a declaration of communicant status, a clerk in Holy Orders, etc to be appointed to discharge a registered patron's functions).

(3) The 1986 Measure applies to R as it applies to an individual appointed by the registered patron of the benefice under section 8(1)(b) or (3) of that Measure to discharge his functions as patron.

(4) 'The 1986 Measure' means the Patronage (Benefices) Measure 1986 (No 3).

Schedule 3
International Protection of Adults

Section 63

PART 1
PRELIMINARY

Introduction

1 This Part applies for the purposes of this Schedule.

The Convention

2 (1) 'Convention' means the Convention referred to in section 63.

(2) 'Convention country' means a country in which the Convention is in force.

(3) A reference to an Article or Chapter is to an Article or Chapter of the Convention.

(4) An expression which appears in this Schedule and in the Convention is to be construed in accordance with the Convention.

Countries, territories and nationals

3 (1) 'Country' includes a territory which has its own system of law.

(2) Where a country has more than one territory with its own system of law, a reference to the country, in relation to one of its nationals, is to the territory with which the national has the closer, or the closest, connection.

Adults with incapacity

4 (1) 'Adult' means (subject to sub-paragraph (2) a person who –

(a) as a result of an impairment or insufficiency of his personal faculties, cannot protect his interests, and
(b) has reached 16.

(2) But "adult" does not include a child to whom either of the following applies –

(a) the Convention on Jurisdiction, Applicable Law, Recognition, Enforcement and Co-Operation in respect of Parental Responsibility and Measures for the Protection of Children that was signed at The Hague on 19 October 1996;
(b) Council Regulation (EC) No. 2201/2003 concerning jurisdiction and the recognition and enforcement of judgments in matrimonial matters and the matters of parental responsibility.

Protective measures

5 (1) 'Protective measure' means a measure directed to the protection of the person or property of an adult; and it may deal in particular with any of the following –

(a) the determination of incapacity and the institution of a protective regime,
(b) placing the adult under the protection of an appropriate authority,
(c) guardianship, curatorship or any corresponding system,
(d) the designation and functions of a person having charge of the adult's person or property, or representing or otherwise helping him,
(e) placing the adult in a place where protection can be provided,
(f) administering, conserving or disposing of the adult's property,
(g) authorising a specific intervention for the protection of the person or property of the adult.

(2) Where a measure of like effect to a protective measure has been taken in relation to a person before he reaches 16, this Schedule applies to the measure in so far as it has effect in relation to him once he has reached 16.

Central Authority

6 (1) Any function under the Convention of a Central Authority is exercisable in England and Wales by the Lord Chancellor.

(2) A communication may be sent to the Central Authority in relation to England and Wales by sending it to the Lord Chancellor.

PART 2
JURISDICTION OF COMPETENT AUTHORITY

Scope of jurisdiction

7 (1) The court may exercise its functions under this Act (in so far as it cannot otherwise do so) in relation to –

    (a)   an adult habitually resident in England and Wales,

    (b)   an adult's property in England and Wales,

    (c)   an adult present in England and Wales or who has property there, if the matter is urgent, or

    (d)   an adult present in England and Wales, if a protective measure which is temporary and limited in its effect to England and Wales is proposed in relation to him.

(2) An adult present in England and Wales is to be treated for the purposes of this paragraph as habitually resident there if –

    (a)   his habitual residence cannot be ascertained,

    (b)   he is a refugee, or

    (c)   he has been displaced as a result of disturbance in the country of his habitual residence.

8 (1) The court may also exercise its functions under this Act (in so far as it cannot otherwise do so) in relation to an adult if sub-paragraph (2) or (3) applies in relation to him.

(2) This sub-paragraph applies in relation to an adult if –

    (a)   he is a British citizen,

    (b)   he has a closer connection with England and Wales than with Scotland or Northern Ireland, and

    (c)   Article 7 has, in relation to the matter concerned, been complied with.

(3) This sub-paragraph applies in relation to an adult if the Lord Chancellor, having consulted such persons as he considers appropriate, agrees to a request under Article 8 in relation to the adult.

Exercise of jurisdiction

9 (1) This paragraph applies where jurisdiction is exercisable under this Schedule in connection with a matter which involves a Convention country other than England and Wales.

(2) Any Article on which the jurisdiction is based applies in relation to the matter in so far as it involves the other country (and the court must, accordingly, comply with any duty conferred on it as a result).

(3) Article 12 also applies, so far as its provisions allow, in relation to the matter in so far as it involves the other country.

10 A reference in this Schedule to the exercise of jurisdiction under this Schedule is to the exercise of functions under this Act as a result of this Part of this Schedule.

PART 3
APPLICABLE LAW

Applicable law

11 In exercising jurisdiction under this Schedule, the court may, if it thinks that the matter has a substantial connection with a country other than England and Wales, apply the law of that other country.

12 Where a protective measure is taken in one country but implemented in another, the conditions of implementation are governed by the law of the other country.

Lasting powers of attorney, etc

13 (1) If the donor of a lasting power is habitually resident in England and Wales at the time of granting the power, the law applicable to the existence, extent, modification or extinction of the power is –

(a) the law of England and Wales, or
(b) if he specifies in writing the law of a connected country for the purpose, that law.

(2) If he is habitually resident in another country at that time, but England and Wales is a connected country, the law applicable in that respect is –

(a) the law of the other country, or
(b) if he specifies in writing the law of England and Wales for the purpose, that law.

(3) A country is connected, in relation to the donor, if it is a country –

(a) of which he is a national,
(b) in which he was habitually resident, or
(c) in which he has property.

(4) Where this paragraph applies as a result of sub-paragraph (3)(c), it applies only in relation to the property which the donor has in the connected country.

(5) The law applicable to the manner of the exercise of a lasting power is the law of the country where it is exercised.

(6) In this Part of this Schedule, 'lasting power' means –

(a) a lasting power of attorney (see section 9),
(b) an enduring power of attorney within the meaning of Schedule 4, or
(c) any other power of like effect.

14 (1) Where a lasting power is not exercised in a manner sufficient to guarantee the protection of the person or property of the donor, the court, in exercising jurisdiction under this Schedule, may disapply or modify the power.

(2) Where, in accordance with this Part of this Schedule, the law applicable to the power is, in one or more respects, that of a country other than England and Wales, the court must, so far as possible, have regard to the law of the other country in that respect (or those respects).

15 Regulations may provide for Schedule 1 (lasting powers of attorney: formalities) to apply with modifications in relation to a lasting power which comes within paragraph 13(6)(c) above.

Protection of third parties

16 (1) This paragraph applies where a person (a 'representative') in purported exercise of an authority to act on behalf of an adult enters into a transaction with a third party.

(2) The validity of the transaction may not be questioned in proceedings, nor may the third party be held liable, merely because –

   (a)   where the representative and third party are in England and Wales when entering into the transaction, sub-paragraph (3) applies;
   (b)   where they are in another country at that time, sub-paragraph (4) applies.

(3) This sub-paragraph applies if –

   (a)   the law applicable to the authority in one or more respects is, as a result of this Schedule, the law of a country other than England and Wales, and
   (b)   the representative is not entitled to exercise the authority in that respect (or those respects) under the law of that other country.

(4) This sub-paragraph applies if –

   (a)   the law applicable to the authority in one or more respects is, as a result of this Part of this Schedule, the law of England and Wales, and
   (b)   the representative is not entitled to exercise the authority in that respect (or those respects) under that law.

(5) This paragraph does not apply if the third party knew or ought to have known that the applicable law was –

   (a)   in a case within sub-paragraph (3), the law of the other country;
   (b)   in a case within sub-paragraph (4), the law of England and Wales.

Mandatory rules

17 Where the court is entitled to exercise jurisdiction under this Schedule, the mandatory provisions of the law of England and Wales apply, regardless of any system of law which would otherwise apply in relation to the matter.

Public policy

18 Nothing in this Part of this Schedule requires or enables the application in England and Wales of a provision of the law of another country if its application would be manifestly contrary to public policy.

PART 4
RECOGNITION AND ENFORCEMENT

Recognition

19 (1) A protective measure taken in relation to an adult under the law of a country other than England and Wales is to be recognised in England and Wales if it was taken on the ground that the adult is habitually resident in the other country.

(2) A protective measure taken in relation to an adult under the law of a Convention country other than England and Wales is to be recognised in England and Wales if it was taken on a ground mentioned in Chapter 2 (jurisdiction).

(3) But the court may disapply this paragraph in relation to a measure if it thinks that –

    (a) the case in which the measure was taken was not urgent,

    (b) the adult was not given an opportunity to be heard, and

    (c) that omission amounted to a breach of natural justice.

(4) It may also disapply this paragraph in relation to a measure if it thinks that –

    (a) recognition of the measure would be manifestly contrary to public policy,

    (b) the measure would be inconsistent with a mandatory provision of the law of England and Wales, or

    (c) the measure is inconsistent with one subsequently taken, or recognised, in England and Wales in relation to the adult.

(5) And the court may disapply this paragraph in relation to a measure taken under the law of a Convention country in a matter to which Article 33 applies, if the court thinks that that Article has not been complied with in connection with that matter.

20 (1) An interested person may apply to the court for a declaration as to whether a protective measure taken under the law of a country other than England and Wales is to be recognised in England and Wales.

(2) No permission is required for an application to the court under this paragraph.

21 For the purposes of paragraphs 19 and 20, any finding of fact relied on when the measure was taken is conclusive.

Enforcement

22 (1) An interested person may apply to the court for a declaration as to whether a protective measure taken under the law of, and enforceable in, a country other than England and Wales is enforceable, or to be registered, in England and Wales in accordance with Court of Protection Rules.

(2) The court must make the declaration if –

  (a) the measure comes within sub-paragraph (1) or (2) of paragraph 19, and
  (b) the paragraph is not disapplied in relation to it as a result of sub-paragraph (3), (4) or (5).

(3) A measure to which a declaration under this paragraph relates is enforceable in England and Wales as if it were a measure of like effect taken by the court.

Measures taken in relation to those aged under 16

23 (1) This paragraph applies where –

  (a) provision giving effect to, or otherwise deriving from, the Convention in a country other than England and Wales applies in relation to a person who has not reached 16, and
  (b) a measure is taken in relation to that person in reliance on that provision.

(2) This Part of this Schedule applies in relation to that measure as it applies in relation to a protective measure taken in relation to an adult under the law of a Convention country other than England and Wales.

Supplementary

24 The court may not review the merits of a measure taken outside England and Wales except to establish whether the measure complies with this Schedule in so far as it is, as a result of this Schedule, required to do so.

25 Court of Protection Rules may make provision about an application under paragraph 20 or 22.

PART 5
CO-OPERATION

Proposal for cross-border placement

26 (1) This paragraph applies where a public authority proposes to place an adult in an establishment in a Convention country other than England and Wales.

(2) The public authority must consult an appropriate authority in that other country about the proposed placement and, for that purpose, must send it –

  (a) a report on the adult, and

(b) a statement of its reasons for the proposed placement.

(3) If the appropriate authority in the other country opposes the proposed placement within a reasonable time, the public authority may not proceed with it.

27 A proposal received by a public authority under Article 33 in relation to an adult is to proceed unless the authority opposes it within a reasonable time.

Adult in danger etc

28 (1) This paragraph applies if a public authority is told that an adult –

(a) who is in serious danger, and
(b) in relation to whom the public authority has taken, or is considering taking, protective measures,

is, or has become resident, in a Convention country other than England and Wales.

(2) The public authority must tell an appropriate authority in that other country about –

(a) the danger, and
(b) the measures taken or under consideration.

29 A public authority may not request from, or send to, an appropriate authority in a Convention country information in accordance with Chapter 5 (co-operation) in relation to an adult if it thinks that doing so –

(a) would be likely to endanger the adult or his property, or
(b) would amount to a serious threat to the liberty or life of a member of the adult's family.

PART 6
GENERAL

Certificates

30 A certificate given under Article 38 by an authority in a Convention country other than England and Wales is, unless the contrary is shown, proof of the matters contained in it.

Powers to make further provision as to private international law

31 Her Majesty may by Order in Council confer on the Lord Chancellor, the court or another public authority functions for enabling the Convention to be given effect in England and Wales.

32 (1) Regulations may make provision –

(a) giving further effect to the Convention, or
(b) otherwise about the private international law of England and Wales in relation to the protection of adults.

(2) The regulations may –

    (a) confer functions on the court or another public authority;
    (b) amend this Schedule;
    (c) provide for this Schedule to apply with specified modifications;
    (d) make provision about countries other than Convention countries.

Exceptions

33 Nothing in this Schedule applies, and no provision made under paragraph 32 is to apply, to any matter to which the Convention, as a result of Article 4, does not apply.

Regulations and orders

34 A reference in this Schedule to regulations or an order (other than an Order in Council) is to regulations or an order made for the purposes of this Schedule by the Lord Chancellor.

Commencement

35 The following provisions of this Schedule have effect only if the Convention is in force in accordance with Article 57 –

    (a) paragraph 8,
    (b) paragraph 9,
    (c) paragraph 19(2) and (5),
    (d) Part 5,
    (e) paragraph 30.

Schedule 4
Provisions Applying to Existing Enduring Powers of Attorney

Section 66(3)

PART 1
ENDURING POWERS OF ATTORNEY

Enduring power of attorney to survive mental incapacity of donor

1 (1) Where an individual has created a power of attorney which is an enduring power within the meaning of this Schedule –

    (a) the power is not revoked by any subsequent mental incapacity of his,
    (b) upon such incapacity supervening, the donee of the power may not do anything under the authority of the power except as provided by sub-paragraph (2) unless or until the instrument creating the power is registered under paragraph 13, and
    (c) if and so long as paragraph (b) operates to suspend the donee's authority to act under the power, section 5 of the Powers of Attorney Act 1971 (protection of donee and third persons), so far as applicable, applies as if the power had been revoked by the donor's mental incapacity,

and, accordingly, section 1 of this Act does not apply.

(2) Despite sub-paragraph (1)(b), where the attorney has made an application for registration of the instrument then, until it is registered, the attorney may take action under the power –

(a) to maintain the donor or prevent loss to his estate, or
(b) to maintain himself or other persons in so far as paragraph 3(2) permits him to do so.

(3) Where the attorney purports to act as provided by sub-paragraph (2) then, in favour of a person who deals with him without knowledge that the attorney is acting otherwise than in accordance with sub-paragraph (2)(a) or (b), the transaction between them is as valid as if the attorney were acting in accordance with sub-paragraph (2)(a) or (b).

Characteristics of an enduring power of attorney

2 (1) Subject to sub-paragraphs (5) and (6) and paragraph 20, a power of attorney is an enduring power within the meaning of this Schedule if the instrument which creates the power –

(a) is in the prescribed form,
(b) was executed in the prescribed manner by the donor and the attorney, and
(c) incorporated at the time of execution by the donor the prescribed explanatory information.

(2) In this paragraph, 'prescribed' means prescribed by such of the following regulations as applied when the instrument was executed –

(a) the Enduring Powers of Attorney (Prescribed Form) Regulations 1986,
(b) the Enduring Powers of Attorney (Prescribed Form) Regulations 1987,
(c) the Enduring Powers of Attorney (Prescribed Form) Regulations 1990,
(d) the Enduring Powers of Attorney (Welsh Language Prescribed Form) Regulations 2000.

(3) An instrument in the prescribed form purporting to have been executed in the prescribed manner is to be taken, in the absence of evidence to the contrary, to be a document which incorporated at the time of execution by the donor the prescribed explanatory information.

(4) If an instrument differs in an immaterial respect in form or mode of expression from the prescribed form it is to be treated as sufficient in point of form and expression.

(5) A power of attorney cannot be an enduring power unless, when he executes the instrument creating it, the attorney is –

(a) an individual who has reached 18 and is not bankrupt or is not subject to a debt relief order (under Part 7A of the Insolvency Act 1986), or
(b) a trust corporation.

(6) A power of attorney which gives the attorney a right to appoint a substitute or successor cannot be an enduring power.

(7) An enduring power is revoked by the bankruptcy of the donor or attorney [or the making of a debt relief order (under Part 7A of the Insolvency Act 1986) in respect of the donor or attorney].

(8) But where the donor or attorney is bankrupt merely because an interim bankruptcy restrictions order has effect in respect of him or where the donor or attorney is subject to an interim debt relief restrictions order, the power is suspended for so long as the order has effect.

(9) An enduring power is revoked if the court –

    (a)   exercises a power under sections 16 to 20 in relation to the donor, and
    (b)   directs that the enduring power is to be revoked.

(10) No disclaimer of an enduring power, whether by deed or otherwise, is valid unless and until the attorney gives notice of it to the donor or, where paragraph 4(6) or 15(1) applies, to the Public Guardian.

Scope of authority etc of attorney under enduring power

3 (1) If the instrument which creates an enduring power of attorney is expressed to confer general authority on the attorney, the instrument operates to confer, subject to –

    (a)   the restriction imposed by sub-paragraph (3), and
    (b)   any conditions or restrictions contained in the instrument,

authority to do on behalf of the donor anything which the donor could lawfully do by an attorney at the time when the donor executed the instrument.

(2) Subject to any conditions or restrictions contained in the instrument, an attorney under an enduring power, whether general or limited, may (without obtaining any consent) act under the power so as to benefit himself or other persons than the donor to the following extent but no further –

    (a)   he may so act in relation to himself or in relation to any other person if the donor might be expected to provide for his or that person's needs respectively, and
    (b)   he may do whatever the donor might be expected to do to meet those needs.

(3) Without prejudice to sub-paragraph (2) but subject to any conditions or restrictions contained in the instrument, an attorney under an enduring power, whether general or limited, may (without obtaining any consent) dispose of the property of the donor by way of gift to the following extent but no further –

    (a)   he may make gifts of a seasonal nature or at a time, or on an anniversary, of a birth, a marriage or the formation of a civil partnership, to persons (including himself) who are related to or connected with the donor, and

(b) he may make gifts to any charity to whom the donor made or might be expected to make gifts,

provided that the value of each such gift is not unreasonable having regard to all the circumstances and in particular the size of the donor's estate.

PART 2
ACTION ON ACTUAL OR IMPENDING INCAPACITY OF DONOR

Duties of attorney in event of actual or impending incapacity of donor

4 (1) Sub-paragraphs (2) to (6) apply if the attorney under an enduring power has reason to believe that the donor is or is becoming mentally incapable.

(2) The attorney must, as soon as practicable, make an application to the Public Guardian for the registration of the instrument creating the power.

(3) Before making an application for registration the attorney must comply with the provisions as to notice set out in Part 3 of this Schedule.

(4) An application for registration –

(a) must be made in the prescribed form, and
(b) must contain such statements as may be prescribed.

(5) The attorney –

(a) may, before making an application for the registration of the instrument, refer to the court for its determination any question as to the validity of the power, and
(b) must comply with any direction given to him by the court on that determination.

(6) No disclaimer of the power is valid unless and until the attorney gives notice of it to the Public Guardian; and the Public Guardian must notify the donor if he receives a notice under this sub-paragraph.

(7) A person who, in an application for registration, makes a statement which he knows to be false in a material particular is guilty of an offence and is liable –

(a) on summary conviction, to imprisonment for a term not exceeding 12 months or a fine not exceeding the statutory maximum or both;
(b) on conviction on indictment, to imprisonment for a term not exceeding 2 years or a fine or both.

(8) In this paragraph, 'prescribed' means prescribed by regulations made for the purposes of this Schedule by the Lord Chancellor.

PART 3
NOTIFICATION PRIOR TO REGISTRATION

Duty to give notice to relatives

5 Subject to paragraph 7, before making an application for registration the attorney must give notice of his intention to do so to all those persons (if any) who are entitled to receive notice by virtue of paragraph 6.

6 (1) Subject to sub-paragraphs (2) to (4), persons of the following classes ('relatives') are entitled to receive notice under paragraph 5 –

    (a)   the donor's spouse or civil partner,
    (b)   the donor's children,
    (c)   the donor's parents,
    (d)   the donor's brothers and sisters, whether of the whole or half blood,
    (e)   the widow, widower or surviving civil partner of a child of the donor,
    (f)   the donor's grandchildren,
    (g)   the children of the donor's brothers and sisters of the whole blood,
    (h)   the children of the donor's brothers and sisters of the half blood,
    (i)   the donor's uncles and aunts of the whole blood,
    (j)   the children of the donor's uncles and aunts of the whole blood.

(2) A person is not entitled to receive notice under paragraph 5 if –

    (a)   his name or address is not known to the attorney and cannot be reasonably ascertained by him, or
    (b)   the attorney has reason to believe that he has not reached 18 or is mentally incapable.

(3) Except where sub-paragraph (4) applies –

    (a)   no more than 3 persons are entitled to receive notice under paragraph 5, and
    (b)   in determining the persons who are so entitled, persons falling within the class in sub-paragraph (1)(a) are to be preferred to persons falling within the class in sub-paragraph (1)(b), those falling within the class in sub-paragraph (1)(b) are to be preferred to those falling within the class in sub-paragraph (1)(c), and so on.

(4) Despite the limit of 3 specified in sub-paragraph (3), where –

    (a)   there is more than one person falling within any of classes (a) to (j) of sub-paragraph (1), and
    (b)   at least one of those persons would be entitled to receive notice under paragraph 5,

then, subject to sub-paragraph (2), all the persons falling within that class are entitled to receive notice under paragraph 5.

7 (1) An attorney is not required to give notice under paragraph 5 –

    (a)   to himself, or

(b) to any other attorney under the power who is joining in making the application,

even though he or, as the case may be, the other attorney is entitled to receive notice by virtue of paragraph 6.

(2) In the case of any person who is entitled to receive notice by virtue of paragraph 6, the attorney, before applying for registration, may make an application to the court to be dispensed from the requirement to give him notice; and the court must grant the application if it is satisfied –

(a) that it would be undesirable or impracticable for the attorney to give him notice, or
(b) that no useful purpose is likely to be served by giving him notice.

Duty to give notice to donor

8 (1) Subject to sub-paragraph (2), before making an application for registration the attorney must give notice of his intention to do so to the donor.

(2) Paragraph 7(2) applies in relation to the donor as it applies in relation to a person who is entitled to receive notice under paragraph 5.

Contents of notices

9 A notice to relatives under this Part of this Schedule must –

(a) be in the prescribed form,
(b) state that the attorney proposes to make an application to the Public Guardian for the registration of the instrument creating the enduring power in question,
(c) inform the person to whom it is given of his right to object to the registration under paragraph 13(4), and
(d) specify, as the grounds on which an objection to registration may be made, the grounds set out in paragraph 13(9).

10 A notice to the donor under this Part of this Schedule –

(a) must be in the prescribed form,
(b) must contain the statement mentioned in paragraph 9(b), and
(c) must inform the donor that, while the instrument remains registered, any revocation of the power by him will be ineffective unless and until the revocation is confirmed by the court.

Duty to give notice to other attorneys

11 (1) Subject to sub-paragraph (2), before making an application for registration an attorney under a joint and several power must give notice of his intention to do so to any other attorney under the power who is not joining in making the application; and paragraphs 7(2) and 9 apply in relation to attorneys entitled to receive notice by virtue of this paragraph as they apply in relation to persons entitled to receive notice by virtue of paragraph 6.

(2) An attorney is not entitled to receive notice by virtue of this paragraph if –

(a) his address is not known to the applying attorney and cannot reasonably be ascertained by him, or

(b) the applying attorney has reason to believe that he has not reached 18 or is mentally incapable.

Supplementary

12 Despite section 7 of the Interpretation Act 1978 (construction of references to service by post), for the purposes of this Part of this Schedule a notice given by post is to be regarded as given on the date on which it was posted.

PART 4
REGISTRATION

Registration of instrument creating power

13 (1) If an application is made in accordance with paragraph 4(3) and (4) the Public Guardian must, subject to the provisions of this paragraph, register the instrument to which the application relates.

(2) If it appears to the Public Guardian that –

(a) there is a deputy appointed for the donor of the power created by the instrument, and

(b) the powers conferred on the deputy would, if the instrument were registered, to any extent conflict with the powers conferred on the attorney,

the Public Guardian must not register the instrument except in accordance with the court's directions.

(3) The court may, on the application of the attorney, direct the Public Guardian to register an instrument even though notice has not been given as required by paragraph 4(3) and Part 3 of this Schedule to a person entitled to receive it, if the court is satisfied –

(a) that it was undesirable or impracticable for the attorney to give notice to that person, or

(b) that no useful purpose is likely to be served by giving him notice.

(4) Sub-paragraph (5) applies if, before the end of the period of 5 weeks beginning with the date (or the latest date) on which the attorney gave notice under paragraph 5 of an application for registration, the Public Guardian receives a valid notice of objection to the registration from a person entitled to notice of the application.

(5) The Public Guardian must not register the instrument except in accordance with the court's directions.

(6) Sub-paragraph (7) applies if, in the case of an application for registration –

(a) it appears from the application that there is no one to whom notice has been given under paragraph 5, or

(b) the Public Guardian has reason to believe that appropriate inquiries might bring to light evidence on which he could be satisfied that one of the grounds of objection set out in sub-paragraph (9) was established.

(7) The Public Guardian –

(a) must not register the instrument, and
(b) must undertake such inquiries as he thinks appropriate in all the circumstances.

(8) If, having complied with sub-paragraph (7)(b), the Public Guardian is satisfied that one of the grounds of objection set out in sub-paragraph (9) is established –

(a) the attorney may apply to the court for directions, and
(b) the Public Guardian must not register the instrument except in accordance with the court's directions.

(9) A notice of objection under this paragraph is valid if made on one or more of the following grounds –

(a) that the power purported to have been created by the instrument was not valid as an enduring power of attorney,
(b) that the power created by the instrument no longer subsists,
(c) that the application is premature because the donor is not yet becoming mentally incapable,
(d) that fraud or undue pressure was used to induce the donor to create the power,
(e) that, having regard to all the circumstances and in particular the attorney's relationship to or connection with the donor, the attorney is unsuitable to be the donor's attorney.

(10) If any of those grounds is established to the satisfaction of the court it must direct the Public Guardian not to register the instrument, but if not so satisfied it must direct its registration.

(11) If the court directs the Public Guardian not to register an instrument because it is satisfied that the ground in sub-paragraph (9)(d) or (e) is established, it must by order revoke the power created by the instrument.

(12) If the court directs the Public Guardian not to register an instrument because it is satisfied that any ground in sub-paragraph (9) except that in paragraph (c) is established, the instrument must be delivered up to be cancelled unless the court otherwise directs.

Register of enduring powers

14 The Public Guardian has the function of establishing and maintaining a register of enduring powers for the purposes of this Schedule.

PART 5
LEGAL POSITION AFTER REGISTRATION

Effect and proof of registration

15 (1) The effect of the registration of an instrument under paragraph 13 is that –

(a) no revocation of the power by the donor is valid unless and until the court confirms the revocation under paragraph 16(3);

(b) no disclaimer of the power is valid unless and until the attorney gives notice of it to the Public Guardian;

(c) the donor may not extend or restrict the scope of the authority conferred by the instrument and no instruction or consent given by him after registration, in the case of a consent, confers any right and, in the case of an instruction, imposes or confers any obligation or right on or creates any liability of the attorney or other persons having notice of the instruction or consent.

(2) Sub-paragraph (1) applies for so long as the instrument is registered under paragraph 13 whether or not the donor is for the time being mentally incapable.

(3) A document purporting to be an office copy of an instrument registered under this Schedule is, in any part of the United Kingdom, evidence of –

(a) the contents of the instrument, and

(b) the fact that it has been so registered.

(4) Sub-paragraph (3) is without prejudice to section 3 of the Powers of Attorney Act 1971 (proof by certified copies) and to any other method of proof authorised by law.

Functions of court with regard to registered power

16 (1) Where an instrument has been registered under paragraph 13, the court has the following functions with respect to the power and the donor of and the attorney appointed to act under the power.

(2) The court may –

(a) determine any question as to the meaning or effect of the instrument;

(b) give directions with respect to –

(i) the management or disposal by the attorney of the property and affairs of the donor;

(ii) the rendering of accounts by the attorney and the production of the records kept by him for the purpose;

(iii) the remuneration or expenses of the attorney whether or not in default of or in accordance with any provision made by the instrument, including directions for the repayment of excessive or the payment of additional remuneration;

(c) require the attorney to supply information or produce documents or things in his possession as attorney;

(d) give any consent or authorisation to act which the attorney would have to obtain from a mentally capable donor;

(e) authorise the attorney to act so as to benefit himself or other persons than the donor otherwise than in accordance with paragraph 3(2) and (3) (but subject to any conditions or restrictions contained in the instrument);

(f) relieve the attorney wholly or partly from any liability which he has or may have incurred on account of a breach of his duties as attorney.

(3) On application made for the purpose by or on behalf of the donor, the court must confirm the revocation of the power if satisfied that the donor –

(a) has done whatever is necessary in law to effect an express revocation of the power, and

(b) was mentally capable of revoking a power of attorney when he did so (whether or not he is so when the court considers the application).

(4) The court must direct the Public Guardian to cancel the registration of an instrument registered under paragraph 13 in any of the following circumstances –

(a) on confirming the revocation of the power under sub-paragraph (3),

(b) on directing under paragraph 2(9)(b) that the power is to be revoked,

(c) on being satisfied that the donor is and is likely to remain mentally capable,

(d) on being satisfied that the power has expired or has been revoked by the mental incapacity of the attorney,

(e) on being satisfied that the power was not a valid and subsisting enduring power when registration was effected,

(f) on being satisfied that fraud or undue pressure was used to induce the donor to create the power,

(g) on being satisfied that, having regard to all the circumstances and in particular the attorney's relationship to or connection with the donor, the attorney is unsuitable to be the donor's attorney.

(5) If the court directs the Public Guardian to cancel the registration of an instrument on being satisfied of the matters specified in sub-paragraph (4)(f) or (g) it must by order revoke the power created by the instrument.

(6) If the court directs the cancellation of the registration of an instrument under sub-paragraph (4) except paragraph (c) the instrument must be delivered up to the Public Guardian to be cancelled, unless the court otherwise directs.

Cancellation of registration by Public Guardian

17 The Public Guardian must cancel the registration of an instrument creating an enduring power of attorney –

(a) on receipt of a disclaimer signed by the attorney;

(b) if satisfied that the power has been revoked by the death or bankruptcy of the donor or attorney or the making of a debt relief order (under

Part 7A of the Insolvency Act 1986) in respect of the donor or attorney or, if the attorney is a body corporate, by its winding up or dissolution;

(c) on receipt of notification from the court that the court has revoked the power;

(d) on confirmation from the court that the donor has revoked the power.

PART 6
PROTECTION OF ATTORNEY AND THIRD PARTIES

Protection of attorney and third persons where power is invalid or revoked

18 (1) Sub-paragraphs (2) and (3) apply where an instrument which did not create a valid power of attorney has been registered under paragraph 13 (whether or not the registration has been cancelled at the time of the act or transaction in question).

(2) An attorney who acts in pursuance of the power does not incur any liability (either to the donor or to any other person) because of the non-existence of the power unless at the time of acting he knows –

(a) that the instrument did not create a valid enduring power,

(b) that an event has occurred which, if the instrument had created a valid enduring power, would have had the effect of revoking the power, or

(c) that, if the instrument had created a valid enduring power, the power would have expired before that time.

(3) Any transaction between the attorney and another person is, in favour of that person, as valid as if the power had then been in existence, unless at the time of the transaction that person has knowledge of any of the matters mentioned in sub-paragraph (2).

(4) If the interest of a purchaser depends on whether a transaction between the attorney and another person was valid by virtue of sub-paragraph (3), it is conclusively presumed in favour of the purchaser that the transaction was valid if –

(a) the transaction between that person and the attorney was completed within 12 months of the date on which the instrument was registered, or

(b) that person makes a statutory declaration, before or within 3 months after the completion of the purchase, that he had no reason at the time of the transaction to doubt that the attorney had authority to dispose of the property which was the subject of the transaction.

(5) For the purposes of section 5 of the Powers of Attorney Act 1971 (protection where power is revoked) in its application to an enduring power the revocation of which by the donor is by virtue of paragraph 15 invalid unless and until confirmed by the court under paragraph 16 –

(a) knowledge of the confirmation of the revocation is knowledge of the revocation of the power, but

(b) knowledge of the unconfirmed revocation is not.

Further protection of attorney and third persons

19 (1) If –

(a) an instrument framed in a form prescribed as mentioned in paragraph 2(2) creates a power which is not a valid enduring power, and

(b) the power is revoked by the mental incapacity of the donor,

sub-paragraphs (2) and (3) apply, whether or not the instrument has been registered.

(2) An attorney who acts in pursuance of the power does not, by reason of the revocation, incur any liability (either to the donor or to any other person) unless at the time of acting he knows –

(a) that the instrument did not create a valid enduring power, and

(b) that the donor has become mentally incapable.

(3) Any transaction between the attorney and another person is, in favour of that person, as valid as if the power had then been in existence, unless at the time of the transaction that person knows –

(a) that the instrument did not create a valid enduring power, and

(b) that the donor has become mentally incapable.

(4) Paragraph 18(4) applies for the purpose of determining whether a transaction was valid by virtue of sub-paragraph (3) as it applies for the purpose or determining whether a transaction was valid by virtue of paragraph 18(3).

PART 7
JOINT AND JOINT AND SEVERAL ATTORNEYS

Application to joint and joint and several attorneys

20 (1) An instrument which appoints more than one person to be an attorney cannot create an enduring power unless the attorneys are appointed to act –

(a) jointly, or

(b) jointly and severally.

(2) This Schedule, in its application to joint attorneys, applies to them collectively as it applies to a single attorney but subject to the modifications specified in paragraph 21.

(3) This Schedule, in its application to joint and several attorneys, applies with the modifications specified in sub-paragraphs (4) to (7) and in paragraph 22.

(4) A failure, as respects any one attorney, to comply with the requirements for the creation of enduring powers –

(a) prevents the instrument from creating such a power in his case, but

(b) does not affect its efficacy for that purpose as respects the other or others or its efficacy in his case for the purpose of creating a power of attorney which is not an enduring power.

(5) If one or more but not both or all the attorneys makes or joins in making an application for registration of the instrument –

    (a) an attorney who is not an applicant as well as one who is may act pending the registration of the instrument as provided in paragraph 1(2),

    (b) notice of the application must also be given under Part 3 of this Schedule to the other attorney or attorneys, and

    (c) objection may validly be taken to the registration on a ground relating to an attorney or to the power of an attorney who is not an applicant as well as to one or the power of one who is an applicant.

(6) The Public Guardian is not precluded by paragraph 13(5) or (8) from registering an instrument and the court must not direct him not to do so under paragraph 13(10) if an enduring power subsists as respects some attorney who is not affected by the ground or grounds of the objection in question; and where the Public Guardian registers an instrument in that case, he must make against the registration an entry in the prescribed form.

(7) Sub-paragraph (6) does not preclude the court from revoking a power in so far as it confers a power on any other attorney in respect of whom the ground in paragraph 13(9)(d) or (e) is established; and where any ground in paragraph 13(9) affecting any other attorney is established the court must direct the Public Guardian to make against the registration an entry in the prescribed form.

(8) In sub-paragraph (4), 'the requirements for the creation of enduring powers' means the provisions of –

    (a) paragraph 2 other than sub-paragraphs (8) and (9), and

    (b) the regulations mentioned in paragraph 2.

Joint attorneys

21 (1) In paragraph 2(5), the reference to the time when the attorney executes the instrument is to be read as a reference to the time when the second or last attorney executes the instrument.

(2) In paragraph 2(6) to (8), the reference to the attorney is to be read as a reference to any attorney under the power.

(3) Paragraph 13 has effect as if the ground of objection to the registration of the instrument specified in sub-paragraph (9)(e) applied to any attorney under the power.

(4) In paragraph 16(2), references to the attorney are to be read as including references to any attorney under the power.

(5) In paragraph 16(4), references to the attorney are to be read as including references to any attorney under the power.

(6) In paragraph 17, references to the attorney are to be read as including references to any attorney under the power.

Joint and several attorneys

22 (1) In paragraph 2(7), the reference to the bankruptcy of the attorney is to be read as a reference to the bankruptcy of the last remaining attorney under the power; and the bankruptcy of any other attorney under the power causes that person to cease to be an attorney under the power.

(1A) In paragraph 2(7), the reference to the making of a debt relief order (under Part 7A of the Insolvency Act 1986) in respect of the attorney is to be read as a reference to the making of a debt relief order in respect of the last remaining attorney under the power; and the making of a debt relief order in respect of any other attorney under the power causes that person to cease to be an attorney under the power.

(2) In paragraph 2(8), the reference to the suspension of the power is to be read as a reference to its suspension in so far as it relates to the attorney in respect of whom the interim bankruptcy restrictions order has effect.

(2A) In paragraph 2(8), the reference to the suspension of the power is to be read as a reference to its suspension in so far as it relates to the attorney in respect of whom the interim debt relief restrictions order has effect.

(3) The restriction upon disclaimer imposed by paragraph 4(6) applies only to those attorneys who have reason to believe that the donor is or is becoming mentally incapable.

PART 8
INTERPRETATION

23 (1) In this Schedule –

'enduring power' is to be construed in accordance with paragraph 2,
'mentally incapable' or 'mental incapacity', except where it refers to revocation at common law, means in relation to any person, that he is incapable by reason of mental disorder … of managing and administering his property and affairs and 'mentally capable' and 'mental capacity' are to be construed accordingly,
'notice' means notice in writing, and
'prescribed', except for the purposes of paragraph 2, means prescribed by regulations made for the purposes of this Schedule by the Lord Chancellor.

(1A) In sub-paragraph (1), 'mental disorder' has the same meaning as in the Mental Health Act but disregarding the amendments made to that Act by the Mental Health Act 2007.

(2) Any question arising under or for the purposes of this Schedule as to what the donor of the power might at any time be expected to do is to be determined by assuming that he had full mental capacity at the time but otherwise by reference to the circumstances existing at that time.

Schedule 5
Transitional Provisions and Savings

Section 66(4)

PART 1
REPEAL OF PART 7 OF THE MENTAL HEALTH ACT 1983

Existing receivers

1 (1) This paragraph applies where, immediately before the commencement day, there is a receiver ('R') for a person ('P') appointed under section 99 of the Mental Health Act.

(2) On and after that day –

(a) this Act applies as if R were a deputy appointed for P by the court, but with the functions that R had as receiver immediately before that day, and

(b) a reference in any other enactment to a deputy appointed by the court includes a person appointed as a deputy as a result of paragraph (a).

(3) On any application to it by R, the court may end R's appointment as P's deputy.

(4) Where, as a result of section 20(1), R may not make a decision on behalf of P in relation to a relevant matter, R must apply to the court.

(5) If, on the application, the court is satisfied that P is capable of managing his property and affairs in relation to the relevant matter –

(a) it must make an order ending R's appointment as P's deputy in relation to that matter, but

(b) it may, in relation to any other matter, exercise in relation to P any of the powers which it has under sections 15 to 19.

(6) If it is not satisfied, the court may exercise in relation to P any of the powers which it has under sections 15 to 19.

(7) R's appointment as P's deputy ceases to have effect if P dies.

(8) 'Relevant matter' means a matter in relation to which, immediately before the commencement day, R was authorised to act as P's receiver.

(9) In sub-paragraph (1), the reference to a receiver appointed under section 99 of the Mental Health Act includes a reference to a person who by virtue of Schedule 5 to that Act was deemed to be a receiver appointed under that section.

Orders, appointments etc

2 (1) Any order or appointment made, direction or authority given or other thing done which has, or by virtue of Schedule 5 to the Mental Health Act was deemed to have, effect under Part 7 of the Act immediately before the commencement day is to continue to have effect despite the repeal of Part 7.

(2) In so far as any such order, appointment, direction, authority or thing could have been made, given or done under sections 15 to 20 if those sections had then been in force –

(a) it is to be treated as made, given or done under those sections, and
(b) the powers of variation and discharge conferred by section 16(7) apply accordingly.

(3) Sub-paragraph (1) –

(a) does not apply to nominations under section 93(1) or (4) of the Mental Health Act, and
(b) as respects receivers, has effect subject to paragraph 1.

(4) This Act does not affect the operation of section 109 of the Mental Health Act (effect and proof of orders etc) in relation to orders made and directions given under Part 7 of that Act.

(5) This paragraph is without prejudice to section 16 of the Interpretation Act 1978 (general savings on repeal).

Pending proceedings

3 (1) Any application for the exercise of a power under Part 7 of the Mental Health Act which is pending immediately before the commencement day is to be treated, in so far as a corresponding power is exercisable under sections 16 to 20, as an application for the exercise of that power.

(2) For the purposes of sub-paragraph (1) an application for the appointment of a receiver is to be treated as an application for the appointment of a deputy.

Appeals

4 (1) Part 7 of the Mental Health Act and the rules made under it are to continue to apply to any appeal brought by virtue of section 105 of that Act which has not been determined before the commencement day.

(2) If in the case of an appeal brought by virtue of section 105(1) (appeal to nominated judge) the judge nominated under section 93 of the Mental Health Act has begun to hear the appeal, he is to continue to do so but otherwise it is to be heard by a puisne judge of the High Court nominated under section 46.

Fees

5 All fees and other payments which, having become due, have not been paid to the former Court of Protection before the commencement day, are to be paid to the new Court of Protection.

Court records

6 (1) The records of the former Court of Protection are to be treated, on and after the commencement day, as records of the new Court of Protection and are to be dealt with accordingly under the Public Records Act 1958.

(2) On and after the commencement day, the Public Guardian is, for the purpose of exercising any of his functions, to be given such access as he may require to such of the records mentioned in sub-paragraph (1) as relate to the appointment of receivers under section 99 of the Mental Health Act.

Existing charges

7 This Act does not affect the operation in relation to a charge created before the commencement day of –

(a)　so much of section 101(6) of the Mental Health Act as precludes a charge created under section 101(5) from conferring a right of sale or foreclosure during the lifetime of the patient, or

(b)　section 106(6) of the Mental Health Act (charge created by virtue of section 106(5) not to cause interest to fail etc).

Preservation of interests on disposal of property

8 Paragraph 8(1) of Schedule 2 applies in relation to any disposal of property (within the meaning of that provision) by a person living on 1st November 1960, being a disposal effected under the Lunacy Act 1890 as it applies in relation to the disposal of property effected under sections 16 to 20.

Accounts

9 Court of Protection Rules may provide that, in a case where paragraph 1 applies, R is to have a duty to render accounts –

(a)　while he is receiver;

(b)　after he is discharged.

Interpretation

10 In this Part of this Schedule –

(a)　'the commencement day' means the day on which section 66(1)(a) (repeal of Part 7 of the Mental Health Act) comes into force,

(b)　'the former Court of Protection' means the office abolished by section 45, and

(c)　'the new Court of Protection' means the court established by that section.

PART 2
REPEAL OF THE ENDURING POWERS OF ATTORNEY ACT 1985

Orders, determinations, etc

11 (1) Any order or determination made, or other thing done, under the 1985 Act which has effect immediately before the commencement day continues to have effect despite the repeal of that Act.

(2) In so far as any such order, determination or thing could have been made or done under Schedule 4 if it had then been in force –

    (a) it is to be treated as made or done under that Schedule, and

    (b) the powers of variation and discharge exercisable by the court apply accordingly.

(3) Any instrument registered under the 1985 Act is to be treated as having been registered by the Public Guardian under Schedule 4.

(4) This paragraph is without prejudice to section 16 of the Interpretation Act 1978 (general savings on repeal).

Pending proceedings

12 (1) An application for the exercise of a power under the 1985 Act which is pending immediately before the commencement day is to be treated, in so far as a corresponding power is exercisable under Schedule 4, as an application for the exercise of that power.

(2) For the purposes of sub-paragraph (1) –

    (a) a pending application under section 4(2) of the 1985 Act for the registration of an instrument is to be treated as an application to the Public Guardian under paragraph 4 of Schedule 4 and any notice given in connection with that application under Schedule 1 to the 1985 Act is to be treated as given under Part 3 of Schedule 4,

    (b) a notice of objection to the registration of an instrument is to be treated as a notice of objection under paragraph 13 of Schedule 4, and

    (c) pending proceedings under section 5 of the 1985 Act are to be treated as proceedings on an application for the exercise by the court of a power which would become exercisable in relation to an instrument under paragraph 16(2) of Schedule 4 on its registration.

Appeals

13 (1) The 1985 Act and, so far as relevant, the provisions of Part 7 of the Mental Health Act and the rules made under it as applied by section 10 of the 1985 Act are to continue to have effect in relation to any appeal brought by virtue of section 10(1)(c) of the 1985 Act which has not been determined before the commencement day.

(2) If, in the case of an appeal brought by virtue of section 105(1) of the Mental Health Act as applied by section 10(1)(c) of the 1985 Act (appeal to nominated judge), the judge nominated under section 93 of the Mental Health Act has begun to hear the appeal, he is to continue to do so but otherwise the appeal is to be heard by a puisne judge of the High Court nominated under section 46.

Exercise of powers of donor as trustee

14 (1) Section 2(8) of the 1985 Act (which prevents a power of attorney under section 25 of the Trustee Act 1925 as enacted from being an enduring power) is to continue to apply to any enduring power –

    (a) created before 1st March 2000, and

(b) having effect immediately before the commencement day.

(2) Section 3(3) of the 1985 Act (which entitles the donee of an enduring power to exercise the donor's powers as trustee) is to continue to apply to any enduring power to which, as a result of the provision mentioned in sub-paragraph (3), it applies immediately before the commencement day.

(3) The provision is section 4(3)(a) of the Trustee Delegation Act 1999 (which provides for section 3(3) of the 1985 Act to cease to apply to an enduring power when its registration is cancelled, if it was registered in response to an application made before 1st March 2001).

(4) Even though section 4 of the 1999 Act is repealed by this Act, that section is to continue to apply in relation to an enduring power –

(a) to which section 3(3) of the 1985 Act applies as a result of sub-paragraph (2), or

(b) to which, immediately before the repeal of section 4 of the 1999 Act, section 1 of that Act applies as a result of section 4 of it.

(5) The reference in section 1(9) of the 1999 Act to section 4(6) of that Act is to be read with sub-paragraphs (2) to (4).

Interpretation

15 In this Part of this Schedule, 'the commencement day' means the day on which section 66(1)(b) (repeal of the 1985 Act) comes into force.

Schedule 6
Minor and Consequential Amendments

Section 67(1)

Fines and Recoveries Act 1833

1 (1) The Fines and Recoveries Act 1833 is amended as follows.

(2) In section 33 (case where protector of settlement lacks capacity to act), for the words from 'shall be incapable' to 'is incapable as aforesaid' substitute 'lacks capacity (within the meaning of the Mental Capacity Act 2005) to manage his property and affairs, the Court of Protection is to take his place as protector of the settlement while he lacks capacity'.

(3) In sections 48 and 49 (mental health jurisdiction), for each reference to the judge having jurisdiction under Part 7 of the Mental Health Act substitute a reference to the Court of Protection.

Improvement of Land Act 1864

2 In section 68 of the Improvement of Land Act 1864 (apportionment of rentcharges) –

(a) for 'curator, or receiver of' substitute 'or curator of, or a deputy with powers in relation to property and affairs appointed by the Court of Protection for', and

(b) for 'or patient within the meaning of Part VII of the Mental Health Act 1983' substitute 'person who lacks capacity (within the meaning of the Mental Capacity Act 2005) to receive the notice'.

Trustee Act 1925

3 (1) The Trustee Act 1925 is amended as follows.

(2) In section 36 (appointment of new trustee) –

(a) in subsection (6C), for the words from 'a power of attorney' to the end, substitute 'an enduring power of attorney or lasting power of attorney registered under the Mental Capacity Act 2005', and

(b) in subsection (9) –

(i) for the words from 'is incapable' to 'exercising' substitute 'lacks capacity to exercise', and

(ii) for the words from 'the authority' to the end substitute 'the Court of Protection'.

(3) In section 41(1) (power of court to appoint new trustee) for the words from 'is incapable' to 'exercising' substitute 'lacks capacity to exercise'.

(4) In section 54 (mental health jurisdiction) –

(a) for subsection (1) substitute –

'(1) Subject to subsection (2), the Court of Protection may not make an order, or give a direction or authority, in relation to a person who lacks capacity to exercise his functions as trustee, if the High Court may make an order to that effect under this Act.',

(b) in subsection (2) –

(i) for the words from the beginning to 'of a receiver' substitute 'Where a person lacks capacity to exercise his functions as a trustee and a deputy is appointed for him by the Court of Protection or an application for the appointment of a deputy',

(ii) for 'the said authority', in each place, substitute 'the Court of Protection', and

(iii) for 'the patient', in each place, substitute 'the person concerned', and

(c) omit subsection (3).

(5) In section 55 (order made on particular allegation to be conclusive evidence of it) –

(a) for the words from 'Part VII' to 'Northern Ireland' substitute 'sections 15 to 20 of the Mental Capacity Act 2005 or any corresponding provisions having effect in Northern Ireland', and

(b) for paragraph (a) substitute –

'(a) that a trustee or mortgagee lacks capacity in relation to the matter in question;'.

(6) In section 68 (definitions), at the end add –

> '(3) Any reference in this Act to a person who lacks capacity in relation to a matter is to a person –
>> (a)   who lacks capacity within the meaning of the Mental Capacity Act 2005 in relation to that matter, or
>> (b)   in respect of whom the powers conferred by section 48 of that Act are exercisable and have been exercised in relation to that matter.'.

Law of Property Act 1925

4 (1) The Law of Property Act 1925 is amended as follows.

(2) In section 22 (conveyances on behalf of persons who lack capacity) –

- (a)   in subsection (1) –
  - (i)   for the words from 'in a person suffering' to 'is acting' substitute 'either solely or jointly with any other person or persons, in a person lacking capacity (within the meaning of the Mental Capacity Act 2005) to convey or create a legal estate, a deputy appointed for him by the Court of Protection or (if no deputy is appointed', and
  - (ii)   for 'the authority having jurisdiction under Part VII of the Mental Health Act 1983' substitute 'the Court of Protection',
- (b)   in subsection (2), for 'is incapable, by reason of mental disorder, of exercising' substitute 'lacks capacity (within the meaning of that Act) to exercise', and
- (c)   in subsection (3), for the words from 'an enduring power' to the end substitute 'an enduring power of attorney or lasting power of attorney (within the meaning of the 2005 Act) is entitled to act for the trustee who lacks capacity in relation to the dealing.'.

(3) In section 205(1) (interpretation), omit paragraph (xiii).

Administration of Estates Act 1925

5 (1) The Administration of Estates Act 1925 is amended as follows.

(2) In section 41(1) (powers of personal representatives to appropriate), in the proviso –

- (a)   in paragraph (ii) –
  - (i)   for the words from 'is incapable' to 'the consent' substitute 'lacks capacity (within the meaning of the Mental Capacity Act 2005) to give the consent, it', and
  - (ii)   for 'or receiver' substitute 'or a person appointed as deputy for him by the Court of Protection', and
- (b)   in paragraph (iv), for 'no receiver is acting for a person suffering from mental disorder' substitute 'no deputy is appointed for a person who lacks capacity to consent'.

(3) Omit section 55(1)(viii) (definitions of 'person of unsound mind' and 'defective').

National Assistance Act 1948

6 In section 49 of the National Assistance Act 1948 (expenses of council officers acting for persons who lack capacity) –

(a) for the words from 'applies' to 'affairs of a patient' substitute 'applies for appointment by the Court of Protection as a deputy', and

(b) for 'such functions' substitute 'his functions as deputy'.

USA Veterans' Pensions (Administration) Act 1949

7 In section 1 of the USA Veterans' Pensions (Administration) Act 1949 (administration of pensions) –

(a) in subsection (4), omit the words from 'or for whom' to '1983', and

(b) after subsection (4), insert –

'(4A)An agreement under subsection (1) is not to be made in relation to a person who lacks capacity (within the meaning of the Mental Capacity Act 2005) for the purposes of this Act if –

(a) there is a donee of an enduring power of attorney or lasting power of attorney (within the meaning of the 2005 Act), or a deputy appointed for the person by the Court of Protection, and

(b) the donee or deputy has power in relation to the person for the purposes of this Act.

(4B) The proviso at the end of subsection (4) also applies in relation to subsection (4A).'.

Intestates' Estates Act 1952

8 In Schedule 2 to the Intestates' Estates Act 1952 (rights of surviving spouse or civil partner in relation to home), for paragraph 6(1) substitute –

'(1) Where the surviving spouse or civil partner lacks capacity (within the meaning of the Mental Capacity Act 2005) to make a requirement or give a consent under this Schedule, the requirement or consent may be made or given by a deputy appointed by the Court of Protection with power in that respect or, if no deputy has that power, by that court.'.

Variation of Trusts Act 1958

9 In section 1 of the Variation of Trusts Act 1958 (jurisdiction of courts to vary trusts) –

(a) in subsection (3), for the words from 'shall be determined' to the end substitute 'who lacks capacity (within the meaning of the Mental Capacity Act 2005) to give his assent is to be determined by the Court of Protection', and

(b) in subsection (6), for the words from 'the powers' to the end substitute 'the powers of the Court of Protection'.

Administration of Justice Act 1960

10 In section 12(1)(b) of the Administration of Justice Act 1960 (contempt of court to publish information about proceedings in private relating to persons with incapacity) for the words from 'under Part VIII' to 'that Act' substitute 'under the Mental Capacity Act 2005, or under any provision of the Mental Health Act 1983'.

Industrial and Provident Societies Act 1965

11 (*Repealed*)

Compulsory Purchase Act 1965

12 In Schedule 1 to the Compulsory Purchase Act 1965 (persons without power to sell their interests), for paragraph 1(2)(b) substitute –

> '(b) do not have effect in relation to a person who lacks capacity (within the meaning of the Mental Capacity Act 2005) for the purposes of this Act if –
>> (i) there is a donee of an enduring power of attorney or lasting power of attorney (within the meaning of the 2005 Act), or a deputy appointed for the person by the Court of Protection, and
>> (ii) the donee or deputy has power in relation to the person for the purposes of this Act.'.

Leasehold Reform Act 1967

13 (1) For section 26(2) of the Leasehold Reform Act 1967 (landlord lacking capacity) substitute –

> '(2) Where a landlord lacks capacity (within the meaning of the Mental Capacity Act 2005) to exercise his functions as a landlord, those functions are to be exercised –
>> (a) by a donee of an enduring power of attorney or lasting power of attorney (within the meaning of the 2005 Act), or a deputy appointed for him by the Court of Protection, with power to exercise those functions, or
>> (b) if no donee or deputy has that power, by a person authorised in that respect by that court.'.

(2) That amendment does not affect any proceedings pending at the commencement of this paragraph in which a receiver or a person authorised under Part 7 of the Mental Health Act is acting on behalf of the landlord.

Medicines Act 1968

14 In section 72 of the Medicines Act 1968 (pharmacist lacking capacity) –

> (a) in subsection (1)(c), for the words from 'a receiver' to '1959' substitute 'he becomes a person who lacks capacity (within the meaning of the Mental Capacity Act 2005) to carry on the business',
> (b) after subsection (1) insert –
>> '(1A)In subsection (1)(c), the reference to a person who lacks capacity to carry on the business is to a person –

(a)   in respect of whom there is a donee of an enduring power of attorney or lasting power of attorney (within the meaning of the Mental Capacity Act 2005), or

(b)   for whom a deputy is appointed by the Court of Protection, and in relation to whom the donee or deputy has power for the purposes of this Act.',

(c)   in subsection (3)(d) –

(i)   for 'receiver' substitute 'deputy', and

(ii)   after 'guardian' insert 'or from the date of registration of the instrument appointing the donee', and

(d)   in subsection (4)(c), for 'receiver' substitute 'donee, deputy'.

Family Law Reform Act 1969

15 For section 21(4) of the Family Law Reform Act 1969 (consent required for taking of bodily sample from person lacking capacity), substitute –

'(4)   A bodily sample may be taken from a person who lacks capacity (within the meaning of the Mental Capacity Act 2005) to give his consent, if consent is given by the court giving the direction under section 20 or by –

(a)   a donee of an enduring power of attorney or lasting power of attorney (within the meaning of that Act), or

(b)   a deputy appointed, or any other person authorised, by the Court of Protection,

with power in that respect.'.

Local Authority Social Services Act 1970

16 (1) Schedule 1 to the Local Authority Social Services Act 1970 (enactments conferring functions assigned to social services committee) is amended as follows.

(2) In the entry for section 49 of the National Assistance Act 1948 (expenses of local authority officer appointed for person who lacks capacity) for 'receiver' substitute 'deputy'.

(3) At the end, insert –

'Mental Capacity
Act 2005

Section 39	Instructing independent mental capacity advocate before providing accommodation for person lacking capacity.
Section 49	Reports in proceedings.'.

Courts Act 1971

17 In Part 1A of Schedule 2 to the Courts Act 1971 (office-holders eligible for appointment as circuit judges), omit the reference to a Master of the Court of Protection.

Local Government Act 1972

18 (1) Omit section 118 of the Local Government Act 1972 (payment of pension etc where recipient lacks capacity).

(2) Sub-paragraph (3) applies where, before the commencement of this paragraph, a local authority has, in respect of a person referred to in that section as 'the patient', made payments under that section –

(a) to an institution or person having the care of the patient, or
(b) in accordance with subsection (1)(a) or (b) of that section.

(3) The local authority may, in respect of the patient, continue to make payments under that section to that institution or person, or in accordance with subsection (1)(a) or (b) of that section, despite the repeal made by sub-paragraph (1).

Matrimonial Causes Act 1973

19 In section 40 of the Matrimonial Causes Act 1973 (payments to person who lacks capacity) (which becomes subsection (1)) –

(a) for the words from 'is incapable' to 'affairs' substitute '('P') lacks capacity (within the meaning of the Mental Capacity Act 2005) in relation to the provisions of the order',
(b) for 'that person under Part VIII of that Act' substitute 'P under that Act',
(c) for the words from 'such persons' to the end substitute 'such person ('D') as it may direct', and
(d) at the end insert –

'(2) In carrying out any functions of his in relation to an order made under subsection (1), D must act in P's best interests (within the meaning of that Act).'.

Juries Act 1974

20 In Schedule 1 to the Juries Act 1974 (disqualification for jury service), for paragraph 3 substitute –

'3
A person who lacks capacity, within the meaning of the Mental Capacity Act 2005, to serve as a juror.'.

Consumer Credit Act 1974

21 For section 37(1)(c) of the Consumer Credit Act 1974 (termination of consumer credit licence if holder lacks capacity) substitute –

'(c) becomes a person who lacks capacity (within the meaning of the Mental Capacity Act 2005) to carry on the activities covered by the licence.'.

Solicitors Act 1974

22 (1) The Solicitors Act 1974 is amended as follows.

(2) (Repealed).

(3) In section 62(4) (contentious business agreements made by clients) for paragraphs (c) and (d) substitute –

> '(c) as a deputy for him appointed by the Court of Protection with powers in relation to his property and affairs, or
> (d) as another person authorised under that Act to act on his behalf.'.

(4) In paragraph 1(1) of Schedule 1 (circumstances in which Law Society may intervene in solicitor's practice), for paragraph (f) substitute –

> '(f) a solicitor lacks capacity (within the meaning of the Mental Capacity Act 2005) to act as a solicitor and powers under sections 15 to 20 or section 48 of that Act are exercisable in relation to him;'.

Local Government (Miscellaneous Provisions) Act 1976

23 In section 31 of the Local Government (Miscellaneous Provisions) Act 1976 (the title to which becomes 'Indemnities for local authority officers appointed as deputies or administrators'), for the words from 'as a receiver' to '1959' substitute 'as a deputy for a person by the Court of Protection'.

Sale of Goods Act 1979

24 In section 3(2) of the Sale of Goods Act 1979 (capacity to buy and sell) the words 'mental incapacity or' cease to have effect in England and Wales.

Limitation Act 1980

25 In section 38 of the Limitation Act 1980 (interpretation) substitute –

(a) in subsection (2) for 'of unsound mind' substitute 'lacks capacity (within the meaning of the Mental Capacity Act 2005) to conduct legal proceedings', and
(b) omit subsections (3) and (4).

Public Passenger Vehicles Act 1981

26 In section 57(2)(c) of the Public Passenger Vehicles Act 1981 (termination of public service vehicle licence if holder lacks capacity) for the words from 'becomes a patient' to 'or' substitute 'becomes a person who lacks capacity (within the meaning of the Mental Capacity Act 2005) to use a vehicle under the licence, or'.

Judicial Pensions Act 1981

27 In Schedule 1 to the Judicial Pensions Act 1981 (pensions of Supreme Court officers, etc), in paragraph 1, omit the reference to a Master of the Court of

Protection except in the case of a person holding that office immediately before the commencement of this paragraph or who had previously retired from that office or died.

Senior Courts Act 1981

28 In Schedule 2 to the Senior Courts Act 1981 (qualifications for appointment to office in Supreme Court), omit paragraph 11 (Master of the Court of Protection).

Mental Health Act 1983

29 (1) The Mental Health Act is amended as follows.

(2) In section 134(3) (cases where correspondence of detained patients may not be withheld) for paragraph (b) substitute –

> '(b) any judge or officer of the Court of Protection, any of the Court of Protection Visitors or any person asked by that Court for a report under section 49 of the Mental Capacity Act 2005 concerning the patient;'.

(3) In section 139 (protection for acts done in pursuance of 1983 Act), in subsection (1), omit from 'or in, or in pursuance' to 'Part VII of this Act,'.

(4) Section 142 (payment of pension etc where recipient lacks capacity) ceases to have effect in England and Wales.

(5) Sub-paragraph (6) applies where, before the commencement of sub-paragraph (4), an authority has, in respect of a person referred to in that section as 'the patient', made payments under that section –

(a)   to an institution or person having the care of the patient, or
(b)   in accordance with subsection (2)(a) or (b) of that section.

(6) The authority may, in respect of the patient, continue to make payments under that section to that institution or person, or in accordance with subsection (2)(a) or (b) of that section, despite the amendment made by sub-paragraph (4).

(7) In section 145(1) (interpretation), in the definition of 'patient', omit '(except in Part VII of this Act)'.

(8) In section 146 (provisions having effect in Scotland), omit from '104(4)' to 'section),'.

(9) In section 147 (provisions having effect in Northern Ireland), omit from '104(4)' to 'section),'.

Administration of Justice Act 1985

30 In section 18(3) of the Administration of Justice Act 1985 (licensed conveyancer who lacks capacity), for the words from 'that person' to the end substitute 'he becomes a person who lacks capacity (within the meaning of the Mental Capacity Act 2005) to practise as a licensed conveyancer.'.

Insolvency Act 1986

31 (1) The Insolvency Act 1986 is amended as follows.

(2) In section 389A (people not authorised to act as nominee or supervisor in voluntary arrangement), in subsection (3) –

    (a) omit the 'or' immediately after paragraph (b),
    (b) in paragraph (c), omit 'Part VII of the Mental Health Act 1983 or', and
    (c) after that paragraph, insert ', or
    (d) he lacks capacity (within the meaning of the Mental Capacity Act 2005) to act as nominee or supervisor'.

(3) In section 390 (people not qualified to be insolvency practitioners), in subsection (4) –

    (a). omit the 'or' immediately after paragraph (b),
    (b) in paragraph (c), omit 'Part VII of the Mental Health Act 1983 or', and
    (c) after that paragraph, insert ', or
    (d) he lacks capacity (within the meaning of the Mental Capacity Act 2005) to act as an insolvency practitioner.'.

Building Societies Act 1986

32 In section 102D(9) of the Building Societies Act 1986 (references to a person holding an account on trust for another) –

    (a) in paragraph (a), for 'Part VII of the Mental Health Act 1983' substitute 'the Mental Capacity Act 2005', and
    (b) for paragraph (b) substitute –
        '(b) to an attorney holding an account for another person under –
            (i) an enduring power of attorney or lasting power of attorney registered under the Mental Capacity Act 2005, or
            (ii) an enduring power registered under the Enduring Powers of Attorney (Northern Ireland) Order 1987;'.

Public Trustee and Administration of Funds Act 1986

33 In section 3 of the Public Trustee and Administration of Funds Act 1986 (functions of the Public Trustee) –

    (a) for subsections (1) to (5) substitute –

        '(1) The Public Trustee may exercise the functions of a deputy appointed by the Court of Protection.',

    (b) in subsection (6), for 'the 1906 Act' substitute 'the Public Trustee Act 1906', and
    (c) omit subsection (7).

Patronage (Benefices) Measure 1986 (No 3)

34 (1) The Patronage (Benefices) Measure 1986 (No 3) is amended as follows.

(2) In section 5 (rights of patronage exercisable otherwise than by registered patron), after subsection (3) insert –

'(3A)The reference in subsection (3) to a power of attorney does not include an enduring power of attorney or lasting power of attorney (within the meaning of the Mental Capacity Act 2005).'

(3) In section 9 (information to be sent to designated officer when benefice becomes vacant), after subsection (5) insert –

'(5A)Subsections (5B) and (5C) apply where the functions of a registered patron are, as a result of paragraph 10 of Schedule 2 to the Mental Capacity Act 2005 (patron's loss of capacity to discharge functions), to be discharged by an individual appointed by the Court of Protection.
(5B) If the individual is a clerk in Holy Orders, subsection (5) applies to him as it applies to the registered patron.
(5C) If the individual is not a clerk in Holy Orders, subsection (1) (other than paragraph (b)) applies to him as it applies to the registered patron.'

Courts and Legal Services Act 1990

35 (1) The Courts and Legal Services Act 1990 is amended as follows.

(2) In Schedule 11 (judges etc barred from legal practice), for the reference to a Master of the Court of Protection substitute a reference to each of the following –

(a) Senior Judge of the Court of Protection,
(b) President of the Court of Protection,
(c) Vice-President of the Court of Protection.

(3) In paragraph 5(3) of Schedule 14 (exercise of powers of intervention in registered foreign lawyer's practice), for paragraph (f) substitute –
'(f) he lacks capacity (within the meaning of the Mental Capacity Act 2005) to act as a registered foreign lawyer and powers under sections 15 to 20 or section 48 are exercisable in relation to him;'.

Child Support Act 1991

36 In section 50 of the Child Support Act 1991 (unauthorised disclosure of information) –

(a) in subsection (8) –
  (i) immediately after paragraph (a), insert 'or',
  (ii) omit paragraphs (b) and (d) and the 'or' immediately after paragraph (c), and
  (iii) for ', receiver, custodian or appointee' substitute 'or custodian', and
(b) after that subsection, insert –

'(9) Where the person to whom the information relates lacks capacity (within the meaning of the Mental Capacity Act 2005) to consent to its disclosure, the appropriate person is –
(a) a donee of an enduring power of attorney or lasting power of attorney (within the meaning of that Act), or
(b) a deputy appointed for him, or any other person authorised, by the Court of Protection,
with power in that respect.'.

Social Security Administration Act 1992

37 In section 123 of the Social Security Administration Act 1992 (unauthorised disclosure of information) –

(a) in subsection (10), omit –
    (i) in paragraph (b), 'a receiver appointed under section 99 of the Mental Health Act 1983 or',
    (ii) in paragraph (d)(i), 'sub-paragraph (a) of rule 41(1) of the Court of Protection Rules 1984 or',
    (iii) in paragraph (d)(ii), 'a receiver ad interim appointed under sub-paragraph (b) of the said rule 41(1) or', and
    (iv) 'receiver,', and
(b) after that subsection, insert –

'(11) Where the person to whom the information relates lacks capacity (within the meaning of the Mental Capacity Act 2005) to consent to its disclosure, the appropriate person is –
    (a) a donee of an enduring power of attorney or lasting power of attorney (within the meaning of that Act), or
    (b) a deputy appointed for him, or any other person authorised, by the Court of Protection,
with power in that respect.'.

Judicial Pensions and Retirement Act 1993

38 (1) The Judicial Pensions and Retirement Act 1993 is amended as follows.

(2) In Schedule 1 (qualifying judicial offices), in Part 2, under the cross-heading 'Court officers', omit the reference to a Master of the Court of Protection except in the case of a person holding that office immediately before the commencement of this sub-paragraph or who had previously retired from that office or died.

(3) In Schedule 5 (retirement: the relevant offices), omit the entries relating to the Master and Deputy or temporary Master of the Court of Protection, except in the case of a person holding any of those offices immediately before the commencement of this sub-paragraph.

(4) In Schedule 7 (retirement: transitional provisions), omit paragraph 5(5)(i)(g) except in the case of a person holding office as a deputy or temporary Master of the Court of Protection immediately before the commencement of this sub-paragraph.

Leasehold Reform, Housing and Urban Development Act 1993

39 (1) For paragraph 4 of Schedule 2 to the Leasehold Reform, Housing and Urban Development Act 1993 (landlord under a disability), substitute –

  '4

    (1) This paragraph applies where a Chapter I or Chapter II landlord lacks capacity (within the meaning of the Mental Capacity Act 2005) to exercise his functions as a landlord.

(2) For the purposes of the Chapter concerned, the landlord's place is to be taken –

(a) by a donee of an enduring power of attorney or lasting power of attorney (within the meaning of the 2005 Act), or a deputy appointed for him by the Court of Protection, with power to exercise those functions, or

(b) if no deputy or donee has that power, by a person authorised in that respect by that court.'.

(2) That amendment does not affect any proceedings pending at the commencement of this paragraph in which a receiver or a person authorised under Part 7 of the Mental Health Act 1983 is acting on behalf of the landlord.

Goods Vehicles (Licensing of Operators) Act 1995

40 (1) The Goods Vehicles (Licensing of Operators) Act 1995 is amended as follows.

(2) In section 16(5) (termination of licence), for 'he becomes a patient within the meaning of Part VII of the Mental Health Act 1983' substitute 'he becomes a person who lacks capacity (within the meaning of the Mental Capacity Act 2005) to use a vehicle under the licence'.

(3) In section 48 (licence not to be transferable, etc) –

(a) in subsection (2) –

(i) for 'or become a patient within the meaning of Part VII of the Mental Health Act 1983' substitute ', or become a person who lacks capacity (within the meaning of the Mental Capacity Act 2005) to use a vehicle under the licence,', and

(ii) in paragraph (a), for 'became a patient' substitute 'became a person who lacked capacity in that respect', and

(b) in subsection (5), for 'a patient within the meaning of Part VII of the Mental Health Act 1983' substitute 'a person lacking capacity'.

Disability Discrimination Act 1995

41 In section 20(7) of the Disability Discrimination Act 1995 (regulations to disapply provisions about incapacity), in paragraph (b), for 'Part VII of the Mental Health Act 1983' substitute 'the Mental Capacity Act 2005'.

Trusts of Land and Appointment of Trustees Act 1996

42 (1) The Trusts of Land and Appointment of Trustees Act 1996 is amended as follows.

(2) In section 9 (delegation by trustees), in subsection (6), for the words from 'an enduring power' to the end substitute 'an enduring power of attorney or lasting power of attorney within the meaning of the Mental Capacity Act 2005'.

(3) In section 20 (the title to which becomes 'Appointment of substitute for trustee who lacks capacity') –

(a) in subsection (1)(a), for 'is incapable by reason of mental disorder of exercising' substitute 'lacks capacity (within the meaning of the Mental Capacity Act 2005) to exercise', and

(b) in subsection (2) –

    (i) for paragraph (a) substitute –

> '(a) a deputy appointed for the trustee by the Court of Protection,',

    (ii) in paragraph (b), for the words from 'a power of attorney' to the end substitute 'an enduring power of attorney or lasting power of attorney registered under the Mental Capacity Act 2005', and

    (iii) in paragraph (c), for the words from 'the authority' to the end substitute 'the Court of Protection'.

Human Rights Act 1998

43 In section 4(5) of the Human Rights Act 1998 (courts which may make declarations of incompatibility), after paragraph (e) insert –

> '(f) the Court of Protection, in any matter being dealt with by the President of the Family Division, the Vice-Chancellor or a puisne judge of the High Court.'

Access to Justice Act 1999

44 In paragraph 1 of Schedule 2 to the Access to Justice Act 1999 (services excluded from the Community Legal Service), after paragraph (e) insert –

> '(ea) the creation of lasting powers of attorney under the Mental Capacity Act 2005,
> (eb) the making of advance decisions under that Act,'.

Adoption and Children Act 2002

45 In section 52(1)(a) of the Adoption and Children Act 2002 (parental consent to adoption), for 'is incapable of giving consent' substitute 'lacks capacity (within the meaning of the Mental Capacity Act 2005) to give consent'.

Licensing Act 2003

46 (1) The Licensing Act 2003 is amended as follows.

(2) In section 27(1) (lapse of premises licence), for paragraph (b) substitute –

> '(b) becomes a person who lacks capacity (within the meaning of the Mental Capacity Act 2005) to hold the licence,'.

(3) In section 47 (interim authority notice in relation to premises licence) –

(a) in subsection (5), for paragraph (b) substitute –

> '(b) the former holder lacks capacity (within the meaning of the Mental Capacity Act 2005) to hold the licence and that person acts for him under an enduring power of attorney or lasting power of attorney registered under that Act,', and

(b) in subsection (10), omit the definition of 'mentally incapable'.

Courts Act 2003

47 (1) The Courts Act 2003 is amended as follows.

(2) In section 1(1) (the courts in relation to which the Lord Chancellor must discharge his general duty), after paragraph (a) insert –
          '(aa) the Court of Protection,'.

(3) In section 64(2) (judicial titles which the Lord Chancellor may by order alter) –

    (a)   omit the reference to a Master of the Court of Protection, and
    (b)   at the appropriate place insert a reference to each of the following –
        (i)   Senior Judge of the Court of Protection,
        (ii) President of the Court of Protection,
        (iii) Vice-president of the Court of Protection.

Schedule 7
Repeals

Section 67(2)

Short title and chapter	Extent of repeal
Trustee Act 1925	Section 54(3).
Law of Property Act 1925	Section 205(1)(xiii).
Administration of Estates Act 1925	Section 55(1)(viii)
U.S.A. Veterans' Pensions (Administration) Act 1949	In section 1(4), the words from 'or for whom' to '1983'.
Mental Health Act 1959	In Schedule 7, in Part 1, the entries relating to –
	section 33 of the Fines and Recoveries Act 1833,
	section 68 of the Improvement of Land Act 1864,
	section 55 of the Trustee Act 1925,
	section 205(1) of the Law of Property Act 1925,
	section 49 of the National Assistance Act 1948, and
	section 1 of the Variation of Trusts Act 1958.
Courts Act 1971	In Schedule 2, in Part 1A, the words 'Master of the Court of Protection'.
Local Government Act 1972	Section 118.
Limitation Act 1980	Section 38(3) and (4).
Senior Courts Act 1981	In Schedule 2, in Part 2, paragraph 11.

Mental Health Act 1983	Part 7.
	In section 139(1) the words from 'or in, or in pursuance' to 'Part VII of this Act,'.
	In section 145(1), in the definition of 'patient' the words '(except in Part VII of this Act)'.
	In sections 146 and 147 the words from '104(4)' to 'section),'.
	Schedule 3.
	In Schedule 4, paragraphs 1, 2, 4, 5, 7, 9, 14, 20, 22, 25, 32, 38, 55 and 56.
	In Schedule 5, paragraphs 26, 43, 44 and 45.
Enduring Powers of Attorney Act 1985	The whole Act.
Insolvency Act 1986	In section 389A(3) –
	the 'or' immediately after paragraph (b), and in paragraph (c), the words 'Part VII of the Mental Health Act 1983 or'.
	In section 390(4) –
	the 'or' immediately after paragraph (b), and in paragraph (c), the words 'Part VII of the Mental Health Act 1983 or'.
Public Trustee and Administration of Funds Act 1986	Section 2.
	Section 3(7).
Child Support Act 1991	In section 50(8) –
	paragraphs (b) and (d), and the 'or' immediately after paragraph (c).
Social Security Administration Act 1992	In section 123(10) –
	in paragraph (b), 'a receiver appointed under section 99 of the Mental Health Act 1983 or',
	in paragraph (d)(i), 'sub-paragraph (a) of rule 41(1) of the Court of Protection Rules Act 1984 or',
	in paragraph (d)(ii), 'a receiver ad interim appointed under sub-paragraph (b) of the said rule 41(1) or', and

	'receiver,'.
Trustee Delegation Act 1999	Section 4.
	Section 6.
	In section 7(3), the words 'in accordance with section 4 above'.
Care Standards Act 2000	In Schedule 4, paragraph 8.
Licensing Act 2003	In section 47(10), the definition of 'mentally incapable'.
Courts Act 2003	In section 64(2), the words 'Master of the Court of Protection'.

APPENDIX 2

MENTAL CAPACITY ACT 2005: CODE OF PRACTICE

Issued by the Lord Chancellor on 23 April 2007 in accordance with sections 42 and 43 of the Act.

FOREWORD BY LORD FALCONER

The Mental Capacity Act 2005 is a vitally important piece of legislation, and one that will make a real difference to the lives of people who may lack mental capacity. It will empower people to make decisions for themselves wherever possible, and protect people who lack capacity by providing a flexible framework that places individuals at the very heart of the decision-making process. It will ensure that they participate as much as possible in any decisions made on their behalf, and that these are made in their best interests. It also allows people to plan ahead for a time in the future when they might lack the capacity, for any number of reasons, to make decisions for themselves.

The Act covers a wide range of decisions and circumstances, but legislation alone is not the whole story. We have always recognised that the Act needs to be supported by practical guidance, and the Code of Practice is a key part of this. It explains how the Act will operate on a day-to-day basis and offers examples of best practice to carers and practitioners.

Many individuals and organisations have read and commented upon earlier drafts of the Code of Practice and I am very grateful to all those who contributed to this process. This Code of Practice is a better document as a result of this input.

A number of people will be under a formal duty to have regard to the Code: professionals and paid carers for example, or people acting as attorneys or as deputies appointed by the Court of Protection. But for many people, the most important relationships will be with the wide range of less formal carers, the close family and friends who know the person best, some of whom will have been caring for them for many years. The Code is also here to provide help and guidance for them. It will be crucial to the Code's success that all those relying upon it have a document that is clear and that they can understand. I have been particularly keen that we do all we can to achieve this.

The Code of Practice will be important in shaping the way the Mental Capacity Act 2005 is put into practice and I strongly encourage you to take the time to read and digest it.

INTRODUCTION

The Mental Capacity Act 2005, covering England and Wales, provides a statutory framework for people who lack capacity to make decisions for themselves, or who have capacity and want to make preparations for a time when they may lack capacity in the future. It sets out who can take decisions, in which situations, and how they should go about this. The Act received Royal Assent on 7 April 2005 and will come into force during 2007.

The legal framework provided by the Mental Capacity Act 2005 is supported by this Code of Practice (the Code), which provides guidance and information about how the Act works in practice. Section 42 of the Act requires the Lord Chancellor to produce a Code of Practice for the guidance of a range of people with different duties and functions under the Act. Before the Code is prepared, section 43 requires that the Lord Chancellor must have consulted the National Assembly for Wales and such other persons as he considers appropriate. The Code is also subject to the approval of Parliament and must have been placed before both Houses of Parliament for a 40-day period without either House voting against it. This Code of Practice has been produced in accordance with these requirements.

The Code has statutory force, which means that certain categories of people have a legal duty to have regard to it when working with or caring for adults who may lack capacity to make decisions for themselves. These categories of people are listed below.

How should the Code of Practice be used?

The Code of Practice provides guidance to anyone who is working with and/ or caring for adults who may lack capacity to make particular decisions. It describes their responsibilities when acting or making decisions on behalf of individuals who lack the capacity to act or make these decisions for themselves. In particular, the Code of Practice focuses on those who have a duty of care to someone who lacks the capacity to agree to the care that is being provided.

Who is the Code of Practice for?

The Act does not impose a legal duty on anyone to 'comply' with the Code – it should be viewed as guidance rather than instruction. But if they have not followed relevant guidance contained in the Code then they will be expected to give good reasons why they have departed from it.

Certain categories of people are legally required to 'have regard to' relevant guidance in the Code of Practice. That means they must be aware of the Code of Practice when acting or making decisions on behalf of someone who lacks capacity to make a decision for themselves, and they should be able to explain how they have had regard to the Code when acting or making decisions.

The categories of people that are required to have regard to the Code of Practice include anyone who is:

- an attorney under a Lasting Power of Attorney (LPA) (see Chapter 7)
- a deputy appointed by the new Court of Protection (see Chapter 8)
- acting as an Independent Mental Capacity Advocate (see Chapter 10)
- carrying out research approved in accordance with the Act (see Chapter 11)
- acting in a professional capacity for, or in relation to, a person who lacks capacity working
- being paid for acts for or in relation to a person who lacks capacity.
- The last two categories cover a wide range of people. People acting in a professional capacity may include:
- a variety of healthcare staff (doctors, dentists, nurses, therapists, radiologists, paramedics etc)
- social care staff (social workers, care managers, etc)
- others who may occasionally be involved in the care of people who lack capacity to make the decision in question, such as ambulance crew, housing workers, or police officers.

People who are being paid for acts for or in relation to a person who lacks capacity may include:

- care assistants in a care home
- care workers providing domiciliary care services, and
- others who have been contracted to provide a service to people who lack capacity to consent to that service.

However, the Act applies more generally to everyone who looks after, or cares for, someone who lacks capacity to make particular decisions for themselves. This includes family carers or other carers. Although these carers are not legally required to have regard to the Code of Practice, the guidance given in the Code will help them to understand the Act and apply it. They should follow the guidance in the Code as far as they are aware of it.

What does 'lacks capacity' mean?

One of the most important terms in the Code is 'a person who lacks capacity'.

Whenever the term 'a person who lacks capacity' is used, it means **a person who lacks capacity to make a particular decision or take a particular action for themselves at the time the decision or action needs to be taken.**

This reflects the fact that people may lack capacity to make some decisions for themselves, but will have capacity to make other decisions. For example, they may have capacity to make small decisions about everyday issues such as what to wear or what to eat, but lack capacity to make more complex decisions about financial matters.

It also reflects the fact that a person who lacks capacity to make a decision for themselves at a certain time may be able to make that decision at a later date. This may be because they have an illness or condition that means their capacity changes. Alternatively, it may be because at the time the decision needs to be made, they are unconscious or barely conscious whether due to an accident or being under anaesthetic or their ability to make a decision may be affected by the influence of alcohol or drugs.

Finally, it reflects the fact that while some people may always lack capacity to make some types of decisions – for example, due to a condition or severe learning disability that has affected them from birth – others may learn new skills that enable them to gain capacity and make decisions for themselves.

Chapter 4 provides a full definition of what is meant by 'lacks capacity'.

What does the Code of Practice actually cover?

The Code explains the Act and its key provisions.

- Chapter 1 introduces the Mental Capacity Act 2005.
- Chapter 2 sets out the five statutory principles behind the Act and the way they affect how it is put in practice.
- Chapter 3 explains how the Act makes sure that people are given the right help and support to make their own decisions.
- Chapter 4 explains how the Act defines 'a person who lacks capacity to make a decision' and sets out a single clear test for assessing whether a person lacks capacity to make a particular decision at a particular time.
- Chapter 5 explains what the Act means by acting in the best interests of someone lacking capacity to make a decision for themselves, and describes the checklist set out in the Act for working out what is in someone's best interests.
- Chapter 6 explains how the Act protects people providing care or treatment for someone who lacks the capacity to consent to the action being taken.
- Chapter 7 shows how people who wish to plan ahead for the possibility that they might lack the capacity to make particular decisions for

themselves in the future are able to grant Lasting Powers of Attorney (LPAs) to named individuals to make certain decisions on their behalf, and how attorneys appointed under an LPA should act.

- Chapter 8 describes the role of the new Court of Protection, established under the Act, to make a decision or to appoint a decision-maker on someone's behalf in cases where there is no other way of resolving a matter affecting a person who lacks capacity to make the decision in question.

- Chapter 9 explains the procedures that must be followed if someone wishes to make an advance decision to refuse medical treatment to come into effect when they lack capacity to refuse the specified treatment.

- Chapter 10 describes the role of Independent Mental Capacity Advocates appointed under the Act to help and represent particularly vulnerable people who lack capacity to make certain significant decisions. It also sets out when they should be instructed.

- Chapter 11 provides guidance on how the Act sets out specific safeguards and controls for research involving, or in relation to, people lacking capacity to consent to their participation.

- Chapter 12 explains those parts of the Act which can apply to children and young people and how these relate to other laws affecting them.

- Chapter 13 explains how the Act relates to the Mental Health Act 1983.

- Chapter 14 sets out the role of the Public Guardian, a new public office established by the Act to oversee attorneys and deputies and to act as a single point of contact for referring allegations of abuse in relation to attorneys and deputies to other relevant agencies.

- Chapter 15 examines the various ways that disputes over decisions made under the Act or otherwise affecting people lacking capacity to make relevant decisions can be resolved.

- Chapter 16 summarises how the laws about data protection and freedom of information relate to the provisions of the Act.

What is the legal status of the Code?

Where does it apply?

The Act and therefore this Code applies to everyone it concerns who is habitually resident or present in England and Wales. However, it will also be possible for the Court of Protection to consider cases which involve persons who have assets or property outside this jurisdiction, or who live abroad but have assets or property in England or Wales.

What happens if people don't comply with it?

There are no specific sanctions for failure to comply with the Code. But a failure to comply with the Code can be used in evidence before a court or tribunal in any civil or criminal proceedings, if the court or tribunal considers it to be relevant to those proceedings. For example, if a court or tribunal believes that anyone making decisions for someone who lacks capacity has not acted in the best interests of the person they care for, the court can use the person's failure to comply with the Code as evidence. That's why it's important that anyone working with or caring for a person who lacks capacity to make specific decisions should become familiar with the Code.

Where can I find out more?

The Code of Practice is not an exhaustive guide or complete statement of the law. Other materials have been produced by the Department for Constitutional Affairs, the Department of Health and the Office of the Public Guardian to help explain aspects of the Act from different perspectives and for people in different situations. These include guides for family carers and other carers and basic information of interest to the general public. Professional organisations may also produce specialist information and guidance for their members.

The Code also provides information on where to get more detailed guidance from other sources. A list of contact details is provided in Annex A and further information appears in the footnotes to each chapter. References made and any links provided to material or organisations do not form part of the Code and do not attract the same legal status. Signposts to further information are provided for assistance only and references made should not suggest that the Department for Constitutional Affairs endorses such material.

Using the code

References in the Code of Practice

Throughout the Code of Practice, the Mental Capacity Act 2005 is referred to as 'the Act' and any sections quoted refer to this Act unless otherwise stated. References are shown as follows: section 4(1). This refers to the section of the Act. The subsection number is in brackets.

Where reference is made to provisions from other legislation, the full title of the relevant Act will be set out, for example 'the Mental Health Act 1983', unless otherwise stated. (For example, in Chapter 13, the Mental Health Act 1983 is referred to as MHA and the Mental Capacity Act as MCA.) The Code of Practice is sometimes referred to as the Code.

Scenarios used in the Code of Practice

The Code includes many boxes within the text in which there are scenarios, using imaginary characters and situations. These are intended to help illustrate what is meant in the main text. The scenarios should not in any way be taken as templates for decisions that need to be made in similar situations.

Alternative formats and further information

The Code is also available in Welsh and can be made available in other formats on request.

****

1 WHAT IS THE MENTAL CAPACITY ACT 2005?

1.1 The Mental Capacity Act 2005 (the Act) provides the legal framework for acting and making decisions on behalf of individuals who lack the mental capacity to make particular decisions for themselves. Everyone working with and/or caring for an adult who may lack capacity to make specific decisions must comply with this Act when making decisions or acting for that person, when the person lacks the capacity to make a particular decision for themselves. The same rules apply whether the decisions are life-changing events or everyday matters.

1.2 The Act's starting point is to confirm in legislation that it should be assumed that an adult (aged 16 or over) has full legal capacity to make decisions for themselves (the right to autonomy) unless it can be shown that they lack capacity to make a decision for themselves at the time the decision needs to be made. This is known as the presumption of capacity. The Act also states that people must be given all appropriate help and support to enable them to make their own decisions or to maximise their participation in any decision-making process.

1.3 The underlying philosophy of the Act is to ensure that any decision made, or action taken, on behalf of someone who lacks the capacity to make the decision or act for themselves is made in their best interests.

1.4 The Act is intended to assist and support people who may lack capacity and to discourage anyone who is involved in caring for someone who lacks capacity from being overly restrictive or controlling. But the Act also aims to balance an individual's right to make decisions for themselves with their right to be protected from harm if they lack capacity to make decisions to protect themselves.

1.5 The Act sets out a legal framework of how to act and make decisions on behalf of people who lack capacity to make specific decisions for themselves. It sets out some core principles and methods for making decisions and carrying out actions in relation to personal welfare, healthcare and financial matters affecting people who may lack capacity to make specific decisions about these issues for themselves.

1.6 Many of the provisions in the Act are based upon existing common law principles (i.e. principles that have been established through decisions made by courts in individual cases). The Act clarifies and improves upon these principles and builds on current good practice which is based on the principles.

1.7 The Act introduces several new roles, bodies and powers, all of which will support the Act's provisions. These include:

- Attorneys appointed under Lasting Powers of Attorney (see Chapter 7)
- The new Court of Protection, and court-appointed deputies (see Chapter 8)
- Independent Mental Capacity Advocates (see Chapter 10).

The roles, bodies and powers are all explained in more depth in the specific chapters of the Code highlighted above.

What decisions are covered by the Act, and what decisions are excluded?

1.8 The Act covers a wide range of decisions made, or actions taken, on behalf of people who may lack capacity to make specific decisions for themselves. These can be decisions about day-to-day matters – like what to wear, or what to buy when doing the weekly shopping – or decisions about major life-changing events, such as whether the person should move into a care home or undergo a major surgical operation.

1.9 There are certain decisions which can never be made on behalf of a person who lacks capacity to make those specific decisions. This is because they are either so personal to the individual concerned, or governed by other legislation.

1.10 Sections 27–29 and 62 of the Act set out the specific decisions which can never be made or actions which can never be carried out under the Act, whether by family members, carers, professionals, attorneys or the Court of Protection. These are summarised below.

Decisions concerning family relationships (section 27)

Nothing in the Act permits a decision to be made on someone else's behalf on any of the following matters:

- consenting to marriage or a civil partnership
- consenting to have sexual relations
- consenting to a decree of divorce on the basis of two years' separation
- consenting to the dissolution of a civil partnership
- consenting to a child being placed for adoption or the making of an adoption order
- discharging parental responsibility for a child in matters not relating to the child's property, or
- giving consent under the Human Fertilisation and Embryology Act 1990.

Mental Health Act matters (section 28)

Where a person who lacks capacity to consent is currently detained and being treated under Part 4 of the Mental Health Act 1983, nothing in the Act authorises anyone to:

- give the person treatment for mental disorder, or
- consent to the person being given treatment for mental disorder.

Further guidance is given in Chapter 13 of the Code.

Voting rights (section 29)

Nothing in the Act permits a decision on voting, at an election for any public office or at a referendum, to be made on behalf of a person who lacks capacity to vote.

Unlawful killing or assisting suicide (section 62)

For the avoidance of doubt, nothing in the Act is to be taken to affect the law relating to murder, manslaughter or assisting suicide.

1.11 Although the Act does not allow anyone to make a decision about these matters on behalf of someone who lacks capacity to make such a decision for themselves (for example, consenting to have sexual relations), this does not prevent action being taken to protect a vulnerable person from abuse or exploitation.

How does the Act relate to other legislation?

1.12 The Mental Capacity Act 2005 will apply in conjunction with other legislation affecting people who may lack capacity in relation to specific matters. This means that healthcare and social care staff acting under the Act should also be aware of their obligations under other legislation, including (but not limited to) the:
- Care Standards Act 2000
- Data Protection Act 1998
- Disability Discrimination Act 1995
- Human Rights Act 1998
- Mental Health Act 1983
- National Health Service and Community Care Act 1990
- Human Tissue Act 2004.

What does the Act say about the Code of Practice?

1.13 Section 42 of the Act sets out the purpose of the Code of Practice, which is to provide guidance for specific people in specific circumstances.

Section 43 explains the procedures that had to be followed in preparing the Code and consulting on its contents, and for its consideration by Parliament.

Section 42, subsections (4) and (5), set out the categories of people who are placed under a legal duty to 'have regard to' the Code and gives further information about the status of the Code. More details can be found in the Introduction, which explains the legal status of the Code.

2 WHAT ARE THE STATUTORY PRINCIPLES AND HOW SHOULD THEY BE APPLIED?

Section 1 of the Act sets out the five 'statutory principles' – the values that underpin the legal requirements in the Act. The Act is intended to be enabling and supportive of people who lack capacity, not restricting or controlling of their lives. It aims to protect people who lack capacity to make particular decisions, but also to maximise their ability to make decisions, or to participate in decision-making, as far as they are able to do so.

The five statutory principles are:

1. A person must be assumed to have capacity unless it is established that they lack capacity.
2. A person is not to be treated as unable to make a decision unless all practicable steps to help him to do so have been taken without success.
3. A person is not to be treated as unable to make a decision merely because he makes an unwise decision.
4. An act done, or decision made, under this Act for or on behalf of a person who lacks capacity must be done, or made, in his best interests.
5. Before the act is done, or the decision is made, regard must be had to whether the purpose for which it is needed can be as effectively achieved in a way that is less restrictive of the person's rights and freedom of action.

This chapter provides guidance on how people should interpret and apply the statutory principles when using the Act. Following the principles and applying them to the Act's framework for decision-making will help to ensure not only that appropriate action is taken in individual cases, but also to point the way to solutions in difficult or uncertain situations.

> In this chapter, as throughout the Code, a person's capacity (or lack of capacity) refers specifically to their capacity to make a particular decision at the time it needs to be made.

Quick summary

- Every adult has the right to make their own decisions if they have the capacity to do so. Family carers and healthcare or social care staff must assume that a person has the capacity to make decisions, unless it can be established that the person does not have capacity.

- People should receive support to help them make their own decisions. Before concluding that individuals lack capacity to make a particular decision, it is important to take all possible steps to try to help them reach a decision themselves.

- People have the right to make decisions that others might think are unwise. A person who makes a decision that others think is unwise should not automatically be labelled as lacking the capacity to make a decision.

- Any act done for, or any decision made on behalf of, someone who lacks capacity must be in their best interests.

- Any act done for, or any decision made on behalf of, someone who lacks capacity should be an option that is less restrictive of their basic rights and freedoms – as long as it is still in their best interests.

What is the role of the statutory principles?

2.1 The statutory principles aim to:
- protect people who lack capacity and
- help them take part, as much as possible, in decisions that affect them.

They aim to assist and support people who may lack capacity to make particular decisions, not to restrict or control their lives.

2.2 The statutory principles apply to any act done or decision made under the Act. When followed and applied to the Act's decision-making framework, they will help people take appropriate action in individual cases. They will also help people find solutions in difficult or uncertain situations.

How should the statutory principles be applied?

Principle 1: '*A person must be assumed to have capacity unless it is established that he lacks capacity.*' (section 1(2))

2.3 This principle states that every adult has the right to make their own decisions – unless there is proof that they lack the capacity to make a particular decision when it needs to be made. This has been a fundamental principle of the common law for many years and it is now set out in the Act.

2.4 It is important to balance people's right to make a decision with their right to safety and protection when they can't make decisions to protect themselves. But the starting assumption must always be that an individual has the capacity, until there is proof that they do not. Chapter 4 explains the Act's definition of 'lack of capacity' and the processes involved in assessing capacity.

Scenario: Assessing a person's capacity to make decisions

When planning her retirement, Mrs Arnold made and registered a Lasting Power of Attorney (LPA) – a legal process that would allow her son to manage her property and financial affairs if she ever lacked capacity to manage them herself. She has now been diagnosed with dementia, and her son is worried that she is becoming confused about money.

Her son must assume that his mother has capacity to manage her affairs. Then he must consider each of Mrs Arnold's financial decisions as she makes them, giving her any help and support she needs to make these decisions herself.

Mrs Arnold's son goes shopping with her, and he sees she is quite capable of finding goods and making sure she gets the correct change. But when she needs to make decisions about her investments, Mrs Arnold gets confused – even though she has made such decisions in the past. She still doesn't understand after her son explains the different options.

Her son concludes that she has capacity to deal with everyday financial matters but not more difficult affairs at this time. Therefore, he is able to use the LPA for the difficult financial decisions his mother can't make. But Mrs Arnold can continue to deal with her other affairs for as long as she has capacity to do so.

2.5 Some people may need help to be able to make a decision or to communicate their decision. However, this does not necessarily mean that they cannot make that decision – unless there is proof that they do lack capacity to do so. Anyone who believes that a person lacks capacity should be able to prove their case. Chapter 4 explains the standard of proof required.

Principle 2: '*A person is not to be treated as unable to make a decision unless all practicable steps to help him to do so have been taken without success.*' *(section 1(3))*

2.6 It is important to do everything practical (the Act uses the term 'practicable') to help a person make a decision for themselves before concluding that they lack capacity to do so. People with an illness or disability affecting their ability to make a decision should receive support to help them make as many decisions as they can. This principle aims to stop people being automatically labelled as lacking capacity to make particular decisions. Because it encourages individuals to play as big a role as possible in decision-making, it also helps prevent unnecessary interventions in their lives.

2.7 The kind of support people might need to help them make a decision varies. It depends on personal circumstances, the kind of decision that has to be made and the time available to make the decision. It might include:

- using a different form of communication (for example, non-verbal communication)
- providing information in a more accessible form (for example, photographs, drawings, or tapes)
- treating a medical condition which may be affecting the person's capacity or
- having a structured programme to improve a person's capacity to make particular decisions (for example, helping a person with learning disabilities to learn new skills).

Chapter 3 gives more information on ways to help people make decisions for themselves.

Scenario: *Taking steps to help people make decisions for themselves*

Mr Jackson is brought into hospital following a traffic accident. He is conscious but in shock. He cannot speak and is clearly in distress, making noises and gestures.

From his behaviour, hospital staff conclude that Mr Jackson currently lacks capacity to make decisions about treatment for his injuries, and they give him urgent treatment. They hope that after he has recovered from the shock they can use an advocate to help explain things to him.

However, one of the nurses thinks she recognises some of his gestures as sign language, and tries signing to him. Mr Jackson immediately becomes calmer, and the doctors realise that he can communicate in sign language. He can also answer some written questions about his injuries.

The hospital brings in a qualified sign-language interpreter and concludes that Mr Jackson has the capacity to make decisions about any further treatment.

2.8 Anyone supporting a person who may lack capacity should not use excessive persuasion or 'undue pressure'.[1] This might include behaving in a manner which is overbearing or dominating, or seeking to influence the

---

[1] Undue influence in relation to consent to medical treatment was considered in *Re T (Adult: Refusal of Treatment)* [1992] 4 All E R 649, 662 and in financial matters in *Royal Bank of Scotland v Etridge* [2001] UKHL 44.

person's decision, and could push a person into making a decision they might not otherwise have made. However, it is important to provide appropriate advice and information.

Scenario: *Giving appropriate advice and support*

Sara, a young woman with severe depression, is getting treatment from mental health services. Her psychiatrist determines that she has capacity to make decisions about treatment, if she gets advice and support.

Her mother is trying to persuade Sara to agree to electro-convulsive therapy (ECT), which helped her mother when she had clinical depression in the past. However, a friend has told Sara that ECT is 'barbaric'.

The psychiatrist provides factual information about the different types of treatment available and explains their advantages and disadvantages. She also describes how different people experience different reactions or side effects. Sara is then able to consider what treatment is right for her, based on factual information rather than the personal opinions of her mother and friend.

2.9　In some situations treatment cannot be delayed while a person gets support to make a decision. This can happen in emergency situations or when an urgent decision is required (for example, immediate medical treatment). In these situations, the only practical and appropriate steps might be to keep a person informed of what is happening and why.

Principle 3: '*A person is not to be treated as unable to make a decision merely because he makes an unwise decision.*' *(section 1(4))*

2.10　Everybody has their own values, beliefs, preferences and attitudes. A person should not be assumed to lack the capacity to make a decision just because other people think their decision is unwise. This applies even if family members, friends or healthcare or social care staff are unhappy with a decision.

Scenario: *Allowing people to make decisions that others think are unwise*

Mr Garvey is a 40-year-old man with a history of mental health problems. He sees a Community Psychiatric Nurse (CPN) regularly. Mr Garvey decides to spend £2,000 of his savings on a camper van to travel around Scotland for six months. His CPN is concerned that it will be difficult to give Mr Garvey continuous support and treatment while travelling, and that his mental health might deteriorate as a result.　　　　　➙

> However, having talked it through with his CPN, it is clear that Mr Garvey is fully aware of these concerns and has the capacity to make this particular decision. He has decided he would like to have a break and thinks this will be good for him.
>
> Just because, in the CPN's opinion, continuity of care might be a wiser option, it should not be assumed that Mr Garvey lacks the capacity to make this decision for himself.

2.11 There may be cause for concern if somebody:

- repeatedly makes unwise decisions that put them at significant risk of harm or exploitation or
- makes a particular unwise decision that is obviously irrational or out of character.

These things do not necessarily mean that somebody lacks capacity. But there might be need for further investigation, taking into account the person's past decisions and choices. For example, have they developed a medical condition or disorder that is affecting their capacity to make particular decisions? Are they easily influenced by undue pressure? Or do they need more information to help them understand the consequences of the decision they are making?

Scenario: *Decisions that cause concern*

Cyril, an elderly man with early signs of dementia, spends nearly £300 on fresh fish from a door-to-door salesman. He has always been fond of fish and has previously bought small amounts in this way. Before his dementia, Cyril was always very careful with his money and would never have spent so much on fish in one go.

This decision alone may not automatically mean Cyril lacks capacity to manage all aspects of his property and affairs. But his daughter makes further enquiries and discovers Cyril has overpaid his cleaner on several occasions – something he has never done in the past. He has also made payments from his savings that he cannot account for.

His daughter decides it is time to use the registered Lasting Power of Attorney her father made in the past. This gives her the authority to manage Cyril's property and affairs whenever he lacks the capacity to manage them himself. She takes control of Cyril's chequebook to protect him from possible exploitation, but she can still ensure he has enough money to spend on his everyday needs.

Principle 4: '*An act done, or decision made, under this Act for or on behalf of a person who lacks capacity must be done, or made, in his best interests.*' *(section 1(5))*

2.12 The principle of acting or making a decision in the best interests of a person who lacks capacity to make the decision in question is a well-established principle in the common law.[2] This principle is now set out in the Act, so that a person's best interests must be the basis for all decisions made and actions carried out on their behalf in situations where they lack capacity to make those particular decisions for themselves. The only exceptions to this are around research (see Chapter 11) and advance decisions to refuse treatment (see Chapter 9) where other safeguards apply.

2.13 It is impossible to give a single description of what 'best interests' are, because they depend on individual circumstances. However, section 4 of the Act sets out a checklist of steps to follow in order to determine what is in the best interests of a person who lacks capacity to make the decision in question each time someone acts or makes a decision on that person's behalf. See Chapter 5 for detailed guidance and examples.

Principle 5: *'Before the act is done, or the decision is made, regard must be had to whether the purpose for which it is needed can be as effectively achieved in a way that is less restrictive of the person's rights and freedom of action.'* *(section 1(6))*

2.14 Before somebody makes a decision or acts on behalf of a person who lacks capacity to make that decision or consent to the act, they must always question if they can do something else that would interfere less with the person's basic rights and freedoms. This is called finding the 'less restrictive alternative'. It includes considering whether there is a need to act or make a decision at all.

2.15 Where there is more than one option, it is important to explore ways that would be less restrictive or allow the most freedom for a person who lacks capacity to make the decision in question. However, the final decision must always allow the original purpose of the decision or act to be achieved.

2.16 Any decision or action must still be in the best interests of the person who lacks capacity. So sometimes it may be necessary to choose an option that is not the least restrictive alternative if that option is in the person's best interests. In practice, the process of choosing a less restrictive option and deciding what is in the person's best interests will be combined. But both principles must be applied each time a decision or action may be taken on behalf of a person who lacks capacity to make the relevant decision.

Scenario: *Finding a less restrictive option*

Sunil, a young man with severe learning disabilities, also has a very severe and unpredictable form of epilepsy that is associated with drop attacks. This can result in serious injury. A neurologist has advised that, to limit ➙

---

2 See for example *Re MB (Medical Treatment)* [1997] 2 FLR 426, CA; *Re A (Male Sterilisation)* [2000] 1 FLR 549; *Re S (Sterilisation: Patient's Best Interests)* [2000] 2 FLR 389; *Re F (Adult Patient: Sterilisation)* [2001] Fam 15.

the harm that might come from these attacks, Sunil should either be under constant close observation, or wear a protective helmet.

After assessment, it is decided that Sunil lacks capacity to decide on the most appropriate course of action for himself. But through his actions and behaviour, Sunil makes it clear he doesn't like to be too closely observed – even though he likes having company.

The staff of the home where he lives consider various options, such as providing a special room for him with soft furnishings, finding ways to keep him under close observation or getting him to wear a helmet. In discussion with Sunil's parents, they agree that the option that is in his best interests, and is less restrictive, will be the helmet – as it will enable him to go out, and prevent further harm.

3 HOW SHOULD PEOPLE BE HELPED TO MAKE THEIR OWN DECISIONS?

Before deciding that someone lacks capacity to make a particular decision, it is important to take all practical and appropriate steps to enable them to make that decision themselves (statutory principle 2, see Chapter 2). In addition, as section 3(2) of the Act underlines, these steps (such as helping individuals to communicate) must be taken in a way which reflects the person's individual circumstances and meets their particular needs. This chapter provides practical guidance on how to support people to make decisions for themselves, or play as big a role as possible in decision-making.

In this chapter, as throughout the Code, a person's capacity (or lack of capacity) refers specifically to their capacity to make a particular decision at the time it needs to be made.

Quick summary

To help someone make a decision for themselves, check the following points:

Providing relevant information

- Does the person have all the relevant information they need to make a particular decision?
- If they have a choice, have they been given information on all the alternatives?

Communicating in an appropriate way

- Could information be explained or presented in a way that is easier for the person to understand (for example, by using simple language or visual aids)?

- Have different methods of communication been explored if required, including non-verbal communication?

- Could anyone else help with communication (for example, a family member, support worker, interpreter, speech and language therapist or advocate)?

Making the person feel at ease

- Are there particular times of day when the person's understanding is better?

- Are there particular locations where they may feel more at ease?

- Could the decision be put off to see whether the person can make the decision at a later time when circumstances are right for them?

Supporting the person

- Can anyone else help or support the person to make choices or express a view?

How can someone be helped to make a decision?

3.1   There are several ways in which people can be helped and supported to enable them to make a decision for themselves. These will vary depending on the decision to be made, the time-scale for making the decision and the individual circumstances of the person making it.

3.2   The Act applies to a wide range of people with different conditions that may affect their capacity to make particular decisions. So, the appropriate steps to take will depend on:
   - a person's individual circumstances (for example, somebody with learning difficulties may need a different approach to somebody with dementia)
   - the decision the person has to make and
   - the length of time they have to make it.

3.3   Significant, one-off decisions (such as moving house) will require different considerations from day-to-day decisions about a person's care and welfare. However, the same general processes should apply to each decision.

3.4   In most cases, only some of the steps described in this chapter will be relevant or appropriate, and the list included here is not exhaustive. It is up to the people (whether family carers, paid carers, healthcare staff or anyone else) caring for or supporting an individual to consider what is possible and appropriate in individual cases. In all cases it is extremely important to find the most effective way of communicating with the person concerned. Good communication is essential for explaining relevant information in an appropriate way and for ensuring that the steps being taken meet an individual's needs.

3.5 Providing appropriate help with decision-making should form part of care planning processes for people receiving health or social care services. Examples include:
- Person Centred Planning for people with learning disabilities
- the Care Programme Approach for people with mental disorders
- the Single Assessment Process for older people in England, and
- the Unified Assessment Process in Wales.

What happens in emergency situations?

3.6 Clearly, in emergency medical situations (for example, where a person collapses with a heart attack or for some unknown reason and is brought unconscious into a hospital), urgent decisions will have to be made and immediate action taken in the person's best interests. In these situations, it may not be practical or appropriate to delay the treatment while trying to help the person make their own decisions, or to consult with any known attorneys or deputies. However, even in emergency situations, healthcare staff should try to communicate with the person and keep them informed of what is happening.

What information should be provided to people and how should it be provided?

3.7 Providing relevant information is essential in all decision-making. For example, to make a choice about what they want for breakfast, people need to know what food is available. If the decision concerns medical treatment, the doctor must explain the purpose and effect of the course of treatment and the likely consequences of accepting or refusing treatment.

3.8 All practical and appropriate steps must be taken to help people to make a decision for themselves. Information must be tailored to an individual's needs and abilities. It must also be in the easiest and most appropriate form of communication for the person concerned.

What information is relevant?

3.9 The Act cannot state exactly what information will be relevant in each case. Anyone helping someone to make a decision for themselves should therefore follow these steps.
- Take time to explain anything that might help the person make a decision. It is important that they have access to all the information they need to make an informed decision.

- Try not to give more detail than the person needs – this might confuse them. In some cases, a simple, broad explanation will be enough. But it must not miss out important information.
- What are the risks and benefits? Describe any foreseeable consequences of making the decision, and of not making any decision at all.
- Explain the effects the decision might have on the person and those close to them – including the people involved in their care.
- If they have a choice, give them the same information in a balanced way for all the options.
- For some types of decisions, it may be important to give access to advice from elsewhere. This may be independent or specialist advice (for example, from a medical practitioner or a financial or legal adviser). But it might simply be advice from trusted friends or relatives.

Communication – general guidance

3.10 To help someone make a decision for themselves, all possible and appropriate means of communication should be tried.

- Ask people who know the person well about the best form of communication (try speaking to family members, carers, day centre staff or support workers). They may also know somebody the person can communicate with easily, or the time when it is best to communicate with them.
- Use simple language. Where appropriate, use pictures, objects or illustrations to demonstrate ideas.
- Speak at the right volume and speed, with appropriate words and sentence structure. It may be helpful to pause to check understanding or show that a choice is available.
- Break down difficult information into smaller points that are easy to understand. Allow the person time to consider and understand each point before continuing.
- It may be necessary to repeat information or go back over a point several times.
- Is help available from people the person trusts (relatives, friends, GP, social worker, religious or community leaders)? If so, make sure the person's right to confidentiality is respected.
- Be aware of cultural, ethnic or religious factors that shape a person's way of thinking, behaviour or communication. For example, in some cultures it is important to involve the community in decision-making. Some religious beliefs (for example, those of Jehovah's Witnesses or Christian Scientists) may influence the person's approach to medical treatment and information about treatment decisions.
- If necessary, consider using a professional language interpreter. Even if a person communicated in English or Welsh in the past, they may have lost some verbal skills (for example, because of dementia). They

may now prefer to communicate in their first language. It is often more appropriate to use a professional interpreter rather than to use family members.

- If using pictures to help communication, make sure they are relevant and the person can understand them easily. For example, a red bus may represent a form of transport to one person but a day trip to another.
- Would an advocate (someone who can support and represent the person) improve communication in the current situation? (See Chapters 10 and 15 for more information about advocates.)

Scenario: Providing relevant information

Mrs Thomas has Alzheimer's disease and lives n a care home. She enjoys taking part in the activities provided at the home. Today there is a choice between going to a flower show, attending her usual pottery class or watching a DVD. Although she has the capacity to choose, having to decide is making her anxious.

The care assistant carefully explains the different options. She tells Mrs Thomas about the DVD she could watch, but Mrs Thomas doesn't like the sound of it. The care assistant shows her a leaflet about the flower show. She explains the plans for the day, where the show is being held and how long it will take to get there in the mini-van. She has to repeat this information several times, as Mrs Thomas keeps asking whether they will be back in time for supper. She also tells Mrs Thomas that one of her friends is going on the trip.

At first, Mrs Thomas is reluctant to disturb her usual routine. But the care assistant reassures her she will not lose her place at pottery if she misses a class. With this information, Mrs Thomas can therefore choose whether or not to go on the day trip.

Helping people with specific communication or cognitive problems

3.11 Where people have specific communication or cognitive problems, the following steps can help:
- Find out how the person is used to communicating. Do they use picture boards or Makaton (signs and symbols for people with communication or learning difficulties)? Or do they have a way of communicating that is only known to those close to them?
- If the person has hearing difficulties, use their preferred method of communication (for example, visual aids, written messages or sign language). Where possible, use a qualified interpreter.
- Are mechanical devices such as voice synthesisers, keyboards or other computer equipment available to help?

- If the person does not use verbal communication skills, allow more time to learn how to communicate effectively.
- For people who use non-verbal methods of communication, their behaviour (in particular, changes in behaviour) can provide indications of their feelings.
- Some people may prefer to use non-verbal means of communication and can communicate most effectively in written form using computers or other communication technologies. This is particularly true for those with autistic spectrum disorders.
- For people with specific communication difficulties, consider other types of professional help (for example, a speech and language therapist or an expert in clinical neuropsychology).

Scenario: Helping people with specific communication difficulties

David is a deafblind man with learning disabilities who has no formal communication. He lives in a specialist home. He begins to bang his head against the wall and repeats this behaviour throughout the day. He has not done this before.

The staff in the home are worried and discuss ways to reduce the risk of injury. They come up with a range of possible interventions, aimed at engaging him with activities and keeping him away from objects that could injure him. They assess these as less restrictive ways to ensure he is safe. But David lacks the capacity to make a decision about which would be the best option.

The staff call in a specialist in challenging behaviour, who says that David's behaviour is communicative. After investigating this further, staff discover he is in pain because of tooth decay. They consult a dentist about how to resolve this, and the dentist decides it is in David's best interests to get treatment for the tooth decay. After treatment, David's head-banging stops.

What steps should be taken to put a person at ease?

3.12 To help put someone at ease and so improve their ability to make a decision, careful consideration should be given to both location and timing.

Location

3.13 In terms of location, consider the following:

- Where possible, choose a location where the person feels most at ease. For example, people are usually more comfortable in their own home than at a doctor's surgery.
- Would the person find it easier to make their decision in a relevant location? For example, could you help them decide about medical treatment by taking them to hospital to see what is involved?
- Choose a quiet location where the discussion can't be easily interrupted.
- Try to eliminate any background noise or distractions (for example, the television or radio, or people talking).
- Choose a location where the person's privacy and dignity can be properly respected.

Timing

3.14 In terms of timing, consider the following:
- Try to choose the time of day when the person is most alert – some people are better in the mornings, others are more lively in the afternoon or early evening. It may be necessary to try several times before a decision can be made.
- If the person's capacity is likely to improve in the foreseeable future, wait until it has done so – if practical and appropriate. For example, this might be the case after treatment for depression or a psychotic episode. Obviously, this may not be practical and appropriate if the decision is urgent.
- Some medication could affect a person's capacity (for example, medication which causes drowsiness or affects memory). Can the decision be delayed until side effects have subsided?
- Take one decision at a time – be careful to avoid making the person tired or confused.
- Don't rush – allow the person time to think things over or ask for clarification, where that is possible and appropriate.
- Avoid or challenge time limits that are unnecessary if the decision is not urgent. Delaying the decision may enable further steps to be taken to assist people to make the decision for themselves.

Scenario: Getting the location and timing right

Luke, a young man, was seriously injured in a road traffic accident and suffered permanent brain damage. He has been in hospital several months, and has made good progress, but he gets very frustrated at his inability to concentrate or do things for himself.

Luke now needs surgical treatment on his leg. During the early morning ward round, the surgeon tries to explain what is involved in the operation. She asks Luke to sign a consent form, but he gets angry and says he doesn't want to talk about it.

→

His key nurse knows that Luke becomes more alert and capable later in the day. After lunch, she asks him if he would like to discuss the operation again. She also knows that he responds better one-to-one than in a group. So she takes Luke into a private room and repeats the information that the surgeon gave him earlier. He understands why the treatment is needed, what is involved and the likely consequences. Therefore, Luke has the capacity to make a decision about the operation.

Support from other people

3.15 In some circumstances, individuals will be more comfortable making decisions when someone else is there to support them.

- Might the person benefit from having another person present? Sometimes having a relative or friend nearby can provide helpful support and reduce anxiety. However, some people might find this intrusive, and it could increase their anxiety or affect their ability to make a free choice. Find ways of getting the person's views on this, for example, by watching their behaviour towards other people.
- Always respect a person's right to confidentiality.

Scenario: Getting help from other people

Jane has a learning disability. She expresses herself using some words, facial expressions and body language. She has lived in her current community home all her life, but now needs to move to a new group home. She finds it difficult to discuss abstract ideas or things she hasn't experienced. Staff conclude that she lacks the capacity to decide for herself which new group home she should move to.

The staff involve an advocate to help Jane express her views. Jane's advocate spends time with her in different environments. The advocate uses pictures, symbols and Makaton to find out the things that are important to Jane, and speaks to people who know Jane to find out what they think she likes. She then supports Jane to show their work to her care manager, and checks that the new homes suggested for her are able to meet Jane's needs and preferences.

When the care manager has found some suitable places, Jane's advocate visits the homes with Jane. They take photos of the houses to help her distinguish between them. The advocate then uses the photos to help Jane work out which home she prefers. Jane's own feelings can now play an important part in deciding what is in her best interests – and so in the final decision about where she will live.

What other ways are there to enable decision-making?

3.16 There are other ways to help someone make a decision for themselves.
- Many people find it helpful to talk things over with people they trust – or people who have been in a similar situation or faced similar dilemmas. For example, people with learning difficulties may benefit from the help of a designated support worker or being part of a support network.
- If someone is very distressed (for example, following a death of someone close) or where there are long-standing problems that affect someone's ability to understand an issue, it may be possible to delay a decision so that the person can have psychological therapy, if needed.
- Some organisations have produced materials to help people who need support to make decisions and for those who support them. Some of this material is designed to help people with specific conditions, such as Alzheimer's disease or profound learning disability.
- It may be important to provide access to technology. For example, some people who appear not to communicate well verbally can do so very well using computers.

Scenario: *Making the most of technology*

Ms Patel has an autistic spectrum disorder. Her family and care staff find it difficult to communicate with her. She refuses to make eye contact, and gets very upset and angry when her carers try to encourage her to speak.

One member of staff notices that Ms Patel is interested in the computer equipment. He shows her how to use the keyboard, and they are able to have a conversation using the computer. An IT specialist works with her to make sure she can make the most of her computing skills to communicate her feelings and decisions.

---

4 HOW DOES THE ACT DEFINE A PERSON'S CAPACITY TO MAKE A DECISION AND HOW SHOULD CAPACITY BE ASSESSED?

This chapter explains what the Act means by 'capacity' and 'lack of capacity'. It provides guidance on how to assess whether someone has the capacity to make a decision, and suggests when professionals should be involved in the assessment.

In this chapter, as throughout the Code, a person's capacity (or lack of capacity) refers specifically to their capacity to make a particular decision at the time it needs to be made

Quick summary

This checklist is a summary of points to consider when assessing a person's capacity to make a specific decision. Readers should also refer to the more detailed guidance in this chapter and Chapters 2 and 3.

Presuming someone has capacity

- The starting assumption must always be that a person has the capacity to make a decision, unless it can be established that they lack capacity.

Understanding what is meant by capacity and lack of capacity

- A person's capacity must be assessed specifically in terms of their capacity to make a particular decision at the time it needs to be made.

Treating everyone equally

- A person's capacity must not be judged simply on the basis of their age, appearance, condition or an aspect of their behaviour.

Supporting the person to make the decision for themselves

- It is important to take all possible steps to try to help people make a decision for themselves (see Chapter 2, Principle 2, and Chapter 3).

Assessing capacity

Anyone assessing someone's capacity to make a decision for themselves should use the two-stage test of capacity.

- Does the person have an impairment of the mind or brain, or is there some sort of disturbance affecting the way their mind or brain works? (It doesn't matter whether the impairment or disturbance is temporary or permanent.)
- If so, does that impairment or disturbance mean that the person is unable to make the decision in question at the time it needs to be made?

Assessing ability to make a decision

- Does the person have a general understanding of what decision they need to make and why they need to make it?
- Does the person have a general understanding of the likely consequences of making, or not making, this decision?
- Is the person able to understand, retain, use and weigh up the information relevant to this decision?

- Can the person communicate their decision (by talking, using sign language or any other means)? Would the services of a professional (such as a speech and language therapist) be helpful?

Assessing capacity to make more complex or serious decisions

- Is there a need for a more thorough assessment (perhaps by involving a doctor or other professional expert)?

What is mental capacity?

4.1 Mental capacity is the ability to make a decision.
- This includes the ability to make a decision that affects daily life – such as when to get up, what to wear or whether to go to the doctor when feeling ill – as well as more serious or significant decisions.
- It also refers to a person's ability to make a decision that may have legal consequences – for them or others. Examples include agreeing to have medical treatment, buying goods or making a will.

4.2 The starting point must always be to assume that a person has the capacity to make a specific decision (see Chapter 2, Principle 1). Some people may need help to be able to make or communicate a decision (see Chapter 3). But this does not necessarily mean that they lack capacity to do so. What matters is their ability to carry out the processes involved in making the decision – and not the outcome.

What does the Act mean by 'lack of capacity'?

4.3 Section 2(1) of the Act states:

> 'For the purposes of this Act, a person lacks capacity in relation to a matter if at the material time he is unable to make a decision for himself in relation to the matter because of an impairment of, or a disturbance in the functioning of, the mind or brain.'

This means that a person lacks capacity if:
- they have an impairment or disturbance (for example, a disability, condition or trauma) that affects the way their mind or brain works, and
- the impairment or disturbance means that they are unable to make a specific decision at the time it needs to be made.

4.4 An assessment of a person's capacity must be based on their ability to make a specific decision at the time it needs to be made, and not their ability to make decisions in general. Section 3 of the Act defines what it means to be unable to make a decision (this is explained in paragraph 4.14 below).

4.5 Section 2(2) states that the impairment or disturbance does not have to be permanent. A person can lack capacity to make a decision at the time it needs to be made even if:

- the loss of capacity is partial
- the loss of capacity is temporary
- their capacity changes over time.

A person may also lack capacity to make a decision about one issue but not about others.

4.6 The Act generally applies to people who are aged 16 or older. Chapter 12 explains how the Act affects children and young people – in particular those aged 16 and 17 years.

What safeguards does the Act provide around assessing someone's capacity?

4.7 An assessment that a person lacks capacity to make a decision must never be based simply on:
- their age
- their appearance
- assumptions about their condition, or
- any aspect of their behaviour. (section 2(3))

4.8 The Act deliberately uses the word 'appearance', because it covers all aspects of the way people look. So for example, it includes the physical characteristics of certain conditions (for example, scars, features linked to Down's syndrome or muscle spasms caused by cerebral palsy) as well as aspects of appearance like skin colour, tattoos and body piercings, or the way people dress (including religious dress).

4.9 The word 'condition' is also wide-ranging. It includes physical disabilities, learning difficulties and disabilities, illness related to age, and temporary conditions (for example, drunkenness or unconsciousness). Aspects of behaviour might include extrovert (for example, shouting or gesticulating) and withdrawn behaviour (for example, talking to yourself or avoiding eye contact).

Scenario: *Treating everybody equally*

Tom, a man with cerebral palsy, has slurred speech. Sometimes he also falls over for no obvious reason

One day Tom falls in the supermarket. Staff call an ambulance, even though he says he is fine. They think he may need treatment after his fall.

When the ambulance comes, the ambulance crew know they must not make assumptions about Tom's capacity to decide about treatment, based simply on his condition and the effects of his disability. They talk to him and find that he is capable of making healthcare decisions for himself.

What proof of lack of capacity does the Act require?

4.10 Anybody who claims that an individual lacks capacity should be able to provide proof. They need to be able to show, *on the balance of probabilities*, that the individual lacks capacity to make a particular decision, at the time it needs to be made (section 2(4)). This means being able to show that it is more likely than not that the person lacks capacity to make the decision in question.

What is the test of capacity?

To help determine if a person lacks capacity to make particular decisions, the Act sets out a two-stage test of capacity.

Stage 1: Does the person have an impairment of, or a disturbance in the functioning of, their mind or brain?

4.11 Stage 1 requires proof that the person has an impairment of the mind or brain, or some sort of or disturbance that affects the way their mind or brain works. If a person does not have such an impairment or disturbance of the mind or brain, they will not lack capacity under the Act.

4.12 Examples of an impairment or disturbance in the functioning of the mind or brain may include the following:
- conditions associated with some forms of mental illness
- dementia
- significant learning disabilities
- the long-term effects of brain damage
- physical or medical conditions that cause confusion, drowsiness or loss of consciousness
- delirium
- concussion following a head injury, and
- the symptoms of alcohol or drug use.

Scenario: Assessing whether an impairment or disturbance is affecting someone's ability to make a decision

Mrs Collins is 82 and has had a stroke. This has weakened the left-hand side of her body. She is living in a house that has been the family home for years. Her son wants her to sell the house and live with him.

Mrs Collins likes the idea, but her daughter does not. She thinks her mother will lose independence and her condition will get worse. She talks to her mother's consultant to get information that will help stop the sale. But he says that although Mrs Collins is anxious about the physical effects ➙

the stroke has had on her body, it has not caused any mental impairment or affected her brain, so she still has capacity to make her own decision about selling her house.

Stage 2: Does the impairment or disturbance mean that the person is unable to make a specific decision when they need to?

4.13 For a person to lack capacity to make a decision, the Act says their impairment or disturbance must affect their ability to make the specific decision when they need to. But first people must be given all practical and appropriate support to help them make the decision for themselves (see Chapter 2, Principle 2). Stage 2 can only apply if all practical and appropriate support to help the person make the decision has failed. See Chapter 3 for guidance on ways of helping people to make their own decisions.

What does the Act mean by 'inability to make a decision'?

4.14 A person is unable to make a decision if they cannot:
  1. understand information about the decision to be made (the Act calls this 'relevant information')
  2. retain that information in their mind
  3. use or weigh that information as part of the decision-making process, or
  4. communicate their decision (by talking, using sign language or any other means). See section 3(1).

4.15 These four points are explained in more detail below. The first three should be applied together. If a person cannot do any of these three things, they will be treated as unable to make the decision. The fourth only applies in situations where people cannot communicate their decision in any way.

Understanding information about the decision to be made

4.16 It is important not to assess someone's understanding before they have been given relevant information about a decision. Every effort must be made to provide information in a way that is most appropriate to help the person to understand. Quick or inadequate explanations are not acceptable unless the situation is urgent (see Chapter 3 for some practical steps). Relevant information includes:
  •   the nature of the decision
  •   the reason why the decision is needed, and
  •   the likely effects of deciding one way or another, or making no decision at all.

4.17 Section 3(2) outlines the need to present information in a way that is appropriate to meet the individual's needs and circumstances. It also stresses the importance of explaining information using the most effective form of communication for that person (such as simple language, sign language, visual representations, computer support or any other means).

4.18 For example:

- a person with a learning disability may need somebody to read information to them. They might also need illustrations to help them to understand what is happening. Or they might stop the reader to ask what things mean. It might also be helpful for them to discuss information with an advocate.

- a person with anxiety or depression may find it difficult to reach a decision about treatment in a group meeting with professionals. They may prefer to read the relevant documents in private. This way they can come to a conclusion alone, and ask for help if necessary.

- someone who has a brain injury might need to be given information several times. It will be necessary to check that the person understands the information. If they have difficulty understanding, it might be useful to present information in a different way (for example, different forms of words, pictures or diagrams). Written information, audiotapes, videos and posters can help people remember important facts.

4.19 Relevant information must include what the likely consequences of a decision would be (the possible effects of deciding one way or another) – and also the likely consequences of making no decision at all (section 3(4)). In some cases, it may be enough to give a broad explanation using simple language. But a person might need more detailed information or access to advice, depending on the decision that needs to be made. If a decision could have serious or grave consequences, it is even more important that a person understands the information relevant to that decision.

Scenario: *Providing relevant information in an appropriate format*

Mr Leslie has learning disabilities and has developed an irregular heartbeat. He has been prescribed medication for this, but is anxious about having regular blood tests to check his medication levels. His doctor gives him a leaflet to explain:

- the reason for the tests
- what a blood test involves
- the risks in having or not having the tests, and
- that he has the right to decide whether or not to have the test.   →

The leaflet uses simple language and photographs to explain these things. Mr Leslie's carer helps him read the leaflet over the next few days, and checks that he understands it.

Mr Leslie goes back to tell the doctor that, even though he is scared of needles, he will agree to the blood tests so that he can get the right medication. He is able to pick out the equipment needed to do the blood test. So the doctor concludes that Mr Leslie can understand, retain and use the relevant information and therefore has the capacity to make the decision to have the test.

Retaining information

4.20 The person must be able to hold the information in their mind long enough to use it to make an effective decision. But section 3(3) states that people who can only retain information for a short while must not automatically be assumed to lack the capacity to decide – it depends on what is necessary for the decision in question. Items such as notebooks, photographs, posters, videos and voice recorders can help people record and retain information.

Scenario: Assessing a person's ability to retain information

Walter, an elderly man, is diagnosed with dementia and has problems remembering things in the short term. He can't always remember his great-grandchildren's names, but he recognises them when they come to visit. He can also pick them out on photographs.

Walter would like to buy premium bonds (a type of financial investment) for each of his great-grandchildren. He asks his solicitor to make the arrangements. After assessing his capacity to make financial decisions, the solicitor is satisfied that Walter has capacity to make this decision, despite his short-term memory problems.

Using or weighing information as part of the decision-making process

4.21 For someone to have capacity, they must have the ability to weigh up information and use it to arrive at a decision. Sometimes people can understand information but an impairment or disturbance stops them using it. In other cases, the impairment or disturbance leads to a person making a specific decision without understanding or using the information they have been given.[3]

---

[3] This issue has been considered in a number of court cases, including *Re MB* [1997] 2 FLR 426; *R v Collins and Ashworth Hospital Authority ex parte Brady* [2001] 58 BMLR 173.

4.22 For example, a person with the eating disorder anorexia nervosa may understand information about the consequences of not eating. But their compulsion not to eat might be too strong for them to ignore. Some people who have serious brain damage might make impulsive decisions regardless of information they have been given or their understanding of it.

Inability to communicate a decision in any way

4.23 Sometimes there is no way for a person to communicate. This will apply to very few people, but it does include:
- people who are unconscious or in a coma, or
- those with the very rare condition sometimes known as 'locked-in syndrome', who are conscious but cannot speak or move at all.

If a person cannot communicate their decision in any way at all, the Act says they should be treated as if they are unable to make that decision.

4.24 Before deciding that someone falls into this category, it is important to make all practical and appropriate efforts to help them communicate. This might call for the involvement of speech and language therapists, specialists in non-verbal communication or other professionals. Chapter 3 gives advice for communicating with people who have specific disabilities or cognitive problems.

4.25 Communication by simple muscle movements can show that somebody can communicate and may have capacity to make a decision.[4] For example, a person might blink an eye or squeeze a hand to say 'yes' or 'no'. In these cases, assessment must use the first three points listed in paragraph 4.14, which are explained in more depth in paragraphs 4.16–4. 22.

What other issues might affect capacity?

People with fluctuating or temporary capacity

4.26 Some people have fluctuating capacity – they have a problem or condition that gets worse occasionally and affects their ability to make decisions. For example, someone who has manic depression may have a temporary manic phase which causes them to lack capacity to make financial decisions, leading them to get into debt even though at other times they are perfectly able to manage their money. A person with a psychotic illness may have delusions that affect their capacity to make decisions at certain times but disappear at others. Temporary factors may also affect someone's ability to make decisions. Examples include acute illness, severe pain, the effect of medication, or distress after a death or shock. More guidance on how to support someone with fluctuating or temporary

---

[4]   This was demonstrated in the case *Re AK (Adult Patient) (Medical Treatment: Consent)* [2001] 1 FLR 129.

capacity to make a decision can be found in Chapter 3, particularly paragraphs 3.12–3.16. More information about factors that may indicate that a person may regain or develop capacity in the future can be found at paragraph 5.28.

4.27 As in any other situation, an assessment must only examine a person's capacity to make a particular decision when it needs to be made. It may be possible to put off the decision until the person has the capacity to make it (see also guidance on best interests in Chapter 5).

Ongoing conditions that may affect capacity

4.28 Generally, capacity assessments should be related to a specific decision. But there may be people with an ongoing condition that affects their ability to make certain decisions or that may affect other decisions in their life. One decision on its own may make sense, but may give cause for concern when considered alongside others.

4.29 Again, it is important to review capacity from time to time, as people can improve their decision-making capabilities. In particular, someone with an ongoing condition may become able to make some, if not all, decisions. Some people (for example, people with learning disabilities) will learn new skills throughout their life, improving their capacity to make certain decisions. So assessments should be reviewed from time to time. Capacity should always be reviewed:
- whenever a care plan is being developed or reviewed
- at other relevant stages of the care planning process, and
- as particular decisions need to be made.

4.30 It is important to acknowledge the difference between:
- unwise decisions, which a person has the right to make (Chapter 2, principle 3), and
- decisions based on a lack of understanding of risks or inability to weigh up the information about a decision.

Information about decisions the person has made based on a lack of understanding of risks or inability to weigh up the information can form part of a capacity assessment – particularly if someone repeatedly makes decisions that put them at risk or result in harm to them or someone else.

Scenario: Ongoing conditions

Paul had an accident at work and suffered severe head injuries. He was awarded compensation to pay for care he will need throughout his life as a result of his head injury. An application was made to the Court of Protection to consider how the award of compensation should be managed, including whether to appoint a deputy to manage Paul's financial affairs. Paul objected as he believed he could manage his life and should be able to spend his money however he liked.   ➔

He wrote a list of what he intended to spend his money on. This included fully-staffed luxury properties and holiday villas, cars with chauffeurs, jewellery and various other items for himself and his family. But spending money on all these luxury items would not leave enough money to cover the costs of his care in future years.

The court judged that Paul had capacity to make day-to-day financial decisions, but he did not understand why he had received compensation and what the money was supposed to be used for. Nor did he understand how buying luxuries now could affect his future care. The court therefore decided Paul lacked capacity to manage large amounts of money and appointed a deputy to make ongoing financial decisions relating to his care. But it gave him access to enough funds to cover everyday needs and occasional treats.

What other legal tests of capacity are there?

4.31 The Act makes clear that the definition of 'lack of capacity' and the two-stage test for capacity set out in the Act are 'for the purposes of this Act'. This means that the definition and test are to be used in situations covered by this Act. Schedule 6 of the Act also amends existing laws to ensure that the definition and test are used in other areas of law not covered directly by this Act.

For example, Schedule 6, paragraph 20 allows a person to be disqualified from jury service if they lack the capacity (using this Act's definition) to carry out a juror's tasks.

4.32 There are several tests of capacity that have been produced following judgments in court cases (known as common law tests).[5] These cover:

- capacity to make a will[6]
- capacity to make a gift[7]
- capacity to enter into a contract[8]
- capacity to litigate (take part in legal cases),[9] and
- capacity to enter into marriage.[10]

4.33 The Act's new definition of capacity is in line with the existing common law tests, and the Act does not replace them. When cases come before the court on the above issues, judges can adopt the new definition if they think it is appropriate. The Act will apply to all other cases relating to financial, healthcare or welfare decisions.

---

[5] For details, see British Medical Association & Law Society, *Assessment of Mental Capacity: Guidance for Doctors and Lawyers* (BMA, 1995; BMJ Books, 2nd edn, 2004; Law Society Publishing, 3rd edn, 2009).

[6] *Banks v Goodfellow* (1870) LR 5 QB 549.

[7] *Re Beaney (deceased)* [1978] 2 All ER 595.

[8] *Boughton v Knight* (1873) LR 3 PD 64.

[9] *Masterman-Lister v Brutton & Co and Jewell & Home Counties Dairies* [2003] 3 All ER 162, CA.

[10] *E (an Alleged Patient), Re; Sheffield City Council v E & S* [2005] 1 FLR 965.

When should capacity be assessed?

4.34 Assessing capacity correctly is vitally important to everyone affected by the Act. Someone who is assessed as lacking capacity may be denied their right to make a specific decision – particularly if others think that the decision would not be in their best interests or could cause harm. Also, if a person lacks capacity to make specific decisions, that person might make decisions they do not really understand. Again, this could cause harm or put the person at risk. So it is important to carry out an assessment when a person's capacity is in doubt. It is also important that the person who does an assessment can justify their conclusions. Many organisations will provide specific professional guidance for members of their profession.[11]

4.35 There are a number of reasons why people may question a person's capacity to make a specific decision:
- the person's behaviour or circumstances cause doubt as to whether they have the capacity to make a decision
- somebody else says they are concerned about the person's capacity, or
- the person has previously been diagnosed with an impairment or disturbance that affects the way their mind or brain works (see paragraphs 4.11–4.12 above), and it has already been shown they lack capacity to make other decisions in their life.

4.36 The starting assumption must be that the person has the capacity to make the specific decision. If, however, anyone thinks a person lacks capacity, it is important to then ask the following questions:
- Does the person have all the relevant information they need to make the decision?
- If they are making a decision that involves choosing between alternatives, do they have information on all the different options?
- Would the person have a better understanding if information was explained or presented in another way?
- Are there times of day when the person's understanding is better?
- Are there locations where they may feel more at ease?
- Can the decision be put off until the circumstances are different and the person concerned may be able to make the decision?
- Can anyone else help the person to make choices or express a view (for example, a family member or carer, an advocate or someone to help with communication)?

4.37 Chapter 3 describes ways to deal with these questions and suggest steps which may help people make their own decisions. If all practical and appropriate steps fail, an assessment will then be needed of the person's capacity to make the decision that now needs to be made.

---

[11] See for example, British Medical Association & Law Society, *Assessment of Mental Capacity: Guidance for Doctors and Lawyers* (BMA, 1995; BMJ Books, 2nd edn, 2004; Law Society Publishing, 3rd edn, 2009); the Joint Royal Colleges Ambulance Service Liaison Committee Clinical Practice Guidelines (JRCALC, available online at www2.warwick.ac.uk/fac/med/research/hsri/ emergencycare/jrcalc_2006/clinical_guidelines_2006.pdf) and British Psychological Society, *Guidelines on assessing capacity* (BPS, 2006 available online at www.bps.org.uk).

Who should assess capacity?

4.38 The person who assesses an individual's capacity to make a decision will usually be the person who is directly concerned with the individual at the time the decision needs to be made. This means that different people will be involved in assessing someone's capacity to make different decisions at different times.

   For most day-to-day decisions, this will be the person caring for them at the time a decision must be made. For example, a care worker might need to assess if the person can agree to being bathed. Then a district nurse might assess if the person can consent to have a dressing changed.

4.39 For acts of care or treatment (see Chapter 6), the assessor must have a 'reasonable belief' that the person lacks capacity to agree to the action or decision to be taken (see paragraphs 4.44–4.45 for a description of reasonable belief).

4.40 If a doctor or healthcare professional proposes treatment or an examination, they must assess the person's capacity to consent. In settings such as a hospital, this can involve the multi-disciplinary team (a team of people from different professional backgrounds who share responsibility for a patient). But ultimately, it is up to the professional responsible for the person's treatment to make sure that capacity has been assessed.

4.41 For a legal transaction (for example, making a will), a solicitor or legal practitioner must assess the client's capacity to instruct them. They must assess whether the client has the capacity to satisfy any relevant legal test. In cases of doubt, they should get an opinion from a doctor or other professional expert.

4.42 More complex decisions are likely to need more formal assessments (see paragraph 4.54 below). A professional opinion on the person's capacity might be necessary. This could be, for example, from a psychiatrist, psychologist, a speech and language therapist, occupational therapist or social worker. But the final decision about a person's capacity must be made by the person intending to make the decision or carry out the action on behalf of the person who lacks capacity – not the professional, who is there to advise.

4.43 Any assessor should have the skills and ability to communicate effectively with the person (see Chapter 3). If necessary, they should get professional help to communicate with the person.

Scenario: *Getting help with assessing capacity*

Ms Dodd suffered brain damage in a road accident and is unable to speak. At first, her family thought she was not able to make decisions. But they soon discovered that she could choose by pointing at things, such as the clothes she wants to wear or the food she prefers. Her behaviour also indicates that she enjoys attending a day centre, but she refuses to go swimming. Her carers have assessed her as having capacity to make these decisions.   →

Ms Dodd needs hospital treatment but she gets distressed when away from home. Her mother feels that Ms Dodd is refusing treatment by her behaviour, but her father thinks she lacks capacity to say no to treatment that could improve her condition.

The clinician who is proposing the treatment will have to assess Ms Dodd's capacity to consent. He gets help from a member of staff at the day centre who knows Ms Dodd's communication well and also discusses things with her parents. Over several meetings the clinician explains the treatment options to Ms Dodd with the help of the staff member. The final decision about Ms Dodd's capacity rests with the clinician, but he will need to use information from the staff member and others who know Ms Dodd well to make this assessment.

What is 'reasonable belief' of lack of capacity?

4.44 Carers (whether family carers or other carers) and care workers do not have to be experts in assessing capacity. But to have protection from liability when providing care or treatment (see Chapter 6), they must have a 'reasonable belief' that the person they care for lacks capacity to make relevant decisions about their care or treatment (section 5(1)). To have this reasonable belief, they must have taken 'reasonable' steps to establish that that the person lacks capacity to make a decision or consent to an act at the time the decision or consent is needed. They must also establish that the act or decision is in the person's best interests (see Chapter 5).

They do not usually need to follow formal processes, such as involving a professional to make an assessment. However, if somebody challenges their assessment (see paragraph 4.63 below), they must be able to describe the steps they have taken. They must also have objective reasons for believing the person lacks capacity to make the decision in question.

4.45 The steps that are accepted as 'reasonable' will depend on individual circumstances and the urgency of the decision. Professionals, who are qualified in their particular field, are normally expected to undertake a fuller assessment, reflecting their higher degree of knowledge and experience, than family members or other carers who have no formal qualifications. See paragraph 4.36 for a list of points to consider when assessing someone's capacity. The following may also be helpful:

- Start by assuming the person has capacity to make the specific decision. Is there anything to prove otherwise?
- Does the person have a previous diagnosis of disability or mental disorder? Does that condition now affect their capacity to make this decision? If there has been no previous diagnosis, it may be best to get a medical opinion.
- Make every effort to communicate with the person to explain what is happening.
- Make every effort to try to help the person make the decision in question.

- See if there is a way to explain or present information about the decision in a way that makes it easier to understand. If the person has a choice, do they have information about all the options?
- Can the decision be delayed to take time to help the person make the decision, or to give the person time to regain the capacity to make the decision for themselves?
- Does the person understand what decision they need to make and why they need to make it?
- Can they understand information about the decision? Can they retain it, use it and weigh it to make the decision?
- Be aware that the fact that a person agrees with you or assents to what is proposed does not necessarily mean that they have capacity to make the decision.

What other factors might affect an assessment of capacity?

4.46 It is important to assess people when they are in the best state to make the decision, if possible. Whether this is possible will depend on the nature and urgency of the decision to be made. Many of the practical steps suggested in Chapter 3 will help to create the best environment for assessing capacity. The assessor must then carry out the two stages of the test of capacity (see paragraphs 4.11–4.25 above).

4.47 In many cases, it may be clear that the person has an impairment or disturbance in the functioning of their mind or brain which could affect their ability to make a decision. For example, there might be a past diagnosis of a disability or mental disorder, or there may be signs that an illness is returning. Old assumptions about an illness or condition should be reviewed. Sometimes an illness develops gradually (for example, dementia), and it is hard to know when it starts to affect capacity. Anyone assessing someone's capacity may need to ask for a medical opinion as to whether a person has an illness or condition that could affect their capacity to make a decision in this specific case.

Scenario: Getting a professional opinion

Mr Elliott is 87 years old and lives alone. He has poor short-term memory, and he often forgets to eat. He also sometimes neglects his personal hygiene. His daughter talks to him about the possibility of moving into residential care. She decides that he understands the reasons for her concerns as well as the risks of continuing to live alone and, having weighed these up, he has the capacity to decide to stay at home and accept the consequences.

Two months later, Mr Elliott has a fall and breaks his leg. While being treated in hospital, he becomes confused and depressed. He says he wants to go home, but the staff think that the deterioration in his mental health has affected his capacity to make this decision at this time. They think he →

---

cannot understand the consequences or weigh up the risks he faces if he goes home. They refer him to a specialist in old age psychiatry, who assesses whether his mental health is affecting his capacity to make this decision. The staff will then use the specialist's opinion to help their assessment of Mr Elliott's capacity.

4.48 Anyone assessing someone's capacity must not assume that a person lacks capacity simply because they have a particular diagnosis or condition. There must be proof that the diagnosed illness or condition affects the ability to make a decision when it needs to be made. The person assessing capacity should ask the following questions:

- Does the person have a general understanding of what decision they need to make and why they need to make it?
- Do they understand the likely consequences of making, or not making, this decision?
- Can they understand and process information about the decision? And can they use it to help them make a decision?

In borderline cases, or where there is doubt, the assessor must be able to show that it is more likely than not that the answer to these questions is 'no'.

What practical steps should be taken when assessing capacity?

4.49 Anyone assessing someone's capacity will need to decide which of these steps are relevant to their situation.

- They should make sure that they understand the nature and effect of the decision to be made themselves. They may need access to relevant documents and background information (for example, details of the person's finances if assessing capacity to manage affairs). See Chapter 16 for details on access to information.
- They may need other relevant information to support the assessment (for example, healthcare records or the views of staff involved in the person's care).
- Family members and close friends may be able to provide valuable background information (for example, the person's past behaviour and abilities and the types of decisions they can currently make). But their personal views and wishes about what they would want for the person must not influence the assessment.
- They should again explain to the person all the information relevant to the decision. The explanation must be in the most appropriate and effective form of communication for that person.
- Check the person's understanding after a few minutes. The person should be able to give a rough explanation of the information that was explained. There are different methods for people who use nonverbal means of communication (for example, observing behaviour or their ability to recognise objects or pictures).

- Avoid questions that need only a 'yes' or 'no' answer (for example, did you understand what I just said?). They are not enough to assess the person's capacity to make a decision. But there may be no alternative in cases where there are major communication difficulties. In these cases, check the response by asking questions again in a different way.
- Skills and behaviour do not necessarily reflect the person's capacity to make specific decisions. The fact that someone has good social or language skills, polite behaviour or good manners doesn't necessarily mean they understand the information or are able to weigh it up.
- Repeating these steps can help confirm the result.

4.50 For certain kinds of complex decisions (for example, making a will), there are specific legal tests (see paragraph 4.32 above) in addition to the two-stage test for capacity. In some cases, medical or psychometric tests may also be helpful tools (for example, for assessing cognitive skills) in assessing a person's capacity to make particular decisions, but the relevant legal test of capacity must still be fulfilled.

When should professionals be involved?

4.51 Anyone assessing someone's capacity may need to get a professional opinion when assessing a person's capacity to make complex or major decisions. In some cases this will simply involve contacting the person's general practitioner (GP) or family doctor. If the person has a particular condition or disorder, it may be appropriate to contact a specialist (for example, consultant psychiatrist, psychologist or other professional with experience of caring for patients with that condition). A speech and language therapist might be able to help if there are communication difficulties. In some cases, a multi-disciplinary approach is best. This means combining the skills and expertise of different professionals.

4.52 Professionals should never express an opinion without carrying out a proper examination and assessment of the person's capacity to make the decision. They must apply the appropriate test of capacity. In some cases, they will need to meet the person more than once – particularly if the person has communication difficulties. Professionals can get background information from a person's family and carers. But the personal views of these people about what they want for the person who lacks capacity must not influence the outcome of that assessment.

4.53 Professional involvement might be needed if:
- the decision that needs to be made is complicated or has serious consequences
- an assessor concludes a person lacks capacity, and the person challenges the finding
- family members, carers and/or professionals disagree about a person's capacity
- there is a conflict of interest between the assessor and the person being assessed

- the person being assessed is expressing different views to different people – they may be trying to please everyone or telling people what they think they want to hear
- somebody might challenge the person's capacity to make the decision – either at the time of the decision or later (for example, a family member might challenge a will after a person has died on the basis that the person lacked capacity when they made the will)
- somebody has been accused of abusing a vulnerable adult who may lack capacity to make decisions that protect them
- a person repeatedly makes decisions that put them at risk or could result in suffering or damage.

Scenario: Involving professional opinion

Ms Ledger is a young woman with learning disabilities and some autistic spectrum disorders. Recently she began a sexual relationship with a much older man, who is trying to persuade her to move in with him and come off the pill. There are rumours that he has been violent towards her and has taken her bankbook.

Ms Ledger boasts about the relationship to her friends. But she has admitted to her key worker that she is sometimes afraid of the man. Staff at her sheltered accommodation decide to make a referral under the local adult protection procedures. They arrange for a clinical psychologist to assess Ms Ledger's understanding of the relationship and her capacity to consent to it.

4.54 In some cases, it may be a legal requirement, or good professional practice, to undertake a formal assessment of capacity. These cases include:
- where a person's capacity to sign a legal document (for example, a will), could later be challenged, in which case an expert should be asked for an opinion[12]
- to establish whether a person who might be involved in a legal case needs the assistance of the Official Solicitor or other litigation friend (somebody to represent their views to a court and give instructions to their legal representative) and there is doubt about the person's capacity to instruct a solicitor or take part in the case[13]
- whenever the Court of Protection has to decide if a person lacks capacity in a certain matter
- if the courts are required to make a decision about a person's capacity in other legal proceedings[14]

---

[12] *Kenward v Adams* (1975) *The Times*, 29 November.
[13] Civil Procedure Rules 1998, r 21.1.
[14] *Masterman-Lister v Brutton & Co and Jewell & Home Counties Dairies* [2002] EWCA Civ 1889, CA at 54.

- if there may be legal consequences of a finding of capacity (for example, deciding on financial compensation following a claim for personal injury).

Are assessment processes confidential?

4.55 People involved in assessing capacity will need to share information about a person's circumstances. But there are ethical codes and laws that require professionals to keep personal information confidential. As a general rule, professionals must ask their patients or clients if they can reveal information to somebody else – even close relatives. But sometimes information may be disclosed without the consent of the person who the information concerns (for example, to protect the person or prevent harm to other people).[15]

4.56 Anyone assessing someone's capacity needs accurate information concerning the person being assessed that is relevant to the decision the person has to make. So professionals should, where possible, make relevant information available. They should make every effort to get the person's permission to reveal relevant information. They should give a full explanation of why this is necessary, and they should tell the person about the risks and consequences of revealing, and not revealing information. If the person is unable to give permission, the professional might still be allowed to provide information that will help make an accurate assessment of the person's capacity to make the specific decision. Chapter 16 has more detail on how to access information.

What if someone refuses to be assessed?

4.57 There may be circumstances in which a person whose capacity is in doubt refuses to undergo an assessment of capacity or refuses to be examined by a doctor or other professional. In these circumstances, it might help to explain to someone refusing an assessment why it is needed and what the consequences of refusal are. But threats or attempts to force the person to agree to an assessment are not acceptable.

4.58 If the person lacks capacity to agree or refuse, the assessment can normally go ahead, as long as the person does not object to the assessment, and it is in their best interests (see Chapter 5).

4.59 Nobody can be forced to undergo an assessment of capacity. If someone refuses to open the door to their home, it cannot be forced. If there are serious worries about the person's mental health, it may be possible to get a warrant to force entry and assess the person for treatment in hospital – but the situation must meet the requirements of the Mental Health

---

[15]   For example, in the circumstances discussed in *W v Egdell and others* [1990] 1 All ER 835 at 848; *R (S) v Plymouth City Council and C* [2002] EWCA Civ 388 at 49.

Act 1983 (section 135). But simply refusing an assessment of capacity is in no way sufficient grounds for an assessment under the Mental Health Act 1983 (see Chapter 13).

Who should keep a record of assessments?

4.60 Assessments of capacity to take day-to-day decisions or consent to care require no formal assessment procedures or recorded documentation. Paragraphs 4.44–4.45 above explain the steps to take to reach a 'reasonable belief' that someone lacks capacity to make a particular decision. It is good practice for paid care workers to keep a record of the steps they take when caring for the person concerned.

Professional records

4.61 It is good practice for professionals to carry out a proper assessment of a person's capacity to make particular decisions and to record the findings in the relevant professional records.
- A doctor or healthcare professional proposing treatment should carry out an assessment of the person's capacity to consent (with a multi-disciplinary team, if appropriate) and record it in the patient's clinical notes.
- Solicitors should assess a client's capacity to give instructions or carry out a legal transaction (obtaining a medical or other professional opinion, if necessary) and record it on the client's file.
- An assessment of a person's capacity to consent or agree to the provision of services will be part of the care planning processes for health and social care needs, and should be recorded in the relevant documentation. This includes:
- Person Centred Planning for people with learning disabilities
- the Care Programme Approach for people with mental illness
- the Single Assessment Process for older people in England, and
- the Unified Assessment Process in Wales.

Formal reports or certificates of capacity

4.62 In some cases, a more detailed report or certificate of capacity may be required, for example,
- for use in court or other legal processes
- as required by Regulations, Rules or Orders made under the Act.

How can someone challenge a finding of lack of capacity?

4.63 There are likely to be occasions when someone may wish to challenge the results of an assessment of capacity. The first step is to raise the matter with the person who carried out the assessment. If the challenge comes from the individual who is said to lack capacity, they might need support from family, friends or an advocate. Ask the assessor to:

- give reasons why they believe the person lacks capacity to make the decision, and
- provide objective evidence to support that belief.

4.64 The assessor must show they have applied the principles of the Mental Capacity Act (see Chapter 2). Attorneys, deputies and professionals will need to show that they have also followed guidance in this chapter.

4.65 It might be possible to get a second opinion from an independent professional or another expert in assessing capacity. Chapter 15 has other suggestions for dealing with disagreements. But if a disagreement cannot be resolved, the person who is challenging the assessment may be able to apply to the Court of Protection. The Court of Protection can rule on whether a person has capacity to make the decision covered by the assessment (see Chapter 8).

5 WHAT DOES THE ACT MEAN WHEN IT TALKS ABOUT 'BEST INTERESTS'?

One of the key principles of the Act is that any act done for, or any decision made on behalf of a person who lacks capacity must be done, or made, in that person's *best interests*. That is the same whether the person making the decision or acting is a family carer, a paid care worker, an attorney, a court-appointed deputy, or a healthcare professional, and whether the decision is a minor issue – like what to wear – or a major issue, like whether to provide particular healthcare.

As long as these acts or decisions are in the best interests of the person who lacks capacity to make the decision for themselves, or to consent to acts concerned with their care or treatment, then the decision-maker or carer will be protected from liability.

There are exceptions to this, including circumstances where a person has made an advance decision to refuse treatment (see Chapter 9) and, in specific circumstances, the involvement of a person who lacks capacity in research (see Chapter 11). But otherwise the underpinning principle of the Act is that all acts and decisions should be made in the best interests of the person without capacity.

Working out what is in someone else's best interests may be difficult, and the Act requires people to follow certain steps to help them work out whether a particular act or decision is in a person's best interests. In some cases, there may be disagreement about what someone's best interests really are. As long as the person who acts or makes the decision has followed the steps to establish whether a person has capacity, and done everything they reasonably can to work out what someone's best interests are, the law should protect them.

This chapter explains what the Act means by 'best interests' and what things should be considered when trying to work out what is in someone's best interests. It also highlights some of the difficulties that might come up in working out what the best interests of a person who lacks capacity to make the decision actually are.

> In this chapter, as throughout the Code, a person's capacity (or lack of capacity) refers specifically to their capacity to make a particular decision at the time it needs to be made.

Quick summary

A person trying to work out the best interests of a person who lacks capacity to make a particular decision ('lacks capacity') should:

Encourage participation

- do whatever is possible to permit and encourage the person to take part, or to improve their ability to take part, in making the decision

Identify all relevant circumstances

- try to identify all the things that the person who lacks capacity would take into account if they were making the decision or acting for themselves

Find out the person's views

- try to find out the views of the person who lacks capacity, including:
  - the person's past and present wishes and feelings – these may have been expressed verbally, in writing or through behaviour or habits.
  - any beliefs and values (e.g. religious, cultural, moral or political) that would be likely to influence the decision in question.
  - any other factors the person themselves would be likely to consider if they were making the decision or acting for themselves.

Avoid discrimination

- not make assumptions about someone's best interests simply on the basis of the person's age, appearance, condition or behaviour.

Assess whether the person might regain capacity

- consider whether the person is likely to regain capacity (e.g. after receiving medical treatment). If so, can the decision wait until then?

If the decision concerns life-sustaining treatment

- not be motivated in any way by a desire to bring about the person's death. They should not make assumptions about the person's quality of life.

Consult others

- if it is practical and appropriate to do so, consult other people for their views about the person's best interests and to see if they have any information about the person's wishes and feelings, beliefs and values. In particular, try to consult:
  - anyone previously named by the person as someone to be consulted on either the decision in question or on similar issues
  - anyone engaged in caring for the person
  - close relatives, friends or others who take an interest in the person's welfare
  - any attorney appointed under a Lasting Power of Attorney or Enduring Power of Attorney made by the person
  - any deputy appointed by the Court of Protection to make decisions for the person.
- For decisions about major medical treatment or where the person should live and where there is no-one who fits into any of the above categories, an Independent Mental Capacity Advocate (IMCA) must be consulted. (See Chapter 10 for more information about IMCAs.)
- When consulting, remember that the person who lacks the capacity to make the decision or act for themselves still has a right to keep their affairs private – so it would not be right to share every piece of information with everyone.

Avoid restricting the person's rights

- see if there are other options that may be less restrictive of the person's rights.

Take all of this into account

- weigh up all of these factors in order to work out what is in the person's best interests.

What is the best interests principle and who does it apply to?

5.1 The best interests principle underpins the Mental Capacity Act. It is set out in section 1(5) of the Act.

> 'An act done, or decision made, under this Act for or on behalf of a person who lacks capacity must be done, or made, in his best interests.'

The concept has been developed by the courts in cases relating to people who lack capacity to make specific decisions for themselves, mainly decisions concerned with the provision of medical treatment or social care.

5.2 This principle covers all aspects of financial, personal welfare and healthcare decision-making and actions. It applies to anyone making decisions or acting under the provisions of the Act, including:

- family carers, other carers and care workers
- healthcare and social care staff
- attorneys appointed under a Lasting Power of Attorney or registered Enduring Power of Attorney
- deputies appointed by the court to make decisions on behalf of someone who lacks capacity, and
- the Court of Protection.

5.3 However, as Chapter 2 explained, the Act's first key principle is that people must be assumed to have capacity to make a decision or act for themselves unless it is established that they lack it. That means that working out a person's best interests is only relevant when that person has been assessed as lacking, or is reasonably believed to lack, capacity to make the decision in question or give consent to an act being done.

People with capacity are able to decide for themselves what they want to do. When they do this, they might choose an option that other people don't think is in their best interests. That is their choice and does not, in itself, mean that they lack capacity to make those decisions.

Exceptions to the best interests principle

5.4 There are two circumstances when the best interests principle will not apply. The first is where someone has previously made an advance decision to refuse medical treatment while they had the capacity to do so. Their advance decision should be respected when they lack capacity, even if others think that the decision to refuse treatment is not in their best interests (guidance on advance decisions is given in Chapter 9).

The second concerns the involvement in research, in certain circumstances, of someone lacking capacity to consent (see Chapter 11).

What does the Act mean by best interests?

5.5 The term 'best interests' is not actually defined in the Act. This is because so many different types of decisions and actions are covered by the Act, and so many different people and circumstances are affected by it.

5.6 Section 4 of the Act explains how to work out the best interests of a person who lacks capacity to make a decision at the time it needs to be made. This section sets out a checklist of common factors that must always be considered by anyone who needs to decide what is in the best interests of a person who lacks capacity in any particular situation. This checklist is only the starting point: in many cases, extra factors will need to be considered.

5.7 When working out what is in the best interests of the person who lacks capacity to make a decision or act for themselves, decision-makers must take into account all relevant factors that it would be reasonable to consider, not just those that they think are important. They must not act or make a decision based on what they would want to do if they were the person who lacked capacity.

Scenario: *Whose best interests?*

Pedro, a young man with a severe learning disability, lives in a care home. He has dental problems which cause him a lot of pain, but refuses to open his mouth for his teeth to be cleaned.

The staff suggest that it would be a good idea to give Pedro an occasional general anaesthetic so that a dentist can clean his teeth and fill any cavities. His mother is worried about the effects of an anaesthetic, but she hates to see him distressed and suggests instead that he should be given strong painkillers when needed.

While the views of Pedro's mother and carers are important in working out what course of action would be in his best interests, the decision must *not* be based on what would be less stressful for them. Instead, it must focus on Pedro's best interests.

Having talked to others, the dentist tries to find ways of involving Pedro in the decision, with the help of his key worker and an advocate, to try to find out the cause and location of the problem and to explain to him that they are trying to stop the pain. The dentist tries to find out if any other forms of dental care would be better, such as a mouthwash or dental gum.

The dentist concludes that it would be in Pedro's best interests for:

- proper investigation to be carried out under anaesthetic so that immediate treatment can be provided
- options for his future dental care to be reviewed by the care team, involving Pedro as far as possible.

Who can be a decision-maker?

5.8 Under the Act, many different people may be required to make decisions or act on behalf of someone who lacks capacity to make decisions for themselves. The person making the decision is referred to throughout this chapter, and in other parts of the Code, as the 'decision-maker', and it is the decision-maker's responsibility to work out what would be in the best interests of the person who lacks capacity.
- For most day-to-day actions or decisions, the decision-maker will be the carer most directly involved with the person at the time.

- Where the decision involves the provision of medical treatment, the doctor or other member of healthcare staff responsible for carrying out the particular treatment or procedure is the decision-maker.
- Where nursing or paid care is provided, the nurse or paid carer will be the decision-maker.
- If a Lasting Power of Attorney (or Enduring Power of Attorney) has been made and registered, or a deputy has been appointed under a court order, the attorney or deputy will be the decision-maker, for decisions within the scope of their authority.

5.9   What this means is that a range of different decision-makers may be involved with a person who lacks capacity to make different decisions.

5.10 In some cases, the same person may make different types of decision for someone who lacks capacity to make decisions for themselves. For instance, a family carer may carry out certain acts in caring for the person on a day-to-day basis, but if they are also an attorney, appointed under a Lasting Power of Attorney (LPA), they may also make specific decisions concerning the person's property and affairs or their personal welfare (depending on what decisions the LPA has been set up to cover).

5.11 There are also times when a joint decision might be made by a number of people. For example, when a care plan for a person who lacks capacity to make relevant decisions is being put together, different healthcare or social care staff might be involved in making decisions or recommendations about the person's care package. Sometimes these decisions will be made by a team of healthcare or social care staff as a whole. At other times, the decision will be made by a specific individual within the team. A different member of the team may then implement that decision, based on what the team has worked out to be the person's best interests.

5.12 No matter who is making the decision, the most important thing is that the decision-maker tries to work out what would be in the best interests of the person who lacks capacity.

Scenario: *Coming to a joint decision*

Jack, a young man with a brain injury, lacks capacity to agree to a rehabilitation programme designed to improve his condition. But the healthcare and social care staff who are looking after him believe that he clearly needs the programme, and have obtained the necessary funding from the Primary Care Trust.

However, Jack's family want to take him home from hospital as they believe they can provide better care for him at home.

A 'best interests' case conference is held, involving Jack, his parents and other family members and the relevant professionals, in order to decide what course of action would be in the Jack's best interests.   →

> A plan is developed to enable Jack to live at home, but attend the day hospital every weekday. Jack seems happy with the proposals and both the family carers and the healthcare and social care staff are satisfied that the plan is in his best interests.

What must be taken into account when trying to work out someone's best interests?

5.13 Because every case – and every decision – is different, the law can't set out all the factors that will need to be taken into account in working out someone's best interests. But section 4 of the Act sets out some common factors that must always be considered when trying to work out someone's best interests. These factors are summarised in the checklist here:

- Working out what is in someone's best interests cannot be based simply on someone's age, appearance, condition or behaviour. (see paragraphs 5.16–5.17).
- All relevant circumstances should be considered when working out someone's best interests (paragraphs 5.18–5.20).
- Every effort should be made to encourage and enable the person who lacks capacity to take part in making the decision (paragraphs 5.21–5.24).
- If there is a chance that the person will regain the capacity to make a particular decision, then it may be possible to put off the decision until later if it is not urgent (paragraphs 5.25–5.28).
- Special considerations apply to decisions about life-sustaining treatment (paragraphs 5.29–5.36).
- The person's past and present wishes and feelings, beliefs and values should be taken into account (paragraphs 5.37–5.48).
- The views of other people who are close to the person who lacks capacity should be considered, as well as the views of an attorney or deputy (paragraphs 5.49–5.55).

It's important not to take shortcuts in working out best interests, and a proper and objective assessment must be carried out on every occasion. If the decision is urgent, there may not be time to examine all possible factors, but the decision must still be made in the best interests of the person who lacks capacity. Not all the factors in the checklist will be relevant to all types of decisions or actions, and in many cases other factors will have to be considered as well, even though some of them may then not be found to be relevant.

5.14 What is in a person's best interests may well change over time. This means that even where similar actions need to be taken repeatedly in connection with the person's care or treatment, the person's best interests should be regularly reviewed.

5.15 Any staff involved in the care of a person who lacks capacity should make sure a record is kept of the process of working out the best interests of that person for each relevant decision, setting out:

- how the decision about the person's best interests was reached
- what the reasons for reaching the decision were
- who was consulted to help work out best interests, and
- what particular factors were taken into account.

This record should remain on the person's file.

For major decisions based on the best interests of a person who lacks capacity, it may also be useful for family and other carers to keep a similar kind of record.

What safeguards does the Act provide around working out someone's best interests?

5.16   Section 4(1) states that anyone working out someone's best interests must not make unjustified assumptions about what their best interests might be simply on the basis of the person's age, appearance, condition or any aspect of their behaviour. In this way, the Act ensures that people who lack capacity to make decisions for themselves are not subject to discrimination or treated any less favourably than anyone else.

5.17   'Appearance' is a broad term and refers to all aspects of physical appearance, including skin colour, mode of dress and any visible medical problems, disfiguring scars or other disabilities. A person's 'condition' also covers a range of factors including physical disabilities, learning difficulties or disabilities, age-related illness or temporary conditions (such as drunkenness or unconsciousness). 'Behaviour' refers to behaviour that might seem unusual to others, such as talking too loudly or laughing inappropriately.

Scenario: *Following the checklist*

Martina, an elderly woman with dementia, is beginning to neglect her appearance and personal hygiene and has several times been found wandering in the street unable to find her way home. Her care workers are concerned that Martina no longer has capacity to make appropriate decisions relating to her daily care. Her daughter is her personal welfare attorney and believes the time has come to act under the Lasting Power of Attorney (LPA).

She assumes it would be best for Martina to move into a care home, since the staff would be able to help her wash and dress smartly and prevent her from wandering.

However, it cannot be assumed *simply on the basis of her age, condition, appearance or behaviour* either that Martina lacks capacity to make such a decision or that such a move would be in her best interests.   →

Instead, steps must be taken to assess her capacity. If it is then agreed that Martina lacks the capacity to make this decision, all the relevant factors in the best interests' checklist must be considered to try to work out what her best interests would be.

Her daughter must therefore consider:

* Martina's past and present wishes and feelings
* the views of the people involved in her care
* any alternative ways of meeting her care needs effectively which might be less restrictive of Martina's rights and freedoms, such as increased provision of home care or attendance at a day centre.

By following this process, Martina's daughter can then take decisions on behalf of her mother and in her best interests, when her mother lacks the capacity to make them herself, on any matters that fall under the authority of the LPA.

How does a decision-maker work out what 'all relevant circumstances' are?

5.18 When trying to work out someone's best interests, the decision-maker should try to identify all the issues that would be most relevant to the individual who lacks capacity and to the particular decision, as well as those in the 'checklist'. Clearly, it is not always possible or practical to investigate in depth every issue which may have some relevance to the person who lacks capacity or the decision in question. So relevant circumstances are defined in section 4(11) of the Act as those:

> '(a) of which the person making the determination is aware, and (b) which it would be reasonable to regard as relevant.'

5.19 The relevant circumstances will of course vary from case to case. For example, when making a decision about major medical treatment, a doctor would need to consider the clinical needs of the patient, the potential benefits and burdens of the treatment on the person's health and life expectancy and any other factors relevant to making a professional judgement.[16] But it would not be reasonable to consider issues such as life expectancy when working out whether it would be in someone's best interests to be given medication for a minor problem.

5.20 Financial decisions are another area where the relevant circumstances will vary. For example, if a person had received a substantial sum of money as compensation for an accident resulting in brain injury, the decision-maker would have to consider a wide range of circumstances when making decisions about how the money is spent or invested, such as:

---

[16] *An NHS Trust v S* [2003] EWHC 365 (Fam) at 47.

- whether the person's condition is likely to change
- whether the person needs professional care, and
- whether the person needs to live somewhere else to make it easier for them.

These kinds of issues can only be decided on a case-by-case basis.

How should the person who lacks capacity be involved in working out their best interests?

5.21 Wherever possible, the person who lacks capacity to make a decision should still be involved in the decision-making process (section 4(4)).

5.22 Even if the person lacks capacity to make the decision, they may have views on matters affecting the decision, and on what outcome would be preferred. Their involvement can help work out what would be in their best interests.

5.23 The decision-maker should make sure that all practical means are used to enable and encourage the person to participate as fully as possible in the decision-making process and any action taken as a result, or to help the person improve their ability to participate.

5.24 Consulting the person who lacks capacity will involve taking time to explain what is happening and why a decision needs to be made. Chapter 3 includes a number of practical steps to assist and enable decision-making which may be also be helpful in encouraging greater participation. These include:

- using simple language and/or illustrations or photographs to help the person understand the options
- asking them about the decision at a time and location where the person feels most relaxed and at ease
- breaking the information down into easy-to-understand points
- using specialist interpreters or signers to communicate with the person.

This may mean that other people are required to communicate with the person to establish their views. For example, a trusted relative or friend, a full-time carer or an advocate may be able to help the person to express wishes or aspirations or to indicate a preference between different options.

More information on all of these steps can be found in Chapter 3.

Scenario: Involving someone in working out their best interests

The parents of Amy, a young woman with learning difficulties, are going through a divorce and are arguing about who should continue to care for their daughter. Though she cannot understand what is happening, attempts are made to see if Amy can give some indication of where she would prefer to live. →

An advocate is appointed to work with Amy to help her understand the situation and to find out her likes and dislikes and matters which are important to her. With the advocate's help, Amy is able to participate in decisions about her future care.

How do the chances of someone regaining and developing capacity affect working out what is in their best interests?

5.25 There are some situations where decisions may be deferred, if someone who currently lacks capacity may regain the capacity to make the decision for themselves. Section 4(3) of the Act requires the decision-maker to consider:

- whether the individual concerned is likely to regain the capacity to make that particular decision in the future, and
- if so, when that is likely to be.

It may then be possible to put off the decision until the person can make it for themselves.

5.26 In emergency situations – such as when urgent medical treatment is needed – it may not be possible to wait to see if the person may regain capacity so they can decide for themselves whether or not to have the urgent treatment.

5.27 Where a person currently lacks capacity to make a decision relating to their day-to-day care, the person may – over time and with the right support – be able to develop the skills to do so. Though others may need to make the decision on the person's behalf at the moment, all possible support should be given to that person to enable them to develop the skills so that they can make the decision for themselves in the future.

Scenario: Taking a short-term decision for someone who may regain capacity

Mr Fowler has suffered a stroke leaving him severely disabled and unable to speak. Within days, he has shown signs of improvement, so with intensive treatment there is hope he will recover over time. But at present both his wife and the hospital staff find it difficult to communicate with him and have been unable to find out his wishes.

He has always looked after the family finances, so Mrs Fowler suddenly discovers she has no access to his personal bank account to provide the family with money to live on or pay the bills. Because the decision can't be put off while efforts are made to find effective means of communicating with Mr Fowler, an application is made to the Court of Protection for an order that allows Mrs Fowler to access Mr Fowler's money. →

> The decision about longer-term arrangements, on the other hand, can be
> delayed until alternative methods of communication have been tried and
> the extent of Mr Fowler's recovery is known.

5.28 Some factors which may indicate that a person may regain or develop
capacity in the future are:
- the cause of the lack of capacity can be treated, either by medication
  or some other form of treatment or therapy
- the lack of capacity is likely to decrease in time (for example, where it
  is caused by the effects of medication or alcohol, or following a
  sudden shock)
- a person with learning disabilities may learn new skills or be subject
  to new experiences which increase their understanding and ability to
  make certain decisions
- the person may have a condition which causes capacity to come and
  go at various times (such as some forms of mental illness) so it may
  be possible to arrange for the decision to be made during a time when
  they do have capacity
- a person previously unable to communicate may learn a new form of
  communication (see Chapter 3).

How should someone's best interests be worked out when making decisions about life-sustaining treatment?

5.29 A special factor in the checklist applies to decisions about treatment
which is necessary to keep the person alive ('life-sustaining treatment') and
this is set out in section 4(5) of the Act. The fundamental rule is that
anyone who is deciding whether or not life-sustaining treatment is in the
best interests of someone who lacks capacity to consent to or refuse such
treatment must not be motivated by a desire to bring about the person's
death.

5.30 Whether a treatment is 'life-sustaining' depends not only on the type of
treatment, but also on the particular circumstances in which it may be
prescribed. For example, in some situations giving antibiotics may be
life-sustaining, whereas in other circumstances antibiotics are used to treat
a non-life-threatening condition. It is up to the doctor or healthcare
professional providing treatment to assess whether the treatment is
life-sustaining in each particular situation.

5.31 All reasonable steps which are in the person's best interests should be
taken to prolong their life. There will be a limited number of cases where
treatment is futile, overly burdensome to the patient or where there is no
prospect of recovery. In circumstances such as these, it may be that an
assessment of best interests leads to the conclusion that it would be in the
best interests of the patient to withdraw or withhold life-sustaining
treatment, even if this may result in the person's death. The
decision-maker must make a decision based on the best interests of the

person who lacks capacity. They must not be motivated by a desire to bring about the person's death for whatever reason, even if this is from a sense of compassion. Healthcare and social care staff should also refer to relevant professional guidance when making decisions regarding life-sustaining treatment.

5.32 As with all decisions, before deciding to withdraw or withhold life-sustaining treatment, the decision-maker must consider the range of treatment options available to work out what would be in the person's best interests. All the factors in the best interests checklist should be considered, and in particular, the decision-maker should consider any statements that the person has previously made about their wishes and feelings about life-sustaining treatment.

5.33 Importantly, section 4(5) cannot be interpreted to mean that doctors are under an obligation to provide, or to continue to provide, life-sustaining treatment where that treatment is not in the best interests of the person, even where the person's death is foreseen. Doctors must apply the best interests' checklist and use their professional skills to decide whether life-sustaining treatment is in the person's best interests. If the doctor's assessment is disputed, and there is no other way of resolving the dispute, ultimately the Court of Protection may be asked to decide what is in the person's best interests.

5.34 Where a person has made a written statement in advance that requests particular medical treatments, such as artificial nutrition and hydration (ANH), these requests should be taken into account by the treating doctor in the same way as requests made by a patient who has the capacity to make such decisions. Like anyone else involved in making this decision, the doctor must weigh written statements alongside all other relevant factors to decide whether it is in the best interests of the patient to provide or continue life-sustaining treatment.

5.35 If someone has made an advance decision to refuse life-sustaining treatment, specific rules apply. More information about these can be found in Chapter 9 and in paragraph 5.45 below.

5.36 As mentioned in paragraph 5.33 above, where there is any doubt about the patient's best interests, an application should be made to the Court of Protection for a decision as to whether withholding or withdrawing life-sustaining treatment is in the patient's best interests.

How do a person's wishes and feelings, beliefs and values affect working out what is in their best interests?

5.37 Section 4(6) of the Act requires the decision-maker to consider, as far as they are 'reasonably ascertainable':

> '(a) the person's past and present wishes and feelings (and in particular, any relevant written statements made by him when he had capacity),

(b) the beliefs and values that would be likely to influence his decision if he had capacity, and

(c) the other factors that he would be likely to consider if he were able to do so.'

Paragraphs 5.38–5.48 below give further guidance on each of these factors.

5.38   In setting out the requirements for working out a person's 'best interests', section 4 of the Act puts the person who lacks capacity at the centre of the decision to be made. Even if they cannot make the decision, their wishes and feelings, beliefs and values should be taken fully into account – whether expressed in the past or now. But their wishes and feelings, beliefs and values will not necessarily be the deciding factor in working out their best interests. Any such assessment must consider past and current wishes and feelings, beliefs and values alongside all other factors, but the final decision must be based entirely on what is in the person's best interests.

Scenario: Considering wishes and feelings as part of best interests

Andre, a young man with severe learning disabilities who does not use any formal system of communication, cuts his leg while outdoors. There is some earth in the wound. A doctor wants to give him a tetanus jab, but Andre appears scared of the needle and pushes it away. Assessments have shown that he is unable to understand the risk of infection following his injury, or the consequences of rejecting the injection.

The doctor decides that it is in the Andre's best interests to give the vaccination. She asks a nurse to comfort Andre, and if necessary, restrain him while she gives the injection. She has objective reasons for believing she is acting in Andre's best interests, and for believing that Andre lacks capacity to make the decision for himself. So she should be protected from liability under section 5 of the Act (see Chapter 6).

What is 'reasonably ascertainable'?

5.39   How much someone can learn about a person's past and present views will depend on circumstances and the time available. 'Reasonably ascertainable' means considering all possible information in the time available. What is available in an emergency will be different to what is available in a non-emergency. But even in an emergency, there may still be an opportunity to try to communicate with the person or his friends, family or carers (see Chapter 3 for guidance on helping communication).

What role do a person's past and present wishes and feelings play?

5.40 People who cannot express their current wishes and feelings in words may express themselves through their behaviour. Expressions of pleasure or distress and emotional responses will also be relevant in working out what is in their best interests. It is also important to be sure that other people have not influenced a person's views. An advocate could help the person make choices and express their views.

5.41 The person may have held strong views in the past which could have a bearing on the decision now to be made. All reasonable efforts must be made to find out whether the person has expressed views in the past that will shape the decision to be made. This could have been through verbal communication, writing, behaviour or habits, or recorded in any other way (for example, home videos or audiotapes).

5.42 Section 4(6)(a) places special emphasis on written statements the person might have made before losing capacity. These could provide a lot of information about a person's wishes. For example, these statements could include information about the type of medical treatment they would want in the case of future illness, where they would prefer to live, or how they wish to be cared for.

5.43 The decision-maker should consider written statements carefully. If their decision does not follow something a person has put in writing, they must record the reasons why. They should be able to justify their reasons if someone challenges their decision.

5.44 A doctor should take written statements made by a person before losing capacity which request specific treatments as seriously as those made by people who currently have capacity to make treatment decisions. But they would not have to follow a written request if they think the specific treatment would be clinically unnecessary or not appropriate for the person's condition, so not in the person's best interests.

5.45 It is important to note the distinction between a written statement expressing treatment preferences and a statement which constitutes an advance decision to refuse treatment. This is covered by section 24 of the Act, and it has a different status in law. Doctors cannot ignore a written statement that is a valid advance decision to refuse treatment. An advance decision to refuse treatment must be followed if it meets the Act's requirements and applies to the person's circumstances. In these cases, the treatment must not be given (see Chapter 9 for more information). If there is not a valid and applicable advance decision, treatment should be provided based on the person's best interests.

What role do beliefs and values play?

5.46 Everybody's values and beliefs influence the decisions they make. They may become especially important for someone who lacks capacity to make a decision because of a progressive illness such as dementia, for example. Evidence of a person's beliefs and values can be found in things like their:

- cultural background
- religious beliefs
- political convictions, or
- · past behaviour or habits.

Some people set out their values and beliefs in a written statement while they still have capacity.

Scenario: Considering beliefs and values

Anita, a young woman, suffers serious brain damage during a car accident. The court appoints her father as deputy to invest the compensation she received. As the decision-maker he must think about her wishes, beliefs and values before deciding how to invest the money.

Anita had worked for an overseas charity. Her father talks to her former colleagues. They tell him how Anita's political beliefs shaped her work and personal beliefs, so he decides not to invest in the bonds that a financial adviser had recommended, because they are from companies Anita would not have approved of. Instead, he employs an ethical investment adviser to choose appropriate companies in line with her beliefs.

What other factors should a decision-maker consider?

5.47 Section 4(6)(c) of the Act requires decision-makers to consider any other factors the person who lacks capacity would consider if they were able to do so. This might include the effect of the decision on other people, obligations to dependants or the duties of a responsible citizen.

5.48 The Act allows actions that benefit other people, as long as they are in the best interests of the person who lacks capacity to make the decision. For example, having considered all the circumstances of the particular case, a decision might be made to take a blood sample from a person who lacks capacity to consent, to check for a genetic link to cancer within the family, because this might benefit someone else in the family. But it might still be in the best interests of the person who lacks capacity. 'Best interests' goes beyond the person's medical interests.

For example, courts have previously ruled that possible wider benefits to a person who lacks capacity to consent, such as providing or gaining emotional support from close relationships, are important factors in working out the person's own best interests.[17] If it is likely that the person who lacks capacity would have considered these factors themselves, they can be seen as part of the person's best interests.

---

[17] See for example *Re Y (Mental Incapacity: Bone marrow transplant)* [1996] 2 FLR 787; *Re A (Male Sterilisation)* [2000] 1 FLR 549.

Who should be consulted when working out someone's best interests?

5.49 The Act places a duty on the decision-maker to consult other people close to a person who lacks capacity, where practical and appropriate, on decisions affecting the person and what might be in the person's best interests. This also applies to those involved in caring for the person and interested in the person's welfare. Under section 4(7), the decision-maker has a duty to take into account the views of the following people, where it is practical and appropriate to do so:
- anyone the person has previously named as someone they want to be consulted
- anyone involved in caring for the person
- anyone interested in their welfare (for example, family carers, other close relatives, or an advocate already working with the person)
- an attorney appointed by the person under a Lasting Power of Attorney, and
- a deputy appointed for that person by the Court of Protection.

5.50 If there is no-one to speak to about the person's best interests, in some circumstances the person may qualify for an Independent Mental Capacity Advocate (IMCA). For more information on IMCAs, see Chapter 10.

5.51 Decision-makers must show they have thought carefully about who to speak to. If it is practical and appropriate to speak to the above people, they must do so and must take their views into account. They must be able to explain why they did not speak to a particular person – it is good practice to have a clear record of their reasons. It is also good practice to give careful consideration to the views of family carers, if it is possible to do so.

5.52 It is also good practice for healthcare and social care staff to record at the end of the process why they think a specific decision is in the person's best interests. This is particularly important if healthcare and social care staff go against the views of somebody who has been consulted while working out the person's best interests.

5.53 The decision-maker should try to find out:
- what the people consulted think is in the person's best interests in this matter, and
- if they can give information on the person's wishes and feelings, beliefs and values.

5.54 This information may be available from somebody the person named before they lost capacity as someone they wish to be consulted. People who are close to the person who lacks capacity, such as close family members, are likely to know them best. They may also be able to help with communication or interpret signs that show the person's present wishes and feelings. Everybody's views are equally important – even if they do not agree with each other. They must be considered alongside the views of the person who lacks capacity and other factors. See paragraphs 5.62–5.69 below for guidance on dealing with conflicting views.

> ### Scenario: Considering other people's views
>
> Lucia, a young woman with severe brain damage, is cared for at home by her parents and attends a day centre a couple of days each week. The day centre staff would like to take some of the service users on holiday. They speak to Lucia's parents as part of the process of assessing whether the holiday would be in her best interests.
>
> The parents think that the holiday would be good for her, but they are worried that Lucia gets very anxious if she is surrounded by strangers who don't know how to communicate with her. Having tried to seek Lucia's views and involve her in the decision, the staff and parents agree that a holiday would be in her best interests, as long as her care assistant can go with her to help with communication.

5.55 Where an attorney has been appointed under a Lasting Power of Attorney or Enduring Power of Attorney, or a deputy has been appointed by a court, they must make the decisions on any matters they have been appointed to deal with. Attorneys and deputies should also be consulted, if practical and appropriate, on other issues affecting the person who lacks capacity.

For instance, an attorney who is appointed only to look after the person's property and affairs may have information about the person's beliefs and values, wishes and feelings, that could help work out what would be in the person's best interests regarding healthcare or treatment decisions. (See Chapters 7 and 8 for more information about the roles of attorneys and deputies.)

How can decision-makers respect confidentiality?

5.56 Decision-makers must balance the duty to consult other people with the right to confidentiality of the person who lacks capacity. So if confidential information is to be discussed, they should only seek the views of people who it is appropriate to consult, where their views are relevant to the decision to be made and the particular circumstances.

5.57 There may be occasions where it is in the person's best interests for personal information (for example, about their medical condition, if the decision concerns the provision of medical treatment) to be revealed to the people consulted as part of the process of working out their best interests (further guidance on this is given in Chapter 16). Healthcare and social care staff who are trying to determine a person's best interests must follow their professional guidance, as well as other relevant guidance, about confidentiality.

When does the best interests principle apply?

5.58 Section 1(5) of the Act confirms that the principle applies to any act done, or any decision made, on behalf of someone where there is reasonable belief that the person lacks capacity under the Act. This covers informal day-to-day decisions and actions as well as decisions made by the courts.

Reasonable belief about a person's best interests

5.59 Section 4(9) confirms that if someone acts or makes a decision in the reasonable belief that what they are doing is in the best interests of the person who lacks capacity, then – provided they have followed the checklist in section 4 – they will have complied with the best interests principle set out in the Act. Coming to an incorrect conclusion about a person's capacity or best interests does not necessarily mean that the decision-maker would not get protection from liability (this is explained in Chapter 6). But they must be able to show that it was reasonable for them to think that the person lacked capacity and that they were acting in the person's best interests at the time they made their decision or took action.

5.60 Where there is a need for a court decision, the court is likely to require formal evidence of what might be in the person's best interests. This will include evidence from relevant professionals (for example, psychiatrists or social workers). But in most day-to-day situations, there is no need for such formality. In emergency situations, it may not be practical or possible to gather formal evidence.

5.61 Where the court is not involved, people are still expected to have reasonable grounds for believing that they are acting in somebody's best interests. This does not mean that decision-makers can simply impose their own views. They must have objective reasons for their decisions – and they must be able to demonstrate them. They must be able to show they have considered all relevant circumstances and applied all elements of the best interests checklist.

Scenario: Demonstrating reasonable belief

Mrs Prior is mugged and knocked unconscious. She is brought to hospital without any means of identification. She has head injuries and a stab wound, and has lost a lot of blood. In casualty, a doctor arranges an urgent blood transfusion. Because this is necessary to save her life, the doctor believes this is in her best interests.

When her relatives are contacted, they say that Mrs Prior's beliefs meant that she would have refused all blood products. But since Mrs Prior's handbag had been stolen, the doctor had no idea who the woman was nor what her beliefs her. He needed to make an immediate decision and Mrs Prior lacked capacity to make the decision for herself. Therefore he →

had reasonable grounds for believing that his action was in his patient's best interests – and so was protected from liability.

Now that the doctor knows Mrs Prior's beliefs, he can take them into account in future decisions about her medical treatment if she lacks capacity to make them for herself. He can also consult her family, now that he knows where they are.

What problems could arise when working out someone's best interests?

5.62 It is important that the best interests principle and the statutory checklist are flexible. Without flexibility, it would be impossible to prioritise factors in different cases – and it would be difficult to ensure that the outcome is the best possible for the person who lacks capacity to make the particular decision. Some cases will be straightforward. Others will require decision-makers to balance the pros and cons of all relevant factors.[18] But this flexibility could lead to problems in reaching a conclusion about a person's best interests.

What happens when there are conflicting concerns?

5.63 A decision-maker may be faced with people who disagree about a person's best interests. Family members, partners and carers may disagree between themselves. Or they might have different memories about what views the person expressed in the past. Carers and family might disagree with a professional's view about the person's care or treatment needs.

5.64 The decision-maker will need to find a way of balancing these concerns or deciding between them. The first approach should be to review all elements of the best interests checklist with everyone involved. They should include the person who lacks capacity (as much as they are able to take part) and anyone who has been involved in earlier discussions. It may be possible to reach an agreement at a meeting to air everyone's concerns. But an agreement in itself might not be in the person's best interests. Ultimate responsibility for working out best interests lies with the decision-maker.

Scenario: *Dealing with disagreement*

Some time ago, Mr Graham made a Lasting Power of Attorney (LPA) appointing his son and daughter as joint attorneys to manage his finances and property. He now has Alzheimer's disease and has moved into private residential care. The son and daughter have to decide what to do with Mr Graham's house. →

---

18 *Re A (Male Sterilisation)* [2000] 1 FLR 549.

His son thinks it is in their father's best interests to sell it and invest the money for Mr Graham's future care. But his daughter thinks it is in Mr Graham's best interests to keep the property, because he enjoys visiting and spending time in his old home.

After making every effort to get Mr Graham's views, the family meets to discuss all the issues involved. After hearing other family views, the attorneys agree that it would be in their father's best interests to keep the property for so long as he is able to enjoy visiting it.

Family, partners and carers who are consulted

5.65 If disagreement continues, the decision-maker will need to weigh up the views of different parties. This will depend entirely upon the circumstances of each case, the people involved and their relationship with the person who lacks capacity. Sometimes the decision-maker will find that carers have an insight into how to interpret a person's wishes and feelings that can help them reach a decision.

5.66 At the same time, paid care workers and voluntary sector support workers may have specialist knowledge about up-to-date care options or treatments. Some may also have known the person for many years.

5.67 People with conflicting interests should not be cut out of the process (for example, those who stand to inherit from the person's will may still have a right to be consulted about the person's care or medical treatment). But decision-makers must always ensure that the interests of those consulted do not overly influence the process of working out a person's best interests. In weighing up different contributions, the decision-maker should consider:

- how long an individual has known the person who lacks capacity, and
- what their relationship is.

Scenario: Settling disagreements

Robert is 19 and has learning disabilities and autism. He is about to leave his residential special school. His parents want Robert to go to a specialist unit run by a charitable organisation, but he has been offered a place in a local supported living scheme. The parents don't think Robert will get appropriate care there.

The school sets up a 'best interests' meeting. People who attend include Robert, his parents, teachers from his school and professionals involved in preparing Robert's care plan. Robert's parents and teachers know him best. They set out their views and help Robert to communicate where he would like to live. →

> Social care staff identify some different placements within the county. Robert visits these with his parents. After further discussion, everyone agrees that a community placement near his family home would be in Robert's best interests.

Settling disputes about best interests

5.68 If someone wants to challenge a decision-maker's conclusions, there are several options:
- Involve an advocate to act on behalf of the person who lacks capacity to make the decision (see paragraph 5.69 below).
- Get a second opinion.
- Hold a formal or informal 'best interests' case conference.
- Attempt some form of mediation (see Chapter 15).
- Pursue a complaint through the organisation's formal procedures.

Ultimately, if all other attempts to resolve the dispute have failed, the court might need to decide what is in the person's best interests. Chapter 8 provides more information about the Court of Protection.

Advocacy

5.69 An advocate might be useful in providing support for the person who lacks capacity to make a decision in the process of working out their best interests, if:
- the person who lacks capacity has no close family or friends to take an interest in their welfare, and they do not qualify for an Independent Mental Capacity Advocate (see Chapter 10)
- family members disagree about the person's best interests
- family members and professionals disagree about the person's best interests
- there is a conflict of interest for people who have been consulted in the best interests assessment (for example, the sale of a family property where the person lives)
- the person who lacks capacity is already in contact with an advocate
- the proposed course of action may lead to the use of restraint or other restrictions on the person who lacks capacity
- there is a concern about the protection of a vulnerable adult.

6   WHAT PROTECTION DOES THE ACT OFFER FOR PEOPLE PROVIDING CARE OR TREATMENT?

Section 5 of the Act allows carers, healthcare and social care staff to carry out certain tasks without fear of liability. These tasks involve the personal care, healthcare or treatment of people who lack capacity to consent to them. The aim is to give legal backing for acts that need to be carried out in the best interests of the person who lacks capacity to consent.[19]

This chapter explains:

- how the Act provides protection from liability
- how that protection works in practice
- where protection is restricted or limited, and
- when a carer can use a person's money to buy goods or services without formal permission.

> In this chapter, as throughout the Code, a person's capacity (or lack of capacity) refers specifically to their capacity to make a particular decision at the time it needs to be made.

Quick summary

The following steps list all the things that people providing care or treatment should bear in mind to ensure they are protected by the Act.

Acting in connection with the care or treatment of someone who lacks capacity to consent

- Is the action to be carried out in connection with the care or treatment of a person who lacks capacity to give consent to that act?
- Does it involve major life changes for the person concerned? If so, it will need special consideration.
- Who is carrying out the action? Is it appropriate for that person to do so at the relevant time?

Checking whether the person has capacity to consent

- Have all possible steps been taken to try to help the person make a decision for themselves about the action?
- Has the two-stage test of capacity been applied?
- Are there reasonable grounds for believing the person lacks capacity to give permission?

Acting in the person's best interests

- Has the best interests checklist been applied and all relevant circumstances considered?

---

[19] The provisions of section 5 are based on the common law 'doctrine of necessity' as set out in *Re F (Mental Patient: Sterilisation)* [1990] 2 AC 1.

- Is a less restrictive option available?
- Is it reasonable to believe that the proposed act is in the person's best interests?

Understanding possible limitations on protection from liability

- If restraint is being considered, is it necessary to prevent harm to the person who lacks capacity, and is it a proportionate response to the likelihood of the person suffering harm – and to the seriousness of that harm?
- Could the restraint be classed as a 'deprivation of the person's liberty'?
- Does the action conflict with a decision that has been made by an attorney or deputy under their powers?

Paying for necessary goods and services

- If someone wishes to use the person's money to buy goods or pay for services for someone who lacks capacity to do so themselves, are those goods or services necessary and in the person's best interests?
- Is it necessary to take money from the person's bank or building society account or to sell the person's property to pay for goods or services? If so, formal authority will be required.

What protection do people have when caring for those who lack capacity to consent?

6.1   Every day, millions of acts are done to and for people who lack capacity either to:
- take decisions about their own care or treatment, or
- consent to someone else caring for them.

Such acts range from everyday tasks of caring (for example, helping someone to wash) to life-changing events (for example, serious medical treatment or arranging for someone to go into a care home).

In theory, many of these actions could be against the law. Legally, people have the right to stop others from interfering with their body or property unless they give permission. But what happens if someone lacks capacity to give permission? Carers who dress people who cannot dress themselves are potentially interfering with someone's body without their consent, so could theoretically be prosecuted for assault. A neighbour who enters and cleans the house of a person who lacks capacity could be trespassing on the person's property.

6.2   Section 5 of the Act provides 'protection from liability'. In other words, it protects people who carry out these actions. It stops them being prosecuted for acts that could otherwise be classed as civil wrongs or crimes. By protecting family and other carers from liability, the Act allows necessary caring acts or treatment to take place as if a person who lacks capacity to consent had consented to them. People providing care of this sort do not therefore need to get formal authority to act.

6.3 Importantly, section 5 does not give people caring for or treating someone the power to make any other decisions on behalf of those who lack capacity to make their own decisions. Instead, it offers protection from liability so that they can act in connection with the person's care or treatment. The power to make decisions on behalf of someone who lacks capacity can be granted through other parts of the Act (such as the powers granted to attorneys and deputies, which are explained in Chapters 7 and 8).

What type of actions might have protection from liability?

6.4 Section 5(1) provides possible protection for actions carried out *in connection with care or treatment*. The action may be carried out on behalf of someone who is believed to lack capacity to give permission for the action, so long as it is in that person's best interests (see Chapter 5). The Act does not define 'care' or 'treatment'. They should be given their normal meaning. However, section 64(1) makes clear that treatment includes diagnostic or other procedures.

6.5 Actions that might be covered by section 5 include:

Personal care
- helping with washing, dressing or personal hygiene
- helping with eating and drinking
- helping with communication
- helping with mobility (moving around)
- helping someone take part in education, social or leisure activities
- going into a person's home to drop off shopping or to see if they are alright
- doing the shopping or buying necessary goods with the person's money
- arranging household services (for example, arranging repairs or maintenance for gas and electricity supplies)
- providing services that help around the home (such as homecare or meals on wheels)
- undertaking actions related to community care services (for example, day care, residential accommodation or nursing care) – but see also paragraphs 6.7–6.14 below
- helping someone to move home (including moving property and clearing the former home).

Healthcare and treatment
- carrying out diagnostic examinations and tests (to identify an illness, condition or other problem)
- providing professional medical, dental and similar treatment
- giving medication

- taking someone to hospital for assessment or treatment
- providing nursing care (whether in hospital or in the community)
- carrying out any other necessary medical procedures (for example, taking a blood sample) or therapies (for example, physiotherapy or chiropody)
- providing care in an emergency.

6.6 These actions only receive protection from liability if the person is reasonably believed to lack capacity to give permission for the action. The action must also be in the person's best interests and follow the Act's principles (see paragraph 6.26 onwards).

6.7 Some acts in connection with care or treatment may cause major life changes with significant consequences for the person concerned. Those requiring particularly careful consideration include a change of residence, perhaps into a care home or nursing home, or major decisions about healthcare and medical treatment. These are described in the following paragraphs.

A change of residence

6.8 Sometimes a person cannot get sufficient or appropriate care in their own home, and they may have to move – perhaps to live with relatives or to go into a care home or nursing home. If the person lacks capacity to consent to a move, the decision-maker(s) must consider whether the move is in the person's best interests (by referring to the best interests checklist in Chapter 5 and in particular the person's past and present wishes and feelings, as well as the views of other relevant people). The decision-maker(s) must also consider whether there is a less restrictive option (see Chapter 2, principle 5).

This may involve speaking to:
- anyone currently involved in the person's care
- family carers and other family members close to the person and interested in their welfare
- others who have an interest in the person's welfare
- anyone the person has previously named as someone to be consulted, and
- an attorney or deputy who has been legally appointed to make particular decisions on their behalf.

6.9 Some cases will require an Independent Mental Capacity Advocate (IMCA). The IMCA represents and supports the person who lacks capacity and they will provide information to make sure the final decision is in the person's best interests (see Chapter 10). An IMCA is needed when there is no-one close to the person who lacks capacity to give an opinion about what is best for them, and:
- an NHS body is proposing to provide serious medical treatment or
- an NHS body or local authority is proposing to arrange accommodation in hospital or a care home or other longer-term accommodation and

> – the person will stay in hospital longer than 28 days, or
> – they will stay in a care home for more than eight weeks.

There are also some circumstances where an IMCA may be appointed on a discretionary basis. More guidance is available in Chapter 10.

6.10 Sometimes the final outcome may not be what the person who lacks capacity wanted. For example, they might want to stay at home, but those caring for them might decide a move is in their best interests. In all cases, those making the decision must first consider other options that might restrict the person's rights and freedom of action less (see Chapter 2, principle 5).

6.11 In some cases, there may be no alternative but to move the person. Such a move would normally require the person's formal consent if they had capacity to give, or refuse, it. In cases where a person lacks capacity to consent, section 5 of the Act allows carers to carry out actions relating to the move – as long as the Act's principles and the requirements for working out best interests have been followed. This applies even if the person continues to object to the move.

However, section 6 places clear limits on the use of force or restraint by only permitting restraint to be used (for example, to transport the person to their new home) where this is necessary to protect the person from harm and is a proportionate response to the risk of harm (see paragraphs 6.40–6.53). Any action taken to move the person concerned or their property could incur liability unless protected under section 5.

6.12 If there is a serious disagreement about the need to move the person that cannot be settled in any other way, the Court of Protection can be asked to decide what the person's best interests are and where they should live. For example, this could happen if members of a family disagree over what is best for a relative who lacks capacity to give or deny permission for a move.

6.13 In some circumstances, being placed in a hospital or care home may deprive the person of their liberty (see paragraphs 6.49–6.53). If this is the case, there is no protection from liability – even if the placement was considered to be in the best interests of the person (section 6(5)). It is up to the decision-maker to first look at a range of alternative and less restrictive options to see if there is any way of avoiding taking away the person's liberty.

6.14 If there is no alternative way of caring for the person, specific authority will be required to keep the person in a situation which deprives them of their liberty. For instance, sometimes the Court of Protection might be prepared to grant an order of which a consequence is the deprivation of a person's liberty – if it is satisfied that this is in the person's best interests. In other cases, if the person needs treatment for a mental disorder and meets the criteria for detention under the Mental Health Act 1983, this may be used to admit or keep the person in hospital (see Chapter 13).

Healthcare and treatment decisions

6.15 Section 5 also allows actions to be taken to ensure a person who lacks capacity to consent receives necessary medical treatment. This could involve taking the person to hospital for out-patient treatment or arranging for admission to hospital. Even if a person who lacks capacity to consent objects to the proposed treatment or admission to hospital, the action might still be allowed under section 5 (but see paragraphs 6.20 and 6.22 below). But there are limits about whether force or restraint can be used to impose treatment (see paragraphs 6.40–6.53).

6.16 Major healthcare and treatment decisions – for example, major surgery or a decision that no attempt is to be made to resuscitate the patient (known as 'DNR' decisions) – will also need special consideration. Unless there is a valid and applicable advance decision to refuse the specific treatment, healthcare staff must carefully work out what would be in the person's best interests (see Chapter 5). As part of the process of working this out, they will need to consider (where practical and appropriate):
- the past and present wishes and feelings, beliefs and values of the person who lacks capacity to make the treatment decision, including any advance statement the person wrote setting out their wishes when they had capacity
- the views of anyone previously named by the person as someone to be consulted
- the views of anyone engaged in caring for the person
- the views of anyone interested in their welfare, and
- the views of any attorney or deputy appointed for the person.

In specific cases where there is no-one else available to consult about the person's best interests, an IMCA must be appointed to support and represent the person (see paragraph 6.9 above and Chapter 10).

Healthcare staff must also consider whether there are alternative treatment options that might be less intrusive or restrictive (see Chapter 2, principle 5). When deciding about the provision or withdrawal of life-sustaining treatment, anyone working out what is in the best interests of a person who lacks capacity must not be motivated by a desire to bring about the person's death (see Chapter 5).

6.17 Multi-disciplinary meetings are often the best way to decide on a person's best interests. They bring together healthcare and social care staff with different skills to discuss the person's options and may involve those who are closest to the person concerned. But final responsibility for deciding what is in a person's best interest lies with the member of healthcare staff responsible for the person's treatment. They should record their decision, how they reached it and the reasons for it in the person's clinical notes. As long as they have recorded objective reasons to show that the decision is in the person's best interests, and the other requirements of section 5 of the Act are met, all healthcare staff taking actions in connection with the particular treatment will be protected from liability.

6.18 Some treatment decisions are so serious that the court has to make them – unless the person has previously made a Lasting Power of Attorney appointing an attorney to make such healthcare decisions for them (see Chapter 7) or they have made a valid advance decision to refuse the proposed treatment (see Chapter 9). The Court of Protection must be asked to make decisions relating to:[20]

- the proposed withholding or withdrawal of artificial nutrition and hydration (ANH) from a patient in a permanent vegetative state (PVS)
- cases where it is proposed that a person who lacks capacity to consent should donate an organ or bone marrow to another person
- the proposed non-therapeutic sterilisation of a person who lacks capacity to consent (for example, for contraceptive purposes)
- cases where there is a dispute about whether a particular treatment will be in a person's best interests.

See paragraphs 8.18–8.24 for more details on these types of cases.

6.19 This last category may include cases that introduce ethical dilemmas concerning untested or innovative treatments (for example, new treatments for variant Creutzfeldt-Jakob Disease (CDJ)) where it is not known if the treatment will be effective, or certain cases involving a termination of pregnancy. It may also include cases where there is conflict between professionals or between professionals and family members which cannot be resolved in any other way.

Where there is conflict, it is advisable for parties to get legal advice, though they may not necessarily be able to get legal aid to pay for this advice. Chapter 8 gives more information about the need to refer cases to court for a decision.

Who is protected from liability by section 5?

6.20 Section 5 of the Act is most likely to affect:
- family carers and other kinds of carers
- care workers
- healthcare and social care staff, and
- others who may occasionally be involved in the care or treatment of a person who lacks capacity to consent (for example, ambulance staff, housing workers, police officers and volunteer support workers).

6.21 At any time, it is likely that several people will be carrying out tasks that are covered by section 5 of the Act. Section 5 does not:
- give one person more rights than another to carry out tasks
- specify who has the authority to act in a specific instance
- allow somebody to make decisions relating to subjects other than the care or treatment of the person who lacks capacity, or

---

[20] The procedures resulting from those court judgements are set out in a Practice Note from the Official Solicitor (available at www.officialsolicitor.gov.uk) and will be set out in a Practice Direction from the new Court of Protection.

- allow somebody to give consent on behalf of a person who lacks capacity to do so.

6.22 To receive protection from liability under section 5, all actions must be related to the care or treatment of the person who lacks capacity to consent. Before taking action, carers must first reasonably believe that:

- the person lacks the capacity to make that particular decision at the time it needs to be made, and
- the action is in the person's best interests.

This is explained further in paragraphs 6.26–6.34 below.

Scenario: Protecting multiple carers

Mr Rose, an older man with dementia, gets help from several people. His sister sometimes cooks meals for him. A district nurse visits him to change the dressing on a pressure sore, and a friend often takes Mr Rose to the park, guiding him when they cross the road. Each of these individuals would be protected from liability under section 5 of the Act – but only if they take reasonable steps to check that he lacks capacity to consent to the actions they take and hold a reasonable belief that the actions are in Mr Rose's best interests.

6.23 Section 5 may also protect carers who need to use the person's money to pay for goods or services that the person needs but lacks the capacity to purchase for themselves. However, there are strict controls over who may have access to another person's money. See paragraphs 6.56–6.66 for more information.

6.24 Carers who provide personal care services must not carry out specialist procedures that are normally done by trained healthcare staff. If the action involves medical treatment, the doctor or other member of healthcare staff with responsibility for the patient will be the decision-maker who has to decide whether the proposed treatment is in the person's best interests (see Chapter 5). A doctor can delegate responsibility for giving the treatment to other people in the clinical team who have the appropriate skills or expertise. People who do more than their experience or qualifications allow may not be protected from liability.

Care planning

6.25 Decisions about a person's care or treatment are often made by a multi-disciplinary team (a team of professionals with different skills that contribute to a person's care), by drawing up a care plan for the person. The preparation of a care plan should always include an assessment of the person's capacity to consent to the actions covered by the care plan, and confirm that those actions are agreed to be in the person's best interests. Healthcare and social care staff may then be able to assume that any actions they take under the care plan are in the person's best interests, and therefore receive protection from liability under section 5. But a person's capacity and best interests must still be reviewed regularly.

What steps should people take to be protected from liability?

6.26 As well as taking the following steps, somebody who wants to be protected from liability should bear in mind the statutory principles set out in section 1 of the Act (see Chapter 2).

6.27 First, reasonable steps must be taken to find out whether a person has the capacity to make a decision about the proposed action (section 5(1)(a)). If the person has capacity, they must give their consent for anyone to take an action on their behalf, so that the person taking the action is protected from liability. For guidance on what is classed as 'reasonable steps', see paragraphs 6.29–6.34. But reasonable steps must always include:

- taking all practical and appropriate steps to help people to make a decision about an action themselves, and
- applying the two-stage test of capacity (see Chapter 4).

The person who is going to take the action must have a 'reasonable belief' that the individual lacks capacity to give consent for the action at the time it needs to be taken.

6.28 Secondly, the person proposing to take action must have reasonable grounds for believing that the action is in the best interests of the person who lacks capacity. They should apply all elements of the best interests checklist (see Chapter 5), and in particular

- consider whether the person is likely to regain capacity to make this decision in the future. Can the action wait until then?
- consider whether a less restrictive option is available (Chapter 2, principle 5), and
- have objective reasons for thinking an action is in the best interests of the person who lacks capacity to consent to it.

What is 'reasonable'?

6.29 As explained in Chapter 4, anyone assessing a person's capacity to make decisions for themselves or give consent must focus wholly on whether the person has capacity to make a specific decision at the time it needs to be made and not the person's capacity to make decisions generally. For example, a carer helping a person to dress can assess a person's capacity to agree to their help by explaining the different options (getting dressed or staying in nightclothes), and the consequences (being able to go out, or staying in all day).

6.30 Carers do not have to be experts in assessing capacity. But they must be able to show that they have taken *reasonable steps* to find out if the person has the capacity to make the specific decision. Only then will they have *reasonable grounds for believing* the person lacks capacity in relation to that particular matter. See paragraphs 4.44–4.45 for guidance on what is classed as 'reasonable' – although this will vary, depending on circumstances.

6.31 For the majority of decisions, formal assessment processes are unlikely to be required. But in some circumstances, professional practice requires some formal procedures to be carried out (for example, where consent to medical treatment is required, the doctor will need to assess – and record the person's capacity to consent). Under section 5, carers and professionals will be protected from liability as long as they are able to provide some objective reasons that explain why they believe that the person lacks capacity to consent to the action. If somebody challenges their belief, both carers and professionals will be protected from liability as long as they can show that they took steps to find out whether the person has capacity and that they have a reasonable belief that the person lacks capacity.

6.32 Similarly, carers, relatives and others involved in caring for someone who lacks capacity must have *reasonable grounds for believing* that their action is in the person's best interests. They must not simply impose their own views. They must be able to show that they considered all relevant circumstances and applied the best interests checklist. This includes showing that they have tried to involve the person who lacks capacity, and find out their wishes and feelings, beliefs and values. They must also have asked other people's opinions, where practical and appropriate. If somebody challenges their decision, they will be protected from liability if they can show that it was reasonable for them to believe that their action was in the person's best interests – in all the circumstances of that particular case.

6.33 If healthcare and social care staff are involved, their skills and knowledge will affect what is classed as 'reasonable'. For example, a doctor assessing somebody's capacity to consent to treatment must demonstrate more skill than someone without medical training. They should also record in the person's healthcare record the steps they took and the reasons for the finding. Healthcare and social care staff should apply normal clinical and professional standards when deciding what treatments to offer. They must then decide whether the proposed treatment is in the best interests of the person who lacks capacity to consent. This includes considering all relevant circumstances and applying the best interests checklist (see Chapter 5).

6.34 Healthcare and social care staff can be said to have 'reasonable grounds for believing' that a person lacks capacity if:
• they are working to a person's care plan, and
• the care planning process involved an assessment of the person's capacity to make a decision about actions in the care plan.
It is also reasonable for them to assume that the care planning process assessed a person's best interests. But they should still make every effort to communicate with the person to find out if they still lack capacity and the action is still in their best interests.

Scenario: *Working with a care plan*

Margaret, an elderly woman, has serious mental health and physical problems. She lives in a nursing home and a care plan has been prepared by the multi-disciplinary team, in consultation with her relatives in deciding what course of action would be in Margaret's best interests. The care plan covers the medication she has been prescribed, the physiotherapy she needs, help with her personal care and other therapeutic activities such as art therapy.

Although attempts were made to involve Margaret in the care planning process, she has been assessed by the doctor responsible for her care as lacking capacity to consent to most aspects of her care plan. The care plan can be relied on by the nurse or care assistant who administers the medication, by the physiotherapist and art therapist, and also by the care assistant who helps with Margaret's personal care, providing them with reasonable grounds for believing that they are acting in her best interests.

However, as each act is performed, they must all take reasonable steps to communicate with Margaret to explain what they are doing and to ascertain whether she has the capacity to consent to the act in question. If they think she does, they must stop the treatment unless or until Margaret agrees that it should continue.

What happens in emergency situations?

6.35 Sometimes people who lack capacity to consent will require emergency medical treatment to save their life or prevent them from serious harm. In these situations, what steps are 'reasonable' will differ to those in non-urgent cases. In emergencies, it will almost always be in the person's best interests to give urgent treatment without delay. One exception to this is when the healthcare staff giving treatment are satisfied that an advance decision to refuse treatment exists (see paragraph 6.37).

What happens in cases of negligence?

6.36 Section 5 does not provide a defence in cases of negligence – either in carrying out a particular act or by failing to act where necessary. For example, a doctor may be protected against a claim of battery for carrying out an operation that is in a person's best interests. But if they perform the operation negligently, they are not protected from a charge of negligence. So the person who lacks capacity has the same rights in cases of negligence as someone who has consented to the operation.

What is the effect of an advance decision to refuse treatment?

6.37 Sometimes people will make an advance decision to refuse treatment while they still have capacity to do so and before they need that particular treatment. Healthcare staff must respect this decision if it is valid and applies to the proposed treatment.

6.38 If healthcare staff are satisfied that an advance decision is valid and applies to the proposed treatment, they are not protected from liability if they give any treatment that goes against it. But they are protected from liability if they did not know about an advance decision or they are not satisfied that the advance decision is valid and applies in the current circumstances (section 26(2)). See Chapter 9 for further guidance.

What limits are there on protection from liability?

6.39 Section 6 imposes some important limitations on acts which can be carried out with protection from liability under section 5 (as described in the first part of this chapter). The key areas where acts might not be protected from liability are where there is inappropriate use of restraint or where a person who lacks capacity is deprived of their liberty.

Using restraint

6.40 Section 6(4) of the Act states that someone is using restraint if they:
- use force – or threaten to use force – to make someone do something that they are resisting, or
- restrict a person's freedom of movement, whether they are resisting or not.

6.41 Any action intended to restrain a person who lacks capacity will not attract protection from liability unless the following two conditions are met:
- the person taking action must reasonably believe that restraint is *necessary* to prevent *harm* to the person who lacks capacity, and
- the amount or type of restraint used and the amount of time it lasts must be a *proportionate response* to the likelihood and seriousness of harm.

See paragraphs 6.44–6.48 for more explanation of the terms *necessary, harm* and a *proportionate response*.

6.42 Healthcare and social care staff should also refer to:

- professional and other guidance on restraint or physical intervention, such as that issued by the Department of Health[21] or Welsh Assembly Government,[22] and
- limitations imposed by regulations and standards, such as the national minimum standards for care services (see Chapter 14).

6.43 In addition to the requirements of the Act, the common law imposes a duty of care on healthcare and social care staff in respect of all people to whom they provide services. Therefore if a person who lacks capacity to consent has challenging behaviour, or is in the acute stages of illness causing them to act in way which may cause harm to others, staff may, under the common law, take appropriate and necessary action to restrain or remove the person, in order to prevent harm, both to the person concerned and to anyone else.

However, within this context, the common law would not provide sufficient grounds for an action that would have the effect of depriving someone of their liberty (see paragraphs 6.49–6.53).

When might restraint be 'necessary'?

6.44 Anybody considering using restraint must have objective reasons to justify that restraint is necessary. They must be able to show that the person being cared for is likely to suffer harm unless proportionate restraint is used. A carer or professional must not use restraint just so that they can do something more easily. If restraint is necessary to prevent harm to the person who lacks capacity, it must be the minimum amount of force for the shortest time possible.

Scenario: Appropriate use of restraint

Derek, a man with learning disabilities, has begun to behave in a challenging way. Staff at his care home think he might have a medical condition that is causing him distress. They take him to the doctor, who thinks that Derek might have a hormone imbalance. But the doctor needs to take a blood test to confirm this, and when he tries to take the test Derek attempts to fight him off.

The results might be negative – so the test might not be necessary. But the doctor decides that a test is in Derek's best interests, because failing to treat a problem like a hormone imbalance might make it worse. It is therefore in Derek's best interests to restrain him to take the blood test. →

---

[21] For guidance on using restraint with people with learning disabilities and autistic spectrum disorder, see *Guidance for restrictive physical interventions* (published by the Department of Health and Department for Education and Skills and available at www.dh.gov.uk/assetRoot/ 04/06/84/61/04068461.pdf).

[22] In Wales, the relevant guidance is the Welsh Assembly Government's *Framework for restrictive physical intervention policy and practice* (available at www.childrenfirst.wales.gov.uk/content/ framework/phys-int-e.pdf).

> The temporary restraint is in proportion to the likely harm caused by failing to treat a possible medical condition.

What is 'harm'?

6.45 The Act does not define 'harm', because it will vary depending on the situation. For example,

- a person with learning disabilities might run into a busy road without warning, if they do not understand the dangers of cars
- a person with dementia may wander away from home and get lost, if they cannot remember where they live
- a person with manic depression might engage in excessive spending during a manic phase, causing them to get into debt
- a person may also be at risk of harm if they behave in a way that encourages others to assault or exploit them (for example, by behaving in a dangerously provocative way).

6.46 Common sense measures can often help remove the risk of harm (for example, by locking away poisonous chemicals or removing obstacles). Also, care planning should include risk assessments and set out appropriate actions to try to prevent possible risks. But it is impossible to remove all risk, and a proportionate response is needed when the risk of harm does arise.

What is a 'proportionate response'?

6.47 A 'proportionate response' means using the least intrusive type and minimum amount of restraint to achieve a specific outcome in the best interests of the person who lacks capacity. On occasions when the use of force may be necessary, carers and healthcare and social care staff should use the minimum amount of force for the shortest possible time.

For example, a carer may need to hold a person's arm while they cross the road, if the person does not understand the dangers of roads. But it would not be a proportionate response to stop the person going outdoors at all. It may be appropriate to have a secure lock on a door that faces a busy road, but it would not be a proportionate response to lock someone in a bedroom all the time to prevent them from attempting to cross the road.

6.48 Carers and healthcare and social care staff should consider less restrictive options before using restraint. Where possible, they should ask other people involved in the person's care what action they think is necessary to protect the person from harm. For example, it may be appropriate to get an advocate to work with the person to see if they can avoid or minimise the need for restraint to be used.

Scenario: *Avoiding restraint*

Oscar has learning disabilities. People at the college he attends sometimes cannot understand him, and he gets frustrated. Sometimes he hits the wall and hurts himself.

Staff don't want to take Oscar out of class, because he says he enjoys college and is learning new skills. They have allowed his support worker to sit with him, but he still gets upset. The support worker could try to hold Oscar back. But she thinks this is too forceful, even though it would stop him hurting himself.

Instead, she gets expert advice from members of the local community team. Observation helps them understand Oscar's behaviour better. They come up with a support strategy that reduces the risk of harmful behaviour and is less restrictive of his freedom.

When are acts seen as depriving a person of their liberty?

6.49 Although section 5 of the Act permits the use of restraint where it is necessary under the above conditions, section 6(5) confirms that there is no protection under the Act for actions that result in someone being deprived of their liberty (as defined by Article 5(1) of the European Convention on Human Rights). This applies not only to public authorities covered by the Human Rights Act 1998 but to everyone who might otherwise get protection under section 5 of the Act. It also applies to attorneys or deputies – they cannot give permission for an action that takes away a person's liberty.

6.50 Sometimes there is no alternative way to provide care or treatment other than depriving the person of their liberty. In this situation, some people may be detained in hospital under the Mental Health Act 1983– but this only applies to people who require hospital treatment for a mental disorder (see Chapter 13). Otherwise, actions that amount to a deprivation of liberty will not be lawful unless formal authorisation is obtained.

6.51 In some cases, the Court of Protection might grant an order that permits the deprivation of a person's liberty, if it is satisfied that this is in a person's best interests.

6.52 It is difficult to define the difference between actions that amount to a restriction of someone's liberty and those that result in a deprivation of liberty. In recent legal cases, the European Court of Human Rights said that the difference was 'one of degree or intensity, not one of nature or substance'.[23] There must therefore be particular factors in the specific

---

[23] *HL v The United Kingdom* (Application no, 45508/99). Judgment 5 October 2004, para 89.

situation of the person concerned which provide the 'degree' or 'intensity' to result in a deprivation of liberty. In practice, this can relate to:

- the type of care being provided
- how long the situation lasts
- its effects, or
- the way in a particular situation came about.[24]

The European Court of Human Rights has identified the following as factors contributing to deprivation of liberty in its judgments on cases to date:

- restraint was used, including sedation, to admit a person who is resisting
- professionals exercised complete and effective control over care and movement for a significant period
- professionals exercised control over assessments, treatment, contacts and residence
- the person would be prevented from leaving if they made a meaningful attempt to do so
- a request by carers for the person to be discharged to their care was refused
- the person was unable to maintain social contacts because of restrictions placed on access to other people
- the person lost autonomy because they were under continuous supervision and control.[25]

6.53 The Government has announced that it intends to amend the Act to introduce new procedures and provisions for people who lack capacity to make relevant decisions but who need to be deprived of their liberty, in their best interests, otherwise than under the Mental Health Act 1983 (the so-called 'Bournewood provisions'). This chapter will be fully revised in due course to reflect those changes. Information about the Government's current proposals in respect of the Bournewood safeguards is available on the Department of Health website. This information includes draft illustrative Code of Practice guidance about the proposed safeguards. See paragraphs 13.52–13.55 for more details.

How does section 5 apply to attorneys and deputies?

6.54 Section 5 does not provide protection for actions that go against the decision of someone who has been authorised to make decisions for a person who lacks capacity to make such decision for themselves. For instance, if someone goes against the decision of an attorney acting under

---

[24] In *HL v UK* (also known as the 'Bournewood' case), the European Court said that 'the key factor in the present case [is] that the health care professionals treating and managing the applicant exercised complete and effective control over his care and movements'. They found 'the concrete situation was that the applicant was under continuous supervision and control and was not free to leave.'

[25] These are listed in the Department of Health's draft illustrative Code of Practice guidance about the proposed safeguards. www.dh.gov.uk/assetRoot/04/14/17/64/04141764.pdf.

a Lasting Power of Attorney (LPA) (see Chapter 7) or a deputy appointed by the Court of Protection (see Chapter 8), they will not be protected under section 5.

6.55 Attorneys and deputies must only make decisions within the scope of the authority of the LPA or court order. Sometimes carers or healthcare and social care staff might feel that an attorney or deputy is making decisions they should not be making, or that are not in a person's best interests. If this is the case, and the disagreement cannot be settled any other way, either the carers, the staff or the attorney or deputy can apply to the Court of Protection. If the dispute concerns the provision of medical treatment, medical staff can still give life-sustaining treatment, or treatment which stops a person's condition getting seriously worse, while the court is coming to a decision (section 6(6)).

Who can pay for goods or services?

6.56 Carers may have to spend money on behalf of someone who lacks capacity to purchase necessary goods or services. For example, they may need to pay for a milk delivery or for a chiropodist to provide a service at the person's home. In some cases, they might have to pay for more costly arrangements such as house repairs or organising a holiday. Carers are likely to be protected from liability if their actions are properly taken under section 5, and in the best interests of the person who lacks capacity.

6.57 In general, a contract entered into by a person who lacks capacity to make the contract cannot be enforced if the other person knows, or must be taken to have known, of the lack of capacity. Section 7 of the Act modifies this rule and states that where the contract is for 'necessary' goods or services for a person who lacks capacity to make the arrangements for themselves, that person must pay a reasonable price for them.

What are necessary goods and services?

6.58 'Necessary' means something that is suitable to the person's condition in life (their place in society, rather than any mental or physical condition) and their actual requirements when the goods or services are provided (section 7(2)). The aim is to make sure that people can enjoy a similar standard of living and way of life to those they had before lacking capacity. For example, if a person who now lacks capacity previously chose to buy expensive designer clothes, these are still necessary goods – as long as they can still afford them. But they would not be necessary for a person who always wore cheap clothes, no matter how wealthy they were.

6.59 Goods are not necessary if the person already has a sufficient supply of them. For example, buying one or two new pairs of shoes for a person who lacks capacity could be necessary. But a dozen pairs would probably not be necessary.

How should payments be arranged?

6.60 If a person lacks capacity to arrange for payment for necessary goods and services, sections 5 and 8 allow a carer to arrange payment on their behalf.

6.61 The carer must first take reasonable steps to check whether a person can arrange for payment themselves, or has the capacity to consent to the carer doing it for them. If the person lacks the capacity to consent or pay themselves, the carer must decide what goods or services would be necessary for the person and in their best interests. The carer can then lawfully deal with payment for those goods and services in one of three ways:

- If neither the carer nor the person who lacks capacity can produce the necessary funds, the carer may promise that the person who lacks capacity will pay. A supplier may not be happy with this, or the carer may be worried that they will be held responsible for any debt. In such cases, the carer must follow the formal steps in paragraphs 6. 62–6.66 below.
- If the person who lacks capacity has cash, the carer may use that money to pay for goods or services (for example, to pay the milkman or the hairdresser).
- The carer may choose to pay for the goods or services with their own money. The person who lacks capacity must pay them back. This may involve using cash in the person's possession or running up an IOU. (This is not appropriate for paid care workers, whose contracts might stop them handling their clients' money.) The carer must follow formal steps to get money held in a bank or building society account (see paragraphs 6.63–6.66 below).

6.62 Carers should keep bills, receipts and other proof of payment when paying for goods and services. They will need these documents when asking to get money back. Keeping appropriate financial records and documentation is a requirement of the national minimum standards for care homes or domiciliary care agencies.

Access to a person's assets

6.63 The Act does not give a carer or care worker access to a person's income or assets. Nor does it allow them to sell the person's property.

6.64 Anyone wanting access to money in a person's bank or building society will need formal legal authority. They will also need legal authority to sell a person's property. Such authority could be given in a Lasting Power of Attorney (LPA) appointing an attorney to deal with property and affairs, or in an order of the Court of Protection (either a single decision of the court or an order appointing a deputy to make financial decisions for the person who lacks capacity to make such decisions).

> ### Scenario: *Being granted access to a person's assets*
>
> A storm blew some tiles off the roof of a house owned by Gordon, a man with Alzheimer's disease. He lacks capacity to arrange for repairs and claim on his insurance. The repairs are likely to be costly.
>
> Gordon's son decides to organise the repairs, and he agrees to pay because his father doesn't have enough cash available. The son could then apply to the Court of Protection for authority to claim insurance on his father's behalf and for him to be reimbursed from his father's bank account to cover the cost of the repairs once the insurance payment had been received.

6.65 Sometimes another person will already have legal control of the finances and property of a person who lacks capacity to manage their own affairs. This could be an attorney acting under a registered EPA or an appropriate LPA (see Chapter 7) or a deputy appointed by the Court of Protection (see Chapter 8). Or it could be someone (usually a carer) that has the right to act as an 'appointee' (under Social Security Regulations) and claim benefits for a person who lacks capacity to make their own claim and use the money on the person's behalf. But an appointee cannot deal with other assets or savings from sources other than benefits.

6.66 Section 6(6) makes clear that a family carer or other carer cannot make arrangements for goods or services to be supplied to a person who lacks capacity if this conflicts with a decision made by someone who has formal powers over the person's money and property, such as an attorney or deputy acting within the scope of their authority. Where there is no conflict and the carer has paid for necessary goods and services the carer may ask for money back from an attorney, a deputy or where relevant, an appointee.

7 WHAT DOES THE ACT SAY ABOUT LASTING POWERS OF ATTORNEY?

This chapter explains what Lasting Powers of Attorney (LPAs) are and how they should be used. It also sets out:

- how LPAs differ from Enduring Powers of Attorney (EPAs)
- the types of decisions that people can appoint attorneys to make (attorneys are also called 'donees' in the Act)
- situations in which an LPA can and cannot be used
- the duties and responsibilities of attorneys
- the standards required of attorneys, and
- measures for dealing with attorneys who don't meet appropriate standards.

This chapter also explains what should happen to EPAs that were made before the Act comes into force.

> In this chapter, as throughout the Code, a person's capacity (or lack of capacity) refers specifically to their capacity to make a particular decision at the time it needs to be made.

Quick summary

Anyone asked to be an attorney should:

- consider whether they have the skills and ability to act as an attorney (especially if it is for a property and affairs LPA)
- ask themselves whether they actually want to be an attorney and take on the duties and responsibilities of the role.

Before acting under an LPA, attorneys must:

- make sure the LPA has been registered with the Public Guardian
- take all practical and appropriate steps to help the donor make the particular decision for themselves.

When acting under an LPA:

- make sure that the Act's statutory principles are followed
- check whether the person has the capacity to make that particular decision for themselves. If they do:
  - a personal welfare LPA cannot be used – the person must make the decision
  - a property and affairs LPA can be used even if the person has capacity to make the decision, unless they have stated in the LPA that they should make decisions for themselves when they have capacity to do so.

At all times, remember:

- anything done under the authority of the LPA must be in the person's best interests
- anyone acting as an attorney must have regard to guidance in this Code of Practice that is relevant to the decision that is to be made
- attorneys must fulfil their responsibilities and duties to the person who lacks capacity.

What is a Lasting Power of Attorney (LPA)?

7.1 Sometimes one person will want to give another person authority to make a decision on their behalf. A power of attorney is a legal document that allows them to do so. Under a power of attorney, the chosen person (the attorney or donee) can make decisions that are as valid as one made by the person (the donor).

7.2 Before the Enduring Powers of Attorney Act 1985, every power of attorney automatically became invalid as soon as the donor lacked the capacity to make their own decision. But that Act introduced the Enduring Power of Attorney (EPA). An EPA allows an attorney to make decisions about property and financial affairs even if the donor lacks capacity to manage their own affairs.

7.3 The Mental Capacity Act replaces the EPA with the Lasting Power of Attorney (LPA). It also increases the range of different types of decisions that people can authorise others to make on their behalf. As well as property and affairs (including financial matters), LPAs can also cover personal welfare (including healthcare and consent to medical treatment) for people who lack capacity to make such decisions for themselves.

7.4 The donor can choose one person or several to make different kinds of decisions. See paragraphs 7.21–7.31 for more information about personal welfare LPAs. See paragraphs 7.32–7.42 for more information about LPAs on property and affairs.

How do LPAs compare to EPAs?

7.5 There are a number of differences between LPAs and EPAs. These are summarised as follows:
- EPAs only cover property and affairs. LPAs can also cover personal welfare.
- Donors must use the relevant specific form (prescribed in regulations) to make EPAs and LPAs. There are different forms for EPAs, personal welfare LPAs and property and affairs LPAs.
- EPAs must be registered with the Public Guardian when the donor can no longer manage their own affairs (or when they start to lose capacity). But LPAs can be registered at any time before they are used – before or after the donor lacks capacity to make particular decisions that the LPA covers. If the LPA is not registered, it can't be used.
- EPAs can be used while the donor still has capacity to manage their own property and affairs, as can property and affairs LPAs, so long as the donor does not say otherwise in the LPA. But personal welfare LPAs can only be used once the donor lacks capacity to make the welfare decision in question.
- Once the Act comes into force, only LPAs can be made but existing EPAs will continue to be valid. There will be different laws and procedures for EPAs and LPAs.

- Attorneys making decisions under a registered EPA or LPA must follow the Act's principles and act in the best interests of the donor.
- The duties under the law of agency apply to attorneys of both EPAs and LPAs (see paragraphs 7.58–7.68 below).
- Decisions that the courts have made about EPAs may also affect how people use LPAs.
- Attorneys acting under an LPA have a legal duty to have regard to the guidance in this Code of Practice. EPA attorneys do not. But the Code's guidance will still be helpful to them.

How does a donor create an LPA?

7.6 The donor must also follow the right procedures for creating and registering an LPA, as set out below. Otherwise the LPA might not be valid. It is not always necessary to get legal advice. But it is a good idea for certain cases (for example, if the donor's circumstances are complicated).

7.7 Only adults aged 18 or over can make an LPA, and they can only make an LPA if they have the capacity to do so. For an LPA to be valid:
- the LPA must be a written document set out in the statutory form prescribed by regulations[26]
- the document must include prescribed information about the nature and effect of the LPA (as set out in the regulations)
- the donor must sign a statement saying that they have read the prescribed information (or somebody has read it to them) and that they want the LPA to apply when they no longer have capacity
- the document must name people (not any of the attorneys) who should be told about an application to register the LPA, or it should say that there is no-one they wish to be told
- the attorneys must sign a statement saying that they have read the prescribed information and that they understand their duties – in particular the duty to act in the donor's best interests
- the document must include a certificate completed by an independent third party,[27] confirming that:
  - in their opinion, the donor understands the LPA's purpose
  - nobody used fraud or undue pressure to trick or force the donor into making the LPA and
  - there is nothing to stop the LPA being created.

---

[26] The prescribed forms will be available from the Office of the Public Guardian (OPG) or from legal stationers.

[27] Details of who may and who may not be a certificate provider will be available in regulations. The OPG will produce guidance for certificate providers on their role.

Who can be an attorney?

7.8 A donor should think carefully before choosing someone to be their attorney. An attorney should be someone who is trustworthy, competent and reliable. They should have the skills and ability to carry out the necessary tasks.

7.9 Attorneys must be at least 18 years of age. For property and affairs LPAs, the attorney could be either:

- an individual (as long as they are not bankrupt at the time the LPA is made), or
- a trust corporation (often parts of banks or other financial institutions).

If an attorney nominated under a property and affairs LPA becomes bankrupt at any point, they will no longer be allowed to act as an attorney for property and affairs. People who are bankrupt can still act as an attorney for personal welfare LPAs.

7.10 The donor must name an individual rather than a job title in a company or organisation, (for example, 'The Director of Adult Services' or 'my solicitor' would not be sufficient). A paid care worker (such as a care home manager) should not agree to act as an attorney, apart from in unusual circumstances (for example, if they are the only close relative of the donor).

7.11 Section 10(4) of the Act allows the donor to appoint two or more attorneys and to specify whether they should act 'jointly', 'jointly and severally', or 'jointly in respect of some matters and jointly and severally in respect of others'.

- Joint attorneys must always act together. All attorneys must agree decisions and sign any relevant documents.
- Joint and several attorneys can act together but may also act independently if they wish. Any action taken by any attorney alone is as valid as if they were the only attorney.

7.12 The donor may want to appoint attorneys to act jointly in some matters but jointly and severally in others. For example, a donor could choose to appoint two or more financial attorneys jointly and severally. But they might say then when selling the donor's house, the attorneys must act jointly. The donor may appoint welfare attorneys to act jointly and severally but specify that they must act jointly in relation to giving consent to surgery. If a donor who has appointed two or more attorneys does not specify how they should act, they must always act jointly (section 10(5)).

7.13 Section 10(8) says that donors may choose to name replacement attorneys to take over the duties in certain circumstances (for example, in the event of an attorney's death). The donor may name a specific attorney to be replaced, or the replacements can take over from any attorney, if necessary. Donors cannot give their attorneys the right to appoint a substitute or successor.

How should somebody register and use an LPA?

7.14 An LPA must be registered with the Office of the Public Guardian (OPG) before it can be used. An unregistered LPA will not give the attorney any legal powers to make a decision for the donor. The donor can register the LPA while they are still capable, or the attorney can apply to register the LPA at any time.

7.15 There are advantages in registering the LPA soon after the donor makes it (for example, to ensure that there is no delay when the LPA needs to be used). But if this has not been done, an LPA can be registered after the donor lacks the capacity to make a decision covered by the LPA.

7.16 If an LPA is unregistered, attorneys must register it before making any decisions under the LPA. If the LPA has been registered but not used for some time, the attorney should tell the OPG when they begin to act under it – so that the attorney can be sent relevant, up-to-date information about the rules governing LPAs.

7.17 While they still have capacity, donors should let the OPG know of permanent changes of address for the donor or the attorney or any other changes in circumstances. If the donor no longer has capacity to do this, attorneys should report any such changes to the OPG. Examples include an attorney of a property and affairs LPA becoming bankrupt or the ending of a marriage between the donor and their attorney. This will help keep OPG records up to date, and will make sure that attorneys do not make decisions that they no longer have the authority to make.

What guidance should an attorney follow?

7.18 Section 9(4) states that attorneys must meet the requirements set out in the Act. Most importantly, they have to follow the statutory principles (section 1) and make decisions in the best interests of the person who lacks capacity (section 4). They must also respect any conditions or restrictions that the LPA document contains. See Chapter 2 for guidance on how to apply the Act's principles.

7.19 Chapter 3 gives suggestions of ways to help people make their own decisions in accordance with the Act's second principle. Attorneys should also refer to the guidance in Chapter 4 when assessing the donor's capacity to make particular decisions, and in particular, should follow the steps suggested for establishing a 'reasonable belief' that the donor lacks capacity (see paragraphs 4.44–4.45). Assessments of capacity or best interests must not be based merely on:
- a donor's age or appearance, or
- unjustified assumptions about any condition they might have or their behaviour.

7.20 When deciding what is in the donor's best interests, attorneys should refer to the guidance in Chapter 5. In particular, they must consider the donor's past and present wishes and feelings, beliefs and values. Where practical and appropriate, they should consult with:

- anyone involved in caring for the donor
- close relatives and anyone else with an interest in their welfare
- other attorneys appointed by the donor.

See paragraphs 7.52–7.68 for a description of an attorney's duties.

Scenario: *Making decisions in a donor's best interests*

Mr Young has been a member of the Green Party for a long time. He has appointed his solicitor as his attorney under a property and affairs LPA. But Mr Young did not state in the LPA that investments made on his behalf must be ethical investments. When the attorney assesses his client's best interests, however, the attorney considers the donor's past wishes, values and beliefs. He makes sure that he only invests in companies that are socially and environmentally responsible.

What decisions can an LPA attorney make?

Personal welfare LPAs

7.21 LPAs can be used to appoint attorneys to make decisions about personal welfare, which can include healthcare and medical treatment decisions. Personal welfare LPAs might include decisions about:

- where the donor should live and who they should live with
- the donor's day-to-day care, including diet and dress
- who the donor may have contact with
- consenting to or refusing medical examination and treatment on the donor's behalf
- arrangements needed for the donor to be given medical, dental or optical treatment
- assessments for and provision of community care services
- whether the donor should take part in social activities, leisure activities, education or training
- the donor's personal correspondence and papers
- rights of access to personal information about the donor, or
- complaints about the donor's care or treatment.

7.22 The standard form for personal welfare LPAs allows attorneys to make decisions about anything that relates to the donor's personal welfare. But donors can add restrictions or conditions to areas where they would not wish the attorney to have the power to act. For example, a donor might only want an attorney to make decisions about their social care and not their healthcare. There are particular rules for LPAs authorising an attorney to make decisions about life-sustaining treatment (see paragraphs 7.30–7.31 below).

7.23 A general personal welfare LPA gives the attorney the right to make all of the decisions set out above although this is not a full list of the actions they can take or decisions they can make. However, a personal welfare LPA can only be used at a time when the donor lacks capacity to make a specific welfare decision.

Scenario: Denying attorneys the right to make certain decisions

Mrs Hutchison is in the early stages of Alzheimer's disease. She is anxious to get all her affairs in order while she still has capacity to do so. She makes a personal welfare LPA, appointing her daughter as attorney. But Mrs Hutchison knows that her daughter doesn't always get on with some members of the family – and she wouldn't want her daughter to stop those relatives from seeing her.

She states in the LPA that her attorney does not have the authority to decide who can contact her or visit her. If her daughter wants to prevent anyone having contact with Mrs Hutchison, she must ask the Court of Protection to decide.

7.24 Before making a decision under a personal welfare LPA, the attorney must be sure that:
- the LPA has been registered with the OPG
- the donor lacks the capacity to make the particular decision or the attorney reasonably believes that the donor lacks capacity to take the decisions covered by the LPA (having applied the Act's principles), and
- they are making the decision in the donor's best interests.

7.25 When healthcare or social care staff are involved in preparing a care plan for someone who has appointed a personal welfare attorney, they must first assess whether the donor has capacity to agree to the care plan or to parts of it. If the donor lacks capacity, professionals must then consult the attorney and get their agreement to the care plan. They will also need to consult the attorney when considering what action is in the person's best interests.

Personal welfare LPAs that authorise an attorney to make healthcare decisions

7.26 A personal welfare LPA allows attorneys to make decisions to accept or refuse healthcare or treatment unless the donor has stated clearly in the LPA that they do not want the attorney to make these decisions.

7.27 Even where the LPA includes healthcare decisions, attorneys do not have the right to consent to or refuse treatment in situations where:
- **the donor has capacity to make the particular healthcare decision (section 11(7)(a))**

An attorney has no decision-making power if the donor can make their own treatment decisions.

- **the donor has made an advance decision to refuse the proposed treatment (section 11(7)(b))**

    An attorney cannot consent to treatment if the donor has made a valid and applicable advance decision to refuse a specific treatment (see Chapter 9). But if the donor made an LPA after the advance decision, and gave the attorney the right to consent to or refuse the treatment, the attorney can choose not to follow the advance decision.

- **a decision relates to life-sustaining treatment (section 11(7)(c))**

    An attorney has no power to consent to or refuse life-sustaining treatment, unless the LPA document expressly authorises this (See paragraphs 7.30–7.31 below.)

- **the donor is detained under the Mental Health Act (section 28)**

    An attorney cannot consent to or refuse treatment for a mental disorder for a patient detained under the Mental Health Act 1983 (see also Chapter 13).

7.28 LPAs cannot give attorneys the power to demand specific forms of medical treatment that healthcare staff do not believe are necessary or appropriate for the donor's particular condition.

7.29 Attorneys must always follow the Act's principles and make decisions in the donor's best interests. If healthcare staff disagree with the attorney's assessment of best interests, they should discuss the case with other medical experts and/or get a formal second opinion. Then they should discuss the matter further with the attorney. If they cannot settle the disagreement, they can apply to the Court of Protection (see paragraphs 7.45–7.49 below). While the court is coming to a decision, healthcare staff can give life-sustaining treatment to prolong the donor's life or stop their condition getting worse.

Personal welfare LPAs that authorise an attorney to make decisions about life-sustaining treatment

7.30 An attorney can only consent to or refuse life-sustaining treatment on behalf of the donor if, when making the LPA, the donor has specifically stated in the LPA document that they want the attorney to have this authority.

7.31 As with all decisions, an attorney must act in the donor's best interests when making decisions about such treatment. This will involve applying the best interests checklist (see Chapter 5) and consulting with carers, family members and others interested in the donor's welfare. In particular, the attorney must not be motivated in any way by the desire to bring about the donor's death (see paragraphs 5.29–5.36). Anyone who doubts that the attorney is acting in the donor's best interests can apply to the Court of Protection for a decision.

Scenario: Making decisions about life-sustaining treatment

Mrs Joshi has never trusted doctors. She prefers to rely on alternative therapies. Because she saw her father suffer after invasive treatment for cancer, she is clear that she would refuse such treatment herself.

She is diagnosed with cancer and discusses her wishes with her husband. Mrs Joshi knows that he would respect her wishes if he ever had to make a decision about her treatment. She makes a personal welfare LPA appointing him as her attorney with authority to make all her welfare and healthcare decisions. She includes a specific statement authorising him to consent to or refuse life-sustaining treatment.

He will then be able to consider her views and make decisions about treatment in her best interests if she later lacks capacity to make those decisions herself.

Property and affairs LPAs

7.32 A donor can make an LPA giving an attorney the right to make decisions about property and affairs (including financial matters). Unless the donor states otherwise, once the LPA is registered, the attorney is allowed to make all decisions about the donor's property and affairs even if the donor still has capacity to make the decisions for themselves. In this situation, the LPA will continue to apply when the donor no longer has capacity.

7.33 Alternatively a donor can state in the LPA document that the LPA should only apply when they lack capacity to make a relevant decision. It is the donor's responsibility to decide how their capacity should then be assessed. For example, the donor may trust the attorney to carry out an assessment, or they may say that the LPA only applies if their GP or another doctor confirms in writing that they lack capacity to make specific decisions about property or finances. Financial institutions may wish to see the written confirmation before recognising the attorney's authority to act under the LPA.

7.34 The fact that someone has made a property and affairs LPA does not mean that they cannot continue to carry out financial transactions for themselves. The donor may have full capacity, but perhaps anticipates that they may lack capacity at some future time. Or they may have fluctuating or partial capacity and therefore be able to make some decisions (or at some times), but need an attorney to make others (or at other times). The attorney should allow and encourage the donor to do as much as possible, and should only act when the donor asks them to or to make those decisions the donor lacks capacity to make. However, in other cases, the donor may wish to hand over responsibility for all decisions to the attorney, even those they still have capacity to make.

7.35 If the donor restricts the decisions an attorney can make, banks may ask the attorney to sign a declaration that protects the bank from liability if the attorney misuses the account.[28]

7.36 If a donor does not restrict decisions the attorney can make, the attorney will be able to decide on any or all of the person's property and financial affairs. This might include:

- buying or selling property
- opening, closing or operating any bank, building society or other account
- giving access to the donor's financial information
- claiming, receiving and using (on the donor's behalf) all benefits, pensions, allowances and rebates (unless the Department for Work and Pensions has already appointed someone and everyone is happy for this to continue)
- receiving any income, inheritance or other entitlement on behalf of the donor
- dealing with the donor's tax affairs
- paying the donor's mortgage, rent and household expenses
- insuring, maintaining and repairing the donor's property
- investing the donor's savings
- making limited gifts on the donor's behalf (but see paragraphs 7.40–7.42 below)
- paying for private medical care and residential care or nursing home fees
- applying for any entitlement to funding for NHS care, social care or adaptations
- using the donor's money to buy a vehicle or any equipment or other help they need
- repaying interest and capital on any loan taken out by the donor.

7.37 A general property and affairs LPA will allow the attorney to carry out any or all of the actions above (although this is not a full list of the actions they can take). However, the donor may want to specify the types of powers they wish the attorney to have, or to exclude particular types of decisions. If the donor holds any assets as trustee, they should get legal advice about how the LPA may affect this.

7.38 The attorney must make these decisions personally and cannot generally give someone else authority to carry out their duties (see paragraphs 7.61–7.62 below). But if the donor wants the attorney to be able to give authority to a specialist to make specific decisions, they need to state this clearly in the LPA document (for example, appointing an investment manager to make particular investment decisions).

7.39 Donors may like to appoint someone (perhaps a family member or a professional) to go through their accounts with the attorney from time to time. This might help to reassure donors that somebody will check their

---

[28] See British Banking Association's guidance for bank staff on *'Banking for mentally incapacitated and learning disabled customers'*.

financial affairs when they lack capacity to do so. It may also be helpful for attorneys to arrange a regular check that everything is being done properly. The donor should ensure that the person is willing to carry out this role and is prepared to ask for the accounts if the attorney does not provide them. They should include this arrangement in the signed LPA document. The LPA should also say whether the person can charge a fee for this service.

What gifts can an attorney make under a property and affairs LPA?

7.40 An attorney can only make gifts of the donor's money or belongings to people who are related to or connected with the donor (including the attorney) on specific occasions, including:
- births or birthdays
- weddings or wedding anniversaries
- civil partnership ceremonies or anniversaries, or
- any other occasion when families, friends or associates usually give presents (section 12(3)(b)).

7.41 If the donor previously made donations to any charity regularly or from time to time, the attorney can make donations from the person's funds. This also applies if the donor could have been expected to make such payments (section 12(2)(b)). But the value of any gift or donation must be reasonable and take into account the size of the donor's estate. For example, it would not be reasonable to buy expensive gifts at Christmas if the donor was living on modest means and had to do without essential items in order to pay for them.

7.42 The donor cannot use the LPA to make more extensive gifts than those allowed under section 12 of the Act. But they can impose stricter conditions or restrictions on the attorney's powers to make gifts. They should state these restrictions clearly in the LPA document when they are creating it. When deciding on appropriate gifts, the attorney should consider the donor's wishes and feelings to work out what would be in the donor's best interests. The attorney can apply to the Court of Protection for permission to make gifts that are not included in the LPA (for example, for tax planning purposes).

Are there any other restrictions on attorneys' powers?

7.43 Attorneys are not protected from liability if they do something that is intended to restrain the donor, unless:
- the attorney reasonably believes that the donor lacks capacity to make the decision in question, and
- the attorney reasonably believes that restraint is necessary to prevent harm to the donor, and

- the type of restraint used is in proportion to the likelihood and the seriousness of the harm.

If an attorney needs to make a decision or take action which may involve the use of restraint, they should take account of the guidance set out in Chapter 6.

7.44 Attorneys have no authority to take actions that result in the donor being deprived of their liberty. Any deprivation of liberty will only be lawful if this has been properly authorised and there is other protection available for the person who lacks capacity. An example would be the protection around detention under the Mental Health Act 1983 (see Chapter 13) or a court ruling. Chapter 6 gives more guidance on working out whether an action is restraint or a deprivation of liberty.

What powers does the Court of Protection have over LPAs?

7.45 The Court of Protection has a range of powers to:
- determine whether an LPA is valid
- give directions about using the LPA, and
- to remove an attorney (for example, if the attorney does not act in the best interests of the donor).

Chapter 8 gives more information about the Court of Protection's powers.

7.46 If somebody has doubts over whether an LPA is valid, they can ask the court to decide whether the LPA:
- meets the Act's requirements
- has been revoked (cancelled) by the donor, or
- has come to an end for any other reason.

7.47 The court can also stop somebody registering an LPA or rule that an LPA is invalid if:
- the donor made the LPA as a result of undue pressure or fraud, or
- the attorney behaves, has behaved or is planning to behave in a way that goes against their duties or is not in the donor's best interests.

7.48 The court can also clarify an LPA's meaning, if it is not clear, and it can tell attorneys how they should use an LPA. If an attorney thinks that an LPA does not give them enough powers, they can ask the court to extend their powers – if the donor no longer has capacity to authorise this. The court can also authorise an attorney to give a gift that the Act does not normally allow (section 12(2)), if it is in the donor's best interests.

7.49 All attorneys should keep records of their dealings with the donor's affairs (see also paragraph 7.67 below). The court can order attorneys to produce records (for example, financial accounts) and to provide specific reports, information or documentation. If somebody has concerns about an attorney's payment or expenses, the court could resolve the matter.

What responsibilities do attorneys have?

7.50 A donor cannot insist on somebody agreeing to become an attorney. It is down to the proposed attorney to decide whether to take on this responsibility. When an attorney accepts the role by signing the LPA document, this is confirmation that they are willing to act under the LPA once it is registered. An attorney can withdraw from the appointment if they ever become unable or unwilling to act, but if the LPA has been registered they must follow the correct procedures for withdrawing. (see paragraph 7.66 below).

7.51 Once the attorney starts to act under an LPA, they must meet certain standards. If they don't carry out the duties below, they could be removed from the role. In some circumstances they could face charges of fraud or negligence.

What duties does the Act impose?

7.52 Attorneys acting under an LPA have a duty to:
- follow the Act's statutory principles (see Chapter 2)
- make decisions in the donor's best interests
- have regard to the guidance in the Code of Practice
- only make those decisions the LPA gives them authority to make.

Principles and best interests

7.53 Attorneys must act in accordance with the Act's statutory principles (section 1) and in the best interests of the donor (the steps for working out best interests are set out in section 4). In particular, attorneys must consider whether the donor has capacity to make the decision for themselves. If not, they should consider whether the donor is likely to regain capacity to make the decision in the future. If so, it may be possible to delay the decision until the donor can make it.

The Code of Practice

7.54 As well as this chapter, attorneys should pay special attention to the following guidance set out in the Code:
- Chapter 2, which sets out how the Act's principles should be applied
- Chapter 3, which describes the steps which can be taken to try to help the person make decisions for themselves
- Chapter 4, which describes the Act's definition of lack of capacity and gives guidance on assessing capacity, and
- Chapter 5, which gives guidance on working out the donor's best interests.

7.55 In some circumstances, attorneys might also find it useful to refer to guidance in:

- Chapter 6, which explains when attorneys who have caring responsibilities may have protection from liability and gives guidance on the few circumstances when the Act allows restraint in connection with care and treatment
- Chapter 8, which gives a summary of the Court of Protection's powers relating to LPAs
- Chapter 9, which explains how LPAs may be affected if the donor has made an advance decision to refuse treatment, and
- Chapter 15, which describes ways to settle disagreements.

Only making decisions covered by an LPA

7.56 A personal welfare attorney has no authority to make decisions about a donor's property and affairs (such as their finances). A property and affairs attorney has no authority in decisions about a donor's personal care. (But the same person could be appointed in separate LPAs to carry out both these roles.) Under any LPA, the attorney will have authority in a wide range of decisions. But if a donor includes restrictions in the LPA document, this will limit the attorney's authority (section 9(4)(b)). If the attorney thinks that they need greater powers, they can apply to the Court of Protection which may decide to give the attorney the authority required or alternatively to appoint the attorney as a deputy with the necessary powers (see Chapter 8).

7.57 It is good practice for decision-makers to consult attorneys about any decision or action, whether or not it is covered by the LPA. This is because an attorney is likely to have known the donor for some time and may have important information about their wishes and feelings. Researchers can also consult attorneys if they are thinking about involving the donor in research (see Chapter 11).

Scenario: Consulting attorneys

Mr Varadi makes a personal welfare LPA appointing his son and daughter as his joint attorneys. He also makes a property and affairs LPA, appointing his son and his solicitor to act jointly and severally. He registers the property and affairs LPA straight away, so his attorneys can help with financial decisions.

Two years later, Mr Varadi has a stroke, is unable to speak and has difficulty communicating his wishes. He also lacks the capacity to make decisions about treatment. The attorneys apply to register the personal welfare LPA. Both feel that they should delay decisions about Mr Varadi's future care, because he might regain capacity to make the decisions himself. But they agree that some decisions cannot wait.

Although the solicitor has no authority to make welfare decisions, the welfare attorneys consult him about their father's best interests. They →

> speak to him about immediate treatment decisions and their suggestion to delay making decisions about his future care. Similarly, the property and affairs attorneys consult the daughter about the financial decisions that Mr Varadi does not have the capacity to make himself.

What are an attorney's other duties?

7.58 An attorney appointed under an LPA is acting as the chosen agent of the donor and therefore, under the law of agency, the attorney has certain duties towards the donor. An attorney takes on a role which carries a great deal of power, which they must use carefully and responsibly. They have a duty to:

- apply certain standards of care and skill (duty of care) when making decisions
- carry out the donor's instructions
- not take advantage of their position and not benefit themselves, but benefit the donor (fiduciary duty)
- not delegate decisions, unless authorised to do so
- act in good faith
- respect confidentiality
- comply with the directions of the Court of Protection
- not give up the role without telling the donor and the court.

In relation to property and affairs LPAs, they have a duty to:

- keep accounts
- keep the donor's money and property separate from their own.

Duty of care

7.59 'Duty of care' means applying a certain standard of care and skill – depending on whether the attorney is paid for their services or holds relevant professional qualifications.

- Attorneys who are not being paid must apply the same care, skill and diligence they would use to make decisions about their own life. An attorney who claims to have particular skills or qualifications must show greater skill in those particular areas than someone who does not make such claims.
- If attorneys are being paid for their services, they should demonstrate a higher degree of care and skill.
- Attorneys who undertake their duties in the course of their professional work (such as solicitors or corporate trustees) must display professional competence and follow their profession's rules and standards.

Fiduciary duty

7.60 A fiduciary duty means attorneys must not take advantage of their position. Nor should they put themselves in a position where their personal interests conflict with their duties. They also must not allow any other influences to affect the way in which they act as an attorney. Decisions should always benefit the donor, and not the attorney. Attorneys must not profit or get any personal benefit from their position, apart from receiving gifts where the Act allows it, whether or not it is at the donor's expense.

Duty not to delegate

7.61 Attorneys cannot usually delegate their authority to someone else. They must carry out their duties personally. The attorney may seek professional or expert advice (for example, investment advice from a financial adviser or advice on medical treatment from a doctor). But they cannot, as a general rule, allow someone else to make a decision that they have been appointed to make, unless this has been specifically authorised by the donor in the LPA.

7.62 In certain circumstances, attorneys may have limited powers to delegate (for example, through necessity or unforeseen circumstances, or for specific tasks which the donor would not have expected the attorney to attend to personally). But attorneys cannot usually delegate any decisions that rely on their discretion.

Duty of good faith

7.63 Acting in good faith means acting with honesty and integrity. For example, an attorney must try to make sure that their decisions do not go against a decision the donor made while they still had capacity (unless it would be in the donor's best interests to do so).

Duty of confidentiality

7.64 Attorneys have a duty to keep the donor's affairs confidential, unless:
  • before they lost capacity to do so, the donor agreed that some personal or financial information may be revealed for a particular purpose (for example, they have named someone they want to check their financial accounts), or
  • there is some other good reason to release it (for example, it is in the public interest or the best interests of the person who lacks capacity, or there is a risk of harm to the donor or others).
  In the latter circumstances, it may be advisable for the attorney to get legal advice. Chapter 16 gives more information about confidentiality.

Duty to comply with the directions of the Court of Protection

7.65 Under sections 22 and 23 of the Act, the Court of Protection has wide-ranging powers to decide on issues relating to the operation or validity of an LPA. It can also:
- give extra authority to attorneys
- order them to produce records (for example, financial accounts), or
- order them to provide specific information or documentation to the court.

Attorneys must comply with any decision or order that the court makes.

Duty not to disclaim without notifying the donor and the OPG

7.66 Once someone becomes an attorney, they cannot give up that role without notifying the donor and the OPG. If they decide to give up their role, they must follow the relevant guidance available from the OPG.

Duty to keep accounts

7.67 Property and affairs attorneys must keep accounts of transactions carried out on the donor's behalf. Sometimes the Court of Protection will ask to see accounts. If the attorney is not a financial expert and the donor's affairs are relatively straightforward, a record of the donor's income and expenditure (for example, through bank statements) may be enough. The more complicated the donor's affairs, the more detailed the accounts may need to be.

Duty to keep the donor's money and property separate

7.68 Property and affairs attorneys should usually keep the donor's money and property separate from their own or anyone else's. There may be occasions where donors and attorneys have agreed in the past to keep their money in a joint bank account (for example, if a husband is acting as his wife's attorney). It might be possible to continue this under the LPA. But in most circumstances, attorneys must keep finances separate to avoid any possibility of mistakes or confusion.

How does the Act protect donors from abuse?

What should someone do if they think an attorney is abusing their position?

7.69 Attorneys are in a position of trust, so there is always a risk of them abusing their position. Donors can help prevent abuse by carefully choosing a suitable and trustworthy attorney. But others have a role to play in looking out for possible signs of abuse or exploitation, and reporting any concerns to the OPG. The OPG will then follow this up in co-operation with relevant agencies.

7.70 Signs that an attorney may be exploiting the donor (or failing to act in the donor's best interests) include:

- stopping relatives or friends contacting the donor – for example, the attorney may prevent contact or the donor may suddenly refuse visits or telephone calls from family and friends for no reason
- sudden unexplained changes in living arrangements (for example, someone moves in to care for a donor they've had little contact with)
- not allowing healthcare or social care staff to see the donor
- taking the donor out of hospital against medical advice, while the donor is having necessary medical treatment
- unpaid bills (for example, residential care or nursing home fees)
- an attorney opening a credit card account for the donor
- spending money on things that are not obviously related to the donor's needs
- the attorney spending money in an unusual or extravagant way
- transferring financial assets to another country.

7.71 Somebody who suspects abuse should contact the OPG immediately. The OPG may direct a Court of Protection Visitor to visit an attorney to investigate. In cases of suspected physical or sexual abuse, theft or serious fraud, the person should contact the police. They might also be able to refer the matter to the relevant local adult protection authorities.

7.72 In serious cases, the OPG will refer the matter to the Court of Protection. The court may revoke (cancel) the LPA or (through the OPG) prevent it being registered, if it decides that:

- the LPA does not meet the legal requirements for creating an LPA
- the LPA has been revoked or come to an end for any other reason
- somebody used fraud or undue pressure to get the donor to make the LPA
- the attorney has done something that they do not have authority to do, or
- the attorney has behaved or is planning to behave in a way that is not in the donor's best interests.

The court might then consider whether the authority previously given to an attorney can be managed by:

- the court making a single decision, or
- appointing a deputy.

What should an attorney do if they think someone else is abusing the donor?

7.73 An attorney who thinks someone else is abusing or exploiting the donor should report it to the OPG and ask for advice on what action they should take. They should contact the police if they suspect physical or sexual abuse, theft or serious fraud. They might also be able to refer the matter to local adult protection authorities.

7.74 Chapter 13 gives more information about protecting vulnerable people from abuse, ill treatment or neglect. It also discusses the duties and responsibilities of the various agencies involved, including the OPG and local authorities. In particular, it is a criminal offence (with a maximum penalty of five years' imprisonment, a fine, or both) for anyone (including attorneys) to wilfully neglect or ill-treat a person in their care who lacks capacity to make decisions for themselves (section 44).

What happens to existing EPAs once the Act comes into force?

7.75 Once the Act comes into force, it will not be possible to make new EPAs. Only LPAs can then be made.

7.76 Some donors will have created EPAs before the Act came into force with the expectation that their chosen attorneys will manage their property and affairs in the future, whether or not they have capacity to do so themselves.

7.77 If donors still have capacity after the Act comes into force, they can cancel the EPA and make an LPA covering their property and affairs. They should also notify attorneys and anyone else aware of the EPA (for example, a bank) that they have cancelled it.

7.78 Some donors will choose not to cancel their EPA or they may already lack the capacity to do so. In such cases, the Act allows existing EPAs, whether registered or not, to continue to be valid so that attorneys can meet the donor's expectations (Schedule 4). An EPA must be registered with the OPG when the attorney thinks the donor lacks capacity to manage their own affairs, or is beginning to lack capacity to do so.

7.79 EPA attorneys may find guidance in this chapter helpful. In particular, all attorneys must comply with the duties described in paragraphs 7.58–7.68 above. EPA attorneys can also be found liable under section 44 of the new Act, which sets out the new criminal offences of ill treatment and wilful neglect. The OPG has produced guidance on EPAs (see Annex A for details of publications and contact information).

8   WHAT IS THE ROLE OF THE COURT OF PROTECTION AND COURT-APPOINTED DEPUTIES?

This chapter describes the role of the Court of Protection and the role of court-appointed deputies. It explains the powers that the court has and how to make an application to the court. It also looks at how the court appoints a deputy to act and make decisions on behalf of someone who lacks capacity to make those decisions. In particular, it gives guidance on a deputy's duties and the consequences of not carrying them out responsibly.

The Office of the Public Guardian (OPG) produces detailed guidance for deputies. See the Annex for more details of the publications and how to get them. Further details on the court's procedures are given in the Court of Protection Rules and Practice Directions issued by the court.

> In this chapter, as throughout the Code, a person's capacity (or lack of capacity) refers specifically to their capacity to make a particular decision at the time it needs to be made.

Quick summary

The Court of Protection has powers to:

- decide whether a person has capacity to make a particular decision for themselves
- make declarations, decisions or orders on financial or welfare matters affecting people who lack capacity to make such decisions
- appoint deputies to make decisions for people lacking capacity to make those decisions
- decide whether an LPA or EPA is valid, and
- remove deputies or attorneys who fail to carry out their duties.

Before accepting an appointment as a deputy, a person the court nominates should consider whether:

- they have the skills and ability to carry out a deputy's duties (especially in relation to property and affairs)
- they actually want to take on the duties and responsibilities.

Anyone acting as a deputy must:

- make sure that they only make those decisions that they are authorised to make by the order of the court
- make sure that they follow the Act's statutory principles, including:
  - considering whether the person has capacity to make a particular decision for themselves. If they do, the deputy should allow them to do so unless the person agrees that the deputy should make the decision
  - taking all possible steps to try to help a person make the particular decision
- always make decisions in the person's best interests
- have regard to guidance in the Code of Practice that is relevant to the situation

- fulfil their duties towards the person concerned (in particular the duty of care and fiduciary duties to respect the degree of trust placed in them by the court).

What is the Court of Protection?

8.1 Section 45 of the Act sets up a specialist court, the Court of Protection, to deal with decision-making for adults (and children in a few cases) who may lack capacity to make specific decisions for themselves. The new Court of Protection replaces the old court of the same name, which only dealt with decisions about the property and financial affairs of people lacking capacity to manage their own affairs. As well as property and affairs, the new court also deals with serious decisions affecting healthcare and personal welfare matters. These were previously dealt with by the High Court under its inherent jurisdiction.

8.2 The new Court of Protection is a superior court of record and is able to establish precedent (it can set examples for future cases) and build up expertise in all issues related to lack of capacity. It has the same powers, rights, privileges and authority as the High Court. When reaching any decision, the court must apply all the statutory principles set out in section 1 of the Act. In particular, it must make a decision in the best interests of the person who lacks capacity to make the specific decision. There will usually be a fee for applications to the court.[29]

How can somebody make an application to the Court of Protection?

8.3 In most cases concerning personal welfare matters, the core principles of the Act and the processes set out in Chapters 5 and 6 will be enough to:
- help people take action or make decisions in the best interests of someone who lacks capacity to make decisions about their own care or treatment, or
- find ways of settling disagreements about such actions or decisions.

But an application to the Court of Protection may be necessary for:
- particularly difficult decisions
- disagreements that cannot be resolved in any other way (see Chapter 15), or
- situations where ongoing decisions may need to be made about the personal welfare of a person who lacks capacity to make decisions for themselves.

8.4 An order of the court will usually be necessary for matters relating to the property and affairs (including financial matters) of people who lack capacity to make specific financial decisions for themselves, unless:
- their only income is state benefits (see paragraph 8.36 below), or

---

[29] Details of the fees charged by the court, and the circumstances in which the fees may be waived or remitted, are available from the Office of the Public Guardian (OPG).

- they have previously made an Enduring Power of Attorney (EPA) or a Lasting Power of Attorney (LPA) to give somebody authority to manage their property and affairs (see Chapter 7).

8.5 Receivers appointed by the court before the Act commences will be treated as deputies. But they will keep their existing powers and duties. They must meet the requirements set out in the Act and, in particular, follow the statutory principles and act in the best interests of the person for whom they have been appointed. They must also have regard to guidance in this chapter and other parts of the Code of Practice. Further guidance for receivers is available from the OPG.

Cases involving young people aged 16 or 17

8.6 Either a court dealing with family proceedings or the Court of Protection can hear cases involving people aged 16 or 17 who lack capacity. In some cases, the Court of Protection can hear cases involving people younger than 16 (for example, when somebody needs to be appointed to make longer-term decisions about their financial affairs). Under section 21 of the Mental Capacity Act, the Court of Protection can transfer cases concerning children to a court that has powers under the Children Act 1989. Such a court can also transfer cases to the Court of Protection, if necessary. Chapter 12 gives more detail on cases where this might apply.

Who should make the application?

8.7 The person making the application will vary, depending on the circumstances. For example, a person wishing to challenge a finding that they lack capacity may apply to the court, supported by others where necessary. Where there is a disagreement among family members, for example, a family member may wish to apply to the court to settle the disagreement – bearing in mind the need, in most cases, to get permission beforehand (see paragraphs 8.11–8.12 below).

8.8 For cases about serious or major decisions concerning medical treatment (see paragraphs 8.18–8.24 below), the NHS Trust or other organisation responsible for the patient's care will usually make the application. If social care staff are concerned about a decision that affects the welfare of a person who lacks capacity, the relevant local authority should make the application.

8.9 For decisions about the property and affairs of someone who lacks capacity to manage their own affairs, the applicant will usually be the person (for example, family carer) who needs specific authority from the court to deal with the individual's money or property.

8.10 If the applicant is the person who is alleged to lack capacity, they will always be a party to the court proceedings. In all other cases, the court will decide whether the person who lacks, or is alleged to lack, capacity should be involved as a party to the case. Where the person is a party to the case, the court may appoint the Official Solicitor to act for them.

Who must ask the court for permission to make an application?

8.11 As a general rule, potential applicants must get the permission of the Court of Protection before making an application (section 50). People who the Act says do not need to ask for permission include:
- a person who lacks, or is alleged to lack, capacity in relation to a specific decision or action (or anyone with parental responsibility, if the person is under 18 years)
- the donor of the LPA an application relates to – or their attorney
- a deputy who has been appointed by the court to act for the person concerned, and
- a person named in an existing court order relating to the application.

The Court of Protection Rules also set out specific types of cases where permission is not required.

8.12 When deciding whether to give permission for an application, the court must consider:
- the applicant's connection to the person the application is about
- the reasons for the application
- whether a proposed order or direction of the court will benefit the person the application is about, and
- whether it is possible to get that benefit another way.

Scenario: Considering whether to give permission for an application

Sunita, a young Asian woman, has always been close to her older brother, who has severe learning disabilities and lives in a care home. Two years ago, Sunita married a non-Asian man, and her family cut off contact with her. She still wants to visit her brother and to be consulted about his care and what is in his best interests. But the family is not letting her. The Court of Protection gives Sunita permission to apply to the court for an order allowing her contact with her brother.

What powers does the Court of Protection have?

8.13 The Court of Protection may:
- make declarations, decisions and orders on financial and welfare matters affecting people who lack, or are alleged to lack, capacity (the lack of capacity must relate to the particular issue being presented to the court)
- appoint deputies to make decisions for people who lack capacity to make those decisions
- remove deputies or attorneys who act inappropriately.

The Court can also hear cases about LPAs and EPAs. The court's powers concerning EPAs are set out in Schedule 4 of the Act.

8.14 The court must always follow the statutory principles set out in section 1 of the Act (see Chapter 2) and make the decision in the best interests of the person concerned (see Chapter 5).

What declarations can the court make?

8.15 Section 15 of the Act provides the court with powers to make a declaration (a ruling) on specific issues. For example, it can make a declaration as to whether a person has capacity to make a particular decision or give consent for or take a particular action. The court will require evidence of any assessment of the person's capacity and may wish to see relevant written evidence (for example, a diary, letters or other papers). If the court decides the person has capacity to make that decision, they will not take the case further. The person can now make the decision for themselves.

8.16 Applications concerning a person's capacity are likely to be rare – people can usually settle doubts and disagreements informally (see Chapters 4 and 15). But an application may be relevant if:
- a person wants to challenge a decision that they lack capacity
- professionals disagree about a person's capacity to make a specific (usually serious) decision
- there is a dispute over whether the person has capacity (for example, between family members).

8.17 The court can also make a declaration as to whether a specific act relating to a person's care or treatment is lawful (either where somebody has carried out the action or is proposing to). Under section 15, this can include an omission or failure to provide care or treatment that the person needs.

This power to decide on the lawfulness of an act is particularly relevant for major medical treatment cases where there is doubt or disagreement over whether the treatment would be in the person's best interests. Healthcare staff can still give life-sustaining treatment, or treatment which stops a person's condition getting seriously worse, while the court is coming to a decision.

Serious healthcare and treatment decisions

8.18 Prior to the Act coming into force, the courts decided that some decisions relating to the provision of medical treatment were so serious that in each case, an application should be made to the court for a declaration that the proposed action was lawful before that action was taken. Cases involving any of the following decisions should therefore be brought before a court:

- decisions about the proposed withholding or withdrawal of artificial nutrition and hydration (ANH) from patients in a permanent vegetative state (PVS)
- cases involving organ or bone marrow donation by a person who lacks capacity to consent
- cases involving the proposed non-therapeutic sterilisation of a person who lacks capacity to consent to this (e.g. for contraceptive purposes) and
- all other cases where there is a doubt or dispute about whether a particular treatment will be in a person's best interests.

8.19 The case law requirement to seek a declaration in cases involving the withholding or withdrawing of artificial nutrition and hydration to people in a permanent vegetative state is unaffected by the Act[30] and as a matter of practice, these cases should be put to the Court of Protection for approval.

8.20 Cases involving organ or bone marrow donation by a person who lacks capacity to consent should also be referred to the Court of Protection. Such cases involve medical procedures being performed on a person who lacks capacity to consent but which would benefit a third party (though would not necessarily directly or physically benefit the person who lacks capacity). However, sometimes such procedures may be in the person's overall best interests (see Chapter 5). For example, the person might receive emotional, social and psychological benefits as a result of the help they have given, and in some cases the person may experience only minimal physical discomfort.

8.21 A prime example of this is the case of *Re Y*[31] where it was found to be in Y's best interests for her to donate bone marrow to her sister. The court decided that it was in Y's best interests to continue to receive strong emotional support from her mother, which might be diminished if her sister's health were to deteriorate further, or she were to die.

Further details on this area are available in Department of Health or Welsh Assembly guidance.[32]

8.22 Non-therapeutic sterilisation is the sterilisation for contraceptive purposes of a person who cannot consent. Such cases will require a careful assessment of whether such sterilisation would be in the best interests of the person who lacks capacity and such cases should continue to be referred to the court.[33] The court has also given guidance on when certain termination of pregnancy cases should be brought before the court.[34]

---

[30] *Airedale NHS Trust v Bland* [1993] AC 789.

[31] *Re Y (Mental incapacity: Bone marrow transplant)* [1996] 2 FLR 787.

[32] Reference Guide to Consent for Examination or Treatment, Department of Health, March 2001: www.dh.gov.uk/PublicationsAndStatistics/Publications/PublicationsPolicyAnd Guidance/PublicationsPolicyAndGuidanceArticle/fs/en?CONTENT_ID=4006757&chk=snmdw8.

[33] See e.g. *Re A (medical treatment: male sterilisation)* (1999) 53 BMLR 66 where a mother applied for a declaration that a vasectomy was in the best interests of A, her son, (who had Down's syndrome and was borderline between significant and severe impairment of

8.23 Other cases likely to be referred to the court include those involving ethical dilemmas in untested areas (such as innovative treatments for variant CJD), or where there are otherwise irresolvable conflicts between healthcare staff, or between staff and family members.

8.24 There are also a few types of cases that should generally be dealt with by the court, since other dispute resolution methods are unlikely to be appropriate (see Chapter 15). This includes, for example, cases where it is unclear whether proposed serious and/or invasive medical treatment is likely to be in the best interests of the person who lacks capacity to consent.

What powers does the court have to make decisions and appoint deputies?

8.25 In cases of serious dispute, where there is no other way of finding a solution or when the authority of the court is needed in order to make a particular decision or take a particular action, the court can be asked to make a decision to settle the matter using its powers under section 16.

However, if there is a need for ongoing decision-making powers and there is no relevant EPA or LPA, the court may appoint a deputy to make future decisions. It will also state what decisions the deputy has the authority to make on the person's behalf.

8.26 In deciding what type of order to make, the court must apply the Act's principles and the best interests checklist. In addition, it must follow two further principles, intended to make any intervention as limited as possible:

- Where possible, the court should make the decision itself in preference to appointing a deputy.
- If a deputy needs to be appointed, their appointment should be as limited in scope and for as short a time as possible.

What decisions can the court make?

8.27 In some cases, the court must make a decision, because someone needs specific authority to act and there is no other route for getting it. These include cases where:

- there is no EPA or property and affairs LPA in place and someone needs to make a financial decision for a person who lacks capacity to make that decision (for example, the decision to terminate a tenancy agreement), or
- it is necessary to make a will, or to amend an existing will, on behalf of a person who lacks capacity to do so.

---

intelligence), in the absence of his consent. After balancing the burdens and benefits of the proposed vasectomy to A, the Court of Appeal held that the vasectomy would not be in A's best interests.

34   *D v An NHS Trust (Medical Treatment: Consent: Termination)* [2004] 1 FLR 1110.

8.28 Examples of other types of cases where a court decision might be appropriate include cases where:

- there is genuine doubt or disagreement about the existence, validity or applicability of an advance decision to refuse treatment (see Chapter 9)
- there is a major disagreement regarding a serious decision (for example, about where a person who lacks capacity to decide for themselves should live)
- a family carer or a solicitor asks for personal information about someone who lacks capacity to consent to that information being revealed (for example, where there have been allegations of abuse of a person living in a care home)
- someone suspects that a person who lacks capacity to make decisions to protect themselves is at risk of harm or abuse from a named individual (the court could stop that individual contacting the person who lacks capacity).

8.29 Anyone carrying out actions under a decision or order of the court must still also follow the Act's principles.

Scenario: *Making a decision to settle disagreements*

Mrs Worrell has Alzheimer's disease. Her son and daughter argue over which care home their mother should move to. Although Mrs Worrell lacks the capacity to make this decision herself, she has enough money to pay the fees of a care home.

Her solicitor acts as attorney in relation to her financial affairs under a registered EPA. But he has no power to get involved in this family dispute – nor does he want to get involved.

The Court of Protection makes a decision in Mrs Worrell's best interests, and decides which care home can best meet her needs. Once this matter is resolved, there is no need to appoint a deputy.

What powers does the court have in relation to LPAs?

8.30 The Court of Protection can determine the validity of an LPA or EPA and can give directions as to how an attorney should use their powers under an LPA (see Chapter 7). In particular, the court can cancel an LPA and end the attorney's appointment. The court might do this if the attorney was not carrying out their duties properly or acting in the best interests of the donor. The court must then decide whether it is necessary to appoint a deputy to take over the attorney's role.

What are the rules for appointing deputies?

8.31 Sometimes it is not practical or appropriate for the court to make a single declaration or decision. In such cases, if the court thinks that somebody needs to make future or ongoing decisions for someone whose condition makes it likely they will lack capacity to make some further decisions in the future, it can appoint a deputy to act for and make decisions for that person. A deputy's authority should be as limited in scope and duration as possible (see paragraphs 8.35–8.39 below).

How does the court appoint deputies?

8.32 It is for the court to decide who to appoint as a deputy. Different skills may be required depending on whether the deputy's decisions will be about a person's welfare (including healthcare), their finances or both. The court will decide whether the proposed deputy is reliable and trustworthy and has an appropriate level of skill and competence to carry out the necessary tasks.

8.33 In the majority of cases, the deputy is likely to be a family member or someone who knows the person well. But in some cases the court may decide to appoint a deputy who is independent of the family (for example, where the person's affairs or care needs are particularly complicated). This could be, for example, the Director of Adult Services in the relevant local authority (but see paragraph 8.60 below) or a professional deputy. The OPG has a panel of professional deputies (mainly solicitors who specialise in this area of law) who may be appointed to deal with property and affairs if the court decides that would be in the person's best interests.

When might a deputy need to be appointed?

8.34 Whether a person who lacks capacity to make specific decisions needs a deputy will depend on:
- the individual circumstances of the person concerned
- whether future or ongoing decisions are likely to be necessary, and
- whether the appointment is for decisions about property and affairs or personal welfare.

Property and affairs

8.35 The court will appoint a deputy to manage a person's property and affairs (including financial matters) in similar circumstances to those in which they would have appointed a receiver in the past. If a person who lacks capacity to make decisions about property and affairs has not made an EPA or LPA, applications to the court are necessary:
- for dealing with cash assets over a specified amount that remain after any debts have been paid

- for selling a person's property, or
- where the person has a level of income or capital that the court thinks a deputy needs to manage.

8.36 If the only income of a person who lacks capacity is social security benefits and they have no property or savings, there will usually be no need for a deputy to be appointed. This is because the person's benefits can be managed by an appointee, appointed by the Department for Work and Pensions to receive and deal with the benefits of a person who lacks capacity to do this for themselves. Although appointees are not covered by the Act, they will be expected to act in the person's best interests and must do so if they are involved in caring for the person. If the court does appoint a property and affairs deputy for someone who has an appointee, it is likely that the deputy would take over the appointee's role.

8.37 Anybody considered for appointment as a property and affairs deputy will need to sign a declaration giving details of their circumstances and ability to manage financial affairs. The declaration will include details of the tasks and duties the deputy must carry out. The deputy must assure the court that they have the skills, knowledge and commitment to carry them out.

Personal welfare (including healthcare)

8.38 Deputies for personal welfare decisions will only be required in the most difficult cases where:
- important and necessary actions cannot be carried out without the court's authority, or
- there is no other way of settling the matter in the best interests of the person who lacks capacity to make particular welfare decisions.

8.39 Examples include when:
- someone needs to make a series of linked welfare decisions over time and it would not be beneficial or appropriate to require all of those decisions to be made by the court. For example, someone (such as a family carer) who is close to a person with profound and multiple learning disabilities might apply to be appointed as a deputy with authority to make such decisions
- the most appropriate way to act in the person's best interests is to have a deputy, who will consult relevant people but have the final authority to make decisions
- there is a history of serious family disputes that could have a detrimental effect on the person's future care unless a deputy is appointed to make necessary decisions
- the person who lacks capacity is felt to be at risk of serious harm if left in the care of family members. In these rare cases, welfare decisions may need to be made by someone independent of the family, such as a local authority officer. There may even be a need for an additional court order prohibiting those family members from having contact with the person.

Who can be a deputy?

8.40 Section 19(1) states that deputies must be at least 18 years of age. Deputies with responsibility for property and affairs can be either an individual or a trust corporation (often parts of banks or other financial institutions). No-one can be appointed as a deputy without their consent.

8.41 Paid care workers (for example, care home managers) should not agree to act as a deputy because of the possible conflict of interest – unless there are exceptional circumstances (for example, if the care worker is the only close relative of the person who lacks capacity). But the court can appoint someone who is an office-holder or in a specified position (for example, the Director of Adult Services of the relevant local authority). In this situation, the court will need to be satisfied that there is no conflict of interest before making such an appointment (see paragraphs 8.58–8.60).

8.42 The court can appoint two or more deputies and state whether they should act 'jointly', 'jointly and severally' or 'jointly in respect of some matters and jointly and severally in respect of others' (section 19 (4)(c)).

- Joint deputies must always act together. They must all agree decisions or actions, and all sign any relevant documents.
- Joint and several deputies can act together, but they may also act independently if they wish. Any action taken by any deputy alone is as valid as if that person were the only deputy.

8.43 Deputies may be appointed jointly for some issues and jointly and severally for others. For example, two deputies could be appointed jointly and severally for most decisions, but the court might rule that they act jointly when selling property.

Scenario: Acting jointly and severally

Toby had a road accident and suffered brain damage and other disabilities. He gets financial compensation but lacks capacity to manage this amount of money or make decisions about his future care. His divorced parents are arguing about where their son should live and how his compensation money should be used. Toby has always been close to his sister, who is keen to be involved but is anxious about dealing with such a large amount of money.

The court decides where Toby will live. It also appoints his sister and a solicitor as joint and several deputies to manage his property and affairs. His sister can deal with any day-to-day decisions that Toby lacks capacity to make, and the solicitor can deal with more complicated matters.

What happens if a deputy can no longer carry out their duties?

8.44 When appointing a deputy, the court can also appoint someone to be a successor deputy (someone who can take over the deputy's duties in certain situations). The court will state the circumstances under which this could occur. In some cases it will also state a period of time in which the successor deputy can act. Appointment of a successor deputy might be useful if the person appointed as deputy is already elderly and wants to be sure that somebody will take over their duties in the future, if necessary.

Scenario: *Appointing a successor deputy*

Neil, a man with Down's syndrome, inherits a lot of money and property. His parents were already retired when the court appointed them as joint deputies to manage Neil's property and affairs. They are worried about what will happen to Neil when they cannot carry out their duties as deputies any more. The court agrees to appoint other relatives as successor deputies. They will then be able to take over as deputies after the parents' death or if his parents are no longer able to carry out the deputy's role.

Can the court protect people lacking capacity from financial loss?

8.45 Under section 19(9)(a) of the Act the court can ask a property and affairs deputy to provide some form of security (for example, a guarantee bond) to the Public Guardian to cover any loss as a result of the deputy's behaviour in carrying out their role. The court can also ask a deputy to provide reports and accounts to the Public Guardian, as it sees fit.

Are there any restrictions on a deputy's powers?

8.46 Section 20 sets out some specific restrictions on a deputy's powers. In particular, a deputy has no authority to make decisions or take action:
- if they do something that is intended to restrain the person who lacks capacity – apart from under certain circumstances (guidance on the circumstances when restraint might be permitted is given in Chapter 6)[35]
- if they think that the person concerned has capacity to make the particular decision for themselves
- if their decision goes against a decision made by an attorney acting under a Lasting Power of Attorney granted by the person before they lost capacity, or
- to refuse the provision or continuation of life-sustaining treatment for a person who lacks capacity to consent – such decisions must be taken by the court.

---

[35] It is worth noting that there is a drafting error in section 20 of the Act. The word 'or' in section 20(11)(a) should have been 'and' in order to be consistent with sections 6(3)(a) and 11(4)(a). The Government will make the necessary amendment to correct this error at the earliest available legislative opportunity.

If a deputy thinks their powers are not enough for them to carry out their duties effectively, they can apply to the court to change their powers. See paragraph 8.54 below.

What responsibilities do deputies have?

8.47 Once a deputy has been appointed by the court, the order of appointment will set out their specific powers and the scope of their authority. On taking up the appointment, the deputy will assume a number of duties and responsibilities and will be required to act in accordance with certain standards. Failure to comply with the duties set out below could result in the Court of Protection revoking the order appointing the deputy and, in some circumstances, the deputy could be personally liable to claims for negligence or criminal charges of fraud.

8.48 Deputies should always inform any third party they are dealing with that the court has appointed them as deputy. The court will give the deputy official documents to prove their appointment and the extent of their authority.

8.49 A deputy must act whenever a decision or action is needed and it falls within their duties as set out in the court order appointing them. A deputy who fails to act at all in such situations could be in breach of duty.

What duties does the Act impose?

8.50 Deputies must:
- follow the Act's statutory principles (see Chapter 2)
- make decisions or act in the best interests of the person who lacks capacity
- have regard to the guidance in this Code of Practice
- only make decisions the Court has given them authority to make.

Principles and best interests

8.51 Deputies must act in accordance with the Act's statutory principles (section 1) and in particular the best interests of the person who lacks capacity (the steps for working out best interests are set out in section 4). In particular, deputies must consider whether the person has capacity to make the decision for themselves. If not, they should consider whether the person is likely to regain capacity to make the decision in the future. If so, it may be possible to delay the decision until the person can make it.

The Code of Practice

8.52 As well as this chapter, deputies should pay special attention to the following guidance set out in the Code:
- Chapter 2, which sets out how the Act's principles should be applied

- Chapter 3, which describes the steps which can be taken to try to help the person make decisions for themselves
- Chapter 4, which describes the Act's definition of lack of capacity and gives guidance on assessing capacity, and
- Chapter 5, which gives guidance on working out someone's best interests.

8.53 In some situations, deputies might also find it useful to refer to guidance in:

- Chapter 6, which explains when deputies who have caring responsibilities may have protection from liability and gives guidance on the few circumstances when the Act allows restraint in connection with care and treatment, and
- Chapter 15, which describes ways to settle disagreements.

Only making decisions the court authorises a deputy to make

8.54 A deputy has a duty to act only within the scope of the actual powers given by the court, which are set out in the order of appointment. It is possible that a deputy will think their powers are not enough for them to carry out their duties effectively. In this situation, they must apply to the court either to:

- ask the court to make the decision in question, or
- ask the court to change the deputy's powers.

What are a deputy's other duties?

8.55 Section 19(6) states that a deputy is to be treated as 'the agent' of the person who lacks capacity when they act on their behalf. Being an agent means that the deputy has legal duties (under the law of agency) to the person they are representing. It also means that when they carry out tasks within their powers, they are not personally liable to third parties.

8.56 Deputies must carry out their duties carefully and responsibly. They have a duty to:

- act with due care and skill (duty of care)
- not take advantage of their situation (fiduciary duty)
- indemnify the person against liability to third parties caused by the deputy's negligence
- not delegate duties unless authorised to do so
- act in good faith
- respect the person's confidentiality, and
- comply with the directions of the Court of Protection.

Property and affairs deputies also have a duty to:

- keep accounts, and
- keep the person's money and property separate from own finances.

Duty of care

8.57 'Duty of care' means applying a certain standard of care and skill – depending on whether the deputy is paid for their services or holds relevant professional qualifications.

- Deputies who are not being paid must use the same care, skill and diligence they would use when making decisions for themselves or managing their own affairs. If they do not, they could be held liable for acting negligently. A deputy who claims to have particular skills or qualifications must show greater skill in those particular areas than a person who does not make such claims.
- If deputies are being paid for their services, they are expected to demonstrate a higher degree of care or skill when carrying out their duties.
- Deputies whose duties form part of their professional work (for example, solicitors or accountants) must display normal professional competence and follow their profession's rules and standards.

Fiduciary duty

8.58 A fiduciary duty means deputies must not take advantage of their position. Nor should they put themselves in a position where their personal interests conflict with their duties. For example, deputies should not buy property that they are selling for the person they have been appointed to represent. They should also not accept a third party commission in any transactions. Deputies must not allow anything else to influence their duties. They cannot use their position for any personal benefit, whether or not it is at the person's expense.

8.59 In many cases, the deputy will be a family member. In rare situations, this could lead to potential conflicts of interests. When making decisions, deputies should follow the Act's statutory principles and apply the best interests checklist and not allow their own personal interests to influence the decision.

8.60 Sometimes the court will consider appointing the Director of Adult Services in England or Director of Social Services in Wales of the relevant local authority as a deputy. The court will need to be satisfied that the authority has arrangements to avoid possible conflicts of interest. For example where the person for whom a financial deputy is required receives community care services from the local authority, the court will wish to be satisfied that decisions about the person's finances will be made in the best interests of that person, regardless of any implications for the services provided.

Duty not to delegate

8.61 A deputy may seek professional or expert advice (for example, investment advice from a financial adviser or a second medical opinion from a doctor). But they cannot give their decision-making responsibilities to someone else. In certain circumstances, the court will authorise the delegation of specific tasks (for example, appointing a discretionary investment manager for the conduct of investment business).

8.62 In certain circumstances, deputies may have limited powers to delegate (for example, through necessity or unforeseen circumstances, or for specific tasks which the court would not have expected the deputy to attend to personally). But deputies cannot usually delegate any decisions that rely on their discretion. If the deputy is the Director of Adult Services in England or Director of Social Services in Wales, or a solicitor, they can delegate specific tasks to other staff. But the deputy is still responsible for any actions or decisions taken, and can therefore be held accountable for any errors that are made.

Duty of good faith

8.63 Acting in good faith means acting with honesty and integrity. For example, a deputy must try to make sure that their decisions do not go against a decision the person made while they still had capacity (unless it would be in the person's best interests to do so).

Duty of confidentiality

8.64 Deputies have a duty to keep the person's affairs confidential, unless:
- before they lost capacity to do so, the person agreed that information could be revealed where necessary
- there is some other good reason to release information (for example, it is in the public interest or in the best interests of the person who lacks capacity, or where there is a risk of harm to the person concerned or to other people).

In the latter circumstances, it is advisable for the deputy to contact the OPG for guidance or get legal advice. See Chapter 16 for more information about revealing personal information.

Duty to comply with the directions of the Court of Protection

8.65 The Court of Protection may give specific directions to deputies about how they should use their powers. It can also order deputies to provide reports (for example, financial accounts or reports on the welfare of the person who lacks capacity) to the Public Guardian at any time or at such intervals as the court directs. Deputies must comply with any direction of the court or request from the Public Guardian.

Duty to keep accounts

8.66 A deputy appointed to manage property and affairs is expected to keep, and periodically submit to the Public Guardian, correct accounts of all their dealings and transactions on the person's behalf.

Duty to keep the person's money and property separate

8.67 Property and affairs deputies should usually keep the person's money and property separate from their own or anyone else's. This is to avoid any possibility of mistakes or confusion in handling the person's affairs. Sometimes there may be good reason not to do so (for example, a husband might be his wife's deputy and they might have had a joint account for many years).

Changes of contact details

8.68 A deputy should inform the OPG of any changes of contact details or circumstances (for the deputy or the person they are acting for). This will help make sure that the OPG has up-to-date records. It will also allow the court to discharge people who are no longer eligible to act as deputies.

Who is responsible for supervising deputies?

8.69 Deputies are accountable to the Court of Protection. The court can cancel a deputy's appointment at any time if it decides the appointment is no longer in the best interests of the person who lacks capacity.

8.70 The OPG is responsible for supervising and supporting deputies. But it must also protect people lacking capacity from possible abuse or exploitation. Anybody who suspects that a deputy is abusing their position should contact the OPG immediately. The OPG may instruct a Court of Protection Visitor to visit a deputy to investigate any matter of concern. It can also apply to the court to cancel a deputy's appointment.

8.71 The OPG will consider carefully any concerns or complaints against deputies. But if somebody suspects physical or sexual abuse or serious fraud, they should contact the police and/or social services immediately, as well as informing the OPG. Chapter 14 gives more information about the role of the OPG. It also discusses the protection of vulnerable people from abuse, ill treatment or wilful neglect and the responsibilities of various relevant agencies.

9 WHAT DOES THE ACT SAY ABOUT ADVANCE DECISIONS TO REFUSE TREATMENT?

This chapter explains what to do when somebody has made an advance decision to refuse treatment. It sets out:

- what the Act means by an 'advance decision'
- guidance on making, updating and cancelling advance decisions
- how to check whether an advance decision exists
- how to check that an advance decision is valid and that it applies to current circumstances
- the responsibilities of healthcare professionals when an advance decision exists
- how to handle disagreements about advance decisions.

In this chapter, as throughout the Code, a person's capacity (or lack of capacity) refers specifically to their capacity to make a particular decision at the time it needs to be made.

Quick summary

- An advance decision enables someone aged 18 and over, while still capable, to refuse specified medical treatment for a time in the future when they may lack the capacity to consent to or refuse that treatment.
- An advance decision to refuse treatment must be valid and applicable to current circumstances. If it is, it has the same effect as a decision that is made by a person with capacity: healthcare professionals must follow the decision.
- Healthcare professionals will be protected from liability if they:
  - stop or withhold treatment because they reasonably believe that an advance decision exists, and that it is valid and applicable
  - treat a person because, having taken all practical and appropriate steps to find out if the person has made an advance decision to refuse treatment, they do not know or are not satisfied that a valid and applicable advance decision exists.
- People can only make an advance decision under the Act if they are 18 or over and have the capacity to make the decision. They must say what treatment they want to refuse, and they can cancel their decision – or part of it – at any time.
- If the advance decision refuses life-sustaining treatment, it must:
  - be in writing (it can be written by a someone else or recorded in healthcare notes)
  - be signed and witnessed, and
  - state clearly that the decision applies even if life is at risk.

- To establish whether an advance decision is valid and applicable, healthcare professionals must try to find out if the person:
  - has done anything that clearly goes against their advance decision
  - has withdrawn their decision
  - has subsequently conferred the power to make that decision on an attorney, or
  - would have changed their decision if they had known more about the current circumstances.
- Sometimes healthcare professionals will conclude that an advance decision does not exist, is not valid and/or applicable – but that it is an expression of the person's wishes. The healthcare professional must then consider what is set out in the advance decision as an expression of previous wishes when working out the person's best interests (see Chapter 5).
- Some healthcare professionals may disagree in principle with patients' decisions to refuse life-sustaining treatment. They do not have to act against their beliefs. But they must not simply abandon patients or act in a way that that affects their care.
- Advance decisions to refuse treatment for mental disorder may not apply if the person who made the advance decision is or is liable to be detained under the Mental Health Act 1983.

How can someone make an advance decision to refuse treatment?

What is an advance decision to refuse treatment?

9.1 It is a general principle of law and medical practice that people have a right to consent to or refuse treatment. The courts have recognised that adults have the right to say in advance that they want to refuse treatment if they lose capacity in the future – even if this results in their death. A valid and applicable advance decision to refuse treatment has the same force as a contemporaneous decision. This has been a fundamental principle of the common law for many years and it is now set out in the Act. Sections 24–26 of the Act set out the when a person can make an advance decision to refuse treatment. This applies if:
   - the person is 18 or older, and
   - they have the capacity to make an advance decision about treatment. Information on advance decisions to refuse treatment made by young people (under the age of 18) will be available at www.dh.gov.uk/consent

9.2 Healthcare professionals must follow an advance decision if it is valid and applies to the particular circumstances. If they do not, they could face criminal prosecution (they could be charged for committing a crime) or civil liability (somebody could sue them).

9.3 Advance decisions can have serious consequences for the people who make them. They can also have an important impact on family and friends, and professionals involved in their care. Before healthcare professionals can apply an advance decision, there must be proof that the decision:

- exists
- is valid, and
- is applicable in the current circumstances.

These tests are legal requirements under section 25(1). Paragraphs 9.38–9.44 explain the standard of proof the Act requires.

Who can make an advance decision to refuse treatment?

9.4   It is up to individuals to decide whether they want to refuse treatment in advance. They are entitled to do so if they want, but there is no obligation to do so. Some people choose to make advance decisions while they are still healthy, even if there is no prospect of illness. This might be because they want to keep some control over what might happen to them in the future. Others may think of an advance decision as part of their preparations for growing older (similar to making a will). Or they might make an advance decision after they have been told they have a specific disease or condition.

Many people prefer not to make an advance decision, and instead leave healthcare professionals to make decisions in their best interests at the time a decision needs to be made. Another option is to make a Lasting Power of Attorney. This allows a trusted family member or friend to make personal welfare decisions, such as those around treatment, on someone's behalf, and in their best interests if they ever lose capacity to make those decisions themselves (see paragraph 9.33 below and Chapter 7).

9.5   People can only make advance decisions to refuse treatment. Nobody has the legal right to demand specific treatment, either at the time or in advance. So no-one can insist (either at the time or in advance) on being given treatments that healthcare professionals consider to be clinically unnecessary, futile or inappropriate. But people can make a request or state their wishes and preferences in advance. Healthcare professionals should then consider the request when deciding what is in a patient's best interests (see Chapter 5) if the patient lacks capacity.

9.6   Nobody can ask for and receive procedures that are against the law (for example, help with committing suicide). As section 62 sets out, the Act does not change any of the laws relating to murder, manslaughter or helping someone to commit suicide.

Capacity to make an advance decision

9.7   For most people, there will be no doubt about their capacity to make an advance decision. Even those who lack capacity to make some decisions may have the capacity to make an advance decision. In some cases it may be helpful to get evidence of a person's capacity to make the advance decision (for example, if there is a possibility that the advance decision may be challenged in the future). It is also important to remember that capacity can change over time, and a person who lacks capacity to make a decision now might be able to make it in the future.

Chapter 3 explains how to assess a person's capacity to make a decision.

Scenario: Respecting capacity to make an advance decision

Mrs Long's family has a history of polycystic ovary syndrome. She has made a written advance decision refusing any treatment or procedures that might affect her fertility. The document states that her ovaries and uterus must not be removed. She is having surgery to treat a blocked fallopian tube and, during the consent process, she told her doctor about her advance decision.

During surgery the doctor discovers a solid mass that he thinks might be cancerous. In his clinical judgement, he thinks it would be in Mrs Long's best interests for him to remove the ovary. But he knows that Mrs Long had capacity when she made her valid and applicable advance decision, so he must respect her rights and follow her decision. After surgery, he can discuss the matter with Mrs Long and advise her about treatment options.

9.8   In line with principle 1 of the Act, that 'a person must be assumed to have capacity unless it is established that he lacks capacity', healthcare professionals should always start from the assumption that a person who has made an advance decision had capacity to make it, unless they are aware of reasonable grounds to doubt the person had the capacity to make the advance decision at the time they made it. If a healthcare professional is not satisfied that the person had capacity at the time they made the advance decision, or if there are doubts about its existence, validity or applicability, they can treat the person without fear of liability. It is good practice to record their decisions and the reasons for them. The Act does not require them to record their assessment of the person's capacity at the time the decision was made, but it would be good practice to do so.

9.9   Healthcare professionals may have particular concerns about the capacity of someone with a history of suicide attempts or suicidal thoughts who has made an advance decision. It is important to remember that making an advance decision which, if followed, may result in death does not necessarily mean a person is or feels suicidal. Nor does it necessarily mean the person lacks capacity to make the advance decision. If the person is clearly suicidal, this may raise questions about their capacity to make an advance decision at the time they made it.

What should people include in an advance decision?

9.10 There are no particular formalities about the format of an advance decision. It can be written or verbal, unless it deals with life-sustaining treatment, in which case it must be written and specific rules apply (see paragraphs 9.24–9.28 below).

9.11 An advance decision to refuse treatment:
- must state precisely what treatment is to be refused – a statement giving a general desire not to be treated is not enough
- may set out the circumstances when the refusal should apply – it is helpful to include as much detail as possible
- will only apply at a time when the person lacks capacity to consent to or refuse the specific treatment.

Specific rules apply to life-sustaining treatment.

9.12 People can use medical language or everyday language in their advance decision. But they must make clear what their wishes are and what treatment they would like to refuse.

9.13 An advance decision refusing all treatment in any situation (for example, where a person explains that their decision is based on their religion or personal beliefs) may be valid and applicable.

9.14 It is recommended that people who are thinking about making an advance decision get advice from:
- healthcare professionals (for example, their GP or the person most closely involved with current healthcare or treatment), or
- an organisation that can provide advice on specific conditions or situations (they might have their own format for recording an advance decision).

But it is up to the person whether they want to do this or not. Healthcare professionals should record details of any discussion on healthcare records.

9.15 Some people may also want to get legal advice. This will help them make sure that they express their decision clearly and accurately. It will also help to make sure that people understand their advance decision in the future.

9.16 It is a good idea to try to include possible future circumstances in the advance decision. For example, a woman may want to state in the advance decision whether or not it should still apply if she later becomes pregnant. If the document does not anticipate a change in circumstance, healthcare professionals may decide that it is not applicable if those particular circumstances arise.

9.17 If an advance decision is recorded on a patient's healthcare records, it is confidential. Some patients will tell others about their advance decision (for example, they might tell healthcare professionals, friends or family). Others will not. People who do not ask for their advance decision to be recorded on their healthcare record will need to think about where it should be kept and how they are going to let people know about their decision.

Written advance decisions

9.18 A written document can be evidence of an advance decision. It is helpful to tell others that the document exists and where it is. A person may want to carry it with them in case of emergency, or carry a card, bracelet or other indication that they have made an advance decision and explaining where it is kept.

9.19 There is no set form for written advance decisions, because contents will vary depending on a person's wishes and situation. But it is helpful to include the following information:
- full details of the person making the advance decision, including date of birth, home address and any distinguishing features (in case healthcare professionals need to identify an unconscious person, for example)
- the name and address of the person's GP and whether they have a copy of the document
- a statement that the document should be used if the person ever lacks capacity to make treatment decisions
- a clear statement of the decision, the treatment to be refused and the circumstances in which the decision will apply
- the date the document was written (or reviewed)
- the person's signature (or the signature of someone the person has asked to sign on their behalf and in their presence)
- the signature of the person witnessing the signature, if there is one (or a statement directing somebody to sign on the person's behalf).

See paragraphs 9.24–9.28 below if the advance decision deals with life-sustaining treatment.

9.20 Witnessing the person's signature is not essential, except in cases where the person is making an advance decision to refuse life-sustaining treatment. But if there is a witness, they are witnessing the signature and the fact that it confirms the wishes set out in the advance decision. It may be helpful to give a description of the relationship between the witness and person making the advance decision. The role of the witness is to witness the person's signature, it is not to certify that the person has the capacity to make the advance decision – even if the witness is a healthcare professional or knows the person.

9.21 It is possible that a professional acting as a witness will also be the person who assesses the person's capacity. If so, the professional should also make a record of the assessment, because acting as a witness does not prove that there has been an assessment.

Verbal advance decisions

9.22 There is no set format for verbal advance decisions. This is because they will vary depending on a person's wishes and situation. Healthcare professionals will need to consider whether a verbal advance decision exists and whether it is valid and applicable (see paragraphs 9.38– 9.44).

9.23 Where possible, healthcare professionals should record a verbal advance decision to refuse treatment in a person's healthcare record. This will produce a written record that could prevent confusion about the decision in the future. The record should include:

- a note that the decision should apply if the person lacks capacity to make treatment decisions in the future
- a clear note of the decision, the treatment to be refused and the circumstances in which the decision will apply
- details of someone who was present when the oral advance decision was recorded and the role in which they were present (for example, healthcare professional or family member), and
- whether they heard the decision, took part in it or are just aware that it exists.

What rules apply to advance decisions to refuse life-sustaining treatment?

9.24 The Act imposes particular legal requirements and safeguards on the making of advance decisions to refuse life-sustaining treatment. Advance decisions to refuse life-sustaining treatment must meet specific requirements:

- They must be put in writing. If the person is unable to write, someone else should write it down for them. For example, a family member can write down the decision on their behalf, or a healthcare professional can record it in the person's healthcare notes.
- The person must sign the advance decision. If they are unable to sign, they can direct someone to sign on their behalf in their presence.
- The person making the decision must sign in the presence of a witness to the signature. The witness must then sign the document in the presence of the person making the advance decision. If the person making the advance decision is unable to sign, the witness can witness them directing someone else to sign on their behalf. The witness must then sign to indicate that they have witnessed the nominated person signing the document in front of the person making the advance decision.
- The advance decision must include a clear, specific written statement from the person making the advance decision that the advance decision is to apply to the specific treatment even if life is at risk.
- If this statement is made at a different time or in a separate document to the advance decision, the person making the advance decision (or someone they have directed to sign) must sign it in the presence of a witness, who must also sign it.

9.25 Section 4(10) states that life-sustaining treatment is treatment which a healthcare professional who is providing care to the person regards as necessary to sustain life. This decision will not just depend on the type of treatment. It will also depend on the circumstances in which the healthcare professional is giving it. For example, in some situations antibiotics may be life-sustaining, but in others they can be used to treat conditions that do not threaten life.

9.26 Artificial nutrition and hydration (ANH) has been recognised as a form of medical treatment. ANH involves using tubes to provide nutrition and fluids to someone who cannot take them by mouth. It bypasses the natural mechanisms that control hunger and thirst and requires clinical monitoring. An advance decision can refuse ANH. Refusing ANH in an advance decision is likely to result in the person's death, if the advance decision is followed.

9.27 It is very important to discuss advance decisions to refuse life-sustaining treatment with a healthcare professional. But it is not compulsory. A healthcare professional will be able to explain:

- what types of treatment may be life-sustaining treatment, and in what circumstances
- the implications and consequences of refusing such treatment (see also paragraph 9.14).

9.28 An advance decision cannot refuse actions that are needed to keep a person comfortable (sometimes called basic or essential care). Examples include warmth, shelter, actions to keep a person clean and the offer of food and water by mouth. Section 5 of the Act allows healthcare professionals to carry out these actions in the best interests of a person who lacks capacity to consent (see Chapter 6). An advance decision can refuse artificial nutrition and hydration.

When should someone review or update an advance decision?

9.29 Anyone who has made an advance decision is advised to regularly review and update it as necessary. Decisions made a long time in advance are not automatically invalid or inapplicable, but they may raise doubts when deciding whether they are valid and applicable. A written decision that is regularly reviewed is more likely to be valid and applicable to current circumstances – particularly for progressive illnesses. This is because it is more likely to have taken on board changes that have occurred in a person's life since they made their decision.

9.30 Views and circumstances may change over time. A new stage in a person's illness, the development of new treatments or a major change in personal circumstances may be appropriate times to review and update an advance decision.

How can someone withdraw an advance decision?

9.31 Section 24(3) allows people to cancel or alter an advance decision at any time while they still have capacity to do so. There are no formal processes to follow. People can cancel their decision verbally or in writing, and they can destroy any original written document. Where possible, the person who made the advance decision should tell anybody who knew about their advance decision that it has been cancelled. They can do this at any time. For example, they can do this on their way to the operating theatre or immediately before being given an anaesthetic. Healthcare professionals should record a verbal cancellation in healthcare records. This then forms a written record for future reference.

How can someone make changes to an advance decision?

9.32 People can makes changes to an advance decision verbally or in writing (section 24(3)) whether or not the advance decision was made in writing. It is good practice for healthcare professionals to record a change of decision in the person's healthcare notes. But if the person wants to change an advance decision to include a refusal of life-sustaining treatment, they must follow the procedures described in paragraphs 9.24–9.28.

How do advance decisions relate to other rules about decision-making?

9.33 A valid and applicable advance decision to refuse treatment is as effective as a refusal made when a person has capacity. Therefore, an advance decision overrules:
- the decision of any personal welfare Lasting Power of Attorney (LPA) made before the advance decision was made. So an attorney cannot give consent to treatment that has been refused in an advance decision made after the LPA was signed
- the decision of any court-appointed deputy (so a deputy cannot give consent to treatment that has been refused in an advance decision which is valid and applicable)
- the provisions of section 5 of the Act, which would otherwise allow healthcare professionals to give treatment that they believe is in a person's best interests.

9.34 An LPA made after an advance decision will make the advance decision invalid, if the LPA gives the attorney the authority to make decisions about the same treatment (see paragraph 9.40).

9.35 The Court of Protection may make declarations as to the existence, validity and applicability of an advance decision, but it has no power to overrule a valid and applicable advance decision to refuse treatment.

9.36 Where an advance decision is being followed, the best interests principle (see Chapter 5) does not apply. This is because an advance decision reflects the decision of an adult with capacity who has made the decision for themselves. Healthcare professionals must follow a valid and applicable advance decision, even if they think it goes against a person's best interests.

Advance decisions regarding treatment for mental disorder

9.37 Advance decisions can refuse any kind of treatment, whether for a physical or mental disorder. But generally an advance decision to refuse treatment for mental disorder can be overruled if the person is detained in hospital under the Mental Health Act 1983, when treatment could be given compulsorily under Part 4 of that Act. Advance decisions to refuse treatment for other illnesses or conditions are not affected by the fact that the person is detained in hospital under the Mental Health Act. For further information see Chapter 13.

How can somebody decide on the existence, validity and applicability of advance decisions?

Deciding whether an advance decision exists

9.38 It is the responsibility of the person making the advance decision to make sure their decision will be drawn to the attention of healthcare professionals when it is needed. Some people will want their decision to be recorded on their healthcare records. Those who do not will need to find other ways of alerting people that they have made an advance decision and where somebody will find any written document and supporting evidence. Some people carry a card or wear a bracelet. It is also useful to share this information with family and friends, who may alert healthcare professionals to the existence of an advance decision. But it is not compulsory. Providing their GP with a copy of the written document will allow them to record the decision in the person's healthcare records.

9.39 It is important to be able to establish that the person making the advance decision was 18 or over when they made their decision, and that they had the capacity to make that decision when they made it, in line with the two-stage test for capacity set out in Chapter 3. But as explained in paragraphs 9.7–9.9 above, healthcare professionals should always start from the assumption that the person had the capacity to make the advance decision.

Deciding whether an advance decision is valid

9.40 An existing advance decision must still be valid at the time it needs to be put into effect. Healthcare professionals must consider the factors in section 25 of the Act before concluding that an advance decision is valid. Events that would make an advance decision invalid include those where:
- the person withdrew the decision while they still had capacity to do so
- after making the advance decision, the person made a Lasting Power of Attorney (LPA) giving an attorney authority to make treatment decisions that are the same as those covered by the advance decision (see also paragraph 9.33)

- the person has done something that clearly goes against the advance decision which suggests that they have changed their mind.

Scenario: Assessing whether an advance decision is valid

A young man, Angus, sees a friend die after prolonged hospital treatment. Angus makes a signed and witnessed advance decision to refuse treatment to keep him alive if he is ever injured in this way. The advance decision includes a statement that this will apply even if his life is at risk.

A few years later, Angus is seriously injured in a road traffic accident. He is paralysed from the neck down and cannot breathe without the help of a machine. At first he stays conscious and gives permission to be treated. He takes part in a rehabilitation programme. Some months later he loses consciousness.

At this point somebody finds his written advance decision, even though Angus has not mentioned it during his treatment. His actions before his lack of capacity obviously go against the advance decision. Anyone assessing the advance decision needs to consider very carefully the doubt this has created about the validity of the advance decision, and whether the advance decision is valid and applicable as a result.

Deciding whether an advance decision is applicable

9.41 To be applicable, an advance decision must apply to the situation in question and in the current circumstances. Healthcare professionals must first determine if the person still has capacity to accept or refuse treatment at the relevant time (section 25(3)). If the person has capacity, they can refuse treatment there and then. Or they can change their decision and accept treatment. The advance decision is not applicable in such situations.

9.42 The advance decision must also apply to the proposed treatment. It is not applicable to the treatment in question if (section 25(4)):
- the proposed treatment is not the treatment specified in the advance decision
- the circumstances are different from those that may have been set out in the advance decision, or
- there are reasonable grounds for believing that there have been changes in circumstance, which would have affected the decision if the person had known about them at the time they made the advance decision.

9.43 So when deciding whether an advance decision applies to the proposed treatment, healthcare professionals must consider:
- how long ago the advance decision was made, and

- whether there have been changes in the patient's personal life (for example, the person is pregnant, and this was not anticipated when they made the advance decision) that might affect the validity of the advance decision, and
- whether there have been developments in medical treatment that the person did not foresee (for example, new medications, treatment or therapies).

9.44 For an advance decision to apply to life-sustaining treatment, it must meet the requirements set out in paragraphs 9.24–9.28.

Scenario: Assessing if an advance decision is applicable

Mr Moss is HIV positive. Several years ago he began to have AIDS-related symptoms. He has accepted general treatment, but made an advance decision to refuse specific retro-viral treatments, saying he didn't want to be a 'guinea pig' for the medical profession. Five years later, he is admitted to hospital seriously ill and keeps falling unconscious.

The doctors treating Mr Moss examine his advance decision. They are aware that there have been major developments in retro-viral treatment recently. They discuss this with Mr Moss's partner and both agree that there are reasonable grounds to believe that Mr Moss may have changed his advance decision if he had known about newer treatment options. So the doctors decide the advance decision does not apply to the new retro-virals and give him treatment.

If Mr Moss regains his capacity, he can change his advance decision and accept or refuse future treatment.

What should healthcare professionals do if an advance decision is not valid or applicable?

9.45 If an advance decision is not valid or applicable to current circumstances:
- healthcare professionals must consider the advance decision as part of their assessment of the person's best interests (see Chapter 5) if they have reasonable grounds to think it is a true expression of the person's wishes, and
- they must not assume that because an advance decision is either invalid or not applicable, they should always provide the specified treatment (including life-sustaining treatment) – they must base this decision on what is in the person's best interests.

What happens to decisions made before the Act comes into force?

9.46 Advance decisions made before the Act comes into force may still be valid and applicable. Healthcare professionals should apply the rules in the Act to advance decisions made before the Act comes into force, subject to the transitional protections that will apply to advance decisions that refuse life-sustaining treatment. Further guidance will be available at www.dh.gov.uk/consent.

What implications do advance decisions have for healthcare professionals?

What are healthcare professionals' responsibilities?

9.47 Healthcare professionals should be aware that:
- a patient they propose to treat may have refused treatment in advance, and
- valid and applicable advance decisions to refuse treatment have the same legal status as decisions made by people with capacity at the time of treatment.

9.48 Where appropriate, when discussing treatment options with people who have capacity, healthcare professionals should ask if there are any specific types of treatment they do not wish to receive if they ever lack capacity to consent in the future.

9.49 If somebody tells a healthcare professional that an advance decision exists for a patient who now lacks capacity to consent, they should make reasonable efforts to find out what the decision is. Reasonable efforts might include having discussions with relatives of the patient, looking in the patient's clinical notes held in the hospital or contacting the patient's GP.

9.50 Once they know a verbal or written advance decision exists, healthcare professionals must determine whether:
- it is valid (see paragraph 9.40), and
- it is applicable to the proposed treatment (see paragraphs 9.41–9.44).

9.51 When establishing whether an advance decision applies to current circumstances, healthcare professionals should take special care if the decision does not seem to have been reviewed or updated for some time. If the person's current circumstances are significantly different from those when the decision was made, the advance decision may not be applicable. People close to the person concerned, or anyone named in the advance decision, may be able to help explain the person's prior wishes.

9.52 If healthcare professionals are satisfied that an advance decision to refuse treatment exists, is valid and is applicable, they must follow it and not provide the treatment refused in the advance decision.

9.53 If healthcare professionals are not satisfied that an advance decision exists that is both valid and applicable, they can treat the person without fear of liability. But treatment must be in the person's best interests (see Chapter 5). They should make clear notes explaining why they have not followed an advance decision which they consider to be invalid or not applicable.

9.54 Sometimes professionals can give or continue treatment while they resolve doubts over an advance decision. It may be useful to get information from someone who can provide information about the person's capacity when they made the advance decision. The Court of Protection can settle disagreements about the existence, validity or applicability of an advance decision. Section 26 of the Act allows healthcare professionals to give necessary treatment, including life-sustaining treatment, to stop a person's condition getting seriously worse while the court decides.

Do *advance decisions apply in emergencies?*

9.55 A healthcare professional must provide treatment in the patient's best interests, unless they are satisfied that there is a advance decision that is:
- valid, and
- applicable in the circumstances.

9.56 Healthcare professionals should not delay emergency treatment to look for an advance decision if there is no clear indication that one exists. But if it is clear that a person has made an advance decision that is likely to be relevant, healthcare professionals should assess its validity and applicability as soon as possible. Sometimes the urgency of treatment decisions will make this difficult.

When can healthcare professionals be found liable?

9.57 Healthcare professionals must follow an advance decision if they are satisfied that it exists, is valid and is applicable to their circumstances. Failure to follow an advance decision in this situation could lead to a claim for damages for battery or a criminal charge of assault.

9.58 But they are protected from liability if they are not:
- aware of an advance decision, or
- satisfied that an advance decision exists, is valid and is applicable to the particular treatment and the current circumstances (section 26(2)).

If healthcare professionals have genuine doubts, and are therefore not 'satisfied', about the existence, validity or applicability of the advance decision, treatment can be provided without incurring liability.

9.59 Healthcare professionals will be protected from liability for failing to provide treatment if they 'reasonably believe' that a valid and applicable advance decision to refuse that treatment exists. But they must be able to demonstrate that their belief was reasonable (section 26(3)) and point to reasonable grounds showing why they believe this. Healthcare professionals can only base their decision on the evidence that is available at the time they need consider an advance decision.

9.60 Some situations might be enough in themselves to raise concern about the existence, validity or applicability of an advance decision to refuse treatment. These could include situations when:

- a disagreement between relatives and healthcare professionals about whether verbal comments were really an advance decision
- evidence about the person's state of mind raises questions about their capacity at the time they made the decision (see paragraphs 9.7–9.9)
- evidence of important changes in the person's behaviour before they lost capacity that might suggest a change of mind.

In cases where serious doubt remains and cannot be resolved in any other way, it will be possible to seek a declaration from the court.

What if a healthcare professional has a conscientious objection to stopping or providing life-sustaining treatment?

9.61 Some healthcare professionals may disagree in principle with patients' rights to refuse life-sustaining treatment. The Act does not change the current legal situation. They do not have to do something that goes against their beliefs. But they must not simply abandon patients or cause their care to suffer.

9.62 Healthcare professionals should make their views clear to the patient and the healthcare team as soon as someone raises the subject of withholding, stopping or providing life-sustaining treatment. Patients who still have capacity should then have the option of transferring their care to another healthcare professional, if it is possible to do this without affecting their care.

9.63 In cases where the patient now lacks capacity but has made a valid and applicable advance decision to refuse treatment which a doctor or health professional cannot, for reasons of conscience, comply with, arrangements should be made for the management of the patient's care to be transferred to another healthcare professional.[36] Where a transfer cannot be agreed, the Court of Protection can direct those responsible for the person's healthcare (for example, a Trust, doctor or other health professional) to make arrangements to take over responsibility for the person's healthcare (section 17(1)(e)).

What happens if there is a disagreement about an advance decision?

9.64 It is ultimately the responsibility of the healthcare professional who is in charge of the person's care when the treatment is required to decide

---

[36] *Re B (Adult: Refusal of Medical Treatment)* [2002] EWHC 429 (Fam) at para 100(viii).

whether there is an advance decision which is valid and applicable in the circumstances. In the event of disagreement about an advance decision between healthcare professionals, or between healthcare professionals and family members or others close to the person, the senior clinician must consider all the available evidence. This is likely to be a hospital consultant or the GP where the person is being treated in the community.

9.65 The senior clinician may need to consult with relevant colleagues and others who are close to or familiar with the patient. All staff involved in the person's care should be given the opportunity to express their views. If the person is in hospital, their GP may also have relevant information.

9.66 The point of such discussions should not be to try to overrule the person's advance decision but rather to seek evidence concerning its validity and to confirm its scope and its applicability to the current circumstances. Details of these discussions should be recorded in the person's healthcare records. Where the senior clinician has a reasonable belief that an advance decision to refuse medical treatment is both valid and applicable, the person's advance decision should be complied with.

When can somebody apply to the Court of Protection?

9.67 The Court of Protection can make a decision where there is genuine doubt or disagreement about an advance decision's existence, validity or applicability. But the court does not have the power to overturn a valid and applicable advance decision.

9.68 The court has a range of powers (sections 16–17) to resolve disputes concerning the personal care and medical treatment of a person who lacks capacity (see Chapter 8). It can decide whether:
- a person has capacity to accept or refuse treatment at the time it is proposed
- an advance decision to refuse treatment is valid
- an advance decision is applicable to the proposed treatment in the current circumstances.

9.69 While the court decides, healthcare professionals can provide life-sustaining treatment or treatment to stop a serious deterioration in their condition. The court has emergency procedures which operate 24 hours a day to deal with urgent cases quickly. See Chapter 8 for guidance on applying to the court.

10 WHAT IS THE NEW INDEPENDENT MENTAL CAPACITY ADVOCATE SERVICE AND HOW DOES IT WORK?

This chapter describes the new Independent Mental Capacity Advocate (IMCA) service created under the Act. The purpose of the IMCA service is to help particularly vulnerable people who lack the capacity to make important decisions about serious medical treatment and changes of accommodation, and who have no family or friends that it would be appropriate to consult about those decisions. IMCAs will work with and support people who lack capacity, and represent their views to those who are working out their best interests.

The chapter provides guidance both for IMCAs and for everyone who may need to instruct an IMCA. It explains how IMCAs should be appointed. It also explains the IMCA's duties and the situations when an IMCA should be instructed. Both IMCAs and decision-makers are required to have regard to the Code of Practice.

> In this chapter, as throughout the Code, a person's capacity (or lack of capacity) refers specifically to their capacity to make a particular decision at the time it needs to be made.

Quick summary

Understanding the role of the IMCA service

- The aim of the IMCA service is to provide independent safeguards for people who lack capacity to make certain important decisions and, at the time such decisions need to be made, have no-one else (other than paid staff) to support or represent them or be consulted.
- IMCAs must be independent.

Instructing and consulting an IMCA

- An IMCA must be instructed, and then consulted, for people lacking capacity who have no-one else to support them (other than paid staff), whenever:
  - an NHS body is proposing to provide serious medical treatment, or
  - an NHS body or local authority is proposing to arrange accommodation (or a change of accommodation) in hospital or a care home, and
  - the person will stay in hospital longer than 28 days, or
  - they will stay in the care home for more than eight weeks.
- An IMCA may be instructed to support someone who lacks capacity to make decisions concerning:
  - care reviews, where no-one else is available to be consulted
  - adult protection cases, whether or not family, friends or others are involved

Ensuring an IMCA's views are taken into consideration

- The IMCA's role is to support and represent the person who lacks capacity. Because of this, IMCAs have the right to see relevant healthcare and social care records.

- Any information or reports provided by an IMCA must be taken into account as part of the process of working out whether a proposed decision is in the person's best interests.

What is the IMCA service?

10.1 Sections 35–41 of the Act set up a new IMCA service that provides safeguards for people who:
- lack capacity to make a specified decision at the time it needs to be made
- are facing a decision on a long-term move or about serious medical treatment and
- have nobody else who is willing and able to represent them or be consulted in the process of working out their best interests.

10.2 Regulations made under the Act also state that IMCAs may be involved in other decisions, concerning:
- a care review, or
- an adult protection case.

In adult protection cases, an IMCA may be appointed even where family members or others are available to be consulted.

10.3 Most people who lack capacity to make a specific decision will have people to support them (for example, family members or friends who take an interest in their welfare). Anybody working out a person's best interests must consult these people, where possible, and take their views into account (see Chapter 5). But if a person who lacks capacity has nobody to represent them or no-one who it is appropriate to consult, an IMCA must be instructed in prescribed circumstances. The prescribed circumstances are:
- providing, withholding or stopping serious medical treatment
- moving a person into long-term care in hospital or a care home (see 10.11 for definition), or
- moving the person to a different hospital or care home.

The only exception to this can be in situations where an urgent decision is needed. Further details on the situations where there is a duty to instruct an IMCA are given in paragraphs 10.40–10.58.

In other circumstances, an IMCA *may* be appointed for the person (see paragraphs 10.59–10.68). These include:
- care reviews or
- adult protection cases.

10.4 The IMCA will:
- be independent of the person making the decision
- provide support for the person who lacks capacity
- represent the person without capacity in discussions to work out whether the proposed decision is in the person's best interests

- provide information to help work out what is in the person's best interests (see Chapter 5), and
- raise questions or challenge decisions which appear not to be in the best interests of the person.

The information the IMCA provides must be taken into account by decision-makers whenever they are working out what is in a person's best interests. See paragraphs 10.20–10.39 for more information on an IMCA's role. For more information on who is a decision-maker, see Chapter 5.

10.5 The IMCA service will build on good practice in the independent advocacy sector. But IMCAs have a different role from many other advocates. They:

- provide statutory advocacy
- are instructed to support and represent people who lack capacity to make decisions on specific issues
- have a right to meet in private the person they are supporting
- are allowed access to relevant healthcare records and social care records
- provide support and representation specifically while the decision is being made, and
- act quickly so their report can form part of decision-making.

Who is responsible for delivering the service?

10.6 The IMCA service is available in England and Wales. Both countries have regulations for setting up and managing the service.

- England's regulations[37] are available at www.opsi.gov.uk/si/si200618. htm and www.opsi.gov.uk/si/dsis2006.htm.
- The regulations for Wales[38] are available at www.new.wales.gov.uk/consultations/closed/healandsoccarecloscons/.

Guidance has been issued to local health boards and local authorities involved in commissioning IMCA services for their area.

---

[37] *The Mental Capacity Act 2005 (Independent Mental Capacity Advocate) (General) Regulations 2006* (SI 2006/1832). The 'General Regulations'. These regulations set out the details on how the IMCA will be appointed, the functions of the IMCA, including their role in challenging the decision-maker and include definitions of 'serious medical treatment' and 'NHS body'.

The Mental Capacity Act 2005 (Independent Mental Capacity Advocate) (Expansion of Role) Regulations 2006 (SI 2006/2883). The 'Expansion Regulations'. These regulations specify the circumstances in which local authorities and NHS bodies may provide the IMCA service on a discretionary basis. These include involving the IMCA in a care review and in adult protection cases.

[38] *The Mental Capacity Act 2005 (Independent Mental Capacity Advocate) (Wales) Regulations 2007* (SI 2007/852 (W.77)). These regulations will remain in draft form until they are made by the National Assembly for Wales. The target coming into force date is 1 October 2007. Unlike the two sets of English regulations there will be one set only for Wales. Although the Welsh regulations will remain in draft form until the coming into force date, these have been drafted to give effect to similar and corresponding provisions to the regulations in England.

10.7 In England the Secretary of State for Health delivers the service through local authorities, who work in partnership with NHS organisations. Local authorities have financial responsibility for the service. In Wales the National Assembly for Wales delivers the service through local health boards, who have financial responsibility for the service and work in partnership with local authority social services departments and other NHS organisations. The service is commissioned from independent organisations, usually advocacy organisations.

10.8 Local authorities or NHS organisations are responsible for instructing an IMCA to represent a person who lacks capacity. In these circumstances they are called the 'responsible body'.

10.9 For decisions about serious medical treatment, the responsible body will be the NHS organisation providing the person's healthcare or treatment. But if the person is in an independent or voluntary sector hospital, the responsible body will be the NHS organisation arranging and funding the person's care, which should have arrangements in place with the independent or voluntary sector hospital to ensure an IMCA is appointed promptly.

10.10 For decisions about admission to accommodation in hospital for 28 days or more, the responsible body will be the NHS body that manages the hospital. For admission to an independent or voluntary sector hospital for 28 days or more, the responsible body will be the NHS organisation arranging and funding the person's care. The independent or voluntary hospital must have arrangements in place with the NHS organisation to ensure that an IMCA can be appointed without delay.

10.11 For decisions about moves into long-term accommodation[39] (for eight weeks or longer), or about a change of accommodation, the responsible body will be either:

- the NHS body that proposes the move or change of accommodation (e.g. a nursing home), or
- the local authority that has carried out an assessment of the person under the NHS and Community Care Act 1990 and decided the move may be necessary.

10.12 Sometimes NHS organisations and local authorities will make decisions together about moving a person into long-term care. In these cases, the organisation that must instruct the IMCA is the one that is ultimately responsible for the decision to move the person. The IMCA to be instructed is the one who works wherever the person is at the time that the person needs support and representation.

What are the responsible body's duties?

10.13 The responsible body:

---

[39] This may be accommodation in a care home, nursing home, ordinary and sheltered housing, housing association or other registered social housing or in private sector housing provided by a local authority or in hostel accommodation.

- *must* instruct an IMCA to support and represent a person in the situations set out in paragraphs 10.40–10.58
- *may* decide to instruct an IMCA in situations described in paragraphs 10.59–10.68
- *must*, in all circumstances when an IMCA is instructed, take properly into account the information that the IMCA provides when working out whether the particular decision (such as giving, withholding or stopping treatment, changing a person's accommodation, or carrying out a recommendation following a care review or an allegation requiring adult protection) is in the best interests of the person who lacks capacity.

10.14 The responsible body should also have procedures, training and awareness programmes to make sure that:
- all relevant staff know when they need to instruct an IMCA and are able to do so promptly
- all relevant staff know how to get in touch with the IMCA service and know the procedure for instructing an IMCA
- they record an IMCA's involvement in a case and any information the IMCA provides to help decision-making
- they also record how a decision-maker has taken into account the IMCA's report and information as part of the process of working out the person's best interests (this should include reasons for disagreeing with that advice, if relevant)
- they give access to relevant records when requested by an IMCA under section 35(6)(b) of the Act
- the IMCA gets information about changes that may affect the support and representation the IMCA provides
- decision-makers let all relevant people know when an IMCA is working on a person's case, and
- decision-makers inform the IMCA of the final decision taken and the reason for it.

10.15 Sometimes an IMCA and staff working for the responsible body might disagree. If this happens, they should try to settle the disagreement through discussion and negotiation as soon as possible. If they cannot do this, they should then follow the responsible body's formal procedures for settling disputes or complaints (see paragraphs 10.34 to 10.39 below).

10.16 In some situations the IMCA may challenge a responsible body's decision, or they may help somebody who is challenging a decision. The General Regulations in England and the Regulations in Wales set out when this may happen (see also Chapter 15). If there is no other way of resolving the disagreement, the decision may be challenged in the Court of Protection.

Who can be an IMCA?

10.17 In England, a person can only be an IMCA if the local authority approves their appointment. In Wales, the local health board will provide approval. Qualified employees of an approved organisation can act as IMCAs. Local authorities and health boards will usually commission independent advocacy organisations to provide the IMCA service. These organisations will work to appropriate organisational standards set through the contracting/commissioning process.

10.18 Individual IMCAs must:
- have specific experience
- have IMCA training
- have integrity and a good character, and
- be able to act independently.

All IMCAs must complete the IMCA training in order that they can work as an independent mental capacity advocate. A national advocacy qualification is also being developed, which will include the IMCA training.

Before a local authority or health board appoints an IMCA, they must carry out checks with the Criminal Records Bureau (CRB) to get a criminal record certificate or enhanced criminal record certificate for that individual.[40]

10.19 IMCAs must be independent. People cannot act as IMCAs if they:
- care for or treat (in a paid or professional capacity) the person they will be representing (this does not apply if they are an existing advocate acting for that person), or
- have links to the person instructing them, to the decision-maker or to other individuals involved in the person's care or treatment that may affect their independence.

What is an IMCA's role?

10.20 An IMCA must decide how best to represent and support the person who lacks capacity that they are helping. They:
- must confirm that the person instructing them has the authority to do so
- should interview or meet in private the person who lacks capacity, if possible
- must act in accordance with the principles of the Act (as set out in section 1 of the Act and Chapter 2 of the Code) and take account of relevant guidance in the Code
- may examine any relevant records that section 35(6) of the Act gives them access to
- should get the views of professionals and paid workers providing care or treatment for the person who lacks capacity
- should get the views of anybody else who can give information about the wishes and feelings, beliefs or values of the person who lacks capacity

---

[40] IMCAs were named as a group that is subject to mandatory checking under the new vetting and barring system in the Safeguarding Vulnerable Groups Act 2006. Roll-out of the bulk of the scheme will take place in 2008.

- should get hold of any other information they think will be necessary
- must find out what support a person who lacks capacity has had to help them make the specific decision
- must try to find out what the person's wishes and feelings, beliefs and values would be likely to be if the person had capacity
- should find out what alternative options there are
- should consider whether getting another medical opinion would help the person who lacks capacity, and
- must write a report on their findings for the local authority or NHS body.

10.21   Where possible, decision-makers should make decisions based on a full understanding of a person's past and present wishes. The IMCA should provide the decision-maker with as much of this information as possible – and anything else they think is relevant. The report they give the decision-maker may include questions about the proposed action or may include suggested alternatives, if they think that these would be better suited to the person's wishes and feelings.

10.22   Another important part of the IMCA's role is communicating their findings. Decision-makers should find the most effective way to enable them to do this. In some of the IMCA pilot areas,[41] hospital discharge teams added a 'Need to instruct an IMCA?' question on their patient or service user forms. This allowed staff to identify the need for an IMCA as early as possible, and to discuss the timetable for the decision to be made. Some decisions need a very quick IMCA response, others will allow more time. In the pilot areas, IMCA involvement led to better informed discharge planning, with a clearer focus on the best interests of a person who lacked capacity. It did not cause additional delays in the hospital discharge.

Representing and supporting the person who lacks capacity

10.23   IMCAs should take account of the guidance in Chapter 5.
- IMCAs should find out whether the decision-maker has given all practical and appropriate support to help the person who lacks capacity to be involved as much as possible in decision-making. If the person has communication difficulties, the IMCA should also find out if the decision-maker has obtained any specialist help (for example, from a speech and language therapist).
- Sometimes an IMCA may find information to suggest a person might regain capacity in the future, either so they can make the decision themselves or be more involved in decision-making. In such a situation, the IMCA can ask the decision-maker to delay the decision, if it is not urgent.
- The IMCA will need to get as much information as possible about the person's wishes, feelings, beliefs and values – both past and

---

[41]   For further information see www.dh.gov.uk/imca.

present. They should also consider the person's religion and any cultural factors that may influence the decision.

10.24 Sometimes a responsible body will not have time to instruct an IMCA (for example in an emergency or if a decision is urgent). If this is the case, this should be recorded, with the reason an IMCA has not been instructed. Where the decision concerns a move of accommodation, the local authority must appoint an IMCA as soon as possible afterwards. Sometimes the IMCA will not have time to carry out full investigations. In these situations, the IMCA must make a judgement about what they can achieve in the time available to support and represent the person who lacks capacity.

10.25 Sometimes an IMCA might not be able to get a good picture of what the person might want. They should still try to make sure the decision-maker considers all relevant information by:
- raising relevant issues and questions, and
- providing additional, relevant information to help the final decision.

Finding and evaluating information

10.26 Section 35(6) provides IMCAs with certain powers to enable them to carry out their duties. These include:
- the right to have an interview in private with the person who lacks capacity, and
- the right to examine, and take copies of, any records that the person holding the record thinks are relevant to the investigation (for example, clinical records, care plans, social care assessment documents or care home records).

10.27 The IMCA may also need to meet professionals or paid carers providing care or treatment for the person who lacks capacity. These people can help assess the information in case records or other sources. They can also comment on possible alternative courses of action. Ultimately, it is the decision-maker's responsibility to decide whether a proposed course of action is in the person's best interests. However, the Act requires the decision-maker to take account of the reports made and information given by the IMCA. In most cases a decision on the person's best interests will be made through discussion involving all the relevant people who are providing care or treatment, as well as the IMCA.

Finding out the person's wishes and feelings, beliefs and values

10.28 The IMCA needs to try and find out what the person's wishes and feelings might be, and what their underlying beliefs and values might also be. The IMCA should try to communicate both verbally and non-verbally with the person who may lack capacity, as appropriate. For example, this might mean using pictures or photographs. But there will be cases where the person cannot communicate at all (for example, if they are unconscious). The IMCA may also talk to other professionals or paid carers directly involved in providing present or past care or treatment. The IMCA might also need to examine health and social care records and any written statements of preferences the person may have made while they still had capacity to do so.

Chapter 5 contains further guidance on finding out the views of people who lack capacity. Chapter 3 contains further guidance on helping someone to make their own decision.

Considering alternative courses of action

10.29 The IMCA will need to check whether the decision-maker has considered all possible options. They should also ask whether the proposed option is less restrictive of the person's rights or future choices or would allow them more freedom (Chapter 2, principle 5).

10.30 The IMCA may wish to discuss possible options with other professionals or paid carers directly involved in providing care or treatment for the person. But they must respect the confidentiality of the person they are representing.

Scenario: *Using an IMCA*

Mrs Nolan has dementia. She is being discharged from hospital. She has no close family or friends. She also lacks the capacity to decide whether she should return home or move to a care home. The local authority instructs an IMCA.

Mrs Nolan tells the IMCA that she wants to go back to her own home, which she can remember and describe. But the hospital care team thinks she needs additional support, which can only be provided in a care home.

The IMCA reviewed all the assessments of Mrs Nolan's needs, spoke to people involved in her care and wrote a report stating that Mrs Nolan had strong and clear wishes. The IMCA also suggested that a care package could be provided to support Mrs Nolan if she were allowed to return home. The care manager now has to decide what is in Mrs Nolan's best interests. He must consider the views of the hospital care team and the IMCA's report.

Getting a second medical opinion

10.31 For decisions about serious medical treatment, the IMCA may consider seeking a second medical opinion from a doctor with appropriate expertise. This puts a person who lacks the capacity to make a specific decision in the same position as a person who has capacity, who has the right to request a second opinion.

What happens if the IMCA disagrees with the decision-maker?

10.32 The IMCA's role is to support and represent their client. They may do this through asking questions, raising issues, offering information and writing a report. They will often take part in a meeting involving different healthcare and social care staff to work out what is in the person's best interests. There may sometimes be cases when an IMCA thinks that a decision-maker has not paid enough attention to their report and other relevant information and is particularly concerned about the decision made. They may then need to challenge the decision.

10.33 An IMCA has the same rights to challenge a decision as any other person caring for the person or interested in his welfare. The right of challenge applies both to decisions about lack of capacity and a person's best interests.

10.34 Chapter 15 sets out how disagreements can be settled. The approach will vary, depending on the type and urgency of the disagreement. It could be a formal or informal approach.

Disagreements about health care or treatment
- Consult the Patient Advice and Liaison Service (England)
- Consult the Community Health Council (Wales)
- Use the NHS Complaints Procedure
- Refer the matter to the local continuing care review panel
- Engage the services of the Independent Complaints Advocacy Service (England) or another advocate.

Disagreements about social care
- Use the care home's complaints procedure (if the person is in a care home)
- Use the local authority complaints procedure.

10.35 Before using these formal methods, the IMCA and the decision-maker should discuss the areas they disagree about – particularly those that might have a serious impact on the person the IMCA is representing. The IMCA and decision-maker should make time to listen to each other's views and to understand the reason for the differences. Sometimes these discussions can help settle a disagreement.

10.36 Sometimes an IMCA service will have a steering group, with representatives from the local NHS organisations and the local authority. These representatives can sometimes negotiate between two differing views. Or they can clarify policy on a certain issue. They should also be involved if an IMCA believes they have discovered poor practice on an important issue.

10.37 IMCAs may use complaints procedures as necessary to try to settle a disagreement – and they can pursue a complaint as far as the relevant ombudsman if needed. In particularly serious or urgent cases, an IMCA may seek permission to refer a case to the Court of Protection for a decision. The Court will make a decision in the best interests of the person who lacks capacity.

10.38 The first step in making a formal challenge is to approach the Official Solicitor (OS) with the facts of the case. The OS can decide to apply to the court as a litigation friend (acting on behalf of the person the IMCA is representing). If the OS decides not to apply himself, the IMCA can ask for permission to apply to the Court of Protection. The OS can still be asked to act as a litigation friend for the person who lacks capacity.

10.39 In extremely serious cases, the IMCA might want to consider an application for judicial review in the High Court. This might happen if the IMCA thinks there are very serious consequences to a decision that has been made by a public authority. There are time limits for making an application, and the IMCA would have to instruct solicitors – and may be liable for the costs of the case going to court. So IMCAs should get legal advice before choosing this approach. The IMCA can also ask the OS to consider making the claim.

What decisions require an IMCA?

10.40 There are three types of decisions which require an IMCA to be instructed for people who lack capacity. These are:
- decisions about providing, withholding or stopping serious medical treatment
- decisions about whether to place people into accommodation (for example a care home or a long stay hospital), and
- decisions about whether to move people to different long stay accommodation.

For these decisions all local authorities and all health bodies must refer the same kinds of decisions to an IMCA for anyone who lacks capacity and qualifies for the IMCA service.

10.41 There are two further types of decisions where the responsible body has the power to instruct an IMCA for a person who lacks capacity. These are decisions relating to:
- care reviews and
- adult protection cases.

In such cases, the relevant local authority or NHS body must decide in each individual case whether it would be of particular benefit to the person who lacks capacity to have an IMCA to support them. The factors which should be considered are explained in paragraphs 10.59–10.68.[42]

Decisions about serious medical treatment

10.42 Where a serious medical treatment decision is being considered for a person who lacks the capacity to consent, and who qualifies for additional safeguards, section 37 of the Act imposes a duty on the NHS body to

---

[42] See Chapter 11 for information about the role of 'consultees' when research is proposed involving a person who lacks capacity to make a decision about whether to agree to take part in research. In certain situations IMCAs may be involved as consultees for research purposes.

instruct an IMCA. NHS bodies must instruct an IMCA whenever they are proposing to take a decision about 'serious medical treatment', or proposing that another organisation (such as a private hospital) carry out the treatment on their behalf, if:

- the person concerned does not have the capacity to make a decision about the treatment, and
- there is no-one appropriate to consult about whether the decision is in the person's best interests, other than paid care staff.

10.43 Regulations for England and Wales set out the definition of 'serious medical treatment' for decisions that require an IMCA. It includes treatments for both mental and physical conditions.

Serious medical treatment is defined as treatment which involves giving new treatment, stopping treatment that has already started or withholding treatment that could be offered in circumstances where:

- if a single treatment is proposed there is a fine balance between the likely benefits and the burdens to the patient and the risks involved
- a decision between a choice of treatments is finely balanced, or
- what is proposed is likely to have serious consequences for the patient.

10.44 'Serious consequences' are those which could have a serious impact on the patient, either from the effects of the treatment itself or its wider implications. This may include treatments which:

- cause serious and prolonged pain, distress or side effects
- have potentially major consequences for the patient (for example, stopping life-sustaining treatment or having major surgery such as heart surgery), or
- have a serious impact on the patient's future life choices (for example, interventions for ovarian cancer).

10.45 It is impossible to set out all types of procedures that may amount to 'serious medical treatment', although some examples of medical treatments that might be considered serious include:

- chemotherapy and surgery for cancer
- electro-convulsive therapy
- therapeutic sterilisation
- major surgery (such as open-heart surgery or brain/neuro-surgery)
- major amputations (for example, loss of an arm or leg)
- treatments which will result in permanent loss of hearing or sight
- withholding or stopping artificial nutrition and hydration, and
- termination of pregnancy.

These are illustrative examples only, and whether these or other procedures are considered serious medical treatment in any given case, will depend on the circumstances and the consequences for the patient. There are also many more treatments which will be defined as serious medical treatments under the Act's regulations. Decision-makers who are not sure whether they need to instruct an IMCA should consult their colleagues.

10.46 The only situation in which the duty to instruct an IMCA need not be followed, is when an urgent decision is needed (for example, to save the person's life). This decision must be recorded with the reason for the non-referral. Responsible bodies will however still need to instruct an IMCA for any serious treatment that follows the emergency treatment.

10.47 While a decision-maker is waiting for the IMCA's report, they must still act in the person's best interests (for example, to give treatment that stops the person's condition getting worse).

Scenario: *Using an IMCA for serious medical treatment*

Mr Jones had a fall and suffered serious head injuries. Hospital staff could not find any family or friends. He needed urgent surgery, but afterwards still lacked capacity to accept or refuse medical treatment.

The hospital did not involve an IMCA in the decision to operate, because it needed to make an emergency decision. But it did instruct an IMCA when it needed to carry out further serious medical treatment.

The IMCA met with Mr Jones looked at his case notes and reviewed the options with the consultant. The decision-maker then made the clinical decision about Mr Jones' best interests taking into account the IMCA's report.

10.48 Some decisions about medical treatment are so serious that the courts need to make them (see Chapter 8). But responsible bodies should still instruct an IMCA in these cases. The OS may be involved as a litigation friend of the person who lacks capacity.

10.49 Responsible bodies do not have to instruct an IMCA for patients detained under the Mental Health Act 1983, if:
- the treatment is for mental disorder, and
- they can give it without the patient's consent under that Act.

10.50 If serious medical treatment proposed for the detained patient is not for their mental disorder, the patient then has a right to an IMCA – as long as they meet the Mental Capacity Act's requirements. So a detained patient without capacity to consent to cancer treatment, for example, should qualify for an IMCA if there are no family or friends whom it would be appropriate to consult.

Decisions about accommodation or changes of residence

10.51 The Act imposes similar duties on NHS bodies and local authorities who are responsible for long-term accommodation decisions for a person who lacks the capacity to agree to the placement and who qualifies for the additional safeguard of an IMCA. The right to an IMCA applies to decisions about long-term accommodation in a hospital or care home if it is:
- provided or arranged by the NHS, or

- residential care that is provided or arranged by the local authority or provided under section 117 of the Mental Health Act 1983, or
- a move between such accommodation.

10.52 Responsible bodies have a duty to instruct an IMCA if:
- an NHS organisation proposes to place a person who lacks capacity in a hospital – or to move them to another hospital – for longer than 28 days, or
- an NHS organisation proposes to place a person who lacks capacity in a care home – or to move them to a different care home – for what is likely to be longer than eight weeks.

In either situation the other qualifying conditions apply. So, if the accommodation is for less than 28 days in a hospital or less than 8 weeks in a care home, then an IMCA need not be appointed.

10.53 The duty also applies if a local authority carries out an assessment under section 47 of the NHS and Community Care Act 1990, and it decides to:
- provide care services for a person who lacks capacity in the form of residential accommodation in a care home or its equivalent (see paragraph 10.11) which is likely to be longer than eight weeks, or
- move a person who lacks capacity to another care home or its equivalent for a period likely to exceed eight weeks.

10.54 In some cases, a care home may decide to de-register so that they can provide accommodation and care in a different way. If a local authority makes the new arrangements, then an IMCA should still be instructed if a patient lacks capacity and meets the other qualifying conditions.

10.55 Sometimes a person's placement will be longer than expected. The responsible body should involve an IMCA as soon as they realise the stay will be longer than 28 days or eight weeks, as appropriate.

10.56 People who fund themselves in long-term accommodation have the same rights to an IMCA as others, if the local authority:
- carries out an assessment under section 47 of the NHS and Community Care Act 1990, and
- decides it has a duty to the person (under either section 21 or 29 of the National Assistance Act 1947 or section 117 of the Mental Health Act 1983).

10.57 Responsible bodies can only put aside the duty to involve an IMCA if the placement or move is urgent (for example, an emergency admission to hospital or possible homelessness). The decision-maker must involve an IMCA as soon as possible after making an emergency decision, if:
- the person is likely to stay in hospital for longer than 28 days, or
- they will stay in other accommodation for longer than eight weeks.

10.58 Responsible bodies do not have to involve IMCAs if the person in question is going to be required to stay in the accommodation under the Mental Health Act 1983. But if a person is discharged from detention, they have a right to an IMCA in future accommodation decisions (if they meet the usual conditions set out in the Act).

When can a local authority or NHS body decide to instruct an IMCA?

10.59 The Expansion Regulations have given local authorities and NHS bodies the power to apply the IMCA role to two further types of decisions:
- a care review, and
- adult protection cases that involve vulnerable people.

10.60 In these situations, the responsible body must consider in each individual case whether to instruct an IMCA. Where an IMCA is instructed:
- the decision-maker must be satisfied that having an IMCA will be of particular benefit to the person who lacks capacity
- the decision-maker must also follow the best interests checklist, including getting the views of anyone engaged in caring for a person when assessing their best interests, and
- the decision-maker must consider the IMCA's report and related information when making a decision.

10.61 Responsible bodies are expected to take a strategic approach in deciding when they will use IMCAs in these two additional situations. They should establish a policy locally for determining these decisions, setting out the criteria for appointing an IMCA including the issues to be taken into account when deciding if an IMCA will be of particular benefit to the person concerned. However, decision-makers will need to consider each case separately to see if the criteria are met. Local authorities or NHS bodies may want to publish their approach for ease of access, setting out the ways they intend to use these additional powers and review it periodically.

Involving an IMCA in care reviews

10.62 A responsible body can instruct an IMCA to support and represent a person who lacks capacity when:
- they have arranged accommodation for that person
- they aim to review the arrangements (as part of a care plan or otherwise), and
- there are no family or friends who it would be appropriate to consult.

10.63 Section 7 of the Local Authority Social Services Act 1970 sets out current requirements for care reviews. It states that there should be a review 'within three months of help being provided or major changes made to services'. There should then be a review every year – or more often, if needed.

10.64 Reviews should relate to decisions about accommodation:
- for someone who lacks capacity to make a decision about accommodation
- that will be provided for a continuous period of more than 12 weeks

- that are not the result of an obligation under the Mental Health Act 1983, and
- that do not relate to circumstances where sections 37 to 39 of the Act would apply.

10.65 Where the person is to be detained or required to live in accommodation under the Mental Health Act 1983, an IMCA will not be needed since the safeguards available under that Act will apply.

Involving IMCAs in adult protection cases

10.66 Responsible bodies have powers to instruct an IMCA to support and represent a person who lacks capacity where it is alleged that:
- the person is or has been abused or neglected by another person, or
- the person is abusing or has abused another person.

The responsible bodies can only instruct an IMCA if they propose to take, or have already taken, protective measures. This is in accordance with adult protection procedures set up under statutory guidance.[43]

10.67 In adult protection cases (and no other cases), access to IMCAs is not restricted to people who have no-one else to support or represent them. People who lack capacity who have family and friends can still have an IMCA to support them in the adult protection procedures.

10.68 In some situations, a case may start out as an adult protection case where a local authority may consider whether or not to involve an IMCA under the criteria they have set – but may then become a case where the allegations or evidence give rise to the question of whether the person should be moved in their best interests. In these situations the case has become one where an IMCA must be involved if there is no-one else appropriate to support and represent the person in this decision.

Who qualifies for an IMCA?

10.69 Apart from the adult protection cases discussed above, IMCAs are only available to people who:
- lack capacity to make a specific decision about serious medical treatment or long-term accommodation, *and*
- have no family or friends who are available and appropriate to support or represent them apart from professionals or paid workers providing care or treatment, *and*

---

[43] Published guidance: No secrets: Guidance on developing and implementing multi-agency policies and procedures to protect vulnerable adults from abuse for England (on the Department of Health website) and In safe hands in Wales.
No secrets applies to adults aged 18 or over. The Children Act 1989 applies to 16 and 17 year olds who may be facing abuse. Part V of the Act covers the Protection of Children, which includes at section 47 the duty to investigate by a local authority in order to decide whether they should take any action to safeguard or promote a child's welfare where he or she requires protection or may suffer harm. See also Chapter 12 of this Code.

- have not previously named someone who could help with a decision, *and*
- have not made a Lasting Power of Attorney or Enduring Power of Attorney (see paragraph 10.70 below).

10.70 The Act says that IMCAs cannot be instructed if:
- a person who now lacks capacity previously named a person that should be consulted about decisions that affect them, and that person is available and willing to help
- the person who lacks capacity has appointed an attorney, either under a Lasting Power of Attorney or an Enduring Power of Attorney, and the attorney continues to manage the person's affairs
- the Court of Protection has appointed a deputy, who continues to act on the person's behalf.

10.71 However, where a person has no family or friends to represent them, but does have an attorney or deputy who has been appointed solely to deal with their property and affairs, they should not be denied access to an IMCA. The Government is seeking to amend the Act at the earliest opportunity to ensure that, in such circumstances, an IMCA should always be appointed to represent the person's views when they lack the capacity to make decisions relating to serious medical treatment or long-term accommodation moves.

10.72 A responsible body can still instruct an IMCA if the Court of Protection is deciding on a deputy, but none is in place when a decision needs to be made.

Scenario: *Qualifying for an IMCA*

Ms Lewis, a woman with a history of mental health problems has lived in a care home for several years. Her home will soon close, and she has no-one who could help her. She has become very anxious and now lacks capacity to make a decision about future accommodation. The local authority instructs an IMCA to support her. The IMCA visits Ms Lewis, talks to staff who have been involved in her care and reviews her case notes.

In his report, the IMCA includes the information that Ms Lewis is very close to another client in the care home. The IMCA notes that they could move together – if it is also in the interests of the other client. The local authority now has to decide on the best interests of the client, considering the information that the IMCA has provided.

Will IMCAs be available to people in prisons?

10.73 IMCAs should be available to people who are in prison and lack capacity to make decisions about serious medical treatment or long-term accommodation.

Who is it 'appropriate to consult'?

10.74 The IMCA is a safeguard for those people who lack capacity, who have no-one close to them who 'it would be appropriate to consult'. (This is apart from adult protection cases where this criterion does not apply.) The safeguard is intended to apply to those people who have little or no network of support, such as close family or friends, who take an interest in their welfare or no-one willing or able to be formally consulted in decision-making processes.

10.75 The Act does not define those 'whom it would be appropriate to consult' and the evaluation of the IMCA pilots reported that decision-makers in the local authority and in the NHS, whose decision it is to determine this, sometimes found it difficult to establish when an IMCA was required.[44] Section 4(7) provides that consultation about a person's best interests shall include among others, anyone:
- named by the person as someone to be consulted on a relevant decision
- engaged in caring for them, or
- interested in their welfare (see Chapter 4).

10.76 The decision-maker must determine if it is possible and practical to speak to these people, and those described in paragraph 10.70 when working out whether the proposed decision is in the person's best interests. If it is not possible, practical and appropriate to consult anyone, an IMCA should be instructed.

10.77 There may be situations where a person who lacks capacity has family or friends, but it is not practical or appropriate to consult them. For example, an elderly person with dementia may have an adult child who now lives in Australia, or an older person may have relatives who very rarely visit. Or, a family member may simply refuse to be consulted. In such cases, decision-makers must instruct an IMCA – for serious medical treatment and care moves and record the reason for the decision.

10.78 The person who lacks capacity may have friends or neighbours who know their wishes and feelings but are not willing or able to help with the specific decision to be made. They may think it is too much of a responsibility. If they are elderly and frail themselves, it may be too difficult for them to attend case conferences and participate formally. In this situation, the responsible body should instruct an IMCA, and the IMCA may visit them and enable them to be involved more informally.

10.79 If a family disagrees with a decision-maker's proposed action, this is not grounds for concluding that there is nobody whose views are relevant to the decision.

10.80 A person who lacks capacity and already has an advocate may still be entitled to an IMCA. The IMCA would consult with the advocate. Where

---

[44] see www.dh.gov.uk/PolicyAndGuidance/HealthAndSocialCareTopics/SocialCare/IMCA/fs/en

that advocate meets the appointment criteria for the IMCA service, they may be appointed to fulfil the IMCA role for this person in addition to their other duties.

11   HOW DOES THE ACT AFFECT RESEARCH PROJECTS INVOLVING A PERSON WHO LACKS CAPACITY?

It is important that research involving people who lack capacity can be carried out, and that is carried out properly. Without it, we would not improve our knowledge of what causes a person to lack or lose capacity, and the diagnosis, treatment, care and needs of people who lack capacity.

This chapter gives guidance on involving people who lack capacity to consent to take part in research. It sets out:

* what the Act means by 'research'
* the requirements that people must meet if their research project involves somebody who lacks capacity
* the specific responsibilities of researchers, and
* how the Act applies to research that started before the Act came into force.

This chapter only deals with research in relation to adults. Further guidance will be provided on how the Act applies in relation to research involving those under the age of 18.

> In this chapter, as throughout the Code, a person's capacity (or lack of capacity) refers specifically to their capacity to make a particular decision at the time it needs to be made.

Quick summary

The Act's rules for research that includes people who lack capacity to consent to their involvement cover:

* when research can be carried out
* the ethical approval process
* respecting the wishes and feelings of people who lack capacity
* other safeguards to protect people who lack capacity
* how to engage with a person who lacks capacity
* how to engage with carers and other relevant people.

This chapter also explains:

- the specific rules that apply to research involving human tissue and
- what to do if research projects have already been given the go-ahead.

The Act applies to all research that is intrusive. 'Intrusive' means research that would be unlawful if it involved a person who had capacity but had not consented to take part. The Act does not apply to research involving clinical trials (testing new drugs).

Why does the Act cover research?

11.1 Because the Act is intended to assist and support people who may lack capacity, the Act protects people who take part in research projects but lack capacity to make decisions about their involvement. It makes sure that researchers respect their wishes and feelings. The Act does not apply to research that involves clinical trials of medicines – because these are covered by other rules.[45]

How can research involving people who lack capacity help?

A high percentage of patients with Down's syndrome lack capacity to agree or refuse to take part in research. Research involving patients with Down's syndrome has shown that they are more likely than other people to get pre-senile dementia. Research has also shown that when this happens the pathological changes that occur in a person with Down's syndrome (changes affecting their body and brain) are similar to those that occur in someone with Alzheimer's disease. This means that we now know that treatment similar to that used for memory disorders in patients with Alzheimer's is appropriate to treat dementia in those with Down's syndrome.

What is 'research'?

11.2 The Act does not have a specific definition for 'research'. The Department of Health and National Assembly for Wales publications *Research governance framework for health and social care* both state:

> 'research can be defined as the attempt to derive generalisable new knowledge by addressing clearly defined questions with systematic and rigorous methods.'[46]

Research may:
- provide information that can be applied generally to an illness, disorder or condition

---

[45] The Medicines for Human Use (Clinical Trials) Regulations 2004.

[46] www.dh.gov.uk/PublicationsAndStatistics/Publications/PublicationsPolicyAndGuidance/ PublicationsPolicyAndGuidanceArticle/fx/en?CONTENT_ID=4008777&chk=dMRd/5 and www.word.wales.gov.uk/content/governance/governance-e.htm.

- demonstrate how effective and safe a new treatment is
- add to evidence that one form of treatment works better than another
- add to evidence that one form of treatment is safer than another, or
- examine wider issues (for example, the factors that affect someone's capacity to make a decision).

11.3 Researchers must state clearly if an activity is part of someone's care and not part of the research. Sometimes experimental medicine or treatment may be performed for the person's benefit and be the best option for their care. But in these cases, it may be difficult to decide whether treatment is research or care. Where there is doubt, the researcher should seek legal advice.

What assumptions can a researcher make about capacity?

11.4 Researchers should assume that a person has capacity, unless there is proof that they lack capacity to make a specific decision (see Chapter 3). The person must also receive support to try to help them make their own decision (see Chapter 2). The person whose capacity is in question has the right to make decisions that others might not agree with, and they have the right not to take part in research.

What research does the Act cover?

11.5 It is expected that most of the researchers who ask for their research to be approved under the Act will be medical or social care researchers. However, the Act can cover more than just medical and social care research. Intrusive research which does not meet the requirements of the Act cannot be carried out lawfully in relation to people who lack capacity.

11.6 The Act applies to research that:
- is 'intrusive' (if a person taking part had capacity, the researcher would need to get their consent to involve them)
- involves people who have an impairment of, or a disturbance in the functioning of, their mind or brain which makes them unable to decide whether or not to agree to take part in the research (ie they lack capacity to consent), and
- is not a clinical trial covered under the Medicines for Human Use (Clinical Trials) Regulations 2004.

11.7 There are circumstances where no consent is needed to lawfully involve a person in research. These apply to all persons, whether they have capacity or not:
- Sometimes research only involves data that has been anonymised (it cannot be traced back to individuals). Confidentiality and data protection laws do not apply in this case.
- Under the Human Tissue Act 2004, research that deals only with human tissue that has been anonymised does not require consent (see paragraphs 11.37–11.40). This applies to both those who have

capacity and those who do not. But the research must have ethical approval, and the tissue must come from a living person.[47]
- If researchers collected human tissue samples before 31 August 2006, they do not need a person's consent to work on them. But they will normally have to get ethical approval.
- Regulations[48] made under section 251 of the NHS Act 2006 (formerly known as section 60 of the Health and Social Care Act 2001[49]) allow people to use confidential patient information without breaking the law on confidentiality by applying to the Patient Information Advisory Group for approval on behalf of the Secretary of State.[50]

Who is responsible for making sure research meets the Act's requirements?

11.8 Responsibility for meeting the Act's requirements lies with:
- the 'appropriate body', as defined in regulations made by the Secretary of State (for regulations applying in England) or the National Assembly for Wales (for regulations applying in Wales) (see paragraph 11.10), and
- the researchers carrying out the research (see paragraphs 11.20–11. 40).

How can research get approval?

11.9 Research covered by the Act cannot include people who lack capacity to consent to the research unless:
- it has the approval of 'the appropriate body', and
- it follows other requirements in the Act to:
  - consider the views of carers and other relevant people
  - treat the person's interests as more important than those of science and society, and
  - respect any objections a person who lacks capacity makes during research.

11.10 An 'appropriate body' is an organisation that can approve research projects. In England, the 'appropriate body' must be a research ethics

---

[47] Human Tissue Act 2004, s 1(9).

[48] Health Service (Control of Patient Information) Regulations 2002 Section I. 2002/1438.

[49] Section 60 of the Health and Social Care Act 2001 was included in the NHS Act 2006 which consolidated all the previous health legislation still in force.

[50] The Patient Information Advisory Group considers applications on behalf of the Secretary of State to allow the common law duty of confidentiality to be aside. It was established under section 61of the Health and Social Care Act 2006 (now known as section 252 of the NHS Act 2006). Further information can be found at www.advisorybodies.doh.gov.uk/PIAG.

committee recognised by the Secretary of State.[51] In Wales, the 'appropriate body' must be a research ethics committee recognised by the Welsh Assembly Government.

11.11 The appropriate body can only approve a research project if the research is linked to:

- an impairing condition that affects the person who lacks capacity, or
- the treatment of that condition (see paragraph 11.17)

and:

- there are reasonable grounds for believing that the research would be less effective if only people with capacity are involved, and
- the research project has made arrangements to consult carers and to follow the other requirements of the Act.

11.12 Research must also meet one of two requirements:

1. The research must have some chance of benefiting the person who lacks capacity, as set out in paragraph 11.14 below. The benefit must be in proportion to any burden caused by taking part, or
2. The aim of the research must be to provide knowledge about the cause of, or treatment or care of people with, the same impairing condition – or a similar condition.

If researchers are relying on the second requirement, the Act sets out further requirements that must be met:

- the risk to the person who lacks capacity must be negligible
- there must be no significant interference with the freedom of action or privacy of the person who lacks capacity, and
- nothing must be done to or in relation to the person who lacks capacity which is unduly invasive or restrictive (see paragraphs 11. 16–11.19 below).

11.13 An impairing condition:

- is caused by (or may be caused by) an impairment of, or disturbance in the functioning of, the person's mind or brain
- causes (or may cause) an impairment or disturbance of the mind or brain, or
- contributes to (or may contribute to) an impairment or disturbance of the mind or brain.

Balancing the benefit and burden of research

11.14 Potential benefits of research for a person who lacks capacity could include:

- developing more effective ways of treating a person or managing their condition
- improving the quality of healthcare, social care or other services that they have access to
- discovering the cause of their condition, if they would benefit from that knowledge, or

---

[51]   Mental Capacity Act 2005 (Appropriate Body) (England) Regulations 2006.

- reducing the risk of the person being harmed, excluded or disadvantaged.

11.15 Benefits may be direct or indirect (for example, the person might benefit at a later date if policies or care packages affecting them are changed because of the research). It might be that participation in the research itself will be of benefit to the person in particular circumstances. For example, if the research involves interviews and the person has the opportunity to express their views, this could be considered of real benefit to a particular individual.

Providing knowledge about causes, treatment or care of people with the same impairing condition or a similar condition

11.16 It is possible for research to be carried out which doesn't actually benefit the person taking part, as long as it aims to provide knowledge about the causes, treatment or care of people with the same impairing condition, or a similar condition. *'Care'* and *'treatment'* are not limited to medical care and treatment. For example, research could examine how day-to-day life in prison affects prisoners with mental health conditions.

11.17 It is the person's actual condition that must be the same or similar in research, not the underlying cause. A *'similar condition'* may therefore have a different cause to that suffered by the participant. For example, research into ways of supporting people with learning disabilities to live more independently might involve a person with a learning disability caused by a head trauma. But its findings might help people with similar learning disabilities that have different causes.

Scenario: Research that helps find a cause or treatment

Mr Neal has Down's syndrome. For many years he has lived in supported housing and worked in a local supermarket. But several months ago, he became aggressive, forgetful and he started to make mistakes at work. His consultant believes that this may indicate the start of Alzheimer's disease.

Mr Neal's condition is now so bad that he does not have capacity to consent to treatment or make other decisions about his care. A research team is researching the cause of dementia in people with Down's syndrome. They would like to involve Mr Neal. The research satisfies the Act's requirement that it is intended to provide knowledge of the causes or treatment of that condition, even though it may not directly benefit Mr Neal. So the approving body might give permission – if the research meets other requirements.

11.18 Any risk to people involved in this category of research must be 'negligible' (minimal). This means that a person should suffer no harm or distress by taking part. Researchers must consider risks to psychological wellbeing as well as physical wellbeing. This is particularly relevant for research related to observations or interviews.

11.19 Research in this category also must not affect a person's freedom of action or privacy in a significant way, and it should not be unduly invasive or restrictive. What will be considered as unduly invasive will be different for different people and different types of research. For example, in psychological research some people may think a specific question is intrusive, but others would not. Actions will not usually be classed as unduly invasive if they do not go beyond the experience of daily life, a routine medical examination or a psychological examination.

Scenario: Assessing the risk to research participants

A research project is studying:

- how well people with a learning disability make financial decisions, and

- communication techniques that may improve their decision-making capacity.

Some of the participants lack capacity to agree to take part. The Research Ethics Committee is satisfied that some of these participants may benefit from the study because their capacity to make financial decisions may be improved. For those who will not gain any personal benefit, the Committee is satisfied that:

- the research meets the other conditions of the Act

- the research methods (psychological testing and different communication techniques) involve no risk to participants, and

- the research could not have been carried out as effectively with people who have capacity.

What responsibilities do researchers have?

11.20 Before starting the research, the research team must make arrangements to:
- obtain approval for the research from the 'appropriate body'
- get the views of any carers and other relevant people before involving a person who lacks capacity in research (see paragraphs 11.22–11. 28). There is an exception to this consultation requirement in situations where urgent treatment needs to be given or is about to be given
- respect the objections, wishes and feelings of the person, and
- place more importance on the person's interests than on those of science and society.

11.21 The research proposal must give enough information about what the team will do if a person who lacks capacity needs urgent treatment during research and it is not possible to speak to the person's carer or someone else who acts or makes decisions on behalf of the person (see paragraphs 11.32–11.36).

Consulting carers

11.22 Once it has been established that a person lacks capacity to agree to participate, then before they are included in research the researcher must consult with specified people in accordance with section 32 of the Act to determine whether the person should be included in the research.

Who can researchers consult?

11.23 The researcher should as a matter of good practice take reasonable steps to identify someone to consult. That person (the consultee) must be involved in the person's care, interested in their welfare and must be willing to help. They must not be a professional or paid care worker. They will probably be a family member, but could be another person.

11.24 The researcher must take into account previous wishes and feelings that the person might have expressed about who they would, or would not, like involved in future decisions.

11.25 A person is not prevented from being consulted if they are an attorney authorised under a registered Lasting Power of Attorney or are a deputy appointed by the Court of Protection. But that person must not be acting in a professional or paid capacity (for example, person's solicitor).

11.26 Where there is no-one who meets the conditions mentioned at paragraphs 11.23 and 11.25, the researcher must nominate a person to be the consulted. In this situation, they must follow guidance from the Secretary of State for Health in England or the National Assembly for Wales (the guidance will be available from mid-2007). The person who is nominated must have no connection with the research project.

11.27 The researcher must provide the consultee with information about the research project and ask them:
- for advice about whether the person who lacks capacity should take part in the project, and
- what they think the person's feelings and wishes would be, if they had capacity to decide whether to take part.

11.28 Sometimes the consultee will say that the person would probably not take part in the project or that they would ask to be withdrawn. In this situation, the researcher must not include the person in the project, or they should withdraw them from it. But if the project has started, and the person is getting treatment as part of the research, the researcher may decide that the person should not be withdrawn if the researcher reasonably believes that this would cause a significant risk to the person's health. The researcher may decide that the person should continue with the research while the risk exists. But they should stop any parts of the study that are not related to the risk to the person's health.

What other safeguards does the Act require?

11.29 Even when a consultee agrees that a person can take part in research, the researcher must still consider the person's wishes and feelings.

11.30 Researchers must not do anything the person who lacks capacity objects to. They must not do anything to go against any advance decision to refuse treatment or other statement the person has previously made expressing preferences about their care or treatment. They must assume that the person's interests in this matter are more important than those of science and society.

11.31 A researcher must withdraw someone from a project if:
- they indicate in any way that they want to be withdrawn from the project (for example, if they become upset or distressed), or
- any of the Act's requirements are no longer met.

What happens if urgent decisions are required during the research project?

11.32 Anyone responsible for caring for a person must give them urgent treatment if they need it. In some circumstances, it may not be possible to separate the research from the urgent treatment.

11.33 A research proposal should explain to the appropriate body how researchers will deal with urgent decisions which may occur during the project, when there may not be time to carry out the consultations required under the Act. For example, after a patient has arrived in intensive care, the doctor may want to chart the course of an injury by taking samples or measurements immediately and then taking further samples after some type of treatment to compare with the first set.

11.34 Special rules apply where a person who lacks capacity is getting, or about to get, urgent treatment and researchers want to include them in a research project. If in these circumstances a researcher thinks that it is necessary to take urgent action for the purposes of the research, and they think it is not practical to consult someone about it, the researcher can take that action if:
- they get agreement from a registered medical practitioner not involved with the research, or
- they follow a procedure that the appropriate body agreed to at approval stage.

11.35 The medical practitioner may have a connection to the person who lacks capacity (for example, they might be their doctor). But they must not be involved in the research project in any way. This is to avoid conflicts of interest.

11.36 This exception to the duty to consult only applies:
- for as long as the person needs urgent treatment, and
- when the researcher needs to take action urgently for research to be valid.

It is likely to be limited to research into procedures or treatments used in emergencies. It does not apply where the researcher simply wants to act quickly.

What happens for research involving human tissue?

11.37 A person with capacity has to give their permission for someone to remove tissue from their body (for example, taking a biopsy (a sample) for diagnosis or removal of tissue in surgery). The Act allows the removal of tissue from the body of a person who lacks capacity, if it is in their best interests (see Chapter 5).

11.38 People with capacity must also give permission for the storage or use of tissue for certain purposes, set out in the Human Tissue Act 2004, (for example, transplants and research). But there are situations in which permission is not required by law:
- research where the samples are anonymised and the research has ethical approval[52]
- clinical audit
- education or training relating to human health
- performance assessment
- public health monitoring, and
- quality assurance.

11.39 If an adult lacks capacity to consent, the Human Tissue Act 2004 says that tissue can be stored or used without seeking permission if the storage or use is:
- to get information relevant to the health of another individual (for example, before conducting a transplant), as long as the researcher or healthcare professional storing or using the human tissue believes they are doing it in the best interests of the person who lacks capacity to consent
- for a clinical trial approved and carried out under the Medicines for Human Use (Clinical Trials) Regulations 2004, or
- for intrusive research:
  - after the Mental Capacity Act comes into force
  - that meets the Act's requirements, and
  - that has ethical approval.

11.40 Tissue samples that were obtained before 31 August 2006 are existing holdings under the Human Tissue Act. Researchers can work with these

---

[52] Section 1(9) of the Human Tissue Act 2004.

tissues without seeking permission. But they will still need to get ethical approval. Guidance is available in the Human Tissue Authority Code of Practice on consent.[53]

What should happen to research that started before the Act came into force?

What if a person has capacity when research starts but loses capacity?

11.41 Some people with capacity will agree to take part in research but may then lose capacity before the end of the project. In this situation, researchers will be able to continue research as long as they comply with the conditions set out in the Mental Capacity Act 2005 (Loss of Capacity During Research Project) (England) Regulations 2007 or equivalent Welsh regulations.

The regulations only apply to tissue and data collected before the loss of capacity from a person who gave consent before 31 March 2008 to join a project that starts before 1 October 2007.

11.42 The regulations do not cover research involving direct intervention (for example, taking of further blood pressure readings) or the taking of further tissue after loss of capacity. Such research must comply with sections 30 to 33 of the Act to be lawful.

11.43 Where the regulations do apply, research can only continue if the project already has procedures to deal with people who lose capacity during the project. An appropriate body must have approved the procedures. The researcher must follow the procedures that have been approved.

11.44 The researcher must also:
- seek out the views of someone involved in the person's care or interested in their welfare and if a carer can't be found they must nominate a consultee (see paragraphs 11.22–11.28)
- respect advance decisions and expressed preferences, wishes or objections that the person has made in the past, and
- treat the person's interests as more important than those of science and society.

The appropriate body must be satisfied that the research project has reasonable arrangements to meet these requirements.

11.45 If at any time the researcher believes that procedures are no longer in place or the appropriate body no longer approves the research, they must stop research on the person immediately.

11.46 Where regulations do apply, research does not have to:
- be linked to an impairing condition of the person
- have the potential to benefit that person, or

---

[53] www.hta.gov.uk.

- aim to provide knowledge relevant to others with the same or a similar condition.

What happens to existing projects that a person never had capacity to agree to?

11.47 There are no regulations for projects that:
- started before the Act comes into force, and
- a person never had the capacity to agree to.

Projects that already have ethical approval will need to obtain approval from an appropriate body under sections 30 and 31 of the Mental Capacity Act and to comply with the requirements of sections 32 and 33 of that Act by 1 October 2008. Research that does not have ethical approval must get approval from an appropriate body by 1 October 2007 to continue lawfully. This is the case in England and it is expected that similar arrangements will apply in Wales.

12   HOW DOES THE ACT APPLY TO CHILDREN AND YOUNG PEOPLE?

This chapter looks at the few parts of the Act that may affect children under 16 years of age. It also explains the position of young people aged 16 and 17 years and the overlapping laws that affect them.

This chapter does not deal with research. Further guidance will be provided on how the Act applies in relation to research involving those under the age of 18.

Within this Code of Practice, 'children' refers to people aged below 16. 'Young people' refers to people aged 16–17. This differs from the Children Act 1989 and the law more generally, where the term 'child' is used to refer to people aged under 18.

> In this chapter, as throughout the Code, a person's capacity (or lack of capacity) refers specifically to their capacity to make a particular decision at the time it needs to be made.

Quick summary

Children under 16

- The Act does not generally apply to people under the age of 16.
- There are two exceptions:
  - The Court of Protection can make decisions about a child's property or finances (or appoint a deputy to make these decisions) if the child

lacks capacity to make such decisions within section 2(1) of the Act and is likely to still lack capacity to make financial decisions when they reach the age of 18 (section 18(3)).
  – Offences of ill treatment or wilful neglect of a person who lacks capacity within section 2(1) can also apply to victims younger than 16 (section 44).

Young people aged 16–17 years

- Most of the Act applies to young people aged 16–17 years, who may lack capacity within section 2(1) to make specific decisions.
- There are three exceptions:
  – Only people aged 18 and over can make a Lasting Power of Attorney (LPA).
  – Only people aged 18 and over can make an advance decision to refuse medical treatment.
  – The Court of Protection may only make a statutory will for a person aged 18 and over.

Care or treatment for young people aged 16–17

- People carrying out acts in connection with the care or treatment of a young person aged 16–17 who lacks capacity to consent within section 2(1) will generally have protection from liability (section 5), as long as the person carrying out the act:
  – has taken reasonable steps to establish that the young person lacks capacity
  – reasonably believes that the young person lacks capacity and that the act is in the young person's best interests, and
  – follows the Act's principles.
- When assessing the young person's best interests (see Chapter 5), the person providing care or treatment must consult those involved in the young person's care and anyone interested in their welfare – if it is practical and appropriate to do so. This may include the young person's parents. Care should be taken not to unlawfully breach the young person's right to confidentiality (see Chapter 16).
- Nothing in section 5 excludes a person's civil liability for loss or damage, or his criminal liability, resulting from his negligence in carrying out the act.

Legal proceedings involving young people aged 16-17

- Sometimes there will be disagreements about the care, treatment or welfare of a young person aged 16 or 17 who lacks capacity to make relevant decisions. Depending on the circumstances, the case may be heard in the family courts or the Court of Protection.

- The Court of Protection may transfer a case to the family courts, and vice versa.

Does the Act apply to children?

12.1 Section 2(5) of the Act states that, with the exception of section 2(6), as explained below, no powers under the Act may be exercised in relation to a child under 16.

12.2 Care and treatment of children under the age of 16 is generally governed by common law principles. Further information is provide at www.dh.gov.uk/consent.

Can the Act help with decisions about a child's property or finances?

12.3 Section 2(6) makes an exception for some decisions about a child's property and financial affairs. The Court of Protection can make decisions about property and affairs of those under 16 in cases where the person is likely to still lack capacity to make financial decisions after reaching the age of 18. The court's ruling will still apply when the person reaches the age of 18, which means there will not be a need for further court proceedings once the person reaches the age of 18.

12.4 The Court of Protection can:
- make an order (for example, concerning the investment of an award of compensation for the child), and/or
- appoint a deputy to manage the child's property and affairs and to make ongoing financial decisions on the child's behalf.

In making a decision, the court must follow the Act's principles and decide in the child's best interests as set out in Chapter 5 of the Code.

Scenario: *Applying the Act to children*

Tom was nine when a drunk driver knocked him off his bicycle. He suffered severe head injuries and permanent brain damage. He received a large amount of money in compensation. He is unlikely to recover enough to be able to make financial decisions when he is 18. So the Court of Protection appoints Tom's father as deputy to manage his financial affairs in order to pay for the care Tom will need in the future.

What if somebody mistreats or neglects a child who lacks capacity?

12.5 Section 44 covers the offences of ill treatment or wilful neglect of a person who lacks capacity to make relevant decisions (see Chapter 14). This section also applies to children under 16 and young people aged 16 or 17.

But it only applies if the child's lack of capacity to make a decision for themselves is caused by an impairment or disturbance that affects how their mind or brain works (see Chapter 4). If the lack of capacity is solely the result of the child's youth or immaturity, then the ill treatment or wilful neglect would be dealt with under the separate offences of child cruelty or neglect.

Does the Act apply to young people aged 16–17?

12.6 Most of the Act applies to people aged 16 years and over. There is an overlap with the Children Act 1989. For the Act to apply to a young person, they must lack capacity to make a particular decision (in line with the Act's definition of lack of capacity described in Chapter 4). In such situations either this Act or the Children Act 1989 may apply, depending upon the particular circumstances.

However, there may also be situations where neither of these Acts provides an appropriate solution. In such cases, it may be necessary to look to the powers available under the Mental Health Act 1983 or the High Court's inherent powers to deal with cases involving young people.

12.7 There are currently no specific rules for deciding when to use either the Children Act 1989 or the Mental Capacity Act 2005 or when to apply to the High Court. But, the examples below show circumstances where this Act may be the most appropriate (see also paragraphs 12.21–12.23 below).

- In unusual circumstances it might be in a young person's best interests for the Court of Protection to make an order and/or appoint a property and affairs deputy. For example, this might occur when a young person receives financial compensation and the court appoints a parent or a solicitor as a property and affairs deputy.
- It may be appropriate for the Court of Protection to make a welfare decision concerning a young person who lacks capacity to decide for themselves (for example, about where the young person should live) if the court decides that the parents are not acting in the young person's best interests.
- It might be appropriate to refer a case to the Court of Protection where there is disagreement between a person interested in the care and welfare of a young person and the young person's medical team about the young person's best interests or capacity.

Do any parts of the Act not apply to young people aged 16 or 17?

LPAs

12.8 Only people aged 18 or over can make a Lasting Power of Attorney (LPA) (section 9(2)(c)).

Advance decisions to refuse treatment

12.9 Information on decisions to refuse treatment made in advance by young people under the age of 18 will be available at www.dh.gov.uk/consent.

Making a will

12.10 The law generally does not allow anyone below the age of 18 to make a will. So section 18(2) confirms that the Court of Protection can only make a statutory will on behalf of those aged 18 and over.

What does the Act say about care or treatment of young people aged 16 or 17?

Background information concerning competent young people

12.11 The Family Law Reform Act 1969 presumes that young people have the legal capacity to agree to surgical, medical or dental treatment.[54] This also applies to any associated procedures (for example, investigations, anaesthesia or nursing care).

12.12 It does not apply to some rarer types of procedure (for example, organ donation or other procedures which are not therapeutic for the young person) or research. In those cases, anyone under 18 is presumed to lack legal capacity, subject to the test of 'Gillick competence' (testing whether they are mature and intelligent enough to understand a proposed treatment or procedure).[55]

12.13 Even where a young person is presumed to have legal capacity to consent to treatment, they may not necessarily be able to make the relevant decision. As with adults, decision-makers should assess the young person's capacity to consent to the proposed care or treatment (see Chapter 4). If a young person lacks capacity to consent within section 2(1) of the Act because of an impairment of, or a disturbance in the functioning of, the mind or brain then the Mental Capacity Act will apply in the same way as it does to those who are 18 and over. If however they are unable to make the decision for some other reason, for example because they are overwhelmed by the implications of the decision, the Act will not apply to them and the legality of any treatment should be assessed under common law principles.

---

[54] Family Law Reform Act 1969, s 8(1).

[55] In the case of *Gillick v West Norfolk and Wisbech Area Health Authority* [1986] 1 AC 112 the court found that a child below 16 years of age will be competent to consent to medical treatment if they have sufficient intelligence and understanding to understand what is proposed. This test applies in relation to all people under 18 where there is no presumption of competence in relation to the procedure – for example where the procedure is not one referred to in section 8 of the Family Law Reform Act 1969, eg organ donation.

12.14 If a young person has capacity to agree to treatment, their decision to consent must be respected. Difficult issues can arise if a young person has legal and mental capacity and refuses consent – especially if a person with parental responsibility wishes to give consent on the young person's behalf. The Family Division of the High Court can hear cases where there is disagreement. The Court of Protection has no power to settle a dispute about a young person who is said to have the mental capacity to make the specific decision.

12.15 It may be unclear whether a young person lacks capacity within section 2(1) of the Act. In those circumstances, it would be prudent for the person providing care or treatment for the young person to seek a declaration from the court.

If the young person lacks capacity to make care or treatment decisions

12.16 Under the common law, a person with parental responsibility for a young person is generally able to consent to the young person receiving care or medical treatment where they lack capacity under section 2(1) of the Act. They should act in the young person's best interests.

12.17 However if a young person lacks the mental capacity to make a specific care or treatment decision within section 2(1) of the Act, healthcare staff providing treatment, or a person providing care to the young person, can carry out treatment or care with protection from liability (section 5) whether or not a person with parental responsibility consents.[56] They must follow the Act's principles and make sure that the actions they carry out are in the young person's best interests. They must make every effort to work out and consider the young person's wishes, feelings, beliefs and values – both past and present – and consider all other factors in the best interests checklist (see Chapter 5).

12.18 When assessing a young person's best interests, healthcare staff must take into account the views of anyone involved in caring for the young person and anyone interested in their welfare, where it is practical and appropriate to do so. This may include the young person's parents and others with parental responsibility for the young person. Care should be taken not to unlawfully breach the young person's right to confidentiality (see Chapter 16).

12.19 If a young person has said they do not want their parents to be consulted, it may not be appropriate to involve them (for example, where there have been allegations of abuse).

12.20 If there is a disagreement about whether the proposed care or treatment is in the best interests of a young person, or there is disagreement about whether the young person lacks capacity and there is no other way of

---

[56] Nothing in section 5 excludes a person's civil liability for loss or damage, or his criminal liability, resulting from his negligence in doing the Act.

resolving the matter, it would be prudent for those in disagreement to seek a declaration or other order from the appropriate court (see paragraphs 12.23–12.25 below).

Scenario: *Working out a young person's best interests*

Mary is 16 and has Down's syndrome. Her mother wants Mary to have dental treatment that will improve her appearance but is not otherwise necessary.

To be protected under section 5 of the Act, the dentist must consider whether Mary has capacity to agree to the treatment and what would be in her best interests. He decides that she is unable to understand what is involved or the possible consequences of the proposed treatment and so lacks capacity to make the decision.

But Mary seems to want the treatment, so he takes her views into account in deciding whether the treatment is in her best interests. He also consults with both her parents and with her teacher and GP to see if there are other relevant factors to take into account.

He decides that the treatment is likely to improve Mary's confidence and self-esteem and is in her best interests.

12.21 There may be particular difficulties where young people with mental health problems require in-patient psychiatric treatment, and are treated informally rather than detained under the Mental Health Act 1983. The Mental Capacity Act and its principles apply to decisions related to the care and treatment of young people who lack mental capacity to consent, including treatment for mental disorder. As with any other form of treatment, somebody assessing a young person's best interests should consult anyone involved in caring for the young person or anyone interested in their welfare, as far as is practical and appropriate. This may include the young person's parents or those with parental responsibility for the young person.

But the Act does not allow any actions that result in a young person being deprived of their liberty (see Chapter 6). In such circumstances, detention under the Mental Health Act 1983 and the safeguards provided under that Act might be appropriate (see also Chapter 13).

12.22 People may disagree about a young person's capacity to make the specific decision or about their best interests, or it may not be clear whether they lack capacity within section 2(1) or for some other reason. In this situation, legal proceedings may be necessary if there is no other way of settling the disagreement (see Chapters 8 and 15). If those involved in caring for the young person or who are interested in the young person's welfare do not agree with the proposed treatment, it may be necessary for an interested party to make an application to the appropriate court.

What powers do the courts have in cases involving young people?

12.23 A case involving a young person who lacks mental capacity to make a specific decision could be heard in the family courts (probably in the Family Division of the High Court) or in the Court of Protection.

12.24 If a case might require an ongoing order (because the young person is likely to still lack capacity when they are 18), it may be more appropriate for the Court of Protection to hear the case. For one-off cases not involving property or finances, the Family Division may be more appropriate.

12.25 So that the appropriate court hears a case, the Court of Protection can transfer cases to the family courts, and vice versa (section 21).

Scenario: Hearing cases in the appropriate court

Shola is 17. She has serious learning disabilities and lacks the capacity to decide where she should live. Her parents are involved in a bitter divorce. They cannot agree on several issues concerning Shola's care – including where she should live. Her mother wants to continue to look after Shola at home. But her father wants Shola to move into a care home.

In this case, it may be more appropriate for the Court of Protection to deal with the case. This is because an order made in the Court of Protection could continue into Shola's adulthood. However an order made by the family court under the Children Act 1989 would end on Shola's eighteenth birthday.

---

13   WHAT IS THE RELATIONSHIP BETWEEN THE MENTAL CAPACITY ACT AND THE MENTAL HEALTH ACT 1983?

This chapter explains the relationship between the Mental Capacity Act 2005 (MCA) and the Mental Health Act 1983 (MHA). It:

- sets out when it may be appropriate to detain someone under the MHA rather than to rely on the MCA

- describes how the MCA affects people lacking capacity who are also subject to the MHA

- explains when doctors cannot give certain treatments for a mental disorder (in particular, psychosurgery) to someone who lacks capacity to consent to it, and

- sets out changes that the Government is planning to make to both Acts.

It does not provide a full description of the MHA. The MHA has its own Memorandum to explain the Act and its own Code of Practice to guide people about how to use it.[57]

> In this chapter, as throughout the Code, a person's capacity (or lack of capacity) refers specifically to their capacity to make a particular decision at the time it needs to be made.

Quick summary

- Professionals may need to think about using the MHA to detain and treat somebody who lacks capacity to consent to treatment (rather than use the MCA), if:
    - it is not possible to give the person the care or treatment they need without doing something that might deprive them of their liberty
    - the person needs treatment that cannot be given under the MCA (for example, because the person has made a valid and applicable advance decision to refuse an essential part of treatment)
    - the person may need to be restrained in a way that is not allowed under the MCA
    - it is not possible to assess or treat the person safely or effectively without treatment being compulsory (perhaps because the person is expected to regain capacity to consent, but might then refuse to give consent)
    - the person lacks capacity to decide on some elements of the treatment but has capacity to refuse a vital part of it – and they have done so, or
    - there is some other reason why the person might not get treatment, and they or somebody else might suffer harm as a result.
- Before making an application under the MHA, decision-makers should consider whether they could achieve their aims safely and effectively by using the MCA instead.
- Compulsory treatment under the MHA is not an option if:
    - the patient's mental disorder does not justify detention in hospital, or
    - the patient needs treatment only for a physical illness or disability.
- The MCA applies to people subject to the MHA in the same way as it applies to anyone else, with four exceptions:
    - if someone is detained under the MHA, decision-makers cannot normally rely on the MCA to give treatment for mental disorder or make decisions about that treatment on that person's behalf

---

[57]   Department of Health & Welsh Office, *Mental Health Act 1983 Code of Practice* (TSO, 1999), www.dh.gov.uk/assetRoot/04/07/49/61/04074961.pdf.

- – if somebody can be treated for their mental disorder without their consent because they are detained under the MHA, healthcare staff can treat them even if it goes against an advance decision to refuse that treatment
- – if a person is subject to guardianship, the guardian has the exclusive right to take certain decisions, including where the person is to live, and
- – Independent Mental Capacity Advocates do not have to be involved in decisions about serious medical treatment or accommodation, if those decisions are made under the MHA.
- Healthcare staff cannot give psychosurgery (i.e. neurosurgery for mental disorder) to a person who lacks capacity to agree to it. This applies whether or not the person is otherwise subject to the MHA.

Who does the MHA apply to?

13.1 The MHA provides ways of assessing, treating and caring for people who have a serious mental disorder that puts them or other people at risk. It sets out when:
- people with mental disorders can be detained in hospital for assessment or treatment
- people who are detained can be given treatment for their mental disorder without their consent (it also sets out the safeguards people must get in this situation), and
- people with mental disorders can be made subject to guardianship or after-care under supervision to protect them or other people.

13.2 Most of the MHA does not distinguish between people who have the capacity to make decisions and those who do not. Many people covered by the MHA have the capacity to make decisions for themselves. Most people who lack capacity to make decisions about their treatment will never be affected by the MHA, even if they need treatment for a mental disorder.

13.3 But there are cases where decision-makers will need to decide whether to use the MHA or MCA, or both, to meet the needs of people with mental health problems who lack capacity to make decisions about their own treatment.

What are the MCA's limits?

13.4 Section 5 of the MCA provides legal protection for people who care for or treat someone who lacks capacity (see Chapter 6). But they must follow the Act's principles and may only take action that is in a person's best interests (see Chapter 5). This applies to care or treatment for physical and mental conditions. So it can apply to treatment for people with mental disorders, however serious those disorders are.

13.5 But section 5 does have its limits. For example, somebody using restraint only has protection if the restraint is:

- necessary to protect the person who lacks capacity from harm, and
- in proportion to the likelihood and seriousness of that harm.

13.6 There is no protection under section 5 for actions that deprive a person of their liberty (see Chapter 6 for guidance). Similarly, the MCA does not allow giving treatment that goes against a valid and applicable advance decision to refuse treatment (see Chapter 9).

13.7 None of these restrictions apply to treatment for mental disorder given under the MHA – but other restrictions do.

When can a person be detained under the MHA?

13.8 A person may be taken into hospital and detained for assessment under section 2 of the MHA for up to 28 days if:

- they have a mental disorder that is serious enough for them to be detained in a hospital for assessment (or for assessment followed by treatment) for at least a limited period, and
- they need to be detained to protect their health or safety, or to protect others.

13.9 A patient may be admitted to hospital and detained for treatment under section 3 of the MHA if:

- they have a mental illness, severe mental impairment, psychopathic disorder or mental impairment (the MHA sets out definitions for these last three terms)
- their mental disorder is serious enough to need treatment in hospital
- treatment is needed for the person's health or safety, or for the protection of other people – and it cannot be provided without detention under this section, and
- (if the person has a mental impairment or psychopathic disorder) treatment is likely to improve their condition or stop it getting worse.

13.10 Decision-makers should consider using the MHA if, in their professional judgment, they are not sure it will be possible, or sufficient, to rely on the MCA. They do not have to ask the Court of Protection to rule that the MCA does not apply before using the MHA.

13.11 If a clinician believes that they can safely assess or treat a person under the MCA, they do not need to consider using the MHA. In this situation, it would be difficult to meet the requirements of the MHA anyway.

13.12 It might be necessary to consider using the MHA rather than the MCA if:

- it is not possible to give the person the care or treatment they need without carrying out an action that might deprive them of their liberty
- the person needs treatment that cannot be given under the MCA (for example, because the person has made a valid and applicable advance decision to refuse all or part of that treatment)

- the person may need to be restrained in a way that is not allowed under the MCA
- it is not possible to assess or treat the person safely or effectively without treatment being compulsory (perhaps because the person is expected to regain capacity to consent, but might then refuse to give consent)
- the person lacks capacity to decide on some elements of the treatment but has capacity to refuse a vital part of it – and they have done so, or
- there is some other reason why the person might not get the treatment they need, and they or somebody else might suffer harm as a result.

13.13 But it is important to remember that a person cannot be treated under the MHA unless they meet the relevant criteria for being detained. Unless they are sent to hospital under Part 3 of the MHA in connection with a criminal offence, people can only be detained where:
- the conditions summarised in paragraph 13.8 or 13.9 are met
- the relevant people agree that an application is necessary (normally two doctors and an approved social worker), and
- (in the case of section 3) the patient's nearest relative has not objected to the application.

'Nearest relative' is defined in section 26 of the MHA. It is usually, but not always, a family member.

Scenario: *Using the MHA*

Mr Oliver has a learning disability. For the last four years, he has had depression from time to time, and has twice had treatment for it at a psychiatric hospital. He is now seriously depressed and his care workers are worried about him.

Mr Oliver's consultant has given him medication and is considering electro-convulsive therapy. The consultant thinks this care plan will only work if Mr Oliver is detained in hospital. This will allow close observation and Mr Oliver will be stopped if he tries to leave. The consultant thinks an application should be made under section 3 of the MHA.

The consultant also speaks to Mr Oliver's nearest relative, his mother. She asks why Mr Oliver needs to be detained when he has not needed to be in the past. But after she hears the consultant's reasons, she does not object to the application. An approved social worker makes the application and obtains a second medical recommendation. Mr Oliver is then detained and taken to hospital for his treatment for depression to begin.

13.14 Compulsory treatment under the MHA is not an option if:
- the patient's mental disorder does not justify detention in hospital, or

- the patient needs treatment only for a physical illness or disability.

13.15 There will be some cases where a person who lacks capacity cannot be treated either under the MHA or the MCA – even if the treatment is for mental disorder.

Scenario: *Deciding whether to use the MHA or MCA*

Mrs Carter is in her 80s and has dementia. Somebody finds her wandering in the street, very confused and angry. A neighbour takes her home and calls her doctor. At home, it looks like she has been deliberately smashing things. There are cuts on her hands and arms, but she won't let the doctor touch them, and she hasn't been taking her medication.

Her doctor wants to admit her to hospital for assessment. Mrs Carter gets angry and says that they'll never keep her in hospital. So the doctor thinks that it might be necessary to use the MHA. He arranges for an approved social worker to visit. The social worker discovers that Mrs Carter was expecting her son this morning, but he has not turned up. They find out that he has been delayed, but could not call because Mrs Carter's telephone has become unplugged.

When she is told that her son is on his way, Mrs Carter brightens up. She lets the doctor treat her cuts – which the doctor thinks it is in her best interests to do as soon as possible. When Mrs Carter's son arrives, the social worker explains the doctor is very worried, especially that Mrs Carter is not taking her medication. The son explains that he will help his mother take it in future. It is agreed that the MCA will allow him to do that. The social worker arranges to return a week later and calls the doctor to say that she thinks Mrs Carter can get the care she needs without being detained under the MHA. The doctor agrees.

How does the MCA apply to a patient subject to guardianship under the MHA?

13.16 Guardianship gives someone (usually a local authority social services department) the exclusive right to decide where a person should live – but in doing this they cannot deprive the person of their liberty. The guardian can also require the person to attend for treatment, work, training or education at specific times and places, and they can demand that a doctor, approved social worker or another relevant person have access to the person wherever they live. Guardianship can apply whether or not the person has the capacity to make decisions about care and treatment. It does not give anyone the right to treat the person without their permission or to consent to treatment on their behalf.

13.17 An application can be made for a person who has a mental disorder to be received into guardianship under section 7 of the MHA when:

- the situation meets the conditions summarised in paragraph 13.18
- the relevant people agree an application for guardianship should be made (normally two doctors and an approved social worker), and
- the person's nearest relative does not object.

13.18 An application can be made in relation to any person who is 16 years or over if:

- they have a mental illness, severe mental impairment, psychopathic disorder or mental impairment that is serious enough to justify guardianship (see paragraph 13.20 below), and
- guardianship is necessary in the interests of the welfare of the patient or to protect other people.

13.19 Applicants (usually approved social workers) and doctors supporting the application will need to determine whether they could achieve their aims without guardianship. For patients who lack capacity, the obvious alternative will be action under the MCA.

13.20 But the fact that the person lacks capacity to make relevant decision is not the only factor that applicants need to consider. They need to consider all the circumstances of the case. They may conclude that guardianship is the best option for a person with a mental disorder who lacks capacity to make those decisions if, for example:

- they think it is important that one person or authority should be in charge of making decisions about where the person should live (for example, where there have been long-running or difficult disagreements about where the person should live)
- they think the person will probably respond well to the authority and attention of a guardian, and so be more prepared to accept treatment for the mental disorder (whether they are able to consent to it or it is being provided for them under the MCA), or
- they need authority to return the person to the place they are to live (for example, a care home) if they were to go absent.

Decision-makers must never consider guardianship as a way to avoid applying the MCA.

13.21 A guardian has the exclusive right to decide where a person lives, so nobody else can use the MCA to arrange for the person to live elsewhere. Somebody who knowingly helps a person leave the place a guardian requires them to stay may be committing a criminal offence under the MHA. A guardian also has the exclusive power to require the person to attend set times and places for treatment, occupation, education or training. This does not stop other people using the MCA to make similar arrangements or to treat the person in their best interests. But people cannot use the MCA in any way that conflicts with decisions which a guardian has a legal right to make under the MHA. See paragraph 13.16 above for general information about a guardian's powers.

How does the MCA apply to a patient subject to after-care under supervision under the MHA?

13.22 When people are discharged from detention for medical treatment under the MHA, their responsible medical officer may decide to place them on after-care under supervision. The responsible medical officer is usually the person's consultant psychiatrist. Another doctor and an approved social worker must support their application.

13.23 After-care under supervision means:
- the person can be required to live at a specified place (where they can be taken to and returned, if necessary)
- the person can be required to attend for treatment, occupation, education or training at a specific time and place (where they can be taken, if necessary), and
- their supervisor, any doctor or approved social worker or any other relevant person must be given access to them wherever they live.

13.24 Responsible medical officers can apply for after-care under supervision under section 25A of the MHA if:
- the person is 16 or older and is liable to be detained in a hospital for treatment under section 3 (and certain other sections) of the MHA
- the person has a mental illness, severe mental impairment, psychopathic disorder or mental impairment
- without after-care under supervision the person's health or safety would be at risk of serious harm, they would be at risk of serious exploitation, or other people's safety would be at risk of serious harm, and
- after-care under supervision is likely to help make sure the person gets the after-care services they need.

'Liable to be detained' means that a hospital is allowed to detain them. Patients who are liable to be detained are not always actually in hospital, because they may have been given permission to leave hospital for a time.

13.25 After-care under supervision can be used whether or not the person lacks capacity to make relevant decisions. But if a person lacks capacity, decision-makers will need to decide whether action under the MCA could achieve their aims before making an application. The kinds of cases in which after-care under supervision might be considered for patients who lack capacity to take decisions about their own care and treatment are similar to those for guardianship.

How does the Mental Capacity Act affect people covered by the Mental Health Act?

13.26 There is no reason to assume a person lacks capacity to make their own decisions just because they are subject (under the MHA) to:
- detention
- guardianship, or

- after-care under supervision.

13.27 People who lack capacity to make specific decisions are still protected by the MCA even if they are subject to the MHA (this includes people who are subject to the MHA as a result of court proceedings). But there are four important exceptions:

- if someone is liable to be detained under the MHA, decision-makers cannot normally rely on the MCA to give mental health treatment or make decisions about that treatment on someone's behalf

- if somebody can be given mental health treatment without their consent because they are liable to be detained under the MHA, they can also be given mental health treatment that goes against an advance decision to refuse treatment

- if a person is subject to guardianship, the guardian has the exclusive right to take certain decisions, including where the person is to live, and

- Independent Mental Capacity Advocates do not have to be involved in decisions about serious medical treatment or accommodation, if those decisions are made under the MHA.

What are the implications for people who need treatment for a mental disorder?

13.28 Subject to certain conditions, Part 4 of the MHA allows doctors to give patients who are liable to be detained treatment for mental disorders without their consent – whether or not they have the capacity to give that consent. Paragraph 13.31 below lists a few important exceptions.

13.29 Where Part 4 of the MHA applies, the MCA cannot be used to give medical treatment for a mental disorder to patients who lack capacity to consent. Nor can anyone else, like an attorney or a deputy, use the MCA to give consent for that treatment. This is because Part 4 of the MHA already allows clinicians, if they comply with the relevant rules, to give patients medical treatment for mental disorder even though they lack the capacity to consent. In this context, medical treatment includes nursing and care, habilitation and rehabilitation under medical supervision.

13.30 But clinicians treating people for mental disorder under the MHA cannot simply ignore a person's capacity to consent to treatment. As a matter of good practice (and in some cases in order to comply with the MHA) they will always need to assess and record:
- whether patients have capacity to consent to treatment, and
- if so, whether they have consented to or refused that treatment.
For more information, see the MHA Code of Practice.

13.31 Part 4 of the MHA does not apply to patients:
- admitted in an emergency under section 4(4)(a) of the MHA, following a single medical recommendation and awaiting a second recommendation

- temporarily detained (held in hospital) under section 5 of the MHA while awaiting an application for detention under section 2 or section 3
- remanded by a court to hospital for a report on their medical condition under section 35 of the MHA
- detained under section 37(4), 135 or 136 of the MHA in a place of safety, or
- who have been conditionally discharged by the Mental Health Review Tribunal (and not recalled to hospital).

13.32 Since the MHA does not allow treatment for these patients without their consent, the MCA applies in the normal way, even if the treatment is for mental disorder.

13.33 Even when the MHA allows patients to be treated for mental disorders, the MCA applies in the normal way to treatment for physical disorders. But sometimes healthcare staff may decide to focus first on treating a detained patient's mental disorder in the hope that they will get back the capacity to make a decision about treatment for the physical disorder.

13.34 Where people are subject to guardianship or after-care under supervision under the MHA, the MCA applies as normal to all treatment. Guardianship and after-care under supervision do not give people the right to treat patients without consent.

Scenario: Using the MCA to treat a patient who is detained under the MHA

Mr Peters is detained in hospital under section 3 of the MHA and is receiving treatment under Part 4 of the MHA. Mr Peters has paranoid schizophrenia, delusions, hallucinations and thought disorder. He refuses all medical treatment. Mr Peters has recently developed blood in his urine and staff persuaded him to have an ultrasound scan. The scan revealed suspected renal carcinoma.

His consultant believes that he needs a CT scan and treatment for the carcinoma. But Mr Peters refuses a general anaesthetic and other medical procedures. The consultant assesses Mr Peters as lacking capacity to consent to treatment under the MCA's test of capacity. The MHA is not relevant here, because the CT scan is not part of Mr Peters' treatment for mental disorder.

Under section 5 of the MCA, doctors can provide treatment without consent. But they must follow the principles of the Act and believe that treatment is in Mr Peters' best interests.

How does the Mental Health Act affect advance decisions to refuse treatment?

13.35 The MHA does not affect a person's advance decision to refuse treatment, unless Part 4 of the MHA means the person can be treated for mental disorder without their consent. In this situation healthcare staff can treat patients for their mental disorder, even if they have made an advance decision to refuse such treatment.

13.36 But even then healthcare staff must treat a valid and applicable advance decision as they would a decision made by a person with capacity at the time they are asked to consent to treatment. For example, they should consider whether they could use a different type of treatment which the patient has not refused in advance. If healthcare staff do not follow an advance decision, they should record in the patient's notes why they have chosen not to follow it.

13.37 Even if a patient is being treated without their consent under Part 4 of the MHA, an advance decision to refuse other forms of treatment is still valid. Being subject to guardianship or after-care under supervision does not affect an advance decision in any way. See Chapter 9 for further guidance on advance decisions to refuse treatment.

Scenario: Deciding on whether to follow an advance decision to refuse treatment

Miss Khan gets depression from time to time and has old physical injuries that cause her pain. She does not like the side effects of medication, and manages her health through diet and exercise. She knows that healthcare staff might doubt her decision-making capacity when she is depressed. So she makes an advance decision to refuse all medication for her physical pain and depression.

A year later, she gets major depression and is detained under the MHA. Her GP (family doctor) tells her responsible medical officer (RMO) at the hospital about her advance decision. But Miss Khan's condition gets so bad that she will not discuss treatment. So the RMO decides to prescribe medication for her depression, despite her advance decision. This is possible because Miss Khan is detained under the MHA.

The RMO also believes that Miss Khan now lacks capacity to consent to medication for her physical pain. He assesses the validity of the advance decision to refuse medication for the physical pain. Her GP says that Miss Khan seemed perfectly well when she made the decision and seemed to understand what it meant. In the GP's view, Miss Khan had the capacity to make the advance decision. The RMO decides that the advance decision is valid and applicable, and does not prescribe medication for Miss Khan's pain – even though he thinks it would be in →

---

her best interests. When Miss Khan's condition improves, the consultant will be able to discuss whether she would like to change her mind about treatment for her physical pain.

Does the MHA affect the duties of attorneys and deputies?

13.38 In general, the MHA does not affect the powers of attorneys and deputies. But there are two exceptions:
- they will not be able to give consent on a patient's behalf for treatment under Part 4 of the MHA, where the patient is liable to be detained under the MHA (see 13.28–13.34 above), and
- they will not be able to take decisions:
  - about where a person subject to guardianship should live, or
  - that conflict with decisions that a guardian has a legal right to make.

13.39 Being subject to the MHA does not stop patients creating new Lasting Powers of Attorney (if they have the capacity to do so). Nor does it stop the Court of Protection from appointing a deputy for them.

13.40 In certain cases, people subject to the MHA may be required to meet specific conditions relating to:
- leave of absence from hospital
- after-care under supervision, or
- conditional discharge.

Conditions vary from case to case, but could include a requirement to:
- live in a particular place
- maintain contact with health services, or
- avoid a particular area.

13.41 If an attorney or deputy takes a decision that goes against one of these conditions, the patient will be taken to have gone against the condition. The MHA sets out the actions that could be taken in such circumstances. In the case of leave of absence or conditional discharge, this might involve the patient being recalled to hospital.

13.42 Attorneys and deputies are able to exercise patients' rights under the MHA on their behalf, if they have the relevant authority. In particular, some personal welfare attorneys and deputies may be able to apply to the Mental Health Review Tribunal (MHRT) for the patient's discharge from detention, guardianship or after-care under supervision.

13.43 The MHA also gives various rights to a patient's nearest relative. These include the right to:
- insist that a local authority social services department instructs an approved social worker to consider whether the patient should be made subject to the MHA
- apply for the patient to be admitted to hospital or guardianship
- object to an application for admission for treatment
- order the patient's discharge from hospital (subject to certain conditions) and

- order the patient's discharge from guardianship.

13.44 Attorneys and deputies may not exercise these rights, unless they are themselves the nearest relative. If the nearest relative and an attorney or deputy disagree, it may be helpful for them to discuss the issue, perhaps with the assistance of the patient's clinicians or social worker. But ultimately they have different roles and both must act as they think best. An attorney or deputy must act in the patient's best interests.

13.45 It is good practice for clinicians and others involved in the assessment or treatment of patients under the MHA to try to find out if the person has an attorney or deputy. But this may not always be possible. So attorneys and deputies should contact either:

- the healthcare professional responsible for the patient's treatment (generally known as the patient's RMO)
- the managers of the hospital where the patient is detained
- the person's guardian (normally the local authority social services department), or
- the person's supervisor (if the patient is subject to after-care under supervision).

Hospitals that treat detained patients normally have a Mental Health Act Administrator's office, which may be a useful first point of contact.

Does the MHA affect when Independent Mental Capacity Advocates must be instructed?

13.46 As explained in Chapter 10, there is no duty to instruct an Independent Mental Capacity Advocate (IMCA) for decisions about serious medical treatment which is to be given under Part 4 of the MHA. Nor is there a duty to do so in respect of a move into accommodation, or a change of accommodation, if the person in question is to be required to live in it because of an obligation under the MHA. That obligation might be a condition of leave of absence or conditional discharge from hospital or a requirement imposed by a guardian or a supervisor.

13.47 However, the rules for instructing an IMCA for patients subject to the MHA who might undergo serious medical treatment not related to their mental disorder are the same as for any other patient.

13.48 The duty to instruct an IMCA would also apply as normal if accommodation is being planned as part of the after-care under section 117 of the MHA following the person's discharge from detention (and the person is not going to be required to live in it as a condition of after-care under supervision). This is because the person does not have to accept that accommodation.

What is the effect of section 57 of the Mental Health Act on the MCA?

13.49 Section 57 of the MHA states that psychosurgery (neurosurgery for mental disorder) requires:
- the consent of the patient, and
- the approval of an independent doctor and two other people appointed by the Mental Health Act Commission.

Psychosurgery is any surgical operation that destroys brain tissue or the function of brain tissue.

13.50 The same rules apply to other treatments specified in regulations under section 57. Currently, the only treatment included in regulations is the surgical implantation of hormones to reduce a man's sex drive.

13.51 The combined effect of section 57 of the MHA and section 28 of the MCA is, effectively, that a person who lacks the capacity to consent to one of these treatments for mental disorder may never be given it. Healthcare staff cannot use the MCA as an alternative way of giving these kinds of treatment. Nor can an attorney or deputy give permission for them on a person's behalf.

What changes does the Government plan to make to the MHA and the MCA?

13.52 The Government has introduced a Mental Health Bill into Parliament in order to modernise the MHA. Among the changes it proposes to make are:
- some amendments to the criteria for detention, including a new requirement that appropriate medical treatment be available for patients before they can be detained for treatment
- the introduction of supervised treatment in the community for suitable patients following a period of detention and treatment in hospital. This will help make sure that patients get the treatment they need and help stop them relapsing and returning to hospital
- the replacement of the approved social worker with the approved mental health professional. This will open up the possibility of approved mental healthcare professionals being drawn from other disciplines as well as social work. Other changes will open up the possibility of clinicians who are not doctors being approved to take on the role of the responsible medical officer. This role will be renamed the responsible clinician.
- provisions to make it possible for patients to apply to the county court for an unsuitable nearest relative to be replaced, and
- the abolition of after-care under supervision.

13.53 The Bill will also amend the MCA to introduce new procedures and provisions to make relevant decisions but who need to be deprived of their liberty, in their best interests, otherwise than under the Mental Health Act 1983 (the so-called 'Bournewood provisions').[58]

13.54 This chapter, as well as Chapter 6, will be fully revised in due course to reflect those changes. Information about the Government's current proposals in respect of the Bournewood safeguards is available on the Department of Health website. This information includes draft illustrative Code of Practice guidance about the proposed safeguards.[59]

13.55 In the meantime, people taking decisions under both the MCA and the MHA must base those decisions on the Acts as they stand now.

14 WHAT MEANS OF PROTECTION EXIST FOR PEOPLE WHO LACK CAPACITY TO MAKE DECISIONS FOR THEMSELVES?

This chapter describes the different agencies that exist to help make sure that adults who lack capacity to make decisions for themselves are protected from abuse. It also explains the services those agencies provide and how they supervise people who provide care for or make decisions on behalf of people who lack capacity. Finally, it explains what somebody should do if they suspect that somebody is abusing a vulnerable adult who lacks capacity.

> In this chapter, as throughout the Code, a person's capacity (or lack of capacity) refers specifically to their capacity to make a particular decision at the time it needs to be made.

Quick summary

- Always report suspicions of abuse of a person who lacks capacity to the relevant agency.

Concerns about an appointee

- When someone is concerned about the collection or use of social security benefits by an appointee on behalf a person who lacks capacity, they should contact the local Jobcentre Plus. If the appointee is for someone who is over the age of 60, contact The Pension Service.

Concerns about an attorney or deputy

---

[58] This refers to the European Court of Human Rights judgment (5 October 2004) in the case of *HL v The United Kingdom* (Application no, 45508/99).
[59] See www.dh.gov.uk/PublicationsAndStatistics/Publications/PublicationsPolicy AndGuidance/PublicationsPolicyAndGuidanceArticle/fs/ en?CONTENT_ID=4141656&chk=jlw07L.

- If someone is concerned about the actions of an attorney or deputy, they should contact the Office of the Public Guardian.

Concerns about a possible criminal offence

- If there is a good reason to suspect that someone has committed a crime against a vulnerable person, such as theft or physical or sexual assault, contact the police.
- In addition, social services should also be contacted, so that they can support the vulnerable person during the investigation.

Concerns about possible ill-treatment or wilful neglect

- The Act introduces new criminal offences of ill treatment or wilful neglect of a person who lacks capacity to make relevant decisions (section 44).
- If someone is not being looked after properly, contact social services.
- In serious cases, contact the police.

Concerns about care standards

- In cases of concern about the standard of care in a care home or an adult placement scheme, or about the care provided by a home care worker, contact social services.
- It may also be appropriate to contact the Commission for Social Care Inspection (in England) or the Care and Social Services Inspectorate for Wales.

Concerns about healthcare or treatment

- If someone is concerned about the care or treatment given to the person in any NHS setting (such as an NHS hospital or clinic) contact the managers of the service.
- It may also be appropriate to make a formal complaint through the NHS complaints procedure (see Chapter 15).

What is abuse?

14.1 The word 'abuse' covers a wide range of actions. In some cases, abuse is clearly deliberate and intentionally unkind. But sometimes abuse happens because somebody does not know how to act correctly – or they haven't got appropriate help and support. It is important to prevent abuse, wherever possible. If somebody is abused, it is important to investigate the abuse and take steps to stop it happening.

14.2 Abuse is anything that goes against a person's human and civil rights. This includes sexual, physical, verbal, financial and emotional abuse. Abuse can be:

- a single act
- a series of repeated acts
- a failure to provide necessary care, or
- neglect.

Abuse can take place anywhere (for example, in a person's own home, a care home or a hospital).

14.3 The main types of abuse are:

Type of abuse	Examples
Financial	<ul><li>theft</li><li>fraud</li><li>undue pressure</li><li>misuse of property, possessions or benefits</li><li>dishonest gain of property, possessions or benefits.</li></ul>
Physical	<ul><li>slapping, pushing, kicking or other forms of violence</li><li>misuse of medication (for example, increasing dosage to make someone drowsy)</li><li>inappropriate punishments (for example, not giving someone a meal because they have been 'bad').</li></ul>
Sexual	<ul><li>rape</li><li>sexual assault</li><li>sexual acts without consent (this includes if a person is not able to give consent or the abuser used pressure).</li></ul>
Psychological	<ul><li>emotional abuse</li><li>threats of harm, restraint or abandonment</li><li>refusing contact with other people</li><li>intimidation</li><li>threats to restrict someone's liberty.</li></ul>
Neglect and acts of omission	<ul><li>ignoring the person's medical or physical care needs</li><li>failing to get healthcare or social care</li><li>withholding medication, food or heating.</li></ul>

14.4 The Department of Health and the National Assembly for Wales have produced separate guidance on protecting vulnerable adults from abuse.

No secrets[60] (England) and *In safe hands*[61] (Wales) both define vulnerable adults as people aged 18 and over who:

- need community care services due to a mental disability, other disability, age or illness, and
- may be unable to take care of themselves or protect themselves against serious harm or exploitation.

This description applies to many people who lack capacity to make decisions for themselves.

14.5 Anyone who thinks that someone might be abusing a vulnerable adult who lacks capacity should:

- contact the local social services (see paragraphs 14.27–14.28 below)
- contact the Office of the Public Guardian (see paragraph 14.8 below), or
- seek advice from a relevant telephone helpline[62] or through the Community Legal Service.[63]

Full contact details are provided in Annex A.

14.6 In most cases, local adult protection procedures will say who should take action (see paragraphs 14.28–14.29 below). But some abuse will be a criminal offence, such as physical assault, sexual assault or rape, theft, fraud and some other forms of financial exploitation. In these cases, the person who suspects abuse should contact the police urgently. The criminal investigation may take priority over all other forms of investigation. So all agencies will have to work together to plan the best way to investigate possible abuse.

14.7 The Fraud Act 2006 (due to come into force in 2007) creates a new offence of 'fraud by abuse of position'. This new offence may apply to a range of people, including:

- attorneys under a Lasting Power of Attorney (LPA) or an Enduring Power of Attorney (EPA), or
- deputies appointed by the Court of Protection to make financial decisions on behalf of a person who lacks capacity.

Attorneys and deputies may be guilty of fraud if they dishonestly abuse their position, intend to benefit themselves or others, and cause loss or expose a person to the risk of loss. People who suspect fraud should report the case to the police.

---

[60] Department of Health and Home Office, *No secrets: Guidance on developing and implementing multi-agency policies and procedures to protect vulnerable adults from abuse*, (2000) www.dh.gov.uk/assetRoot/04/07/45/40/04074540.pdf.

[61] National Assembly for Wales, *In safe hands: Implementing adult protection procedures in Wales* (update 2003) available to order from http://welshgovernmentpublications.soutron.net/publications/ (Note: new website address inserted by authors).

[62] For example, the Action on Elder Abuse (0808 808 8141), Age Concern (0800 009966) or CarersLine (0808 808 7777).

[63] Community Legal Service Direct www.clsdirect.org.uk.

How does the Act protect people from abuse?

The Office of the Public Guardian

14.8 Section 57 of the Act creates a new Public Guardian, supported by staff of the Office of the Public Guardian (OPG). The Public Guardian helps protect people who lack capacity by:
- setting up and managing a register of LPAs
- setting up and managing a register of EPAs
- setting up and managing a register of court orders that appoint deputies
- supervising deputies, working with other relevant organisations (for example, social services, if the person who lacks capacity is receiving social care)
- sending Court of Protection Visitors to visit people who may lack capacity to make particular decisions and those who have formal powers to act on their behalf (see paragraphs 14.10–14.11 below)
- receiving reports from attorneys acting under LPAs and from deputies
- providing reports to the Court of Protection, as requested, and
- dealing with representations (including complaints) about the way in which attorneys or deputies carry out their duties.

14.9 Section 59 of the Act creates a Public Guardian Board to oversee and review how the Public Guardian carries out these duties.

Court of Protection Visitors

14.10 The role of a Court of Protection Visitor is to provide independent advice to the court and the Public Guardian. They advise on how anyone given power under the Act should be, and is, carrying out their duties and responsibilities. There are two types of visitor: General Visitors and Special Visitors. Special visitors are registered medical practitioners with relevant expertise. The court or Public Guardian can send whichever type of visitor is most appropriate to visit and interview a person who may lack capacity. Visitors can also interview attorneys or deputies and inspect any relevant healthcare or social care records. Attorneys and deputies must co-operate with the visitors and provide them with all relevant information. If attorneys or deputies do not co-operate, the court can cancel their appointment, where it thinks that they have not acted in the person's best interests.

Scenario: Using a General Visitor

Mrs Quinn made an LPA appointing her nephew, Ian, as her financial attorney. She recently lost capacity to make her own financial decisions, and Ian has registered the LPA. He has taken control of Mrs Quinn's financial affairs. ➞

> But Mrs Quinn's niece suspects that Ian is using Mrs Quinn's money to pay off his own debts. She contacts the OPG, which sends a General Visitor to visit Mrs Quinn and Ian. The visitor's report will assess the facts. It might suggest the case go to court to consider whether Ian has behaved in a way which:
>
> • goes against his authority under the LPA, or
> • is not in Mrs Quinn's best interests.
>
> The Public Guardian will decide whether the court should be involved in the matter. The court will then decide if it requires further evidence. If it thinks that Ian is abusing his position, the court may cancel the LPA.

14.11 Court of Protection Visitors have an important part to play in investigating possible abuse. But their role is much wider than this. They can also check on the general wellbeing of the person who lacks capacity, and they can give support to attorneys and deputies who need help to carry out their duties.

How does the Public Guardian oversee LPAs?

14.12 An LPA is a private arrangement between the donor and the attorney (see Chapter 7). Donors should only choose attorneys that they can trust. The OPG provides information to help potential donors understand:
• the impact of making an LPA
• what they can give an attorney authority to do
• what to consider when choosing an attorney.

14.13 The Public Guardian must make sure that an LPA meets the Act's requirements. Before registering an LPA, the OPG will check documentation. For property and affairs LPAs, it will check whether an attorney appointed under the LPA is bankrupt since this would revoke the authority.

14.14 The Public Guardian will not usually get involved once somebody has registered an LPA – unless someone is worried about how an attorney is carrying out their duties. If concerns are raised about an attorney, the OPG works closely with organisations such as local authorities and NHS Trusts to carry out investigations.

How does the Public Guardian supervise deputies?

14.15 Individuals do not choose who will act as a deputy for them. The court will make the decision. There are measures to make sure that the court appoints an appropriate deputy. The OPG will then supervise deputies and support them in carrying out their duties, while also making sure they do not abuse their position.

14.16 When a case comes before the Court of Protection, the Act states that the court should make a decision to settle the matter rather than appoint a deputy, if possible. Deputies are most likely to be needed for financial matters where someone needs continued authority to make decisions about the person's money or other assets. It will be easier for the courts to make decisions in cases where a one-off decision is needed about a person's welfare, so there are likely to be fewer personal welfare deputies. But there will be occasions where ongoing decisions about a person's welfare will be required, and so the court will appoint a personal welfare deputy (see Chapter 8).

Scenario: *Appointing deputies*

Peter was in a motorbike accident that left him permanently and seriously brain-damaged. He has minimal awareness of his surroundings and an assessment has shown that he lacks capacity to make most decisions for himself.

Somebody needs to make several decisions about what treatment Peter needs and where he should be treated. His parents feel that healthcare staff do not always consider their views in decisions about what treatment is in Peter's best interests. So they make an application to the court to be appointed as joint personal welfare deputies.

There will be many care or treatment decisions for Peter in the future. The court decides it would not be practical to make a separate decision on each of them. It also thinks Peter needs some continuity in decision-making. So it appoints Peter's parents as joint personal welfare deputies.

14.17 The OPG may run checks on potential deputies if requested to by the court. It will carry out a risk assessment to determine what kind of supervision a deputy will need once they are appointed.

14.18 Deputies are accountable to the court. The OPG supervises the deputy's actions on the court's behalf, and the court may want the deputy to provide financial accounts or other reports to the OPG. The Public Guardian deals with complaints about the way deputies carry out their duties. It works with other relevant agencies to investigate them. Chapter 8 gives detailed information about the responsibilities of deputies.

What happens if someone says they are worried about an attorney or deputy?

14.19 Many people who lack capacity are likely to get care or support from a range of agencies. Even when an attorney or deputy is acting on behalf of a person who lacks capacity, the other carers still have a responsibility to the person to provide care and act in the person's best interests. Anybody who is caring for a person who lacks capacity, whether in a paid or unpaid role, who is worried about how attorneys or deputies carry out their duties should contact the Public Guardian.

14.20 The OPG will not always be the most appropriate organisation to investigate all complaints. It may investigate a case jointly with:

- healthcare or social care professionals
- social services
- NHS bodies
- the Commission for Social Care Inspection in England or the Care and Social Services Inspectorate for Wales (CSSIW)[64]
- the Healthcare Commission in England or the Healthcare Inspectorate for Wales, and
- in some cases, the police.

14.21 The OPG will usually refer concerns about personal welfare LPAs or personal welfare deputies to the relevant agency. In certain circumstances it will alert the police about a case. When it makes a referral, the OPG will make sure that the relevant agency keeps it informed of the action it takes. It will also make sure that the court has all the information it needs to take possible action against the attorney or deputy.

14.22 Examples of situations in which a referral might be necessary include where:

- someone has complained that a welfare attorney is physically abusing a donor – the OPG would refer this case to the relevant local authority adult protection procedures and possibly the police
- the OPG has found that a solicitor appointed as a financial deputy for an elderly woman has defrauded her estate – the OPG would refer this case to the police and the Law Society Consumer Complaints Service.

How does the Act deal with ill treatment and wilful neglect?

14.23 The Act introduces two new criminal offences: ill treatment and wilful neglect of a person who lacks capacity to make relevant decisions (section 44). The offences may apply to:

- anyone caring for a person who lacks capacity – this includes family carers, healthcare and social care staff in hospital or care homes and those providing care in a person's home
- an attorney appointed under an LPA or an EPA, or
- a deputy appointed for the person by the court.

14.24 These people may be guilty of an offence if they ill-treat or wilfully neglect the person they care for or represent. Penalties will range from a fine to a sentence of imprisonment of up to five years – or both.

---

[64] In April 2007, the Care Standards Inspectorate for Wales (CSIW) and the Social Services Inspectorate for Wales (SSIW) came together to form the Care and Social Services Inspectorate for Wales.

14.25 Ill treatment and neglect are separate offences.[65] For a person to be found guilty of ill treatment, they must either:
- have deliberately ill-treated the person, or
- be reckless in the way they were ill-treating the person or not.

It does not matter whether the behaviour was likely to cause, or actually caused, harm or damage to the victim's health.

14.26 The meaning of 'wilful neglect' varies depending on the circumstances. But it usually means that a person has deliberately failed to carry out an act they knew they had a duty to do.

Scenario: *Reporting abuse*

Norma is 95 and has Alzheimer's disease. Her son, Brendan, is her personal welfare attorney under an LPA. A district nurse has noticed that Norma has bruises and other injuries. She suspects Brendan may be assaulting his mother when he is drunk. She alerts the police and the local Adult Protection Committee.

Following a criminal investigation, Brendan is charged with ill-treating his mother. The Public Guardian applies to the court to cancel the LPA. Social services start to make alternative arrangements for Norma's care.

What other measures protect people from abuse?

14.27 Local agencies have procedures that allow them to work together (called multi-agency working) to protect vulnerable adults – in care settings and elsewhere. Most areas have Adult Protection Committees. These committees:
- create policy (including reporting procedures)
- oversee investigations and other activity between agencies
- carry out joint training, and
- monitor and review progress.

Other local authorities have developed multi-agency Adult Protection Procedures, which are managed by a dedicated Adult Protection Co-ordinator.

14.28 Adult Protection Committees and Procedures (APCP) involve representatives from the NHS, social services, housing, the police and other relevant agencies. In England, they are essential points of contact for anyone who suspects abuse or ill treatment of a vulnerable adult. They can also give advice to the OPG if it is uncertain whether an intervention is necessary in a case of suspected abuse. In Wales, APCPs are not necessarily points of contact themselves, but they publish details of points of contact.

---

[65]   *R v Newington* (1990) 91 Cr App R 247, CA.

Who should check that staff are safe to work with vulnerable adults?

14.29　Under the Safeguarding Vulnerable Groups Act 2006, criminal record checks are now compulsory for staff who:
- have contact with service users in registered care homes
- provide personal care services in someone's home, and
- are involved in providing adult placement schemes.

14.30　Potential employers must carry out a pre-employment criminal record check with the Criminal Records Bureau (CRB) for all potential new healthcare and social care staff. This includes nursing agency staff and home care agency staff.

See Annex A for sources of more detailed information.

14.31　The Protection of Vulnerable Adults (POVA) list has the names of people who have been barred from working with vulnerable adults (in England and Wales). Employers providing care in a residential setting or a person's own home must check whether potential employees are on the list.[66] If they are on the list, they must:
- refuse to employ them, or
- employ them in a position that does not give them regular contact with vulnerable adults.

It is an offence for anyone on the list to apply for a care position. In such cases, the employer should report the person making the application.

Who is responsible for monitoring the standard of care providers?

14.32　All care providers covered by the Care Standards Act 2000 must register with the Commission for Social Care Inspection in England (CSCI) or the Care and Social Services Inspectorate for Wales (CSSIW).[67] These agencies make sure that care providers meet certain standards. They require care providers to have procedures to protect people from harm or abuse. These agencies can take action if they discover dangerous or unsafe practices that could place people at risk.

14.33　Care providers must also have effective complaints procedures. If providers cannot settle complaints, CSCI or CSSIW can look into them.

14.34　CSCI or CSSIW assesses the effectiveness of local adult protection procedures. They will also monitor the arrangements local councils make in response to the Care Standards Act.

---

[66] https://www.gov.uk/government/uploads/system/uploads/attachment_data/file/215956/dh_121571.pdf.

[67] See note 64 above regarding the merger of the Care Standards Inspectorate for Wales and the Social Services Inspectorate for Wales.

What is an appointee, and who monitors them?

14.35 The Department for Work and Pensions (DWP) can appoint someone (an appointee) to claim and spend benefits on a person's behalf[68] if that person:
- gets social security benefits or pensions
- lacks the capacity to act for themselves
- has not made a property and affairs LPA or an EPA, and
- the court has not appointed a property and affairs deputy.

14.36 The DWP checks that an appointee is trustworthy. It also investigates any allegations that an appointee is not acting appropriately or in the person's interests. It can remove an appointee who abuses their position. Concerns about appointees should be raised with the relevant DWP agency (the local Jobcentre Plus, or if the person is aged 60 or over, The Pension Service).

Are there any other means of protection that people should be aware of?

14.37 There are a number of additional means that exist to protect people who lack capacity to make decisions for themselves. Healthcare and social care staff, attorneys and deputies should be aware of:
- National Minimum Standards (for example, for healthcare, care homes, and home care agencies) which apply to both England and Wales (see paragraph 14.38)
- National Service Frameworks, which set out national standards for specific health and care services for particular groups (for example, for mental health services[69] or services for older people[70])
- complaints procedures for all NHS bodies and local councils (see Chapter 15)
- Stop Now Orders (also known as Enforcement Orders) that allow consumer protection bodies to apply for court orders to stop poor trading practices (for example, unfair door-step selling or rogue traders).[71]
- The Public Interest Disclosure Act 1998, which encourages people to report malpractice in the workplace and protects people who report malpractice from being sacked or victimised.

14.38 Information about all national minimum standards are available on the CSCI[72] and Healthcare Commission websites[73] and the Welsh Assembly

---

[68] www.dwp.gov.uk/publications/dwp/2005/gl21_apr.pdf.

[69] www.dh.gov.uk/assetRoot/04/07/72/09/04077209.pdf and www.wales.nhs.uk/sites3/page.cfm?orgid=438&pid=11071.

[70] www.dh.gov.uk/assetRoot/04/07/12/83/04071283.pdf and www.wales.nhs.uk/sites3/home.cfm?orgid=439&redirect=yes&CFID=298511&CFTOKEN=6985382.

[71] www.oft.gov.uk/Business/Legal/Stop+Now+Regulations.htm

[72] www.csci.org.uk/information_for_service_providers/national_minimum_standards/default.htm.

Government website. Chapter 15 gives guidance on complaints procedures. Individual local authorities will have their own complaints system in place.

15 WHAT ARE THE BEST WAYS TO SETTLE DISAGREEMENTS AND DISPUTES ABOUT ISSUES COVERED IN THE ACT?

Sometimes people will disagree about:

- a person's capacity to make a decision
- their best interests
- a decision someone is making on their behalf, or
- an action someone is taking on their behalf.

It is in everybody's interests to settle disagreements and disputes quickly and effectively, with minimal stress and cost. This chapter sets out the different options available for settling disagreements. It also suggests ways to avoid letting a disagreement become a serious dispute. Finally, it sets out when it might be necessary to apply to the Court of Protection and when somebody can get legal funding.

> In this chapter, as throughout the Code, a person's capacity (or lack of capacity) refers specifically to their capacity to make a particular decision at the time it needs to be made.

Quick summary

- When disagreements occur about issues that are covered in the Act, it is usually best to try and settle them before they become serious.
- Advocates can help someone who finds it difficult to communicate their point of view. (This may be someone who has been assessed as lacking capacity.)
- Some disagreements can be effectively resolved by mediation.
- Where there is a concern about healthcare or social care provided to a person who lacks capacity, there are formal and informal ways of complaining about the care or treatment.
- The Health Service Ombudsman or the Local Government Ombudsman (in England) or the Public Services Ombudsman (in Wales) can be asked to investigate some problems that have not been resolved through formal complaints procedures.

---

[73] www.healthcarecommission.org.uk/_db/_documents/The_annual_health_check_in_2006_2007_assessing_and_rating_the_NHS_200609225143.pdf.

- Disputes about the finances of a person who lacks capacity should usually be referred to the Office of the Public Guardian (OPG).
- When other methods of resolving disagreements are not appropriate, the matter can be referred to the Court of Protection.
- There are some decisions that are so serious that the Court of Protection should always make them.

What options are there for settling disagreements?

15.1 Disagreements about healthcare, social or other welfare services may be between:
- people who have assessed a person as lacking capacity to make a decision and the person they have assessed (see Chapter 4 for how to challenge an assessment of lack of capacity)
- family members or other people concerned with the care and welfare of a person who lacks capacity
- family members and healthcare or social care staff involved in providing care or treatment
- healthcare and social care staff who have different views about what is in the best interests of a person who lacks capacity.

15.2 In general, disagreements can be resolved by either formal or informal procedures, and there is more information on both in this chapter. However, there are some disagreements and some subjects that are so serious they can only be resolved by the Court of Protection.

15.3 It is usually best to try and settle disagreements before they become serious disputes. Many people settle them by communicating effectively and taking the time to listen and to address worries. Disagreements between family members are often best settled informally, or sometimes through mediation. When professionals are in disagreement with a person's family, it is a good idea to start by:
- setting out the different options in a way that is easy to understand
- inviting a colleague to talk to the family and offer a second opinion
- offering to get independent expert advice
- using an advocate to support and represent the person who lacks capacity
- arranging a case conference or meeting to discuss matters in detail
- listening to, acknowledging and addressing worries, and
- where the situation is not urgent, allowing the family time to think it over.

Further guidance on how to deal with problems without going to court may also be found in the Community Legal Services Information Leaflet 'Alternatives to Court'.[74]

---

[74] CLS (Community Legal Services) Direct Information Leaflet Number 23, www.clsdirect.org.uk/ legalhelp/leaflet23.jsp?lang=en.

When is an advocate useful?

15.4 An advocate helps communicate the feelings and views of someone who has communication difficulties. The definition of advocacy set out in the Advocacy Charter adopted by most advocacy schemes is as follows: 'Advocacy is taking action to help people say what they want, secure their rights, represent their interests and obtain services they need. Advocates and advocacy schemes work in partnership with the people they support and take their side. Advocacy promotes social inclusion, equality and social justice.'[75]

An advocate may be able to help settle a disagreement simply by presenting a person's feelings to their family, carers or professionals. Most advocacy services are provided by the voluntary sector and are arranged at a local level. They have no link to any agency involved with the person.

15.5 Using advocates can help people who find it difficult to communicate (including those who have been assessed as lacking capacity) to:
- say what they want
- claim their rights
- represent their interests, and
- get the services they need.

15.6 Advocates may also be involved in supporting the person during mediation (see paragraphs 15.7–15.13 below) or helping with complaints procedures. Sometimes people who lack capacity or have been assessed as lacking capacity have a legal right to an advocate, for example:
- when making a formal complaint against the NHS (see paragraph 15.18), and
- where the Act requires the involvement of an Independent Mental Capacity Advocate (IMCA) (see Chapter 10).

When is mediation useful?

15.7 A mediator helps people to come to an agreement that is acceptable to all parties. Mediation can help solve a problem at an early stage. It offers a wider range of solutions than the court can – and it may be less stressful for all parties, more cost-effective and quicker. People who come to an agreement through mediation are more likely to keep to it, because they have taken part in decision-making.

15.8 Mediators are independent. They have no personal interest in the outcome of a case. They do not make decisions or impose solutions. The mediator will decide whether the case is suitable for mediation. They will consider the likely chances of success and the need to protect the interests of the person who lacks capacity.

15.9 Any case that can be settled through negotiation is likely to benefit from mediation. It is most suitable when people are not communicating well or not understanding each other's point of view. It can improve relationships

---

[75] Advocacy across London, *Advocacy Charter* (2002).

and stop future disputes, so it is a good option when it is in the person's interests for people to have a good relationship in the future.

Scenario: Using mediation

Mrs Roberts has dementia and lacks capacity to decide where she should live. She currently lives with her son. But her daughter has found a care home where she thinks her mother will get better care. Her brother disagrees.

Mrs Roberts is upset by this family dispute, and so her son and daughter decide to try mediation. The mediator believes that Mrs Roberts is able to communicate her feelings and agrees to take on the case. During the sessions, the mediator helps them to focus on their mother's best interests rather than imposing their own views. In the end, everybody agrees that Mrs Roberts should continue to live with her son. But they agree to review the situation again in six months to see if the care home might then be better for her.

15.10   In mediation, everybody needs to take part as equally as possible so that a mediator can help everyone involved to focus on the person's best interests. It might also be appropriate to involve an advocate to help communicate the wishes of the person who lacks capacity.

15.11   The National Mediation Helpline[76] helps callers to identify an effective means of resolving their difficulty without going to court. It will arrange an appointment with a trained and accredited mediator. The Family Mediation Helpline[77] can provide information on family mediation and referrals to local family mediation services. Family mediators are trained to deal with the emotional, practical and financial needs of those going through relationship breakdown.

15.12   Healthcare and social care staff may also take part in mediation processes. But it may be more appropriate to follow the relevant healthcare or social care complaints procedures (see paragraphs 15.14–15. 32).

15.13   In certain situations (mainly family mediation), legal aid may be available to fund mediation for people who meet the qualifying criteria (see paragraphs 15.38–15.44).

How can someone complain about healthcare?

15.14   There are formal and informal ways of complaining about a patient's healthcare or treatment. Healthcare staff and others need to know which methods are suitable in which situations.

---

[76]   National Mediation Helpline, Tel: 0845 60 30 809, www.nationalmediationhelpline.com.
[77]   Family Mediation Helpline, Tel: 0845 60 26 627, www.familymediationhelpline.co.uk.

15.15 In England, the Patient Advice and Liaison Service (PALS) provides an informal way of dealing with problems before they reach the complaints stage. PALS operate in every NHS and Primary Care Trust in England. They provide advice and information to patients (or their relatives or carers) to try to solve problems quickly. They can direct people to specialist support services (for example, advocates, mental health support teams, social services or interpreting services). PALS do not investigate complaints. Their role is to explain complaints procedures and direct people to the formal NHS complaints process, if necessary. NHS complaints procedures deal with complaints about something that happened in the past that requires an apology or explanation. A court cannot help in this situation, but court proceedings may be necessary in some clinical negligence cases (see paragraph 15.22).

15.16 In Wales, complaints advocates based at Community Health Councils provide advice and support to anyone with concerns about treatment they have had.

Disagreements about proposed treatments

15.17 If a case is not urgent, the supportive atmosphere of the PALS may help settle it. In Wales, the local Community Health Council may be able to help. But urgent cases about proposed serious treatment may need to go to the Court of Protection (see paragraphs 15.35–15.36).

Scenario: Disagreeing about treatment or an assessment

Mrs Thompson has Alzheimer's and does not want a flu jab. Her daughter thinks she should have the injection. The doctor does not want to go against the wishes of his patient, because he believes she has capacity to refuse treatment.

Mrs Thompson's daughter goes to PALS. A member of staff gives her information and advice about what is meant by capacity to consent to or refuse treatment, and tells her how to find out about the flu jab. The PALS staff speak to the doctor, and then they explain his clinical assessment to Mrs Thompson's daughter.

The daughter is still unhappy. PALS staff advise her that the Independent Complaints Advocacy Service can help if she wishes to make a formal complaint.

The formal NHS complaints procedure

15.18 The formal NHS complaints procedure deals with complaints about NHS services provided by NHS organisations or primary care practitioners. As a first step, people should try to settle a disagreement through an informal discussion between:

- the healthcare staff involved
- the person who may lack capacity to make the decision in question (with support if necessary)
- their carers, and
- any appropriate relatives.

If the person who is complaining is not satisfied, the Independent Complaints Advocacy Service (ICAS) may help. In Wales, the complaints advocates based at Community Health Councils will support and advise anyone who wants to make a complaint.

15.19 In England, if the person is still unhappy after a local investigation, they can ask for an independent review by the Healthcare Commission. If the patient involved in the complaint was or is detained under the Mental Health Act 1983, the Mental Health Act Commission can be asked to look into the complaint. If people are still unhappy after this stage, they can go to the Health Service Ombudsman. More information on how to make a complaint in England is available from the Department of Health.

15.20 In Wales, if patients are still unhappy after a local investigation, they can ask for an independent review of their complaint by independent lay reviewers. After this, they can take their case to the Public Services Ombudsman for Wales. People can take their complaint direct to the Ombudsman if:

- the complaint is about care or treatment that took place after 1 April 2006, and
- they have tried to settle the problem locally first.

The Mental Health Act Commission may also investigate complaints about the care or treatment of detained patients in Wales, if attempts have been made to settle the complaint locally without success.

15.21 Regulations about first trying to settle complaints locally do not apply to NHS Foundation Trusts. But these Trusts are covered by the independent review stage operated by the Healthcare Commission and by the Health Service Ombudsman. People who have a complaint about an NHS Foundation Trust should contact the Trust for advice on how to make a complaint.

Cases of clinical negligence

15.22 The NHS Litigation Authority oversees all clinical negligence cases brought against the NHS in England. It actively encourages people to try other forms of settling complaints before going to court. The National Assembly for Wales also encourages people to try other forms of settling complaints before going to court.

How can somebody complain about social care?

15.23 The social services complaints procedure has been reformed. The reformed procedure came into effect on 1 September 2006 in England and on 1 April 2006 in Wales.

15.24 A service provider's own complaints procedure should deal with complaints about:
- the way in which care services are delivered
- the type of services provided, or
- a failure to provide services.

15.25 Care agencies contracted by local authorities or registered with the Commission for Social Care Inspection (CSCI) in England or Care and Social Services Inspectorate for Wales (CSSIW) are legally obliged to have their own written complaints procedures. This includes residential homes, agencies providing care in people's homes, nursing agencies and adult placement schemes. The procedures should set out how to make a complaint and what to do with a complaint that cannot be settled locally.

Local authority complaints procedures

15.26 For services contracted by a local authority, it may be more appropriate to use the local authority's complaints procedure. A simple example would be a situation where a local authority places a person in a care home and the person's family are not happy with the placement. If their complaint is not about the services the home provides (for example, it might be about the local authority's assessment of the person's needs), it might be more appropriate to use the local authority's complaints procedure.

15.27 As a first step, people should try to settle a disagreement through an informal discussion, involving:
- the professionals involved
- the person who may lack capacity to make the decision in question (with support if necessary)
- their carers, and
- any appropriate relatives.

15.28 If the person making the complaint is not satisfied, the local authority will carry out a formal investigation using its complaints procedure. In England, after this stage, a social service Complaints Review Panel can hear the case. In Wales complaints can be referred to the National Assembly for Wales for hearing by an independent panel.

Other complaints about social care

15.29 People can take their complaint to the CSCI in England or the CSSIW in Wales, if:
- the complaint is about regulations or national minimum standards not being met, and

- the complainants are not happy with the provider's own complaints procedure or the response to their complaint.

15.30 If a complaint is about a local authority's administration, it may be referred to the Commission for Local Administration in England (the Local Government Ombudsman) or the Public Services Ombudsman for Wales.

What if a complaint covers healthcare and social care?

15.31 Taking a complaint through NHS or local authority complaints procedures can be a complicated process – especially if the complaint covers a number of service providers or both healthcare and social care. In such situations, local authorities and the NHS must work together and agree which organisation will lead in handling the complaint. If a person is not happy with the outcome, they can take their case to the Health Service Ombudsman or to the Local Government Ombudsman (in England). There is guidance which sets out how organisations should work together to handle complaints that cover healthcare and social care (in England *Learning from Complaints* and in Wales *Listening and learning*). The Public Services Ombudsman for Wales handles complaints that cover both healthcare and social care.

Who can handle complaints about other welfare issues?

15.32 The Independent Housing Ombudsman deals with complaints about registered social landlords in England. This applies mostly to housing associations. But it also applies to many landlords who manage homes that were formerly run by local authorities and some private landlords. In Wales, the Public Services Ombudsman for Wales deals with complaints about registered social landlords. Complaints about local authorities may be referred to the Local Government Ombudsman in England or the Public Services Ombudsman for Wales. They look at complaints about decisions on council housing, social services, Housing Benefit and planning applications. More information about complaints to an Ombudsman is available on the relevant websites (see Annex A).

What is the best way to handle disagreement about a person's finances?

15.33 Some examples of disagreements about a person's finances are:
- disputes over the amount of money a person who lacks capacity should pay their carer
- disputes over whether a person who lacks capacity should sell their house

- somebody questioning the actions of a carer, who may be using the money of a person who lacks capacity inappropriately or without proper authority
- somebody questioning the actions of an attorney appointed under a Lasting Power of Attorney or an Enduring Power of Attorney or a deputy appointed by the court.

15.34 In all of the above circumstances, the most appropriate action would usually be to contact the Office of the Public Guardian (OPG) for guidance and advice. See Chapter 14 for further details on the role of the OPG.

How can the Court of Protection help?

15.35 The Court of Protection deals with all areas of decision-making for adults who lack capacity to make particular decisions for themselves (see Chapter 8 for more information about its roles and responsibilities). But the court is not always the right place to settle problems involving people who lack capacity. Other forms of settling disagreements may be more appropriate and less distressing.

15.36 There are some decisions that are so serious that the court should always make them. There are also other types of cases that the court should deal with when another method would generally not be suitable. See Chapter 8 for more information about both kinds of cases.

Right of Appeal

15.37 Section 53 of the Act describes the rights of appeal against any decision taken by the Court of Protection. There are further details in the Court of Protection Rules. It may be advisable for anyone who wishes to appeal a decision made by the court to seek legal advice.

Will public legal funding be available?

15.38 Depending on their financial situation, once the Act comes into force people may be entitled to:
- publicly funded legal advice from accredited solicitors or advice agencies
- legal representation before the new Court of Protection (in the most serious cases).

Information about solicitors and organisations who give advice on different areas of law is available from Community Legal Services Direct

(CLS Direct).[78] Further information about legal aid and public funding can be obtained from the Legal Services Commission.[79] See Annex A for full contact details.

15.39 People who lack capacity to instruct a solicitor or conduct their own case will need a litigation friend. This person could be a relative, friend, attorney or the Official Solicitor (when no-one else is available). The litigation friend is able to instruct the solicitor and conduct the case on behalf of a person who lacks capacity to give instructions. If the person qualifies for public legal funding, the litigation friend can claim funding on their behalf.

When can someone get legal help?

15.40 Legal help is a type of legal aid (public funding) that pays for advice and assistance on legal issues, including those affecting a person who lacks capacity. But it does not provide representation for a full court hearing, although there is a related form of funding called 'help at court' under which a legal representative can speak in court on a client's behalf on an informal basis. To qualify for legal help, applicants must show that:
- they get specific social security benefits, or they earn less than a specific amount and do not have savings or other financial assets in excess of a specific amount
- they would benefit sufficiently from legal advice to justify the amount it costs, and
- they cannot get another form of funding.

15.41 Legal help can include:
- help from a solicitor or other representative in writing letters
- in exceptional circumstances, getting a barrister's opinion, and
- assistance in preparing for Court of Protection hearings.

15.42 People cannot get legal help for making a Lasting Power of Attorney or an advance decision to refuse treatment. But they can get general help and information from the OPG. The OPG cannot give legal or specialist advice. For example, they will not be able to advise someone on what powers they should delegate to their attorney under an LPA.

When can someone get legal representation?

15.43 Public funding for legal representation in the Court of Protection will be available from solicitors with a relevant contract – but only for the most serious cases. To qualify, applicants will normally face the same test as for legal help to qualify financially (paragraph 15.40). They will generally have to satisfy more detailed criteria than applicants for legal help, relating, for instance, to their prospects of being successful, to whether legal representation is necessary and to the cost benefit of being

---

[78] CLS Direct, Tel: 0845 345 4 345, www.clsdirect.org.uk.
[79] www.legalservices.gov.uk.

represented. They will also have to establish that the case could not be brought or funded in another way and that there are not alternatives to court proceedings that should be explored first.

15.44 Serious personal welfare cases that were previously heard by the High Court will continue to have public funding for legal representation when they are transferred to the Court of Protection. These cases will normally be related to personal liberty, serious welfare decisions or medical treatment for a person who lacks capacity. But legal representation may also be available in other types of cases, depending on the particular circumstances.

16 WHAT RULES GOVERN ACCESS TO INFORMATION ABOUT A PERSON WHO LACKS CAPACITY?

This chapter gives guidance on:

- what personal information about someone who lacks capacity people involved in their care have the right to see, and
- how they can get hold of that information.

This chapter is only a general guide. It does not give detailed information about the law. Nor does it replace professional guidance or the guidance of the Information Commissioner's Office on the Data Protection Act 1998 (this guidance is available on its website, see Annex A). Where necessary, people should take legal advice.

This chapter is mainly for people such as family carers and other carers, deputies and attorneys, who care for or represent someone who lacks capacity to make specific decisions and in particular, lacks capacity to allow information about them to be disclosed. Professionals have their own codes of conduct, and they may have the support of experts in their organisations.

> In this chapter, as throughout the Code, a person's capacity (or lack of capacity) refers specifically to their capacity to make a particular decision at the time it needs to be made.

Quick summary

Questions to ask when requesting personal information about someone who may lack capacity

- Am I acting under a Lasting Power of Attorney or as a deputy with specific authority?

- Does the person have capacity to agree that information can be disclosed? Have they previously agreed to disclose the information?
- What information do I need?
- Why do I need it?
- Who has the information?
- Can I show that:
  - I need the information to make a decision that is in the best interests of the person I am acting for, and
  - the person does not have the capacity to act for themselves?
- Do I need to share the information with anyone else to make a decision that is in the best interests of the person who lacks capacity?
- Should I keep a record of my decision or action?
- How long should I keep the information for?
- Do I have the right to request the information under section 7 of the Data Protection Act 1998?

Questions to ask when considering whether to disclose information

- Is the request covered by section 7 of the Data Protection Act 1998? Is the request being made by a formally authorised representative?

If not:

- Is the disclosure legal?
- Is the disclosure justified, having balanced the person's best interests and the public interest against the person's right to privacy?

Questions to ask to decide whether the disclosure is legal or justified

- Do I (or does my organisation) have the information?
- Am I satisfied that the person concerned lacks capacity to agree to disclosure?
- Does the person requesting the information have any formal authority to act on behalf of the person who lacks capacity?
- Am I satisfied that the person making the request:
  - is acting in the best interests of the person concerned?
  - needs the information to act properly?
  - will respect confidentiality?
  - will keep the information for no longer than necessary?
- Should I get written confirmation of these things?

What laws and regulations affect access to information?

16.1 People caring for, or managing the finances of, someone who lacks capacity may need information to:
- assess the person's capacity to make a specific decision
- determine the person's best interests, and
- make appropriate decisions on the person's behalf.

16.2 The information they need varies depending on the circumstances. For example:
- a daughter providing full-time care for an elderly parent will make decisions based on her own experience and knowledge of her parent
- a deputy may need information from other people. For instance, if they were deciding whether a person needs to move into a care home or whether they should sell the person's home, they might need information from family members, the family doctor, the person's bank and their solicitor to make sure they are making the decision in the person's best interests.

16.3 Much of the information needed to make decisions under the Act is sensitive or confidential. It is regulated by:
- the Data Protection Act 1998
- the common law duty of confidentiality
- professional codes of conduct on confidentiality, and
- the Human Rights Act 1998 and European Convention on Human Rights, in particular Article 8 (the right to respect for private and family life), which means that it is only lawful to reveal someone's personal information if:
  - there is a legitimate aim in doing so
  - a democratic society would think it necessary to do so, and
  - the kind and amount of information disclosed is in relation to the need.

What information do people generally have a right to see?

16.4 Section 7 of the Data Protection Act 1998 gives everyone the right to see personal information that an organisation holds about them. They may also authorise someone else to access their information on their behalf. The person holding the information has a legal duty to release it. So, where possible, it is important to try to get a person's consent before requesting to see information about them.

16.5 A person may have the capacity to agree to someone seeing their personal information, even if they do not have the capacity to make other decisions. In some situations, a person may have previously given consent (while they still had capacity) for someone to see their personal information in the future.

16.6 Doctors and lawyers cannot share information about their clients, or that clients have given them, without the client's consent. Sometimes it is fair to assume that a doctor or lawyer already has someone's consent (for example, patients do not usually expect healthcare staff or legal professionals to get consent every time they share information with a colleague – but staff may choose to get clients' consent in writing when they begin treating or acting for that person). But in other circumstances, doctors and lawyers must get specific consent to 'disclose' information (share it with someone else).

16.7 If someone's capacity changes from time to time, the person needing the information may want to wait until that person can give their consent. Or they may decide that it is not necessary to get access to information at all, if the person will be able to make a decision on their own in the future.

16.8 If someone lacks the capacity to give consent, someone else might still be able to see their personal information. This will depend on:
- whether the person requesting the information is acting as an agent (a representative recognised by the law, such as a deputy or attorney) for the person who lacks capacity
- whether disclosure is in the best interests of the person who lacks capacity, and
- what type of information has been requested.

When can attorneys and deputies ask to see personal information?

16.9 An attorney acting under a valid LPA or EPA (and sometimes a deputy) can ask to see information concerning the person they are representing, as long as the information applies to decisions the attorney has the legal right to make.

16.10 In practice, an attorney or deputy may only require limited information and may not need to make a formal request. In such circumstances, they can approach the information holder informally. Once satisfied that the request comes from an attorney or deputy (having seen appropriate authority), the person holding information should be able to release it. The attorney or deputy can still make a formal request for information in the future.

16.11 The attorney or deputy must treat the information confidentially. They should be extremely careful to protect it. If they fail to do so, the court can cancel the LPA or deputyship.

16.12 Before the Act came into effect, only a few receivers were appointed with the general authority to manage a person's property and affairs. So they needed specific authority from the Court of Protection to ask for access to the person's personal information. Similarly, a deputy who only has authority to act in specific areas only has the right to ask for information relating to decisions in those specific areas. For information relating to other areas, the deputy will need to apply to the Court of Protection.

16.13 Requests for personal information must be in writing, and there might be a fee. Information holders should release it promptly (always within 40 calendar days). Fees may be particularly high for getting copies of healthcare records – particularly where information may be in unusual formats (for example, x-rays). The maximum fee is currently £50. Complaints about a failure to comply with the Data Protection Act 1998 should be directed to the Information Commissioner's Office (see Annex A for contact details).

What limitations are there?

16.14 Attorneys and deputies should only ask for information that will help them make a decision they need to make on behalf of the person who lacks capacity. For example, if the attorney needs to know when the person should take medication, they should not ask to see the entire healthcare record. The person who releases information must make sure that an attorney or deputy has official authority (they may ask for proof of identity and appointment). When asking to see personal information, attorneys and deputies should bear in mind that their decision must always be in the best interests of the person who lacks capacity to make that decision.

16.15 The attorney or deputy may not know the kind of information that someone holds about the person they are representing. So sometimes it might be difficult for them to make a specific request. They might even need to see all the information to make a decision. But again, the 'best interests' principle applies.

Scenario: Giving attorneys access to personal information

Mr Yapp is in the later stages of Alzheimer's disease. His son is responsible for Mr Yapp's personal welfare under a Lasting Power of Attorney. Mr Yapp has been in residential care for a number of years. But his son does not think that the home is able to meet his father's current needs as his condition has recently deteriorated.

The son asks to see his father's records. He wants specific information about his father's care, so that he can make a decision about his father's best interests. But the manager of the care home refuses, saying that the Data Protection Act stops him releasing personal information.

Mr Yapp's son points out that he can see his father's records, because he is his personal welfare attorney and needs the information to make a decision. The Data Protection Act 1998 requires the care home manager to provide access to personal data held on Mr Yapp.

16.16 The deputy or attorney may find that some information is held back (for example, when this contains references to people other than the person who lacks capacity). This might be to protect another person's privacy, if that person is mentioned in the records. It is unlikely that information relating to another person would help an attorney make a decision on behalf of the person who lacks capacity. The information holder might also be obliged to keep information about the other person confidential. There might be another reason why the person does not want information about them to be released. Under these circumstances, the attorney does not have the right to see that information.

16.17 An information holder should not release information if doing so would cause serious physical or mental harm to anyone – including the person the information is about. This applies to information on health, social care and education records.

16.18 The Information Commissioner's Office can give further details on:
  • how to request personal information
  • restrictions on accessing information, and
  • how to appeal against a decision not to release information.

When can someone see information about healthcare or social care?

16.19 Healthcare and social care staff may disclose information about somebody who lacks capacity only when it is in the best interests of the person concerned to do so, or when there is some other, lawful reason for them to do so.

16.20 The Act's requirement to consult relevant people when working out the best interests of a person who lacks capacity will encourage people to share the information that makes a consultation meaningful. But people who release information should be sure that they are acting lawfully and that they can justify releasing the information. They need to balance the person's right to privacy with what is in their best interests or the wider public interest (see paragraphs 16.24–16.25 below).

16.21 Sometimes it will be fairly obvious that staff should disclose information. For example, a doctor would need to tell a new care worker about what drugs a person needs or what allergies the person has. This is clearly in the person's best interests.

16.22 Other information may need to be disclosed as part of the process of working out someone's best interests. A social worker might decide to reveal information about someone's past when discussing their best interests with a close family member. But staff should always bear in mind that the Act requires them to consider the wishes and feelings of the person who lacks capacity.

16.23 In both these cases, staff should only disclose as much information as is relevant to the decision to be made.

Scenario: Sharing appropriate information

Mr Jeremy has learning disabilities. His care home is about to close down. His care team carries out a careful assessment of his needs. They involve him as much as possible, and use the support of an Independent Mental Capacity Advocate. Following the assessment, he is placed with carers under an adult placement scheme.

The carers ask to see Mr Jeremy's case file, so that they can provide him with appropriate care in his best interests. The care manager seeks Mr Jeremy's consent to disclosure of his notes, but believes that Mr Jeremy lacks capacity to make this decision. She recognises that it is appropriate to provide the carers with sufficient information to enable them to act in Mr Jeremy's best interests. But it is not appropriate for them to see all the information on the case file. Much of it is not relevant to his current care needs. The care manager therefore only passes on relevant information from the file.

16.24 Sometimes a person's right to confidentiality will conflict with broader public concerns. Information can be released if it is in the public interest, even if it is not in the best interests of the person who lacks capacity. It can be difficult to decide in these cases, and information holders should consider each case on its merits. The NHS Code on Confidentiality gives examples of when disclosure is in the public interest. These include situations where disclosing information could prevent, or aid investigation of, serious crimes, or to prevent serious harm, such as spread of an infectious disease. It is then necessary to judge whether the public good that would be achieved by the disclosure outweighs both the obligation of confidentiality to the individual concerned and the broader public interest in the provision of a confidential service.

16.25 For disclosure to be in the public interest, it must be proportionate and limited to the relevant details. Healthcare or social care staff faced with this decision should seek advice from their legal advisers. It is not just things for 'the public's benefit' that are in the public interest – disclosure for the benefit of the person who lacks capacity can also be in the public interest (for example, to stop a person who lacks capacity suffering physical or mental harm).

What financial information can carers ask to see?

16.26 It is often more difficult to get financial information than it is to get information on a person's welfare. A bank manager, for example, is less likely to:

- know the individual concerned
- be able to make an assessment of the person's capacity to consent to disclosure, and
- be aware of the carer's relationship to the person.

So they are less likely than a doctor or social worker to be able to judge what is in a person's best interests and are bound by duties to keep clients' affairs confidential. It is likely that someone wanting financial information will need to apply to the Court of Protection for access to that information. This clearly does not apply to an attorney or a deputy appointed to manage the person's property and affairs, who will generally have the authority (because of their appointment) to obtain all relevant information about the person's property and affairs.

Is information still confidential after someone shares it?

16.27 Whenever a carer gets information, they should treat the information in confidence, and they should not share it with anyone else (unless there is a lawful basis for doing so). In some circumstances, the information holder might ask the carer to give a formal confirmation that they will keep information confidential.

16.28 Where the information is in written form, carers should store it carefully and not keep it for longer than necessary. In many cases, the need to keep the information will be temporary. So the carer should be able to reassure the information holder that they will not keep a permanent record of the information.

What is the best way to settle a disagreement about personal information?

16.29 A carer should always start by trying to get consent from the person whose information they are trying to access. If the person lacks capacity to consent, the carer should ask the information holder for the relevant information and explain why they need it. They may need to remind the information holder that they have to make a decision in the person's best interests and cannot do so without the relevant information.

16.30 This can be a sensitive area and disputes will inevitably arise. Healthcare and social care staff have a difficult judgement to make. They might feel strongly that disclosing the information would not be in the best interests of the person who lacks capacity and would amount to an invasion of their privacy. This may be upsetting for the carer who will probably have good motives for wanting the information. In all cases, an assessment of the interests and needs of the person who lacks capacity should determine whether staff should disclose information.

16.31 If a discussion fails to settle the matter, and the carer still is not happy, there are other ways to settle the disagreement (see Chapter 15). The carer may need to use the appropriate complaints procedure. Since the complaint involves elements of data protection and confidentiality, as well as best interests, relevant experts should help deal with the complaint.

16.32 In cases where carers and staff cannot settle their disagreement, the carer can apply to the Court of Protection for the right to access to the specific information. The court would then need to decide if this was in the best interests of the person who lacks capacity to consent. In urgent cases, it might be necessary for the carer to apply directly to the court without going through the earlier stages.

KEY WORDS AND PHRASES USED IN THE CODE

The table below is not a full index or glossary. Instead, it is a list of key terms used in the Code or the Act, and the main references to them. References in bold indicate particularly valuable content for that term.

Acts in connection with care or treatment	Tasks carried out by carers, healthcare or social care staff which involve the personal care, healthcare or medical treatment of people who lack capacity to consent to them – referred to in the Act as 'section 5 acts'.	**Chapter 6** 2.13–2.14, 4.39 Best interests and _ 5.10, 5,39 Deprivation of liberty and_ 6.39. 6.49–6.52
Advance decision to refuse treatment	A decision to refuse specified treatment made in advance by a person who has capacity to do so. This decision will then apply at a future time when that person lacks capacity to consent to, or refuse, the specified treatment. This is set out in Section 24(1) of the Act. Specific rules apply to advance decisions to refuse life-sustaining treatment.	**Chapter 9 (all)** Best interests and _ 5.5, 5.35, 5.45 Protection from liability and _ 6.37–6.38 LPAs and _ 7.55 Deputies and _ 8.28 Research and _ 11.30 Young people and _ 12.9 Mental Health Act 13.35–13.37

Adult protection procedures	Procedures devised by local authorities, in conjunction with other relevant agencies, to investigate and deal with allegations of abuse or ill treatment of vulnerable adults, and to put in place safeguards to provide protection from abuse.	**Chapter 14** 14.6, 14.22, 14.27–28, 14.34 IMCAs and _ 10.66–10.67
After-care under supervision	Arrangements for supervision in the community following discharge from hospital of certain patients previously detained under the Mental Health Act 1983.	**Chapter 13** **13.22–13.25,** 13.34, 13.37, 13.40, 13.42, 13.45, 13.48, 13.52
Agent	A person authorised to act on behalf of another person under the law of agency. Attorneys appointed under an LPA or EPA are agents and court-appointed deputies are deemed to be agents and must undertake certain duties as agents.	LPAs and _ 7.58–7.68 Deputies and _ 8.55–8.68
Appointee	Someone appointed under Social Security Regulations to claim and collect social security benefits or pensions on behalf of a person who lacks capacity to manage their own benefits. An appointee is permitted to use the money claimed to meet the person's needs.	Role of _ 6:65–6.66 Deputies and _ 8.56 Concerns about _ 14:35–14.36
Appropriate body	A committee which is established to advise on, or on matters which include, the ethics of intrusive research in relation to people who lack capacity to consent to it, and is recognised for those purposes by the Secretary of State (in England) or the National Assembly for Wales (in Wales).	**Chapter 11** 11.8–11.11, 11.20, 11.33–11.34, 11.43–11.47.
Approved Social Worker (ASW)	A specially trained social worker with responsibility for assessing a person's needs for care and treatment under the Mental Health Act 1983. In particular, an ASW assesses whether the person should be admitted to hospital for assessment and/or treatment.	**Chapter 13** 13.16, 13.22–13.23, 13.43, 13.52

Artificial Nutrition and Hydration (ANH)	Artificial nutrition and hydration (ANH) has been recognised as a form of medical treatment. ANH involves using tubes to provide nutrition and fluids to someone who cannot take them by mouth. It bypasses the natural mechanisms that control hunger and thirst and requires clinical monitoring.	**9.26** 5.34 6.18 8.18
Attorney	Someone appointed under either a Lasting Power of Attorney (LPA) or an Enduring Power of Attorney (EPA), who has the legal right to make decisions within the scope of their authority on behalf of the person (the donor) who made the Power of Attorney.	**Chapter 7** Best interests principle and _ 5.2, 5.13, 5.49, 5.55 Protection from liability as _ 6.54–6.55 Court of Protection and _ 8.30 Advance decisions and _ 9.33 Mental Health Act and _ 13.38–13.45 Public Guardian and _ 14.7–14.14 Legal help and _ 15.39–15.42 Accessing personal information as _ 16.9–16.16

Best interests	Any decisions made, or anything done for a person who lacks capacity to make specific decisions, must be in the person's best interests. There are standard minimum steps to follow when working out someone's best interests. These are set out in section 4 of the Act, and in the non-exhaustive checklist in 5.13.	**Chapter 2 (Principle 4) Chapter 5** Protection from liability and _ 6.4–6.18 Reasonable belief and _ 6.32–6.36 Deprivation of liberty and _ 6.51–6.53 Acting as an attorney and _ 7.19–7.20, 7.29, 7.53 Court of Protection and _ 8.14–8.26 Acting as a deputy and _ 8.50–8.52 Advance decisions and _ 9.4–9.5
Bournewood provisions	A name given to some proposed new procedures and safeguards for people who lack capacity to make relevant decisions but who need to be deprived of their liberty, in their best interests, otherwise than under the Mental Health Act 1983. The name refers to a case which was eventually decided by the European Court of Human Rights.	6.53–6.54 13.53–13.54
Capacity	The ability to make a decision about a particular matter at the time the decision needs to be made. The legal definition of a person who lacks capacity is set out in section 2 of the Act.	**Chapter 4**

Carer	Someone who provides *unpaid* care by looking after a friend or neighbour who needs support because of sickness, age or disability. In this document, the role of the carer is different from the role of a professional care worker.	**Acting as decision-maker 5.8–5.10 Protection from liability 6.20–6.24** Assessing capacity as _ 4.44–4.45 Acting with reasonable belief 6.29–6.34 Paying for goods and services 6.56–6.66 Accessing information 16.26–16.32
Care worker	Someone employed to provide personal care for people who need help because of sickness, age or disability. They could be employed by the person themselves, by someone acting on the person's behalf or by a care agency.	Assessing capacity as _4.38, 4.44–4.45 Protection from liability 6.20 Paying for goods and services 6.56–6.66 Acting as an attorney 7.10 Acting as a deputy 8.41
Children Act 1989	A law relating to children and those with parental responsibility for children.	**Chapter 12**
Complaints Review Panel	A panel of people set up to review and reconsider complaints about health or social care services which have not been resolved under the first stage of the relevant complaints procedure.	15.28

Consultee	A person who is consulted, for example about the involvement in a research project of a person who lacks capacity to consent to their participation in the research.	11.23, 11.28–29, 11.44
Court of Protection	The specialist Court for all issues relating to people who lack capacity to make specific decisions. The Court of Protection is established under section 45 of the Act.	**Chapter 8** _ must always make decisions about these issues 6.18 Decisions about life-sustaining treatment 5.33–5.36 LPAs and _ 7.45–7.49 Advance decisions and _ 9.35, 9.54, 9.67–9.69 Decisions regarding children and young people 12.3–12.4, 12.7, 12.10, 12.23–12.25 Access to legal help 15.40–15.44
Court of Protection Visitor	Someone who is appointed to report to the Court of Protection on how attorneys or deputies are carrying out their duties. Court of Protection Visitors are established under section 61 of the Act. They can also be directed by the Public Guardian to visit donors, attorney and deputies under section 58 (1) (d).	**14.10–14.11** Attorneys and _ 7.71 Deputies and _ 8.71

Criminal Records Bureau (CRB)	An Executive Agency of the Home Office which provides access to criminal record information. Organisations in the public, private and voluntary sectors can ask for the CRB to check candidates for jobs to see if they have any criminal records which would make them unsuitable for certain work, especially that involves children or vulnerable adults. For some jobs, a CRB check is mandatory.	Checking healthcare and social care staff 14.29–14.30 Checking IMCAs 10.18
Data Protection Act 1998	A law controlling the handling of, and access to, personal information, such as medical records, files held by public bodies and financial information held by credit reference agencies.	**Chapter 16**
Decision-maker	Under the Act, many different people may be required to make decisions or act on behalf of someone who lacks capacity to make decisions for themselves. The person making the decision is referred to throughout the Code, as the 'decision-maker', and it is the decision-maker's responsibility to work out what would be in the best interests of the person who lacks capacity.	**Chapter 5** Working with IMCAs 10.4, 10.21–10.29 Applying the MHA 13.3, 13.10, 13.27
Declaration	A kind of order made by the Court of Protection. For example, a declaration could say whether a person has or lacks capacity to make a particular decision, or declaring that a particular act would or would not be lawful. The Court's power to make declarations is set out in section 15 of the Act	**8.13–8.19** Advance decisions and _ 9.35
Deprivation of liberty	Deprivation of liberty is a term used in the European Convention on Human Rights about circumstances when a person's freedom is taken away. Its meaning in practice is being defined through case law.	**6.49–6.54** Protection from liability 6.13–6.14 Attorneys and _ 7.44 Mental Health Act and _ 13.12, 13.16

Deputy	Someone appointed by the Court of Protection with ongoing legal authority as prescribed by the Court to make decisions on behalf of a person who lacks capacity to make particular decisions as set out in Section 16(2) of the Act.	Chapter 8 Best interests principle and _ 5.2, 5.13, 5.49, 5.55 Protection from liability as _ 6.54–6.55 Attorneys becoming _ 7.56 Advance decisions and _ 9.33 IMCAs and _ 10.70–72 Acting for children and young people 12.4, 12.7 Public Guardian and _ 14.15–14.18 Complaints about 14.19–14.25 Accessing personal information as _ 16.9–16.16
Donor	A person who makes a Lasting Power of Attorney or Enduring Power of Attorney	Chapter 7
Enduring Power of Attorney (EPA)	A Power of Attorney created under the Enduring Powers of Attorney Act 1985 appointing an attorney to deal with the donor's property and financial affairs. Existing EPAs will continue to operate under Schedule 4 of the Act, which replaces the EPA Act 1985.	Chapter 7 See also LPA

Family carer	A family member who looks after a relative who needs support because of sickness, age or disability. It does not mean a professional care-worker employed by a disabled person or a care assistant in a nursing home, for example.	See carer
Family Division of the High Court	The Division of the High Court that has the jurisdiction to deal with all matrimonial and civil partnership matters, family disputes, matters relating to children and some disputes about medical treatment.	12.14, 12.23
Fiduciary duty	Anyone acting under the law of agency will have this duty. In essence, it means that any decision taken or act done as an agent (such as an attorney or deputy) must not benefit themselves, but must benefit the person for whom they are acting.	_ for attorneys 7.58 _ for deputies 8.58
Guardian-ship	Arrangements, made under the Mental Health Act 1983, for a guardian to be appointed for a person with mental disorder to help ensure that the person gets the care they need in the community.	**13.16–13.21** 13.1, 13.25–13.27, 13.54
Health Service Ombudsman	An independent person whose organisation investigates complaints about National Health Service (NHS) care or treatment in England which have not been resolved through the NHS complaints procedure.	15.19, 15.21, 15.31
Human Rights Act 1998	A law largely incorporating into UK law the substantive rights set out in the European Convention on Human Rights.	6.49 16.3
Human Tissue Act 2004	A law to regulate issues relating to whole body donation and the taking, storage and use of human organs and tissue.	11.7 11.38–11.39

Ill treatment	Section 44 of the Act introduces a new offence of ill treatment of a person who lacks capacity by someone who is caring for them, or acting as a deputy or attorney for them. That person can be guilty of ill treatment if they have deliberately ill-treated a person who lacks capacity, or been reckless as to whether they were ill-treating the person or not. It does not matter whether the behaviour was likely to cause, or actually caused, harm or damage to the victim's health.	14.23–14.26
Independent Complaints Advocacy Service (ICAS)	In England, a service to support patients and their carers who wish to pursue a complaint about their NHS treatment or care.	15.18
Independent Mental Capacity Advocate (IMCA)	Someone who provides support and representation for a person who lacks capacity to make specific decisions, where the person has no-one else to support them. The IMCA service is established under section 35 of the Act and the functions of IMCAs are set out in section 36. It is not the same as an ordinary advocacy service.	**Chapter 10** Consulting to work out best interests 5.51 Involvement in changes of residence 6.9 Involvement in serious medical decisions 6.16 MHA and _ 13.46–13.48
Information Commission-er's Office	An independent authority set up to promote access to official information and to protect personal information. It has powers to ensure that the laws about information, such as the Data Protection Act 1998, are followed.	16.13 16.18

| Lasting Power of Attorney (LPA) | A Power of Attorney created under the Act (see Section 9(1)) appointing an attorney (or attorneys) to make decisions about the donor's personal welfare (including healthcare) and/or deal with the donor's property and affairs. | **Chapter 7** Best interests principle and _ 5.2, 5.13, 5.49, 5.55 Protection from liability as _ 6.54–6.55 Court of Protection and _ 8.30 Advance decisions and _ 9.33 Mental Health Act and _ 13.38–13.45 Public Guardian and _ 14.7–14.14 Legal help and _ 15.39–15.42 Accessing personal information as _ 16.9–16.16 |

Life-sustaining treatment	Treatment that, in the view of the person providing healthcare, is necessary to keep a person alive See Section 4(10) of the Act.	**Providing or stopping _ in best interests 5.29–5.36 Advance decisions to refuse _ 9.10–9.11, 9.19–9.20, 9.24–9.28** Protection from liability when providing _ 6.16, 6.55 Attorneys and _ 7.22, 7.27, 7.29-7.30 Deputies and _ 8.17, 8.46 Conscientious objection to stopping _ 9.61–9.63 IMCAs and _ 10.44
Litigation friend	A person appointed by the court to conduct legal proceedings on behalf of, and in the name of, someone who lacks capacity to conduct the litigation or to instruct a lawyer themselves.	4.54 10.38 15.39
Local Government Ombudsman	In England, an independent organisation that investigates complaints about councils and local authorities on most council matters including housing, planning, education and social services.	15.30–15.32
Makaton	A language programme using signs and symbols, for the teaching of communication, language and literacy skills for people with communication and learning difficulties.	3.11

Mediation	A process for resolving disagreements in which an impartial third party (the mediator) helps people in dispute to find a mutually acceptable resolution.	15.7–15.13
Mental capacity	See capacity	
Mental Health Act 1983	A law mainly about the compulsory care and treatment of patients with mental health problems. In particular, it covers detention in hospital for mental health treatment.	**Chapter 13** Deprivation of liberty other than in line with _ 6.50–6.53, 7.44 Attorneys and _ 7.27 Advance decisions and _9.37 IMCAs and 10.44, 10.51, 10.56–10.58 Children and young people and _ 12.6, 12.21 Complaints regarding _ 15.19
Mental Health Review Tribunal	An independent judicial body with powers to direct the discharge of patients who are detained under the Mental Health Act 1983.	13.31 13.42
NHS Litigation Authority	A Special Health Authority (part of the NHS), responsible for handling negligence claims made against NHS bodies in England.	15.22

Office of the Public Guardian (OPG)	The Public Guardian is an officer established under Section 57 of the Act. The Public Guardian will be supported by the Office of the Public Guardian, which will supervise deputies, keep a register of deputies, Lasting Powers of Attorney and Enduring Powers of Attorney, check on what attorneys are doing, and investigate any complaints about attorneys or deputies. The OPG replaces the Public Guardianship Office (PGO) that has been in existence for many years.	**14.8–14.22** Registering LPAs with _ 7.14–7.17 Supervision of attorneys by _ 7.69–7.74 Registering EPAs with _ 7.78 Guidance for EPAs _ 7.79 Guidance for receivers_ 8.5 Panel of deputies of _ 8.35 Supervision of deputies by _ 8.69–8.77
Official Solicitor	Provides legal services for vulnerable persons, or in the interests of achieving justice. The Official Solicitor represents adults who lack capacity to conduct litigation in county court or High Court proceedings in England and Wales, and in the Court of Protection.	Helping with formal assessment of capacity 4.54 Acting in applications to the Court of Protection 8.10 Acting as litigation friend 10.38, 15.39
Patient Advice and Liaison Service (PALS)	In England, a service providing information, advice and support to help NHS patients, their families and carers. PALS act on behalf of service users when handling patient and family concerns and can liaise with staff, managers and, where appropriate, other relevant organisations, to find solutions.	15.15–15.17

Permanent vegetative state (PVS)	A condition caused by catastrophic brain damage whereby patients in PVS have a permanent and irreversible lack of awareness of their surroundings and no ability to interact at any level with those around them.	6.18 8.18
Personal welfare	Personal welfare decisions are any decisions about person's healthcare, where they live, what clothes they wear, what they eat and anything needed for their general care and well-being. Attorneys and deputies can be appointed to make decisions about personal welfare on behalf of a person who lacks capacity. Many acts of care are to do with personal welfare.	_ LPAs 7.21–7.31 _ deputies 8.38–8.39 Advance decisions about _ 9.4, 9.35 Role of High Court in decisions about _ 15.44
Property and affairs	Any possessions owned by a person (such as a house or flat, jewellery or other possessions), the money they have in income, savings or investments and any expenditure. Attorneys and deputies can be appointed to make decisions about property and affairs on behalf of a person who lacks capacity.	_ LPAs 7.32–7.42 _ deputies 8.34–8.37 Restrictions on _ LPA 7.56 Duties of _ attorney 7.58, 7.67–7.68 _ EPAs 7.76–7.77 OPG panel of _ deputies 8.35 Duties of _ deputy 8.56, 8.67–8.68 _ of children and young people 12.3–12.4, 12.7
Protection from liability	Legal protection, granted to anyone who has acted or made decisions in line with the Act's principles.	Chapter 6

Protection of Vulnerable Adults (POVA) list	A register of individuals who have abused, neglected or otherwise harmed vulnerable adults in their care or placed vulnerable adults at risk of harm. Providers of care must not offer such individuals employment in care positions.	14.31
Public Services Ombudsman for Wales	An independent body that investigates complaints about local government and NHS organisations in Wales, and the National Assembly for Wales, concerning matters such as housing, planning, education, social services and health services.	15.20 15.30–15.32
Receiver	Someone appointed by the former Court of Protection to manage the property and affairs of a person lacking capacity to manage their own affairs. Existing receivers continue as deputies with legal authority to deal with the person's property and affairs.	8.5 8.35
Restraint	See Section 6(4) of the Act. The use or threat of force to help do an act which the person resists, or the restriction of the person's liberty of movement, whether or not they resist. Restraint may only be used where it is necessary to protect the person from harm and is proportionate to the risk of harm.	**6.39–6.44, 6.47–53** Use of _ in moves between accommoda-tion 6.11 Use of _ in healthcare and treatment decisions 6.15 Attorneys and _ 7.43-7.44 Deputies and _ 8.46 MHA and _ 13.5

Statutory principles	The five key principles are set out in Section 1 of the Act. They are designed to emphasise the fundamental concepts and core values of the Act and to provide a benchmark to guide decision-makers, professionals and carers acting under the Act's provisions. The principles generally apply to all actions and decisions taken under the Act.	**Chapter 2**
Two-stage test of capacity	Using sections 2 and 3 of the Act to assess whether or not a person has capacity to make a decision for themselves at that time.	**4.10–4.13** Protection from liability 6.27 Applying _ to advance decisions 9.39
Wilful neglect	An intentional or deliberate omission or failure to carry out an act of care by someone who has care of a person who lacks (or whom the person reasonably believes lacks) capacity to care for themselves. Section 44 introduces a new offence of wilful neglect of a person who lacks capacity.	14.23–14.26
Written statements of wishes and feelings	Written statements the person might have made before losing capacity about their wishes and feelings regarding issues such as the type of medical treatment they would want in the case of future illness, where they would prefer to live, or how they wish to be cared for. They should be used to help find out what someone's wishes and feelings might be, as part of working out their best interests. They are not the same as advance decisions to refuse treatment and are not binding.	5.34 5.37 5.42–5.44

ANNEX A

The following list provides contact details for some organisations that provide information, guidance or materials related to the Code of Practice and the Mental Capacity Act. The list is not exhaustive: many other organisations may also produce their own materials.

British Banking Association

[Provides a leaflet for customers on *'Banking for people who lack capacity to make decisions (England and Wales)'*. Available from www.bba.org.uk/publications/entry/banking-for-people-who-lack-capacity-to-make-decisions-england-and-wales/leaflets/]

Note—Words in square brackets have been amended by the authors to reflect changes to website addresses.

web: www.bba.org.uk
telephone: 020 7216 8800

British Medical Association

[Co-authors (with the Law Society) of *Assessment of Mental Capacity: A Practical Guide for Doctors and Lawyers* (Third edition) (London: The Law Society, 2010). See www.bma.org.uk/ap.nsf/Content/Assessmentmental?OpenDocument& Highlight=2,mental, capacity

Available from The Law Society (www.lawsocietyshop.org.uk/ecom_lawsoc/public/saleproduct.jsf?catalogueCode=9781853287787), price £41.95]

Note—Words in square brackets have been amended by the authors to reflect changes to website addresses.

web: www.bma.org.uk
telephone: 020 7387 4499

British Psychological Society

Publishers of *Guidelines on assessing capacity* – professional guidance available online to members.

web: www.bps.org.uk
telephone: (0)116 254 9568

Commission for Social Care Inspection

The Commission for Social Care Inspection (CSCI) registers, inspects and reports on social care services in England.

web: www.csci.org.uk
telephone: 0845 015 0120 / 0191 233 3323
textphone: 0845 015 2255 / 0191 233 3588

Criminal Records Bureau (CRB)

The CRB runs criminal records checks on people who apply for jobs working with children and vulnerable adults.

web: www.crb.org.uk
telephone: 0870 90 90 811

Department for Constitutional Affairs

The government department with responsibility for the Mental Capacity Act and the Code of Practice. Also publishes guidance for specific audiences www.dca.gov.uk/legal-policy/mental-capacity/guidance.htm

Department of Health

Publishes guidance for healthcare and social care staff in England. Key publications referenced in the Code include:

* on using restraint with people with learning disabilities and autistic spectrum disorder, see *Guidance for restrictive physical interventions* www.dh.gov.uk/
     assetRoot/04/06/84/61/04068461.pdf
* on adult protection procedures, see *No secrets: Guidance on developing and implementing multi-agency policies and procedures to protect vulnerable adults from abuse* www.dh.gov.uk/assetRoot/04/07/45/44/04074544.pdf
* on consent to examination and treatment, including advance decisions to refuse treatment www.dh/gov.uk/consent
* [on the Deprivation of Liberty safeguards, a supplement to this Code of Practice   www.dh.gov.uk/en/Publicationsandstatistics/Publications/PublicationsPolicyAndGuidance/DH_085476]
* on IMCAs and the IMCA pilots www.dh.gov.uk/imca
* [DH also is responsible for the *Mental Health Act 1983 Code of Practice* (TSO 2008) www.dh.gov.uk/prod_consum_dh/groups/dh_digitalassets/@dh/@en/documents/digitalasset/dh_087073.pdf]

Note—Words in square brackets have been amended by the authors to reflect changes to website addresses.

Direct.gov

Provides free legal information to people living in England and Wales to help them deal with legal problems.

web: www.direct.gov.uk/en/Governmentcitizensandrights/
                  Mentalcapacityandthelaw/index.htm

Note—Community Legal Services Direct no longer exists. The authors have added in this new entry in light of this.

Family Mediation Helpline

Provides general information on family mediation and contact details for mediation services in your local area.

Web: www.familymediationhelpline.co.uk
telephone: 0845 60 26 627

Healthcare Commission

The health watchdog in England, undertaking reviews and investigations into the provision of NHS and private healthcare services.

Web: www.healthcarecommission.org.uk
telephone: 0845 601 3012
switchboard: 020 7448 9200

Healthcare Inspectorate for Wales

Undertakes reviews and investigations into the provision of NHS funded care, either by or for Welsh NHS organisations.

Web: www.hiw.org.uk
email: hiw@wales.gsi.gov.uk
telephone: 029 2092 8850

Housing Ombudsman Service

The Housing Ombudsman Service considers complaints against member organisations, and deals with other housing disputes.

Web: www.ihos.org.uk
email: info@housing-ombudsman.org.uk
telephone: 020 7421 3800

Information Commissioner's Office

The Information Commissioner's Office is the UK's independent authority set up to promote access to official information and to protect personal information.

Web: www.ico.gov.uk
telephone   08456 30 60 60
helpline:

Legal Services Commission

Looks after legal aid in England and Wales, and provides information, advice and legal representation.

Web: www.legalservices.gov.uk

See also Community Legal Services Direct.

Local Government Ombudsman

The Local Government Ombudsmen investigate complaints about councils and certain other bodies.

Web: www.lgo.org.uk
telephone: 0845 602 1983

National Mediation Helpline

Provides access to a simple, low cost method of resolving a wide range of disputes.

The National Mediation Helpline is operated on behalf of the Department for Constitutional Affairs (DCA) in conjunction with the Civil Mediation Council (CMC).

Web: www.nationalmediationhelpline.com
telephone: 0845 60 30 809

Office of the Public Guardian

The new Public Guardian is established under the Act and will be supported by the Office of the Public Guardian, which will replace the current Public Guardianship Office (PGO). The OPG will be an executive agency of the Department for Constitutional Affairs. Amongst its other roles, it provides forms for LPAs and EPAs.

Web: From October 2007, a new website will be created at
              www.publicguardian.gov.uk

Official Solicitor

Provides legal services for vulnerable people and is able to represent people who lack capacity and act as a litigation friend.

Web: www.officialsolicitor.gov.uk
telephone: 020 7911 7127

Patient Advice and Liaison Service (PALS)

Provides information about the NHS and help resolve concerns or problems with the NHS, including support when making complaints.

Web: www.pals.nhs.uk

The site includes contact details for local PALS offices around the country.

Patient Information Advisory Group

Considers applications on behalf of the Secretary of State to allow the common law duty of confidentiality to be aside.

Web: www.advisorybodies.doh.gov.uk/PIAG

Public Service Ombudsman for Wales

Investigates complaints about local authorities and NHS organisations in Wales, and about the National Assembly Government for Wales.

Web: www.ombudsman-wales.org.uk
telephone: 01656 641 150

Welsh Assembly Government

Produces key pieces of guidance for healthcare and social care staff, including:

* *In safe hands – Implementing Adult Protection Procedures in Wales* (update 2003) [http://welshgovernmentpublications.soutron.net/publications/]
* *Framework for restrictive physical intervention policy and practice* (available for order from [http://welshgovernmentpublications.soutron.net/publications/])

Hard copies of this publication are available from TSO

For more information on the Mental Capacity Act contact [the Office of the Public Guardian]:

9am – 5pm, Mon – Fri

Note—Words in square brackets have been amended by the authors to reflect changes to website addresses.

Telephone: [0300 456 0300]
or   +44 207 664 7000 (for callers outside UK)
Text Phone: [0115 934 2778]

Fax:	0870 739 5780 (UK callers)
Email:	[customerservices@publicguardian.gsi.gov.uk]
Website:	[www.justice.gov.uk/about/opg.htm]
Post:	[Office of the Public Guardian PO Box 15118 Birmingham B16 6GX]

Note—Words in square brackets have been amended by the authors to reflect changes to contact information.

APPENDIX 3

MENTAL CAPACITY ACT 2005: DEPRIVATION OF LIBERTY SAFEGUARDS CODE OF PRACTICE SUPPLEMENTING THE MAIN MENTAL CAPACITY ACT 2005 CODE OF PRACTICE[1]

Issued by the Lord Chancellor on 26 August 2008 in accordance with sections 42 and 43 of the Act.

FOREWORD BY IVAN LEWIS AND EDWINA HART MBE

The Mental Capacity Act 2005 ('the Act') provides a statutory framework for acting and making decisions on behalf of individuals who lack the mental capacity to do so for themselves. It introduced a number of laws to protect these individuals and ensure that they are given every chance to make decisions for themselves. The Act came into force in October 2007.

The Government has added new provisions to the Act: the deprivation of liberty safeguards. The safeguards focus on some of the most vulnerable people in our society: those who for their own safety and in their own best interests need to be accommodated under care and treatment regimes that may have the effect of depriving them of their liberty, but who lack the capacity to consent.

The deprivation of a person's liberty is a very serious matter and should not happen unless it is absolutely necessary, and in the best interests of the person concerned. That is why the safeguards have been created: to ensure that any decision to deprive someone of their liberty is made following defined processes and in consultation with specific authorities.

---

[1]   As was anticipated in the Code of Practice (at para 2), and discussed in detail in Chapter 6 above, the case law upon deprivation of liberty has moved on substantially since it was issued in August 2008. It is likely that the Code of Practice will require updating in light of the decision of the Supreme Court in the conjoined appeals against the decisions of the Court of Appeal in *Cheshire West and Chester Council v P* [2011] EWCA Civ 1257, [2012] COPLR 37 and *P and Q v Surrey County Council* [2011] EWCA Civ 190, [2011] COPLR Con Vol 931. Further, it will also require updating to take into account the abolition of Primary Care Trusts with effect from 1 April 2013 (which means that local authorities will assume the responsibilities of supervisory bodies for those detained in hospital as well as in care homes). A decision has been taken not to annotate this document on a 'running' basis, but it now must be approached with some caution as a guide to the current state of the law.

The new provisions in the Act set out the legal framework of the deprivation of liberty safeguards. This Code of Practice is formally issued by the Lord Chancellor as a Code of Practice under the Mental Capacity Act 2005. It provides guidance and information for those implementing the deprivation of liberty safeguards legislation on a daily basis. In some cases, this will be paid staff, in others those who have been appointed in law to represent individuals who lack capacity to make decisions for themselves (such as deputies or donees of a Lasting Power of Attorney).

Because of this broad audience, the Code of Practice has been written so as to make it as user-friendly as possible – like the main Mental Capacity Act 2005 Code of Practice, issued in April 2007. We are grateful to all those who commented on earlier drafts of the Code to help it achieve that goal.

Ivan Lewis
Edwina Hart

INTRODUCTION

The Mental Capacity Act 2005 ('the Act'), covering England and Wales, provides a statutory framework for acting and making decisions on behalf of people who lack the capacity to make those decisions for themselves. These can be small decisions – such as what clothes to wear – or major decisions, such as where to live.

In some cases, people lack the capacity to consent to particular treatment or care that is recognised by others as being in their best interests, or which will protect them from harm. Where this care might involve depriving vulnerable people of their liberty in either a hospital or a care home, extra safeguards have been introduced, in law, to protect their rights and ensure that the care or treatment they receive is in their best interests.

This Code of Practice helps explain how to identify when a person is, or is at risk of, being deprived of their liberty and how deprivation of liberty may be avoided. It also explains the safeguards that have been put in place to ensure that deprivation of liberty, where it does need to occur, has a lawful basis. In addition, it provides guidance on what someone should do if they suspect that a person who lacks capacity is being deprived of their liberty unlawfully.

These safeguards are an important way of protecting the rights of many vulnerable people and should not be viewed negatively. Depriving someone of their liberty can be a necessary requirement in order to provide effective care or treatment. By following the criteria set out in the safeguards, and explained in this Code of Practice, the decision to deprive someone of their liberty can be made lawfully and properly.

How does this Code of Practice relate to the main Mental Capacity Act 2005 Code of Practice?

This document adds to the guidance in the main Mental Capacity Act 2005 Code of Practice ('the main Code'), which was issued in April 2007, and should be used in conjunction with the main Code. It focuses specifically on the deprivation of liberty safeguards added to the Act. These can be found in sections 4A and 4B of, and Schedules A1 and 1A to, the Act.

Though these safeguards were mentioned in the main Code (particularly in Chapters 6 and 13), they were not covered in any detail. That was because, at the time the main Code was published, the deprivation of liberty safeguards were still going through the Parliamentary process as part of the Mental Health Bill.[2]

Although the main Code does not cover the deprivation of liberty safeguards, the principles of that Code, and much of its content, are directly relevant to the deprivation of liberty safeguards. It is important that both the Act and the main Code are adhered to whenever capacity and best interests issues, and the deprivation of liberty safeguards, are being considered. The deprivation of liberty safeguards are in addition to, and do not replace, other safeguards in the Act.

How should this Code of Practice be used?

This Code of Practice provides guidance to anyone working with and/or caring for adults who lack capacity, but it particularly focuses on those who have a 'duty of care' to a person who lacks the capacity to consent to the care or treatment that is being provided, where that care or treatment may include the need to deprive the person of their liberty. This Code of Practice is also intended to provide information for people who are, or could become, subject to the deprivation of liberty safeguards, and for their families, friends and carers, as well as for anyone who believes that someone is being deprived of their liberty unlawfully.

In this Code of Practice, as throughout the main Code, references to 'lack of capacity' refer to the capacity to make a particular decision at the time it needs to be made. In the context of the deprivation of liberty safeguards, the capacity is specifically the capacity to decide whether or not to consent to care or treatment which involves being kept in a hospital or care home in circumstances that amount to a deprivation of liberty, at the time that decision needs to be made.

---

[2] The Mental Health Bill was used as a vehicle to amend the Mental Capacity Act 2005 in order to introduce the deprivation of liberty safeguards. The Bill became the Mental Health Act 2007 following completion of its Parliamentary passage.

What is the legal status of this Code of Practice?

As with the main Code, this Code of Practice is published by the Lord Chancellor, under sections 42 and 43 of the Mental Capacity Act 2005. The purpose of the main Code is to provide guidance and information about how the Act works in practice.

Both this Code and the main Code have statutory force, which means that certain people are under a legal duty to have regard to them. More details can be found in the Introduction to the main Code, which explains the legal status of the Code and who should have regard to it.

In addition to those for whom the main Code is intended, this Code of Practice specifically focuses on providing guidance for:

- people exercising functions relating to the deprivation of liberty safeguards, and
- people acting as a relevant person's representative[3] under the deprivation of liberty safeguards (see Chapter 7).

Scenarios used in this Code of Practice

This Code of Practice includes boxes within the main text containing scenarios, using imaginary characters and situations. These are intended to help illustrate what is meant in the main text. They should not in any way be taken as templates for decisions that need to be made in similar situations. Decisions must always be made on the facts of each individual case.

Alternative formats and further information

This Code of Practice is also available in Welsh and can be made available in other formats on request.

1 WHAT ARE THE DEPRIVATION OF LIBERTY SAFEGUARDS AND WHY WERE THEY INTRODUCED?

The deprivation of liberty safeguards were introduced to provide a legal framework around the deprivation of liberty. Specifically, they were introduced to prevent breaches of the European Convention on Human Rights (ECHR) such as the one identified by the judgment of the European Court of Human Rights (ECtHR) in the case of *HL v the United Kingdom*[4] (commonly referred to as the 'Bournewood' judgment). The case concerned an autistic man (HL)

---

3 A 'relevant person' is a person who is, or may become, deprived of their liberty in accordance with the deprivation of liberty safeguards.

4 (2004) Application No: 00045508/99.

with a learning disability, who lacked the capacity to decide whether he should be admitted to hospital for specific treatment. He was admitted on an informal basis under common law in his best interests, but this decision was challenged by HL's carers. In its judgment, the ECtHR held that this admission constituted a deprivation of HL's liberty and, further, that:

- the deprivation of liberty had not been in accordance with 'a procedure prescribed by law' and was, therefore, in breach of Article 5(1) of the ECHR, and

- there had been a contravention of Article 5(4) of the ECHR because HL had no means of applying quickly to a court to see if the deprivation of liberty was lawful.

To prevent further similar breaches of the ECHR, the Mental Capacity Act 2005 has been amended to provide safeguards for people who lack capacity specifically to consent to treatment or care in either a hospital or a care home[5] that, in their own best interests, can only be provided in circumstances that amount to a deprivation of liberty, and where detention under the Mental Health Act 1983 is not appropriate for the person at that time. These safeguards are referred to in this Code of Practice as 'deprivation of liberty safeguards'.

What are the deprivation of liberty safeguards?

1.1 The deprivation of liberty safeguards provide legal protection for those vulnerable people who are, or may become, deprived of their liberty within the meaning of Article 5 of the ECHR in a hospital or care home, whether placed under public or private arrangements. They do not apply to people detained under the Mental Health Act 1983. The safeguards exist to provide a proper legal process and suitable protection in those circumstances where deprivation of liberty appears to be unavoidable, in a person's own best interests.

1.2 Every effort should be made, in both commissioning and providing care or treatment, to prevent deprivation of liberty. If deprivation of liberty cannot be avoided, it should be for no longer than is necessary.

1.3 The safeguards provide for deprivation of liberty to be made lawful through 'standard' or 'urgent' authorisation processes. These processes are designed to prevent arbitrary decisions to deprive a person of liberty and give a right to challenge deprivation of liberty authorisations.

1.4 The deprivation of liberty safeguards mean that a 'managing authority' (i.e. the relevant hospital or care home – see paragraph 3.1) must seek authorisation from a 'supervisory body' in order to be able lawfully to deprive someone of their liberty. Before giving such an authorisation, the

---

[5]   Throughout this document, the term 'care home' means a care home registered under the Care Standards Act 2000.

supervisory body must be satisfied that the person has a mental disorder[6] and lacks capacity to decide about their residence or treatment. The supervisory body could be a primary care trust, a local authority, Welsh Ministers or a local health board (LHB) (see paragraph 3.3).

1.5 A decision as to whether or not deprivation of liberty arises will depend on all the circumstances of the case (as explained more fully in Chapter 2). It is neither necessary nor appropriate to apply for a deprivation of liberty authorisation for everyone who is in hospital or a care home simply because the person concerned lacks capacity to decide whether or not they should be there. In deciding whether or not an application is necessary, a managing authority should carefully consider whether any restrictions that are, or will be, needed to provide ongoing care or treatment amount to a deprivation of liberty when looked at together.

1.6 The deprivation of liberty safeguards cover:
- how an application for authorisation should be applied for
- how an application for authorisation should be assessed
- the requirements that must be fulfilled for an authorisation to be given
- how an authorisation should be reviewed
- what support and representation must be provided for people who are subject to an authorisation, and
- how people can challenge authorisations.

Who is covered by these safeguards?

1.7 The safeguards apply to people in England and Wales who have a mental disorder and lack capacity to consent to the arrangements made for their care or treatment, but for whom receiving care or treatment in circumstances that amount to a deprivation of liberty may be necessary to protect them from harm and appears to be in their best interests. A large number of these people will be those with significant learning disabilities, or older people who have dementia or some similar disability, but they can also include those who have certain other neurological conditions (for example as a result of a brain injury).

1.8 In order to come within the scope of a deprivation of liberty authorisation, a person must be detained in a hospital or care home, for the purpose of being given care or treatment in circumstances that amount to a deprivation of liberty. The authorisation must relate to the individual concerned and to the hospital or care home in which they are detained.

1.9 For the purposes of Article 5 of the ECHR, there is no distinction in principle between depriving a person who lacks capacity of their liberty

---

[6]   As defined in section 1 of the Mental Health Act 1983, a mental disorder is any disorder or disability of the mind, apart from dependence on alcohol and drugs. This includes all learning disabilities. The distinction in the Mental Health Act 1983 between learning disabilities depending on whether or not they are associated with abnormally aggressive or seriously irresponsible behaviour is not relevant.

for the purpose of treating them for a physical condition, and depriving them of their liberty for treatment of a mental disorder. There will therefore be occasions when people who lack capacity to consent to admission are taken to hospital for treatment of physical illnesses or injuries, and then need to be cared for in circumstances that amount to a deprivation of liberty. In these circumstances, a deprivation of liberty authorisation must be applied for. Consequently, this Code of Practice must be followed and applied in acute hospital settings as well as care homes and mental health units.

1.10 It is important to bear in mind that, while the deprivation of liberty might be for the purpose of giving a person treatment, a deprivation of liberty authorisation does not itself authorise treatment. Treatment that is proposed following authorisation of deprivation of liberty may only be given with the person's consent (if they have capacity to make the decision) or in accordance with the wider provisions of the Mental Capacity Act 2005. More details of this are contained in paragraphs 5.10 to 5.13 of this Code.

1.11 The safeguards cannot apply to people while they are detained in hospital under the Mental Health Act 1983. The safeguards can, however, apply to a person who has previously been detained in hospital under the Mental Health Act 1983. There are other cases in which people who are – or could be – subject to the Mental Health Act 1983 will not meet the eligibility requirement for the safeguards. Chapter 13 of the main Code contains guidance on the relationship between the Mental Capacity Act 2005 and the Mental Health Act 1983 generally, as does the Code of Practice to the Mental Health Act 1983 itself. Paragraphs 4.40 to 4.57 of the present Code explain the relationship of the deprivation of liberty safeguards to the Mental Health Act 1983, and in particular how to assess if a person is eligible to be deprived of their liberty under the safeguards.

1.12 The safeguards relate only to people aged 18 and over. If the issue of depriving a person under the age of 18 of their liberty arises, other safeguards must be considered – such as the existing powers of the court, particularly those under section 25 of the Children Act 1989, or use of the Mental Health Act 1983.

When can someone be deprived of their liberty?

1.13 Depriving someone who lacks the capacity to consent to the arrangements made for their care or treatment of their liberty is a serious matter, and the decision to do so should not be taken lightly. The deprivation of liberty safeguards make it clear that a person may only be deprived of their liberty:
- in their own best interests to protect them from harm
- if it is a proportionate response to the likelihood and seriousness of the harm, and
- if there is no less restrictive alternative.

1.14 Under no circumstances must deprivation of liberty be used as a form of punishment, or for the convenience of professionals, carers or anyone else. Deprivation of liberty should not be extended due to delays in moving people between care or treatment settings, for example when somebody awaits discharge after completing a period of hospital treatment.

Are there any cultural considerations in implementing the safeguards?

1.15 The deprivation of liberty safeguards should not impact in any different way on different racial or ethnic groups, and care should be taken to ensure that the provisions are not operated in a manner that discriminates against particular racial or ethnic groups. It is up to managing authorities and supervisory bodies to ensure that their staff are aware of their responsibilities in this regard and of the need to ensure that the safeguards are operated fairly and equitably.

1.16 Assessors who carry out deprivation of liberty assessments to help decide whether a person should be deprived of their liberty (see Chapter 4) should have the necessary skills and experience to take account of people's diverse backgrounds. Accordingly, they will need to have an understanding of, and respect for, the background of the relevant person. Supervisory bodies must take these factors into account when appointing assessors and must seek to appoint the most suitable available person for each case.

1.17 Interpreters should be available, where necessary, to help assessors to communicate not only with the relevant person but also with people with an interest in their care and treatment. An interpreter should be suitably qualified and experienced to enable them to provide effective language and communication support in the particular case concerned, and to offer appropriate assistance to the assessors involved. Information should be made available in other languages where relevant.

1.18 Any decision about the instruction of Independent Mental Capacity Advocates (see paragraphs 3.22 to 3.28) or relevant person's representatives (see Chapter 7) should take account of the cultural, national, racial or ethnic background of the relevant person.

Where do the safeguards apply?

1.19 Although the Bournewood judgment was specifically about a patient who lacked capacity to consent to admission to hospital for mental health treatment, the judgment has wider implications that extend to people who lack capacity and who might be deprived of their liberty either in a hospital or in a care home.

1.20 It will only be lawful to deprive somebody of their liberty elsewhere (for example, in their own home, in supported living arrangements other than in a care home, or in a day centre) when following an order of the Court of Protection on a personal welfare matter. In such a case, the Court of

Protection order itself provides a legal basis for the deprivation of liberty. This means that a separate deprivation of liberty authorisation under the processes set out in this Code of Practice is not required. More information about applying to the Court of Protection regarding personal welfare matters is given in Chapter 10.

How do the safeguards apply to privately arranged care or treatment?

1.21 Under the Human Rights Act 1998, the duty to act in accordance with the ECHR applies only to public authorities. However, all states that have signed up to the ECHR are obliged to make sure that the rights set out in the ECHR apply to all of their citizens. The Mental Capacity Act 2005 therefore makes it clear that the deprivation of liberty safeguards apply to both publicly and privately arranged care or treatment.

How do the safeguards relate to the rest of the Mental Capacity Act 2005?

1.22 The deprivation of liberty safeguards are in addition to, and do not replace, other safeguards in the Mental Capacity Act 2005. This means that decisions made, and actions taken, for a person who is subject to a deprivation of liberty authorisation must fulfil the requirements of the Act in the same way as for any other person. In particular, any action taken under the deprivation of liberty safeguards must be in line with the principles of the Act:

- A person must be assumed to have capacity to make a decision unless it is established that they lack the capacity to make that decision.
- A person is not to be treated as unable to make a decision unless all practicable steps to help them to do so have been taken without success.
- A person is not to be treated as unable to make a decision merely because they make an unwise decision.
- An act done, or decision made, under the Act for or on behalf of a person who lacks capacity must be done, or made, in their best interests.
- Before the act is done, or the decision is made, regard must be had to whether the purpose for which it is needed can be as effectively achieved in a way that is less restrictive of the person's rights and freedom of action.

These principles are set out in Chapter 2 of the main Code and explained in more detail in Chapters 3 to 6 of the same document. Paragraph 5.13 of the main Code contains a checklist of factors that need to be taken into account in determining a person's best interests.

2   WHAT IS DEPRIVATION OF LIBERTY?

There is no simple definition of deprivation of liberty. The question of whether the steps taken by staff or institutions in relation to a person amount to a deprivation of that person's liberty is ultimately a legal question, and only the courts can determine the law. This guidance seeks to assist staff and institutions in considering whether or not the steps they are taking, or proposing to take, amount to a deprivation of a person's liberty. The deprivation of liberty safeguards give best interests assessors the authority to make recommendations about proposed deprivations of liberty, and supervisory bodies the power to give authorisations that deprive people of their liberty.

This chapter provides guidance for staff and institutions on how to assess whether particular steps they are taking, or proposing to take, might amount to a deprivation of liberty, based on existing case law. It also considers what other factors may be taken into account when considering the issue of deprivation of liberty, including, importantly, what is permissible under the Mental Capacity Act 2005 in relation to restraint or restriction. Finally, it provides a summary of some of the most important cases to date.

Further legal developments may occur after this guidance has been issued, and healthcare and social care staff need to keep themselves informed of legal developments that may have a bearing on their practice.

What does case law say to date?

2.1   The European Court of Human Rights (ECtHR) has drawn a distinction between the deprivation of liberty of an individual (which is unlawful, unless authorised) and restrictions on the liberty of movement of an individual.

2.2   The ECtHR made it clear that the question of whether someone has been deprived of liberty depends on the particular circumstances of the case. Specifically, the ECtHR said in its October 2004 judgment in *HL v the United Kingdom*:

> 'to determine whether there has been a deprivation of liberty, the starting-point must be the specific situation of the individual concerned and account must be taken of a whole range of factors arising in a particular case such as the type, duration, effects and manner of implementation of the measure in question. The distinction between a deprivation of, and restriction upon, liberty is merely one of degree or intensity and not one of nature or substance.'

2.3   The difference between deprivation of liberty and restriction upon liberty is one of degree or intensity. It may therefore be helpful to envisage a scale, which moves from 'restraint' or 'restriction' to 'deprivation of liberty'. Where an individual is on the scale will depend on the concrete circumstances of the individual and may change over time. For more information on how the Act defines restraint, see paragraphs 2.8–2.12.

2.4 Although the guidance in this chapter includes descriptions of past decisions of the courts, which should be used to help evaluate whether deprivation of liberty may be occurring, each individual case must be assessed on its own circumstances. No two cases are likely to be identical, so it is important to be aware of previous court judgments and the factors that the courts have identified as important.

2.5 The ECtHR and UK courts have determined a number of cases about deprivation of liberty. Their judgments indicate that the following factors can be relevant to identifying whether steps taken involve more than restraint and amount to a deprivation of liberty. It is important to remember that this list is not exclusive; other factors may arise in future in particular cases.

- Restraint is used, including sedation, to admit a person to an institution where that person is resisting admission.
- Staff exercise complete and effective control over the care and movement of a person for a significant period.
- Staff exercise control over assessments, treatment, contacts and residence.
- A decision has been taken by the institution that the person will not be released into the care of others, or permitted to live elsewhere, unless the staff in the institution consider it appropriate.
- A request by carers for a person to be discharged to their care is refused.
- The person is unable to maintain social contacts because of restrictions placed on their access to other people.
- The person loses autonomy because they are under continuous supervision and control.

There is more information on some relevant cases at the end of this chapter (paragraphs 2.17–2.23).

How can deprivation of liberty be identified?

2.6 In determining whether deprivation of liberty has occurred, or is likely to occur, decision-makers need to consider all the facts in a particular case. There is unlikely to be any simple definition that can be applied in every case, and it is probable that no single factor will, in itself, determine whether the overall set of steps being taken in relation to the relevant person amount to a deprivation of liberty. In general, the decision-maker should always consider the following:

- All the circumstances of each and every case
- What measures are being taken in relation to the individual? When are they required? For what period do they endure? What are the effects of any restraints or restrictions on the individual? Why are they necessary? What aim do they seek to meet?

- What are the views of the relevant person, their family or carers? Do any of them object to the measures?
- How are any restraints or restrictions implemented? Do any of the constraints on the individual's personal freedom go beyond 'restraint' or 'restriction' to the extent that they constitute a deprivation of liberty?
- Are there any less restrictive options for delivering care or treatment that avoid deprivation of liberty altogether?
- Does the cumulative effect of all the restrictions imposed on the person amount to a deprivation of liberty, even if individually they would not?

What practical steps can be taken to reduce the risk of deprivation of liberty occurring?

2.7 There are many ways in which providers and commissioners of care can reduce the risk of taking steps that amount to a deprivation of liberty, by minimising the restrictions imposed and ensuring that decisions are taken with the involvement of the relevant person and their family, friends and carers. The processes for staff to follow are:
- Make sure that all decisions are taken (and reviewed) in a structured way, and reasons for decisions recorded.
- Follow established good practice for care planning.
- Make a proper assessment of whether the person lacks capacity to decide whether or not to accept the care or treatment proposed, in line with the principles of the Act (see Chapter 3 of the main Code for further guidance).
- Before admitting a person to hospital or residential care in circumstances that may amount to a deprivation of liberty, consider whether the person's needs could be met in a less restrictive way. Any restrictions placed on the person while in hospital or in a care home must be kept to the minimum necessary, and should be in place for the shortest possible period.
- Take proper steps to help the relevant person retain contact with family, friends and carers. Where local advocacy services are available, their involvement should be encouraged to support the person and their family, friends and carers.
- Review the care plan on an ongoing basis. It may well be helpful to include an independent element, possibly via an advocacy service, in the review.

What does the Act mean by 'restraint'?

2.8 Section 6(4) of the Act states that someone is using restraint if they:
- use force – or threaten to use force – to make someone do something that they are resisting, or

- restrict a person's freedom of movement, whether they are resisting or not.

2.9   Paragraphs 6.40 to 6.48 of the main Code contain guidance about the appropriate use of restraint. Restraint is appropriate when it is used to prevent harm to the person who lacks capacity and it is a proportionate response to the likelihood and seriousness of harm. Appropriate use of restraint falls short of deprivation of liberty.

2.10 Preventing a person from leaving a care home or hospital unaccompanied because there is a risk that they would try to cross a road in a dangerous way, for example, is likely to be seen as a proportionate restriction or restraint to prevent the person from coming to harm. That would be unlikely, in itself, to constitute a deprivation of liberty. Similarly, locking a door to guard against immediate harm is unlikely, in itself, to amount to a deprivation of liberty.

2.11 The ECtHR has also indicated that the duration of any restrictions is a relevant factor when considering whether or not a person is deprived of their liberty. This suggests that actions that are immediately necessary to prevent harm may not, in themselves, constitute a deprivation of liberty.

2.12 However, where the restriction or restraint is frequent, cumulative and ongoing, or if there are other factors present, then care providers should consider whether this has gone beyond permissible restraint, as defined in the Act. If so, then they must either apply for authorisation under the deprivation of liberty safeguards (as explained in Chapter 3) or change their care provision to reduce the level of restraint.

How does the use of restraint apply within a hospital or when taking someone to a hospital or a care home?

Within a hospital

2.13 If a person in hospital for mental health treatment, or being considered for admission to a hospital for mental health treatment, needs to be restrained, this is likely to indicate that they are objecting to treatment or to being in hospital. The care providers should consider whether the need for restraint means the person is objecting (see paragraph 4.46 of this Code for guidance on how to decide whether a person is objecting for this purpose). A person who objects to mental health treatment, and who meets the criteria for detention under the Mental Health Act 1983, is normally ineligible for an authorisation under the deprivation of liberty safeguards. If the care providers believe it is necessary to detain the person, they may wish to consider use of the Mental Health Act 1983.

Taking someone to a hospital or a care home

2.14 Transporting a person who lacks capacity from their home, or another location, to a hospital or care home will not usually amount to a deprivation of liberty (for example, to take them to hospital by ambulance in an emergency.) Even where there is an expectation that the person will be deprived of liberty within the care home or hospital, it is unlikely that the journey itself will constitute a deprivation of liberty so that an authorisation is needed before the journey commences. In almost all cases, it is likely that a person can be lawfully taken to a hospital or a care home under the wider provisions of the Act, as long as it is considered that being in the hospital or care home will be in their best interests.

2.15 In a very few cases, there may be exceptional circumstances where taking a person to a hospital or a care home amounts to a deprivation of liberty, for example where it is necessary to do more than persuade or restrain the person for the purpose of transportation, or where the journey is exceptionally long. In such cases, it may be necessary to seek an order from the Court of Protection to ensure that the journey is taken on a lawful basis.

How should managing authorities avoid unnecessary applications for standard authorisations?

2.16 While it is unlawful to deprive a person of their liberty without authorisation, managing authorities should take into consideration that unnecessary applications for standard authorisations in cases that do not in fact involve depriving a person of liberty may place undue stress upon the person being assessed and on their families or carers. Moreover, consideration must always be given to the possibility of less restrictive options for delivering care or treatment that avoid deprivation of liberty altogether.

Examples of case law

2.17 To provide further guidance, the following paragraphs contain short descriptions of what appear to be the significant features of recent or important cases in England and Wales and the ECtHR dealing with deprivation of liberty. Remember that:
- these descriptions are for guidance only
- only the courts can authoritatively determine the law; and
- the courts are likely to give judgments in cases after this guidance is issued. Staff will need to keep up to date and take account of further relevant legal developments.

Cases where the courts found that the steps taken did not involve a deprivation of liberty

2.18 *LLBC v TG* (judgment of High Court of 14 November 2007)
TG was a 78-year-old man with dementia and cognitive impairment. TG was resident in a care home, but was admitted to hospital with

pneumonia and septicaemia. While he was in hospital, there was a dispute between the local authority and TG's daughter and granddaughter about TG's future. The daughter and granddaughter wanted TG to live with them, but the local authority believed that TG needed 24-hour care in a residential care home.

The council obtained an order from the court, directing that TG be delivered to the care home identified as appropriate by the council. Neither the daughter nor granddaughter was informed that a court hearing was taking place. That order was subsequently changed and TG was able to live with his daughter and granddaughter.

TG's daughter and granddaughter claimed that the period of time he had spent at the care home amounted to a deprivation of his liberty.

The judge considered that there was no deprivation of liberty, but the case was borderline. The key factors in his decision included:

- The care home was an ordinary care home where only ordinary restrictions of liberty applied.
- The family were able to visit TG on a largely unrestricted basis and were entitled to take him out from the home for outings.
- TG was personally compliant and expressed himself as happy in the care home. He had lived in a local authority care home for over three years and was objectively content with his situation there.
- There was no occasion where TG was objectively deprived of his liberty.

The judge said:

> 'Whilst I agree that the circumstances of the present case may be near the borderline between mere restrictions of liberty and Article 5 detention, I have come to the conclusion that, looked at as a whole and having regard to all the relevant circumstances, the placement of TG in Towerbridge falls short of engaging Article 5.'

2.19 *Nielsen v Denmark (ECtHR; (1988) 11 EHRR 175)*

The mother of a 12-year-old boy arranged for his admission to the state hospital's psychiatric ward. The boy had a nervous disorder and required treatment in the form of regular talks and environmental therapy. The treatment given, and the conditions under which it was administered, was appropriate. The duration of treatment was 5½ months. The boy, however, applied to the ECtHR, feeling that he had been deprived of his liberty.

The restrictions placed on the applicant's freedom of movement and contacts with the outside world were not much different from restrictions that might be imposed on a child in an ordinary hospital. The door of the ward was locked to prevent children exposing themselves to danger or running around disturbing other patients. The applicant was free to leave the ward with permission and to go out if accompanied by a member of staff. He was able to visit his family and friends, and towards the end of his stay to go to school.

The Court held:

'The restrictions imposed on the applicant were not of a nature or degree similar to the cases of deprivation of liberty specified in paragraph (1) of Article 5. In particular, he was not detained as a person of unsound mind. ... Indeed, the restrictions to which the applicant was subject were no more than the normal requirements for the care of a child of 12 years of age receiving treatment in hospital. The conditions in which the applicant stayed thus did not, in principle, differ from those obtaining in many hospital wards where children with physical disorders are treated.'

It concluded:

'the hospitalisation of the applicant did not amount to a deprivation of liberty within the meaning of Article 5, but was a responsible exercise by his mother of her custodial rights in the interests of the child.'

2.20 *HM v Switzerland (ECtHR; (2002) 38 EHRR 314)*

An 84-year-old woman was placed indefinitely in a nursing home by state authorities. She had had the possibility of staying at home and being cared for there, but she and her son had refused to co-operate with the relevant care association, and her living conditions had subsequently deteriorated. The state authorities placed her in the home in order to provide her with necessary medical care and satisfactory living conditions and hygiene.

The woman was not placed in the secure ward of the home but was free to move within the home and to have social contacts with the outside world. She was initially undecided as to what solution she preferred and, after moving into the home, the applicant had agreed to stay there. However, she subsequently applied to the courts saying that she had been deprived of her liberty.

The Court held that she had not been deprived of her liberty:

'Bearing these elements in mind, in particular the fact that [the authorities] had ordered the applicant's placement in the nursing home in her own interests in order to provide her with the necessary medical care and satisfactory living conditions and standards of hygiene, and also taking into consideration the comparable circumstances of *Nielsen v Denmark* [see case summary above], the Court concludes that in the circumstances of the present case the applicant's placement in the nursing home did not amount to a deprivation of liberty within the meaning of Article 5(1), but was a responsible measure taken by the competent authorities in the applicant's best interests.'

Cases where the courts have found that the steps taken involve a deprivation of liberty

2.21 *DE and JE v Surrey County Council (SCC)* (High Court judgment of 29 December 2006)

DE was a 76-year-old man who, following a major stroke, had become blind and had significant short-term memory impairment. He also had dementia and lacked capacity to decide where he should live, but was still often able to express his wishes with some clarity and force.

DE was married to JE. In August 2003, DE was living at home with JE. There was an occasion when JE felt that she could not care for DE, and placed him on a chair on the pavement in front of the house and called the police. The local authority then placed him in two care homes, referred to in the judgment of the court as the X home and the Y home.

Within the care homes, DE had a very substantial degree of freedom and lots of contact with the outside world. He was never subject to physical or chemical restraint.

DE repeatedly expressed the wish to live with JE, and JE also wanted DE to live with her. SCC would not agree to DE returning to live with, or visit, JE and made it clear that if JE were to persist in an attempt to remove DE, SCC would contact the police. DE and JE applied to the courts that this was a deprivation of his liberty.

In his judgment, Justice Munby said:

'The fundamental issue in this case ... is whether DE has been and is deprived of his liberty to leave the X home and whether DE has been and is deprived of his liberty to leave the Y home. And when I refer to leaving the X home and the Y home, I do not mean leaving for the purpose of some trip or outing approved by SCC or by those managing the institution; I mean leaving in the sense of removing himself permanently in order to live where and with whom he chooses, specifically removing himself to live at home with JE.'

He then said:

'DE was not and is not "free to leave", and was and is, in that sense, completely under the control of [the local authority], because, as [counsel for DE] put it, it was and is [the local authority] who decides the essential matters of where DE can live, whether he can leave and whether he can be with JE.'

He concluded:

'The simple reality is that DE will be permitted to leave the institution in which [the local authority] has placed him and be released to the care of JE only as and when, – if ever; probably never, – [the local authority] considers it appropriate. [The local authority's] motives may be the purest, but in my judgment, [it] has been and is continuing to deprive DE of his liberty.'

2.22   *HL v United Kingdom (ECtHR; (2004) 40 EHRR 761)*

A 48-year-old man who had had autism since birth was unable to speak and his level of understanding was limited. He was frequently agitated and had a history of self-harming behaviour. He lacked the capacity to consent to treatment.

For over 30 years, he was cared for in Bournewood Hospital. In 1994, he was entrusted to carers and for three years he lived successfully with his carers. Following an incident of self-harm at a day centre on 22 July 1997, the applicant was taken to Bournewood Hospital where he was re-admitted informally (not under the Mental Health Act 1983).

The carers wished to have the applicant released to their care, which the hospital refused. The carers were unable to visit him.

In its judgment in *HL v the United Kingdom*, the ECtHR said that:

> 'the key factor in the present case [is] that the health care professionals treating and managing the applicant exercised complete and effective control over his care and movements from the moment he presented acute behavioural problems on July 22, 1997 to the date when he was compulsorily detained on October 29, 1997.

> 'His responsible medical officer (Dr M) was clear that, had the applicant resisted admission or tried to leave thereafter, she would have prevented him from doing so and would have considered his involuntary committal under s. 3 of the 1983 Act; indeed, as soon as the Court of Appeal indicated that his appeal would be allowed, he was compulsorily detained under the 1983 Act. The correspondence between the applicant's carers and Dr M reflects both the carer's wish to have the applicant immediately released to their care and, equally, the clear intention of Dr M and the other relevant health care professionals to exercise strict control over his assessment, treatment, contacts and, notably, movement and residence; the applicant would only be released from hospital to the care of Mr and Mrs E as and when those professionals considered it appropriate. ... it was clear from the above noted correspondence that the applicant's contact with his carers was directed and controlled by the hospital, his carers visiting him for the first time after his admission on 2 November 1997.

> 'Accordingly, the concrete situation was that the applicant was under continuous supervision and control and was not free to leave.'

2.23 *Storck v Germany (ECtHR; (2005) 43 EHRR 96)*

A young woman was placed by her father in a psychiatric institution on occasions in 1974 and 1975. In July 1977, at the age of 18, she was placed again in a psychiatric institution. She was kept in a locked ward and was under the continuous supervision and control of the clinic personnel and was not free to leave the clinic during her entire stay of 20 months. When she attempted to flee, she was shackled. When she succeeded one time, she was brought back by the police. She was unable to maintain regular contact with the outside world.

She applied to the courts on the basis that she had been deprived of her liberty. There was a dispute about whether she consented to her confinement.

The Court noted:

> 'the applicant, on several occasions, had tried to flee from the clinic. She had to be shackled in order to prevent her from absconding and had to be brought back to the clinic by the police when she managed to escape on one occasion. Under these circumstances, the Court is unable to discern any factual basis for the assumption that the applicant – presuming that she had the capacity to consent – agreed to her continued stay in the clinic. In the alternative, assuming that the applicant was no longer capable of consenting

following her treatment with strong medication, she cannot, in any event, be considered to have validly agreed to her stay in the clinic.'

2.24 These cases reinforce the need to carefully consider all the specific circumstances of the relevant individual before deciding whether or not a person is being deprived of their liberty. They also underline the vital importance of involving family, friends and carers in this decision-making process: a significant feature of a number of the cases that have come before the courts is a difference of opinion or communication issue between the commissioners or providers of care and family members and carers.

3 HOW AND WHEN CAN DEPRIVATION OF LIBERTY BE APPLIED FOR AND AUTHORISED?

There are some circumstances in which depriving a person, who lacks capacity to consent to the arrangements made for their care or treatment, of their liberty is necessary to protect them from harm, and is in their best interests.

Deprivation of liberty can be authorised by supervisory bodies (primary care trusts (PCTs), local authorities, Welsh Ministers or local health boards (LHBs). To obtain authorisation to deprive someone of their liberty, managing authorities have to apply for an authorisation following the processes set out in this chapter.[7] Once an application has been received, the supervisory body must then follow the assessment processes set out in Chapter 4 before it can authorise deprivation of liberty. It should be borne in mind that a deprivation of liberty authorisation does not, in itself, give authority to treat someone. This issue is covered in paragraphs 5.10 to 5.13.

In the vast majority of cases, it should be possible to plan in advance so that a standard authorisation can be obtained before the deprivation of liberty begins. There may, however, be some exceptional cases where the need for the deprivation of liberty is so urgent that it is in the best interests of the person for it to begin while the application is being considered. In that case, the care home or hospital may give an urgent authorisation for up to seven days (see Chapter 6).

How, in summary, can deprivation of liberty be authorised?

3.1 A **managing authority** has responsibility for applying for authorisation of deprivation of liberty for any person who may come within the scope of the deprivation of liberty safeguards:

---

[7]   If a person is lawfully deprived of liberty in a care home or hospital as **a consequence of an order of the Court of Protection**, there is no need to apply for an authorisation. However, once the order of the Court of Protection has expired, for lawful deprivation of liberty to continue authorisation must be obtained by following the processes set out in this chapter.

- In the case of an NHS hospital, the managing authority is the NHS body responsible for the running of the hospital in which the relevant person is, or is to be, a resident.
- In the case of a care home or a private hospital, the managing authority will be the person registered, or required to be registered, under part 2 of the Care Standards Act 2000 in respect of the hospital or care home.

3.2 If a healthcare or social care professional thinks that an authorisation is needed, they should inform the managing authority. This might be as a result of a care review or needs assessment but could happen at any other time too. (See Chapter 9 for guidance on action to take if there is a concern that a person is already being deprived of their liberty, without authorisation.)

3.3 A **supervisory body** is responsible for considering requests for authorisations, commissioning the required assessments (see Chapter 4) and, where all the assessments agree, authorising the deprivation of liberty:

- Where the deprivation of liberty safeguards are applied to a person in a hospital situated in England, the supervisory body will be:
  - if a PCT commissions[8] the relevant care or treatment (or it is commissioned on the PCT's behalf), that PCT
  - if the Welsh Ministers or an LHB commissions the relevant care and treatment in England, the Welsh Ministers, or
  - in any other case, the PCT for the area in which the hospital is situated.
- Where the deprivation of liberty safeguards are applied to a person in a hospital situated in Wales, the supervisory body will be the Welsh Ministers or an LHB **unless** a PCT commissions the relevant care and treatment in Wales, in which case the PCT will be the supervisory body.
- Where the deprivation of liberty safeguards are applied to a person in a care home, whether situated in England or Wales, the supervisory body will be the local authority for the area in which the person is ordinarily resident. However, if the person is not ordinarily resident in the area of any local authority (for example a person of no fixed abode), the supervisory body will be the local authority for the area in which the care home is situated.[9]

---

[8] Guidance on establishing the responsible commissioner can be found at http://www.dh.gov.uk/en/Publicationsandstatistics/Publications/PublicationsPolicyAndGuidance/DH_078466.

[9] To work out the place of ordinary residence, the usual mechanisms under the National Assistance Act 1948 apply (see www.dh.gov.uk/en/Publicationsandstatistics/Publications/PublicationsPolicyAndGuidance/DH_113627 – new website address inserted by the authors). Any unresolved questions about the ordinary residence of a person will be handled by the Secretary of State or by the Welsh Ministers. Until a decision is made, the local authority that received the application must act as the supervisory body. After the decision is made, the local authority of ordinary residence must become the supervisory body. Regulations 17 to 19 of the Mental Capacity (Deprivation of Liberty: Standard Authorisations, Assessments and Ordinary Residence) Regulations 2008 set out, for England, arrangements that are to have effect while

3.4   There are two types of authorisation: standard and urgent. A managing authority must request a standard authorisation when it appears likely that, at some time during the next 28 days, someone will be accommodated in its hospital or care home in circumstances that amount to a deprivation of liberty within the meaning of Article 5 of the European Convention on Human Rights. The request must be made to the supervisory body. Whenever possible, authorisation should be obtained in advance. Where this is not possible, and the managing authority believes it is necessary to deprive someone of their liberty in their best interests **before** the standard authorisation process can be completed, the managing authority must itself give an urgent authorisation and then obtain standard authorisation within seven calendar days (see Chapter 6).

3.5   The flowchart at Annex 1 gives an overview of how the deprivation of liberty safeguards process should operate.

How should managing authorities decide whether to apply for an authorisation?

3.6   Managing authorities should have a procedure in place that identifies:
- whether deprivation of liberty is or may be necessary in a particular case
- what steps they should take to assess whether to seek authorisation
- whether they have taken all practical and reasonable steps to avoid a deprivation of liberty
- what action they should take if they do need to request an authorisation
- how they should review cases where authorisation is or may be necessary, and
- who should take the necessary action.

A flowchart that can be used to help develop such a procedure is at Annex 2.

What is the application process?

3.7   A managing authority must apply for a standard authorisation. The application should be made in writing to the supervisory body. A standard form is available for this purpose.

3.8   In England, the request from a managing authority for a standard authorisation must include:
- the name and gender of the relevant person
- the age of the relevant person or, where this is not known, whether the managing authority reasonably believes that the relevant person is aged 18 years or older

---

any question as to the ordinary residence of a person is determined in a case in which a local authority has received a request for a standard authorisation or a request to decide whether there is an unauthorised deprivation of liberty.

- the address at which the relevant person is currently located, and the telephone number at the address
- the name, address and telephone number of the managing authority and the name of the person within the managing authority who is dealing with the request
- the purpose for which the authorisation is requested
- the date from which the authorisation is sought, and
- whether the managing authority has given an urgent authorisation and, if so, the date on which it expires.

3.9 A request for a standard authorisation must also include, if it is available or could reasonably be obtained by the managing authority:

- any medical information relating to the relevant person's health that the managing authority reasonably considers to be relevant to the proposed restrictions to their liberty
- the diagnosis of the mental disorder (within the meaning of the Mental Health Act 1983 but disregarding any exclusion for persons with learning disability) from which the relevant person is suffering
- any relevant care plans and needs assessments
- the racial, ethnic or national origins of the relevant person
- whether the relevant person has any special communication needs
- details of the proposed restrictions on the relevant person's liberty
- whether it is necessary for an Independent Mental Capacity Advocate (IMCA) to be instructed
- where the purpose of the proposed restrictions to the relevant person's liberty is to give treatment, whether the relevant person has made an advance decision that may be valid and applicable to some or all of that treatment
- whether there is an existing standard authorisation in relation to the detention of the relevant person and, if so, the date of the expiry of that authorisation
- whether the relevant person is subject to any requirements of the Mental Health Act 1983, and
- the name, address and telephone number of:
  - anyone named by the relevant person as someone to be consulted about their welfare
  - anyone engaged in caring for the person or interested in their welfare
  - any donee of a Lasting Power of Attorney ('donee') granted by the person
  - any deputy appointed for the person by the court, and
  - any IMCA who has already been instructed.

If there is an existing authorisation, information that has not changed does not have to be resupplied.

3.10 In Wales, the request from a managing authority for a standard authorisation must include:

- the name of the relevant person
- the name, address and telephone number of the managing authority

- the reasons why the managing authority considers that the relevant person is being or will be detained in circumstances which amount to a deprivation of liberty
- the reasons why the managing authority considers that the relevant person satisfies the qualifying requirements
- details of any urgent authorisation
- information or documents in support of why the relevant person satisfies the qualifying requirements
- the name, address and telephone number of any person who has an interest in the welfare of the relevant person, and
- details of any relevant valid and applicable advance decision.

Where should applications be sent?

3.11 If the application is being made by a care home, the application must be sent to the local authority for the area in which the relevant person is ordinarily resident. If the relevant person is not ordinarily resident in the area of any local authority (for example, is of no fixed abode), if the care home does not know where the person currently lives, or if the person does not live in England or Wales, the application should be sent to the local authority in whose area the care home is located.

3.12 When the application is being made by a hospital:
- if the care is commissioned by a PCT, the application should be sent to that PCT
- if the care is commissioned by the Welsh Ministers, the application should be sent to the LHB for the area in which the relevant person is ordinarily resident
- if the care is commissioned by an LHB, the application should be sent to that LHB, and
- in any other case (for example, care that is commissioned privately), the application should be sent to the PCT for the area in which the relevant hospital is situated.

3.13 An application sent to the wrong supervisory body can be passed on to the correct supervisory body without the managing authority needing to reapply. But the managing authority should make every effort to establish which is the correct supervisory body to minimise delays in handling the application. (Footnote 8 explains how place of ordinary residence is determined and how disputes about the place of ordinary residence will be resolved.)

3.14 The managing authority must keep a written record of each request made for a standard authorisation and the reasons for making the request.

Who should be informed that an application has been made?

3.15 The managing authority should tell the relevant person's family, friends and carers, and any IMCA already involved in the relevant person's case, that it has applied for an authorisation of deprivation of liberty, unless it is impractical or impossible to do so, or undesirable in terms of the interests of the relevant person's health or safety. Anyone who is engaged in caring for the relevant person or interested in their welfare, or who has been named by them as a person to consult, must be given the opportunity to input their views on whether deprivation of liberty is in the best interests of the relevant person, as part of the best interests assessment (see paragraphs 4.58 to 4.76), as far as is practical and appropriate. The views of the relevant person about who to inform and consult should be taken into account.

3.16 The managing authority must notify the supervisory body if it is satisfied that there is no one who should be consulted in determining the relevant person's best interests, except those providing care and treatment for the relevant person in a professional capacity or for remuneration. In such a case, the supervisory body must instruct an IMCA to represent and support the relevant person before any assessments take place (see paragraphs 3.22 to 3.27 regarding the rights and role of an IMCA instructed in these circumstances).

What action does the supervisory body need to take when it receives an application for authorisation?

3.17 When it receives an application for authorisation of deprivation of liberty, the supervisory body must, as soon as is practical and possible:
- consider whether the request is appropriate and should be pursued, and
- seek any further information that it requires from the managing authority to help it with the decision.

If the supervisory body has any doubts about proceeding with the request, it should seek to resolve them with the managing authority.

3.18 Supervisory bodies should have a procedure in place that identifies the action they should take, who should take it and within what timescale. As far as practical and possible, they should communicate the procedure to managing authorities and give them the relevant contact details for making an application. The flowchart at Annex 3 summarises the process that a supervisory body should follow on receipt of a request from a managing authority for a standard deprivation of liberty authorisation.

Can an application for authorisation be made in advance?

3.19 A standard authorisation comes into force when it is given, or at any later time specified in the authorisation. Paragraph 3.4 refers to the timescales for initially applying for authorisations: 28 days are allowed so that authorisations can usually be sought as part of care planning (such as planning of discharge from hospital). There is no statutory limit on how far in advance of the expiry of one authorisation a fresh authorisation can be sought. Clearly, however, an authorisation should not be applied for too far in advance as this may prevent an assessor from making an accurate assessment of what the person's circumstances will be at the time the authorisation will come into force.

3.20 If a supervisory body considers that an application for an authorisation has been made too far in advance, it should raise the matter with the managing authority. The outcome may be an agreement with the managing authority that the application should be withdrawn, to be resubmitted at a more appropriate time.

What happens when the managing authority and the supervisory body are the same organisation?

3.21 In some cases, a single organisation will be both supervisory body and managing authority – for example, where a local authority itself provides a residential care home, rather than purchasing the service from another organisation. This does not prevent it from acting in both capacities. However, in England the regulations specify that in such a situation the best interests assessor cannot be an employee of the supervisory body/managing authority, or providing services to it. For example, in a case involving a local authority care home, the best interests assessor could be an NHS employee or an independent practitioner. (See paragraphs 4.13 and 4.60 for full details of who can be a best interests assessor.) There are similar provisions for Wales.

When should an IMCA be instructed?

3.22 If there is nobody appropriate to consult, other than people engaged in providing care or treatment for the relevant person in a professional capacity[10] or for remuneration, the managing authority must notify the supervisory body when it submits the application for the deprivation of liberty authorisation. The supervisory body must then instruct an IMCA straight away to represent the person. It is particularly important that the IMCA is instructed quickly if an urgent authorisation has been given, so that they can make a meaningful input at a very early stage in the process. (See paragraph 3.28 for other stages in the deprivation of liberty safeguards process when an IMCA must or may be instructed.)

3.23 Chapter 10 of the main Code ('What is the new Independent Mental Capacity Advocate service and how does it work?') describes the wider rights and role of an IMCA. Supervisory bodies should follow the guidance in that chapter in identifying an IMCA who is suitably qualified to represent the relevant person. However, it is also important to note that an IMCA instructed at this initial stage of the deprivation of liberty safeguards process has additional rights and responsibilities compared to

---

[10] A friend or family member is **not** considered to be acting in a professional capacity simply because they have been appointed as the person's representative for a previous authorisation.

an IMCA more generally instructed under the Mental Capacity Act 2005. IMCAs in this context have the right to:

- as they consider appropriate, give information or make submissions to assessors, which assessors must take into account in carrying out their assessments
- receive copies of any assessments from the supervisory body
- receive a copy of any standard authorisation given by the supervisory body
- be notified by the supervisory body if they are unable to give a standard authorisation because one or more of the deprivation of liberty assessments did not meet the qualifying requirements
- receive a copy of any urgent authorisation from the managing authority
- receive from the managing authority a copy of any notice declining to extend the duration of an urgent authorisation
- receive from the supervisory body a copy of any notice that an urgent authorisation has ceased to be in force, and
- apply to the Court of Protection for permission to take the relevant person's case to the Court in connection with a matter relating to the giving or refusal of a standard or urgent authorisation (in the same way as any other third party can).

The assessment and authorisation processes are described in Chapters 4 and 5.

3.24 IMCAs will need to familiarise themselves with the relevant person's circumstances and to consider what they may need to tell any of the assessors during the course of the assessment process. They will also need to consider whether they have any concerns about the outcome of the assessment process.

3.25 Differences of opinion between an IMCA and an assessor should ideally be resolved while the assessment is still in progress. Where there are significant disagreements between an IMCA and one or more of the assessors that cannot be resolved between them, the supervisory body should be informed before the assessment is finalised. The supervisory body should then consider what action might be appropriate, including perhaps convening a meeting to discuss the matter. Wherever possible, differences of opinion should be resolved informally in order to minimise the need for an IMCA to make an application to the Court of Protection. However, an IMCA should not be discouraged from making an application to the Court of Protection should they consider it necessary. (Chapter 15 of the main Code ('What are the best ways to settle disagreements and disputes about issues covered in the Act?') contains general guidance about the resolution of disputes arising under the Act.)

3.26 An IMCA will also need to consider whether they have any concerns about the giving of an urgent authorisation (see Chapter 6), and whether it would be appropriate to challenge the giving of such an authorisation via the Court of Protection.

3.27 Once a relevant person's representative is appointed (see Chapter 7), the duties imposed on the IMCA cease to apply. The IMCA may, however, still apply to the Court of Protection for permission to take the relevant person's case to the Court in connection with the giving of a standard authorisation; but, in doing so, the IMCA must take account of the views of the relevant person's representative.

Other circumstances in which an IMCA *must or may be* instructed

3.28 An IMCA must also be instructed during gaps in the appointment of a relevant person's representative (for instance, if a new representative is being sought – see paragraphs 7.34 to 7.36). In addition, an IMCA may be instructed at any time where:

- the relevant person does not have a paid 'professional' representative
- the relevant person or their representative requests that an IMCA is instructed to help them, or
- a supervisory body believes that instructing an IMCA will help to ensure that the person's rights are protected (see paragraphs 7.37 to 7.41).

4 WHAT IS THE ASSESSMENT PROCESS FOR A STANDARD AUTHORISATION OF DEPRIVATION OF LIBERTY?

When a supervisory body gives a standard authorisation of deprivation of liberty, the managing authority may lawfully deprive the relevant person of their liberty in the hospital or care home named in the authorisation.

This chapter describes the assessments that have to be undertaken in order for a standard authorisation to be given. It also sets out who is eligible to undertake the assessments.

What assessments are required before giving a standard authorisation?

4.1 As soon as the supervisory body has confirmed that the request for a standard authorisation should be pursued, it must obtain the relevant assessments to ascertain whether the qualifying requirements of the deprivation of liberty safeguards are met. The supervisory body has a legal responsibility to select assessors who are both suitable and eligible. Assessments must be completed within 21 days for a standard deprivation of liberty authorisation, or, where an urgent authorisation has been given, before the urgent authorisation expires.

4.2 The assessments (described in paragraphs 4.23 to 4.76) are:

- age assessment (paragraphs 4.23 and 4.24)
- no refusals assessment (paragraphs 4.25 to 4.28).
- mental capacity assessment (paragraphs 4.29 to 4.32)
- mental health assessment (paragraphs 4.33 to 4.39)
- eligibility assessment (paragraphs 4.40 to 4.57), and
- best interests assessment (paragraphs 4.58 to 4.76).

Standard forms are available for completion by each of the assessors.

4.3 If the person being assessed is not currently in the supervisory body's area, the supervisory body should seek, as far as is practical and possible, to arrange to use assessors based near where the person currently is.

Using equivalent assessments

4.4 The Act states that where an 'equivalent assessment' to any of these assessments has already been obtained, it may be relied upon instead of obtaining a fresh assessment.

4.5 An equivalent assessment is an assessment:
- that has been carried out in the last 12 months, not necessarily for the purpose of a deprivation of liberty authorisation (where the required assessment is an age assessment, there is no time limit on the use of an equivalent assessment)
- that meets all the requirements of the deprivation of liberty assessment,
- of which the supervisory body is satisfied that there is no reason to believe that it is no longer accurate, and
- of which the supervisory body has a written copy.

An example would be a recent assessment carried out for the purposes of the Mental Health Act 1983, which could serve as an equivalent to a mental health assessment.

4.6 Great care should be taken in deciding to use an equivalent assessment and this should not be done routinely. The older the assessment is, even if it took place within the last 12 months, the less likely it is to represent a valid equivalent assessment (unless it is an age assessment). For example, only a very recent mental capacity assessment would be appropriate where capacity is known to fluctuate, since one of the principles of the Act is that a person must be assumed to have capacity unless it is established that they lack capacity.

4.7 If an equivalent best interests assessment is used, the supervisory body must also take into account any information given, or submissions made, by the relevant person's representative or an Independent Mental Capacity Advocate (IMCA) instructed under the deprivation of liberty safeguards.

4.8 Supervisory bodies should record the reasons why they have used any equivalent assessment. A standard form is available for this purpose.

When must assessments take place?

4.9   The regulations for England[11] specify that all assessments required for a standard authorisation must be completed within 21 calendar days from the date on which the supervisory body receives a request from a managing authority. The regulations for Wales specify that all assessments required for a standard authorisation must be completed within 21 days from the date the assessors were instructed by the supervisory body.

4.10 However, if an urgent authorisation is already in force, the assessments must be completed before the urgent authorisation expires. The regulations for Wales specify that, where the managing authority has given itself an urgent authorisation and applies for a standard authorisation, the assessors must complete the assessments within five days of the date of instruction.

4.11 Urgent authorisations may be given by managing authorities for an initial period not exceeding seven days. If there are exceptional reasons why it has not been possible to deal with the request for a standard authorisation within the period of the urgent authorisation, they may be extended **by the supervisory body** for up to a further seven days. It is for the supervisory body to decide what constitutes an 'exceptional reason', taking into account all the circumstances of an individual case.

4.12 Supervisory bodies must keep a record of all requests for standard authorisations that they receive and should acknowledge the receipt of requests from managing authorities for standard authorisations.

How should assessors be selected?

4.13 The six assessments do not have to be completed by different assessors. In fact, it is highly unlikely that there will be six separate assessors – not least because it is desirable to minimise the burden on the person being assessed. However, each assessor must make their own decisions, and to ensure that an appropriate degree of objectivity is brought to the assessment process:

- there **must** be a minimum of two assessors
- the mental health and best interests assessors **must** be different people
- the best interests assessor can be an employee of the supervisory body or managing authority, but **must not** be involved in the care or treatment of the person they are assessing nor in decisions about their care
- a potential best interests assessor should not be used if they are in a line management relationship with the professional proposing the deprivation of liberty or the mental health assessor
- none of the assessors may have a financial interest in the case of the person they are assessing (a person is considered to have a financial

---

[11]   The Mental Capacity (Deprivation of Liberty: Standard Authorisations, Assessments and Ordinary Residence) Regulations 2008.

      interest in a case where that person is a partner, director, other office-holder or major shareholder of the managing authority that has made the application for a standard authorisation)
- an assessor **must not** be a relative of the person being assessed, nor of a person with a financial interest in the person's care. For this purpose, a 'relative' is:
  - a. a spouse, ex-spouse, civil partner or ex-civil partner
  - b. a person living with the relevant person as if they were a spouse or a civil partner
  - c. a parent or child
  - d. a brother or sister
  - e. a child of a person falling within definitions a, b or d
  - f. a grandparent or grandchild
  - g. a grandparent-in-law or grandchild-in-law
  - h. an aunt or uncle
  - i. a sister-in-law or brother-in-law
  - j. a son-in-law or daughter-in-law
  - k. a first cousin, or
  - l. a half-brother or half-sister.

  These relationships include step-relationships
- where the managing authority and supervisory body are both the same body (see paragraph 3.21), the supervisory body may not select to carry out a best interests assessment a person who is employed by the body, or providing services to it, and
- the supervisory body should seek to avoid appointing assessors in any other possible conflict of interests situations that might bring into question the objectivity of an assessment.

4.14 Other relevant factors for supervisory bodies to consider when appointing assessors include:
- the reason for the proposed deprivation of liberty
- whether the potential assessor has experience of working with the service user group from which the person being assessed comes (for example, older people, people with learning disabilities, people with autism, or people with brain injury)
- whether the potential assessor has experience of working with people from the cultural background of the person being assessed, and
- any other specific needs of the person being assessed, for example communication needs.

4.15 Supervisory bodies should ensure that sufficient assessors are available to meet their needs, and must be satisfied in each case that the assessors have the skills, experience, qualifications and training required by regulations to perform the function effectively. The regulations also require supervisory bodies to be satisfied that there is an appropriate criminal record certificate issued in respect of an assessor. It will be useful to keep a record of qualified assessors and their experience and availability. Supervisory bodies should consider making arrangements to ensure that assessors have the necessary opportunities to maintain their skills and knowledge (of legal developments, for example) and share, audit and review their practice.

4.16 Assessors act as individual professionals and are personally accountable for their decisions. Managing authorities and supervisory bodies must not dictate or seek to influence their decisions.

4.17 There is no reason in principle why interviews, examinations and fact-finding required as part of any deprivation of liberty safeguards assessment cannot serve more than one purpose, in order to avoid unnecessary burdens both on the person being assessed and on staff. However, if this does happen, all purposes of the interview or examination should be made clear to the relevant person, and to any family members, friends, carers or advocates supporting them.

Protection against liability

4.18 Nobody can or should carry out an assessment unless they are protected against any liabilities that might arise in connection with carrying out the assessment. Individual assessors will need to satisfy themselves, and any supervisory body that selects them as an assessor, that they are appropriately covered by either employers' or personal insurance.

What is the assessment process?

4.19 As indicated in paragraph 4.2, there are six assessments that must be conducted before a supervisory body can give an authorisation.

4.20 The assessments are set out in the order in which it will normally be most appropriate to complete them. In particular, it is recommended that the best interests assessment, which is likely to be the most time-consuming, is not started until there is a reasonable expectation that the other five qualifying requirements will be met.

4.21 But, ultimately, it is for the supervisory body to decide on the order in which the assessments should be undertaken and, in the light of the time available to complete the overall assessment process, the extent to which they should be undertaken to separate or simultaneous timescales. The supervisory body's decision about how many assessors will undertake the assessments (see paragraph 4.13) will also be a relevant factor.

4.22 The following paragraphs explain the assessment process.

Age assessment

4.23 The purpose of the age assessment is simply to confirm whether the relevant person is aged 18 or over. This is because, as paragraph 1.12 explains, the deprivation of liberty safeguards apply only to people aged 18 or over. For people under the age of 18, a different safeguards process applies. In most cases, this is likely to be a fairly straightforward assessment. If there is any doubt, age should be established by a birth certificate or other evidence that the assessor considers reliable. Where it is not possible to verify with any certainty whether a person is aged 18 or over, the assessor should base the assessment on the best of their knowledge and belief.

4.24 This assessment can be undertaken by anybody whom the supervisory body is satisfied is eligible to be a best interests assessor.

No refusals assessment

4.25 The purpose of the no refusals assessment is to establish whether an authorisation to deprive the relevant person of their liberty would conflict with other existing authority for decision-making for that person.

4.26 The following are instances of a conflict that would mean that a standard authorisation could not be given:
- If the relevant person has made **an advance decision to refuse treatment** that remains valid and is applicable to some or all of the treatment that is the purpose for which the authorisation is requested, then a standard authorisation cannot be given. See sections 24 to 26 of the Mental Capacity Act 2005 and Chapter 9 of the main Code ('What does the Act say about advance decisions to refuse treatment?') for more information about advance decisions and when they are valid and applicable. Remember too that the deprivation of liberty authorisation does not, in itself, provide authority to treat the person (see paragraphs 5.10 to 5.13 of this Code).
- If any part of the proposal to deprive the person of their liberty (including any element of the care plan) would be in conflict with a **valid decision of a donee or a deputy** made within the scope of their authority, then a standard authorisation cannot be given. For example, if a donee or deputy decides that it would not be in the best interests of the relevant person to be in a particular care home, and that decision is within the scope of their authority, then the care plan will need to be reviewed with the donee or deputy.

4.27 If there is any such conflict, the no refusals assessment qualifying requirement will not be met and a standard authorisation for deprivation of liberty cannot be given.

4.28 The no refusals assessment can be undertaken by anybody that the supervisory body is satisfied is eligible to be a best interests assessor.

Mental capacity assessment

4.29 The purpose of the mental capacity assessment is to establish whether the relevant person lacks capacity to decide whether or not they should be accommodated in the relevant hospital or care home to be given care or treatment. The assessment refers specifically to the relevant person's capacity to make this decision at the time it needs to be made. The starting assumption should always be that a person has the capacity to make the decision.

4.30 Sections 1 to 3 of the Act set out how a person's capacity to make decisions should be determined. Chapter 4 of the main Code ('How does the Act define a person's capacity to make a decision and how should capacity be assessed?') gives further guidance on ways to assess capacity. When assessing the capacity of a person being considered for the deprivation of liberty safeguards, these guidelines should be followed.

4.31 The regulations for England specify that the mental capacity assessment can be undertaken by anyone who is eligible to act as a mental health or best interests assessor. In deciding who to appoint for this assessment, the supervisory body should take account of the need for understanding and practical experience of the nature of the person's condition and its impact on decision-making.

4.32 Supervisory bodies may wish to consider using an eligible assessor who already knows the relevant person to undertake this assessment, if they think it would be of benefit. This will primarily arise if somebody involved in the person's care is considered best placed to carry out a reliable assessment, using their knowledge of the person over a period of time. It may also help in reducing any distress that might be caused to the person if they were assessed by somebody they did not know.

Mental health assessment

4.33 The purpose of the mental health assessment is to establish whether the relevant person has a mental disorder within the meaning of the Mental Health Act 1983. That means any disorder or disability of mind, apart from dependence on alcohol or drugs. It includes all learning disabilities. This is not an assessment to determine whether the person requires mental health treatment.

4.34 A distinction can be drawn between the mental health assessment and the mental capacity assessment:
- Although a person must have an impairment or disturbance of the functioning of the mind or brain in order to lack capacity, it does not follow that they automatically have a mental disorder within the meaning of the Mental Health Act 1983.
- The objective of the mental health assessment is to ensure that the person is medically diagnosed as being of 'unsound mind' and so comes within the scope of Article 5 of the European Convention on Human Rights.

4.35 In both England and Wales, the regulations specify that:
- the mental health assessment must be carried out by a doctor, and
- the assessing doctor has to either be approved under section 12 of the Mental Health Act 1983, or be a registered medical practitioner with

at least three years' post-registration experience in the diagnosis or treatment of mental disorder, such as a GP with a special interest. This includes doctors who are automatically treated as being section 12 approved because they are approved clinicians under the Mental Health Act 1983.

4.36 To be eligible to undertake assessments, in England a doctor will need to have completed the standard training for deprivation of liberty mental health assessors. Except in the 12 month period beginning with the date the doctor has successfully completed the standard training, the regulations for England also require the supervisory body to be satisfied that the doctor has, in the 12 months prior to selection, completed further training relevant to their role as a mental health assessor. In Wales, a doctor will need to have completed appropriate training and have appropriate skills and experience.

4.37 Supervisory bodies must consider the suitability of the assessor for the particular case (for example, whether they have experience relevant to the person's condition).

4.38 As with the mental capacity assessment, supervisory bodies may wish to consider using an eligible assessor who already knows the relevant person to undertake this assessment, if they think it would be of benefit.

4.39 The mental health assessor is required to consider how the mental health of the person being assessed is likely to be affected by being deprived of their liberty, and to report their conclusions to the best interests assessor. The mental health and best interests assessments cannot be carried out by the same person.

Eligibility assessment

4.40 This assessment relates specifically to the relevant person's status, or potential status, under the Mental Health Act 1983.

4.41 A person is not eligible for a deprivation of liberty authorisation if:
- they are detained as a hospital in-patient under the Mental Health Act 1983, or
- the authorisation, if given, would be inconsistent with an obligation placed on them under the Mental Health Act 1983, such as a requirement to live somewhere else. This will only affect people who are on leave of absence from detention under the Mental Health Act 1983 or who are subject to guardianship, supervised community treatment or conditional discharge.

4.42 Where the proposed authorisation relates to a care home, or to deprivation of liberty in a hospital for non-mental health treatment, the eligibility assessment will simply be a matter of checking that authorisation would not be inconsistent with an obligation placed on the person under the Mental Health Act 1983.

4.43 When a person is subject to guardianship under the Mental Health Act 1983, their guardian can decide where they are to live, but cannot authorise deprivation of liberty and cannot require them to live somewhere where they are deprived of liberty unless that deprivation of liberty is authorised.

4.44 Occasionally, a person who is subject to guardianship and who lacks capacity to make the relevant decisions may need specific care or treatment in a care home or hospital that cannot be delivered without deprivation of liberty. This may be in a care home in which they are already living or in which the guardian thinks they ought to live, or it may be in a hospital where they need to be for physical health care. It may also apply if they need to be in hospital for mental health care. The process for obtaining a deprivation of liberty authorisation and the criteria to be applied are the same as for any other person.

4.45 If the proposed authorisation relates to deprivation of liberty in a hospital **wholly or partly for the purpose of treatment of mental disorder**, then the relevant person will not be eligible if:
- they object to being admitted to hospital, or to some or all the treatment they will receive there for mental disorder, **and**
- they meet the criteria for an application for admission under section 2 or section 3 of the Mental Health Act 1983 (unless an attorney or deputy, acting within their powers, had consented to the things to which the person is objecting).

4.46 In many cases, the relevant person will be able to state an objection. However, where the person is unable to communicate, or can only communicate to a limited extent, assessors will need to consider the person's behaviour, wishes, feelings, views, beliefs and values, both present and past, so far as they can be ascertained (see paragraphs 5.37 to 5.48 of the main Code for guidance on how to do this). If there is reason to think that a person would object if able to do so, then the person should be assumed to be objecting. Occasionally, it may be that the person's behaviour initially suggests an objection, but that this objection is in fact not directed at the treatment at all. In that case, the person should **not** be taken to be objecting.

4.47 Assessors should always bear in mind that their job is simply to establish whether the person objects to treatment or to being in hospital: whether that objection is reasonable or not is not the issue.

4.48 Even where a person does not object and a deprivation of liberty authorisation is possible, it should not be assumed that such an authorisation is invariably the correct course. There may be other factors that suggest that the Mental Health Act 1983 should be used (for example, where it is thought likely that the person will recover relevant capacity and will then refuse to consent to treatment, or where it is important for the hospital managers to have a formal power to retake a person who goes absent without leave). Further guidance on this is given in the Mental Health Act 1983 Code of Practice.

4.49 The eligibility assessor is not required to decide (or even consider) whether an application under the Mental Health Act 1983 would be in the person's best interests.

4.50 If the proposed authorisation relates to deprivation of liberty in a hospital **wholly or partly for the purpose of treatment of mental disorder**, then the person will also not be eligible if they are:

- currently on leave of absence from detention under the Mental Health Act 1983
- subject to supervised community treatment, or
- subject to conditional discharge,

in which case powers of recall under the Mental Health Act 1983 should be used.

4.51 People on leave of absence from detention under the Mental Health Act 1983 or subject to supervised community treatment or conditional discharge are, however, eligible for the deprivation of liberty safeguards if they require treatment in hospital for a physical disorder.

Who can conduct an eligibility assessment?

4.52 The regulations for England specify that the eligibility assessment must be completed by:

- a mental health assessor who is also a section 12 doctor, or
- a best interests assessor who is also an approved mental health professional (AMHP).

4.53 The assessment cannot be carried out by a non-section 12 doctor, even if they are qualified to be a mental health assessor, nor by a non-AMHP, even if they are qualified to be a best interests assessor. This will ensure that the eligibility assessor is sufficiently familiar with the Mental Health Act 1983, which will be particularly important in cases in which it appears that the powers available under the Mental Health Act 1983 may be more appropriate than the deprivation of liberty safeguards.

4.54 The eligibility assessment will often be carried out by the best interests assessor but, where this is not the case, the eligibility assessor must request the best interests assessor to provide any relevant eligibility information that the best interests assessor may have, and the best interests assessor must comply with this request.

What happens when people are assessed as ineligible?

4.55 If the eligibility assessor believes that the relevant person is not eligible, but (on the basis of the report of the best interests assessor) that they should nevertheless be deprived of liberty in their best interests, the eligibility assessor should immediately inform the supervisory body.

4.56 In the case of someone already subject to the Mental Health Act 1983, the eligibility assessor should inform the supervisory body with a view to contact being made with the relevant responsible clinician (i.e. the clinician in overall charge of the person's treatment) or, if the person is subject to guardianship, the relevant local social services authority. Otherwise, the assessor or supervisory body should take steps to arrange for the person to be assessed further with a view to an application being made for admission to hospital under the Mental Health Act 1983. Assessors will need to be familiar with local arrangements for doing this.

4.57 In some cases, even before the eligibility assessment is undertaken, it may be known that there is a chance that the person will have to be assessed with a view to an application under the Mental Health Act 1983 because the eligibility assessment might conclude that they are ineligible for a deprivation of liberty authorisation. In such cases, steps should be taken, where practical and possible, to arrange assessments in a way that minimises the number of separate interviews or examinations the person has to undergo.

Best interests assessment

4.58 The purpose of the best interests assessment is to establish, firstly, whether deprivation of liberty is occurring or is going to occur and, if so, whether:

- it is in the best interests of the relevant person to be deprived of liberty
- it is necessary for them to be deprived of liberty in order to prevent harm to themselves, and
- deprivation of liberty is a proportionate response to the likelihood of the relevant person suffering harm and the seriousness of that harm.

4.59 The best interests assessor is the person who is responsible for assessing what is in the best interests of a relevant person.

4.60 In both England and Wales, the best interests assessment must be undertaken by an AMHP, social worker, nurse, occupational therapist or chartered psychologist with the skills and experience specified in the regulations. In England, this includes at least two years' post-registration experience. In England, the supervisory body must also be satisfied that the assessor:

- is not suspended from the register or list relevant to the person's profession
- has successfully completed training that has been approved[12] by the Secretary of State to be a best interests assessor
- except in the 12 month period beginning with the date the person has successfully completed the approved training, has, in the 12 months prior to selection, completed further training relevant to their role as a best interests assessor, and
- has the skills necessary to obtain, evaluate and analyse complex evidence and differing views and to weigh them appropriately in decision-making.

4.61 Section 4 of the Mental Capacity Act 2005 sets out the best interests principles that apply for the purpose of the Act. Chapter 5 of the main

---

[12] Approved courses can be found at: http://www.dh.gov.uk/en/SocialCare/ Deliveringadultsocialcare/MentalCapacity/MentalCapacityActDeprivationofLibertySafeguards/ index.htm.

Code ('What does the Act mean when it talks about "best interests"?') explains this in more detail, and, in particular, paragraph 5.13 of the main Code includes a checklist of factors that need to be taken into account in working out what is in a person's best interests. These principles and guidance apply equally to working out a person's best interests for the purpose of the deprivation of liberty safeguards. However, when it comes to best interests around deprivation of liberty, additional factors apply, including:

- whether any harm to the person could arise if the deprivation of liberty does not take place
- what that harm would be
- how likely that harm is to arise (i.e. is the level of risk sufficient to justify a step as serious as depriving a person of liberty?)
- what other care options there are which could avoid deprivation of liberty, and
- if deprivation of liberty is currently unavoidable, what action could be taken to avoid it in future.

Establishing whether deprivation of liberty is occurring

4.62 The first task of a best interests assessor is to establish whether deprivation of liberty is occurring, or is likely to occur, since there is no point in the assessment process proceeding further if deprivation of liberty is not at issue. If the best interests assessor concludes that deprivation of liberty is **not** occurring and is not likely to occur, they should state in their assessment report to the supervisory body that deprivation of liberty is not in the person's best interests because there is obviously a less restrictive option available. The best interests requirement will therefore not be met in such a case.

4.63 To establish whether deprivation of liberty is occurring, or is likely to occur, the best interests assessor must consult the managing authority of the hospital or care home where the person is, or will be, accommodated and examine any relevant needs assessments and care plans prepared for the person. The best interests assessor must consider whether the care plan and the manner in which it is being, or will be, implemented constitutes a deprivation of liberty. If not, then no deprivation of liberty authorisation is required for that care plan.

4.64 The managing authority and supervisory body must provide the best interests assessor with any needs assessments or care plans that they have undertaken or which have been undertaken on their behalf.

The best interests assessment process

4.65 If the best interests assessor considers that deprivation of liberty is occurring, or is likely to occur, they should start a full best interests assessment. In line with section 4(7) of the Act this involves seeking the views of a range of people connected to the relevant person to find out whether they believe that depriving the relevant person of their liberty is, or would be, in the person's best interests to protect them from harm or to enable them to follow the care plan proposed. The best interests assessor should, as far as is practical and possible, seek the views of:

- anyone the person has previously named as someone they want to be consulted
- anyone involved in caring for the person
- anyone interested in the person's welfare (for example, family carers, other close relatives, or an advocate already working with the person), and
- any donee or deputy who represents the person.

4.66 This may mean that the best interests assessor needs to explain key aspects of the care plan and what it aims to do to the people being consulted. The best interests assessor should then take the views received into account as far as is practical and appropriate. It is essential that the best interests assessor provides an independent and objective view of whether or not there is a genuine justification for deprivation of liberty, taking account of all the relevant views and factors.

4.67 The best interests assessor must state in their assessment the name and address of every interested person whom they have consulted in carrying out the assessment.

4.68 Family and friends may not be confident about expressing their views: it is the responsibility of the best interests assessor to enable them to do so – using support to meet communication or language needs as necessary.

Scenario: Consulting around best interests

Mr Simpson is 60 and has dementia with particularly poor short-term memory, which clinicians agree is most likely to be related to chronic excessive alcohol intake. After initial treatment in hospital, he has been admitted to a care home – a decision which he consented to.

However, though he had the mental capacity to consent to hospital admission, he has no insight into his dementia. He is unable to understand the health and safety implications of continuing to drink, and will do so heavily whenever he has access to alcohol and the money to buy it.

Although Mr Simpson had no access to alcohol in hospital, there is a pub within walking distance of the care home, which he visits and drinks in. When he returns to the home intoxicated, his behaviour can be very distressing and potentially dangerous to other residents. The care home staff believe that if this continues, there may be no other option than to return him to hospital under the Mental Health Act 1983.

The care home staff have asked Mr Simpson to drink only in moderation, but this has not proved successful; and the landlord has been asked not to serve him more than one drink but has refused to do so. The manager of the home is now considering a care plan to prevent Mr Simpson from →

leaving the home without an escort, and to prevent visits from friends who bring alcohol. He believes this would be in Mr Simpson's best interests.

As the pub is open all day, if this new care plan was adopted, Mr Simpson would be stopped from going out at all without an escort, even though he often goes to the shops and the park as well as the pub. Staffing levels are such that an escort would only be available on some days and for limited periods.

Mr Simpson's daughter, his closest relative, is concerned that these restrictions are excessive and would amount to a deprivation of liberty. She believes that having a drink and socialising in the pub is her father's 'only remaining pleasure', and is sure that, if he still had capacity, he would choose to carry on drinking, regardless of the health risks.

She requests a best interests meeting to consider whether a less restrictive care plan could still meet his needs.

At this meeting, Mr Simpson's community mental health nurse confirms that Mr Simpson is likely to lack capacity in relation to this particular issue, and advises that if he continues to drink to excess his dementia is likely to advance rapidly and his life expectancy will be reduced. However, small amounts of alcohol will not be significantly harmful.

The consensus is that the proposed restrictions would severely limit Mr Simpson's ability to maintain social contact and to carry on the life he has been used to, and that this would amount to deprivation of liberty. Bearing in mind his daughter's view, it is felt that it would not be in Mr Simpson's best interests to prevent him from having any alcohol at all. However, in view of the health risks and the likelihood that he would otherwise have to be detained in hospital, it would be in Mr Simpson's best interests to ensure that he does not get intoxicated. (The possibility of limiting his access to his money would be unacceptable since he retains the capacity to decide how to spend it in other ways.)

Discussion then focuses on ways of minimising restrictions so that he is still able to visit the pub, but drinks in moderation. The care home key worker says that when she has gone to the pub with Mr Simpson he has been fully co-operative and has had just one drink before coming back with her. It is therefore agreed that the home will provide an escort for him to visit the pub at least three times a week, and the shops and the park at other times, and that his daughter will be able to take him out at any time.

It is agreed that care home staff (in consultation with his daughter) will review Mr Simpson's care plan in two months' time and, if it is felt that ➡

> increased restrictions are required, consider whether it is then necessary to request an authorisation for deprivation of liberty.

4.69 The best interests assessor must involve the relevant person in the assessment process as much as is possible and practical, and help them to participate in decision-making. The relevant person should be given the support needed to participate, using non-verbal means of communication where needed (see paragraphs 3.10 and 3.11 of the main Code) or the support of speech and language therapists. It may also help to involve others whom the relevant person already trusts and who are used to communicating with the relevant person.

4.70 The best interests assessor will need to consider the conclusions of the mental health assessor about how the person being assessed is likely to be affected by being deprived of their liberty. If the proposed care would involve the person being moved, then the assessor should consider the impact of the upheaval and of the journey itself on the person.

4.71 If the best interests assessment supports deprivation of liberty in the care home or hospital in question, the assessor must state what the maximum authorisation period should be in the case concerned. This must not exceed 12 months. The assessor should set out the reasons for selecting the period stated. This decision will be based on the information obtained during the consultation process – but should also reflect information from the person's care plan about how long any treatment or care will be required in circumstances that amount to a deprivation of liberty. It should also take into account any available indication of how likely it is that the relevant person's circumstances will change, including the expected progression of the illness or disability. The underlying principle is that deprivation of liberty should be for the minimum period necessary so, for the maximum 12-month period to apply, the assessor will need to be confident that there is unlikely to be a change in the person's circumstances that would affect the authorisation within that timescale.

The report of the best interests assessor

4.72 The best interests assessor must provide a report that explains their conclusion and their reasons for it. If they do not support deprivation of liberty, then their report should aim to be as useful as possible to the commissioners and providers of care in deciding on future action (for example, recommending an alternative approach to treatment or care in which deprivation of liberty could be avoided). It may be helpful for the best interests assessor to discuss the possibility of any such alternatives with the providers of care **during the assessment process.**

4.73 If the best interests assessor does not support deprivation of liberty, it would be good practice for their report to be included in the relevant person's care plan or case notes, to ensure that any views about how deprivation of liberty can be avoided are made clear to the providers of care and all relevant staff on an ongoing basis.

4.74 The best interests assessor may recommend that conditions should be attached to the authorisation. For example, they may make recommendations around contact issues, issues relevant to the person's culture or other major issues related to the deprivation of liberty, which – if not dealt with – would mean that the deprivation of liberty would cease to be in the person's best interests. The best interests assessor may also recommend conditions in order to work towards avoiding deprivation of liberty in future. But it is not the best interests assessor's role to specify conditions that do not directly relate to the issue of deprivation of liberty.

4.75 Conditions should not be a substitute for a properly constructed care plan (see paragraph 2.7 on good practice for care planning). In recommending conditions, best interests assessors should aim to impose the minimum necessary constraints, so that they do not unnecessarily prevent or inhibit the staff of the hospital or care home from responding appropriately to the person's needs, whether they remain the same or vary over time. It would be good practice for the best interests assessor to discuss any proposed conditions with the relevant personnel at the home or hospital before finalising the assessment, and to make clear in their report whether the rejection or variation of recommended conditions by the supervisory body would significantly affect the other conclusions they have reached.

4.76 Where possible, the best interests assessor should recommend someone to be appointed as the relevant person's representative (see Chapter 7). The assessor should be well placed, as a result of the consultation process, to identify whether there is anybody suitable to take on this role. The appointment of the relevant person's representative cannot take place unless and until an authorisation is given. However, by identifying someone to take on this role at an early stage, the best interests assessor can help to ensure that a representative is appointed as soon as possible.

Scenario: Application for standard authorisation

Mrs Jackson is 87 years old and lives by herself in an isolated bungalow in a rural area. Over the past few years, staff at her local health centre have become increasingly concerned about her wellbeing and ability to look after herself. Her appearance has become unkempt, she does not appear to be eating properly and her house is dirty.

The community mental health team have attempted to gain her trust, but she is unwilling to engage with them. She has refused care workers entry to her home and declined their help with personal hygiene and household chores.

Because it is believed that she is a potential risk to herself, she is admitted to psychiatric hospital under section 2 of the Mental Health Act 1983 for assessment of her mental disorder.　　　　　　　　　　　　　　　　➙

Following the assessment, it is felt that Mrs Jackson requires further treatment for mental disorder. An application is made for her detention to be continued under section 3 of the Mental Health Act 1983. She is prescribed antipsychotic medication, but this seems to have little effect on her behaviour. She remains extremely suspicious of people to the point of being delusional. She is assessed as potentially having mild dementia, most probably of the Alzheimer type, but because there is no obvious benefit from anti-dementia medication, further treatment for mental disorder is felt unnecessary.

Mrs Jackson insists that she wishes to return to her own home, but given past failed attempts to gain her acceptance of support at home and her likely future mental deterioration, transfer to a care home is believed to be most appropriate.

A best interests meeting is held by the mental health team to consider her future care and placement, and the team's approved social worker and the instructed IMCA are invited. The meeting concludes that Mrs Jackson does not have sufficient mental capacity to make an informed decision on her stated wish to return home. There is no advance decision in existence, no Lasting Power of Attorney or court deputy appointed and no practical way of contacting her immediate family.

An appropriate care home is identified. A care plan is developed to give Mrs Jackson as much choice and control over her daily living as possible. However, it is felt that the restrictions still necessary to ensure Mrs Jackson's wellbeing will be so intense and of such duration that a request for a standard deprivation of liberty authorisation should be made by the care home manager (the relevant managing authority).

The best interests assessor agrees that the proposed course of action is in Mrs Jackson's best interests and recommends a standard authorisation for six months in the first instance.

What guidelines are there relating to the work of assessors?

Access to records

4.77 All assessors may, at any reasonable time, examine and take copies of:
- any health record
- any record of, or held by, a local authority that was compiled in accordance with a social services function, and
- any record held by a care home

which they consider may be relevant to their assessment. Assessors should list in their assessment report what records they examined.

Recording and reporting assessments

4.78 As soon as possible after carrying out their assessments, assessors must keep a written record of the assessment and must give copies of their assessment report(s) to the supervisory body. The supervisory body must in turn give copies of the assessment report(s) to:
- the managing authority
- the relevant person and their representative, and
- any IMCA instructed

at the same time that it gives them copies of the deprivation of liberty authorisation or notification that an authorisation is not to be given (see paragraphs 5.7 and 5.18 respectively).

5 WHAT SHOULD HAPPEN ONCE THE ASSESSMENTS ARE COMPLETE?

If all the assessments in the standard authorisation assessment process indicate that the relevant person meets all the qualifying requirements, then the supervisory body will give a deprivation of liberty authorisation. If any of the qualifying requirements are not met, however, different actions will need to be taken, depending on the circumstances of the individual case.

This chapter identifies potential outcomes of the assessment process and offers guidance on what should happen next.

What action should the supervisory body take if the assessments conclude that the person meets the requirements for authorisation?

5.1 If all the assessments conclude that the relevant person meets the requirements for authorisation, and the supervisory body has written copies of all the assessments, it must give a standard authorisation. A standard form is available for this purpose.

5.2 The supervisory body cannot give a standard authorisation if any of the requirements are not fulfilled.

5.3 The supervisory body must set the period of the authorisation, which may not be longer than that recommended by the best interests assessor (see paragraph 4.71).

5.4 When the supervisory body gives a standard authorisation, it must do so in writing and must state the following:
- the name of the relevant person
- the name of the relevant hospital or care home
- the period during which the authorisation is to be in force (which may not exceed the period recommended by the best interests assessor)

- the purpose for which the authorisation is given (i.e. why the person needs to be deprived of their liberty)
- any conditions subject to which the authorisation is given (see paragraph 5.5), and
- the reason why each qualifying requirement is met.

5.5 The supervisory body may attach conditions to the authorisation. Before deciding whether to give the authorisation subject to conditions, the supervisory body must consider any recommendations made by the best interests assessor (see paragraph 4.74). Where the supervisory body does not attach conditions as recommended by the best interests assessor, it should discuss the matter with the best interests assessor in case the rejection or variation of the conditions would significantly affect the other conclusions the best interests assessor reached in their report.

5.6 It is the responsibility of the supervisory body to appoint a representative for the relevant person (see Chapter 7).

5.7 As soon as possible after giving the authorisation, the supervisory body must give a copy of the authorisation to:
- the managing authority
- the relevant person
- the relevant person's representative
- any Independent Mental Capacity Advocate (IMCA) involved, and
- every interested person named by the best interests assessor in their report as somebody they have consulted in carrying out their assessment.

The supervisory body must also keep a written record of any standard authorisation that it gives and of the matters referred to in paragraph 5.4.

5.8 The managing authority must take all practical and possible steps to ensure that the relevant person understands the effect of the authorisation and their rights around it. These include their right to challenge the authorisation via the Court of Protection, their right to request a review, and their right to have an IMCA instructed, along with the process for doing so (see paragraphs 7.37 to 7.41). Appropriate information must be given to the relevant person both orally and in writing. Any written information must also be given to the relevant person's representative. This must happen as soon as possible and practical after the authorisation is given.

How long can an authorisation last?

5.9 A deprivation of liberty should last for the shortest period possible. The best interests assessor should only recommend authorisation for as long as the relevant person is likely to meet all the qualifying requirements. The authorisation may be for quite a short period. A short period may, for example, be appropriate if:
- the reason that the deprivation of liberty is in the person's best interests is because their usual care arrangements have temporarily broken down, or

- there are likely to be changes in the person's mental disorder in the relatively near future (for example, if the person is in rehabilitation following brain injury).

What restrictions exist on authorisations?

5.10 A deprivation of liberty authorisation – whether urgent or standard – relates solely to the issue of deprivation of liberty. It does not give authority to treat people, nor to do anything else that would normally require their consent. The arrangements for providing care and treatment to people in respect of whom a deprivation of liberty authorisation is in force are subject to the wider provisions of the Mental Capacity Act 2005.

5.11 This means that any treatment can only be given to a person who has not given their consent if:
- it is established that the person lacks capacity to make the decision concerned
- it is agreed that the treatment will be in their best interests, having taken account of the views of the person and of people close to them, and, where relevant in the case of serious medical treatment, of any IMCA involved
- the treatment does not conflict with a valid and applicable advance decision to refuse treatment, and
- the treatment does not conflict with a decision made by a donee of Lasting Power of Attorney or a deputy acting within the scope of their powers.

5.12 In deciding what is in a person's best interests, section 4 of the Act applies in the same way as it would if the person was not deprived of liberty. The guidance in Chapter 5 of the main Code on assessing best interests is also relevant.

5.13 Life-sustaining treatment, or treatment to prevent a serious deterioration in the person's condition, may be provided while a decision in respect of any relevant issue is sought from the Court of Protection. The need to act in the best interests of the person concerned will continue to apply in the meantime.

Can a person be moved to a different location under a standard authorisation?

5.14 If a person who is subject to a standard authorisation moves to a different hospital or care home, the managing authority of the new hospital or care home must request a new standard authorisation. The application should be made **before** the move takes place.

5.15 If the move has to take place so urgently that this is impossible, the managing authority of the new hospital or care home will need to give an urgent authorisation (see Chapter 6).

5.16 The only exception is if the care regime in the new facility will not involve deprivation of liberty.

5.17 These arrangements are not an alternative to applying the provisions of sections 38 and 39 of the Act regarding change of residence.

What happens if an assessment concludes that one of the requirements is not met?

5.18 If any of the assessments conclude that one of the requirements is not met, then the assessment process should stop immediately and authorisation may not be given. The supervisory body should:

- inform anyone still engaged in carrying out an assessment that they are not required to complete it
- notify the managing authority, the relevant person, any IMCA involved and every interested person consulted by the best interests assessor that authorisation has not been given (a standard form is available for this purpose), and
- provide the managing authority, the relevant person and any IMCA involved with copies of those assessments that have been carried out. This must be done as soon as possible, because in some cases different arrangements will need to be made for the person's care.

5.19 If the reason the standard authorisation cannot be given is because the eligibility requirement is not met, it may be necessary to consider making the person subject to the Mental Health Act 1983. If this is the case, it may be possible to use the same assessors to make that decision, thereby minimising the assessment processes.

What are the responsibilities of the managing authority and the commissioners of care if a request for an authorisation is turned down?

5.20 The managing authority is responsible for ensuring that it does not deprive a person of their liberty without an authorisation. The managing authority must comply with the law in this respect: where a request for an authorisation is turned down, it will need to review the relevant person's actual or proposed care arrangements to ensure that a deprivation of liberty is not allowed to either continue or commence.

5.21 Supervisory bodies and other commissioners of care will need to purchase care packages in a way that makes it possible for managing authorities to comply with the outcome of the deprivation of liberty safeguards assessment process when a request for a standard authorisation is turned down.

5.22 The actions that both managing authorities and commissioners of care should consider if a request for an authorisation is turned down will depend on the reason why the authorisation has not been given:

- If the best interests assessor concluded that the relevant person was not in fact being, or likely to be, deprived of liberty, no action is likely to be necessary.
- If the best interests assessor concluded that the proposed or actual deprivation of liberty was not in the relevant person's best interests, the managing authority, in conjunction with the commissioner of the care, will need to consider how the care plan could be changed to avoid deprivation of liberty. (See, for example, the guidance on practical ways to reduce the risk of deprivation of liberty in paragraph 2.7.) They should examine carefully the reasons given in the best interests assessor's report, and may find it helpful to discuss the matter with the best interests assessor. Where appropriate, they should also discuss the matter with family and carers. If the person is not yet a resident in the care home or hospital, the revised care plan may not involve admission to that facility unless the conditions of care are adapted to be less restrictive and deprivation of liberty will not occur.
- If the mental capacity assessor concluded that the relevant person **has** capacity to make decisions about their care, the care home or hospital will need to consider, in conjunction with the commissioner of the care, how to support the person to make such decisions.
- If the relevant person was identified as not eligible to be subject to a deprivation of liberty authorisation, it may be appropriate to assess whether an application should be made to detain the person under the Mental Health Act 1983.
- If the relevant person does not have a mental disorder as defined in the Mental Health Act 1983, the care plan will need to be modified to avoid a deprivation of liberty, since there would be no lawful basis for depriving a person of liberty in those circumstances.
- Where there is a valid refusal by a donee or deputy, or an applicable and valid advance decision (see paragraphs 4.25 to 4.28), alternative care arrangements will need to be made. If there is a question about the refusal, a decision may be sought from the Court of Protection.
- If the person is under 18, use of the Children Act 1989 may be considered.

5.23 Working out what action should be taken where a request for a standard deprivation of liberty authorisation is turned down in respect of a 'self-funder' may present particular problems, because the managing authority may not be able to make alternative care arrangements without discussing them with those controlling the funding, whether relatives of the person concerned or others. The desired outcome should be the provision of a care regime that does not constitute deprivation of liberty.

5.24 Where the best interests assessor comes to the conclusion that the best interests requirement is not met, but it appears to the assessor that the person being assessed is already being deprived of their liberty, the assessor must inform the supervisory body and explain in their report why they have reached that conclusion. The supervisory body must then inform the managing authority to review the relevant person's care plan immediately so that unauthorised deprivation of liberty does not continue. Any necessary changes must be made urgently to stop what would be an unlawful deprivation of liberty. The steps taken to stop the deprivation of liberty should be recorded in the care plan. Where possible, family, friends and carers should be involved in deciding how to prevent the unauthorised deprivation of liberty from continuing. If the supervisory body has any doubts about whether the matter is being satisfactorily resolved within an appropriately urgent timescale, it should alert the inspection body (see Chapter 11).

6 WHEN CAN URGENT AUTHORISATIONS OF DEPRIVATION OF LIBERTY BE GIVEN?

Wherever possible, applications for deprivation of liberty authorisations should be made before the deprivation of liberty commences. However, where deprivation of liberty unavoidably needs to commence before a standard authorisation can be obtained, an urgent authorisation can be given which will make the deprivation of liberty lawful for a short period of time.

This chapter contains guidance on the rules around urgent authorisations.

When can an urgent authorisation be given?

6.1 A managing authority can itself give an urgent authorisation for deprivation of liberty where:
- it is required to make a request to the supervisory body for a standard authorisation, but believes that the need for the person to be deprived of their liberty is so urgent that deprivation needs to begin before the request is made, or
- it has made a request for a standard authorisation, but believes that the need for a person to be deprived of liberty has now become so urgent that deprivation of liberty needs to begin before the request is dealt with by the supervisory body.

This means that an urgent authorisation can never be given without a request for a standard authorisation being made simultaneously. Therefore, before giving an urgent authorisation, a managing authority will need to have a reasonable expectation that the six qualifying requirements for a standard authorisation are likely to be met.

6.2 Urgent authorisations should normally only be used in response to sudden unforeseen needs. However, they can also be used in care planning (for example, to avoid delays in transfer for rehabilitation, where delay would reduce the likely benefit of the rehabilitation).

6.3 However, an urgent authorisation should not be used where there is no expectation that a standard deprivation of liberty authorisation will be needed. Where, for example:

- a person who lacks capacity to make decisions about their care and treatment has developed a mental disorder as a result of a physical illness, and
- the physical illness requires treatment in hospital in circumstances that amount to a deprivation of liberty, and
- the treatment of that physical illness is expected to lead to rapid resolution of the mental disorder such that a standard deprivation of liberty authorisation would not be required,

it would not be appropriate to give an urgent authorisation simply to legitimise the short-term deprivation of liberty.

6.4 Similarly, an urgent deprivation of liberty authorisation should not be given when a person is, for example, in an accident and emergency unit or a care home, and it is anticipated that within a matter of a few hours or a few days the person will no longer be in that environment.

6.5 Any decision to give an urgent authorisation and take action that deprives a person of liberty must be in the person's best interests, as set out in section 4 of the Mental Capacity Act 2005. Where restraint is involved, all actions must comply with the additional conditions in section 6 of the Act (see Chapter 6 of the main Code).

6.6 The managing authority must decide the period for which the urgent authorisation is given, but this must not exceed seven days (see paragraphs 6.20 to 6.28 regarding the possible extension of the seven-day period). The authorisation must be in writing and must state:
- the name of the relevant person
- the name of the relevant hospital or care home
- the period for which the authorisation is to be in force, and
- the purpose for which the authorisation is given.

A standard form is available for a managing authority to use to notify a supervisory body that it has given an urgent authorisation.

6.7 Supervisory bodies and managing authorities should have a procedure in place that identifies:
- what actions should be taken when an urgent authorisation needs to be made
- who should take each action, and
- within what timescale.

What records should be kept about urgent authorisations?

6.8 The managing authority must keep a written record of any urgent authorisations given, including details of why it decided to give an urgent authorisation. They must give a copy of the authorisation to the relevant person and any IMCA instructed, and place a copy in the relevant person's records. The managing authority must also seek to ensure that, as far as possible, the relevant person understands the effect of the authorisation and the right to challenge the authorisation via the Court of Protection. Appropriate information must be given both orally and in writing.

6.9   The managing authority should, as far as possible and appropriate, notify the relevant person's family, friends and carers when an urgent authorisation is given in order to enable them to offer informed support to the person.

6.10 The processes surrounding the giving and receiving of urgent authorisations should be clearly recorded, and regularly monitored and audited, as part of a managing authority's or supervisory body's governance structure.

Who should be consulted before giving an urgent authorisation?

6.11 If the managing authority is considering depriving a person of liberty in an emergency and giving an urgent authorisation, they must, as far as is practical and possible, take account of the views of anyone engaged in caring for the relevant person or interested in their welfare. The aim should be to consult carers and family members at as early a stage as possible so that their views can be properly taken into account before a decision to give an urgent authorisation is taken.

6.12 The steps taken to involve family, friends or carers should be recorded in the relevant person's records, along with their views. The views of the carers will be important because their knowledge of the person will put them in a good position to gauge how the person will react to the deprivation of their liberty, and the effect it will have on their mental state. It may also be appropriate to consult any staff who may have some involvement in the person's case.

6.13 The ultimate decision, though, will need to be based on a judgement of what is in the relevant person's best interests. The decision-maker from the managing authority will need to be able to show that they have made a reasonable decision based on their professional judgement and taking account of all the relevant factors. This is an important decision, because it could mean the deprivation of a person's liberty without, at this stage, the full deprivation of liberty safeguards assessment process having taken place. The decision should therefore be taken at a senior level within the managing authority.

Scenario: Urgent authorisation followed by short-term standard authorisation

Mr Baker is 75, widowed and lives near his only family – his daughter. He is admitted to hospital having been found by his daughter on his kitchen floor. He is uncharacteristically confused and is not able to give a reliable history of what has happened. He has a routine physical examination, as well as blood and urine investigations, and is diagnosed as having a urinary tract infection. He is given antibiotics, but his nursing care is complicated by his fluctuating confusion. Once or twice he removes his clothes and walks through the ward naked, and at times he tries to leave the ward, unaware that he is in hospital, and believing that he is late for →

an important work meeting. During more lucid moments, however, he knows where he is and accepts the need for investigation and treatment in hospital.

The responsible consultant, in consultation with ward nursing staff and Mr Baker's daughter, feels that it would be in his best interests to place him in a side room to protect his dignity, and restrict his movements to ensure he remains on the ward.

However, after two days, his confusion appears to worsen: he starts having hallucinations and has to be restrained more often by staff to prevent him leaving the ward. After assessment by a doctor from the liaison psychiatry team, Mr Baker is prescribed antipsychotic medication for his own and other patients' safety. He does not resist taking this medication. The likely benefits and possible side effects are discussed with his daughter and, on balance, the medication is felt to be in his best interests in order to continue his medical investigations.

Staff become concerned about the level of restriction of liberty Mr Baker is now subject to. In particular, they are concerned about the duration of the restrictions; the fact that Mr Baker no longer has lucid intervals when he can give his consent to ongoing care and treatment in hospital; and the physical restraint that is still being required on occasion.

After discussion between the ward manager and Mr Baker's daughter, the managing authority gives an urgent authorisation and submits a request for a standard authorisation to the supervisory body (PCT). A best interests assessor is appointed, and the liaison psychiatrist provides the mental health and mental capacity assessments. In making all the deprivation of liberty safeguards assessments to see whether the qualifying requirements are met, it is considered that although restraint is being used, this does not mean he is objecting having regard to all the circumstances, so he is not ineligible and a standard authorisation is given.

Can a person be moved into care under an urgent authorisation?

6.14 There may be cases in which managing authorities are considering giving an urgent authorisation to enable them to move the relevant person to a new type of care. This may occur, for example, when considering whether to admit a person living at home or with relatives into a hospital care regime that would deprive them of their liberty, and when the need for admission appears to be so urgent that there would not be enough time to follow the standard authorisation process.

6.15 For some people, such a change of location may have a detrimental effect on their mental health, which might significantly distort the way they come across during any assessment process. In such a case, managing authorities should consider whether giving the urgent authorisation and admitting the person to hospital would outweigh the benefits of leaving the person in their existing location, where any assessment of their needs might be more accurate. This will involve looking carefully at the existing care arrangements and consulting with any carers involved, to establish whether or not the person could safely and beneficially be cared for in their home environment while the assessment process takes place. Where the relevant person is already known to statutory care providers, for example the community mental health team or social services, it will be important to involve them in this decision-making process. The relevant person's GP may also be an important source of knowledge about the person's situation, and may be able to offer a valuable opinion when the appropriateness of moving the person into a different care setting is under consideration.

What happens at the end of an urgent authorisation period?

6.16 An urgent authorisation will terminate at the end of the period for which it is given. As noted above, this is normally a maximum of seven days, but in exceptional circumstances an urgent authorisation can be extended to a maximum of 14 days **by the supervisory body**, as explained in paragraphs 6.20 to 6.28.

6.17 An urgent authorisation will terminate before this time if the standard authorisation applied for is given.

6.18 An urgent authorisation will also terminate if a managing authority receives notice from the supervisory body that the standard authorisation will not be given. It will not then be lawful to continue to deprive the relevant person of their liberty.

6.19 The supervisory body must inform the relevant person and any IMCA instructed that the urgent authorisation has ended. This notification can be combined with the notification to them of the outcome of the application for standard authorisation.

Scenario: *Considering an urgent authorisation*

Mr Watson is 35. He has autism and learning disabilities. He lives in the family home with his parents. Although he is well settled and generally calm at home, Mr Watson sometimes becomes disturbed when in an unfamiliar and crowded environment.

While his parents are away for a couple of days, and Mr Watson is in the care of a paid carer, he has an accident at home. His carer is concerned that he may have broken his arm and takes him to the A&E department at the local hospital, where it is decided that his arm needs to be X-rayed to check for a break. The outcome is that there is no break, just bad bruising, so there is no medical need to admit him.   →

However, because of the pain he is in and the crowded environment, Mr Watson has become very agitated to the extent that hospital security personnel feel a need to control him physically. The carer tries to restrain him and lead him outside where she says he is likely to be more settled and calm down.

Because restraint is being used, the A&E doctor wonders whether it his duty to use an urgent authorisation or other measure to detain Mr Watson in hospital if he believes it is in his best interests.

He consults a liaison psychiatry nurse, who reassures him that such restraint is permitted under the Mental Capacity Act 2005 where it is necessary to prevent harm to the person himself and so long as it is a proportionate response. The nurse assists the carer with gentle restraint to take Mr Watson to a quieter area. She suggests the doctor phone Mr Watson's parents for further information, and obtains painkillers for Mr Watson.

The doctor speaks to Mr Watson's parents, who believe that Mr Watson does not have the mental capacity to decide on his care and treatment in the current circumstances. They have experienced similar situations many times, and are confident that Mr Watson will calm down once he is back in his home environment. They state that if any more detailed assessment of his mental state is required it should take place there, in the company of the carer whom they know and trust. They reassure the doctor that Mr Watson is highly unlikely to present a danger to himself, his carer or the general public.

The doctor decides that it will be in Mr Watson's best interests to return home with his carer.

How and when can an urgent authorisation be extended?

6.20 If there are exceptional reasons why the request for a standard authorisation cannot be dealt with within the period of the original urgent authorisation, the managing authority may ask the supervisory body to extend the duration of the urgent authorisation for a maximum of a further seven days. The managing authority must keep a written record of the reason for making the request and must notify the relevant person, in writing, that they have made the request. Standard forms are available for managing authorities to request the extension of an urgent authorisation from a supervisory body and for supervisory bodies to record their decision in response to such a request.

6.21 Unless the duration of the urgent authorisation is extended by the supervisory body, or a standard authorisation is given before the urgent authorisation expires, the authority to deprive the person of liberty will cease once the urgent authorisation period has expired. It is therefore essential that any request for an extension of an urgent authorisation is made promptly. This will necessitate good communication between the managing authority and the supervisory body regarding the progress of the standard authorisation assessment process. Particular care may need to be taken where an urgent authorisation is due to expire over the weekend or on a bank holiday, when appropriate people at the managing authority and supervisory body may not be immediately available.

6.22 The supervisory body may only extend the duration of the urgent authorisation if:

- the managing authority has made a request for a standard authorisation
- there are exceptional reasons why it has not yet been possible to make a standard authorisation, and
- it is essential for the deprivation of liberty to continue while the supervisory body makes its decision.

6.23 Extensions can only be granted for exceptional reasons. An example of when an extension would be justified might be where:

- it was not possible to contact a person whom the best interests assessor needed to contact
- the assessment could not be relied upon without their input, and
- extension for the specified period would enable them to be contacted.

6.24 It is for the supervisory body to decide what constitutes an 'exceptional reason', but because of the seriousness of the issues involved, the supervisory body's decision must be soundly based and defensible. It would not, for example, be appropriate to use staffing shortages as a reason to extend an urgent authorisation.

6.25 An urgent authorisation can only be extended once.

6.26 The supervisory body must notify the managing authority of the length of any extension granted and must vary the original urgent authorisation so that it states the extended duration. The supervisory body must also keep a written record of the outcome of the request and the period of the extension.

6.27 The managing authority must give a copy of the varied urgent authorisation to the relevant person and any IMCA instructed, and must seek to ensure that, as far as possible, the relevant person understands the effect of the varied authorisation and the right to challenge the authorisation via the Court of Protection. The appropriate information must be given both orally and in writing.

6.28 If the supervisory body decides not to extend the urgent authorisation, it must inform the managing authority of its decision and the reasons for it. The managing authority must give a copy of the notice to the relevant person and any IMCA involved.

7 WHAT IS THE ROLE OF THE RELEVANT PERSON'S REPRESENTATIVE?

Once a standard deprivation of liberty authorisation has been given, supervisory bodies must appoint the relevant person's representative as soon as possible and practical to represent the person who has been deprived of their liberty.

This chapter explains the role of the relevant person's representative and gives guidance on their selection and appointment.

What is the role of the relevant person's representative?

7.1 The supervisory body must appoint a relevant person's representative for every person to whom they give a standard authorisation for deprivation of liberty. It is important that the representative is appointed at the time the authorisation is given or as soon as possible and practical thereafter.

7.2 The role of the relevant person's representative, once appointed, is:
- to maintain contact with the relevant person, and
- to represent and support the relevant person in all matters relating to the deprivation of liberty safeguards, including, if appropriate, triggering a review, using an organisation's complaints procedure on the person's behalf or making an application to the Court of Protection.

This is a crucial role in the deprivation of liberty process, providing the relevant person with representation and support that is independent of the commissioners and providers of the services they are receiving.

7.3 The best interests principle of the Act applies to the relevant person's representative in the same way that it applies to other people acting or making decisions for people who lack capacity.

How should managing authorities work with the relevant person's representative?

7.4 As soon as possible and practical after a standard deprivation of liberty authorisation is given, the managing authority must seek to ensure that the relevant person and their representative understand:
- the effect of the authorisation
- their right to request a review (see Chapter 8)
- the formal and informal complaints procedures that are available to them
- their right to make an application to the Court of Protection to seek variation or termination of the authorisation (see Chapter 10), and

- their right, where the relevant person does not have a paid 'professional' representative, to request the support of an Independent Mental Capacity Advocate (IMCA) (see paragraphs 7.37 to 7.41).

7.5 When providing information to the person and their representative, the managing authority should take account of the communication and language needs of both the person and their representative. Provision of information should be seen as an ongoing responsibility, rather than a one-off activity.

Who can be the relevant person's representative?[13]

7.6 To be eligible to be the relevant person's representative, a person must be:
- 18 years of age or over
- able to keep in contact with the relevant person, and
- willing to be appointed.

The person must not be:
- financially interested in the relevant person's managing authority (a person is considered to be financially interested where that person is a partner, director, other office-holder or major shareholder of the managing authority)
- a relative of a person who has a financial interest in the relevant person's managing authority (paragraph 4.13 explains what is meant by 'relative')
- employed by, or providing services to, the care home in which the person relevant person is residing
- employed by the hospital in a role that is, or could be, related to the treatment or care of the relevant person, or
- employed to work in the relevant person's supervisory body in a role that is, or could be, related to the relevant person's case.

7.7 The appointment of the relevant person's representative is in addition to, and does not affect, any appointment of a donee or deputy. Similarly, the functions of the representative are in addition to, and do not affect, the authority of any donee, the powers of any deputy or any powers of the court. A donee or deputy may themselves be appointed as the relevant person's representative if they meet the eligibility criteria set out in paragraph 7.6.

7.8 There is no presumption that the relevant person's representative should be the same as the person who is their nearest relative for the purposes of the Mental Health Act 1983, even where the relevant person is likely to be subject simultaneously to an authorisation under these safeguards and a provision of the Mental Health Act 1983. This is because the relevant

---

[13] Requirements relating to the eligibility, selection and appointment of relevant person's representatives are covered in regulations. The regulations for England are The Mental Capacity (Deprivation of Liberty: Appointment of Relevant Person's Representative) Regulations 2008. The regulations for Wales are The Mental Capacity (Deprivation of Liberty: Appointment of Relevant Person's Representative) (Wales) Regulations 2008.

person's representative is not selected in the same way as the nearest relative under the Mental Health Act 1983, nor do they perform the same role. However, there is nothing to stop the relevant person's representative being the same as their nearest relative under the Mental Health Act 1983.

When should the relevant person's representative be identified?

7.9   The process of identifying a representative must begin as soon as possible.

7.10   Normally, this should be when the best interests assessor is appointed – even if one or more of the other assessments has not yet been completed. This is because the best interests assessor must, as part of the assessment process, identify if there is anyone they would recommend to become the relevant person's representative. The best interests assessor should discuss the representative role with the people interviewed as part of the assessment.

7.11   This does leave a risk that the process to identify a representative might begin in cases where authorisation is not given. Nevertheless, it is important that the process begins, so that the representative can be appointed immediately the authorisation is given or as soon as possible and practical thereafter.

How should the relevant person's representative be selected?

7.12   The best interests assessor should first establish whether the relevant person has the capacity to select their own representative and, if so, invite them to do so. If the relevant person has capacity and selects an eligible person (according to the criteria set out in paragraph 7.6), the best interests assessor must recommend that person to the supervisory body for appointment.

7.13   Alternatively, if the relevant person lacks capacity and there is a donee or deputy with the appropriate authority, the donee or deputy may select the person to be recommended as the relevant person's representative, again subject to the criteria set out in paragraph 7.6. If a donee or deputy selects an eligible person, then the best interests assessor must recommend that person to the supervisory body for appointment.

7.14   It is up to the best interests assessor to confirm whether any representative proposed by the relevant person, a donee or a deputy is eligible. If the best interests assessor decides that a proposed representative is not eligible, they must advise the person who made the selection and invite them to make a further selection.

7.15   If neither the relevant person, nor a donee or deputy, selects an eligible person, then the best interests assessor must consider whether they are able to identify someone eligible who could act as the relevant person's representative.

7.16   In making a recommendation, the assessor should consider, and balance, factors such as:

- Does the relevant person have a preference?
- If they do not have the capacity to express a preference now, is there any written statement made by the relevant person when they had capacity that indicates who they may now want to be their representative?
- Will the proposed representative be able to keep in contact with the relevant person?
- Does the relevant person appear to trust and feel comfortable with the proposed representative?
- Would the proposed representative be able to represent the relevant person effectively?
- Is the proposed representative likely to represent the relevant person's best interests?

In most cases, the best interests assessor will be able to check at the same time that the proposed representative is willing to take on the role.

7.17 It should not be assumed that the representative needs to be someone who supports the deprivation of liberty.

7.18 The best interests assessor must not select a representative where the relevant person, if they have the capacity to do so, or a donee or a deputy acting within the scope of their authority, states they are not content with that selection.

7.19 If the best interests assessor is unable to recommend anybody to be the relevant person's representative, they must notify the supervisory body accordingly. The supervisory body must then itself identify an eligible person to be appointed as the representative. In doing so, the supervisory body may select a person who:
- would be performing the role in a professional capacity
- has satisfactory skills and experience to perform the role
- is not a family member, friend or carer of the relevant person
- is not employed by, or providing services to, the relevant person's managing authority, where the relevant person's managing authority is a care home
- is not employed to work in the relevant person's managing authority in a role that is, or could be, related to the relevant person's case, where the relevant person's managing authority is a hospital
- is not employed to work in the supervisory body that is appointing the representative in a role that is, or could be, related to the relevant person's case, and
- the supervisory body is satisfied that an appropriate criminal record certificate has been issued in respect of.

7.20 The supervisory body may pay a person they select to be the relevant person's representative in the circumstances set out in paragraph 7.19. This service could be commissioned, for example, through an advocacy services provider, ensuring that the service provides effective independent representation for the relevant person.

7.21 When selecting a suitable representative for the relevant person, the best interests assessor or supervisory body should pay particular attention to the communication and cultural needs of the relevant person.

How should the relevant person's representative be appointed?

7.22 The supervisory body must invite, in writing, the person recommended by the best interests assessor to become the relevant person's representative. If the best interests assessor does not recommend anyone, then the supervisory body should identify and appoint someone to undertake the role. If the person is willing to become the representative, the supervisory body must formally appoint them. If the person refuses, a further eligible person must be identified and invited to become the representative. This process must continue until an eligible person is appointed.

7.23 The appointment of the relevant person's representative by the supervisory body must be in writing and set out the role and responsibilities of the relevant person's representative. The letter of appointment should also state the name of the appointed person and the date of expiry of the appointment, which must be for the period of the standard authorisation that has been given. The supervisory body must send copies of the written appointment to:
- the appointed person
- the relevant person
- any donee or deputy of the relevant person
- any IMCA involved
- every interested person named by the best interests assessor in their report as somebody they have consulted in carrying out their assessment, and
- the managing authority of the relevant hospital or care home.

7.24 The relevant person's representative must confirm to the supervisory body in writing that they are willing to accept the appointment and have understood their roles and responsibilities in respect of the relevant person.

How should the work of the relevant person's representative be supported and monitored?

7.25 It is important that the representative has sufficient contact with the relevant person to ensure that the relevant person's best interests are being safeguarded. In order to fulfil their role, therefore, the representative will need to be able to have face-to-face contact with the relevant person. That means that the care home or hospital should accommodate visits by the representative at reasonable times. The name of the person's representative should be recorded in the person's health and social care records.

7.26 Managing authorities and supervisory bodies should inform the relevant person's representative about sources of support and information available to help them in the role, including how to access the support of an IMCA (see paragraphs 7.37 to 7.41).

7.27 If the representative has insufficient contact with the relevant person, for whatever reason, the person may effectively be unable to access important review and appeal rights. For this reason, if the representative does not maintain an appropriate level of contact with the person, the managing authority will need to consider informing the supervisory body. When the managing authority is reviewing the person's care plan, it should consider whether the representative is in sufficient contact with the relevant person to offer effective support. Records kept by managing authorities about frequency of contact will support this consideration.

7.28 Because the appropriate levels and methods of contact between a relevant person and their representative will vary from case to case, this is a matter about which the managing authority will need to exercise discretion. If the managing authority has any concerns, it may be best to raise the matter with the representative initially to see whether any perceived problems can be resolved informally. If after this the representative still does not maintain what the managing authority considers to be an appropriate level of contact with the relevant person, then the managing authority should notify the supervisory body.

When can the appointment of the relevant person's representative be terminated?

7.29 The appointment of the relevant person's representative will be terminated in any of the following circumstances:
- The standard authorisation comes to an end and a new authorisation is not applied for or, if applied for, is not given.
- The relevant person, if they have capacity to do so, objects to the representative continuing in their role and a different person is selected to be their representative instead.
- A donee or deputy, if it is within their authority to do so and the relevant person lacks the capacity to decide, objects to the representative continuing in their role and a different person is selected to be the representative instead.
- The supervisory body becomes aware that the representative is no longer willing or eligible to continue in the role.
- The supervisory body becomes aware that the relevant person's representative is not keeping in touch with the person, is not representing and supporting them effectively or is not acting in the person's best interests.
- The relevant person's representative dies.

7.30 If the supervisory body becomes aware that the representative may not be keeping in touch with the person, is not acting in the relevant person's best interests, or is no longer eligible, it should contact the representative to clarify the position before deciding whether to terminate the appointment.

7.31 When the appointment of the relevant person's representative ends, the supervisory body must give notice to all those listed in paragraph 7.23. This notice should be given as soon as possible, stating when the appointment ended and the reason why.

7.32 When the appointment of a relevant person's representative ends but the lawful deprivation of liberty continues, the supervisory body must appoint a suitable replacement to be the relevant person's representative as soon as possible and practical after they become aware of the vacancy. As before, a person qualified to be a best interests assessor should make a recommendation to the supervisory body and the supervisory body should take account of any such recommendations.

7.33 If the reason for the termination of the former representative's appointment is that they are no longer eligible, the views of the former representative on who might replace them should be sought. The person identified as most suitable should then be invited to accept the appointment. This process should continue until an eligible person is willing to accept appointment.

What happens when there is no relevant person's representative available?

7.34 A person who is being deprived of their liberty will be in a particularly vulnerable position during any gaps in the appointment of the relevant person's representative, since there may be nobody to represent their interests or to apply for a review on their behalf. In these circumstances, if there is nobody who can support and represent the person (other than a person engaged in providing care and treatment for the relevant person in a professional capacity or for remuneration), the managing authority must notify the supervisory body, who must instruct an IMCA to represent the relevant person until a new representative is appointed.

7.35 The role of an IMCA instructed in these circumstances is essentially the same as that of the relevant person's representative. The role of the IMCA in this situation ends when the new relevant person's representative is appointed.

7.36 At any time when the relevant person does not have a representative, it will be particularly important for supervisory bodies to consider exercising their discretion to carry out a review if there is any significant change in the person's circumstances.

When should an IMCA be instructed?

7.37 Both the person who is deprived of liberty under a standard authorisation and their representative have a statutory right of access to an IMCA. It is the responsibility of the supervisory body to instruct an IMCA if the relevant person or their representative requests one. The intention is to provide extra support to the relevant person or a family member or friend acting as their representative if they need it, and to help them make use of the review process or access the Court of Protection safeguards. Where the relevant person has a paid 'professional' representative (see paragraphs 7.19 and 7.20), the need for additional advocacy support should not arise and so there is no requirement for an IMCA to be provided in those circumstances.

7.38 The role of the IMCA is to help represent the relevant person and, in particular, to assist the relevant person and their representative to understand the effect of the authorisation, what it means, why it has been given, why the relevant person meets the criteria for authorisation, how long it will last, any conditions to which the authorisation is subject and how to trigger a review or challenge in the Court of Protection. The IMCA can also provide support with a review (see Chapter 8) or with an application to the Court of Protection (see Chapter 10), for example to help the person to communicate their views.

7.39 The IMCA will have the right to make submissions to the supervisory body on the question of whether a qualifying requirement should be reviewed, or to give information, or make submissions, to any assessor carrying out a review assessment. Both the person and their representative must be told about the IMCA service and how to request an IMCA.

7.40 An IMCA must be instructed whenever requested by the relevant person or their representative. A request may be made more than once during the period of the authorisation. For example, help may be sought at the start of the authorisation and then again later in order to request a review.

7.41 In addition, if the supervisory body has reason to believe that the review and Court of Protection safeguards might not be used without the support of an IMCA, then they must instruct an IMCA. For example, if the supervisory body is aware that the person has selected a representative who needs support with communication, it should consider whether an IMCA is needed.

8   WHEN SHOULD AN AUTHORISATION BE REVIEWED AND WHAT HAPPENS WHEN IT ENDS?

When a person is deprived of their liberty, the managing authority has a duty to monitor the case on an ongoing basis to see if the person's circumstances change – which may mean they no longer need to be deprived of their liberty.

The managing authority must set out in the care plan clear roles and responsibilities for monitoring and confirm under what circumstances a review is necessary. For example, if a person's condition is changing frequently, then their situation should be reviewed more frequently.

This chapter explains the duties of managing authorities and supervisory bodies in relation to reviewing cases, and what happens when an authorisation ends. The review process is set out in flowchart form at Annex 4.

When should a standard authorisation be reviewed?

8.1 A standard authorisation can be reviewed at any time. The review is carried out by the supervisory body.

8.2 There are certain statutory grounds for carrying out a review. If the statutory grounds for a review are met, the supervisory body must carry out a review. If a review is requested by the relevant person, their representative or the managing authority, the supervisory body must carry out a review. Standard letters are available for the relevant person or their representative to request a review. There is also a standard form available for the managing authority to request a review. A supervisory body can also decide to carry out a review at its own discretion.

8.3 The statutory grounds for a review are:
- The relevant person no longer meets the age, no refusals, mental capacity, mental health or best interests requirements.
- The relevant person no longer meets the eligibility requirement because they now object to receiving mental health treatment in hospital and they meet the criteria for an application for admission under section 2 or section 3 of the Mental Health Act 1983 (see paragraphs 4.45 to 4.48).
- There has been a change in the relevant person's situation and, because of the change, it would be appropriate to amend an existing condition to which the authorisation is subject, delete an existing condition or add a new condition.
- The reason(s) the person now meets the qualifying requirement(s) is(are) different from the reason(s) given at the time the standard authorisation was given.

8.4 Different arrangements apply if the person no longer meets the eligibility requirement because they have been detained under the Mental Health Act, or become subject to a requirement under that Act that conflicts with the authorisation. (See paragraphs 8.19 to 8.21 regarding the short-term suspension of a standard authorisation.)

8.5 A managing authority must request a review if it appears to it that one or more of the qualifying requirements is no longer met, or may no longer be met.

What happens when a review is going to take place?

8.6 The supervisory body must tell the relevant person, their representative and the managing authority if they are going to carry out a review. This must be done either before the review begins or as soon as possible and practical after it has begun. A standard form is available for this purpose.

8.7   The relevant person's records must include information about any formal reviews that have been requested, when they were considered, and the outcome. These records must be retained by the supervisory body.

8.8   Deprivation of liberty can be ended before a formal review. An authorisation only **permits** deprivation of liberty: it does not mean that a person **must be** deprived of liberty where circumstances no longer necessitate it. If a care home or hospital decides that deprivation of liberty is no longer necessary then they must end it immediately, by adjusting the care regime or implementing whatever other change is appropriate. The managing authority should then apply to the supervisory body to review and, if appropriate, formally terminate the authorisation.

How should standard authorisations be reviewed?

8.9   When a supervisory body receives a request for a review, it must first decide which, if any, of the qualifying requirements need to be reviewed. A standard form is available for recording this decision.

8.10 If the supervisory body concludes that none of the qualifying requirements need to be reviewed, no further action is necessary. For example, if there has been a very recent assessment or review and no new evidence has been submitted to show that the relevant person does not meet the criteria, or that circumstances have changed, no review is required.

8.11 If it appears that one or more of the qualifying requirements should be reviewed, the supervisory body must arrange for a separate review assessment to be carried out for each of these requirements.

8.12 The supervisory body must record when a review is requested, what it decides to do (whether it decides to carry out a review or not) and the reasons for its decision.

8.13 In general, review processes should follow the standard authorisation processes – so supervisory bodies should conduct the assessments outlined in Chapter 4 of this Code of Practice for each of the qualifying requirements that need to be reviewed.

8.14 Where the supervisory body decides that the best interests requirement should be reviewed solely because details of the **conditions** attached to the authorisation need to be changed, and the review request does not include evidence that there is a significant change in the relevant person's overall circumstances, there is no need for a full reassessment of best interests. The supervisory body can simply vary the conditions attached to the authorisation as appropriate. In deciding whether a full reassessment is necessary, the supervisory body should consider whether the grounds for the authorisation, or the nature of the conditions, are being contested by anyone as part of the review request.

8.15 If the review relates to any of the other requirements, or to a significant change in the person's situation under the best interests requirement, the supervisory body must obtain a new assessment.

8.16 If the assessment shows that the requirement is still met, the supervisory body must check whether the reason that it is met has changed from the reason originally stated on the authorisation. If it has, the supervisory body should make any appropriate amendments to the authorisation. In addition, if the review relates to the best interests requirement, the supervisory body must consider whether any conditions should be changed following the new assessment.

Scenario: *The review process*

Jo is 29 and sustained severe brain damage in a road traffic collision that killed her parents. She has great difficulty in verbal and written communication. Jo can get very frustrated and has been known to lash out at other people in the nursing care home where she now lives. At first, she regularly attempted to leave the home, but the view of the organisation providing Jo's care was that such a move would place her at serious risk, so she should be prevented from leaving.

Jo was assessed under the deprivation of liberty safeguards and an authorisation was made for six months. That authorisation is not due to end for another three months. However, Jo has made huge progress at the home and her representative is no longer sure that the restrictions are necessary. Care home staff, however, do not think that her improvement reduces the best interests requirement of the deprivation of liberty authorisation.

Jo is assisted by her representative to request a review, in the form of a letter with pictures. The pictures appear to describe Jo's frustration with the legal processes that she perceives are preventing her from moving into her own accommodation.

The supervisory body appoints a best interests assessor to coordinate the review. The best interests assessor considers which of the qualifying requirements needs to be reviewed and by whom. It appears that the best interests assessment, as well as possibly the mental health and mental capacity assessments, should be reviewed.

To assess Jo's mental capacity and her own wishes for the best interests assessment, the best interests assessor feels that specialist help would be beneficial. A speech and language therapist meets with Jo and uses a visual communication system with her. Using this system, the therapist is able to say that in her view Jo is unlikely to have capacity to make the decision to leave the care home. The mental health assessment also confirmed that Jo was still considered to have a mental disorder.

The best interests assessor was uncertain, however, whether it was still in Jo's best interests to remain under the deprivation of liberty authorisation. It was not possible to coordinate full updated assessments from the →

rehabilitation team, who knew her well, in the time limits required. So, because the care home believed that the standard authorisation was still required, and it was a complex case, the best interests assessor recommended to the supervisory body that two conditions should be applied to the standard authorisation:

- assessments must be carried out by rehabilitation specialists on Jo's clinical progress, and
- a full case review should be held within one month.

At this review meeting, to which Jo's representative and the best interests assessor were invited, it was agreed that Jo had made such good progress that deprivation of liberty was no longer necessary, because the risks of her having increased freedom had reduced. The standard authorisation was therefore terminated, and a new care plan was prepared which focused on working towards more independent living.

What happens if any of the requirements are not met?

8.17 If any of the requirements are not met, then the authorisation must be terminated immediately.

8.18 The supervisory body must give written notice of the outcome of a review and any changes that have been made to the deprivation of liberty authorisation to:
- the managing authority and the care home or hospital itself
- the relevant person
- the relevant person's representative, and
- any Independent Mental Capacity Advocate (IMCA) involved.

Short-term suspension of authorisation

8.19 There are separate review arrangements for cases in which the eligibility requirement ceases to be met for a short period of time for reasons other than that the person is objecting to receiving mental health treatment in hospital. For example, if the relevant person is detained as a hospital in-patient under the Mental Health Act 1983, the managing authority must notify the supervisory body, who will suspend the authorisation.

8.20 If the relevant person then becomes eligible again within 28 days, the managing authority must notify the supervisory body who will remove the suspension. If no such notice is given within 28 days, then the authorisation will be terminated. Standard forms are available for managing authorities to notify supervisory bodies about the need for suspension of an authorisation, or that a suspension should be lifted.

8.21 If the person ceases to meet the eligibility requirement because they begin to object to receiving mental health treatment in hospital and they meet the criteria for an application for admission under section 2 or section 3 of the Mental Health Act 1983, a review should be started immediately (see paragraph 8.3).

Is a review necessary when the relevant person's capacity fluctuates?

8.22 Guidance about people with fluctuating or temporary capacity is contained in paragraphs 4.26 and 4.27 of the main Code. In the context of deprivation of liberty safeguards, where a relevant person's capacity to make decisions about the arrangements made for their care and treatment fluctuates on a short-term basis, a balance needs to be struck between:

- the need to review and terminate an authorisation if a person regains capacity, and
- spending time and resources constantly reviewing, terminating and then seeking fresh deprivation of liberty authorisations as the relevant person's capacity changes.

8.23 Each case must be treated on its merits. Managing authorities should keep all cases under review: where a person subject to an authorisation is deemed to have regained the capacity to decide about the arrangements made for their care and treatment, the managing authority must assess whether there is consistent evidence of the regaining of capacity on a longer-term basis. This is a clinical judgement that will need to be made by a suitably qualified person.

8.24 Where there is consistent evidence of regaining capacity on this longer-term basis, deprivation of liberty should be lifted immediately, and a formal review and termination of the authorisation sought. However, it should be borne in mind that a deprivation of liberty authorisation carries with it certain safeguards that the relevant person will lose if the authorisation is terminated. Where the regaining of capacity is likely to be temporary, and the authorisation will be required again within a short period of time, the authorisation should be left in place, but with the situation kept under ongoing review.

Scenario: Fluctuating capacity

Walter, an older man with severe depression, is admitted to hospital from a care home. He seems confused and bewildered, but does not object. His family are unable to look after him at home, but they would prefer him to go into a different care home rather than stay in hospital. However, there is no alternative placement available, so when the assessment concludes that Walter lacks capacity to make decisions about his care and treatment, the only option seems to be that he should stay on the ward,

Because the care regime in the ward is extremely restrictive – Walter is not allowed to leave the hospital and his movement within the hospital is ➡

restricted for his own safety – ward staff think that they need to apply for a deprivation of liberty authorisation which is subsequently given.

However, over time Walter starts to experience lucid passages, during which he expresses relief at being on the ward rather than in the care home. A review meeting is convened and the participants agree that Walter now sometimes has capacity to make decisions about the arrangements made for his care and treatment. As this capacity fluctuates, it is decided, in consultation with his family, that the deprivation of liberty authorisation should remain in place for the time being.

Walter remains on the ward and his progress is such that his family feel they could look after him at home. Walter seems happy with this proposal and the consultant psychiatrist with responsibility for his care agrees to this. The deprivation of liberty authorisation is reviewed and terminated.

What happens when an authorisation ends?

8.25 When an authorisation ends, the managing authority cannot lawfully continue to deprive a person of their liberty.

8.26 If the managing authority considers that a person will still need to be deprived of liberty after the authorisation ends, they need to request a further standard authorisation to begin immediately after the expiry of the existing authorisation.

8.27 There is no statutory time limit on how far in advance of the expiry of one authorisation the managing authority can apply for a renewal authorisation. It will need to be far enough in advance for the renewal authorisation to be given before the existing authorisation ends (but see paragraphs 3.19 and 3.20 about not applying for authorisations too far in advance).

8.28 Once underway, the process for renewing a standard authorisation is the same as that for obtaining an original authorisation, and the same assessment processes must take place. However, the need to instruct an IMCA will not usually arise because the relevant person should at this stage have a representative appointed.

8.29 When the standard authorisation ends, the supervisory body must inform in writing:
- the relevant person
- the relevant person's representative
- the managing authority, and
- every interested person named by the best interests assessor in their report as somebody they have consulted in carrying out their assessment.

9 WHAT HAPPENS IF SOMEONE THINKS A PERSON IS BEING DEPRIVED OF THEIR LIBERTY WITHOUT AUTHORISATION?

It is a serious issue to deprive someone of their liberty without authorisation if they lack the capacity to consent. If anyone believes that a person is being deprived of their liberty without authorisation, they should raise this with the relevant authorities.

If the conclusion is that the person is being deprived of their liberty unlawfully, this will normally result in a change in their care arrangements, or in an application for a deprivation of liberty authorisation being made.

This chapter explains the process for reporting concerns and for assessing whether unauthorised deprivation of liberty is occurring. The flowchart at Annex 3 summarises the process that a supervisory body should follow when it receives a request from somebody other than the managing authority to examine whether or not there is a current unauthorised deprivation of liberty.

What action should someone take if they think a person is being deprived of their liberty without authorisation?

9.1 If the relevant person themselves, any relative, friend or carer or any other third party (such as a person carrying out an inspection visit or a member of an advocacy organisation) believes that a person is being deprived of liberty without the managing authority having applied for an authorisation, they should draw this to the attention of the managing authority. A standard letter is available for this purpose. In the first instance, they should ask the managing authority to apply for an authorisation if it wants to continue with the care regime, or to change the care regime immediately. Given the seriousness of deprivation of liberty, a managing authority must respond within a reasonable time to the request. This would normally mean within 24 hours.

9.2 It may be possible for the managing authority to resolve the matter informally with the concerned person. For example, the managing authority could discuss the case with the concerned person, and perhaps make some adjustment to the care arrangements so that concerns that a deprivation of liberty may be occurring are removed. However, if the managing authority is unable to resolve the issue with the concerned person quickly, they should submit a request for a standard authorisation to the supervisory body.

9.3 If the concerned person has raised the matter with the managing authority, and the managing authority does not apply for an authorisation within a reasonable period, the concerned person can ask the supervisory body to decide whether there is an unauthorised deprivation of liberty. They should:

- tell the supervisory body the name of the person they are concerned about and the name of the hospital or care home, and
- as far as they are able, explain why they think that the person is deprived of their liberty.

A standard letter is available for this purpose.

9.4 In such circumstances, the supervisory body must select and appoint a person who is suitable and eligible to carry out a best interests assessment to consider whether the person is deprived of liberty.

9.5 The supervisory body does not, however, need to arrange such an assessment where it appears to the supervisory body that:

- the request they have received is frivolous or vexatious (for example, where the person is very obviously not deprived of their liberty) or where a very recent assessment has been carried out and repeated requests are received, or
- the question of whether or not there is an unauthorised deprivation of liberty has already been decided, and since that decision, there has been no change of circumstances that would merit the question being considered again.

The supervisory body should record the reasons for their decisions. A standard form is available for this purpose.

9.6 The supervisory body must notify the person who raised the concern, the relevant person, the managing authority of the relevant hospital or care home and any IMCA involved:

- that it has been to asked to assess whether or not there is an unauthorised deprivation of liberty
- whether or not it has decided to commission an assessment, and
- where relevant, who has been appointed as assessor.

What happens if somebody informs the supervisory body directly that they think a person is being deprived of their liberty without authorisation?

9.7 If a person raises concerns about a potential unauthorised deprivation of liberty directly with the supervisory body, the supervisory body should immediately arrange a preliminary assessment to determine whether a deprivation of liberty is occurring. The supervisory body should then immediately notify the managing authority, rather than asking the concerned person to contact the managing authority themselves, to ask them to request a standard authorisation in respect of the person who is possibly deprived of liberty. The supervisory body should agree with the managing authority what is a reasonable period within which a standard authorisation should be requested (unless the managing authority is able to resolve the matter informally with the concerned person as described in paragraph 9.2). If the managing authority does not submit an application within the agreed period, and the matter has not been resolved informally, the supervisory body should follow the process set out in paragraphs 9.3 to 9.6 to assess whether unlawful deprivation of liberty is occurring. Even if the concerned person prefers to deal directly with the managing authority, the supervisory body should monitor what happens very closely to ensure that no unlawful deprivation of liberty may be occurring without proper action being taken.

How will the assessment of unlawful deprivation of liberty be conducted?

9.8 An assessment of whether an unlawful deprivation of liberty is occurring must be carried out within seven calendar days. Although the assessment must be completed by somebody who is suitable and eligible to carry out a best interests assessment, it is not a best interests assessment as such. The purpose of the assessment is simply to establish whether unlawful deprivation of liberty is occurring.

9.9 The person nominated to undertake the assessment must consult the managing authority of the relevant hospital or care home, and examine any relevant needs assessments and care plans to consider whether they constitute a deprivation of liberty. They should also speak to the person who raised the concern about why they believe that the relevant person is being deprived of their liberty and consult, as far as is possible, with the relevant person's family and friends. If there is nobody appropriate to consult among family and friends, they should inform the supervisory body who must arrange for an IMCA to be instructed to support and represent the person. A standard form is available for the assessor to record the outcome of their assessment.

What happens once the assessment has been conducted?

9.10 There are three possible outcomes of this assessment. The assessor may conclude that:
- the person is not being deprived of their liberty
- the person is being lawfully deprived of their liberty because authorisation exists (this, though, is an unlikely outcome since the supervisory body should already be aware if any authorisation exists, thus rendering any assessment in response to a third party request unnecessary), or
- the person is being deprived of their liberty unlawfully.

9.11 The supervisory body must notify the following people of the outcome of the assessment:
- the concerned third party who made the request
- the relevant person
- the managing authority of the relevant hospital or care home, and
- any IMCA involved.

A standard form is available for this purpose.

9.12 If the outcome of the assessment is that there is an unauthorised deprivation of liberty, then the full assessment process should be completed as if a standard authorisation for deprivation of liberty had been applied for – unless the managing authority changes the care arrangements so that it is clear that there is no longer any deprivation of liberty.

9.13 If, having considered what could be done to avoid deprivation of liberty, the managing authority decides that the need to continue the deprivation of liberty is so urgent that the care regime should continue while the assessments are carried out, it must give an urgent authorisation and seek a standard authorisation within seven days. The managing authority must supply the supervisory body with the same information it would have had to include in a request for a standard authorisation.

9.14 If the concerned person does not accept the outcome of their request for assessment, they can apply to the Court of Protection to hear their case. See Chapter 10 for more details of the role of the Court of Protection.

10   WHAT IS THE COURT OF PROTECTION AND WHEN CAN PEOPLE APPLY TO IT?

To comply with Article 5(4) of the European Convention on Human Rights, anybody deprived of their liberty in accordance with the safeguards described in this Code of Practice is entitled to the right of speedy access to a court that can review the lawfulness of their deprivation of liberty. The Court of Protection, established by the Mental Capacity Act 2005, is the court for this purpose. Chapter 8 of the main Code provides more details on its role, powers and responsibilities.

When can people apply to the Court of Protection about the deprivation of liberty safeguards and who can apply?

Applying before an authorisation is given

10.1 The relevant person, or someone acting on their behalf, may make an application to the Court of Protection **before** a decision has been reached on an application for authorisation to deprive a person of their liberty. This might be to ask the court to declare whether the relevant person has capacity, or whether an act done or proposed to be done in relation to that person is lawful (this may include whether or not the act is or would be in the best interests of the relevant person). It is up to the Court of Protection to decide whether or not to consider such an application in advance of the decision on authorisation.

Applying after an authorisation has been given

10.2 Once a standard authorisation has been given, the relevant person or their representative has the right to apply to the Court of Protection to determine any question relating to the following matters:
- whether the relevant person meets one or more of the qualifying requirements for deprivation of liberty
- the period for which the standard authorisation is to be in force
- the purpose for which the standard authorisation is given, or
- the conditions subject to which the standard authorisation is given.

10.3 Where an urgent authorisation has been given, the relevant person or certain persons acting on their behalf, such as a donee or deputy, has the right to apply to the Court of Protection to determine any question relating to the following matters:
- whether the urgent authorisation should have been given
- the period for which the urgent authorisation is to be in force, or
- the purpose for which the urgent authorisation has been given.

10.4 Where a standard or urgent authorisation has been given, any other person may also apply to the Court of Protection for permission to take the relevant person's case to court to determine whether an authorisation should have been given. However, the Court of Protection has discretion to decide whether or not to consider an application from these people.

10.5 Wherever possible, concerns about the deprivation of liberty should be resolved informally or through the relevant supervisory body's or managing authority's complaints procedure, rather than through the Court of Protection. Chapter 15 of the main Code ('What are the best ways to settle disagreements and disputes about issues covered in the Act?') contains general guidance on how to settle disputes about issues covered in the Mental Capacity Act 2005. The review processes covered in Chapter 8 of this Code also provide a way of resolving disputes or concerns, as explained in that chapter.

10.6 The aim should be to limit applications to the Court of Protection to cases that genuinely need to be referred to the court. However, with deprivation of liberty at stake, people should not be discouraged from making an application to the Court of Protection if it proves impossible to resolve concerns satisfactorily through other routes in a timely manner.

How should people apply to the Court of Protection?

10.7 Guidance on the court's procedures, including how to make an application, is given in the Court of Protection Rules and Practice Directions issued by the court.[14]

---

[14] There will usually be a fee for applications to the court. Details of the fees charged by the court and the circumstances in which fees may be waived or remitted are available from the Office of the Public Guardian (http://www.publicguardian.gov.uk/).

10.8 The following people have an automatic right of access to the Court of Protection and do not have to obtain permission from the court to make an application:

- a person who lacks, or is alleged to lack, capacity in relation to a specific decision or action
- the donor of a Lasting Power of Attorney to whom an application relates, or their donee
- a deputy who has been appointed by the court to act for the person concerned
- a person named in an existing court order[15] to which the application relates, and
- the person appointed by the supervisory body as the relevant person's representative.

10.9 All other applicants must obtain the permission of the court before making an application. (See section 50 of the Mental Capacity Act 2005, as amended.) This can be done by completing the appropriate application form.

What orders can the Court of Protection make?

10.10 The court may make an order:

- varying or terminating a standard or urgent authorisation, or
- directing the supervisory body (in the case of a standard authorisation) or the managing authority (in the case of an urgent authorisation) to vary or terminate the authorisation.

What is the role of the Court of Protection in respect of people lacking capacity who are deprived of their liberty in settings other than hospitals or care homes?

10.11 The deprivation of liberty safeguards relate only to circumstances where a person is deprived of their liberty in a hospital or care home. Depriving a person who lacks capacity to consent to the arrangements made for their care or treatment of their liberty in other settings (for example in a person's own home, in supported living arrangements other than in care homes or in a day centre) will only be lawful following an order of the Court of Protection on a best interests personal welfare matter (see paragraph 6.51 of the main Code).

10.12 In such a case, application to the Court of Protection should be made before deprivation of liberty begins. A Court of Protection order will then itself provide a legal basis for the deprivation of liberty. A separate deprivation of liberty authorisation under the processes set out in this Code will not be required.

---

15 Examples of existing court orders include orders appointing a deputy or declarations made by the court in relation to treatment issues.

Is legal aid available to support applications to the Court of Protection in deprivation of liberty safeguards cases?

10.13 Legal aid will be available both for advice and representation before the Court of Protection.

11 HOW WILL THE SAFEGUARDS BE MONITORED?

The deprivation of a person's liberty is a significant issue. The deprivation of liberty safeguards are designed to ensure that a person who lacks capacity to consent to the arrangements made for their care or treatment is suitably protected against arbitrary detention. In order to provide reassurance that the safeguards processes are being correctly operated, it is important for there to be an effective mechanism for monitoring the implementation of the safeguards.

Who will monitor the safeguards?

11.1 Regulations[16] will confer the responsibility for the inspection process of the operation of the deprivation of liberty safeguards in England on a new regulator, the Care Quality Commission, bringing together functions from the existing Commission for Social Care Inspection, the Healthcare Commission and the Mental Health Act Commission. The new body will be established during 2008, subject to the passage of the relevant legislation through Parliament, and is expected to be fully operational by 2009/10 in line with the deprivation of liberty safeguards coming into force.

11.2 In Wales, the functions of monitoring the operation of the deprivation of liberty safeguards will fall to Welsh Ministers. These functions will be performed on their behalf by Healthcare Inspectorate Wales and the Care and Social Services Inspectorate Wales.

What will the inspection bodies do and what powers will they have?

11.3 The inspection bodies for care homes and hospitals will be expected to:
- monitor the manner in which the deprivation of liberty safeguards are being operated by:
  - visiting hospitals and care homes in accordance with their existing visiting programme
  - interviewing people accommodated in hospitals and care homes to the extent that they consider it necessary to do so, and

---

[16] Draft regulations for England will be consulted upon later. Welsh Ministers are currently considering how they will use their regulation-making powers for Wales.

- requiring the production of, and inspecting, relevant records relating to the care or treatment of people accommodated in hospitals and care homes
- report annually, summarising their activity and their findings about the operation of the deprivation of liberty safeguards. In England this report will be made to the Secretary of State for Health, and in Wales the report will be made to the Welsh Ministers. It will be for each monitoring body to decide whether there should be a deprivation of liberty safeguards specific report or whether the report should form part of a wider report on the monitoring body's activities.

11.4 The inspection bodies will have the power to require supervisory bodies and managing authorities of hospitals or care homes to disclose information to them.

11.5 The inspection process will not cover the revisiting of individual assessments (other than by way of a limited amount of sampling).

11.6 The inspection process will not constitute an alternative review or appeal process. However, if the inspection body comes across a case where they believe deprivation of liberty may be occurring without an authorisation, they should inform the supervisory body in the same way as any other third party may do.

11.7 The inspection bodies will look at the deprivation of liberty protocols and procedures in place within managing authorities and supervisory bodies. The aim is to use a small amount of sampling to evaluate the effect of these protocols and procedures on individual cases. Monitoring should take place at a time when the monitoring body is visiting the care home or in-patient setting as part of routine operations, not as an exception.

11.8 Supervisory bodies and managing authorities should keep their protocols and procedures under review and supervisory bodies should assess the nature of the authorisations they are giving in light of their local population. This information may be relevant to policy decisions about commissioning care and support services.

CHECKLISTS

Key points for care homes and hospitals (managing authorities)

- Managing authorities need to adapt their care planning processes to incorporate consideration of whether a person has capacity to consent to the services which are to be provided and whether their actions are likely to result in a deprivation of liberty.

- A managing authority must not, except in an urgent situation, deprive a person of liberty unless a standard authorisation has been given by the supervisory body for that specific situation, and remains in force.

- It is up to the managing authority to request such authorisation and implement the outcomes.

- Authorisation should be obtained from the supervisory body in advance of the deprivation of liberty, except in circumstances considered to be so urgent that the deprivation of liberty needs to begin immediately. In such cases, authorisation must be obtained within seven calendar days of the start of the deprivation of liberty.

- A managing authority must ensure that they comply with any conditions attached to the authorisation.

- A managing authority should monitor whether the relevant person's representative maintains regular contact with the person.

- Authorisation of deprivation of liberty should only be sought if it is genuinely necessary for a person to be deprived of liberty in their best interests in order to keep them safe. It is not necessary to apply for authorisations for all admissions to hospitals and care homes simply because the person concerned lacks capacity to decide whether to be admitted.

Key points for local authorities and NHS bodies (supervisory bodies)

- Supervisory bodies will receive applications from managing authorities for standard authorisations of deprivation of liberty. Deprivation of liberty cannot lawfully begin until the supervisory body has given authorisation, or the managing authority has itself given an urgent authorisation.

- Before an authorisation for deprivation of liberty may be given, the supervisory body must have obtained written assessments of the relevant person in order to ensure that they meet the qualifying requirements (including that the deprivation of liberty is necessary to protect them from harm and will be in their best interests).

- Supervisory bodies will need to ensure that sufficient assessors are available to meet the needs of their area and that these assessors have the skills, qualifications, experience and training to perform the function.

- Authorisation may not be given unless all the qualifying requirements are met.

- In giving authorisation, the supervisory body must specify its duration, which may not exceed 12 months and may not be for longer than recommended by the best interests assessor. Deprivation of liberty should not continue for longer than is necessary.

- The supervisory body may attach conditions to the authorisation if it considers it appropriate to do so.

- The supervisory body must give notice of its decision in writing to specified people, and notify others.

- The supervisory body must appoint a relevant person's representative to represent the interests of every person for whom they give a standard authorisation for deprivation of liberty.

- When an authorisation is in force, the relevant person, the relevant person's representative and any IMCA representing the individual have a right at any time to request that the supervisory body reviews the authorisation.

Key points for managing authorities and supervisory bodies

In addition to the above, both managing authorities and supervisory bodies should be aware of the following key points:

- An authorisation may last for a maximum period of 12 months.

- Anyone engaged in caring for the person, anyone named by them as a person to consult, and anyone with an interest in the person's welfare must be consulted in decision-making.

- Before the current authorisation expires, the managing authority may seek a fresh authorisation for up to another 12 months, provided it is established, on the basis of further assessment, that the requirements continue to be met.

- The authorisation should be reviewed, and if appropriate revoked, before it expires if there has been a significant change in the person's circumstances. To this end, the managing authority will be required to ensure that the continued deprivation of liberty of a person remains necessary in the best interests of the person.

- A decision to deprive a person of liberty may be challenged by the relevant person, or by the relevant person's representative, by an application to the Court of Protection. However, managing authorities and supervisory bodies should always be prepared to try to resolve disputes locally and informally. No one should be forced to apply to the court because of failure or unwillingness on the part of a managing authority or supervisory body to engage in constructive discussion.

- If the court is asked to decide on a case where there is a question about whether deprivation of liberty is lawful or should continue to be authorised, the managing authority can continue with its current care regime where it is necessary:
  - for the purpose of giving the person life-sustaining treatment, or
  - to prevent a serious deterioration in their condition while the court makes its decision.

- The complete process of assessing and authorising deprivation of liberty should be clearly recorded, and regularly monitored and audited, as part of an organisation's governance structure.

- Management information should be recorded and retained, and used to measure the effectiveness of the deprivation of liberty processes. This information will also need to be shared with the inspection bodies.

ANNEXES

Annex 1

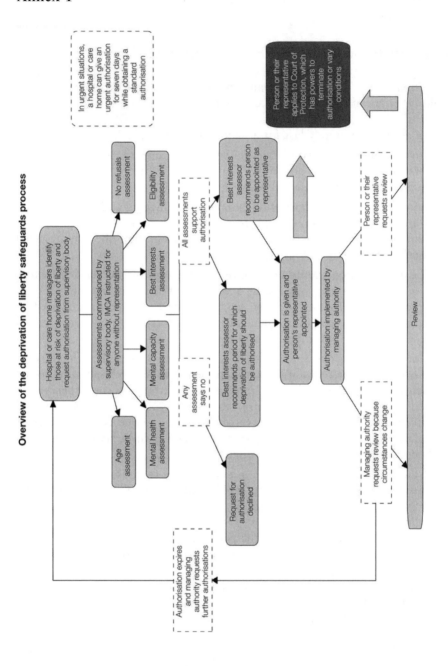

Annex 2

What should a managing authority consider before applying for authorisation of deprivation of liberty?

These questions are relevant **both** at admission **and** when reviewing the care of patients and residents. By considering the following questions in the following or der, a managing authority will be helped to know whether an application for authorisation is required.

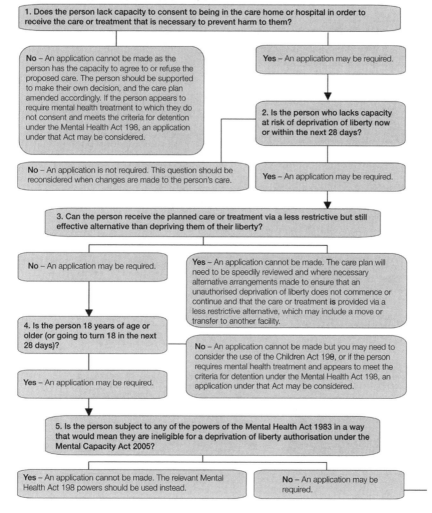

1. Does the person lack capacity to consent to being in the care home or hospital in order to receive the care or treatment that is necessary to prevent harm to them?

No – An application cannot be made as the person has the capacity to agree to or refuse the proposed care. The person should be supported to make their own decision, and the care plan amended accordingly. If the person appears to require mental health treatment to which they do not consent and meets the criteria for detention under the Mental Health Act 198, an application under that Act may be considered.

Yes – An application may be required.

2. Is the person who lacks capacity at risk of deprivation of liberty now or within the next 28 days?

No – An application is not required. This question should be reconsidered when changes are made to the person's care.

Yes – An application may be required.

3. Can the person receive the planned care or treatment via a less restrictive but still effective alternative than depriving them of their liberty?

No – An application may be required.

Yes – An application cannot be made. The care plan will need to be speedily reviewed and where necessary alternative arrangements made to ensure that an unauthorised deprivation of liberty does not commence or continue and that the care or treatment **is** provided via a less restrictive alternative, which may include a move or transfer to another facility.

4. Is the person 18 years of age or older (or going to turn 18 in the next 28 days)?

No – An application cannot be made but you may need to consider the use of the Children Act 198, or if the person requires mental health treatment and appears to meet the criteria for detention under the Mental Health Act 198, an application under that Act may be considered.

Yes – An application may be required.

5. Is the person subject to any of the powers of the Mental Health Act 1983 in a way that would mean they are ineligible for a deprivation of liberty authorisation under the Mental Capacity Act 2005?

Yes – An application cannot be made. The relevant Mental Health Act 198 powers should be used instead.

No – An application may be required.

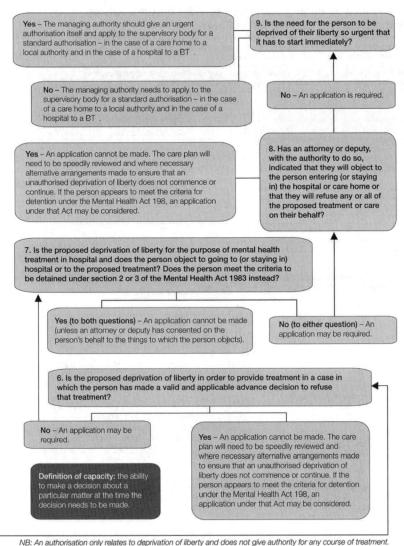

Yes – The managing authority should give an urgent authorisation itself and apply to the supervisory body for a standard authorisation – in the case of a care home to a local authority and in the case of a hospital to a PCT.

9. Is the need for the person to be deprived of their liberty so urgent that it has to start immediately?

No – The managing authority needs to apply to the supervisory body for a standard authorisation – in the case of a care home to a local authority and in the case of a hospital to a PCT.

No – An application is required.

Yes – An application cannot be made. The care plan will need to be speedily reviewed and where necessary alternative arrangements made to ensure that an unauthorised deprivation of liberty does not commence or continue. If the person appears to meet the criteria for detention under the Mental Health Act 198, an application under that Act may be considered.

8. Has an attorney or deputy, with the authority to do so, indicated that they will object to the person entering (or staying in) the hospital or care home or that they will refuse any or all of the proposed treatment or care on their behalf?

7. Is the proposed deprivation of liberty for the purpose of mental health treatment in hospital and does the person object to going to (or staying in) hospital or to the proposed treatment? Does the person meet the criteria to be detained under section 2 or 3 of the Mental Health Act 1983 instead?

Yes (to both questions) – An application cannot be made (unless an attorney or deputy has consented on the person's behalf to the things to which the person objects).

No (to either question) – An application may be required.

6. Is the proposed deprivation of liberty in order to provide treatment in a case in which the person has made a valid and applicable advance decision to refuse that treatment?

No – An application may be required.

Definition of capacity: the ability to make a decision about a particular matter at the time the decision needs to be made.

Yes – An application cannot be made. The care plan will need to be speedily reviewed and where necessary alternative arrangements made to ensure that an unauthorised deprivation of liberty does not commence or continue. If the person appears to meet the criteria for detention under the Mental Health Act 198, an application under that Act may be considered.

NB: An authorisation only relates to deprivation of liberty and does not give authority for any course of treatment.

Annex 3

Supervisory body action on receipt of a request from:

a) **a managing authority for a standard deprivation of liberty authorisation**

b) **somebody other than a managing authority (an eligible person) to determine whether or not there is a current unauthorised deprivation of liberty**

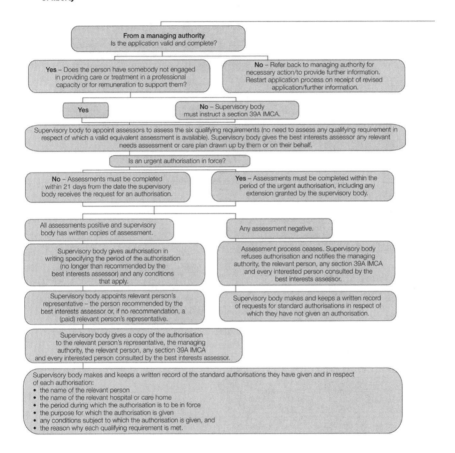

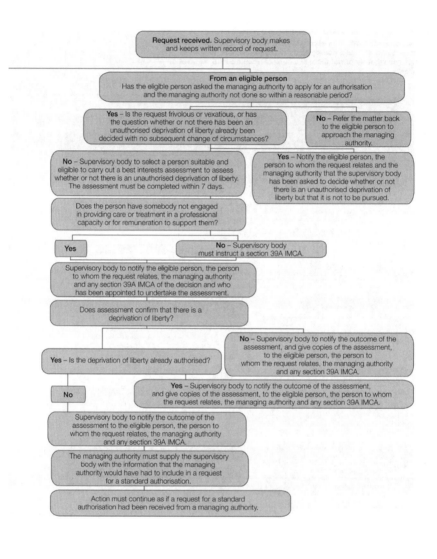

Annex 4

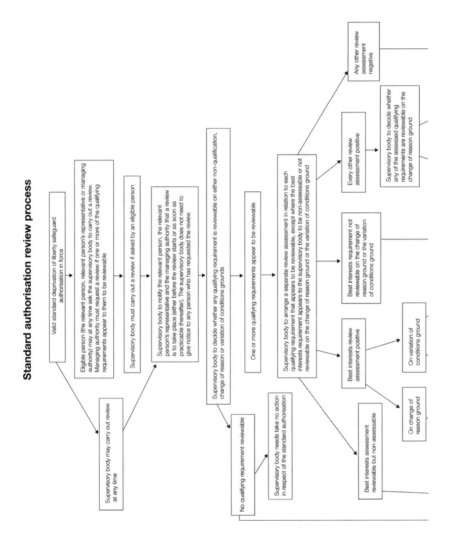

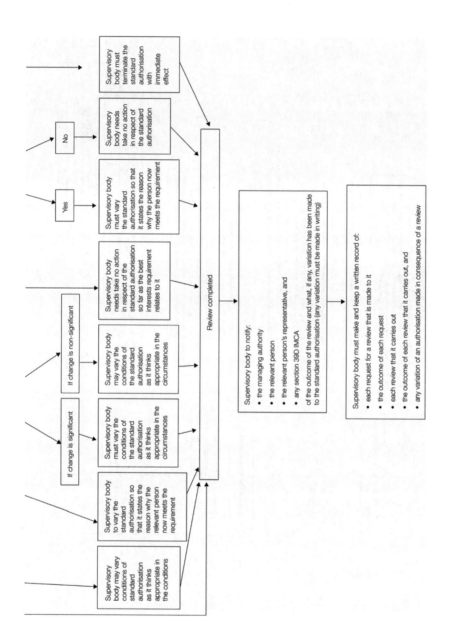

KEY WORDS AND PHRASES USED IN THE CODE OF PRACTICE

The table below is not a full index or glossary. Instead, it is a list of key terms used in this Code of Practice. References in bold indicate particularly valuable content for that term.

Advance decision to refuse treatment	A decision to refuse specified treatment made in advance by a person who has capacity to do so. This decision will then apply at a future time when that person lacks capacity to consent to, or refuse, the specified treatment. Specific rules apply to advance decisions to refuse life sustaining treatment.	4.26
Advocacy	Independent help and support with understanding issues and putting forward a person's own views, feelings and ideas.	2.7
Age assessment	An assessment, for the purpose of the deprivation of liberty safeguards, of whether the relevant person has reached age 18.	**4.23–4.24**
Approved mental health professional	A social worker or other professional approved by a local social services authority to act on behalf of a local social services authority in carrying out a variety of functions.	4.52, 4.53, 4.60
Assessor	A person who carries out a deprivation of liberty safeguards assessment.	**Chapter 4 (all)** 1.16–1.17, 3.21, 5.22, 9.10 Best interests, and appointing a relevant person's representative: 7.10–7.23

Best interests assessment	An assessment, for the purpose of the deprivation of liberty safeguards, of whether deprivation of liberty is in a detained person's best interests, is necessary to prevent harm to the person and is a proportionate response to the likelihood and seriousness of that harm.	**4.58–4.76** Best interests, and appointing a relevant person's representative: 7.10–7.23
Bournewood judgment	The commonly used term for the October 2004 judgment by the European Court of Human Rights in the case of *HL v the United Kingdom* that led to the introduction of the deprivation of liberty safeguards.	**Introduction to Chapter 1** 1.19, 2.2, 2.22
Capacity	Short for mental capacity. The ability to make a decision about a particular matter at the time the decision needs to be made. A legal definition is contained in section 2 of the Mental Capacity Act 2005.	Throughout
Care home	A care facility registered under the Care Standards Act 2000.	Throughout
Care Quality Commission	The new integrated regulator for health and adult social care that, subject to the passage of legislation, will take over regulation of health and adult social care from 1 April 2009.	Chapter 11
Carer	Someone who provides unpaid care by looking after a friend or neighbour who needs support because of sickness, age or disability. In this document, the term carer does not mean a paid care worker.	Throughout
Children Act 1989	A law relating to children and those with parental responsibility for children.	1.12, 5.22
Conditions	Requirements that a supervisory body may impose when giving a standard deprivation of liberty authorisation, after taking account of any recommendations made by the best interests assessor.	**4.74–4.75** 5.5 Review of: 8.14, 8.16

Consent	Agreeing to a course of action – specifically in this document, to a care plan or treatment regime. For consent to be legally valid, the person giving it must have the capacity to take the decision, have been given sufficient information to make the decision, and not have been under any duress or inappropriate pressure.	Throughout
Court of Protection	The specialist court for all issues relating to people who lack capacity to make specific decisions.	**Chapter 10**
Deprivation of liberty	Deprivation of liberty is a term used in the European Convention on Human Rights about circumstances when a person's freedom is taken away. Its meaning in practice is being defined through case law.	**Chapter 2** Throughout
Deprivation of liberty safeguards	The framework of safeguards under the Mental Capacity Act 2005 for people who need to be deprived of their liberty in a hospital or care home in their best interests for care or treatment and who lack the capacity to consent to the arrangements made for their care or treatment.	Throughout
Deprivation of liberty safeguards assessment	Any one of the six assessments that need to be undertaken as part of the standard deprivation of liberty authorisation process.	**Chapter 4**
Deputy	Someone appointed by the Court of Protection with ongoing legal authority, as prescribed by the Court, to make decisions on behalf of a person who lacks capacity to make particular decisions.	4.26, 4.65, 5.11, 5.22, 7.7, 7.13–7.15, 7.18, 7.23, 7.29, 10.3, 10.8
Donee	Someone appointed under a Lasting Power of Attorney who has the legal right to make decisions within the scope of their authority on behalf of the person (the donor) who made the Lasting Power of Attorney.	3.9, 4.26, 4.65, 5.11, 5.22, 7.7, 7.13–7.15, 7.18, 7.23, 7.29, 10.3, 10.8

Eligibility assessment	An assessment, for the purpose of the deprivation of liberty safeguards, of whether or not a person is rendered ineligible for a standard deprivation of liberty authorisation because the authorisation would conflict with requirements that are, or could be, placed on the person under the Mental Health Act 1983.	**4.40–4.57**
European Convention on Human Rights	A convention drawn up within the Council of Europe setting out a number of civil and political rights and freedoms, and setting up a mechanism for the enforcement of the obligations entered into by contracting states.	Chapter 1, Chapter 2
European Court of Human Rights	The court to which any contracting state or individual can apply when they believe that there has been a violation of the European Convention on Human Rights.	Introduction to Chapter 1, 2.1–2.2
Guardianship under the Mental Health Act 1983	The appointment of a guardian to help and supervise patients in the community for their own welfare or to protect other people. The guardian may be either a local authority or a private individual approved by the local authority.	4.43, 4.44
Independent Mental Capacity Advocate (IMCA)	Someone who provides support and representation for a person who lacks capacity to make specific decisions, where the person has no-one else to support them. The IMCA service was established by the Mental Capacity Act 2005 and is not the same as an ordinary advocacy service.	**3.22–3.28, 7.34–7.41** 3.16, 4.7, 5.7–5.8, 5.18, 6.8, 6.19, 6.27–6.28, 7.4, 7.23, 7.26, 8.18, 8.28, 9.6, 9.9
Lasting Power of Attorney	A Power of Attorney created under the Mental Capacity Act 2005 appointing an attorney (donee), or attorneys, to make decisions about the donor's personal welfare, including health care, and/or deal with the donor's property and affairs.	10.8

Life-sustaining treatment	Treatment that, in the view of the person providing health care, is necessary to keep a person alive.	5.13
Local authority	In the deprivation of liberty safeguards context, the local council responsible for social services in any particular area of the country.	1.4, 2.18, 2.21, 3.3, 3.11, 3.21, 4.77
Local health board (LHB)	Local health boards cover the same geographic areas as local authorities in Wales. They work alongside their respective local authorities in planning long-term strategies for dealing with issues of health and wellbeing in their areas.	1.4, 3.3
Main Code	The Code of Practice for the Mental Capacity Act 2005.	Throughout
Managing authority	The person or body with management responsibility for the hospital or care home in which a person is, or may become, deprived of their liberty.	**1.4–1.5, 3.1** Throughout
Maximum authorisation period	The maximum period for which a supervisory body may give a standard deprivation of liberty authorisation, which must not exceed the period recommended by the best interests assessor, and which cannot be for more than 12 months.	4.71
Mental Capacity Act 2005	Legislation that governs decision-making for people who lack capacity to make decisions for themselves or who have capacity and want to make preparations for a time when they may lack capacity in the future. It sets out who can take decisions, in which situations, and how they should go about this.	Throughout

Mental capacity assessment	An assessment, for the purpose of the deprivation of liberty safeguards, of whether a person lacks capacity in relation to the question of whether or not they should be accommodated in the relevant hospital or care home for the purpose of being given care or treatment.	4.29–4.32
Mental disorder	Any disorder or disability of the mind, apart from dependence on alcohol or drugs. This includes all learning disabilities.	1.4, 1.7, 1.9, 3.9, 4.33–4.35, 4.45, 4.50, 5.9, 5.22, 6.3
Mental Health Act 1983	Legislation mainly about the compulsory care and treatment of patients with mental health problems. It covers detention in hospital for mental health treatment, supervised community treatment and guardianship.	**4.33–4.57** 1.1, 1.11–1.12, 2.13, 4.5, 5.19, 5.22, 7.8, 8.3, 8.19–8.21
Mental health assessment	An assessment, for the purpose of the deprivation of liberty safeguards, of whether a person has a mental disorder.	**4.33–4.39**
No refusals assessment	An assessment, for the purpose of the deprivation of liberty safeguards, of whether there is any other existing authority for decision-making for the relevant person that would prevent the giving of a standard deprivation of liberty authorisation. This might include any valid advance decision, or valid decision by a deputy or donee appointed under a Lasting Power of Attorney.	**4.25–4.28**
Qualifying requirement	Any one of the six qualifying requirements (age, mental health, mental capacity, best interests, eligibility and no refusals) that need to be assessed and met in order for a standard deprivation of liberty authorisation to be given.	4.1
Relevant hospital or care home	The hospital or care home in which the person is, or may become, deprived of their liberty.	Throughout

Relevant person	A person who is, or may become, deprived of their liberty in a hospital or care home.	Throughout
Relevant person's representative	A person, independent of the relevant hospital or care home, appointed to maintain contact with the relevant person, and to represent and support the relevant person in all matters relating to the operation of the deprivation of liberty safeguards.	**Chapter 7**
Restraint	The use or threat of force to help carry out an act that the person resists. Restraint may only be used where it is necessary to protect the person from harm and is proportionate to the risk of harm.	2.8–2.15
Restriction of liberty	An act imposed on a person that is not of such a degree or intensity as to amount to a deprivation of liberty.	Chapter 2
Review	A formal, fresh look at a relevant person's situation when there has been, or may have been, a change of circumstances that may necessitate an amendment to, or termination of, a standard deprivation of liberty authorisation.	**Chapter 8**
Standard authorisation	An authorisation given by a supervisory body, after completion of the statutory assessment process, giving lawful authority to deprive a relevant person of their liberty in the relevant hospital or care home.	**Chapter 4** Throughout
Supervised community treatment	Arrangements under which people can be discharged from detention in hospital under the Mental Health Act 1983, but remain subject to the Act in the community rather than in hospital. Patients on supervised community treatment can be recalled to hospital if treatment in hospital is necessary again.	4.41, 4.50, 4.51

Supervisory body	A primary care trust, local authority, Welsh Ministers or a local health board that is responsible for considering a deprivation of liberty request received from a managing authority, commissioning the statutory assessments and, where all the assessments agree, authorising deprivation of liberty.	**1.4, 3.3** Throughout
Unauthorised deprivation of liberty	A situation in which a person is deprived of their liberty in a hospital or care home without the deprivation being authorised by either a standard or urgent deprivation of liberty authorisation.	Chapter 9
Urgent authorisation	An authorisation given by a managing authority for a maximum of seven days, which may subsequently be extended by a maximum of a further seven days by a supervisory body, that gives the managing authority lawful authority to deprive a person of their liberty in a hospital or care home while the standard deprivation of liberty authorisation process is undertaken.	**Chapter 6** Throughout

INDEX

References are to paragraph numbers.